The Concise OXFORD SCHOOL THESAURUS

Compiled by

Alan Spooner

OXFORD UNIVERSITY PRESS

Oxford University Press, Great Clarendon Street, Oxford OX2 6DP

Oxford New York
Athens Auckland Bangkok Bogotá Buenos Aires Calcutta
Cape Town Chennai Dar es Salaam Delhi Florence Hong Kong Istanbul
Karachi Kuala Lumpur Madrid Melbourne Mexico City Mumbai
Nairobi Paris São Paolo Singapore Taipei Tokyo Toronto Warsaw

and associated companies in
Berlin Ibadan

Oxford is a trade mark of Oxford University Press

This edition based on The Oxford School Thesaurus
3   5   7   9   10   8   6   4   2

A CIP catalogue record for this book is available from the British Library

ISBN 0-19-910431-X

Typeset by Selwood Systems, Midsomer Norton

Printed in England by Clays, Bungay

OWLS
OXFORD ENGLISH
DICTIONARY
WORD AND
LANGUAGE
SERVICE

Do you have a query about words, their origin, meaning, use, spelling,
pronunciation, or any other aspect of the English Language?
Then write to OWLS at Oxford University Press,
Great Clarendon Street, Oxford OX2 6DP.

All queries will be answered using the full resources of the
Oxford Dictionary Department

Preface

This thesaurus offers, in an accessible form, the main features of larger thesauruses. Entries are arranged in single alphabetical sequence; example sentences and phrases are given to suggest how words may be used in context; there is access to a wide range of synonyms and (via cross-references) antonyms; cross-references are unambiguously signalled; and word-family lists are included in addition to synonym lists. This volume is designed as a compact, self-explanatory, and, I hope, thought-provoking thesaurus for use in school or at home.

Alan Spooner, January 1997

Before you use this thesaurus . . .

What is a thesaurus for?

The English language has many words which are similar in meaning. Words which mean the same, or nearly the same, are called synonyms. Most entries in this thesaurus give lists of synonyms for the headword (the word you have looked up). They also often suggest an entry to look up if you want opposites of the headword. Some entries provide useful families of words: words which are not synonyms, but which are related in other ways (names of colours, different foods, various sports, and so on).

Careful use of a thesaurus can help you in several ways:
It can increase your knowledge of words by giving lists of words to think about and discuss.
It may help you to avoid using the same word again and again by reminding you of other words that could be used.
It can suggest words which may be more appropriate or more exact than the word you first thought of.
Sometimes a thesaurus is useful just to jog your memory about a word that you can't quite recall.

Your main use of this thesaurus will most likely be to look for answers to the question, What's another word for . . .? When you use a thesaurus, however, remember that synonyms don't necessarily mean exactly the same as each other. Don't exchange a synonym for a word in a particular sentence without giving it careful thought. Which word you choose will depend on what you are writing about, why you are writing, who is likely to read it, how formal or informal you want it to sound, and so on. For example, glamorous, handsome, and picturesque are all synonyms of beautiful, but none of them is suitable as a synonym for beautiful in the phrase 'a beautiful baby'. Sometimes you'll decide that, after all, it's best to use the word you first thought of!

How is the thesaurus arranged?

Headwords
The first word of each entry (the headword) is printed in bold type. It is followed by a part of speech label (noun, verb, etc.) to show its grammatical function. All the headwords are arranged in alphabetical order.

Numbers
When the headword can be used in more than one sense, numbers identify the main meanings or uses of the word.

Opposites
If you want opposites of the headword (sometimes called antonyms), we give a simple cross-reference so that you know where to find them.

OPPOSITES: SEE optimistic.

pest noun
1 *Don't be a pest!* annoyance, bother, curse, irritation, nuisance, [*informal*] pain in the neck, trial, vexation.
2 *garden pests.* [*informal*] bug, [*informal*] creepy-crawly, insect, parasite, [*plural*] vermin.

pester verb
Don't pester me while I'm busy! annoy, badger, bait, besiege, bother, harass, harry, [*informal*] hassle, molest, nag, plague, torment, trouble, worry.

pet noun

CREATURES COMMONLY KEPT AS PETS:
budgerigar, canary, cat, dog, ferret, fish, gerbil, goldfish, guinea-pig, hamster, mouse, parrot, pigeon, rabbit, rat, tortoise.
OTHER ANIMALS: SEE **animal** noun.

pet verb
Our dog loves you to pet him. caress, cuddle, fondle, kiss, pat, stroke, SEE **touch** verb.

petition noun
a petition to the government. appeal, entreaty, list of signatures, plea, request, suit, supplication.

petty adjective
1 *petty crime.* insignificant, minor, small, trifling, trivial, SEE **unimportant**.
OPPOSITES: SEE **important**.
2 *a petty attitude.* grudging, nit-picking, SEE **small-minded**, ungenerous.

pharmacy noun
Get your medicine from the pharmacy. chemists, dispensary, [*American*] drugstore.

phase noun
a phase of your life. a phase of an activity. development, period, season, spell, stage, step, SEE **time** noun.

phenomenal adjective
The winner of the qui had a phenomenal memory. amazing, exceptional, extraordinary, [*informal*] fantastic, incredible, notable, outstanding, remarkable, [*informal*] sensational, singular, unbelievable, unusual, [*informal*] wonderful.
OPPOSITES: SEE **ordinary**.

phenomenon noun

Usage warnings
If you need to be careful about how you use a word (because it is normally informal, old-fashioned, etc.) there is a warning before the word.

Word families
Lists of words which are not synonyms but which are related in some other way are displayed between horizontal ruled lines.

Illustrative examples
Sentences or phrases printed in italics illustrate how the headword can be used.

Synonyms
Most entries include one or more lists of synonyms (that is, words which are similar, but not necessarily exactly the same, in meaning).

Aa

abandon verb
1 *to abandon ship.* desert, evacuate, forsake, leave, quit, vacate, withdraw from.
2 *to abandon a friend.* desert, drop, forsake, jilt, leave behind, leave in the lurch, maroon, renounce, repudiate, strand, wash your hands of.
3 *to abandon a plan.* cancel, [*slang*] chuck in, discard, discontinue, [*informal*] ditch, drop, finish, forgo, give up, postpone, scrap.
4 *to abandon a right.* cede, drop, forfeit, forgo, give up, relinquish, renounce, resign, surrender, waive, yield.

abbreviate verb SEE **abridge**.

aberration noun SEE **abnormality**.

abhorrent adjective
Torture is abhorrent to civilized people. abominable, detestable, disgusting, distasteful, execrable, hateful, horrible, horrid, horrifying, loathsome, nauseating, obnoxious, odious, offensive, repellent, repugnant, repulsive, revolting.

abide verb
1 [*old-fashioned*] *Abide with me.* SEE **stay**.
2 *I can't abide cigarette smoke.* accept, bear, endure, put up with, stand, [*informal*] stomach, suffer, tolerate.
to abide by *Abide by the rules.* accept, act in accordance with, adhere to, carry out, conform to, follow, keep to, obey, observe, stand by, submit to.

ability noun
1 *The rich have the ability to buy what they want.* capability, capacity, chance, means, opportunity, potential, potentiality, power, resources, scope, way, wherewithal.
2 *She has the ability to be a good artist.* aptitude, bent, brains, calibre, capability, cleverness, competence, expertise, facility, faculty, flair, genius, gift, intelligence, knack, [*informal*] know-how, knowledge, power, proficiency, prowess, qualification, skill, strength, talent, training.

able adjective
1 *I'm able to stay.* allowed, at liberty (to), authorized, available, eligible, equipped, fit, free, permitted, prepared, ready, willing.
OPPOSITES: **unable**.
2 *She's an able player.* accomplished, adept, capable, clever, competent, effective, efficient, experienced, expert, gifted, [*informal*] handy, intelligent, masterly, practised, proficient, qualified, skilful,

skilled, strong, talented, trained.
OPPOSITES: SEE **incompetent**.

abnormal adjective
abnormal behaviour. aberrant, anomalous, atypical, [*informal*] bent, bizarre, curious, deviant, eccentric, erratic, exceptional, extraordinary, freak, funny, heretical, irregular, [*informal*] kinky, odd, peculiar, perverse, perverted, queer, singular, strange, unaccountable, uncharacteristic, uncommon, unexpected, unnatural, unpredictable, unrepresentative, untypical, unusual, wayward, weird.
OPPOSITES: SEE **normal**.

abnormality noun
aberration, anomaly, deformity, deviation, eccentricity, idiosyncrasy, irregularity, oddity, peculiarity, perversity, singularity, strangeness, waywardness.

abolish verb
to abolish a law. abrogate, annul, cancel, destroy, do away with, eliminate, end, eradicate, finish, [*informal*] get rid of, invalidate, nullify, overturn, put an end to, quash, repeal, remove, rescind, revoke, suppress, terminate, withdraw.
OPPOSITES: SEE **create**.

abominable adjective
abominable tortures. abhorrent, appalling, atrocious, awful, base, beastly, brutal, contemptible, cruel, despicable, detestable, disgusting, distasteful, dreadful, execrable, foul, hateful, heinous, horrible, horrid, horrifying, inhuman, loathsome, nasty, nauseating, obnoxious, odious, offensive, repellent, repugnant, repulsive, revolting, terrible, unpleasant, vile.
OPPOSITES: SEE **humane**.

abortion noun
Her pregnancy ended in an abortion. miscarriage, premature birth, termination of pregnancy.

abortive adjective
an abortive attempt. fruitless, futile, ineffective, ineffectual, pointless, stillborn, unavailing, unfruitful, unproductive, unsuccessful, useless, vain.
OPPOSITES: SEE **successful**.

about-turn noun
His sudden about-turn surprised me. about-face, change of direction, reversal, U-turn, volte-face.

abrasive adjective
an abrasive manner. biting, caustic, galling, grating, harsh, hurtful, irritating, rough, sharp, SEE **unkind**.
OPPOSITES: SEE **kind** adjective.

abridge verb
The play was abridged for TV. abbreviate, compress, condense, curtail, cut, digest, edit, precis, prune, reduce, shorten, summarize, truncate.
OPPOSITES: SEE **expand**.

abridgement noun
an abridgement of a book. abbreviation, condensation, digest, precis, short version, summary, synopsis.

abrupt adjective
1 *an abrupt ending.* hasty, headlong, hurried, precipitate, quick, rapid, sudden, swift, unexpected, unforeseen, unpredicted.
2 *an abrupt drop.* precipitous, sharp, sheer, steep.
OPPOSITES: SEE **gradual**.
3 *an abrupt manner.* blunt, brusque, curt, discourteous, gruff, impolite, rude, unceremonious, uncivil, ungracious.
OPPOSITES: SEE **polite**.

abscond verb SEE **escape** verb.

absent adjective
absent from work. away, [*slang*] bunking off, missing, playing truant, [*informal*] skiving.
OPPOSITES: SEE **present** adjective.

absent-minded adjective
careless, forgetful, heedless, impractical, inattentive, scatterbrained, thoughtless, unheeding, unthinking, vague.
OPPOSITES: SEE **alert** adjective.

absolute adjective
1 *absolute silence. absolute happiness. an absolute certainty.* categorical, certain, complete, conclusive, decided, definite, downright, entire, full, genuine, implicit (*implicit faith*), inalienable (*an inalienable right*), indubitable, infallible, [*informal*] out-and-out, perfect, positive, pure, sheer, stark (*stark reality*), supreme, sure, thorough, total, unadulterated, unalloyed, unambiguous, unconditional, unequivocal, unmitigated, unmixed, unqualified, unquestionable, unreserved, unrestricted, utter.
2 *an absolute ruler.* almighty, autocratic, despotic, dictatorial, omnipotent, sovereign, totalitarian, tyrannical, undemocratic, unrestricted.

absolve verb SEE **forgive**.

absorb verb
1 *Our bodies absorb nutrients from our food.* assimilate, consume, devour, digest, drink in, fill up with, hold, imbibe, incorporate, [*formal*] ingest, receive, retain, soak up, suck up, take in, utilize.
OPPOSITES: SEE **emit**.

2 *Buffers absorb the shock of impact.* cushion, deaden, lessen, reduce, soften.
3 *The game totally absorbed us.* captivate, engage, engross, enthral, fascinate, interest, involve, occupy, preoccupy, rivet.

absorbed adjective SEE **interested**.

absorbent adjective
Absorbent substances soak up liquids. absorptive, permeable, pervious, porous, spongy.

absorbing adjective SEE **interesting**.

abstain verb
to abstain from *to abstain from alcohol.* avoid, cease, decline, deny yourself, desist from, eschew, forgo, give up, go without, refrain from, refuse, reject, renounce, resist, shun, stop.

abstemious adjective
an abstemious way of life. ascetic, austere, frugal, moderate, restrained, self-denying, self-disciplined, sober, sparing, teetotal [= *abstaining from alcohol*], temperate.
OPPOSITES: SEE **self-indulgent**.

abstract adjective
abstract ideas. abstruse, academic, general, hypothetical, indefinite, intangible, intellectual, metaphysical, philosophical, theoretical, unpractical, unreal, unrealistic.
OPPOSITES: SEE **concrete**.

absurd adjective
1 *an absurd explanation.* anomalous, illogical, incongruous, irrational, SEE **mad**, meaningless, nonsensical, paradoxical, preposterous, senseless, silly, stupid, unreasonable, untenable.
OPPOSITES: SEE **sensible**.
2 *absurd antics.* amusing, comic, crazy, [*informal*] daft, farcical, foolish, funny, grotesque, humorous, laughable, ludicrous, ridiculous, zany.
OPPOSITES: SEE **serious**.

abundant adjective
an abundant supply of food. an abundant growth of weeds. ample, bounteous, bountiful, copious, excessive, flourishing, full, generous, lavish, liberal, luxuriant, overflowing, plenteous, plentiful, prodigal, profuse, rampant, rank, rich, well-supplied.
OPPOSITES: SEE **scarce**.

abuse noun
1 *Politicians should beware of the abuse of power.* misuse.
2 *We deplore the physical abuse of any human being.* assault, cruel treatment, ill-treatment, maltreatment.
3 *They yelled abuse at us.* curses, insults, invective, obscenities, slander.

abuse verb
1 *to abuse a thing, a machine, or a person*
[*physically*]. batter, damage, harm, hurt, ill-
treat, injure, maltreat, manhandle, misuse,
molest, spoil, treat roughly.
2 *to abuse a person* [*verbally*]. affront, be
rude to, [*informal*] call someone names,
castigate, criticize, curse, defame, denigrate,
disparage, insult, inveigh against, libel,
malign, revile, slander, [*informal*] slate,
[*informal*] smear, sneer at, swear at,
traduce, upbraid, vilify, vituperate, wrong.

abusive adjective
abusive language. acrimonious, angry,
censorious, contemptuous, critical, cruel,
defamatory, denigrating, derisive,
derogatory, disparaging, harsh, hurtful,
impolite, insulting, libellous, obscene,
offensive, opprobrious, pejorative, rude,
scathing, scurrilous, slanderous,
vituperative.
OPPOSITES: SEE **friendly**, **polite**.

abysmal adjective
[*informal*] *The film was so abysmal that I
fell asleep.* appalling, awful, SEE **bad**,
dreadful, terrible, worthless.

abyss noun
a bottomless abyss. chasm, crater, fissure,
gap, gulf, hole, opening, pit, rift, void.

academic adjective
1 *A university is an academic institution.*
educational, pedagogical, scholastic.
2 *an academic student.* bookish, brainy,
clever, erudite, highbrow, intelligent,
learned, scholarly, studious, well-read.
OPPOSITES: SEE **stupid**.
3 *academic studies.* abstract, intellectual,
pure (*pure science*), theoretical.
OPPOSITES: SEE **applied**.
4 *Ideas about time-travelling are purely
academic.* conjectural, hypothetical,
impractical, notional, speculative,
unpractical.
OPPOSITES: SEE **practical**.

accelerate verb
1 *The bus accelerated.* [*informal*] get a move
on, go faster, hasten, pick up speed, quicken,
speed up.
2 *The factory must accelerate production.*
[*formal*] expedite, promote, spur on, step
up, stimulate.

accent noun
1 *an Irish accent.* brogue, cadence, dialect,
enunciation, inflection, intonation,
pronunciation, sound, tone.
2 *Play the first note with a strong accent.*
accentuation, beat, emphasis, force, pulse,
rhythm, stress.

accept verb
1 *I accepted her gift.* acquire, get, [*informal*]
jump at, receive, take, welcome.
2 *She accepts responsibility.* acknowledge,
admit, assume, bear, suffer, undertake.
3 *He accepted my arguments.* abide by, accede
to, acquiesce in, adopt, agree to, approve,
believe in, be reconciled to, consent to, defer
to, grant, recognize, resign yourself to,
[*informal*] stomach, submit to, [*informal*]
swallow, take in, tolerate, [*informal*] wear,
yield to.
OPPOSITES: SEE **reject**.

acceptable adjective
1 *an acceptable gift.* agreeable, appreciated,
gratifying, pleasant, pleasing, welcome,
worthwhile.
2 *an acceptable standard of work.* adequate,
admissible, appropriate, moderate,
passable, satisfactory, suitable, tolerable,
unexceptionable.
OPPOSITES: SEE **unacceptable**.

acceptance noun
*I wrote a letter of acceptance when he offered
me the job.* acquiescence, agreement,
approval, consent, willingness.
OPPOSITES: SEE **refusal**.

accepted adjective
an accepted fact. acknowledged, agreed,
canonical, indisputable, recognized,
standard, undeniable, undisputed,
unquestioned.
OPPOSITES: SEE **controversial**.

access noun SEE **entrance** noun.

accessible adjective
Make sure the first aid box is accessible. at
hand, available, convenient, [*informal*] get-
at-able, [*informal*] handy, reachable, within
reach.
OPPOSITES: SEE **inaccessible**.

accident noun
1 *a tragic accident.* calamity, catastrophe,
collision, [*usually joking*] contretemps,
crash, derailment, disaster, misadventure,
mischance, misfortune, mishap, [*informal*]
pile-up, [*slang*] shunt, wreck.
2 *an unforeseen accident. It happened by
accident.* chance, coincidence, contingency,
fate, fluke, fortune, hazard, luck, [*informal*]
pot luck, serendipity.

accidental adjective
an accidental mistake. adventitious,
arbitrary, casual, chance, coincidental,
[*informal*] fluky, fortuitous, fortunate,
haphazard, inadvertent, lucky, random,
unconscious, unexpected, unforeseen,
unfortunate, unintended, unintentional,
unlooked for, unplanned, unpremeditated.
OPPOSITES: SEE **intentional**.

acclaim verb SEE **praise** verb.

accommodate verb
1 *If you need anything, we'll try to accommodate you.* aid, assist, furnish, help, oblige, provide, serve, supply.
2 *The hostel can accommodate thirty guests.* billet, board, cater for, entertain, harbour, hold, house, lodge, provide for, [*informal*] put up, quarter, shelter, take in.

accommodation noun
holiday accommodation. temporary accommodation. board, housing, lodgings, pied-à-terre, shelter.

KINDS OF ACCOMMODATION: apartment, barracks, bed and breakfast, [*informal*] bedsit, bedsittcr, billet, boarding house, [*informal*] digs, flat, guest house, hall of residence, SEE **home**, hostel, hotel, married quarters, motel, rooms, self-catering, timeshare, youth hostel.

accompany verb
A friend accompanied me. attend, chaperon, conduct, convoy, escort, follow, go with, guard, guide, look after, partner, [*informal*] tag along with, travel with, usher.

accompanying adjective
associated, attendant, concomitant, connected, related.

accomplice noun
The thief had an accomplice. abettor, accessory, associate, collaborator, confederate, conspirator, SEE **helper**, [*informal*] henchman, partner.

accomplish verb
We accomplished our task. achieve, attain, bring off, carry out, complete, conclude, consummate, discharge, do successfully, effect, execute, finish, fulfil, perform, realize, succeed in.

accomplished adjective SEE **skilful**.

accomplishment noun SEE **skill**.

account noun
1 *The waiter gave us our account.* bill, check, invoice, receipt, reckoning, [*informal*] score, statement, tally.
2 *Money is of little account compared with your health.* advantage, benefit, concern, consequence, consideration, importance, interest, merit, profit, significance, standing, use, value, worth.
3 *I wrote an account of my trip.* chronicle, commentary, description, diary, disquisition, explanation, history, log, memoir, narration, narrative, portrayal, record, report, story, tale, version, [*informal*] write-up.

account verb
Can you account for his odd behaviour? clarify, elucidate, explain, give reasons for, justify, make excuses for, rationalize, vindicate.

accumulate verb
1 *I accumulate a lot of rubbish.* agglomerate, aggregate, amass, assemble, bring together, collect, gather, heap up, hoard, mass, pile up, [*informal*] stash away, stockpile, store up.
OPPOSITES: SEE **disperse**.
2 *The interest on your savings will accumulate.* accrue, build up, grow, increase, multiply.
OPPOSITES: SEE **decrease** verb.

accumulation noun
an accumulation of odds and ends. [*informal*] build-up, collection, conglomeration, heap, hoard, mass, pile, stock, store, supply.

accurate adjective
1 *an accurate description.* authentic, close, factual, faithful, faultless, reliable, right, sound, strict, true, truthful, veracious.
2 *accurate measurements.* careful, correct, exact, meticulous, minute, perfect, precise, scrupulous.
3 *accurate aim.* certain, [*informal*] spot-on, sure, unerring.
OPPOSITES: SEE **inaccurate**.

accusation noun
She denied the accusation completely. allegation, alleged offence, charge, complaint, indictment, summons.

accuse verb
to accuse someone of a crime. blame, bring charges against, censure, charge, condemn, denounce, impeach, impugn, incriminate, indict, inform against, make allegations against, prosecute, summons, tax.
OPPOSITES: SEE **defend**.

accustomed adjective
We had our accustomed bedtime drink. common, conventional, customary, established, expected, familiar, habitual, normal, ordinary, prevailing, regular, routine, set, traditional, usual, wonted.
to get accustomed *You'll soon get accustomed to new surroundings.* acclimatize, adapt, adjust, become conditioned, become hardened, become inured, become seasoned, become trained, familiarize yourself (with), get broken in, get used (to), orientate yourself.

ache noun
Exercise made the ache worse. anguish, discomfort, hurt, pang, SEE **pain** noun, smart, soreness, suffering, throbbing, twinge.

ache verb
The swollen ankle ached when I walked. be painful, be sore, hurt, smart, sting, suffer, throb.

achieve verb
1 *to achieve an ambition.* accomplish, attain, bring off, carry out, complete, conclude, consummate, discharge, do successfully, effect, execute, finish, fulfil, manage, perform, succeed in.
2 *They achieved fame overnight.* acquire, earn, gain, get, obtain, procure, reach, score (*They scored a great success*), strike, win.

achievement noun SEE **feat, success.**

aching adjective SEE **painful.**

acid adjective
Lemons taste acid. sharp, sour, stinging, tangy, tart, vinegary.

acknowledge verb
1 *I acknowledge that you are right.* accede, accept, admit, affirm, agree, allow, concede, confess, confirm, declare, endorse, grant, own, profess, yield.
OPPOSITES: SEE **deny.**
2 *Please acknowledge my letter.* answer, notice, react to, reply to, respond to, return (*a signal or greeting*).
3 *He acknowledged me with a smile.* greet, hail, recognize, salute, [*informal*] say hullo to.

acquaint verb
to acquaint with *She acquainted us with her discovery.* advise of, announce, apprise of, brief about, disclose, divulge, enlighten about, inform of, make familiar with, notify, reveal, tell about.

acquaintance noun SEE **friend.**

acquiesce verb SEE **agree.**

acquire verb SEE **get.**

acquisition noun
a new acquisition for the library. accession, addition, [*informal*] buy, gain, possession, prize, property, purchase.

acquisitive adjective SEE **greedy.**

acquit verb
The judge acquitted the prisoner. absolve, clear, declare innocent, discharge, dismiss, [*formal*] exculpate, excuse, exonerate, free, [*informal*] let off, liberate, release, reprieve, set free, vindicate.
to acquit yourself *We acquitted ourselves well in the competition.* act, behave, conduct yourself, operate, perform, work.

acrid adjective
an acrid smell of burning. bitter, caustic, harsh, pungent, sharp, unpleasant.

acrimonious adjective
acrimonious insults. abusive, acerbic, angry, bad-tempered, biting, bitter, caustic, censorious, churlish, cutting, hostile, hot-tempered, ill-natured, ill-tempered, irascible, mordant, peevish, petulant, pungent, SEE **quarrelsome**, rancorous, sarcastic, sharp, spiteful, tart, testy, venomous, virulent, waspish.
OPPOSITES: SEE **peaceable.**

act noun
1 *a brave act.* action, deed, effort, enterprise, exploit, feat, operation, proceeding, step, undertaking.
2 *an act of parliament.* bill [= *draft of an act before it is passed*], decree, edict, law, order, regulation, statute.
3 *an act in a concert.* item, performance, routine, sketch, turn.

act verb
1 *He acted like a baby.* behave, conduct yourself, seem to be.
2 *The medicine didn't act.* function, have an effect, operate, serve, take effect, work.
3 *to act a role. to act in a play.* appear (as), assume the character of, characterize, enact, imitate, impersonate, mime, mimic, perform, personify, play, portray, pose as, represent, simulate.

action noun
1 *a brave action. a prompt action.* act, deed, effort, endeavour, enterprise, exploit, feat, measure, performance, proceeding, process, step, undertaking, work.
2 *a holiday packed with action.* activity, drama, energy, excitement, exercise, exertion, liveliness, movement, vigour, vitality.

activate verb
to activate a fire-alarm. to activate someone's enthusiasm. actuate, animate, arouse, energize, excite, fire, galvanize, [*informal*] get going, initiate, mobilize, motivate, prompt, rouse, set in motion, set off, start, stimulate, stir, trigger off.

active adjective
1 *an active person. an active scene.* agile, animated, bustling, busy, energetic, enterprising, enthusiastic, functioning, live, lively, militant, nimble, [*informal*] on the go, spirited, sprightly, vigorous, vital, vivacious.
2 *an active supporter.* assiduous, busy, committed, dedicated, devoted, diligent, employed, engaged, enthusiastic, hardworking, industrious, involved,

occupied, sedulous, staunch, working, zealous.
OPPOSITES: SEE **inactive**.
3 *an active volcano.* erupting, smoking, smouldering.
OPPOSITES: SEE **extinct**.

activity noun
1 *The market-place was full of activity.* action, animation, bustle, commotion, excitement, hurly-burly, hustle, industry, life, liveliness, motion, movement, stir.
2 *spare-time activities.* hobby, interest, job, labour, occupation, pastime, project, pursuit, scheme, task, undertaking, venture, work.

actor, **actress** nouns
artist, artiste, SEE **entertainer**, lead, leading lady, performer, player, star, supporting actor, trouper, walk-on part.

actual adjective
I saw the actual place where it happened. authentic, bona fide, certain, confirmed, definite, existing, factual, genuine, indisputable, legitimate, real, realistic, tangible, true, truthful, unquestionable, verifiable.
OPPOSITES: SEE **imaginary**.

acute adjective
1 *an acute mind.* analytical, astute, canny, SEE **clever**, incisive, intelligent, keen, observant, penetrating, perceptive, perspicacious, quick, sharp, shrewd, [*informal*] smart, subtle.
OPPOSITES: SEE **dull**, **stupid**.
2 *acute pain.* exquisite, extreme, fierce, intense, keen, piercing, racking, severe, sharp, shooting, sudden, violent.
OPPOSITES: SEE **mild**.
3 *an acute problem.* compelling, crucial, decisive, immediate, important, overwhelming, pressing, serious, urgent, vital.
OPPOSITES: SEE **continual**.
4 *an acute illness.* critical, sudden.
OPPOSITES: SEE **chronic**.
5 *an acute angle.* pointed, sharp.
OPPOSITE: obtuse.

adapt verb
1 *to adapt yourself to new ways.* acclimatize, accommodate, accustom, adjust, attune, fit, habituate, harmonize, orientate, reconcile, suit, tailor, turn.
2 *to adapt something for a new purpose.* alter, amend, change, convert, metamorphose, modify, process, rearrange, rebuild, reconstruct, refashion, remake, remodel, reorganize, reshape, transform, vary.

add verb
to add one thing to another. annex, append, attach, combine, integrate, join, put

together, [*informal*] tack on, unite.
OPPOSITES: SEE **deduct**.
to add up 1 *Add up the scores.* calculate, compute, count, do a sum, reckon up, [*informal*] tot up, work out. 2 [*informal*] *Her story doesn't add up.* be convincing, be reasonable, [*informal*] hold water, make sense, [*informal*] ring true.
to add up to *What does the cost add up to?* amount to, come to, make, total.

addiction noun
alcoholism [= *addiction to alcohol*], compulsion, craving, dependence, fixation, habit, obsession.

addition noun
accession (*to a library*), accessory, accretion, addendum (*to a document*), additive, adjunct, admixture, afterthought, amplification, annexe (*to a building*), appendage, appendix (*to a book*), appurtenance, attachment, continuation, development, enlargement, expansion, extension, extra, increase, increment (*to salary*), postscript (*to a letter*), supplement.

additional adjective
additional resources. added, extra, further, increased, more, new, other, spare, supplementary.

address noun
1 *the address on an envelope.* directions.
2 *The vicar delivered an address.* discourse, [*formal*] disquisition, harangue, [*now often joking*] homily, lecture, [*formal*] oration, sermon, speech, talk.

address verb
A stranger addressed me. accost, apostrophize, approach, [*informal*] buttonhole, engage in conversation, greet, hail, salute, speak to, talk to.
to address yourself to *Address yourself to your work.* apply yourself to, attend to, concentrate on, devote yourself to, engage in, focus on, get involved in, settle down to, tackle, undertake.

adept adjective SEE **skilful**.

adequate adjective
an adequate standard of work. acceptable, competent, fair, good enough, passable, presentable, respectable, satisfactory, sufficient, suitable, tolerable.
OPPOSITES: SEE **inadequate**.

adhere verb SEE **stick** verb.

adjoining adjective
the garden adjoining ours. abutting, adjacent to, alongside, beside, bordering, closest to, contiguous with, juxtaposed to, nearest, neighbouring, next to, touching.

adjourn verb
to adjourn a meeting. break off, defer, discontinue, dissolve, interrupt, postpone, prorogue (*parliament*), put off, stop temporarily, suspend.

adjournment noun
an adjournment of a meeting. break, delay, interruption, pause, postponement, prorogation, recess, stay, stoppage, suspension.

adjust verb
1 *I adjusted the TV picture.* alter, amend, arrange, balance, change, modify, position, put right, rectify, regulate, set, temper, tune, vary.
2 *I adjusted myself to my new work.* acclimatize, accommodate, accustom, adapt, convert, fit, habituate, harmonize, modify, reconcile, refashion, remake, remodel, reorganize, reshape, tailor.

ad-lib adjective
ad-lib remarks. extempore, impromptu, improvised, impulsive, made-up, [*informal*] off the cuff, [*informal*] off the top of your head, spontaneous, unplanned, unprepared, unrehearsed.

ad-lib verb
I had to ad-lib when I lost my notes. extemporize, improvise, make it up, [*informal*] play it by ear.

administer verb
1 *The Head administers the school.* administrate, command, conduct the affairs of, control, direct, govern, head, lead, look after, manage, organize, oversee, preside over, regulate, rule, run, superintend, supervise.
2 *A nurse administered my medicine.* apply, deal out, dispense, distribute, dole out, give, hand out, measure out, mete out, provide, supply.

administrator noun
bureaucrat, civil servant, executive, SEE **manager**, organizer.

admirable adjective
She has many admirable qualities. commendable, creditable, deserving, enjoyable, estimable, excellent, exemplary, fine, SEE **good**, honourable, laudable, likeable, lovable, marvellous, meritorious, pleasing, praiseworthy, valued, wonderful, worthy.
OPPOSITES: SEE **contemptible**.

admiration noun
Her skill won our admiration. appreciation, approval, commendation, esteem, hero-worship, high regard, honour, praise, respect.
OPPOSITES: SEE **contempt**.

admire verb
1 *I admire her skill.* applaud, approve of, esteem, have a high opinion of, hero-worship, [*formal*] laud, look up to, marvel at, praise, respect, revere, think highly of, value, wonder at.
2 *We admired the view.* appreciate, be delighted by, enjoy, like, love.
OPPOSITES: SEE **despise**.

admiring adjective
admiring glances. appreciative, approving, complimentary, flattering, respectful.
OPPOSITES: SEE **contemptuous**.

admission noun
1 *Admission is by ticket.* access, admittance, entrance, entry.
2 *an admission of guilt.* acceptance, acknowledgement, affirmation, avowal, confession, declaration, profession, revelation.
OPPOSITES: SEE **denial**.

admit verb
1 *to admit someone to hospital.* accept, allow in, grant access, let in, provide a place (in), receive, take in.
OPPOSITES: SEE **exclude**.
2 *to admit your guilt.* accept, acknowledge, agree, allow, concede, confess, declare, disclose, divulge, grant, own up, profess, recognize, reveal, say reluctantly.
OPPOSITES: SEE **deny**.

adolescence noun
boyhood, girlhood, growing up, puberty, [*informal*] your teens, youth.

adolescent adjective
adolescent behaviour. [These words are often used by adults to suggest that they are superior to young people.] boyish, girlish, immature, juvenile, puerile, teenage, youthful.

adolescent noun
boy, girl, [*formal*] juvenile, minor, [*informal*] teenager, youngster, youth.

adopt verb
1 *We adopted their suggestion.* accept, appropriate, approve, back, champion, choose, embrace, endorse, espouse, follow, [*informal*] go for, support, take up.
2 *We adopted a stray cat.* befriend, foster, patronize, stand by, take in, [*informal*] take under your wing.

adorable adjective SEE **lovable**.

adore verb
She adores her grandad. dote on, glorify, idolize, love, revere, venerate, worship.
OPPOSITES: SEE **hate** verb.

adorn verb SEE **decorate**.

adult adjective
developed, full-size, fully grown, grown-up,
marriageable, mature, of age.
OPPOSITES: SEE **immature**.

adulterate verb
*He adulterated the expensive wine with a
cheaper brand.* contaminate, corrupt,
debase, defile, dilute, [*informal*] doctor,
pollute, taint, thin, water down, weaken.

advance noun
You can't stop the advance of science.
development, evolution, forward movement,
growth, headway, progress.

advance verb
1 *As the army advanced, the enemy fled.*
approach, bear down, come near, forge
ahead, gain ground, go forward, make
headway, make progress, [*informal*] make
strides, move forward, press ahead, press
on, proceed, progress, [*informal*] push on.
OPPOSITES: SEE **retreat** verb.
2 *Computer technology has advanced
enormously.* develop, evolve, grow, improve,
increase, prosper, thrive.
OPPOSITES: SEE **regress**.
3 *Passing your exams will advance your
career.* accelerate, assist, benefit, boost,
expedite, facilitate, further, help the
progress of, promote.
OPPOSITES: SEE **hinder**.

advanced adjective
1 *advanced technology.* latest, modern,
sophisticated, ultra-modern, up-to-date.
OPPOSITES: SEE **obsolete**.
2 *advanced ideas.* avant-garde,
contemporary, experimental, forward-
looking, futuristic, imaginative, innovative,
inventive, new, novel, original, pioneering,
precocious, progressive, revolutionary,
trend-setting, unconventional, unheard of,
[*informal*] way-out.
OPPOSITES: SEE **old-fashioned**.
3 *advanced mathematics.* complex,
complicated, difficult, hard, higher.
OPPOSITES: SEE **elementary**.
4 *advanced for her age.* grown-up, mature,
sophisticated, well-developed.

advantage noun
We had the advantage of a following wind.
aid, asset, assistance, benefit, boon,
convenience, favour, gain, help, profit,
service, use, usefulness.
OPPOSITES: SEE **handicap** noun.
to take advantage of SEE **exploit** verb.

advantageous adjective SEE **helpful**.

adventure noun
1 *a dangerous adventure.* enterprise,
escapade, exploit, gamble, incident,
occurrence, operation, risk, undertaking,
venture.
2 *a sense of adventure.* danger, excitement,
hazard.

adventurous adjective
1 *adventurous explorers.* bold, daring,
enterprising, heroic, intrepid, valiant,
venturesome.
2 *an adventurous life.* challenging,
dangerous, eventful, exciting, perilous,
risky.
OPPOSITES: SEE **unadventurous**.

adverse adjective
1 *an adverse report.* antagonistic, attacking,
censorious, critical, derogatory,
disapproving, hostile, hurtful, inimical,
negative, uncomplimentary, unfavourable,
unfriendly, unkind, unsympathetic.
2 *adverse conditions, adverse effects.*
contrary, deleterious, detrimental,
disadvantageous, harmful, inappropriate,
inauspicious, opposing, prejudicial,
uncongenial, unfortunate, unpropitious.
OPPOSITES: SEE **favourable**.

adversity noun SEE **misfortune**.

advertise verb
announce, broadcast, display, flaunt, make
known, market, merchandise, notify,
[*informal*] plug, proclaim, promote,
promulgate, publicize, [*informal*] push,
show off, [*informal*] spotlight, tout.

advertisement noun
[*informal*] ad, [*informal*] advert,
announcement, bill, [*informal*] blurb,
[*informal*] break [*on TV*], classified
advertisement [*in newspaper*], commercial
[*on TV*], display, hand-out, leaflet, notice,
placard, [*informal*] plug, poster, promotion,
publicity, [*old-fashioned or joking*] puff,
sign, [*informal*] small ad.

advice noun
He gave me some advice. admonition, caution,
counsel, guidance, help, opinion,
recommendation, suggestion, tip, warning.

advisable adjective
The doctor said a rest was advisable. prudent,
recommended, wise.
OPPOSITES: SEE **inadvisable**.

advise verb
1 *The doctor advised her to rest.* admonish,
advocate, caution, counsel, encourage,
[*formal*] enjoin, [*formal*] exhort, instruct,
prescribe, recommend, suggest, urge, warn.
2 *They advised us that the plane would be
delayed.* SEE **inform**.

advocate verb SEE **recommend**.

aerodrome noun
airfield, airport, airstrip, landing-strip.

aeroplane noun SEE **aircraft**.

aesthetic adjective SEE **artistic**.

affable adjective SEE **friendly**.

affair noun
1 *business affairs.* activity, business, concern, interest, matter, operation, project, question, subject, topic, transaction, undertaking.
2 *The crash was a mysterious affair.* circumstance, episode, event, happening, incident, occasion, occurrence, thing.
3 *a passionate affair.* attachment, intrigue, involvement, liaison, love affair, relationship, romance.

affect verb
[Don't confuse *affect* with *effect.*]
1 *Acid rain affects trees. The storm affected the train service.* act on, alter, attack, change, have an effect on, have an impact on, [*informal*] hit, impinge on, influence, modify, pertain to, relate to, transform.
2 *The bad news affected us.* agitate, concern, disturb, grieve, impress, move, perturb, stir, touch, trouble, upset.

affectation noun
[Don't confuse *affectation* with *affection.*]
Her posh accent is pure affectation. insincerity, mannerism, SEE **pretence**, pretension.

affected adjective
an affected way of talking. SEE **pretentious**.

affection noun
We can show affection by hugs and kisses. amity, attachment, devotion, feeling, fondness, friendliness, friendship, liking, love, partiality, regard, [*informal*] soft spot, tenderness, warmth.
OPPOSITES: SEE **hatred**.

affectionate adjective SEE **loving**.

affiliate verb
Our club is affiliated to a national organization. ally, amalgamate, associate, band together, combine, connect, couple, federate, incorporate, join, join forces, link up, merge, syndicate, unite.

affirm verb SEE **declare**.

affirmative adjective
an affirmative answer. agreeing, assenting, concurring, confirming, consenting, positive, saying 'yes'.
OPPOSITES: SEE **negative**.

afflict verb
He is afflicted by illness. A plague of locusts afflicted the land. annoy, bedevil, beset, burden, cause suffering, distress, harass, harm, hurt, oppress, pain, pester, plague, rack, torment, torture, trouble, try, vex, worry, wound.

affluent adjective
1 *an affluent life-style.* comfortable, expensive, gracious, lavish, luxurious, opulent, pampered, self-indulgent, sumptuous.
2 *an affluent businessman.* flourishing, [*informal*] flush, [*slang*] loaded, moneyed, [*often joking*] plutocratic, prosperous, rich, wealthy, [*informal*] well-heeled, well-off, well-to-do.
OPPOSITES: SEE **poor**.

afford verb
Can you afford the cost? find enough, manage to give, spare, [*informal*] stand.

afraid adjective
I was afraid of the danger. aghast, agitated, alarmed, anxious, apprehensive, cowardly, cowed, daunted, diffident, faint-hearted, fearful, frightened, hesitant, horrified, intimidated, jittery, nervous, pusillanimous, reluctant, scared, terrified, timid, timorous, uneasy, unheroic, [*informal*] yellow.
OPPOSITES: SEE **brave**, **confident**.
to be afraid dread, fear, quake, tremble, worry.

afterthought noun
addendum, addition, appendix, extra, postscript.

age noun
1 *What is your age?* date of birth.
2 *Age is catching up on me.* decrepitude, dotage, old age, senility.
3 *the Victorian age.* days, epoch, era, generation, period, time.

age verb
1 *He's aged since we last saw him.* decline, degenerate, look older.
2 *Wine needs to age.* develop, grow older, mature, mellow, ripen.

aged adjective SEE **old**.

agenda noun
[In Latin, *agenda* is plural = *things to be done*, but in English it is often used as if it were singular.] list, plan, programme, schedule, timetable.

agent noun
He employs an agent to act on his behalf. broker, delegate, emissary, executor, [*old-fashioned*] functionary, go-between, intermediary, mediator, middleman, negotiator, representative, trustee.

aggravate verb
[Some people think that the informal use of *aggravate* = *annoy* is incorrect.] 1 *The medicine only aggravated the pain.* add to,

augment, compound, exacerbate, exaggerate, heighten, increase, inflame, intensify, magnify, make more serious, make worse, worsen.
OPPOSITES: SEE **alleviate**.
2 [*informal*] *Their teasing aggravated us.* annoy, bother, exasperate, irk, irritate, [*informal*] needle, nettle, [*informal*] peeve, provoke, trouble, vex.

aggression noun SEE **attack** noun, **hostility**.

aggressive adjective
aggressive behaviour. antagonistic, assertive, attacking, bellicose, belligerent, bullying, [*slang*] butch, contentious, destructive, hostile, jingoistic, [*slang*] macho, militant, offensive, provocative, pugnacious, pushful, [*informal*] pushy, quarrelsome, violent, warlike, zealous.
OPPOSITES: SEE **friendly**.

aggressor noun SEE **attacker**.

agile adjective
acrobatic, active, adroit, deft, fleet, graceful, limber, lissom, lithe, lively, mobile, nimble, quick-moving, sprightly, spray, supple, swift.
OPPOSITES: SEE **clumsy, slow** adjective.

agitate verb
1 *The wind agitated the surface of the water.* beat, churn, convulse, ferment, froth up, ruffle, shake, stimulate, stir, toss, work up.
2 *The storm agitated the animals.* alarm, arouse, confuse, disconcert, disturb, excite, fluster, incite, perturb, rouse, stir up, trouble, unsettle, upset, worry.
OPPOSITES: SEE **calm** verb.

agitated adjective
anxious, confused, distraught, disturbed, edgy, excited, feverish, fidgety, flustered, nervous, restive, restless, ruffled, [*informal*] tossing and turning, unsettled, upset.
OPPOSITES: SEE **serene**.

agnostic noun
doubter, sceptic.
COMPARE: atheist, believer.

agonize verb
I agonized over the decision. be in agony [SEE **agony**], SEE **hurt**, labour, struggle, suffer, worry, wrestle.

agonizing adjective SEE **painful**.

agony noun
anguish, distress, pain, suffering, torment, torture.

agree verb
1 *I agree to pay my share. He agreed to my proposal.* accede (to), accept, acknowledge, acquiesce (in), admit, allow, assent (to), be willing, concede, consent (to), [*formal*] covenant, grant, make a contract, pledge yourself, promise, undertake.

2 *I'm glad that we agree. We both added the figures up, but our answers didn't agree.* accord, be unanimous, be united, coincide, concur, conform, correspond, fit, get on, harmonize, match, [*informal*] see eye to eye, suit (*each other*).
OPPOSITES: SEE **disagree**.
to agree with *I don't agree with capital punishment.* advocate, argue for, [*informal*] back, defend, support.

agreeable adjective SEE **pleasant**.

agreement noun
1 *There's a large measure of agreement between us.* accord, affinity, compatibility, compliance, concord, conformity, congruence, consensus, consent, consistency, correspondence, harmony, similarity, solidarity, sympathy, unanimity, unity.
OPPOSITES: SEE **disagreement**.
2 *The two sides signed an agreement.* acceptance, alliance, armistice, arrangement, bargain, bond, compact, concordat, contract, convention, covenant, deal, [*French*] entente, pact, pledge, protocol, settlement, treaty, truce, understanding.

agriculture noun
[*formal*] agronomy, crofting, cultivation, farming, growing, husbandry, tilling.

aid noun
Poorer countries need aid from richer ones. advice, assistance, backing, benefit, collaboration, co-operation, contribution, donation, encouragement, guidance, help, loan, patronage, prop, relief, sponsorship, subsidy, succour, support.

aid verb
to aid the poor. to aid a partner. abet, assist, back, benefit, collaborate with, co-operate with, contribute to, encourage, help, [*informal*] lend a hand to, promote, prop up, [*informal*] rally round, relieve, subsidize, [*formal*] succour, support, sustain.

ailment noun SEE **illness**.

aim noun
What's your aim in life? ambition, aspiration, cause, design, desire, destination, direction, dream, end, goal, hope, intention, mark, object, objective, plan, purpose, target, wish.

aim verb
1 *to aim a missile at someone.* address, beam, direct, level, line up, point, send, sight, take aim, train, turn, zero in on.
2 *to aim to do something.* aspire, attempt, design, endeavour, essay, intend, mean, plan, propose, resolve, seek, strive, try, want, wish.

air noun
1 *the air above us.* airspace, atmosphere, ether, heavens, sky, [*poetic*] welkin.
2 *We went out to get some air.* breath of air, breeze, draught, oxygen, waft, wind, [*poetic*] zephyr.
3 *She has the air of one who gets her own way.* ambience, appearance, aspect, aura, bearing, character, demeanour, effect, feeling, impression, look, manner, mien, mood, quality, style.

air verb
1 *to air a room. to air clothes.* aerate, dry off, freshen, ventilate.
2 *to air opinions.* SEE **express** verb.

aircraft noun
aeroplane, [*old-fashioned*] flying-machine, plane.

KINDS OF AIRCRAFT: airliner, airship, balloon, biplane, bomber, delta wing, dirigible, fighter, flying boat, glider, gunship, hang-glider, helicopter, jet, jumbo jet, jump-jet, microlight, monoplane, seaplane, STOL (short take-off and landing), supersonic aircraft, turboprop, VTOL (vertical take-off and landing).

PARTS OF AIRCRAFT: aileron, cabin, cargo hold, cockpit, elevator, fin, flap, fuselage, jet engine, joy-stick, passenger cabin, propeller, rotor, rudder, tail, tail-plane, undercarriage, wing.

---

airman noun
aviator, flier, pilot.

airport noun
aerodrome, airfield, air strip, heliport, landing-strip, runway.

airy adjective
an airy room. blowy, breezy, draughty, fresh, open, spacious, ventilated.
OPPOSITES: SEE **stuffy**.

aisle noun
corridor, gangway, passage, passageway.

alarm noun
1 *Did you hear the alarm?* alarm-clock, alert, bell, fire-alarm, gong, signal, siren, tocsin, warning.
2 *We were filled with alarm.* anxiety, apprehension, consternation, dismay, distress, fear, fright, nervousness, panic, terror, trepidation, uneasiness.

alarm verb
The noise alarmed us. agitate, daunt, dismay, distress, disturb, frighten, panic, [*informal*] put the wind up, scare, shock, startle, surprise, terrify, unnerve, upset, worry.
OPPOSITES: SEE **reassure**.

alcoholic adjective
alcoholic drink. brewed, distilled, fermented, [*informal*] hard, intoxicating, [*old-fashioned*] spirituous, [*informal*] strong.

alcoholic noun
addict, dipsomaniac, SEE **drunkard**, hard drinker, inebriate, toper.
OPPOSITES: SEE **teetotaller**.

alert adjective
Stay alert! alive (to), attentive, awake, careful, circumspect, heedful, lively, observant, on the alert, on the lookout, [*informal*] on the qui vive, on your guard, perceptive, quick, ready, sharp-eyed, vigilant, wary, watchful, wide awake.
OPPOSITES: SEE **dull** adjective, **inattentive**.

alert verb
We alerted them to the danger. caution, forewarn, give the alarm, inform, make aware, notify, signal, tip off, warn.

alibi noun SEE **excuse** noun.

alien adjective
alien beings. exotic, extra-terrestrial, foreign, outlandish, remote, strange, unfamiliar.

alien noun SEE **foreigner**.

alight adjective
ablaze, afire, aflame, bright, burning, fiery, ignited, illuminated, lit up, on fire, shining.

alight verb
1 *to alight from a bus.* descend, disembark, dismount, get down, get off.
2 *The bird alighted on a branch.* come down, come to rest, land, perch, settle, touch down.

align verb
1 *I aligned the marker pegs.* arrange in line, line up, place in line, straighten up.
2 *He aligns himself with the socialists.* affiliate, agree, ally, associate, co-operate, join, side, sympathize.

alike adjective
These paintings are alike. akin, analogous, close, cognate, comparable, corresponding, equivalent, identical, indistinguishable, like, parallel, related, resembling, similar, the same, twin, uniform.

alive adjective
Are the goldfish still alive? SEE **active**, animate, breathing, existing, extant, flourishing, in existence, live, living, [*old-fashioned*] quick, surviving.
OPPOSITES: SEE **dead**.

allay verb
to allay someone's fears. alleviate, assuage, calm, check, compose, diminish, ease, lessen, lull, mitigate, moderate, mollify,

pacify, quell, quench (*your thirst*), quiet,
quieten, reduce, relieve, slake (*your thirst*),
soften, soothe, subdue.
OPPOSITES: SEE **increase, stimulate.**

allegation noun
*The allegations against him were never
proved.* accusation, assertion, charge, claim,
declaration, statement, testimony.

allege verb
She alleged that he was a thief. adduce,
affirm, assert, [*formal*] asseverate, attest,
aver, avow, claim, contend, declare, [*formal*]
depose, insist, maintain, make a charge,
[*formal*] plead, state.

allergic adjective
[*informal*] *I'm allergic to work.* antagonistic,
antipathetic, averse, disinclined, hostile,
incompatible (with), opposed.

alleviate verb
to alleviate suffering. abate, allay,
ameliorate, assuage, check, diminish, ease,
lessen, lighten, make lighter, mitigate,
moderate, pacify, palliate, quell, quench
(*your thirst*), reduce, relieve, slake (*your
thirst*), soften, soothe, subdue, temper.
OPPOSITES: SEE **aggravate.**

alliance noun
an alliance between two countries or parties.
affiliation, agreement, association, bloc,
bond, cartel, coalition, combination,
compact, concordat, confederation,
connection, consortium, covenant, entente,
federation, guild, league, marriage, pact,
partnership, relationship, syndicate, treaty,
understanding, union.

allot verb
We allotted fair shares to all. allocate, allow,
apportion, assign, award, deal out,
[*informal*] dish out, [*informal*] dole out,
dispense, distribute, divide out, give out,
grant, mete out, ration, set aside, share out.

allow verb
1 *We don't allow smoking.* approve,
authorize, bear, endure, enable, grant
permission for, let, license, permit,
[*informal*] put up with, sanction, [*informal*]
stand, suffer, support, tolerate.
OPPOSITES: SEE **forbid.**
2 *The shop allowed £40 for our old gas fire.*
allot, allocate, deduct, give, grant, provide,
remit, set aside.

allowance noun
1 *a daily allowance of food.* allocation,
allotment, amount, measure, portion, quota,
ration, share.
2 *I can just live on my allowance.* annuity,
grant, SEE **payment**, pension, pocket money,
subsistence.

3 *They offered us an allowance for our old
cooker.* deduction, discount, rebate,
reduction, remittance, subsidy.

alloy noun
an alloy of two metals. amalgam, blend,
combination, composite, compound, fusion,
mixture.
VARIOUS METAL ALLOYS: SEE **metal.**

all right [Although *alright* is common, *all
right* is still the better spelling.] *Are you all
right? The food's all right.* SEE **healthy, safe,
satisfactory.**

allude verb
to allude to *Please don't allude to her illness.*
hint at, make an allusion to, mention, refer
to, speak of, suggest, touch on.

allure verb
allured by a smell of cooking. attract, beguile,
bewitch, cajole, charm, coax, decoy, draw,
entice, fascinate, inveigle, lead on, lure,
magnetize, persuade, seduce, tempt.

ally noun
abettor, accessory, accomplice, associate,
collaborator, colleague, companion,
confederate, friend, helper, helpmate,
[*informal*] mate, partner.
OPPOSITES: SEE **enemy.**

ally verb
With which side do you ally yourself? affiliate,
amalgamate, associate, band together,
collaborate, combine, confederate, co-
operate, form an alliance (SEE **alliance**),
fraternize, join, join forces, league,
[*informal*] link up, marry, merge, side,
[*informal*] team up, unite.

almost adverb
about, all but, approximately, around, as
good as, just about, nearly, not quite,
practically, virtually.

alone adjective
She lives alone. apart, desolate, forlorn,
friendless, isolated, lonely, lonesome, on
your own, separate, single, solitary, solo,
unaccompanied.

aloof adjective
He's hard to know—he's so aloof. cold, cool,
dispassionate, distant, formal, frigid,
haughty, inaccessible, indifferent, remote,
reserved, reticent, self-contained, self-
possessed, [*informal*] standoffish,
supercilious, unapproachable,
unconcerned, undemonstrative,
unforthcoming, unfriendly, unresponsive,
unsociable, unsympathetic.
OPPOSITES: SEE **approachable.**

aloud adverb
to read aloud. audibly, clearly, distinctly, out loud.
OPPOSITES: SEE **silently**.

alright SEE **all right**.

also adverb
additionally, besides, furthermore, in addition, moreover, [*joking*] to boot, too.

alter verb
adapt, adjust, amend, become different, SEE **change** verb, convert, edit, emend, enlarge, make different, modify, reconstruct, reduce, reform, remake, remodel, reorganize, reshape, revise, transform, vary.

alteration noun
adaptation, adjustment, amendment, SEE **change** noun, difference, modification, reorganization, transformation.

alternate verb
Two actors will alternate in the leading role. act alternately, come alternately, follow each other, interchange, oscillate, replace each other, rotate, [*informal*] see-saw, substitute for each other, take turns.

alternative noun
1 *I had no alternative.* choice, option.
2 *There are alternatives to coal.* back-up, replacement, substitute.

altitude noun
elevation, height.

altogether adverb
I'm not altogether satisfied. absolutely, completely, entirely, fully, perfectly, quite, thoroughly, totally, utterly, wholly.

always adverb
consistently, constantly, continually, continuously, endlessly, eternally, everlastingly, evermore, forever, [*informal*] for ever and ever, invariably, perpetually, persistently, regularly, repeatedly, unceasingly, unfailingly, unremittingly.

amalgamate verb
Two teams amalgamated. We amalgamated two teams. affiliate, ally, associate, band together, coalesce, combine, come together, confederate, form an alliance, fuse, integrate, join, join forces, league, [*informal*] link up, marry, merge, put together, synthesize, [*informal*] team up, unite.

amateur adjective
an amateur player. an amateur worker. inexperienced, unpaid, unqualified, untrained.
OPPOSITES: SEE **professional**.

amateur noun
unpaid amateurs. dabbler, dilettante, enthusiast, layman, non-professional.
OPPOSITES: SEE **professional**.

amateurish adjective
amateurish work. clumsy, crude, [*informal*] do-it-yourself, incompetent, inept, inexpert, [*informal*] rough-and-ready, second-rate, shoddy, unpolished, unprofessional, unskilful, unskilled, untrained.
OPPOSITES: SEE **skilled**.

amaze verb
astonish, astound, bewilder, confound, confuse, daze, disconcert, dumbfound, [*informal*] flabbergast, perplex, [*informal*] rock, shock, stagger, startle, stun, stupefy, surprise.

amazed adjective
astonished, astounded, confused, dazed, dumbfounded, [*informal*] flabbergasted, non-plussed, speechless, staggered, stumped, stunned, surprised, [*informal*] thunderstruck.

amazing adjective
awe-inspiring, breathtaking, exceptional, extraordinary, [*informal*] fantastic, incredible, miraculous, notable, phenomenal, prodigious, remarkable, [*informal*] sensational, special, staggering, stunning, stupendous, unusual, [*informal*] wonderful.

ambassador noun
attaché, chargé d'affaires, consul, diplomat, emissary, envoy, legate (*of the pope*), nuncio (*of the pope*), plenipotentiary, representative.

ambiguous adjective
an ambiguous message. ambivalent, confusing, enigmatic, equivocal, indefinite, indeterminate, puzzling, uncertain, unclear, vague, woolly.
OPPOSITES: SEE **definite**.

ambition noun
1 *She's got the ambition to succeed.* drive, enterprise, enthusiasm, [*informal*] push, pushfulness, self-assertion, thrust, zeal.
2 *Her ambition is to run in the Olympics.* aim, aspiration, desire, dream, goal, hope, ideal, intention, object, objective, target, wish.

ambitious adjective
1 *You must be ambitious to succeed in business.* assertive, committed, eager, energetic, enterprising, enthusiastic, go-ahead, [*informal*] go-getting, hard-working, industrious, keen, [*informal*] pushy, zealous.
OPPOSITES: SEE **apathetic**.
2 *She has ambitious ideas.* [*informal*] big,

far-reaching, grand, grandiose, large-scale,
SEE **unrealistic**.
OPPOSITES: SEE **modest**.

ambush noun
The patrol set up an ambush. ambuscade,
attack, snare, surprise attack, trap.

ambush verb
The patrol ambushed the outlaws. attack,
ensnare, entrap, intercept, pounce on,
surprise, swoop on, trap, waylay.

amenable adjective
He was quite amenable to our suggestions.
accommodating, acquiescent, adaptable,
agreeable, biddable, complaisant, compliant,
co-operative, deferential, docile, open-
minded, persuadable, responsive,
submissive, tractable, willing.
OPPOSITES: SEE **obstinate**.

amend verb
*I hope that naughty dog will soon amend its
ways.* adapt, adjust, alter, change, correct,
emend, improve, mend, modify, put right,
rectify, reform, remedy, revise.

amiable, **amicable** adjectives SEE **friendly**.

ammunition noun
buckshot, bullet, cartridge, grenade, missile,
projectile, round, shell, shrapnel.

amorous adjective
amorous advances. affectionate, ardent,
carnal, doting, enamoured, erotic, fond,
impassioned, loving, lustful, passionate,
[*slang*] randy, sexual, [*informal*] sexy.

amount noun
1 *a cheque for the full amount.* aggregate,
entirety, quantum, reckoning, sum, total,
whole.
2 *a large amount of rubbish.* bulk, lot, mass,
measure, SEE **quantity**, supply, volume.

amount verb
to amount to *What does it all amount to?* add
up to, aggregate, be equivalent to, come to,
equal, make, mean, total.

ample adjective
an ample supply of food. abundant, big,
bountiful, capacious, commodious,
considerable, copious, extensive, generous,
great, large, lavish, liberal, munificent,
plentiful, profuse, roomy, spacious,
substantial, voluminous.
OPPOSITES: SEE **inadequate**.

amplify verb
1 *I amplified what I had written in my notes.*
add to, augment, broaden, develop, dilate
upon, elaborate, enlarge, expand, expatiate
on, extend, fill out, lengthen, make fuller,
make longer, supplement.
OPPOSITES: SEE **condense**.
2 *to amplify sound.* boost, heighten, increase,

intensify, make louder, magnify, raise the
volume.
OPPOSITES: SEE **decrease**.

amputate verb
to amputate a limb. chop off, cut off, dock (*a
dog's tail*), lop off (*a branch*), poll or pollard
(*a tree*), remove, sever, truncate.

amuse verb
1 *A comedian tries to amuse people.* cheer up,
delight, divert, enliven, entertain, gladden,
make laugh, raise a smile, [*informal*] tickle.
2 *The crossword amused me for a while.*
absorb, beguile, engross, interest, involve,
occupy, please.
OPPOSITES: SEE **bore** verb.

amusement noun
1 *We tried not to show our amusement.*
hilarity, laughter, merriment, mirth.
2 *What's your chief amusement?* delight,
distraction, diversion, enjoyment,
entertainment, fun, game, hobby, interest,
joke, leisure activity, pastime, play,
pleasure, recreation, sport.

amusing adjective
diverting, enjoyable, entertaining, SEE **funny**,
pleasing.

anaemic adjective
bloodless, colourless, feeble, frail, pale,
pallid, pasty, sallow, sickly, wan, weak.

analogy noun
*To explain the circulation of the blood she
used the analogy of a central heating system.*
comparison, likeness, metaphor, parallel,
resemblance, similarity, simile.

analyse verb
We analysed the results of our experiment.
break down, dissect, evaluate, examine,
interpret, investigate, scrutinize, separate
out, study.

analysis noun
What did your analysis of the figures show?
breakdown, enquiry, evaluation,
examination, interpretation, investigation,
[*informal*] post-mortem, scrutiny, study,
test.

analytical adjective
an analytical mind. analytic, critical,
[*informal*] in-depth (*an in-depth
investigation*), inquiring, investigative,
logical, methodical, penetrating,
questioning, rational, searching,
systematic.
OPPOSITES: SEE **superficial**.

anarchy noun
There would be anarchy if we had no police.
bedlam, chaos, confusion, disorder,

disorganization, insurrection, lawlessness, misgovernment, misrule, mutiny, pandemonium, riot.

ancestor noun
antecedent, forebear, forefather, forerunner, precursor, predecessor, progenitor.
OPPOSITES: SEE **descendant**.

ancestry noun
Their family is of German ancestry. blood, derivation, descent, extraction, family, genealogy, heredity, line, lineage, origin, parentage, pedigree, roots, stock.

anchor verb
1 *to anchor a ship.* berth, make fast, moor, tie up.
2 *to anchor something firmly.* SEE **fix**.

anchorage noun
a safe anchorage for ships. harbour, haven, marina, moorings, port, refuge, sanctuary, shelter.

ancient adjective
1 *ancient buildings.* aged, [*often joking*] antediluvian, antiquated, antique, archaic, fossilized, obsolete, old, old-fashioned, outmoded, out-of-date, passé, [*often joking*] superannuated, venerable.
2 *ancient times.* bygone, early, [*poetic*] immemorial (*time immemorial*), [*old-fashioned*] olden, past, prehistoric, primeval, primitive, primordial, remote, [*old-fashioned*] of yore.
OPPOSITES: SEE **modern**.

angel noun
archangel, cherub, divine messenger, seraph.

angelic adjective
1 *an angelic expression. angelic music.* beatific, SEE **beautiful**, blessed, celestial, cherubic, divine, ethereal, heavenly, holy, seraphic, spiritual.
2 *angelic behaviour.* exemplary, SEE **good**, innocent, pious, pure, saintly, unworldly, virtuous.
OPPOSITES: SEE **devilish**.

anger noun
filled with anger. angry feelings [SEE **angry**], annoyance, bitterness, [*old-fashioned*] choler, exasperation, fury, hostility, indignation, [*old-fashioned*] ire, irritability, outrage, passion, pique, rage, [*formal*] rancour, resentment, tantrum, temper, vexation, wrath.

anger verb
Don't anger the bull! [*informal*] aggravate, SEE **annoy**, antagonize, [*slang*] bug, displease, enrage, exasperate, incense, incite, inflame, infuriate, irritate, madden, make angry [SEE **angry**], [*informal*] needle,

provoke, [*informal*] rile, [*informal*] rub up the wrong way, vex.
OPPOSITES: SEE **pacify**.

angle noun
1 *an angle between two walls or lines.* bend, corner, crook, nook.
2 *The speaker took an interesting angle on the topic.* approach, outlook, perspective, point of view, position, slant, standpoint, viewpoint.

angry adjective
[*informal*] aerated, annoyed, apoplectic, bad-tempered, bitter, [*informal*] bristling, [*informal*] choked, [*old-fashioned*] choleric, SEE **cross** adjective, disgruntled, enraged, exasperated, fiery, fuming, furious, heated, hostile, [*informal*] hot under the collar, ill-tempered, incensed, indignant, infuriated, [*informal*] in high dudgeon, irascible, irate, livid, mad, [*informal*] miffed, outraged, [*informal*] peeved, piqued, provoked, [*informal*] put out, raging, [*informal*] ratty, raving, resentful, riled, seething, [*slang*] shirty, [*informal*] sore, vexed, [*informal*] ugly (*in an ugly mood*), wild, wrathful.
OPPOSITES: SEE **calm** adjective.
an angry person [*informal*] cross-patch, [*informal*] sourpuss, [*informal*] spitfire.
to be angry, **to become angry** [*informal*] be in a paddy, [*informal*] blow up, boil, bristle, flare up, [*informal*] fly off the handle, fulminate (= *talk angrily*), fume, [*informal*] get steamed up, lose your temper, rage, rant, rave, [*informal*] see red, seethe, snap, storm.
to make someone angry SEE **anger** verb.

anguish noun
agony, anxiety, distress, grief, heartache, misery, pain, sorrow, suffering, torment, torture, tribulation, woe.

animal noun
beast, being, brute, creature, [*formal*], [*plural*] fauna, [*plural*] wildlife.
KINDS OF ANIMAL: amphibian, arachnid, biped, SEE **bird**, carnivore, SEE **fish**, herbivore, hibernating animal, SEE **insect**, invertebrate, mammal, marsupial, mollusc, monster, nocturnal animal, omnivore, pet, predator, quadruped, SEE **reptile**, rodent, scavenger, vertebrate.

SOME LIVING ANIMALS: aardvark, antelope, ape, armadillo, baboon, badger, bear, beaver, bison, buffalo, camel, caribou, cat, chamois, cheetah, chimpanzee, chinchilla, chipmunk, coypu, deer, dog, dolphin, donkey, dormouse, dromedary.
elephant, elk, ermine, ferret, fox, frog, gazelle, gerbil, gibbon, giraffe, gnu, goat, gorilla, grizzly bear, guinea-pig, hamster,

hare, hedgehog, hippopotamus, horse, hyena, ibex, impala, jackal, jaguar, jerboa. kangaroo, koala, lemming, lemur, leopard, lion, llama, lynx, marmoset, marmot, marten, mink, mongoose, monkey, moose, mouse, musquash, ocelot, octopus, opossum, orang-utan, otter, panda, panther, pig, platypus, polar bear, pole-cat, porcupine, porpoise.
rabbit, rat, reindeer, rhinoceros, roe, salamander, scorpion, seal, sea-lion, sheep, shrew, skunk, snake, spider, squirrel, stoat, tapir, tiger, toad, vole, wallaby, walrus, weasel, whale, wilde-beest, wolf, wolverine, wombat, yak, zebra.

FEMALE ANIMALS: bitch (*dog, wolf*), cow (*cattle, elephant, whale, etc.*), doe (*deer, hare, rabbit*), ewe (*sheep*), filly (*horse*), hen (*bird*), hind (*deer*), nanny goat, lioness, mare (*horse*), sow (*pig*), tigress, vixen (*fox*).

MALE ANIMALS: billy goat, buck (*deer, hare, rabbit*), bull (*cattle, elephant, whale*), cob (*swan*), cock (*bird*), dog (*dog, fox, wolf*), drake (*duck*), gander (*goose*), hart (*deer*), ram (*sheep*), stag (*deer*), stallion (*horse*), steer (*cattle*), tom (*cat*).

YOUNG ANIMALS: calf (*cattle*), chick, colt (*male horse*), cub (*fox, lion, etc.*), cygnet (*swan*), duckling, fawn (*deer*), filly (*female horse*), fledgling (*bird*), foal (*horse*), fry (*fish*), gosling (*goose*), heifer (*cow*), kid (*goat*), kitten (*cat*), lamb (*sheep*), leveret (*hare*), piglet, pup (*dog, seal, etc.*), whelp (*dog*).

GROUPS OF ANIMALS: brood (*of chicks*), covey (*of partridges*), flock (*of birds, sheep*), gaggle (*of geese*), herd (*of cattle*), leap (*of leopards*), litter (*of puppies*), pack (*of wolves*), pride (*of lions*), school (*of porpoises*), shoal (*of fish*), swarm (*of bees*).

SOME EXTINCT ANIMALS: brontosaurus, dinosaur, dodo, mastodon, pterodactyl, pterosaur, quagga.

---

animate adjective
Animals are animate, stones are not. alive, breathing, conscious, feeling, live, living, sentient.
OPPOSITES: SEE **inanimate**.

animate verb
The captain tried to animate her weary team. activate, arouse, brighten up, [*informal*] buck up, cheer up, encourage, energize, enliven, excite, exhilarate, fire, galvanize, incite, inspire, invigorate, kindle, liven up, make lively, move, [*informal*] pep up, [*informal*] perk up, quicken, rejuvenate, revitalize, revive, rouse, spark, spur, stimulate, stir, urge, vitalize.

animated adjective
animated chatter. active, alive, bright, brisk, bubbling, busy, cheerful, eager, ebullient, energetic, enthusiastic, excited, exuberant, gay, impassioned, lively, passionate, quick, spirited, sprightly, vibrant, vigorous, vivacious, zestful.
OPPOSITES: SEE **lethargic**.

animosity noun
animosity between two fighters. acerbity, acrimony, animus, antagonism, antipathy, asperity, aversion, bad blood, bitterness, dislike, enmity, grudge, hate, hatred, hostility, ill will, loathing, malevolence, malice, malignancy, malignity, odium, rancour, resentment, sarcasm, sharpness, sourness, spite, unfriendliness, venom, vindictiveness, virulence.

annex verb
to annex territory. acquire, appropriate, conquer, occupy, purloin (*goods or property*), seize, take over, usurp (*someone's position or authority*).

annihilate verb
Nuclear weapons could annihilate the world. abolish, destroy, eliminate, eradicate, erase, exterminate, extinguish, [*formal*] extirpate, [*informal*] finish off, [*informal*] kill off, [*informal*] liquidate, [*formal*] nullify, obliterate, raze, slaughter, wipe out.

annihilation noun SEE **destruction**.

anniversary noun
annual celebration.
SPECIAL ANNIVERSARIES: bicentenary, birthday, centenary, coming-of-age, jubilee, silver/golden/diamond/ruby wedding.

annotation noun
I wrote annotations in the margin of the book. comment, commentary, [*formal*] elucidation, explanation, footnote, gloss, interpretation, note.

announce verb
1 *The boss announced his decision.* advertise, broadcast, declare, disclose, divulge, intimate, notify, proclaim, promulgate, publish, report, reveal, state.
2 *The DJ announced the next record.* introduce, lead into, preface, present.

announcement noun
advertisement, bulletin, [*official*] communiqué, declaration, [*formal*] intimation, notification, [*official*] proclamation, [*formal*] promulgation, publication, report, revelation, statement.

announcer noun
broadcaster, commentator, compère, [*poetic*] harbinger, herald, messenger, newscaster, newsreader, reporter, town crier.

annoy verb
[*informal*] aggravate, SEE **anger** verb,
antagonize, [*informal*] badger, be an
annoyance to, bother, [*slang*] bug, chagrin,
displease, exasperate, [*informal*] get on
your nerves, grate, harass, harry, irk,
irritate, jar, madden, make cross, molest,
[*informal*] needle, [*informal*] nettle, offend,
[*joking*] peeve, pester, pique, [*informal*]
plague, provoke, rankle, [*informal*] rile,
[*informal*] rub up the wrong way, ruffle,
tease, trouble, try (*He tries me sorely*),
upset, vex, worry.
OPPOSITES: SEE **please**.

annoyance noun
Her annoyance was obvious. SEE **anger** noun,
chagrin, crossness, displeasure,
exasperation, irritation, pique, vexation.

annoyed adjective
SEE **angry**, chagrined, cross, displeased,
exasperated, [*informal*] huffy, irritated,
jaundiced, [*informal*] mad, [*informal*]
miffed, [*informal*] needled, [*informal*]
nettled, offended, [*informal*] peeved,
piqued, [*informal*] riled, [*informal*] shirty,
[*informal*] sore, upset, vexed.
OPPOSITES: SEE **pleased**.

annoying adjective
[*informal*] aggravating, displeasing,
exasperating, galling, grating, irksome,
irritating, jarring, maddening, offensive,
provocative, provoking, tiresome,
troublesome, trying, upsetting, vexatious,
vexing, worrying.

annul verb SEE **abolish**.

anoint verb
1 *to anoint a king.* bless, consecrate,
dedicate, hallow, sanctify.
2 *to anoint a wound with ointment.*
embrocate, grease, lubricate, oil, rub,
smear.

anonymous adjective
1 *an anonymous poet.* incognito, nameless,
unacknowledged, unidentified, unknown,
unnamed, unspecified, unsung.
2 *an anonymous letter.* unattributed,
unsigned.

answer noun
1 *an answer to a question.* acknowledgement,
[*informal*] comeback, reaction, rejoinder,
reply, response, retort, [*joking*] riposte.
2 *an answer to a problem.* explanation,
outcome, solution.

answer verb
1 *I answered her question.* acknowledge,
give an answer to, react to, reply to,
respond to.
2 *"I'm quite well," I answered.* rejoin, reply,
respond, retort, return.

3 *The dictionary answered our problem.*
explain, resolve, solve.
4 *How did she answer the accusation?* refute.

antagonize verb
*Don't antagonize the neighbours by making
a noise.* alienate, anger, annoy, embitter,
estrange, irritate, make an enemy of, offend,
provoke, upset.
OPPOSITES: SEE **please**.

antedate verb
*The pottery we found antedates the fragments
in the museum.* be older than, come before,
go before, precede, predate.

anthem noun
canticle, chant, chorale, hymn, introit,
paean, psalm.

anthology noun
an anthology of poems. collection,
compendium, compilation, digest,
miscellany, selection, treasury.

anticipate verb
1 *I anticipated his blow and fended it off.*
forestall, pre-empt.
2 [*informal*] *I anticipate that the result will
be a draw.* expect, forecast, foresee, foretell,
hope, predict. [Many people think this is an
incorrect use of *anticipate*.]

anticlimax noun
*It was an anticlimax when they abandoned
the game.* bathos, [*informal*] come-down,
[*informal*] damp squib, disappointment,
[*informal*] let-down.

antics noun
The children laughed at the clown's antics.
buffoonery, capers, clowning, escapades,
foolery, fooling, [*informal*] larking about,
pranks, [*informal*] skylarking, tomfoolery,
tricks.

antidote noun
antitoxin, corrective, countermeasure, cure,
neutralizing agent, remedy.

antiquarian noun
antiquary, antiques expert, collector, dealer.

antiquated adjective
antiquated ideas. an antiquated machine.
aged, anachronistic, ancient, antediluvian,
antique, archaic, dated, obsolete, SEE **old**, old-
fashioned, out-dated, outmoded, out-of-date,
passé, [*informal*] past it, [*informal*]
prehistoric, [*informal*] primeval, primitive,
quaint, [*joking*] superannuated,
unfashionable.
OPPOSITES: SEE **new**.

antique adjective
antique furniture. ancient, antiquarian, SEE
antiquated, historic, old-fashioned,
traditional, veteran (*cars*), vintage (*cars*).

antique noun
bygone, curio, curiosity.

antiseptic adjective
1 *an antiseptic dressing.* aseptic, clean,
disinfected, germfree, hygienic, medicated,
sanitized, sterile, sterilized, unpolluted.
2 *antiseptic ointment.* disinfectant,
germicidal, sterilizing.

antisocial adjective
antisocial behaviour. antisocial hooligans.
alienated, anarchic, disagreeable,
disorderly, disruptive, misanthropic, nasty,
obnoxious, offensive, rebellious, rude,
troublesome, uncooperative, undisciplined,
unfriendly, unruly, unsociable.
OPPOSITES: SEE **friendly, sociable.**

antithesis noun SEE **opposite** noun.

antonym noun
opposite.

anxiety noun
1 *anxiety about the future.* apprehension,
concern, disquiet, distress, doubt, dread,
fear, foreboding, fretfulness, misgiving,
nervousness, qualm, scruple, strain, stress,
tension, uncertainty, unease, worry.
OPPOSITES: SEE **calmness.**
2 *anxiety to do your best.* desire, eagerness,
enthusiasm, impatience, keenness,
willingness.

anxious
1 *anxious about the future.* afraid, agitated,
alarmed, apprehensive, concerned,
distressed, disturbed, edgy, fearful,
[*informal*] fraught, fretful, [*informal*]
jittery, nervous, [*informal*] nervy,
overwrought, perturbed, solicitous, tense,
troubled, uneasy, upset, worried.
OPPOSITES: SEE **calm** adjective, **carefree.**
2 *anxious to do your best.* avid, careful,
desirous, [*informal*] dying, eager,
impatient, intent, [*informal*] itching, keen,
willing, yearning.

apathetic adjective
You won't succeed if you are apathetic. cool,
dispassionate, emotionless, impassive,
inactive, indifferent, lethargic, listless,
passive, phlegmatic, sluggish, tepid, torpid,
unambitious, uncommitted, unconcerned,
unenthusiastic, unfeeling, uninterested,
uninvolved, unmotivated.
OPPOSITES: SEE **enthusiastic.**

apathy noun
coolness, inactivity, indifference, lassitude,
lethargy, listlessness, passivity, torpor.
OPPOSITES: SEE **enthusiasm.**

aperture noun SEE **opening** noun.

apex noun
1 *the apex of a pyramid or mountain.*
crest, crown, head, peak, pinnacle, point,
summit, tip, top, vertex.
OPPOSITES: SEE **bottom** noun.
2 *the apex of her career.* acme, apogee, climax,
consummation, crowning moment,
culmination, height, zenith.
OPPOSITES: SEE **nadir.**

apologetic adjective
He was apologetic about his mistake. contrite,
penitent, regretful, remorseful, repentant,
rueful, sorry.
OPPOSITES: SEE **unrepentant.**

apologize verb
He apologized for being rude. be penitent,
express regret, make an apology, repent, say
sorry.

apology noun
He made an apology for his rudeness.
acknowledgement, confession, defence,
excuse, explanation, justification, plea.

appal verb
Their injuries appalled us. alarm, disgust,
dismay, distress, frighten, harrow, horrify,
nauseate, outrage, revolt, shock, sicken,
terrify, unnerve.

appalling adjective
1 *appalling injuries. appalling behaviour.*
alarming, atrocious, disgusting, distressing,
dreadful, frightening, frightful, gruesome,
harrowing, horrendous, horrible, horrific,
horrifying, nauseating, outrageous,
revolting, shocking, sickening, terrifying,
unnerving.
2 [*informal*] *an appalling piece of work.* SEE
bad.

apparatus noun
appliance, contraption, device, equipment,
gadget, [*informal*] gear, instrument,
machine, machinery, mechanism,
[*informal*] setup, system, [*informal*] tackle,
tool.

apparent adjective
There was no apparent reason for the crash.
blatant, clear, conspicuous, detectable,
discernible, evident, manifest, noticeable,
observable, obvious, ostensible, overt,
patent, perceptible, recognizable, self-
explanatory, unconcealed, visible.
OPPOSITES: SEE **concealed.**

apparition noun
chimera, ghost, hallucination, illusion,
manifestation, phantasm, phantom,
presence, shade, spectre, spirit, [*informal*]
spook, vision, wraith.

appeal noun
1 *an appeal for help.* call, cry, entreaty,
petition, request, supplication.
2 *She had a great appeal for the audience.*
allure, attractiveness, charisma, charm,
[*informal*] pull, seductiveness.

appeal verb
to appeal for aid. ask earnestly, beg, beseech, call, canvass, cry out, entreat, implore, invoke, petition, plead, pray, request, solicit, supplicate.
to appeal to *His good looks don't appeal to me.* SEE **attract**.

appealing adjective SEE **attractive**.

appear verb
Our visitors appeared. A light appeared upstairs. Snowdrops appear in the spring. arise, arrive, attend, begin, be seen, [*informal*] bob up, come, come into view, [*informal*] crop up, enter, develop, emerge, [*informal*] heave into sight, loom, materialize, occur, show, [*informal*] show up, spring up, surface, turn up.

appearance noun
1 *His early appearance surprised us.* SEE **arrival**.
2 *He has the appearance of one who's had no sleep.* aspect, exterior, impression, likeness, SEE **look** noun, semblance.

appease verb
They offered a sacrifice to appease the gods. assuage, calm, conciliate, humour, mollify, pacify, placate, propitiate, quiet, reconcile, satisfy, soothe, [*informal*] sweeten, tranquillize, win over.
OPPOSITES: SEE **anger** verb.

appendage noun SEE **addition**.

appendix noun
an appendix to a book. addendum, addition, annexe, codicil (*to a will*), epilogue, postscript, rider, supplement.

appetite noun
an appetite for food. an appetite for adventure. craving, demand, desire, eagerness, greed, hankering, hunger, keenness, longing, lust, passion, predilection, relish, [*informal*] stomach, taste, thirst, urge, willingness, wish, yearning, [*informal*] yen, zeal, zest.

appetizing adjective
appetizing food. delicious, [*informal*] mouthwatering, tasty, tempting.
WORDS TO DESCRIBE HOW THINGS TASTE: SEE **taste** verb.

applaud verb
to applaud a performance. acclaim, approve, [*informal*] bring the house down, cheer, clap, commend, compliment, congratulate, eulogize, extol, give an ovation, [*formal*] laud, praise, salute.
OPPOSITES: SEE **criticize**.

applause noun
approval, clapping, ovation, plaudits, SEE **praise** noun.

applicant noun
an applicant for a job. aspirant, candidate, competitor, entrant, interviewee, participant, postulant [= *applicant to join a religious order*.]

applied adjective
applied science. practical, utilitarian.
OPPOSITES: SEE **pure**.

apply verb
1 *Apply ointment to the wound.* administer, bring into contact, lay on, put on, spread.
2 *The rules apply to everyone.* appertain, be relevant, pertain, refer, relate.
3 *Apply your skill.* bring into use, employ, exercise, implement, practise, use, utilize, wield.
to apply for *I applied for a refund.* ask formally for, [*informal*] put in for, request, solicit, sue for.

appoint verb
1 *to appoint a time for a meeting.* arrange, decide on, determine, fix, ordain, settle.
2 *Who did they appoint to do the job?* choose, co-opt, delegate, depute, designate, detail, elect, make an appointment, name, nominate, [*informal*] plump for, select, settle on, vote for.

appointment noun
1 *an appointment with the dentist.* arrangement, assignation, consultation, date, engagement, fixture, interview, meeting, rendezvous, session, [*old-fashioned*] tryst.
2 *the appointment of a new member of staff.* choice, choosing, commissioning, election, naming, nomination, selection.
3 *Did you apply for the appointment?* job, office, place, position, post, situation.

apposite adjective SEE **relevant**.

appreciable adjective SEE **considerable**.

appreciate verb
1 *I appreciate what she did for me.* admire, approve of, be grateful for, be sensitive to, cherish, enjoy, esteem, like, prize, regard highly, respect, sympathize with, treasure, value, welcome.
OPPOSITES: SEE **despise**.
2 *I appreciate that you can't afford much.* acknowledge, apprehend, comprehend, know, realize, recognize, see, understand.
OPPOSITES: SEE **disregard**.
3 *The value of property may appreciate.* build up, escalate, gain, go up, grow, improve, increase, inflate, mount, rise, soar, strengthen.
OPPOSITES: SEE **depreciate**.

appreciative adjective SEE **admiring, grateful**.

apprehensive adjective SEE **anxious**.

apprentice noun
beginner, learner, novice, probationer, pupil, starter, [*joking*] tiro, trainee.

approach noun
1 *Footsteps signalled their approach.* advance, advent, arrival, coming, nearing.
OPPOSITES: SEE **retreat** noun.
2 *The easiest approach is from the west.* access, doorway, entrance, entry, passage, road, way in.
3 *She has a positive approach to her work.* attitude, course, manner, means, method, mode, procedure, style, system, technique, way.
4 *I made an informal approach to the bank manager.* appeal, application, invitation, offer, overture, proposal, proposition.

approach verb
1 *The lion approached its prey.* advance on, bear down on, catch up with, come near, draw near, gain on, move towards, near.
2 *We approached the job cheerfully.* SEE **begin, undertake**.
3 *I approached the bank manager for a loan.* SEE **contact** verb.

approachable adjective
an approachable person. accessible, affable, agreeable, congenial, cordial, friendly, informal, kind, [*informal*] matey, open, sociable, sympathetic, [*informal*] unstuffy, welcoming, well-disposed.
OPPOSITES: SEE **aloof, formal**.

appropriate adjective
appropriate clothes. an appropriate moment to ask a question. applicable, apposite, [*joking*] apropos, apt, becoming, befitting, correct, deserved, due, felicitous, fit, fitting, germane, happy, just, [*old-fashioned*] meet, opportune, pertinent, proper, relevant, right, seasonable, seemly, suitable, tactful, tasteful, timely, well-judged, well-suited, well-timed.
OPPOSITES: SEE **inappropriate**.

appropriate verb
to appropriate someone else's property. commandeer, confiscate, gain control of, [*informal*] hijack, requisition, seize, steal, take, take over, usurp.

approval noun
1 *We cheered to show our approval.* acclaim, acclamation, admiration, applause, appreciation, approbation, commendation, esteem, favour, liking, plaudits, praise, regard, respect, support.
OPPOSITES: SEE **disapproval**.
2 *The committee gave its approval to our plan.*

acceptance, acquiescence, agreement, assent, authorization, [*informal*] blessing, confirmation, consent, endorsement, [*informal*] go-ahead, [*informal*] green light, licence, mandate, [*informal*] OK, permission, ratification, sanction, seal (*of approval*), stamp (*of approval*), support, [*informal*] thumbs up, validation.
OPPOSITES: SEE **refusal, veto**.

approve verb
The boss approved my request for leave. accede to, accept, agree to, allow, assent to, authorize, [*informal*] back, [*informal*] bless, confirm, consent to, countenance, endorse, give in to, pass, permit, ratify, [*informal*] rubber-stamp, sanction, sign, subscribe to, support, tolerate, uphold, validate.
OPPOSITES: SEE **refuse** verb, **veto**.
to approve of *She approves of what I did.* acclaim, admire, applaud, appreciate, commend, esteem, favour, like, love, praise, respect, value, welcome.
OPPOSITES: SEE **condemn**.

approximate adjective
an approximate calculation. close, estimated, inexact, near, rough.
OPPOSITES: SEE **exact** adjective.

approximate verb
to approximate to *Does the price approximate to what you expected?* approach, be close to, be similar to, border on, come near to, equal roughly, look like, resemble.

approximately adverb
about, round, circa (*born circa 1750*), close to, just about, loosely, more or less, nearly, [*informal*] nigh on, [*informal*] or thereabouts, [*informal*] pushing, roughly, round about.

apt adjective
1 *an apt remark.* SEE **appropriate** adjective.
2 *apt to fall asleep.* SEE **likely**.
3 *an apt pupil.* SEE **clever**.

aptitude noun SEE **ability**.

arable adjective
arable land. cultivated.
OPPOSITES: SEE **pasture**.

arbitrary adjective
1 *an arbitrary decision.* capricious, casual, chance, fanciful, illogical, indiscriminate, irrational, random, subjective, unplanned, unpredictable, unreasonable, whimsical, wilful.
OPPOSITES: SEE **methodical, rational**.
2 *an arbitrary show of force.* absolute, autocratic, despotic, dictatorial, high-handed, imperious, summary, tyrannical, tyrannous.

arbitrate verb
to arbitrate in a dispute. adjudicate, decide
the outcome, intercede, judge, make peace,
mediate, negotiate, pass judgement, referee,
settle, umpire.

arbitration noun
*The arbitration of an independent judge
settled the dispute.* adjudication, decision,
[*informal*] good offices, intercession,
judgement, mediation, negotiation,
settlement.

arbitrator noun
adjudicator, arbiter, go-between,
intermediary, judge, mediator, middleman,
negotiator, ombudsman, peacemaker,
referee, [*informal*] trouble-shooter, umpire.

arch noun
arc, archway, bridge, SEE **curve** noun, vault.

arch verb
The cat arched its back. arc, bend, bow,
curve.

archaic adjective SEE **old-fashioned**.

archetype noun
classic, example, ideal, model, original,
paradigm, pattern, precursor, prototype,
standard.

archives noun
*Historians searched the archives for
information.* annals, chronicles, documents,
history, libraries, memorials, museums,
papers, records, registers.

archivist noun
curator, historian, researcher.

ardent adjective
ardent kisses. SEE **fervent**.

arduous adjective
arduous work. back-breaking, daunting,
demanding, difficult, exhausting, fatiguing,
formidable, gruelling, hard, harsh, heavy,
herculean, [*informal*] killing, laborious,
onerous, punishing, rigorous, severe,
strenuous, taxing, tough, uphill, wearisome.
OPPOSITES: SEE **easy**.

area noun
1 *an area of land or water.* breadth, expanse,
extent, patch, sector, sheet, space, stretch,
surface, tract, width.
2 *an urban area.* district, environment,
environs, locality, neighbourhood, part,
precinct, province, region, sector, terrain,
territory, vicinity, zone.
3 *an area of study.* field, sphere, subject.

arena noun
a sports arena. amphitheatre, field, ground,
park, pitch, playing area, ring, rink,
stadium.

arguable adjective SEE **debatable**.

argue verb
1 *Whenever I make a suggestion you argue!*
[*informal*] bandy words, bicker, demur,
differ, disagree, dispute, dissent,
expostulate, fall out, feud, fight, have an
argument [SEE **argument**], object, protest,
quarrel, remonstrate, squabble, take
exception, wrangle.
OPPOSITES: SEE **agree**.
2 *He argued over the price.* bargain, haggle.
3 *The lawyer argued that the accused was
innocent.* assert, claim, contend,
demonstrate, maintain, prove, reason, show,
suggest.

argument noun
1 *a violent argument.* altercation, clash,
controversy, difference, disagreement,
dispute, expostulation, feud, fight, quarrel,
remonstration, row, [*informal*] set-to,
squabble, wrangle.
2 *a civilized argument.* consultation, debate,
defence, deliberation, [*formal*] dialectic,
discussion, exposition, polemic, reasoning.
3 *Did you follow the argument of the lecture?*
abstract, case, contention, gist, hypothesis,
idea, line of reasoning, outline, plot,
summary, synopsis, theme, thesis, view.

argumentative adjective SEE **quarrelsome**.

arid adjective
1 *arid desert.* barren, desert, dry, fruitless,
infertile, lifeless, parched, sterile, torrid,
unproductive, waste, waterless.
OPPOSITES: SEE **fruitful**.
2 *an arid subject.* boring, dreary, dull,
pointless, tedious, uninspired,
uninteresting, vapid.
OPPOSITES: SEE **interesting**.

arise verb
1 *Perhaps the matter won't arise.* SEE **appear**,
come up, crop up.
2 *We arose at dawn.* SEE **rise** verb.

aristocratic adjective
an old aristocratic family. [*informal*] blue-
blooded, courtly, élite, gentle, highborn,
lordly, noble, patrician, princely, royal,
thoroughbred, titled, upperclass.

arm noun
appendage, bough, branch, extension, limb,
offshoot, projection.

arm verb
We armed ourselves with sticks. equip,
fortify, furnish, provide, supply.

armed services

VARIOUS GROUPS OF FIGHTING MEN: air
force, army, battalion, brigade, cavalry,
cohort, company, corps, fleet, foreign legion,

garrison, infantry, legion, militia, navy, patrol, platoon, rearguard, regiment, reinforcements, squad, squadron, task-force, vanguard.
SERVICEMEN & WOMEN INCLUDE: aircraftman, aircraftwoman, cavalryman, commando, infantryman, marine, mercenary, paratrooper, recruit, sailor, soldier, [plural] troops.
SEE ALSO: **fighter, officer, rank** noun.

armistice noun
An armistice ended the fighting. agreement, cease-fire, entente, league, moratorium, pact, peace, suspension of hostilities, treaty, truce, understanding.

armour noun
a knight's armour. chainmail, mail, protection.
PARTS OF MEDIEVAL ARMOUR: breastplate, gauntlet, greave, habergeon, helmet, visor.

armoury noun
an armoury of weapons. ammunition-dump, arsenal, depot, magazine, ordnance depot, stockpile.

army noun SEE armed services.
RANKS IN THE ARMY: SEE **rank** noun.

aroma noun
bouquet, fragrance, odour, perfume, scent, smell, whiff.

arouse verb
The controversial plan aroused strong feelings. SEE **cause** verb, kindle, quicken, provoke, spark off, stimulate, stir up, [informal] whip up.
OPPOSITES: SEE **allay**.

arrange verb
1 *to arrange flowers. to arrange information.* adjust, align, array, categorize, classify, collate, display, dispose, distribute, grade, group, lay out, line up, marshal, order, organize, [informal] pigeon-hole, position, put in order, put out, range, rank, set out, sift, sort, sort out, space out, systematize, tabulate, tidy up.
2 *to arrange an outing.* contrive, coordinate, devise, fix, manage, organize, plan, prepare, see to, settle, set up.

arrangement noun
1 *the arrangement of the furniture in a room. the arrangement of words on a page.* adjustment, alignment, SEE **array** noun, design, display, disposition, distribution, grouping, layout, marshalling, organization, planning, setting out, spacing, tabulation.
2 *a business arrangement.* agreement, bargain, compact, contract, deal, pact, scheme, settlement, terms, understanding.
3 *a musical arrangement.* adaptation,

harmonization, orchestration, setting, version.

array noun
a gleaming array of vintage cars. arrangement, assemblage, SEE **collection**, demonstration, display, exhibition, formation, [informal] line-up, muster, panoply, parade, presentation, show, spectacle.

arrest verb
1 *A landslide arrested our progress.* bar, block, check, delay, end, halt, hinder, impede, inhibit, interrupt, obstruct, prevent, retard, slow, stem, stop.
2 *The police arrested the suspect.* apprehend, [informal] book, capture, catch, [informal] collar, detain, [informal] have up (*They had me up for speeding*), hold, [informal] nab, [informal] nick, [informal] pinch, restrain, [informal] run in, seize, take into custody, take prisoner.

arrival noun
1 *A crowd awaited the star's arrival.* advent, appearance, approach, coming, entrance, homecoming, landing, return, touchdown.
2 *Have you met the new arrivals yet?* caller, newcomer, visitor.

arrive verb
When is she due to arrive? appear, come, disembark, drive up, enter, get in, land, [informal] roll in, [informal] roll up, show up, touch down, turn up.
to arrive at *We arrived at the terminus.* attain, come to, get to, [informal] make, reach.

arrogant adjective
an arrogant manner. boastful, bumptious, cavalier, [informal] cocky, conceited, condescending, disdainful, haughty, [informal] high and mighty, high-handed, imperious, insolent, lordly, overbearing, pompous, presumptuous, proud, scornful, self-important, snobbish, [informal] stuck-up, supercilious, superior, vain.
OPPOSITES: SEE **modest**.

arsonist noun
fire-raiser, incendiary, pyromaniac.

art noun
1 artistry, artwork, craft, craftsmanship, draughtsmanship.

ARTS AND CRAFTS INCLUDE: architecture, batik, cameo, caricature, carpentry, cartoon, cloisonné, collage, commercial art, crochet, draughtsmanship, drawing, embroidery, enamelling, engraving, etching, fashion design, graphics, handicraft, illustration, jewellery, knitting, linocut, lithography, marquetry, metalwork, mobiles, modelling, monoprint, mosaic, needlework, origami, SEE **painting**, patchwork, photography, portraiture, pottery, print, printing, SEE **sculpture**, sewing, sketching, spinning, stencilling, stone carving, weaving, wicker-work, woodcut, woodwork.

2 *There's an art in lighting a bonfire.* aptitude, cleverness, craft, dexterity, expertise, facility, knack, proficiency, skilfulness, skill, talent, technique, touch, trick.

artful adjective
[*usually uncomplimentary*] *That was an artful trick!* astute, canny, clever, crafty, cunning, deceitful, designing, devious, [*informal*] fly, [*informal*] foxy, ingenious, knowing, scheming, shrewd, skilful, sly, smart, subtle, tricky, wily.
OPPOSITES: SEE **ingenuous**.

article noun
1 *Have you any unwanted articles for the jumble sale?* SEE **thing**.
2 *Did you read my article in the magazine?* SEE **writing**.

articulate adjective
an articulate speaker. clear, coherent, comprehensible, distinct, eloquent, expressive, fluent, [*uncomplimentary*] glib, intelligible, lucid, understandable, vocal.
OPPOSITES: SEE **inarticulate**.

artificial adjective
1 *an artificial beard. an artificial cheeriness.* affected, assumed, bogus, contrived, counterfeit, factitious, fake, false, feigned, imitation, mock, [*informal*] phoney, [*informal*] put on, pretended, pseudo, sham, simulated, spurious, unreal.
OPPOSITES: SEE **genuine**.
2 *artificial fertilizers.* fabricated, made-up, man-made, manufactured, synthetic, unnatural.
OPPOSITES: SEE **natural**.

artist noun
1 craftsman, craftswoman, designer.

ARTISTS AND CRAFTSMEN INCLUDE:
architect, blacksmith, caricaturist, carpenter, cartoonist, commercial artist, draughtsman, draughtswoman, engraver, goldsmith, graphic designer, illustrator, mason, miniaturist, old master, painter, photographer, portrait painter, potter, printer, sculptor, silversmith, smith, weaver.

2 *a music-hall artist.* SEE **performer**.

artistic adjective
an artistic arrangement of flowers. aesthetic, attractive, beautiful, creative, cultured,

decorative, imaginative, ornamental, tasteful.
OPPOSITES: SEE **crude, ugly**.

ascend verb
1 *to ascend a hill.* climb, come up, go up, mount, move up, scale.
2 *The plane ascended.* defy gravity, fly up, levitate, lift off, rise, soar, take off.
3 *The road ascends to the church.* slope up.
OPPOSITES: SEE **descend**.

ascent noun
a steep ascent. ascension, climb, elevation, gradient, hill, incline, ramp, rise, slope.
OPPOSITES: SEE **descent**.

ascertain verb
We ascertained that our passports were in order. confirm, determine, discover, establish, find out, identify, learn, make certain, make sure, settle, verify.

ascribe verb SEE **attribute**.

ash noun
ash from a fire. burnt remains, cinders, clinker, embers.

ashamed adjective
1 *ashamed of doing wrong.* apologetic, blushing, chagrined, chastened, conscience-stricken, contrite, discomfited, distressed, guilty, humbled, humiliated, mortified, penitent, red-faced, remorseful, repentant, rueful, shamefaced, sorry, upset.
OPPOSITES: SEE **unrepentant**.
2 *too ashamed to take his clothes off.* abashed, bashful, demure, diffident, embarrassed, modest, prudish, self-conscious, sheepish, shy.
OPPOSITES: SEE **shameless**.

ask verb
1 *to ask a question. to ask for help.* appeal, apply, badger, beg, beseech, [*formal*] catechize, crave, demand, enquire, entreat, implore, importune, inquire, interrogate, petition, plead, pose a question, pray, press, query, question, quiz, request, seek, solicit, sue, supplicate.
2 *to ask someone to a party.* [*old-fashioned*] bid, invite, [*formal*] request the pleasure of the company of.
to ask for *He asked for trouble!* attract, cause, court, encourage, generate, incite, provoke, [*informal*] stir up, tempt.

asleep adjective
asleep in bed. comatose, [*informal*] dead to the world, dormant, dozing, [*informal*] fast off, [*informal*] having a nap, hibernating, inactive, inattentive, napping, resting, sedated, sleeping, slumbering, snoozing, [*informal*] sound off, unconscious, under sedation.
OPPOSITES: SEE **awake**.

aspect noun
1 *There's an aspect of this affair I don't understand.* angle, circumstance, detail, facet, feature, side, standpoint.
2 *The place had a peaceful aspect. He had a belligerent aspect.* air, appearance, attitude, bearing, countenance, demeanour, expression, face, look, manner, mien, visage.
3 *The house has a southern aspect.* direction, orientation, outlook, position, prospect, situation, view.

aspiration noun SEE **ambition**.

aspire verb
to aspire to *He aspires to the top position in the business.* aim for, crave, desire, dream of, have ambitions to or for, hope for, long for, pursue, seek, set your sights on, strive after, want, wish for, yearn for.

aspiring adjective
an aspiring politician. budding, [*informal*] hopeful, intending, potential, [*informal*] would-be.

assail verb
They assailed us with missiles. assault, SEE **attack** verb, bombard, pelt, set on.

assassinate verb SEE **kill**.

assassination noun SEE **murder** noun.

assault noun, verb SEE **attack** noun, verb.

assemble verb
1 *A crowd assembled.* accumulate, collect, come together, congregate, converge, crowd together, flock together, gather, group, herd, join up, meet, rally round, swarm, throng round.
2 *We assembled our luggage. The general assembled his troops.* amass, bring together, convene, gather, get together, marshal, mobilize, muster, pile up, rally, round up.
OPPOSITES: SEE **disperse**.
3 *These cars are assembled in Britain.* build, construct, erect, fabricate, fit together, make, manufacture, piece together, produce, put together.
OPPOSITES: SEE **dismantle**.

assembly noun
1 *a political assembly.* conclave, conference, congregation [= *assembly for worship*], congress, convention, convocation, council, gathering, SEE **meeting**, parliament, rally, synod [= *church assembly*].
2 *an assembly of people.* SEE **crowd** noun.

assent noun
We need the Head's assent before we do anything. acceptance, accord, acquiescence, agreement, approbation, approval, compliance, consent, [*informal*] go-ahead, permission, sanction, willingness.
OPPOSITES: SEE **refusal**.

assent verb
He assented to our proposals. accede, accept, acquiesce, agree, approve, be willing, comply, concede, concur, consent, express agreement, give assent, say 'yes', submit, yield.

assert verb
The accused asserted that he was innocent. affirm, allege, argue, asseverate, attest, claim, contend, declare, emphasize, insist, maintain, proclaim, profess, protest, state, stress, swear, testify.
to assert yourself *Don't give in: assert yourself!* be assertive [SEE **assertive**], be resolute, insist, make demands, persist, stand firm, [*informal*] stick to your guns.

assertive adjective
His assertive personality dominated the meeting. aggressive, assured, authoritative, bold, confident, decided, decisive, dogmatic, domineering, emphatic, firm, forceful, insistent, [*uncomplimentary*] opinionated, positive, [*uncomplimentary*] pushy, self-assured, strong, strong-willed, [*uncomplimentary*] stubborn, uncompromising.
OPPOSITES: SEE **submissive**.

assess verb
The garage assessed the damage to the car. appraise, assay (*quality of metals*), calculate, compute, consider, determine, estimate, evaluate, fix, gauge, judge, price, reckon, review, [*informal*] size up, value, weigh up, work out.

asset noun
Good health is a great asset. advantage, aid, blessing, benefit, boon, [*informal*] godsend, good, help, profit, support.
assets capital, estate, funds, goods, holdings, means, money, possessions, property, resources, savings, securities, wealth, [*informal*] worldly goods.

assign verb
1 *He assigned the most responsible jobs to experienced people.* allocate, allot, apportion, consign, dispense, distribute, give, hand over, share out.
2 *He assigned me to the sweeping up.* appoint, choose, consign, delegate, designate, nominate, put down, select, specify, stipulate.
3 *I assign my success to pure luck.* accredit, ascribe, attribute, credit.

assignment noun
We were given a hard assignment. duty, errand, job, mission, post, project, responsibility, task, work.

assist verb
We'll do the job more quickly if you assist us.
abet, advance, aid, back, benefit, boost,
collaborate, co-operate, facilitate, further,
help, [*informal*] lend a hand, [*informal*]
rally round, reinforce, relieve, second,
serve, succour, support, sustain.
OPPOSITES: SEE **hinder**.

assistance noun
aid, backing, collaboration, co-operation,
contribution, encouragement, help,
patronage, sponsorship, subsidy, succour,
support.
OPPOSITES: SEE **hindrance**.

assistant noun
abettor, accessory, accomplice, acolyte, aide,
ally, associate, auxiliary, backer,
collaborator, colleague, companion,
confederate, deputy, helper, helpmate,
[*informal*] henchman, mainstay,
[*uncomplimentary*] minion, partner,
[*informal*] right-hand man or woman,
second, second-in-command, stand-by,
subordinate, supporter.

associate verb
1 *I hope you don't associate with that mob!*
ally yourself, be friends, consort, fraternize,
[*informal*] gang up, mix, side, socialize.
2 *I don't associate sunbathing with the North
Pole.* bracket together, connect, put
together, relate, [*informal*] tie up.

association noun
1 *The association between us lasted many
years.* SEE **friendship**, **relationship**.
2 *an association of youth clubs.* affiliation,
alliance, amalgamation, body, brotherhood,
cartel, clique, club, coalition, combination,
company, confederation, consortium, co-
operative, corporation, federation,
fellowship, group, league, marriage, merger,
organization, partnership, party, society,
syndicate, trust, union.

assorted adjective SEE various.

assortment noun
an assortment of sandwiches. array, choice,
collection, diversity, medley, mélange,
miscellany, mixture, selection, variety.

assume verb
1 *I assume you'd like some tea.* believe,
deduce, expect, guess, [*informal*] have a
hunch, have no doubt, imagine, infer,
presume, presuppose, suppose, surmise,
suspect, take for granted, think, understand.
2 *The new boss assumes his duties next week.*
accept, embrace, take on, undertake.
3 *She assumed a disguise.* acquire, adopt,
don, dress up in, feign, put on, wear.

assumption noun
*My assumption is that we can average 40
miles an hour.* belief, conjecture,
expectation, guess, hypothesis, premise or
premiss, supposition, surmise, theory.

assure verb
1 *He assured me the work would be done by
Friday.* SEE **promise** verb.
2 *He wanted to assure himself that all was
well.* SEE **reassure**.

astonish verb
amaze, astound, baffle, bewilder, confound,
daze, [*informal*] dazzle, dumbfound,
electrify, flabbergast, leave speechless,
nonplus, shock, stagger, startle, stun,
stupefy, surprise, take aback, take by
surprise, [*informal*] take your breath away,
[*slang*] wow.

astound verb SEE astonish.

astray adverb
to go astray. adrift, amiss, awry, lost, off
course, [*informal*] off the rails, wide of the
mark, wrong.

astronaut noun
cosmonaut, space-traveller.

astronomy noun
star-gazing.

SOME ASTRONOMICAL TERMS: asteroid,
comet, constellation, cosmos, eclipse,
galaxy, meteor, meteorite, moon, nebula,
nova, planet, pulsar, quasar, satellite,
shooting star, space, sun, supernova,
universe, world.

---

astute adjective
an astute tactician. an astute move. acute,
adroit, artful, canny, clever, crafty,
cunning, discerning, [*informal*] fly,
[*informal*] foxy, ingenious, intelligent,
knowing, observant, perceptive,
perspicacious, sagacious, sharp, shrewd,
sly, subtle, wily.
OPPOSITES: SEE **stupid**.

asylum noun
The travellers sought asylum from the storm.
cover, haven, refuge, retreat, safety,
sanctuary, shelter.

asymmetrical adjective
asymmetrical shapes. awry, crooked,
distorted, irregular, lop-sided, unbalanced,
uneven, [*informal*] wonky.
OPPOSITES: SEE **symmetrical**.

atheist noun
pagan, unbeliever.
OPPOSITES: SEE **believer**.

athletic adjective
an athletic person. athletic pursuits.
acrobatic, active, energetic, fit, in condition,
muscular, powerful, robust, sinewy,
[*informal*] sporty, [*informal*] strapping,
strong, sturdy, vigorous, well-built, wiry.
OPPOSITES: SEE **feeble**.

athletics noun
OTHER SPORTS: SEE **sport**.

VARIOUS ATHLETIC EVENTS: cross-country,
decathlon, discus, field events, high jump,
hurdles, javelin, long jump, marathon,
pentathlon, pole-vault, relay race, running,
shot, sprinting, triple jump.

---

atmosphere noun
1 *We still let harmful gases escape into the
atmosphere.* aerospace, air, ether, heavens,
ionosphere, sky, stratosphere,
troposphere.
2 *There was a happy atmosphere at the party.*
ambience, aura, character, climate,
environment, feeling, mood, spirit, tone,
undercurrent, [*informal*] vibes, vibrations.

atom noun
[*informal*] bit, crumb, grain, iota, jot,
molecule, morsel, particle, scrap, speck, spot,
trace.

atone verb
to atone for be punished for, compensate
for, do penance for, expiate, make amends
for, make reparation for, make up for, pay
for, pay the penalty for, pay the price for,
recompense for, redeem yourself, redress (*to
redress a wrong*).

atrocious adjective
an atrocious attack. abominable, barbaric,
bloodthirsty, brutal, brutish, callous, cruel,
diabolical, evil, execrable, fiendish, grim,
hateful, heartless, hideous, horrifying,
inhuman, merciless, monstrous, outrageous,
sadistic, savage, terrible, vicious, vile,
villainous, wicked.

attach verb
1 *to attach one thing to another.* add, affix,
anchor, append, bind, combine, connect,
couple, SEE **fasten**, fix, join, link, secure,
stick, tie, unite, weld.
2 *to attach importance to something.* ascribe,
assign, associate, attribute, impute, place,
put, relate to.
OPPOSITES: SEE **detach**.

attached adjective
The twins are very attached to each other.
affectionate, close, dear, devoted, fond,
friendly, loving, loyal, warm.

attack noun
1 *an attack against the enemy.* aggression,
ambush, assault, [*legal*] battery, blitz,
bombardment, broadside, cannonade,
charge, counter-attack, foray, incursion,
invasion, offensive, onslaught, raid, rush,
sortie, strike.
2 *She was upset by his attack on her character.*
abuse, censure, criticism, diatribe,
impugnment, invective, outburst, tirade.
3 *a heart attack. an attack of coughing.* bout,
convulsion, fit, outbreak, paroxysm,
seizure, spasm, stroke, [*informal*] turn.

attack verb
1 *to attack an enemy.* ambush, assail, assault,
[*informal*] beat up, [*informal*] blast,
bombard, charge, counterattack, descend on,
[*informal*] do over, fall on, fly at, invade,
jump on, lash out at, [*informal*] lay into,
mob, mug, [*informal*] pitch into, pounce on,
raid, rush, set about, set on, storm, strike at,
[*informal*] wade into.
2 *He attacked her reputation.* abuse, censure,
criticize, denounce, impugn, inveigh
against, libel, malign, round on, slander,
snipe at, traduce, vilify.
OPPOSITES: SEE **defend**.

attacker noun
aggressor, assailant, critic, detractor,
enemy, SEE **fighter**, intruder, invader,
mugger, opponent, persecutor, raider,
slanderer.

attacking adjective SEE **aggressive**.

attain verb
to attain your objective. accomplish, achieve,
acquire, arrive at, complete, earn, fulfil,
gain, get, grasp, [*informal*] make, obtain,
[*informal*] pull (it) off, procure, reach,
realize, secure, touch, win.

attempt noun
You made a good attempt. assault (*an assault
on a mountain*), bid, endeavour, [*informal*]
go (*Let me have a go*), start, try.

attempt verb
We attempted to beat the record. aim, aspire,
do your best, endeavour, essay, exert
yourself, [*informal*] have a go, make an
assault, make a bid, make an effort, put
yourself out, seek, [*informal*] spare no effort,
strive, [*informal*] sweat blood, tackle, try,
undertake, venture.

attend verb
1 *Attend to what I say.* concentrate on, follow
carefully, hear, heed, listen, mark, mind,
note, notice, observe, pay attention, think
about, watch.
2 *I attended an interview.* appear at, be
present at, go to, present yourself at, visit.
3 *The bride was attended by two bridesmaids.*
accompany, assist, chaperon, escort, follow,

guard, usher, wait on.
to attend to *Nurses attended to the wounded.*
care for, help, look after, make
arrangements for, mind, minister to, nurse,
see to, take care of, tend.

attention noun
1 *Give proper attention to your work.*
alertness, awareness, care, concentration,
concern, diligence, heed, notice, recognition,
thought, vigilance.
2 *Thank you for your kind attention.*
attentiveness, civility, consideration,
courtesy, gallantry, good manners,
kindness, politeness, regard, respect,
thoughtfulness.

attentive adjective SEE **alert** adjective,
polite.

attire noun
accoutrements, apparel, array, clothes,
clothing, costume, dress, finery, garb,
garments, [*informal*] gear, [*old-fashioned*]
habit, outfit, [*old-fashioned*] raiment, wear,
weeds (*widow's weeds*).

attitude noun
1 *a light-hearted attitude.* air, approach,
bearing, behaviour, demeanour,
disposition, frame of mind, manner, mien,
mood, posture, stance.
2 *What's your attitude towards smoking?*
belief, feeling, opinion, outlook, position,
standpoint, thought, view.

attract verb
Baby animals attract crowds at the zoo.
Magnets attract iron. allure, appeal to,
beguile, bewitch, bring in, captivate, charm,
decoy, drag, draw, enchant, entice,
fascinate, induce, interest, inveigle, lure,
magnetize, pull, seduce, tempt, tug at.
OPPOSITES: SEE **repel**.

attractive adjective
an attractive person. an attractive dress.
agreeable, alluring, adorable, appealing,
artistic, beautiful, bewitching, [*informal*]
bonny, captivating, [*informal*] catchy
(*tune*), charming, [*informal*] cute, desirable,
enchanting, endearing, engaging, enticing,
fascinating, fetching, glamorous, good-
looking, gorgeous, handsome, hypnotic,
interesting, inviting, irresistible, lovable,
lovely, magnetic, personable, pleasant,
pleasing, [*usually negative*] prepossessing
(*not very prepossessing*), pretty, quaint,
seductive, stunning, [*informal*] taking,
tempting, winsome.
OPPOSITES: SEE **repulsive**.

attribute verb
To what do you attribute your success?
accredit, ascribe, assign, blame, charge,
credit, impute, put down, refer, trace back.

atypical adjective SEE **abnormal**,
uncharacteristic, unrepresentative.
OPPOSITES: SEE **typical**.

audacious adjective SEE **bold**.

audacity noun
1 *We admired her audacity.* SEE **bravery**.
2 [*uncomplimentary*] *I was amazed that she
had the audacity to ask for money.* [*informal*]
cheek, effrontery, forwardness,
impertinence, impudence,
presumptuousness, rashness, [*informal*]
sauce, temerity.

audible adjective
an audible voice. clear, detectable, distinct,
high, loud, noisy, strong, recognizable.
OPPOSITES: SEE **inaudible**.

audience noun
assembly, congregation, crowd, gathering,
the house (*in a theatre*), listeners, meeting,
onlookers, ratings [= *numbers in a TV
audience*], spectators, [*informal*] turn-out,
viewers.

audio equipment noun

AUDIO EQUIPMENT: amplifier, cassette
recorder, earphones, gramophone,
headphones, hi-fi, high-fidelity equipment,
juke-box, loudspeaker, microphone, music-
centre, personal stereo, pick-up, [*old-
fashioned*] phonograph, radio, [*old-
fashioned*] radiogram, recorder, record-
player, stereo, stylus, tape-deck, tape-
recorder, tuner, turntable, [*informal*]
walkman.

---

audio-visual adjective

TEACHING AND STUDY AIDS: SEE **audio
equipment**, epidiascope, film-projector,
interactive video, language laboratory,
microfiche-reader, microfilm-reader,
overhead-projector, slide-projector, tape-
slide equipment, television, VCR, video,
video-disc equipment.

---

augment verb
to augment your resources. add to, amplify,
boost, eke out, enlarge, expand, extend, fill
out, grow, increase, intensify, magnify,
make larger, multiply, raise, reinforce,
strengthen, supplement, swell.
OPPOSITES: SEE **decrease** verb.

augur verb
The signs augur well for tomorrow's weather.
bode, forebode, foreshadow, forewarn, give
an omen, herald, portend, predict, promise,
prophesy, signal.

auspicious adjective
auspicious signs. [*informal*] hopeful,
positive, promising.
OPPOSITES: SEE **ominous**.

austere adjective
1 *an austere person.* cold, exacting,
forbidding, formal, grave, hard, harsh, self-
disciplined, serious, severe, stern,
[*informal*] straightlaced, strict.
OPPOSITES: SEE **genial**.
2 *an austere life-style.* abstemious, ascetic,
chaste, economical, frugal, hermit-like,
parsimonious, puritanical, restrained,
rigorous, self-denying, sober, spartan,
thrifty, unpampered.
OPPOSITES: SEE **lavish**.
3 *an austere building.* modest, plain, simple,
unadorned, unfussy.
OPPOSITES: SEE **elaborate**.

authentic adjective
1 *an authentic antique.* actual, bona fide,
certain, genuine, legitimate, original, real,
true, valid.
OPPOSITES: SEE **fake** adjective.
2 *an authentic account.* accurate,
authoritative, dependable, factual, honest,
reliable, truthful, veracious.
OPPOSITES: SEE **false**.

author noun
1 *the author of a book, etc.* composer, creator,
dramatist, novelist, playwright, poet,
scriptwriter, SEE **writer**.
2 *the author of an idea.* architect, begetter,
designer, father, founder, initiator,
inventor, maker, mover, organizer,
originator, parent, planner, prime mover,
producer.

authoritarian adjective SEE **bossy**.

authoritative adjective SEE **definitive**.

authority noun
1 *I have the boss's authority to park here.*
approval, authorization, consent, licence,
mandate, permission, permit, sanction,
warrant.
2 *If you're the boss, you can assert your
authority.* charge, command, control,
domination, force, influence, jurisdiction,
might, power, prerogative, right,
sovereignty, supremacy, sway, weight.
3 *He's an authority on steam trains.*
[*informal*] boffin, connoisseur (of), expert,
specialist.
the authorities administration,
government, management, officialdom,
[*informal*] the powers that be.

authorize verb
*The director authorized the purchase of a
computer.* accede to, agree to, allow,
approve, [*informal*] back, commission,

consent to, empower, endorse, entitle,
legalize, license, mandate, [*informal*] OK,
pass, permit, ratify, [*informal*] rubber-
stamp, sanction, sign the order or warrant,
validate.

automated adjective
an automated production-line. SEE **automatic**,
computerized, electronic, programmable,
programmed, robotic.

automatic adjective
1 *an automatic reaction.* habitual, impulsive,
instinctive, involuntary, natural, reflex,
spontaneous, unconscious, unintentional,
unthinking.
2 *an automatic machine.* automated,
computerized, mechanical, programmed,
robotic, self-regulating, unmanned.

autonomous adjective
an autonomous country. free, independent,
self-determining, self-governing, sovereign.

auxiliary adjective
auxiliary engines. additional, ancillary,
assisting, [*informal*] back-up, emergency,
extra, helping, reserve, secondary, spare,
subsidiary, substitute, supplementary,
supporting, supportive.

available adjective
available cash. accessible, at hand,
convenient, disposable, free, handy,
obtainable, procurable, ready, to hand,
uncommitted, unengaged, unused, usable.
OPPOSITES: SEE **inaccessible**.

avaricious adjective SEE **greedy, miserly**.

avenge verb
to avenge a wrong someone has done to you.
exact punishment for, [*informal*] get your
own back for, repay, requite, take revenge
for.

average adjective
[*informal*] *an average sort of day.* common,
commonplace, everyday, indifferent,
mediocre, medium, middling, moderate,
normal, ordinary, passable, regular,
[*informal*] run of the mill, [*informal*] so-so,
typical, usual.
OPPOSITES: SEE **extraordinary**.

average noun
the mathematical average. mean, mid-point.

average verb
equalize, even out, normalize, standardize.

aversion noun SEE **hostility**.

avert verb
to avert disaster. to avert a blow. change the
course of, deflect, draw off, fend off, parry,
prevent, stave off, turn aside, turn away,
ward off.

avid adjective SEE **eager, greedy**.

avoid verb
to avoid a blow. to avoid a subject. to avoid work. abstain from, be absent from, [*informal*] beg the question, [*informal*] bypass, circumvent, dodge, [*informal*] duck, elude, escape, eschew, evade, fend off, find a way round, get out of the way of, [*informal*] get round, [*informal*] give a wide berth to, help (*I couldn't help hearing*), ignore, keep away from, keep clear of, refrain from, run away from, shirk, shun, sidestep, skirt round, [*informal*] skive [= *avoid work*], steer clear of.
OPPOSITES: SEE **seek**.

await verb
I await your reply. be ready for, expect, hope for, lie in wait for, look out for, wait for.

awake adjective
Are you awake? alert, attentive, aware, conscious, lively, observant, on the lookout, open-eyed, ready, restless, sleepless, vigilant, wakeful, watchful, wide awake.
OPPOSITES: SEE **asleep**.

awaken verb
The alarm awakened us. The TV programme awakened my interest. alert, animate, arouse, awake, call, excite, kindle, revive, rouse, stimulate, stir up, wake, waken.
OPPOSITES: SEE **calm** verb, **sedate** verb.

award verb
They awarded him first prize. accord, allot, assign, bestow, confer, endow, give, grant, hand over, present.

aware adjective
aware of *Are you aware of the rules?* acquainted with, alive to, appreciative of, attentive to, cognisant of, conscious of, conversant with, familiar with, heedful of, informed about, knowledgeable about, mindful of, observant of, responsive to, sensible of, sensitive to, versed in.
OPPOSITES: SEE **ignorant, insensitive**.

awe noun
We watched in awe as the volcano erupted. admiration, amazement, apprehension, dread, fear, respect, reverence, terror, veneration, wonder.

awe-inspiring adjective
The erupting volcano was an awe-inspiring sight. amazing, awesome, [*old-fashioned*] awful, breathtaking, dramatic, grand, imposing, impressive, magnificent, [*informal*] marvellous, overwhelming, solemn, [*informal*] stunning, stupendous, sublime, [*informal*] wonderful, [*poetic*] wondrous.
OPPOSITES: SEE **insignificant**.

awesome adjective SEE **awe-inspiring**.

awful adjective
1 [*old-fashioned*] *The erupting volcano was an awful sight.* SEE **awe-inspiring**.
2 *awful handwriting.* SEE **bad**.
3 *an awful crime.* SEE **hateful**.

awkward adjective
1 *an awkward thing to handle.* bulky, cumbersome, inconvenient, unmanageable, unwieldy.
OPPOSITES: SEE **convenient**.
2 *awkward with your hands.* blundering, bungling, clumsy, gauche, gawky, [*informal*] ham-fisted, inept, inexpert, maladroit, uncoordinated, ungainly, unskilful.
OPPOSITES: SEE **skilful**.
3 *an awkward problem.* annoying, difficult, perplexing, thorny, [*informal*] ticklish, troublesome, trying, vexatious, vexing.
OPPOSITES: SEE **straightforward**.
4 *an awkward silence.* embarrassing, uncomfortable, uneasy.
OPPOSITES: SEE **reassuring**.
5 *an awkward customer.* [*informal*] bloody-minded, disobliging, exasperating, obstinate, perverse, [*informal*] prickly, rude, stubborn, touchy, uncooperative.
OPPOSITES: SEE **co-operative**.
6 *an awkward pupil.* [*slang*] bolshie, defiant, disobedient, intractable, misbehaving, naughty, rebellious, refractory, undisciplined, unruly, wayward.
OPPOSITES: SEE **well-behaved**.

axe noun
battleaxe, chopper, cleaver, hatchet, tomahawk.

axe verb
They axed our bus service. The firm axed 20 workers. cancel, cut, discharge, discontinue, dismiss, eliminate, get rid of, [*informal*] give the chop to, make redundant, [*euphemistic*] rationalize, remove, sack, terminate, withdraw.

Bb

baby noun
babe, child, infant, papoose, toddler, [*uncomplimentary*] weakling.

babyish adjective
[All these words are uncomplimentary. Compare *childlike*.] childish, immature, infantile, juvenile, puerile.
OPPOSITES: SEE **mature**.

back adjective
the back legs of an animal. dorsal (*dorsal
fin*), end, hind, hinder, hindmost, last, rear,
rearmost.
OPPOSITES: SEE **front** adjective.

back noun
1 *the back of a train.* end, rear, tail-end.
2 *the back of a ship.* stern.
3 *the back of an envelope.* reverse, verso.
4 *the back of an animal.* hindquarters,
posterior, rear, spine, tail.
OPPOSITES: SEE **front** noun.

back verb
1 *to back into a corner.* back away, back off,
back-pedal, backtrack, [*informal*] beat a
retreat, give way, go backwards, move back,
recede, recoil, retire, retreat, reverse.
OPPOSITES: SEE **advance** verb.
2 *to back a plan.* SEE **support** verb.
3 *to back horses.* SEE **gamble** verb.
to back down SEE **retreat** verb.
to back out SEE **withdraw.**

backbone noun
spine, the vertebrae.

backer noun
SEE **sponsor** noun.

background noun
1 *the background of a picture.* context,
setting, surroundings.
2 *the background to the Second World War.*
circumstances, context, history, [*informal*]
lead-up.
3 *a family with a military background.*
breeding, culture, education, experience,
[*formal*] milieu, tradition, upbringing.

backing noun
1 *We had the backing of the Principal.* aid,
assistance, encouragement, endorsement,
help, loan, patronage, sponsorship, subsidy,
support.
2 *a musical backing.* accompaniment,
orchestration, scoring.

backward adjective
1 *a backward movement.* regressive,
retrograde, retrogressive, reverse.
OPPOSITES: SEE **forward.**
2 *a backward pupil.* handicapped, immature,
late-starting, retarded, slow, SEE **stupid**,
subnormal, underdeveloped, undeveloped.
OPPOSITES: SEE **precocious.**
3 *Don't be backward—ask for his autograph.*
afraid, bashful, coy, diffident, hesitant,
inhibited, modest, reluctant, reserved,
reticent, self-effacing, shy, timid,
unforthcoming.
OPPOSITES: SEE **confident.**

bacon noun
gammon, ham, rashers.

bacteria noun SEE **microorganism.**

bad adjective
[We use the word *bad* to describe almost
anything we don't like. There are, therefore,
hundreds of possible synonyms, depending
on the context in which the word is used. We
give synonyms here for some main senses of
the word, but you can look in other places for
synonyms to suit particular contexts. For
example, in the case of *bad handwriting*, you
might find synonyms under *illegible*; in the
case of *bad visibility*, under *foggy*; and so on.]
1 *a bad man. a bad deed.* abhorrent, base,
beastly, blameworthy, corrupt, criminal, SEE
cruel, dangerous, delinquent, deplorable,
depraved, detestable, evil, guilty, immoral,
infamous, malevolent, malicious, malignant,
mean, mischievous, nasty, naughty,
offensive, regrettable, reprehensible, rotten,
shameful, sinful, unworthy, vicious, vile,
villainous, wicked, wrong.
2 *a bad accident. a bad illness.* appalling,
awful, calamitous, dire, disastrous,
distressing, dreadful, frightful, ghastly,
grave, hair-raising, hideous, horrible,
painful, serious, severe, shocking, terrible,
unfortunate, SEE **unpleasant**, violent.
3 *bad behaviour. a bad driver. bad work.*
abominable, abysmal, appalling, awful,
cheap, [*informal*] chronic, defective,
deficient, diabolical, disgraceful, dreadful,
egregious, execrable, faulty, feeble,
[*informal*] grotty, hopeless, imperfect,
inadequate, incompetent, incorrect,
ineffective, inefficient, inferior, [*informal*]
lousy, pitiful, poor, [*informal*] ropy, shoddy,
[*informal*] sorry (*in a sorry state*),
substandard, unsound, unsatisfactory,
useless, weak, worthless.
4 *bad conditions.* adverse, deleterious,
detrimental, discouraging, [*informal*]
frightful, harmful, harsh, hostile,
inappropriate, inauspicious, prejudicial,
uncongenial, unfortunate, unhelpful,
unpropitious.
5 *bad eggs. a bad smell.* decayed,
decomposing, diseased, foul, loathsome,
mildewed, mouldy, nauseating, noxious,
objectionable, obnoxious, odious, offensive,
polluted, putrid, rancid, repellent,
repulsive, revolting, rotten, sickening,
smelly, sour, spoiled, tainted, vile.
6 *Smoking is bad for you.* SEE **harmful.**
7 *I felt so bad I went to bed.* SEE **ill.**
8 *I feel bad about not phoning.* SEE **sorry.**

badge noun
an identifying badge. chevron, crest, device,
emblem, insignia, logo, mark, medal,
rosette, sign, symbol, token.

bad-tempered adjective
acrimonious, angry, cantankerous,
churlish, crabbed, cross, [*informal*]
crotchety, disgruntled, dyspeptic, gruff,
grumbling, grumpy, hot-tempered, ill-
humoured, ill-tempered, irascible, irritable,
moody, morose, peevish, petulant,
quarrelsome, querulous, rude, short-
tempered, shrewish, snappy, [*informal*]
stroppy, sulky, sullen, testy, truculent.
OPPOSITES: SEE **good-tempered**.

baffle verb
The problem baffled us. [*informal*]
bamboozle, bemuse, bewilder, confound,
confuse, defeat, [*informal*] floor, [*informal*]
flummox, foil, frustrate, mystify, perplex,
puzzle, [*informal*] stump, thwart.

baffling adjective
a baffling problem. bewildering, confusing,
extraordinary, frustrating, inexplicable,
inscrutable, insoluble, mysterious,
mystifying, perplexing, puzzling,
unfathomable.
OPPOSITES: SEE **straightforward**.

bag noun
basket, carrier, carrier-bag, case, SEE
container, handbag, holdall, sack, satchel,
shopping-bag, shoulder-bag.

baggage noun
accoutrements (*of a soldier*), bags,
belongings, cases, [*informal*] gear, [*joking*]
impedimenta, luggage, paraphernalia,
suitcases, trunks.

bait noun
allurement, attraction, bribe, carrot, decoy,
enticement, inducement, lure, temptation.

balance noun
1 *weighed in the balance.* scales, weighing-
machine.
2 *to lose your balance.* equilibrium,
equipoise, poise, stability, steadiness.
3 *We want to get a balance of girls and boys.*
correspondence, equality, equivalence,
evenness, parity, symmetry.
4 *I spend half my wages and put the balance
in the bank.* difference, remainder, residue,
rest, surplus.

balance verb
1 *If I carry one bag in each hand, they balance
each other.* counteract, counterbalance,
counterpoise, equalize, even up, level, make
steady, match, neutralize, offset, parallel,
stabilize, steady.
2 *He balanced ten baskets on his head.* keep,
keep balanced, keep in equilibrium, poise,
steady, support.

balanced adjective
1 *a balanced shape.* even, regular,
symmetrical.

2 *a balanced argument.* even-handed, fair,
impartial.
3 *a balanced personality.* equable, sane,
stable.
OPPOSITES: SEE **unbalanced**.

bale noun
bunch, bundle, pack, package, truss.

bale verb
to bale out *to bale out of an aircraft.* eject,
escape, jump out, parachute down.

ball noun
1 drop, globe, globule, orb, shot, sphere,
spheroid.
2 *Cinderella went to a ball.* dance, disco,
party, social.

ballerina noun
ballet-dancer, dancer.

ballot noun
election, plebiscite, poll, referendum, vote.

balmy adjective
a balmy evening. gentle, mild, peaceful,
pleasant, soft, soothing, summery.

ban noun
a ban on smoking. embargo, moratorium,
prohibition, veto.

ban verb
to ban smoking. banish, bar, debar, disallow,
exclude, forbid, [*formal*] interdict, make
illegal, ostracize, outlaw, prevent, prohibit,
proscribe, put a ban on [SEE **ban** noun],
restrict, stop, suppress, veto.
OPPOSITES: SEE **permit** verb.

banal adjective
an exciting film spoiled by a banal ending.
boring, clichéd, cliché-ridden,
commonplace, [*informal*] corny, dull,
hackneyed, obvious, ordinary, over-used,
pedestrian, platitudinous, predictable,
stereotyped, trite, unimaginative,
uninteresting, unoriginal, vapid.
OPPOSITES: SEE **interesting**.

band noun
1 *a band of colour.* belt, hoop, line, loop,
ribbon, ring, strip, stripe, swathe.
2 *a band of devoted followers.* association,
body, clique, club, company, crew, flock,
gang, group, herd, horde, party, society,
troop.
3 *a concert band.* ensemble, group,
orchestra.
OTHER MUSICAL GROUPS: SEE **music**.

bandit noun
brigand, buccaneer, desperado, footpad,
gangster, gunman, highwayman, hijacker,
marauder, outlaw, pirate, robber, thief.

bandy adjective
bandy-legged, bowed, bow-legged.

bandy verb
Various ideas were bandied about. exchange, interchange, pass, swap, throw, toss.

bang noun
1 *a bang on the head.* blow, [*informal*] box, bump, collision, cuff, hit, knock, punch, slam, smack, stroke, thump, [*slang*] wallop, whack.
2 *a loud bang.* blast, boom, clap, crash, explosion, pop, report, thud, thump.

bang verb
VARIOUS SOUNDS: SEE **sound** noun.

banish verb
1 *He was banished to an island.* deport, eject, evict, exile, expatriate, expel, outlaw, send away, ship away, transport.
2 *Would you want to banish bad news from the papers?* ban, bar, [*informal*] black, debar, eliminate, exclude, forbid, get rid of, make illegal, ostracize, oust, prohibit, proscribe, put an embargo on, remove, restrict, stop, suppress, veto.
OPPOSITES: SEE **reinstate**.

bank noun
1 *a grassy bank.* dike, earthwork, embankment, mound, rampart, ridge.
2 *a river bank.* brink, edge, margin, shore, side.
3 *a steep bank.* camber, [*formal*] declivity, gradient, incline, ramp, rise, slope, tilt.
4 *a bank of navigational instruments.* array, collection, display, file, group, line, rank, row, series.

bank verb
1 *The plane banked.* cant, heel, incline, lean, list, pitch, slant, slope, tilt, tip.
2 *I banked my wages.* deposit, keep in a bank, save.

bankrupt adjective
a bankrupt business. failed, [*slang*] gone bust, insolvent, ruined.

banner noun
banners fluttering in the wind. colours, ensign, flag, pennant, pennon, standard, streamer.

banquet noun
[*informal*] binge, [*slang*] blow-out, dinner, feast, SEE **meal**, [*formal*] repast, [*informal*] spread.

banter noun
good-humoured banter. badinage, chaffing, joking, [*formal*] persiflage, pleasantry, raillery, repartee, ribbing, ridicule, teasing, word-play.

bar noun
1 *iron bars.* beam, girder, pole, rail, railing, rod, shaft, stake, stick, strut.
2 *a bar of chocolate, soap, etc.* block, cake, chunk, hunk, ingot, lump, nugget, piece, slab, wedge.
3 *a bar to invaders.* barricade, barrier, check, deterrent, hindrance, impediment, obstacle, obstruction.
4 *a bar for refreshments.* café, canteen, counter, inn, lounge (*coffee lounge*), pub, saloon, tavern.

bar verb
1 *She was barred from the club.* ban, banish, debar, exclude, forbid to enter, keep out, ostracize, outlaw, prevent from entering, prohibit, proscribe.
2 *A fallen tree barred our way.* arrest, block, check, deter, halt, hinder, impede, obstruct, prevent, stop, thwart.

barbarian noun
[Compare *barbaric, barbarous. Barbarian* originally referred to any foreigner with different customs, etc. *Barbarian* and the synonyms given here are especially insulting when used to refer to foreigners.] heathen, hun, pagan, Philistine, savage, vandal.

barbaric adjective
a barbaric attack. barbarous, brutal, SEE **cruel**, inhuman, primitive, savage, uncivilized, wild.
OPPOSITES: SEE **civilized, humane**.

bare adjective
1 *bare legs. a bare patch.* bald, denuded, exposed, naked, nude, stark-naked, stripped, unclad, unclothed, uncovered, undressed.
2 *a bare landscape.* barren, bleak, desolate, featureless, open, treeless, unwooded, windswept.
3 *bare trees.* defoliated, leafless.
4 *a bare room.* austere, empty, plain, simple, unfurnished, vacant.
5 *a bare wall.* blank, clean, unadorned, undecorated, unmarked.
6 *the bare facts.* explicit, honest, literal, plain, straightforward, unconcealed, undisguised, unembellished.
7 *the bare necessities.* basic, essential, just adequate, just sufficient, minimum.

bare verb
to bare your private thoughts. betray, communicate, disclose, expose, lay bare, make known, publish, reveal, show, uncover, unveil.

bargain noun
1 *I made a bargain with the salesman.* agreement, arrangement, compact, contract, deal, negotiation, pact, pledge,

promise, settlement, transaction, treaty, understanding.
2 *The coat I bought was a bargain.*
discounted item, [*informal*] give-away, good buy, loss-leader, reduced item, [*informal*] snip, special offer.

bargain verb
to bargain about the price. argue, barter, discuss (*terms*), do a deal, haggle, negotiate.
to bargain on *I didn't bargain on him bringing his family.* anticipate, be prepared for, contemplate, expect, foresee, imagine, plan for, reckon on.

bark verb
1 *to bark your shin.* abrade, chafe, graze, rub, score, scrape, scratch.
2 *The dog barked fiercely.* growl, yap.

barracks noun
military barracks. accommodation, billet, camp, garrison, lodging, quarters.

barrage noun
1 *a barrage across a river.* barrier, dam, embankment, wall.
2 *a barrage of artillery fire.* assault, attack, battery, bombardment, cannonade, fusillade, gunfire, onslaught, salvo, storm, volley.

barrel noun
butt, cask, drum, hogshead, keg, tub, tun, water-butt.

barren adjective
1 *barren desert.* arid, bare, desert, desolate, dried-up, empty, infertile, lifeless, non-productive, treeless, useless, uncultivated, unproductive, untilled, waste.
2 *a barren tree.* fruitless, unfruitful.
3 *a barren woman.* childless, infertile, sterile, sterilized.
OPPOSITES: SEE **fertile**.

barricade noun
a barricade across a road. barrier, blockade, bulwark, fence, obstacle, obstruction, palisade, stockade.

barrier noun
1 *a barrier to keep spectators off the track.* bar, barricade, fence, hurdle, obstacle, obstruction, railing, wall.
2 *a barrier across a river.* barrage, boom, dam.
3 *a barrier to progress.* check, drawback, handicap, hindrance, impediment, limitation, restriction, stumbling-block.

barter verb
bargain, deal, exchange, negotiate, swap, trade, traffic.

base adjective
a base crime. contemptible, cowardly, depraved, despicable, detestable,

dishonourable, evil, ignoble, immoral, low, mean, scandalous, selfish, shameful, sordid, vile, wicked.
OPPOSITES: SEE **sublime**.

base noun
1 *the base of a wall. a base on which to build.* basis, bed, bedrock, bottom, core, essentials, foot, footing, foundation, fundamentals, groundwork, pedestal, plinth, rest, stand, substructure, support.
2 *the base of an expedition.* camp, depot, headquarters, post, station.

base verb
The building was based on rock. The story was based on fact. build, construct, establish, found, ground, locate, set up, station.

bashful adjective
Don't be bashful—speak up for yourself. abashed, backward, blushing, coy, demure, diffident, embarrassed, faint-hearted, inhibited, modest, nervous, reserved, reticent, retiring, self-conscious, self-effacing, sheepish, shy, timid, timorous, unforthcoming.
OPPOSITES: SEE **assertive**.

basic adjective
the basic facts. basic needs. central, chief, crucial, elementary, essential, foremost, fundamental, important, intrinsic, key, main, necessary, primary, principal, radical, underlying, vital.
OPPOSITES: SEE **unimportant**.

basin noun
bowl, dish, sink, stoup.

basis noun
the basis on which something is built. the basis of a rumour. base, core, footing, foundation, ground, premise, principle, starting-point, support.

bask verb
to bask in the sun. to bask in applause. enjoy, expose yourself (to), feel pleasure, glory, lie, lounge, luxuriate, relax, sunbathe, wallow.

basket noun
bag, hamper, pannier, punnet, shopping-basket, skip, trug.

bat noun
Hit the ball with the bat. club, racket, racquet.

batch noun
a batch of cakes. SEE **group** noun.

bath noun
1 *a bath of water.* SEE **container**.
2 *to have a bath.* douche, jacuzzi, sauna, shower, [*informal*] soak, [*informal*] tub, wash.

bathe verb
1 *to bathe a wound.* clean, cleanse, immerse, moisten, rinse, soak, steep, swill, wash.
2 *to bathe in the sea.* go swimming, paddle, plunge, splash about, swim, [*informal*] take a dip.

bathos noun
anticlimax, [*informal*] come-down, disappointment, [*informal*] let-down.
OPPOSITES: SEE **climax**.

bathroom noun

BATHROOM FITTINGS: bath, bidet, extractor fan, jacuzzi, lavatory, medicine cabinet, mirror, shaver-point, shower, taps, tiles, toilet, towel-rail, ventilator, washbasin.

OTHER THINGS YOU FIND IN A BATHROOM: bath-mat, bath salts, comb, SEE **cosmetics**, curlers, flannel, foam bath, hairbrush, hair-drier, loofah, nail-brush, nail-scissors, pumice-stone, razor, scales, shampoo, shaver, soap, sponge, toiletries, toilet-roll, toothbrush, towel, tweezers.

---

baton noun
SEE **stick** noun.

batter verb
to batter on a door. SEE **beat** verb, bludgeon, cudgel, keep hitting, pound.

battery noun
1 *a battery of guns.* artillery-unit, emplacement, SEE **group** noun.
2 *an electric battery.* accumulator, cell.
3 [*legal*] *assault and battery.* assault, attack, [*informal*] beating-up, blows, onslaught, thrashing, violence.

battle noun
Many died in the battle. action, air-raid, Armageddon, attack, blitz, brush, campaign, clash, combat, conflict, confrontation, contest, crusade, [*informal*] dogfight (= *air battle*), dispute, encounter, engagement, fight, fray, hostilities, offensive, pitched battle, pre-emptive strike, [*informal*] punch-up, row, scrap, [*informal*] shoot-out, siege, skirmish, strife, struggle, war, warfare.

battle verb
They battled to control the fire. SEE **fight** verb, **struggle** verb.

bawdy adjective
SEE **obscene**.

bay noun
1 *a sandy bay.* bight, cove, creek, estuary, fjord, gulf, harbour, indentation, inlet, ria, sound.
2 *an unloading bay.* alcove, booth, compartment, niche, nook, opening, recess.

bazaar noun
a fund-raising bazaar. auction, boot-sale, bring-and-buy, fair, fête, jumble sale, market, sale.

be verb
1 *To be, or not to be?* be alive, breathe, endure, exist, live.
2 *Will you be here long?* continue, dwell, inhabit, keep going, last, occupy a position, persist, remain, stay, survive.
3 *When will your next holiday be?* arise, befall, come about, happen, occur, take place.
4 *She wants to be a writer.* become, develop into.

beach noun
a sandy beach. coast, coastline, foreshore, sand, sands, seashore, seaside, shore, [*poetic*] strand.

beacon noun
bonfire, flare, lighthouse, signal.

bead noun
1 *pretty beads.* SEE **jewellery**.
2 *beads of sweat.* blob, drip, drop, droplet, globule, pearl.

beaker noun
a beaker of water. cup, glass, goblet, jar, mug, tankard, tumbler, wine-glass.

beam noun
1 *a wooden beam.* bar, boom, girder, joist, plank, post, rafter, spar, stanchion, support, timber.
2 *a beam of light.* gleam, ray, shaft, stream.

beam verb
1 *to beam radio waves towards a satellite.* aim, broadcast, direct, emit, radiate, send out, shine, transmit.
2 *to beam happily.* grin, laugh, look radiant, radiate happiness, smile.
OPPOSITES: SEE **glower**.

bean noun
legume, pulse.

KINDS OF BEAN: broad bean, butter-bean, French bean, haricot, kidney bean, runner bean, soya bean.

---

bear verb
1 *The rope won't bear my weight.* carry, hold, prop up, support, take.
2 *The gravestone bears an inscription.* display, exhibit, have, possess, show.
3 *They bore the coffin into the church.* bring, carry, convey, deliver, fetch, move, take, transfer, transport.
4 *I can't bear pain.* abide, accept, brook, cope with, endure, live with, permit, put up with, [*informal*] stand, [*informal*] stomach,

suffer, sustain, tolerate, undergo.
5 *The bitch bore six puppies. The tree bore a lot of fruit.* breed, [*old-fashioned*] bring forth, develop, give birth to [SEE **birth**], produce, yield.

bearing noun
1 *a military bearing.* air, appearance, behaviour, carriage, demeanour, deportment, look, manner, mien, poise, posture, presence, style.
2 *Your evidence has no bearing on the case.* connection, import, pertinence, reference, relationship, relevance, significance.
bearings *I lost my bearings in the fog.* aim, course, direction, line, location, orientation, path, position, road, sense of direction, tack, track, way, whereabouts.

beast noun
wild beasts. SEE **animal** noun, brute, creature, monster.

beat noun
1 *music with a strong beat.* accent, pulse, rhythm, stress, throb.
2 *a policeman's beat.* course, itinerary, journey, path, rounds, route, way.

beat verb
1 *to beat with a stick.* batter, bludgeon, buffet, cane, clout, cudgel, flail, flog, hammer, SEE **hit** verb, knock about, lash, [*informal*] lay into, manhandle, pound, punch, scourge, strike, [*informal*] tan, thrash, thump, trounce, [*informal*] wallop, whack, whip.
2 *to beat eggs.* agitate, blend, froth up, knead, mix, pound, stir, whip, whisk.
3 *My heart beat faster.* flutter, palpitate, pound, pulsate, race, thump.
4 *Our opponents beat us.* best, conquer, crush, defeat, excel, get the better of, [*informal*] lick, master, outclass, outdistance, outdo, outpace, outrun, outwit, overcome, overpower, overthrow, overwhelm, rout, subdue, surpass, [*informal*] thrash, top, trounce, vanquish, win against, worst.

beautiful adjective
[*Beautiful* has many shades of meaning. The words given here are only a selection of the synonyms you could use.] *a beautiful bride. beautiful pictures. beautiful scenery.* admirable, aesthetic, alluring, appealing, artistic, attractive, bewitching, brilliant, captivating, charming, [*old-fashioned*] comely, dainty, delightful, elegant, exquisite, [*old-fashioned*] fair, fascinating, fetching, fine, good-looking, glamorous, glorious, gorgeous, graceful, handsome, imaginative, irresistible, lovely, magnificent, neat, picturesque, pleasing, pretty, quaint, radiant, ravishing, scenic,

seductive, sensuous, spectacular, splendid, stunning, superb, tempting.
OPPOSITES: SEE **ugly**.

beautify verb
The church was beautified with flowers. adorn, deck, decorate, embellish, make beautiful, ornament, prettify, [*uncomplimentary*] tart up.
OPPOSITES: SEE **disfigure**.

beauty noun
the beauty of the landscape. allure, appeal, attractiveness, charm, elegance, fascination, glamour, glory, grace, handsomeness, loveliness, magnificence, prettiness, radiance, splendour.
OPPOSITES: SEE **ugliness**.

become verb
1 *Little puppies become big dogs!* change into, develop into, grow into, turn into.
2 *That colour becomes you.* be appropriate to, be becoming to, befit, enhance, fit, flatter, harmonize with, set off, suit.

becoming adjective
a becoming dress. appropriate, apt, attractive, befitting, charming, decent, decorous, fit, fitting, flattering, [*old-fashioned*] meet, pleasing, proper, seemly, suitable, tasteful.

bed noun
1 *a bed to sleep in.*

KINDS OF BED: air-bed, berth, bunk, cot, couch, couchette, cradle, crib, divan, four-poster, hammock, pallet, palliasse, truckle bed, water-bed.

PARTS OF A BED: bedpost, bedstead, headboard, mattress, springs.

THINGS YOU USE TO MAKE A BED: bed linen, bedspread, blanket, bolster, continental quilt, counterpane, coverlet, duvet, eiderdown, electric blanket, mattress, pillow, pillowcase, pillowslip, quilt, sheet, sleeping-bag.

---

2 *a bed of concrete.* base, foundation, groundwork, layer, substratum.
3 *a river bed.* bottom, channel, course, watercourse.
4 *a flower bed.* border, garden, patch, plot.

bedraggled adjective
bedraggled from the rain. dirty, dishevelled, messy, scruffy, sodden, soiled, stained, unkempt, untidy, wet.

bedroom noun
dormitory, sleeping quarters.

bee noun
bumble-bee, drone, honey-bee, queen, worker.
a home for bees apiary, beehive, hive.

beer noun
ale, [*informal*] bitter, lager, [*informal*] mild, stout.

befall verb
[*old-fashioned*] *Who knows what may befall?* be the outcome, [*old-fashioned*] betide, chance, come about, [*informal*] crop up, eventuate, happen, occur, take place, [*informal*] transpire.

before adverb
earlier, in advance, previously, sooner.

beg verb
1 *to beg for food.* ask for alms, [*informal*] cadge, scrounge, sponge.
2 *to beg for a favour.* ask, beseech, crave, entreat, implore, importune, petition, plead, pray, request, [*formal*] supplicate.

beggar noun
destitute person, down-and-out, homeless person, mendicant, pauper, poor person, ragamuffin, tramp, vagrant.

begin verb
1 *to begin something new.* activate, attack, be first with, broach, commence, conceive, create, embark on, enter into, found, [*informal*] get cracking on, [*informal*] get something going, inaugurate, initiate, inspire, instigate, introduce, kindle, launch, launch into, lay the foundations of, move into, open up, originate, pioneer, precipitate, provoke, set in motion, set about, set up, [*informal*] spark off, start, take the initiative, take up, touch off, trigger off, undertake.
OPPOSITES: SEE **finish** verb.
2 *How did your new idea begin?* appear, arise, break out, come into existence, crop up, emerge, get going, happen, materialize, originate, spring up.
OPPOSITES: SEE **end** verb.

beginner noun
1 *Who was the beginner of it all?* creator, founder, initiator, inspiration, instigator, originator, pioneer.
2 *I'm only a beginner.* apprentice, fresher (*at university or college*), greenhorn, initiate, learner, novice, recruit, starter, tiro, trainee.

beginning noun
1 *the beginning of life. the beginning of a new career.* birth, commencement, conception, creation, dawn, embryo, emergence, establishment, foundation, genesis, germ, inauguration, inception, initiation, instigation, introduction, launch, onset, opening, origin, outset, point of departure, rise, source, start, starting-point, threshold.
2 *the beginning of a book.* preface, prelude, prologue.
OPPOSITES: SEE **end** noun.

begrudge verb
Don't begrudge his just reward. be bitter about, covet, envy, grudge, mind, object to, resent.

behave verb
1 *Try to behave well.* acquit yourself, act, conduct yourself, function, operate, perform, react, respond, run, work.
2 *I wish those kids would behave!* be good, be on best behaviour, be virtuous.

behaviour noun
Their behaviour was excellent. actions, attitude, bearing, comportment, conduct, courtesy, dealings, demeanour, deportment, manners, performance, reaction, response, ways.

behead verb
decapitate, guillotine.

being noun
1 *She loves him with all her being.* actuality, essence, existence, life, living, reality, solidity, soul, spirit, substance.
2 *a mortal being.* animal, creature, individual, person.

belated adjective
belated thanks. behindhand, delayed, last-minute, late, overdue, posthumous, tardy, unpunctual.
OPPOSITES: SEE **prompt** adjective.

belch verb
1 *Cucumber makes me belch.* break wind, [*informal*] burp, emit wind.
2 *The chimney belched smoke.* discharge, emit, erupt, fume, gush, send out, smoke, spew out, vomit.

belief noun
1 *belief in Santa Claus.* certainty, confidence, credence, reliance, sureness, trust.
OPPOSITES: SEE **disbelief, scepticism.**
2 *religious belief.* assurance, attitude, conviction, creed, doctrine, dogma, ethos, faith, feeling, ideology, morality, notion, opinion, persuasion, principles, religion, standards, tenets, theories, views.

believe verb
1 *I believe all he says.* accept, be certain about, count on, credit, depend on, endorse, have faith in, reckon on, rely on, subscribe to, [*informal*] swallow, swear by, trust.
OPPOSITES: SEE **disbelieve.**
2 *I believe she cheated.* assume, consider, [*informal*] dare say, feel, gather, guess, imagine, judge, know, maintain, [*formal*] postulate, presume, speculate, suppose, take it for granted, think.

believer noun
a religious believer. adherent, devotee, disciple, fanatic, follower, proselyte, supporter, upholder, zealot.
OPPOSITES: SEE **agnostic, atheist.**

bell noun
Did you hear the bell? alarm, carillon, chime, knell, peal, signal.
RELEVANT VERBS: chime, clang, clink, jangle, jingle, peal, ping, resonate, resound, reverberate, ring, sound the knell, strike, tinkle, toll.

belligerent adjective
a belligerent fighter. aggressive, antagonistic, argumentative, bellicose, bullying, combative, contentious, defiant, fierce, hostile, martial, militant, militaristic, provocative, pugnacious, quarrelsome, unfriendly, violent, warlike, warmongering, warring.
OPPOSITES: SEE **peaceable**.

belong verb
1 *This book belongs to me.* be owned by, go with, pertain to, relate to.
2 *I belong to the squash club.* be affiliated with, be a member of, be connected with, [*informal*] be in with, subscribe to.
3 *I don't feel I belong here.* be at home, feel welcome, have a place.

belongings noun
[*old-fashioned*] chattels, effects, [*informal*] gear, goods, [*joking*] impedimenta, possessions, property, things.

belt noun
1 *a belt round the waist.* cummerbund, girdle, girth (*on a horse*), sash, strap, waistband.
2 *a fan-belt.* band, circle, loop.
3 *a belt of woodland.* area, district, line, stretch, strip, swathe, tract, zone.

bench noun
1 *a park bench.* form, pew, seat, settle.
2 *the magistrate's bench.* court, courtroom, judge, magistrate, tribunal.
3 *a carpenter's bench.* counter, table, work-bench, work-table.

bend noun
a bend in the road. angle, arc, bow, corner, crank, crook, curvature, curve, loop, turn, twist, zigzag.

bend verb
1 *to bend wire.* arch, bow, buckle, coil, contort, curl, curve, distort, flex, fold, loop, mould, refract (*light rays*), shape, turn, twist, warp, wind.
2 *Wire bends.* be flexible, [*informal*] give, yield.
to bend down bow, crouch, duck, kneel, lean, stoop.

benefactor noun
An anonymous benefactor paid for my trip. backer, [*uncomplimentary*] do-gooder, donor, [*informal*] fairy godmother, patron, philanthropist, promoter, sponsor, supporter, well-wisher.

beneficial adjective
beneficial to health. advantageous, benign, constructive, favourable, good, healthy, helpful, improving, nourishing, nutritious, profitable, rewarding, salutary, useful, valuable, wholesome.
OPPOSITES: SEE **harmful**.

beneficiary noun
a beneficiary under a will. heir, heiress, inheritor, legatee, recipient, successor (*to a title*).

benefit noun
1 *the benefits of living in the country.* advantage, asset, blessing, [*old-fashioned*] boon, convenience, gain, good thing, help, privilege, prize, profit, use.
OPPOSITES: SEE **handicap** noun.
2 *unemployment benefit.* allowance, assistance, [*informal*] dole, [*informal*] hand-out, grant, income support, payment, social security, welfare.

benefit verb
The money will benefit the poor. advance, advantage, aid, assist, better, boost, do good to, enhance, further, help, improve, profit, promote, serve.
OPPOSITES: SEE **hinder**.

benevolent adjective
a benevolent sponsor. altruistic, caring, charitable, considerate, friendly, generous, good, helpful, humane, humanitarian, SEE **kind** adjective, kindly, liberal, magnanimous, merciful, philanthropic, supportive, sympathetic, warm-hearted.
OPPOSITES: MALEVOLENT, SEE **malicious**.

bent adjective
1 *bent wire. a bent back.* angled, arched, bowed, buckled, coiled, contorted, crooked, curved, distorted, folded, hunched, looped, twisted, warped.
OPPOSITES: SEE **straight**.
2 [*informal*] *a bent businessman.* corrupt, criminal, dishonest, immoral, untrustworthy, wicked.
OPPOSITES: SEE **honest**.

bequeath verb
She bequeathed her money to her grandchildren. endow, hand down, leave, pass on, settle, will.

bequest noun
He received a bequest under his grandmother's will. endowment, gift, inheritance, legacy, settlement.

bereavement noun
a bereavement in the family. death, loss.

berserk adjective
The dog went berserk when a wasp stung him. [*informal*] beside yourself, crazy, demented, deranged, frantic, frenetic, frenzied, furious,

infuriated, insane, mad, maniacal, rabid, violent, wild.
to go berserk lose control, rampage, rave, run amok, run riot, [*informal*] see red.

berth noun
1 *a sleeping-berth.* SEE **bed**, bunk, hammock.
2 *a berth for a ship.* anchorage, dock, harbour, haven, landing-stage, moorings, pier, port, quay, slipway, wharf.

berth verb
The ship berthed. anchor, dock, drop anchor, land, moor, tie up.

besiege verb
1 *The Greeks besieged Troy for 10 long years.* beleaguer, beset, blockade, cut off, encircle, encompass, isolate, surround.
2 *The superstar was besieged by reporters.* SEE **pester**.

best adjective
my best friend. best quality. first-class, foremost, incomparable, leading, matchless, optimum, outstanding, pre-eminent, supreme, top, unequalled, unrivalled, unsurpassed.

bestial adjective
bestial cruelty. animal, beast-like, beastly, brutal, brutish, inhuman, SEE **savage** adjective, subhuman.

bet noun
1 *I had a bet that she would win.* [*informal*] flutter, gamble, [*informal*] punt, speculation, wager.
2 *How much was the bet?* bid, stake.

bet verb
He bet everything he had. I bet occasionally. bid, gamble, do the pools, enter a lottery, [*informal*] have a flutter, hazard, lay bets, [*informal*] punt, risk, speculate, stake, venture, wager.

betray verb
1 *to betray someone.* abandon, be a Judas to, be a traitor to, cheat, conspire against, deceive, desert, double-cross, [*informal*] grass on, inform on, jilt (*a lover*), let down, [*informal*] rat on, [*informal*] sell down the river, sell out, [*informal*] shop, [*informal*] tell tales about, [*informal*] turn Queen's evidence on.
2 *to betray a secret.* disclose, divulge, expose, give away, indicate, let out, let slip, manifest, reveal, show, tell.

better adjective
Are you better after your flu? back to normal, convalescent, cured, fitter, healed, healthier, improved, [*informal*] none the worse, [*informal*] on the mend, progressing, recovered, recovering, restored, well.

beware verb
to beware of *Beware of the bull.* avoid, be alert to (SEE **alert**), be cautious about, guard against, heed, keep clear of, look out for, mind, shun, steer away from, take heed of, take precautions against, watch out for.

bewilder verb
baffle, [*informal*] bamboozle, bemuse, confound, confuse, daze, disconcert, disorientate, distract, floor, [*informal*] flummox, mislead, muddle, mystify, perplex, puzzle, stump, stun.

bewitch verb
SEE **charm** verb.

bias noun
1 *She has a bias towards science.* aptitude, bent, inclination, leaning, liking, partiality, penchant, predilection, predisposition, preference, proclivity, proneness, propensity, tendency.
2 *The ref was guilty of bias.* bigotry, chauvinism, favouritism, imbalance, injustice, nepotism, one-sidedness, partiality, partisanship, prejudice, racism, sexism, unfairness.

biased adjective
a biased decision. a biased referee. bigoted, blinkered, chauvinistic, distorted, influenced, interested (*an interested party*), loaded, one-sided, partial, partisan, prejudiced, racist, sexist, slanted, tendentious, unfair, unjust, warped.
OPPOSITES: SEE **unbiased**.

bicycle noun
[*informal*] bike, cycle, penny-farthing, [*informal*] push-bike, racer, tandem, [*informal*] two-wheeler.

bid noun
1 *a bid at an auction.* offer, price, proposal, proposition, tender.
2 *a bid to beat a record.* attempt, [*informal*] crack, effort, endeavour, [*informal*] go, try, venture.

bid verb
1 *to bid at an auction.* make an offer, offer, proffer, propose, tender.
2 [*formal or old-fashioned*] *He bade them enter.* SEE **command** verb.

big adjective
1 *a big amount. a big woman. a big box.* [*informal*] almighty, ample, bulky, burly, capacious, colossal, commodious, considerable, elephantine, enormous, extensive, SEE **fat** adjective, gargantuan, giant, gigantic, grand, great, heavy, hefty, high, huge, [*informal*] hulking, husky, immeasurable, immense, impressive, incalculable, infinite, [*informal*] jumbo, large, lofty, mammoth, massive, mighty,

monstrous, monumental, mountainous,
prodigious, roomy, sizeable, spacious,
substantial, tall, titanic, towering,
[*informal*] tremendous, vast, voluminous,
weighty.
2 *a big decision. the big match.* grave,
important, influential, leading, main, major,
momentous, notable, powerful, prime,
principal, prominent, serious, significant.

bigoted adjective
SEE **prejudiced**.

bilious adjective
He's feeling bilious. SEE **ill**, liverish,
nauseated, queasy, sick.

bill noun
1 *a bill showing what you pay.* account,
invoice, receipt, statement.
2 *a bill advertising a sale.* advertisement,
broadsheet, bulletin, circular, handbill,
handout, leaflet, notice, placard, poster,
sheet.
3 a *Parliamentary bill.* draft law, proposed
law. [*A bill* becomes an *Act* when passed.]
4 *a bird's bill.* beak, mandible.

billow verb
The sheets billowed on the washing-line.
balloon, belly, bulge, fill out, heave, puff out,
rise, roll, surge, swell, undulate.

bin noun
CONTAINERS: SEE **container**.

bind verb
1 *to bind something with string.* attach,
clamp, connect, SEE **fasten**, hitch, join, lash,
link, rope, secure, strap, tie, truss.
2 *Loyalty to our leader bound us together.*
combine, fuse, hold together, unify, unite,
weld.
3 *The nurse bound the wound.* bandage,
cover, dress, encase, swathe, wrap.
4 *I was bound by oath to tell the truth.* compel,
constrain, force, necessitate, oblige,
require.

binding adjective
a binding agreement. compulsory,
contractual, formal, irrevocable, legally
enforceable, mandatory, necessary,
obligatory, permanent, required, [*informal*]
signed and sealed, statutory, unalterable,
unavoidable, unbreakable.

biography noun
autobiography, history, life, life-story,
memoirs, recollections.

biology noun
botany, life science, nature study, zoology.

bird noun
[*childish*] birdie, [*joking*] feathered friend,
fowl.
female bird hen.

male bird cock, drake (*duck*), gander
(*goose*).
young bird chick, cygnet (*swan*), duckling,
fledgling, gosling (*goose*), nestling.
a home for birds aviary, cage, nest, nesting-
box.
the study of birds ornithology.

KINDS OF BIRD: gamebird, seabird, wader,
waterfowl, wildfowl.

VARIOUS BIRDS: albatross, auk, bittern,
blackbird, budgerigar, bullfinch, bunting,
bustard, buzzard, canary, carrion
crow, cassowary, chaffinch, chicken,
chiff-chaff, chough, cockatoo, coot,
cormorant, corncrake, crane, crow, cuckoo,
curlew, dabchick, dipper, dove, duck,
dunnock.

eagle, egret, emu, falcon, finch,
flamingo, flycatcher, fulmar, goldcrest,
goldfinch, goose, grebe, greenfinch, grouse,
gull, hawk, hedge-sparrow, heron, hoopoe,
hornbill, humming bird, ibis, jackdaw, jay,
kestrel, kingfisher, kite, kiwi, kookaburra,
lapwing, lark, linnet.

macaw, magpie, martin, mynah bird,
moorhen, nightingale, nightjar, nuthatch,
oriole, osprey, ostrich, ousel, owl, parakeet,
parrot, partridge, peacock, peewit, pelican,
penguin, peregrine, petrel, pheasant,
pigeon, pipit, plover, ptarmigan, puffin,
quail, raven, redbreast, redstart, robin,
rook.

sandpiper, seagull, shearwater, shelduck,
shrike, skua, skylark, snipe, sparrow,
sparrowhawk, spoonbill, starling,
stonechat, stork, swallow, swan, swift, teal,
tern, thrush, tit, toucan, turkey, turtle-dove,
vulture, wagtail, warbler, waxwing,
wheatear, woodcock, woodpecker, wren,
yellowhammer.

PARTS OF A BIRD: beak, bill, claw, crest,
down, feathers, mandible, plumage, tail,
talon, wing.

GROUPS OF BIRDS: brood (*of chicks*), covey
(*of partridges*), flock, gaggle (*of geese*).

birth noun
1 *the birth of a baby.* breech birth, Caesarian,
childbirth, confinement, delivery, labour,
nativity (*of Christ*), [*formal*] parturition.
MEDICAL SPECIALIST IN CHILDBIRTH: obstetrician.
2 *of noble birth.* ancestry, background, blood,
breeding, derivation, descent, extraction,
family, genealogy, line, lineage, parentage,
pedigree, race, stock, strain.
3 *the birth of a new idea.* SEE **beginning**.
to give birth (to) bear, SEE **begin**, calve,
farrow, foal.

biscuit noun
[*American*] cookie, cracker, crispbread, digestive, ginger-nut, pretzel, rusk, shortbread, wafer.

bisect verb
The lines bisect each other. cross, cut in half, divide, halve, intersect.

bit noun
1 *a bit of chocolate. a bit of stone.* atom, block, chip, chunk, crumb, division, dollop, fraction, fragment, grain, helping, hunk, iota, lump, morsel, part, particle, piece, portion, scrap, section, segment, share, slab, slice, snippet, speck.
2 *Can you wait a bit?* instant, [*informal*] jiffy, minute, moment, second, [*informal*] tick, time, while.

bite noun
1 *a nasty bite.* nip, pinch, sting, SEE **wound** noun.
2 *a bite to eat.* bit, morsel, mouthful, nibble, piece, snack, taste.

bite verb
champ, chew, crunch, cut into, gnaw, [*formal*] masticate, munch, nibble, nip, rend, snap, tear at, wound.

bitter adjective
1 *a bitter taste.* acid, acrid, harsh, sharp, sour, unpleasant.
OPPOSITES: SEE **mild**, **sweet** adjective.
2 *a bitter experience.* calamitous, dire, distasteful, distressing, galling, hateful, heartbreaking, painful, poignant, sorrowful, unhappy, unwelcome, upsetting.
OPPOSITES: SEE **pleasant**.
3 *bitter remarks.* acerbic, acrimonious, angry, cruel, cynical, embittered, envious, hostile, jaundiced, jealous, malicious, rancorous, resentful, savage, sharp, spiteful, stinging, vicious, violent, waspish.
OPPOSITES: SEE **kind** adjective.
4 *a bitter wind.* biting, SEE **cold** adjective, fierce, freezing, perishing, piercing, raw.
OPPOSITES: SEE **gentle**.

bizarre adjective SEE **odd**.

black adjective
blackish, coal-black, SEE **dark**, dusky, ebony, funereal, gloomy, inky, jet, jet-black, moonless, murky, pitch-black, pitch-dark, raven, sable, sooty, starless, unlit.

blacklist verb
ban, bar, blackball, boycott, debar, disallow, exclude, ostracize, preclude, proscribe, repudiate, snub, veto.

blackmail noun
extortion.

blade noun
dagger, edge, knife, razor, scalpel, SEE **sword**, vane.

blame noun
I accepted the blame. accountability, accusation, castigation, censure, charge, complaint, condemnation, criticism, culpability, fault, guilt, imputation, incrimination, liability, onus, [*informal*] rap, recrimination, reprimand, reproach, reproof, responsibility, [*informal*] stick, stricture.

blame verb
They blamed me for the accident. accuse, admonish, censure, charge, chide, condemn, criticize, denounce, [*informal*] get at, hold responsible, incriminate, rebuke, reprehend, reprimand, reproach, reprove, round on, scold, tax, upbraid.
OPPOSITES: SEE **excuse** verb.

blameless adjective
SEE **innocent**.

bland adjective
1 *a bland flavour.* boring, flat, insipid, mild, nondescript, smooth, tasteless, unappetizing, uninteresting, watery, weak.
OPPOSITES: SEE **sharp**, **tasty**.
2 *a bland personality. bland remarks.* affable, amiable, banal, calm, characterless, dull, gentle, [*informal*] smooth, soft, soothing, suave, trite, unexciting, uninspiring, uninteresting, vapid, weak, [*informal*] wishy-washy.
OPPOSITES: SEE **interesting**.

blank adjective
1 *blank paper. blank tape.* clean, clear, empty, plain, spotless, unmarked, unused, void.
2 *a blank look.* apathetic, baffled, baffling, dead, [*informal*] deadpan, emotionless, expressionless, featureless, glazed, immobile, impassive, inane, inscrutable, lifeless, poker-faced, uncomprehending, unresponsive, vacant, vacuous.

blank noun
1 *My mind was a blank.* emptiness, nothingness, [*formal*] vacuity, vacuum, void.
2 *Fill in the blanks.* break, gap, space.

blasphemous adjective
blasphemous language. godless, impious, irreligious, irreverent, profane, sacrilegious, ungodly, wicked.
OPPOSITES: SEE **reverent**.

blast noun
1 *a blast of air.* SEE **wind** noun.
2 *a bomb blast.* SEE **explosion**.

blatant adjective
a blatant mistake. blatant rudeness. apparent, bare-faced, bold, brazen, conspicuous, evident, flagrant, glaring, obtrusive, obvious, open, overt, shameless,

stark, unconcealed, undisguised, unmistakable, visible.
OPPOSITES: SEE **concealed**.

blaze noun SEE **fire** noun.

bleach verb
blanch, discolour, etiolate (*leaves of a plant*), fade, lighten, pale, peroxide (*hair*), whiten.

bleak adjective
a bleak hillside. a bleak outlook. bare, barren, blasted, cheerless, SEE **cold** adjective, comfortless, depressing, desolate, dismal, dreary, exposed, grim, hopeless, joyless, uncomfortable, unpromising, windswept, wintry.

bleary adjective
bleary eyes. bleary vision. blurred, [*informal*] blurry, cloudy, dim, filmy, fogged, foggy, fuzzy, hazy, indistinct, misty, murky, obscured, smeary, unclear, watery.
OPPOSITES: SEE **clear** adjective.

blemish noun
1 *a blemish in your work.* blot, defect, eyesore, fault, flaw, imperfection, mark, mess, smudge, speck, stain, ugliness.
2 *a blemish on the skin.* birthmark, blackhead, blister, blotch, callus, corn, deformity, disfigurement, freckle, mole, naevus, pimple, pustule, scar, spot, verruca, wart, whitlow, [*slang*] zit.

blend noun
a blend of various ingredients. alloy (*of metals*), amalgam, amalgamation, combination, composite, compound, concoction, fusion, mélange, mix, mixture, synthesis, union.

blend verb
1 *to blend into a crowd.* amalgamate, coalesce, combine, fuse, harmonize, integrate, intermingle, intermix, merge, mingle, synthesize, unite.
2 *to blend ingredients for a cake.* beat, compound, mix, stir together, whip, whisk.

bless verb
1 *to bless someone or something to make it holy.* anoint, consecrate, dedicate, grace, hallow, make sacred, ordain, sanctify.
OPPOSITES: SEE **condemn**, **desecrate**.
2 *to bless God's name.* exalt, extol, glorify, magnify, praise.
OPPOSITES: SEE **curse** verb.

blessed adjective
God's blessed name. adored, divine, hallowed, holy, revered, sacred, sanctified.

blessing noun
1 *The priest pronounced a blessing.* benediction, grace, prayer.
OPPOSITES: SEE **curse** noun.
2 *Our parents gave their blessing to our*

marriage. approbation, approval, backing, [*formal*] concurrence, consent, leave, permission, sanction, support.
OPPOSITES: SEE **disapproval**.
3 *Central heating is a blessing in the winter.* advantage, asset, benefit, [*old-fashioned*] boon, comfort, convenience, godsend, help.
OPPOSITES: SEE **evil** noun.

blight noun
blight in the potatoes. a blight on society. affliction, ailment, [*old-fashioned*] bane, cancer, canker, curse, decay, disease, evil, illness, infestation, [*old-fashioned*] pestilence, plague, pollution, rot, scourge, sickness.

blind adjective
1 WORDS TO DESCRIBE PEOPLE WITH IMPAIRED VISION: astigmatic, blinded, boss-eyed, colour-blind, cross-eyed, eyeless, long-sighted, myopic, near-sighted, short-sighted, sightless, suffering from cataract or glaucoma, unseeing, visually handicapped.
2 *blind devotion. blind to his faults.* blinkered, heedless, ignorant, inattentive, indifferent, insensible, insensitive, mindless, oblivious, prejudiced, unaware, unobservant.
OPPOSITES: SEE **aware**.

blink verb
blinking lights. flash, flicker, flutter, gleam, glimmer, twinkle, wink.

bliss noun
a life of bliss. delight, ecstasy, euphoria, felicity, gladness, happiness, heaven, joy, paradise, pleasure, rapture.
OPPOSITES: SEE **misery**.

blissful adjective
SEE **happy**.

bloated adjective
starving children with bloated stomachs. dilated, distended, enlarged, inflated, swollen.

block noun
1 *a block of chocolate. a block of wood.* bar, brick, cake, chock, chunk, hunk, ingot, lump, mass, piece, slab.
2 *a mental block. a block in the system.* barrier, blockage, delay, hang-up, hindrance, impediment, jam, obstacle, obstruction, resistance, stoppage.

block verb
1 *The drain was blocked with leaves.* [*informal*] bung up, choke, clog, close, congest, constrict, dam, fill, jam, obstruct, plug, stop up.
2 *A parked car blocked our way.* bar, barricade, impede, obstruct.
3 *The boss blocked our plan.* deter, halt, hamper, hinder, hold back, prevent,

prohibit, resist, [*informal*] scotch, [*informal*] stonewall, stop, thwart.

blockage noun
a blockage in a drain. barrier, block, bottleneck, congestion, constriction, delay, hang-up, hindrance, impediment, jam, obstacle, obstruction, resistance, stoppage.

blood noun
gore.

bloodshed noun
The battlefield was a scene of appalling bloodshed. bloodletting, butchery, carnage, killing, massacre, murder, slaughter, slaying.

bloodthirsty adjective
barbaric, brutal, SEE **cruel**, ferocious, fierce, inhuman, murderous, pitiless, ruthless, sadistic, savage, vicious, violent, warlike.

bloody adjective
1 *a bloody wound.* bleeding, blood-stained, raw.
2 *a bloody battle.* SEE **fierce**, gory, sanguinary.

bloom noun
1 *I cut my best blooms for the flower-show.* blossom, bud, flower.
2 *the bloom of youth.* beauty, blush, flush, glow, prime.

bloom verb
Most flowers bloom in summer. be healthy, blossom, [*poetic*] blow, bud, burgeon, develop, flourish, flower, grow, open, prosper, sprout, thrive.
OPPOSITES: SEE **fade**.

blossom noun
[*Blossom often refers to a mass of flowers rather than a single flower.*] *apple blossom.* blooms, buds, florets, flowers.

blot noun
1 *a blot of ink.* blob, blotch, mark, smear, smudge, [*informal*] splodge, spot, stain.
2 *a blot on the landscape.* blemish, defect, eyesore, fault, flaw, ugliness.

blot verb
to blot a page. bespatter, mar, mark, smudge, spoil, spot, stain.
to blot out *The fog blotted out the view.* cancel, conceal, cover, delete, eclipse, erase, expunge, hide, mask, obliterate, obscure, rub out, wipe out.

blotchy adjective
a blotchy skin. blemished, marked, patchy, smudged, spotty, uneven.

blow noun
1 *a blow on the head.* bang, bash, [*informal*] belt, [*informal*] biff, box (*on the ears*), buffet, bump, clip, clout, clump, [*formal*] concussion, hit, jolt, knock, punch, rap,

slap, [*informal*] slosh, smack, [*informal*] sock, stroke, swat, swipe, thump, wallop, [*informal*] wap, welt, whack.
2 *The loss of her purse was a terrible blow.* affliction, [*informal*] bombshell, calamity, disappointment, disaster, misfortune, shock, surprise, upset.

blow verb
The heater blows out hot air. blast, breathe, exhale, fan, puff, waft, whirl, whistle.
to blow up 1 *to blow up tyres.* dilate, expand, fill, inflate, pump up. 2 *to blow up a photo.* enlarge. 3 *to blow up with explosive.* blast, bomb, burst, detonate, dynamite, erupt, explode, go off, set off, shatter.

blue adjective
SHADES OF BLUE: aquamarine, azure, cerulean, cobalt, indigo, navy, sapphire, sky-blue, turquoise, ultramarine.

blueprint noun
a blueprint for a new invention. basis, design, draft, model, outline, pattern, pilot, plan, project, proposal, prototype, scheme.

blunder noun
I made a terrible blunder. [*informal*] boob, [*informal*] botch, [*informal*] clanger, [*slang*] cock-up, error, fault, faux pas, gaffe, howler, indiscretion, miscalculation, misjudgement, mistake, slip, slip-up, [*formal*] solecism.

blunder verb
Someone has blundered! be clumsy, [*informal*] botch (something) up, bumble, bungle, [*informal*] drop a clanger, err, [*informal*] foul (something) up, [*slang*] goof, go wrong, [*informal*] make a hash (of something), make a mistake, mess (something) up, miscalculate, misjudge, [*informal*] put your foot in it, slip up, stumble.

blunt adjective
1 *a blunt knife. a blunt instrument.* dull, rounded, thick, unpointed, unsharpened.
OPPOSITES: SEE **sharp**.
2 *a blunt remark. a blunt manner.* abrupt, bluff, brusque, candid, curt, direct, downright, forthright, frank, honest, insensitive, outspoken, plain-spoken, SEE **rude**, straightforward, tactless, unceremonious.
OPPOSITES: SEE **polite, tactful**.

blunt verb
to blunt your awareness. to blunt your hunger. abate, allay, anaesthetize, dampen, deaden, desensitize, dull, lessen, numb, soften, take the edge off, weaken.
OPPOSITES: SEE **sharpen**.

blurred adjective
a blurred memory. a blurred photo. bleary, blurry, clouded, cloudy, confused, dim, faint, foggy, fuzzy, hazy, ill-defined, indefinite, indistinct, misty, nebulous, out of focus, smoky, unclear, unfocused, vague.
OPPOSITES: SEE **clear** adjective.

blurt verb
to blurt out be indiscreet, [*informal*] blab, burst out with, come out with, cry out, disclose, divulge, exclaim, [*informal*] give the game away, let out, let slip, reveal, [*informal*] spill the beans, tell.

blustering adjective
I don't like his blustering manner. angry, boasting, boisterous, bragging, bullying, crowing, defiant, domineering, hectoring, noisy, ranting, self-assertive, showing-off, storming, swaggering, threatening, vaunting, violent.
OPPOSITES: SEE **modest**.

blustery adjective
gusty, squally, SEE **windy**.

board noun
1 *wooden boards.* blockboard, chipboard, clapboard, panel, plank, plywood, sheet, slab, slat, timber, weather board.
2 *the managing board.* committee, council, department, directorate, jury, panel.

board verb
1 *The fire victims were boarded in a hotel.* accommodate, billet, house, lodge, put up, quarter.
2 *We boarded the plane an hour before take-off.* catch, embark (on), enter, get on, go on board.

boast verb
[*slang*] be all mouth, [*informal*] blow your own trumpet, bluster, brag, crow, exaggerate, gloat, praise yourself, [*slang*] shoot a line, show off, [*informal*] sing your own praises, swagger, [*informal*] swank, talk big, vaunt.

boastful adjective
[*informal*] big headed, bragging, [*informal*] cocky, conceited, egotistical, proud, puffed up, swaggering, swanky, swollen-headed, vain, [*formal*] vainglorious.
OPPOSITES: SEE **modest**.

boat noun
VARIOUS BOATS: SEE **vessel**.

boatman noun
bargee, ferryman, gondolier, lighterman, oarsman, rower, SEE **sailor**, waterman, yachtsman.

bob verb
Something bobbed up and down in the water. be agitated, bounce, dance, hop, jerk, jig about, jolt, jump, leap, move about, nod, oscillate, shake, toss about, twitch.

body noun
1 *the human body.* anatomy, being, build, figure, form, frame, individual, physique, shape, substance.
2 *a blow to the body.* torso, trunk.
3 *a dead body.* cadaver, carcass, corpse, mortal remains, mummy, relics, remains, [*slang*] stiff.
4 *the governing body.* association, band, committee, company, corporation, SEE **group** noun, society.
5 *a large body of material.* accumulation, agglomeration, collection, corpus, mass.

PARTS OF THE HUMAN BODY: abdomen, Adam's apple, ankle, anus, aorta, arm, armpit, artery, backbone, bladder, bone, bowel, brain, breast, buttocks, calf, cartilage, cheek, chest, chin, clavicle, coccyx, cranium, duodenum, ear, eardrum, elbow, epiglottis, eye, Fallopian tube, finger, foot, forehead.
genitals, gland, groin, gullet, gums, gut, hand, haunch, head, heart, heel, hip, instep, intestines, jaw, jugular, kidney, knee, kneecap, knuckle, larynx, leg, lip, liver, loins, lung, mastoid, midriff, mouth, muscle, navel, neck, nerves, nipple, nose.
oesophagus, ovary, pancreas, pelvis, pituitary, pore, prostate, rectum, rib, shin, shoulder, sinew, sinus, skeleton, skin, skull, spine, spleen, stomach, temple, tendon, testicle, thigh, thorax, throat, thyroid, tongue, tonsil, tooth, trachea, uterus, vein, vertebrae, waist, windpipe, womb, wrist.

SOME BODILY FLUIDS AND CHEMICALS: bile, blood, hormone, saliva.

---

bodyguard noun
defender, guard, minder, protector.

bog noun
fen, marsh, marshland, mire, morass, mudflats, peat bog, quagmire, quicksands, salt-marsh, [*old-fashioned*] slough, swamp, wetlands.

boil noun
a boil on the skin. abscess, blister, carbuncle, chilblain, eruption, gathering, gumboil, inflammation, pimple, pock, pustule, sore, spot, tumour, ulcer, [*slang*] zit.

boil verb
1 *I boiled the water. I boiled the potatoes.* bring to boiling point, SEE **cook** verb, heat, simmer, stew.

2 *Is the water boiling yet?* bubble, effervesce, foam, seethe, steam.

boisterous adjective
1 *boisterous weather.* SEE **windy**.
2 *boisterous behaviour.* animated, cheerful, disorderly, exuberant, irrepressible, lively, loud, noisy, obstreperous, riotous, rollicking, rough, rowdy, tumultuous, unrestrained, unruly, uproarious, wild.
OPPOSITES: SEE **calm** adjective.

bold adjective
1 [*complimentary*] *a bold explorer.* adventurous, audacious, brave, confident, courageous, daring, dauntless, enterprising, fearless, forceful, gallant, heroic, intrepid, [*informal*] plucky, self-confident, valiant, valorous, venturesome.
OPPOSITES: SEE **cowardly**, **nervous**.
2 [*uncomplimentary*] *a bold request.* brash, brazen, cheeky, forward, fresh, impertinent, impudent, insolent, pert, presumptuous, rude, saucy, shameless, unashamed.
OPPOSITES: SEE **polite**.
3 *bold colours. bold writing.* big, bright, clear, conspicuous, eye-catching, large, obvious, prominent, pronounced, showy, striking, strong, vivid.
OPPOSITES: SEE **inconspicuous**.

boldness noun SEE **bravery**.

bolt noun
1 *a bolt on a door.* bar, catch, fastening, latch, lock.
2 *nuts and bolts.* peg, pin, rivet, rod, screw.

bolt verb
1 *Bolt the door.* bar, close, fasten, latch, lock, secure.
2 *The animals bolted.* abscond, dart away, dash away, escape, flee, fly, SEE **run**, rush off.
3 *Don't bolt your food.* devour, eat hastily, gobble, gulp, guzzle, stuff, wolf.

bomb noun
OTHER WEAPONS: SEE **weapon**.

bombard verb
1 *to bombard someone with missiles.* assail, assault, attack, beset, blast, blitz, bomb, fire at, pelt, pound, shell, shoot at, strafe.
2 *to bombard someone with questions.* badger, harass, importune, pester, plague.

bombardment noun
a bombardment of missiles. attack, barrage, blast, blitz, broadside, burst, cannonade, discharge, fusillade, hail, salvo, volley.

bond noun
1 *The captive tried to undo his bonds.* chain, cord, fastening, fetters, handcuffs, manacles, rope, shackles.
2 *There's a bond between the twins.*

affiliation, affinity, attachment, connection, link, relationship, tie, unity.
3 *His word is his bond.* agreement, compact, contract, covenant, guarantee, legal document, pledge, promise, word.

bonus noun
1 *I got £25 as a Christmas bonus.* bounty, commission, dividend, gift, gratuity, payment, [*informal*] perk, reward, supplement, tip.
2 *an unexpected bonus.* addition, advantage, benefit, extra, [*informal*] plus.

bony adjective
a bony figure. angular, emaciated, gangling, gawky, lanky, lean, scraggy, scrawny, skinny, thin, ungainly.
OPPOSITES: SEE **graceful**, **plump**.

boo verb
SEE **jeer**.

book noun
SEE **booklet**, copy, edition, hardback, paperback, publication, [*old-fashioned*] tome, volume, work.

VARIOUS KINDS OF BOOK: album, annual, anthology, atlas, bestiary, [*old-fashioned*] chap-book, compendium, concordance, diary, dictionary, digest, directory, encyclopaedia, fiction, gazetteer, guidebook, handbook, hymnal, hymnbook, jotter, ledger, lexicon, SEE **magazine**, manual, manuscript, missal, nonfiction, notebook, omnibus, picture-book, prayer-book, primer, psalter, reading book, reference book, score (*musical score*), scrap-book, scroll, sketch-book, textbook, thesaurus, vade mecum.

PARTS OF A BOOK: appendix, bibliography, [*informal*] blurb, chapter, contents page, cover, dust-jacket, epilogue, foreword, frontispiece, illustrations, index, introduction, plates, preface, prologue, text, title, title page.

VARIOUS KINDS OF WRITING: SEE **writing**.

---

book verb
1 *The policeman booked him for speeding.* SEE **arrest**, take your name, write down details.
2 *We booked tickets for the play.* buy, order, reserve.
3 *I've booked the disco for the party.* arrange, engage, organize, sign up.

booklet noun
brochure, leaflet, pamphlet, paperback.

boom noun
1 *the boom of big guns.* bang, blast, crash, explosion, reverberation, roar, SEE **sound** noun.
2 *a boom in trade.* bonanza, boost, expansion,

growth, improvement, increase, SEE
prosperity, spurt, upsurge, upturn.
OPPOSITES: SEE **slump** noun.

boost verb
Advertising boosts sales. advance, aid, assist,
augment, bolster, build up, buoy up,
encourage, enhance, enlarge, expand, foster,
further, give an impetus to [SEE **impetus**],
heighten, help, improve, increase, inspire,
lift, promote, push up, raise, sustain.
OPPOSITES: SEE **depress, hinder**.

booth noun
a telephone booth. a voting booth. carrel,
compartment, cubicle, hut, kiosk, stall,
stand.

booty noun
The escaping thieves dropped their booty.
contraband, gains, haul, loot, pickings,
pillage, plunder, spoils, [*informal*] swag,
takings, trophies, winnings.

border noun
1 *the border of a tablecloth. the border of a
lake.* brim, brink, edge, edging, frame,
frieze, frill, fringe, hem, margin, perimeter,
periphery, rim, surround, verge.
2 *You mustn't cross the border.* borderline,
boundary, frontier, limit.

border verb
Our garden borders the railway. abut on,
adjoin, be adjacent to, be alongside, join,
share a border with, touch.

borderline noun
SEE **boundary**.

bore verb
1 *to bore a hole.* burrow, drill, mine,
penetrate, perforate, pierce, sink, tunnel.
OPPOSITES: SEE **fill**.
2 *to bore an audience.* alienate, [*informal*]
leave people cold, tire, [*informal*] turn off,
weary.
OPPOSITES: SEE **interest** verb.

boring adjective
a boring book. boring work. arid,
commonplace, dreary, dry, dull, flat,
humdrum, long-winded, monotonous,
repetitious, repetitive, stale, tedious,
tiresome, trite, uneventful, unexciting,
uninspiring, uninteresting, vapid,
wearisome, wordy.
OPPOSITES: SEE **interesting**.

borrow verb
to borrow a pen. to borrow someone's ideas.
adopt, appropriate, be lent, [*informal*]
cadge, copy, crib, make use of, pirate,
plagiarize, [*informal*] scrounge, take, use,
usurp.
OPPOSITES: SEE **lend**.

bossy adjective
We resented her bossy manner. aggressive,
assertive, authoritarian, autocratic,
bullying, despotic, dictatorial, domineering,
exacting, hectoring, high-handed,
imperious, lordly, magisterial, masterful,
SEE **officious**, oppressive, overbearing,
peremptory, [*informal*] pushy, self-
assertive, tyrannical.
OPPOSITES: SEE **servile**.

bother noun
1 *There was some bother in the youth club.*
ado, difficulty, disorder, disturbance, fuss,
[*informal*] hassle, problem, [*informal*] to-
do, SEE **trouble** noun.
2 *Is the dog a bother to you?* annoyance,
inconvenience, irritation, nuisance, pest,
trouble, worry.

bother verb
1 *Do the wasps bother you?* annoy, concern,
dismay, disturb, exasperate, harass,
[*informal*] hassle, inconvenience, irk,
irritate, molest, nag, pester, plague, trouble,
upset, vex, worry.
2 *Don't bother to wash up.* be concerned, be
worried, care, mind, take trouble.

bottle noun
KINDS OF BOTTLE: carafe, carboy, decanter,
flagon, flask, jar, jeroboam, magnum, phial,
pitcher, vial, wine-bottle.

bottom adjective
1 *the bottom rung of a ladder.* deepest, lowest.
2 *bottom marks.* least, minimum.
OPPOSITES: SEE **top** adjective.

bottom noun
1 *the bottom of a wall.* base, foot, foundation,
pedestal, substructure, underside.
2 *the bottom of the sea.* bed, depths, floor,
underneath.
3 *She was at the bottom of her fortunes.* lowest
point, nadir.
4 *We tried to get to the bottom of his problem.*
basis, essence, grounds, heart, origin, root,
source.
5 *A wasp stung me on the bottom.* [*vulgar*]
arse, backside, behind, [*informal*] bum,
buttocks, [*formal or joking*] posterior, rear,
rump, seat, [*informal*] sit-upon.

boulder noun
a beach strewn with boulders. rock, stone.

bounce verb
The ball bounced up and down. bob, bound,
bump, jump, leap, move about, rebound,
recoil, ricochet, spring.

bound adjective
1 *Our friends are bound to help.* certain,
committed, compelled, destined, doomed,
duty-bound, fated, forced, obliged, pledged,
required, sure.

2 *His wrists were bound with rope.*
connected, hitched together, joined, lashed
together, linked, roped, strapped, tied,
trussed up.
bound for *The rocket was bound for the
moon.* aimed at, directed towards, going to,
heading for, making for, off to, travelling
towards.

bound verb
A dog bounded across the lawn. bob, bounce,
caper, frisk, gambol, hop, hurdle, jump,
leap, pounce, skip, spring, vault.

boundary noun
The fence marks the boundary. border,
borderline, bounds, brink, circumference,
confines, demarcation, edge, end, extremity,
fringe, frontier, interface, limit, margin,
perimeter, threshold, verge.

boundless adjective
boundless energy. endless, everlasting,
immeasurable, incalculable, inexhaustible,
infinite, limitless, unbounded, unflagging,
unlimited, untold, vast.

bounty noun
*The rich are not always known for their
bounty.* alms, altruism, benevolence,
charity, generosity, giving, kindness,
largesse, liberality, philanthropy,
unselfishness.

bouquet noun
a bouquet of flowers. arrangement, bunch,
buttonhole, corsage, garland, nosegay, posy,
spray, wreath.

bout noun
1 *a bout of coughing.* attack, fit, period, run,
spell, stint, stretch, time, turn.
2 *a boxing bout.* battle, combat, competition,
contest, encounter, engagement, fight,
match, round, struggle.

bow verb
to bow as a sign of respect. bend, bob, curtsy,
genuflect, incline, nod, stoop.

bowl noun
a bowl of soup. basin, dish, tureen.

bowl verb
He bowled a faster ball. fling, hurl, lob, pitch,
throw, toss.

box noun
carton, case, casket, chest, coffer, coffin,
crate, pack, package, tea chest, trunk.
OTHER CONTAINERS: SEE **container**.

boy noun
[*uncomplimentary*] brat, [*informal*] kid, lad,
schoolboy, son, [*joking*] stripling,
[*uncomplimentary*] urchin, youngster,
youth.

boycott noun
a boycott of imported goods. ban, blacklist,
embargo, prohibition.

boycott verb
to boycott a meeting. to boycott goods. avoid,
black, blackball, blacklist, exclude,
[*informal*] give the cold-shoulder to, ignore,
make unwelcome, ostracize, outlaw,
prohibit, spurn, stay away from.

boyish adjective
SEE **youthful**.

bracing adjective
SEE **invigorating**.

brag verb
I don't think you should brag about winning.
[*informal*] blow your own trumpet, boast,
crow, gloat, show off, swank, talk big.

brain noun
Use your brain! brains, [*informal*] grey
matter, intellect, intelligence, mind,
[*informal*] nous, reason, sense,
understanding, wisdom, wit.
RELATED ADJECTIVE: cerebral.

brainwash verb
to brainwash political prisoners. condition,
indoctrinate, re-educate.

branch noun
1 *a branch of a tree.* arm, bough, limb,
offshoot, prong.
2 *a branch of the armed services. a branch of
a subject.* department, division, part, office,
ramification, section, subdivision, wing.

brand noun
a brand of margarine. kind, label, line, make,
sort, trademark, type, variety.

brand verb
1 *to brand cattle with a hot iron.* burn,
identify, label, mark, scar, stamp.
2 *to brand someone as a trouble-maker.*
censure, denounce, discredit, give (someone)
the reputation of, stigmatize, vilify.

brandish verb
SEE **wave** verb.

brass noun
OTHER METALS: SEE **metal**.

BRASS INSTRUMENTS: bugle, cornet,
euphonium, flugelhorn, horn, trombone,
trumpet, tuba.

brave adjective
a brave act. a brave person. adventurous,
audacious, bold, chivalrous, cool,
courageous, daring, dauntless, fearless,
gallant, game, heroic, indomitable, intrepid,
lion-hearted, [*uncomplimentary*] macho,
[*sexist*] manly, noble, plucky, resolute,

spirited, stalwart, stoical, tough, unafraid, uncomplaining, undaunted, unshrinking, valiant, valorous, venturesome.
OPPOSITES: SEE **cowardly**.

bravery noun
Everyone praised her bravery. audacity, boldness, [*informal*] bottle, bravado [= *outward show of bravery*], courage, daring, determination, fearlessness, fortitude, gallantry, [*informal*] grit, [*informal*] guts, heroism, [*informal*] nerve, [*informal*] pluck, prowess, resolution, spirit, [*slang*] spunk, stoicism, valour.
OPPOSITES: SEE **cowardice**.

brawl noun
a brawl in the street. affray, altercation, [*informal*] bust-up, clash, [*informal*] dust-up, SEE **fight** noun, fracas, fray, [*informal*] free-for-all, mêlée, [*informal*] punch-up, scrap, scuffle, [*informal*] set-to, tussle.

brawl verb
SEE **fight** verb.

breach noun
1 *a breach of the rules.* breaking, contravention, failure, infringement, offence (against), transgression, violation.
2 *a breach between friends.* alienation, break, difference, disagreement, drifting apart, estrangement, quarrel, rift, [*formal*] schism (*in a church, etc.*), separation, split.
3 *a breach in a sea wall.* aperture, chasm, crack, fissure, gap, hole, opening, rent, rupture, space, split.

bread noun
WAYS IN WHICH BREAD IS SOLD: brioche, cob, croissant, French bread, loaf, roll, stick of bread, toast.

break noun
1 *a break in a pipe.* breach, breakage, burst, chink, cleft, crack, crevice, cut, fissure, fracture, gap, gash, hole, leak, opening, rent, rift, rupture, slit, split, tear.
2 *a break in work.* [*informal*] breather, breathing-space, hiatus, interlude, intermission, interval, [*informal*] let-up, lull, pause, respite, rest, tea-break.

break verb
1 *to break in half. to break into pieces.* breach, burst, [*informal*] bust, chip, crack, crumple, crush, damage, demolish, SEE **destroy**, fracture, fragment, knock down, ruin, shatter, shiver, smash, [*informal*] smash to smithereens, snap, splinter, split, squash, wreck.
2 *to break the law. to break a promise.* contravene, disobey, disregard, flout, go back on, infringe, transgress, violate.
3 *to break a record. to break the speed limit.* beat, better, do more than, exceed, excel, go beyond, outdo, outstrip, pass, surpass.

breakdown noun
1 *a mental breakdown. a mechanical breakdown.* collapse, disintegration, failure, fault (*a mechanical fault*), hitch, [*formal*] malfunction, stoppage.
2 *a breakdown of the figures.* analysis, classification, dissection, itemization.

breakthrough noun
a scientific breakthrough. advance, development, discovery, find, improvement, innovation, invention, leap forward, progress, revolution, success.

breakwater noun
groyne, jetty, mole, pier, sea-defence.

breast noun
bosom, bust, chest, front.

breath noun
a breath of wind. breeze, pant, puff, sigh, waft, whiff, whisper.

breathe verb
1 *to breathe fresh air.* exhale, inhale, pant, puff, respire.
2 *Don't breathe a word of this!* hint, let out, SEE **speak**, whisper.

breathless adjective
Running makes me breathless. exhausted, gasping, out of breath, panting, puffing, tired out, wheezy.

breed noun
1 *a breed of dog.* kind, pedigree, sort, species, strain, type, variety.
2 *a breed of people.* ancestry, clan, family, line, nation, progeny, race, stock.

breed verb
1 *Mice breed rapidly.* bear young ones, beget young ones, increase, multiply, procreate, produce young, propagate (*plants*), raise young ones, reproduce.
2 *Familiarity breeds contempt.* arouse, cause, create, cultivate, develop, engender, foster, generate, induce, nourish, nurture, occasion.

breeze noun SEE **wind** noun.

breezy adjective
airy, draughty, fresh, SEE **windy**.

brevity noun
Owing to the brevity of the speeches, we finished early. briefness, compression, conciseness, curtness, economy, incisiveness, pithiness, shortness, succinctness, terseness.

brew verb
1 *to brew beer. to brew tea.* ferment, infuse, make, steep, stew.
2 *They're brewing mischief.* concoct, contrive, [*informal*] cook up, develop,

devise, foment, hatch, plan, plot, prepare,
scheme, stir up.

bribe noun
[*slang*] backhander, bribery, [*informal*]
carrot, enticement, [*slang*] graft, gratuity,
incentive, inducement, [*informal*] payola,
protection money, [*informal*] sweetener,
tip.

bribe verb
Don't try to bribe the vicar. buy off, corrupt,
entice, [*informal*] grease the palm of,
influence, offer a bribe to [SEE **bribe** noun],
pervert, reward, [*formal*] suborn, tempt,
tip.

brick noun
bricks used in building. block, breeze-block,
building block, flagstone, paving stone, set
or sett, stone.

bridge noun
a bridge over a river. arch, crossing, span,
way over.

KINDS OF BRIDGE: aqueduct, Bailey bridge,
causeway, drawbridge, flyover, footbridge,
overpass, pontoon bridge, suspension
bridge, swing bridge, subway, underpass,
viaduct.

bridge verb
to bridge a gap. connect, cross, fill, join, link,
span, straddle, traverse, unite.

brief adjective
1 *a brief visit. a brief journey.* cursory, fast,
SEE **fleeting**, hasty, limited, little,
momentary, passing, quick, sharp, short,
short-lived, temporary, transient.
OPPOSITES: SEE **long** adjective.
2 *a brief summary of a story. a brief comment.*
abbreviated, abridged, compact,
compressed, concise, condensed, crisp, curt,
curtailed, incisive, laconic, pithy,
shortened, succinct, terse, thumbnail [*a
thumbnail sketch*].
OPPOSITES: SEE **wordy**.

brief noun
1 *We were given the brief for our next job.*
advice, briefing, data, description,
directions, information, instructions,
orders, outline, plan.
2 *a barrister's brief.* argument, case, defence,
dossier, summary.

brief verb
*The captain briefed her team before the
match.* advise, direct, [*informal*] fill
(someone) in, give (someone) the facts,
guide, inform, instruct, prepare, [*informal*]
put (someone) in the picture, prime.

bright adjective
1 *bright colours. a bright day.* blazing,
brilliant, burnished, clear, dazzling, flashy,
gaudy, glaring, gleaming, glistening,
glittering, glowing, intense, light (*a light
room*), luminous, lustrous, pellucid, radiant,
resplendent, scintillating, shimmering,
shining, shiny, showy, sparkling, sunny,
twinkling, vivid.
OPPOSITES: SEE **dark, dull** adjective.
2 *a bright manner.* SEE **cheerful**.
3 *a bright idea.* SEE **clever**.

brighten verb
1 *Some fresh paint will brighten this place
up.* cheer, enliven, gladden, illuminate, light
up, perk up, revitalize, smarten up.
2 *The weather brightened.* become sunny,
clear up, lighten.

brilliant adjective
1 *brilliant light.* blazing, bright, dazzling,
glaring, gleaming, glittering, glorious,
resplendent, scintillating, shining, showy,
sparkling, splendid, vivid.
OPPOSITES: SEE **dull** adjective.
2 *a brilliant scientist.* SEE **clever**.
3 *a brilliant game.* SEE **excellent**.

brim noun
filled to the brim. brink, circumference, edge,
limit, lip, margin, perimeter, periphery,
rim, top, verge.

bring verb
1 *Did you bring the shopping home?* bear,
carry, convey, deliver, fetch, take, transfer,
transport.
2 *Bring your friends in.* accompany, conduct,
escort, guide, lead, usher.
3 *Their performance brought great applause.*
attract, cause, create, draw, engender,
generate, get, give rise to, induce, lead to,
occasion, produce, prompt, provoke, result
in.
to bring about *The head teacher brought
about changes.* achieve, cause, create, effect,
engineer, manage.
to bring in 1 *The charity appeal brought in
many donations.* accrue, earn, gross, net,
profit, realize, yield. 2 *The manufacturer is
bringing in a new model.* initiate, introduce,
make available, start.
to bring off *It was a difficult play to bring
off.* accomplish, be successful in, do
successfully, succeed in.
to bring on 1 *The warmth brings on the
flowers.* accelerate, advance, encourage,
speed up. 2 *Stress brings on his asthma.*
aggravate, cause, give rise to, induce, lead
to, occasion, precipitate, provoke.
to bring out 1 *We brought out a poetry
magazine.* issue, print, produce, publish,
release. 2 *Her description brings out the
funny side.* accentuate, dwell on, emphasize,

feature, foreground, highlight, make obvious, play up, point up, show clearly, spotlight, stress, underline.
to bring up *Parents bring up children.* care for, educate, foster, look after, nurture, raise, rear, teach, train.

brink noun
the brink of the lake. bank, border, boundary, brim, circumference, edge, fringe, limit, lip, margin, perimeter, periphery, rim, skirt, threshold, verge.

brisk adjective
brisk exercise. a brisk manner. active, alert, animated, bright, businesslike, bustling, busy, crisp, decisive, energetic, fast, invigorating, keen, lively, nimble, quick, rapid, [*informal*] snappy, [*informal*] spanking (*at a spanking pace*), speedy, spirited, sprightly, spry, vigorous.
OPPOSITES: SEE **leisurely**.

bristly adjective
SEE **hairy**.

brittle adjective
brittle bones. brittle toffee. breakable, crackly, crisp, crumbling, delicate, easily broken, fragile, frail.
OPPOSITES: SEE **flexible, resilient**.

broad adjective
1 *a broad path. a broad expanse of countryside.* ample, capacious, expansive, extensive, great, large, open, roomy, spacious, sweeping, vast, wide.
OPPOSITES: SEE **narrow, small**.
2 *a broad outline of a story.* general, imprecise, indefinite, inexact, non-specific, undetailed, vague.
OPPOSITES: SEE **specific**.
3 *She had broad tastes in music.* all-embracing, catholic, comprehensive, eclectic, encyclopaedic, universal, wide-ranging.
4 *Her broad sense of humour made him blush.* bawdy, [*slang*] blue, coarse, earthy, improper, impure, indecent, indelicate, racy, ribald, suggestive, vulgar.

broadcast verb
1 *They broadcast the concert on TV.* relay, send out, televise, transmit.
2 *I'll tell you a secret if you promise not to broadcast it.* advertise, announce, circulate, [*formal*] disseminate, make known, make public, proclaim, [*formal*] promulgate, publish, report, scatter about, spread.

broadcaster noun
anchor-man, announcer, commentator, compère, disc jockey, DJ, SEE **entertainer**, linkman, newsreader, presenter.

broaden verb
to broaden your interests. branch out (into something), build up, develop, diversify, enlarge, expand, extend, increase, open up, spread, widen.

broad-minded adjective
a broad-minded outlook. all-embracing, balanced, broad, catholic, comprehensive, cosmopolitan, eclectic, enlightened, liberal, open-minded, permissive, tolerant, unbiased, unbigoted, unprejudiced, unshockable, wide-ranging.
OPPOSITES: SEE **narrow-minded**.

brochure noun
a travel brochure. booklet, broadsheet, catalogue, circular, folder, handbill, leaflet, pamphlet, prospectus.

brooch noun
badge, clasp, clip.

brood noun
a mother and her brood. clutch (*of eggs*), children, issue, family, litter (*of pups*), offspring, progeny, young.

brood verb
1 *The hen was brooding her clutch of eggs.* hatch, incubate, sit on.
2 *Don't brood over past mistakes.* agonize, dwell (on), fret, meditate (on), mope, mull over, muse (on), ponder, reflect (on), sulk (about), think (about).

brook noun
beck, burn, channel, [*poetic*] rill, rivulet, stream, watercourse.

broom noun
Sweep the floor with a broom. besom, brush.

brown adjective
SHADES OF BROWN: beige, bronze, buff, chestnut, chocolate, dun, fawn, khaki, ochre, russet, sepia, tan, tawny, terracotta, umber.

brown verb
1 *Brown the topping under the grill.* grill, toast.
2 *Do you brown quickly in the sun?* bronze, burn, colour, tan.

browse verb
1 *The cattle browsed in the meadow.* crop grass, eat, feed, graze, pasture.
2 *I was browsing in a book.* dip in, flick through, leaf through, look through, peruse, read here and there, scan, skim, thumb through.

bruise noun
black eye, bump, [*formal*] contusion, discoloration, [*informal*] shiner. SEE ALSO: **wound** noun.

bruise verb
blacken, crush, damage, discolour, injure, knock, mark, SEE **wound** verb.

brush noun
1 *a brush to sweep with.* besom, broom.
2 *a brush with the police.* SEE **conflict** noun.

brush verb
Brush your hair. comb, groom, tidy.
to brush up *to brush up your facts.* go over, improve, read up, refresh your memory of, relearn, revise, study, [*informal*] swot up.

brusque adjective
SEE **curt**.

brutal adjective
a brutal murder. atrocious, barbarous, beastly, bestial, bloodthirsty, bloody, brutish, callous, cold-blooded, cruel, dehumanized, ferocious, heartless, inhuman, inhumane, merciless, murderous, pitiless, remorseless, ruthless, sadistic, savage, uncivilized, unfeeling, vicious, violent, wild.
OPPOSITES: SEE **gentle, humane**.

brute noun
1 SEE **animal** noun, beast, creature, dumb animal.
2 *The executioner was a cruel brute.* barbarian, bully, devil, lout, monster, SEE **ruffian**, sadist, savage, swine.

brutish adjective
We were horrified by their brutish behaviour. animal, barbaric, barbarous, beastly, bestial, boorish, brutal, coarse, cold-blooded, crude, SEE **cruel**, [*informal*] gross, inhuman, insensitive, loutish, mindless, savage, senseless, stupid, subhuman, uncouth, unintelligent, unthinking.
OPPOSITES: SEE **humane**.

bubble noun
ball, blister, hollow, [*formal*] vesicle.
bubbles *soap bubbles. bubbles in champagne.* effervescence, fizz, foam, froth, head, lather, suds.

bubble verb
The water bubbled. boil, effervesce, fizz, fizzle, foam, froth, gurgle, seethe, sparkle.

bubbly adjective
bubbly drinks. carbonated, effervescent, fizzy, foaming, seething, sparkling.
OPPOSITE: flat.

buck verb
The horse bucked. bound, jerk, jump, leap, prance, spring, start, vault.
to buck up 1 [*informal*] *Buck up—we're late!* SEE **hurry**. 2 [*informal*] *After I lost the game, she tried to buck me up.* animate, cheer up, encourage, enliven, gladden, hearten, inspire, make cheerful, please, revitalize, revive.

bucket noun
can, pail.

buckle noun
the buckle of a belt. catch, clasp, clip, fastener, fastening, hasp.

buckle verb
1 *Buckle your safety belts.* clasp, clip, do up, fasten, hitch up, hook up, secure.
2 *The framework buckled under the weight.* bend, bulge, cave in, collapse, contort, crumple, curve, dent, distort, fold, twist, warp.

bud verb
The trees are budding early this year. begin to grow, burgeon, develop, shoot, sprout.

budge verb
1 *The stubborn donkey wouldn't budge.* change position, give way, move, shift, stir, yield.
2 *We couldn't budge him.* alter, change, dislodge, influence, move, persuade, propel, push, remove, shift, sway.

budget noun
Don't spend more than your budget allows. accounts, allocation of funds, allowance, estimate, financial planning, funds, means, resources.

budget verb
We've budgeted for a new carpet next year. allocate money, allot resources, allow (for), estimate expenditure, plan your spending, provide (for), ration your spending.

buff verb
Buff up the paintwork with a soft cloth. burnish, clean, polish, rub, shine, smooth.

buffet noun
1 *We went to the buffet for a snack.* bar, café, cafeteria, counter, snack-bar.
2 *They prepared a buffet for the party.* SEE **meal**.

bug noun
1 [*informal*] *Birds help to control bugs in the garden.* SEE **pest**.
2 [*informal*] *I had a bug which made me ill.* SEE **micro-organism**.
3 *a bug in a computer program.* breakdown, defect, error, failing, fault, flaw, [*informal*] gremlin, imperfection, [*formal*] malfunction, mistake, [*informal*] snarl-up, virus.

bug verb
Spies had bugged the telephone. intercept, interfere with, listen in to, tap.

build verb
to build a shed. assemble, construct, erect,
fabricate, form, [*informal*] knock together,
make, put together, put up, raise, rear (*They
reared a monument*), set up.
to build up 1 *He built up a large collection
of records.* accumulate, amass, assemble,
begin, bring together, collect, create,
develop, enlarge, expand, raise. 2 *The
excitement built up to a climax.* augment,
escalate, grow, increase, intensify, rise,
strengthen.

builder noun
bricklayer, construction worker, labourer.

building noun
construction, edifice, erection, piece of
architecture, [*informal*] pile, premises,
structure.

VARIOUS BUILDINGS: arcade, art gallery,
barn, barracks, basilica, boat-house,
brewery, broiler-house, bungalow, cabin,
castle, cathedral, chapel, château, SEE
church, cinema, clinic, college, complex,
cottage, crematorium, dovecote, factory,
farmhouse, filling-station, flats, fort,
fortress.
garage, gazebo, granary, grandstand,
gymnasium, hall, hangar, hotel, SEE **house**,
inn, library, lighthouse, mansion,
mausoleum, mill, monastery, monument,
mosque, museum, observatory, orphanage,
outbuilding, outhouse.
pagoda, palace, pavilion, pier, pigsty, police
station, post office, power-station, prison,
pub, public house, restaurant, school, shed,
SEE **shop**, silo, skyscraper, slaughterhouse,
stable, storehouse, studio, summerhouse,
synagogue, temple, theatre, tower, villa,
warehouse, waterworks, windmill,
woodshed.

ARCHITECTURAL FEATURES:
arch, balcony, baluster, balustrade,
banister, basement, battlement, bay
window, belfry, boss, bow window,
brickwork, buttress, capital, ceiling, cellar,
chimney, cloister, colonnade, column,
coping, corbel, cornice, corridor, courtyard,
coving, crypt.
dome, dormer window, drawbridge,
dungeon, eaves, finial, floor, foundation,
foyer, gable, gallery, gateway, gutter, joist,
keep, lobby, masonry, minaret, mullion.
parapet, pediment, pilaster, pillar, pinnacle,
porch, portal, portcullis, quadrangle, rafter,
rampart, roof, room, sill, spire, staircase,
steeple, tower, tracery, turret, vault,
veranda, wall, window, window-sill.

SOME BUILDING MATERIALS: asbestos,
asphalt, brick, cement, concrete,
fibre-board, fibreglass, glass, hardboard,
metal, mortar, paint, perspex, plaster,
plasterboard, plastic, plywood, polystyrene,
polythene, putty, PVC, rubber, slate, stone,
tar, tile, timber, vinyl, wood.

bulb noun
1 corm, tuber.

SOME FLOWERS THAT GROW FROM BULBS:
amaryllis, bluebell, crocus, daffodil, freesia,
hyacinth, lily, snowdrop, tulip.

2 *an electric bulb.* lamp, light.

bulge noun
*The bruise made a discoloured bulge under
his skin.* bump, [*formal*] distension, hump,
knob, lump, projection, [*formal*] protrusion,
protuberance, rise, swelling.

bulge verb
The sails bulged in the wind. belly, billow,
dilate, distend, enlarge, expand, project,
protrude, stick out, swell.

bulk noun
1 *The bulk of the aircraft amazed us.*
amplitude, bigness, body, dimensions,
extent, immensity, largeness, magnitude,
mass, size, substance, volume, weight.
2 *We did the bulk of the work ourselves.*
[*informal*] best part, greater part, majority,
preponderance.

bulky adjective
a bulky parcel. SEE **big**.

bulletin noun
a news bulletin. announcement,
communication, communiqué, dispatch,
message, news-flash, notice, proclamation,
report, statement.

bullfighter noun
matador, toreador.

bullion noun
gold bullion. bar, ingot, nugget, solid gold or
silver, etc.

bully verb
to bully younger children. bludgeon,
browbeat, coerce, cow, domineer, frighten,
hector, intimidate, oppress, persecute,
[*informal*] push around, terrorize, threaten,
torment, tyrannize.

bump noun
1 *a bump in the car.* bang, blow, collision,
crash, hit, knock, smash, thud, thump.
2 *a bump on the head.* bulge, [*formal*]
distension, hump, knob, lump, projection,
[*formal*] protrusion, protuberance, rise,
swelling.

bump verb
1 *He bumped us deliberately.* bang, collide with, crash into, jar, knock, ram, slam, smash into, strike, thump, wallop. SEE ALSO: **hit** verb.
2 *We bumped up and down on the rough road.* bounce, jerk, jolt, shake.

bumptious adjective
SEE **conceited**.

bumpy adjective
1 *a bumpy ride.* bouncy, jerky, jolting, rough.
2 *a bumpy surface.* irregular, knobbly, lumpy, uneven.

bunch noun
1 *a bunch of carrots. a bunch of keys.* batch, bundle, clump, cluster, collection, heap, lot, number, pack, quantity, set, sheaf, tuft.
2 *a bunch of flowers.* bouquet, posy, spray.
3 [*informal*] *a bunch of friends.* band, crew, crowd, flock, gang, gathering, group, mob, party, team, troop.

bunch verb
My friends bunched together in a corner. assemble, cluster, collect, congregate, crowd, flock, gather, group, herd, huddle, mass, pack.
OPPOSITES: SEE **scatter**.

bundle noun
a bundle of papers. bag, bale, bunch, carton, collection, pack, package, packet, parcel, sheaf, truss (*truss of hay*).

bung noun
the bung of a barrel. cork, plug, stopper.

bungle verb
If you bungle a job, you must do it again! blunder, botch, [*slang*] cock up, [*informal*] foul up, fluff, [*informal*] make a hash of, [*informal*] make a mess of, [*informal*] mess up, mismanage, [*informal*] muff, ruin, spoil.

buoyant adjective
1 *A boat must be made of buoyant material.* floating, light.
2 *We were in a buoyant mood after winning our match.* SEE **cheerful**.

burden noun
1 *a heavy burden.* cargo, encumbrance, load, weight.
2 *the burden of responsibility.* affliction, anxiety, care, duty, handicap, millstone, obligation, onus, problem, responsibility, sorrow, trial, trouble, worry.

burden verb
For years she was burdened by illness. afflict, bother, encumber, hamper, handicap, load (with), [*informal*] lumber (with), oppress, overload (with), [*informal*] saddle (with), strain, tax, trouble, worry.

burdensome adjective
a burdensome task. difficult, exacting, hard, heavy, irksome, onerous, taxing, tiring, troublesome, trying, wearisome, wearying, worrying.
OPPOSITES: SEE **easy**.

bureau noun
1 *a writing bureau.* desk.
2 *an information bureau.* agency, counter, department, office, service.

bureaucracy noun
They'd do things quicker if there was less bureaucracy! administration, officialdom, paperwork, [*informal*] red tape, regulations.

burglar noun
cat-burglar, house-breaker, intruder, robber, thief.

burglary noun
break-in, forcible entry, house-breaking, larceny, pilfering, robbery, stealing, theft, thieving.

burgle verb
to burgle a house. break in, pilfer, rob, steal from, thieve from.

burial noun
a burial service. entombment, funeral, interment, obsequies.

burly adjective
a burly figure. athletic, beefy, big, brawny, heavy, hefty, hulking, husky, muscular, powerful, stocky, stout, [*informal*] strapping, strong, sturdy, thickset, tough, well-built.
OPPOSITES: SEE **thin** adjective.

burn noun
1 *The victim's body was covered with burns.* blister, charring.
2 *a Scottish burn.* SEE **stream** noun.

burn verb
1 *The bonfire burned all day.* be alight, blaze, flame, flare, flash, flicker, glow, smoke, smoulder.
2 *The incinerator burns anything.* carbonize, consume, cremate, destroy by fire, ignite, incinerate, kindle, light, reduce to ashes, set fire to.
3 *The heat burnt his skin.* blister, brand, char, scald, scorch, sear, shrivel, singe, sting, toast.
OTHER RELATED WORDS: SEE **fire** noun, verb.

burning adjective
1 *a burning building.* ablaze, afire, alight, blazing, flaming, glowing, incandescent, lit up, on fire, raging, smouldering.
2 *a burning pain.* biting, blistering, boiling, fiery, hot, inflamed, scalding, scorching, searing, smarting, stinging.
3 *a burning substance* [= *a substance which*

burns you]. acid, caustic, corrosive.
4 *a burning smell* [= *a smell of burning*].
acrid, pungent, reeking, scorching, smoky.
5 *a burning desire.* acute, ardent, consuming,
eager, fervent, flaming, frenzied, heated,
impassioned, intense, passionate, red-hot,
vehement.
6 *a burning question.* crucial, important,
pertinent, pressing, relevant, urgent, vital.

burrow noun
an animal's burrow. (*a fox's or badger's*)
earth, excavation, hole, retreat, (*a badger's*)
set, shelter, tunnel, (*a rabbit's*) warren.

burrow verb
The rabbits burrowed under the fence. delve,
dig, excavate, mine, tunnel.

burst verb
1 *The door burst open. They burst open the
door.* be forced open, break, crack,
disintegrate, erupt, explode, force open, give
way, open suddenly, part suddenly,
puncture, rupture, shatter, split, tear.
2 *He burst into the room.* SEE **rush** verb.

bury verb
to bury something in the ground. conceal,
cover, embed, enclose, engulf, entomb, hide,
immerse, implant, insert, inter, lay to rest,
plant, put away, secrete, sink, submerge.

bus noun
[*old-fashioned*] charabanc, coach, double-
decker, minibus, [*old-fashioned*] omnibus.

bush noun SEE **shrub**.

bushy adjective
a bushy beard. bristling, bristly, dense,
fluffy, fuzzy, hairy, luxuriant, rough,
shaggy, spreading, sticking out, tangled,
thick, thick-growing, unruly, untidy.

business noun
1 *I have urgent business to see to.* affair,
concern, duty, issue, matter, problem,
question, responsibility, subject, task, topic.
2 *What sort of business do you want to go
into?* calling, career, craft, employment,
industry, job, line of work, occupation,
profession, pursuit, trade, vocation, work.
3 *The new shop does a lot of business.* buying
and selling, commerce, dealings, industry,
marketing, merchandising, selling, trade,
trading, transactions.
4 *He works for a sports equipment business.*
company, concern, corporation, enterprise,
establishment, firm, organization,
[*informal*] outfit, practice, [*informal*] set-
up, venture.

businesslike adjective
efficient, hard-headed, methodical, orderly,
practical, professional, prompt, systematic,
well-organized.

businessman, businesswoman nouns
dealer, entrepreneur, executive, financier,
industrialist, magnate, manager, merchant,
trader, tycoon.

bustle noun SEE **activity**.

bustle verb
*He bustled about the kitchen preparing
dinner.* dart, dash, fuss, hasten, hurry,
hustle, make haste, move busily, rush,
scamper, scramble, scurry, scuttle,
[*informal*] tear, whirl.

busy adjective
1 *busy in the garden. busy at work.* active,
assiduous, bustling about, diligent,
employed, energetic, engaged, engrossed,
[*informal*] hard at it, industrious, involved,
occupied, [*informal*] on the go, pottering,
slaving, tireless, [*informal*] up to your eyes,
working.
OPPOSITES: SEE **idle** adjective.
2 *It's busy in town on Saturdays.* bustling,
frantic, full of people, hectic, lively.
OPPOSITES: SEE **quiet**.

busybody noun
gossip, inquisitive person [SEE **inquisitive**],
meddler, [*informal*] Nosy Parker,
scandalmonger, snooper, spy.
to be a busybody SEE **interfere**.

butt noun
1 *a rifle butt.* haft, handle, shaft, stock.
2 *a water butt.* barrel, cask, water-butt.
OTHER CONTAINERS: SEE **container**.
3 *a cigar butt.* end, remains, remnant, stub.
4 *the butt of someone's ridicule.* mark, object,
subject, target, victim.
butts rifle-range, shooting-gallery, shooting-
range.

butt verb
It's not nice to be butted by a goat. buffet,
bump, jab, knock, poke, prod, punch, push,
ram, shove, strike, thump. SEE ALSO: **hit** verb.
to butt in SEE **interrupt**.

buttocks noun
[*impolite*] arse, backside, behind, bottom,
[*sometimes impolite*] bum, haunches,
hindquarters, [*joking*] posterior, rear,
rump, seat.

buttress noun
a buttress supporting the church wall. pier,
prop, reinforcement, support.

buy verb
to buy a TV set. acquire, gain, get, get on
hire purchase, [*informal*] invest in, obtain,
pay for, procure, purchase.
OPPOSITES: SEE **sell**.

buyer noun
customer, purchaser, shopper.
OPPOSITES: SEE **seller**.

bypass verb
Her case was so urgent that they bypassed the usual admission procedure. avoid, circumvent, dodge, evade, find a way round, get out of, go round, ignore, neglect, omit.

by-product noun
Becoming a baseball fan was a by-product of my research into sport on TV. adjunct, complement, consequence, corollary, repercussion, result, side-effect.

bystander noun
The police asked bystanders to describe the accident. eye-witness, looker-on, observer, onlooker, passer-by, spectator, watcher, witness.

Cc

cabin noun
1 *a cabin in the hills.* chalet, hut, lodge, shack, shanty, shed, shelter.
2 *a cabin on a ship.* berth, compartment, deck-house, quarters.

cable noun
1 *an anchor cable.* chain, cord, hawser, line, mooring, rope.
2 *electric cable.* flex, lead, wire.
3 *They sent a message by cable.* message, telegram, wire.

cache noun
a cache of stores. depot, dump, hiding-place, hoard, repository, reserve, stockpile, storehouse, supply.

cacophony noun
a noisy cacophony. atonality, caterwauling, din, discord, disharmony, dissonance, harshness, jangle, noise, racket, row, rumpus, tumult.
OPPOSITES: SEE **harmony**.

cadet noun
a cadet in the armed forces. beginner, learner, recruit, trainee.

cadge verb
The cat from next door cadges for food. ask, beg, scrounge, sponge.

café noun
bar, bistro, buffet, cafeteria, canteen, coffee bar, restaurant, snack-bar, take-away, tea-room.

cage noun
an animal's cage. a bird's cage. aviary, coop, enclosure, hutch, pen, pound.

cake noun
1 *cake for tea.*

KINDS OF CAKE: bun, doughnut, éclair, flan, fruit cake, gateau, gingerbread, macaroon, Madeira, madeleine, meringue, muffin, sandwich, scone, shortbread, simnel cake, sponge, teacake.

---

2 *a cake of soap.* block, lump, mass, piece, slab.

calamitous adjective
a calamitous mistake. cataclysmic, catastrophic, deadly, devastating, dire, disastrous, dreadful, fatal, ghastly, ruinous, serious, terrible, tragic, unfortunate, unlucky, woeful.

calamity noun
The fire was a terrible calamity. accident, affliction, cataclysm, catastrophe, disaster, misadventure, mischance, misfortune, mishap, tragedy, tribulation.

calculate verb
to calculate figures. add up, assess, compute, count, determine, do sums, enumerate, estimate, figure out, find out, gauge, judge, reckon, total, value, weigh, work out.

calculated adjective
SEE **deliberate**.

calculating adjective
SEE **crafty**.

calibre noun
1 *the calibre of a rifle.* bore, diameter, gauge, measure, size.
2 *They ought to win with players of such high calibre.* ability, capacity, character, distinction, excellence, genius, gifts, merit, proficiency, quality, skill, stature, talent, worth.

call noun
1 *a call for help.* cry, exclamation, scream, shout, yell.
2 *a bugle call.* signal, summons.
3 *Grandad made an unexpected call.* stay, stop, visit.

call verb
1 *He called in a loud voice.* clamour, cry out, exclaim, shout, yell.
2 *Grandad called on us.* drop in, visit.
3 *What did they call him?* baptize, christen, dub, name.
4 *What do you call your story?* entitle.
5 *On Saturdays mum calls me at nine.* arouse, awaken, get someone up, rouse, wake, waken.
6 *The boss called me to his office.* convene, gather, invite, order, summon.
7 *I tried to call, but the phone was dead.*

contact, dial, phone, ring, telephone.
to call for 1 *This calls for a celebration!*
demand, entail, necessitate, need, occasion,
require. 2 *They don't deliver, so we must call
for it.* collect, come for, fetch, pick up.
to call off *The weather was so bad we had to
call the game off.* abandon, adjourn, cancel,
discontinue, drop, end, halt, postpone.

calling noun
your calling in life. business, career,
employment, job, line of work, occupation,
profession, trade, vocation, work.

callous adjective
a callous murder. cold, cold-blooded, SEE
cruel, dispassionate, hard-bitten, [*informal*]
hard-boiled, hard-hearted, heartless,
inhuman, insensitive, merciless, pitiless,
ruthless, [*informal*] thick-skinned,
uncaring, unconcerned, unemotional,
unfeeling, unsympathetic.
OPPOSITES: SEE **kind** adjective.

callus noun SEE **blemish**.

calm adjective
1 *calm water. calm weather.* airless, even,
flat, glassy, [*poetic*] halcyon (*halcyon days*),
like a millpond, motionless, placid, quiet,
slow-moving, smooth, still, unclouded,
unruffled, unwrinkled, windless.
OPPOSITES: SEE **stormy**.
2 *a calm mood. a calm temperament.*
collected, [*uncomplimentary*] complacent,
composed, cool, dispassionate, equable,
impassive, imperturbable, [*informal*] laid-
back, level-headed, moderate, pacific,
[*uncomplimentary*] passionless, patient,
peaceful, quiet, relaxed, restful, restrained,
sedate, self-possessed, sensible, serene,
tranquil, unemotional, unexcitable,
[*informal*] unflappable, unhurried,
unperturbed, untroubled.
OPPOSITES: SEE **anxious**, **excitable**.

calm noun
1 *the calm after a storm.* calmness, peace,
quietness, stillness, tranquillity.
OPPOSITES: SEE **storm** noun.
2 *I admired his calm.* SEE **calmness**.

calm verb
to calm an angry person. appease, compose,
control, cool down, lull, mollify, pacify,
placate, quieten, settle down, sober down,
soothe, tranquillize.
OPPOSITES: SEE **upset** verb.

calmness noun
I was amazed by his calmness in the crisis.
[*uncomplimentary*] complacency,
composure, equability, equanimity,
imperturbability, level-headedness, peace

of mind, sang-froid, self-possession,
serenity, [*informal*] unflappability.
OPPOSITES: SEE **anxiety**.

camouflage noun
They used branches of trees as camouflage.
blind, cloak, concealment, cover, disguise,
front, guise, mask, protective colouring,
screen, veil.

camouflage verb
We camouflaged our hide-out. cloak, conceal,
cover up, disguise, hide, mask, obscure,
screen, veil.

camp noun
a scout camp. bivouac, camping-ground,
camp-site, encampment.

campaign noun
*a military campaign. a campaign to save the
whale.* action, battle, crusade, drive, fight,
movement, offensive, operation, push,
struggle, war.

can noun
a can of lager. canister, jar, tin.

canal noun
channel, waterway.

cancel verb
1 *to cancel a sporting fixture.* abandon, drop,
give up, postpone, scrap, [*informal*] scrub.
2 *to cancel an instruction. to cancel a debt.*
abolish, abort, [*formal*] abrogate (*a law*),
annul, countermand, cross out, delete,
eliminate, erase, expunge, invalidate,
nullify, override, overrule, quash, repeal,
repudiate, rescind, revoke, wipe out.
to cancel out compensate for, counterbalance, make up for, neutralize, offset,
outweigh, wipe out.

cancer noun
canker (*of a plant or tree*), carcinoma,
growth, malignancy, melanoma, tumour.

carcinogenic adjective
producing cancer.

candid adjective
a candid opinion. blunt, direct, fair,
forthright, frank, honest, just, [*informal*]
no-nonsense, open, outspoken, plain,
sincere, straightforward, true, truthful,
unbiased, undisguised, unflattering,
unprejudiced.
OPPOSITES: SEE **devious**, **insincere**.

candidate noun
a candidate for a job or an examination.
applicant, aspirant, competitor, contender,
contestant, entrant, [*informal*] possibility,
pretender (*to the throne*), runner, [*old-
fashioned*] suitor (*for a woman's hand in
marriage*).

cane noun
a cane to support a tomato plant. bamboo, rod, stick.

canoe noun
dug-out, kayak.
OTHER CRAFT: SEE **vessel**.

canopy noun
There was a waterproof canopy over the platform. awning, cover, covering, shade, shelter, umbrella.

canteen noun
We had a snack in the canteen. bar, buffet, café, cafeteria, coffee-bar, restaurant, snack-bar.

canvass noun
a canvass of public opinion. census, enquiry (into), examination, investigation, market research (into), opinion poll, poll, probe (into), scrutiny, survey.

canvass verb
to canvass for votes. ask for, campaign (for), [*informal*] drum up, electioneer, seek, solicit.

canyon noun
a deep canyon. defile, gorge, pass, ravine, valley.

cap noun
1 KINDS OF HAT: SEE **hat**.
2 *the cap off a ketchup bottle.* covering, lid, top.

capable adjective
a capable mathematician. able, accomplished, clever, competent, effective, efficient, experienced, expert, gifted, [*informal*] handy, intelligent, masterly, practised, proficient, qualified, skilful, skilled, talented, trained.
OPPOSITES: SEE **incompetent**.
capable of *She's capable of turning up without warning.* adept at, apt to, disposed to, equal to, liable to.

capacity noun
1 *the capacity of a container.* dimensions, magnitude, size, volume.
2 *your mental capacity. your physical capacity.* ability, capability, competence, SEE **intelligence**, power, skill, talent.
3 *In his capacity as captain he's got a right to tell us what to do.* appointment, function, job, office, position, post, role.

cape noun
1 *a waterproof cape.* cloak, coat, cope, mantle, robe, shawl, wrap.
2 *the Cape of Good Hope.* head, headland, peninsula, point, promontory.

capital adjective
1 *the capital city.* chief, controlling, first, foremost, leading, main, pre-eminent, primary, principal.
2 *a capital offence.* punishable by death.
3 *a capital letter.* big, block, initial, large, upper-case.

capital noun
1 *Paris is the capital of France.* chief city, centre of government.
2 *capital to start a new business.* assets, cash, finance, funds, investments, principal, money, property, [*slang*] the ready, resources, riches, savings, stock, wealth, [*informal*] the wherewithal.

capitulate verb
They capitulated after a long fight. be defeated, desist, fall, give in, submit, succumb, surrender, [*informal*] throw in the towel, yield.
OPPOSITES: SEE **persevere**.

capricious adjective
a capricious wind. a capricious personality. changeable, erratic, fanciful, fickle, fitful, flighty, impulsive, inconstant, mercurial, moody, quirky, uncertain, unpredictable, unreliable, variable, wayward, whimsical.
OPPOSITES: SEE **steady** adjective.

capsize verb
The boat capsized. flip over, invert, keel over, overturn, tip over, turn over, [*informal*] turn turtle, turn upside down.

capsule noun
The doctor gave her some capsules. lozenge, medicine, pill, tablet.

captain noun
1 *the captain of a team.* boss, chief, head, leader.
2 *an army captain. a naval captain.* SEE **rank** noun.
3 *the captain of a ship. the captain of an aircraft.* commander, master, officer in charge, pilot, skipper.

captivate verb
The music captivated us. Her beauty captivated him. attract, beguile, bewitch, charm, delight, enamour, enchant, enrapture, ensnare, enthral, entrance, fascinate, hypnotize, infatuate, mesmerize, seduce, [*informal*] steal your heart, [*informal*] turn your head.
OPPOSITES: SEE **repel**.

captive adjective
captive animals. caged, captured, chained, confined, detained, enslaved, ensnared, fettered, gaoled, imprisoned, incarcerated, jailed, restricted, secure, taken prisoner.
OPPOSITES: SEE **free** adjective.

captive noun
captives in prison. convict, detainee, hostage, internee, prisoner.

captivity noun
His enemies kept him in captivity. bondage, confinement, custody, detention, duress (*under duress*), imprisonment, incarceration, internment [don't confuse with *interment*], SEE **prison**, protective custody, remand (*on remand*), restraint (*under restraint*), servitude, slavery.
OPPOSITES: SEE **freedom**.

capture verb
1 *to capture a criminal.* apprehend, arrest, [*informal*] bag, bind, catch, [*informal*] collar, corner, [*informal*] get, [*informal*] nab, overpower, secure, seize, take prisoner, SEE **trap** verb.
2 *to capture a castle.* SEE **conquer**.

car noun
automobile, [*informal*] banger [= *old car*], [*joking*] bus, [*joking*] jalopy, motor, motor car, [*informal*] wheels.

KINDS OF CAR: convertible, coupé, Dormobile, estate, fastback, hatchback, jeep, Land Rover, limousine, Mini, patrol car, police car, saloon, shooting brake, sports car, tourer.

OTHER VEHICLES: SEE **vehicle**.

---

carcass noun
1 *the carcass of an animal.* body, cadaver, corpse, meat, remains.
2 *the rusting carcass of an old car.* framework, hulk, remains, shell, skeleton, structure.

card noun
a piece of card. cardboard, SEE **paper**, pasteboard.

VARIOUS MESSAGE CARDS: birthday card, Christmas card, congratulations card, Easter card, get well card, greetings card, invitation, notelet, picture postcard, postcard, sympathy card, Valentine, visiting card.

---

care noun
1 *Drive with care.* attention. carefulness, caution, circumspection, concentration, concern, diligence, exactness, forethought, heed, interest, meticulousness, pains, prudence, solicitude, thoroughness, thought, vigilance, watchfulness.
OPPOSITES: SEE **carelessness**.
2 *He doesn't have a care in the world!* anxiety, burden, concern, difficulty, hardship, problem, responsibility, sorrow, stress, tribulation, trouble, vexation, woe, worry.
3 *She left the baby in my care.* charge, control, custody, guardianship, keeping,
management, protection, safe-keeping, [*formal*] ward.

care verb
If you saw their suffering, you would care about them. be troubled, bother, concern yourself, mind, worry.
to care for 1 *He cares for his dog.* attend to, cherish, guard, keep, [*informal*] keep an eye on, look after, mind, mother, nurse, protect, supervise, take care of, tend, watch over. 2 *Do you care for me?* SEE **love** verb.

career noun
a career in industry. business, calling, employment, job, livelihood, occupation, profession, trade, vocation, work.
VARIOUS CAREERS: SEE **job**.

carefree adjective
1 *a carefree attitude.* casual, cheerful, cheery, contented, debonair, easy, easy-going, happy, happy-go-lucky, [*informal*] laid-back, light-hearted, relaxed, unconcerned, unworried.
OPPOSITES: SEE **anxious, tense** adjective.
2 *a carefree holiday.* leisured, peaceful, quiet, relaxing, restful, trouble-free, untroubled.

careful adjective
1 *a careful worker. careful work.* accurate, conscientious, deliberate, diligent, exhaustive, fastidious, judicious, methodical, meticulous, neat, orderly, organized, painstaking, particular, precise, punctilious, responsible, rigorous, scrupulous, systematic, thorough.
2 *Be careful not to upset anyone.* alert, attentive, cautious, chary, circumspect, heedful, mindful, observant, prudent, solicitous, thoughtful, vigilant, wary, watchful.
OPPOSITES: SEE **careless**.

careless adjective
1 *careless driving. careless talk.* absent-minded, heedless, ill-considered, imprudent, inattentive, incautious, inconsiderate, irresponsible, negligent, rash, reckless, thoughtless, uncaring, unguarded, unthinking, unwary.
2 *careless work.* casual, confused, cursory, disorganized, hasty, imprecise, inaccurate, jumbled, messy, perfunctory, scatter-brained, shoddy, slapdash, slipshod, [*informal*] sloppy, slovenly, thoughtless, untidy.
OPPOSITES: SEE **careful**.

carelessness noun
haste, inattention, irresponsibility, negligence, recklessness, [*informal*] sloppiness, slovenliness, thoughtlessness, untidiness.
OPPOSITES: SEE **care** noun.

caress verb
to caress someone lovingly. cuddle, embrace, fondle, hug, kiss, make love to, [*slang*] neck with, nuzzle, pat, pet, rub against, smooth, stroke, touch.

caretaker noun
custodian, janitor, keeper, porter, superintendent, warden, watchman.

cargo noun
The cargo was transported in large containers. consignment, freight, goods, [*formal*] lading (*bill of lading*), load, merchandise, payload, shipment.

caricature noun
[Don't confuse with *character*.] *She drew a wickedly funny caricature of the teacher.* cartoon, parody, satire, [*informal*] send-up, [*informal*] take-off, travesty.

caring adjective SEE **kind** adjective.

carnage noun
a scene of carnage. blood-bath, bloodshed, butchery, havoc, holocaust, killing, massacre, pogrom, shambles, slaughter.

carnal adjective
carnal desires. animal, bodily, erotic, fleshly, SEE **lustful**, natural, physical, sensual, sexual.

carnival noun
a bank-holiday carnival. celebration, fair, festival, festivity, fête, fiesta, fun and games, gala, jamboree, merrymaking, pageant, parade, procession, revelry, show, spectacle.

carnivorous adjective
flesh-eating, meat-eating.

carp verb
to carp about small problems. [*informal*] belly-ache, cavil, SEE **complain**, find fault, [*informal*] go on, grumble, object, quibble, [*informal*] split hairs.

carpentry noun
joinery, woodwork.

carriage noun
1 OTHER VEHICLES: SEE **vehicle**.
2 *Military men have an upright carriage.* bearing, comportment, demeanour, gait, manner, mien, posture.

carry verb
1 bring, fetch, haul, lift, [*informal*] lug, manhandle, move, remove, shoulder, take, transfer.
2 *Aircraft carry passengers and goods.* convey, ferry, ship, transport.
3 *Telegraph wires carry signals.* communicate, relay, transmit.
4 *The rear axle carries the greatest weight.* bear, hold up, support.

5 *Murder carries a heavy penalty.* demand, entail, involve, lead to, occasion, require, result in.
to carry on *We carried on in spite of the rain.* continue, go on, keep on, last, persevere, persist, remain, stay, [*informal*] stick it out, survive.
to carry out *We carried out her orders.* accomplish, achieve, complete, do, enforce, execute, finish, perform.

cart noun
barrow, dray, truck, wagon, wheelbarrow.

carton noun
box, case, pack, package, packet.

cartoon noun
1 *a cartoon in the newspaper.* caricature, comic strip, drawing, SEE **picture** noun, sketch.
2 *a cartoon on TV.* animation, SEE **film** noun.

cartridge noun
1 *a cartridge of film. a cartridge of ink.* canister, capsule, case, cassette, cylinder, tube.
2 *a cartridge for a rifle.* magazine, round, shell.

carve verb
1 *to carve meat.* SEE **cut** verb, slice.
2 *to carve a statue.* chisel, hew, [*informal*] sculpt.

carving noun
SEE **sculpture** noun.

cascade noun
cataract, torrent, waterfall.

case noun
1 *a packing case. a display-case.* box, cabinet, carton, casket, chest, crate, SEE **luggage**, pack, packaging, suitcase, trunk.
OTHER CONTAINERS: SEE **container**.
2 *an obvious case of favouritism.* example, illustration, instance, occurrence, specimen, state of affairs.
3 *Normally everyone has to help with the washing up, but in her case we made an exception.* circumstances, condition, context, plight, predicament, situation, state.
4 *The judge said he'd never known a case like this one.* argument, inquiry, investigation, law suit.

cash noun
bank notes, change, coins, currency, [*informal*] dough, funds, hard money, money, notes, [*informal*] the ready, [*informal*] the wherewithal.

cashier noun
accountant, banker, check-out (person), clerk, [*formal*] teller, treasurer.

cask noun
a cask of rum. barrel, butt, hogshead, tub, tun, vat.

cast noun
1 *a plaster cast.* SEE **sculpture** noun.
2 *the cast of a play.* characters, company, dramatis personae, troupe.

cast verb
1 *to cast coins into a well.* bowl, chuck, drop, fling, hurl, impel, launch, lob, pelt, pitch, project, scatter, shy, sling, throw, toss.
2 *The sculptor cast his statue in bronze.* form, mould, shape.

castigate verb
censure, chasten, chastize, [*old-fashioned*] chide, SEE **criticize**, discipline, lash, punish, rebuke, reprimand, scold.

castle noun
château, citadel, fort, fortress, palace, stronghold, tower.

PARTS OF A CASTLE: bailey, barbican, battlement, buttress, courtyard, donjon, drawbridge, dungeon, gate, keep, magazine, moat, motte, parapet, portcullis, rampart, tower, turret, wall.

---

casual adjective
1 *a casual meeting.* accidental, chance, fortuitous, incidental, random, unexpected, unforeseen, unintentional, unplanned, unpremeditated.
OPPOSITES: SEE **deliberate**.
2 *casual conversation. a casual attitude.* apathetic, blasé, careless, [*informal*] couldn't-care-less, easy-going, [*informal*] free-and-easy, lackadaisical, [*informal*] laid back, lax, negligent, nonchalant, offhand, relaxed, [*informal*] slap-happy, [*informal*] throwaway (*a throwaway remark*), unconcerned, unenthusiastic, unimportant, unprofessional.
OPPOSITES: SEE **committed, enthusiastic**.
3 *casual clothes.* informal.
OPPOSITE: formal.

casualty noun
It was a nasty accident, but there were few casualties. dead person, death, fatality, injured person, injury, loss, victim, wounded person.

cat noun
kitten, [*informal*] moggy, [*informal*] pussy, tabby, tom, tomcat.
RELATED ADJECTIVES: [*informal*] catty [= *spiteful*], feline [= *characteristic of a cat.*]

catalogue noun
a shopping catalogue. a library catalogue. brochure, directory, index, inventory, list, record, register, roll, schedule, table.

catalogue verb
to catalogue a record collection. classify, codify, file, index, list, make an inventory of, record, register, tabulate.

cataract noun
cascade, falls, rapids, torrent, waterfall.

catastrophe noun
The flood was a catastrophe for farmers. blow, calamity, cataclysm, crushing blow, débâcle, devastation, disaster, fiasco, holocaust, mischance, misfortune, mishap, ruin, ruination, tragedy, upheaval.

catch noun
1 *an angler's catch.* bag, booty, haul, net, prey.
2 *The price is so low that there must be a catch.* difficulty, disadvantage, drawback, obstacle, problem, snag, trap, trick.
3 *a catch on a door.* bolt, clasp, clip, fastener, fastening, hasp, hook, latch, lock.
catch-22 SEE **dilemma**.

catch verb
1 *to catch a fish.* ensnare, entrap, hook, net, snare, trap.
2 *to catch a ball.* clutch, grab, grasp, grip, hang on to, hold, seize, snatch, take.
3 *to catch a thief.* apprehend, arrest, capture, [*informal*] cop, corner, detect, discover, expose, [*informal*] nab, [*informal*] nobble, stop, surprise, take by surprise, unmask.
4 *to catch a bus.* be in time for, get on.
5 *to catch an illness.* become infected by, contract, get.

catching adjective
a catching disease. communicable, contagious, infectious, spreading, transmittable.
OPPOSITE: non-infectious.

catchy adjective
a catchy tune. attractive, haunting, memorable, popular, singable, tuneful.

categorical adjective
a categorical denial. absolute, certain, complete, decided, definite, direct, downright, emphatic, explicit, forceful, [*informal*] out-and-out, positive, strong, total, unambiguous, unconditional, unequivocal, unmitigated, unqualified, unreserved, utter, vigorous.
OPPOSITES: SEE **tentative, uncertain**.

category noun
class, classification, division, grade, group, heading, kind, order, rank, section, set, sort, type.

cater verb
We catered for twelve people at Christmas. cook, make arrangements, provide, supply.

catholic adjective
catholic tastes in music. all-embracing,
broad, broad-minded, comprehensive,
cosmopolitan, eclectic, general, liberal,
universal, varied, wide, wide-ranging.

cattle plural noun
bulls, bullocks, calves, cows, heifers,
livestock, oxen, steers.

cause noun
1 *What was the cause of the trouble?* basis,
beginning, genesis, grounds, motivation,
motive, occasion, origin, reason, root,
source, spring, stimulus.
2 *Who was the cause of it all?* agent, author,
[*old-fashioned*] begetter, creator, initiator,
inspiration, inventor, originator, producer.
3 *Do you know the cause of his absence?*
explanation, excuse, pretext, reason.
4 *We were collecting for a good cause.* aim,
belief, end, object, purpose, undertaking.

cause verb
1 *It'll cause trouble if we don't share things
fairly.* arouse, begin, bring about, create,
effect, effectuate, engender, foment,
generate, give rise to, incite, kindle, lead to,
occasion, precipitate, produce, provoke,
result in, set off, trigger off, [*informal*] whip
up.
2 *His illness caused him to retire.* compel,
force, induce, motivate.

caustic adjective
1 *caustic substances.* acid, astringent,
burning, corrosive.
2 *caustic criticism.* acidulous, biting, bitter,
cutting, mordant, pungent, sarcastic,
scathing, severe, sharp, stinging, virulent,
waspish.

caution noun
1 *Proceed with caution.* alertness,
attentiveness, care, carefulness,
circumspection, discretion, forethought,
heed, heedfulness, prudence, vigilance,
wariness, watchfulness.
2 *They let me off with a caution.* admonition,
[*informal*] dressing-down, reprimand,
[*informal*] talking-to, [*informal*] ticking-off,
warning.

caution verb
1 *They cautioned us about the dangers of
drugs.* advise, alert, counsel, forewarn,
inform, [*informal*] tip off, warn.
2 *The police cautioned me.* admonish,
censure, give a warning, reprehend,
reprimand, [*informal*] tell off, [*informal*]
tick off.

cautious adjective
1 *a cautious driver.* alert, attentive, careful,
heedful, prudent, scrupulous, vigilant,
watchful.
OPPOSITES: SEE **careless, reckless**.

2 *a cautious remark. a cautious attempt.*
[*informal*] cagey, calculating, chary,
circumspect, deliberate, discreet, gingerly (*a
gingerly approach*), grudging, guarded,
hesitant, judicious, non-committal,
restrained, suspicious, tactful, tentative,
unadventurous, wary, watchful.
OPPOSITES: SEE **forthright, impetuous**.

cavalcade noun
march-past, parade, procession, spectacle,
troop (*of horses*).

cave noun
cavern, cavity, den, grotto, hole, pothole,
underground chamber.
the study of caves speleology.

cave verb
to cave in SEE **collapse**.

cavity noun
cave, crater, dent, hole, hollow, pit.

cease verb
Cease work! break off, call a halt to,
conclude, cut off, desist (from), discontinue,
end, finish, halt, [*informal*] kick (*to kick a
habit*), [*informal*] knock off (*to knock off
work*), [*informal*] lay off, [*informal*] pack in,
refrain from, stop, terminate.
OPPOSITES: SEE **begin, persevere**.

ceaseless adjective
Their ceaseless noise annoyed the neighbours.
chronic, constant, continual, continuous,
endless, everlasting, incessant,
interminable, never-ending, non-stop,
permanent, perpetual, persistent, relentless,
unending, unremitting, untiring.

celebrate verb
1 *Let's celebrate!* be happy, have a celebration
[SEE **celebration**], let yourself go, [*informal*]
live it up, make merry, rejoice, revel.
2 *to celebrate an anniversary.* commemorate,
keep, observe, remember, solemnize.

celebrated adjective
a celebrated actor. acclaimed, distinguished,
eminent, exalted, famous, glorious,
illustrious, legendary, notable, noted,
[*uncomplimentary*] notorious, outstanding,
popular, prominent, renowned, revered,
well-known.

celebration noun

KINDS OF CELEBRATION: anniversary,
banquet, binge, birthday, carnival,
commemoration, feast, festival, festivity,
fête, gala, jamboree, [*joking*] jollification,
jubilee, merry-making, orgy, party,
[*informal*] rave-up, [*formal*] remembrance,
reunion, [*informal*] shindig, wedding.

celebrity noun
a TV celebrity. big name, [*informal*] bigwig, dignitary, famous person [SEE **famous**], idol, notability, personality, public figure, star, superstar, VIP, [*joking*] worthy.

celestial adjective
1 *celestial regions.* cosmic, galactic, interplanetary, interstellar, starry, stellar, universal.
2 *celestial music.* angelic, blissful, divine, ethereal, godlike, heavenly, seraphic, sublime, supernatural, transcendental, visionary.

celibate adjective
a celibate life. chaste, continent, single, virgin, unmarried, unwedded.

cell noun
a prison cell. a cell of a honeycomb. cavity, compartment, cubicle, den, enclosure, living space, prison, room, space, unit.

cellar noun
basement, crypt, vault, wine-cellar.

cemetery noun
burial-ground, churchyard, graveyard, [*formal*] necropolis [= *ancient cemetery*].

censor verb
[Do not confuse with verb *censure*.] 1 [= *to remove certain parts only*] *They censored the violent film.* amend, bowdlerize, [*informal*] clean up, cut, edit, expurgate.
2 [= *to remove completely*] *They censored the violence.* ban, cut out, exclude, forbid, prohibit, remove.

censure noun
He deserved the referee's censure for that foul. accusation, admonition, blame, castigation, condemnation, criticism, denunciation, diatribe, disapproval, [*informal*] dressing-down, harangue, rebuke, reprimand, reproach, reprobation, reproof, [*informal*] slating, stricture, [*informal*] talking-to, [*informal*] telling-off, tirade, verbal attack, vituperation.

censure verb
[Do not confuse with verb *censor*.] *The referee censured him.* admonish, berate, blame, [*informal*] carpet, castigate, caution, chide, condemn, criticize, denounce, lecture, rebuke, reproach, reprove, scold, take (someone) to task, [*slang*] tear (someone) off a strip, [*informal*] tell off, [*informal*] tick off, upbraid.

central adjective
1 *the central part of town.* focal, inner, innermost, interior, middle.
2 *the central facts.* chief, crucial, essential, focal, fundamental, important, key, main, major, overriding, pivotal, primary, principal, vital.
OPPOSITES: SEE **peripheral**.

centre noun
the centre of a circle. the centre of town. bull's-eye, core, focus, heart, hub, inside, interior, kernel, middle, mid-point, nucleus, pivot.

cereal noun
corn, grain.
CEREALS INCLUDE: barley, corn on the cob, maize, millet, oats, rice, rye, sweetcorn, wheat.

ceremonial adjective
a ceremonial occasion. dignified, formal, [*in church*] liturgical, majestic, official, ritual, ritualistic, solemn, stately.
OPPOSITES: SEE **informal**.

ceremony noun
1 *a ceremony to mark an anniversary.* celebration, commemoration, [*informal*] do, event, formal occasion, function, occasion, parade, reception, rite, ritual, service [*church service*].
2 *a quiet wedding without a lot of ceremony.* ceremonial, decorum, etiquette, formality, grandeur, pageantry, pomp, pomp and circumstance, protocol, ritual, spectacle.

certain adjective
1 *I was certain I would win.* adamant, assured, confident, convinced, determined, firm, positive, resolved, satisfied, sure, undoubting, unshakable.
2 *a certain fact. certain proof.* absolute, authenticated, categorical, certified, clear, clear-cut, conclusive, convincing, definite, dependable, established, genuine, incontestable, incontrovertible, indubitable, infallible, irrefutable, known, official, plain, reliable, settled, sure, true, trustworthy, unarguable, undeniable, undisputed, undoubted, unmistakable, unquestionable, valid, verifiable.
3 *She faced certain disaster.* destined, fated, guaranteed, imminent, inescapable, inevitable, inexorable, predictable, unavoidable.
OPPOSITES: SEE **uncertain**.
4 *If the watch doesn't go, they are certain to refund your money.* bound, compelled, obliged, required, sure.
to be certain SEE **know**.
to make certain SEE **ensure**.

certainty noun
1 *I saw it happen, so I can speak with certainty.* assertiveness, assurance, authority, [*formal*] certitude, confidence, conviction, knowledge, positiveness, proof, sureness, truth, validity.
2 *It was a certainty that we'd quarrel sooner or later.* certain fact, [*informal*] foregone

conclusion, foreseeable outcome, inevitability, necessity, [*informal*] sure thing.

certificate noun
a certificate of airworthiness. authorization, award, credentials, degree, diploma, document, guarantee, licence, pass, permit, qualification, warrant.

certify verb
The doctor certified that I was fit to go to work. affirm, attest, authenticate, authorize, [*formal*] avow, confirm, declare, endorse, guarantee, notify, sign, testify, verify, vouch, witness.

chain noun
1 *iron chains.* bonds, coupling, fetters, handcuffs, irons, links, manacles, shackles.
2 *a chain of events. a human chain.* column, concatenation, cordon, line, progression, row, sequence, series, string, succession, train.

chain verb
The slaves were chained. bind, [*old-fashioned*] clap in irons, SEE **fasten**, fetter, handcuff, link, manacle, shackle, tether, tie.

chair noun
FURNITURE YOU SIT ON: SEE **seat** noun.

chairman noun
the chairman of a committee. chair, chairperson, chairwoman, convener, director, organizer, president, speaker.

challenge verb
1 *to challenge an intruder.* accost, confront, [*informal*] have a go at, take on, tax.
2 *to challenge someone to a duel.* dare, defy, [*old-fashioned*] demand satisfaction, provoke, summon.
3 *to challenge a decision.* argue against, dissent from, dispute, impugn, object to, oppose, protest against, query, question.

challenging adjective
a challenging task. SEE **difficult**, inspiring, stimulating, testing, thought-provoking, worthwhile.
OPPOSITES: SEE **easy**.

champion adjective
a champion athlete. great, leading, record-breaking, supreme, top, unrivalled, victorious, winning, world-beating.

champion noun
1 *The final game decides who is the champion.* conqueror, hero, medallist, prize-winner, record-breaker, superman, superwoman, title-holder, victor, winner.
2 *a great champion of civil rights.* backer, defender, guardian, patron, protector, supporter, upholder, vindicator.
3 [*old-fashioned*] *The lord sent his champion*

into the lists. challenger, contender, contestant, fighter, knight, warrior.

championship noun
a snooker championship. competition, contest, tournament.

chance adjective
a chance meeting. accidental, [*formal*] adventitious, casual, coincidental, [*informal*] fluky, fortuitous, fortunate, haphazard, inadvertent, incidental, lucky, random, unexpected, unforeseen, unfortunate, unintentional, unlooked for, unplanned, unpremeditated.
OPPOSITES: SEE **planned**.

chance noun
1 *It happened by chance.* accident, coincidence, destiny, fate, fluke, fortune, gamble, hazard, luck, misfortune, serendipity.
2 *a chance of rain.* danger, liability, likelihood, possibility, probability, prospect, risk.
3 *Now it's your chance to try.* occasion, opportunity, time, turn.

change noun
1 *a change in the weather. a change of policy. a change in the shape or appearance of something.* adaptation, adjustment, alteration, break, conversion, deterioration, development, difference, diversion, improvement, innovation, metamorphosis, modification, modulation, mutation, new look, rearrangement, refinement, reformation, reorganization, revolution, shift, substitution, swing, transfiguration, transformation, transition, translation, [*joking*] transmogrification, transmutation, transposition, [*informal*] turn-about, U-turn, variation, vicissitude, variety.
2 *Have you any change?* cash, coins, money, notes.

change verb
1 *to change your mind. to change your way of life. to change the shape or appearance of something.* acclimatize, accommodate, accustom, adapt, adjust, affect, alter, amend, convert, diversify, influence, modify, process, rearrange, reconstruct, refashion, reform, remodel, reorganize, reshape, restyle, tailor, transfigure, transform, translate, [*joking*] transmogrify, transmute, vary.
2 *to change clothes. to change places.* alternate, displace, exchange, replace, substitute, switch, swop, transpose.
3 *to change money.* barter, convert, trade in.
4 *Over a period, things do change.* alter, be transformed, [*informal*] chop and change, develop, fluctuate, metamorphose, move on, mutate, shift, vary.

changeable adjective
changeable weather. changeable moods.
capricious, chequered (*a chequered career*),
erratic, fickle, fitful, fluctuating, fluid,
inconsistent, inconstant, irregular,
mercurial, mutable, shifting,
temperamental, uncertain, unpredictable,
unreliable, unstable, unsteady, [*informal*]
up and down, vacillating, variable, varying,
volatile, wavering.
OPPOSITES: SEE **constant, steady** adjective.

channel noun
1 *a channel to take away water. a navigable
channel.* canal, conduit, course, dike, ditch,
duct, groove, gully, gutter, overflow, pipe,
sound, strait, SEE **stream** noun, trough,
water-course, waterway.
2 *a channel of communication.* avenue,
means, medium, path, route, way.
3 *a TV channel.* [*informal*] side (*Which side
is the news on?*), station, waveband,
wavelength.

chaos noun
anarchy, bedlam, confusion, disorder,
disorganization, lawlessness, mayhem,
muddle, pandemonium, shambles, tumult.
OPPOSITES: SEE **order** noun.

chaotic adjective
1 *My room's in a chaotic state.* confused,
deranged, disordered, disorderly,
disorganized, haphazard, [*informal*]
haywire, [*informal*] higgledy-piggledy,
jumbled, muddled, [*informal*] shambolic,
[*informal*] topsy-turvy, untidy, [*informal*]
upside-down.
OPPOSITES: SEE **neat, orderly**.
2 *During the famine, the country was in a
chaotic state.* anarchic, lawless, rebellious,
riotous, tumultuous, uncontrolled,
ungovernable, unruly.
OPPOSITES: SEE **law-abiding, organized**.

chapter noun
1 *a chapter of a book.* act (*of a play*), canto
(*of a poem*), division, episode, instalment,
part, scene (*of a play*), section, subdivision.
2 *When you leave school you start a new
chapter of your life.* SEE **part** noun.

char verb
The fire charred the woodwork. blacken,
brown, burn, carbonize, scorch, sear, singe.

character noun
1 *This brand of tea has a character all of its
own.* SEE **characteristic** noun,
distinctiveness, flavour, idiosyncrasy,
individuality, integrity, peculiarity,
quality, stamp, taste, uniqueness.
2 *She has a forceful character.* attitude,
constitution, disposition, individuality,
make-up, manner, nature, personality,
reputation, temper, temperament.

3 *She's a well-known character.* figure,
human being, individual, person,
personality, [*informal*] type.
4 *She made us laugh—she's such a character!*
[*informal*] case, comedian, comic, eccentric,
[*informal*] nut-case, oddity,
[*uncomplimentary slang*] weirdo.
5 *a character in a play.* part, persona,
portrayal, role.
6 *the characters of the alphabet.* cipher,
figure, [*plural*] hieroglyphics (*Egyptian
hieroglyphics*), ideogram, letter, mark, rune,
sign, symbol, type.

characteristic adjective
I recognized his characteristic walk.
distinctive, distinguishing, essential,
idiosyncratic, individual, particular,
peculiar, recognizable, singular, special,
specific, symptomatic, unique.

characteristic noun
He has some odd characteristics. attribute,
distinguishing feature, feature, hallmark,
idiosyncrasy, peculiarity, symptom, trait.

charge noun
1 *an increase in charges.* cost, expenditure,
expense, fare, fee, payment, postage, price,
rate, terms, toll, value.
2 *They left the dog in my charge.* care,
command, control, custody, keeping,
protection, responsibility, safe-keeping,
trust.
3 *a criminal charge.* accusation, allegation,
imputation, indictment.
4 *Some of the horses fell in the charge.* assault,
attack, incursion, invasion, offensive,
onslaught, raid, rush, sortie, strike.

charge verb
1 *What do they charge for a coffee?* ask for,
exact, levy, make you pay, require.
2 *They charged me with the duty of cleaning
the hall.* burden, command, commit,
empower, entrust, give, impose on.
3 *What crime did they charge him with?*
accuse, blame, [*formal*] impeach, [*formal*]
indict, prosecute, tax.
4 *The cavalry charged the enemy line.* assail,
assault, attack, [*informal*] fall on, rush, set
on, storm, [*informal*] wade into.

charitable adjective
SEE **generous, kind**.

charity noun
1 *He helped us out of charity, not self-interest.*
affection, altruism, benevolence, bounty,
caring, compassion, consideration,
generosity, goodness, helpfulness,
humanity, kindness, love, mercy,
philanthropy, sympathy, tender-
heartedness, unselfishness, warm-
heartedness.
OPPOSITES: SEE **selfishness**.

2 *The animals' hospital depends on our charity.* [*old-fashioned*] alms or alms-giving, bounty, donations, financial support, gifts, [*informal*] hand-outs, largesse, offerings, patronage, self-sacrifice.
3 *We collected for charity.* a good cause, the needy, the poor.

charm noun
1 *Everyone falls for his charm!* allure, appeal, attractiveness, charisma, fascination, hypnotic power, lovable nature, lure, magic, magnetism, power, pull, seductiveness, sex appeal.
2 *magic charms.* curse, enchantment, incantation, SEE **magic**, mumbo-jumbo, sorcery, spell, witchcraft, wizardry.
3 *a charm on a silver chain.* amulet, lucky charm, mascot, ornament, talisman, trinket.

charm verb
He charmed us with his singing. allure, attract, beguile, bewitch, cajole, captivate, cast a spell on, decoy, delight, enchant, enrapture, entrance, fascinate, hold spellbound, intrigue, lure, mesmerize, please, seduce, soothe.

charming adjective
charming manners. alluring, SEE **attractive**, disarming, endearing, lovable, seductive, winning, winsome.

chart noun
1 *a weather chart.* map, sketch-map.
2 *an information chart.* diagram, graph, plan, table.

charter verb
to charter an aircraft. employ, engage, hire, lease, rent.

chase verb
The dog chased a rabbit. drive, follow, hound, hunt, pursue, track, trail.

chasm noun
a deep chasm. abyss, canyon, cleft, crater, crevasse, drop, fissure, gap, gulf, hole, hollow, opening, pit, ravine, rift, split, void.

chastise verb
SEE **punish**.

chastity noun
sexual chastity. abstinence, celibacy, continence, innocence, maidenhood, purity, sinlessness, virginity, virtue.

chat noun, verb
SEE **talk** noun, verb.

chatty adjective
SEE **talkative**.

chauvinism noun
[*Chauvinism* means *exaggerated patriotism*, but is now also used to mean *sexism*.] SEE **patriotism**, sexism, SEE **prejudice** noun.

cheap adjective
1 *a cheap buy. a cheap price.* bargain, budget, cut-price, [*informal*] dirt-cheap, discount, economical, economy, fair, inexpensive, [*informal*] knock-down, low-priced, reasonable, reduced, [*informal*] rock-bottom, sale, under-priced.
OPPOSITES: SEE **expensive**.
2 *cheap quality.* inferior, poor, second-rate, shoddy, tatty, tawdry, tinny, worthless.
OPPOSITES: SEE **superior**.
3 *cheap humour. cheap insults.* contemptible, crude, despicable, facile, glib, ill-bred, ill-mannered, mean, silly, tasteless, unworthy, vulgar.
OPPOSITES: SEE **worthy**.

cheat noun
1 *Don't trust him—he's a cheat.* charlatan, cheater, [*informal*] conman, counterfeiter, crafty person, deceiver, double-crosser, extortioner, forger, fraud, hoaxer, impersonator, impostor, [*informal*] phoney, [*informal*] quack, racketeer, rogue, [*informal*] shark, swindler, trickster, [*informal*] twister.
2 *The whole thing was a cheat.* artifice, bluff, chicanery, [*informal*] con, confidence trick, deceit, deception, [*slang*] fiddle, fraud, hoax, imposture, lie, misrepresentation, pretence, [*informal*] put-up job, [*informal*] racket, [*informal*] rip-off, ruse, sham, swindle, [*informal*] swizz, treachery, trick.

cheat verb
1 *He cheated me by selling me an unroadworthy car.* bamboozle, beguile, bilk, [*informal*] con, deceive, defraud, [*slang*] diddle, [*informal*] do, double-cross, dupe, [*slang*] fiddle, [*informal*] fleece, fool, hoax, hoodwink, outwit, [*informal*] rip off, rob, [*informal*] short-change, swindle, take in, trick.
2 *to cheat in an examination.* copy, crib, plagiarize.

check noun
1 *We reached our destination without any check.* SEE **interruption**.
2 *I took the car to the garage for a check.* check-up, examination, [*informal*] going-over, inspection, investigation, [*informal*] once-over, scrutiny, test.

check verb
1 *to check someone's progress. to check a horse.* arrest, bar, block, bridle, control, curb, delay, foil, govern, halt, hamper, hinder, hold back, impede, inhibit, keep in check, obstruct, regulate, rein, repress, restrain, retard, slow, slow down, stem (*to stem the tide*), stop, stunt (*to stunt growth*), thwart.
2 *We checked our answers. They checked the locks on the doors.* [*American*] check out,

compare, cross-check, examine, inspect, investigate, monitor, research, scrutinize, test, verify.

cheeky adjective
a cheeky manner. a cheeky remark. arrogant, audacious, bold, brazen, cool, discourteous, disrespectful, flippant, forward, impertinent, impolite, impudent, insolent, insulting, irreverent, mocking, pert, presumptuous, rude, [*informal*] saucy, shameless, [*informal*] tongue-in-cheek.
OPPOSITES: SEE **respectful**.

cheer noun
Give the winners a hearty cheer! acclamation, applause, cry of approval, encouragement, hurrah, ovation, shout of approval.

cheer verb
1 *We cheered the winners.* acclaim, applaud, clap, shout.
OPPOSITES: SEE **jeer**.
2 *The good news cheered us.* comfort, console, delight, divert, encourage, entertain, exhilarate, gladden, make cheerful, please, solace, uplift.
OPPOSITES: SEE **sadden**.
to cheer up *The weather cheered up. Cheer up—we're nearly home!* become more cheerful, brighten, [*informal*] buck up, make more cheerful, [*informal*] perk up, [*slang*] snap out of it, take heart.

cheerful adjective
a cheerful mood. animated, bright, buoyant, cheery, [*informal*] chirpy, contented, convivial, delighted, elated, festive, gay, genial, glad, gleeful, good-humoured, SEE **happy**, hearty, jaunty, jocund, jolly, jovial, joyful, joyous, jubilant, laughing, light (*a light heart*), light-hearted, lively, merry, optimistic, [*informal*] perky, pleased, rapturous, sparkling, spirited, sprightly, sunny, warm-hearted.
OPPOSITES: SEE **sad**.

cheerfulness noun
animation, brightness, cheeriness, elation, festivity, gaiety, good-humour, SEE **happiness**, jollity, laughter, merriment, optimism, sprightliness.
OPPOSITES: SEE **depression**.

cheerless adjective
a cheerless rainy day. bleak, comfortless, dark, depressing, desolate, dingy, disconsolate, dismal, drab, dreary, dull, forbidding, forlorn, frowning, funereal, gloomy, grim, joyless, lack-lustre, melancholy, miserable, mournful, sad, sober, sombre, sullen, sunless, uncongenial, unhappy, uninviting, unpleasant, unpromising, woeful, wretched.
OPPOSITES: SEE **cheerful**.

chemical noun
compound, element, substance.

SOME CHEMICALS: acid, alcohol, alkali, ammonia, arsenic, chlorine, fluoride, litmus.

CHEMICAL ELEMENTS AND THEIR SYMBOLS:
actinium *Ac*, aluminium *Al*, americium *Am*, antimony *Sb*, argon *Ar*, arsenic *As*, astatine *At*, barium *Ba*, berkelium *Bk*, beryllium *Be*, bismuth *Bi*, boron *B*, bromine *Br*, cadmium *Cd*, caesium *Cs*, calcium *Ca*, californium *Cf*, carbon *C*, cerium *Ce*, chlorine *Cl*, chromium *Cr*, cobalt *Co*, copper *Cu*, curium *Cm*, dysprosium *Dy*, einsteinium *Es*, erbium *Er*, europium *Eu*.
fermium *Fm*, fluorine *F*, francium *Fr*, gadolinium *Gd*, gallium *Ga*, germanium *Ge*, gold *Au*, hafnium *Hf*, helium *He*, holmium *Ho*, hydrogen *H*, indium *In*, iodine *I*, iridium *Ir*, iron *Fe*, krypton *Kr*, lanthanum *La*, lawrencium *Lr*, lead *Pb*, lithium *Li*, lutetium *Lu*, magnesium *Mg*, manganese *Mn*, mendelevium *Md*, mercury *Hg*, molybdenum *Mo*.
neodymium *Nd*, neon *Ne*, neptunium *Np*, nickel *Ni*, niobium *Nb*, nitrogen *N*, nobelium *No*, osmium *Os*, oxygen *O*, palladium *Pd*, phosphorus *P*, platinum *Pt*, plutonium *Pu*, polonium *Po*, potassium *K*, praseodymium *Pr*, promethium *Pm*, protactinium *Pa*, radium *Ra*, radon *Rn*, rhenium *Re*, rhodium *Rh*, rubidium *Rb*, ruthenium *Ru*.
samarium *Sm*, scandium *Sc*, selenium *Se*, silicon *Si*, silver *Ag*, sodium *Na*, strontium *Sr*, sulphur *S*, tantalum *Ta*, technetium *Tc*, tellurium *Te*, terbium *Tb*, thallium *Tl*, thorium *Th*, thulium *Tm*, tin *Sn*, titanium *Ti*, tungsten *W*, uranium *U*, vanadium *V*, xenon *Xe*, ytterbium *Yb*, yttrium *Y*, zinc *Zn*, zirconium *Zr*.

---

chemist noun
I went to the chemist's for some medicine. [*old-fashioned*] apothecary, [*American*] drug-store, pharmacist.

cherish verb
I cherish the present you gave me. be fond of, care for, foster, keep safe, look after, love, nourish, nurse, prize, protect, treasure, value.

chest noun
1 *a tool chest.* box, case, casket, coffer, crate, strongbox, trunk.
2 *a person's chest.* breast, rib-cage.
RELATED ADJECTIVE: pectoral.

chew verb
to chew food. bite, champ, crunch, SEE **eat**, gnaw, masticate, munch, nibble.

chewy adjective
1 *chewy toffee.* elastic, flexible, [*formal*] malleable, pliant, springy, sticky, stiff.
OPPOSITES: SEE **brittle**.
2 *chewy meat.* gristly, leathery, rubbery, tough.
OPPOSITES: SEE **tender**.

chicken noun
bantam, broiler, chick, cockerel, fowl, hen, pullet, rooster.

chief adjective
1 *the chief guest.* first, greatest, highest, major, most honoured, most important, principal.
2 *the chief cook.* arch (*the arch enemy*), head, in charge, leading, most experienced, oldest, senior, supreme, top, unequalled, unrivalled.
3 *the chief facts.* basic, cardinal, central, dominant, especial, essential, foremost, fundamental, high-priority, indispensable, key, main, necessary, outstanding, overriding, paramount, predominant, primary, prime, salient, significant, substantial, uppermost, vital, weighty.
OPPOSITES: SEE **unimportant**.

chief noun
Who's the chief around here? administrator, authority-figure, [*informal*] bigwig, [*informal*] boss, captain, chairperson, chieftain, commander, commanding officer, commissioner, controller, director, employer, executive, foreman, [*informal*] gaffer, [*American*] godfather [= *chief criminal*], governor, head, leader, manager, master, mistress, officer, organizer, overseer, owner, president, principal, proprietor, responsible person, [*uncomplimentary*] ring-leader, ruler, superintendent, supervisor, [*informal*] supremo.

chiefly adverb
especially, essentially, generally, mainly, mostly, predominantly, primarily, principally, usually.

child noun
1 *a growing child.* [*informal*] babe, baby, [*Scottish*] bairn, [*informal, from Italian*] bambino, boy, [*uncomplimentary*] brat, girl, [*uncomplimentary*] guttersnipe, infant, [*formal*] juvenile, [*informal*] kid, [*formal*] minor, [*informal*] nipper, offspring, toddler, [*informal*] tot, [*uncomplimentary*] urchin, youngster, youth.
2 *a child of wealthy parents.* daughter, descendant, heir, issue, offspring, progeny, son.

childhood noun
adolescence, babyhood, boyhood, girlhood, infancy, minority, schooldays, [*informal*] your teens, youth.

childish adjective
[*Childish* is a word used by adults to describe behaviour or qualities they disapprove of, whereas *childlike* is used to describe qualities people generally approve of.] *It's childish to make rude noises.* babyish, foolish, immature, infantile, juvenile, puerile, silly.
OPPOSITES: SEE **mature**.

childlike adjective
[See note under *childish*.] *a childlike trust in people's goodness.* artless, frank, guileless, ingenuous, innocent, naïve, natural, simple, trustful, unaffected, unsophisticated.
OPPOSITES: SEE **artful**.

chill verb
1 *The wind chilled us to the bone.* cool, freeze, make cold.
OPPOSITES: SEE **warm** verb.
2 *to chill food.* keep cold, refrigerate.

chilly adjective
1 *a chilly evening.* cold, cool, crisp, fresh, frosty, icy, [*informal*] nippy, [*informal*] parky, raw, sharp, wintry.
OPPOSITES: SEE **warm** adjective.
2 *a chilly greeting.* aloof, cool, dispassionate, frigid, hostile, ill-disposed, remote, reserved, [*informal*] standoffish, unforthcoming, unfriendly, unresponsive, unsympathetic, unwelcoming.
OPPOSITES: SEE **friendly**.

chimney noun
flue, funnel, smokestack.

china noun
crockery, earthenware, porcelain, SEE **pottery**.

chip noun
1 *I knocked a chip off the cup.* bit, flake, fleck, fragment, piece, scrap, shaving, shiver, slice, sliver, splinter, wedge.
2 *I noticed a chip in the cup.* crack, damage, flaw, gash, nick, notch, scratch, snick.

chip verb
I chipped the cup. break, crack, damage, gash, nick, notch, scratch, splinter.

chivalrous adjective
a chivalrous knight. bold, brave, chivalric, courageous, courteous, courtly, gallant, generous, gentlemanly, heroic, honourable, knightly, noble, polite, respectable, true, trustworthy, valiant, valorous, worthy.
OPPOSITES: SEE **dishonourable**.

choice noun
1 *The choice was between two good candidates.* alternative, choosing, dilemma, need to choose, option.
2 *The older candidate was our choice.* decision, election, liking, nomination, pick, preference, say, vote.

3 *The greengrocer has a good choice of vegetables.* array, assortment, diversity, miscellany, mixture, range, selection, variety.

choir noun
choral society, chorus, vocal ensemble.

choke verb
1 *This collar is choking me.* asphyxiate, smother, stifle, strangle, suffocate, throttle.
2 *The firemen choked in the smoke.* gag, gasp, retch, suffocate.
3 *The roads were choked with traffic.* block, [*informal*] bung up, clog, close, congest, fill, jam, obstruct, smother, stop up.

choose verb
1 *They choose a new leader. I chose a green anorak.* adopt, appoint, decide on, distinguish, draw lots for, elect, fix on, identify, isolate, name, nominate, opt for, pick out, [*informal*] plump for, select, settle on, show a preference for, single out, vote for.
2 *I chose to do it myself.* decide, determine, prefer, resolve.

chop verb
to chop wood. cleave, SEE **cut** verb, hack, hew, slash, split.
to chop down cut down, fell.

chopper noun
1 axe, cleaver.
2 helicopter.

choppy adjective
a choppy sea. rippled, roughish, ruffled, turbulent, uneven, wavy.
OPPOSITES: SEE **smooth**.

chore noun
chores around the house. boring work (SEE **boring**), burden, drudgery, duty, errand, job, task, work.

chorus noun
1 choir, choral society, vocal ensemble.
2 *We all sang the chorus.* refrain, response.

chronic adjective
a chronic illness. ceaseless, constant, continual, continuous, deep-rooted, everlasting, habitual, incessant, incurable, ineradicable, ingrained, lifelong, lingering, permanent, persistent, unending.
OPPOSITES: SEE **acute, temporary**.

chronicle noun
a chronicle of events. account, annals, diary, history, journal, narrative, record, saga, story.

chronological adjective
chronological order. consecutive, sequential.

chuck verb
[*informal*] *Stop chucking rubbish in the water.* cast, ditch, dump, fling, heave, hurl,

jettison, lob, pitch, shy, sling, throw, toss.
to chuck away, to chuck out
discard, dispose of, reject, scrap, throw away.

chunk noun
SEE **lump**.

church noun

CHURCH BUILDINGS: abbey, basilica, cathedral, chapel, convent, monastery, nunnery, parish church, priory.

PARTS OF A CHURCH: aisle, belfry, buttress, chancel, chapel, cloister, crypt, dome, gargoyle, nave, porch, precinct, sacristy, sanctuary, spire, steeple, tower, transept, vestry.

THINGS YOU FIND IN A CHURCH: altar, Bible, candle, communion-table, crucifix, font, hymn-book, lectern, memorial tablet, pew, prayer-book, pulpit.

WORDS TO DO WITH CHURCH: Advent, angel, Ascension Day, Ash Wednesday, baptism, benediction, christening, Christmas, communion, confirmation, Easter, Good Friday, gospel, hymn, incense, Lent, martyr, mass, Nativity, New Testament, Old Testament, Palm Sunday, patron saint, Pentecost, prayer, preaching, psalm, requiem, Resurrection, sabbath, sacrament, saint, scripture, sermon, service, Whitsun, worship.

PEOPLE CONNECTED WITH CHURCH: archbishop, bishop, cardinal, chaplain, choirboy, choirgirl, churchwarden, clergyman, cleric, congregation, curate, deacon, deaconess, elder, evangelist, friar, layman, minister, missionary, monk, nonconformist, nun, padre, parson, pastor, Pope, preacher, prelate, priest, rector, sexton, sidesman, verger, vicar.

---

churchyard noun
burial-ground, cemetery, graveyard.

chutney noun
pickle, relish.

cinder noun
a cinder from a fire. ash, clinker, ember.

cinema noun
films, [*informal*] the movies, the pictures.

circle noun
1 *a perfect circle.* ring.
2 *a large circle of friends.* association, band, body, clique, club, company, fellowship, fraternity, gang, SEE **group** noun, party, set, society.

LINES AND SHAPES IN RELATION TO
A CIRCLE: arc, chord, diameter, radius,
sector, segment, tangent.

VARIOUS CIRCULAR SHAPES OR
MOVEMENTS: band, belt, circlet, circuit,
circulation, circumference,
circumnavigation, coil, cordon, curl, curve,
cycle, disc, ellipse, girdle, globe, gyration,
hoop, lap, loop, orb, orbit,
oval, revolution, rotation, round,
sphere, spiral, tour, turn, wheel, whirl,
whorl.

circle verb
1 VARIOUS WAYS TO MAKE A CIRCLE OR TO MOVE
IN A CIRCLE: circulate, circumnavigate,
circumscribe, coil, compass, corkscrew,
curl, curve, encircle, girdle, gyrate,
hem in, loop, orbit, pirouette, pivot,
reel, revolve, ring, rotate, spin, spiral,
surround, swirl, swivel, tour, wheel, whirl,
wind.
2 *Trees circled the lawn.* encircle, enclose,
encompass, girdle, hem in, ring, skirt,
surround.

circuit noun
1 SEE **circle** noun.
2 *I completed one circuit in record time.* lap,
orbit, revolution.

circuitous adjective
a circuitous route. curving, devious, indirect,
labyrinthine, meandering, oblique,
rambling, roundabout, serpentine, tortuous,
twisting, winding, zigzag.
OPPOSITES: SEE **direct** adjective.

circular adjective
1 *a circular shape.* elliptical, oval, round.
2 *a circular argument.* cyclic, repeating,
repetitive.

circular noun
an advertising circular. advertisement,
leaflet, letter, notice, pamphlet.

circulate verb
We circulated a notice about our sale.
[*formal*] disseminate, distribute, issue,
[*formal*] promulgate, publicize, publish,
send round, spread about.

circulation noun
1 *the circulation of the blood.* flow, movement,
pumping, recycling.
2 *the circulation of information.*
broadcasting, dissemination, distribution,
spread, transmission.
3 *the circulation of a newspaper.* distribution,
sales-figures.

circumference noun
*It's a mile round the circumference of
the field.* border, boundary, circuit, edge,

exterior, fringe, limit, margin, outline,
outside, perimeter, periphery, rim,
verge.

circumstances noun
[*usually plural*] *Don't jump to conclusions
before you know the circumstances.*
background, causes, conditions,
considerations, context, contingencies,
details, facts, factors, influences,
particulars, position, situation,
surroundings.

circus noun
big top.

WORDS TO DO WITH A CIRCUS: acrobat,
clown, contortionist, juggler, lion-tamer,
ring, ringmaster, tightrope, trainer, trapeze,
trapeze-artist.

cite verb
*She cited several authorities to support her
case.* adduce, advance, [*informal*] bring up,
enumerate, mention, name, quote,
[*informal*] reel off, refer to, specify.

citizen noun
the citizens of a town or country. [*old-
fashioned*] burgess, commoner, denizen,
householder, inhabitant, national, native,
passport-holder, ratepayer, resident,
subject, taxpayer, voter.

citrus fruit noun
VARIOUS CITRUS FRUITS: clementine,
grapefruit, lemon, lime, mandarin, orange,
satsuma, tangerine.

city noun
London is a large city. conurbation,
metropolis, town.
RELATED ADJECTIVE: urban.

civil adjective
1 *I know you're angry, but try to be civil.*
affable, civilized, considerate, courteous,
obliging, SEE **polite**, respectful, well-bred,
well-mannered.
OPPOSITES: SEE **rude**.
2 *civil defence. civil liberties.* communal,
national, public, social, state.

civilization noun
the civilization of the ancient Egyptians.
achievements, attainments, culture,
organization, refinement, sophistication,
urbanity, urbanization.

civilized adjective
a civilized nation. civilized behaviour.
cultivated, cultured, democratic, developed,
educated, enlightened, orderly, polite,
sophisticated, urbane, well-behaved, well-
run.
OPPOSITES: SEE **uncivilized**.

claim verb
1 *I claimed my reward.* ask for, collect, demand, exact, insist on, request, require, take.
2 *He claims that he's an expert.* affirm, allege, argue, assert, attest, contend, declare, insist, maintain, pretend, profess, state.

clairvoyant noun
fortune-teller, oracle, prophet, seer, sibyl, soothsayer.

clamber verb
We clambered over the rocks. climb, crawl, move awkwardly, scramble.

clammy adjective
a clammy atmosphere. clammy hands. damp, dank, humid, moist, muggy, slimy, sticky, sweaty.

clamour noun
The starlings made a clamour. babel, commotion, din, hubbub, hullabaloo, noise, outcry, racket, row, screeching, shouting, storm (*a storm of protest*), uproar.

clamour verb
They clamoured for attention. call out, cry out, exclaim, shout, yell.

clap verb
1 *We clapped her performance.* applaud.
2 *He clapped me on the shoulder.* SEE **hit** verb, pat, slap, smack.

clarify verb
1 *Clarify what you want us to do.* define, elucidate, explain, gloss, illuminate, make clear, throw light on.
OPPOSITES: SEE **confuse**.
2 *I passed the wine through a filter to clarify it.* cleanse, clear, filter, purify, refine.

clash verb
1 *The cymbals clashed.*
VARIOUS SOUNDS: SEE **sound** noun.
2 *The rival gangs clashed. The colours clash.*
SEE **conflict** verb.
3 *My interview clashes with my dentist's appointment.* SEE **coincide**.

clasp verb
1 *to clasp things together.* SEE **fasten**.
2 *to clasp someone in your arms.* cling to, clutch, embrace, enfold, grasp, grip, hold, hug, squeeze.
3 *to clasp your hands.* hold together, wring.

class noun
1 *in a class of its own.* category, classification, division, genre, genus, grade, group, kind, league, order, quality, rank, set, sort, species, sphere, type.
2 *social class.* caste, degree, grouping, standing, station, status.

TERMS SOMETIMES USED TO LABEL SOCIAL CLASSES: aristocracy, bourgeoisie, commoners, the commons, gentry, lower class, middle class, nobility, proletariat, ruling class, serfs, upper class, upper-middle class, the workers, working class.

3 *a class in a school.* band, form, group, set, stream.

classic adjective
[It is useful to distinguish between *classic* = *excellent or typical of its kind*, and *classical* = *of the ancient Greeks and Romans*, or *classical* = *having an elegant style like that associated with classical times.*] 1 *a classic goal.* admirable, consummate, copybook, excellent, exceptional, exemplary, fine, first-class, first-rate, flawless, SEE **good**, ideal, [*informal*] immaculate, masterly, memorable, model, perfect, superlative, supreme, [*informal*] vintage.
OPPOSITES: SEE **commonplace**.
2 *classic works of literature.* abiding, ageless, deathless, enduring, established, immortal, lasting, time-honoured, undying.
OPPOSITES: SEE **ephemeral**.
3 *a classic case of chicken-pox.* archetypal, characteristic, regular, standard, typical, usual.
OPPOSITES: SEE **unusual**.

classical adjective
[See note under *classic.*] 1 *classical civilizations.* ancient, Attic, Greek, Hellenic, Latin, Roman.
2 *a classical style of architecture.* austere, dignified, elegant, pure, restrained, simple, symmetrical, well-proportioned.
3 *classical music.* established, harmonious, highbrow.

classified adjective
classified information. confidential, [*informal*] hush-hush, private, restricted, secret, sensitive, top secret.

classify verb
We classified the plants according to the shape of their leaves. arrange, catalogue, categorize, class, grade, group, order, organize, [*informal*] pigeon-hole, put into sets, sort, systematize, tabulate.

clause noun
a clause in a legal document. article, condition, item, paragraph, part, passage, provision, proviso, section, subsection.

claw verb
The animal clawed at its attacker. graze, injure, lacerate, maul, rip, scrape, scratch, tear.

clean adjective
1 *a clean floor. clean clothes.* dirt-free, hygienic, immaculate, laundered, perfect,

polished, sanitary, scrubbed, spotless, tidy, unsoiled, unstained, washed, wholesome.
2 *clean water.* clarified, clear, decontaminated, distilled, fresh, pure, purified, sterilized, unadulterated, unpolluted.
3 *clean paper.* blank, new, plain, uncreased, unmarked, untouched, unused.
4 *a clean edge. a clean incision.* neat, regular, smooth, straight, tidy.
5 *a clean fight.* chivalrous, fair, honest, honourable, sporting, sportsmanlike.
OPPOSITES: SEE **dirty** adjective.

clean verb

VARIOUS WAYS TO CLEAN THINGS: bath, bathe, brush, buff, cleanse, decontaminate, deodorize, disinfect, dry-clean, dust, filter, flush, groom, hoover, launder, mop, polish, purge, purify, rinse, sand-blast, sanitize, scour, scrape, scrub, shampoo, shower, soap, sponge, spring-clean, spruce up, sterilize, swab, sweep, swill, vacuum, wash, wipe, wring out.
OPPOSITES: SEE **contaminate, dirty** verb.

clear adjective
1 *clear water.* clean, colourless, crystalline, glassy, limpid, pellucid, pure, transparent.
OPPOSITES: SEE **opaque**.
2 *a clear sky.* bright, cloudless, sunny, starlit, unclouded.
OPPOSITES: SEE **cloudy**.
3 *a clear conscience.* blameless, easy, guiltless, innocent, quiet, satisfied, sinless, undisturbed, untarnished, untroubled, unworried.
OPPOSITES: SEE **troubled**.
4 *a clear outline. a clear signal. clear handwriting.* bold, clean, definite, distinct, explicit, focused, legible, obvious, plain, positive, recognizable, sharp, simple, unambiguous, unmistakable, visible, well-defined.
OPPOSITES: SEE **indistinct**.
5 *a clear sound.* audible, clarion (*a clarion call*), distinct, penetrating, sharp.
OPPOSITES: SEE **muffled**.
6 *a clear explanation.* clear-cut, coherent, comprehensible, intelligible, lucid, perspicuous, unambiguous, understandable, unequivocal, well-presented.
OPPOSITES: SEE **confused**.
7 *a clear case of cheating.* apparent, blatant, conspicuous, evident, glaring, indisputable, manifest, noticeable, obvious, palpable, perceptible, plain, pronounced, straightforward, unconcealed, undisguised.
OPPOSITES: SEE **debatable**.
8 *a clear road. a clear space.* empty, free, open, passable, uncluttered, uncrowded,

unhampered, unhindered, unimpeded, unobstructed.
OPPOSITES: SEE **congested**.

clear verb
1 *The fog cleared.* disappear, evaporate, fade, melt away, vanish.
2 *Wait for the water to clear. The weather cleared.* become clear, brighten, clarify, lighten, uncloud.
3 *I cleared the misty windows.* clean, make clean, make transparent, polish, wipe.
4 *I cleared the weeds from my garden.* disentangle, eliminate, get rid of, remove, strip.
5 *She cleared the blocked drainpipe.* clean out, free, loosen, open up, unblock, unclog.
6 *The court cleared him of all blame.* absolve, acquit, [*formal*] exculpate, excuse, exonerate, free, [*informal*] let off, liberate, release, vindicate.
7 *If the alarm goes, clear the building.* empty, evacuate.
8 *The horse cleared the fence.* bound over, jump, leap over, pass over, spring over, vault.
to clear up 1 *Clear up the mess.* clean, remove, put right, put straight, tidy.
2 *I asked her to clear up a difficulty.* answer, clarify, elucidate, explain, make clear, resolve, solve.

clear-cut adjective
Her proposal was clear-cut. clear, coherent, definite, distinct, explicit, intelligible, lucid, plain, positive, precise, specific, straightforward, unambiguous, understandable, unequivocal, well-defined, well-presented.

clearing noun
a clearing in the forest. gap, glade, opening, space.

clement adjective
clement weather. balmy, calm, favourable, gentle, mild, peaceful, pleasant, temperate, warm.

clench verb
1 *to clench your teeth. to clench your fist.* clamp up, close tightly, double up, grit (your teeth), squeeze tightly.
2 *to clench something in your hand.* clasp, grasp, grip, hold.

clergyman noun
VARIOUS CLERGYMEN: archbishop, bishop, canon, cardinal, chaplain, cleric, curate, deacon, deaconess, dean, evangelist, minister, ordained person, padre, parson, pastor, preacher, prelate, priest, rector, vicar.

clerical adjective
1 *clerical work.* office, secretarial.
2 [= *of clerics, of clergymen*] *clerical duties.* ecclesiastical, pastoral, priestly, spiritual.

clerk noun

VARIOUS PEOPLE DOING CLERICAL WORK:
assistant, bookkeeper, computer operator,
copyist, filing clerk, office boy, office girl,
office worker, [*informal*] pen-pusher,
receptionist, recorder, scribe, secretary,
shorthand-typist, stenographer, typist,
word-processor operator.

clever adjective
a clever child. a clever idea. able, academic,
accomplished, acute, adroit, apt, artful,
artistic, astute, brainy, bright, brilliant,
canny, capable, [*uncomplimentary*] crafty,
[*uncomplimentary*] cunning, [*informal*]
cute, [*informal*] deep (*She's a deep one!*), deft,
dextrous, discerning, expert, gifted,
[*informal*] handy, imaginative, ingenious,
intellectual, intelligent, inventive,
judicious, keen, knowing, knowledgeable,
precocious, quick, quick-witted, rational,
resourceful, sagacious, sensible, sharp,
shrewd, skilful, skilled, [*uncomplimentary*]
slick, smart, subtle, talented,
[*uncomplimentary*] wily, wise, witty.
OPPOSITES: SEE **stupid, unskilful**.

cliché noun
He talks uninterestingly in boring clichés.
banality, commonplace, familiar phrase,
hackneyed expression, platitude, well-worn
phrase.

client noun
a client of the bank. [*plural*] clientele [=
clients], consumer, customer, patron, user.

cliff noun
bluff, crag, escarpment, precipice, rock-face,
sheer drop.

climate noun
1 SEE **weather** noun.
2 *a climate of opinion.* ambience, atmosphere,
disposition, environment, feeling, mood,
spirit, temper, trend.

climax noun
1 *The music built up to a climax.* crisis,
culmination, head, highlight, high point,
peak, summit.
OPPOSITES: SEE **bathos**.
2 *a sexual climax.* orgasm.

climb noun
a steep climb. ascent, gradient, hill, incline,
rise, slope.

climb verb
1 *She climbed the rope.* ascend, clamber up,
go up, mount, move up, scale, swarm up.
2 *The plane climbed steeply.* defy gravity,
levitate, lift off, soar, take off.
3 *The road climbs steeply.* incline, rise, slope
up.

4 *They climbed the mountain.* conquer, reach
the top of.

climber noun
1 mountaineer, rock-climber.
2 [= *climbing plant*]

CLIMBING PLANTS INCLUDE: clematis,
creeper, honeysuckle, hops, ivy, runner
bean, vine.

clinch verb
to clinch a deal. agree, close, conclude,
confirm, decide, make certain of, ratify,
settle, shake hands on, sign, verify.

cling verb
1 *Ivy clings to the wall.* adhere, fasten on,
stick.
2 *The baby clung to its mother.* clasp, clutch,
embrace, grasp, hug.

clinic noun
health centre, infirmary, medical centre,
sick-bay, surgery.

clip noun
1 *a paper clip.*
VARIOUS FASTENERS: SEE **fasten**.
2 *a clip from a film.* excerpt, extract,
fragment, passage, quotation, section,
trailer.

clip verb
1 *to clip papers together.* SEE **fasten**, pin,
staple.
2 *to clip a hedge.* crop, SEE **cut** verb, dock,
prune, shear, snip, trim.
3 *to clip someone on the ear.* SEE **hit** verb.

cloak noun
She wrapped a cloak around her. cape, coat,
cope, mantle, wrap.

clock noun

INSTRUMENTS USED TO MEASURE TIME:
alarm-clock, chronometer, digital clock,
grandfather clock, hour-glass, pendulum
clock, sundial, watch.

clog verb
The drain was clogged with leaves. block,
[*informal*] bung up, choke, close, congest,
dam, fill, jam, obstruct, plug, stop up.

close adjective
1 *a close position.* adjacent, adjoining, at
hand, handy (for), near, neighbouring,
point-blank (*point-blank range*).
OPPOSITES: SEE **distant**.
2 *a close relationship.* affectionate, attached,
dear, devoted, familiar, fond, friendly,
intimate, loving, [*informal*] thick.
OPPOSITES: SEE **unfriendly**.

close 72 cloud

3 *a close comparison.* alike, analogous, comparable, compatible, corresponding, related, resembling, similar.
OPPOSITES: SEE **dissimilar.**
4 *a close crowd.* compact, congested, cramped, crowded, dense, [*informal*] jam-packed, packed, thick.
OPPOSITES: SEE **thin** adjective.
5 *a close examination.* attentive, careful, concentrated, detailed, minute, painstaking, precise, rigorous, searching, thorough.
OPPOSITES: SEE **cursory.**
6 *close about her private life.* confidential, private, reserved, reticent, secretive, taciturn.
OPPOSITES: SEE **frank.**
7 *close with money.* illiberal, mean, [*informal*] mingy, miserly, niggardly, parsimonious, penurious, stingy, tight, tightfisted, ungenerous.
OPPOSITES: SEE **generous.**
8 *a close atmosphere.* airless, fuggy, humid, muggy, oppressive, stifling, stuffy, suffocating, sweltering, unventilated, warm.
OPPOSITES: SEE **airy.**

close verb
1 *Close the door.* bolt, fasten, lock, seal, secure, shut.
2 *The road was closed.* bar, barricade, block, obstruct, stop up.
3 *We closed the party with "Auld lang syne".* complete, conclude, culminate, discontinue, end, finish, stop, terminate, [*informal*] wind up.
4 *Close the gap.* fill, join up, make smaller, reduce, shorten.

clot verb
When you cut yourself, blood clots and forms a scab. coagulate, coalesce, congeal, curdle, make lumps, set, solidify, stiffen, thicken.

cloth noun
cloth to make clothes and curtains. fabric, material, stuff, textile.

SOME KINDS OF CLOTH: astrakhan, bouclé, brocade, broderie anglaise, buckram, calico, cambric, candlewick, canvas, cashmere, cheesecloth, chenille, chiffon, chintz, corduroy, cotton, crepe, cretonne, damask, denim, dimity, drill, drugget.
elastic, felt, flannel, flannelette, gaberdine, gauze, georgette, gingham, hessian, holland, lace, lamé, lawn, linen, lint, mohair, moiré, moquette, muslin, nankeen, nylon, oilcloth, oilskin, organdie, organza, patchwork, piqué, plaid, plissé, plush, polycotton, polyester, poplin.
rayon, sackcloth, sacking, sailcloth, sarsenet, sateen, satin, satinette, seersucker, serge, silk, stockinet, taffeta, tapestry, tartan, terry, ticking, tulle, tussore, tweed, velour, velvet, velveteen, viscose, voile, winceyette, wool, worsted.

clothe verb
She always clothes her children nicely. array, attire, cover, deck, drape, dress, garb, outfit, robe, swathe, wrap up.
to clothe yourself in don, dress in, put on, wear.

clothed adjective
warmly clothed. [*old-fashioned*] apparelled, attired, clad, dressed, fitted out, [*informal*] turned out (*well turned out*), wrapped up.

clothes noun
apparel, attire, [*informal*] clobber, clothing, costume, dress, finery [= *best clothes*], garb, garments, [*informal*] gear, [*informal*] get-up, outfit, [*old-fashioned*] raiment, [*informal*] rigout, trousseau [= *a bride's clothes*], underclothes, uniform, vestments [= *priest's clothes*], wardrobe, wear (*leisure wear*), weeds (*widow's weeds*).
RELATED ADJECTIVE: sartorial.

VARIOUS GARMENTS: anorak, apron, belt, bib, blazer, blouse, bodice, breeches, caftan, cagoule, cape, cardigan, cassock, chemise, chuddar, cloak, coat, cravat, crinoline, culottes, cummerbund, décolletage, doublet, dress, dressing-gown, duffel coat, dungarees, frock.
gaiters, garter, gauntlet, glove, gown, greatcoat, gym-slip, habit (*a monk's habit*), SEE **hat**, housecoat, jacket, jeans, jerkin, jersey, jodhpurs, jumper, kilt, knickers, leg-warmers, leotard, livery, loincloth, lounge suit.
mackintosh, mantle, miniskirt, mitten, muffler, necktie, négligé, night-clothes, night-dress, oilskins, overalls, overcoat, pants, parka, pinafore, poncho, pullover, pyjamas, raincoat, robe, rompers.
sari, sarong, scarf, shawl, shirt, SEE **shoe**, shorts, singlet, skirt, slacks, smock, sock, sou'wester, spats, stocking, stole, suit, surplice, sweater, sweat-shirt, tail-coat, tie, tights, trousers, trunks, t-shirt, tunic, tutu, SEE **underclothes**, uniform, waistcoat, wet-suit, wind-cheater, wrap, yashmak.

cloud noun
1 *clouds in the sky.*
KINDS OF CLOUD: altocumulus, altostratus, cirrocumulus, cirrostratus, cirrus, cumulonimbus, cumulus, mackerel sky, nimbostratus, rain cloud, storm cloud, stratocumulus, stratus.
2 *a cloud of steam.* billow, haze, mass, mist, puff.

cloud verb
Mist clouded our view. blur, conceal, cover, darken, dull, eclipse, enshroud, hide, mantle, mist up, obfuscate, obscure, screen, shroud, veil.

cloudless adjective
a cloudless sky. bright, clear, starlit, sunny, unclouded.
OPPOSITES: SEE **cloudy**.

cloudy adjective
1 *a cloudy sky.* dark, dismal, dull, gloomy, grey, leaden, lowering, overcast, sullen, sunless.
OPPOSITES: SEE **cloudless**.
2 *cloudy windows.* blurred, blurry, dim, misty, opaque, steamy, unclear.
3 *cloudy liquid.* hazy, milky, muddy, murky.
OPPOSITES: SEE **clear** adjective.

clown noun
buffoon, comedian, comic, fool, jester, joker.

cloying adjective
sweet, syrupy.
OPPOSITES: SEE **refreshing**.

club noun
1 *a club to hit someone with.* bat, baton, bludgeon, cosh, cudgel, stick, truncheon.
2 *a football club. a book club.* association, circle, company, group, league, order, organization, party, set, society, union.

clue noun
I don't know the answer—give me a clue. hint, idea, indication, inkling, key, lead, pointer, sign, suggestion, tip.

clump noun
a clump of daffodils. a clump of trees. bunch, bundle, cluster, collection, SEE **group** noun, mass, shock (*a shock of hair*), thicket, tuft.

clumsy adjective
1 *clumsy movements. a clumsy person.* awkward, blundering, bumbling, bungling, fumbling, gangling, gawky, graceless, [*informal*] hamfisted, heavy-handed, hulking, inelegant, lumbering, maladroit, shambling, uncoordinated, ungainly, ungraceful, unskilful.
OPPOSITES: SEE **dainty**, **skilful**.
2 *a clumsy raft.* amateurish, badly made, bulky, cumbersome, heavy, inconvenient, inelegant, large, ponderous, rough, shapeless, unmanageable, unwieldy.
OPPOSITES: SEE **neat**.
3 *He made a clumsy remark about her illness.* boorish, gauche, ill-judged, inappropriate, indelicate, indiscreet, inept, insensitive, tactless, uncouth, undiplomatic, unsubtle, unsuitable.
OPPOSITES: SEE **tactful**.

a clumsy person botcher, bungler, [*informal*] butterfingers, fumbler.

cluster noun
a cluster of trees. a cluster of people. assembly, batch, bunch, clump, collection, crowd, gathering, SEE **group** noun, knot.

clutch verb
He clutched the rope. catch, clasp, cling to, grab, grasp, grip, hang on to, hold on to, seize, snatch.

clutter noun
We'll have to clear up all this clutter. confusion, disorder, jumble, junk, litter, lumber, mess, mix-up, muddle, odds and ends, rubbish, untidiness.

clutter verb
Her belongings clutter up my bedroom. be scattered about, fill, lie about, litter, make untidy, [*informal*] mess up, muddle, strew.

coach noun
1 *a motor coach.* bus, [*old-fashioned*] charabanc.
OTHER VEHICLES: SEE **vehicle**.
2 *a football coach.* instructor, teacher, trainer.

coach verb
to coach a football team. instruct, prepare, teach, train, tutor.

coagulate verb
clot, congeal, curdle, [*informal*] jell, solidify, stiffen, thicken.

coarse adjective
1 *coarse cloth. coarse sand.* bristly, gritty, hairy, harsh, lumpy, rough, scratchy, sharp, stony.
OPPOSITES: SEE **fine**.
2 *coarse language.* bawdy, blasphemous, boorish, common, crude, earthy, foul, immodest, impolite, improper, impure, indecent, indelicate, offensive, ribald, rude, smutty, uncouth, unrefined, vulgar.
OPPOSITES: SEE **polite**.

coast noun
beach, coastline, seaboard, sea-shore, seaside, shore.

coast verb
to coast down a hill on a bike. cruise, drift, free-wheel, glide, sail.

coastal adjective
a coastal town. maritime, nautical, naval, seaside.

coat noun
1 [= *a coat you wear*]

KINDS OF COAT YOU CAN WEAR: anorak, blazer, cagoule, cardigan, dinner-jacket, doublet, duffel coat, greatcoat, jacket, jerkin, mackintosh, overcoat, raincoat, tail-coat, tunic, tuxedo, waistcoat, wind-cheater.

2 *an animal's coat.* fleece, fur, hair, hide, pelt, skin.
3 *a coat of paint.* coating, cover, covering, film, finish, glaze, layer, membrane, patina, sheet, veneer, wash.
coat of arms badge, crest, emblem, heraldic device, shield.

coat verb
SEE **cover** verb.

coax verb
We coaxed the animal back into its cage. allure, beguile, cajole, decoy, entice, induce, inveigle, persuade, tempt, wheedle.

cobbler noun
shoemaker, shoe-mender, shoe-repairer.

code noun
1 *The Highway Code. a code of conduct.* etiquette, laws, manners, regulations, rule-book, rules, system.
2 *a message in code.* cipher, Morse code, secret language, semaphore, sign-system, signals.

coerce verb
I was coerced into joining the gang. bludgeon, browbeat, bully, compel, constrain, dragoon, force, frighten, intimidate, press-gang, pressurize, terrorize.

coercion noun
We prefer you to work voluntarily rather than by coercion. brow-beating, brute force, bullying, compulsion, conscription [*into the armed services*], constraint, duress, force, intimidation, physical force, pressure, [*informal*] strong-arm tactics, threats.

cogent adjective
a cogent argument. compelling, conclusive, convincing, effective, forceful, forcible, indisputable, irresistible, persuasive, potent, powerful, rational, strong, unanswerable, weighty, well-argued.

cohere verb
When you squeeze a handful of snow, the flakes cohere to make a snowball. bind, cake, cling together, coalesce, combine, consolidate, fuse, hang together, hold together, join, stick together, unite.

coherent adjective
a coherent argument. coherent speech. articulate, clear, cohering, cohesive,

connected, consistent, convincing, intelligible, logical, lucid, orderly, organized, rational, reasonable, reasoned, sound, structured, systematic, understandable, well-structured.
OPPOSITES: SEE **incoherent**.

coil noun

VARIOUS COILED SHAPES OR MOVEMENTS: circle, convolution, corkscrew, curl, helix, kink, loop, ring, roll, screw, spiral, twirl, twist, vortex, whirl, whorl.

coil verb
The sailor coiled the rope. The snake coiled round a branch. bend, curl, entwine, loop, roll, snake, spiral, turn, twine, twirl, twist, wind, writhe.

coin noun
a fifty pence coin. bit, piece.
coins *I haven't any coins, only notes.* change, coppers, loose change, silver, small change.

coin verb
1 *It's a serious offence to coin money.* forge, make, mint, mould, stamp.
2 *We coined a new name for our group.* conceive, concoct, create, devise, dream up, fabricate, hatch, introduce, invent, make up, originate, produce, think up.

coincide verb
1 *My birthday coincides with a bank holiday.* clash, coexist, fall together, happen together, synchronize.
2 *Our answers coincided.* accord, agree, be identical, be in unison, be the same, concur, correspond, harmonize, match, square, tally.

coincidence noun
We met by coincidence. accident, chance, fluke, luck.

cold adjective
1 *cold weather. a cold wind. a cold place.* arctic, biting, bitter, bleak, chill, chilly, cool, crisp, cutting, draughty, freezing, fresh, frosty, glacial, icy, inclement, keen, [*informal*] nippy, numbing, [*informal*] parky, penetrating, perishing, piercing, polar, raw, shivery, Siberian, snowy, unheated, wintry.
OPPOSITES: SEE **hot**.
2 *cold hands.* blue with cold, chilled, dead, frostbitten, frozen, numbed, shivering, shivery.
OPPOSITES: SEE **warm** adjective.
3 *a cold attitude. a cold heart.* aloof, callous, cold-blooded, cool, cruel, distant, frigid, hard, hard-hearted, heartless, indifferent, inhospitable, inhuman, insensitive, passionless, phlegmatic, reserved, standoffish, stony, uncaring, unconcerned,

undemonstrative, unemotional,
unenthusiastic, unfeeling, unfriendly,
unkind, unresponsive, unsympathetic.
OPPOSITES: SEE **kind** adjective, **passionate**.

cold noun
1 *Our cat doesn't like the cold.* chill, coldness,
coolness, freshness, iciness, low
temperature, wintriness.
OPPOSITES: SEE **heat** noun.
2 *She's got a nasty cold.* chill, cough.

SYMPTOMS OF A COLD: catarrh, coughing,
runny nose, sneezing, sniffing, snuffling.

---

cold-blooded adjective
a cold-blooded killing. barbaric, brutal,
callous, cold, cold-hearted, SEE **cruel**,
dispassionate, hard-hearted, heartless,
impassive, inhuman, insensitive, merciless,
pitiless, ruthless, savage, unemotional,
unfeeling.
OPPOSITES: SEE **humane**.

collaborate verb
1 *The work gets done more quickly when we
collaborate.* band together,
[*uncomplimentary*] collude,
[*uncomplimentary*] connive, co-operate,
join forces, [*informal*] pull together, team
up, work together.
2 *to collaborate with an enemy.* be a
collaborator, join the opposition, [*informal*]
rat, turn traitor.

collaborator noun
1 *I need a collaborator to help me.* accomplice
(*in wrongdoing*), ally, assistant, associate,
co-author, colleague, confederate, fellow
worker, helper, helpmate, partner, [*joking*]
partner-in-crime.
2 *a collaborator with the enemy.* blackleg,
[*informal*] Judas, quisling, [*informal*] scab,
traitor, turncoat.

collapse noun
*An earthquake caused the collapse of the
hotel.* break-up, cave-in, destruction,
downfall, end, fall, ruin, ruination,
subsidence, wreck.

collapse verb
1 *Many buildings collapsed in the
earthquake.* buckle, cave in, crumble,
crumple, disintegrate, fall apart, fall in, fold
up, give in, [*informal*] go west, sink,
subside, tumble down.
2 *People collapsed in the heat.* be ill,
[*informal*] bite the dust, faint, fall down,
founder, [*informal*] go under.
3 *Ice-cream sales collapsed in the cold
weather.* become less, crash, deteriorate,
drop, fail, slump, worsen.

collapsible adjective
a tripod with collapsible legs. adjustable,
folding, retractable, telescopic.

collect verb
1 *Squirrels collect nuts.* accumulate,
agglomerate, aggregate, amass, bring
together, garner, gather, harvest, heap,
hoard, lay up, pile up, put by, reserve, save,
scrape together, stockpile, store.
2 *A crowd collected to watch the fire.*
assemble, cluster, come together,
congregate, convene, converge, crowd,
forgather, group, muster, rally round.
OPPOSITES: SEE **disperse**.
3 *We collected a large sum for charity.* be
given, raise, secure, take.
4 *I collected the bread from the baker's.*
acquire, bring, fetch, get, obtain.

collection noun
1 accumulation, array, assortment, cluster,
conglomeration, heap, hoard, mass, pile, set,
stack.

VARIOUS COLLECTIONS OF PEOPLE AND
THINGS: anthology (*of poems, etc.*), arsenal
(*of weapons*), assembly (*of people*), batch (*of
cakes, etc.*), company, congregation (*of
worshippers*), crowd, gathering, SEE **group**
noun, library (*of books*), stockpile (*of
weapons*).

---

2 *a collection for charity.* [*old-fashioned*] alms-
giving, flag-day, free-will offering, offertory,
voluntary contributions, [*informal*] whip-
round.

collective adjective
a collective decision. combined, common,
composite, co-operative, corporate,
democratic, group, joint, shared, unified,
united.
OPPOSITES: SEE **individual** adjective.

college noun
academy, conservatory, institute,
polytechnic, school (*art school, etc.*),
university.

collide verb
to collide with *The car collided with the gate-
post.* bump into, cannon into, crash into, SEE
hit verb, knock, meet, run into, slam into,
smash into, strike, touch.

collision noun
a collision on the motorway. accident, bump,
clash, crash, head-on collision, impact,
knock, pile-up, scrape, smash.

colloquial adjective
colloquial language. chatty, conversational,
everyday, informal, slangy, [*formal*]
vernacular.
OPPOSITES: SEE **formal**.

colonize verb
to colonize a territory. found a colony in, move into, occupy, people, populate, settle in, subjugate.

colony noun
1 *At one time Britain had colonies all over the world.* dependency, dominion, possession, protectorate, province, settlement, territory.
2 *a colony of ants.* SEE **group** noun.

colossal adjective
A colossal statue towered above us. SEE **big**, elephantine, enormous, gargantuan, giant, gigantic, huge, immense, mammoth, massive, mighty, monstrous, monumental, prodigious, titanic, towering, vast.
OPPOSITES: SEE **small**.

colour noun
1 coloration, colouring, hue, shade, tincture, tinge, tint, tone.

SUBSTANCES WHICH GIVE COLOUR:
cochineal, colourant, colouring, cosmetics, dye, make-up, SEE **paint** noun, pigment, pigmentation, stain, tincture, woad.

VARIOUS COLOURS: amber, azure, beige, black, blue, brindled, bronze, brown, buff, carroty, cherry, chestnut, chocolate, cobalt, cream, crimson, dun, fawn, gilt, gold, golden, green, grey, indigo, ivory, jet-black, khaki, lavender, maroon, mauve, navy blue, ochre, olive, orange, pink, puce, purple, red, rosy, russet, sandy, scarlet, silver, tan, tawny, turquoise, vermilion, violet, white, yellow.

---

2 *colour in your cheeks.* bloom, blush, flush, glow, rosiness, ruddiness.
colours *the colours of a regiment.* banner, ensign, flag, standard.

colour verb
1 *to colour a picture.* colourwash, dye, paint, shade, stain, tinge, tint.
2 *His fair skin colours easily.* blush, bronze, brown, burn, flush, redden, tan.
OPPOSITES: SEE **fade**.
3 *An umpire shouldn't let her prejudices colour her decisions.* affect, bias, distort, impinge on, influence, pervert, prejudice, slant, sway.

colourful adjective
1 *colourful flowers. a colourful scene.* bright, brilliant, chromatic, gaudy, iridescent, multicoloured, psychedelic, showy, vibrant.
OPPOSITES: SEE **colourless**, **pale** adjective.
2 *a colourful description.* exciting, florid, graphic, picturesque, rich, stimulating, striking, telling, vivid.
OPPOSITES: SEE **dull** adjective.

3 *a colourful personality.* dashing, distinctive, dynamic, SEE **eccentric**, energetic, flamboyant, flashy, glamorous, interesting, lively, publicity-seeking, unusual, vigorous.
OPPOSITES: SEE **restrained**.

colourless adjective
1 *a colourless substance.* albino, black, faded, grey, monochrome, neutral, SEE **pale** adjective, [*informal*] washed-out, white.
2 *a colourless personality. a colourless scene.* boring, characterless, dingy, dismal, dowdy, drab, dreary, dull, insipid, lacklustre, shabby, tame, uninteresting, vacuous, vapid.
OPPOSITES: SEE **colourful**.

column noun
1 *columns supporting a roof.* pilaster, pile, pillar, pole, post, prop, shaft, support, upright.
2 *I write a column in a local newspaper.* article, feature, leader, leading article, piece.
3 *a column of figures. a column of writing.* vertical division, vertical section.
4 *a column of soldiers.* cavalcade, file, line, procession, queue, rank, row, string, train.

comb verb
1 *to comb your hair.* arrange, groom, neaten, smarten up, spruce up, tidy, untangle.
2 *I combed the house in search of my pen.* hunt through, ransack, rummage through, scour, search thoroughly.

combat noun
a fierce combat. action, battle, bout, clash, conflict, contest, duel, encounter, engagement, fight, SEE **martial (martial arts)**, skirmish, struggle, war, warfare.

combat verb
to combat crime. battle against, contend against, contest, counter, defy, face up to, fight, grapple with, oppose, resist, stand up to, strive against, struggle against, tackle, withstand.

combination noun
a combination of things. a combination of people. aggregate, alliance, alloy, amalgam, amalgamation, association, blend, coalition, compound, concoction, concurrence, confederacy, confederation, conjunction, consortium, conspiracy, federation, fusion, link-up, marriage, merger, mix, mixture, partnership, syndicate, synthesis, unification, union.

combine verb
1 *to combine resources.* add together, amalgamate, bind, blend, bring together, compound, fuse, integrate, intertwine, interweave, join, link, [*informal*] lump together, marry, merge, mingle, mix, pool, put together, synthesize, unify, unite.

2 *to combine as a team.* associate, band together, club together, coalesce, connect, co-operate, gang together, join forces, team up.

come verb
1 *Visitors are coming tomorrow.* appear, arrive, visit.
2 *Spring came suddenly this year.* advance, draw near, materialize, occur.
3 *Tell me when we come to my station.* approach, arrive at, get to, near, reach.
to come about SEE **happen.**
to come across SEE **find.**
to come round SEE **recover.**

comedian noun
buffoon, clown, comic, SEE **entertainer**, fool, humorist, jester, joker, wag.

comedy noun
buffoonery, clowning, facetiousness, farce, hilarity, humour, jesting, joking, satire, slapstick, wit.

comfort noun
1 *to live in comfort.* affluence, contentment, cosiness, ease, luxury, opulence, relaxation, well-being.
2 *We tried to give the injured woman some comfort.* aid, cheer, consolation, encouragement, help, moral support, reassurance, relief, solace, succour, sympathy.
OPPOSITES: SEE **discomfort.**

comfort verb
He was upset, so we tried to comfort him. assuage, calm, cheer up, console, ease, encourage, gladden, hearten, help, reassure, relieve, solace, soothe, succour, sympathize with.

comfortable adjective
1 *a comfortable chair. a comfortable place to rest.* [*informal*] comfy, convenient, cosy, easy, padded, reassuring, relaxing, roomy, snug, soft, upholstered, warm.
2 *comfortable clothes.* informal, loose-fitting, well-fitting, well-made.
3 *a comfortable life-style.* affluent, agreeable, contented, happy, homely, luxurious, pleasant, prosperous, relaxed, restful, serene, well-off.
OPPOSITES: SEE **uncomfortable.**

comic adjective
a comic situation. comic remarks. absurd, amusing, comical, diverting, droll, facetious, farcical, funny, hilarious, humorous, hysterical, jocular, joking, laughable, ludicrous, [*informal*] priceless, [*informal*] rich (*That's rich!*), ridiculous, SEE **sarcastic**, sardonic, satirical, side-splitting, silly, uproarious, waggish, witty.

command noun
1 *Do you always obey commands?* behest, bidding, commandment (*the Ten Commandments*), decree, directive, edict, injunction, instruction, order, requirement, ultimatum, writ.
2 *She has command of the whole expedition.* authority (over), charge, control, direction, government, management, power (over), rule (over), supervision, sway (over).

command verb
1 *He commanded us to stop.* adjure, bid, charge, compel, decree, demand, direct, enjoin, instruct, ordain, order, require.
2 *A captain commands his ship.* administer, be in charge of, control, direct, govern, head, lead, manage, reign over, rule, supervise.

commander noun
captain, SEE **chief** noun, commanding-officer, general, head, leader, officer-in-charge.

commemorate verb
a ceremony to commemorate those who died in war. be a memorial to, be a reminder of, celebrate, honour, keep alive the memory of, pay your respects to, pay tribute to, remember, salute, solemnize.

commence verb
SEE **begin.**

commend verb
The boss commended our effort. acclaim, applaud, approve of, compliment, congratulate, eulogize, extol, praise, recommend.
OPPOSITES: SEE **criticize.**

comment verb
1 *I heard several comments about the way we played.* animadversion [= *hostile comment*], criticism, mention, observation, opinion, reference, remark, statement.
2 *Teachers write comments on pupils' work.* annotation, footnote, gloss, note.

comment verb
I commented that the weather had been bad. explain, interject, interpose, mention, note, observe, remark, say.

commentary noun
1 *a commentary on a football match.* account, broadcast, description, report.
2 *We wrote a commentary on the novel we were studying.* analysis, criticism, critique, discourse, elucidation, explanation, interpretation, notes, review, treatise.

commentator noun
a radio commentator. announcer, broadcaster, journalist, reporter.

commerce noun
A healthy economy depends on commerce.
business, buying and selling, dealings,
financial transactions, marketing,
merchandising, trade, trading, traffic.

commercial adjective
1 *commercial dealings.* business, economic,
financial, mercantile.
2 *a commercial success.* financially
successful, monetary, money-making,
pecuniary, profitable, profit-making.

commercial noun
a TV commercial. [*informal*] ad, [*informal*]
advert, advertisement, [*informal*] break
(*commercial break*), [*informal*] plug.

commiserate verb
We commiserated with the losers. comfort,
condole, console, express sympathy for, feel
for, SEE **sympathize**.
OPPOSITES: SEE **congratulate**.

commission noun
1 *a commission in the armed services.*
appointment, promotion, warrant.
VARIOUS RANKS: SEE **rank** noun.
2 *a commission to paint a portrait.* booking,
order, request.
3 *a commission to investigate a complaint.* SEE
committee.
4 *a salesperson's commission on a sale.*
allowance, [*informal*] cut, fee, percentage,
[*informal*] rake-off, reward.

commit verb
1 *to commit a crime.* be guilty of, carry
out, do, enact, execute, perform,
perpetrate.
2 *to commit valuables to someone's
safekeeping.* consign, deliver, deposit,
entrust, give, hand over.
to commit yourself *I committed myself to
help with the jumble sale.* contract,
covenant, guarantee, pledge, promise,
undertake, vow.

commitment noun
1 *The builder had a commitment to finish the
work on time.* assurance, duty, guarantee,
liability, pledge, promise, undertaking, vow,
word.
2 *The Green party has a commitment to
conservation.* adherence, dedication,
determination, involvement, loyalty.
3 *I checked my diary to see if I had any
commitments.* appointment, arrangement,
engagement.

committed adjective
a committed member of a political party.
active, ardent, [*informal*] card-carrying,
dedicated, devoted, earnest, enthusiastic,
fervent, firm, keen, passionate, resolute,
single-minded, staunch, unwavering,
wholehearted, zealous.
OPPOSITES: SEE **apathetic**.

committee noun

GROUPS WHICH MAKE DECISIONS, ETC.:
advisory group, assembly, board, cabinet,
caucus, commission, convention, council,
discussion group, junta, jury, panel,
parliament, quango, synod, think-tank,
working party.
SEE ALSO: **meeting**.

common adjective
1 *common knowledge.* accepted, collective,
communal, general, joint, mutual, open,
popular, public, shared, universal.
OPPOSITES: SEE **individual** adjective.
2 *a common happening.* average, [*informal*]
common or garden, SEE **commonplace**,
conventional, customary, daily, everyday,
familiar, frequent, habitual, normal,
ordinary, popular, prevalent, regular,
routine, [*informal*] run-of-the-mill,
standard, traditional, typical, unsurprising,
usual, well-known, widespread.
OPPOSITES: SEE **unusual**.
3 [*informal*] *common behaviour.* boorish,
churlish, coarse, crude, disreputable, ill-
bred, loutish, low, plebeian, rude, uncouth,
unrefined, vulgar, [*informal*] yobbish.
OPPOSITES: SEE **refined**.

commonplace adjective
*a commonplace event. a commonplace
remark.* banal, boring, SEE **common**
adjective, familiar, forgettable, hackneyed,
humdrum, mediocre, obvious, ordinary,
pedestrian, plain, platitudinous,
predictable, routine, standard, trite,
undistinguished, unexceptional, unexciting,
unremarkable, unsurprising.
OPPOSITES: SEE **distinguished**, **memorable**.

commotion noun
a commotion in the street. [*informal*] ado,
agitation, [*informal*] bedlam, [*informal*]
brouhaha, bother, brawl, [*informal*] bust-
up, chaos, clamour, confusion, contretemps,
din, disorder, disturbance, excitement,
ferment, flurry, fracas, fray, furore, fuss,
hubbub, hullabaloo, hurly-burly, incident,
[*informal*] kerfuffle, noise, [*informal*]
palaver, pandemonium, [*informal*] punch-
up, quarrel, racket, riot, row, rumpus,
[*informal*] shemozzle, sensation, [*informal*]
stir, [*informal*] to-do, tumult, turbulence,
turmoil, unrest, upheaval, uproar, upset.

communal adjective
communal washing facilities. collective,
common, general, joint, mutual, open,
public, shared.
OPPOSITES: SEE **private**.

communicate verb
1 *to communicate information.* advise, announce, broadcast, convey, declare, disclose, disseminate, divulge, express, impart, indicate, inform, intimate, make known, mention, [*in computing*] network, notify, pass on, proclaim, promulgate, publish, put across, relay, report, reveal, say, show, speak, spread, state, write.
2 *to communicate with other people.* commune, confer, contact [= *communicate with*], converse, correspond, discuss, get in touch, interrelate, make contact, speak, talk, write (to).
3 *to communicate a disease.* give, infect someone with, pass on, spread, transfer, transmit.

communication noun
Animals have various methods of communication. communicating, communion, contact, [*old-fashioned*] intercourse, understanding one another.

METHODS OF HUMAN COMMUNICATION: announcement, bulletin, cable, SEE **card**, communiqué, computer, conversation, correspondence, dialogue, directive, dispatch, document, FAX, gossip, [*informal*] grapevine, information, intelligence, intercom, intimation, SEE **letter**, the media [SEE BELOW], [*informal*] memo, memorandum, message, news, note, notice, proclamation, radar, report, rumour, satellite, signal, speaking, statement, talk, telegram, telegraph, telephone, teleprinter, transmission, walkie-talkie, wire, word, writing.

THE MASS MEDIA: advertising, broadcasting, cable television, newspapers, the press, radio, telecommunications, television.

---

communicative adjective
a communicative person. frank, informative, open, out-going, sociable, SEE **talkative**.
OPPOSITES: SEE **secretive**.

community noun
Most people like to live in a community. colony, commonwealth, commune, country, SEE **group** noun, kibbutz, nation, society, state.

commute verb
1 *to commute a prison sentence.* adjust, alter, curtail, decrease, lessen, lighten, mitigate, reduce, shorten.
2 *to commute into the city.* SEE **travel** verb.

compact adjective
1 *compact soil.* close-packed, compacted, compressed, dense, firm, heavy, solid, tight-packed.
OPPOSITES: SEE **loose**.

2 *a compact encyclopaedia.* abbreviated, abridged, brief, compendious, compressed, concentrated, condensed, short, small, succinct, terse.
OPPOSITES: SEE **diffuse** adjective.
3 *a compact tool-box.* handy, neat, portable, small.
OPPOSITES: SEE **large, spacious**.

companion noun
He took a companion with him. accomplice, assistant, associate, colleague, comrade, confederate, confidant, consort, [*informal*] crony, escort, fellow, follower, SEE **friend**, SEE **helper**, [*informal*] henchman, mate, partner, stalwart.

company noun
1 *We enjoy other people's company.* companionship, fellowship, friendship, society.
2 [*informal*] *We've got company coming on Sunday.* callers, guests, visitors.
3 *a company of friends.* assemblage, band, body, circle, community, coterie, crew, crowd, entourage, gang, gathering, throng, troop.
4 *a theatrical company.* association, club, ensemble, group, society, troupe.
5 *a trading company.* business, cartel, concern, conglomerate, consortium, corporation, establishment, firm, house, line, organization, partnership, [*informal*] set-up, syndicate, union.

comparable adjective
I got better quality at a comparable price. The work she does is not comparable to yours. analogous, cognate, commensurate, compatible, corresponding, equal, equivalent, parallel, proportionate, related, similar.
OPPOSITES: SEE **dissimilar**.

compare verb
1 *Compare these sets of figures.* check, contrast, correlate, draw parallels between, juxtapose, make connections between, match, parallel, relate, set side by side, weigh.
2 *You can't compare the two teams.* equate, liken.
3 *Their team cannot compare with ours.* compete with, emulate, equal, match, rival, vie with.

comparison noun
analogy, contrast, correlation, difference, distinction, juxtaposition, likeness, parallel, resemblance, similarity.

compartment noun
a compartment to keep belongings in. a compartment to sleep in. alcove, area, bay, berth, booth, cell, chamber, [*informal*]

cubby-hole, cubicle, division, kiosk, locker, niche, nook, pigeon-hole, section, space, subdivision.

compatible adjective
1 *People who live together must be compatible.* SEE **friendly**, harmonious, like-minded.
2 *The work he did was not compatible with his terms of employment.* accordant, congruent, consistent, consonant, matching, reconcilable.
OPPOSITES: SEE **incompatible**.

compel verb
You can't compel me to join in. bind, SEE **bully** verb, coerce, constrain, dragoon, drive, exact, force, impel, make, necessitate, oblige, order, press, press-gang, pressurize, require, [*informal*] shanghai, urge.

compensate verb
to compensate someone for damage. atone, [*informal*] cough up, [*formal*] indemnify, make amends, make reparation, make up, offset, pay back, pay compensation [SEE **compensation**], recompense, redress, reimburse, repay.

compensation noun
How much compensation did they get? amends, damages, [*formal*] indemnity, recompense, refund, reimbursement, reparation, repayment, restitution.

compete verb
to compete in a sport. be a contestant, enter, participate, perform, take part, take up the challenge.
to compete against be in competition with [SEE **competition**], challenge, conflict with, contend against, emulate, SEE **fight** verb, oppose, rival, strive against, struggle with, undercut, vie with.

competent adjective
a competent builder. a competent performance. able, acceptable, accomplished, adept, adequate, capable, clever, effective, effectual, efficient, experienced, expert, fit, [*informal*] handy, practical, proficient, qualified, satisfactory, skilful, skilled, trained, workmanlike.
OPPOSITES: SEE **incompetent**.

competition noun
1 *The competition between contestants was fierce.* competitiveness, conflict, contention, emulation, rivalry, struggle.
2 *a football competition. a prize competition.* challenge, championship, contest, event, game, heat, match, quiz, race, rally, series, tournament, trial.

competitive adjective
1 *competitive games.* aggressive, antagonistic, combative, contentious, cut-throat, hard-fought, keen, lively, sporting, well-fought.
OPPOSITES: SEE **co-operative**.
2 *competitive prices.* average, comparable with others, fair, moderate, reasonable, similar to others.
OPPOSITES: SEE **exorbitant**.

competitor noun
the competitors in a quiz. adversary, antagonist, candidate, challenger, contender, contestant, entrant, finalist, opponent, participant, rival.

compile verb
to compile a magazine. arrange, assemble, collect together, compose, edit, gather together, marshal, organize, put together.

complacent adjective
You can't be complacent when the job is only half-finished. confident, contented, pleased with yourself, self-congratulatory, self-righteous, self-satisfied, smug, unconcerned, untroubled.
OPPOSITES: SEE **anxious**.

complain verb
We complained about the awful service. [*informal*] beef, [*slang*] bind, carp, cavil, find fault (with), fuss, [*informal*] gripe, [*informal*] grouch, grouse, grumble, lament, moan, object, protest, whine, [*informal*] whinge.
OPPOSITES: SEE **approve (approve of)**.

complaint noun
1 *We had complaints about the noise.* accusation, [*informal*] beef, charge, condemnation, criticism, grievance, [*informal*] gripe, grouse, grumble, moan, objection, protest, stricture, whine, whinge.
2 *Flu is a common complaint in winter.* affliction, ailment, disease, disorder, SEE **illness**, indisposition, infection, malady, malaise, sickness, upset.

complement verb
[Do not confuse with *compliment*.] *Her guitar-playing complemented his singing perfectly.* complete, make complete, make perfect, make whole, top up.

complete adjective
1 *the complete story.* comprehensive, entire, exhaustive, full, intact, total, unabbreviated, unabridged, unedited, unexpurgated, whole.
2 *a complete job of work.* accomplished, achieved, completed, concluded, ended, faultless, finished, perfect.
OPPOSITES: SEE **incomplete**.
3 *complete disaster. complete rubbish.* absolute, arrant, downright, extreme, [*informal*] out-and-out, outright, pure, rank, sheer, thorough, thoroughgoing, total, unmitigated, unmixed, unqualified, utter, [*informal*] wholesale.

complete verb
to complete a job of work. accomplish, achieve, carry out, clinch, close, conclude, do, end, finalize, finish, fulfil, perfect, perform, round off, terminate, [*informal*] wind up.

complex adjective
a complex substance. a complex task. complicated, composite, compound, convoluted, elaborate, [*informal*] fiddly, heterogeneous, intricate, involved, manifold, mixed, multifarious, multiple, multiplex, sophisticated.

complexion noun
a healthy complexion. appearance, colour, colouring, look, pigmentation, skin, texture.

WORDS TO DESCRIBE COMPLEXIONS: black, brown, clear, dark, fair, freckled, pasty, ruddy, sickly, spotty, swarthy, tanned, white.

---

complicate verb
Don't complicate things by asking for food that's not on the menu. compound, confuse, elaborate, make complicated (SEE **complicated**), mix up, muddle, tangle.
OPPOSITES: SEE **simplify**.

complicated adjective
a complicated task. a complicated plan. complex, convoluted, difficult, elaborate, entangled, hard, intricate, involved, knotty (*a knotty problem*), perplexing, problematical, sophisticated, tangled, tortuous, [*informal*] tricky, twisted, twisting.
OPPOSITES: SEE **straightforward**.

compliment noun
[Do not confuse with *complement*.] [*often plural*] *Give our compliments to the chef.* accolade, admiration, appreciation, approval, commendation, congratulations, [*formal*] encomium, [*formal*] eulogy, [*formal or joking*] felicitations, flattery, honour, [*formal*] panegyric, plaudits, praise, testimonial, tribute.
OPPOSITES: SEE **insult** noun.

compliment verb
[Do not confuse with *complement*.] *to compliment someone on their performance.* applaud, commend, congratulate, [*informal*] crack up, eulogize, extol, [*formal*] felicitate, give credit, [*formal*] laud, praise, salute, speak highly of.
OPPOSITES: SEE **criticize, insult** verb.

complimentary adjective
1 *complimentary remarks.* admiring, appreciative, approving, commendatory, congratulatory, eulogistic, favourable, flattering, fulsome, generous, laudatory, rapturous, supportive.
OPPOSITES: SEE **critical, insulting**.
2 *complimentary tickets.* free, [*informal*] give-away, gratis.

comply verb
to comply with *I complied with the rules.* accede to, acquiesce in, agree to, assent to, conform to, consent to, defer to, fall in with, follow, fulfil, obey, observe, perform, satisfy, submit to, yield to.
OPPOSITES: SEE **defy**.

component noun
components of a car. bit, constituent part, element, essential part, ingredient, item, part, piece, [*informal*] spare, spare part, unit.

compose verb
1 *The village was composed of small huts.* build, compile, constitute, construct, fashion, form, frame, make, put together.
2 *Mozart composed a lot of music.* arrange, create, devise, imagine, make up, produce, write.
3 *Have a cup of tea and compose yourself.* calm, control, pacify, quieten, soothe, tranquillize.
to be composed of *A hockey team is composed of 11 players.* comprehend, consist of, comprise, contain, embody, embrace, include, incorporate, involve.

composed adjective SEE **calm** adjective.

composition noun
1 *the composition of a team. the composition of a chemical.* constitution, content, establishment, formation, formulation, [*informal*] make-up, structure.
2 *a musical composition.* [*formal*] opus, piece, work.
VARIOUS COMPOSITIONS: SEE **music**.

compound noun
1 *a chemical compound.* alloy, amalgam, blend, combination, composite, composition, fusion, synthesis. SEE ALSO: **mixture**: but note that in chemical terms *compound* and *mixture* are not the same.
2 *a compound for animals.* [*American*] corral, enclosure, pen, run.

comprehend verb
Can you comprehend what I'm saying? appreciate, conceive, discern, fathom, follow, grasp, know, perceive, realize, see, [*informal*] twig, understand.

comprehensible adjective
a comprehensible explanation. clear, easy, intelligible, lucid, meaningful, plain, self-

explanatory, simple, straightforward, understandable.
OPPOSITES: SEE **incomprehensible**.

comprehension noun
SEE **understanding**.

comprehensive adjective
a comprehensive account of a subject. all-embracing, broad, catholic, compendious, complete, detailed, encyclopaedic, exhaustive, extensive, full, inclusive, thorough, total, universal, wide-ranging.
OPPOSITES: SEE **selective**.

compress verb
to compress ideas into a few words. to compress things into a small space. abbreviate, abridge, compact, concentrate, condense, constrict, contract, cram, crush, flatten, [*informal*] jam, précis, press, shorten, squash, squeeze, stuff, summarize, telescope, truncate.
OPPOSITES: SEE **expand**.

comprise verb
This album comprises the best hits of the year. be composed of, consist of, contain, cover, embody, embrace, include, incorporate, involve.

compromise noun
The two sides reached a compromise. bargain, concession, [*informal*] give-and-take, [*informal*] halfway house, middle course, middle way, settlement.

compromise verb
1 *The two sides compromised.* concede a point, go to arbitration, make concessions, meet halfway, negotiate a settlement, reach a formula, settle, [*informal*] split the difference, strike a balance.
2 *He compromised his reputation by getting involved in a scandal.* discredit, dishonour, imperil, jeopardize, prejudice, risk, undermine, weaken.

compromising adjective
a compromising situation. damaging, discreditable, disgraceful, dishonourable, embarrassing, ignoble, improper, questionable, scandalous, unworthy.

compulsion noun
1 *Slaves work by compulsion, not by choice.* being compelled, coercion, duress (*under duress*), force, necessity, restriction, restraint.
2 *an irresistible compulsion to eat.* addiction, drive, habit, impulse, pressure, urge.
OPPOSITES: SEE **option**.

compulsive adjective
1 *a compulsive urge.* besetting, compelling, driving, instinctive, involuntary, irresistible, overpowering, overwhelming, powerful, uncontrollable, urgent.

2 *a compulsive eater.* addicted, habitual, incorrigible, incurable, obsessive, persistent.

compulsory adjective
The wearing of seat-belts is compulsory. binding, de rigueur, imperative, imposed, incumbent, inescapable, mandatory, obligatory, official, required, stipulated, unavoidable.
OPPOSITES: SEE **optional**.

compute verb
to compute figures. add up, assess, calculate, count, estimate, evaluate, measure, reckon, total, work out.

computer noun
mainframe, [*informal*] micro, microcomputer, mini-computer, personal computer, PC, word-processor.

SOME TERMS USED IN COMPUTING: bit, byte, chip, cursor, data, database, data-processing, desk-top publishing, [*adjective*] digital, disc, disc-drive, firmware, floppy-disc, hard copy, hard disc, hardware, input, interface, joystick, keyboard, machine-code, [*adjective*] machine-readable, memory, menu, micro, microchip, micro-processor, monitor, mouse, network, output, printer, printout, processor, program, retrieval, robotics, silicon chip, software, spreadsheet, terminal, VDU, virus, window, word-processing.

---

concave adjective
SEE **curved**, dished.
OPPOSITES: SEE **convex**.

conceal verb
blot out, bury, camouflage, cloak, cover up, disguise, envelop, hide, hush up, keep dark, keep quiet, keep secret, mask, obscure, screen, suppress, veil.
OPPOSITES: SEE **reveal**.

concealed adjective
camouflaged, cloaked, disguised, furtive, hidden, SEE **invisible**, secret, unobtrusive.
OPPOSITES: SEE **obvious, visible**.

concede verb
1 *I conceded that I was wrong.* acknowledge, admit, agree, allow, confess, grant, make a concession, own, profess, recognize.
2 *After a long fight he conceded.* capitulate, [*informal*] cave in, cede, [*informal*] give in, resign, submit, surrender, yield.

conceited adjective
arrogant, [*informal*] bigheaded, boastful, bumptious, [*informal*] cocky, egocentric, egotistic, egotistical, haughty, [*informal*] high and mighty, immodest, overweening, pleased with yourself, proud, self-satisfied,

[*informal*] snooty, [*informal*] stuck-up,
[*informal*] swollen-headed, supercilious,
vain, vainglorious.
OPPOSITES: SEE **modest**.

conceive verb
1 *to conceive a baby*. become pregnant.
2 *to conceive an idea*. [*informal*] bring up,
conjure up, create, design, devise,
[*informal*] dream up, envisage, form,
formulate, germinate, hatch, imagine,
invent, make-up, originate, plan, produce,
realize, suggest, think up, visualize, work
out.

concentrate verb
1 *Please concentrate on your work*. apply
yourself (to), attend (to), be absorbed (in),
be attentive (to), engross yourself (in), focus
(on), think (about), work hard (at).
OPPOSITE: be inattentive (SEE **inattentive**).
2 *The crowds concentrated in the middle of
town*. accumulate, centre, cluster, collect,
congregate, converge, crowd, gather, mass.
OPPOSITES: SEE **disperse**.
3 *to concentrate a liquid*. condense, reduce,
thicken.
OPPOSITES: SEE **dilute** verb.

conception noun
1 *She has no conception of how difficult it is*.
SEE **idea**.
2 *the conception of a baby*. begetting,
beginning, conceiving, fathering,
fertilization, impregnation.

concern noun
1 *concern for others*. attention, care,
consideration, heed, interest, involvement,
responsibility, solicitude.
2 *It's no concern of theirs*. affair, business,
matter.
3 *a matter of great concern to us all*. anxiety,
worry.
4 *a business concern*. company, corporation,
enterprise, establishment, firm,
organization.

concern verb
Road safety concerns us all. affect, be
important to, be relevant to, interest,
involve, matter to, [*formal*] pertain to, refer
to, relate to.

concerned adjective
[The meaning of *concerned* varies according
to whether the word comes before or after
the noun it describes: compare the examples
given here.] 1 *The concerned parents asked
for news of their children*. SEE **anxious**,
bothered, caring, distressed, disturbed,
fearful, solicitous, touched, troubled,
unhappy, upset, worried.
OPPOSITES: UNCONCERNED, SEE **callous**.
2 *If you want the truth, talk to the people*

concerned. connected, implicated,
interested, involved, relevant, referred to.

concerning preposition
information concerning our holiday. about,
apropos of, germane to, involving, re,
regarding, relating to, relevant to, with
reference to, with regard to.

concerted adjective
a concerted effort. collaborative, collective,
combined, co-operative, joint, mutual,
shared, united.

concise adjective
a concise dictionary. *a concise account*.
abbreviated, abridged, brief, compact,
compendious, compressed, concentrated,
condensed, laconic, pithy, short, small,
succinct, terse.
OPPOSITES: SEE **diffuse** adjective.

conclude verb
1 *The concert concluded with an encore*. cease,
close, complete, culminate, end, finish,
round off, stop, terminate.
2 *When you didn't arrive, we concluded that
the car had broken down*. assume, decide,
deduce, gather, infer, judge, reckon,
suppose, surmise, SEE **think**.

conclusion noun
1 *the conclusion of a journey*. *the conclusion
of a concert*. close, completion, culmination,
end, finale, finish, peroration, rounding-off,
termination.
2 *Now that you've heard the evidence, what's
your conclusion?* answer, assumption, belief,
decision, deduction, inference,
interpretation, judgement, opinion,
outcome, resolution, result, solution,
upshot, verdict.

conclusive adjective
conclusive evidence. convincing, decisive,
definite, persuasive, unambiguous,
unanswerable, unequivocal.
OPPOSITES: SEE **inconclusive**.

concoct verb
to concoct excuses. *to concoct something to
eat*. SEE **cook** verb, cook up, contrive,
counterfeit, devise, fabricate, feign,
formulate, hatch, invent, make up, plan,
prepare, put together, think up.

concrete adjective
concrete evidence. actual, definite, existing,
factual, firm, material, objective, palpable,
physical, real, solid, substantial, tactile,
tangible, touchable, visible.
OPPOSITES: SEE **abstract** adjective.

concurrent adjective
You can't attend two concurrent events!
coexisting, coinciding, concomitant,

contemporaneous, contemporary, overlapping, parallel, simultaneous, synchronous.

condemn verb
1 *We condemn violence. We condemn criminals.* blame, castigate, censure, criticize, damn, decry, denounce, deplore, disapprove of, disparage, rebuke, reprehend, reprove, revile, [*informal*] slam, [*informal*] slate, upbraid.
OPPOSITES: SEE **commend**.
2 *They were condemned by the evidence. The judge condemned them.* convict, find guilty, judge, pass judgement, prove guilty, punish, sentence.
OPPOSITES: SEE **acquit**.

condense verb
1 *to condense a book.* abbreviate, abridge, compress, contract, curtail, précis, reduce, shorten, summarize, synopsize.
OPPOSITES: SEE **expand**.
2 *to condense a liquid.* concentrate, distil, reduce, solidify, thicken.
OPPOSITES: SEE **dilute** verb.
3 *Steam condenses on a cold window.* become liquid, form condensation.
OPPOSITES: SEE **evaporate**.

condescending adjective
a condescending attitude. disdainful, haughty, imperious, lofty, patronizing, [*informal*] snooty, supercilious, superior.

condition noun
1 *in good condition, in bad condition.* case, circumstance, fettle (*in fine fettle*), fitness, health, [*informal*] nick, order, shape, situation, state, [*informal*] trim.
2 *a medical condition.* SEE **illness**.
3 *conditions of membership.* limitation, obligation, proviso, qualification, requirement, restriction, stipulation, terms.

conditional adjective
a conditional agreement. conditional surrender. dependent, limited, provisional, qualified, restricted, safeguarded, [*informal*] with strings attached.
OPPOSITES: SEE **unconditional**.

condone verb
Do you condone his sin? allow, connive at, disregard, endorse, excuse, forgive, ignore, let someone off, overlook, pardon, tolerate.

conducive adjective
Warm, wet weather is conducive to the growth of weeds. advantageous, beneficial, encouraging, favourable, helpful, supportive.

conduct noun
1 *good conduct.* actions, attitude, bearing, behaviour, demeanour, manner, ways.
2 *the conduct of the nation's affairs.* administration, control, direction, discharge, handling, leading, management, organization, running, supervision.

conduct verb
1 *The curator conducted us round the museum.* accompany, convey, escort, guide, lead, pilot, steer, take, usher.
2 *The chairman conducted the meeting well.* administer, be in charge of, chair, command, control, direct, govern, handle, head, lead, look after, manage, organize, oversee, preside over, regulate, rule, run, superintend, supervise.

confer verb
1 *to confer an honour on someone.* accord, award, bestow, give, grant, honour with, impart, invest, present.
2 *You may not confer with each other during the exam!* compare notes, consult, converse, debate, deliberate, discourse, discuss, exchange ideas, [*informal*] put your heads together, seek advice, talk, talk things over.

conference noun
consultation, convention, council, deliberation, discussion, SEE **meeting**, symposium.

confess verb
to confess guilt. acknowledge, admit (to), be truthful (about), [*informal*] come clean (about), concede, [*informal*] make a clean breast (of), own up (to), SEE **reveal**, unbosom yourself, unburden yourself.

confession noun
a confession of guilt. acknowledgement, admission, declaration, disclosure, profession, revelation.

confide verb
to confide in consult, have confidence in, open your heart to, speak confidentially to, [*informal*] spill the beans to, [*informal*] tell all to, tell secrets to, trust, unbosom yourself to.

confidence noun
1 *to face the future with confidence.* certainty, credence, faith, hope, optimism, positiveness, reliance, trust.
OPPOSITES: SEE **doubt** noun.
2 *I wish I had her confidence.* aplomb, assurance, boldness, composure, conviction, firmness, nerve, panache, self-assurance, self-confidence, self-possession, self-reliance, spirit, verve.

confident adjective
1 *confident of success.* certain, convinced, hopeful, optimistic, positive, sanguine, sure, trusting.
OPPOSITES: SEE **doubtful**.
2 *a confident person.* assertive, assured, bold, [*uncomplimentary*] cocksure, composed, definite, fearless, secure, self-assured, self-confident, self-possessed, self-reliant, unafraid.
OPPOSITES: SEE **diffident**.

confidential adjective
confidential information. classified, [*informal*] hush-hush, intimate, [*informal*] off the record, personal, private, restricted, secret, suppressed, top secret.
OPPOSITES: SEE **public** adjective.

confine verb
The police confined the home supporters at one end of the ground. bind, cage, circumscribe, constrain, [*informal*] coop up, cordon off, cramp, curb, detain, enclose, gaol, hem in, [*informal*] hold down, immure, imprison, incarcerate, intern, isolate, keep, limit, localize, restrain, restrict, rope off, shut in, shut up, surround, wall up.
OPPOSITES: SEE **free** verb.

confirm verb
1 *The strange events confirmed his belief in the supernatural.* authenticate, back up, bear out, corroborate, demonstrate, endorse, establish, fortify, give credence to, justify, lend force to, prove, reinforce, settle, show, strengthen, substantiate, support, underline, vindicate, witness to.
OPPOSITES: SEE **disprove**.
2 *We shook hands to confirm the deal.* [*informal*] clinch, formalize, guarantee, make legal, make official, ratify, validate, verify.
OPPOSITES: SEE **cancel**.

confiscate verb
The police confiscated his air gun. appropriate, impound, remove, seize, sequester, take away, take possession of.

conflict noun
1 *conflict between rivals.* antagonism, antipathy, contention, difference, disagreement, discord, dissension, friction, hostility, opposition, strife, unrest, variance (*to be at variance*).
2 *conflict on the battlefield.* action, battle, brawl, brush, clash, combat, confrontation, contest, encounter, engagement, feud, fight, quarrel, [*informal*] set-to, skirmish, struggle, war, warfare.

conflict verb
1 *Her account of events conflicts with mine.* [*informal*] be at odds, be at variance, be incompatible, clash, compete, contend, contradict, contrast, differ, disagree, oppose each other.
2 SEE **fight** verb, **quarrel** verb.

conform verb
The club has strict rules and will throw you out if you don't conform. acquiesce, be good, behave conventionally, comply, [*informal*] do what you are told, fit in, [*informal*] keep in step, obey, [*informal*] see eye to eye, [*informal*] toe the line.
to conform to *to conform to the rules.* abide by, accord with, agree with, be in accordance with, coincide with, comply with, concur with, correspond to, fit in with, follow, harmonize with, keep to, match, obey, square with, submit to, suit.
OPPOSITES: SEE **differ**, **disobey**.

confront verb
to confront your enemies. accost, argue with, attack, brave, challenge, defy, face up to, oppose, resist, stand up to, take on, withstand.
OPPOSITES: SEE **avoid**.

confuse verb
1 *Don't confuse the system.* disarrange, disorder, jumble, mingle, mix up, muddle, tangle.
2 *The complicated rules confused us.* agitate, baffle, bemuse, bewilder, confound, disconcert, disorientate, distract, [*informal*] flummox, fluster, mislead, mystify, perplex, puzzle, [*informal*] rattle.

confused adjective
1 *a confused argument.* aimless, chaotic, disconnected, disjointed, disordered, disorderly, disorganized, garbled, [*informal*] higgledy-piggledy, incoherent, irrational, jumbled, misleading, mixed up, muddled, muddle-headed, obscure, rambling, [*informal*] topsy-turvy, unclear, unsound, woolly.
OPPOSITES: SEE **orderly**.
2 *a confused state of mind.* addled, addle-headed, baffled, bewildered, dazed, disorientated, distracted, flustered, fuddled, [*informal*] in a tizzy, inebriated, muddle-headed, [*informal*] muzzy, non-plussed, perplexed, puzzled.
OPPOSITES: SEE **sane**.

confusion noun
1 [*informal*] ado, anarchy, bedlam, bother, chaos, clutter, commotion, confusion, din, disorder, disorganization, disturbance, fuss, hubbub, hullabaloo, jumble, maelstrom, [*informal*] mayhem, mêlée, mess, [*informal*] mix-up, muddle, pandemonium, racket, riot, rumpus, shambles, tumult, turbulence, turmoil, upheaval, uproar, welter, whirl.
2 *I saw the confusion on their faces.* bemusement, bewilderment, disorientation,

distraction, mystification, perplexity, puzzlement.

congeal verb
Blood congeals to form a clot. Water congeals to ice. clot, coagulate, coalesce, condense, curdle, freeze, harden, [*informal*] jell, set, solidify, stiffen, thicken.

congenial adjective
congenial company. congenial surroundings. acceptable, agreeable, amicable, companionable, compatible, SEE **friendly**, genial, kindly, SEE **pleasant**, suitable, sympathetic, understanding, well-suited.
OPPOSITES: SEE **uncongenial**.

congenital adjective
congenital deafness. hereditary, inborn, inbred, inherent, inherited, innate, natural.

congested adjective
a congested road. a congested space. blocked, clogged, crowded, full, jammed, obstructed, overcrowded, stuffed.
OPPOSITES: SEE **clear** adjective.

congratulate verb
We congratulated the winners. applaud, SEE **compliment** verb, felicitate, praise.
OPPOSITES: SEE **commiserate**, **reprimand** verb.

congregate verb
On summer evenings, we congregate in the park. accumulate, assemble, cluster, collect, come together, convene, converge (on), crowd, forgather, gather, get together, group, mass, meet, muster, rally, rendezvous, swarm, throng.

conjure verb
The wizard conjured stones to move. bewitch, charm, compel, enchant, invoke, raise, rouse, summon.
SEE ALSO: **magic** noun (**to do magic**).

conjuring noun
The entertainer didn't fool us with his conjuring. illusions, legerdemain, SEE **magic** noun, sleight of hand, tricks, wizardry.

connect verb
1 *to connect things together.* attach, combine, couple, engage, fasten, fix, interlock, join, link, tie.
OPPOSITES: SEE **disconnect**.
2 *to connect ideas in your mind.* associate, bracket together, compare, make a connection between, put together, relate, tie up.

connection noun
I don't see the connection. affinity, association, bond, coherence, contact, correlation, correspondence, interrelationship, join, link, relationship, [*informal*] tie-up, unity.
OPPOSITES: SEE **separation**.

connotation noun
What are the connotations of the word "food"? association, implication, insinuation, reverberation, suggested meaning, undertone.

conquer verb
1 *to conquer a territory.* annex, capture, occupy, overrun, possess, quell, seize, subject, subjugate, take, win.
2 *to conquer an opponent.* beat, best, checkmate, crush, defeat, get the better of, humble, [*informal*] lick, master, outdo, overcome, overpower, overthrow, overwhelm, rout, silence, subdue, succeed against, [*informal*] thrash, triumph over, vanquish, worst.
3 *to conquer a mountain.* climb, reach the top of.

conquest noun
the conquest of a territory. annexation, appropriation, capture, defeat, invasion, occupation, overthrow, subjection, subjugation, [*informal*] takeover, triumph (over), victory (over), win (against).

conscience noun
Vegetarians have a conscience about eating animals. compunction, ethics, misgivings, morals, principles, qualms, reservations, scruples, standards.

conscientious adjective
a conscientious worker. accurate, attentive, careful, diligent, dutiful, exact, hard-working, honest, meticulous, painstaking, particular (*She's particular about details*), punctilious, responsible, scrupulous, serious, thorough.
OPPOSITES: SEE **careless**.

conscious adjective
1 *In spite of the knock on his head, he remained conscious.* alert, awake, aware, compos mentis, sensible.
OPPOSITES: SEE **unconscious**.
2 *a conscious act. a conscious foul.* calculated, deliberate, intended, intentional, knowing, planned, premeditated, self-conscious, studied, voluntary, waking, wilful.
OPPOSITES: SEE **accidental**.

consecrated adjective
The churchyard is consecrated ground. blessed, hallowed, holy, religious, revered, sacred, sanctified.

consecutive adjective
She was away for three consecutive days. continuous, following, one after the other, running (*three days running*), sequential, succeeding, successive.

consent verb
They consented to come with us. agree, undertake.
OPPOSITES: SEE **refuse** verb.

to consent to *She consented to my request.* allow, approve of, authorize, comply with, concede, grant, permit.

consequence noun
1 *The flood was a consequence of all that snow.* aftermath, by-product, corollary, effect, end, [*informal*] follow-up, issue, outcome, repercussion, result, sequel, side-effect, upshot.
2 *The loss of one penny is of no consequence.* account, concern, importance, moment, note, significance, value, weight.

conservation noun
the conservation of the environment. careful management, economy, maintenance, preservation, protection, safeguarding, saving, upkeep.

conservationist noun
ecologist, environmentalist, [*informal*] green, preservationist.

conservative adjective
1 *conservative ideas.* conventional, die-hard, hidebound, moderate, narrow-minded, old-fashioned, reactionary, sober, traditional, unadventurous.
OPPOSITES: SEE **progressive**.
2 *a conservative estimate.* cautious, moderate, reasonable, understated, unexaggerated.
OPPOSITES: SEE **extreme** adjective.
3 *conservative politics.* right-of-centre, right-wing, Tory.

conservative noun
conformist, die-hard, reactionary, [*political*] right-winger, [*political*] Tory, traditionalist.

conserve verb
to conserve energy. be economical with, hold in reserve, keep, look after, maintain, preserve, protect, safeguard, save, store up, use sparingly.
OPPOSITES: SEE **waste** verb.

consider verb
1 *to consider a problem.* cogitate, contemplate, deliberate, discuss, examine, meditate on, mull over, muse, ponder, reflect on, ruminate, study, think about, [*informal*] turn over, weigh up.
2 *I consider that he was right.* believe, deem, judge, reckon.

considerable adjective
a considerable amount of rain. a considerable margin. appreciable, big, biggish, comfortable, fairly important, fairly large, noteworthy, noticeable, perceptible, reasonable, respectable, significant, sizeable, substantial, [*informal*] tidy (*a tidy amount*), tolerable, worthwhile.
OPPOSITES: SEE **negligible**.

considerate adjective
It was considerate to lend your umbrella. altruistic, attentive, caring, charitable, friendly, gracious, helpful, kind, kind-hearted, obliging, polite, sensitive, solicitous, sympathetic, tactful, thoughtful, unselfish.
OPPOSITES: SEE **selfish**.

consignment noun
a consignment of goods. batch, cargo, delivery, load, lorry-load, shipment, van-load.

consist verb
to consist of *What does this fruit salad consist of? What does the job consist of?* add up to, amount to, be composed of, be made of, comprise, contain, embody, include, incorporate, involve.

consistent adjective
1 *a consistent player. a consistent temperature.* constant, dependable, faithful, predictable, regular, reliable, stable, steady, unchanging, unfailing, uniform, unvarying.
2 *His story is consistent with hers.* accordant, compatible, congruous, consonant, in accordance, in agreement, in harmony, of a piece.
OPPOSITES: SEE **inconsistent**.

console verb
to console someone who is unhappy. calm, cheer, comfort, ease, encourage, hearten, relieve, solace, soothe, sympathize with.

consolidate verb
This season she consolidated her reputation as our best athlete. make secure, make strong, reinforce, stabilize, strengthen.

consort verb
to consort with *to consort with criminals.* accompany, associate with, befriend, be friends with, be seen with, fraternize with, [*informal*] gang up with, keep company with, mix with.

conspicuous adjective
a conspicuous landmark. a conspicuous mistake. apparent, blatant, clear, discernible, dominant, evident, flagrant, glaring, impressive, manifest, notable, noticeable, obvious, patent, perceptible, prominent, pronounced, self-evident, showy, striking, unconcealed, unmistakable, visible.
OPPOSITES: SEE **inconspicuous**.

conspiracy noun
a conspiracy to defraud. cabal, collusion, [*informal*] frame-up, insider dealing, intrigue, [*often joking*] machinations, plot, [*informal*] racket, scheme, treason.

conspire verb
Several men conspired to defraud the company. be in league, collude, combine, co-operate, hatch a plot, have designs, intrigue, plot, scheme.

constant adjective
1 *a constant cough. a constant rhythm.* ceaseless, chronic, consistent, continual, continuous, endless, eternal, everlasting, fixed, incessant, invariable, never-ending, non-stop, permanent, perpetual, persistent, predictable, regular, relentless, repeated, stable, steady, sustained, unbroken, unchanging, unending, unflagging, uniform, uninterrupted, unremitting, unvarying, unwavering.
OPPOSITES: SEE **changeable, irregular**.
2 *a constant friend.* dedicated, dependable, determined, devoted, faithful, firm, loyal, reliable, staunch, steadfast, true, trustworthy, trusty.
OPPOSITES: SEE **fickle, unreliable**.

constitute verb
1 *In soccer, eleven players constitute a team.* compose, comprise, form, make up.
2 *We constituted a committee to organize a jumble sale.* appoint, bring together, create, establish, found, inaugurate, make, set up.

constriction noun
a constriction in the throat. SEE **blockage**, narrowing, pressure, [*formal*] stricture, tightness.

construct verb
to construct a shelter. assemble, build, create, engineer, erect, [*formal*] fabricate, fashion, fit together, form, [*informal*] knock together, make, manufacture, pitch (*a tent*), produce, put together, put up, set up.
OPPOSITES: SEE **demolish**.

construction noun
1 *The construction of a shelter took an hour.* assembly, building, creation, erecting, erection, manufacture, production, putting-up, setting-up.
2 *The shelter was a flimsy construction.* building, edifice, erection, structure.

constructive adjective
a constructive suggestion. advantageous, beneficial, co-operative, creative, helpful, positive, practical, useful, valuable, worthwhile.
OPPOSITES: SEE **destructive**.

construe verb SEE **interpret**.

consul noun SEE **official** noun.

consult verb
Please consult me before you do anything. ask, confer (with), debate (with), discuss (with), exchange views (with), [*informal*]

put your heads together (with), question, refer (to), seek advice (from), speak (to).

consume verb
1 *to consume food.* devour, digest, eat, [*informal*] gobble up, [*informal*] guzzle, swallow.
2 *to consume your energy. to consume your savings.* absorb, deplete, drain, eat into, employ, exhaust, expend, swallow up, use up, utilize.

contact noun
1 *an electrical contact.* connection, join, touch, union.
2 *contact between people.* SEE **communication, meeting**.

contact verb
I'll contact you when I have some news. approach, call, call on, communicate with, correspond with, [*informal*] drop a line to, get hold of, get in touch with, notify, phone, ring, speak to, talk to.

contagious adjective
a contagious disease. catching, communicable, infectious, spreading, transmittable.
OPPOSITE: non-infectious.

contain verb
This box contains odds and ends. This book contains helpful information. be composed of, comprise, consist of, embody, embrace, hold, include, incorporate, involve.

container noun
holder, receptacle, repository, vessel.

SOME CONTAINERS: bag, barrel, basin, basket, bath, beaker, billy-can, bin, SEE **bottle**, bowl, box, briefcase, bucket, butt, caddy, can, canister, carton, cartridge, case, cask, casket, casserole, cauldron, chest, churn, cistern, coffer, coffin, crate, creel, cup.

decanter, dish, drum, dustbin, envelope, flask, glass, goblet, hamper, handbag, haversack, hod, hogshead, holdall, holster, jar, jerry-can, jug, keg, kettle, knapsack, luggage, money-box, mould, mug, pail, pan, pannier, pitcher, pocket, portmanteau, pot, pouch, punnet, purse.

rucksack, sachet, sack, satchel, saucepan, scuttle, skip, suitcase, tank, tankard, tea-chest, teapot, test tube, thermos, tin, trough, trunk, tub, tumbler, urn, vacuum flask, vase, vat, wallet, water-butt, watering-can, wine-glass.

---

contaminate verb
Chemicals contaminated the water.
adulterate, defile, foul, infect, poison,
pollute, soil, taint.
OPPOSITES: SEE **purify**.

contemplate verb
1 *We contemplated the view.* eye, gaze at, look
at, observe, regard, stare at, survey, view,
watch.
2 *We contemplated what to do next.* cogitate,
consider, deliberate, examine, mull over,
plan, reflect on, study, think about, work
out.
3 *I contemplate taking a holiday soon.*
envisage, expect, intend, propose.
4 *She sat quietly and contemplated.*
[*informal*] day-dream, meditate, muse,
ponder, reflect, ruminate, think.

contemporary adjective
1 [= *belonging to the same time as other things
you are referring to*] *contemporary events.*
coinciding, concurrent, contemporaneous,
simultaneous, synchronous, topical.
2 [= *belonging to the present time*]
contemporary music. current, fashionable,
the latest, modern, newest, present-day,
[*informal*] trendy, up-to-date, [*informal*]
with-it.

contempt noun
*Our contempt for their bad behaviour was
obvious.* derision, detestation, disdain,
disgust, dislike, disparagement, disrespect,
SEE **hatred**, loathing, ridicule, scorn.
OPPOSITES: SEE **admiration**.

contemptible adjective
a contemptible crime. base, beneath
contempt, despicable, detestable,
discreditable, disgraceful, dishonourable,
disreputable, hateful, ignominious,
inferior, loathsome, [*informal*] low-down,
mean, odious, pitiful, [*informal*] shabby,
shameful, worthless, wretched.
OPPOSITES: SEE **admirable**.

contemptuous adjective
a contemptuous sneer. arrogant,
condescending, derisive, disdainful,
dismissive, disrespectful, haughty,
[*informal*] holier-than-thou, insolent,
insulting, jeering, patronizing, sarcastic,
scathing, scornful, sneering, [*informal*]
snooty, supercilious, withering.
OPPOSITES: SEE **admiring**.

contend verb
1 *We had to contend with strong opposition.*
compete, contest, dispute, SEE **fight** verb,
grapple, oppose, SEE **quarrel** verb, rival,
strive, struggle, vie.
2 *I contended that I was right.* affirm, allege,
argue, assert, claim, declare, maintain.

content noun
Butter has a high fat content. constituent,
element, ingredient, part.

contented adjective
a contented expression. cheerful,
comfortable, complacent, content, fulfilled,
gratified, SEE **happy**, peaceful, pleased,
relaxed, satisfied, serene, smiling, smug,
uncomplaining, untroubled, well-fed.
OPPOSITES: SEE **dissatisfied**.

contentious adjective
1 *a contentious crowd of objectors.* SEE
quarrelsome.
2 *a contentious problem.* SEE **controversial**.

contentment noun
a smile of contentment. comfort, content,
contentedness, ease, fulfilment, SEE
happiness, relaxation, satisfaction, serenity,
smugness, tranquillity, well-being.
OPPOSITES: SEE **dissatisfaction**.

contest noun
a sporting contest. bout, challenge,
championship, [*informal*] clash, combat,
competition, conflict, confrontation, duel,
encounter, SEE **fight** noun, game, match,
[*informal*] set-to, struggle, tournament,
trial.

contest verb
1 *to contest a title.* compete for, contend for,
fight for [SEE **fight** verb], [*informal*] make a
bid for, strive for, struggle for, take up the
challenge of, vie for.
2 *to contest a decision.* argue against,
challenge, debate, dispute, doubt, oppose,
query, question, refute, resist.

contestant noun
a contestant in a competition. candidate,
competitor, contender, entrant, participant,
player.

context noun
*Words only have meaning if you put them in
a context.* background, frame of reference,
framework, milieu, position, situation,
surroundings.

continual adjective
*a continual process of change. continual
bickering.* constant, continuing, SEE
continuous, endless, eternal, everlasting,
frequent, interminable, lasting, limitless,
ongoing, perennial, permanent, perpetual,
persistent, recurrent, regular, relentless,
repeated, unending, unremitting.
OPPOSITES: SEE **occasional**, **temporary**.

continuation noun
1 *the continuation of a journey.* carrying on,
continuance, continuing, extension,
maintenance, prolongation, protraction,
resumption.

2 *a continuation of a book.* addition,
appendix, postscript, sequel, supplement.

continue verb
1 *We continued the search while it was light.*
carry on, keep going, keep up, persevere
with, proceed with, prolong, pursue,
[*informal*] stick at, sustain.
2 *We'll continue work after lunch.*
recommence, restart, resume.
3 *This rain can't continue for long.* carry on,
endure, go on, keep on, last, linger, live on,
persist, remain, stay, survive.
4 *Continue the line to the edge of the paper.*
extend, lengthen.

continuous adjective
continuous bad weather. exhausted by
continuous effort. ceaseless, chronic (*chronic*
illness), SEE **continual**, incessant, never-
ending, non-stop, [*informal*] round-the-
clock, [*informal*] solid (*I worked for 3 solid*
hours), sustained, unbroken, unceasing,
uninterrupted.

contract noun
a business contract. agreement, bargain,
bond, commitment, compact, concordat,
covenant, deal, indenture, lease, pact,
settlement, treaty, understanding,
undertaking.

contract verb
1 *Most substances contract as they cool.*
become denser, become smaller, close up,
condense, decrease, diminish, draw
together, dwindle, fall away, lessen, narrow,
reduce, shrink, shrivel, slim down, thin out,
wither.
OPPOSITES: SEE **expand**.
2 *A local firm contracted to build our*
extension. agree, arrange, close a deal,
covenant, negotiate a deal, promise, sign an
agreement, undertake.
3 *She contracted a mysterious illness.* become
infected by, catch, develop, get.

contradict verb
It's considered rude to contradict other
people's views. challenge, confute,
controvert, disagree with, dispute, gainsay,
impugn, oppose, speak against.
OPPOSITES: SEE **confirm**.

contradictory adjective
contradictory opinions. antithetical,
conflicting, contrary, discrepant, different,
incompatible, inconsistent, irreconcilable,
opposed, opposite.
OPPOSITES: SEE **consistent**.

contraption noun
apparatus, contrivance, device, gadget,
invention, machine, mechanism.

contrary adjective
1 [pronounced *con*trary] *She spoke for the*
motion, and I put the contrary view.
contradictory, conflicting, converse,
different, opposed, opposite, other, reverse.
OPPOSITES: SEE **similar**.
2 [pronounced *con*trary] *contrary winds.*
adverse, hostile, inimical, opposing,
unfavourable, unhelpful.
OPPOSITES: SEE **favourable**.
3 [pronounced con*trary*] *a contrary child.*
awkward, cantankerous, defiant, difficult,
disobedient, disobliging, intractable,
obstinate, perverse, rebellious, [*informal*]
stroppy, stubborn, uncooperative, wayward,
wilful.
OPPOSITES: SEE **co-operative**.

contrast noun
a contrast between two things. antithesis,
comparison, difference, differentiation,
disparity, dissimilarity, distinction,
divergence, foil (*act as a foil to*), opposition.
OPPOSITES: SEE **similarity**.

contrast verb
1 *The teacher contrasted the work of the two*
students. compare, differentiate between,
discriminate between, distinguish between,
emphasize differences between, make a
distinction between, set one against the
other.
2 *His style contrasts with mine.* be set off (by),
clash (with), deviate (from), differ (from).

contrasting adjective
contrasting colours. contrasting opinions.
antithetical, clashing, conflicting, different,
dissimilar, incompatible, opposite.
OPPOSITES: SEE **similar**.

contribute verb
to contribute money to charity. bestow,
donate, [*informal*] fork out, give, provide,
put up, sponsor (*to sponsor an event or a*
person), subscribe, supply.
to contribute to *Good weather contributed*
to our enjoyment. add to, encourage, SEE **help**
verb, reinforce, support.

contribution noun
1 *a contribution to charity.* donation, fee, gift,
grant, [*informal*] handout, offering,
payment, sponsorship, subscription.
2 *The weather made an important*
contribution to our enjoyment. addition,
encouragement, SEE **help** noun, input,
support.

contributor noun
1 *a contributor to charity.* backer, benefactor,
donor, giver, helper, patron, sponsor,
subscriber, supporter.
2 *a contributor to a magazine.* columnist,
correspondent, free-lance, journalist,
reporter, writer.

control noun

Who is in control? A teacher needs good control in the classroom. administration, authority, charge, command, direction, discipline, government, guidance, influence, jurisdiction, management, mastery, orderliness, organization, oversight, power, regulation, restraint, rule, strictness, supervision, supremacy.

control verb

1 *The government controls the country's affairs. Managers control the workforce.* administer, [*informal*] be at the helm of, be in charge of, [*informal*] boss, command, conduct, cope with, deal with, direct, dominate, engineer, govern, guide, handle, have control of, lead, look after, manage, manipulate, order about, oversee, regiment, regulate, rule, run, superintend, supervise.
2 *They built a dam to control the floods.* check, confine, contain, curb, hold back, keep in check, master, repress, restrain, subdue, suppress.

controversial adjective

a controversial decision. arguable, contentious, controvertible, debatable, disputable, doubtful, [*formal*] polemical, problematical, questionable.
OPPOSITES: SEE **straightforward**.

controversy noun

controversy about the building of a motorway. altercation, argument, contention, debate, disagreement, dispute, dissension, issue, [*formal*] polemic, quarrel, war of words, wrangle.

convalescent adjective

convalescent after an operation. getting better, improving, making progress, [*informal*] on the mend, recovering, recuperating.

convene verb

1 *The chairman convened a meeting.* bring together, call, [*formal*] convoke, summon.
2 *The meeting convened at two o'clock.* SEE **assemble**.

convenient adjective

a convenient shop. a convenient tool. a convenient moment. accessible, appropriate, at hand, available, handy, helpful, labour-saving, nearby, neat, opportune, suitable, timely, usable, useful.
OPPOSITES: SEE **inconvenient**.

conventional adjective

1 *conventional behaviour. conventional ideas.* accepted, accustomed, common, commonplace, correct, customary, decorous, everyday, expected, habitual, mainstream, normal, ordinary, orthodox, prevalent, regular, routine, [*informal*] run-of-the-mill, standard, straight, traditional,

unsurprising, usual.
OPPOSITES: SEE **unconventional**.
2 [*uncomplimentary*] *Don't be so conventional!* bourgeois, conservative, formal, hackneyed, hidebound, pedestrian, rigid, stereotyped, [*informal*] stuffy, unadventurous, unimaginative, unoriginal.

converge verb

Motorways converge in one mile. coincide, combine, come together, join, meet, merge.
OPPOSITES: SEE **disperse**, **diverge**.

conversation noun

[*informal*] chat, [*informal*] chinwag, [*formal*] colloquy, communication, [*formal*] conference, dialogue, discourse, discussion, exchange of views, gossip, [*informal*] heart-to-heart, [*formal*] intercourse, [*informal*] natter, phone-call, [*informal*] powwow, SEE **talk** noun, tête-à-tête.

convert verb

1 *We converted the attic to a games-room.* SEE **adapt**.
2 *She converted me to a new way of thinking.* change, change someone's mind, convince, persuade, re-educate, reform, regenerate, rehabilitate, save (= *convert to Christianity*), win over.

convex adjective

bulging, SEE **curved**, domed.
OPPOSITES: SEE **concave**.

convey verb

1 *to convey goods.* bear, bring, carry, conduct, deliver, export, ferry, fetch, forward, import, move, send, shift, ship, take, transfer, transport.
2 *What does his message convey to you?* communicate, disclose, impart, imply, indicate, mean, reveal, signify, tell.

convict noun

Convicts were transported to Australia. condemned person, criminal, culprit, felon, malefactor, prisoner, wrongdoer.

convict verb

to convict someone of a crime. condemn, declare guilty, prove guilty, sentence.
OPPOSITES: SEE **acquit**.

conviction noun

1 *He spoke with conviction.* assurance, certainty, confidence, firmness.
2 *She has strong religious convictions.* belief, creed, faith, opinion, persuasion, principle, tenet, view.

convince verb

He convinced the jury. He convinced them that he was innocent. assure, [*informal*] bring round, convert, persuade, prove to, reassure, satisfy, sway, win over.

convincing adjective
convincing evidence. conclusive, decisive, definite, persuasive, unambiguous, unarguable, unequivocal.
OPPOSITES: SEE **inconclusive**.

convulsion noun
1 *The doctor treated him for convulsions.* attack, fit, involuntary movement, paroxysm, seizure, spasm.
2 *a volcanic convulsion.* disturbance, eruption, outburst, tremor, turbulence, upheaval.

convulsive adjective
convulsive movements. jerky, shaking, spasmodic, [*informal*] twitchy, uncontrolled, uncoordinated, violent, wrenching.

cook verb
to cook a meal. concoct, heat up, make, prepare, warm up.
RELATED ADJECTIVES: culinary, gastronomic, SEE **taste** verb.

WAYS TO COOK FOOD: bake, barbecue, boil, braise, brew, broil, casserole, coddle (*eggs*), fry, grill, pickle, poach, roast, sauté, scramble (*eggs*), simmer, steam, stew, toast.

OTHER THINGS TO DO IN COOKING: baste, blend, chop, grate, freeze, infuse, knead, mix, peel, sieve, sift, stir, whisk.

SOME COOKING UTENSILS: baking-tin, basin, billy-can, blender, bowl, bread-board, breadknife, carving knife, casserole, cauldron, chafing dish, chip-pan, coffee grinder, colander, corkscrew, SEE **crockery**, SEE **cutlery**, deep-fat-fryer, dish, food-processor, frying-pan, jug, kettle, ladle, liquidizer, microwave, mincer, mixer, pan, pepper-mill, percolator, plate, pot, pressure-cooker, rolling-pin, rôtisserie, salt-cellar, sauce-pan, scales, skewer, spatula, spit, strainer, timer, tin-opener, toaster, whisk, wok, wooden spoon.

OTHER KITCHEN EQUIPMENT: SEE **kitchen**.

---

cooking noun
baking, catering, cookery, cuisine.

cool adjective
1 *cool weather.* chilly, SEE **cold** adjective, coldish.
2 *a cool drink.* chilled, iced, refreshing.
OPPOSITES: SEE **hot**.
3 *a cool reaction to danger.* SEE **brave**, calm, collected, composed, dignified, elegant, [*informal*] laid-back, level-headed, quiet, relaxed, self-possessed, sensible, serene, unflustered, unruffled, urbane.
OPPOSITES: SEE **frantic**.
4 *cool feelings.* aloof, apathetic, dispassionate, distant, frigid, half-hearted, indifferent, lukewarm, negative, offhand, reserved, [*informal*] stand-offish, unconcerned, unemotional, unenthusiastic, unfriendly, unresponsive, unwelcoming.
OPPOSITES: SEE **passionate**.

cool verb
1 *to cool food.* chill, freeze, ice, refrigerate.
OPPOSITES: SEE **heat** verb.
2 *to cool someone's enthusiasm.* abate, allay, assuage, calm, dampen, lessen, moderate, [*informal*] pour cold water on, quiet, temper.
OPPOSITES: SEE **inflame**.

co-operate verb
We need two people to co-operate on this job. aid each other, assist each other, collaborate, combine, conspire (= *co-operate in wrongdoing*), help each other, [*informal*] join forces, [*informal*] pitch in, [*informal*] play ball, [*informal*] pull together, support each other, work as a team, work together.

co-operation noun
aid, assistance, collaboration, co-operative effort [SEE **co-operative**], co-ordination, help, joint action, team-work.
OPPOSITES: SEE **competition**.

co-operative adjective
1 *As everyone was co-operative, we finished early.* accommodating, comradely, constructive, hard-working, helpful to each other, keen, obliging, supportive, united, willing, working as a team.
OPPOSITES: SEE **competitive, uncooperative**.
2 *a co-operative effort,* collective, combined, communal, concerted, co-ordinated, corporate, joint, shared.
OPPOSITES: SEE **individual** adjective.

cope verb
Shall I help you, or can you cope? carry on, get by, make do, manage, survive, win through.
to cope with *She coped with her illness cheerfully.* contend with, deal with, endure, handle, look after, suffer, tolerate.

copious adjective
copious supplies of food. abundant, ample, bountiful, extravagant, generous, great, huge, inexhaustible, large, lavish, liberal, luxuriant, overflowing, plentiful, profuse, unsparing, unstinting.
OPPOSITES: SEE **scarce**.

copy noun
a copy of a letter. a copy of a work of art. carbon-copy, clone, counterfeit, double, duplicate, facsimile, fake, forgery, imitation, likeness, model, pattern, photocopy, print, replica, representation, reproduction, tracing, transcript, twin, Xerox.

copy verb
1 *to copy a work of art. to copy someone's ideas.* borrow, counterfeit, crib, duplicate, emulate, follow, forge, imitate, photocopy, plagiarize, print, repeat, reproduce, simulate, transcribe, xerox.
2 *to copy someone's voice or mannerisms.* ape, imitate, impersonate, mimic, parrot.

cord noun
a length of cord. cable, catgut, lace, line, rope, strand, string, twine, wire.

cordon noun
a cordon of policemen. barrier, chain, fence, line, ring, row.

core noun
1 *the core of an apple. the core of the earth.* centre, heart, inside, middle, nucleus.
2 *the core of a problem.* central issue, crux, essence, kernel, [*slang*] nitty-gritty, nub.

corner noun
1 *a corner where lines or surfaces meet.* angle, crook (*the crook of your arm*), joint.
2 *a quiet corner.* hideaway, hiding-place, hole, niche, nook, recess, retreat.
3 *the corner of the road.* bend, crossroads, intersection, junction, turn, turning.

corner verb
After a chase, they cornered him. capture, catch, trap.

corporation noun
1 *a business corporation.* company, concern, enterprise, firm, organization.
2 *the city corporation.* council, local government.

corpse noun
body, cadaver, carcass, remains, skeleton.

correct adjective
1 *the correct time. correct information.* accurate, authentic, exact, factual, faithful, faultless, flawless, genuine, precise, reliable, right, strict, true.
OPPOSITES: SEE **inaccurate, wrong**.
2 *the correct thing to do.* acceptable, appropriate, fitting, just, normal, proper, regular, standard, suitable, tactful, unexceptionable, well-mannered.
OPPOSITES: SEE **inappropriate, wrong**.

correct verb
1 *to correct a fault.* adjust, alter, cure, [*informal*] debug (*to debug a computer system*), put right, rectify, redress, remedy, repair.
2 *to correct pupils' homework.* assess, mark.

correspond verb
1 *Her story corresponds with mine.* accord, agree, be consistent, coincide, concur, conform, correlate, fit, harmonize, match, parallel, square, tally.

2 *I corresponded with a girl in Paris.* communicate with, send letters to, write to.

correspondence noun
A secretary deals with his boss's correspondence. letters, memoranda, [*informal*] memos, messages, notes, writings.

corresponding adjective
When I got a more responsible job I expected a corresponding rise in pay. analogous, appropriate, commensurate, complementary, correlative, equivalent, matching, parallel, reciprocal, related, similar.

corrode verb
1 *Acid may corrode metal.* consume, eat away, erode, oxidize, rot, rust, tarnish.
2 *Many metals corrode.* crumble, deteriorate, disintegrate, tarnish.

corrugated adjective
a corrugated surface. creased, [*informal*] crinkly, [*formal*] fluted, furrowed, lined, puckered, ribbed, ridged, wrinkled.

corrupt adjective
1 *a corrupt judge. corrupt practices.* [*informal*] bent, bribable, criminal, crooked, dishonest, dishonourable, false, fraudulent, unethical, unprincipled, unscrupulous, unsound, untrustworthy.
2 *corrupt behaviour. a corrupt individual.* debauched, decadent, degenerate, depraved, [*informal*] dirty, dissolute, evil, immoral, iniquitous, low, perverted, profligate, rotten, sinful, venal, vicious, wicked.
OPPOSITES: SEE **honest**.

corrupt verb
1 *to corrupt an official. to corrupt the course of justice.* bribe, divert, [*informal*] fix, influence, pervert, suborn, subvert.
2 *to corrupt the innocent.* debauch, deprave, lead astray, make corrupt [SEE **corrupt** adjective], tempt, seduce.

cosmetics noun
make-up, toiletries.

VARIOUS COSMETICS: cream, deodorant, eye-shadow, lipstick, lotion, mascara, nail varnish, perfume, powder, scent, talc, talcum powder.

---

cosmopolitan adjective
Big cities usually have a cosmopolitan atmosphere. international, multicultural, sophisticated, urbane.
OPPOSITES: SEE **provincial**.

cosmos noun
galaxy, universe.

cost noun
the cost of a ticket. amount, charge,
expenditure, expense, fare, figure, outlay,
payment, price, rate, value.

cost verb
This watch costs £10. be valued at, be worth,
fetch, go for, realize, sell for, [*informal*] set
you back.

costume noun
actors' costumes. [*formal*] apparel, attire, SEE
clothes, clothing, dress, fancy-dress, garb,
garments, [*informal*] get-up, livery, outfit,
period dress, [*old-fashioned*] raiment, robes,
uniform, vestments.

cosy adjective
a cosy room. a cosy atmosphere. comfortable,
[*informal*] comfy, homely, intimate,
reassuring, relaxing, restful, secure, snug,
soft, warm.
OPPOSITES: SEE **uncomfortable**.

council noun
1 *a council of war.* SEE **assembly**.
2 *the town council.* corporation.

counsel verb
*The careers officer counselled me about a
possible career.* advise, give help, guide,
have a discussion with, listen to your views.

count verb
1 *Count your money.* add up, calculate, check,
compute, enumerate, estimate, figure out,
keep account of, [*informal*] notch up,
number, reckon, score, take stock of, tell,
total, [*informal*] tot up, work out.
2 *It's taking part that counts, not winning.*
be important, have significance, matter,
signify.
to count on *You can count on my support.*
bank on, believe in, depend on, expect, have
faith in, rely on, swear by, trust.

countenance noun
a sad countenance. air, appearance, aspect,
demeanour, expression, face, features, look,
visage.

counter noun
1 *a counter in a shop or café.* bar, sales-point,
service-point.
2 *You play ludo with counters.* disc, token.

counteract verb
a treatment to counteract poison. act against,
be an antidote to, cancel out, fight against,
foil, invalidate, militate against, negate,
neutralize, offset, oppose, resist, thwart,
withstand, work against.

counterfeit adjective
counterfeit money. a counterfeit work of art.
artificial, bogus, copied, ersatz, fake, false,

feigned, forged, fraudulent, imitation,
pastiche, phoney, [*childish*] pretend, sham,
simulated, spurious.
OPPOSITES: SEE **genuine**.

counterfeit verb
1 *to counterfeit money.* copy, fake, forge.
2 *to counterfeit an illness.* feign, imitate,
pretend, sham, simulate.

counterpart noun
*The sales manager phoned his counterpart in
the rival firm.* corresponding person or
thing, equivalent, match, opposite number,
parallel person or thing.

countless adjective
countless stars. a countless number. endless,
immeasurable, incalculable, infinite,
innumerable, many, measureless, myriad,
numberless, numerous, unnumbered, untold.

country noun
1 *the countries of the world.* canton,
commonwealth, domain, empire, kingdom,
land, nation, people, principality, realm,
state, territory.
POLITICAL SYSTEMS FOUND IN VARIOUS COUNTRIES:
democracy, dictatorship, monarchy,
republic.
2 *There's some attractive country near here.*
countryside, green belt, landscape, scenery.
RELATED ADJECTIVES: SEE **rural**.

couple verb
1 *to couple two things together.* combine,
connect, fasten, hitch, join, link, match,
pair, unite, yoke.
2 *to couple sexually.* SEE **mate** verb.

courage noun
audacity, boldness, [*informal*] bottle,
bravery, daring, dauntlessness,
determination, fearlessness, fibre (*moral
fibre*), firmness, fortitude, gallantry,
[*informal*] grit, [*informal*] guts, heroism,
indomitability, intrepidity, mettle,
[*informal*] nerve, [*informal*] pluck, prowess,
resolution, spirit, [*slang*] spunk, [*formal*]
stoicism, valour.
OPPOSITES: SEE **cowardice**.

courageous adjective
audacious, bold, brave, cool, daring,
dauntless, determined, fearless, gallant,
game, heroic, indomitable, intrepid, lion-
hearted, noble, plucky, resolute, spirited,
stalwart, stoical, tough, unafraid,
uncomplaining, undaunted, unshrinking,
valiant, valorous.
OPPOSITES: SEE **cowardly**.

courier noun
1 *A courier delivers packages.* carrier,
messenger, runner.
2 *A courier helps tourists.* guide,
representative.

course noun
1 *a normal course of events.* advance, continuation, development, movement, passage, passing, progress, progression, succession.
2 *a ship's course.* bearings, direction, path, route, way.
3 *a course of treatment at hospital.* programme, schedule, sequence, series.
4 *a course in college.* curriculum, syllabus.

court noun
1 SEE **courtyard**.
2 *a monarch's court.* entourage, followers, palace, retinue.
3 *a court of law.* [*old-fashioned*] assizes, bench, court martial, high court, law-court, magistrates' court.

court verb
1 *to court attention.* [*informal*] ask for (*She's just asking for attention*), attract, invite, provoke, seek, solicit.
2 [*old-fashioned*] *to court a boyfriend or girlfriend.* date, [*informal*] go out with, make advances to, make love to [SEE **love** noun], try to win, woo.

courteous adjective
SEE **polite**.

courtyard noun
court, enclosure, forecourt, patio, [*informal*] quad, quadrangle, yard.

cover noun
1 *a cover to keep the rain off.* canopy, cloak, clothes, clothing, coat, SEE **covering**, roof, screen, shield, tarpaulin.
2 *a jam-pot cover.* cap, lid, top.
3 *a cover for papers or a book.* binding, case, dust-jacket, envelope, file, folder, portfolio, wrapper.
4 *cover from a storm.* hiding-place, refuge, sanctuary, shelter.
5 *A helicopter gave them cover from the air.* defence, guard, protection, support.
6 *the cover of an assumed identity.* camouflage, concealment, cover-up, deception, disguise, façade, front, mask, pretence, veneer.

cover verb
1 *A cloth covered the table. Cloud covers the hills. Fresh paint will cover the graffiti.* blot out, bury, camouflage, cap, carpet, cloak, clothe, cloud, coat, conceal, curtain, disguise, drape, dress, encase, enclose, enshroud, envelop, face, hide, hood, mantle, mask, obscure, overlay, overspread, plaster, protect, screen, shade, sheathe, shield, shroud, spread over, surface, tile, veil, veneer, wrap up.
2 *Will £10 cover your expenses?* be enough for, match, meet, pay for, suffice for.
3 *An encyclopaedia covers many subjects.* comprise, contain, deal with, embrace, encompass, include, incorporate, involve, treat.

covering noun
a light covering of snow. blanket, cap, carpet, casing, cladding, cloak, coating, cocoon, cover, facing, film, layer, mantle, pall, sheath, sheet, shroud, skin, surface, tarpaulin, veil, veneer, wrapping.

covetous adjective
SEE **greedy**.

cowardice noun
cowardliness, desertion, evasion, faint-heartedness, SEE **fear** noun, [*informal*] funk, shirking, spinelessness, timidity.
OPPOSITES: SEE **bravery**.

cowardly adjective
a cowardly person. a cowardly action. abject, afraid, base, chicken-hearted, cowering, craven, dastardly, faint-hearted, fearful, [*informal*] gutless, [*old-fashioned*] lily-livered, pusillanimous, spineless, submissive, timid, timorous, unheroic, [*informal*] yellow.
OPPOSITES: SEE **brave**.

cower verb
The naughty dog cowered in a corner. cringe, crouch, flinch, grovel, hide, quail, shiver, shrink, skulk, tremble.

coy adjective
Don't be coy: come and be introduced. bashful, coquettish, demure, diffident, embarrassed, modest, reserved, retiring, self-conscious, sheepish, shy, timid.
OPPOSITES: SEE **forward** adjective.

crack noun
1 *the crack of a whip.*
VARIOUS SOUNDS: SEE **sound** noun.
2 *a crack on the head.* SEE **hit**.
3 [*informal*] *a witty crack.* SEE **joke** noun.
4 *a crack in a cup. a crack in a rock.* break, chink, chip, cleavage, cleft, cranny, craze, crevice, fissure, flaw, fracture, gap, opening, rift, split.

crack verb
1 *The whip cracked.*
VARIOUS SOUNDS: SEE **sound** noun.
2 *to crack a cup. to crack a nut.* break, chip, fracture, snap, splinter, split.

craft noun
1 *the craft of thatching.* art, handicraft, job, skilled work, technique, trade.
VARIOUS CRAFTS: SEE **art**.
2 *I admired the thatcher's craft.* SEE **craftsmanship**.
3 *He wins by craft rather than by honest effort.* SEE **deceit**.
4 *All sorts of craft were in the harbour.* SEE **vessel**.

craftsmanship noun
artistry, cleverness, craft, dexterity, expertise, handiwork, knack, [*informal*] know-how, SEE **skill**, workmanship.

crafty adjective
a crafty deception. artful, astute, calculating, canny, clever, cunning, deceitful, designing, devious, [*informal*] dodgy, [*informal*] foxy, SEE **furtive**, guileful, ingenious, knowing, machiavellian, scheming, shrewd, sly, [*informal*] sneaky, tricky, wily.

craggy adjective
a craggy pinnacle. jagged, rocky, rough, rugged, steep, uneven.

cram verb
1 *to cram into a confined space.* compress, crowd, crush, fill, force, jam, overcrowd, overfill, pack, press, squeeze, stuff.
2 *to cram for an examination.* SEE **study** verb.

cramped adjective
cramped accommodation. crowded, narrow, restricted, tight, uncomfortable.
OPPOSITES: SEE **roomy**.

crane noun
a crane for loading freight. davit, derrick, hoist.

crash noun
1 *a loud crash.*
VARIOUS SOUNDS: SEE **sound** noun.
2 *a rail crash. a crash on the motorway.* accident, bump, collision, derailment, impact, knock, pile-up, smash, wreck.
3 *a crash on the stockmarket.* collapse, depression, fall.

crash verb
1 *to crash into someone.* bump, collide, SEE **hit** verb, knock, lurch, pitch, smash.
2 *to crash to the ground.* collapse, fall, plunge, topple.

crate noun
We packed our belongings in crates. box, carton, case, packing-case, tea-chest.

crater noun
The explosion left a crater. abyss, cavity, chasm, hole, hollow, opening, pit.

craving noun
SEE **desire** noun.

crawl verb
I crawled along a narrow ledge. clamber, creep, edge, inch, slither, wriggle.

craze noun
the latest craze. diversion, enthusiasm, fad, fashion, infatuation, mania, novelty, obsession, passion, pastime, rage, trend, vogue.

crazy adjective
1 *The dog went crazy when it was stung by a wasp.* berserk, crazed, delirious, demented, deranged, frantic, frenzied, hysterical, insane, lunatic, SEE **mad**, [*informal*] potty, [*informal*] scatty, unbalanced, unhinged, wild.
OPPOSITES: SEE **sane**.
2 *a crazy comedy.* absurd, confused, daft, eccentric, farcical, foolish, idiot, illogical, irrational, ludicrous, nonsensical, preposterous, ridiculous, senseless, silly, stupid, unreasonable, weird, zany.
OPPOSITES: SEE **sensible**.
3 [*informal*] *crazy about snooker.* SEE **enthusiastic**.

creamy adjective
a creamy liquid. milky, oily, rich, smooth, thick, velvety.

crease noun
a crease in a piece of cloth. corrugation, crinkle, fold, furrow, groove, line, pleat, pucker, ridge, ruck, tuck, wrinkle.

crease verb
to crease a piece of paper. crimp, crinkle, crumple, crush, fold, furrow, pleat, pucker, ridge, ruck, rumple, wrinkle.

create verb
to create something new. to create trouble. [*old-fashioned*] beget, SEE **begin**, breed, bring about, bring into existence, build, cause, conceive, concoct, constitute, construct, design, devise, engender, establish, form, found, generate, give rise to, hatch, institute, invent, make, make up, manufacture, occasion, originate, produce, set up, shape, think up.
OPPOSITES: SEE **destroy**.
to create a work of art compose, draw, embroider, engrave, model, paint, print, sculpt, sketch, throw (*pottery*), weave, write.

creation noun
1 *the creation of the world.* beginning, birth, building, conception, constitution, construction, establishing, formation, foundation, generation, genesis, inception, institution, making, origin, procreation, production, shaping.
OPPOSITES: SEE **destruction**.
2 *The dress is her own creation.* achievement, brainchild, concept, effort, handiwork, invention, product, work of art.

creative adjective
a creative imagination. artistic, clever, fecund, fertile, imaginative, inspired, inventive, original, positive, productive, resourceful, talented.
OPPOSITES: SEE **destructive**.

creator noun
1 *the creator of an empire. the creator of a TV programme.* architect, begetter, builder, designer, deviser, discoverer, initiator, inventor, maker, manufacturer, originator, parent, producer.
2 *the creator of a work of art.* artist, author, composer, craftsman, painter, photographer, potter, sculptor, smith, weaver, writer.

creature noun
animal, beast, being, brute, mortal being.

credible adjective
[Do not confuse with *creditable*.] *The report about Martian visitors is not credible.* believable, conceivable, convincing, imaginable, likely, persuasive, plausible, possible, reasonable, tenable, thinkable, trustworthy.
OPPOSITES: SEE **incredible**.

credit noun
Her success brought credit to the school. approval, commendation, distinction, esteem, fame, glory, honour, [*informal*] kudos, merit, praise, prestige, recognition, reputation, status.
OPPOSITES: SEE **dishonour**.

credit verb
1 *You won't credit her far-fetched story.* accept, believe, [*informal*] buy, count on, depend on, endorse, have faith in, reckon on, rely on, subscribe to, [*informal*] swallow, swear by, trust.
OPPOSITES: SEE **disbelieve**.
2 *I credited you with more sense.* attribute to, ascribe to, assign to, attach to.
3 *The bank credited £10 to my account.* add, enter.
OPPOSITES: SEE **debit**.

creditable adjective
[Do not confuse with *credible*.] *a creditable performance.* admirable, commendable, estimable, excellent, good, honourable, laudable, meritorious, praiseworthy, respectable, well thought of, worthy.
OPPOSITES: SEE **unworthy**.

credulous adjective
You must be credulous if she fooled you with that story. easily taken in, [*informal*] green, gullible, innocent, naïve, [*informal*] soft, trusting, unsuspecting.
OPPOSITES: SEE **sceptical**.

creed noun
a religious creed. beliefs, convictions, doctrine, dogma, faith, principles, tenets.

creep verb
1 *to creep along the ground.* crawl, edge, inch, move slowly, slink, slither, worm, wriggle, writhe.

2 *to creep quietly past.* move quietly, slip, sneak, steal, tiptoe.

crest noun
1 *a crest on a bird's head.* comb, plume, tuft.
2 *the crest of a hill.* apex, brow, crown, head, peak, ridge, summit, top.
3 *the school crest.* badge, emblem, insignia, seal, sign, symbol.

crib verb
to crib in a test. cheat, copy, plagiarize.

crime noun
The law punishes crime. delinquency, dishonesty, [*old-fashioned*] felony, illegality, law-breaking, misconduct, misdeed, misdemeanour, offence, racket, sin, transgression of the law, wrongdoing.

VARIOUS CRIMES: abduction, arson, blackmail, burglary, extortion, hijacking, hold-up, hooliganism, kidnapping, manslaughter, misappropriation, mugging, murder, pilfering, poaching, rape, robbery, shop-lifting, smuggling, stealing, theft, vandalism.

criminal adjective
a criminal act. [*informal*] bent, corrupt, [*informal*] crooked, [*formal*] culpable, dishonest, felonious, illegal, illicit, indictable, nefarious, [*informal*] shady, unlawful, SEE **wrong** adjective.
OPPOSITES: SEE **lawful**.

criminal noun
The law punishes criminals. convict, [*informal*] crook, culprit, delinquent, felon, hooligan, law-breaker, [*formal*] malefactor, offender, outlaw, recidivist, [*old-fashioned*] transgressor, villain, wrongdoer.

VARIOUS CRIMINALS: assassin, bandit, blackmailer, brigand, buccaneer, burglar, desperado, gangster, gunman, highwayman, hijacker, kidnapper, mugger, murderer, outlaw, pickpocket, pirate, poacher, racketeer, rapist, receiver, robber, shop-lifter, smuggler, swindler, terrorist, thief, thug, vandal.

cringe verb
to cringe in fear. blench, cower, crouch, dodge, duck, flinch, grovel, quail, quiver, recoil, shrink back, shy away, tremble, wince.

cripple verb
1 *to cripple a person.* disable, dislocate (*a joint*), fracture (*a bone*), hamper, hamstring, incapacitate, lame, maim, mutilate, paralyse, weaken.

2 *to cripple a machine.* damage, make useless, put out of action, sabotage, spoil.

crippled adjective
1 *a crippled person.* deformed, SEE **disabled**, handicapped, hurt, incapacitated, injured, invalid, lame, maimed, mutilated, paralysed.
2 *a crippled vehicle.* damaged, immobilized, out of action, sabotaged, useless.

crisis noun
1 *the crisis of a story.* climax.
2 *We had a crisis when we found a gas leak.* danger, difficulty, emergency, predicament, problem.

crisp adjective
crisp biscuits. brittle, crackly, crispy, crunchy, fragile, hard and dry.
OPPOSITES: SEE **soft**.

critic noun
1 *a music critic.* analyst, authority, commentator, judge, pundit, reviewer.
2 *a critic of the government.* attacker, detractor.

critical adjective
1 *Critical* can mean either (a) *unfavourable* (a *critical review of the dreadful new LP*) or (b) *showing careful judgement* (a *critical analysis of Shakespeare's plays*).
(a) = *unfavourable.* captious, censorious, criticizing [SEE **criticize**], deprecatory, derogatory, fault-finding, hypercritical, [*informal*] nit-picking, scathing, slighting, uncomplimentary, unfavourable.
OPPOSITES: SEE **complimentary**.
(b) = *showing careful judgement.* analytical, discerning, discriminating, intelligent, judicious, perceptive.
OPPOSITES: SEE **undiscriminating**.
2 *a critical decision.* crucial, SEE **dangerous**, decisive, important, key, momentous, vital.
OPPOSITES: SEE **unimportant**.

criticism noun
1 *unfair criticism of our behaviour.* censure, diatribe, disapproval, disparagement, judgement, reprimand, reproach, stricture, tirade, verbal attack.
2 *literary criticism.* analysis, appraisal, appreciation, assessment, commentary, critique, elucidation, evaluation, notice (a *favourable notice in the papers*), [*informal*] puff [= *a flattering notice*], review.

criticize verb
She criticized us for being noisy. She criticized our efforts. belittle, berate, blame, carp, [*informal*] cast aspersions on, castigate, censure, [*old-fashioned*] chide, condemn, decry, disapprove of, disparage, fault, find fault with, [*informal*] flay, impugn, [*informal*] knock, [*informal*] lash, [*informal*] pan, [*informal*] pick holes in, [*informal*] pitch into, [*informal*] rap, rate,

rebuke, reprimand, satirize, scold, [*informal*] slam, [*informal*] slate, snipe at.
OPPOSITES: SEE **praise** verb.

crockery noun
ceramics, china, crocks, dishes, earthenware, porcelain, pottery, tableware.

VARIOUS ITEMS OF CROCKERY: basin, bowl, coffee-cup, coffee-pot, cup, dinner plate, dish, jug, milk-jug, mug, plate, [*American*] platter, pot, sauceboat, saucer, serving dish, side plate, soup bowl, sugar-bowl, teacup, teapot, [*old-fashioned*] trencher, tureen.

---

crook noun
1 *the crook of your arm.* angle, bend, corner, hook.
2 [*informal*] *The cops got the crooks.* SEE **criminal** noun.

crooked adjective
1 *The picture hangs crooked.* angled, askew, awry, lopsided, offcentre.
2 *a crooked road. a crooked tree.* bent, bowed, curved, curving, deformed, misshapen, tortuous, twisted, twisty, winding, zigzag.
3 *a crooked salesman.* SEE **criminal** adjective.

crop noun
a crop of fruit. gathering, harvest, produce, sowing, vintage, yield.

crop verb
1 *Animals crop grass.* bite off, browse, eat, graze, nibble.
2 *A barber crops hair.* clip, SEE **cut** verb, shear, snip, trim.
to crop up *A difficulty cropped up.* appear, arise, come up, emerge, happen, occur, spring up, turn up.

cross adjective
She's always cross when she comes in from work. SEE **angry**, annoyed, bad-tempered, cantankerous, crotchety, [*informal*] grumpy, ill-tempered, irascible, irate, irritable, peevish, short-tempered, testy, tetchy, upset, vexed.
OPPOSITES: SEE **even-tempered**.

cross noun
1 *marked with a cross.* intersecting lines, X.
RELATED ADJECTIVE [= *cross-shaped*]: cruciform.
2 *a cross I have to bear.* affliction, burden, difficulty, grief, misfortune, problem, sorrow, trial, tribulation, trouble, worry.
3 *a cross between two breeds. a cross between soup and stew.* amalgam, blend, combination, cross-breed, half-way house, hybrid, mixture, mongrel [= *a cross between two breeds of dog*].

cross verb
1 *lines which cross.* criss-cross, intersect, intertwine, meet, zigzag.
2 *to cross a river.* bridge, ford, go across, pass over, span, traverse.

cross-breed noun
hybrid, mongrel.

crouch verb
They crouched in the bushes. bend, bow, cower, cringe, duck, kneel, squat, stoop.

crowd noun
1 *a crowd of people.* army, assembly, bunch, circle, cluster, collection, company, crush, flock, gathering, SEE **group** noun, horde, host, mass, mob, multitude, pack, rabble, swarm, throng.
2 *a football crowd.* audience, gate, spectators.

crowd verb
We crowded together. They crowded us into a small room. assemble, bundle, compress, congregate, cram, crush, flock, gather, herd, huddle, jostle, mass, muster, overcrowd, pack, [*informal*] pile, press, push, squeeze, swarm, throng.

crowded adjective
a crowded room. congested, cramped, full, jammed, jostling, overcrowded, overflowing, packed, swarming, teeming, thronging.
OPPOSITES: SEE **empty** adjective.

crown noun
1 *a monarch's crown.* coronet, diadem, tiara.
2 *the crown of a hill.* apex, brow, crown, head, peak, ridge, summit, top.

crown verb
1 *to crown a monarch.* anoint, appoint, enthrone, install.
2 *to crown your efforts with success.* cap, complete, conclude, consummate, finish off, perfect, round off, top.

crowning adjective
her crowning achievement. culminating, deserved, final, highest, hoped for, perfect, successful, supreme, top, ultimate.

crucial adjective
a crucial decision. a crucial part of an argument. central, critical, decisive, important, major, momentous, pivotal, serious.
OPPOSITES: SEE **peripheral**.

crude adjective
1 *crude oil.* natural, raw, unprocessed, unrefined.
2 *crude workmanship.* amateurish, awkward, bungling, clumsy, inartistic, incompetent, inelegant, inept, makeshift, primitive, rough, rudimentary, unpolished, unrefined, unskilful, unworkmanlike.

3 *crude language.* SEE **indecent**.
OPPOSITES: SEE **refined**.

cruel adjective
a cruel action. a cruel person. atrocious, barbaric, barbarous, beastly, blood-thirsty, bloody, brutal, callous, cold-blooded, diabolical, ferocious, fierce, flinty, grim, hard, hard-hearted, harsh, heartless, hellish, implacable, inexorable, inhuman, inhumane, malevolent, merciless, murderous, pitiless, relentless, remorseless, ruthless, sadistic, savage, spiteful, stern, stony-hearted, tyrannical, unfeeling, unjust, unkind, unmerciful, unrelenting, vengeful, vicious, violent.
OPPOSITES: SEE **kind** adjective.

crumb noun
a crumb of bread. bit, fragment, grain, morsel, particle, scrap, shred, speck.

crumble verb
1 *Rotten wood crumbles.* break up, decay, decompose, deteriorate, disintegrate, fall apart, [*of rubber*] perish.
2 *He crumbled the cake onto his plate.* break into pieces, crush, fragment, grind, pound, powder, pulverize.

crumple verb
Don't crumple your clothes! crease, crush, dent, fold, pucker, rumple, wrinkle.

crunch verb
The dog crunched up a bone. break, champ, chew, crush, grind, masticate, munch, scrunch, smash, squash.

crusade noun
a crusade against drugs. campaign, drive, movement, struggle, war.

crush verb
1 *to crush a finger in the door.* break, bruise, crumple, crunch, grind, SEE **injure**, mangle, mash, pound, press, pulp, pulverize, smash, squash, squeeze.
2 *to crush your opponents.* conquer, defeat, humiliate, mortify, overcome, overpower, overthrow, overwhelm, quash, quell, rout, subdue, thrash, vanquish.

crust noun
the crust of a loaf. the crust of the earth. coat, coating, covering, incrustation, outer layer, outside, rind, scab, shell, skin, surface.

crux noun
the crux of a problem. centre, core, crucial issue, essence, heart, nub.

cry noun
a bird's cry. a cry of pain. battlecry, bellow, call, caterwaul, [*formal*] ejaculation, exclamation, hoot, howl, outcry, roar, scream, screech, shout, shriek, yell, yelp.

cry verb
1 *It was so sad it made me cry.* blubber, grizzle, shed tears, snivel, sob, wail, weep, whimper, whinge.
2 *Who cried out?* bawl, bellow, call, caterwaul, clamour, exclaim, roar, scream, screech, shout, shriek, yell, yelp.

cryptic adjective
a cryptic message. coded, concealed, enigmatic, hidden, mysterious, obscure, occult, perplexing, puzzling, secret, unclear, unintelligible, veiled.
OPPOSITES: SEE **intelligible**.

cube noun
cuboid, hexahedron.
RELATED ADJECTIVES: cubical, cuboidal.

cuddle verb
to cuddle a baby. caress, clasp lovingly, dandle, embrace, fondle, hold closely, huddle against, hug, kiss, nestle against, nurse, pet, snuggle against.

cudgel noun
armed with cudgels. baton, bludgeon, cane, club, cosh, stick, truncheon.

cue noun
Don't miss your cue to speak. hint, prompt, reminder, sign, signal.

culminate verb
The gala culminated in a firework display. build up to, climax, close, conclude, end, finish, reach a finale, rise to a peak, terminate.

culpable adjective
culpable negligence. blameworthy, criminal, SEE **deliberate** adjective, guilty, knowing, liable, punishable, reprehensible, wrong.
OPPOSITES: SEE **innocent**.

culprit noun
They punished the culprit. SEE **criminal** noun, delinquent, felon, malefactor, miscreant, offender, trouble-maker, wrongdoer.

cult noun
1 *a religious cult.* SEE **denomination**.
2 *The new pop-idol inspired a cult.* craze, enthusiasts [SEE **enthusiast**], fan-club, fashion, following, party, school, trend, vogue.

cultivate verb
1 *to cultivate land.* dig, farm, fertilize, hoe, manure, mulch, plough, prepare, rake, till, turn, work.
2 *to cultivate crops.* grow, plant, produce, raise, sow, take cuttings, tend.
3 *to cultivate good relations with your neighbours.* court, develop, encourage, foster, further, improve, promote, pursue, try to achieve.

cultivated adjective
1 *a cultivated way of speaking.* SEE **cultured**.
2 *cultivated land.* agricultural, farmed, farming, planted, prepared, tilled.

cultivation noun
the cultivation of the land. agriculture, agronomy, culture, farming, gardening, horticulture, husbandry.

cultural adjective
The festival included sporting and cultural events. aesthetic, artistic, civilized, civilizing, educational, elevating, enlightening, highbrow, improving, intellectual.

culture noun
a nation's culture. art, background, civilization, customs, education, learning, traditions.

cultured adjective
a cultured person. artistic, civilized, cultivated, educated, erudite, highbrow, knowledgeable, scholarly, well-bred, well-educated, well-read.
OPPOSITES: SEE **ignorant**.

cumulative adjective
the cumulative effect of something. accumulating, building up, developing.

cunning adjective
1 *a cunning deception.* artful, SEE **crafty**, devious, dodgy, guileful, insidious, knowing, machiavellian, sly, subtle, tricky, wily.
2 *a cunning way to do something.* adroit, astute, SEE **clever**, ingenious, skilful.

cunning noun
1 [*uncomplimentary*] *Foxes have a reputation for cunning.* artfulness, chicanery, craftiness, deceit, deception, deviousness, duplicity, guile, slyness, trickery.
2 *The inventor showed great cunning in solving the problem.* cleverness, expertise, ingenuity.

cup noun

THINGS TO DRINK FROM: beaker, bowl, chalice, glass, goblet, mug, tankard, teacup, tumbler, wineglass.

cupboard noun

VARIOUS KINDS OF CUPBOARD: cabinet, chiffonier, closet, dresser, filing-cabinet, food-cupboard, larder, locker, sideboard, wardrobe.

curable adjective
a curable disease. operable, remediable, treatable.
OPPOSITES: SEE **incurable**.

curb verb
to curb someone's enthusiasm. bridle, check, contain, control, deter, hamper, hinder, hold back, impede, inhibit, limit, moderate, repress, restrain, restrict, subdue, suppress.
OPPOSITES: SEE **encourage**.

cure noun
a cure for a cold. antidote, corrective, medicine, nostrum, palliative, panacea [= *a cure for everything*], prescription, remedy, restorative, solution, therapy, treatment.

cure verb
1 *The pill cured my headache.* alleviate, counteract, ease, heal, help, palliate, relieve, remedy, treat.
OPPOSITES: SEE **aggravate**.
2 *I cured the fault in the car.* correct, [*informal*] fix, mend, put right, rectify, repair, solve.

curiosity noun
I couldn't restrain my curiosity. inquisitiveness, interest, meddling, nosiness, prying.

curious adjective
1 *curious questions.* inquiring, inquisitive, interested, [*informal*] nosy, prying, puzzled.
OPPOSITES: SEE **indifferent**.
to be curious SEE **pry**.
1 *a curious smell.* abnormal, bizarre, extraordinary, funny, mysterious, odd, peculiar, puzzling, queer, rare, strange, surprising, unconventional, unexpected, unusual.
OPPOSITES: SEE **normal**.

curl verb
The snake curled round a branch. bend, SEE **circle** verb, coil, corkscrew, curve, entwine, loop, spiral, turn, twine, twist, wind, wreathe, writhe.

curly adjective
curly hair. crimped, curled, curling, frizzy, fuzzy, kinky, permed, wavy.
OPPOSITES: SEE **straight**.

current adjective
1 *current fashions.* contemporary, fashionable, modern, prevailing, prevalent, [*informal*] trendy, up-to-date.
OPPOSITES: SEE **old-fashioned**.
2 *a current passport.* usable, valid.
OPPOSITES: SEE **invalid**.
3 *the current government.* existing, extant, present, reigning.

current noun
a current of air or water. course, draught, drift, flow, jet, river, stream, tide.

curriculum noun
the school curriculum. course, programme of study, syllabus.

curse noun
1 *I let out a curse.* blasphemy, exclamation, expletive, imprecation, malediction, oath, obscenity, profanity, swearword.
OPPOSITES: SEE **blessing**.
2 *Pollution is a curse in modern society.* SEE **evil** noun.

curse verb
I cursed when I hit my finger. blaspheme, damn, fulminate, swear, utter curses [SEE **curse** noun].

cursory adjective
a cursory inspection. brief, careless, casual, desultory, fleeting, hasty, hurried, perfunctory, quick, slapdash, superficial.
OPPOSITES: SEE **thorough**.

curt adjective
a curt answer. abrupt, brief, brusque, gruff, laconic, monosyllabic, offhand, rude, sharp, short, succinct, tart, terse, uncommunicative, ungracious.
OPPOSITES: SEE **expansive**.

curtail verb
to curtail a debate. abbreviate, abridge, break off, contract, cut short, decrease, [*informal*] dock, guillotine, halt, lessen, lop, prune, reduce, restrict, shorten, stop, terminate, trim, truncate.
OPPOSITES: SEE **extend**.

curtain noun
Close the curtains. blind, drape, drapery, hanging, screen.

curve noun
arc, arch, bend, bow, bulge, camber, SEE **circle** noun, convolution, corkscrew, crescent, curl, curvature, cycloid, loop, meander, spiral, swirl, trajectory, turn, twist, undulation, whorl.

curved adjective
arched, bent, bowed, bulging, cambered, coiled, concave, convex, convoluted, crescent, crooked, curled, [*formal*] curvilinear, curving, curvy, looped, meandering, rounded, serpentine, shaped, sinuous, snaking, spiral, sweeping, swelling, tortuous, turned, twisted, undulating, whorled, winding.

cushion verb
to cushion the impact of a collision. absorb, bolster, deaden, lessen, mitigate, muffle, protect from, reduce the effect of, soften, support.

custodian noun
the custodian of a museum. caretaker,
curator, guardian, keeper, overseer,
superintendent, warden, warder, [*informal*]
watch-dog, watchman.

custody noun
1 *The animals were left in my custody.* care,
charge, guardianship, keeping, observation,
possession, preservation, protection, safe-
keeping.
2 *He was kept in police custody.* captivity,
confinement, detention, imprisonment,
incarceration, remand [*on remand = in
custody*].

custom noun
1 *It's our custom to give presents at
Christmas.* convention, etiquette, fashion,
form, formality, habit, institution, manner,
observance, policy, practice, procedure,
routine, tradition, way.
2 *The shop offers discounts to attract custom.*
business, buyers, customers, patronage,
support, trade.

customary adjective
It was customary to give a tip to the waiter.
accepted, accustomed, common,
conventional, established, expected,
fashionable, general, habitual, normal,
ordinary, popular, prevailing, regular,
routine, traditional, typical, usual, wonted.
OPPOSITES: SEE **unusual**.

customer noun
a shop's customers. buyer, client, consumer,
patron, purchaser, shopper.
OPPOSITES: SEE **seller**.

cut noun
1 *a cut on the finger. a cut in a piece of wood.*
gash, graze, groove, [*formal*] incision, SEE
injury, [*formal*] laceration, nick, notch, rent,
rip, slash, slice, slit, snick, snip, split, stab,
tear, wound.
2 *a cut in prices.* cut-back, decrease, fall,
lowering, reduction, saving.

cut verb
1 VARIOUS WAYS TO CUT THINGS: amputate
(*a limb*), axe, carve, chip, chisel, chop,
cleave, clip, crop, dissect, dock, engrave
(*an inscription on something*), fell (*a tree*),
gash, gouge, grate (*into small pieces*),
graze, guillotine, hack, hew, incise, lacerate,
lop, mince, mow (*grass*), nick, notch, pare
(*skin off fruit*), pierce, poll, pollard
(*a tree*), prune (*a growing plant*), reap
(*corn*), saw, scalp, score, sever, shave,
shear, shred, slash, slice, slit, snick, snip,
split, stab, trim, whittle (*wood with a
knife*), wound.
TOOLS FOR CUTTING: SEE **cutter**.
2 *to cut a long story.* abbreviate, abridge,
bowdlerize, censor, condense, curtail,

digest, edit, précis, shorten, summarize,
truncate.
3 *to cut expenditure.* SEE **reduce**.

cutlery noun
[*informal*] eating irons.

ITEMS OF CUTLERY: breadknife, butter knife,
carving knife, cheese knife, dessert-spoon,
fish knife, fish fork, fork, knife, ladle, salad
servers, spoon, steak knife, tablespoon,
teaspoon.

---

cutter noun

VARIOUS TOOLS FOR CUTTING: axe, billhook,
chisel, chopper, clippers, guillotine, SEE
knife noun, lawnmower, SEE **saw**, scalpel,
scissors, scythe, secateurs, shears, sickle.

---

cutting adjective
cutting remarks. acute, biting, caustic, SEE
hurtful, incisive, keen, mordant, sarcastic,
satirical, sharp, trenchant.

cycle noun
1 *a cycle of events.* circle, repetition,
revolution, rotation, round, sequence,
series.
2 *A cycle is a cheap form of transport.*

KINDS OF CYCLE: bicycle, [*informal*] bike,
moped, [*informal*] motor bike, motor cycle,
mountain bike, penny-farthing, scooter,
tandem, tricycle.

---

cyclic adjective
a cyclic process. circular, recurring,
repeating, repetitive, rotating.

cynical adjective
a cynical outlook. doubting, [*informal*] hard,
misanthropic, negative, pessimistic,
questioning, sceptical, sneering.
OPPOSITES: SEE **optimistic**.

Dd

daily adjective
a daily occurrence. diurnal, everyday, SEE
regular.

dainty adjective
1 *dainty embroidery.* charming, delicate,
exquisite, fine, meticulous, neat, nice,
pretty, skilful.

OPPOSITES: SEE **clumsy**.
2 *a dainty eater*. choosy, discriminating, fastidious, finicky, fussy, well-mannered.
OPPOSITES: SEE **messy**.

dally verb
Don't dally: we must move on. dawdle, delay, [*informal*] dilly-dally, hang about, idle, linger, loaf, loiter, play about, procrastinate, saunter, [*old-fashioned*] tarry, waste time.

dam noun
a dam across a river. bank, barrage, barrier, dike, embankment, wall, weir.

dam verb
to dam the flow of a river. block, check, hold back, obstruct, restrict, stanch, stem, stop.

damage noun
Did the accident cause any damage? destruction, devastation, harm, havoc, hurt, SEE **injury**, loss, mutilation, sabotage.

damage verb
1 *A gale damaged the tree. Frost can damage water-pipes*. break, buckle, burst, [*informal*] bust, crack, SEE **destroy**, [*informal*] do a mischief to, fracture, harm, hurt, impair, injure, mutilate, [*informal*] play havoc with, ruin, rupture, strain, warp, weaken, wound, wreck.
2 *Someone damaged the paintwork*. blemish, chip, deface, disfigure, flaw, mar, mark, sabotage, scar, scratch, spoil, vandalize.
3 *Corrosion damaged the engine*. cripple, disable, immobilize, incapacitate, make inoperative, make useless.

damaged adjective
damaged goods. broken, faulty, flawed, hurt, injured, misused, shop-soiled, unsound.
OPPOSITES: SEE **undamaged**.

damaging adjective
the damaging effects of war. calamitous, deleterious, destructive, detrimental, disadvantageous, evil, harmful, injurious, negative, pernicious, prejudicial, ruinous, unfavourable.
OPPOSITES: SEE **constructive**.

damp adjective
1 *damp clothes. a damp room*. clammy, dank, dripping, moist, perspiring, soggy, sticky, sweaty, unaired, unventilated, wet.
2 *damp weather*. dewy, drizzly, foggy, humid, misty, muggy, raining, wet.
OPPOSITES: SEE **dry** adjective.

damp, dampen verbs
1 *to damp a cloth*. SEE **moisten**.
2 *to damp someone's enthusiasm*. SEE **discourage**.

dance noun
1 choreography, dancing.
RELATED ADJECTIVE: choreographic.

2 *We went to a dance*. ball, barn-dance, [*Scottish & Irish*] ceilidh, [*informal*] disco, discothèque, [*informal*] hop, [*informal*] knees-up, party, SEE **social** noun, square dance.

KINDS OF DANCING: aerobics, ballet, ballroom dancing, break-dancing, country dancing, disco dancing, flamenco dancing, folk dancing, Latin American dancing, limbo dancing, morris dancing, old-time dancing, tap-dancing.

VARIOUS DANCES: bolero, cancan, conga, fandango, fling, foxtrot, gavotte, hornpipe, jig, mazurka, minuet, polka, polonaise, quadrille, quickstep, reel, rumba, square dance, tango, waltz.

---

dance verb
We danced all night. I danced for joy. caper, cavort, frisk, frolic, gambol, hop about, jig about, jive, jump about, leap, prance, rock, skip, [*joking*] trip the light fantastic, whirl.

danger noun
1 *a danger of frost*. chance, liability, possibility, risk, threat.
2 *He faced the danger bravely*. crisis, distress, hazard, insecurity, jeopardy, menace, peril, pitfall, trouble, uncertainty.
OPPOSITES: SEE **safety**.

dangerous adjective
1 *dangerous driving. a dangerous situation*. alarming, breakneck (*speed*), [*informal*] chancy, critical, explosive (*an explosive situation*), grave, [*slang*] hairy, hazardous, insecure, menacing, [*informal*] nasty, perilous, precarious, reckless (*driving*), risky, uncertain, unsafe.
OPPOSITES: SEE **safe**.
2 *dangerous lions. dangerous criminals*. desperate, SEE **ruthless**, treacherous, unmanageable, unpredictable, violent, volatile, wild.
OPPOSITES: SEE **tame** adjective.
3 *dangerous chemicals*. destructive, harmful, noxious, toxic.
OPPOSITES: SEE **harmless**.

dangle verb
A rope dangled above my head. be suspended, droop, flap, hang, sway, swing, trail, wave about.

dappled adjective
dappled with patches of light. blotchy, brindled, dotted, flecked, freckled, marbled, motley, mottled, particoloured, patchy, pied, speckled, spotted, stippled, streaked, varicoloured, variegated.

dare verb
1 *Would you dare to make a parachute jump?* gamble, have the courage, risk, take a

chance, venture.
2 *He dared me to jump.* challenge, defy, provoke, taunt.

daring adjective
a daring explorer. a daring feat.
adventurous, audacious, bold, SEE **brave**, brazen, [*informal*] cool, dauntless, fearless, hardy, intrepid, plucky, reckless, unafraid, valiant, venturesome.
OPPOSITES: SEE **timid**.

dark adjective
1 *a dark room. a dark sky.* black, blackish, cheerless, clouded, coal-black, dim, dingy, dismal, drab, dull, dusky, funereal, gloomy, glowering, glum, grim, inky, moonless, murky, overcast, pitch-black, pitch-dark, [*poetic*] sable, shadowy, shady, sombre, starless, sullen, sunless, unilluminated, unlit.
OPPOSITES: SEE **bright**.
2 *dark colours.* dense, heavy, strong.
OPPOSITES: SEE **pale** adjective.

darken verb
1 *The sky darkened.* become overcast, cloud over.
2 *Clouds darkened the sky.* blacken, dim, eclipse, obscure, overshadow, shade.
OPPOSITES: SEE **brighten**.

darling noun
beloved, dear, dearest, love, loved one, sweetheart.

dart verb
to dart about. bound, SEE **dash** verb, fling, flit, fly, hurtle, leap, move suddenly, shoot, spring, [*informal*] whiz, [*informal*] zip.

dash noun
1 *a dash to the finishing-post.* chase, race, run, rush, sprint, spurt.
2 [= *punctuation mark*] hyphen.

dash verb
1 *to dash home.* bolt, chase, dart, fly, hasten, hurry, move quickly, race, run, rush, speed, sprint, tear, [*informal*] zoom.
2 *to dash your foot against a rock.* SEE **hit** verb, knock, smash, strike.

data noun
[*Data* is a plural word. We don't say *Have you a data?* but *Have you any data?* It is, however, often used with a singular verb: *The data is in a computer file* rather than *The data are . . .*] details, evidence, facts, figures, information, statistics.

date noun
1 *the date of my birthday.* SEE **time**.
2 *a date with a friend.* appointment, assignation, engagement, fixture, meeting, rendezvous.

daunt verb
I was daunted by the size of the task. alarm, depress, deter, discourage, dishearten, dismay, SEE **frighten**, intimidate, overawe, put off, unnerve.
OPPOSITES: SEE **encourage**.

dawdle verb
Don't dawdle: we haven't got all day. be slow, dally, delay, [*informal*] dilly-dally, hang about, idle, lag behind, linger, loaf about, loiter, move slowly, straggle, [*informal*] take your time, trail behind.
OPPOSITES: SEE **hurry** verb.

dawn noun
1 daybreak, first light, [*informal*] peep of day, sunrise.
OPPOSITES: SEE **dusk**.
2 *the dawn of a new age.* SEE **beginning**.

day noun
1 *There are seven days in a week.*

VARIOUS TIMES OF THE DAY: afternoon, dawn, daybreak, dusk, evening, [*poetic*] eventide, gloaming, midday, midnight, morning, night, nightfall, noon, sunrise, sunset, twilight.

---

2 *Most people are awake during the day.* daylight, daytime, light.
OPPOSITES: SEE **night**.
3 *Things were different in grandad's day.* age, epoch, era, period, time.

daydream noun
a daydream about being rich and famous. dream, fantasy, hope, illusion, meditation, pipe-dream, reverie, vision, wool-gathering.

dead adjective
1 *a dead animal. a dead body.* cold, dead and buried, deceased, departed, inanimate, inert, killed, late (*the late king*), lifeless, perished, rigid, stiff.
OPPOSITES: SEE **alive, living**.
2 *a dead language. a dead species.* died out, extinct, obsolete.
OPPOSITES: SEE **existing**.
3 *dead with cold.* deadened, insensitive, numb, paralysed, without feeling.
OPPOSITES: SEE **sensitive**.
4 *a dead battery. a dead engine.* burnt out, defunct, flat, inoperative, not going, not working, no use, out of order, unresponsive, used up, useless, worn out.
OPPOSITES: SEE **operational**.
a dead person body, cadaver, carcass, corpse, [*informal*] goner, mortal remains, [*slang*] stiff.

deaden verb
1 *to deaden a sound. to deaden a blow.* check, cushion, damp, hush, lessen, muffle, mute, quieten, reduce, smother, soften, stifle,

suppress, weaken.
OPPOSITES: SEE **amplify**.
2 *to deaden a pain. to deaden feeling.*
alleviate, anaesthetize, blunt, desensitize,
dull, numb, paralyse.
OPPOSITES: SEE **aggravate, intensify**.

deadlock noun
Negotiations reached deadlock. halt,
impasse, stalemate, standstill, stop.
OPPOSITES: SEE **progress** noun.

deadly adjective
a deadly illness. deadly poison. dangerous,
destructive, fatal, SEE **harmful**, lethal,
mortal, noxious, terminal.
OPPOSITES: SEE **harmless**.

deafening adjective
a deafening roar. SEE **loud**.

deal noun
1 *a business deal.* agreement, arrangement,
bargain, contract, pact, settlement,
transaction, understanding.
2 *a great deal of trouble.* amount, quantity,
volume.

deal verb
1 *to deal cards.* allot, apportion, assign,
dispense, distribute, divide, [*informal*] dole
out, give out, share out.
2 *to deal someone a blow on the head.*
administer, apply, deliver, give, inflict,
mete out.
3 *to deal in stocks and shares.* buy and sell,
do business, trade, traffic.
to deal with 1 *I'll deal with this problem.*
attend to, come to grips with, control, cope
with, get over, grapple with, handle, look
after, manage, overcome, see to, SEE **solve**,
sort out, surmount, tackle, take action on. 2
I want a book that deals with insects. be
concerned with, cover, explain, treat.

dealer noun
a car dealer. a dealer in antiques. merchant,
retailer, shopkeeper, stockist, supplier,
trader, tradesman, wholesaler.

dear adjective
1 *dear friends.* beloved, close, darling,
intimate, SEE **lovable**, loved, valued.
OPPOSITES: SEE **hateful**.
2 *dear goods.* costly, exorbitant, expensive,
over-priced, [*informal*] pricey.
OPPOSITES: SEE **cheap**.

death noun
1 *We mourn the death of a friend.* [*formal*]
decease, demise, dying [SEE **die** verb], end,
loss, passing.
2 *The accident resulted in several deaths.*
casualty, fatality.

debase verb
*They debased that lovely music by using it in
an advert.* commercialize, degrade, demean,

depreciate, devalue, lower the tone of,
pollute, reduce the value of, ruin, soil, spoil,
sully, vulgarize.

debatable adjective
a debatable question. arguable, contentious,
controversial, controvertible, disputable,
doubtful, dubious, moot (*a moot point*), open
to question, problematical, questionable,
uncertain.
OPPOSITES: SEE **indisputable**.

debate noun
a debate about animal rights. SEE **argument**,
conference, consultation, controversy,
deliberation, [*formal*] dialectic, discussion,
[*formal*] disputation, dispute, [*formal*]
polemic.

debate verb
We debated the pros and cons of the matter.
argue, consider, deliberate, discuss, dispute,
[*informal*] mull over, question, reflect on,
weigh up.

debit verb
The bank debited £10 from my account.
cancel, remove, subtract, take away.
OPPOSITES: SEE **credit** verb.

debris noun
debris from a crashed aircraft. bits, detritus,
flotsam [= *floating debris*], fragments, litter,
pieces, remains, rubbish, rubble, ruins,
waste, wreckage.

debt noun
1 *Can you pay off your debt?* account, arrears,
bill, debit, dues, score (*I have a score to
settle*), what you owe.
2 *I owe you a great debt for your kindness.*
duty, indebtedness, obligation.

decadent adjective
a decadent society. SEE **corrupt** adjective,
declining, degenerate, immoral.
OPPOSITES: SEE **moral** adjective.

decay verb
1 *Dead plants and animals decay.* break
down, decompose, degenerate, fester, go
bad, moulder, putrefy, rot, shrivel, waste
away, wither.
2 *Most substances decay in time.* corrode,
crumble, deteriorate, disintegrate, dissolve,
fall apart, oxidize, perish, spoil.

deceit noun
We saw through his deceit. artifice, bluff,
cheating, chicanery, [*informal*] con,
craftiness, cunning, deceitfulness,
deception, dishonesty, dissimulation,
double-dealing, duplicity, feint, [*informal*]
fiddle, fraud, guile, hoax, imposture,
insincerity, lie, lying, misrepresentation,
pretence, ruse, sham, stratagem,
subterfuge, swindle, treachery, trick,

trickery, underhandedness,
untruthfulness, wile.
OPPOSITES: SEE **honesty**.

deceitful adjective
a deceitful person. a deceitful trick. cheating,
crafty, cunning, deceiving, deceptive,
designing, dishonest, double-dealing, false,
fraudulent, furtive, hypocritical, insincere,
lying, secretive, shifty, sneaky, treacherous,
[*informal*] tricky, [*informal*] two-faced,
underhand, unfaithful, untrustworthy,
wily.
OPPOSITES: SEE **honest**.

deceive verb
*I had no intention to deceive. His disguise
deceived me.* [*informal*] bamboozle, be an
impostor, beguile, betray, blind, bluff, cheat,
[*informal*] con, defraud, delude, [*informal*]
diddle, double-cross, dupe, fool, [*informal*]
fox, [*informal*] have on, hoax, hoodwink
[*informal*] kid, [*informal*] lead on, lie,
mislead, mystify, [*informal*] outsmart,
outwit, pretend, swindle, [*informal*] take for
a ride, [*informal*] take in, trick.

decent adjective
decent behaviour. decent language.
acceptable, appropriate, becoming,
befitting, chaste, courteous, decorous,
delicate, fitting, honourable, modest, polite,
presentable, proper, pure, respectable,
seemly, sensitive, suitable.
OPPOSITES: SEE **indecent**.

deception noun
I was taken in by the deception. bluff, cheat,
cheating, chicanery, [*informal*] con,
confidence trick, cover-up, craftiness,
cunning, deceit, deceitfulness, dishonesty,
dissimulation, double-dealing, duplicity,
fake, feint, [*informal*] fiddle, fraud, hoax,
imposture, lie, lying, misrepresentation,
pretence, ruse, sham, stratagem,
subterfuge, swindle, treachery, trick,
trickery, underhandedness,
untruthfulness, wile.

deceptive adjective
a deceptive argument. deceptive appearances.
delusive, fallacious, false, fraudulent,
illusory, insincere, misleading, specious,
spurious, treacherous, unreliable.
OPPOSITES: SEE **genuine**.

decide verb
Please decide what to do. adjudicate, choose,
conclude, determine, elect, fix on, judge,
make up your mind, opt for, pick, resolve,
select, settle.

decimate verb
[Originally *decimate* meant *to kill one in ten.*
Now it usually means *to kill a large number.*]
SEE **destroy**.

decision noun
The judge announced his decision.
conclusion, findings, judgement, outcome,
result, ruling, verdict.

decisive adjective
1 *decisive evidence.* conclusive, convincing,
crucial, final, influential, positive,
significant.
OPPOSITES: SEE **inconclusive**.
2 *a decisive person. decisive action.* decided,
SEE **definite**, determined, firm, forceful,
forthright, incisive, resolute, strong-
minded, unhesitating.
OPPOSITES: SEE **hesitant**.

declaration noun
a formal declaration of intentions.
affirmation, announcement, assertion,
avowal, confirmation, deposition,
disclosure, edict, manifesto, proclamation,
profession, pronouncement, protestation,
revelation, statement, testimony.

declare verb
He declared that he would never steal again.
affirm, announce, assert, attest, avow,
certify, claim, confirm, contend, disclose,
emphasize, insist, maintain, make known,
proclaim, profess, pronounce, protest,
report, reveal, SEE **say**, show, state, swear,
testify, witness.

decline noun
*a decline in productivity. a decline in
population.* decrease, degeneration,
deterioration, downturn, drop, fall, falling
off, loss, recession, reduction, slump,
worsening.

decline verb
1 *to decline an invitation.* forgo, refuse,
reject, turn down.
OPPOSITES: SEE **accept**.
2 *His health declined.* decrease, degenerate,
deteriorate, die away, diminish, drop away,
dwindle, ebb, fail, fall off, flag, lessen, sink,
wane, weaken, wilt, worsen.
OPPOSITES: SEE **improve**.

decode verb
to decode a cryptic message. [*informal*] crack,
decipher, explain, figure out, interpret,
make out, read, solve, understand,
unscramble.

decorate verb
1 *to decorate a room with flowers.* adorn,
array, beautify, [*old-fashioned*] bedeck,
deck, embellish, festoon, garnish, make
beautiful, ornament, [*uncomplimentary*]
prettify, [*uncomplimentary*] tart up.
2 *to decorate a room with a new colour scheme.*
colour, [*informal*] do up, paint, paper,
refurbish, renovate, wallpaper.
3 *to decorate someone for bravery.* give a
medal to, honour, reward.

decoration noun
1 *beautiful decorations.* accessory, adornment, arabesque, elaboration, embellishment, embroidery, filigree, finery, flourish, frill, ornament, ornamentation, tracery, [*plural*] trappings, trimming.
2 *a decoration for bravery.* award, badge, medal, ribbon, star.

decorative adjective
decorative details. elaborate, fancy, non-functional, ornamental, ornate.
OPPOSITES: SEE **functional**.

decorous adjective
decorous behaviour. appropriate, becoming, befitting, correct, SEE **decent**, dignified, fitting, presentable, proper, refined, respectable, sedate, staid, suitable, well-behaved.
OPPOSITES: SEE **improper**.

decoy verb
attract, bait, draw, entice, inveigle, lead, lure, seduce, tempt.

decrease noun
a decrease in wages. contraction, cut, cut-back, decline, diminuendo [= *decrease in loudness*], downturn, drop, fall, falling off, reduction.
OPPOSITES: SEE **increase** noun.

decrease verb
1 *We decreased speed.* abate, curtail, cut, lessen, lower, reduce, slacken.
2 *Our speed decreased.* contract, decline, die away, diminish, dwindle, fall off, lessen, peter out, shrink, slim down, subside, [*informal*] tail off, taper off, wane.
OPPOSITES: SEE **increase** verb.

decree noun
an official decree. act, command, declaration, edict, fiat, law, order, ordinance, proclamation, regulation, ruling, statute.

decree verb
The government decrees what we must pay in taxes. command, decide, declare, determine, dictate, direct, ordain, order, prescribe, proclaim, pronounce, rule.

decrepit adjective
a decrepit old car. battered, broken down, derelict, dilapidated, feeble, frail, infirm, SEE **old**, ramshackle, tumbledown, weak, worn out.

dedicate verb
1 *The church is dedicated to St Paul.* consecrate, hallow, sanctify, set apart.
2 *I dedicate my poem to my father's memory.* address, inscribe.
3 *He dedicates himself to his work.* commit, devote, give (yourself) completely, pledge.

dedicated adjective
dedicated fans. committed, devoted, enthusiastic, faithful, keen, loyal, single-minded, zealous.

dedication noun
1 *I admire her dedication to the job.* adherence, allegiance, commitment, devotion, faithfulness, loyalty, single-mindedness.
2 *the dedication in a book.* inscription.

deduce verb
The policeman deduced that I was involved. conclude, draw the conclusion, extrapolate, gather, infer, [*informal*] put two and two together, reason, work out.

deduct verb
to deduct tax from your pay. [*informal*] knock off, subtract, take away.
OPPOSITES: SEE **add**.

deduction noun
1 [In this sense, *deduction* is related to the verb *deduct*.] *a deduction off your bill.* allowance, decrease, discount, reduction, subtraction.
2 [In this sense, *deduction* is related to the verb *deduce*.] *My deduction was correct.* conclusion, inference, reasoning.

deed noun
1 *a heroic deed.* achievement, act, action, adventure, effort, endeavour, enterprise, exploit, feat, performance, stunt, undertaking.
2 *the deeds of a house.* contract, documents, [*formal*] indenture, papers, records, [*formal*] title.

deep adjective
1 *a deep pit.* bottomless, fathomless, unfathomable, unplumbed.
2 *deep feelings.* earnest, extreme, genuine, heartfelt, intense, serious, sincere.
OPPOSITES: SEE **shallow**.
3 *deep in thought.* absorbed, concentrating, engrossed, immersed, lost, preoccupied, rapt, thoughtful.
4 *a deep subject.* abstruse, arcane, SEE **difficult**, esoteric, intellectual, learned, obscure, profound, recondite.
OPPOSITES: SEE **easy**.
5 *deep sleep.* heavy, sound.
6 *a deep colour.* dark, rich, strong, vivid.
OPPOSITES: SEE **pale** adjective.
7 *a deep voice.* bass, booming, growling, low, low-pitched, resonant, reverberating, sonorous.
OPPOSITES: SEE **high**.

deer noun

DEER AND SIMILAR ANIMALS: antelope,
[*male*] buck, caribou, chamois, [*female*] doe,
elk, fallow deer, gazelle, gnu, [*male*] hart,
[*female*] hind, impala, moose, reindeer, roe,
[*male*] roebuck, [*male*] stag, wildebeest.

---

deface verb
Vandals defaced the statue. damage, disfigure,
injure, mar, mutilate, spoil, vandalize.

defeat noun
a humiliating defeat. beating, conquest,
downfall, [*informal*] drubbing, failure,
humiliation, [*informal*] licking, overthrow,
[*informal*] put-down, rebuff, repulse,
reverse, rout, setback, subjugation,
thrashing, trouncing.
OPPOSITES: SEE **victory**.

defeat verb
to defeat an opponent. beat, best, checkmate,
[*informal*] clobber, confound, conquer,
crush, [*informal*] flatten, foil, frustrate, get
the better of, [*informal*] lay low, [*informal*]
lick, master, outdo, outvote, outwit,
overcome, overpower, overthrow,
overwhelm, put down, quell, repulse, rout,
ruin, [*informal*] smash, subdue, subjugate,
suppress, [*informal*] thrash, thwart,
triumph over, trounce, vanquish, win a
victory over.

defeated adjective
the defeated team. beaten, bottom, last,
losing, unsuccessful, vanquished.
OPPOSITES: SEE **victorious**.

defect noun
a defect in a piece of work. blemish, bug (*in
a computer program*), deficiency, error,
failing, fault, flaw, imperfection,
inadequacy, lack, mark, mistake,
shortcoming, spot, stain, want, weakness.

defence noun
1 *What was the accused woman's defence?*
alibi, apology, case, excuse, explanation,
justification, plea, testimony, vindication.
2 *a defence against attack.* SEE **barricade**,
cover, deterrence, fortification, guard,
protection, rampart, safeguard, security,
shelter, shield.

defend verb
1 *to defend yourself against attackers.* cover,
fortify, guard, keep safe, preserve, protect,
safeguard, screen, secure, shelter, shield,
[*informal*] stick up for.
OPPOSITES: SEE **attack** verb.
2 *He defended himself in court.* champion,
justify, plead for, speak up for, stand up for,
support, uphold, vindicate.
OPPOSITES: SEE **accuse**.

defensive adjective
1 *a defensive style of play.* cautious,
defending, protective, wary, watchful.
OPPOSITES: SEE **aggressive**.
2 *defensive remarks.* apologetic, faint-
hearted, self-justifying.
OPPOSITES: SEE **assertive**.

defer verb
*We deferred the remaining business until next
week.* adjourn, delay, hold over, postpone,
prorogue (*parliament*), put off, [*informal*]
shelve, suspend.

defiant adjective
a defiant attitude. aggressive, challenging,
disobedient, insolent, insubordinate,
mutinous, obstinate, rebellious,
recalcitrant, refractory, stubborn,
truculent, uncooperative, unyielding.
OPPOSITES: SEE **co-operative**.

deficient adjective
Their diet is deficient in vitamins. defective,
imperfect, inadequate, incomplete,
insufficient, lacking, meagre, scanty, scarce,
short, unsatisfactory, wanting, weak.

deficit noun
The company had a deficit in their accounts.
loss, shortfall.
OPPOSITES: SEE **excess**.

defile verb
I felt defiled by the filth. contaminate,
corrupt, degrade, desecrate, dirty,
dishonour, infect, make dirty [SEE **dirty**
adjective], poison, pollute, soil, stain, sully,
taint, tarnish.

define verb
1 *A thesaurus simply lists words, whereas a
dictionary defines them.* clarify, explain,
formulate, give the meaning of, interpret.
2 *The fence defines the extent of our land.*
bound, be the boundary of, circumscribe,
demarcate, determine, limit, mark out,
outline.

definite adjective
1 *definite opinions. a definite manner.*
assured, categorical, certain, clear-cut,
confident, cut-and-dried, decided,
determined, emphatic, exact, explicit, fixed,
incisive, particular, precise, settled, specific,
sure, unambiguous, unequivocal.
OPPOSITES: SEE **indefinite**.
2 *definite signs of improvement.* apparent,
clear, discernible, distinct, marked,
noticeable, obvious, perceptible, plain,
positive, pronounced, unmistakable.
OPPOSITES: SEE **imperceptible**.

definitely adverb
I'll definitely come tomorrow. beyond doubt,
certainly, doubtless, for certain,
indubitably, positively, surely,
unquestionably, without doubt, without fail.

definition noun
1 *a dictionary definition.* elucidation, explanation, interpretation.
2 *the definition of a photograph.* clarity, clearness, focus, precision, sharpness.

definitive adjective
[Do not confuse with *definite.*] *the definitive account of someone's life.* agreed, authoritative, conclusive, correct, final, last (*He's written the last word on the subject*), official, permanent, reliable, settled, standard.
OPPOSITES: SEE **provisional**.

deflect verb
to deflect a blow. avert, divert, fend off, head off, intercept, parry, prevent, turn aside, ward off.

deformed adjective
a deformed tree. bent, buckled, contorted, SEE **crippled**, crooked, defaced, disfigured, distorted, gnarled, grotesque, malformed, mangled, misshapen, mutilated, twisted, ugly, warped.

defraud verb
SEE **cheat** verb, [*informal*] diddle, embezzle, [*informal*] fleece, rob, swindle.

deft adjective
deft movements. adept, adroit, agile, clever, dextrous, expert, handy, neat [*informal*] nifty, nimble, proficient, quick, skilful.
OPPOSITES: SEE **clumsy**.

defy verb
1 *to defy someone in authority.* confront, disobey, face up to, flout, refuse to obey, resist, stand up to, withstand.
OPPOSITES: SEE **obey**.
2 *I defy you to produce evidence.* challenge, dare.

degenerate verb
His behaviour degenerated. become worse, decline, deteriorate, regress, retrogress, sink, slip, weaken, worsen.
OPPOSITES: SEE **improve**.

degrade verb
Bad living conditions degrade people. brutalize, cheapen, corrupt, debase, dehumanize, demean, deprave, desensitize, harden, humiliate, lower, make uncivilized.

degrading adjective
a degrading experience. brutalizing, cheapening, corrupting, dehumanizing, demeaning, depraving, dishonourable, humiliating, ignoble, lowering, shameful, undignified, unworthy.
OPPOSITES: SEE **uplifting**.

degree noun
1 *a high degree of skill.* calibre, extent, grade, intensity, level, measure, order, standard.
2 *of high degree. of low degree.* class, position, rank, standing, station, status.

dehydrate verb
Take care not to dehydrate in the heat. desiccate, dry out, dry up.

deify verb
idolize, treat as a god, venerate, worship.

deign verb
He doesn't deign to talk to unimportant people like me. condescend, demean yourself, lower yourself, stoop.

deity noun
pagan deities. divinity, god, goddess, godhead, idol, immortal, power, spirit.

dejected adjective
a dejected mood. SEE **depressed**.

delay noun
a delay in proceedings. check, filibuster, hitch, hold-up, moratorium, pause, postponement, set-back, wait.

delay verb
1 *The fog delayed the traffic.* bog down, cause a delay, check, detain, halt, hinder, hold up, impede, keep back, keep waiting, make late, obstruct, retard, set back, slow down, stop.
2 *to delay a meeting.* defer, hold over, postpone, put back, put off, suspend.
3 *You'll lose your chance if you delay.* be late, [*informal*] bide your time, dawdle, [*informal*] dilly-dally, hang back, hesitate, lag, linger, loiter, pause, [*informal*] play for time, procrastinate, stall, [*old-fashioned*] tarry, temporize, wait.

delegate noun
a delegate at a conference. agent, ambassador, envoy, legate, messenger, representative, spokesperson.

delegate verb
They delegated me to speak on their behalf. appoint, assign, authorize, charge, commission, depute, empower, entrust, mandate, nominate.

delete verb
to delete someone from a list. blot out, cancel, cross out, edit out, efface, erase, expunge, obliterate, remove, rub out, strike out, wipe out.

deliberate adjective
1 *deliberate insults.* calculated, conscious, contrived, culpable, intended, intentional, knowing, organized, planned, pre-arranged, premeditated, prepared, studied, wilful.
OPPOSITES: SEE **unintentional**.
2 *deliberate movements.* careful, cautious, circumspect, considered, methodical,

painstaking, slow, thoughtful, unhurried.
OPPOSITES: SEE **hasty**.

delicacy noun
1 *We admired the delicacy of the craftsmanship.* accuracy, care, cleverness, daintiness, exquisiteness, fineness, fragility, intricacy, precision.
2 *She described the unpleasant details with great delicacy.* discrimination, finesse, sensitivity, subtlety, tact.
3 *The table was loaded with delicacies.* rarity, speciality, treat.

delicate adjective
1 *delicate material. delicate plants.* dainty, diaphanous, easily damaged, fine, flimsy, fragile, frail, gauzy, slender, tender.
OPPOSITES: SEE **strong**.
2 *a delicate touch.* gentle, feathery, light, soft.
OPPOSITES: SEE **clumsy**.
3 *delicate workmanship.* accurate, careful, clever, deft, exquisite, intricate, precise, skilled.
OPPOSITES: SEE **crude**.
4 *a delicate flavour. delicate colours.* faint, gentle, mild, muted, pale, slight, subtle.
OPPOSITES: SEE **harsh**.
5 *delicate machinery.* complex, easily broken, fragile, intricate, sensitive.
OPPOSITES: SEE **robust**.
6 *a delicate constitution.* feeble, puny, sickly, unhealthy, weak.
OPPOSITES: SEE **healthy**.
7 *a delicate problem.* awkward, confidential, embarrassing, private, problematical, prudish, ticklish, touchy.
OPPOSITES: SEE **straightforward**.

delicious adjective
delicious food. appetizing, choice, delectable, enjoyable, luscious, [*informal*] mouth-watering, palatable, savoury, [*informal*] scrumptious, succulent, tasty.
OPPOSITES: SEE **unpleasant**.

delight noun
A hot bath is a great delight. bliss, ecstasy, enchantment, enjoyment, [*formal*] felicity, gratification, happiness, joy, paradise, pleasure, rapture.

delight verb
The music delighted us. amuse, bewitch, captivate, charm, cheer, divert, enchant, enrapture, entertain, enthral, entrance, fascinate, gladden, please, ravish, thrill, transport.
OPPOSITES: SEE **dismay** verb.

delightful adjective
SEE **pleasant**.

delinquent noun
a juvenile delinquent. criminal, culprit, defaulter, hooligan, law-breaker, miscreant, offender, [*informal*] tear-away, vandal, wrongdoer, young offender.

delirious adjective
delirious with joy. [*informal*] beside yourself, crazy, demented, deranged, SEE **drunk**, ecstatic, excited, feverish, frantic, frenzied, hysterical, irrational, light-headed, SEE **mad**, wild.
OPPOSITES: SEE **sane, sober**.

deliver verb
1 *to deliver letters or goods to an address.* bear, bring, convey, distribute, give out, hand over, make over, present, supply, take round, transfer, transport, turn over.
2 *to deliver a lecture.* give, make, read, SEE **speak**.
3 *to deliver a blow.* aim, deal, SEE **hit** verb, launch, strike, throw (*a punch*).

delivery noun
1 *a delivery of vegetables.* batch, consignment, distribution, shipment.
2 *the delivery of a message.* conveyance, dispatch, transmission.

deluge noun
We got soaked in the deluge. downpour, flood, inundation, rainfall, rainstorm, rush, spate.

deluge verb
They deluged me with questions. drown, engulf, flood, inundate, overwhelm, submerge, swamp.

delusion noun
a misleading delusion. deception, dream, fantasy, hallucination, illusion, mirage, misconception, mistake.

delve verb
to delve into the past. burrow, dig, explore, investigate, probe, research, search.

demand noun
The manager agreed to the workers' demands. claim, command, desire, expectation, importunity, insistence, need, order, request, requirement, requisition, want.

demand verb
1 *I demanded a refund.* call for, claim, command, exact, expect, insist on, order, request, require, requisition, want.
2 *"What do you want?" she demanded.* SEE **ask**.

demanding adjective
1 *a demanding child.* SEE **importunate**.
2 *a demanding task.* SEE **difficult**.

demean verb
She demeans herself by doing his dirty work. abase, cheapen, debase, degrade, disgrace, humble, humiliate, lower, make (yourself) cheap, [*informal*] put (yourself) down, sacrifice (your) pride, undervalue.

demeanour noun
SEE **attitude, behaviour**.

demented noun
SEE **crazy**.

demise noun
SEE **death**.

democratic adjective
democratic government. chosen, elected,
elective, popular, representative.

demolish verb
to demolish old buildings. break down,
bulldoze, SEE **destroy**, dismantle, flatten,
knock down, level, pull down, raze, tear
down, undo, wreck.
OPPOSITES: SEE **build**.

demon noun
devil, fiend, goblin, imp, spirit.

demonstrable adjective
a demonstrable fact. certain, clear, evident,
incontrovertible, irrefutable, palpable,
positive, provable, undeniable, verifiable.

demonstrate verb
1 *to demonstrate how to do something.*
describe, display, embody, establish,
exemplify, exhibit, explain, expound,
illustrate, indicate, manifest, prove,
represent, show, substantiate, teach, typify.
2 *to demonstrate in the streets.* lobby, march,
parade, picket, protest.

demonstration noun
1 *a demonstration of how to do something.*
confirmation, description, display,
evidence, exhibition, experiment,
expression, illustration, indication,
manifestation, presentation, proof,
representation, show, test, trial.
2 *a political demonstration.* [*informal*] demo,
march, parade, picket, protest, rally, sit-in,
vigil.

demonstrative adjective
a demonstrative person. affectionate,
effusive, emotional, fulsome, loving, open,
uninhibited, unreserved, unrestrained.
OPPOSITES: SEE **reserved**.

demote verb
*The boss demoted her to a less responsible
position.* downgrade, put down, reduce,
relegate.
OPPOSITES: SEE **promote**.

demure adjective
a demure expression. bashful, coy, diffident,
modest, prim, quiet, reserved, reticent,
retiring, sedate, shy, sober, staid.
OPPOSITES: SEE **bumptious**.

den noun
a den in the garden. hide-away, hide-out,
hiding-place, hole, lair, private place,
retreat, sanctuary, secret place, shelter.

denial noun
The jury didn't believe his denial of guilt.
abnegation, disclaimer, negation, rejection,
renunciation, repudiation.
OPPOSITES: SEE **admission**.

denigrate verb
It was unkind to denigrate her achievement.
be contemptuous of, belittle, blacken the
reputation of, criticize, decry, disparage,
impugn, malign, [*informal*] run down, sneer
at, speak slightingly of, traduce, vilify.
OPPOSITES: SEE **praise** verb.

denomination noun
1 *a Christian denomination.* church,
communion, creed, cult, persuasion, sect.

VARIOUS CHRISTIAN DENOMINATIONS:
Anglican, Baptist, Congregational,
Episcopalian, Lutheran, Methodist,
Moravian, Orthodox, Presbyterian,
Protestant, Revivalist, Roman Catholic,
United Reformed.
COMPARE: ecumenical.

2 *I need coins of the right denomination for
the slot machine.* category, class,
designation, size, type, value.

denote verb
What does this word denote? be the sign for,
express, indicate, SEE **mean** verb, signify,
stand for.
COMPARE: connote.

denounce verb
to denounce a traitor. to denounce wickedness.
accuse, attack verbally, blame, brand,
censure, complain about, condemn, declaim
against, decry, fulminate against,
[*informal*] hold forth against, inform
against, inveigh against, report, reveal,
stigmatize, [*informal*] tell of.
OPPOSITES: SEE **praise** verb.

dense adjective
1 *dense fog. a dense liquid.* concentrated,
heavy, opaque, thick, viscous.
OPPOSITES: SEE **thin** adjective.
2 *a dense crowd. dense undergrowth.* compact,
close, impenetrable, [*informal*] jam-packed,
lush, massed, packed, solid.
OPPOSITES: SEE **sparse**.
3 *a dense pupil.* crass, dim, dull, foolish,
obtuse, slow, stupid, [*informal*] thick,
unintelligent.
OPPOSITES: SEE **clever**.

dent noun
a dent in a flat surface. concavity,
depression, dimple, dint, dip, hollow,
indentation, pit.

dent verb
I dented the car. bend, buckle, crumple, knock in, push in.

denude verb
to denude a hillside of vegetation. bare, defoliate, deforest, expose, make naked, remove, strip, unclothe, uncover.
OPPOSITES: SEE **clothe**.

denunciation noun
We were amazed to hear the witness's denunciation of the accused. accusation, censure, condemnation, denouncing, incrimination, invective, stigmatization, verbal attack.
OPPOSITES: SEE **praise** noun.

deny verb
1 *to deny an accusation.* contradict, disagree with, disclaim, disown, dispute, oppose, rebuff, refute, reject, repudiate.
OPPOSITES: SEE **acknowledge**.
2 *Her indulgent parents don't deny her anything.* begrudge, deprive of, refuse.
OPPOSITES: SEE **give**.

depart verb
1 *to depart on a journey.* begin a journey, [*informal*] clear off, decamp, disappear, embark, emigrate, escape, exit, go away, leave, make off, [*informal*] make tracks, migrate, [*informal*] push off, quit, retire, retreat, [*slang*] scram, set off, set out, start, take your leave, vanish, withdraw.
OPPOSITES: SEE **arrive**.
2 *to depart from your script.* deviate, digress, diverge, stray from.
OPPOSITE: stick to.

department noun
1 *a government department. a department in a large shop.* branch, division, office, part, section, sector, subdivision, unit.
2 [*informal*] *Ask someone else—it's not my department.* area, domain, field, function, job, line, province, responsibility, specialism, sphere.

departure noun
disappearance, embarkation, escape, exit, exodus, going, retirement, retreat, withdrawal.
OPPOSITES: SEE **arrival**.

depend verb
to depend on 1 *My success will depend on good luck.* be dependent on [SEE **dependent**], hinge on, rest on. 2 *I depend on you to be good.* bank on, count on, need, rely on, trust.

dependable adjective
a dependable worker. conscientious, consistent, faithful, honest, regular,

reliable, safe, sound, steady, true, trustworthy, unfailing.
OPPOSITES: SEE **unreliable**.

dependent adjective
[Do not confuse with noun *dependant = a person who depends on your support.*]
dependent on 1 *Everything is dependent on the weather.* conditional on, connected with, controlled by, determined by, liable to, relative to, subject to, vulnerable to.
2 *dependent on drugs.* addicted to, enslaved by, [*informal*] hooked on, reliant on.

depict verb
to depict a scene. delineate, describe, draw, illustrate, narrate, outline, paint, picture, portray, represent, reproduce, show, sketch.

deplete verb
The holiday has depleted our savings. consume, cut, decrease, drain, lessen, reduce, use up.
OPPOSITES: SEE **increase** verb.

deplorable adjective
deplorable behaviour. SEE **bad**, blameworthy, discreditable, disgraceful, disreputable, lamentable, regrettable, reprehensible, scandalous, shameful, shocking, unfortunate, unworthy.
OPPOSITES: SEE **praiseworthy**.

deplore verb
1 *We deplore suffering.* grieve for, lament, mourn, regret.
2 *We deplore vandalism.* SEE **condemn**, deprecate, disapprove of.

deploy verb
The boss deployed the workers effectively. arrange, bring into action, distribute, manage, position, use systematically, utilize.

deport verb
They used to deport people for minor crimes. banish, exile, expatriate, expel, remove, send abroad.

depose verb
to depose a monarch. demote, dethrone, dismiss, displace, get rid of, oust, remove, [*informal*] topple.

deposit noun
1 *a deposit on a car.* down-payment, initial payment, part-payment, payment, retainer, security, stake.
2 *a deposit in the bottom of a container.* accumulation, dregs, layer, lees, precipitate, sediment, silt, sludge.

deposit verb
1 *Deposit the dirty plates by the hatch.* [*informal*] dump, lay down, leave, [*informal*] park, place, put down, set down.
2 *I deposited my money in the bank.* bank, pay in, save.

3 *The flood deposited a layer of mud.* precipitate.

depot noun
1 *a stores depot.* arsenal [= *arms depot*], base, cache, depository, dump, hoard, store, storehouse.
2 *a bus depot.* garage, headquarters, station, terminus.

depraved adjective
a depraved person. depraved behaviour. SEE **bad**, corrupt, degenerate, dissolute, evil, immoral, lewd, perverted, profligate, reprobate, sinful, vicious, vile, wicked.
OPPOSITES: SEE **moral** adjective.

depreciate verb
[Do not confuse with *depreciate* = *deplore*.]
The value of antiques is not likely to depreciate. become less, decrease, deflate, drop, fall, go down, lessen, lower, reduce, slump, weaken.
OPPOSITES: SEE **appreciate**.

depress verb
1 *The weather depressed us.* discourage, dishearten, dispirit, enervate, grieve, lower the spirits of, make sad [SEE **sad**], sadden, tire, upset, weary.
OPPOSITES: SEE **cheer** verb.
2 *Bad news depresses the stock market.* bring down, deflate, make less active, push down, undermine, weaken.
OPPOSITES: SEE **boost** verb.

depressed adjective
broken-hearted, crestfallen, dejected, desolate, despairing, despondent, disappointed, disconsolate, discouraged, disheartened, dismal, dismayed, dispirited, doleful, [*informal*] down, downcast, down-hearted, friendless, gloomy, glum, hopeless, [*informal*] in the doldrums, [*informal*] in the dumps, languishing, [*informal*] low, melancholy, miserable, morose, pessimistic, sad, suicidal, unhappy, weary, woebegone, wretched.
OPPOSITES: SEE **cheerful**.

depressing adjective
SEE **sad**.

depression noun
1 *a mood of depression.* [*informal*] blues, dejection, desolation, despair, despondency, doldrums (*in the doldrums*), gloom, glumness, heaviness, hopelessness, low spirits, melancholy, misery, pessimism, sadness, unhappiness, weariness.
OPPOSITES: SEE **cheerfulness.**.
2 *an economic depression.* decline, hard times, recession, slump.
OPPOSITES: SEE **boom** noun.
3 *a meteorological depression.* area of low pressure, cyclone, low.
OPPOSITES: anticyclone.

4 *a depression in the ground.* cavity, concavity, dent, dimple, dip, excavation, hole, hollow, indentation, pit, rut, sunken area.

deprive verb
to deprive of deny, dispossess of, prevent from using, refuse, rob of, starve of, strip of, take away.

deprived adjective
deprived families. disadvantaged, needy, SEE **poor**.

deputize verb
to deputize for *I deputized for the manager when she was ill.* act as deputy for [SEE **deputy**], cover for, do the job of, replace, represent, stand in for, substitute for, take over from, understudy [= *deputize for an actor*].

deputy noun
The mayor was ill, so his deputy conducted the ceremony. agent, assistant, delegate, [*informal*] fill-in, locum, proxy, relief, representative, reserve, replacement, second-in-command, [*informal*] stand-in, substitute, supply, surrogate, understudy, [*informal*] vice [and words with prefix *vice-*, e.g. *vice-captain*, etc.].

derailment noun
SEE **accident**.

deranged adjective SEE **mad**.

derelict adjective
derelict buildings. abandoned, broken down, decrepit, deserted, desolate, dilapidated, forlorn, forsaken, neglected, ruined, tumbledown.

derivation noun
SEE **origin**.

derive verb
1 *I derive pleasure from my garden.* acquire, gain, get, obtain, receive.
2 *He derived his ideas from a text book.* borrow, collect, crib, draw, glean, [*informal*] lift, pick up, procure, take.

derogatory adjective
SEE **uncomplimentary**.

descend verb
1 *to descend a hill. to descend by parachute.* come down, climb down, drop down, fall down [SEE **fall** verb], go down, move down, sink down.
2 *The hill descends gradually.* dip, drop, fall, incline, slant, slope.
OPPOSITES: SEE **ascend**.

descendant noun
a descendant of a Victorian scientist. heir, successor.
descendants children, family, issue, line,

lineage, offspring, posterity, progeny, [*formal*] scion.
OPPOSITES: SEE **ancestor**.

descent noun
1 *a steep descent*. declivity, dip, drop, fall, incline, slant, slope, way down.
OPPOSITES: SEE **ascent**.
2 *aristocratic descent*. ancestry, background, blood, derivation, extraction, family, genealogy, heredity, lineage, origin, parentage, pedigree, stock, strain.

describe verb
1 *An eyewitness described what happened*. delineate, depict, detail, explain, express, narrate, outline, recount, relate, report, sketch, tell about.
2 *The novelist describes her as a tyrant*. characterize, portray, present, represent, speak of.

description noun
a vivid description. account, characterization, commentary, delineation, depiction, explanation, narration, outline, portrait, portrayal, report, representation, sketch, story, word-picture.

descriptive adjective
descriptive writing. colourful, detailed, explanatory, expressive, graphic, illustrative, pictorial, vivid.

desecrate verb
to desecrate a holy place. abuse, contaminate, debase, defile, pollute, profane, treat blasphemously or disrespectfully or irreverently, vandalize, violate.

desert adjective
1 *desert conditions*. arid, barren, dry, infertile, sterile, uncultivated, waterless, wild.
OPPOSITES: SEE **fertile**.
2 *a desert island*. desolate, isolated, lonely, solitary, unfrequented, uninhabited.

desert verb
1 *to desert your friends*. abandon, betray, forsake, give up, jilt, [*informal*] leave in the lurch, maroon (*maroon someone on an island*), [*informal*] rat on, renounce, strand, [*informal*] walk out on, [*informal*] wash your hands of.
2 *to desert a sinking ship*. abandon, leave, quit, vacate.
3 *The soldiers deserted*. abscond, decamp, defect, go absent, run away.

deserter noun
a deserter from the army. a deserter from a cause. absentee, apostate, backslider, betrayer, defector, disloyal person [SEE **disloyal**], fugitive, outlaw, renegade, runaway, traitor, truant (*from school*), turncoat.

deserve verb
to deserve a reward. be good enough for, be worthy of, earn, justify, merit, rate, warrant.

deserving adjective
a deserving winner. a deserving cause. admirable, commendable, creditable, good, laudable, meritorious, praiseworthy, worth supporting, worthy.
OPPOSITES: SEE **unworthy**.

design noun
1 *a design for a new car*. blueprint, drawing, model, pattern, plan, prototype, sketch.
2 *an old design*. model, style, type, version.
3 *a jazzy design of dots and lines*. arrangement, composition, configuration, pattern.
4 *I wandered about without any design*. aim, end, goal, intention, object, objective, purpose, scheme.

design verb
Architects design buildings. We designed this book to help you find words. conceive, construct, contrive, create, devise, draft, draw, draw up, fashion, intend, invent, make, plan, plot, project, propose, scheme, sketch.

designer noun
author, contriver, creator, deviser, inventor, originator.

desirable adjective
SEE **attractive**, **sexy**.

desire noun
1 *a desire to do good*. ache, ambition, craving, fancy, hankering, [*informal*] itch, longing, urge, want, wish, yearning, [*informal*] yen.
2 *desire for food or drink*. appetite, gluttony, hunger, thirst.
3 *desire for money*. avarice, covetousness, cupidity, greed, miserliness, rapacity.
4 *sexual desire*. ardour, lasciviousness, libido, love, lust, passion.

desire verb
What do you most desire? ache for, covet, crave, fancy, hanker after, [*informal*] have a yen for, hunger for, [*informal*] itch for, like, long for, lust after, need, pine for, prefer, [*informal*] set your heart on, thirst for, want, wish for, yearn for.

desolate adjective
1 *a desolate place*. abandoned, bare, barren, benighted, bleak, cheerless, depressing, deserted, dismal, dreary, empty, forsaken, gloomy, [*informal*] god-forsaken, inhospitable, isolated, lonely, remote, unfrequented, uninhabited, wild, windswept.
OPPOSITES: SEE **idyllic**.
2 *He was desolate when his dog died*. bereft,

companionless, dejected, SEE **depressed**, disconsolate, distressed, forlorn, forsaken, inconsolable, lonely, melancholy, neglected, sad, solitary, wretched.
OPPOSITES: SEE **cheerful**.

despair noun
a state of despair. anguish, dejection, depression, desperation, despondency, gloom, hopelessness, melancholy, SEE **misery**, pessimism, wretchedness.
OPPOSITES: SEE **hope** noun.

despair verb
give up, [*informal*] lose heart, lose hope.
OPPOSITES: SEE **hope** verb.

desperate adjective
1 *The starving refugees were desperate.* beyond hope, despairing, hopeless, inconsolable.
2 *a desperate situation.* acute, bad, critical, drastic, grave, irretrievable, serious, severe, urgent.
3 *desperate criminals.* dangerous, impetuous, reckless, violent, wild.

despise verb
be contemptuous of, condemn, deride, disapprove of, disdain, feel contempt for, SEE **hate** verb, have a low opinion of, look down on, [*informal*] put down, scorn, sneer at, spurn, undervalue.
OPPOSITES: SEE **admire**.

destination noun
the destination of a journey. goal, objective, purpose, target, terminus.

destined adjective
1 *My plans were destined to fail.* bound, certain, doomed, fated.
2 *I foresaw the destined outcome.* inescapable, inevitable, intended, ordained, predestined, predetermined, preordained, unavoidable.

destiny noun
chance, doom, fate, fortune, karma, kismet, lot (*Accept your lot*), luck, providence.

destitute adjective
destitute beggars. bankrupt, deprived, down-and-out, homeless, impecunious, impoverished, indigent, insolvent, needy, penniless, SEE **poor**, poverty-stricken, [*informal*] skint.
OPPOSITES: SEE **wealthy**.

destroy verb
abolish, annihilate, blast, break down, crush, decimate [see note under *decimate*], SEE **defeat** verb, demolish, devastate, devour, dismantle, eliminate, SEE **end** verb, eradicate, erase, exterminate, extinguish, extirpate, finish off, flatten, get rid of, SEE **kill**, knock down, lay waste (to), level, liquidate, make useless, pull down, put out of existence, raze, ruin, sabotage, scuttle,

shatter, smash, stamp out, undo, uproot, vaporize, wipe out, wreck.
OPPOSITES: SEE **create**.

destruction noun
We deplore the destruction of wildlife. annihilation, damage, decimation [see note under *decimate*], demolition, depredation, devastation, elimination, end, eradication, erasure, extermination, extinction, extirpation, havoc, holocaust, SEE **killing**, liquidation, overthrow, pulling down, ruin, shattering, smashing, undoing, uprooting, wiping out, wrecking.
OPPOSITES: SEE **conservation**, **creation**.

destructive adjective
a destructive storm. destructive criticism. adverse, antagonistic, baleful, baneful, calamitous, catastrophic, damaging, dangerous, deadly, deleterious, detrimental, devastating, disastrous, fatal, harmful, injurious, internecine, lethal, malignant, negative, pernicious, pestilential, ruinous, violent.
OPPOSITES: SEE **constructive**.

detach verb
to detach one thing from another. cut loose, cut off, disconnect, disengage, disentangle, divide, free, isolate, part, release, remove, segregate, separate, sever, take off, tear off, uncouple, undo, unfasten, unfix, unhitch.
OPPOSITES: SEE **attach**.

detached adjective
1 *a detached house.* free-standing, separate, unconnected.
COMPARE: semi-detached, terraced.
2 *a detached point of view.* aloof, cool, disinterested, dispassionate, impartial, impassive, independent, neutral, non-partisan, non-party, objective, unbiased, uncommitted, unconcerned, unemotional, uninvolved, unprejudiced.
OPPOSITES: SEE **committed**.

detail noun
Her account was accurate in every detail. aspect, circumstance, complexity, complication, fact, factor, feature, ingredient, intricacy, item, [*plural*] minutiae, nicety, particular, point, refinement, respect, specific.

detailed adjective
a detailed description. complete, complex, [*uncomplimentary*] fussy, giving all details, [*uncomplimentary*] hair-splitting, intricate, minute, specific.
OPPOSITES: SEE **general**.

detain verb
1 *The police detained the suspect.* arrest, capture, confine, gaol, hold, hold in custody, imprison, intern, restrain.
OPPOSITES: SEE **release** verb.

2 *What detained you? Who detained you?*
buttonhole, delay, hinder, hold up, impede,
keep, keep waiting, prevent, retard, slow,
stop, waylay.

detect verb
to detect a fault. become aware of, diagnose,
discern, discover, expose, feel, [*informal*]
ferret out, find, hear, identify, note, notice,
observe, perceive, recognize, reveal, scent,
see, sense, sight, smell, sniff out, spot, spy,
taste, track down, uncover, unearth,
unmask.

detective noun
investigator, SEE **policeman**, [*informal*]
private eye, sleuth.

detention noun
SEE **imprisonment**.

deter verb
How can we deter the wretched starlings?
check, daunt, discourage, dismay, dissuade,
frighten off, hinder, impede, intimidate,
obstruct, prevent, put off, repel, send away,
stop, [*informal*] turn off, warn off.
OPPOSITES: SEE **encourage**.

deteriorate verb
*His work deteriorated. The buildings
deteriorated.* crumble, decay, decline,
degenerate, depreciate, disintegrate, fall off,
get worse, [*informal*] go downhill, lapse,
relapse, slip, weaken, worsen.
OPPOSITES: SEE **improve**.

determination noun
Marathon runners show great determination.
[*informal*] backbone, commitment, courage,
dedication, doggedness, drive, firmness,
fortitude, [*informal*] grit, [*informal*] guts,
perseverance, persistence, pertinacity,
resolution, resolve, single-mindedness,
spirit, steadfastness, [*uncomplimentary*]
stubbornness, tenacity, will-power.

determined adjective
1 *He's determined he will succeed.* adamant,
bent (*on succeeding*), certain, convinced,
decided, definite, firm, insistent, intent (*on
succeeding*), resolved, sure.
OPPOSITES: SEE **doubtful**.
2 *a determined woman.* assertive, decisive,
dogged, [*uncomplimentary*] obstinate,
persistent, pertinacious, purposeful,
resolute, single-minded, steadfast, strong-
minded, strong-willed, [*uncomplimentary*]
stubborn, sworn (*sworn enemies*), tenacious,
tough, unwavering.
OPPOSITES: SEE **irresolute**.

deterrent noun
*I put a net over my strawberries as a deterrent
to the birds.* barrier, caution, check, curb,
difficulty, discouragement, disincentive,

dissuasion, hindrance, impediment,
obstacle, restraint, threat, [*informal*] turn-
off, warning.
OPPOSITES: SEE **encouragement**.

detest verb SEE **hate** verb.

detour noun
I wasted time making a detour. deviation,
diversion, indirect route, roundabout route.

detrimental adjective
SEE **harmful**.

devastate verb
1 *A hurricane devastated the town.* damage
severely, demolish, destroy, flatten, lay
waste, level, overwhelm, ravage, raze, ruin,
wreck.
2 [*informal*] *We were devastated by the bad
news.* SEE **dismay** verb.

develop verb
1 *People develop. Plans develop.* advance, age,
evolve, get better, grow, flourish, improve,
mature, move on, progress, ripen.
OPPOSITES: SEE **regress**.
2 *A storm developed.* arise, [*informal*] blow
up, come into existence, [*informal*] get up,
work up.
3 *She developed a cold. He developed a posh
accent.* acquire, contract, cultivate, evolve,
foster, get, pick up.
4 *Develop your ideas.* amplify, augment,
elaborate, enlarge on.
5 *Our business will develop next year.* branch
out, build up, diversify, enlarge, expand,
extend, increase, swell.

development noun
1 *the development of science. the development
of trade.* advance, betterment, enlargement,
evolution, expansion, extension, [*informal*]
forward march, furtherance, growth,
improvement, increase, progress,
promotion, regeneration, reinforcement,
spread.
2 [*informal*] *We'll let you know of any
developments.* change, gain, happening,
incident, occurrence, outcome, result,
upshot.
3 *The land is earmarked for industrial
development.* building, conversion,
exploitation, use.

deviate verb
to deviate from the usual path. depart,
digress, diverge, err, go astray, go round,
make a detour, stray, swerve, turn aside,
vary, veer, wander.

device noun
1 *a clever device for opening wine-bottles.*
apparatus, appliance, contraption,
contrivance, gadget, implement, instrument,
invention, machine, tool, utensil.
2 *a device to distract our attention.* dodge,

expedient, gambit, gimmick, manœuvre, plan, ploy, ruse, scheme, stratagem, stunt, tactic, trick, wile.
3 *a heraldic device.* badge, crest, design, figure, logo, motif, shield, sign, symbol, token.

devilish adjective
demoniac, demoniacal, diabolic, diabolical, SEE **evil** adjective, fiendish, hellish, infernal, satanic, wicked.
OPPOSITES: SEE **angelic**.

devious adjective
1 *a devious route.* circuitous, crooked, deviating, indirect, periphrastic, rambling, roundabout, tortuous, wandering, winding.
OPPOSITES: SEE **direct** adjective.
2 *a devious person. a devious explanation.* calculating, cunning, deceitful, SEE **dishonest**, evasive, insincere, misleading, scheming, [*informal*] slippery (*a slippery customer*), sly, sneaky, treacherous, underhand, wily.
OPPOSITES: SEE **straightforward**.

devise verb
to devise a plan. conceive, concoct, contrive, design, engineer, form, formulate, imagine, invent, make up, plan, plot, prepare, project, scheme, think out, think up.

devoted adjective
SEE **loyal**.

devotion noun
SEE **love** noun, **piety**.

diabolical adjective
SEE **devilish**.

diagnose verb
to diagnose an illness. detect, determine, distinguish, find, identify, isolate, name, pinpoint, recognize.

diagnosis noun
What's the doctor's diagnosis? analysis, conclusion, explanation, identification, interpretation, opinion, pronouncement, verdict.

diagram noun
an explanatory diagram. chart, drawing, figure, flow-chart, graph, illustration, outline, picture, plan, representation, sketch, table.

dial noun
the dials on a dashboard. clock, digital display, face, instrument, pointer, speedometer.

dial verb
to dial a number. call, phone, ring, telephone.

dialect noun
a London dialect. a local dialect. accent, brogue, idiom, jargon, language, patois, pronunciation, register, speech, tongue, vernacular.

dialogue noun
a dialogue between two people. [*informal*] chat, [*informal*] chinwag, [*formal*] colloquy, conversation, debate, discourse, discussion, duologue, exchange, interchange, [*old-fashioned*] intercourse, [*formal*] oral communication, talk.

diaphanous adjective
diaphanous fabric. airy, SEE **delicate**, filmy, fine, gauzy, light, see-through, sheer, thin, translucent.

diary noun
a daily diary of events. appointment book, chronicle, engagement book, journal, log, record.

dictate verb
1 *I dictated while he wrote it down.* read aloud, speak slowly.
2 *Should parents dictate what their children do?* command, decree, direct, enforce, give orders, impose, [*informal*] lay down the law, make the rules, ordain, order, prescribe.

dictator noun
autocrat, [*informal*] Big Brother, despot, SEE **ruler**, tyrant.

dictatorial adjective
a dictatorial ruler. absolute, authoritarian, autocratic, [*informal*] bossy, despotic, dogmatic, dominant, domineering, illiberal, imperious, intolerant, oppressive, overbearing, repressive, totalitarian, tyrannical, undemocratic.
OPPOSITES: SEE **democratic**.

dictionary noun
VARIOUS WORD-LISTS: concordance, glossary, lexicon, thesaurus, vocabulary, wordbook.

die verb
1 *All mortal creatures die.* [*informal*] bite the dust, [*informal*] breathe your last, cease to exist, come to the end, [*formal*] decease, depart, [*formal*] expire, fall (*to fall in war*), [*informal*] give up the ghost, pass away, [*slang*] kick the bucket, pass away, [*informal*] peg out, perish, [*slang*] snuff it, starve [= *die of hunger*].
2 *The flowers died.* droop, fade, wilt, wither.
3 *The flames died.* become less, decline, decrease, disappear, dwindle, ebb, end, fail, fizzle out, go out, languish, lessen, peter out, stop, subside, vanish, wane, weaken.

diet noun
1 *a healthy diet.* fare, SEE **food**, nourishment, nutriment, nutrition.
2 *a slimmer's diet.* abstinence, fast, rations, self-denial.

differ verb
1 *My feelings differ from yours.* be different, contrast (with), deviate, diverge, vary.
OPPOSITES: SEE **conform**.

2 *We differed about where to go.* argue, be at odds with each other, clash, conflict, contradict each other, disagree, dispute, dissent, fall out, oppose each other, quarrel, take issue with each other.
OPPOSITES: SEE **agree**.

difference noun
1 *a difference in price. a difference in meaning.* comparison, contrast, differential, differentiation, discrepancy, disparity, dissimilarity, distinction, diversity, incompatibility, incongruity, inconsistency, nuance, unlikeness, variety.
OPPOSITES: SEE **similarity**.
2 *a difference in our plans.* alteration, change, development, deviation, modification, variation.
3 *a difference of opinion.* argument, clash, conflict, controversy, debate, disagreement, disharmony, dispute, dissent, quarrel, strife, tiff, wrangle.
OPPOSITES: SEE **agreement**.

different adjective
1 *different colours. different opinions.* assorted, clashing, conflicting, contradictory, contrasting, deviating, discordant, discrepant, disparate, dissimilar, distinguishable, divergent, diverse, heterogeneous, ill-matched, incompatible, inconsistent, miscellaneous, mixed, multifarious, numerous, opposed, opposite, [*informal*] poles apart, several, sundry, unlike, varied, various.
OPPOSITES: SEE **identical**, **similar**.
2 *I'm always getting different ideas.* altered, changed, changing, fresh, new, original, revolutionary.
3 *It's different to have jam with fried potatoes.* abnormal, anomalous, atypical, bizarre, eccentric, extraordinary, irregular, strange, uncommon, unconventional, unorthodox, unusual.
OPPOSITES: SEE **conventional**.
4 *Everyone's handwriting is different.* distinct, distinctive, individual, particular, peculiar, personal, separate, singular, special, specific, unique.

difficult adjective
1 *a difficult problem.* abstruse, advanced, baffling, complex, complicated, deep, [*informal*] dodgy, enigmatic, hard, intractable, intricate, involved, [*informal*] knotty, [*informal*] nasty, obscure, perplexing, problematical, thorny, ticklish, tricky.
2 *a difficult climb. a difficult task.* arduous, awkward, burdensome, challenging, demanding, exacting, exhausting, formidable, gruelling, heavy, herculean, [*informal*] killing, laborious, onerous, punishing, rigorous, severe, strenuous,

taxing, tough, uphill.
OPPOSITES: SEE **easy**.

difficulty noun
a difficulty to overcome. adversity, challenge, complication, dilemma, embarrassment, enigma, [*informal*] fix (*I'm in a bit of a fix*), [*informal*] hang-up, hardship, [*informal*] hiccup, hindrance, hurdle, impediment, jam, obstacle, perplexity, plight, predicament, problem, puzzle, quandary, snag, [*informal*] spot (*I'm in a bit of spot*), [*informal*] stumbling-block, tribulation, trouble, [*informal*] vexed question.

diffident adjective
a diffident manner. backward, bashful, coy, distrustful, doubtful, fearful, hesitant, hesitating, inhibited, insecure, introvert, meek, modest, nervous, private, reluctant, reserved, retiring, self-effacing, sheepish, shrinking, shy, tentative, timid, timorous, unadventurous, unassuming, underconfident, unsure, withdrawn.
OPPOSITES: SEE **confident**.

diffuse adjective
a diffuse piece of writing. digressive, discursive, long-winded, loose, meandering, prolix, rambling, vague, verbose, [*informal*] waffly, wandering, wordy.
OPPOSITES: SEE **concise**.

dig verb
1 *to dig a hole.* burrow, delve, excavate, gouge out, hollow out, mine, quarry, scoop, tunnel.
2 *to dig the garden.* cultivate, fork over, [*informal*] grub up, till, trench, turn over.
3 *to dig out information.* find, probe, research, search.
4 *to dig someone in the back.* jab, nudge, poke, prod, punch, shove, thrust.
to dig up disinter, exhume.

digest verb
1 *to digest food.* absorb, assimilate, dissolve, SEE **eat**, [*formal*] ingest, process, utilize.
2 *to digest information.* consider, ponder, study, take in, understand.

digit noun
1 *Add up the digits.* figure, integer, number, numeral.
2 *We have five digits on each hand and foot.* finger, toe.

dignified adjective
dignified behaviour. a dignified ceremony. becoming, calm, decorous, elegant, formal, grave, imposing, impressive, majestic, noble, proper, refined, sedate, serious, sober, solemn, stately, tasteful, upright.
OPPOSITES: SEE **undignified**.

dignity noun
They behaved with dignity. calmness, decorum, eminence, formality, glory,

grandeur, gravity, greatness, honour, importance, majesty, nobility, pride, propriety, respectability, seriousness, solemnity, stateliness.

digress verb
to digress from your subject. depart, deviate, diverge, go off at a tangent, ramble, stray, veer, wander.

dilapidated adjective
a dilapidated building. broken down, crumbling, decayed, decrepit, derelict, falling down, in disrepair, in ruins, neglected, ramshackle, rickety, ruined, [*informal*] run-down, tottering, tumbledown, uncared for.
OPPOSITES: SEE **well-maintained**.

dilemma noun
caught in a dilemma. [*informal*] catch-22, difficulty, doubt, embarrassment, [*informal*] fix, [*informal*] jam, [*informal*] mess, [*informal*] pickle, plight, predicament, problem, quandary, [*informal*] spot (*I'm in a bit of a spot*).

diligent adjective
a diligent worker. assiduous, busy, careful, conscientious, devoted, earnest, energetic, hardworking, indefatigable, industrious, painstaking, persevering, persistent, pertinacious, scrupulous, sedulous, studious, thorough, tireless.
OPPOSITES: SEE **lazy**.

dilute verb
You dilute orange squash with water. adulterate, make less concentrated, reduce the strength of, thin, water down, weaken.
OPPOSITES: SEE **concentrate**.

dim adjective
1 *a dim outline in the mist.* bleary, blurred, cloudy, dark, dingy, dull, faint, foggy, fuzzy, gloomy, grey, hazy, indistinct, misty, murky, obscure, pale, shadowy, unclear, vague.
OPPOSITES: SEE **bright, clear** adjective.
2 [*informal*] *You are dim if you can't understand that!* SEE **stupid**.

dim verb
1 *Cloud dimmed the sky.* blacken, cloud, darken, dull, make dim, mask, obscure.
2 *The lights dimmed.* become dim, fade, go out, lose brightness, lower.
OPPOSITES: SEE **brighten**.

diminish verb
Our enthusiasm diminished as time went on. become less, contract, decline, decrease, depreciate, dwindle, lessen, peter out, reduce, shrink, shrivel, subside, wane.
OPPOSITES: SEE **increase**.

din noun
a deafening din. clamour, clatter, commotion, crash, hubbub, hullabaloo, noise, outcry, pandemonium, racket, row, rumpus, shouting, tumult, uproar.

dingy adjective
dingy colours. a dingy room. colourless, dark, depressing, dim, dirty, discoloured, dismal, drab, dreary, dull, faded, gloomy, grimy, murky, old, seedy, shabby, soiled, worn.
OPPOSITES: SEE **bright**.

dining-room noun
cafeteria, carvery, refectory, restaurant.

dinner noun
banquet, feast, SEE **meal**.

dip noun
1 *a dip in the sea.* bathe, dive, immersion, plunge, soaking, swim.
2 *a dip in the ground.* concavity, declivity, dent, depression, fall, hole, hollow, incline, slope.

dip verb
1 *to dip something in liquid.* douse, drop, duck, dunk, immerse, lower, plunge, submerge.
2 *to dip down.* descend, dive, go down, slope down, slump, subside.

diplomacy noun
She showed great diplomacy in ending the dispute. delicacy, discretion, finesse, skill, tact, tactfulness.

diplomat noun
1 ambassador, consul, government representative, negotiator, politician.
2 [used loosely] *Being a diplomat, she smoothed over their differences.* diplomatic person [SEE **diplomatic**], peacemaker, tactician.

diplomatic adjective
a diplomatic reply. careful, considerate, delicate, discreet, judicious, polite, politic, prudent, sensitive, subtle, tactful, thoughtful, understanding.
OPPOSITES: SEE **tactless**.

dire adjective
1 *a dire calamity.* SEE **dreadful**.
2 *a dire warning.* SEE **ominous**.
3 *dire need.* SEE **urgent**.

direct adjective
1 *a direct route.* nonstop, shortest, straight, undeviating, unswerving.
OPPOSITES: SEE **indirect**.
2 *a direct answer.* blunt, candid, explicit, frank, honest, outspoken, plain, point-blank, sincere, straightforward, unambiguous, uncomplicated, unequivocal.
OPPOSITES: SEE **evasive**.
3 *direct opposites. a direct contradiction.*

absolute, categorical, complete, decided, diametrical, exact, head-on, [*informal*] out-and-out, utter.

direct verb
1 *to direct someone to the station.* guide, indicate the way, point, route, show the way, tell the way.
2 *to direct a letter.* address.
3 *to direct an attack on someone.* aim, point, target, train (on), turn (on).
4 *to direct a project.* administer, be in charge of, command, conduct (*an orchestra*), control, govern, handle, lead, manage, mastermind, oversee, produce (*a play*), regulate, rule, run, stage-manage, superintend, supervise, take charge of.
5 *He directed us to begin.* advise, bid, charge, command, enjoin, instruct, order, tell.

direction noun
1 *Which direction did he take?* aim approach, bearing (*compass-bearing*), course, orientation, path, point of the compass, road, route, tack, track, way.
2 [*usually plural*] *The kit comes with directions for assembly.* guidance, guidelines, instructions, orders, plans.

director noun
SEE **chief** noun.

directory noun
a telephone directory. catalogue, index, list, register.

dirt noun
Clean up the dirt. dust, filth, garbage, grime, impurity, mess, mire, muck, pollution, refuse, rubbish, slime, sludge, smut, stain, tarnish.

dirty adjective
1 *a dirty room. dirty clothes.* black, dingy, dusty, filthy, foul, grimy, grubby, marked, messy, mucky, muddy, nasty, scruffy, shabby, smeary, soiled, sooty, sordid, squalid, stained, sullied, tarnished, travel-stained, uncared for, unclean, unwashed.
OPPOSITES: SEE **clean** adjective.
2 *dirty water.* cloudy, impure, muddy, murky, polluted, untreated.
OPPOSITES: SEE **pure.**
3 *dirty tactics.* SEE **corrupt** adjective. dishonest, illegal, [*informal*] low-down, mean, rough, treacherous, unfair, ungentlemanly, unsporting.
OPPOSITES: SEE **honest, sporting.**

dirty verb
Try not to dirty your clothes. SEE **defile,** foul, make dirty [SEE **dirty** adjective], mark, [*informal*] mess up, smear, smudge, soil, spatter, spot, stain, streak, sully, tarnish.
OPPOSITES: SEE **clean** verb.

disability noun
a physical disability. affliction, complaint, disablement, handicap, impairment, incapacity, infirmity, weakness.

disable verb
1 *The accident temporarily disabled her.* cripple, debilitate, enfeeble, [*informal*] hamstring, handicap, immobilize, impair, incapacitate, injure, lame, maim, paralyse, weaken.
2 *The storm disabled the generators.* damage, make useless, put out of action, stop working.

disabled adjective
a disabled person. bedridden, crippled, deformed, handicapped, having a disability, immobilized, incapacitated, infirm, lame, limbless, maimed, mutilated, paralysed, paraplegic, weak, weakened.
disabled person amputee, cripple, invalid, paraplegic.

disadvantage noun
It's a disadvantage to be small if you play basketball. drawback, handicap, hardship, hindrance, impediment, inconvenience, liability, [*informal*] minus, nuisance, privation, snag, trouble, weakness.

disagree verb
argue, bicker, clash, conflict, differ, dissent, fall out, quarrel, squabble, wrangle.
OPPOSITES: SEE **agree.**
to disagree with *He disagrees with everything I say.* argue with, be at variance with, contradict, counter, deviate from, dissent from, object to, oppose, take issue with.

disagreeable adjective
SEE **unpleasant.**

disagreement noun
There was a disagreement between them. altercation, argument, clash, conflict, controversy, debate, difference of opinion, disharmony, dispute, dissension, dissent, divergence, inconsistency, lack of sympathy, misunderstanding, opposition, quarrel, squabble, [*informal*] tiff, variance, wrangle.
OPPOSITES: SEE **agreement.**

disappear verb
1 *The fog disappeared.* become invisible [SEE **invisible**], cease to exist, clear, disperse, dissolve, dwindle, ebb, evaporate, fade, melt away, recede, vanish, wane.
2 *He disappeared round the corner.* depart, escape, flee, fly, go, pass, run away, walk away, withdraw.
OPPOSITES: SEE **appear.**

disappoint verb
The weather disappointed us. be worse than expected, chagrin, [*informal*] dash (a person's) hopes, disillusion, dismay,

displease, fail to satisfy, frustrate, [*informal*] let down, upset, thwart, vex.
OPPOSITES: SEE **delight** verb, **satisfy**.

disappointed adjective
a disappointed man. crestfallen, dejected, discontented, disenchanted, disgruntled, disillusioned, dissatisfied, downcast, downhearted, frustrated, let down, SEE **sad**, unhappy.
OPPOSITES: SEE **contented**.

disapproval noun
Her frown showed her disapproval. anger, censure, condemnation, criticism, disapprobation, disfavour, dislike, displeasure, dissatisfaction, hostility, reprimand, reproach.
OPPOSITES: SEE **approval**.

disapprove verb
to disapprove of *They all disapprove of smoking.* be displeased by, blame, censure, condemn, criticize, denounce, deplore, deprecate, dislike, disparage, frown on, jeer at [SEE **jeer**], look askance at, make unwelcome, object to, regret, reject, take exception to, [*informal*] take a dim view of.
OPPOSITES: SEE **approve**.

disapproving adjective
a disapproving look. [*informal*] black (*I gave him a black look*), censorious, critical, deprecatory, disparaging, reproachful, slighting, unfavourable, unfriendly.
OPPOSITES: SEE **favourable**.

disarm verb
1 *to disarm your opponent.* make powerless, take weapons away from.
2 *to disarm after a war.* demobilize, disband your troops.

disaster noun
1 *a sudden disaster.* accident, blow, calamity, cataclysm, catastrophe, crash, misadventure, mischance, misfortune, mishap, reverse, tragedy.
2 [*informal*] *Our play was a disaster.* débâcle, failure, fiasco, [*informal*] flop, [*informal*] mess-up, [*informal*] washout.
OPPOSITES: SEE **success**.

disastrous adjective
a disastrous fire. a disastrous failure. SEE **bad**, calamitous, cataclysmic, catastrophic, crippling, destructive, devastating, dire, dreadful, fatal, ruinous, terrible, tragic.
OPPOSITES: SEE **successful**.

disbelief noun
distrust, doubt, incredulity, mistrust, scepticism, suspicion.
OPPOSITES: SEE **belief**.

disbelieve verb
Don't think I disbelieve your story. be sceptical of, discount, discredit, doubt, have no faith in, mistrust, reject, suspect.
OPPOSITES: SEE **believe**.

disc noun
1 circle, counter, plate, token.
2 *a recorded disc.* album, compact disc, digital recording, LP, SEE **record** noun, single.
3 *a computer disc.* diskette, floppy disc, hard disc.

discard verb
I discarded some old clothes. cast off, [*informal*] chuck away, dispense with, dispose of, [*informal*] ditch, dump, eliminate, get rid of, jettison, reject, scrap, shed, throw away.

discern verb
We discerned a change in the weather. become aware of, be sensitive to, detect, discover, discriminate, distinguish, make out, mark, notice, observe, perceive, recognize, see, spy.

discharge verb
1 *The chimney discharged thick smoke.* belch, eject, emit, expel, exude, give off, give out, pour out, produce, release, secrete, send out.
2 *to discharge a gun.* detonate, explode, fire, let off, shoot.
3 *to discharge an employee from a job.* dismiss, fire, make redundant, remove, sack, throw out.
4 *to discharge a prisoner.* absolve, acquit, allow to leave, clear, dismiss, excuse, exonerate, free, let off, liberate, pardon, release.

disciple noun
The great teacher had many disciples. acolyte, admirer, apostle, devotee, follower, pupil, student, supporter.

disciplinarian noun
a strict disciplinarian. authoritarian, autocrat, despot, [*informal*] hard-liner, [*informal*] hard task-master, martinet, [*informal*] slave-driver, [*informal*] stickler (*a stickler for good manners*), tyrant.

discipline noun
firm discipline. control, management, obedience, order, orderliness, self-control, strictness, system, training.

discipline verb
1 *You must discipline a young dog.* break in, control, drill, educate, instruct, restrain, train.
2 *We disciplined those who disobeyed.* chasten, chastise, correct, penalize, punish, reprimand, reprove, scold.

disciplined adjective
a disciplined army. SEE **obedient**, orderly,
well-behaved, well-trained.
OPPOSITES: SEE **undisciplined**.

disclaim verb
to disclaim responsibility. deny, disown,
forswear, reject, renounce, repudiate.
OPPOSITES: SEE **acknowledge**.

disclose verb SEE **reveal**.

discomfort noun
the discomfort of a hard chair. ache, distress,
hardship, irritation, pain, soreness,
uncomfortableness, uneasiness.
OPPOSITES: SEE **comfort** noun.

disconcert verb
Bright light disconcerted her. agitate,
bewilder, confuse, discomfit, disturb,
fluster, nonplus, perplex, [*informal*] put off
(*It puts me off*), [*informal*] rattle, ruffle,
throw off balance, trouble, unsettle, upset,
worry.
OPPOSITES: SEE **reassure**.

disconnect verb
to disconnect a telephone. break off, cut off,
detach, disengage, sever, take away,
uncouple, unhitch, unplug.

discord noun
1 *discord between friends.* argument, clash,
conflict, contention, difference of opinion,
disagreement, disharmony, dispute, friction,
SEE **quarrel** noun.
OPPOSITES: SEE **agreement**.
2 *discords in music.* cacophony, discordant
sound [SEE **discordant**], jangle, SEE **noise**.
OPPOSITES: SEE **harmony**.

discordant adjective
1 *discordant sounds.* atonal, cacophonous,
clashing, dissonant, grating, grinding,
harsh, jangling, jarring, shrill, strident,
tuneless, unmusical.
OPPOSITES: SEE **harmonious**.
2 *discordant opinions. a discordant voice.*
conflicting, contrary, differing, disagreeing,
incompatible, inconsistent, opposite, SEE
quarrelsome.

discount noun
a discount on the full price. abatement,
allowance, concession, cut, deduction,
[*informal*] mark-down, rebate, reduction.

discourage verb
1 *The threat of violence discouraged us.* cow,
damp (*It damped our enthusiasm*), dampen,
daunt, demoralize, depress, disenchant,
dishearten, dismay, dispirit, frighten,
hinder, inhibit, intimidate, [*informal*] put
down, [*informal*] put off, scare, [*informal*]
throw cold water on, unman, unnerve.

2 *How can we discourage vandals?* check,
deflect, deter, dissuade, prevent, put an end
to, repress, restrain, stop.
OPPOSITES: SEE **encourage**.

discouragement noun
*The loud music was a discouragement to
conversation.* constraint, [*informal*]
damper, deterrent, disincentive, hindrance,
impediment, obstacle, restraint, setback.
OPPOSITES: SEE **encouragement**.

discover verb
*We discovered a secret spot. I discovered some
new facts.* ascertain, come across, detect,
[*informal*] dig up, [*informal*] dredge up,
explore, find, hit on, identify, learn, light
upon, locate, notice, observe, perceive,
recognize, reveal, search out, see, spot,
[*slang*] suss out, track down, uncover,
unearth.
OPPOSITES: SEE **hide** verb.

discoverer noun
*the discoverer of penicillin. discoverers of new
lands.* creator, explorer, finder, initiator,
inventor, originator, pioneer, traveller.

discovery noun
a new discovery. breakthrough, disclosure,
exploration, [*informal*] find, innovation,
invention, revelation.

discredit verb
1 *to discredit someone.* attack, defame,
disgrace, dishonour, ruin the reputation of,
slander, slur, smear, vilify.
2 *to discredit someone's story.* challenge,
disbelieve, dispute, [*informal*] explode,
prove false, refuse to believe, show up.

discreet adjective
[Do not confuse with *discrete* = *distinct*.] *I
asked a few discreet questions.* careful,
cautious, circumspect, considerate, delicate,
diplomatic, guarded, judicious, polite,
politic, prudent, sensitive, tactful,
thoughtful, wary.
OPPOSITES: SEE **indiscreet**.

discrepancy noun
a discrepancy between two versions of a story.
conflict, SEE **difference**, disparity,
dissimilarity, divergence, incompatibility,
incongruity, inconsistency.
OPPOSITES: SEE **similarity**.

discretion noun
Handle confidential matters with discretion.
SEE **diplomacy**, good sense, judgement,
maturity, prudence, responsibility,
sensitivity, tact, wisdom.

discriminate verb
1 *Can you discriminate between butter and
margarine?* differentiate, distinguish, make
a distinction, tell apart.

2 *It's wrong to discriminate against people because of their religion, colour, or sex.* be biased, be intolerant, be prejudiced, show discrimination [SEE **discrimination**].

discriminating adjective
a discriminating judge of wine. choosy, critical, discerning, fastidious, [*uncomplimentary*] fussy, particular, perceptive, selective.
OPPOSITES: SEE **undiscriminating**.

discrimination noun
1 *She shows discrimination in her choice of music.* discernment, good taste, insight, judgement, perceptiveness, refinement, selectivity, subtlety, taste.
2 *racial discrimination. positive discrimination.* bias, bigotry, chauvinism, favouritism, intolerance, male chauvinism, prejudice, racialism, racism, sexism, unfairness.

discuss verb
to discuss a problem. argue about, confer about, consider, consult about, debate, deliberate, examine, [*informal*] put heads together about, talk about, [*informal*] weigh up the pros and cons of, write about.

discussion noun
a lively discussion. argument, SEE **conference**, consideration, consultation, conversation, debate, deliberation, dialogue, discourse, examination, exchange of views, symposium, talk.

disdainful adjective
SEE **scornful**.

disembark verb
to disembark from a ship. alight, go ashore, land.
OPPOSITES: SEE **embark**.

disembodied adjective
a disembodied voice. bodiless, SEE **ghostly**, immaterial, incorporeal, insubstantial, intangible, unreal.

disentangle verb
1 *to disentangle a knot.* sort out, straighten, undo, unknot, unravel, untangle, untie, untwist.
2 *The fish disentangled itself from the net.* disengage, extricate, free, liberate, release, rescue, separate.
OPPOSITES: SEE **tangle**.

disfigure verb
He was disfigured in a fire. damage, deface, deform, make ugly [SEE **ugly**], mar, mutilate, scar, spoil.
OPPOSITES: SEE **beautify**.

disgrace noun
He never got over the disgrace of his court-case. blot on your name, [*formal*]

contumely, degradation, discredit, dishonour, embarrassment, humiliation, ignominy, opprobrium, scandal, shame, slur, stain, stigma.

disgraceful adjective
disgraceful behaviour. SEE **bad**.

disgruntled adjective
SEE **dissatisfied**.

disguise noun
I didn't recognize him in that disguise. camouflage, cloak, costume, cover, fancy-dress, front, [*informal*] get-up, impersonation, make-up, mask, pretence, smoke-screen.

disguise verb
1 *to disguise your looks.* blend into the background, camouflage, dress up, make inconspicuous, mask, screen, shroud, veil.
2 *to disguise your feelings.* conceal, cover up, falsify, gloss over, hide, misrepresent.
to disguise yourself as counterfeit, dress up as, imitate, impersonate, mimic, pretend to be, [*informal*] take off.

disgust noun
I couldn't hide my disgust at the rotten food. abhorrence, antipathy, aversion, contempt, detestation, dislike, distaste, hatred, loathing, nausea, repugnance, repulsion, revulsion.
OPPOSITES: SEE **liking**.

disgust verb
The rotten food disgusted me. appal, be distasteful to, displease, horrify, nauseate, offend, outrage, put off, repel, revolt, shock, sicken, [*informal*] turn your stomach.
OPPOSITES: SEE **please**.

disgusting adjective
disgusting food, disgusting cruelty. loathsome, nauseating, offensive, repugnant, repulsive, revolting, sickening, SEE **unpleasant**.

dish noun
1 *an earthenware dish.* basin, bowl, casserole, SEE **container**, plate, [*old-fashioned*] platter, tureen.
2 *Stew is a nutritious dish.* concoction, food, item on the menu, recipe.

dishearten verb
The feeble applause disheartened us. depress, deter, SEE **discourage**, dismay, put off, sadden.
OPPOSITES: SEE **encourage**.

dishevelled adjective
dishevelled hair. bedraggled, disarranged, disordered, messy, ruffled, rumpled,

[*informal*] scruffy, slovenly, tangled, tousled, uncombed, unkempt, untidy.
OPPOSITES: SEE **neat**.

dishonest adjective
a dishonest deal. a dishonest salesman.
[*informal*] bent, cheating, corrupt, criminal, crooked, deceitful, deceiving, devious, disreputable, fake, false, fraudulent, immoral, insincere, lying, mendacious, misleading, [*formal*] perfidious, [*informal*] shady, [*informal*] slippery, specious, swindling, thieving, [*informal*] underhand, unethical, unprincipled, unscrupulous, untrustworthy, untruthful.
OPPOSITES: SEE **honest**.

dishonesty noun
corruption, crookedness, deceit, deviousness, falsity, immorality, insincerity, mendacity, perfidy, speciousness.
OPPOSITES: SEE **honesty**.

dishonour noun
There's no dishonour in losing. blot on your reputation, degradation, discredit, disgrace, humiliation, ignominy, indignity, [*formal*] opprobrium, reproach, scandal, shame, slur, stain, stigma.
OPPOSITES: SEE **honour** noun.

dishonourable adjective
dishonourable behaviour. base, blameworthy, compromising, SEE **corrupt** adjective, despicable, discreditable, disgraceful, disgusting, dishonest, disreputable, ignoble, ignominious, improper, infamous, mean, outrageous, reprehensible, scandalous, shabby, shameful, shameless, treacherous, unchivalrous, unethical, unprincipled, unscrupulous, untrustworthy, unworthy, wicked.
OPPOSITES: SEE **honourable**.

disillusion verb
They became disillusioned about the glory of war. disabuse, disappoint, disenchant, SEE **enlighten**, reveal the truth to, undeceive.

disinfect verb
to disinfect a wound. cauterize, chlorinate (*water*), clean, cleanse, decontaminate, fumigate (*a room*), purify, sanitize, sterilize.
OPPOSITES: SEE **infect**.

disinherit verb
to disinherit an heir. cut off, cut you out of a will, deprive you of your inheritance or birthright.

disintegrate verb
The wreck disintegrated. The team disintegrated when the captain quitted.
become disunited, break into pieces, break

up, crack up, crumble, decay, decompose, degenerate, deteriorate, fall apart, lose coherence, rot, shatter, smash up, splinter.

disinterested adjective
SEE **unbiased**.

disjointed adjective
a disjointed story. aimless, broken up, confused, desultory, disconnected, dislocated, disordered, disunited, incoherent, jumbled, loose, mixed up, muddled, rambling, unconnected, uncoordinated, wandering.
OPPOSITES: SEE **coherent**.

dislike noun
I tried to hide my dislike of the food.
antagonism (to), antipathy (to), aversion (to), contempt (for), detestation, disapproval, disgust (for), distaste (for), SEE **hatred**, loathing, revulsion (from).
OPPOSITES: SEE **liking**.

dislike verb
I dislike shopping. avoid, despise, detest, disapprove of, feel dislike [SEE **dislike** noun], SEE **hate** verb, loathe, scorn, [*informal*] take against.
OPPOSITES: SEE **like**.

disloyal adjective
a disloyal ally. faithless, false, insincere, perfidious, seditious, subversive, treacherous, treasonable, [*informal*] two-faced, unfaithful, unreliable, untrustworthy.
OPPOSITES: SEE **loyal**.

disloyalty noun
We couldn't forgive his disloyalty. betrayal, double-dealing, duplicity, faithlessness, falseness, inconstancy, infidelity, perfidy, treachery, treason, unfaithfulness.
OPPOSITES: SEE **loyalty**.

dismal adjective
SEE **gloomy**.

dismantle verb
to dismantle a building or machine.
demolish, knock down, strike, strip down, take apart, take down.
OPPOSITES: SEE **assemble**.

dismay noun
We listened with dismay to the bad news.
agitation, alarm, anxiety, apprehension, astonishment, consternation, depression, disappointment, discouragement, distress, dread, SEE **fear** noun, gloom, horror, pessimism, surprise.

dismay verb
The bad news dismayed us. alarm, appal, daunt, depress, devastate, disappoint, discourage, disgust, dishearten, dispirit,

distress, SEE **frighten**, horrify, scare, shock, unnerve.
OPPOSITES: SEE **encourage**.

dismiss verb
1 *to dismiss a class.* free, let go, release, send away.
2 *to dismiss employees.* [*informal*] axe, banish, [*formal*] cashier, disband, discharge, [*informal*] fire, give notice to, [*informal*] give them their cards, [*informal*] give the push to, lay off, make redundant, sack, [*informal*] send packing.
3 *to dismiss an idea.* discard, discount, disregard, drop, get rid of, give up, [*informal*] pooh-pooh, reject, repudiate, set aside, shelve, wave aside.

dismount verb
to dismount from a horse. alight, descend, get off.

disobedient adjective
a disobedient dog. a disobedient class. badly behaved, contrary, defiant, disorderly, disruptive, fractious, headstrong, insubordinate, intractable, mutinous, SEE **naughty**, obstinate, obstreperous, perverse, rebellious, recalcitrant, refractory, riotous, self-willed, stubborn, uncontrollable, undisciplined, ungovernable, unmanageable, unruly, wayward, wild, wilful.
OPPOSITES: SEE **obedient**.

disobey verb
1 *to disobey the rules.* break, contravene, defy, disregard, flout, ignore, infringe, rebel against, resist, transgress, violate.
2 *Soldiers must never disobey.* be disobedient, mutiny, protest, rebel, revolt, rise up, strike.
OPPOSITES: SEE **obey**.

disorder noun
1 *disorder in the streets.* anarchy, brawl, clamour, commotion, disorderliness, disturbance, fighting, fracas, fuss, hubbub, lawlessness, quarrelling, rioting, rumpus, tumult, uproar.
OPPOSITES: SEE **peace**.
2 *the disorder on my desk.* chaos, confusion, disarray, disorganization, jumble, mess, muddle, shambles, untidiness.
OPPOSITES: SEE **tidiness**.

disorderly adjective
SEE **disobedient**.

disorganized adjective
disorganized work. careless, chaotic, confused, disorderly, haphazard, illogical, jumbled, messy, muddled, scatter-brained, [*informal*] slapdash, [*informal*] slipshod, [*informal*] sloppy, slovenly, unmethodical, unplanned, unstructured, unsystematic, untidy.
OPPOSITES: SEE **neat, systematic**.

disown verb
I'll disown you if you misbehave. cast off, disclaim knowledge of, renounce, repudiate.

disparaging adjective
SEE **uncomplimentary**.

dispassionate adjective
a dispassionate look at a problem. calm, cool, SEE **impartial**, level-headed, unemotional.
OPPOSITES: SEE **emotional**.

dispatch noun
A messenger brought dispatches. bulletin, communiqué, letter, message, report.

dispatch verb
1 *to dispatch a parcel.* consign, convey, forward, post, send, transmit.
2 *to dispatch a wounded animal.* dispose of, finish off, SEE **kill**, put an end to.

dispel verb
SEE **disperse**.

dispense verb
1 *to dispense charity.* allocate, allot, apportion, deal out, distribute, dole out, give out, mete out, provide, share.
2 *to dispense medicine.* make up, prepare, supply.
to dispense with *We dispensed with the formalities.* abolish, cancel, dispose of, do without, get rid of, jettison, make unnecessary, relinquish, remove.

disperse verb
1 *to disperse a crowd.* break up, disband, dismiss, dispel, dissipate, divide up, drive away, send away, send in different directions, separate.
2 *The crowd dispersed.* disappear, dissolve, melt away, scatter, spread out, vanish.
OPPOSITES: SEE **collect**.

displace verb
1 *Vibration displaced part of the mechanism.* disarrange, dislocate, dislodge, disturb, misplace, move, put out of place, shift.
2 *Newcomers displace older players.* crowd out, depose, dispossess, oust, replace, succeed, supersede, supplant.

display noun
a gymnastics display. demonstration, exhibition, pageant, parade, presentation, show, spectacle.

display verb
to display your knowledge. air, demonstrate, disclose, exhibit, flaunt, flourish, give evidence of, parade, present, produce, put on show, reveal, show, show off, vaunt.
OPPOSITES: SEE **hide** verb.

displease verb SEE **annoy**.

disposable adjective
1 *disposable income*. at your disposal,
available, usable.
2 *a disposable razor*. expendable,
replaceable, [*informal*] throwaway.

dispose verb
A general disposes his troops for battle.
arrange, array, group, place, position, set
out.
to dispose of *to dispose of rubbish*. deal
with, destroy, discard, dump, get rid of, give
away, jettison, scrap, sell, throw away.

disproportionate adjective
*Little jobs can use up a disproportionate
amount of time*. excessive, inordinate,
unbalanced, uneven, unreasonable.
OPPOSITES: SEE **proportionate**.

disprove verb
to disprove an allegation. confute,
controvert, discredit, [*informal*] explode,
invalidate, negate, rebut, refute, show to be
wrong.
OPPOSITES: SEE **prove**.

dispute noun
a dispute between rivals. SEE **debate** noun,
quarrel noun.

dispute verb
1 *We disputed the rights and wrongs of the
affair*. SEE **debate** verb.
2 *No one disputed the referee's decision*. argue
against, challenge, contest, contradict,
controvert, deny, doubt, impugn, oppose,
quarrel with, question.
OPPOSITES: SEE **accept**.

disqualify verb
to disqualify someone from driving. debar,
declare ineligible [SEE **ineligible**], preclude,
prohibit.

disregard verb
to disregard advice. brush aside, despise,
discount, dismiss, disobey, disparage,
[*informal*] fly in the face of, forget, ignore,
[*informal*] make light of, neglect, overlook,
pay no attention to, [*informal*] pooh-pooh,
reject, shrug off, slight, snub, turn a blind
eye to.
OPPOSITES: SEE **heed**.

disreputable adjective
1 *a disreputable firm*. dishonest,
dishonourable, [*informal*] dodgy, dubious,
infamous, questionable, [*informal*] shady,
suspect, suspicious, unreliable, unsound,
untrustworthy.
OPPOSITES: SEE **reputable**.
2 *a disreputable appearance*. raffish,
unconventional.
OPPOSITES: SEE **respectable**.

disrespectful adjective SEE **rude**.

disrupt verb
A fire-practice disrupted work. break the
routine of, break up, confuse, dislocate,
disturb, interfere with, interrupt, intrude
on, spoil, throw into disorder, unsettle,
upset.

disruptive adjective
SEE **disobedient**.

dissatisfaction noun
I expressed dissatisfaction at the poor service.
annoyance, chagrin, disappointment,
discontentment, dismay, displeasure,
disquiet, exasperation, frustration,
irritation, mortification, regret,
unhappiness.
OPPOSITES: SEE **satisfaction**.

dissatisfied adjective
dissatisfied customers. disaffected,
disappointed, discontented, disgruntled,
displeased, [*informal*] fed up, frustrated,
unfulfilled, SEE **unhappy**, unsatisfied.
OPPOSITES: SEE **contented**.

dissent verb
SEE **disagree**.

dissident noun
[*uncomplimentary*] agitator, dissenter,
independent thinker, non-conformer,
protester, [*uncomplimentary*] rebel,
[*informal*] refusenik.

dissimilar adjective
dissimilar clothes. dissimilar personalities.
contrasting, different, disparate, distinct,
distinguishable, divergent, diverse,
heterogeneous, incompatible, opposite,
unlike, unrelated, various.
OPPOSITES: SEE **similar**.

dissolute adjective
SEE **immoral**.

dissolve verb
1 [It's useful to note a distinction between
dissolve = disperse in a liquid (*Sugar
dissolves in tea*) and *melt = become liquid by
heating* (*Ice melts*).] become liquid,
deliquesce, diffuse, disappear, disintegrate,
disperse, liquefy.
2 *to dissolve a partnership*. break up, bring
to an end, cancel, dismiss, divorce, end,
sever, split up, suspend, terminate,
[*informal*] wind up.

dissuade verb
to dissuade from advise against, argue
(someone) out of, deter from, discourage
from, persuade (someone) not to, put off,
remonstrate (with someone) against, warn
against.
OPPOSITES: SEE **persuade**.

distance noun
1 *the distance between two points.* breadth, extent, gap, [*informal*] haul (*a long haul*), interval, journey, length, measurement, mileage, range, reach, separation, space, span, stretch, width.
2 *He keeps his distance.* aloofness, coolness, isolation, remoteness, separation, [*informal*] standoffishness, unfriendliness.

distance verb
to distance yourself from someone. be unfriendly (with), keep away, keep your distance, remove, separate, set yourself apart, stay away.

distant adjective
1 *distant places.* far, faraway, far-flung, [*informal*] god-forsaken, inaccessible, outlying, out-of-the-way, remote.
OPPOSITES: SEE **close** adjective.
2 *a distant manner.* aloof, cool, formal, haughty, reserved, reticent, unenthusiastic, unfriendly, withdrawn.
OPPOSITES: SEE **friendly**.

distasteful adjective
SEE **unpleasant**.

distended adjective
SEE **swollen**.

distil verb
to distil water. to distil spirit from wine. extract, purify, refine, vaporize and condense.

distinct adjective
1 [See note under *distinctive*.] *distinct footprints in the mud. a distinct sound.* apparent, clear, clear-cut, definite, evident, noticeable, obvious, patent, plain, recognizable, sharp, unambiguous, unmistakable, visible, well-defined.
OPPOSITES: SEE **indistinct**.
2 *Organize your ideas into distinct sections.* contrasting, detached, different, discrete, dissimilar, distinguishable, individual, separate, special, unconnected.

distinction noun
1 *I can't see any distinction between the twins.* contrast, difference, differentiation, discrimination, dissimilarity, distinctiveness, individuality, particularity, peculiarity.
OPPOSITES: SEE **similarity**.
2 *I had the distinction of being first home.* celebrity, credit, eminence, excellence, fame, glory, greatness, honour, importance, merit, prestige, renown, reputation, superiority.

distinctive adjective
[Do not confuse with *distinct*. *Distinct handwriting* is *clear writing*; *distinctive handwriting* is *writing you don't confuse with*

someone else's.] characteristic, different, distinguishing, idiosyncratic, individual, inimitable, original, peculiar, personal, singular, special, striking, typical, uncommon, unique.

distinguish verb
1 *Can you distinguish between butter and margarine?* SEE **choose**, decide, differentiate, discriminate, judge, make a distinction, separate, tell apart.
2 *In the dark we couldn't distinguish who she was.* ascertain, determine, discern, know, make out, perceive, pick out, recognize, see, single out, tell.

distinguished adjective
1 *distinguished work.* acclaimed, conspicuously good, SEE **excellent**, exceptional, first-rate, outstanding.
OPPOSITES: SEE **ordinary**.
2 *a distinguished actor.* celebrated, eminent, famed, famous, foremost, great, illustrious, important, leading, notable, noted, prominent, renowned, well-known.
OPPOSITES: SEE **unknown**.

distort verb
1 *to distort a shape.* bend, buckle, contort, deform, twist, warp, wrench.
2 *to distort the truth.* exaggerate, falsify, garble, misrepresent, pervert, slant, twist.

distract verb
Don't distract the driver. bewilder, confuse, disconcert, divert, harass, perplex, puzzle, sidetrack, trouble, worry.

distraction noun
1 *The TV is a distraction when I'm working.* bewilderment, cause of confusion, SEE **distress** noun, interference, interruption, upset.
2 *He's always looking for some new distraction.* amusement, diversion, enjoyment, entertainment, fun, interest, pastime, pleasure, recreation.

distress noun
It was painful to see her distress. adversity, affliction, anguish, anxiety, danger, desolation, difficulty, discomfort, dismay, fright, grief, heartache, misery, pain, poverty, privation, sadness, sorrow, suffering, torment, tribulation, trouble, worry, wretchedness.

distress verb
The bad news distressed us. afflict, alarm, bother, [*informal*] cut up, dismay, disturb, frighten, grieve, harrow, hurt, make miserable, pain, perplex, perturb, sadden, scare, shake, shock, terrify, torment, torture, trouble, upset, worry, wound.
OPPOSITES: SEE **comfort** verb.

distribute verb
1 *They distributed free samples.* allocate, allot, assign, circulate, deal out, deliver, [*informal*] dish out, dispense, dispose of, divide out, [*informal*] dole out, give out, hand round, issue, mete out, share out, take round.
2 *Distribute the seeds evenly.* arrange, disperse, disseminate, scatter, spread, strew.

district noun
a rural district. an urban district. area, community, locality, neighbourhood, parish, part, province, quarter (*of a town*), region, sector, vicinity, ward, zone.

distrust verb
I distrust dogs that bark. be sceptical about, be wary of, disbelieve, doubt, have misgivings about, have qualms about, mistrust, question, suspect.
OPPOSITES: SEE **trust** verb.

distrustful adjective
SEE **suspicious**.

disturb verb
1 *Don't disturb her if she's asleep.* agitate, alarm, annoy, bother, discompose, disrupt, distract, distress, excite, fluster, frighten, perturb, pester, ruffle, scare, shake, startle, stir up, trouble, unsettle, upset, worry.
2 *Don't disturb the papers on my desk.* confuse, disorder, [*informal*] mess about with, move, muddle, rearrange, reorganize.

disunited adjective
The committee was disunited on the main issue. divided, polarized, split.
OPPOSITES: SEE **united**.

disunity noun
difference of opinion, disagreement, division, polarization.
OPPOSITES: SEE **solidarity**.

disused adjective
a disused railway line. abandoned, closed, dead, discarded, discontinued, idle, neglected, obsolete, superannuated, unused, withdrawn.
OPPOSITES: SEE **operational**.

ditch noun
a drainage ditch. aqueduct, channel, dike, drain, gully, gutter, moat, trench, watercourse.

dive verb
to dive into water. to dive down. crash-dive, descend, dip, drop, jump, leap, nosedive, pitch, plummet, plunge, sink, submerge, subside, swoop.

diverge noun
1 *to diverge from the path.* branch, deviate, divide, fork, go off at a tangent, part, radiate, separate, split.
2 *Our views diverge.* SEE **differ**.

diverse adjective
SEE **various**.

diversify verb
The shop has diversified into a wider range of goods. branch out, expand, spread out.

diversion noun
1 *a traffic diversion.* detour, deviation.
2 *We organized diversions for the guests.* amusement, distraction, entertainment, game, hobby, pastime, play, recreation, relaxation, sport.

diversity noun
SEE **variety**.

divert verb
1 *They diverted the plane to another airport.* change direction, redirect, re-route, shunt (*a train*), switch.
2 *She diverted us with funny stories.* amuse, cheer up, delight, distract, entertain, keep happy, recreate, regale.

divide verb
1 *The path divides. We divided into two groups.* branch, break up, diverge, fork, move apart, part, polarize, split.
OPPOSITES: SEE **converge**.
2 *We divided the food between us.* allocate, allot, apportion, deal out, dispense, distribute, give out, halve, parcel out, pass round, share out.
OPPOSITES: SEE **gather**.
3 *I divided the potatoes according to size.* arrange, categorize, classify, grade, group, sort out, separate, subdivide.
OPPOSITES: SEE **mix**.

divine adjective
divine beings. angelic, celestial, god-like, heavenly, holy, immortal, mystical, religious, sacred, spiritual, superhuman, supernatural, transcendental.

division noun
1 *the division of land into building plots.* allocation, apportionment, cutting up, dividing, partition, splitting.
2 *a division of opinion.* disagreement, discord, disunity, feud, SEE **quarrel** noun, rupture, schism (*in the church*), split.
3 *a box with divisions for various tools.* compartment, part, section, segment.
4 *a division between two rooms or territories.* boundary, demarcation, divider, dividing wall, fence, partition, screen.
5 *a division of an organization.* branch, department, section, subdivision, unit.

divorce noun
Their marriage ended in divorce. annulment, [*informal*] break-up, [*formal*] decree nisi, separation, [*informal*] split-up.

dizzy adjective
I feel dizzy when I look from a height.
bewildered, confused, dazed, faint, giddy,
light-headed, muddled, reeling, shaky,
swimming, unsteady.

do verb
[The verb *do* can mean many things. The
words given here are only a few of the
synonyms you could use.] 1 *to do a job.*
accomplish, achieve, carry out, commit,
complete, execute, finish, fulfil, organize,
perform, undertake.
2 *to do the garden.* arrange, attend to, cope
with, deal with, handle, look after, manage,
work at.
3 *to do sums.* answer, give your mind to,
puzzle out, solve, think out, work out.
4 *to do good.* bring about, cause, effect,
implement, initiate, instigate, produce,
result in.
5 *Will £10 do?* be acceptable, be enough, be
satisfactory, be sufficient, be suitable,
satisfy, serve, suffice.
6 *Do as you like.* act, behave, conduct
yourself, perform.

docile adjective
a docile animal. SEE **obedient**.

dock noun

PLACES WHERE SHIPS UNLOAD, ETC.: berth,
boat-yard, dockyard, dry-dock, harbour,
haven, jetty, landing-stage, marina, pier,
port, quay, slipway, wharf.

doctor noun
general practitioner, [*informal*] GP, medical
officer or MO, medical practitioner,
physician, [*uncomplimentary*] quack,
surgeon.

doctrine noun
religious doctrines. axiom, belief, conviction,
creed, dogma, maxim, orthodoxy, precept,
principle, teaching, tenet.

document noun

VARIOUS DOCUMENTS: certificate, charter,
deed, diploma, form, instrument, legal
document, licence, manuscript or
MS, passport, policy (*insurance policy*), printout, record, typescript, visa, warrant, will.

documentary adjective
1 *documentary evidence.* authenticated,
recorded, written.
2 *a documentary film.* factual, non-fiction.

dodge noun
a clever dodge. device, knack, manœuvre,
ploy, ruse, scheme, stratagem, trick,
[*informal*] wheeze.

dodge verb
1 *to dodge a snowball.* avoid, duck, elude,
evade, fend off, move out of the way of,
swerve away from, turn away from, veer
away from.
2 *to dodge work.* shirk, [*informal*] skive,
[*informal*] wriggle out of.
3 *to dodge a question.* equivocate, fudge,
hedge, side-step.

dog noun
bitch, [*childish*] bow-wow,
[*uncomplimentary*] cur, dingo, hound,
mongrel, pedigree, pup, puppy, whelp.
RELATED ADJECTIVES: canine, doglike.

SOME BREEDS OF DOG: Alsatian, basset,
beagle, bloodhound, borzoi, boxer, bulldog,
bull-terrier, cairn terrier, chihuahua, chow,
cocker spaniel, collie, corgi, dachshund,
Dalmatian, foxhound, foxterrier, Great
Dane, greyhound, husky, Labrador, mastiff,
Pekingese or Pekinese, Pomeranian, poodle,
pug, retriever, Rottweiler, setter, sheepdog,
spaniel, terrier, whippet.

dogma noun
religious dogma. article of faith, belief,
conviction, creed, doctrine, orthodoxy,
precept, principle, teaching, tenet, truth.

dogmatic adjective
*You won't argue him out of his dogmatic
position.* assertive, authoritarian,
authoritative, categorical, certain,
dictatorial, doctrinaire, [*informal*] hard-
line, hidebound, imperious, SEE **inflexible**,
intolerant, legalistic, narrow-minded,
obdurate, obstinate, opinionated, pontifical,
positive.
OPPOSITES: SEE **unbiased**.

domestic adjective
1 *domestic arrangements.* family, household,
private.
OPPOSITES: SEE **public** adjective.
2 *domestic air services.* inland, internal,
national.
OPPOSITES: SEE **foreign**.

domesticated adjective
domesticated animals. house-trained, tame,
tamed, trained.
OPPOSITES: SEE **wild**.

domesticity noun
a simple life of domesticity. family life, home-
making, house-keeping, staying at home.

dominant adjective
1 *a dominant influence. the dominant issues.* chief, commanding, dominating, influential, leading, main, major, powerful, predominant, presiding, prevailing, primary, principal, ruling, supreme, uppermost.
2 *a dominant feature in the landscape.* biggest, SEE **conspicuous**, eye-catching, highest, imposing, largest, obvious, outstanding, tallest, widespread.

dominate verb
1 *The captain dominated the game.* be the dominant person in [SEE **dominant**], control, direct, govern, influence, lead, manage, master, monopolize, rule, take control of, tyrannize.
2 *A castle dominates our town.* be the dominant thing in [SEE **dominant**], dwarf, look down on, overshadow, tower over.

donate verb SEE **give**.

donation noun SEE **gift**.

donor noun
a donor to a charity. benefactor, contributor, giver, philanthropist, provider, sponsor.
OPPOSITE: recipient.

doomed adjective
1 *doomed to die.* condemned, fated, intended.
2 *The voyage was doomed from the start.* accursed, bedevilled, hopeless, ill-fated, ill-starred, luckless.

door noun
barrier, doorway, [*informal*] SEE **entrance** noun, SEE **exit**, French window, gate, gateway, opening, portal, postern, revolving door, swing door.

dormant adjective
1 *Many living things are dormant in winter.* asleep, comatose, hibernating, resting, sleeping.
OPPOSITES: SEE **awake**.
2 *a dormant illness. a dormant volcano.* inactive, inert, latent, passive, quiescent, quiet.

dormitory noun
bedroom, sleeping-quarters.

dose noun
a dose of medicine. dosage, measure, portion, prescribed amount, quantity.

dot noun
Join up the dots. full stop, mark, point, speck, spot.

dot verb
Sheep dot the hillside. fleck, mark with dots, punctuate, scatter with dots, speckle, spot.

double adjective
a double railway-track. doubled, dual, [*in music*] duple, duplicated, paired, twin, twofold.

double noun
I saw your double in town. clone, copy, duplicate, [*informal*] lookalike, [*informal*] spitting image, twin.

double verb
We must double our efforts. duplicate, increase, multiply by two, reduplicate, repeat.
to double back backtrack, do a U-turn, retrace your steps, return, turn back.
to double up *She doubled up with pain.* bend over, collapse, crumple up, fold over, fold up.

doubt noun
1 *I had my doubts.* agnosticism [= *religious doubts*], anxiety, cynicism, disbelief, distrust, fear, hesitation, incredulity, indecision, misgiving, mistrust, qualm, reservation, scepticism, suspicion, worry.
OPPOSITES: SEE **confidence**.
2 *There's some doubt about the arrangements.* ambiguity, confusion, difficulty, dilemma, perplexity, problem, query, question, uncertainty.
OPPOSITES: SEE **certainty**.

doubt verb
1 *I doubt whether he can afford it.* be dubious about, feel uncertain about [SEE **uncertain**], hesitate, lack confidence.
OPPOSITE: be confident [SEE **confident**].
2 *I doubt her honesty.* be sceptical about, disbelieve, distrust, fear, mistrust, query, question, suspect.
OPPOSITES: SEE **trust** verb.

doubtful adjective
1 *I'm doubtful about her honesty.* agnostic, cynical, disbelieving, distrustful, dubious, hesitant, incredulous, sceptical, suspicious, uncertain, unclear, unconvinced, undecided, unsure.
OPPOSITES: SEE **certain**.
2 *a doubtful decision.* ambiguous, debatable, dubious, equivocal, [*informal*] iffy, inconclusive, problematical, questionable, suspect, vague, worrying.
OPPOSITES: SEE **indisputable**.

dowdy adjective
dowdy clothes. colourless, dingy, drab, dull, [*informal*] frumpish, old-fashioned, shabby, [*informal*] sloppy, slovenly, [*informal*] tatty, unattractive, unstylish.
OPPOSITES: SEE **smart** adjective, **stylish**.

downhearted adjective
SEE **depressed**.

downward adjective
a downward path. descending, downhill, easy, falling, going down, slanting, sloping.
OPPOSITES: SEE **upward**.

downy adjective
downy material. feathery, fleecy, fluffy, furry, fuzzy, soft, velvety, woolly.

doze verb
SEE **sleep** verb.

drab adjective
drab colours. cheerless, colourless, dingy, dismal, dowdy, dreary, dull, flat, gloomy, grey, grimy, lacklustre, shabby, sombre, unattractive, uninteresting.
OPPOSITES: SEE **bright**.

draft noun
[Don't confuse with *draught*.] 1 *a draft of an essay.* first version, notes, outline, plan, rough version, sketch.
2 *a bank draft.* cheque, order, postal order.

draft verb
to draft an essay. outline, plan, prepare, sketch out, work out, write a draft of.

drag verb
1 *The tractor dragged a load of logs.* draw, haul, lug, pull, tow, trail, tug.
OPPOSITES: SEE **push**.
2 *Time drags if you're bored.* be boring, crawl, creep, go slowly, linger, loiter, lose momentum, move slowly, pass slowly.

drain noun
a drain to take away water. channel, conduit, culvert, dike, ditch, SEE **drainage**, drainpipe, duct, gutter, outlet, pipe, sewer, trench, watercourse.

drain verb
1 *to drain marshland.* dry, dry out, remove water from.
2 *to drain oil from an engine.* bleed, clear, draw off, empty, remove, take off, tap.
3 *The water drained through the sieve.* leak out, ooze, seep, strain, trickle.
4 *The exercise drained my energy.* consume, deplete, SEE **exhaust** verb, sap, spend, use up.

drainage noun
mains drainage. sanitation, sewage system, sewers, waste disposal.

drama noun
1 *theatrical drama.* acting, dramatics, histrionics, improvisation, melodrama, play, show, stagecraft, SEE **theatre**, theatricals.
2 *a real-life drama.* action, crisis, SEE **excitement**, suspense, turmoil.

dramatic adjective
1 *a dramatic performance.* SEE **theatrical**.
2 *a dramatic rescue.* SEE **exciting**.

dramatize verb
1 *to dramatize a novel for TV.* adapt, make into a play, rewrite.
2 *Don't dramatize a quite ordinary event.* exaggerate, make too much of, overdo, overstate.

drastic adjective
a drastic remedy. desperate, dire, extreme, harsh, severe.

draught noun
[Don't confuse with *draft*.] 1 *a draught of air.* breeze, current, movement, puff, wind.
2 *a draught of ale.* drink, pull, swallow.

draw noun
a prize draw. competition, lottery, raffle.

draw verb
1 *The horse drew the cart.* drag, haul, lug, pull, tow, tug.
2 *to draw a big crowd.* allure, attract, bring in, coax, entice, invite, lure, persuade, pull in, win over.
3 *to draw a tooth. to draw money from a bank. to draw a sword.* extract, remove, take out, unsheathe (*a sword*), withdraw.
4 *to draw names from a hat.* choose, pick, select.
5 *to draw a diagram.* depict, doodle, map out, mark out, outline, paint, pen, pencil, portray, represent, sketch, trace.
6 *to draw a conclusion.* arrive at, come to, deduce, formulate, infer, work out.
7 *The two teams drew 1–1.* be equal, finish equal, tie.
to draw up 1 *The bus drew up.* brake, halt, pull up, stop. 2 *The lawyer drew up a contract.* compose, make, prepare, write out.

drawing noun
cartoon, design, graphics, illustration, outline, SEE **picture** noun, sketch.

drawing-room noun
living-room, lounge, sitting-room.

dread noun, verb
SEE **fear** noun, verb.

dreadful adjective
1 *a dreadful accident.* alarming, appalling, awful, dire, distressing, fearful, frightening, frightful, ghastly, grisly, gruesome, harrowing, horrible, horrifying, indescribable, monstrous, shocking, terrible, tragic, unspeakable, upsetting.
2 [*informal*] *dreadful weather.* SEE **bad**.

dream noun
1 *Odd things happen in dreams.* delusion, fantasy, hallucination, illusion, nightmare,

reverie, trance, vision.
2 *a dream of fame and riches.* ambition, aspiration, day-dream, ideal, pipedream, wish.

dream verb
I dreamed I could fly. daydream, fancy, fantasize, hallucinate, have a vision, imagine, think.
to dream up SEE **invent**.

dregs noun
dregs at the bottom of a cup. deposit, grounds (*of coffee*), lees (*of wine*), remains, sediment.

drench verb
The rain drenched us. douse, drown, flood, inundate, saturate, soak, souse, steep, wet thoroughly.

dress noun
1 *formal dress.* apparel, attire, SEE **clothes**, clothing, costume, garb, garments, [*informal*] gear, outfit, [*old-fashioned*] raiment.
2 *a woman's dress.* frock, gown, robe, shift.

dress verb
1 *Dad dressed the children.* attire, clothe, cover, provide clothes for, put clothes on. OPPOSITES: SEE **undress**.
2 *A nurse dressed my wound.* attend to, bandage, bind up, care for, put a dressing on, tend, treat.

dribble verb
1 *He dribbled over his food.* drool, slaver, slobber.
2 *Rain dribbled down the window.* drip, flow, leak, ooze, run, seep, trickle.

drift noun
1 *a drift of snow.* accumulation, bank, heap, mound, pile, ridge.
2 *the drift of a speech.* SEE **gist**.

drift verb
1 *The boat drifted downstream.* be carried, coast, float, move slowly.
2 *We had nowhere to go, so we drifted about.* meander, move casually, ramble, stray, walk aimlessly, wander.
3 *The snow drifted.* accumulate, gather, make drifts, pile up.

drill noun
military drill. discipline, exercise, instruction, practice, [*slang*] square-bashing, training.

drill verb
1 *to drill through something.* bore, penetrate, perforate, pierce.
2 *to drill soldiers.* discipline, exercise, instruct, rehearse, train.

drink noun
alcohol, beverage, [*informal*] bevvy, [*informal*] booze, [*joking*] grog, [*informal*] gulp, liquor, [*informal*] nightcap, [*informal*] nip, [*often plural*] refreshment, sip, swallow, swig, [*joking*] tipple (*What's your tipple?*).

SOME NON-ALCOHOLIC DRINKS: barley-water, cocoa, coffee, cordial, juice, lemonade, lime-juice, milk, mineral water, nectar, orangeade, pop, sherbet, sodawater, squash, tea, water.
SOME ALCOHOLIC DRINKS: ale, beer, bourbon, brandy, champagne, chartreuse, cider, cocktail, Cognac, crème de menthe, gin, Kirsch, lager, mead, perry, [*informal*] plonk, port, punch, rum, schnapps, shandy, sherry, vermouth, vodka, whisky, wine.
CONTAINERS YOU DRINK FROM: beaker, cup, glass, goblet, mug, tankard, tumbler, wine-glass.

drink verb
[*informal*] booze, gulp, guzzle, [*formal*] imbibe, [*informal*] knock back, lap, partake of, [*old-fashioned*] quaff, sip, suck, swallow, swig, [*informal*] swill.

drip noun
a drip of oil. bead, dribble, drop, leak, splash, spot, sprinkling, trickle.

drip verb
Water dripped into the basin. dribble, drizzle, drop, fall in drips, leak, plop, splash, sprinkle, trickle, weep.

drive noun
1 *a drive in the country.* excursion, jaunt, journey, outing, ride, run, trip.
2 *the drive to succeed.* ambition, determination, energy, enterprise, enthusiasm, initiative, keenness, motivation, persistence, [*informal*] push, zeal.
3 *a publicity drive.* campaign, crusade, effort.

drive verb
1 *to drive a spade into the ground.* bang, dig, hammer, hit, impel, knock, plunge, prod, push, ram, sink, stab, strike, thrust.
2 *to drive someone to take action.* coerce, compel, constrain, force, oblige, press, urge.
3 *to drive a car. to drive sheep.* control, direct, guide, handle, herd, manage, pilot, propel, send, steer.
to drive out SEE **expel**.

driver noun
chauffeur, motorist.

droop verb
The flag drooped. be limp, bend, dangle, fall, flop, hang, sag, slump, wilt, wither.

drop noun
1 *a drop of liquid.* bead, blob, bubble, dab, drip, droplet, globule, pearl, spot, tear.
2 *a drop of whisky.* dash, [*informal*] nip, small quantity, [*informal*] tot.
3 *a drop of 2 metres.* descent, dive, fall, plunge, SEE **precipice**.
4 *a drop in prices.* cut, decrease, reduction, slump.
OPPOSITES: SEE **rise** noun.

drop verb
1 *to drop to the ground.* collapse, descend, dip, dive, fall, go down, jump down, lower, nosedive, plummet, [*informal*] plump, plunge, sink, slump, subside, swoop, tumble.
2 *to drop someone from a team.* eliminate, exclude, leave out, omit.
3 *to drop a friend.* abandon, desert, [*informal*] dump, forsake, give up, jilt, leave, reject.
4 *to drop a plan.* discard, scrap, shed.

drown verb
1 *The flood drowned everything in the area.* SEE **flood** verb.
2 *The music drowned our conversation.* be louder than, overpower, overwhelm, silence.

drowsy adjective SEE **sleepy**.

drug noun
1 *a medicinal drug.* cure, medicament, medication, medicine, painkiller, [*old-fashioned*] physic, remedy, sedative, stimulant, tonic, tranquillizer, treatment.
2 *an addictive drug.* [*informal*] dope, narcotic, opiate.

VARIOUS DRUGS: barbiturate, caffeine, cannabis, cocaine, digitalis, hashish, heroin, insulin, laudanum, marijuana, morphia, nicotine, opium, phenobarbitone, quinine.

drug verb
anaesthetize, [*informal*] dope, dose, give a drug to, [*informal*] knock out, medicate, poison, stupefy, treat.

drum noun
1 [= *percussion instrument*]
VARIOUS DRUMS: bass-drum, bongo-drums, kettledrum, side-drum, snare-drum, tambour, tenor-drum, [*plural*] timpani, tom-tom.
OTHER PERCUSSION INSTRUMENTS: SEE **percussion**.
2 *a drum of oil.* SEE **barrel**.

drunk adjective
The revellers got drunk. delirious, fuddled, inebriated, intoxicated, over-excited, riotous, uncontrollable, unruly.
SOME OF THE MANY SLANG SYNONYMS ARE: blotto, boozed-up, canned, legless, merry,

paralytic, pickled, plastered, sozzled, tiddly, tight, tipsy.
OPPOSITES: SEE **sober**.

drunkard noun
alcoholic, [*informal*] boozer, dipsomaniac, drunk, [*informal*] tippler, toper, [*slang*] wino.
OPPOSITES: SEE **teetotaller**.

dry adjective
1 *dry desert.* arid, barren, dehydrated, desiccated, moistureless, parched, thirsty, waterless.
OPPOSITES: SEE **wet** adjective.
2 *dry wine.*
OPPOSITES: SEE sweet.
3 *a dry book.* boring, dreary, dull, tedious, tiresome, uninteresting.
OPPOSITES: SEE **interesting**.
4 *a dry sense of humour.* [*informal*] dead-pan, droll, expressionless, laconic, lugubrious, unsmiling.
OPPOSITES: SEE **lively**.

dry verb
[Also **to dry out**, **to dry up**] become dry, dehumidify, dehydrate, desiccate, go hard, make dry, parch, shrivel, towel (*to towel yourself dry*), wilt, wither.
OPPOSITES: SEE **wet** verb.

dual adjective
dual controls. binary, coupled, double, duplicate, linked, paired, twin.

dubious adjective
1 *I was dubious about her honesty.* SEE **doubtful**.
2 *a dubious character.* [*informal*] fishy, [*informal*] shady, suspect, suspicious, unreliable, untrustworthy.

duck noun
drake, duckling.

duck verb
1 *I ducked when he threw a stone.* avoid, bend, bob down, crouch, dip down, dodge, evade, sidestep, stoop, swerve, take evasive action.
2 *They ducked me in the pool.* immerse, plunge, push under, submerge.

due adjective
1 *Subscriptions are now due.* in arrears, outstanding, owed, owing, payable, unpaid.
2 *I gave the matter due consideration.* adequate, appropriate, decent, deserved, fitting, just, mature, merited, proper, requisite, right, rightful, sufficient, suitable, well-earned.
3 *Is the bus due?* expected, scheduled.

due noun
Give him his due. deserts, entitlement, merits, reward, rights.

duel noun, verb SEE **fight** noun, verb.

dull adjective
1 *dull colours*. dim, dingy, dowdy, drab, dreary, faded, flat, gloomy, lacklustre, lifeless, matt (*matt paint*), plain, shabby, sombre, subdued.
OPPOSITES: SEE **bright**.
2 *a dull sky*. cloudy, dismal, grey, heavy, leaden, murky, overcast, sullen, sunless.
OPPOSITES: SEE **clear** adjective.
3 *a dull sound*. deadened, indistinct, muffled, muted.
OPPOSITES: SEE **distinct**.
4 *a dull pupil*. dense, dim, dim-witted, obtuse, slow, SEE **stupid**, [*informal*] thick, unimaginative, unintelligent, unresponsive.
OPPOSITES: SEE **clever**.
5 *a dull edge to a knife*. blunt, blunted, unsharpened.
OPPOSITES: SEE **sharp**.
6 *a dull conversation*. boring, commonplace, dry, monotonous, prosaic, stodgy, tame, tedious, unexciting, uninteresting.
OPPOSITES: SEE **interesting**.

dumb adjective
dumb with amazement. inarticulate, [*informal*] mum, mute, silent, speechless, tongue-tied, unable to speak.

dummy noun
1 *The revolver was a dummy*. copy, counterfeit, duplicate, imitation, model, sham, substitute, toy.
2 *a ventriloquist's dummy*. doll, figure, manikin, puppet.

dump noun
1 *a rubbish dump*. junk yard, rubbish-heap, tip.
2 *an ammunition dump*. cache, depot, hoard, store.

dump verb
1 *to dump rubbish*. discard, dispose of, [*informal*] ditch, get rid of, jettison, reject, scrap, throw away.
2 [*informal*] *Dump your things on the table*. deposit, drop, empty out, let fall, offload, [*informal*] park, place, put down, throw down, tip, unload.

dungeon noun
[*old-fashioned*] gaol, lock-up, pit, prison, underground chamber, vault.

dupe verb SEE **trick** verb.

duplicate adjective
a duplicate key. alternative, copied, corresponding, identical, matching, second, twin.

duplicate noun
a duplicate of an original document. carbon copy, clone, copy, double, facsimile, imitation, likeness, photocopy, photostat, replica, reproduction, twin, Xerox.

duplicate verb
1 *to duplicate documents*. copy, photocopy, print, reproduce, Xerox.
2 *If you both do it, you duplicate the work*. do again, double, repeat.

durable adjective
SEE **lasting**.

dusk noun
evening, gloaming, gloom, sundown, sunset, twilight.
OPPOSITES: SEE **dawn**.

dust noun
chalk dust. dirt, grime, grit, particles, powder.

dusty adjective
1 *a dusty substance. dusty soil*. chalky, crumbly, dry, fine, friable, gritty, powdery, sandy, sooty.
2 *a dusty room*. dirty, filthy, grimy, grubby, mucky, uncleaned, unswept.

dutiful adjective
a dutiful worker. careful, compliant, conscientious, devoted, diligent, faithful, hard-working, loyal, obedient, punctilious, reliable, responsible, scrupulous, thorough, trustworthy.
OPPOSITES: SEE **irresponsible**.

duty noun
1 *a sense of duty towards your employer*. allegiance, faithfulness, loyalty, obedience, obligation, responsibility, service.
2 *household duties*. assignment, business, [*informal*] chore, function, job, office, role, task, work.
3 *customs duty*. charge, customs, dues, levy, tariff, tax, toll.

dwarf adjective
SEE **small**.

dwell verb
to dwell in SEE **inhabit**.

dwindle verb
SEE **decrease** verb.

dynamic adjective
a dynamic leader. active, committed, driving, energetic, enterprising, enthusiastic, forceful, [*informal*] go-ahead, [*uncomplimentary*] go-getting, highly motivated, lively, powerful, pushful,

[*uncomplimentary*] pushy, spirited, vigorous.
OPPOSITES: SEE **apathetic**.

Ee

eager adjective
an eager pupil. eager to hear the news. agog, anxious (*anxious to please*), ardent, avid, bursting, committed, [*formal*] desirous, earnest, enthusiastic, excited, fervent, impatient, intent, interested, keen, [*informal*] keyed up, motivated, passionate, [*informal*] raring (*raring to go*), voracious, zealous.
OPPOSITES: SEE **apathetic**.

eagerness noun
I began the work with great eagerness. alacrity, ardour, commitment, desire, earnestness, enthusiasm, excitement, fervour, impatience, intentness, interest, keenness, longing, motivation, passion, thirst (*thirst for knowledge*), zeal.

early adjective
1 *early flowers.* advanced, first, forward.
OPPOSITES: SEE **late**.
COMPARE: punctual.
2 *an early baby.* premature.
OPPOSITES: SEE **overdue**.
3 *early civilizations. an early computer.* ancient, antiquated, SEE **old**, primitive.
OPPOSITES: SEE **advanced, recent**.

earn verb
1 *to earn money.* [*informal*] bring in, [*informal*] clear (*He clears £300 a week*), fetch in, get, [*informal*] gross, make, net, obtain, realize, receive, [*informal*] take home, work for.
2 *to earn success.* attain, deserve, gain, merit, warrant, win.

earnest adjective
1 *an earnest request.* grave, heartfelt, impassioned, serious, sincere, solemn, thoughtful, well-meant.
OPPOSITES: SEE **frivolous**.
2 *an earnest worker.* committed, conscientious, determined, devoted, diligent, eager, hard-working, industrious, involved, purposeful.
OPPOSITES: SEE **casual, half-hearted**.

earth noun
1 *the planet Earth.* SEE **planet**.
2 *fertile earth.* clay, dirt, ground, humus, land, loam, soil, topsoil.

earthquake noun
quake, shock, tremor, upheaval.
RELATED ADJECTIVE: seismic.

ease noun
1 *The plumber did the job with ease.* dexterity, easiness, effortlessness, facility, nonchalance, simplicity, skill, speed, straightforwardness.
OPPOSITES: SEE **difficulty**.
2 *Now she's retired and leads a life of ease.* aplomb, calmness, comfort, composure, contentment, enjoyment, happiness, leisure, luxury, peace, quiet, relaxation, repose, rest, serenity, tranquillity.
OPPOSITES: SEE **stress** noun.

ease verb
1 *to ease pain.* allay, alleviate, assuage, calm, comfort, lessen, lighten, mitigate, moderate, pacify, quell, quieten, relieve, soothe, tranquillize.
OPPOSITES: SEE **aggravate**.
2 *to ease pressure or tension.* decrease, reduce, relax, slacken, take off.
OPPOSITES: SEE **increase** verb.
3 *to ease something into position.* edge, guide, inch, manoeuvre, move gradually, slide, slip.

easy adjective
1 *easy work.* [*informal*] cushy, effortless, light, painless, pleasant, undemanding.
2 *an easy machine to use. easy instructions to follow.* clear, elementary, facile, fool-proof, [*informal*] idiot-proof, manageable, plain, simple, straightforward, uncomplicated, understandable, user-friendly.
3 *an easy person to get on with.* accommodating, affable, amenable, docile, SEE **easygoing**, friendly, informal, natural, open, tolerant, unexacting.
OPPOSITES: SEE **difficult**.
4 *an easy life. easy conditions.* carefree, comfortable, contented, cosy, leisurely, peaceful, relaxed, relaxing, restful, serene, soft, tranquil, unhurried, untroubled.
OPPOSITES: SEE **stressful**.

easygoing adjective
an easygoing attitude. calm, carefree, SEE **casual**, cheerful, even-tempered, [*informal*] free and easy, genial, [*informal*] happy-go-lucky, indulgent, informal, [*informal*] laid-back, lax, lenient, liberal, nonchalant, patient, permissive, placid, relaxed, tolerant, unexcitable, unruffled.
OPPOSITES: SEE **strict, tense** adjective.

eat verb
to eat food. consume, devour, digest, feed on, [*formal*] ingest, live on, [*old-fashioned*] partake of, swallow, take.

VARIOUS WAYS TO EAT: bite, bolt, champ, chew, crunch, gnaw, gobble, gorge yourself, gormandize, graze, gulp, guzzle, [*informal*] make a pig of yourself, [*formal*] masticate, munch, nibble, overeat, peck, [*informal*] scoff, [*informal*] slurp, [*informal*] stuff yourself, taste, [*informal*] tuck in, [*informal*] wolf it down.

---

to eat away. *The river ate the bank away.* crumble, erode, wear away.

eatable adjective
Is the food eatable? digestible, edible, fit to eat, good, palatable, safe to eat, wholesome.
OPPOSITES: SEE **inedible**.

eccentric adjective
eccentric behaviour. aberrant, abnormal, absurd, bizarre, cranky, curious, freakish, [*informal*] funny, grotesque, idiosyncratic, ludicrous, SEE **mad**, odd, outlandish, out of the ordinary, peculiar, preposterous, queer, quirky, ridiculous, singular, strange, unconventional, unusual, [*informal*] way-out, [*informal*] weird, [*informal*] zany.
OPPOSITES: SEE **conventional**.

eccentric noun
[All these synonyms are used *informally*] character (*She's a bit of a character*), crackpot, crank, freak, oddity, weirdie, weirdo.

echo verb
1 *The sound echoed across the valley.* resound, reverberate, ring, sound again.
2 *The parrot echoed what I said.* ape, copy, imitate, mimic, reiterate, repeat, reproduce, say again.

eclipse verb
1 *to eclipse a light.* block out, blot out, cloud, cover, darken, extinguish, obscure, veil.
2 *to eclipse someone else's achievement.* dim, excel, outdo, outshine, overshadow, put into the shade, surpass.

economic adjective
[= *to do with economics.* Don't confuse with *economical.*] *economic affairs.* budgetary, business, financial, fiscal, monetary, money-making, trading.

economical adjective
[= *to do with saving money.* Don't confuse with *economic.*] 1 *Cycling is more economical than going by bus.* careful, cost-effective, [*uncomplimentary*] SEE **miserly**, parsimonious, prudent, sparing, thrifty.
OPPOSITES: SEE **wasteful**.
2 *Beans make an economical meal.* cheap, [*informal*] cheese-paring, frugal,

inexpensive, low-priced, reasonable.
OPPOSITES: SEE **expensive**.

economize verb
If you're poor you have to economize. be economical [SEE **economical**], cut back, save, [*informal*] scrimp, skimp, spend less, [*informal*] tighten your belt.
OPPOSITES: SEE **squander**.

economy noun
1 *economy in the use of your money.* frugality, [*uncomplimentary*] meanness, [*uncomplimentary*] miserliness, parsimony, providence, prudence, thrift.
OPPOSITE: wastefulness.
2 *I cancelled the holiday as an economy.* cut (*a cut in expenditure*), saving.
3 *the national economy.* budget, economic affairs [SEE **economic**], wealth.

ecstatic adjective
an ecstatic welcome. blissful, delighted, delirious, elated, enraptured, enthusiastic, euphoric, exultant, fervent, frenzied, gleeful, SEE **happy**, joyful, overjoyed, [*informal*] over the moon, rapturous.

eddy verb
The water eddied between the rocks. move in circles, swirl, whirl.

edge noun
1 *the edge of a knife.* acuteness, keenness, sharpness.
2 *the edge of a cup.* brim, brink, lip, rim.
3 *the edge of an area.* border, boundary, circumference, frame, kerb (*of a street*), limit, margin, outline, outlying parts, outskirts (*of a town*), perimeter, periphery, side, suburbs (*of a town*), verge.
4 *the edge of a dress.* edging, fringe, hem, selvage.

edible adjective
I don't think conkers are edible. digestible, eatable, fit to eat, good to eat, palatable, safe to eat, wholesome.
OPPOSITES: SEE **inedible**.

edit verb
to edit a film, book, etc. adapt, alter, assemble, compile, get ready, modify, organize, prepare, put together, supervise the production of.

VARIOUS WAYS TO EDIT A PIECE OF WRITING, ETC.: abridge, amend, annotate, bowdlerize, censor, condense, correct, cut, dub (*sound*), emend, format, polish, proof-read, rearrange, rephrase, revise, rewrite, select, shorten, splice (*film*).

---

edition noun
1 *a Christmas edition of a magazine.* copy, issue, number.

2 *a first edition of a book.* impression, printing, publication, version.

educate verb
to educate people about hygiene. to educate students. bring up, civilize, coach, counsel, discipline, drill, edify, guide, improve, indoctrinate, inform, instruct, lecture, rear, school, teach, train, tutor.

educated adjective
an educated person. civilized, cultivated, cultured, enlightened, erudite, informed, knowledgeable, learned, literate, numerate, sophisticated, well-bred, well-read.

education noun
coaching, curriculum, enlightenment, guidance, indoctrination, instruction, schooling, syllabus, teaching, training, tuition.

PLACES WHERE YOU ARE EDUCATED: academy, college, conservatory, kindergarten, play-group, SEE **school**, sixth-form college, tertiary college, university.

PEOPLE WHO EDUCATE: coach, counsellor, demonstrator, don, governess, guru, headteacher, instructor, lecturer, pedagogue, professor, SEE **teacher**, trainer, tutor.

eerie adjective
eerie sounds in the night. creepy, SEE **frightening**, ghostly, mysterious, [*informal*] scary, [*informal*] spooky, strange, uncanny, unearthly, unnatural, weird.

effect noun
1 *One effect of overeating may be obesity.* aftermath, consequence, impact, influence, issue, outcome, repercussion, result, sequel, upshot.
2 *The rosy lighting gave an effect of warmth.* feeling, illusion, impression, sense.

effect verb
[Do not confuse with *affect*.] *to effect changes.* achieve, bring about, bring in, carry out, cause, create, [*formal*] effectuate, enforce, execute, implement, initiate, make, put into effect.

effective adjective
1 *an effective cure for colds.* effectual, [*formal*] efficacious, efficient, potent, powerful, real, strong, worthwhile.
2 *an effective goalkeeper.* able, capable, competent, impressive, productive, proficient, successful, useful.
3 *an effective argument.* cogent, compelling, convincing, meaningful, persuasive, striking, telling.
OPPOSITES: SEE **ineffective**.

effeminate adjective
[*Effeminate* and its synonyms have sexist overtones, and are usually uncomplimentary. Compare *feminine*.] *effeminate behaviour.* camp, effete, girlish, [*informal*] pansy, [*informal*] sissy, unmanly, weak, womanish.

effervescent adjective
effervescent drinks. bubbling, bubbly, carbonated, fizzy, foaming, sparkling.

efficient adjective
an efficient worker. an efficient use of resources. able, capable, competent, cost-effective, economic, effective, effectual, efficacious, impressive, productive, proficient, successful, thrifty, useful.
OPPOSITES: SEE **inefficient**.

effort noun
1 *strenuous effort.* diligence, endeavour, exertion, industry, labour, pains, strain, stress, striving, struggle, toil, [*old-fashioned*] travail, trouble, work.
2 *a real effort to win.* attempt, endeavour, go, try.

effortless adjective
SEE **easy**.

egoism noun
egocentricity, self-centredness, self-importance, selfishness, self-love, self-regard.

egotism noun
SEE **pride**.

egotistical adjective
SEE **conceited**.

eject verb
1 *to eject someone from a building or country.* banish, [*informal*] boot out, deport, discharge, dismiss, drive out, evict, exile, expel, get rid of, [*informal*] kick out, oust, remove, sack, send out, throw out, turn out.
2 *to eject smoke or liquid.* belch, discharge, disgorge, ejaculate [= *eject semen*], emit, spew, spout, vomit.

elaborate adjective
1 *an elaborate plan.* complex, complicated, detailed, intricate, involved, thorough, well worked out.
2 *elaborate carvings.* baroque, decorative, fancy, fantastic, fussy, grotesque, intricate, ornamental, ornate, rococo, showy.
OPPOSITES: SEE **simple**.

elaborate verb
to elaborate a simple story. add to, amplify, complicate, decorate, develop, embellish, expand, expatiate on, fill out, give details of, improve on, ornament.
OPPOSITES: SEE **simplify**.

elapse verb
Many days elapsed before we met again. go
by, lapse, pass.

elastic adjective
elastic material. bendy, ductile, flexible,
plastic, pliable, pliant, rubbery, [*informal*]
springy, [*informal*] stretchy, yielding.
OPPOSITES: SEE **brittle, rigid.**

elderly adjective SEE **old.**

elect adjective
[Note: *elect* goes *after* the noun it describes.]
the president elect. [also going *after* the noun]
designate, to be; [going *before* the noun]
chosen, elected [SEE **elect** verb], prospective.

elect verb
to elect a leader. adopt, appoint, choose,
name, nominate, opt for, pick, select, vote
for.

election noun
the election of a leader. ballot, choice, poll,
selection, vote.

electorate noun
constituents, electors, voters.

electrical adjective
electrical equipment. battery-operated,
electric, mains-operated.

SOME ITEMS OF ELECTRICAL EQUIPMENT:
accumulator, adaptor, battery, bell, bulb,
cable, capacitor, charger, circuit, dynamo,
electric heater, electric motor, electrode,
electromagnet, electrometer, electrophorus,
electroscope, element, flex, fuse, generator,
insulation, lead, light, meter, plug, power-
point, socket, switch, terminal, torch,
transformer, wiring.

---

electricity noun
Is the electricity on? current, power, power
supply.

electrifying adjective
an electrifying performance. amazing,
astonishing, astounding, electric, exciting,
hair-raising, stimulating, thrilling.

elegant adjective
an elegant building. elegant clothes. artistic,
SEE **beautiful,** chic, courtly, dignified,
fashionable, graceful, gracious, handsome,
modish, noble, [*informal*] posh, refined,
smart, sophisticated, splendid, stately,
stylish, tasteful.
OPPOSITES: SEE **inelegant.**

elegy noun
dirge, lament, requiem.

element noun
1 *an element of truth in her story.* component,
constituent, factor, feature, fragment, hint,

ingredient, part, small amount, trace.
2 *Ducks are in their element swimming in a
pond.* domain, environment, habitat,
sphere.

elementary adjective
an elementary problem. basic, early, SEE **easy,**
first (*the first stages*), fundamental, initial,
primary, principal, rudimentary, simple,
straightforward, uncomplicated.
OPPOSITES: SEE **advanced, complex.**

elevate verb
SEE **raise.**

elevated adjective
SEE **high.**

eligible adjective
eligible to apply for a job. acceptable,
allowed, appropriate, authorized,
competent, equipped, fit, proper, qualified,
suitable, worthy.
OPPOSITES: SEE **ineligible.**

eliminate verb
1 *to eliminate mistakes. to eliminate ants from
your garden.* abolish, annihilate, delete,
destroy, dispense with, do away with, eject,
end, eradicate, exterminate, finish off, get
rid of, SEE **kill,** put an end to, remove, stamp
out.
2 *Our team was eliminated from the
competition.* cut out, drop, exclude, knock
out, leave out, omit, reject.

élite noun
*These experienced workers are the élite of
their profession.* aristocracy, the best, first-
class people, flower, meritocracy, nobility,
top people.

élitist adjective
SEE **snobbish.**

eloquent adjective
[See note at *loquacious.*] *an eloquent speaker.*
articulate, expressive, fluent, forceful,
[*uncomplimentary*] glib, moving,
persuasive, plausible, powerful,
unfaltering.
OPPOSITES: SEE **inarticulate.**

elude verb
to elude capture. avoid, circumvent, dodge,
escape, evade, foil, get away from.

elusive adjective
1 *an elusive criminal.* [*informal*] always on
the move, evasive, fugitive, hard to find.
2 *The poem's meaning is elusive.* ambiguous,
baffling, deceptive, hard to pin down,
indefinable, puzzling, shifting.

emaciated adjective
emaciated bodies. anorexic, bony,
cadaverous, gaunt, haggard, skeletal,
skinny, starved, SEE **thin** adjective,
undernourished, wasted away.

emancipate verb
to emancipate slaves. deliver from slavery, discharge, enfranchise, free, give rights to, liberate, release, set free.
OPPOSITES: SEE **enslave**.

embankment noun
bank, causeway, dam, earthwork, mound, rampart.

embark verb
1 *to embark on a ship.* board, depart, go aboard, leave, set out.
OPPOSITES: SEE **disembark**.
2 *to embark on a project.* begin, commence, start, undertake.

embarrass verb
They embarrassed me by telling everyone my secret. chagrin, confuse, disconcert, disgrace, distress, fluster, humiliate, make (someone) blush, make (someone) feel embarrassed [SEE **embarrassed**], mortify, [*informal*] put (someone) on the spot, shame, upset.

embarrassed adjective
an embarrassed silence. abashed, ashamed, awkward, bashful, confused, disconcerted, distressed, flustered, humiliated, mortified, [*informal*] red in the face, self-conscious, shamed, shy, uncomfortable, upset.

embarrassing adjective
an embarrassing mistake. awkward, disconcerting, distressing, humiliating, shameful, touchy, tricky, uncomfortable, uneasy, upsetting.

embellish verb
SEE **ornament** verb.

embezzle verb
to embezzle funds. appropriate, misappropriate, SEE **steal**, take fraudulently.

embittered adjective
embittered by failure. bitter, disillusioned, envious, resentful, sour.

emblem noun
The olive branch is an emblem of peace. badge, crest, device, image, insignia, mark, regalia, seal, sign, symbol, token.

embody verb
SEE **include**.

embrace verb
1 *She embraced him lovingly.* clasp, cling to, cuddle, enfold, fondle, grasp, hold, hug, kiss, snuggle up to.
2 *She's quick to embrace new ideas.* accept, espouse, receive, take on, welcome.
3 *The syllabus embraces all aspects of the subject.* bring together, comprise, embody, enclose, gather together, include, incorporate, involve, take in.

embryonic adjective
an embryonic organism. an embryonic idea. early, immature, just beginning, rudimentary, underdeveloped, undeveloped, unformed.

emerge verb
He didn't emerge from his bedroom until noon. SEE **appear**, arise, come out, [*old-fashioned*] issue forth, [*informal*] pop up, surface.

emergency noun
She always keeps calm in an emergency. crisis, danger, difficulty, predicament, serious situation.

emigrant noun
OPPOSITE: immigrant.

emigrate verb
to emigrate to another country. leave, quit, set out.

eminent adjective
1 *an eminent actor.* august, celebrated, distinguished, esteemed, familiar, famous, great, illustrious, important, notable, noteworthy, renowned, well-known.
OPPOSITES: SEE **unknown**.
2 *an eminent landmark.* conspicuous, elevated, high, noticeable, obvious, outstanding, prominent, visible.
OPPOSITES: SEE **inconspicuous**.

emit verb
Chimneys emit smoke. Transmitters emit radio signals. belch, discharge, eject, exhale, expel, give off, give out, issue, radiate, send out, spew out, transmit.
OPPOSITES: SEE **absorb, receive**.

emotion noun
His voice was full of emotion. agitation, excitement, feeling, fervour, passion, sentiment, warmth. SEE ALSO: **anger** noun, **love** noun.

emotional adjective
an emotional farewell. an emotional speech. demonstrative, SEE **emotive**, fervent, fiery, heated, impassioned, intense, moving, passionate, romantic, touching, warm-hearted. SEE ALSO: **angry, loving**.
OPPOSITES: SEE **unemotional**.

emotive adjective
emotive language. affecting, biased, SEE **emotional**, inflammatory, loaded, moving, pathetic, poignant, prejudiced, provocative, sentimental, stirring, subjective, tear-jerking, touching.
OPPOSITES: SEE **dispassionate**.

emphasis noun
She put special emphasis on certain words. accent, attention, force, importance, intensity, priority, prominence, strength, stress, urgency, weight.

emphasize verb
She emphasized the important points. accent, accentuate, dwell on, focus on, foreground, give emphasis to, highlight, impress, insist on, [*informal*] play up, [*informal*] press home, spotlight, stress, underline.

empirical adjective
empirical knowledge. gained through experience, observed, practical.
OPPOSITES: SEE **theoretical**.

employ verb
1 *to employ workers.* engage, give work to, have on your payroll, hire, pay, take on, use the services of.
2 *to employ modern methods.* apply, use, utilize.

employed adjective
active, busy, earning, engaged, hired, involved, occupied, working.
OPPOSITES: SEE **unemployed**.

employer noun
boss, chief, [*informal*] gaffer, head, manager, owner, taskmaster.

employment noun
What's her employment? business, calling, craft, job, line, living, occupation, profession, trade, vocation, work.

empty adjective
1 *empty space. an empty room. an empty van.* bare, blank, clean, clear, deserted, desolate, forsaken, hollow, unfilled, unfurnished, uninhabited, unladen, unoccupied, unused, vacant, void.
OPPOSITES: SEE **full**.
2 *empty threats. empty compliments.* futile, idle, impotent, ineffective, insincere, meaningless, pointless, purposeless, senseless, silly, unreal, worthless.
OPPOSITES: SEE **effective**.

empty verb
Empty your cup. Empty the building. clear, drain, evacuate, exhaust, pour out, unload, vacate, void.
OPPOSITES: SEE **fill**.

enable verb
1 *The extra money enabled us to have a holiday.* aid, assist, equip, help, make it possible, provide the means.
2 *A passport enables you to travel to certain countries.* allow, authorize, empower, entitle, license, permit, qualify, sanction.
OPPOSITES: SEE **prevent**.

enchant verb
The ballet enchanted us. allure, bewitch, captivate, charm, delight, enrapture, enthral, entrance, fascinate, spellbind.

enclose verb
1 *to enclose animals within a fence.* cage, confine, cordon off, encircle, encompass, envelop, fence in, hedge in, hem in, imprison, pen, restrict, ring, shut in, surround, wall in.
2 *to enclose something in an envelope, box, etc.* box, case, cocoon, conceal, contain, cover, encase, enfold, insert, package, parcel up, secure, sheathe, wrap.

enclosed adjective
an enclosed space. confined, contained, encircled, fenced, limited, restricted, shut in, surrounded, walled.
OPPOSITES: SEE **open** adjective.

enclosure noun
1 *an enclosure for animals.* arena, cage, compound, coop, corral, court, courtyard, farmyard, field, fold, paddock, pen, pound, ring, run, sheepfold, stockade, sty.
2 *an enclosure in an envelope.* contents, inclusion, insertion.

encounter noun
1 *a friendly encounter.* meeting.
2 *a violent encounter.* battle, brush (*a brush with the authorities*), clash, collision, confrontation, dispute, SEE **fight** noun, struggle.

encounter verb
I encountered fierce opposition. clash with, come upon, confront, contend with, [*informal*] cross swords with, face, grapple with, happen upon, have an encounter with, meet, [*informal*] run into.

encourage verb
1 *We encouraged our team.* abet, animate, applaud, cheer, [*informal*] egg on, embolden, give hope to, hearten, incite, inspire, rally, reassure, rouse, spur on, support.
2 *Advertising encourages sales.* aid, be conducive to, be an incentive to, boost, engender, foster, further, generate, help, increase, induce, promote, stimulate.
3 *Encourage people to stop smoking.* advocate, invite, persuade, prompt, urge.
OPPOSITES: SEE **discourage**.

encouragement noun
We need a little encouragement. applause, approval, boost, cheer, incentive, inspiration, reassurance, [*informal*] shot in the arm, stimulation, support.

encouraging adjective
encouraging news. auspicious, cheering, comforting, favourable, heartening, hopeful, optimistic, promising, reassuring.

encroach verb
to encroach on someone's territory. enter, impinge, SEE **intrude**, invade, trespass, violate.

end noun
1 *the end of the garden.* boundary, edge, limit.
2 *the end of an event.* cessation, close, coda
(*of a piece of music*), completion, conclusion,
culmination, curtain (*of a play*), denouement
(*of a plot*), ending, finale, finish, [*informal*]
pay-off, resolution.
3 *the end of a journey.* destination,
expiration, home, termination, terminus.
4 *the end of a queue.* back, rear, tail.
5 *the end of a walking-stick.* ferrule, point,
tip.
6 *the end of life.* SEE **death,** demise, destiny,
destruction, doom, extinction, fate, passing,
ruin.
7 *an end in view.* aim, aspiration,
consequence, design, effect, intention,
objective, outcome, plan, purpose, result,
upshot.
OPPOSITES: SEE **beginning.**

end verb
1 *to end your work.* break off, bring to an
end, complete, conclude, cut off,
discontinue, [*informal*] drop, halt, put an
end to, [*informal*] round off.
2 *to end a life.* abolish, destroy, eliminate,
exterminate, [*informal*] get rid of, SEE **kill,**
[*informal*] put an end to, ruin, scotch (*to
scotch a rumour*).
3 *When does term end?* break up, cease, close,
come to an end, culminate, expire, finish,
reach a climax, stop, terminate.
OPPOSITES: SEE **begin.**

endanger verb
Bad driving endangers others. expose to risk,
imperil, jeopardize, put at risk, threaten.
OPPOSITES: SEE **protect.**

endearing adjective
endearing ways. appealing, attractive,
charming, disarming, enchanting,
engaging, lovable, sweet, winning.
OPPOSITES: SEE **repulsive.**

endeavour verb SEE **try** verb.

endless adjective
1 *endless space.* boundless, everlasting,
immeasurable, infinite, limitless,
measureless, never-ending, unbounded,
unlimited.
2 *an endless afterlife.* eternal, immortal,
undying.
3 *an endless supply.* ceaseless, constant,
continual, continuous, everlasting,
incessant, inexhaustible, interminable,
perpetual, persistent, unbroken, unending,
unfailing, uninterrupted.

endorse verb
1 *to endorse a cheque.* sign.
2 *to endorse someone's opinion.* agree with,
approve of, condone, SEE **confirm,** subscribe
to.

endurance noun
The big climb was a test of endurance. ability
to endure [SEE **endure**], determination,
fortitude, patience, perseverance,
persistence, pertinacity, resolution,
stamina, staying-power, strength, tenacity.

endure verb
1 *to endure pain. to endure a storm.* bear,
cope with, experience, go through, put up
with, stand, [*informal*] stick, [*informal*]
stomach, submit to, suffer, tolerate, undergo,
weather, withstand.
2 *Life on earth will endure for a long time
yet.* carry on, continue, exist, last, live on,
persevere, persist, prevail, remain, stay,
survive.

enemy noun
adversary, antagonist, assailant, attacker,
competitor, foe, opponent, opposition, the
other side, rival, [*informal*] them (*us and
them*).
OPPOSITES: SEE **ally** noun, **friend.**

energetic adjective
an energetic person. an energetic game.
active, animated, brisk, dynamic,
enthusiastic, fast, forceful, hard-working,
high-powered, indefatigable, lively,
powerful, quick-moving, spirited, strenuous,
tireless, unflagging, vigorous.
OPPOSITES: SEE **lethargic.**

energy noun
1 *She has tremendous energy.* animation,
drive, dynamism, enthusiasm, fire, force,
[*informal*] get-up-and-go, [*informal*] go
(*She's got lots of go*), life, liveliness, might,
spirit, stamina, strength, verve, vigour,
[*informal*] vim, vitality, vivacity, zeal, zest.
OPPOSITES: SEE **lethargy.**
2 *Industry needs a reliable supply of energy.*
fuel, power.

enforce verb
to enforce the rules. administer, apply, carry
out, execute, implement, impose, inflict,
insist on, put into effect.
OPPOSITES: SEE **waive.**

engage verb
1 *to engage workers.* SEE **employ.**
2 *to engage to do something.* SEE **promise** verb.
3 *Cog-wheels engage.* bite, fit together,
interlock.

engaged adjective
1 *engaged to be married.* [*formal*] affianced,
betrothed, [*old-fashioned*] promised.
OPPOSITES: SEE **unattached.**
2 *engaged in your work.* absorbed, active,
busy, committed, employed, engrossed,
immersed, involved, occupied, preoccupied,
tied up.
OPPOSITES: SEE **idle.**
3 *an engaged telephone-line. an engaged*

lavatory. being used, busy, occupied, unavailable.
OPPOSITES: SEE **available**.

engagement 1 *The couple announced their engagement.* betrothal, promise to marry, [*old-fashioned*] troth.
2 *a business engagement.* appointment, arrangement, commitment, date, fixture, meeting, obligation.

engine noun

KINDS OF ENGINE: diesel engine, electric motor, internal-combustion engine, jet engine, outboard-motor, steam-engine, turbine, turbo-jet, turbo-prop.

---

engineering noun
There are many branches of *engineering*, including: aeronautical, chemical, civil, computer, electrical, electronic, manufacturing, marine, mechanical, plant.

enhance verb
SEE **improve**.

enigmatic adjective
SEE **puzzling**.

enjoy verb
1 *We enjoy outings. I enjoyed her paintings.* admire, appreciate, be pleased by, delight in, indulge in, like, love, luxuriate in, rejoice in, relish, revel in, savour, take pleasure from or in.
2 *Visitors can enjoy the college facilities.* benefit from, experience, have, take advantage of, use.
to enjoy yourself celebrate, [*informal*] gad about, [*informal*] have a fling, have a good time.

enjoyable adjective
an enjoyable party. enjoyable food. agreeable, amusing, SEE **delicious**, delightful, gratifying, likeable, [*informal*] nice, pleasant, pleasurable, rewarding, satisfying.
OPPOSITES: SEE **unpleasant**.

enlarge verb
amplify (*sound*), augment, blow up (*a tyre, a photograph*), broaden (*the river broadened*), build up, develop, dilate (*the pupil of an eye*), diversify (*your interests*), elaborate (*a story or argument*), elongate, expand, extend, fill out, get bigger, grow, increase, inflate (*a balloon, a tyre*), lengthen, magnify, make bigger, multiply, stretch, swell, wax (*the moon waxes and wanes*), widen.
OPPOSITES: SEE **decrease** verb, **shrink**.

enlist verb
1 *to enlist troops.* conscript, engage, enrol, muster, recruit.

2 *The men enlisted in the army.* enrol, enter, join up, register, sign on, volunteer.
3 *to enlist someone's help.* SEE **obtain**.

enormous adjective SEE **big**, colossal, elephantine, gargantuan, giant, gigantic, huge, hulking, immense, [*informal*] jumbo, mammoth, massive, mighty, monstrous, mountainous, titanic, towering, tremendous, vast.
OPPOSITES: SEE **small**.

enough adjective
enough food. adequate, ample, as much as necessary, sufficient.

enquire verb
ask, beg, demand, entreat, implore, inquire, query, question, quiz, request.
to enquire about [*informal*] go into, investigate, probe, research, scrutinize.

enquiry noun
SEE **investigation**.

enrage verb SEE **anger** verb.

enrol verb
SEE **enlist**.

enslave verb
disenfranchise, dominate, make slaves of, subject, subjugate, take away the rights of.
OPPOSITES: SEE **liberate**.

ensure verb
[Do not confuse with *insure*.] *Ensure that you lock the door.* confirm, guarantee, make certain, make sure, secure.

entail verb SEE **involve**.

enter verb
1 *to enter a room.* arrive at, come in, go in, move into.
OPPOSITES: SEE **leave** verb.
2 *The bullet entered his leg.* cut into, dig into, penetrate, pierce, push into.
3 *to enter a competition.* engage in, enlist in, enrol in, [*informal*] go in for, join, participate in, sign up for, take part in, take up, volunteer for.
OPPOSITES: SEE **withdraw**.
4 *to enter a name on a list.* add, inscribe, insert, note down, put down, record, register, set down, sign, write.

enterprise noun
1 *a bold enterprise.* adventure, business, effort, endeavour, operation, project, undertaking, venture.
2 *She shows enterprise.* SEE **initiative**.

enterprising adjective
Some enterprising girls organized a sponsored walk. adventurous, ambitious, bold, courageous, daring, eager, energetic, enthusiastic, [*informal*] go-ahead, hard-

working, imaginative, industrious, intrepid, keen, pushful, [*uncomplimentary*] pushy, resourceful, spirited, venturesome.
OPPOSITES: SEE **unadventurous**.

entertain verb
1 *to entertain someone with stories*. amuse, cheer up, delight, divert, keep amused, make laugh, occupy, please, regale, [*informal*] tickle.
OPPOSITES: SEE **bore** verb.
2 *to entertain friends at Christmas*. accommodate, be the host or hostess to, cater for, give hospitality to, [*informal*] put up, receive, welcome.
3 *She wouldn't entertain the idea*. accept, agree to, approve, consent to, consider, contemplate, take seriously.

entertainer noun
performer.

VARIOUS ENTERTAINERS: acrobat, actor, actress, ballerina, broadcaster, busker, clown, comedian, comic, compère, conjuror, contortionist, co-star, dancer, disc jockey, DJ, jester, juggler, lion-tamer, magician, matador, minstrel, musician, question-master, singer, star, stunt man, superstar, toreador, trapeze artist, trouper, ventriloquist.

---

entertainment noun
amusement, distraction, diversion, enjoyment, fun, night-life, pastime, play, pleasure, recreation, sport.

VARIOUS KINDS OF ENTERTAINMENT: aerobatics, air-show, ballet, bullfight, cabaret, casino, ceilidh, cinema, circus, comedy, concert, dance, disco, discothèque, drama, fair, firework display, flower show, gymkhana, motor show, SEE **music**, musical, night-club, opera, pageant, pantomime, play, radio, recital, recitation, revue, rodeo, show, son et lumière, SEE **sport**, tap-dancing, tattoo, television, theatre, variety show, waxworks, zoo.

---

enthralling adjective
SEE **exciting**.

enthusiasm noun
1 *To be successful you need enthusiasm*. ambition, ardour, commitment, drive, eagerness, excitement, fervour, keenness, panache, spirit, verve, zeal, zest.
OPPOSITES: SEE **apathy**.
2 *Her current enthusiasm is judo*. craze, [*informal*] fad, diversion, hobby, interest, passion, pastime.

enthusiast noun
a pop music enthusiast. addict, admirer, aficionado, [*informal*] buff, devotee, fan, fanatic, [*informal*] fiend, [*informal*] freak, lover, supporter.

enthusiastic adjective
an enthusiastic supporter. ardent, avid, [*informal*] crazy, devoted, eager, earnest, ebullient, energetic, excited, exuberant, fervent, fervid, hearty, impassioned, keen, lively, [*informal*] mad keen, optimistic, passionate, positive, rapturous, raring (*raring to go*), spirited, unstinting, vigorous, wholehearted, zealous.
OPPOSITES: SEE **apathetic**.
to be enthusiastic enthuse, get excited, [*informal*] go into raptures, [*informal*] go overboard, rave.

entice verb
SEE **lure** verb.

entire adjective
SEE **whole**.

entitle verb
1 *The voucher entitles you to a refund. Her success entitles her to feel proud*. accredit, allow, authorize, empower, enable, justify, license, permit, warrant.
2 *What did you entitle your story?* call, christen, designate, dub, name, style, title.

entitlement noun
an entitlement to an inheritance. claim, ownership, prerogative, right, title.

entrance noun
1 *You pay at the entrance,* access, door, doorway, entry, gate, gateway, [*formal*] ingress, opening, portal, turnstile, way in.
OPPOSITES: SEE **exit** noun.
2 *I looked up at their entrance*. SEE **arrival**.
entrance hall ante-room, foyer, lobby, porch, vestibule.

entrant noun
an entrant in a competition. applicant, candidate, competitor, contender, contestant, entry, participant, player, rival.

entreat verb
SEE **request** verb.

entrust verb
They entrusted me with the money. put in charge of, trust.

entry noun
1 *Please don't block the entry*. SEE **entrance** noun.
2 *an entry in a diary*. insertion, item, jotting, note, record.
3 *an entry in a competition*. SEE **entrant**.

envelop verb SEE **cover** verb, **wrap** verb.

envelope noun
cover, sheath, wrapper, wrapping.

enviable adjective
an enviable salary. attractive, desirable,
favourable.

envious adjective
envious of her success. begrudging, bitter,
covetous, dissatisfied, [*informal*] green with
envy, grudging, jaundiced, jealous,
resentful.

environment noun
a natural environment. conditions, context,
habitat, location, setting, situation,
surroundings, territory.

envisage noun
SEE **visualize**.

envy noun
feelings of envy. bitterness, covetousness,
cupidity, dissatisfaction, ill-will, jealousy,
resentment.

envy verb
He envies her success. begrudge, grudge,
resent.

ephemeral adjective
Most newspapers are of ephemeral interest.
brief, evanescent, fleeting, impermanent,
momentary, passing, short-lived, temporary,
transient, transitory.
OPPOSITES: SEE **eternal**, **lasting**.

epidemic noun
an epidemic of measles. outbreak, plague.

epilogue noun
afterword, postscript.
OPPOSITES: SEE **prelude**.

episode noun
1 *a happy episode in my life.* SEE **event**.
2 *an episode of a serial.* chapter, instalment,
part, passage, scene, section.

epithet noun
description, designation, name, [*informal*]
tag, title.

epitome noun
She's the epitome of kindness. embodiment,
essence, personification, quintessence,
representation, type.

equal adjective
equal opportunities. equal quantities.
corresponding, egalitarian, equivalent,
even, fair, identical, level, like, matched,
matching, proportionate, the same,
symmetrical, uniform.

equality noun
equality of opportunity. balance,
correspondence, evenhandedness, fairness,
parity, similarity, uniformity.
OPPOSITES: SEE **inequality**.

equalize verb
to equalize scores. balance, even up, level,
make equal, match, [*informal*] square.

equip verb
*to equip workers with tools. to equip a room
with furniture.* arm (*troops*), fit out, furnish,
[*informal*] kit out, provide, stock, supply.

equipment noun
equipment you need for a job. accoutrements,
apparatus, furnishings, [*informal*] gear,
[*informal*] hardware, implements,
instruments, kit, machinery, materials,
outfit, paraphernalia, plant, [*informal*] rig,
[*informal*] stuff, supplies, tackle, [*informal*]
things, tools.

equivalent adjective
SEE **equal**.

equivocal adjective
SEE **ambiguous**.

era noun
SEE **period**.

eradicate, **erase** verbs
SEE **remove**.

erect adjective
SEE **upright**.

erect verb
to erect a tent. to erect a flag pole. build,
construct, elevate, lift up, make upright [SEE
upright], pitch (*a tent*), put up, raise, set up.

erode verb
Water erodes the topsoil. corrode, destroy,
eat away, grind down, wear away.

erotic adjective
SEE **amorous**.

errand noun
an errand to the shops. assignment, job,
journey, mission, task, trip.

erratic adjective
an erratic performance. capricious,
changeable, fickle, fitful, fluctuating,
inconsistent, irregular, shifting, spasmodic,
sporadic, uneven, unpredictable,
unreliable, unstable, unsteady, variable,
wandering, wayward.
OPPOSITES: SEE **consistent**.

erroneous adjective SEE **wrong** adjective.

error noun
factual errors. a fatal error on the motorway.
[*informal*] bloomer, blunder, [*informal*]
boob, fallacy, falsehood, fault, flaw,
[*informal*] howler, inaccuracy,

inconsistency, inexactitude, lapse, misapprehension, miscalculation, misconception, mistake, misunderstanding, omission, oversight, sin, [*informal*] slip-up, [*formal*] solecism, transgression, [*old-fashioned*] trespass, wrongdoing.

erupt verb
Smoke erupted from the volcano. be discharged, be omitted, belch, break out, burst out, explode, gush, issue, pour out, shoot out, spew, spout, spurt, vomit.

escalate verb
Fighting escalated as more people joined in. become worse, build up, expand, grow, increase, intensify, multiply, rise, spiral, step up.

escapade noun
a childish escapade. adventure, exploit, [*informal*] lark, mischief, practical joke, prank, scrape, stunt.

escape noun
1 *an escape from gaol.* bolt, break-out, flight, flit, get-away, retreat, running away.
2 *an escape of gas.* discharge, emission, leak, leakage, seepage.
3 *an escape from reality.* avoidance, distraction, diversion, escapism, evasion, relaxation, relief.

escape verb
1 *The prisoner escaped.* abscond, bolt, break free, break out, [*informal*] do a bunk, elope, flee, get away, [*informal*] give someone the slip, run away, [*slang*] scarper, slip away, [*informal*] slip the net.
2 *Oil escaped from a crack.* discharge, drain, leak, ooze, pour out, run out, seep.

escort noun
1 *a protective escort.* bodyguard, convoy, guard, guide, pilot.
2 *escorts to the queen.* attendant, entourage, retinue, train.
3 *an escort at a dance.* chaperon, companion, partner.

escort verb
to escort someone to a party. to escort a prisoner. accompany, chaperon, guard, [*informal*] keep an eye on, [*informal*] keep tabs on, look after, protect, stay with, usher, watch.

espionage noun SEE spying.

essence noun
1 *the essence of a problem. the essence of someone's personality.* centre, character, core, crux, essential quality [SEE **essential**], heart, kernel, life, meaning, nature, pith, quintessence, soul, spirit.
2 *peppermint essence.* concentrate, decoction, elixir, extract, fragrance, perfume, scent, tincture.

essential adjective
1 *essential information for travellers.* basic, chief, crucial, elementary, fundamental, important, indispensable, irreplaceable, key, main, necessary, primary, principal, requisite, vital.
OPPOSITES: SEE **inessential**.
2 *essential features.* characteristic, inherent, innate, intrinsic, quintessential.

establish verb
1 *to establish a business.* base, begin, construct, create, found, inaugurate, initiate, institute, introduce, organize, originate, set up, start.
2 *to establish yourself as leader.* confirm, ensconce, entrench, install, secure, settle.
3 *to establish the facts.* agree, authenticate, certify, confirm, corroborate, decide, demonstrate, fix, prove, ratify, show to be true, substantiate, verify.

established adjective
an established business. an established favourite on TV. established habits. accepted, confirmed, deep-rooted, deep-seated, entrenched, fixed, indelible, ineradicable, ingrained, long-lasting, long-standing, permanent, proved, proven, recognized, reliable, respected, rooted, secure, settled, traditional, well-known, well-tried.
OPPOSITES: SEE **new, untried**.

establishment noun
1 *the establishment of a new club.* composition, constitution, creation, formation, foundation, inauguration, inception, institution, introduction.
2 *a well-run establishment.* business, concern, factory, household, shop.

estate noun
1 *a housing estate.* area, development.
2 *an estate left in a will.* assets, effects, fortune, goods, inheritance, lands, possessions, property, wealth.

esteem verb
SEE **respect** verb.

estimate noun
1 *What's your estimate of the situation?* appraisal, assessment, conjecture, estimation, evaluation, guess, judgement, opinion, surmise.
2 *an estimate of what a job will cost.* calculation, [*informal*] guesstimate, price, quotation, reckoning, specification, valuation.

estimate verb
to estimate how much something will cost. appraise, assess, calculate, compute, conjecture, consider, count up, evaluate, gauge, guess, judge, project, reckon, surmise, think out, weigh up, work out.

eternal adjective
eternal life. deathless, endless, everlasting, heavenly, immeasurable, immortal, infinite, lasting, limitless, measureless, timeless, unchanging, undying, unending, unlimited.
OPPOSITES: SEE **ephemeral**.

eternity noun
an eternity in heaven. afterlife, eternal life [SEE **eternal**], immortality, infinity, perpetuity.

ethical adjective SEE **moral** adjective.

ethnic adjective
ethnic music. cultural, folk, national, racial, traditional, tribal.

etiquette noun
It's polite to observe correct etiquette. ceremony, civility, conventions, courtesy, decency, decorum, formalities, manners, politeness, propriety, protocol, rules of behaviour, standards of behaviour.

evacuate verb
1 *to evacuate people from a building or an area.* clear, move out, remove, send away.
2 *to evacuate a building or an area.* abandon, decamp from, desert, empty, forsake, leave, quit, relinquish, vacate, withdraw from.

evade verb
to evade your responsibilities. avoid, [*informal*] chicken out of, circumvent, dodge, duck, elude, escape from, fend off, shirk, shun, sidestep, [*informal*] skive, steer clear of, turn your back on.
OPPOSITES: SEE **accept**.

evaporate verb
Dew evaporates in the morning. disappear, disperse, dissipate, dissolve, dry up, melt away, vanish, vaporize.
OPPOSITES: SEE **condense**.

evasive adjective
an evasive answer. ambiguous, deceptive, devious, disingenuous, equivocal, inconclusive, indecisive, indirect, misleading, non-committal, oblique, prevaricating, shifty, uninformative.
OPPOSITES: SEE **straightforward**.

even adjective
1 *an even surface.* flat, flush, horizontal, level, smooth, straight, true, unbroken, unruffled.
OPPOSITES: SEE **rough**.
2 *an even temper.* SEE **even-tempered**.
3 *the even ticking of a clock.* balanced, consistent, equalized, metrical, monotonous, proportional, regular, rhythmical, steady, symmetrical, unvarying.
OPPOSITES: SEE **irregular**.
4 *even scores.* equal, identical, level, the same.
OPPOSITES: SEE **unequal**.

even verb
to even out *I evened out the wrinkled carpet.* flatten, level, smooth, straighten.
to even up *The next goal evened up the scores.* balance, equalize, level, [*informal*] square.

evening noun
dusk, [*poetic*] eventide, [*poetic*] gloaming, nightfall, sundown, sunset, twilight.

event noun
1 *an unexpected event.* affair, business, chance, circumstance, contingency, episode, eventuality, experience, happening, incident, occurrence.
2 *a special event.* activity, ceremony, entertainment, function, occasion.
3 *a sporting event.* bout, championship, competition, contest, engagement, fixture, game, match, meeting, tournament.

even-tempered adjective
an even-tempered character. calm, composed, cool, equable, even, impassive, imperturbable, peaceable, peaceful, placid, reliable, serene, stable, steady, tranquil, unexcitable.
OPPOSITES: SEE **excitable**.

eventual adjective
the eventual result. concluding, consequent, ensuing, final, last, overall, resulting, ultimate.

everlasting adjective
SEE **eternal**.

everyday adjective
an everyday happening. SEE **ordinary, usual**.

evict verb
to evict a tenant. [*formal*] dispossess, eject, expel, [*slang*] give (someone) the boot, [*informal*] kick out, oust, put out, remove, throw out, [*informal*] turf out, turn out.

evidence noun
legal evidence. scientific evidence. confirmation, corroboration, data, demonstration, documentation, facts, grounds, information, proof, sign, statistics, substantiation, testimony.
to give evidence SEE **testify**.

evident adjective
It's evident that he doesn't like work. apparent, certain, clear, discernible, manifest, noticeable, obvious, palpable, patent, perceptible, plain, self-explanatory, unambiguous, undeniable, unmistakable, visible.
OPPOSITES: SEE **unclear**.

evil adjective
1 *an evil deed. an evil person.* amoral, atrocious, SEE **bad**, base, black-hearted, blasphemous, corrupt, criminal, cruel, dark (*dark deeds*), depraved, devilish, diabolical,

dishonest, fiendish, foul, harmful, hateful, heinous, hellish, immoral, impious, infamous, iniquitous, irreligious, machiavellian, malevolent, malicious, malignant, nefarious, pernicious, perverted, reprobate, satanic, sinful, sinister, treacherous, ungodly, unprincipled, unrighteous, vicious, vile, villainous, wicked, wrong.
OPPOSITES: SEE **good**.
2 *an evil smell. an evil mood.* foul, nasty, pestilential, poisonous, troublesome, SEE **unpleasant**, unspeakable, vile.
OPPOSITES: SEE **pleasant**.

evil noun
1 *the fight against evil.* amorality, blasphemy, corruption, SEE **crime**, criminality, cruelty, depravity, dishonesty, fiendishness, heinousness, immorality, impiety, iniquity, [*old-fashioned*] knavery, malevolence, malice, mischief, pain, sin, sinfulness, suffering, treachery, turpitude, ungodliness, unrighteousness, vice, viciousness, villainy, wickedness, wrongdoing.
2 *Pollution is one of the evils of our world.* affliction, bane, calamity, catastrophe, curse, disaster, enormity, harm, ill, misfortune, sin, wrong.

evocative adjective
an evocative description. atmospheric, convincing, descriptive, emotive, graphic, imaginative, provoking, realistic, stimulating, suggestive, vivid.

evoke verb
to evoke a response. arouse, awaken, call up, conjure up, elicit, excite, inspire, kindle, produce, provoke, raise, stimulate, stir up, suggest, summon up.

evolution noun
the evolution of life. the evolution of an idea. development, emergence, growth, improvement, maturing, progress, unfolding.

evolve verb
Animals evolved from simple forms of life. derive, descend, develop, emerge, grow, improve, mature, modify gradually, progress.

exact adjective
1 *exact measurements.* accurate, correct, dead (*the dead centre*), faultless, meticulous, precise, right, specific, [*informal*] spot-on, strict.
2 *an exact account.* detailed, faithful, scrupulous, true, truthful, veracious.
3 *an exact copy.* flawless, identical, indistinguishable, perfect.

exaggerate verb
1 *to exaggerate a difficulty.* amplify, enlarge, inflate, magnify, make too much of, maximize, overdo, over-emphasize, overestimate, overstate, [*informal*] pile it on, [*informal*] play up.
OPPOSITES: SEE **underestimate**.
2 *to exaggerate someone's mannerisms.* burlesque, caricature, overact, parody, [*informal*] take off.

exaggerated adjective
exaggerated mannerisms. burlesque, [*informal*] camp, SEE **excessive**, extravagant, hyperbolical, inflated, overdone, [*informal*] over the top.

examination noun
1 *an examination of our finances.* analysis, appraisal, audit, [*informal*] post-mortem, review, scrutiny, study, survey.
2 *a school examination.* assessment, catechism [= *questions and answers about religious knowledge*], exam, oral [= *oral examination*], paper, test, viva or [*Latin*] viva voce.
3 *a medical examination.* [*informal*] check-up, inspection, investigation, probe, scan.
4 *an examination by the police.* cross-examination, enquiry, inquiry, inquisition, interrogation, questioning, trial.

examine verb
1 *to examine evidence.* analyse, appraise, audit (*accounts*), check, [*informal*] check out, explore, inquire into, inspect, investigate, probe, scrutinize, sift, sort out, study, [*slang*] suss out, test, vet, weigh up.
2 *to examine a witness.* catechize, cross-examine, cross-question, [*informal*] grill, interrogate, question.

example noun
1 *Give an example of what you mean.* case, illustration, instance, occurrence, sample, specimen.
2 *She's an example to us all.* ideal, lesson, model, paragon, pattern, prototype.

exasperate verb
SEE **anger** verb, **annoy**.

excavate verb
SEE **dig**.

exceed verb
to exceed the speed limit. to exceed a particular number. beat, better, excel, go over, outdo, outnumber, outstrip, pass, surpass, top.

exceedingly adverb
exceedingly good cake. amazingly, especially, exceptionally, excessively, extraordinarily, extremely, outstandingly, specially, unusually, very.

excel verb
1 *Their team excelled ours in every event.*
beat, better, do better than, eclipse,
exceed, outclass, outdo, outshine, surpass,
top.
2 *She's a good all-round player, but she excels
in tennis.* be excellent [SEE **excellent**], do best,
shine, stand out.

excellent adjective
an excellent player. excellent food. [*informal*]
ace, [*informal*] brilliant, [*old-fashioned*]
capital, champion, choice, [*slang*] cracking,
distinguished, esteemed, estimable,
exceptional, extraordinary, [*informal*]
fabulous, [*informal*] fantastic, fine, first-
class, first-rate, SEE **good**, gorgeous, great,
high-class, impressive, magnificent,
marvellous, notable, outstanding,
remarkable, [*informal*] smashing, splendid,
sterling, [*informal*] stunning, [*informal*]
super, superb, superlative, supreme,
surpassing, [*informal*] tip-top, [*informal*]
top-notch, top-ranking, [*informal*]
tremendous, unequalled, wonderful.
OPPOSITES: SEE **bad, mediocre**.

exception noun
1 *an exception from a list.* exclusion,
omission, rejection.
2 *an exception from what is normal.*
abnormality, anomaly, departure,
deviation, eccentricity, freak, irregularity,
oddity, peculiarity, quirk, rarity.

exceptional adjective
*exceptional weather. an exceptional stroke of
bad luck.* aberrant, abnormal, anomalous,
atypical, curious, deviant, eccentric,
extraordinary, memorable, notable, odd,
peculiar, phenomenal, quirky, rare,
remarkable, singular, special, strange,
surprising, uncommon, unconventional,
unexpected, unheard of, unparalleled,
unprecedented, unpredictable, unusual.
OPPOSITES: SEE **normal**.

excerpt noun
We read excerpts from '1984'. [*formal*]
citation, clip, extract, fragment, highlight,
part, passage, quotation, section, selection.

excess noun
1 *an excess of food.* abundance, glut, over-
indulgence, superabundance, superfluity,
surfeit.
OPPOSITES: SEE **scarcity**.
2 *an excess of income over expenditure.* profit,
surplus.
OPPOSITES: SEE **deficit**.

excessive adjective
1 *excessive zeal.* disproportionate,
exaggerated, extreme, fanatical, SEE **great**,
immoderate, inordinate, intemperate,

needless, overdone, profuse, undue,
unnecessary.
2 *excessive amounts of food.* extravagant, SEE
huge, prodigal, profligate, superfluous,
unneeded, wasteful.
OPPOSITES: SEE **inadequate, moderate**
adjective.
3 *excessive prices.* SEE **exorbitant**,
extortionate, unrealistic, unreasonable.

exchange noun
1 *an exchange of prisoners.* replacement,
substitution, [*informal*] swap, switch.
2 *exchange of goods.* bargain, barter, deal,
trade-in, traffic.

exchange verb
to exchange one thing for another. barter,
change, convert (*convert pounds into
dollars*), interchange, reciprocate, replace,
substitute, [*informal*] swap or swop, switch,
trade, trade in, traffic.

excitable adjective
an excitable crowd. [*informal*] bubbly,
chattery, emotional, SEE **excited**, explosive,
fiery, highly strung, hot-tempered,
irrepressible, lively, SEE **nervous**,
passionate, quick-tempered, restive,
temperamental, unstable, volatile.
OPPOSITES: SEE **even-tempered**.

excite verb
The smell of food excited the animals. agitate,
animate, discompose, disturb, electrify,
exhilarate, [*informal*] get going, inflame,
intoxicate, make excited [SEE **excited**], move,
provoke, rouse, stimulate, stir up, thrill,
titillate, [*informal*] turn on, upset.
OPPOSITES: SEE **calm** verb.

excited adjective
an excited crowd. an excited reaction.
agitated, animated, aroused, boisterous,
delirious, disturbed, SEE **eager**, elated,
enthusiastic, SEE **excitable**, exuberant,
feverish, frantic, frenzied, heated,
[*informal*] het up, hysterical, impassioned,
lively, moved, nervous, overwrought,
restless, roused, spirited, stimulated,
stirred, thrilled, vivacious, wild, [*informal*]
worked up.
OPPOSITES: SEE **apathetic, subdued**.

excitement noun
1 *feelings of excitement.* agitation, animation,
delirium, discomposure, eagerness,
enthusiasm, heat (*the heat of the moment*),
intensity, [*informal*] kicks, passion,
stimulation, suspense, tension, thrill.
2 *A crowd watched the excitement.* action,
activity, adventure, SEE **commotion**, drama,
furore, fuss, unrest.

exciting adjective
an exciting discovery. amazing, cliff-hanging,
dramatic, electrifying, enthralling,

eventful, exhilarating, fast-moving, gripping, hair-raising, inspiring, interesting, intoxicating, moving, [*informal*] nail-biting, provocative, rousing, sensational, stimulating, stirring, suspenseful, thrilling, titillating.
OPPOSITES: SEE **boring**.

exclaim verb
call, cry out, [*old-fashioned*] ejaculate, SEE **say**, shout, utter an exclamation [SEE **exclamation**], [*formal*] vociferate, [*informal*] yell.

exclamation noun
call, cry, [*old-fashioned*] ejaculation, expletive, interjection, oath, shout, swear word.

exclude verb
to exclude someone from a conversation. to exclude illegal imports. ban, banish, bar, blacklist, debar, disallow, disown, eject, except, excommunicate *(from the church)*, expel, forbid, [*formal*] interdict, keep out, leave out, lock out, omit, ostracize, oust, outlaw, prohibit, proscribe, put an embargo on, refuse, reject, SEE **remove**, repudiate, rule out, shut out, veto.
OPPOSITES: SEE **include**.

exclusive adjective
1 *an exclusive contract*. limiting, restrictive, sole, unique, unshared.
2 *an exclusive club*. classy, closed, fashionable, [*informal*] members only, [*slang*] posh, private, select, selective, snobbish, [*informal*] trendy, [*informal*] up-market.

excrete verb
defecate, eliminate waste matter, evacuate the bowels, go to the lavatory, relieve yourself.

excursion noun
an excursion to the seaside. expedition, jaunt, journey, outing, ramble, tour, trip.

excuse noun
a feeble excuse. alibi, defence, explanation, extenuation, justification, mitigation, plea, pretext, reason, vindication.

excuse verb
1 *to excuse bad behaviour*. condone, explain, forgive, ignore, justify, overlook, pardon, sanction, tolerate, vindicate.
2 *The judge excused the prisoner*. absolve, acquit, discharge, [*formal*] exculpate, exonerate, free, let off, liberate, release.

execute verb
1 *to execute a manœuvre*. accomplish, achieve, carry out, complete, do, effect, enact, finish, implement, perform.
2 *to execute a criminal*. SEE **kill**, SEE **punish**, put to death.

METHODS USED TO EXECUTE PEOPLE:
behead, burn, crucify, decapitate, electrocute, garotte, gas, guillotine, hang, lynch, shoot, stone.

exemplary adjective
exemplary behaviour. SEE **admirable**, faultless, flawless, ideal, model, perfect, unexceptionable.

exempt adjective
exempt from paying tax. excepted, excluded, excused, free, immune, let off, released, spared.

exercise noun
1 *Exercise helps to keep you fit*. action, activity, aerobics, effort, exertion, games, gymnastics, PE, sport, [*informal*] work-out.
2 *army exercises. exercises on the piano*. discipline, drill, manœuvre, operation, practice, training.

exercise verb
1 *to exercise self-control. to exercise power*. apply, bring to bear, display, employ, exert, expend, show, use, utilize, wield.
2 *to exercise your body*. discipline, drill, exert, jog, keep fit, practise, train, [*informal*] work out.

exertion noun
SEE **effort**.

exhaust noun
exhaust from a car. discharge, emission, fumes, gases, smoke.

exhaust verb
1 *to exhaust your resources. to exhaust your energy*. consume, deplete, drain, dry up, empty, finish off, sap, spend, use up, void.
2 *to exhaust yourself*. SEE **tire**.

exhausted adjective
1 *an exhausted oil-well*. drained, dry, empty, finished, used up.
2 *exhausted after a hard game*. breathless, [*informal*] done in, fatigued, gasping, [*slang*] knackered, panting, puffed out, [*informal*] shattered, SEE **tired**, weary, [*informal*] whacked, worn out.

exhausting adjective
exhausting work. arduous, backbreaking, crippling, demanding, difficult, fatiguing, gruelling, hard, laborious, punishing, sapping, severe, strenuous, taxing, tiring, wearying.
OPPOSITES: SEE **refreshing**.

exhaustion noun
debility, fatigue, tiredness, weakness, weariness.

exhaustive adjective
an exhaustive search. all-out, careful, SEE **comprehensive**, intensive, meticulous, thorough.

exhibit verb
1 *to exhibit paintings.* arrange, display, present, put up, set up, show.
2 *to exhibit your knowledge.* air, demonstrate, [*uncomplimentary*] flaunt, indicate, manifest, [*uncomplimentary*] parade, reveal, [*uncomplimentary*] show off.
OPPOSITES: SEE **hide** verb.

exhibition noun
an art exhibition. demonstration, display, presentation, show.

exile noun
1 *Exile can be a harsh punishment.* banishment, deportation, expatriation, expulsion.
2 *an exile from your own country.* exiled person, deportee, émigré, expatriate, outcast, refugee, wanderer.

exile verb
to exile someone. banish, deport, drive out, eject, expatriate, expel, send away.

exist verb
1 *Do dragons exist?* be, be in existence, occur.
2 *We can't exist without food.* continue, endure, hold out, keep going, last, live, remain alive, subsist, survive.

existence noun
1 *I don't believe in the existence of ghosts.* actuality, being, life, living, reality.
2 *We depend on the environment for our existence.* continuance, survival.

existing adjective
existing species. actual, alive, continuing, corporeal, current, enduring, existent, extant, factual, in existence, living, material, ongoing, present, real, remaining, surviving.
OPPOSITES: SEE **non-existent**.

exit noun
1 *Pass through the exit.* barrier, SEE **door**, doorway, egress, gate, gateway, opening, portal, way out.
2 *We made a hurried exit.* SEE **departure**.

exorbitant adjective
exorbitant prices. excessive, expensive, extortionate, extravagant, high, outrageous, overpriced, prohibitive, [*informal*] sky-high, [*informal*] steep, [*informal*] stiff, [*informal*] swingeing, top, unrealistic, unreasonable.
OPPOSITES: SEE **competitive**.

exotic adjective
exotic places. alien, different, exciting, faraway, foreign, remote, romantic, unfamiliar, wonderful.
OPPOSITES: SEE **familiar**.

expand verb
1 *to expand a business. to expand a story.* amplify, augment, broaden, build up, develop, diversify, elaborate, enlarge, extend, fill out, increase, make bigger, make longer.
OPPOSITES: SEE **reduce**.
2 *Metal expands in the heat.* become bigger, dilate, grow, increase, lengthen, open out, stretch, swell, thicken, widen.
OPPOSITES: SEE **contract** verb.

expanse noun
an expanse of water or land. area, breadth, extent, range, sheet, stretch, surface, sweep, tract.

expansive adjective
an expansive talker. affable, communicative, friendly, genial, open, outgoing, sociable, SEE **talkative**, well-disposed.
OPPOSITES: SEE **curt**, **unfriendly**.

expect verb
1 *We expected 100 guests.* anticipate, await, bank on, bargain for, count on, envisage, forecast, foresee, hope for, imagine, look forward to, predict, prophesy, reckon on, wait for.
2 *We expect good behaviour.* consider necessary, demand, insist on, rely on, require, want.

expected adjective
an expected increase in prices. awaited, forecast, foreseen, planned, predictable, predicted, unsurprising.
OPPOSITES: SEE **unexpected**.

expectant adjective
SEE **pregnant**.

expedient adjective
It was expedient to retire gracefully. advantageous, advisable, appropriate, convenient, desirable, helpful, judicious, opportune, politic, practical, pragmatic, profitable, prudent, sensible, suitable, to your advantage, useful, worthwhile.

expedition noun
an expedition to foreign parts. crusade, exploration, SEE **journey** noun, mission, pilgrimage, quest, raid, safari, voyage.

expel verb
1 *to expel a pupil from a school.* ban, banish, cast out, [*informal*] chuck out, dismiss, drive out, eject, evict (*from your home*), exile (*from your country*), exorcise (*evil spirits*), oust, remove, send away, throw out, [*informal*] turf out.

2 *to expel exhaust fumes.* belch, discharge, emit, exhale, give out, send out, spew out.

expense noun
the expense of running a car. charges, cost, expenditure, outgoings, outlay, overheads, payment, price, spending.

expensive adjective
expensive presents. costly, dear, SEE **exorbitant**, extravagant, generous (*a generous gift*), high-priced, [*informal*] pricey, [*informal*] steep, [*informal*] up-market.
OPPOSITES: SEE **cheap**.

experience noun
1 *You learn by experience.* [*informal*] doing it, familiarity, involvement, observation, participation, practice, taking part.
2 *They want someone with experience.* [*informal*] know-how, knowledge, skill, understanding.
3 *a frightening experience.* adventure, event, happening, incident, occurrence, ordeal.

experienced adjective
1 *an experienced worker.* expert, knowledgeable, practised, professional, qualified, skilled, specialized, trained, well-versed.
OPPOSITES: SEE **inexperienced**.
2 *an experienced man of the world.* knowing, sophisticated, wise, worldly-wise.
OPPOSITES: SEE **innocent**.

experiment noun
1 *scientific experiments.* demonstration, investigation, practical, proof, research, test.
2 *The new bus-service is an experiment.* trial, try-out, venture.

experiment verb
to experiment in a laboratory. do an experiment, investigate, make tests, research, test, try out.

experimental adjective
1 *experimental evidence.* based on experiments, empirical, proved, tested.
2 *an experimental bus-service.* being tested, exploratory, on trial, pilot, provisional, tentative, trial.

expert adjective
an expert craftsman. able, [*informal*] ace, [*informal*] brilliant, capable, SEE **clever**, competent, [*informal*] crack, experienced, knowledgeable, master (*a master craftsman*), masterly, practised, professional, proficient, qualified, skilful, skilled, specialized, trained, well-versed.
OPPOSITES: SEE **amateurish**, **ignorant**.

expert noun
an expert in her subject. [*informal*] ace, authority, connoisseur, [*informal*] dab

hand, genius, [*uncomplimentary*] know-all, master, professional, pundit, specialist, virtuoso [= *an expert musician*], [*uncomplimentary*] wiseacre, [*informal*] wizard.

expertise noun SEE **skill**.

expire verb
1 *The animal expired.* SEE **die**.
2 *My licence expired.* become invalid, come to an end, finish, [*informal*] run out.

explain verb
1 *to explain a problem.* clarify, clear up, decipher, decode, demonstrate, disentangle, elucidate, expound, gloss, illustrate, interpret, resolve, simplify, solve, [*informal*] sort out, spell out, teach, translate, unravel.
2 *to explain a mistake.* account for, excuse, give reasons for, justify, make excuses for, rationalize, vindicate.

explanation noun
1 *an explanation of what happened.* account, clarification, definition, demonstration, description, elucidation, [*formal*] exegesis, explication, exposition, illustration, interpretation, meaning, significance.
2 *the explanation for a mistake.* cause, justification, motivation, motive, reason, vindication.

explanatory adjective
explanatory remarks. descriptive, expository, helpful, illuminating, illustrative, interpretive.

explicit adjective
explicit criticism. clear, definite, detailed, direct, exact, express, frank, graphic, open, outspoken, patent, plain, positive, precise, put into words, said, specific, [*informal*] spelt out, spoken, straightforward, unambiguous, unconcealed, unequivocal, unhidden, unreserved.
OPPOSITES: SEE **implicit**.

explode verb
to explode with a bang. backfire, blast, blow up, burst, detonate, erupt, go off, make an explosion, set off, shatter.

exploit verb
1 *to exploit an advantage.* build on, capitalize on, [*informal*] cash in on, develop, make use of, profit by, work on, use, utilize.
2 *to exploit your employees.* [*informal*] bleed, enslave, ill-treat, impose on, keep down, manipulate, [*informal*] milk, misuse, oppress, [*informal*] rip off, [*informal*] squeeze dry, take advantage of, treat unfairly, withhold rights from.

explore verb
1 *to explore unknown lands.* break new ground, probe, prospect, reconnoitre, scout,

search, survey, tour, travel through.
2 *to explore a problem.* analyse, examine,
inspect, investigate, look into, research,
scrutinize.

explosion noun
a loud explosion. bang, blast, burst, clap (*of
thunder*), crack, detonation, discharge (*of a
gun*), eruption (*of a volcano, of noise*),
outburst (*of laughter*), report.

explosive adjective
explosive substances. an explosive situation.
SEE **dangerous**, highly charged, liable to
explode, sensitive, unstable, volatile.

expose verb
SEE **reveal, uncover.**

express verb
to express ideas. air, SEE **communicate**, give
vent to, phrase, put into words, release,
vent, ventilate, word.

expression noun
1 *a verbal expression.* cliché, formula,
phrase, phraseology, remark, SEE **saying**,
statement, term, turn of phrase, wording.
2 *a facial expression.* air, appearance, aspect,
countenance, face, look, mien.

VARIOUS FACIAL EXPRESSIONS: beam, frown,
glare, glower, grimace, grin, laugh, leer,
long face, pokerface, pout, scowl, smile,
smirk, sneer, wince, yawn.

---

3 *She reads with expression.* emotion, feeling,
intensity, sensibility, sensitivity,
sympathy, understanding.

expressionless adjective
1 *an expressionless face.* blank, [*informal*]
dead-pan, emotionless, empty, glassy (*a
glassy stare*), impassive, inscrutable,
pokerfaced, straight-faced,
uncommunicative, wooden.
2 *an expressionless voice.* boring, dull, flat,
monotonous, uninspiring, unmodulated,
unvarying.
OPPOSITES: SEE **expressive.**

expressive adjective
1 *an expressive look.* meaningful, mobile,
revealing, sensitive, significant, striking,
suggestive, telling.
2 *an expressive voice.* articulate, eloquent,
lively, modulated, varied.
OPPOSITES: SEE **expressionless.**

exquisite adjective
SEE **delicate.**

extemporize verb SEE **improvise.**

extend verb
1 *to extend a meeting.* draw out, keep going,
lengthen, make longer, prolong, protract,
[*informal*] spin out.

OPPOSITES: SEE **shorten.**
2 *to extend a deadline.* defer, delay, postpone,
put back, put off.
3 *to extend your hand.* give, hold out, offer,
present, proffer, put out, raise, reach out,
stick out, stretch out.
4 *to extend a business.* add to, build up,
develop, enlarge, expand, increase, widen
the scope of.
5 *The garden extends to the fence.* continue,
go, reach, spread, stretch.

extension noun
1 *an extension to a building.* SEE **addition.**
2 *an extension of a deadline.* delay,
postponement.

extensive adjective SEE **large.**

extent noun
1 *The map shows the extent of the estate.* area,
bounds, breadth, dimensions, distance,
expanse, length, limit, measurement, reach,
space, spread, width.
2 *After the storm we saw the extent of the
damage.* amount, degree, magnitude,
measure, proportions, quantity, range,
scope, size.

extenuating adjective
extenuating circumstances. SEE **mitigating.**

exterior adjective SEE **outside** adjective.

exterminate verb SEE **destroy.**

external adjective SEE **outside** adjective.

extinct adjective
1 *an extinct volcano.* extinguished, inactive.
OPPOSITES: SEE **active.**
2 *extinct species.* dead, defunct, died out,
exterminated, vanished.
OPPOSITES: SEE **existing.**

extinguish verb
to extinguish a fire. damp down, douse, put
out, quench, slake, smother, snuff (*a
candle*).
OPPOSITES: SEE **light** verb.

extort verb
to extort money from someone. bully, exact,
extract, force, obtain by force.

extra adjective
1 *extra supplies.* added, additional, excess,
further, more, other, reserve, spare,
supplementary, surplus, unneeded, unused,
unwanted.
2 *extra staff.* ancillary, auxiliary,
supernumerary, temporary.

extract noun
1 *beef extract.* concentrate, decoction,
distillation, essence.
2 *an extract from a newspaper.* [*formal*]
citation, [*informal*] clip, clipping, cutting,
excerpt, passage, quotation, selection.

extract verb
1 *to extract a tooth.* draw out, pull out, remove, take out, withdraw.
2 *to extract information from a book.* derive, gather, SEE **obtain**, quote, select.

extraordinary adjective
an extraordinary story. extraordinary behaviour. abnormal, amazing, bizarre, curious, exceptional, fantastic, [*informal*] funny, incredible, marvellous, miraculous, mysterious, mystical, notable, noteworthy, odd, outstanding, peculiar, [*informal*] phenomenal, queer, rare, remarkable, singular, special, strange, striking, stupendous, surprising, [*informal*] unbelievable, uncommon, unheard of, unimaginable, unique, unusual, [*informal*] weird, wonderful.
OPPOSITES: SEE **ordinary**.

extravagant adjective
an extravagant waste of money. excessive, SEE **expensive**, [*informal*] fancy, grandiose, improvident, lavish, outrageous, pretentious, prodigal, profligate, profuse, reckless, self-indulgent, [*informal*] showy, spendthrift, uneconomical, unreasonable, unthrifty, wasteful.
OPPOSITES: SEE **economical**.

extreme adjective
1 *extreme cold. extreme care.* acute, drastic, excessive, greatest, intensest, maximum, severest, utmost.
2 *the extreme edge of the field.* farthest, furthest, furthermost, outermost, ultimate.
3 *extreme opinions.* absolute, avant-garde, exaggerated, extravagant, fanatical, [*informal*] hard-line, immoderate, intemperate, intransigent, militant, obsessive, outrageous, uncompromising, [*informal*] way-out, zealous.

extreme noun
from one extreme to the other. edge, end, extremity, limit, maximum or minimum, opposite, pole, top or bottom, ultimate.

extremist noun
SEE **fanatic**.

extroverted adjective
active, confident, outgoing, positive, SEE **sociable**.
OPPOSITES: SEE **introverted**.

exuberant adjective
1 *an exuberant mood.* animated, boisterous, [*informal*] bubbly, buoyant, cheerful, eager, ebullient, effervescent, elated, energetic, enthusiastic, excited, exhilarated, high-spirited, irrepressible, lively, spirited, sprightly, vivacious.
OPPOSITES: SEE **apathetic**.
2 *an exuberant style of decoration.* baroque, exaggerated, highly decorated, ornate, overdone, rich, rococo.
OPPOSITES: SEE **restrained**.

exultant adjective SEE **joyful**.

eye noun

PARTS OF THE EYE: cornea, eyeball, eyebrow, eyelash, eyelid, iris, pupil, retina, white.
RELATED ADJECTIVES: optical, ophthalmic.

eyesight noun
good eyesight. vision.

WORDS TO DESCRIBE EYESIGHT: astigmatic, long-sighted, myopic, short-sighted.

eye-witness noun
Eye-witnesses described the accident. bystander, looker-on, observer, onlooker, spectator, watcher, witness.

Ff

fabric noun
cloth, material, stuff, textile.
VARIOUS FABRICS: SEE **cloth**.

fabulous adjective
1 *fabulous monsters.* SEE **legendary**.
2 [*informal*] *a fabulous party.* SEE **excellent**.

face noun
1 *a person's face.* air, appearance, countenance, SEE **expression**, features, look, [*slang*] mug, [*old-fashioned*] physiognomy, visage.
2 *the face of a building.* aspect (*a house with a southern aspect*), exterior, façade, front, outside.
3 *A cube has six faces.* facet, side, surface.

face verb
1 *to face one another.* be opposite to, front, look towards, overlook.
2 *to face danger.* come to terms with, confront, cope with, defy, encounter, experience, face up to, meet, oppose, square up to, stand up to, tackle.

facetious adjective
SEE **funny**.

facile adjective
1 [*uncomplimentary*] *a facile solution to a problem.* cheap, easy, effortless, hasty, obvious, quick, simple, superficial, unconsidered.
OPPOSITES: SEE **thorough**.

2 [*uncomplimentary*] *a facile talker*. fluent, glib, insincere, plausible, shallow, slick, [*informal*] smooth.
OPPOSITES: SEE **profound**.

facility noun
1 *The facility with which he did the job surprised us*. SEE **ease** noun.
2 *The crèche is a useful facility for working parents*. amenity, convenience, help, provision, resource, service.

fact noun
a known fact. actuality, certainty, fait accompli, reality, truth.
OPPOSITES: SEE **fiction**.
the facts circumstances, data, details, evidence, information, particulars, statistics.

factor noun
The judge took every factor into account. aspect, cause, circumstance, component, consideration, contingency, detail, determinant, element, fact, influence, item, parameter, particular.

factory noun

PLACES WHERE THINGS ARE MANUFACTURED: assembly line, forge, foundry, manufacturing plant, mill, refinery, shop-floor, workshop.

---

factual adjective
1 *factual information*. accurate, circumstantial, SEE **correct** adjective, demonstrable, empirical, objective, provable, true, well-documented.
OPPOSITES: SEE **false**.
2 *a factual film*. biographical, documentary, historical, real-life, true.
OPPOSITES: SEE **fictional**.
3 *a strictly factual account*. matter-of-fact, plain, prosaic, realistic, unadorned, unemotional, unimaginative.
OPPOSITES: SEE **unrealistic**.

fade verb
1 *Sunlight fades the curtains*. blanch, bleach, discolour, whiten.
OPPOSITES: SEE **brighten**.
2 *Daylight faded*. decline, decrease, dim, diminish, disappear, dwindle, evanesce, fail, melt away, pale, vanish, wane, weaken.
OPPOSITES: SEE **increase** verb.
3 *The flowers faded*. droop, flag, perish, shrivel, wilt, wither.
OPPOSITES: SEE **bloom** verb.

fail verb
1 *The engine failed*. break down, [*informal*] conk out, cut out, give out, give up, [*informal*] miss out, stop working.
OPPOSITES: SEE **succeed**.

2 *The attempt failed. The business failed*. be unsuccessful, close down, come to an end, [*informal*] come to grief, [*informal*] crash, fall through, [*informal*] flop, fold, fold up, founder, go bankrupt, [*informal*] go bust, go out of business, meet with disaster, miscarry, misfire, peter out, stop trading.
OPPOSITES: SEE **succeed**.
3 *The light failed*. decline, diminish, disappear, dwindle, fade, get worse, melt away, vanish, wane, weaken.
OPPOSITES: SEE **improve**.
4 *Don't fail to phone!* forget, neglect, omit.
OPPOSITES: SEE **remember**.
5 *She's upset: she thinks she failed us*. disappoint, [*informal*] let down.
OPPOSITES: SEE **please**.

failure noun
1 *a power failure*. breakdown, collapse, crash, stoppage.
2 *The attempt ended in failure*. defeat, disappointment, downfall, disaster, fiasco, [*informal*] flop, [*informal*] washout.
OPPOSITES: SEE **success**.

faint adjective
1 *a faint picture. faint colours*. blurred, dim, faded, hazy, ill-defined, indistinct, misty, pale, pastel (*pastel colours*), shadowy, unclear, vague.
OPPOSITES: SEE **clear** adjective.
2 *a faint smell*. delicate, slight.
OPPOSITES: SEE **strong**.
3 *a faint sound*. distant, hushed, low, muffled, muted, soft, subdued, thin, weak.
OPPOSITES: SEE **clear** adjective.
4 *to feel faint*. dizzy, exhausted, feeble, giddy, light-headed, unsteady, weak, [*informal*] woozy.

faint verb
become unconscious, black out, collapse, [*informal*] flake out, pass out, swoon.

fair adjective
1 *fair hair*. blond, blonde, flaxen, golden, light, yellow.
2 [*old-fashioned*] *a fair maiden*. SEE **beautiful**.
3 *fair weather*. bright, clear, clement, cloudless, dry, favourable, fine, pleasant, sunny.
4 *a fair referee, a fair decision*. disinterested, even-handed, fair-minded, honest, honourable, impartial, just, lawful, legitimate, non-partisan, open-minded, proper, right, unbiased, unprejudiced, upright.
5 *a fair performance*. acceptable, adequate, average, indifferent, mediocre, middling, moderate, ordinary, passable, reasonable, respectable, satisfactory, [*informal*] so-so, tolerable.

fairly adverb
fairly good. moderately, pretty, quite, rather, reasonably, somewhat, tolerably, up to a point.

faith noun
1 *faith that something will happen.* belief, confidence, trust.
2 *religious faith.* conviction, creed, devotion, SEE **religion**.
OPPOSITES: SEE **disbelief**, **doubt** noun.

faithful adjective
1 *a faithful companion.* close, consistent, constant, dependable, devoted, dutiful, loyal, reliable, staunch, trusty, trustworthy, unswerving.
2 *a faithful account of what happened.* accurate, exact, precise, SEE **true**.

fake adjective
a fake antique. artificial, bogus, counterfeit, ersatz, false, fictitious, forged, imitation, [*slang*] phoney, sham, simulated, synthetic, unreal.
OPPOSITES: SEE **genuine**.

fake noun
The picture was a fake. copy, duplicate, forgery, hoax, imitation, replica, reproduction, sham, simulation.

fake verb
to fake a posh accent. affect, copy, counterfeit, SEE **falsify**, feign, forge, fudge, imitate, pretend, put on, reproduce, sham, simulate.

fall noun
a fall in prices. collapse, crash, decline, decrease, descent, dip, dive, drop, lowering, plunge, reduction, slant, slope, tumble.

fall verb
1 *He fell off the wall.* collapse, [*informal*] come a cropper, crash down, dive, drop down, founder, keel over, overbalance, pitch, plummet, plunge, slump, stumble, topple, tumble.
2 *Silence fell.* come, come about, happen, occur, settle.
3 *The curtains fell in thick folds.* be suspended, cascade, dangle, dip down, hang.
4 *The water-level fell.* become lower, decline, decrease, diminish, dwindle, ebb, go down, lessen, sink, subside.
5 *The road falls to sea-level.* SEE **descend**.

fallacy noun SEE **error**.

fallible adjective
We're fallible, so we make mistakes. erring, frail, human, imperfect, liable to make mistakes, uncertain, unpredictable, unreliable, weak.
OPPOSITES: SEE **infallible**.

false adjective
1 *a false idea.* deceptive, erroneous, fallacious, inaccurate, incorrect, inexact, invalid, misleading, mistaken, spurious, unsound, untrue, wrong.
OPPOSITES: SEE **correct** adjective.
2 *a false friend.* deceitful, dishonest, disloyal, double-dealing, double-faced, faithless, lying, treacherous, unfaithful, unreliable, untrustworthy.
OPPOSITES: SEE **trustworthy**.
3 *false documents.* artificial, bogus, concocted, counterfeit, fake, fictitious, imitation, invented, made-up, mock, [*slang*] phoney, pretended, sham, simulated, synthetic, trumped-up, unfounded, unreal.
OPPOSITES: SEE **authentic**.

falsify verb
to falsify the facts. alter, [*informal*] cook (*cook the books*), distort, exaggerate, SEE **fake** verb, misrepresent, oversimplify, pervert, slant, tamper with, tell lies about, twist.

falter verb
1 *to falter in the face of danger.* become weaker, flag, flinch, hesitate, hold back, lose confidence, pause, quail, stagger, stumble, totter, vacillate, waver.
OPPOSITES: SEE **persevere**.
2 *to falter in your speech.* stammer, stutter.

fame noun
a superstar's fame. celebrity, credit, distinction, eminence, glory, honour, importance, [*informal*] kudos, name, prestige, prominence, public esteem, renown, reputation, repute, [*informal*] stardom.

familiar adjective
1 *a familiar sight.* accustomed, common, conventional, customary, everyday, frequent, mundane, normal, ordinary, regular, routine, stock (*a stock reply*), usual, well-known.
OPPOSITES: SEE **strange**.
2 *a familiar relationship. familiar language.* [*informal*] chatty, close, confidential, [*informal*] free-and-easy, SEE **friendly**, informal, intimate, near, relaxed, unceremonious.
OPPOSITES: SEE **formal**.
familiar with *Are you familiar with this music?* acquainted with, [*informal*] at home with, aware of, conscious of, expert in, informed about, knowledgeable about, trained in, versed in.

family noun
1 [= *children of the same parents*] brood, [*informal*] flesh and blood (*our own flesh and blood*), generation, litter (*a litter of puppies*).
2 [= *the wider set of relations*] clan, kindred,

[old-fashioned] kith and kin, relations, relatives, tribe.
3 [= the line from which a person is descended] the royal family. ancestry, blood, clan, dynasty, extraction, forebears, genealogy, house (a royal house), line, lineage, pedigree, race, strain.
RELATED ADJECTIVE: genealogical.

MEMBERS OF A FAMILY: adopted child, ancestor, aunt, brother, child, cousin, [informal] dad or daddy, daughter, descendant, divorcee, father, [male] fiancé, [female] fiancée, forefather, foster-child, foster-parent, godchild, godparent, grandchild, grandparent, guardian, husband, [informal or American] junior, kinsman or kinswoman, [old-fashioned] mater, mother, [informal] mum or mummy, nephew, next-of-kin, niece, offspring, orphan, parent, [old-fashioned] pater, quadruplet, quintuplet, relation, relative, sextuplet, sibling, sister, son, step-child, step-parent, triplet, twin, uncle, ward, widow, widower, wife.

---

famine noun
The drought caused widespread famine. dearth, hunger, malnutrition, scarcity, shortage, starvation, want.
OPPOSITES: SEE **plenty**.

famished adjective
SEE **hungry**.

famous adjective
a famous person. acclaimed, celebrated, distinguished, eminent, famed, great, historic, honoured, illustrious, important, legendary, lionized, notable, noted, outstanding, prominent, proverbial, renowned, time-honoured, well-known, world-famous.
OPPOSITES: SEE **unknown**.
famous person SEE **celebrity**.

fan noun
1 *an air-conditioning fan.* blower, extractor, propeller, ventilator.
2 *a pop music fan.* SEE **fanatic**.

fanatic noun
1 *a pop music fanatic.* addict, admirer, aficionado, devotee, enthusiast, [informal] fan, [informal] fiend, follower, [informal] freak, lover, supporter.
2 *a political fanatic.* activist, adherent, bigot, extremist, fanatical supporter [SEE **fanatical**], militant, zealot.

fanatical adjective
fanatical political views. bigoted, extreme, fervent, immoderate, irrational, militant,

obsessive, over-enthusiastic, passionate, rabid, single-minded, zealous.
OPPOSITES: SEE **moderate** adjective.

fancy verb
1 *I fancied I saw pink elephants.* SEE **imagine**.
2 *What do you fancy to eat?* SEE **desire** verb.

fantastic adjective
1 *fantastic decoration.* absurd, elaborate, exaggerated, extravagant, fanciful, grotesque, ostentatious, quaint, rococo.
OPPOSITES: SEE **plain** adjective.
2 *a fantastic story about dragons.* amazing, extraordinary, fabulous, far-fetched, imaginative, implausible, incredible, odd, remarkable, strange, unbelievable, unlikely, unrealistic, weird.
OPPOSITES: SEE **realistic**.
3 [informal] *We had a fantastic time.* SEE **excellent**.

fantasy noun
a fantasy about the future. day-dream, delusion, dream, fancy, hallucination, illusion, invention, make-believe, reverie, vision.
OPPOSITES: SEE **reality**.

far adjective
far places. SEE **distant**.

farcical adjective SEE **comic** adjective.

fare noun
the train fare to London. charge, cost, fee, payment, price.

farewell noun
a sad farewell. SEE **goodbye**, [informal] send-off, valediction.

far-fetched adjective
SEE **unlikely**.

farm noun
[old-fashioned] grange.

KINDS OF FARM: arable farm, croft, dairy farm, fish farm, fruit farm, livestock farm, organic farm, plantation, poultry farm, ranch, smallholding.

FARM BUILDINGS, ETC.: barn, barn-yard, byre, cowshed, dairy, Dutch barn, farmhouse, farmstead, farmyard, granary, haystack, milking parlour, outhouse, pigsty, rick, shed, silo, stable, sty.

FARMING EQUIPMENT: baler, combine harvester, cultivator, drill, harrow, harvester, hay fork, hoe, irrigation system, manure spreader, mower, planter, plough, scythe, tedder, tractor, trailer.

FARM WORKERS: [American] cowboy, [old-fashioned] dairymaid, farm manager, farm worker, labourer, [*old-fashioned*] land-girl, shepherd, stock-breeder, [*old-fashioned*] swineherd, [*old-fashioned*] yeoman.

CROPS GROWN ON FARMS: barley, cereals, corn, fodder, SEE **fruit**, maize, oats, potatoes, rape, rye, sugar-beet, sweet corn, SEE **vegetable**, wheat.

FARM ANIMALS: SEE **cattle**, chicken, cow, duck, fatstock, goat, goose, hen, horse, lamb, livestock, pig, SEE **poultry**, sheep, turkey.

farming noun
agriculture, [*formal*] agronomy, crofting, husbandry.
RELATED ADJECTIVES: agricultural.

fascinate verb
1 *He fascinated us with his tales.* attract, beguile, bewitch, captivate, charm, delight, enchant, engross, enthral, entrance, interest, rivet, spellbind.
2 *Some snakes fascinate their prey.* allure, entice, hypnotize, mesmerize.

fascinating adjective
SEE **attractive**.

fashion noun
1 *He behaved in a strange fashion.* manner, method, mode, way.
2 *the latest fashion in clothes.* convention, craze, cut, [*informal*] fad, line, look, pattern, rage (*it's all the rage*), style, taste, trend, vogue.

fashionable adjective
fashionable clothes. chic, contemporary, current, elegant, [*informal*] in (*the in thing*), the latest, modern, modish, popular, smart, [*informal*] snazzy, sophisticated, stylish, tasteful, [*informal*] trendy, up-to-date, [*informal*] with it.
OPPOSITES: SEE **unfashionable**.

fast adjective
1 *a fast pace.* breakneck, brisk, expeditious, express (*express delivery*), hasty, headlong, high-speed, hurried, lively, [*informal*] nippy, precipitate, quick, rapid, smart, [*informal*] spanking, speedy, supersonic, swift, unhesitating.
OPPOSITES: SEE **slow** adjective.
2 *Make the rope fast.* attached, fastened, firm, immobile, immovable, secure, tight.
3 *fast colours.* fixed, indelible, lasting, permanent, stable.

fast verb
to fast on a holy day. abstain, deny yourself, diet, go hungry, go without food, starve.

fasten verb
affix, anchor, attach, batten, bind, bolt, buckle, button, chain, clamp, clasp, cling, close, connect, couple, do up (*do up a button*),

fix, grip, hitch, hook, knot, join, lace, lash, latch on, link, lock, moor (*a boat*), nail, padlock, paste, pin, rivet (*metal plates*), rope, seal, secure, solder, staple, SEE **stick** verb, strap, tack, tape, tether (*an animal*), tie, unite, weld (*metal*).
OPPOSITES: SEE **undo**.

THINGS USED FOR FASTENING: anchor, bolt, buckle, button, catch, chain, clamp, clasp, clip, dowel, dowel-pin, drawing-pin, SEE **glue** noun, hasp, hook, knot, lace, latch, lock, mooring, nail, padlock, painter, peg, pin, rivet, rope, safety-pin, screw, seal, Sellotape, solder, staple, strap, string, tack, tape, tether, tie, toggle, velcro, wedge, zip.

fastener, fastening nouns
connection, connector, coupling, link, linkage.

fastidious adjective
a fastidious eater. choosy, dainty, discriminating, finicky, fussy, particular, [*informal*] pernickety, selective, squeamish.

fat adjective
1 *a fat figure.* chubby, corpulent, dumpy, SEE **enormous**, flabby, fleshy, gross, heavy, obese, overweight, paunchy, plump, podgy, portly, pot-bellied, pudgy, rotund, round, solid, squat, stocky, stout, tubby.
OPPOSITES: SEE **thin** adjective.
2 *fat meat.* fatty, greasy, oily.
OPPOSITES: SEE **lean** adjective.

fat noun

KINDS OF FAT: blubber, butter, dripping, ghee, grease, lard, margarine, oil, suet.

fatal adjective
1 *a fatal dose.* deadly, lethal.
2 *a fatal illness.* final, incurable, malignant, mortal, terminal.
3 *a fatal mistake.* calamitous, destructive, disastrous, vital.

fatality noun
The accident resulted in fatalities. casualty, death, loss.

fate noun
Fate was kind to him. chance, destiny, doom, fortune, karma, kismet, luck, nemesis, predestination, providence, the stars.

fated adjective
I was fated to miss that train. certain, destined, doomed, fore-ordained, intended, predestined, predetermined, preordained, sure.

fatigue noun
overcome with fatigue. debility, exhaustion, feebleness, lethargy, tiredness, weakness, weariness.

fatten verb
to fatten cattle. build up, feed up, make fat.

fault noun
1 *a fault in the engine.* blemish, defect, deficiency, failure, flaw, imperfection, malfunction, snag, weakness.
2 *a fault in your reasoning.* error, fallacy, inaccuracy, miscalculation, mistake.
3 *The mistake was my fault.* blunder, [*informal*] boob, demerit, failing, guilt, indiscretion, lapse, misconduct, misdeed, negligence, offence, omission, oversight, responsibility, shortcoming, sin, slip, [*informal*] transgression, [*old-fashioned*] trespass, wrongdoing.

faultless adjective SEE **perfect** adjective.

faulty adjective
faulty goods, *a faulty argument.* broken, damaged, defective, deficient, flawed, illogical, imperfect, inaccurate, incomplete, incorrect, inoperative, invalid, not working, out of order, unusable, useless.
OPPOSITES: SEE **perfect** adjective.

favour noun
1 *She shows favour towards her friends.* acceptance, approval, bias, favouritism, friendliness, goodwill, grace, liking, preference, support.
2 *He did me a favour.* benefit, courtesy, gift, good deed, good turn, indulgence, kindness, service.

favour verb
1 *She favours the original plan.* approve of, be in sympathy with, champion, choose, commend, esteem, [*informal*] fancy, [*informal*] go for, like, opt for, prefer, show favour to [SEE **favour** noun], think well of, value.
OPPOSITES: SEE **dislike** verb.
2 *The wind favoured our team.* abet, back, be advantageous to, befriend, SEE **help** verb, support.
OPPOSITES: SEE **hinder**.

favourable adjective
1 *a favourable wind. favourable comments.* advantageous, approving, auspicious, beneficial, benign, complimentary, encouraging, following (*a following wind*), friendly, generous, helpful, kind, positive, promising, propitious, reassuring, supportive, sympathetic, understanding, well-disposed.
2 *a favourable reputation.* agreeable, desirable, enviable, good, pleasing, satisfactory.
OPPOSITES: SEE **unfavourable**.

favourite adjective
a favourite toy. best, chosen, dearest, esteemed, liked, popular, preferred, well-liked.

favouritism noun
SEE **bias** noun.

fear noun
trembling with fear. alarm, anxiety, apprehension, awe, concern, consternation, cowardice, dismay, doubt, dread, faint-heartedness, foreboding, fright, [*informal*] funk, horror, misgiving, panic, [*formal*] phobia, qualm, suspicion, terror, timidity, trepidation, uneasiness, worry.
VARIOUS KINDS OF FEAR: SEE **phobia**.
OPPOSITES: SEE **courage**.

fear verb
to fear the worst. be afraid of [SEE **afraid**], dread, suspect, tremble at, worry about.

fearful adjective
1 *fearful about the future.* SEE **afraid**.
2 *a fearful sight.* SEE **frightening**.

fearless adjective
SEE **courageous**.

fearsome adjective
SEE **frightening**.

feasible adjective
1 *a feasible plan.* achievable, attainable, possible, practicable, practical, realizable, viable, workable.
OPPOSITES: SEE **impractical**.
2 *a feasible excuse.* acceptable, credible, likely, plausible, reasonable.
OPPOSITES: SEE **implausible**.

feast noun SEE **meal**.

feat noun
a daring feat. accomplishment, achievement, act, action, attainment, deed, exploit, performance.

feather noun
plume, quill.
feathers down, plumage.

feature noun
1 *The crime had some unusual features.* aspect, characteristic, circumstance, detail, facet, peculiarity, point, quality, trait.
2 *a feature in a newspaper.* article, column, item, piece, report, story.
features *a person's features.* countenance, expression, face, lineaments, look, [*formal*] physiognomy.

feature verb
The play featured a new actor. focus on, give prominence to, highlight, present, promote, show up, [*informal*] spotlight, [*informal*] star.

fee noun
a club membership fee. legal fees. charge,
cost, dues, fare, payment, price,
remuneration, subscription, sum, terms,
toll.

feeble adjective
1 *feeble after illness.* debilitated, delicate,
exhausted, faint, frail, helpless, ill,
inadequate, ineffective, listless, poorly,
powerless, puny, sickly, useless, weak.
OPPOSITES: SEE **strong**.
2 *a feeble character.* effete, feckless, hesitant,
incompetent, indecisive, ineffectual,
irresolute, [*informal*] namby-pamby,
spineless, vacillating, weedy, [*informal*]
wishy-washy.
OPPOSITES: SEE **decisive**.
3 *a feeble excuse.* flimsy, lame, paltry, poor,
tame, thin, unconvincing, weak.
OPPOSITES: SEE **convincing**.

feed verb
1 *to feed your children.* cater for, give food
to, nourish, provide for, provision,
strengthen, suckle.
2 *We fed well.* dine, eat, fare.
to feed on SEE **eat**.

feel verb
1 *to feel the texture of something.* caress,
finger, fondle, handle, hold, manipulate,
maul, [*informal*] paw, stroke, touch.
2 *to feel your way in the dark.* explore, fumble,
grope.
3 *to feel the cold.* be aware of, be conscious
of, detect, experience, know, notice,
perceive, sense, suffer, undergo.
4 *It feels cold.* appear, give the feeling of [SEE
feeling], seem.
5 *I feel it's time to go.* believe, consider, deem,
have a feeling [SEE **feeling**], judge, think.

feeling noun
1 *a feeling in my leg.* sensation, sense of
touch, sensitivity.
2 *feelings of love. feelings of hate.* ardour,
emotion, fervour, passion, sentiment,
warmth.
3 *a feeling that something is wrong.* attitude,
belief, consciousness, guess, hunch, idea,
impression, instinct, intuition, notion,
opinion, perception, thought, view.
4 *a feeling for music.* fondness,
responsiveness, sensibility, sympathy,
understanding.

felicity noun SEE **happiness**.

fell verb
1 *to fell an opponent.* bring down, flatten,
[*informal*] floor, knock down, prostrate.
2 *to fell trees.* chop down, cut down.

female adjective, noun SEE **feminine**.
RELATED ADJECTIVE: gynaecological.
OPPOSITES: SEE **male**.

FEMALE PEOPLE: aunt, [*old-fashioned*]
damsel, daughter, [*old-fashioned*]
débutante, fiancée, girl, girlfriend,
grandmother, lady, [*informal*] lass, lesbian,
[*old-fashioned*] maid, [*old-fashioned*]
maiden, [*old-fashioned*] mistress, mother,
niece, sister, spinster, [*old-fashioned or
insulting*] wench, wife, woman.

FEMALE CREATURES: bitch, cow, doe, ewe,
hen, lioness, mare, nanny-goat, sow, tigress,
vixen.

feminine adjective
feminine behaviour. feminine clothes. [*of
males*] effeminate, female,
[*uncomplimentary*] girlish, ladylike,
womanly.
OPPOSITES: SEE **masculine**.

fence noun
a garden fence. barricade, barrier, fencing,
hedge, hurdle, obstacle, paling, palisade,
railing, rampart, stockade, wall, wire.

fence verb
1 *to fence someone in.* circumscribe, confine,
coop up, encircle, enclose, hedge in,
immure, pen, surround, wall in.
2 *to fence with foils.* SEE **fight** verb.

fend verb
to fend for care for, [*informal*] do for, look
after.
to fend off SEE **repel**.

ferment verb
fermenting wine. bubble, effervesce,
[*informal*] fizz, foam, seethe, work.

ferocious adjective
SEE **fierce**.

ferry verb
to ferry passengers. SEE **convey**, drive, ship,
shuttle, take across, taxi, transport.

fertile adjective
a fertile garden. abundant, fecund,
flourishing, fruitful, lush, luxuriant,
productive, prolific, rich, teeming, well-
manured.
OPPOSITES: SEE **barren**.

fertilize verb
1 *to fertilize flowers or eggs.* impregnate,
inseminate, pollinate.
2 *to fertilize the soil.* add fertilizer to,
cultivate, dress, enrich, feed, make fertile,
manure, mulch, top-dress.

fervent adjective
a fervent supporter. ardent, avid, committed,
devout, eager, earnest, enthusiastic,
excited, fanatical, fervid, fiery, impassioned,
keen, passionate, spirited, vehement,
vigorous, warm, wholehearted, zealous.

fervour noun
The fervour of her speech showed she felt strongly. ardour, eagerness, energy, enthusiasm, excitement, fervency, fire, heat, intensity, keenness, passion, sparkle, spirit, vehemence, vigour, warmth, zeal.

fester verb
The wound festered. become infected, become inflamed, become poisoned, decay, discharge, gather, go bad, go septic, putrefy, suppurate, ulcerate.

festival noun
a bank-holiday festival. anniversary, carnival, celebration, commemoration, fair, feast, festivity, fête, fiesta, gala, holiday, jamboree, jubilee, merry-making.

festive adjective
a festive occasion. cheerful, cheery, convivial, gay, gleeful, happy, jolly, jovial, joyful, joyous, light-hearted, merry, uproarious.

festivities noun
Christmas festivities. celebrations, entertainment, feasting, SEE **festival**, festive occasion [SEE **festive**], [*informal*] jollification, party, revelry, revels.

fetch verb
1 *to fetch things from the shops.* bear, bring, call for, carry, collect, convey, get, import, obtain, pick up, retrieve, transfer, transport.
2 *How much would our car fetch?* be bought for, bring in, earn, go for, make, produce, raise, realize, sell for.

feud noun
a feud between two families. animosity, antagonism, conflict, dispute, enmity, hostility, SEE **quarrel** noun, rivalry, strife, vendetta.

feverish adjective
1 *a feverish illness.* burning, febrile, fevered, flushed, hot, inflamed, trembling.
2 *feverish activity.* agitated, excited, frantic, frenetic, frenzied, hectic, hurried, impatient, restless.

few adjective
We have few buses on Sunday. [*informal*] few and far between, inadequate, infrequent, rare, scarce, sparse, sporadic, [*informal*] thin on the ground, uncommon.
OPPOSITES: SEE **many**.

fibre noun
1 *woven fibres.* filament, hair, strand, thread.
2 *moral fibre.* backbone, SEE **courage**, determination, spirit, tenacity, toughness.

fickle adjective
They have no use for fickle supporters. changeable, changing, disloyal, erratic, faithless, inconsistent, inconstant, mutable,

treacherous, unfaithful, unpredictable, unreliable, unstable, [*informal*] up and down, vacillating, variable, volatile.
OPPOSITES: SEE **constant**, **stable**.

fiction noun
1 *a work of fiction.* VARIOUS KINDS OF WRITING: SEE **writing**.
2 *Her account was a fiction from start to finish.* concoction, deception, fabrication, fantasy, figment of the imagination, flight of fancy, invention, SEE **lie** noun, [*informal*] tall story.
OPPOSITES: SEE **fact**.

fictional adjective
a fictional story. fabulous, fanciful, imaginary, invented, legendary, made-up, make-believe, mythical.
OPPOSITES: SEE **factual**.

fictitious adjective
a fictitious name. apocryphal, assumed, SEE **fake** adjective, false, deceitful, fraudulent, imagined, invented, spurious, unreal, untrue.
OPPOSITES: SEE **genuine**, **true**.

fidelity noun
SEE **loyalty**.

fidget verb
It annoys me when you fidget! be restless, [*informal*] fiddle about, fret, frisk about, jerk about, [*informal*] jiggle, [*informal*] mess about, move restlessly, [*informal*] play about, twitch, worry.

fidgety adjective
fidgety movements. agitated, frisky, impatient, jittery, jumpy, nervous, on edge, restive, restless, twitchy, uneasy.
OPPOSITES: SEE **calm** adjective.

field noun
1 *a farm field.* enclosure, [*poetic*] glebe, green, [*old-fashioned & poetic*] mead, meadow, paddock, pasture.
2 *a games field.* arena, ground, pitch, playing-field, recreation ground, stadium.
3 *Electronics isn't my field.* area, [*informal*] department, domain, province, sphere, subject, territory.

fiendish adjective SEE **evil** adjective, **fierce**.

fierce adjective
1 *a fierce attack. fierce animals.* angry, barbaric, barbarous, bloodthirsty, bloody, brutal, cold-blooded, cruel, dangerous, fearsome, ferocious, fiendish, homicidal, inhuman, merciless, murderous, pitiless, ruthless, sadistic, savage, untamed, vicious, violent, wild.
OPPOSITES: SEE **humane**, **kind** adjective.
2 *fierce opposition.* active, aggressive, competitive, eager, heated, furious, intense,

keen, passionate, relentless, strong, unrelenting.
OPPOSITES: SEE **gentle**.
3 *a fierce fire.* SEE **fiery**.

fiery adjective
1 *a fiery furnace.* ablaze, aflame, blazing, burning, flaming, fierce, glowing, heated, hot, raging, red, red-hot.
2 *a fiery temper.* angry, ardent, choleric, excitable, fervent, furious, hot-headed, intense, irritable, livid, mad, passionate, violent.

fight noun
action, affray, attack, battle, bout, brawl, [*informal*] brush, [*informal*] bust-up, clash, combat, competition, conflict, confrontation, contest, counter-attack, dispute, dogfight, duel, [*informal*] dust-up, encounter, engagement, feud, [*old-fashioned*] fisticuffs, fracas, fray, [*informal*] free-for-all, hostilities, joust, SEE **martial (martial arts)**, match, mêlée, [*informal*] punch-up, SEE **quarrel** noun, raid, riot, rivalry, row, scramble, scrap, scrimmage, scuffle, [*informal*] set-to, skirmish, squabble, strife, struggle, tussle, war, wrangle.

fight verb
1 *to fight against an enemy.* attack, battle, box, brawl, [*informal*] brush, clash, compete, conflict, contend, do battle, duel, engage, exchange blows, fence, feud, grapple, have a fight [SEE **fight** noun], joust, quarrel, row, scrap, scuffle, skirmish, spar, squabble, stand up (to), strive, struggle, [*old-fashioned*] tilt, tussle, wage war, wrestle.
2 *to fight a decision.* campaign against, contest, defy, oppose, protest against, resist, take a stand against.

fighter noun
aggressor, antagonist, attacker, belligerent, campaigner, combatant, contender, contestant, defender.

VARIOUS FIGHTERS: archer, boxer, [*informal*] brawler, champion, duellist, freedom-fighter, gladiator, guerrilla, gunman, knight, marine, marksman, mercenary, partisan, prize-fighter, pugilist, sniper, SEE **soldier**, swordsman, terrorist, warrior, wrestler.

---

figment noun
SEE **invention**.

figurative adjective
figurative language. allegorical, metaphorical, poetic, symbolic.
OPPOSITES: SEE **literal**.

figure noun
1 *the figures 1 to 10.* amount, digit, integer, number, numeral, value.
figures *She's good at figures.* accounts, mathematics, statistics, sums.
1 *a diagrammatic figure.* diagram, drawing, graph, illustration, outline, representation.
2 *a plump figure.* body, build, form, physique, shape, silhouette.
3 *a bronze figure.* SEE **sculpture** noun.
4 *a well-known figure.* SEE **personality**.
figure of speech conceit, emblem, image, [*informal*] manner of speaking, trope.

COMMON FIGURES OF SPEECH: alliteration, anacoluthon, antithesis, assonance, climax, ellipsis, hendiadys, hyperbole, irony, litotes, meiosis, metaphor, metonymy, onomatopoeia, oxymoron, parenthesis, personification, simile, synecdoche, zeugma.

---

file noun
1 *a file for papers.* binder, boxfile, cover, document-case, dossier, folder, portfolio, ring-binder.
2 *single file.* column, line, procession, queue, rank, row, stream, string, train.

fill verb
1 *to fill a container.* cram, flood (*with liquid*), inflate (*with air*), load, pack, refill, replenish, [*informal*] stuff, [*informal*] top up.
OPPOSITES: SEE **empty** verb.
2 *to fill a gap.* block, [*informal*] bung up, clog, close up, crowd, jam, obstruct, plug, seal, stop up.
OPPOSITES: SEE **clear** verb.
3 *to fill a need.* fulfil, furnish, meet, provide, satisfy, supply.
4 *to fill a post.* hold, occupy, take up.

filling noun
the filling in a cushion. contents, insides, padding, stuffing.

film noun
1 *a film of oil.* coat, coating, covering, layer, membrane, sheet, skin, slick, tissue, veil.
2 *a cinema film.* [*old-fashioned*] flick, motion picture, movie, picture, video.

KINDS OF FILM: cartoon, comedy, documentary, epic, feature, horror film, short, western.

---

filter verb
to filter a liquid. clarify, filtrate, percolate, purify, screen, sieve, strain.

filth noun
Clean up this filth! dirt, garbage, grime, SEE **impurity**, muck, mud, pollution, refuse, scum, sewage, slime, sludge.

filthy adjective
filthy shoes. a filthy room. caked, dirty, disgusting, dusty, foul, grimy, grubby, impure, messy, mucky, muddy, nasty, slimy, smelly, soiled, sooty, sordid, squalid, stinking, uncleaned, unwashed.
OPPOSITES: SEE **clean** adjective.

final adjective
the final moments of a game. clinching, closing, concluding, conclusive, decisive, dying, eventual, last, terminal, terminating, ultimate.
OPPOSITES: SEE **introductory**.

finance noun
He works in finance. accounting, banking, business, commerce, investment, stocks and shares.
finances *What's the state of your finances?* assets, bank account, budget, funds, income, money, resources, wealth.

finance verb
The bank helped to finance our business. back, fund, invest in, pay for, provide money for, sponsor, subsidize, support, underwrite.

financial adjective
financial affairs. economic, fiscal, monetary, pecuniary.

find verb
1 *to find something new.* acquire, arrive at, become aware of, chance upon, come across, come upon, dig up, discover, encounter, expose, [*informal*] ferret out, happen on, hit on, learn, light on, locate, meet, note, notice, observe, reach, recognize, spot, stumble on, uncover, unearth.
2 *to find something that was lost.* get back, recover, rediscover, regain, retrieve, trace, track down.
3 *to find a fault.* detect, diagnose, identify.
4 *He found me a job.* give, pass on, procure, provide, supply.

fine adjective
1 *a fine performance.* admirable, commendable, excellent, first-class, SEE **good**.
2 *fine weather.* bright, clear, cloudless, fair, pleasant, sunny.
3 *fine thread. fine china.* delicate, flimsy, fragile, narrow, slender, slim, thin.
4 *fine sand.* minute, powdery.
5 *fine embroidery.* beautiful, dainty, delicate, exquisite, skilful.
6 *a fine distinction.* discriminating, fine-drawn, subtle.

finger noun
digit, fingertip, index finger, little finger, middle finger, ring finger.

finish noun
1 *the finish of a race.* cessation, close, completion, conclusion, culmination, end, ending, finale, resolution, result, termination.
2 *a shiny finish on the metalwork.* appearance, gloss, lustre, polish, shine, smoothness, surface, texture.
3 *Their performance lacked finish.* completeness, perfection, polish.

finish verb
1 *to finish a job.* accomplish, achieve, break off, bring to an end, cease, complete, conclude, discontinue, end, finalize, halt, perfect, reach the end of, round off, sign off, stop, terminate, [*informal*] wind up.
2 *to finish your rations.* consume, drink up, eat up, empty, exhaust, expend, get through, [*informal*] polish off, [*informal*] say goodbye to, use up.
3 [*informal*] *The effort finished me.* exhaust, tire out, wear out.
to finish off annihilate, destroy, dispatch, exterminate, SEE **kill**.

finite adjective
finite resources. a finite number. calculable, definable, defined, fixed, known, limited, measurable, numbered, restricted.
OPPOSITES: SEE **infinite**.

fire noun
blaze, burning, combustion, conflagration, flames, holocaust, inferno, pyre.

KINDS OF FIRE OR HEATING APPARATUS: boiler, bonfire, brazier, central heating, convector, electric fire, SEE **fireworks**, forge, furnace, gas fire, immersion-heater, incinerator, kiln, oven, radiator, stove.

---

fire verb
1 *The vandals fired a barn.* burn, ignite, kindle, light, put a light to, set alight, set fire to.
2 *to fire pottery.* bake, heat.
3 *to fire your imagination.* animate, enliven, excite, incite, inflame, inspire, rouse, stimulate, stir.
4 *to fire a gun or missile.* detonate, discharge, explode, launch, let off, set off, shoot, trigger off.
5 *to fire someone from a job.* dismiss, make redundant, sack, throw out.
to fire at *I fired at the target.* aim at, bombard, [*informal*] let fly at, shell, shoot at.

firearm noun SEE **gun**.

fireworks noun
pyrotechnics.

VARIOUS FIREWORKS: banger, Catherine wheel, cracker, rocket, Roman candle, sparkler, squib.

---

firm adjective
1 *firm ground.* compact, compressed, congealed, dense, hard, rigid, solid, stable, stiff, unyielding.
OPPOSITES: SEE **soft**.
2 *a firm fit.* anchored, fast, fixed, immovable, secure, steady, tight.
3 *firm convictions.* adamant, decided, determined, dogged, obstinate, persistent, resolute, unshakeable, unwavering.
4 *a firm arrangement.* agreed, settled, unchangeable.
5 *a firm friend.* constant, dependable, devoted, faithful, loyal, reliable.

firm noun
a business firm. business, company, concern, corporation, establishment, organization.

first adjective
1 *first signs of spring.* earliest, foremost, initial, leading, soonest.
2 *the first thing to consider.* basic, cardinal, chief, fundamental, key, main, paramount, predominant, primary, prime, principal, uppermost.
3 *first steps in arithmetic.* elementary, introductory, preliminary, rudimentary.
4 *the first version of something.* archetypal, eldest, embryonic, oldest, original, primeval.

first-class, first-rate adjectives
SEE **excellent**.

fish noun
OTHER CREATURES: SEE **animal** noun.

VARIOUS FISH: brill, brisling, carp, catfish, chub, cod, coelacanth, conger, cuttlefish, dab, dace, eel, flounder, goldfish, grayling, gudgeon, haddock, hake, halibut, herring, jellyfish, lamprey, ling, mackerel, minnow, mullet, perch, pike, pilchard, piranha, plaice, roach, salmon, sardine, sawfish, shark, skate, sole, sprat, squid, starfish, stickleback, sturgeon, swordfish, [*informal*] tiddler, trout, tuna, turbot, whitebait, whiting.

---

fisher noun
angler, fisherman, trawlerman.

fishing noun
angling, trawling.
RELATED ADJECTIVE: piscatorial.

fit adjective
1 *The house isn't fit to live in.* adapted, adequate, equipped, good enough, satisfactory, sound.
2 *Her rude song isn't fit for your ears!* apposite, appropriate, apt, becoming, befitting, decent, fitting, proper, right, seemly, suitable.
3 *Are you fit to play?* able, capable, competent, in good form, healthy, prepared, ready, strong, well enough.
OPPOSITES: SEE **unfit**.

fit noun
a fit of coughing. attack, bout, convulsion, eruption, explosion, outbreak, outburst, paroxysm, seizure, spasm, spell.

fit verb
1 *My jeans don't fit me.* be the right shape and size for.
2 *Fit the pieces together.* arrange, assemble, build, construct, dovetail, install, interlock, join, match, position, put in place, put together.
3 *Wear clothes to fit the occasion.* accord with, become, be fitting for [SEE **fitting**], conform with, correspond with or to, go with, harmonize with, suit.

fitting adjective
a fitting memorial. apposite, appropriate, apt, becoming, befitting, decent, due, fitting, proper, right, seemly, suitable, timely.
OPPOSITES: SEE **inappropriate**.

fix noun
I got into a fix. corner, difficulty, dilemma, [*informal*] hole, [*informal*] jam, mess, plight, predicament, problem, quandary.

fix verb
1 *to fix something into place.* attach, bind, connect, embed, SEE **fasten**, implant, install, join, link, make firm, plant, position, secure, stabilize, stick.
2 *to fix a price. to fix a time.* agree, appoint, arrange, arrive at, confirm, decide, establish, finalize, name, ordain, settle, sort out, specify.
3 [*informal*] *to fix a broken window.* make good, mend, put right, repair.

fixture noun
a home fixture. date, engagement, game, match, meeting.

fizz verb
bubble, effervesce, fizzle, foam, froth, hiss, sizzle.

fizzy adjective
fizzy drinks. bubbly, effervescent, foaming, sparkling.
OPPOSITES: SEE **still** adjective.

flabby adjective
[*informal*] *flabby muscles.* SEE **fat** adjective, feeble, flaccid, floppy, limp, loose, out of condition, slack, weak.
OPPOSITES: SEE **firm** adjective.

flag noun
decorated with flags. banner, bunting, colours, ensign, pennant, pennon, standard, streamer.

flag verb
1 *Our interest flagged.* SEE **decline** verb.
2 *The police flagged me down.* SEE **signal** verb.

flagrant adjective
SEE **obvious**.

flake noun
flakes of old paint. flakes of flint. bit, chip, leaf, scale, shaving, slice, splinter, wafer.

flamboyant adjective
SEE **showy**.

flame noun
SEE **fire** noun.

flap verb
The sail flapped in the wind. beat, flutter, sway, swing, thrash about, wag, wave about.

flare verb
blaze, SEE **burn** verb, erupt, flame.

flash verb
Lights flashed on and off. flicker, glare, glint, SEE **light** noun (**to give light**), sparkle, twinkle.

flat adjective
1 *The snooker-table must be flat.* horizontal, level, levelled.
OPPOSITES: SEE **vertical**.
2 *lying flat in bed.* outstretched, prone, prostrate, recumbent, spread-eagled, spread out, supine.
OPPOSITES: SEE **upright**.
3 *a flat sea.* calm, even, smooth, unbroken, unruffled.
OPPOSITES: SEE **uneven**.
4 *a flat voice.* boring, dry, dull, insipid, lacklustre, lifeless, monotonous, spiritless, tedious, unexciting, uninteresting, unmodulated, unvarying.
OPPOSITES: SEE **lively**.
5 *a flat tyre.* burst, deflated, punctured.

flatten verb
1 *to flatten a rough surface.* even out, iron out, level out, press, roll, smooth.
2 *They flattened the flowers.* compress, crush, demolish, SEE **destroy**, devastate, level, raze, run over, squash, trample.

flatter verb
1 be flattering to [SEE **flattering**], [*informal*] butter up, compliment, curry favour with, fawn on, humour, [*informal*] play up to,

praise, [*slang*] suck up to, [*informal*] toady to.
OPPOSITES: SEE **insult** verb.

flattering adjective
flattering remarks. adulatory, complimentary, effusive, fawning, fulsome, ingratiating, insincere, mealy-mouthed, obsequious, servile, sycophantic, unctuous.
OPPOSITES: SEE **insulting, sincere**.

flattery noun
adulation, blandishments, [*informal*] blarney, fawning, [*informal*] flannel, insincerity, obsequiousness, servility, [*informal*] soft soap, sycophancy, unctuousness.

flaunt verb SEE **display** verb.

flavour noun
1 *the flavour of food.* SEE **taste** noun.
2 *a film with an oriental flavour.* atmosphere, character, characteristic, feel, feeling, property, quality, style.

flavouring noun
peppermint flavouring. additive, essence, extract, seasoning.

flaw noun
a flaw in someone's work. a flaw in a piece of china. SEE **blemish**, break, chip, crack, error, fallacy, imperfection, inaccuracy, mistake, shortcoming, slip, split, weakness.

flawless adjective
SEE **perfect** adjective.

flee verb
to flee from invaders. abscond, [*informal*] beat a retreat, bolt, clear off, disappear, escape, fly, hurry off, make off, retreat, run away, [*slang*] scarper, [*informal*] take to your heels, vanish, withdraw.

fleet noun
a fleet of ships. armada, convoy, flotilla, navy, squadron, task force.

fleeting adjective
a fleeting moment. SEE **brief** adjective, ephemeral, evanescent, impermanent, momentary, mutable, passing, short-lived, transitory.
OPPOSITES: SEE **lasting**.

flesh noun
an animal's flesh. carrion [= *dead flesh*], fat, meat, muscle, tissue.

flex noun
a flex for an electric iron. cable, lead, wire.

flexible adjective
1 *flexible wire.* bendable, [*informal*] bendy, floppy, limp, pliable, soft, springy, supple, whippy.
2 *flexible arrangements.* adjustable,

alterable, fluid, mutable, open, provisional, variable.
3 *a flexible person*. accommodating, adaptable, amenable, compliant, open-minded, responsive, tractable, willing to please.
OPPOSITES: SEE **inflexible**.

flicker verb
The candles flickered. blink, flutter, glimmer, quiver, tremble, twinkle, waver.

flight noun
1 *the flight of a missile*. SEE **journey**, trajectory.
2 *a flight from danger*. SEE **escape** noun.

flimsy adjective
1 *the flimsy wings of a butterfly*. brittle, delicate, fine, fragile, frail, insubstantial, light, slight, thin.
OPPOSITES: SEE **substantial**.
2 *a flimsy structure*. decrepit, gimcrack, loose, makeshift, rickety, shaky, tottering, weak, wobbly.
OPPOSITES: SEE **sturdy**.
3 *a flimsy argument*. feeble, implausible, superficial, trivial, unconvincing, unsatisfactory.
OPPOSITES: SEE **convincing**.

flinch verb
to flinch in alarm. blench, cower, cringe, dodge, draw back, duck, falter, jerk away, jump, quail, quake, recoil, shrink back, shy away, start, swerve, wince.

fling verb
SEE **throw** verb.

flippant adjective
SEE **frivolous**.

flirt verb
SEE **love** noun (**to make love**).

flirtatious adjective
amorous, coquettish, flirty, [*uncomplimentary*] promiscuous, teasing.

float verb
1 *to float on water*. bob, drift, sail, swim.
2 *to float in the air*. glide, hang, hover, waft.
OPPOSITES: SEE **sink** verb.

flock noun SEE **group** noun.

flog verb
beat, birch, cane, flagellate, flay, SEE **hit** verb, lash, scourge, thrash, [*slang*] wallop, whack, whip.

flood noun
1 *a flood of water*. deluge, downpour, flash-flood, inundation, overflow, rush, spate, tide, torrent.
OPPOSITES: SEE **drought, trickle**.
2 *a flood of imports*. excess, large

quantity, plethora, superfluity.
OPPOSITES: SEE **scarcity**.

flood verb
The river flooded the town. cover, drown, engulf, fill up, immerse, inundate, overflow, overwhelm, sink, submerge, swamp.

floor noun
1 deck, floorboards.
FLOOR COVERINGS: carpet, lino, linoleum, mat, matting, parquet, rug, tiles.
2 *first floor. top floor*. deck, level, storey, tier.

flop verb
1 *The seedlings flopped in the heat*. collapse, dangle, droop, drop, fall, flag, hang down, sag, slump, wilt.
2 *The business flopped*. SEE **fail**.

floppy adjective
floppy lettuce leaves. droopy, flabby, SEE **flexible**, hanging loose, limp, pliable, soft.
OPPOSITES: SEE **crisp, rigid**.

flounder verb
1 *to flounder in mud*. flail, fumble, grope, move clumsily, stagger, struggle, stumble, tumble, wallow.
2 *to flounder through a speech*. falter, get confused, make mistakes, talk aimlessly.

flourish verb
1 *The plants flourished after the rain. Trade flourished in the sales*. be fruitful, be successful, bloom, blossom, boom, burgeon, develop, do well, flower, grow, increase, [*informal*] perk up, progress, prosper, strengthen, succeed, thrive.
2 *He flourished his umbrella*. brandish, flaunt, gesture with, shake, swing, twirl, wag, wave.

flow noun
a steady flow. cascade, course, current, drift, ebb (*the ebb and flow of the tide*), effusion, flood, gush, outpouring, spate, spurt, stream, tide, trickle.

flow verb
Liquids flow. bleed, cascade, course, dribble, drift, drip, ebb, flood, flush, glide, gush, issue, leak, move in a flow [SEE **flow** noun], ooze, overflow, pour, ripple, roll, run, seep, spill, spring, spurt, squirt, stream, trickle, well, well up.

flower noun
flowers in the garden. bloom, blossom, floret, petal.
a bunch of flowers arrangement, bouquet, garland, posy, spray, wreath.

VARIOUS FLOWERS: begonia, bluebell, buttercup, campanula, campion, candytuft, carnation, catkin, celandine, chrysanthemum, coltsfoot, columbine, cornflower, cowslip, crocus, crowfoot, cyclamen, daffodil, dahlia, daisy, dandelion.

forget-me-not, foxglove, freesia, geranium, gladiolus, gypsophila, harebell, hollyhock, hyacinth, iris, jonquil, kingcup, lilac, lily, lupin, marguerite, marigold, montbretia, nasturtium, orchid.

pansy, pelargonium, peony, periwinkle, petunia, phlox, pink, polyanthus, poppy, primrose, rhododendron, rose, saxifrage, scabious, scarlet pimpernel, snowdrop, speedwell, sunflower, tulip, violet, wallflower, water-lily.

PARTS OF A FLOWER: axil, bract, calyx, carpel, corolla, perianth, pistil, pollen, sepal, stamen, whorl.

---

flower verb
Most plants flower in the summer. bloom, blossom, [*poetic*] blow, SEE **flourish** verb, have flowers, open out.

fluent adjective
a fluent speaker. articulate, effortless, eloquent, [*uncomplimentary*] facile, flowing, [*uncomplimentary*] glib, natural, polished, ready, smooth, voluble, unhesitating.
OPPOSITES: SEE **hesitant**.

fluffy adjective
fluffy toys. downy, feathery, fibrous, fleecy, furry, fuzzy, hairy, silky, soft, velvety, woolly.

fluid adjective
1 *a fluid substance.* aqueous, flowing, gaseous, liquefied, liquid, melted, molten, running, [*informal*] runny, sloppy, watery.
OPPOSITES: SEE **solid**.
2 *fluid movements.* SEE **graceful**.
3 *a fluid situation.* SEE **flexible**.

fluid noun
bodily fluids. fluid substance [SEE **fluid** adjective], gas, liquid, plasma.

flush verb
1 *to flush with embarrassment.* blush, colour, glow, go red, redden.
2 *to flush a lavatory.* cleanse, [*informal*] pull the plug, rinse out, wash out.
3 *to flush a bird from its hiding-place.* chase out, drive out, expel, send up.

fluster verb
SEE **confuse**.

flutter verb
bat (*your eyelids*), flap, flicker, flit, move agitatedly, palpitate, quiver, tremble, vibrate.

fly verb
1 *Most birds fly.* ascend, flit, glide, hover, rise, soar, stay in the air, swoop, take wing.
2 *to fly an aircraft.* aviate, pilot, take off (in), travel (in).
3 *to fly a flag.* display, flap, flutter, hang up, hoist, raise, show, wave.

foam noun
1 bubbles, effervescence, froth, head (*on beer*), lather, scum, spume, suds.
2 *a mattress made of foam.* sponge, spongy rubber.

foam verb
What makes the water foam? boil, bubble, effervesce, fizz, froth, lather, make foam [SEE **foam** noun].

focus noun
1 *Get the camera into focus.* clarity, correct adjustment, sharpness.
2 *The cathedral is the main focus for tourism.* centre, core, focal point, heart, hub, pivot.

focus verb
to focus a camera. adjust the lens.
to focus on *Focus on the main problem.* aim at, centre on, concentrate on, direct attention to, fix attention on, home in on, look at, spotlight, think about.

foe noun
SEE **enemy**.

fog noun
fog on the motorway. bad visibility, cloud, foggy conditions [SEE **foggy**], haze, mist, smog.

foggy adjective
foggy weather. a foggy picture. blurry, clouded, dim, hazy, indistinct, misty, murky, obscure.
OPPOSITES: SEE **clear** adjective.

foil verb
The security officer foiled the thieves. baffle, block, check, frustrate, halt, hamper, hinder, obstruct, outwit, prevent, stop, thwart.

fold noun
a fold in paper or cloth. bend, corrugation, crease, furrow, hollow, knife-edge, line, pleat, wrinkle.

fold verb
1 *to fold in two.* bend, crease, crinkle, double over, jack-knife, overlap, pleat, tuck in, turn over.
2 *to fold in your arms.* clasp, embrace, enclose, enfold, entwine, envelop, hold close, hug, wrap.
3 *to fold an umbrella.* close, collapse, let down, put down.
4 *The business folded.* SEE **fail**.

folk noun
SEE **person**.

follow verb
1 *Follow that car! He follows her everywhere.*
accompany, chase, dog, escort, go after,
hound, hunt, keep pace with, pursue,
shadow, stalk, [*informal*] tag along with,
tail, track, trail.
OPPOSITES: SEE **abandon**.
2 *James I followed Elizabeth I.* come after,
replace, succeed, supersede, supplant, take
the place of.
OPPOSITES: SEE **precede**.
3 *Follow the rules.* attend to, comply with,
heed, keep to, obey, observe, pay attention
to, take notice of.
OPPOSITES: SEE **ignore**.
4 *Try to follow what I say.* comprehend,
grasp, keep up with, understand.
5 *Do you follow snooker?* be a fan of, keep
abreast of, know about, support, take an
interest in.
6 *It's sunny now, but it doesn't follow that
it'll be fine tonight.* be inevitable, come
about, ensue, happen, have the consequence,
mean, result.

follower noun
SEE **disciple**.

following adjective
the following day. coming, consequent,
ensuing, future, later, next, resulting,
subsequent, succeeding.
OPPOSITES: SEE **previous**.

fond adjective
1 *a fond kiss.* SEE **loving**.
2 *a fond hope.* SEE **silly**.
fond of *She's fond of him.* SEE **love** noun (**in
love with**).

food noun
[*old-fashioned*] comestibles, cooking,
cuisine, delicacies, diet, [*informal*]
eatables, [*informal*] eats, fare, feed (*chicken
feed*), fodder (*cattle fodder*), foodstuff, forage
(*forage for horses*), [*informal*] grub, SEE **meal**,
meat (*meat and drink*), nourishment,
[*especially = plant food*] nutriments, [*joking*]
provender, provisions, rations, recipe,
refreshments, sustenance, swill (*pig-swill*),
[*old-fashioned*] tuck, [*old-fashioned*] viands,
[*old-fashioned*] victuals.
RELATED ADJECTIVES: cordon bleu, culinary,
gastronomic, gourmet.

CONSTITUENTS OF FOOD: carbohydrate,
cholesterol, fibre, protein, roughage,
vitamin.

VARIOUS FOODS: bacon, batter, beans,
biryani, SEE **biscuit**, blancmange, bran,
bread, broth, SEE **cake** noun, caviare, SEE
cereal, charlotte, cheese, cheesecake, chilli,

chips, chop suey, chupatti, chutney,
coleslaw, cornflakes, cornflour, cream,
crisps, croquette, crouton, crumpet, curry,
custard.
doughnut, dumplings, egg, SEE **fat** noun, **fish**
noun, flan, flour, fondue, fricassee, fritter,
SEE **fruit**, ghee, gherkin, glucose, goulash,
greens, gruel, haggis, hash, health foods,
honey, hot-pot, ice-cream, icing, jam, jelly,
junket, kebab, kedgeree, kipper, kosher
food.
lasagne, lentils, macaroni, malt, marmalade,
SEE **meat**, milk, mincemeat, mince pies,
moussaka, mousse, muesli, noodles, SEE **nut**,
oatmeal, omelette, paella, pancake, pasta,
pastry, pasty, pâté, pie, pikelet, pizza,
porridge, pudding, quiche, rice, risotto,
rissole, rolypoly, rusk.
sago, SEE **salad**, sandwich, sauerkraut,
sausage, sausage-roll, scampi, schnitzel,
seafood, semolina, smorgasbord, sorbet,
soufflé, soup, soya beans, spaghetti, stew,
stock, sundae, syllabub, syrup, tandoori,
tapioca, tart, toast, treacle, trifle, truffle, SEE
vegetable, vegetarian food, waffle,
wholemeal flour, yam, yeast, yogurt or
yoghurt.

CONDIMENTS, FLAVOURINGS, ETC.: chutney,
colouring, dressing, garlic, gravy, herbs,
ketchup, marinade, mayonnaise, mustard,
pepper, pickle, preservative, relish, salt,
sauce, seasoning, spice, stuffing, sugar,
vanilla, vinegar.

fool noun
I am a fool! [All the synonyms given are
normally used *informally*.] ass, blockhead,
booby, buffoon, dimwit, dope, dunce,
dunderhead, dupe, fathead, half-wit, SEE
idiot, ignoramus, mug, muggins, mutt,
ninny, nit, nitwit, silly person [SEE **silly**],
simpleton, sucker, twerp, wally.

fool verb
to fool someone with a trick. [*informal*]
bamboozle, bluff, cheat, [*informal*] con,
deceive, delude, dupe, [*informal*] have on,
hoax, hoodwink, [*informal*] kid, mislead,
[*informal*] string along, swindle, take in,
trick.

foolish adjective SEE **stupid**.

foot noun
1 *an animal's foot.* claw, hoof, paw, trotter.
2 *the foot of a mountain.* SEE **base** noun.

footwear noun SEE **shoe**.

forbid verb
to forbid smoking. ban, bar, deny (*He denied
me the chance*), deter, disallow, exclude,
make illegal, outlaw, preclude, prevent,

prohibit, proscribe, refuse, rule out, say no to, stop, veto.
OPPOSITES: SEE **allow**.

forbidden adjective
Games are forbidden. against the law, banned, barred, disallowed, SEE **illegal**, outlawed, prohibited, proscribed, taboo, unlawful.
OPPOSITES: SEE **permissible**.

forbidding adjective
forbidding storm clouds. gloomy, grim, menacing, ominous, stern, threatening, SEE **unfriendly**, uninviting, unwelcoming.
OPPOSITES: SEE **friendly**.

force noun
1 *We used force to open the door.* drive, effort, energy, might, power, pressure, strength, vehemence, vigour, weight.
2 *the force of an explosion.* effect, impact, intensity, momentum, shock.
3 *a military force.* army, body, SEE **group** noun, troops.
4 *They took over by force.* aggression, brunt (*We bore the brunt of the attack*), coercion, compulsion, constraint, duress, violence.

force verb
1 *You can't force me to do it.* [*informal*] bulldoze, coerce, compel, constrain, drive, impel, impose on, make, oblige, order, press-gang, pressurize.
2 *We had to force the door.* break open, burst open, prise open, smash, use force on, wrench.

forceful adjective
SEE **powerful**.

foreboding noun
a foreboding that something is wrong. anxiety, augury, dread, fear, feeling, intuition, misgiving, omen, portent, premonition, presentiment, warning, worry.

forecast noun
a weather forecast. augury, expectation, outlook, prediction, prognosis, prognostication, projection, prophecy.

forecast verb
SEE **foretell**.

foreign adjective
1 *foreign places.* distant, exotic, far-away, outlandish, remote, strange, unfamiliar, unknown.
2 *foreign tourists.* alien, external, immigrant, incoming, international, outside, overseas, visiting.
OPPOSITES: SEE **native**.
3 *foreign goods.* imported.
OPPOSITE: indigenous.

foreigner noun
alien, immigrant, newcomer, outsider, overseas visitor, stranger.

foremost adjective SEE **chief** adjective.

forerunner noun
SEE **predecessor**.

foresee verb
I foresaw what would happen. anticipate, envisage, expect, forecast, foretell, have a foretaste of, predict, prognosticate, prophesy.

foreshadow verb
SEE **foretell**.

foresight noun
She commended my foresight in bringing an umbrella. anticipation, caution, farsightedness, forethought, looking ahead, perspicacity, planning, preparation, prudence, readiness.

forest noun
coppice, copse, jungle, plantation, trees, woodland, woods.
RELATED ADJECTIVES: arboreal, silvan.

foretaste noun
a foretaste of things to come. example, SEE **forewarning**, preview, sample, specimen, trailer, [*informal*] try-out.

foretell verb
The omens foretold what would happen. augur, [*old-fashioned*] bode, forebode, forecast, foreshadow, forewarn, give a foretaste of, herald, portend, presage, prognosticate, prophesy, signify.

forewarning noun
I had no forewarning of trouble. advance warning, augury, foreknowledge, foretaste, indication, omen, premonition, [*informal*] tip-off.

foreword noun
introduction, prologue.

forfeit noun
He had to pay a forfeit. damages, fine, penalty.

forfeit verb
Because he broke the rules, he forfeited his winnings. abandon, give up, let go, lose, pay up, relinquish, renounce, surrender.

forge verb
1 *to forge metal.* beat into shape, cast, hammer out, mould, shape, work.
2 *to forge money.* coin, copy, counterfeit, fake, falsify, imitate, make illegally.

forgery noun
The painting was a forgery. copy, counterfeit, [*informal*] dud, fake, fraud, imitation, [*informal*] phoney, replica, reproduction.

forget verb
1 *I forget things.* be forgetful [SEE **forgetful**], be oblivious (of), disregard, fail to remember, ignore, leave out, lose track (of), miss out, neglect, omit, overlook, skip, suffer from amnesia, unlearn.
OPPOSITES: SEE **remember**.
2 *I forgot my money.* abandon, be without, leave behind.
OPPOSITES: SEE **bring**.

forgetful adjective
absent-minded, [*formal*] amnesiac, careless, inattentive, neglectful, negligent, oblivious, unconscious, unmindful, unreliable, vague, [*informal*] woolly-minded.

forgetfulness noun
absent-mindedness, [*formal*] amnesia, negligence, oblivion, unconsciousness.

forgivable adjective
a forgivable lapse. allowable, excusable, justifiable, negligible, pardonable, petty, understandable, venial (*a venial sin*).
OPPOSITES: SEE **unforgivable**.

forgive verb
1 *to forgive a person for doing wrong.* [*formal*] absolve, [*formal*] exculpate, excuse, exonerate, let off, pardon, spare.
2 *to forgive a crime.* condone, overlook.

forgiveness noun
absolution, exoneration, mercy, pardon.
OPPOSITES: SEE **retribution**.

forgiving adjective
a forgiving nature. SEE **kind** adjective, merciful, tolerant, understanding.
OPPOSITES: SEE **vengeful**.

fork verb
The road forks. SEE **divide**.

forked adjective
a forked stick. branched, divided, split, V-shaped.

forlorn adjective SEE **sad**.

form noun
1 *human form.* anatomy, body, build, figure, frame, outline, physique, shape, silhouette.
2 *What form did it take?* appearance, arrangement, cast, character, configuration, design, format, framework, genre, guise, kind, manifestation, manner, model, mould, nature, pattern, plan, semblance, sort, species, structure, style, system, type, variety.
3 *your form in school.* class, group, level, set, stream, tutor-group.
4 [*informal*] *It's good form to shake hands.* behaviour, convention, custom, etiquette, fashion, manners, practice.

5 *an application form.* document, paper.
6 *an athlete's form.* condition, fettle (*in fine fettle*), fitness, health, performance, spirits.

form verb
1 *A sculptor forms her material.* cast, construct, design, forge, give form to, model, mould, shape.
2 *We formed a society.* bring into existence, bring together, constitute, create, establish, found, make, organize, produce.
3 *They form a good team.* act as, compose, comprise, make up, serve as.
4 *Icicles formed under the bridge.* appear, come into existence, develop, grow, materialize, take shape.

formal adjective
1 *a formal occasion. formal behaviour.* aloof, ceremonial, ceremonious, conventional, cool, correct, dignified, [*informal*] dressed-up, official, orthodox. [*informal*] posh, [*uncomplimentary*] pretentious, proper, reserved, ritualized, solemn, sophisticated, stately, [*informal*] starchy, stiff, stiff-necked, unbending, unfriendly.
2 *formal language.* academic, impersonal, legal, official, precise, specialist, stilted, technical.
3 *a formal design.* calculated, geometrical, orderly, regular, rigid, symmetrical.
OPPOSITES: SEE **informal**.

former adjective
earlier, opening, SEE **previous**.
OPPOSITES: SEE **latter**.

formidable adjective
a formidable task. SEE **difficult**.

formula noun
1 *a verbal formula.* form of words, ritual, rubric, spell, wording.
2 *a formula for success.* blueprint, method, prescription, procedure, recipe, rule, way.

formulate verb
to formulate a plan. create, define, devise, evolve, express clearly, form, invent, plan, set out in detail, specify, systematize, work out.

forsake verb
SEE **abandon, renounce**.

fort noun
camp, castle, citadel, fortification, fortress, garrison, stronghold, tower.

forthright adjective
forthright views. blunt, candid, direct, SEE **frank**, outspoken, plain-speaking, straightforward, unequivocal.
OPPOSITES: SEE **cautious**.

fortify verb
1 *to fortify a town.* defend, garrison, protect, reinforce, secure against attack.

2 *to fortify yourself for difficulties ahead.*
boost, cheer, encourage, hearten,
invigorate, lift the morale of, reassure,
stiffen the resolve of, strengthen.

fortitude noun
SEE **courage**.

fortunate adjective
SEE **lucky**.

fortune noun
1 *good fortune. bad fortune.* accident, chance,
destiny, fate, kismet, luck, providence.
2 *He left his fortune to a charity.* affluence,
assets, estate, inheritance, millions,
[*informal*] pile (*She made a pile*),
possessions, property, prosperity, riches,
treasure, wealth.

forward adjective
1 *a forward movement.* front, frontal, leading,
onward, progressive.
OPPOSITES: SEE **backward**.
2 *forward planning.* advance, early, forward-
looking, future.
3 [*uncomplimentary*] *too forward for his age.*
assertive, bold, brazen, cheeky, familiar,
[*informal*] fresh, impertinent, impudent,
insolent, over-confident, precocious,
presumptuous, pushful, [*informal*] pushy,
shameless, uninhibited.
OPPOSITES: SEE **diffident**.

forward verb
1 *to forward a letter.* post on, re-address, send
on.
2 *to forward goods.* dispatch, expedite,
freight, send, ship, transmit, transport.

foster verb
1 *to foster a happy atmosphere.* cultivate,
encourage, promote, stimulate.
2 *to foster a child.* adopt, bring up, care for,
look after, nourish, nurse, raise, rear, take
care of. [The legal meaning of *adopt* and
foster is not the same.]

foul adjective
1 *a foul mess. foul air.* contaminated, SEE **dirty**
adjective, disagreeable, disgusting, filthy,
hateful, impure, infected, loathsome, nasty,
nauseating, noisome, obnoxious, offensive,
polluted, putrid, repulsive, revolting, rotten,
smelly, squalid, stinking, unclean, SEE
unpleasant, vile.
OPPOSITES: SEE **pure**.
2 *a foul crime.* abhorrent, abominable,
atrocious, SEE **cruel**, evil, monstrous,
villainous, wicked.
3 *foul language.* abusive, blasphemous,
coarse, common, crude, improper, indecent,
insulting, SEE **obscene**, offensive, rude,
uncouth, vulgar.
4 *foul weather.* foggy, rainy, rough, stormy,
violent, windy.
5 *a foul tackle.* against the rules, illegal,
prohibited, unfair.

found verb
1 *to found a business.* begin, create, endow,
establish, fund, [*informal*] get going,
inaugurate, initiate, institute, organize,
provide money for, raise, set up, start.
2 *a building founded on solid rock.* base,
build, construct, erect.

foundation noun
1 *the foundation of a new association.*
beginning, establishment, inauguration,
initiation, institution, setting up, starting.
2 *the foundation of a building.* base, basis,
bottom, cornerstone, foot, footing,
substructure, underpinning.
3 [*plural*] *the foundations of science.* basic
principles [SEE **principle**], elements,
essentials, fundamentals, origins,
rudiments.

fountain noun
a fountain of water. fount, jet, spout, spray,
spring, well.

fowl noun
bird, chicken, hen.

fox noun
[*female*] vixen.

fraction noun
I could afford only a fraction of the amount.
division, part, portion, section, subdivision.

fracture noun
a fracture in a bone. break, breakage, chip,
cleft, crack, fissure, gap, opening, rent, rift,
split.

fracture verb
to fracture a bone. break, cause a fracture
in, chip, crack, split, suffer a fracture in.

fragile adjective
Egg-shell is fragile. breakable, brittle, SEE
delicate, easily damaged, feeble, frail,
insubstantial, slight, thin, weak.
OPPOSITES: SEE **strong**.

fragment noun
1 *a fragment of broken pottery.* atom, bit,
chip, crumb, part, particle, piece, remnant,
scrap, shiver, shred, sliver, snippet, speck.
2 [*plural*] *smashed into fragments.* debris,
shivers, [*informal*] smithereens.

fragmentary adjective
fragmentary evidence. [*informal*] bitty,
broken, disintegrated, disjointed,
fragmented, in bits, incoherent, incomplete,
in fragments [SEE **fragment** noun], partial,
scattered, scrappy, uncoordinated.
OPPOSITES: SEE **complete** adjective.

fragrant adjective
SEE **smelling**.

frail adjective
1 *a frail person.* delicate, feeble, SEE **ill**,
infirm, [*uncomplimentary*] puny, slight,

unsteady, vulnerable, weak,
[*uncomplimentary*] weedy.
2 *a frail structure.* flimsy, SEE **fragile**,
insubstantial, rickety, unsound.
OPPOSITES: SEE **strong**.

frame noun
1 *the frame of a building.* bodywork,
construction, framework, scaffolding, shell,
skeleton, structure.
2 *a frame for a picture.* border, case, casing,
edge, edging, mount, mounting.

framework noun
bare bones, frame, outline, plan, shell,
skeleton, structure, trellis.

frank adjective
a frank reply, a frank discussion. blunt,
candid, direct, downright, explicit,
forthright, genuine, [*informal*] heart-to-
heart, honest, ingenuous, [*informal*] no-
nonsense, open, outright, outspoken, plain,
plainspoken, revealing, serious, sincere,
straight from the heart, straightforward, to
the point, trustworthy, truthful,
unconcealed, undisguised, unreserved.
OPPOSITES: SEE **insincere**.

frantic adjective
frantic activity. frantic with worry. berserk,
[*informal*] beside yourself, crazy, delirious,
demented, deranged, desperate, distraught,
excitable, feverish, [*informal*] fraught,
frenetic, frenzied, furious, hectic, hysterical,
mad, overwrought, rabid, uncontrollable,
violent, wild, worked up.
OPPOSITES: SEE **calm** adjective.

fraud noun
1 *His fraud landed him in gaol.* chicanery,
[*informal*] con-trick, deceit, deception,
dishonesty, double-dealing, duplicity,
forgery, imposture, [*informal*] sharp
practice, swindling, trickery.
2 *The "special offer" was a fraud.* cheat,
counterfeit, fake, hoax, pretence,
[*informal*] put-up job, ruse, sham, swindle,
trick.
3 *The salesman was a fraud.* charlatan, cheat,
[*informal*] con-man, hoaxer, impostor,
[*slang*] phoney, [*informal*] quack, swindler.

fraudulent adjective
a fraudulent business deal. bogus, cheating,
corrupt, counterfeit, criminal, [*informal*]
crooked, deceitful, devious, [*informal*] dirty,
dishonest, false, illegal, lying, [*slang*]
phoney, sham, specious, swindling,
underhand, unscrupulous.
OPPOSITES: SEE **honest**.

frayed adjective
a frayed collar. rough at the edges, tattered,
threadbare, untidy, worn.

freak adjective
freak weather conditions. aberrant,
abnormal, atypical, exceptional,

extraordinary, odd, peculiar, queer,
unaccountable, unforeseeable,
unpredictable, unusual.
OPPOSITES: SEE **normal**.

freak noun
1 *a freak of Nature.* aberration, abnormality,
abortion, anomaly, irregularity, monster,
monstrosity, mutant, oddity, quirk, sport,
variant.
2 [*informal*] *a keep-fit freak.* SEE **fanatic**.

free adjective
1 *free to come and go.* able, allowed, at leisure,
at liberty, disengaged, idle, loose, not
working, permitted, uncommitted,
unconstrained, unfixed, unrestrained,
unrestricted, untrammelled.
2 *free from slavery.* emancipated, liberated,
released.
3 *a free country.* democratic, independent,
self-governing, sovereign.
4 *a free gift.* complimentary, gratis, without
charge.
5 *Is the bathroom free?* available, open,
unoccupied, vacant.
OPPOSITES: SEE **captive** adjective, **engaged**.

free verb
1 *to free someone from prison.* deliver,
emancipate, liberate, loose, make free,
ransom, release, rescue, save, set free, turn
loose, unchain, unfetter, unleash, unlock,
unloose.
OPPOSITES: SEE **confine**.
2 *to free an accused person.* absolve, acquit,
clear, discharge, [*formal*] exculpate,
exonerate, let go, let off, pardon, prove
innocent, relieve, spare.
OPPOSITES: SEE **condemn**.
3 *to free tangled ropes.* clear, disengage,
disentangle, extricate, loose, undo, unknot,
untangle, untie.
OPPOSITES: SEE **tangle** verb.

freedom noun
freedom to do as you please. autonomy,
discretion, independence, latitude, leeway,
liberty, licence, opportunity, privilege.
OPPOSITES: SEE **restriction**.

freeze verb
1 *Water freezes at 0°C.* become ice, become
solid, congeal, ice over.
2 *The wind froze us to the bone.* chill, cool,
make cold, numb.
3 *to freeze food.* chill, deep-freeze, dry-freeze,
refrigerate.
4 *to freeze prices.* fix, hold, keep as they are,
peg.

freezing adjective
SEE **cold** adjective.

freight noun
Some aircraft carry freight. cargo,
consignment, goods, load, merchandise,
shipment.

frenzy noun
a frenzy of excitement. delirium, fit, fury,
hysteria, insanity, lunacy, madness, mania,
outburst, paroxysm, passion.

frequent adjective
1 *frequent trains. frequent headaches.*
constant, continual, countless, incessant,
many, numerous, recurrent, recurring,
regular, repeated.
2 *a frequent visitor.* common, customary,
familiar, habitual, ordinary, persistent,
regular.
OPPOSITES: SEE **infrequent, rare**.

fresh adjective
1 *fresh evidence. fresh ideas. fresh bread.*
additional, different, extra, just arrived,
new, recent, unfamiliar, up-to-date.
OPPOSITES: SEE **stale**.
2 *fresh water.* clear, drinkable, potable, pure,
refreshing, sweet, uncontaminated.
OPPOSITES: SEE **salt**.
3 *fresh air. a fresh atmosphere.* airy, bracing,
breezy, circulating, clean, cool, draughty,
invigorating, unpolluted, ventilated.
OPPOSITES: SEE **stuffy**.
4 *fresh food.* healthy, natural, newly
gathered, raw, unprocessed, untreated,
wholesome.
OPPOSITES: SEE **preserved, processed**.
5 *fresh sheets on the bed.* clean, crisp,
laundered, untouched, unused, washed-and-
ironed.
OPPOSITES: SEE **dirty** adjective.
6 *fresh colours. fresh paint.* bright, clean,
glowing, just painted, renewed, restored,
sparkling, unfaded, vivid.
OPPOSITES: SEE **dingy**.
7 *fresh after a shower.* alert, energetic,
healthy, invigorated, lively, [*informal*]
perky, rested, revived, sprightly, spry,
tingling, vigorous, vital.
OPPOSITES: SEE **weary** adjective.

friction noun
1 *Bike brakes work by friction against the
wheel.* abrasion, chafing, resistance,
rubbing, scraping.
2 *There was some friction between the two
sides.* SEE **conflict** noun.

friend noun
acquaintance, ally, associate, [*informal*]
buddy, [*informal*] chum, companion,
comrade, [*male*] confidant, [*female*]
confidante, [*informal*] crony, SEE **lover**,
[*informal*] mate, [*informal*] pal, partner,
pen-friend, playfellow, playmate, supporter,
well-wisher.
OPPOSITES: SEE **enemy**.
to be friends associate, consort, fraternize,
[*informal*] go around, [*informal*] hob-nob,
keep company, mix.
to make friends with befriend, [*informal*]

chat up, [*informal*] gang up with, get to
know, make the acquaintance of, [*informal*]
pal up with.

friendliness noun
goodwill, hospitality, kindness, sociability,
warmth.

friendly adjective
a friendly person. a friendly welcome. affable,
affectionate, agreeable, amiable, amicable,
approachable, attached, benevolent, benign,
[*informal*] chummy, civil, close,
companionable, compatible, comradely,
conciliatory, congenial, convivial, cordial,
expansive, SEE **familiar**, favourable, genial,
good-natured, gracious, helpful, hospitable,
intimate, kind, kind-hearted, likeable, SEE
loving, [*informal*] matey, neighbourly,
outgoing, [*informal*] pally, sociable,
sympathetic, tender, [*informal*] thick
(*They're very thick with each other*), warm,
welcoming, well-disposed.
OPPOSITES: SEE **unfriendly**.

friendship noun
She values our friendship. affection, alliance,
amity, association, attachment,
camaraderie, closeness, comradeship,
familiarity, fellowship, fondness,
friendliness, goodwill, harmony, hospitality,
SEE **love** noun, rapport, relationship.
OPPOSITES: SEE **hostility**.

fright noun
1 *The explosion gave them a fright.* jolt, scare,
shock, surprise.
2 *You could see the fright in their faces.* alarm,
consternation, dismay, dread, fear, horror,
panic, terror, trepidation.

frighten verb
The hooligans frightened the passers-by.
alarm, appal, browbeat, bully, cow, curdle
the blood of, daunt, dismay, horrify,
intimidate, make afraid, menace, persecute,
[*informal*] petrify, [*informal*] put the wind
up, scare, shake, shock, startle, terrify,
terrorize, threaten, unnerve.
OPPOSITES: SEE **reassure**.

frightened adjective
afraid, alarmed, apprehensive, [*informal*]
chicken, cowed, dismayed, fearful,
horrorstruck, intimidated, panicky, panic-
stricken, [*informal*] petrified, scared,
terrified, terror-stricken, trembling,
unnerved, [*informal*] windy.

frightening adjective
alarming, appalling, awful, blood-curdling,
[*informal*] creepy, dire, dreadful, eerie,
fearful, fearsome, formidable, frightful,
ghastly, ghostly, grim, hair-raising,
horrific, horrifying, intimidating, menacing,

scary, sinister, spine-chilling, [*informal*]
spooky, terrifying, traumatic, uncanny,
unnerving, upsetting, weird, worrying.

frightful adjective
1 *a frightful accident.* SEE **frightening**,
ghastly, grisly, gruesome, harrowing,
hideous, horrible, horrid, macabre,
shocking, terrible.
2 [*informal*] *frightful weather.* SEE **bad**.

frigid adjective
SEE **unemotional**.

frill noun
SEE **fringe**.

fringe noun
1 *a fringe round the edge of a curtain.* border,
edging, flounce, frill, gathering, trimming,
valance.
2 *the fringe of a town.* borders, edge, limits,
margin, outskirts, periphery.

frisky adjective
frolicsome, high-spirited, jaunty, lively,
perky, playful, skittish, spirited, sprightly.

frivolity noun
We enjoy a bit of frivolity on holiday.
facetiousness, fun, fun-and-games, gaiety,
joking, levity, light-heartedness, nonsense,
playing about, silliness, triviality.

frivolous adjective
frivolous questions. frivolous behaviour.
facetious, flighty, flippant, foolish, jocular,
joking, petty, pointless, ridiculous, shallow,
silly, stupid, superficial, trifling, trivial,
unimportant, unserious, vacuous,
worthless.
OPPOSITES: SEE **serious**.

frolic verb
caper, cavort, dance, frisk about, gambol,
have fun, hop about, jump about, lark
around, leap about, play about, prance,
rollick, romp, skip, sport.

front adjective
the front row. first, foremost, leading, most
advanced.
OPPOSITES: SEE **back** adjective.

front noun
1 bow (*of a ship*), façade (*of a house*), face,
facing, forefront, foreground (*of a picture*),
frontage (*of a building*), head, nose, van,
vanguard (*of an army*).
OPPOSITES: SEE **back** noun.
2 *Troops were sent to the front.* battle area,
danger zone, front line.
3 *His cheerfulness was only a front.*
appearance, blind, [*informal*] cover-up,
disguise, mask, pretence, show.

frontier noun
a national frontier. border, borderline,
boundary, limit.

froth noun
bubbles, effervescence, foam, head (*on beer*),
lather, scum, spume, suds.

frown verb
[*informal*] give a dirty look, glare, glower,
grimace, knit your brow, look sullen, lour,
lower, scowl.
to frown on SEE **disapprove**.

fruit noun
berry.

VARIOUS FRUITS: apple, apricot, avocado,
banana, bilberry, blackberry, cherry, citrus
fruit, coconut, crab-apple, cranberry,
currant, damson, date, fig, gooseberry,
grape, grapefruit, greengage, guava, hip,
kiwi fruit, lemon, lime, litchi or lichee,
loganberry, mango, medlar, melon,
mulberry, nectarine, olive, orange, papaw
or pawpaw, peach, pear, pineapple, plum,
pomegranate, prune, quince, raisin,
raspberry, rhubarb, satsuma, sloe,
strawberry, sultana, tangerine, tomato,
ugli.

fruitful adjective
1 *a fruitful crop. a fruitful garden.* abundant,
copious, fertile, flourishing, lush, plenteous,
productive, profuse, prolific, rich.
OPPOSITES: SEE **unproductive**.
2 *a fruitful search.* effective, gainful,
profitable, rewarding, successful, useful,
worthwhile.
OPPOSITES: SEE **fruitless**.

fruitless adjective
a fruitless search. abortive, disappointing,
futile, pointless, profitless, unavailing,
unfruitful, unproductive, unprofitable,
unrewarding, unsuccessful, useless, vain.
OPPOSITES: SEE **fruitful**.

frustrate verb
The police frustrated an attempted robbery.
baffle, baulk, block, check, defeat,
discourage, foil, halt, hinder, inhibit,
prevent, [*informal*] scotch, stop, thwart.
OPPOSITES: SEE **fulfil**.

fuel noun

KINDS OF FUEL: anthracite, butane, Calor
Gas, charcoal, coal, coke, derv, diesel,
electricity, gas, gasoline, logs, methylated
spirit, nuclear fuel, oil, paraffin, peat,
petrol, propane.

fugitive noun
a fugitive from justice. deserter, escapee,
escaper, refugee, renegade, runaway.

fulfil verb
1 *to fulfil an ambition.* accomplish, achieve, bring about, carry out, complete, effect, make it come true, perform, realize.
2 *to fulfil certain requirements.* answer, comply with, conform to, execute, implement, meet, respond to, satisfy.
OPPOSITES: SEE **frustrate**.

full adjective
1 *a full cup. a full cinema.* brimming, bursting, [*informal*] chock-a-block, [*informal*] chock-full, congested, crammed, crowded, filled, jammed, [*informal*] jam-packed, overflowing, packed, stuffed, topped-up, well-filled, well-stocked.
OPPOSITES: SEE **empty** adjective.
2 *a full stomach.* gorged, replete, sated, satiated, satisfied, well-fed.
OPPOSITES: SEE **hungry**.
3 *the full story. a full investigation.* complete, comprehensive, detailed, entire, exhaustive, total, unabridged, uncensored, uncut, unedited, unexpurgated, whole.
OPPOSITES: SEE **incomplete**.
4 *full price. full speed.* greatest, highest, maximum, top.
OPPOSITES: SEE **minimum**.
5 *a full figure.* ample, buxom, generous, SEE **fat** adjective, large, plump, rounded.
OPPOSITES: SEE **slim** adjective.

fumble verb
He fumbled the ball. grope at, handle awkwardly, mishandle.

fumes plural noun
exhaust, fog, gases, pollution, smog, smoke, vapour.

fun noun
amusement, diversion, enjoyment, entertainment, SEE **frivolity**, games, horseplay, jokes, joking, [*joking*] jollification, laughter, merriment, merrymaking, pastimes, play, pleasure, recreation, romp, [*informal*] skylarking, sport, teasing, tomfoolery.
to make fun of SEE **mock** verb.

function noun
1 *the function of the police.* SEE **job**.
2 *an official function.* SEE **event**.

function verb
The computer doesn't function. SEE **work** verb.

functional adjective
The machine doesn't look elegant—it's purely functional. practical, serviceable, useful, utilitarian.
OPPOSITES: SEE **decorative**.

fund noun
1 *a charitable fund.* [*often plural*] *He invested all his funds.* capital, endowment, SEE **money**, reserves, resources, riches, savings, wealth.

2 *a fund of jokes. a fund of wisdom.* hoard, [*informal*] kitty, mine, pool, reservoir, stock, store, supply, treasure-house.

fundamental adjective
fundamental principles. axiomatic, basic, SEE **elementary**, essential, important, key, main, necessary, primary, prime, principal, underlying.
OPPOSITES: SEE **advanced, inessential**.

funeral noun
burial, cremation, interment, [*informal*] obsequies, Requiem Mass, wake.

WORDS TO DO WITH FUNERALS: bier, catafalque, cemetery, churchyard, cinerary urn, coffin, cortège, cremation, crematorium, grave, graveyard, hearse, memorial, mortuary, mourner, mourning, pall, sarcophagus, tomb, undertaker, wreath.

funereal adjective
dark, depressing, dismal, gloomy, grave, mournful, SEE **sad**, sepulchral, solemn, sombre.
OPPOSITES: SEE **cheerful, lively**.

fun-fair noun

ENTERTAINMENTS AT A FUN-FAIR: amusements, big-dipper, big-wheel, dodgems, merry-go-round, ride, rifle-range, roundabout, side-show, shooting-gallery, switchback.

fungus noun
mould, mushroom, toadstool.

funny adjective
1 *a funny joke.* absurd, amusing, comic, comical, diverting, droll, entertaining, facetious, farcical, hilarious, humorous, hysterical, ironic, jocular, [*informal*] killing, laughable, ludicrous, [*informal*] priceless, ridiculous, risible, sarcastic, satirical, [*informal*] side-splitting, silly, uproarious, witty.
OPPOSITES: SEE **serious**.
2 [*informal*] *a funny pain.* SEE **peculiar**.

fur noun
bristles, coat, down, fleece, hair, hide, pelt, skin, wool.

furious adjective
1 *a furious bull. a furious temper.* SEE **angry**, boiling, enraged, fuming, incensed, infuriated, irate, livid, mad, raging, savage, wrathful.
2 *furious activity.* agitated, frantic, frenzied, intense, tempestuous, tumultuous,

turbulent, violent, wild.
OPPOSITES: SEE **calm** adjective.

furnish verb
1 *to furnish a room.* equip, fit out, fit up.
2 *to furnish someone with information.* give, grant, provide, supply.

furniture noun
antiques, effects, equipment, fittings, furnishings, household goods, [*informal*] moveables, possessions.

ITEMS OF FURNITURE: armchair, bed, bench, bookcase, bunk, bureau, cabinet, chair, chest of drawers, chesterfield, chiffonier, commode, cot, couch, cradle, cupboard, cushion, desk, divan, drawer, dresser, dressing-table, easel, fender, filing-cabinet, fireplace, mantelpiece, ottoman, overmantel, pelmet, pew, pouffe, rocking-chair, seat, settee, sideboard, sofa, stool, suite, table, trestle-table, wardrobe, workbench.

---

furrow noun
channel, corrugation, crease, ditch, drill (*for seeds*), fluting, groove, hollow, line, rut, trench, wrinkle.

furry adjective
furry animals. bristly, downy, feathery, fleecy, fuzzy, hairy, woolly.

further adjective
further information. additional, extra, fresh, more, new, supplementary.

furtive adjective
a furtive look. concealed, conspirational, covert, SEE **crafty**, deceitful, disguised, hidden, mysterious, secretive, shifty, sly, [*informal*] sneaky, stealthy, surreptitious, underhand, untrustworthy.
OPPOSITES: SEE **blatant**.

fury noun
the fury of a storm. SEE **anger** noun, ferocity, fierceness, force, intensity, madness, power, rage, savagery, tempestuousness, turbulence, vehemence, violence, wrath.

fuse verb
to fuse substances together. amalgamate, blend, combine, compound, join, meld, melt, merge, solder, unite, weld.

fuss verb
Please don't fuss! agitate, bother, complain, [*informal*] create, fidget, [*informal*] flap, [*informal*] get worked up, grumble, make a commotion [SEE **commotion**], worry.

fussy adjective
1 *fussy about food.* carping, choosy, difficult, discriminating, [*informal*] faddy, fastidious, [*informal*] finicky, hard to

please, niggling, [*informal*] nit-picking, particular, [*informal*] pernickety, scrupulous, squeamish.
2 *fussy decorations.* complicated, detailed, elaborate, overdone.

futile adjective
a futile attempt to achieve the impossible. abortive, absurd, empty, foolish, forlorn, fruitless, ineffective, ineffectual, pointless, profitless, silly, sterile, unavailing, unproductive, unprofitable, unsuccessful, useless, vain (*a vain attempt*), wasted, worthless.
OPPOSITES: SEE **fruitful**.

future adjective
future events. approaching, awaited, coming, destined, expected, forthcoming, impending, intended, planned, prospective.
OPPOSITES: SEE **past** adjective.

future noun
a bright future. expectations, outlook, prospects, time to come.

fuzzy adjective
1 *a fuzzy beard.* downy, feathery, fleecy, fluffy, frizzy, woolly.
2 *a fuzzy picture.* bleary, blurred, cloudy, dim, faint, hazy, ill-defined, indistinct, misty, out of focus, shadowy, unclear, unfocused, vague.
OPPOSITES: SEE **clear** adjective.

Gg

gadget noun
a gadget for opening tins. appliance, contraption, contrivance, device, implement, instrument, invention, machine, tool, utensil.

gag verb
to gag someone. keep quiet, muzzle, prevent from speaking, silence, stifle, suppress.

gain noun
[*often plural*] *We counted our gains.* achievement, acquisition, advantage, asset, attainment, benefit, dividend, earnings, income, increase, proceeds, profit, return, winnings, yield.
OPPOSITES: SEE **loss**.

gain verb
1 *What do you gain by fighting?* achieve, acquire, bring in, capture, earn, get, make, net, obtain, pick up, procure, profit, realize, receive, win.
OPPOSITES: SEE **lose**.

2 *The explorers gained their objective.* arrive at, attain, get to, reach, secure.

gallant adjective
a gallant knight. attentive, SEE **brave**, chivalrous, courageous, courteous, dashing, fearless, gentlemanly, heroic, honourable, intrepid, magnanimous, noble, polite, valiant.
OPPOSITES: SEE **cowardly, rude**.

gallery noun
the gallery in a theatre. balcony, circle, [*informal*] the gods, upstairs.

gallows noun
sent to the gallows. gibbet, scaffold.

gamble verb
bet, game, [*informal*] have a flutter, risk money, speculate, [*informal*] take a chance, take risks, [*informal*] try your luck, venture, wager.

WAYS OF GAMBLING: backing horses, bingo, cards, dice, drawing lots, lottery, pools, raffle, sweepstake, wager.

PEOPLE WHO GAMBLE: better, gambler, punter, speculator.

PEOPLE WHO SUPERVISE GAMBLING: croupier, bookmaker, turf accountant.

game noun
1 *It's just a game.* amusement, diversion, entertainment, frolic, fun, jest, joke, [*informal*] lark, [*informal*] messing about, pastime, play, playing, recreation, romp, sport.
2 *Shall we play a game?* competition, contest, match, tournament.

SOME GAMES OFTEN PLAYED INDOORS: backgammon, bagatelle, billiards, bingo, cards, charades, chess, crossword puzzle, darts, dice, dominoes, draughts, hoopla, jigsaw puzzle, lotto, ludo, mah-jong, marbles, ping-pong, pool, skittles, snooker, solitaire, spelling-bee, table-tennis, tiddly-winks, tombola.

SOME CHILDREN'S GAMES PLAYED OUT OF DOORS: ball, conkers, hide-and-seek, hopscotch, leapfrog, roller-skating, seesaw, skate-boarding, skating, sledging, sliding, tag.

OTHER OUTDOOR GAMES: SEE **sport**.

gang noun
SEE **group** noun.

gangster noun
bandit, brigand, criminal, crook, desperado, gunman, mugger, robber, ruffian, thug, tough.

gaol noun
[The spellings *gaol* and *jail* are both acceptable. *Gaol* is more common in British official documents; *jail* is more common in America.] borstal, cell, custody, dungeon, guardhouse, jail, [*American*] penitentiary, prison.
OTHER PUNISHMENTS: SEE **punishment**.

gaol verb
He was gaoled for fraud. confine, detain, imprison, incarcerate, intern, [*informal*] send down, send to prison, [*informal*] shut away, shut up.

gaoler noun
guard, prison officer, [*slang*] screw, warder.

gap noun
1 *a gap in a wall.* breach, break, chink, cleft, crack, cranny, crevice, hole, SEE **opening**, rift, space, void.
2 *a gap between events.* breathing-space, discontinuity, hiatus, interlude, intermission, interval, lacuna, lapse, lull, pause, recess, respite, rest.
3 *a gap to be measured.* difference, disparity, distance, interval, space.

gape verb
1 *A chasm gaped.* SEE **open** verb.
2 *He gaped in surprise.* SEE **stare**.

garage noun
car-port, filling-station, petrol station, service station.

garbage noun
SEE **rubbish**.

garbled adjective
SEE **confused**.

garden noun
allotment, patch, plot, yard.
gardens grounds, park.

PARTS OF A GARDEN: arbour, bed, border, compost heap, flower bed, greenhouse, hedge, herbaceous border, hothouse, lawn, orchard, patio, pergola, pond, rockery, rock garden, rose garden, shrubbery, terrace, vegetable garden, walled garden, water garden, window-box.

GARDEN TOOLS AND EQUIPMENT: billhook, broom, cloche, cultivator, dibber, fork, hedge-trimmer, hoe, hose, lawn aerator, lawnmower, lawn-rake, mattock, pruning-knife, rake, riddle, secateurs, shears, shovel, sickle, sieve, spade, sprayer, sprinkler, trowel, watering-can, wheelbarrow.

SOME GARDENING ACTIVITIES: cultivation, digging, hedge-cutting, hoeing, lawn-mowing, manuring, mulching, planting,

pricking-out, pruning, raking, thinning-out, transplanting, watering, weeding.
RELATED ADJECTIVE: horticultural.

gardening noun
cultivation, horticulture.

garish adjective
SEE **gaudy**.

garment noun
SEE **clothes**.

garrison noun
1 *A garrison of troops defended the town.* contingent, detachment, force, unit.
2 *The enemy took the garrison.* barracks, camp, citadel, fort, fortification, fortress, station, stronghold.

gas noun
poisonous gas. exhaust, fumes, vapour.

SOME GASES: carbon dioxide, carbon monoxide, coal gas, helium, hydrogen, laughing-gas, methane, natural gas, nitrogen, nitrous oxide, oxygen, ozone, sulphur dioxide, tear-gas.

gash noun, verb
SEE **cut** noun, verb.

gasp verb
The smoke made them gasp. blow, breathe with difficulty, choke, gulp, pant, puff, wheeze.

gate noun
barrier, door, entrance, entry, exit, gateway, kissing-gate, [*poetic*] portal, portcullis, turnstile, way in, way out, wicket, wicket-gate.

gather verb
1 *to gather in a pile or crowd.* accumulate, amass, assemble, bring together, build up, cluster, collect, come together, concentrate, congregate, convene, crowd, flock together, forgather, get together, group, grow, herd, marshal, mass, meet, mobilize, muster, round up, swarm round, throng.
OPPOSITES: SEE **divide**, **scatter**.
2 *to gather a harvest.* cull, garner, get in, glean, harvest, heap up, hoard, pick, pick up, pile up, pluck, reap, stockpile, store up.
3 *I gather you've been ill.* conclude, deduce, guess, infer, learn, surmise, understand.

gathering noun
a gathering of people. assembly, function, [*informal*] get-together, SEE **group** noun, meeting, party, social.

gaudy adjective
[*uncomplimentary*] *gaudy colours.* bright, flamboyant, flashy, garish, loud (*loud*

colours), lurid, ostentatious, showy, startling, tasteless, tawdry, vivid, vulgar.
OPPOSITES: SEE **tasteful**.

gauge verb SEE **estimate** verb, **measure** verb.

gaunt adjective
1 *gaunt after an illness.* bony, cadaverous, emaciated, haggard, hollow-eyed, lank, lean, pinched, skeletal, skinny, starving, thin, wasted away.
OPPOSITES: SEE **healthy**, **plump**.
2 *a gaunt ruin.* bare, bleak, desolate, forbidding, grim.

gay adjective
1 *gay colours. gay laughter.* animated, bright, carefree, cheerful, colourful, festive, fun-loving, SEE **happy**, jolly, jovial, joyful, lighthearted, lively, merry, sparkling, sunny, vivacious.
2 homosexual, lesbian, [*impolite*] queer.

gaze verb SEE **look** verb.

gear noun
camping gear. accessories, apparatus, baggage, belongings, SEE **clothes**, equipment, [*informal*] get-up, harness, instruments, kit, luggage, paraphernalia, rig, stuff, tackle, things.

gem noun SEE **jewel**.

gender noun SEE **sex**.

general adjective
1 *a general problem. our general experience.* accustomed, collective, common, communal, comprehensive, conventional, customary, everyday, familiar, global, habitual, normal, ordinary, popular, prevailing, regular, shared, typical, universal, usual, widespread.
OPPOSITES: SEE **local**, **special**.
2 *a general idea of where we are going.* approximate, broad, ill-defined, imprecise, indefinite, in outline, loose, unclear, unspecific, vague.
OPPOSITES: SEE **specific**.
general practitioner SEE **doctor**.

generally adverb
as a rule, broadly, chiefly, commonly, in the main, mainly, mostly, normally, on the whole, predominantly, principally, usually.

generate verb
to generate business. beget, breed, bring about, cause, create, engender, give rise to, make, produce, propagate, [*informal*] whip up.

generosity noun
bounty, largess, liberality, munificence, philanthropy.

generous adjective
1 *a generous sponsor.* bounteous, bountiful, charitable, [*informal*] free (*free with her*

money), liberal, munificent, [*informal*] open-handed, philanthropic, unsparing, unstinting.
OPPOSITES: SEE **mean** adjective.
2 *a generous gift.* SEE **expensive**, princely, valuable.
OPPOSITES: SEE **worthless**.
3 *generous portions of food.* abundant, ample, bounteous, copious, SEE **large**, lavish, liberal, plentiful, sizeable, substantial, unstinting.
OPPOSITES: SEE **scanty**.
4 *a generous attitude.* benevolent, big-hearted, forgiving, impartial, kind, magnanimous, open, public-spirited, unmercenary, unprejudiced, unselfish.
OPPOSITES: SEE **selfish**.

genial adjective
a genial welcome. cheerful, easygoing, SEE **friendly**, good-natured, happy, jolly, kindly, pleasant, relaxed, sunny, warm, warm-hearted.
OPPOSITES: SEE **austere, unfriendly**.

genius noun
1 *He has a genius for maths.* aptitude, bent, flair, gift, intellect, knack, talent.
2 *He's a mathematical genius.* academic, [*informal*] egg-head, expert, intellectual, [*uncomplimentary*] know-all, mastermind, thinker.

gentle adjective
1 *a gentle person.* amiable, biddable, compassionate, docile, easygoing, good-tempered, harmless, humane, kind, kindly, lenient, loving, meek, merciful, mild, moderate, obedient, pacific, passive, peace-loving, pleasant, quiet, soft-hearted, sweet-tempered, sympathetic, tame, tender.
OPPOSITES: SEE **violent**.
2 *gentle music. a gentle voice.* low, muted, peaceful, quiet, reassuring, relaxing, soft, soothing.
OPPOSITES: SEE **harsh**.
3 *a gentle wind.* balmy, delicate, faint, light, soft, warm.
OPPOSITES: SEE **strong**.
4 *a gentle hint.* indirect, polite, subtle, tactful.
OPPOSITES: SEE **tactless**.
5 *a gentle hill.* gradual, hardly noticeable, imperceptible, moderate, slight, steady.
OPPOSITES: SEE **steep** adjective.

gentlemanly adjective
SEE **polite**.

genuine adjective
1 *a genuine antique.* actual, authentic, authenticated, bona fide, legitimate, original, real, sterling.
OPPOSITES: SEE **fake** adjective.
2 *genuine feelings.* devout, earnest, frank,

heartfelt, honest, sincere, true, unaffected, unfeigned.
OPPOSITES: SEE **insincere**.

geography noun

MAJOR GEOGRAPHICAL AREAS: Antarctic, Arctic, the continents (Africa, Antarctica, Asia, Australasia, Europe, North America, South America), the oceans (Antarctic, Arctic, Atlantic, Indian, Pacific), the polar regions (North Pole, South Pole), the tropics.

EVERYDAY GEOGRAPHICAL TERMS:
archipelago, bay, canyon, cape, capital, city, climate, continent, contour, conurbation, country, county, creek, dale, delta, downs, east, equator, estate, estuary, fells, fen, fjord, geyser, glacier, glen, gulf, hamlet, heath, hemisphere, highlands, hill.
industry, inlet, island, isthmus, lagoon, lake, land, latitude, longitude, mainland, north, oasis, parish, pass, peninsula, plain, plateau, pole, prairie, province, reef, relief map, river, sea, south, strait, subtropics, suburb, town, tributary, tropics, valley, village, volcano, west, world.

germ noun
1 *the germ of a new organism. the germ of a new idea.* beginning, embryo, genesis, cause, nucleus, origin, seed.
2 *Germs can cause illness.* [*plural*] bacteria, [*informal*] bug, microbe, micro-organism, virus.

germinate verb
Seeds germinate in the right conditions. begin to grow, bud, develop, grow, root, shoot, spring up, sprout, start growing, take root.

gesture noun
an eloquent gesture. action, flourish, gesticulation, indication, motion, movement, sign, signal.

gesture verb
make a gesture, sign, signal.

VARIOUS WAYS TO GESTURE: beckon, bow, gesticulate, motion, nod, point, salute, shake your head, shrug, smile, wave, wink.

get verb
[*Get* can mean many things. We also use *get* in many phrases, the meanings of which depend on their context. For example, *to get on* could mean: *make progress* (*Get on with your work*); *step on a bus* (*Get on before it goes*); *be friendly* (*They get on with each*

other); or *become older* (*Grandad is getting on*). All we can do here is to give a few synonyms for some of the main senses of *get.*] 1 *What can I get for £10?* acquire, be given, buy, come into possession of, gain, get hold of, obtain, procure, purchase, receive.
2 *Try to get him on the phone.* contact, get in touch with, speak to.
3 *Go and get the ball.* bring, fetch, pick up, retrieve.
4 *She got a prize.* earn, take, win.
5 *I got a cold.* catch, contract, develop, suffer from.
6 *They got the thieves.* apprehend, arrest, capture, catch.
7 *Get someone to help.* cause, persuade.
8 *I'll get tea.* make ready, prepare.
9 *I get what you mean.* comprehend, follow, grasp, understand.
10 *When did you get here?* arrive, reach.
11 *How can I get home?* come, go, travel.
12 *It got cold.* become, grow, turn.

ghastly adjective
SEE **frightful**.

ghost noun
apparition, [*informal*] bogy, ghostly apparition [SEE **ghostly**], hallucination, illusion, phantasm, phantom, poltergeist, shade, shadow, spectre, SEE **spirit**, [*informal*] spook, vision, visitant, wraith.

ghostly adjective
a ghostly noise. creepy, disembodied, eerie, frightening, illusory, phantasmal, scary, spectral, [*informal*] spooky, supernatural, uncanny, unearthly, weird.

giant adjective
a giant statue. colossal, elephantine, enormous, gargantuan, gigantic, huge, immense, [*informal*] jumbo, [*informal*] king-size, SEE **large**, mammoth, massive, mighty, monstrous, prodigious, titanic, vast.
OPPOSITES: SEE **small**.

giant noun
colossus, Goliath, giant person [SEE **giant** adjective], leviathan, monster, ogre, Titan, [*informal*] whopper.

gibberish noun
SEE **nonsense**.

giddiness noun
dizziness, faintness, unsteadiness, vertigo.

giddy adjective
a giddy feeling. dizzy, faint, light-headed, reeling, silly, spinning, unbalanced, unsteady.

gift noun
1 *a birthday gift. a gift to charity.* bonus, bounty, contribution, donation, grant,

gratuity, offering, present, tip.
2 *a gift for gymnastics.* ability, aptitude, bent, capability, capacity, flair, genius, knack, talent.

gifted adjective
SEE **talented**.

gigantic adjective SEE **giant** adjective.

giggle verb
SEE **laugh**, snigger, titter.

gimmick noun
a publicity gimmick. device, ploy, stratagem, stunt, trick.

girder noun
a framework of girders. bar, beam, joist, rafter, RSJ.

girdle noun
band, belt, corset, waist-band.

girl noun
[*old-fashioned*] damsel, daughter, débutante, hoyden, lass, [*old-fashioned*] maid, [*old-fashioned*] maiden, schoolgirl, tomboy, virgin, [*old-fashioned or sexist*] wench, SEE **woman**.

girth noun
circumference, measurement round.

gist noun
the gist of a message. direction, drift, essence, general sense, main idea, meaning, nub, point, significance.

give verb
1 *to give money. to give praise.* accord, allocate, allot, allow, apportion, assign, award, bestow, confer, contribute, deal out, [*informal*] dish out, distribute, [*informal*] dole out, donate, endow, entrust, [*informal*] fork out, furnish, give away, give out, grant, hand over, lend, let (someone) have, offer, pass over, pay, present, provide, ration out, render, share out, supply.
OPPOSITES: SEE **take**.
2 *to give information.* deliver, display, express, impart, issue, notify, publish, put across, put into words, reveal, set out, show, tell, transmit.
3 *to give a shout.* let out, utter, voice.
4 *to give punishment.* administer, impose, inflict, mete out.
5 *to give medicine.* dispense, dose with, give out, prescribe.
6 *to give a party.* arrange, organize, provide, put on, run, set up.
7 *to give out heat.* cause, create, emit, engender, generate, give off, produce, release, sent out, throw out.
8 *to give under pressure.* be flexible, bend, buckle, distort, give way, warp, yield.

glad adjective
SEE **pleased**.

glamorous adjective
1 *a glamorous filmstar.* SEE **beautiful**.
2 *a glamorous life in show-business.* alluring,
colourful, dazzling, enviable, exciting,
fascinating, glittering, prestigious, smart,
spectacular, wealthy.

glamour noun
1 SEE **beauty**.
2 *the glamour of show-business.* allure,
appeal, attraction, excitement, fascination,
glitter, high-life, lustre, magic.

glance noun, verb SEE **look** noun, verb.

glare noun
1 *an angry glare.* SEE **expression**.
2 *the glare from a fire.* SEE **light** noun.

glaring adjective SEE **bright**, **obvious**.

glass noun
1 *window glass.* double glazing, glazing,
pane, plate-glass.
2 *a glass of water.* beaker, goblet, tumbler,
wine-glass.
glasses

VARIOUS OPTICAL INSTRUMENTS: bifocals,
binoculars, contact-lenses, eye-glass, field-
glasses, goggles, lorgnette, magnifying glass,
monocle, opera-glasses, pince-nez, reading
glasses, spectacles, sun-glasses, telescope.

---

gleam noun, verb SEE **light** noun.

gleaming adjective
SEE **bright**.

gleeful adjective SEE **joyful**, **triumphant**.

glib adjective
a glib talker. articulate, facile, fluent,
insincere, plausible, quick, ready, slick,
smooth, superficial, SEE **talkative**.
OPPOSITES: SEE **inarticulate**, **sincere**.

glide verb
1 *to glide across ice or snow.* coast, glissade,
move smoothly, skate, ski, skid, skim, slide,
slip.
2 *to glide through the air.* drift, float, fly,
hang, hover, sail, soar.

glimpse noun
a quick glimpse. glance, look, peep, sight,
[*informal*] squint, view.

glimpse verb
I glimpsed someone moving between the trees.
discern, distinguish, espy, get a glimpse of,
make out, notice, observe, see briefly, sight,
spot, spy.

glint noun, verb, **glisten** verb, **glitter**
noun, verb SEE **light** noun.

glittering adjective
a glittering occasion. brilliant, colourful,
glamorous, resplendent, scintillating,
sparkling, SEE **splendid**.

gloat verb
to gloat over a victim. boast, brag, [*informal*]
crow, exult, rejoice, [*informal*] rub it in,
show off, triumph.

global adjective
SEE **universal**.

globe noun
1 *the shape of a globe.* ball, orb, sphere.
2 *the globe we live on.* earth, planet, world.

gloom noun
1 *We could hardly see in the gloom.*
cloudiness, dimness, dullness, dusk, murk,
obscurity, semi-darkness, shade, shadow,
twilight.
2 *a feeling of gloom.* SEE **depression**.

gloomy adjective
1 *a gloomy house. gloomy weather.* cheerless,
cloudy, dark, depressing, dim, dingy,
dismal, dreary, dull, glum, SEE **grim**, heavy,
joyless, murky, overcast, shadowy, sombre.
OPPOSITES: SEE **bright**.
2 *a gloomy person.* SEE **depressed**, lugubrious,
mournful, saturnine.

glorify verb SEE **praise** verb.

glorious adjective
1 *a glorious victory.* celebrated,
distinguished, famous, heroic, illustrious,
noble, noted, renowned, triumphant.
OPPOSITES: SEE **humiliating**.
2 *a glorious sunset.* beautiful, bright,
brilliant, dazzling, excellent, fine, gorgeous,
grand, impressive, lovely, magnificent,
majestic, marvellous, resplendent,
spectacular, splendid, [*informal*] super,
superb, wonderful.

glory noun
1 *the glory of winning an Olympic medal.*
credit, distinction, fame, honour, [*informal*]
kudos, praise, prestige, success, triumph.
2 *glory to God.* adoration, homage, praise,
thanksgiving, veneration, worship.
3 *the glory of the sunrise.* SEE **beauty**,
brightness, brilliance, grandeur,
magnificence, majesty, radiance, splendour.

gloss noun
I polished the table to a high gloss.
brightness, brilliance, burnish, lustre,
polish, sheen, shine, varnish.

glossy adjective
a glossy surface. bright, burnished, glassy,
glazed, gleaming, lustrous, polished,
reflective, shiny, silky, sleek, smooth.
OPPOSITES: SEE **dull** adjective.

glove noun
gauntlet, mitt, mitten.

glow noun
1 *the glow of a light bulb.* SEE **light** noun.
2 *the glow of a fire.* burning, fieriness, heat, incandescence, red-heat, redness.
3 *a glow in your cheeks.* blush, flush, rosiness, warmth.
4 *a glow of excitement.* ardour, enthusiasm, fervour, passion.

glower verb
frown, glare, lour, lower, scowl, stare angrily.

glowing adjective
1 *a glowing light.* bright, fluorescent, hot, incandescent, luminous, phosphorescent, radiant, red, red-hot, white-hot.
2 *a glowing recommendation.* complimentary, enthusiastic, fervent, passionate, warm.

glue noun
[In addition to the words given here, there are many kinds of glue with proprietary names.] adhesive, cement, fixative, gum, paste, sealant, size, wallpaper-paste.

glue verb
to glue things together. affix, bond, cement, fasten, fix, gum, paste, seal, stick.

glum adjective SEE **gloomy**.

glut noun
a glut of fruit. abundance, excess, plenty, superfluity, surfeit, surplus.
OPPOSITES: SEE **scarcity**.

gluttonous adjective
SEE **greedy**.

gnarled adjective
a gnarled old tree. contorted, distorted, knobbly, knotted, lumpy, rough, rugged, twisted.

go verb
1 *Let's go!* advance, begin, be off, commence, decamp, depart, disappear, embark, escape, get away, get going, get moving, get out, get under way, leave, move, [*informal*] nip along, pass along, proceed, retire, retreat, SEE **run** verb, set off, set out, [*informal*] shove off, start, take your leave, SEE **travel** verb, SEE **walk** verb, [*old-fashioned*] wend, withdraw.
2 *How far does this road go?* extend, lead, reach, stretch.
3 *The car won't go.* act, function, operate, perform, run, work.
4 *The firework went bang.* give off, make, produce, sound.
5 *Time goes quickly.* elapse, lapse, pass.
6 *Milk soon goes sour.* become, grow, turn.
7 *The butter goes in the fridge.* belong, feel at

home, have your proper place.
8 *The light goes in the evening.* die, disappear, fade, fail, give way, vanish.
to go away SEE **depart**.
to go into *Don't go into details.* SEE **investigate**.
to go off *A bomb went off.* SEE **explode**.
to go on *How long can you go on?* SEE **continue**.
to go through *She went through a nasty illness.* SEE **suffer**.

goad verb
to goad someone to do something. badger, [*informal*] chivvy, egg on, [*informal*] hassle, needle, prick, prod, prompt, spur, SEE **stimulate**, urge.

goal noun
a goal in life. aim, ambition, aspiration, design, end, intention, object, objective, purpose, target.

gobble verb
to gobble food. bolt, devour, SEE **eat**, gulp, guzzle.

go-between noun
agent, broker, envoy, intermediary, mediator, messenger, middleman.
to act as a go-between SEE **mediate**.

god, goddess nouns
the Almighty, the Creator, deity, divinity, godhead.
the gods the immortals, pantheon, the powers above.
RELIGIOUS TERMS: SEE **religion**.

godsend noun
Her gift of money was a godsend. blessing, miracle, stroke of good luck, windfall.

goggle verb
gape, gawp, SEE **look** verb, stare.

good adjective
[We apply the word *good* to anything we like or approve of. The number of possible synonyms, therefore, is virtually unlimited. We give here some of the more common words which express approval.] 1 [= *good in a general sense*] acceptable, admirable, agreeable, appropriate, approved of, champion, commendable, delightful, enjoyable, esteemed, SEE **excellent**, [*informal*] fabulous, fair, [*informal*] fantastic, fine, gratifying, happy, [*informal*] incredible, lovely, marvellous, nice, outstanding, perfect, [*informal*] phenomenal, pleasant, pleasing, praiseworthy, proper, remarkable, right, satisfactory, [*informal*] sensational, sound, splendid, [*informal*] super, superb, suitable, useful, valid, valuable, wonderful, worthy.
2 *a good person. a good deed.* angelic, benevolent, caring, charitable, chaste,

considerate, decent, dependable, dutiful, ethical, friendly, helpful, holy, honest, honourable, humane, incorruptible, innocent, just, SEE **kind** adjective, law-abiding, loyal, merciful, moral, noble, obedient, personable, pure, reliable, religious, righteous, saintly, sound, [*informal*] straight, thoughtful, true, trustworthy, upright, virtuous, well-behaved, well-mannered, worthy.
3 *a good musician. a good worker.* able, accomplished, capable, SEE **clever**, conscientious, efficient, gifted, proficient, skilful, skilled, talented.
4 *good work.* competent, correct, creditable, efficient, meritorious, neat, orderly, presentable, professional, thorough, well-done.
5 *good food.* delicious, eatable, nourishing, nutritious, tasty, well-cooked, wholesome.
6 *a good book.* classic, exciting, great, interesting, readable, well-written.

goodbye interjection
[Several terms we use when saying goodbye are from foreign languages. Generally, they are used informally.] adieu, adios, arrivederci, auf Wiedersehen, au revoir, bon voyage, ciao, cheerio, farewell, so long.
OPPOSITES: SEE **greeting**.

good-looking adjective SEE **handsome**.

good-natured adjective SEE **good-tempered**.

goods noun
SEE **freight**.

good-tempered adjective
accommodating, amenable, benevolent, benign, cheerful, considerate, cordial, friendly, good-humoured, good-natured, helpful, in a good mood, SEE **kind** adjective, obliging, patient, pleasant, relaxed, sympathetic, thoughtful, willing.
OPPOSITES: SEE **bad-tempered**.

goose noun
gander, gosling.

gorgeous adjective SEE **beautiful**, **magnificent**.

gory adjective
a gory wound. a gory battle. bloodstained, bloody, grisly, gruesome, savage.

gospel noun
preaching the gospel. creed, doctrine, good news, good tidings, message, religion, revelation, teaching, testament.

gossip noun
1 *Don't listen to gossip.* casual talk, chatter, hearsay, prattle, rumour, scandal, [*informal*] tattle, [*informal*] tittle-tattle.
2 *Don't listen to him—he's a real gossip.*

busybody, Nosy Parker, scandal-monger, SEE **talkative** (**talkative person**), tell-tale.

gossip verb
They just stood gossiping. chat, chatter, [*informal*] natter, prattle, spread scandal, SEE **talk** verb, [*informal*] tattle, tell tales, [*informal*] tittle-tattle.

gouge verb
to gouge out a hole. chisel, SEE **cut** verb, dig, hollow, scoop.

gourmet noun
connoisseur, epicure, gastronome.

govern verb
1 *to govern a country.* administer, be in charge of, command, conduct the affairs of, control, direct, guide, head, lead, look after, manage, oversee, preside over, reign, rule, run, steer, superintend, supervise.
2 *to govern your temper.* bridle, curb, check, control, discipline, keep in check, keep under control, master, regulate, restrain, tame.

government noun
Any country needs strong government. administration, bureaucracy, conduct of state affairs, constitution, control, direction, management, regime, regulation, rule, sovereignty, supervision, surveillance.

GROUPS INVOLVED IN GOVERNMENT: Cabinet, constituency, electorate, [*informal*] the Establishment, junta, local authority, ministry, parliament, [*informal*] the powers that be, regime, senate, state.

TYPES OF REGIME: commonwealth, democracy, dictatorship, empire, federation, kingdom, monarchy, oligarchy, republic.

PEOPLE INVOLVED IN GOVERNMENT OR PUBLIC ADMINISTRATION: ambassador, chancellor, Chancellor of the Exchequer, civil servant, consul, councillor, diplomat, elected representative, mayor, Member of Parliament, minister, politician, premier, president, prime minister, SEE **royalty**, Secretary of State (*Home Secretary, Foreign Secretary*, etc.), senator, statesman, stateswoman, viceroy.

---

grab verb
Grab what you can. [*informal*] bag, capture, catch, clutch, [*informal*] collar, get hold of, grasp, hold, [*informal*] nab, pluck, seize, snap up, snatch.

grace noun
1 *grace of movement.* attractiveness, beauty, charm, ease, elegance, fluidity, gracefulness, loveliness, poise, refinement, softness, tastefulness.
2 *God's grace.* beneficence, benevolence, compassion, favour, forgiveness, goodness,

graciousness, kindness, love, mercy.
3 *grace before dinner.* blessing, giving thanks, prayer.

graceful adjective
1 *graceful movements.* agile, balletic, deft, easy, flowing, fluid, natural, nimble, pliant, smooth, supple.
OPPOSITES: SEE **clumsy**.
2 *a graceful figure.* attractive, beautiful, dignified, elegant, slim, slender, willowy.
OPPOSITES: SEE **bony, fat** adjective.

gracious adjective
a gracious lady. affable, agreeable, charitable, compassionate, courteous, dignified, elegant, friendly, good-natured, SEE **kind** adjective, pleasant, polite, with grace.

grade noun
1 *top grade meat.* class, condition, quality, standard.
2 *The examiner re-marked the work and put it up a grade.* category, level, mark, notch, point, position, rank, rung, step.

grade verb
1 *They grade eggs according to size.* arrange, categorize, classify, differentiate, group, range, sort.
2 *Teachers grade students' work.* assess, evaluate, mark, rank, rate.

gradient noun
a steep gradient. ascent, bank, declivity, hill, incline, rise, slope.

gradual adjective
a gradual increase in prices. a gradual slope. continuous, even, gentle, leisurely, moderate, slow, steady, unhurried, unspectacular.
OPPOSITES: SEE **steep, sudden**.

graduate verb
1 *to graduate at a college or university.* become a graduate, be successful, get a degree, pass, qualify.
2 *to graduate a measuring-rod.* calibrate, divide into graded sections, mark off, mark with a scale.

grain noun
1 *the grain harvest.* SEE **cereal**.
2 *a grain of sand. a tiny grain.* bit, crumb, fragment, granule, iota, jot, mite, morsel, particle, seed, speck.
RELATED ADJECTIVE: granular.

grand adjective
1 *a grand occasion. a grand house.* SEE **big**, dignified, glorious, great, important, imposing, impressive, lordly, magnificent, majestic, noble, opulent, [*uncomplimentary*] ostentatious, palatial, posh, [*uncomplimentary*] pretentious, regal, royal, splendid, stately, sumptuous, superb.

OPPOSITES: SEE **modest**.
2 [*often uncomplimentary*] *They're too grand for us.* aristocratic, august, eminent, SEE **grandiose**, haughty, [*informal*] high-and-mighty, patronizing, pompous, upper class, [*informal*] upper crust.
OPPOSITES: SEE **ordinary**.

grandeur noun
SEE **splendour**.

grandiose adjective
[*uncomplimentary*] *grandiose ideas.* affected, exaggerated, extravagant, flamboyant, ostentatious, [*informal*] over the top, pretentious, showy.
OPPOSITES: SEE **unpretentious**.

grandparent noun
[*informal*] gran, [*informal*] grandad, grandfather, grandmother, [*informal*] grandpa, [*informal*] granny.

grant noun
a grant of money. allocation, allowance, annuity, award, benefaction, bursary, donation, expenses, gift, honorarium, investment, loan, scholarship, sponsorship, subsidy.

grant verb
1 *to grant someone a sum of money.* allocate, allow, allot, award, confer, donate, give, pay, provide.
2 *She granted that I was right.* accept, acknowledge, admit, agree, concede, vouchsafe.

granular adjective
a granular substance. crumbly, grainy, granulated, gritty, in grains, rough, sandy.

graph noun
chart, column-graph, diagram, grid, pie chart, table.

graphic adjective
a graphic description. SEE **vivid**.

grapple verb
to grapple with 1 *to grapple with an intruder.* SEE **fight** verb, lay hold of, struggle with, tackle, wrestle with. 2 *to grapple with a problem.* attend to, come to grips with, contend with, cope with, deal with, engage with, get involved with, handle, [*informal*] have a go at, manage, try to solve.
OPPOSITES: SEE **avoid**.

grasp verb
1 *to grasp something in your hands.* catch, clasp, clutch, get hold of, grab, grapple with, grip, hang on to, hold, seize, snatch.
2 *to grasp an idea.* apprehend, comprehend, [*informal*] cotton on to, follow, learn, master, realize, take in, understand.

grass noun

PLANTS RELATED TO GRASS: bamboo, esparto grass, pampas grass, sugar cane.

AREAS OF GRASS: downland, field, grassland, green, lawn, meadow, pasture, playing-field, prairie, recreation ground, savannah, steppe, [*poetic*] sward, turf, veld, village green.

grate verb
1 *to grate cheese.* SEE **cut** verb, shred.
2 *a grating noise.*
VARIOUS SOUNDS: SEE **sound** noun.
3 *His manner grates on me.* SEE **annoy**.

grateful adjective
grateful for the gift. appreciative, indebted, obliged, thankful.
OPPOSITES: SEE **ungrateful**.

gratify verb SEE **please**.

gratitude noun SEE **thanks**.

gratuitous adjective
gratuitous insults. groundless, inappropriate, needless, unasked for, uncalled for, undeserved, unjustifiable, unmerited, unnecessary, unprovoked, unsolicited, unwarranted.
OPPOSITES: SEE **justifiable**.

grave adjective
1 *a grave decision.* crucial, SEE **important**, momentous, pressing, serious, significant, urgent, vital, weighty.
OPPOSITES: SEE **unimportant**.
2 *a grave illness.* acute, critical, dangerous, major, serious, severe, terminal, threatening, worrying.
OPPOSITES: SEE **slight** adjective.
3 *a grave offence.* criminal, indictable, punishable.
OPPOSITES: SEE **minor**.
4 *a grave expression.* dignified, earnest, gloomy, grim, long-faced, pensive, SEE **sad**, sedate, serious, severe, sober, solemn, sombre, subdued, thoughtful, unsmiling.
OPPOSITES: SEE **happy**.

grave noun
graves where people are buried. barrow, burial-place, SEE **gravestone**, mausoleum, sepulchre, tomb, tumulus, vault.

gravel noun
grit, pebbles, shingle, stones.

gravestone noun
headstone, memorial, monument, tombstone.

graveyard noun
burial-ground, cemetery, churchyard.

gravitate verb
We all gravitated towards the food. be attracted to, descend on, head for, make for, move towards.

gravity noun
1 *the gravity of an illness.* acuteness, danger, importance, magnitude, momentousness, seriousness, severity.
2 *the gravity of a state occasion.* ceremony, dignity, earnestness, pomp, sedateness, sobriety, solemnity.
3 *the force of gravity.* gravitation, heaviness, ponderousness, pull, weight.

graze noun
a graze on the knee. abrasion, laceration, raw spot.

graze verb
1 *grazing cattle.* SEE **eat**.
2 *to graze your knee.* [*formal*] abrade, chafe, scrape, scratch, SEE **wound** verb.

greasy adjective
1 *greasy fingers.* fatty, oily, slippery, smeary.
2 *a greasy manner.* fawning, flattering, fulsome, grovelling, ingratiating, [*informal*] smarmy, sycophantic, unctuous.

great adjective
1 *a great mountain. a great ocean.* SEE **big**, colossal, enormous, extensive, huge, immense, large, tremendous.
2 *great pain. great difficulties.* acute, excessive, extreme, intense, SEE **severe**.
3 *a great event.* grand, SEE **important**, large-scale, momentous, serious, significant, spectacular.
4 *a great piece of music.* brilliant, classic, SEE **excellent**, [*informal*] fabulous, famous, [*informal*] fantastic, fine, first-rate, outstanding, wonderful.
5 *a great athlete.* able, celebrated, distinguished, eminent, SEE **famous**, gifted, notable, noted, prominent, renowned, talented, well-known.
6 *a great friend.* SEE **chief** adjective, close, devoted, main, valued.

greed noun
1 *greed for food.* appetite, craving, gluttony, gormandizing, greediness, hunger, intemperance, insatiability, overeating, ravenousness, self-indulgence, voraciousness, voracity.
2 *greed for possessions.* acquisitiveness, avarice, covetousness, cupidity, desire, rapacity, self-interest, selfishness.

greedy adjective
1 *greedy for food.* famished, gluttonous, gormandizing, hungry, insatiable, intemperate, omnivorous, [*informal*] piggish, ravenous, self-indulgent, starving, voracious.
OPPOSITES: SEE **abstemious**.
2 *greedy for possessions.* acquisitive, avaricious, avid, covetous, desirous, eager, grasping, miserly, [*informal*] money-grabbing, rapacious, selfish.

OPPOSITES: SEE **unselfish**.
a greedy person glutton, [*joking*] good trencherman, gormandizer, gourmand, [*informal*] greedy-guts, guzzler, [*informal*] pig.

green adjective
greenish, verdant.

SHADES OF GREEN: emerald, grass-green, jade, khaki, lime, olive, pea-green, turquoise.

---

greet verb
to greet visitors. acknowledge, give a greeting to, hail, receive, salute, say (greeting) to [SEE **greeting**], welcome.

greeting noun
salutation, welcome.
OPPOSITES: SEE **goodbye**.

VARIOUS WORDS OF GREETING: good day, good morning (afternoon, evening), hallo, hello, hullo, how do you do, welcome.

GREETINGS USED ON SPECIAL OCCASIONS: condolences, congratulations, felicitations, happy anniversary (birthday, Christmas, etc.), many happy returns, sympathies, well done.

---

grey adjective
grey hair. grey skies. ashen, blackish, greying, grizzled, grizzly, hoary, leaden, silver, silvery, slate-grey, whitish.

grid noun
1 *an iron grid.* framework, grating, grille, lattice.
2 *Draw the plan on a grid.* graph paper, network of lines, pattern of intersecting lines, squares.

grief noun
the grief of bereavement. affliction, anguish, desolation, distress, heartache, heartbreak, misery, mourning, pain, regret, remorse, sadness, sorrow, suffering, tragedy, [*informal*] trials and tribulations, unhappiness, woe.
OPPOSITES: SEE **happiness**.
to come to grief SEE **fail**.

grieve verb
1 *The uncalled-for criticism grieved her.* afflict, cause grief to [SEE **grief**], depress, dismay, distress, hurt, pain, sadden, upset, wound.
OPPOSITES: SEE **delight** verb.
2 *He grieved terribly when his dog died.* feel grief [SEE **grief**], [*informal*] eat your heart out, fret, go into mourning, lament, mope, mourn, suffer, wail, weep.
OPPOSITES: SEE **rejoice**.

grim adjective
1 *a grim expression.* bad-tempered, cruel, dour, fearsome, fierce, forbidding, frightful, ghastly, gloomy, grisly, gruesome, harsh, hideous, horrible, [*informal*] horrid, menacing, merciless, ominous, relentless, severe, stark, stern, sullen, surly, terrible, threatening, unattractive, unfriendly, unrelenting.
2 *grim weather.* SEE **gloomy**.
OPPOSITES: SEE **cheerful, pleasant**.

grime noun SEE **dirt**.

grimy adjective
grimy windows. SEE **dirty** adjective.

grin verb
beam, SEE **laugh**, smile.

grind verb
1 *to grind coffee, corn, etc.* crush, granulate, grate, mill, pound, powder, pulverize.
2 *to grind your teeth.* gnash, rub together.
3 *to grind a knife.* polish, sharpen, whet.
4 *to grind away. to grind down.* abrade, eat away, erode, file, sand, sandpaper, scrape, smooth, wear away.
5 *to grind people down.* SEE **oppress**.
6 *to grind away at a job.* labour, slave, sweat, toil, SEE **work** verb.

grip noun
a firm grip. clasp, clutch, control, grasp, hand-clasp, hold, purchase, stranglehold.

grip verb
1 *to grip someone's hand.* clasp, clutch, get a grip of [SEE **grip** noun], grab, grasp, hold, seize, take hold of.
2 *to grip someone's attention.* absorb, compel, engross, enthral, fascinate, rivet, spellbind.

grisly adjective
[Don't confuse with *gristly*.] *a grisly accident.* SEE **gruesome**.

gristly adjective
[Don't confuse with *grisly*.] *gristly meat.* leathery, rubbery, tough, unchewable, uneatable.

grit noun
1 *grit in my eye.* dust, gravel, sand.
2 [*informal*] *grit in facing danger.* SEE **courage**.

gritty adjective
something gritty in the food. abrasive, dusty, grainy, granular, gravelly, harsh, rough, sandy.

groan verb
to groan with pain. cry out, moan, sigh, wail.

groom noun
1 [= *person who looks after horses*] ostler, stable-lad, stable-man.

2 [= *man on his wedding day*] bridegroom, husband.

groom verb
1 *to groom a horse. to groom yourself.* brush, clean, make neat, preen, smarten up, spruce up, tidy, [*informal*] titivate.
2 *to groom someone for a job.* coach, educate, get ready, prepare, train up.

groove noun
a groove in a surface. channel, cut, fluting, furrow, gutter, indentation, rut, score, scratch, slot, track.

grope verb
to grope in the dark. to grope for an answer. cast about, feel about, flounder, fumble, search blindly.

gross adjective
1 *a gross figure.* SEE **fat** adjective.
2 *gross manners.* SEE **vulgar.**
3 *gross injustice.* SEE **obvious.**
4 *gross income.* SEE **total** adjective.

grotesque adjective
grotesque carvings. absurd, bizarre, deformed, distorted, fantastic, ludicrous, macabre, malformed, misshapen. monstrous, preposterous, ridiculous, strange, ugly, unnatural, weird.

ground noun
1 *the ground someone owns.* area, land, property, terrain.
2 *fertile ground.* clay, earth, loam, soil.
3 *the grounds of a building.* campus, estate, gardens, park, playing-fields, surroundings.
4 *a sports ground.* arena, field, pitch, stadium.
5 *If you accuse someone, be sure of your ground.* argument, basis, case, cause, evidence, foundation, proof, reason.

ground verb
1 *to ground a ship.* beach, run ashore, shipwreck, strand, wreck.
2 *to ground an aircraft.* keep on the ground, prevent from flying.
3 *On what facts do you ground your argument?* SEE **base** verb.

groundless adjective
a groundless accusation. baseless, false, gratuitous, imaginary, irrational, needless, uncalled for, unfounded, unjustified, unproven, unreasonable, unsubstantiated, unsupported, unwarranted.
OPPOSITES: SEE **justifiable.**

group noun

VARIOUS GROUPS OF PEOPLE: alliance, assembly, association, band, bevy (*of women*), body, brotherhood, [*informal*] bunch, cadre, cartel, caste, caucus, circle (*of friends*), clan, class, [*uncomplimentary*] clique, club, cohort (*of soldiers*), colony, committee, community, company, conclave (*of cardinals*), congregation (*of worshippers*), consortium, contingent, coterie, coven (*of witches*), crew, crowd, delegation, faction (*a break-away faction*), family, federation, force (*of invaders*), fraternity, gang, gathering, guild (*of workers*), horde, host, knot, league, meeting, [*uncomplimentary*] mob, multitude, organization, party, phalanx (*of soldiers*), picket (*of strikers*), platoon, posse (*of law-enforcers*), [*uncomplimentary*] rabble, ring (*of criminals*), sect, [*uncomplimentary*] shower, sisterhood, society, squad, squadron, swarm, team, throng, troop (*of soldiers*), troupe (*of actors*), union.

GROUPS OF ANIMALS, THINGS, ETC.: accumulation, assortment, batch, battery (*of guns*), brood (*of chicks*), bunch, bundle, category, class, clump (*of trees*), cluster, clutch (*of eggs*), collection, combination, conglomeration, constellation (*of stars*), convoy (*of ships*), covey (*of birds*), fleet (*of ships*), flock (*of birds or sheep*), gaggle (*of geese*), galaxy (*of stars*), herd (*of animals*), hoard, host, litter (*of pigs*), mass, pack (*of wolves*), pride (*of lions*), school, set, shoal (*of fish*), species.

GROUPS OF MUSICIANS: SEE **music.**

group verb
1 *to group things together.* arrange, assemble, bring together, categorize, classify, collect, deploy, gather, herd, marshal, order, organize, put into groups [SEE **group** noun], set out, sort.
2 *to group around a leader.* associate, band, cluster, come together, congregate, crowd, flock, gather, get together, herd, make groups [SEE **group** noun], swarm, team up, throng.

grouse verb
SEE **complain.**

grovel verb
Don't grovel—stick up for yourself! abase yourself, be humble, cower, [*informal*] creep, cringe, demean yourself, [*informal*] kowtow, prostrate yourself, snivel, [*informal*] toady.

grow verb
1 *Plants grow well in springtime.* become bigger, burgeon, come to life, develop, emerge, evolve, fill out, flourish, germinate, get bigger, increase in size, lengthen, live, make progress, mature, multiply, mushroom, proliferate, put on growth,

spread, spring up, sprout, survive, swell, thicken up, thrive.
OPPOSITES: SEE **die**.
2 *I grow roses.* cultivate, farm, help along, nurture, produce, propagate, raise.
OPPOSITES: SEE **kill**.
3 *Her business grew. Her confidence grew.* augment, build up, develop, enlarge, expand, extend, improve, increase, progress, prosper.
OPPOSITES: SEE **shrink**.
4 *She grew more confident.* become, turn.
to grow up become adult, mature.

grown-up adjective
adult, fully grown, mature, well-developed.

growth noun
1 *the growth of children.* advance, development, education, getting bigger, growing, maturation, maturing, progress.
2 *the growth of wealth.* accretion, augmentation, enlargement, expansion, improvement, increase, prosperity, success.
3 *growth in the garden.* crop, plants, vegetation.
4 *a growth on the body.* cancer, cyst, excrescence, lump, swelling, tumour.

grubby adjective
grubby clothes. SEE **dirty** adjective.

grudge noun
SEE **resentment**.

grudging adjective
grudging admiration. cautious, envious, guarded, halfhearted, hesitant, jealous, reluctant, resentful, secret, unenthusiastic, ungracious, unkind, unwilling.
OPPOSITES: SEE **enthusiastic**.

gruelling adjective
a gruelling climb. arduous, backbreaking, demanding, difficult, exhausting, fatiguing, hard, laborious, punishing, severe, stiff, strenuous, taxing, tiring, tough, uphill, wearying.
OPPOSITES: SEE **easy**.

gruesome adjective
a gruesome accident. appalling, awful, bloody, disgusting, dreadful, fearful, frightful, ghastly, ghoulish, gory, grim, grisly, hair-raising, hideous, horrible, [*informal*] horrid, horrifying, macabre, revolting, sickening, terrible.

gruff adjective
1 *a gruff voice.* harsh, hoarse, husky, rough.
2 *a gruff manner.* SEE **bad-tempered**.

grumble verb SEE **complain**.

grumpy adjective SEE **bad-tempered**.

guarantee noun
assurance, oath, pledge, promise, surety, warranty.

guarantee verb
1 *to guarantee that a thing works.* assure, certify, give a guarantee, pledge, promise, swear, vouch, vow.
2 *This ticket guarantees your seat.* ensure, make sure of, secure.

guard noun
a prison guard. custodian, escort, lookout, patrol, security-officer, sentinel, sentry, warder, watchman.

guard verb
A mother guards her young. A warder guards prisoners. be on guard over, care for, defend, keep safe, keep watch on, look after, mind, oversee, patrol, police, preserve, prevent from escaping, protect, safeguard, secure, shelter, shield, stand guard over, supervise, tend, watch, watch over.
OPPOSITES: SEE **abandon**, **attack**.

guardian noun
1 *the guardian of a child.* adoptive parent, foster-parent.
2 *a guardian of public morals.* custodian, defender, keeper, minder, preserver, protector, trustee, warden, warder.

guess noun
a guess about the future. assumption, conjecture, estimate, feeling, [*informal*] guesstimate, guesswork, hunch, hypothesis, intuition, opinion, prediction, [*informal*] shot in the dark, speculation, supposition, surmise, suspicion, theory.

guess verb
I guess it will cost a lot. assume, conjecture, divine, estimate, expect, feel, have a hunch, have a theory, [*informal*] hazard a guess, hypothesize, imagine, judge, make a guess [SEE **guess** noun], predict, speculate, suppose, surmise, suspect, think likely.

guest noun
guests at home. caller, company, visitor.

guidance noun
He was new to the job and needed guidance. advice, briefing, counselling, direction, guidelines, guiding, help, instruction, [*informal*] spoon-feeding, [*informal*] taking by the hand, teaching, tips.

guide noun
1 *a guide who shows the way.* courier, escort, leader, pilot.
2 *maps and guides from the bookshop.* atlas, directory, gazetteer, guidebook, handbook.

guide verb
1 *to guide someone on a journey.* conduct, direct, escort, lead, manœuvre, navigate, pilot, steer, supervise.
2 *to guide someone in her studies.* advise, brief, counsel, direct, educate, give guidance to [SEE **guidance**], help along, influence,

[*informal*] take by the hand, teach, train.
OPPOSITES: SEE **mislead**.

guilt noun
1 *The evidence proved his guilt.* blame,
blameworthiness, criminality, culpability,
fault, guiltiness, liability, responsibility,
sinfulness, wickedness.
OPPOSITES: SEE **innocence**.
2 *a look of guilt on her face.* bad conscience,
contrition, dishonour, guilty feelings,
penitence, regret, remorse, self-accusation,
self-reproach, shame.
OPPOSITES: SEE **virtue**.

guiltless adjective
a guiltless conscience. above suspicion,
blameless, clear, faultless, free, honourable,
immaculate, innocent, irreproachable, pure,
sinless, untarnished, untroubled, virtuous.
OPPOSITES: SEE **guilty**.

guilty adjective
1 *guilty of wrongdoing.* at fault, blamable,
blameworthy, culpable, in the wrong, liable,
reprehensible, responsible.
OPPOSITES: SEE **innocent**.
2 *a guilty look.* ashamed, conscience-
stricken, contrite, penitent, regretful,
remorseful, repentant, shamefaced,
sheepish, sorry.
OPPOSITES: SEE **guiltless**.

gullible adjective
He's so gullible he'll believe anything.
credulous, easily taken in, [*informal*] green,
impressionable, innocent, naïve,
suggestible, trusting, unsuspecting.

gun noun
[*plural*] artillery, firearm.

VARIOUS GUNS: airgun, automatic,
blunderbuss, cannon, machine-gun, mortar,
musket, pistol, revolver, rifle, shot-gun,
small-arms, sub-machine-gun, tommy-gun.

PARTS OF A GUN: barrel, bolt, breach, butt,
magazine, muzzle, sights, trigger.

---

gunfire noun
cannonade, firing, gunshots, salvo.

gunman noun
assassin, bandit, criminal, desperado, SEE
fighter, gangster, killer, murderer, sniper,
terrorist.

gush verb
Liquid gushed out. come in a gush, cascade,
flood, flow quickly, overflow, pour, run,
rush, spout, spurt, squirt, stream, well up.
OPPOSITES: SEE **trickle**.

gust noun SEE **wind** noun.

gusty adjective
SEE **windy**.

gut noun
[*often plural*], [*informal*] *a pain in the guts.*
belly, bowels, entrails, [*informal*] innards,
insides, intestines, stomach.
guts [*informal*] *She had guts.* SEE **courage**.

gutter noun
a gutter to carry away water. channel,
conduit, ditch, drain, duct, guttering, sewer,
sluice, trench, trough.

guttural adjective
a guttural voice. SEE **throaty**.

gypsy noun
nomad, Romany, traveller, wanderer.

gyrate verb
circle, pirouette, revolve, rotate, spin, spiral,
turn, twirl, wheel, whirl.

Hh

habit noun
1 *the habit of shaking hands.* convention,
custom, practice, routine, rule, [*old-
fashioned*] wont.
2 *the habit of scratching your head.* manner,
mannerism, propensity, quirk, tendency,
way.
3 *the habit of smoking.* addiction,
compulsion, confirmed habit, craving,
dependence, fixation, obsession, vice.

habitual adjective
1 *my habitual route to work.* accustomed,
common, conventional, customary,
expected, familiar, fixed, frequent, natural,
normal, ordinary, predictable, regular,
routine, standard, traditional, typical,
usual, [*old-fashioned*] wonted.
OPPOSITES: SEE **abnormal**.
2 *a habitual weakness.* addictive, besetting,
chronic, established, ineradicable,
ingrained, obsessive, persistent, recurrent.
3 *a habitual smoker.* addicted, conditioned,
confirmed, dependent, [*informal*] hooked,
inveterate, persistent.
OPPOSITES: SEE **occasional**.

hack verb SEE **cut** verb.

hackneyed adjective
hackneyed language. banal, clichéd, cliché-
ridden, commonplace, conventional,
[*informal*] corny, familiar, feeble, obvious,
overused, pedestrian, platitudinous,

predictable, stale, stereotyped, stock, threadbare, tired, trite, uninspired, unoriginal.
OPPOSITES: SEE **exciting, new.**

haggard adjective
haggard with exhaustion. [*informal*] all skin and bone, careworn, drawn, emaciated, exhausted, gaunt, hollow-eyed, pinched, shrunken, thin, tired out, ugly, unhealthy, wasted, withered, worn out, [*informal*] worried to death.
OPPOSITES: SEE **healthy.**

haggle verb
to haggle over the price. argue, bargain, barter, discuss terms, negotiate, SEE **quarrel** verb, wrangle.

hair noun
1 *hair on an animal's skin.* bristles, fleece, fur, mane.
2 *hair on your head.* curls, hank, locks, [*informal*] mop, shock, tresses.

WORDS TO DESCRIBE THE COLOUR OF HAIR:
auburn, [*male*] blond, [*female*] blonde, brunette, [*informal*] carrotty, dark, fair, flaxen, ginger, SEE **grey**, grizzled, mousy, platinum blonde, redhead.
VARIOUS HAIR-STYLES: SEE **hair-style.**

---

hairdresser noun
barber, [*male*] coiffeur, [*female*] coiffeuse, hair-stylist.

hairless adjective
bald, bare, clean-shaven, naked, shaved, shaven, smooth.
OPPOSITES: SEE **hairy.**

hair-raising adjective
SEE **frightening.**

hair-style noun
coiffure, cut, hair-cut, [*informal*] hair-do, style.

VARIOUS HAIR-STYLES: bob, crew-cut, dreadlocks, fringe, Mohican, [*informal*] perm, permanent wave, pigtail, plaits, pony-tail, quiff, short back and sides, sideboards, sideburns, tonsure, topknot.
FALSE HAIR: hair-piece, toupee, wig.

---

hairy adjective
hairy skin. bearded, bristly, downy, feathery, fleecy, furry, fuzzy, hirsute, long-haired, shaggy, stubbly, woolly.
OPPOSITES: SEE **hairless.**

half-hearted adjective
half-hearted about her work. apathetic, cool, easily distracted, feeble, indifferent, ineffective, lackadaisical, listless,

lukewarm, passive, perfunctory, uncommitted, unenthusiastic, unreliable, wavering, weak, [*informal*] wishy-washy.
OPPOSITES: SEE **committed.**

hall noun
1 *the village hall.* assembly hall, auditorium, concert-hall, theatre.
2 *Wait in the hall.* corridor, entrance-hall, foyer, hallway, lobby, passage, vestibule.

hallucinate verb
day-dream, dream, fantasize, [*informal*] have a trip, have hallucinations, [*informal*] see things, see visions.

hallucination noun
apparition, day-dream, delusion, dream, fantasy, figment of the imagination, illusion, mirage, vision.

halt verb
1 *A traffic-jam halted traffic.* arrest, block, check, curb, impede, obstruct, stop.
2 *Traffic halts at a red light.* come to a halt, come to rest, draw up, pull up, stop, wait.
3 *Work halted when the whistle went.* break off, cease, end, terminate.
OPPOSITES: SEE **start** verb.

halting adjective
halting speech. halting progress. erratic, faltering, hesitant, irregular, stammering, stumbling, stuttering, uncertain, underconfident, unsure.
OPPOSITES: SEE **fluent.**

halve verb
to halve your income. bisect, cut by half, cut in half, decrease, divide into halves, lessen, reduce by half, share equally, split in two.

hammer verb
to hammer on the door. bash, batter, beat, SEE **hit** verb, knock, strike.

hamper verb
1 *Bad weather hampered the work.* curb, curtail, foil, hold up, interfere with, obstruct, prevent, restrict, thwart.
2 *My wellingtons hampered me when I ran.* encumber, entangle, fetter, frustrate, handicap, hinder, hold back, impede, restrain, shackle, slow down, trammel.
OPPOSITES: SEE **help** verb.

hand noun
a human hand. fist, palm.
RELATED ADJECTIVE: manual.
at hand, on hand, to hand available, close by, present, waiting, within reach.
to give a hand SEE **help** verb.

hand verb
to hand something to someone. convey, deliver, give, offer, pass, present, submit.
to hand over 1 *to hand over money.* donate,

[*informal*] fork out, give up, pay, surrender, tender. 2 *to hand over a prisoner.* deliver up, extradite, release, [*informal*] turn over.
to hand round *to hand round the drinks.* circulate, deal out, distribute, give out, pass round, share.

handicap noun
1 *Luggage is a handicap when you run for a train.* difficulty, disadvantage, drawback, encumbrance, hindrance, inconvenience, [*informal*] minus, nuisance, obstacle, problem, restriction, shortcoming, stumbling-block.
OPPOSITES: SEE **advantage**.
2 *Blindness is a handicap.* defect, disability, impairment, impediment, limitation.

handicap verb
A strong wind handicapped the athletes. be a handicap to [SEE **handicap** noun], burden, create problems for, disadvantage, encumber, hamper, hinder, hold back, impede, limit, restrict, retard.
OPPOSITES: SEE **help** verb.

handicapped adjective
handicapped people. disabled, disadvantaged.

SOME WAYS IN WHICH YOU CAN BE HANDICAPPED: autistic, crippled, deaf, disabled, dumb, dyslexic, impaired hearing or sight, lame, limbless, maimed, mute, paralysed, paraplegic, retarded, slow.

---

handiwork noun
Is this your handiwork? achievement, creation, doing, invention, production, responsibility, work.

handle noun
Hold it by the handle. grip, haft, hand-grip, helve, hilt (*of a sword*), knob, stock (*of a rifle*).

handle verb
1 *Take care how you handle small animals.* feel, finger, fondle, grasp, hold, [*informal*] maul, [*informal*] paw, stroke, touch, treat.
2 *to handle a rowdy class. to handle a situation.* conduct, control, cope with, deal with, guide, look after, manage, manipulate, supervise.
3 *The car handles well.* manœuvre, operate, respond, steer, work.
4 *We don't handle second-hand goods.* deal in, do trade in, sell, stock, touch, traffic in.

handsome adjective
1 *a handsome man.* attractive, comely, good-looking, personable.
2 *handsome furniture.* admirable, beautiful, elegant, tasteful, well-made.
OPPOSITES: SEE **ugly**.

3 *a handsome gift. a handsome gesture.* big, big-hearted, bountiful, generous, gracious, large, liberal, magnanimous, munificent, sizeable, unselfish, valuable.
OPPOSITES: SEE **mean** adjective.

handy adjective
1 *a handy tool.* convenient, easy to use, helpful, manageable, practical, serviceable, useful, well-designed, worth having.
OPPOSITES: SEE **awkward**.
2 *Keep your tools handy.* accessible, available, close at hand, easy to reach, get-at-able, nearby, reachable, ready.
OPPOSITES: SEE **inaccessible**.
3 *She's handy with tools.* adept, capable, clever, competent, practical, proficient, skilful.
OPPOSITES: SEE **incompetent**.

hang verb
1 *A flag hangs from a flagpole.* dangle, droop, swing, trail down.
2 *to hang washing on a line. to hang pictures on a wall.* attach, fasten, fix, peg up, pin up, stick up, suspend.
3 *Smoke hung in the air.* drift, float, hover.
4 *to hang criminals.* SEE **execute**.
to hang about *Don't hang about in the cold.* dally, dawdle, linger, loiter.
to hang back *You'll lose your chance if you hang back.* hesitate, pause, wait.
to hang on *Try to hang on until help comes.* carry on, continue, endure, hold on, keep going, persevere, persist, stay with it, stick it out, wait.
to hang on to *Hang on to the rope.* catch, grasp, hold, keep, retain, seize.

hangings noun
hangings on the wall. draperies, drapes, tapestries.

hanker verb
to hanker after SEE **desire** verb.

haphazard adjective
The organization was haphazard. accidental, arbitrary, chaotic, confusing, disorderly, SEE **disorganized**, [*informal*] higgledy-piggledy, [*informal*] hit-or-miss, random, unplanned.
OPPOSITES: SEE **orderly**.

happen verb
Did anything interesting happen? arise, befall, [*old-fashioned*] betide, chance, come about, crop up, emerge, follow, materialize, occur, result, take place, [*informal, sometimes regarded as incorrect*] transpire.
to happen on SEE **find** verb.

happening noun
an unexpected happening. accident, affair, chance, circumstance, event, incident, occasion, occurrence, phenomenon.

happiness noun
bliss, cheer, SEE **cheerfulness**, contentment, delight, ecstasy, elation, euphoria, exhilaration, exuberance, felicity, gaiety, gladness, heaven, high spirits, joy, jubilation, light-heartedness, merriment, pleasure, pride, rapture, well-being.
OPPOSITES: SEE **sorrow** noun.

happy adjective
1 *a happy person. a happy event.* beatific, blessed, blissful, [*poetic*] blithe, SEE **cheerful**, contented, delighted, ecstatic, elated, exultant, felicitous, festive, gay, glad, gleeful, good-humoured, halcyon (*halcyon days*), heavenly, idyllic, jolly, joyful, joyous, laughing, light-hearted, lively, merry, overjoyed, [*informal*] over-the-moon, pleased, proud, radiant, rapturous, relaxed, [*informal*] starry-eyed, thrilled.
OPPOSITES: SEE **unhappy**.
2 *a happy accident.* advantageous, convenient, favourable, fortunate, lucky, opportune, propitious, timely, well-timed.
OPPOSITES: SEE **unlucky**.

harass verb
Dogs mustn't harass the sheep. annoy, badger, bait, bother, disturb, harry, [*informal*] hassle, hound, molest, persecute, pester, [*informal*] plague, torment, trouble, vex, worry.

harassed adjective
a harassed look. [*informal*] at the end of your tether, careworn, distraught, distressed, exhausted, frayed, [*informal*] hassled, irritated, pressured, strained, stressed, tired, troubled, vexed, weary, worn out, worried.
OPPOSITES: SEE **carefree**.

harbour noun
ships tied up in the harbour. anchorage, dock, haven, jetty, landing-stage, marina, moorings, pier, port, quay, shelter, wharf.

harbour verb
1 *to harbour criminals.* conceal, give asylum to, give refuge to, give sanctuary to, hide, protect, shelter, shield.
2 *to harbour a grudge.* cherish, cling on to, hold on to, keep in mind, maintain, nurture, retain.

hard adjective
1 *hard concrete. hard ground.* compact, dense, firm, flinty, impenetrable, inflexible, rigid, rocky, solid, stony, unyielding.
OPPOSITES: SEE **soft**.
2 *hard work.* arduous, back-breaking, exhausting, fatiguing, formidable, gruelling, harsh, heavy, laborious, rigorous, severe, stiff, strenuous, tiring, tough, uphill, wearying.

OPPOSITES: SEE **easy**.
3 *a hard problem.* baffling, complex, complicated, confusing, difficult, intricate, involved, knotty, perplexing, puzzling, [*informal*] thorny.
OPPOSITES: SEE **simple**.
4 *a hard heart. hard feelings.* acrimonious, SEE **angry**, callous, cruel, harsh, heartless, hostile, inflexible, intolerant, merciless, pitiless, rancorous, resentful, ruthless, severe, stern, strict, unbending, unfeeling, unfriendly, unkind.
OPPOSITES: SEE **kind** adjective.
5 *a hard blow.* forceful, heavy, powerful, strong, violent.
OPPOSITES: SEE **light** adjective.
6 *a hard time.* calamitous, disagreeable, intolerable, painful, unhappy, unpleasant.
OPPOSITES: SEE **pleasant**.

harden verb
VARIOUS WAYS SUBSTANCES HARDEN: bake, cake, clot, coagulate, congeal, freeze, gel, jell, ossify, petrify, set, solidify, stiffen, toughen.
OPPOSITES: SEE **soften**.

hardly adverb
hardly visible. barely, faintly, only just, scarcely, with difficulty.

hardship noun
financial hardship. adversity, affliction, austerity, destitution, difficulty, misery, misfortune, need, privation, suffering, [*informal*] trials and tribulations, trouble, unhappiness, want.

hardy adjective
a hardy constitution. hardy plants. fit, healthy, hearty, resilient, robust, rugged, strong, sturdy, tough, vigorous.
OPPOSITES: SEE **tender**.

hark verb SEE **listen**.

harm noun
Did the storm cause any harm? damage, detriment, disservice, SEE **evil** noun, havoc, hurt, inconvenience, injury, loss, mischief, pain, unhappiness, [*informal*] upset, wrong.
OPPOSITES: SEE **benefit** noun.

harm verb
His captors didn't harm him. Chemicals might harm the soil. be harmful to [SEE **harmful**], damage, hurt, ill-treat, impair, injure, maltreat, misuse, ruin, spoil, wound.
OPPOSITES: SEE **benefit** verb.

harmful adjective
a harmful habit. harmful chemicals. bad, damaging, dangerous, deadly, deleterious, destructive, detrimental, evil, hurtful, injurious, malign, noxious, pernicious,

poisonous, prejudicial, unhealthy, unpleasant, unwholesome.
OPPOSITES: SEE **beneficial, harmless**.

harmless adjective
harmless animals. a harmless habit. acceptable, innocent, innocuous, inoffensive, mild, non-addictive, non-toxic, safe, unobjectionable.
OPPOSITES: SEE **harmful**.

harmonious adjective
1 *a harmonious group of friends.* amicable, compatible, congenial, co-operative, friendly, integrated, like-minded, sympathetic.
OPPOSITES: SEE **quarrelsome**.
2 *harmonious music.* concordant, [*informal*] easy on the ear, euphonious, harmonizing, melodious, musical, sweet-sounding, tonal, tuneful.
OPPOSITES: SEE **discordant**.

harmonize verb
I'd like the colours to harmonize. be in harmony [SEE **harmony**], blend, co-ordinate, correspond, go together, match, suit each other, tally, tone in.

harmony noun
1 *living in harmony.* accord, agreement, amity, compatibility, conformity, co-operation, friendliness, goodwill, like-mindedness, peace, rapport, sympathy, understanding.
2 *musical harmony.* assonance, chords, concord, consonance, euphony, tunefulness.
OPPOSITES: SEE **discord**.

harness noun
a horse's harness. equipment, [*informal*] gear, straps, tackle.

PARTS OF A HORSE'S HARNESS: bit, blinker, bridle, collar, crupper, girth, halter, headstall, noseband, pommel, rein, saddle, spurs, stirrups, trace.

---

harness verb
1 *to harness a horse.* saddle.
2 *to harness the forces of nature.* control, domesticate, exploit, keep under control, make use of, mobilize, tame, use, utilize.

harsh adjective
1 *a harsh voice.* croaking, disagreeable, discordant, dissonant, grating, guttural, irritating, jarring, rasping, raucous, rough, shrill, stertorous, strident, unpleasant.
OPPOSITES: SEE **gentle**.
2 *harsh colours. harsh light.* bright, brilliant, dazzling, gaudy, glaring, lurid.
OPPOSITES: SEE **mellow**.

3 *a harsh smell. harsh flavours.* acrid, bitter, unpleasant.
OPPOSITES: SEE **mellow**.
4 *harsh conditions.* arduous, austere, comfortless, difficult, hard, severe, stressful, tough.
OPPOSITES: SEE **easy**.
5 *a harsh texture.* abrasive, bristly, coarse, hairy, rough, scratchy.
OPPOSITES: SEE **smooth** adjective.
6 *harsh criticism.* abusive, bitter, sharp, unkind, unsympathetic.
OPPOSITES: SEE **sympathetic**.
7 *a harsh judge. harsh punishment.* brutal, cruel, Draconian, hard-hearted, merciless, pitiless, severe, stern, strict, unforgiving, unrelenting.
OPPOSITES: SEE **lenient**.

harvest verb
to harvest the corn. bring in, collect, garner, gather, mow, pick, reap, take in.

hassle noun
[*informal*] *I don't want any hassle.* altercation, argument, bother, confusion, difficulty, disagreement, disturbance, fighting, fuss, harassment, inconvenience, making difficulties, nuisance, persecution, problem, SEE **quarrelling**, struggle, trouble, upset.

haste noun
dispatch, hurry, impetuosity, precipitateness, quickness, rush, SEE **speed** noun, urgency.

hasty adjective
1 *a hasty exit. a hasty decision.* abrupt, fast, foolhardy, headlong, hot-headed, hurried, ill-considered, impetuous, impulsive, [*informal*] pell-mell, precipitate, quick, rapid, rash, reckless, speedy, sudden, summary (*summary justice*), swift.
OPPOSITES: SEE **leisurely**.
2 *hasty work.* brief, careless, cursory, hurried, perfunctory, rushed, short, slapdash, superficial, thoughtless.
OPPOSITES: SEE **careful**.

hat noun
head-dress.

VARIOUS HEAD-DRESSES: Balaclava, bearskin, beret, biretta, boater, bonnet, bowler, busby, cap, coronet, crash-helmet, crown, deerstalker, diadem, fez, fillet, headband, helmet, hood, mitre, skull-cap, sombrero, sou'wester, stetson, sun-hat, tiara, top hat, toque, trilby, turban, wig, wimple, yarmulka.

---

hatch verb
1 *to hatch eggs.* brood, incubate.
2 *to hatch a plot.* conceive, concoct, contrive,

[*informal*] cook up, devise, [*informal*] dream up, invent, plan, plot, scheme, think up.

hate noun
What's your pet hate? abomination, aversion, bête noire, dislike, SEE **hatred**, loathing.

hate verb
We hate cruelty. He hates spiders. abhor, abominate, [*informal*] can't bear, [*informal*] can't stand, deplore, despise, detest, dislike, execrate, fear, feel hostility towards, find intolerable, loathe, recoil from, resent, scorn.
OPPOSITES: SEE **like** verb, **love** verb.

hateful adjective
a hateful sin. abhorrent, abominable, accursed, awful, contemptible, cursed, [*informal*] damnable, despicable, detestable, disgusting, execrable, foul, hated, heinous, horrible, loathsome, obnoxious, odious, offensive, repellent, repugnant, repulsive, revolting, SEE **unpleasant**, vile.
OPPOSITES: SEE **lovable**.

hatred noun
He made his hatred obvious. animosity, antagonism, antipathy, aversion, contempt, detestation, dislike, enmity, execration, hate, hostility, ill-will, intolerance, loathing, misanthropy, odium, repugnance, revulsion.
OPPOSITES: SEE **love** noun.

haughty adjective
a haughty manner. arrogant, boastful, bumptious, cavalier, [*informal*] cocky, condescending, disdainful, [*informal*] high-and-mighty, [*informal*] hoity-toity, imperious, lofty, lordly, offhand, pompous, presumptuous, pretentious, proud, self-important, snobbish, [*informal*] snooty, [*informal*] stuck-up, supercilious, superior.
OPPOSITES: SEE **modest**.

haul verb
to haul a sledge. convey, drag, draw, heave, [*informal*] lug, move, pull, tow, trail, tug.

haunt verb
1 *to haunt a place.* frequent, [*informal*] hang around, keep returning to, loiter about, visit frequently.
2 *to haunt the imagination.* linger in, obsess, prey on.

have verb
[*Have* has many meanings. These are only some of the synonyms you can use.] 1 *I have my own radio.* be in possession of, keep, own, possess.
2 *Our house has six rooms.* consist of, contain, embody, hold, include, incorporate, involve.
3 *They had fun. I had a bad time.* endure, enjoy, experience, feel, go through, know, live through, put up with, suffer, tolerate, undergo.
4 *They all had presents.* accept, acquire, be given, gain, get, obtain, procure, receive.
5 *The thieves had everything.* remove, retain, secure, steal, take.
6 *She had the last toffee.* consume, eat.
7 *We had visitors yesterday.* be host to, entertain, put up.
to have to *I'll have to pay for the damage.* be compelled to, be forced to, have an obligation to, must, need to, ought, should.

haven noun
1 *a haven for ships.* SEE **harbour** noun.
2 *The climbers found haven in a mountain hut.* asylum, refuge, retreat, safety, sanctuary, shelter.

havoc noun
The explosion caused havoc. SEE **carnage**, chaos, confusion, damage, destruction, devastation, disorder, disruption, [*informal*] mayhem, ruin, waste, wreckage.

hazard noun. SEE **risk** noun.

hazardous adjective
a hazardous journey. chancy, dangerous, [*informal*] dicey, perilous, precarious, risky, uncertain, unpredictable, unsafe.
OPPOSITES: SEE **safe**.

haze noun
cloud, film, fog, mist, steam, vapour.

hazy adjective
1 *a hazy view.* SEE **misty**.
2 *a hazy understanding.* SEE **vague**.

head noun
1 [= *part of the body*]

PARTS OF YOUR HEAD: brain, brow, cheek, chin, cranium, crown, dimple, ear, eye, forehead, gums, hair, jaw, jowl, lip, mouth, nose, nostril, scalp, skull, teeth, temple, tongue.

OTHER PARTS OF YOUR BODY: SEE **body**.

---

2 *a head for mathematics.* ability, brains, capacity, imagination, intellect, intelligence, mind, understanding.
3 *the head of a mountain.* apex, crown, highest point, summit, top, vertex.
4 *the head of an organization.* boss, SEE **chief** noun, director, employer, leader, manager, ruler.
5 *the head of a school.* headmaster, headmistress, headteacher, principal.
to lose your head SEE **panic** verb.

head verb
1 *to head an expedition.* be in charge of, command, control, direct, govern, guide,

lead, manage, rule, run, superintend, supervise.
2 *to head a ball.* SEE **hit** verb.
3 *to head for home.* aim, go, make, set out, start, steer, turn.
to head off SEE **deflect**.

heading noun
the heading of a leaflet. caption, headline, rubric, title.

headline noun
a newspaper headline. caption, heading, title.

headquarters noun
1 *the headquarters of an expedition.* base, depot, HQ.
2 *the headquarters of a business.* head office, main office.

headstrong adjective
SEE **obstinate**.

heal verb
1 *Wounds heal in time.* get better, knit, mend, recover, unite.
2 *to heal the sick.* cure, make better, remedy, restore, treat.

health noun
1 *your state of health.* condition, constitution, fettle (*in fine fettle*), form (*feeling a bit off-form*), shape (*in good shape*).
2 *We value health.* fitness, robustness, strength, vigour, well-being.

VARIOUS MEDICAL TREATMENTS, ETC.: SEE **medicine**.

VARIOUS ILLNESSES, ETC.: SEE **ill**, **illness**.

---

healthy adjective
1 *a healthy animal. in a healthy condition.* active, [*informal*] blooming, fine, fit, flourishing, good, [*informal*] hale-and-hearty, hearty, [*informal*] in fine fettle, in good shape, lively, perky, robust, sound, strong, sturdy, vigorous, well.
OPPOSITES: SEE **ill**.
2 *healthy surroundings.* bracing, health-giving, hygienic, invigorating, salubrious, sanitary, wholesome.
OPPOSITES: SEE **unhealthy**.

heap noun
a heap of rubbish. SEE **collection**, mass, mound, mountain, pile, stack.
heaps SEE **plenty**.

heap verb
We heaped up the rubbish. bank, SEE **collect**, mass, pile, stack.

hear verb
1 *to hear a sound.* catch, listen to [SEE **listen**], overhear, pick up.
2 *to hear evidence in a lawcourt.* examine,

investigate, judge, try.
3 *to hear news.* be told, discover, find out, gather, learn, receive.

hearing noun
a court hearing. case, inquest, inquiry, trial.

heart noun
1 OTHER PARTS OF YOUR BODY: SEE **body**.
RELATED ADJECTIVE: [= *of the heart*] cardiac.
2 *the heart of a forest. the heart of a problem.* centre, core, crux, focus, hub, inside, kernel, middle, nub, nucleus.
3 *Have you no heart?* affection, compassion, feeling, humanity, kindness, love, sympathy, tenderness, understanding.

heartbreaking adjective
distressing, grievous, heartrending, pitiful, SEE **sad**, tragic.

heartbroken adjective
broken-hearted, dejected, desolate, despairing, dispirited, grieved, inconsolable, miserable, SEE **sad**, [*informal*] shattered.

heartless adjective
heartless cruelty. cold, SEE **cruel**, icy, steely, stony, unemotional.

hearty adjective
1 *a hearty welcome.* enthusiastic, sincere, warm.
2 *a hearty appetite.* big, healthy, robust, strong, vigorous.

heat noun
1 *the heat of a fire.* [*formal*] calorific value, fieriness, glow, hotness, incandescence, warmth.
2 *the heat of summer.* closeness, heatwave, high temperatures, hot weather [SEE **hot**], sultriness, warmth.
OPPOSITES: SEE **cold** noun.
3 *the heat of the moment.* ardour, SEE **excitement**, fervour, feverishness, violence.

heat verb

VERBS SIGNIFYING TO BE HOT, BECOME HOT, OR MAKE HOT: bake, blister, boil, burn, cook, [*informal*] frizzle, fry, grill, SEE **inflame**, make hot [SEE **hot**], melt, reheat, roast, scald, scorch, simmer, sizzle, smoulder, steam, stew, swelter, toast, warm up.
OPPOSITES: SEE **cool** verb.

---

heated adjective
1 *heated food.* SEE **hot**.
2 *a heated argument.* SEE **angry**, **excited**.

heath noun
common land, moor, moorland, open country, wasteland.

heathen adjective
heathen beliefs. atheistic, barbaric, godless, idolatrous, infidel, irreligious, pagan, Philistine, savage, unenlightened.

heave verb
to heave sacks onto a lorry. drag, draw, haul, hoist, lift, lug, pull, raise, SEE **throw**, tow, tug.

heaven noun
after-life, Elysium, eternal rest, next world, nirvana, paradise.
OPPOSITES: SEE **hell**.

heavenly adjective
heavenly music. angelic, beautiful, blissful, celestial, delightful, divine, exquisite, lovely, [*informal*] out of this world, SEE **pleasant**, wonderful.
OPPOSITES: SEE **devilish, unpleasant**.

heavy adjective
1 *a heavy load.* SEE **big**, bulky, burdensome, hefty, immovable, large, leaden, massive, ponderous, unwieldy, weighty.
2 *heavy work.* arduous, demanding, difficult, hard, exhausting, laborious, onerous, strenuous, tough.
3 *heavy rain.* concentrated, dense, penetrating, pervasive, severe, torrential.
4 *a heavy crop. heavy with fruit.* abundant, copious, laden, loaded, profuse, thick.
OPPOSITES: SEE **light** adjective.

heckle verb
to heckle a speaker. barrack, disrupt, harass, interrupt, shout down.

hectic adjective
hectic activity. animated, boisterous, brisk, bustling, busy, chaotic, excited, feverish, frantic, frenetic, frenzied, hurried, lively, mad, restless, riotous, rumbustious, [*informal*] rushed off your feet, turbulent, wild.
OPPOSITES: SEE **leisurely**.

hedge verb
When I asked for an answer, he hedged.
[*informal*] beat about the bush, be evasive, equivocate, [*informal*] hum and haw, quibble, stall, temporize, waffle.
to hedge in circumscribe, confine, encircle, enclose, fence in, hem in, pen, restrict, shield, surround.

hedonistic adjective
epicurean, extravagant, intemperate, luxurious, pleasure-loving, self-indulgent, sensual, sybaritic, voluptuous.
OPPOSITES: SEE **puritanical**.

heed verb
to heed a warning. attend to, concern yourself about, consider, follow, keep to, listen to, mark, mind, note, notice, obey, observe, pay attention to, regard, take notice of.
OPPOSITES: SEE **disregard**.

heedful adjective
heedful of people's needs. attentive, careful, concerned, considerate, mindful, observant, sympathetic, taking notice, vigilant, watchful.
OPPOSITES: SEE **heedless**.

heedless adjective
heedless of other people. careless, inattentive, inconsiderate, neglectful, thoughtless, uncaring, unconcerned, unobservant, unsympathetic.
OPPOSITES: SEE **heedful**.

heel verb
1 *to heel a ball.* SEE **kick** verb.
2 *to heel to one side.* lean, list, slope, tilt.

hefty adjective
a hefty man. beefy, big, brawny, bulky, burly, heavy, heavyweight, hulking, husky, large, mighty, muscular, powerful, robust, solid, [*informal*] strapping (*a strapping lad*), strong, tough.
OPPOSITES: SEE **slight** adjective.

height noun
the height of a mountain. altitude, elevation, tallness, vertical measurement.

heighten verb
1 *to heighten the level of something.* build up, elevate, lift up, make higher, raise.
OPPOSITES: SEE **lower**.
2 *to heighten your enjoyment.* add to, augment, boost, enhance, improve, increase, intensify, magnify, maximize, sharpen, strengthen.
OPPOSITES: SEE **lessen**.

heir, heiress nouns
beneficiary, inheritor, successor.

hell noun
eternal punishment, Hades, infernal regions, lower regions, nether world, underworld.
OPPOSITES: SEE **heaven**.

helmsman noun
boatman, cox, pilot, steersman.

help noun
Give me some help. advice, aid, assistance, avail (*It was of no avail*), backing, benefit, boost, collaboration, contribution, co-operation, friendship, guidance, moral support, relief, succour, support.
OPPOSITES: SEE **hindrance**.

help verb
1 *Help each other. Can I help?* advise, aid, aid and abet, assist, back, befriend, be helpful (to) [SEE **helpful**], boost, collaborate, contribute (to), co-operate, facilitate, forward, further the interests of, [*informal*] give a hand (to), profit, promote, [*informal*] rally round, serve, side (with), [*informal*]

spoon-feed, stand by, succour, support, take pity on.
OPPOSITES: SEE **hinder**.
2 *Some medicine might help your cough.*
alleviate, benefit, cure, ease, improve, lessen, make easier, relieve, remedy.
OPPOSITES: SEE **aggravate**.
3 *I can't help coughing.* SEE **avoid, prevent**.

helper noun
abettor, ally, assistant, collaborator, colleague, deputy, helpmate, partner, [*informal*] right-hand man, second, supporter, [*informal*] willing hands.

helpful adjective
1 *a helpful person.* accommodating, benevolent, caring, considerate, constructive, co-operative, favourable, friendly, helping (*a helping hand*), kind, neighbourly, obliging, practical, supportive, sympathetic, thoughtful.
OPPOSITES: SEE **unhelpful**.
2 *a helpful suggestion.* advantageous, beneficial, informative, instructive, profitable, valuable, useful, worthwhile.
OPPOSITES: SEE **worthless**.
3 *a helpful tool.* SEE **handy**.

helping noun
a helping of food. amount, plateful, portion, ration, serving, share.

helpless adjective
a helpless invalid. defenceless, dependent, destitute, feeble, SEE **handicapped**, impotent, incapable, infirm, powerless, unprotected, vulnerable, weak, [*uncomplimentary*] weedy.
OPPOSITES: SEE **independent**.

hem verb
to hem in SEE **surround**.

herald noun
1 [*old-fashioned*] *the king's herald.*
announcer, courier, messenger, town crier.
2 *The cuckoo is the herald of spring.*
forerunner, harbinger, omen, precursor, sign.

herald verb
The thunder heralded a change in the weather. advertise, announce, SEE **foretell**, indicate, make known, proclaim, promise, publicize.

herb noun
culinary herb.

VARIOUS HERBS: angelica, anise, balm, balsam, basil, borage, camomile, caraway, chervil, chicory, chive, coriander, cumin, dill, fennel, fenugreek, hyssop, liquorice, lovage, marjoram, mint, oregano, parsley, peppermint, rosemary, rue, sage, savory, spearmint, tansy, tarragon, thyme, wintergreen.

herd noun
SEE **group** noun.

hereditary adjective
1 *a hereditary title.* bequeathed, family (*the family name*), handed down, inherited, passed on.
2 *a hereditary disease. hereditary characteristics.* congenital, constitutional, inborn, inbred, inherent, innate, native, natural, transmissible, transmittable.
OPPOSITES: SEE **acquired**.

heretic noun
apostate, blasphemer, dissenter, free-thinker, iconoclast, nonconformist, rebel, renegade, unorthodox thinker.

heritage noun
our national heritage. birthright, culture, history, inheritance, legacy, past, tradition.

hermit noun
monk, recluse, solitary person.

hero, heroine nouns
celebrity, champion, conqueror, daredevil, idol, protagonist [= *leading character in a play*], star, superman, [*informal*] superstar, victor, winner.

heroic adjective
heroic efforts, heroic rescuers. adventurous, bold, brave, chivalrous, courageous, daring, dauntless, doughty, epic, fearless, gallant, herculean, intrepid, lion-hearted, noble, selfless, stout-hearted, superhuman, unafraid, valiant, valorous.
OPPOSITES: SEE **cowardly**.

hesitant adjective
a hesitant speaker. cautious, diffident, dithering, faltering, half-hearted, halting, hesitating, indecisive, irresolute, nervous, [*informal*] shilly-shallying, shy, tentative, timid, uncertain, uncommitted, undecided, underconfident, unsure, vacillating, wary, wavering.
OPPOSITES: SEE **decisive, fluent**.

hesitate verb
I hesitated before jumping into the water. be hesitant [SEE **hesitant**], delay, dither, falter, halt, hang back, [*informal*] hum and haw, pause, put it off, [*informal*] shilly-shally, shrink back, think twice, vacillate, wait, waver.

hesitation noun
caution, indecision, irresolution, nervousness, [*informal*] shilly-shallying, uncertainty, vacillation.

hidden adjective
1 *hidden from view.* concealed, covered, enclosed, invisible, out of sight, private, shrouded, [*informal*] under wraps, unseen, veiled.
OPPOSITES: SEE **visible**.
2 *a hidden meaning.* abstruse, coded, covert, cryptic, dark, implicit, mysterious, mystical, obscure, occult, recondite, secret, unclear.
OPPOSITES: SEE **obvious**.

hide verb
1 *to hide something from view. to hide your feelings.* blot out, bury, camouflage, censor, cloak, conceal, cover, curtain, disguise, eclipse, enclose, mask, obscure, put away, put out of sight, screen, secrete, shelter, shroud, suppress, veil, withhold.
OPPOSITES: SEE **display** verb.
2 *to hide from someone.* disguise yourself, go into hiding, [*informal*] go to ground, keep yourself hidden [SEE **hidden**], [*informal*] lie low, lurk, shut yourself away, take cover.

hideous adjective
a hideous wound. appalling, disgusting, dreadful, frightful, ghastly, grim, grisly, gruesome, macabre, odious, repulsive, revolting, shocking, sickening, terrible, SEE **ugly**.
OPPOSITES: SEE **beautiful**.

hiding-place noun
den, hide, hideaway, [*informal*] hide-out, [*informal*] hidy-hole, lair, refuge, sanctuary.

hierarchy noun
The Principal comes at the top of the college hierarchy. grading, ladder, [*informal*] pecking-order, ranking, scale, sequence, series, social order, system.

high adjective
1 *a high building. a high altitude.* elevated, extending upwards, high-rise, lofty, raised, soaring, tall, towering.
2 *high in rank.* aristocratic, chief, distinguished, eminent, exalted, important, leading, powerful, prominent, royal, top, upper.
3 *high prices.* dear, excessive, exorbitant, expensive, extravagant, unreasonable.
4 *a high wind.* exceptional, extreme, great, intense, stormy, strong.
5 *a high reputation.* favourable, good, noble, respected, virtuous.
6 *a high sound.* high-pitched, piercing, sharp, shrill, soprano, treble.
OPPOSITES: SEE **deep, low** adjective.

highbrow adjective
1 *highbrow literature.* classic, cultural, deep, educational, improving, intellectually demanding, serious.

2 *highbrow music.* classical.
3 *a highbrow person.* academic, bookish, brainy, cultured, intellectual, [*uncomplimentary*] pretentious, sophisticated.

high-class adjective
SEE **excellent**.

highlight noun
the highlight of the evening. best moment, climax, high spot, peak, top point.

highly strung adjective
SEE **nervous**.

high-speed adjective SEE **fast** adjective.

high-spirited adjective SEE **lively**.

hike verb
to hike across the moors. ramble, tramp, trek, SEE **walk** verb.

hilarious adjective SEE **funny**.

hill noun
1 elevation, eminence, foothill, height, hillock, hillside, hummock, knoll, mound, mount, mountain, peak, prominence, ridge, summit.
Words for *hill* used in particular geographical areas: brae, down, fell, [*plural*] Highlands, pike, stack, tor, wold.
2 *a steep hill in the road.* ascent, gradient, incline, rise, slope.

hind, hinder, hindmost adjectives SEE **back** adjective.

hinder verb
Snowdrifts hindered our progress. arrest, bar, be a hindrance to [SEE **hindrance**], check, curb, delay, deter, endanger, frustrate, get in the way of, hamper, handicap, hit, hold back, hold up, impede, keep back, limit, obstruct, oppose, prevent, restrain, restrict, retard, sabotage, slow down, slow up, stand in the way of, stop, thwart.
OPPOSITES: SEE **help** verb.

hindrance noun
Our heavy shoes were more of a hindrance than a help. bar, burden, check, deterrent, difficulty, disadvantage, [*informal*] drag, drawback, encumbrance, handicap, impediment, inconvenience, limitation, obstacle, obstruction, restraint, restriction, stumbling-block.
OPPOSITES: SEE **help** noun.

hinge verb
Everything hinges on your decision. depend, hang, rest, revolve, turn.

hint noun
I don't know the answer: give me a hint. allusion, clue, idea, implication, indication, inkling, innuendo, insinuation, pointer, sign, suggestion, tip, [*informal*] tip-off.

hint verb
She hinted that we'd get a surprise. give a
hint [SEE **hint** noun], imply, indicate,
insinuate, suggest, tip (someone) off.

hire verb
to hire a bus. to hire a hall for a party. book,
charter, engage, lease, pay for the use of,
rent, take on.
to hire out lease out, let, rent out, take
payment for the use of.

hissing adjective
sibilant.

historian noun
antiquarian, archivist, chronicler.

historic adjective
[Note the difference in meaning between
historic and *historical*.] *a historic battle.*
celebrated, eminent, epoch-making, famed,
famous, important, momentous, notable,
outstanding, remarkable, renowned,
significant, well-known.
OPPOSITES: SEE **unimportant**.

historical adjective
[See note under *historic*.] *a historical event.*
actual, authentic, documented, real, real-
life, true, verifiable.
OPPOSITES: SEE **fictitious**.

history noun
1 *Are you interested in history?* bygone days,
heritage, historical events [SEE **historical**],
the past.
2 *I enjoy reading history.* annals, chronicles,
records.

hit verb
1 VARIOUS WAYS TO HIT THINGS: [Many of these
words are normally *informal*.] bang, bash,
baste, batter, beat, belt, biff, birch, buffet,
bump, butt, cane, clap, clip, clobber, clock,
clonk, clout, club, collide with, cosh, crack,
crash into, cudgel, cuff, dash, deliver a blow,
drive (*a ball with a golf-club*), elbow,
flagellate, flail, flick, flip, flog, hammer, head
(*a football*), jab, jar, jog, kick, knee, knock,
lam, lambaste or lambast, lash, nudge, pat,
poke, pound, prod, pummel, punch, punt,
putt (*a golfball*), ram, rap, scourge, slam,
slap, slog, slosh, slug, smack, smash, smite,
sock, spank, stab, strike, stub (*your toe*),
swat, swipe, tan, tap, thrash, thump, thwack,
wallop, whack, wham, whip.
2 *The drought hit the farmers.* affect, attack,
bring disaster to, damage, do harm to, harm,
have an effect on, SEE **hinder**, hurt, make
suffer, ruin.
to hit back SEE **retaliate**.

hoard noun
a hoard of treasure. cache, heap, pile,
stockpile, store, supply, treasure-trove.

hoard verb
Squirrels hoard nuts. accumulate, amass, be
miserly with, collect, gather, keep, lay up,
mass, pile up, put by, save, stockpile, store,
treasure.
OPPOSITES: SEE **squander**.

hoarding noun
a roadside hoarding. advertisement, board,
display, fence, panel.

hoarse adjective
a hoarse voice. croaking, grating, gravelly,
growling, gruff, harsh, husky, rasping,
raucous, rough, throaty.

hoax noun
The alarm was a hoax. cheat, [*informal*] con,
deception, fake, fraud, imposture, joke,
[*informal*] leg-pull, practical joke, spoof,
swindle, trick.

hoax verb
to hoax someone. bluff, [*informal*] con,
deceive, delude, dupe, fool, [*informal*] have
on, hoodwink, lead on, mislead, [*informal*]
pull someone's leg, swindle, [*informal*] take
for a ride, take in, SEE **tease**, trick.

hoaxer noun
SEE **cheat** noun, [*informal*] con-man,
impostor, joker, practical joker, trickster.

hobble verb
limp, totter, SEE **walk** verb.

hobby noun
a spare-time hobby. amateur interest,
diversion, interest, pastime, pursuit,
recreation, relaxation.

hoist noun
block-and-tackle, crane, davit, jack, lift,
pulley, winch, windlass.

hoist verb
to hoist crates onto a ship. heave, lift, lift
with a hoist, pull up, raise, winch up.

hold noun
1 *a firm hold on something.* clasp, clutch,
grasp, grip, purchase.
2 *The blackmailer had a hold over him.*
authority, control, dominance, influence,
power, sway.

hold verb
1 *to hold in your arms or in your hand.* bear,
carry, catch, clasp, cling to, clutch, cradle,
embrace, enfold, grasp, grip, hang on to,
have, hug, keep, possess, retain, seize,
support, take.
2 *to hold a suspect.* arrest, confine, detain,
imprison, keep in custody.
3 *to hold a position. to hold an opinion.*
continue, keep up, maintain, occupy,
preserve, retain, stick to.
4 *to hold a party.* celebrate, conduct,
convene, have, organize.

5 *The jug holds one litre.* contain, enclose, have a capacity of, include.
6 *Will this fine weather hold?* be unaltered, carry on, last, persist, remain unchanged, stay.
to hold back *to hold back tears.* block, check, control, curb, delay, halt, keep back, repress, restrain, retain, stifle, stop, suppress, withhold.
to hold out 1 *to hold out your hand.* extend, offer, reach out, stick out, stretch out. 2 *to hold out against opposition.* be resolute, carry on, endure, hang on, keep going, last, persevere, persist, resist, stand fast.
to hold up *to hold up traffic.* delay, detain, hinder, impede, obstruct, retard, slow down.

hole noun
1 *a hole in the ground.* abyss, burrow, cave, cavern, cavity, chamber, chasm, crater, depression, excavation, fault, fissure, hollow, pit, pocket, pot-hole, shaft, tunnel.
2 *a hole in a fence. a hole in a piece of paper.* aperture, breach, break, chink, crack, cut, eyelet, gap, gash, leak, opening, orifice, perforation, puncture, slit, split, tear, vent.

holiday noun
a holiday from school or from work. bank holiday, break, day off, half-term, leave, rest, sabbatical, time off, vacation.

SOME KINDS OF HOLIDAY: busman's holiday, camping, caravanning, cruise, honeymoon, pony-trekking, safari, seaside holiday, tour, travelling, trip.

HOLIDAY ACCOMMODATION: apartment, boarding-house, camp-site, flat, guesthouse, hostel, hotel, inn, motel, self-catering, villa.

---

holiness noun
devotion, divinity, faith, godliness, piety, [*uncomplimentary*] religiosity, sacredness, saintliness, [*uncomplimentary*] sanctimoniousness, sanctity, venerability.

hollow adjective
a hollow space. cavernous, concave, deep, empty, unfilled, vacant.
OPPOSITES: SEE **solid**.

hollow noun
a hollow in a surface. bowl, cavity, concavity, crater, dent, depression, dimple, dint, dip, dish, hole, indentation, SEE **valley**.

hollow verb
to hollow out burrow, dig, excavate, gouge, scoop.

holy adjective
1 *a holy shrine.* blessed, consecrated, divine, hallowed, heavenly, revered, sacred, sacrosanct, venerable.

2 *holy pilgrims.* dedicated, devoted, devout, faithful, godly, pious, pure, religious, righteous, saintly, [*uncomplimentary*] sanctimonious.
OPPOSITES: SEE **irreligious**.

home noun
1 [= *where I live*] [*old-fashioned*] abode, accommodation, [*formal*] domicile, dwelling, dwelling-place, [*formal*] habitation, SEE **house** noun, household, lodging, residence.
2 [= *where I come from*] birthplace, native land.
3 *a home for the sick or elderly.* [*old-fashioned*] almshouse, convalescent home, hospice, institution, nursing-home.
4 *an animal's home.* habitat, territory.

homeless adjective
homeless families. abandoned, destitute, down-and-out, evicted, forsaken, itinerant, nomadic, outcast, unhoused, wandering.
homeless people beggars, the destitute, the poor, tramps, vagrants.

homely adjective
a homely atmosphere. comfortable, congenial, cosy, easygoing, familiar, friendly, informal, intimate, natural, relaxed, simple, unaffected, unpretentious, unsophisticated.

homicidal adjective
SEE **murderous**.

homicide noun SEE **murder** noun.

homogeneous adjective
a homogeneous group. alike, comparable, compatible, consistent, identical, matching, similar, uniform, unvarying.
OPPOSITES: heterogeneous, SEE **mixed**.

homosexual adjective
[*informal*] camp, gay, lesbian, [*uncomplimentary*] queer.
OPPOSITE: heterosexual.

honest adjective
an honest worker. an honest answer. above-board, blunt, candid, conscientious, direct, equitable, fair, forthright, frank, genuine, good, honourable, impartial, incorruptible, just, law-abiding, legal, legitimate, moral, [*informal*] on the level, open, outspoken, plain, pure, reliable, respectable, scrupulous, sincere, square (*a square deal*), straight, straightforward, trustworthy, trusty, truthful, unbiased, unequivocal, unprejudiced, upright, veracious, virtuous.
OPPOSITES: SEE **dishonest**.
to be honest [*informal*] come clean, [*informal*] put your cards on the table, tell the truth.

honesty noun

1 *I didn't doubt his honesty.* fairness,
goodness, integrity, morality, probity,
rectitude, reliability, scrupulousness, sense
of justice, trustworthiness, truthfulness,
uprightness, veracity, virtue.
2 *I was surprised by the honesty of his
comments.* bluntness, candour, directness,
frankness, outspokenness, plainness,
sincerity, straightforwardness.
OPPOSITES: SEE **dishonesty**.

honour noun

1 *She brought honour to the family.* acclaim,
accolade, compliment, credit, esteem, fame,
good name, [*informal*] kudos, regard,
renown, reputation, repute, respect,
reverence, veneration.
2 *I had the honour of making a speech.*
distinction, duty, importance, privilege.
3 *a sense of honour.* decency, dignity,
honesty, integrity, loyalty, morality,
nobility, principle, rectitude, righteousness,
sincerity, uprightness, virtue.

honour verb

*On Remembrance Sunday we honour those
who died.* acclaim, admire, applaud,
celebrate, commemorate, commend, dignify,
esteem, give credit to, glorify, pay homage
to, pay respects to, pay tribute to, praise,
remember, respect, revere, reverence, show
respect to, sing the praises of, value,
venerate, worship.

honourable adjective

an honourable action. an honourable person.
admirable, chivalrous, creditable, decent,
estimable, ethical, fair, good, high-minded,
SEE **honest**, irreproachable, just, law-
abiding, loyal, moral, noble, principled,
proper, reputable, respectable, respected,
righteous, sincere, [*informal*] straight,
trustworthy, trusty, upright, venerable,
virtuous, worthy.
OPPOSITES: SEE **dishonourable**.

hook verb

1 *to hook a fish.* capture, catch, take.
2 *to hook a trailer to a car.* SEE **fasten**.

hooligan noun

bully, SEE **criminal** noun, delinquent,
hoodlum, lout, mugger, rough, ruffian,
[*informal*] tearaway, thug, tough, trouble-
maker, vandal, [*informal*] yob.

hoop noun

band, circle, girdle, loop, ring.

hooter noun

horn, siren, whistle.

hop verb

bound, caper, dance, jump, leap, limp,
prance, skip, spring.

hope noun

1 *His hope is to become a professional.*
ambition, aspiration, desire, dream, wish.
2 *There's hope of better weather tomorrow.*
assumption, expectation, likelihood,
optimism, prospect.
OPPOSITES: SEE **despair** noun.

hope verb

I hope that I'll win. [*informal*] anticipate, be
hopeful [SEE **hopeful**], believe, desire, expect,
have faith, have hope [SEE **hope** noun], trust,
wish.
OPPOSITES: SEE **despair** verb.

hopeful adjective

1 *in a hopeful mood.* confident, expectant,
optimistic, positive, sanguine.
2 *hopeful signs of success.* auspicious,
cheering, encouraging, favourable,
heartening, promising, propitious,
reassuring.
OPPOSITES: SEE **hopeless**.

hopefully adverb

1 *The hungry dog looked hopefully at the food.*
confidently, expectantly, optimistically, with
hope.
2 [*informal*] *Hopefully, I'll be fit to play.* all
being well, most likely, probably. [Many
people think that this is a wrong use of
hopefully.]

hopeless adjective

1 *hopeless refugees.* beyond hope,
demoralized, despairing, desperate,
disconsolate, pessimistic, wretched.
2 *a hopeless situation.* daunting, depressing,
impossible, incurable, irremediable,
irreparable, irreversible.
OPPOSITES: SEE **hopeful**.
3 [*informal*] *a hopeless footballer.* SEE **bad**,
feeble, inadequate, incompetent, inefficient,
poor, useless, weak, worthless.
OPPOSITES: SEE **competent**.

horde noun

hordes of children from other schools. band,
crowd, gang, SEE **group** noun, mob, swarm,
throng, tribe.

horizontal adjective

a horizontal line. flat, level, lying down.
OPPOSITES: SEE **vertical**.

horrible adjective

[*informal*] *horrible weather. horrible people.*
awful, beastly, disagreeable, dreadful,
ghastly, hateful, horrid, loathsome, nasty,
objectionable, odious, offensive, revolting,
terrible, unkind, SEE **unpleasant**.
OPPOSITES: SEE **pleasant**.

horrific *a horrific accident.* appalling,

atrocious, blood-curdling, disgusting,
dreadful, frightening, frightful, grisly,

gruesome, hair-raising, harrowing, horrendous, horrifying, nauseating, shocking, sickening, spine-chilling, unacceptable, unnerving, unthinkable.

horrify verb
The accident horrified us. alarm, appal, disgust, frighten, harrow, nauseate, scare, shock, sicken, terrify, unnerve.

horror noun
1 *a feeling of horror. a horror of spiders.* abhorrence, antipathy, aversion, detestation, disgust, dislike, dismay, dread, fear, loathing, panic, repugnance, revulsion, terror.
2 *I saw the full horror of the disaster.* awfulness, frightfulness, ghastliness, gruesomeness, hideousness.

horse noun
bronco, carthorse, [*old-fashioned*] charger, cob, colt, filly, foal, [*childish*] gee-gee, gelding, hack, hunter, [*old-fashioned*] jade, mare, mount, mule, mustang, [*informal*] nag, [*old-fashioned*] palfrey, piebald, pony, race-horse, roan, skewbald, stallion, steed, warhorse.
RELATED ADJECTIVES: equestrian, equine.
to ride a horse amble, canter, gallop, trot.

horseman, **horsewoman** nouns
cavalryman, equestrian, jockey, rider.

hospitable adjective
SEE **sociable**.

hospital noun
clinic, convalescent home, hospice, infirmary, nursing home, sanatorium.

hostile adjective
1 *a hostile crowd.* aggressive, SEE **angry**, antagonistic, antipathetic, attacking, averse, bellicose, belligerent, confrontational, ill-disposed, inhospitable, inimical, malevolent, pugnacious, resentful, unfriendly, unwelcoming, warlike.
OPPOSITES: SEE **friendly**.
2 *hostile weather conditions.* adverse, bad, contrary, opposing, unfavourable, unhelpful, unpropitious.
OPPOSITES: SEE **favourable**.

hostility noun
hostility between enemies. aggression, animosity, antagonism, antipathy, aversion, bad feeling, belligerence, confrontation, detestation, dislike, enmity, estrangement, hate, hatred, ill will, incompatibility, malevolence, malice, opposition, pugnacity, resentment, unfriendliness.
OPPOSITES: SEE **friendship**.

hot adjective
1 *hot weather. a hot iron.* baking, blistering, boiling, burning, fiery, flaming, oppressive,

piping hot (*piping hot food*), red-hot, roasting, scalding, scorching, searing, sizzling, steamy, stifling, sultry, summery, sweltering, thermal (*a thermal spring*), torrid, tropical, warm.
OPPOSITES: SEE **cold** adjective.
2 *a hot temper. in hot pursuit.* angry, eager, emotional, excited, feverish, fierce, heated, hotheaded, impatient, impetuous, intense, passionate, violent.
OPPOSITES: SEE **calm** adjective.
3 *a hot taste.* acrid, biting, gingery, peppery, piquant, pungent, spicy, strong.
OPPOSITES: SEE **mild**.

hotheaded adjective SEE **impetuous**.

hot-tempered adjective SEE **bad-tempered**.

house noun
a house to live in. abode, [*formal*] domicile, dwelling, dwelling-place, [*formal*] habitation, home, household, lodging, place (*Come to my place*), quarters, residence.

KINDS OF HOUSE: SEE **accommodation**, apartment, bungalow, chalet, cottage, council house, croft, detached house, farmhouse, flat, grange, hovel, homestead, hut, igloo, lodge, maisonette, manor, manse, mansion, penthouse, [*informal*] prefab, public house, rectory, semi-detached house, shack, shanty, terraced house, thatched house, vicarage, villa.

ROOMS IN A HOUSE: SEE **room**.

---

house verb
to house someone. accommodate, billet, board, [*formal*] domicile, keep, lodge, place, [*informal*] put up, quarter, shelter, take in.

household noun
establishment, family, home, ménage, [*informal*] set-up.

hovel noun
cottage, SEE **house** noun, hut, shack, shanty, shed.

hover verb
1 *to hover in the air.* drift, float, flutter, fly, hang.
2 *to hover about.* be indecisive, dally, dither, [*informal*] hang about, hesitate, linger, loiter, pause, wait about, vacillate, waver.

hub noun
the hub of a wheel. a hub of activity. axis, centre, focal point, heart, middle, pivot.

hubbub noun SEE **commotion**.

huddle verb
to huddle in a corner. cluster, converge, crowd, flock, gather, heap, herd, jumble, pile, press, squeeze, swarm, throng.
OPPOSITES: SEE **scatter**.

hue noun SEE **colour** noun, complexion, dye, nuance, shade, tincture, tinge, tint, tone.

hug verb
to hug baby. clasp, cling to, crush, cuddle, embrace, enfold, fold in your arms, hold close, nurse, squeeze, snuggle against.

huge adjective
Elephants are huge animals. The bank handles huge sums of money. SEE **big**, colossal, enormous, giant, gigantic, great, [*informal*] hulking, immeasurable, immense, imposing, impressive, incalculable, [*informal*] jumbo-sized, large, majestic, mammoth, massive, mighty, [*informal*] monster, monstrous, monumental, mountainous, prodigious, stupendous, titanic, towering, [*informal*] tremendous, vast, weighty, [*informal*] whopping.
OPPOSITES: SEE **small**.

hulk noun
1 *the hulk of an old ship.* body, carcass, frame, hull, shell, wreck.
2 *a clumsy hulk.* clumsy person, lout, lump, oaf.

hum verb
buzz, drone, murmur, purr, sing, SEE **sound** noun, vibrate, whirr.

human adjective
1 *the human race.* anthropoid, mortal.
2 *human feelings.* SEE **humane**, altruistic, kind, merciful, philanthropic, rational, reasonable, sympathetic.
OPPOSITES: SEE **inhuman**.
human beings folk, humanity, mankind, men and women, mortals, people [SEE **person**].

humane adjective
Is it humane to kill animals for food? benevolent, charitable, civilized, compassionate, feeling, forgiving, good, human, humanitarian, kind, kind-hearted, loving, magnanimous, merciful, pitying, sympathetic, tender, understanding, unselfish, warmhearted.
OPPOSITES: SEE **inhumane**.

humble adjective
1 *humble behaviour.* deferential, docile, meek, [*uncomplimentary*] obsequious, polite, respectful, self-effacing, [*uncomplimentary*] servile, submissive, unassertive, unassuming, unpretentious.
OPPOSITES: SEE **proud**.
2 *a humble life-style. humble origins.* commonplace, insignificant, low, lowly, mean, modest, obscure, ordinary, plebeian, poor, simple, undistinguished, unimportant, unremarkable.
OPPOSITES: SEE **important**.

humble verb SEE **humiliate**.

humid adjective
humid weather. clammy, damp, dank, moist, muggy, steamy, sticky, sultry, sweaty.

humiliate verb
They humiliated us by winning 14–0. abase, abash, break (someone's) spirit, bring down, chagrin, chasten, crush, deflate, degrade, demean, discredit, disgrace, embarrass, humble, make ashamed, make (someone) feel humble [SEE **humble** adjective], mortify, [*informal*] put (someone) in their place, shame, [*informal*] take down a peg.

humiliating adjective
a humiliating defeat. chastening, crushing, degrading, demeaning, discreditable, dishonourable, embarrassing, humbling, ignominious, inglorious, mortifying, shaming, undignified.
OPPOSITES: SEE **glorious**.

humiliation noun
chagrin, degradation, dishonour, embarrassment, ignominy, indignity, mortification, shame.

humility noun
deference, humbleness, lowliness, meekness, modesty, self-effacement, unpretentiousness.
OPPOSITES: SEE **pride**.

humorous adjective SEE **funny**.

humour noun
1 *Her humour makes me laugh.* badinage, banter, comedy, facetiousness, jesting, jocularity, jokes, joking, quips, raillery, repartee, [*informal*] sense of fun, wit, witticisms, wittiness.
2 *You're in a good humour!* disposition, frame of mind, mood, spirits, state of mind, temper.

hump noun
a hump in the road. bulge, bump, curve, knob, lump, mound, protuberance, rise, swelling.

hunch noun
I have a hunch that they won't come. feeling, guess, idea, impression, inkling, intuition, suspicion.

hunch verb
to hunch your shoulders. arch, bend, curl, curve, huddle, hump, shrug.

hunger noun
1 *a hunger for food.* appetite, craving, SEE **desire** noun, greed, ravenousness.
2 *Hunger kills millions of people.* deprivation, famine, lack of food, malnutrition, starvation.

hungry adjective
aching, avid, covetous, eager, famished, famishing, greedy, longing, peckish, ravenous, starved, starving, underfed, undernourished, voracious.

hunt noun
a hunt for prey. chase, SEE **hunting**, pursuit, quest, search.

hunt verb
1 *to hunt animals.* chase, course, ferret, hound, poach, pursue, stalk, track down, trail.
2 *to hunt for something you've lost.* ferret out, look for, rummage, search for, seek.

hunter noun
huntsman, predator, trapper.

hunting noun

KINDS OF HUNTING: beagling, deer-stalking, falconry, fox-hunting, hawking, whaling.

hurdle noun
1 *The runners cleared the first hurdle.* barricade, barrier, fence, hedge, jump, obstacle, wall.
2 *There are many hurdles to overcome in life.* difficulty, handicap, hindrance, obstruction, problem, snag, stumbling block.

hurl verb
to hurl something into the air. cast, catapult, chuck, dash, fire, fling, heave, launch, pelt, pitch, project, shy, sling, throw, toss.

hurly-burly noun
SEE **activity**.

hurried adjective
a hurried decision. SEE **hasty**.

hurry verb
1 *to hurry home.* [*informal*] belt, chase, dash, dispatch, [*informal*] fly, [*informal*] get a move on, hasten, hurtle, hustle, move quickly, rush, speed.
OPPOSITE: go slowly.
2 *If you want to finish, you must hurry.* [*informal*] buck up, [*informal*] shift, [*informal*] step on it, work faster.
OPPOSITES: SEE **dawdle**.
3 *to hurry a process.* accelerate, expedite, quicken, speed up.
OPPOSITES: SEE **delay** verb.

hurt verb
1 *Where do you hurt?* ache, be painful [SEE **painful**], smart, sting, suffer pain [SEE **pain** noun], throb, tingle.
2 *Did they hurt you?* abuse, afflict, agonize, bruise, cause pain to [SEE **pain** noun], cripple, cut, damage, disable, harm, injure, maim, misuse, torture, wound.

3 *The insult hurt her.* be hurtful to [SEE **hurtful**], distress, grieve, pain, torment, upset.

hurtful adjective
hurtful remarks. biting, cruel, cutting, damaging, derogatory, distressing, hard to bear, harmful, injurious, malicious, nasty, painful, sarcastic, scathing, spiteful, uncharitable, unkind, upsetting, vicious, wounding.
OPPOSITES: SEE **kind** adjective.

hurtle verb
to hurtle along. to hurtle earthwards. charge, chase, dash, fly, plunge, race, rush, shoot, speed, tear.

hush interjection
be quiet! be silent! [*informal*] hold your tongue! [*informal*] shut up! silence!

hush verb
to hush up *to hush up the facts.* conceal, cover up, hide, keep quiet, keep secret, stifle, suppress.

husky adjective
1 *a husky voice.* SEE **hoarse**.
2 *a big, husky fellow.* SEE **hefty**.

hustle verb
to hustle someone along. bustle, force, hasten, hurry, jostle, push, rush, shove.

hut noun
cabin, den, hovel, lean-to, shack, shanty, shed, shelter.

hybrid noun
a hybrid of two species. amalgam, combination, composite, compound, cross, cross-breed, mixture, mongrel.

hygienic adjective
hygienic conditions in hospital. aseptic, clean, disinfected, germ-free, healthy, pure, salubrious, sanitary, sterilized, unpolluted, wholesome.
OPPOSITES: SEE **unhealthy**.

hypnotic adjective
a hypnotic rhythm. fascinating, irresistible, magnetic, mesmeric, mesmerizing, sleep-inducing, soothing, soporific, spellbinding.

hypnotize verb
bewitch, captivate, dominate, entrance, fascinate, gain power over, magnetize, mesmerize, [*informal*] put to sleep, [*informal*] stupefy.

hypocrisy noun
the hypocrisy of people who say one thing and do another. cant, deceit, deception, double-talk, duplicity, falsity, [*informal*] humbug, inconsistency, insincerity.

hypocritical adjective
[Do not confuse with *hypercritical*.] *It's
hypocritical to say one thing and do another.*
deceptive, false, inconsistent, insincere,
[*informal*] phoney, [*informal*] two-faced.

hypothesis noun
an unproved hypothesis. conjecture, guess,
premise, proposition, supposition, theory,
[*formal*] thesis.

hypothetical adjective
a hypothetical problem. academic,
conjectural, imaginary, putative,
speculative, supposed, suppositional,
theoretical, unreal.

hysteria noun
uncontrollable hysteria in the crowd. frenzy,
hysterics, madness, mania, panic.

hysterical adjective
1 *hysterical fans.* berserk, crazed, delirious,
demented, distraught, frantic, frenzied,
mad, raving, uncontrollable, wild.
2 [*informal*] *a hysterical joke.* comic, crazy,
SEE **funny**, hilarious, [*informal*] killing,
ridiculous, [*informal*] side-splitting,
uproarious.

ice noun

FORMS OF ICE: black ice, floe, frost, glacier,
iceberg, ice-rink, icicle, rime.

---

icy adjective
1 *icy weather.* arctic, SEE **cold** adjective,
freezing, frosty.
2 *icy roads.* frozen, glacial, glassy, greasy,
slippery, [*informal*] slippy.

idea noun
1 *a philosophical idea.* abstraction, attitude,
belief, concept, conception, conjecture,
conviction, hypothesis, notion, opinion,
theory, view.
2 *the main idea of a poem.* intention,
meaning, point, thought.
3 *I have an idea!* brainwave, fancy, guess,
inspiration, plan, proposal, scheme,
suggestion.
4 *The sample gives an idea of what to expect.*
clue, guidelines, impression, inkling,
intimation, model, pattern, perception,
vision.

ideal adjective
1 *ideal conditions.* best, classic, excellent,
faultless, model, optimum, perfect, suitable.
2 *an ideal world.* hypothetical, imaginary,
unattainable, unreal, Utopian, visionary.

idealistic adjective
*I don't think her idealistic plans will ever
materialize.* high-minded, over-optimistic,
quixotic, romantic, starry-eyed, unrealistic.
OPPOSITES: SEE **realistic**.

idealize verb
People idealize their heroes. deify, glamorize,
glorify, [*informal*] put on a pedestal,
romanticize, worship.

identical adjective
identical twins. identical in appearance,
alike, congruent (*congruent triangles*),
corresponding, duplicate, equal,
indistinguishable, interchangeable,
matching, the same, similar, twin.
OPPOSITES: SEE **different**.

identifiable adjective
an identifiable accent. detectable,
discernible, distinctive, distinguishable,
familiar, known, named, noticeable,
perceptible, recognizable, unmistakable.
OPPOSITES: SEE **unidentifiable**.

identify verb
1 *to identify a suspect.* name, pick out,
recognize, single out.
2 *to identify an illness.* detect, diagnose,
discover, distinguish, pinpoint, [*informal*]
put a name to, spot.

identity noun
1 *Can you prove your identity?* [*informal*] ID,
name, nature.
2 *Prisoners sometimes lose their sense of
identity.* character, individuality,
personality, selfhood, uniqueness.

idiomatic adjective
idiomatic expressions. colloquial, natural,
well-phrased.

idiosyncrasy noun
Most of us have a few funny idiosyncrasies.
characteristic, eccentricity, feature, habit,
mannerism, oddity, peculiarity, quirk, trait.

idiosyncratic adjective
idiosyncratic behaviour. characteristic,
distinctive, eccentric, individual, odd,
peculiar, personal, quirky, singular,
unique.
OPPOSITES: SEE **common** adjective.

idiot noun
[These words are used *informally* and are
usually insulting.] ass, blockhead,
bonehead, booby, chump, clot, cretin,
dimwit, dolt, dope, duffer, dumbell,
dummy, dunce, dunderhead, fat-head, fool,

half-wit, ignoramus, imbecile, moron, nincompoop, ninny, nitwit, simpleton, twerp, twit.

idle adjective
1 *The machines lay idle during the strike.* dormant, inactive, inoperative, in retirement, not working, redundant, retired, unemployed, unoccupied, unproductive, unused.
OPPOSITES: SEE **busy, working**.
2 *He lost his job because he was idle.* apathetic, good-for-nothing, indolent, lackadaisical, lazy, shiftless, slothful, slow, sluggish, torpid, uncommitted, work-shy.
OPPOSITES: SEE **enthusiastic**.
3 *idle speculation.* casual, frivolous, futile, pointless, worthless.
OPPOSITES: SEE **serious**.

idle verb
to idle about be lazy [SEE **lazy**], dawdle, do nothing, [*informal*] hang about, [*informal*] kill time, laze, loaf, lounge about, potter, slack, stagnate, take it easy, vegetate.
OPPOSITES: SEE **work** verb.

idol noun
1 *a pagan idol.* deity, god, icon, image, statue.
2 *a pop idol.* favourite, hero, [*informal*] pin-up, star, [*informal*] superstar.

idolize verb
SEE **worship** verb.

idyllic adjective
an idyllic scene. charming, delightful, happy, idealized, lovely, pastoral, peaceful, perfect, unspoiled.
OPPOSITES: SEE **desolate**.

ignite verb
The central-heating boiler won't ignite. burn, catch fire, fire, kindle, light, set alight, set on fire, spark off.

ignoble adjective
ignoble motives. base, churlish, cowardly, despicable, disgraceful, dishonourable, infamous, low, mean, selfish, shabby, uncharitable, unchivalrous, unworthy.
OPPOSITES: SEE **noble** adjective.

ignorance noun
ignorance of the facts. inexperience, innocence, lack of information, unawareness, unconsciousness, unfamiliarity.
OPPOSITES: SEE **knowledge**.

ignorant adjective
1 *ignorant of the facts.* [*informal*] clueless, ill-informed, innocent, lacking knowledge, unacquainted, unaware, unconscious, unfamiliar (with), uninformed.
OPPOSITES: SEE **knowledgeable**.
2 *You'd be ignorant if you didn't go to*

school. illiterate, uncultivated, uneducated, unenlightened, unlettered, unscholarly.
OPPOSITES: SEE **educated**.
3 [*informal*] *He's just plain ignorant!* SEE **stupid**.

ignore verb
to ignore a warning. to ignore your friends. disobey, disregard, leave out, miss out, neglect, omit, overlook, pass over, [*informal*] shut your eyes to, skip, slight, take no notice of, [*informal*] turn a blind eye to.

ill adjective
1 ailing, bedridden, bilious, [*informal*] dicky, diseased, feeble, frail, [*informal*] funny (*feeling a bit funny*), [*informal*] groggy, indisposed, infected, infirm, nauseated, nauseous, [*informal*] off-colour, [*informal*] out of sorts, pasty, poorly, queasy, queer, [*informal*] seedy, sick, sickly, suffering, [*informal*] under the weather, unhealthy, unwell, weak.
OPPOSITES: SEE **healthy**.
2 *ill effects.* SEE **bad**, damaging, detrimental, evil, harmful, injurious, unfavourable, unfortunate, unlucky.
OPPOSITES: SEE **good**.

illegal adjective
illegal activities. illegal trade. actionable, against the law, banned, black-market, criminal, forbidden, SEE **illegitimate**, illicit, invalid, irregular, outlawed, prohibited, proscribed, unauthorized, unconstitutional, unlawful, unlicensed, wrong.
OPPOSITES: SEE **legal**.

illegible adjective
illegible writing. SEE **bad**, indecipherable, indistinct, obscure, unclear, unreadable.
OPPOSITES: SEE **legible**.

illegitimate adjective
1 *an illegitimate course of action.* against the rules, SEE **illegal**, improper, inadmissible, incorrect, invalid, unauthorized, unjustifiable, unreasonable, unwarranted.
2 *an illegitimate child.* bastard, [*old-fashioned*] born out of wedlock, natural.
OPPOSITES: SEE **legitimate**.

illness noun
suffering from an illness. abnormality, affliction, ailment, attack, blight, [*informal*] bug, complaint, condition, contagion, disability, disease, disorder, epidemic, health problem, indisposition, infection, infirmity, malady, malaise, pestilence, plague, sickness, [*informal*] trouble, [*informal*] turn (*He had a nasty turn*), [*informal*] upset, weakness, SEE **wound** noun.

VARIOUS ILLNESSES OR COMPLAINTS:
abscess, acne, allergy, amnesia, anaemia,
appendicitis, arthritis, asthma, bedsore,
beriberi, bilious attack, blister, boil,
bronchitis, brucellosis, bubonic plague,
bunion, cancer, caries, catalepsy, cataract,
catarrh, chicken-pox, chilblains, chill,
cholera, claustrophobia, cold, colic,
 coma, concussion, conjunctivitis,
constipation, convulsion, corns, coronary
thrombosis, cough, cramp, croup,
cystitis.

dandruff, delirium, dermatitis,
diabetes, diarrhoea, diphtheria,
dipsomania, dropsy, dysentery, dyspepsia,
dystrophy, ear-ache, eczema, embolism,
enteritis, epilepsy, fever, fits,
flu, frostbite, gangrene, gastric flu,
glandular fever, goitre, gonorrhoea, gout,
gumboil, haemophilia, haemorrhage,
haemorrhoids, hay fever, headache, hernia,
hypothermia.

impetigo, indigestion, inflammation,
influenza, insomnia, jaundice,
laryngitis, leprosy, leukaemia, lockjaw,
lumbago, malaria, measles, melancholia,
meningitis, mental illness, migraine,
mongolism, multiple sclerosis, mumps,
neuralgia, neuritis, neurosis, paralysis,
paratyphoid, pellagra, peritonitis,
phobia, piles, plague, pleurisy, pneumonia,
polio or poliomyelitis, psychosis,
quinsy.

rabies, rheumatism, rickets, ringworm,
rupture, scabies, scarlet fever,
schizophrenia, sciatica, sclerosis,
scrofula, scurvy, sea-sickness, seizure,
shingles, silicosis, smallpox, spastic,
spina bifida, stomach-ache, stroke, sty,
sunstroke, syphilis, tetanus, thrombosis,
tonsillitis, toothache, tuberculosis, typhoid,
typhus, ulcer, verruca, wart, whooping-
cough.

illogical adjective
an illogical argument. absurd, fallacious,
inconsequential, inconsistent, invalid,
irrational, senseless, SEE **silly**, unreasonable,
unsound.
OPPOSITES: SEE **logical**.

illuminate verb
1 *to illuminate a place with lights.* brighten,
decorate with lights, light up, make
brighter.
2 *to illuminate a problem.* clarify, clear up,
elucidate, enlighten, explain, throw light
on.

illusion noun
an optical illusion. apparition, conjuring
trick, day-dream, deception, delusion,
dream, fancy, fantasy, figment of the
imagination, hallucination, mirage.

illusory adjective
illusory pleasures. deceptive, deluding,
delusive, false, illusive, SEE **imaginary**,
misleading, sham, unreal, untrue.
OPPOSITES: SEE **real**.

illustrate verb
1 *to illustrate a book.* adorn, decorate,
illuminate.
2 *to illustrate a story.* depict, draw pictures
of, picture, portray.
3 *to illustrate how to do something.*
demonstrate, elucidate, exemplify, explain,
show.

illustration noun
1 *illustrations in a picture-book.* decoration,
depiction, diagram, drawing, photograph,
picture, sketch.
2 *This thesaurus gives illustrations of how
words are used.* case, demonstration,
example, instance, specimen.

image noun
1 *an image in a mirror. an image on a screen.*
imitation, likeness, SEE **picture** noun,
projection, reflection.
2 *The temple contained the god's image.*
carving, effigy, figure, icon, idol,
representation, statue.
3 [*informal*] *She's the image of her mother.*
counterpart, double, likeness, spitting-
image, twin.

imaginable adjective
SEE **inconceivable**.

imaginary adjective
The unicorn is an imaginary beast. fabulous,
fanciful, fictional, fictitious, hypothetical,
SEE **illusory**, imagined, insubstantial,
invented, legendary, made up, mythical,
mythological, non-existent, supposed,
unreal, visionary.
OPPOSITES: SEE **real**.

imagination noun
Use your imagination. artistry, cleverness,
creativity, fancy, ingenuity, insight,
inspiration, inventiveness, originality,
resourcefulness, sensitivity, thought,
vision.

imaginative adjective
imaginative paintings. an imaginative story.
artistic, attractive, beautiful, clever,
creative, fanciful, ingenious, inspired,
inventive, original, poetic, resourceful,
sensitive, thoughtful, unusual, visionary,
vivid.
OPPOSITES: SEE **unimaginative**.

imagine verb
1 *Imagine you're on a desert island. Imagine what it would be like.* conceive, conjure up, create, dream up, envisage, fancy, fantasize, invent, make believe, make up, picture, pretend, see, think up, visualize.
2 *I imagine you'd like a drink.* assume, believe, conjecture, guess, infer, presume, suppose, surmise, [*informal*] take it.

imitate verb
1 *to imitate someone's mannerisms. to imitate another person.* ape, caricature, disguise yourself as, echo, guy, impersonate, masquerade as, mimic, parody, parrot, pose as, pretend to be, send up, take off, travesty.
2 *to imitate someone else's example.* copy, emulate, follow, match, model yourself on.

imitation adjective
The actors carried imitation guns. artificial, copied, counterfeit, dummy, ersatz, mock, model, sham, simulated.
OPPOSITES: SEE **real**.

imitation noun
an imitation of the real thing. copy, counterfeit, dummy, duplicate, duplication, fake, forgery, impersonation, impression, likeness, [*informal*] mock-up, model, parody, reflection, replica, reproduction, sham, simulation, [*informal*] take-off, toy, travesty.

imitative adjective
imitative behaviour. an imitative style. conventional, copied, derivative, fake, mock, plagiarized, traditional, unimaginative, unoriginal.
OPPOSITES: SEE **inventive**.

immature adjective
immature behaviour. an immature person. adolescent, babyish, backward, callow, childish, [*informal*] green, inexperienced, infantile, juvenile, puerile, undeveloped, [*of fruit*] unripe, young, youthful.
OPPOSITES: SEE **mature**.

immediate adjective
1 *immediate action.* direct, instant, instantaneous, present, pressing, prompt, quick, speedy, swift, top-priority, unhesitating, urgent.
OPPOSITES: SEE delayed, low-priority.
2 *our immediate neighbours.* adjacent, close, closest, near, nearest, neighbouring, next.
OPPOSITES: SEE **remote**.

immediately adverb
at once, directly, forthwith, instantly, now, promptly, [*informal*] right away, straight away, unhesitatingly.

immense adjective
SEE **huge**.

immerse verb
to immerse something in water. bathe, dip, drench, drown, duck, dunk, lower, plunge, submerge.

immersed adjective
immersed in your work. absorbed, busy, engrossed, interested, involved, occupied, preoccupied, wrapped up.

imminent adjective
imminent disaster. about to happen, approaching, close, coming, foreseeable, impending, looming, near, threatening.

immobile adjective
1 *immobile in deep mud.* fast, firm, fixed, immobilized, immovable, motionless, paralysed, secure, solid, static, stationary, still, stuck, unmoving.
2 *immobile features.* frozen, inexpressive, inflexible, rigid.
OPPOSITES: SEE **mobile**.

immobilize verb
to immobilize a vehicle. cripple, damage, disable, make immobile [SEE **immobile**], paralyse, put out of action, stop.

immoral adjective
immoral behaviour. abandoned, SEE **bad**, base, conscienceless, corrupt, debauched, degenerate, depraved, dishonest, dissipated, dissolute, evil, [*informal*] fast (*fast living*), impure, SEE **indecent**, licentious, loose, low, profligate, promiscuous, sinful, unchaste, unethical, unprincipled, unscrupulous, vicious, villainous, wanton, SEE **wicked**, wrong.
OPPOSITES: SEE **moral** adjective.

immorality noun
SEE **wickedness**.

immortal adjective
immortal souls. an immortal work of art. ageless, deathless, endless, eternal, everlasting, perpetual, timeless, unchanging, undying.
OPPOSITES: SEE **mortal**.

immune adjective
immune to disease. exempt (from), free (from), immunized (against), inoculated (against), invulnerable, protected (from), resistant, safe (from), unaffected (by), vaccinated (against).

immunization noun
inoculation, vaccination.

immutable adjective
immutable truths. constant, dependable, enduring, eternal, fixed, invariable, lasting,

permanent, perpetual, reliable, settled, stable, unalterable, unchangeable.
OPPOSITES: SEE **changeable**.

impact noun
1 *Was the car damaged in the impact?* bang, blow, bump, collision, concussion, contact, crash, knock, smash.
2 *The tragedy had a strong impact on us.* effect, force, impression, influence, repercussions, shock.

impart verb SEE **give**.

impartial adjective
an impartial referee. balanced, detached, disinterested, dispassionate, equitable, even-handed, fair, fair-minded, just, neutral, non-partisan, objective, open-minded, unbiased, uninvolved, unprejudiced.
OPPOSITES: SEE **biased**.

impartiality noun
balance, detachment, disinterest, fairness, justice, lack of bias, neutrality, objectivity, open-mindedness.
OPPOSITES: SEE **prejudice**.

impassable adjective
an impassable road. blocked, closed, obstructed, unusable.

impatient adjective
1 *impatient to start.* anxious, eager, keen, impetuous, precipitate, [*informal*] raring (*raring to go*).
2 *impatient because of the delay.* agitated, chafing, edgy, fidgety, fretful, irritable, nervous, restless, uneasy.
3 *an impatient manner.* abrupt, brusque, curt, hasty, intolerant, quick-tempered, snappy, testy.
OPPOSITES: SEE **patient** adjective.

impede verb SEE **hinder**.

impel verb SEE **propel**, **urge** verb.

impending adjective
SEE **imminent**.

impenetrable adjective
impenetrable forest. dense, impassable, solid, thick.

imperceptible adjective
imperceptible movement. imperceptible sounds. faint, gradual, inaudible, infinitesimal, insignificant, invisible, microscopic, minute, negligible, slight, small, subtle, tiny, undetectable, unnoticeable.
OPPOSITES: SEE **noticeable**.

imperfect adjective
imperfect goods. an imperfect success. broken, damaged, defective, deficient, faulty, flawed, incomplete, incorrect, marred, partial, shop-

soiled, spoilt, unfinished, with imperfections.
OPPOSITES: SEE **perfect** adjective.

imperfection noun
a performance with obvious imperfections. blemish, damage, defect, deficiency, failing, fault, flaw, inadequacy, shortcoming, weakness.
OPPOSITES: SEE **perfection**.

impermanent adjective
an impermanent relationship. destructible, ephemeral, evanescent, fleeting, momentary, passing, short-lived, temporary, transient, transitory, unstable.
OPPOSITES: SEE **permanent**.

impersonal adjective
an impersonal manner. aloof, businesslike, cold, cool, correct, detached, distant, formal, hard, inhuman, official, remote, unapproachable, unemotional, unfriendly, unsympathetic, without emotion.
OPPOSITES: SEE **friendly**.

impersonate verb
SEE **imitate**.

impertinent adjective
impertinent remarks. bold, brazen, cheeky, [*informal*] cocky, [*informal*] cool (*He's a cool customer!*), discourteous, disrespectful, forward, fresh (*Don't get fresh with me!*), impolite, impudent, insolent, insubordinate, insulting, irreverent, pert, SEE **rude**, saucy.
OPPOSITES: SEE **respectful**.

impetuous adjective
an impetuous dash for freedom. careless, eager, hasty, head-long, hot-headed, impulsive, incautious, precipitate, quick, rash, reckless, speedy, thoughtless, spontaneous, [*informal*] tearing (*in a tearing hurry*), unplanned, unpremeditated, unthinking, violent.
OPPOSITES: SEE **cautious**.

impetus noun
Hot weather gives an impetus to swimwear sales. boost, drive, energy, fillip, force, impulse, incentive, momentum, motivation, power, push, spur, stimulus.

impiety noun
blasphemy, godlessness, irreverence, profanity, sacrilege, sinfulness, ungodliness, unrighteousness, wickedness.
OPPOSITES: SEE **piety**.

implausible adjective
an implausible excuse. far-fetched, feeble, improbable, suspect, unconvincing, unlikely, unreasonable, weak.
OPPOSITES: SEE **plausible**.

implement noun
gardening implements. appliance, device, gadget, instrument, tool, utensil.

implement verb
to implement a plan. bring about, carry out, effect, enforce, execute, fulfil, perform, put into practice, realize, try out.

implicate verb
The evidence clearly implicated him in the crime. associate, connect, embroil, entangle, incriminate, inculpate, involve, show involvement in.

implication noun
1 *What was the implication of her comments?* hidden meaning, hint, innuendo, insinuation, overtone, significance.
2 *He was suspected of implication in the crime.* association, connection, entanglement, involvement.

implicit adjective
1 *implicit criticism.* hinted at, implied, indirect, insinuated, tacit, understood, unexpressed, unsaid, unspoken, unstated, unvoiced.
OPPOSITES: SEE **explicit**.
2 *implicit faith in her competence.* SEE **absolute**.

implore verb SEE **ask**.

imply verb
to imply something without saying it directly. hint, indicate, insinuate, intimate, mean, point to, suggest.

impolite adjective SEE **rude**.

import verb
to import goods. bring in, buy in, SEE **convey**, introduce, ship in.
OPPOSITE: export.

important adjective
1 *important facts. an important event.* basic, big, cardinal, central, chief, epoch-making, essential, foremost, fundamental, historic, key, main, major, momentous, newsworthy, noteworthy, once in a lifetime, outstanding, pressing, primary, principal, rare, salient, serious, significant, strategic, urgent, valuable, weighty.
2 *an important person.* celebrated, distinguished, eminent, famous, great, high-ranking, influential, known, leading, notable, powerful, pre-eminent, prominent, renowned, well-known.
OPPOSITES: SEE **unimportant**.

importune verb
He's for ever importuning me for money. SEE **ask**, badger, harass, hound, pester, plague, plead with, press, solicit, urge.

impose verb
to impose a penalty. charge with, decree, dictate, enforce, exact, fix, inflict, insist on, introduce, lay, levy, prescribe, set.
to impose on *I don't want to impose on you.* burden, encumber, place a burden on, [*informal*] saddle, take advantage of.

imposing adjective
an imposing castle. big, dignified, distinguished, grand, grandiose, great, important, impressive, magnificent, majestic, splendid, stately, striking.

impossibility noun
hopelessness, impracticability, unlikelihood.
OPPOSITES: SEE **possibility**.

impossible adjective
an impossible task. hopeless, impracticable, impractical, inconceivable, insoluble, insurmountable, out of the question, overwhelming, unachievable, unattainable, unimaginable, unobtainable, unviable, unworkable.
OPPOSITES: SEE **possible**.

impostor, imposture nouns SEE **cheat** noun.

impotence noun
His impotence to help made him despair. feebleness, inability, inadequacy, incapacity, ineffectuality, powerlessness, weakness.

impotent adjective
impotent to help. feeble, helpless, inadequate, incapable, incompetent, ineffective, ineffectual, powerless, unable, weak.
OPPOSITES: SEE **powerful**.

impractical adjective
an impractical suggestion. academic, idealistic, SEE **impossible**, impracticable, inconvenient, not feasible, romantic, theoretical, unachievable, unrealistic, unworkable.
OPPOSITES: SEE **practical**.

imprecise adjective
1 *imprecise measurements.* approximate, estimated, guessed, inaccurate, inexact, unscientific.
2 *imprecise wording.* ambiguous, SEE **careless**, ill-defined, inexplicit, loose, [*informal*] sloppy, undefined, vague, [*informal*] waffling, [*informal*] woolly.
OPPOSITES: SEE **precise**.

impregnable adjective
an impregnable castle. impenetrable, invincible, invulnerable, safe, secure, strong, unassailable, unconquerable.
OPPOSITES: SEE **vulnerable**.

impress verb
Her hard work impressed me. affect, be
memorable to, excite, influence, inspire,
leave its mark on, move, [*informal*] stick in
the mind of, stir.

impression noun
1 *The film made a big impression on me.*
effect, impact, influence, mark.
2 *I had the impression you were bored.* belief,
consciousness, conviction, fancy, feeling,
hunch, idea, notion, opinion, sense,
suspicion, view.
3 *Granny has clear impressions of her
childhood.* memory, recollection.
4 *Our feet left impressions in the snow.* dent,
hollow, imprint, indentation, mark, print,
stamp.

impressionable adjective
impressionable young children. easily
influenced, gullible, inexperienced, naïve,
receptive, suggestible, susceptible.
OPPOSITES: SEE **knowing**.

impressive adjective
an impressive win. an impressive building.
affecting, SEE **big**, grand, great, important,
imposing, magnificent, majestic,
memorable, moving, powerful, remarkable,
splendid, stately, stirring, striking,
touching.
OPPOSITES: SEE **insignificant**.

imprison verb
to imprison a criminal. cage, commit to
prison, confine, detain, gaol, immure,
incarcerate, intern, jail, keep in custody,
keep under house arrest, [*informal*] keep
under lock and key, lock up, [*informal*] put
away, [*informal*] send down, shut up.
OPPOSITES: SEE **free** verb.

imprisonment noun
confinement, custody, detention, duress
(*under duress*), gaol, house arrest,
incarceration, internment, restraint.

improbable adjective
an improbable story. doubtful, far-fetched,
implausible, incredible, preposterous,
questionable, unbelievable, unconvincing,
unexpected, unlikely.
OPPOSITES: SEE **probable**.

impromptu adjective
impromptu remarks. [*informal*] ad-lib,
extempore, extemporized, improvised,
offhand, [*informal*] off the cuff,
spontaneous, unplanned, unpremeditated,
unprepared, unrehearsed, unscripted.
OPPOSITES: SEE **rehearsed**.

improper adjective
1 *an improper course of action.* ill-timed,
inappropriate, incorrect, inopportune, out
of place, uncalled for, unsuitable,

unwarranted, SEE **wrong** adjective.
2 *improper language.* SEE **indecent**.
OPPOSITES: SEE **proper**.

impropriety noun
*I was surprised by the impropriety of his
remarks.* bad manners, inappropriateness,
indecency, indelicacy, insensitivity,
obscenity, rudeness, vulgarity,
unseemliness.
OPPOSITES: SEE **propriety**.

improve verb
1 *Her work improved.* advance, develop, get
better, move on, progress.
2 *Has he improved since his illness?* get better,
[*informal*] pick up, rally, recover,
recuperate, strengthen, [*informal*] turn the
corner.
OPPOSITES: SEE **decline** verb, **deteriorate**.
3 *The new job improved my finances.*
ameliorate, better, enhance, enrich, make
better.
4 *Improve your manners!* amend, correct,
mend, rectify, refine, reform, revise.
OPPOSITES: SEE **worsen**.
5 *We received a grant to improve our house.*
bring up to date, extend, modernize, rebuild,
renovate, touch up.
OPPOSITES: SEE **damage**, **spoil**.

improvement noun
1 *an improvement in behaviour.* advance,
amelioration, betterment, correction,
development, enhancement, gain, progress,
rally, recovery, reformation, upturn.
2 *improvements to our house.* alteration,
extension, [*informal*] face-lift,
modernization, modification, renovation.

improvise verb
1 *to improvise music.* [*informal*] ad-lib,
extemporize, make up, perform impromptu
[SEE **impromptu**], [*informal*] play it by ear,
vamp.
2 *to improvise a meal.* concoct, invent, make
do, [*informal*] throw together.

impudent adjective
SEE **cheeky**.

impulse noun
1 *What was the impulse behind your decision?*
drive, force, impetus, motive, pressure, push,
stimulus, thrust.
2 *a sudden impulse to do something.* caprice,
desire, instinct, urge, whim.

impulsive adjective
an impulsive action. automatic, hare-
brained, hasty, headlong, hot-headed,
impetuous, impromptu, instinctive,
intuitive, involuntary, madcap, precipitate,
rash, reckless, spontaneous, sudden,
thoughtless, unconscious, unplanned,
unpremeditated, unthinking, wild.
OPPOSITES: SEE **deliberate** adjective.

impure adjective
impure water. adulterated, contaminated, defiled, dirty, SEE **filthy**, foul, infected, polluted, tainted, unclean, unwholesome.

impurity noun
impurities in water. contamination, dirt, SEE **filth**, foreign body, infection, pollution, taint.

inaccessible adjective
an inaccessible spot. cut off, godforsaken, hard to find, inconvenient, isolated, lonely, outlying, out of reach, out-of-the-way, remote, solitary, unfrequented, [*informal*] unget-at-able, unreachable.
OPPOSITES: SEE **accessible**.

inaccurate adjective
inaccurate maths. an inaccurate statement. erroneous, false, faulty, imperfect, imprecise, incorrect, inexact, misleading, mistaken, unfaithful, unreliable, unsound, untrue, vague, wrong.
OPPOSITES: SEE **accurate**.

inactive adjective
Hedgehogs are inactive in winter. asleep, dormant, hibernating, idle, immobile, inanimate, inert, languid, lazy, lethargic, out of action, passive, quiet, sedentary, sleepy, slow, sluggish, somnolent, torpid, unemployed, unoccupied, vegetating.
OPPOSITES: SEE **active**.

inadequate adjective
an inadequate supply. inadequate preparation. deficient, imperfect, ineffective, insufficient, little, meagre, niggardly, [*informal*] pathetic, scanty, [*informal*] skimpy, sparse, unsatisfactory.
OPPOSITES: SEE **adequate**.

inadvertent adjective
SEE **unintentional**.

inadvisable adjective
an inadvisable course of action. foolish, ill-advised, imprudent, misguided, silly, unwise.
OPPOSITES: SEE **advisable**.

inanimate adjective
dead, dormant, inactive, insentient, lifeless, unconscious.
OPPOSITES: SEE **animate** adjective.

inappropriate adjective
an inappropriate gift. inappropriate comments. ill-judged, ill-suited, ill-timed, improper, inapplicable, inapposite, incongruous, incorrect, inopportune, irrelevant, out of place, tactless, tasteless, unbecoming, unfit, unseasonable, unseemly, unsuitable, untimely, wrong.
OPPOSITES: SEE **appropriate**.

inarticulate adjective
an inarticulate speaker. dumb, faltering, halting, hesitant, SEE **incoherent**, mumbling, mute, shy, silent, speechless, stammering, stuttering, tongue-tied, unclear, unintelligible.
OPPOSITES: SEE **articulate** adjective.

inattentive adjective
an inattentive driver. absent-minded, careless, daydreaming, dreaming, heedless, lacking concentration, negligent, preoccupied, unobservant, vague, wandering.
OPPOSITES: SEE **alert** adjective.

inaudible adjective
inaudible sounds. faint, indistinct, low, muffled, mumbled, muted, quiet, silent, unclear, undetectable, unidentifiable, weak.
OPPOSITES: SEE **audible**.

incapable adjective
incapable of doing things for himself. clumsy, helpless, impotent, inadequate, incompetent, ineffective, ineffectual, inept, stupid, unable, useless, weak.
OPPOSITES: SEE **capable**.

incentive noun
an incentive to work. bait, [*informal*] carrot, encouragement, inducement, motivation, reward, stimulus, [*informal*] sweetener.

incessant adjective
an incessant rhythm. incessant demands. ceaseless, chronic, constant, continual, continuous, endless, eternal, everlasting, interminable, never-ending, non-stop, perennial, permanent, perpetual, persistent, relentless, unbroken, unceasing, unending, unremitting.
OPPOSITES: SEE **occasional**, **temporary**.

incident noun
1 *an amusing incident.* affair, circumstance, event, happening, occasion, occurrence.
2 *a nasty incident.* accident, SEE **commotion**, confrontation, disturbance, fight, scene.

incidental adjective
Let's discuss the main point, not incidental issues. attendant, SEE **chance** adjective, inessential, minor, odd, random, secondary, subordinate, subsidiary.
OPPOSITES: SEE **essential**.

incipient adjective
an incipient disease. beginning, developing, early, embryonic, growing, new, rudimentary, starting.
OPPOSITES: SEE **established**.

incision noun SEE **cut** noun.

incite verb
to incite violence. SEE **provoke**.

inclination noun
an inclination to doze off. bent, bias, disposition, fondness, habit, instinct, leaning, liking, partiality, penchant, predilection, predisposition, preference, proclivity, propensity, readiness, tendency, trend, willingness.

incline verb
to incline at an angle. bend, lean, slant, slope, tilt, tip, veer.
to be inclined *I'm inclined to doze off after lunch.* be disposed, be in the habit (of), be liable, have an inclination [SEE **inclination**], like, prefer.

include verb
1 *The programme includes some new songs.* blend in, combine, comprise, consist of, contain, embody, encompass, incorporate, involve, make room for, mix, subsume, take in.
2 *The price includes transport.* add in, allow for, cover, take into account.
OPPOSITES: SEE **exclude**.

incoherent adjective
incoherent messages. an incoherent speaker. confused, disconnected, disjointed, disordered, disorganized, garbled, illogical, SEE **inarticulate**, inconsistent, jumbled, mixed up, muddled, rambling, unclear, unconnected, unintelligible, unstructured, unsystematic.
OPPOSITES: SEE **coherent**.

incombustible adjective
fireproof, fire-resistant, flameproof, non-flammable.
OPPOSITES: SEE **inflammable**.

income noun
earnings, interest, SEE **money**, pay, pension, profits, receipts, revenue, salary, takings, wages.
OPPOSITES: SEE **expense**.

incoming adjective
an incoming aircraft. approaching, arriving, coming, landing, next, returning.
OPPOSITES: SEE **outgoing**.

incomparable adjective
incomparable beauty. SEE **unequalled**.

incompatible adjective
The two accounts are incompatible. at variance, clashing, conflicting, contradictory, contrasting, different, discrepant, incongruous, inconsistent, irreconcilable.
OPPOSITES: SEE **compatible**.

incompetent adjective
incompetent workers. bungling, feckless, helpless, [*informal*] hopeless, inadequate, incapable, ineffective, ineffectual, inefficient, inexperienced, inexpert, stupid, unacceptable, unfit, unqualified, unsatisfactory, unskilful, untrained, useless.
OPPOSITES: SEE **competent**.

incomplete adjective
1 *an incomplete story.* abbreviated, abridged, [*informal*] bitty, edited, expurgated, partial, selective, shortened.
2 *incomplete work.* deficient, faulty, imperfect, insufficient, unfinished, unpolished, wanting.
OPPOSITES: SEE **complete** adjective.

incomprehensible adjective
an incomprehensible message. baffling, beyond your comprehension, cryptic, enigmatic, illegible, impenetrable, indecipherable, meaningless, mysterious, obscure, opaque, perplexing, puzzling, strange, too difficult, unclear, unfathomable, unintelligible.
OPPOSITES: SEE **comprehensible**.

inconceivable adjective
The distances in the universe are inconceivable. implausible, impossible to understand, incredible, [*informal*] mind-boggling, staggering, unbelievable, undreamed of, unimaginable, unthinkable.
OPPOSITES: SEE **credible**.

inconclusive adjective
inconclusive evidence. ambiguous, equivocal, indecisive, indefinite, open, uncertain, unconvincing.
OPPOSITES: SEE **conclusive**.

incongruous adjective
an absurdly incongruous couple. clashing, conflicting, contrasting, discordant, ill-matched, ill-suited, inappropriate, incompatible, inconsistent, irreconcilable, odd, out of place, uncoordinated, unsuited.
OPPOSITES: SEE **matching**.

inconsiderate adjective
an inconsiderate remark. inconsiderate neighbours. careless, cruel, insensitive, negligent, rude, self-centred, selfish, tactless, thoughtless, uncaring, unconcerned, unfriendly, unhelpful, unkind, unsympathetic, unthinking.
OPPOSITES: SEE **considerate**.

inconsistent adjective
1 *He is inconsistent in his views.* capricious, changeable, erratic, fickle, inconstant, patchy, unpredictable, unreliable, unstable, [*informal*] up-and-down, variable.
2 *The stories of the two witnesses are*

inconsistent. SEE **incompatible**.
OPPOSITES: SEE **consistent**.

inconspicuous adjective
an inconspicuous worker. an inconspicuous act of bravery. camouflaged, hidden, insignificant, invisible, modest, ordinary, out of sight, plain, restrained, retiring, self-effacing, unassuming, unobtrusive.
OPPOSITES: SEE **conspicuous**.

inconvenience noun
the inconvenience of having to change buses. annoyance, bother, disadvantage, disruption, drawback, encumbrance, hindrance, irritation, nuisance, trouble.

inconvenient adjective
an inconvenient moment. annoying, awkward, bothersome, cumbersome, difficult, embarrassing, inopportune, irritating, tiresome, troublesome, unsuitable, untimely, untoward, unwieldy.
OPPOSITES: SEE **convenient**.

incorporate verb
SEE **include**.

incorporeal adjective
incorporeal voices. disembodied, ethereal, ghostly, impalpable, insubstantial, intangible, spectral, unreal.
OPPOSITES: SEE **physical**.

incorrect adjective SEE **wrong** adjective.

incorruptible adjective
an incorruptible judge. SEE **good**, honest, honourable, just, moral, sound, [*informal*] straight, true, trustworthy, unbribable, upright.
OPPOSITES: SEE **corrupt** adjective.

increase noun
an increase in the size, length, intensity, etc., of something. addition, amplification, augmentation, boost, build-up, crescendo, development, enlargement, escalation, expansion, extension, gain, growth, increment, inflation, intensification, proliferation, rise, upsurge, upturn.
OPPOSITES: SEE **decrease** noun.

increase verb
1 *to increase the size, length, intensity, etc., of something.* add to, amplify, augment, boost, build up, develop, enlarge, expand, extend, lengthen, magnify, make greater, maximize, multiply, prolong, put up, raise, [*informal*] step up, strengthen, stretch, swell.
2 *My responsibilities have increased.* escalate, gain (*in size, etc.*), get greater, grow, intensify, proliferate, [*informal*] snowball, spread, [*poetic*] wax.
OPPOSITES: SEE **decrease** verb.

incredible adjective
an incredible story. extraordinary, far-fetched, implausible, improbable, inconceivable, miraculous, surprising, unbelievable, unconvincing, unimaginable, unlikely, untenable, unthinkable.
OPPOSITES: SEE **credible**.

incredulous adjective
She was incredulous when told she'd won. disbelieving, distrustful, dubious, questioning, sceptical, suspicious, uncertain, unconvinced.
OPPOSITES: SEE **credulous**.

incriminate verb
to incriminate someone in wrongdoing. accuse, blame, embroil, implicate, inculpate, involve.
OPPOSITES: SEE **excuse** verb.

incur verb
to incur a fine. [*informal*] be on the receiving end of, bring upon yourself, earn, get, provoke, run up, suffer.

incurable adjective
incurable illness. fatal, hopeless, inoperable, irreparable, terminal, untreatable.
OPPOSITES: SEE **curable**.

indebted adjective
I'm indebted to you. [*old-fashioned*] beholden, grateful, obliged, thankful, under an obligation.

indecent adjective
indecent behaviour. indecent language. [*informal*] blue, coarse, crude, dirty, immodest, impolite, improper, impure, indecorous, indelicate, insensitive, naughty, SEE **obscene**, offensive, risqué, rude, [*informal*] sexy, [*informal*] smutty, suggestive, tasteless, titillating, unbecoming, unprintable, unrepeatable, unseemly, vulgar.
OPPOSITES: SEE **decent**.

indecisive adjective
SEE **hesitant**.

indefensible adjective
Her silly behaviour puts her in an indefensible position. unjustifiable, unpardonable, untenable, vulnerable, weak.

indefinite adjective
ambiguous, confused, equivocal, evasive, general, ill-defined, imprecise, inexact, [*informal*] leaving it open, neutral, uncertain, unclear, undefined, unsettled, unspecific, unspecified, unsure, vague.
OPPOSITES: SEE **definite**.

indelible adjective
1 *indelible ink.* fast, fixed, ineradicable, ingrained, lasting, permanent.
2 *indelible memories.* unforgettable.

indentation noun
an indentation in a surface. cut, dent, depression, dimple, dip, hollow, nick, notch, serration.

indented adjective
the indented line of the battlements. crenellated, dented, notched, serrated, toothed, zigzag.

independence noun
We value independence. autonomy, being independent [SEE **independent**], freedom, individualism, liberty, nonconformity, self-government.

independent adjective
1 *an independent country.* autonomous, liberated, neutral, nonaligned, self-determining, self-governing, sovereign.
2 *an independent individual.* carefree, [*informal*] foot-loose, free, individualistic, private, self-reliant, separate, unconventional, untrammelled, without ties.
OPPOSITES: SEE **dependent**.
3 *an independent opinion.* SEE **unbiased**.

indescribable adjective
indescribable beauty. beyond words, indefinable, ineffable, inexpressible, leaving you speechless, stunning, unspeakable, unutterable.

indestructible adjective
1 *indestructible materials.* durable, lasting, permanent, solid, strong, tough, toughened, unbreakable.
OPPOSITES: SEE **impermanent**.
2 *the indestructible spirit of humankind.* enduring, eternal, everlasting, immortal, imperishable.
OPPOSITES: SEE **mortal**.

indeterminate adjective
SEE **uncertain**.

index noun
a library index. alphabetical list, catalogue, directory, register.

indiarubber noun
eraser, rubber.

indicate verb
1 *Indicate where you are going.* describe, display, give an indication of [SEE **indication**], intimate, make known, manifest, point out, reveal, say, show, specify.
2 *A red light indicates danger.* be an indication of [SEE **indication**], betoken, communicate, convey, denote, express, mean, register, signal, signify, spell, stand for, symbolize.

indication noun
He gave no indication of his feelings. clue, evidence, hint, inkling, intimation, omen, portent, sign, signal, suggestion, symptom, token, warning.

indicator noun
The indicators showed that the machine was working normally. clock, dial, display, gauge, index, instrument, marker, meter, pointer, screen, sign, signal, trafficator.

indifferent adjective
[Note: *indifferent* is NOT the opposite of *different*.] 1 *I was indifferent about the result.* aloof, apathetic, blasé, bored, casual, cold, cool, detached, disinterested, dispassionate, half-hearted, incurious, neutral, nonchalant, not bothered, uncaring, unconcerned, unemotional, unenthusiastic, unexcited, unimpressed, uninterested, uninvolved, unmoved.
OPPOSITES: SEE **concerned, enthusiastic**.
2 *The food was indifferent.* commonplace, fair, mediocre, middling, moderate, [*informal*] nothing to write home about, SEE **ordinary**, unexciting.
OPPOSITES: SEE **excellent**.

indigestion noun
dyspepsia, flatulence, heartburn.

indignant adjective
We were indignant about the way they treated us. [*informal*] aerated, SEE **angry**, annoyed, cross, disgruntled, exasperated, furious, heated, infuriated, [*informal*] in high dudgeon, irate, irritated, livid, mad, [*informal*] peeved, provoked, [*informal*] put out, riled, sore, upset, vexed.

indirect adjective
1 *an indirect route.* [*informal*] all round the houses, circuitous, devious, long, meandering, rambling, roundabout, tortuous, winding, zigzag.
2 *an indirect insult.* ambiguous, backhanded, circumlocutory, disguised, equivocal, euphemistic, SEE **evasive**, implicit, implied, oblique.
OPPOSITES: SEE **direct** adjective.

indiscreet adjective
indiscreet remarks. careless, ill-advised, ill-considered, ill-judged, impolite, impolitic, incautious, injudicious, tactless, undiplomatic, unguarded, unthinking, unwise.
OPPOSITES: SEE **discreet**.

indiscriminate adjective
indiscriminate attacks. indiscriminate praise. aimless, desultory, general, haphazard, [*informal*] hit or miss, imperceptive, miscellaneous, mixed, random, uncritical, undifferentiated,

undiscriminating, uninformed, unselective, unsystematic, wholesale.
OPPOSITES: SEE **selective**.

indispensable adjective
indispensable equipment. basic, central, crucial, essential, imperative, key, necessary, needed, required, requisite, vital.
OPPOSITES: SEE **unnecessary**.

indisposed adjective
SEE **ill**.

indisputable adjective
indisputable facts. accepted, acknowledged, axiomatic, certain, clear, evident, incontestable, incontrovertible, indubitable, irrefutable, positive, proved, proven, self-evident, sure, unanswerable, unarguable, undeniable, undisputed, undoubted, unimpeachable, unquestionable.
OPPOSITES: SEE **debatable**.

indistinct adjective
1 *an indistinct image.* bleary, blurred, confused, dim, faint, fuzzy, hazy, ill-defined, indefinite, misty, obscure, shadowy, unclear, vague.
2 *indistinct sounds.* deadened, dull, indistinguishable, muffled, mumbled, slurred, unintelligible.
OPPOSITES: SEE **distinct**.

indistinguishable adjective
indistinguishable twins. identical, interchangeable, the same, twin.
OPPOSITES: SEE **different**.

individual adjective
an individual style. characteristic, different, distinct, distinctive, exclusive, idiosyncratic, particular, peculiar, personal, private, separate, singular, special, specific, unique.
OPPOSITES: SEE **collective**.

indoctrinate verb SEE **teach**.

induce verb
1 *We couldn't induce her to come out.* coax, encourage, incite, influence, persuade, prevail on, [*informal*] talk (someone) into, tempt.
OPPOSITES: SEE **dissuade**.
2 *What induced your cold?* bring on, cause, engender, generate, give rise to, lead to, occasion, produce, provoke.

indulge verb
Older people sometimes indulge children. be indulgent to [SEE **indulgent**], cosset, favour, give in to, gratify the whims of, humour, mollycoddle, pamper, pander to, spoil, [*informal*] spoon-feed, treat.
OPPOSITES: SEE **discipline** verb.
to indulge in SEE **enjoy**.

indulgent adjective
indulgent grandparents. compliant, easygoing, fond, forbearing, forgiving, genial, kind, lenient, liberal, overgenerous, patient, permissive, tolerant.
OPPOSITES: SEE **strict**.

industrious adjective
an industrious worker. assiduous, busy, conscientious, diligent, earnest, energetic, enterprising, hard-working, involved, keen, laborious, persistent, productive, sedulous, tireless, zealous.
OPPOSITES: SEE **lazy**.

industry noun
1 *There's a lot of industry in this town.* business, commerce, manufacturing, trade.
2 *We admired the industry of the volunteers.* activity, application, commitment, determination, diligence, effort, energy, hard work, industriousness, keenness, labour, perseverance, persistence, tirelessness, toil, zeal.
OPPOSITES: SEE **laziness**.

inedible adjective
inedible food. bad for you, harmful, indigestible, nauseating, [*informal*] off (*This meat is off*), poisonous, rotten, tough, uneatable, unpalatable, unwholesome.
OPPOSITES: SEE **edible**.

ineffective adjective
1 *ineffective efforts.* fruitless, futile, [*informal*] hopeless, inept, unconvincing, unproductive, unsuccessful, useless, vain, worthless.
2 *an ineffective salesman.* feckless, feeble, idle, impotent, inadequate, incapable, incompetent, ineffectual, inefficient, powerless, shiftless, unenterprising, weak.
OPPOSITES: SEE **effective**.

inefficient adjective
1 *an inefficient worker.* SEE **ineffective**.
2 *inefficient use of resources.* extravagant, prodigal, uneconomic, wasteful.
OPPOSITES: SEE **efficient**.

inelegant adjective
inelegant movements. inelegant style. awkward, clumsy, crude, gauche, graceless, inartistic, rough, SEE **ugly**, uncouth, ungainly, unpolished, unskilful, unsophisticated, unstylish.
OPPOSITES: SEE **elegant**.

ineligible adjective
ineligible for a job. disqualified, inappropriate, [*informal*] out of the running, [*informal*] ruled out, unacceptable, unfit, unsuitable.
OPPOSITES: SEE **eligible**.

inept adjective
an inept attempt to put things right.
bungling, clumsy, SEE **inappropriate**,
incompetent, maladroit.

inequality noun
inequalities between rich and poor.
difference, disparity, dissimilarity,
imbalance.
OPPOSITES: SEE **equality**.

inertia noun
*The cheering crowd roused us from our
inertia.* apathy, deadness, idleness,
immobility, inactivity, indolence, lassitude,
laziness, lethargy, listlessness, numbness,
passivity, sluggishness, torpor.
OPPOSITES: SEE **activity**.

inescapable adjective
SEE **unavoidable**.

inessential adjective
Leave inessential equipment behind.
dispensable, expendable, minor, needless,
non-essential, optional, ornamental,
secondary, spare, superfluous,
unimportant, unnecessary.
OPPOSITES: SEE **essential**.

inevitable adjective
inevitable disaster. SEE **unavoidable**.

inexact adjective
SEE **imprecise**.

inexcusable adjective
SEE **unforgivable**.

inexhaustible adjective
SEE **infinite**.

inexpensive adjective SEE **cheap**, cut-price,
low-priced, reasonable.
OPPOSITES: SEE **expensive**.

inexperienced adjective
an inexperienced recruit. callow, [*informal*]
green, immature, inexpert, naïve, new,
probationary, raw, unaccustomed,
unskilled, unsophisticated, untried,
[*informal*] wet behind the ears, young.
OPPOSITES: SEE **experienced**.

inexplicable adjective
an inexplicable mystery. baffling, enigmatic,
incomprehensible, insoluble, mysterious,
mystifying, puzzling, strange,
unaccountable, unfathomable, unsolvable.
OPPOSITES: SEE **explicable**.

infallible adjective
an infallible method. certain, dependable,
foolproof, perfect, predictable, reliable,
sound, sure, trustworthy, unbeatable.
OPPOSITES: SEE **fallible**.

infant noun
baby, SEE **child**, [*informal*] toddler.

infantile adjective
[*uncomplimentary*] *infantile behaviour.*
adolescent, babyish, childish, immature,
juvenile, puerile, SEE **silly**.
OPPOSITES: SEE **mature**.

infatuated adjective
besotted, [*informal*] head over heels, in love
[SEE **love** noun], obsessed, [*informal*]
smitten.

infatuation noun
[*informal*] crush, SEE **love** noun, obsession,
passion.

infect verb
1 *to infect the water supply. to infect a wound.*
blight, contaminate, defile, make infected
[SEE **infected**], poison, pollute, spoil, taint.
2 *to infect someone with your laughter.* affect,
influence, inspire, touch.

infected adjective
an infected wound. blighted, contaminated,
festering, inflamed, poisoned, polluted,
putrid, septic, tainted.

infection noun
1 *The infection spread rapidly.* blight,
contagion, contamination, epidemic,
pestilence, pollution, virus.
2 *He's off work with some sort of infection.*
SEE **illness**.

infectious adjective
infectious diseases. catching, communicable,
contagious, spreading, transmissible,
transmittable.

infer verb
[Note: *infer* and *imply* are NOT synonyms.]
*I infer from what you say that you are
unhappy?* assume, conclude, deduce,
extrapolate, gather, guess, reach the
conclusion, understand, work out.

inferior adjective
1 *inferior rank.* junior, lesser, lower, menial,
secondary, second-class, servile,
subordinate, subsidiary.
2 *inferior quality.* SEE **bad**, cheap, indifferent,
mediocre, poor, shoddy, tawdry, [*informal*]
tinny.
OPPOSITES: SEE **superior**.

infertile adjective
SEE **barren**.

infested adjective
infested with mice. alive, crawling, overrun,
plagued, ravaged, swarming, teeming,
verminous.

infidelity noun
1 *infidelity to a leader.* SEE **disloyalty**.
2 *infidelity to a wife or husband.* adultery, unfaithfulness.

infiltrate verb
to infiltrate the enemy's camp. enter secretly, insinuate, intrude, penetrate.

infinite adjective
infinite numbers. infinite patience. boundless, countless, endless, everlasting, SEE **huge**, immeasurable, immense, incalculable, inestimable, inexhaustible, interminable, limitless, never-ending, numberless, uncountable, undefined, unending, unfathomable, unlimited, unnumbered, untold.
OPPOSITES: SEE **finite**.

infirm adjective
Infirm people may need our help. bedridden, crippled, elderly, feeble, frail, SEE **ill**, lame, old, poorly, senile, sickly, unwell, weak.
OPPOSITES: SEE **healthy**.

inflame verb
to inflame violent feelings. SEE **anger** verb, arouse, encourage, excite, fire, foment, ignite, kindle, madden, provoke, rouse, stimulate.
OPPOSITES: SEE **cool** verb.

inflamed adjective
1 *an inflamed wound.* festering, infected, poisoned, red, septic, swollen.
2 *inflamed passions.* angry, enraged, excited, feverish, fiery, heated, hot, passionate, roused.

inflammable adjective
inflammable chemicals. burnable, combustible, flammable, volatile.
OPPOSITES: SEE **incombustible**.

inflammation noun
an inflammation of the skin. abscess, boil, infection, redness, sore, soreness.

inflate verb
1 *to inflate a tyre.* blow up, dilate, distend, puff up, pump up, swell.
2 *to inflate the importance of something.* SEE **exaggerate**.

inflexible adjective
1 *inflexible materials.* firm, hard, hardened, immovable, rigid, solid, stiff, unbending, unyielding.
2 *an inflexible attitude.* entrenched, immutable, intractable, intransigent, obdurate, obstinate, resolute, strict, stubborn, unaccommodating, unalterable, uncompromising, unhelpful.
OPPOSITES: SEE **flexible**.

inflict verb
to inflict punishment or pain. administer, apply, deal out, enforce, force, impose, mete out, perpetrate, wreak.

influence verb
1 *Our trainer influenced the way we played.* affect, change, control, determine, direct, dominate, guide, impinge on, impress, manipulate, modify, motivate, move, persuade, prompt, stir, sway.
2 *Don't try to influence the referee.* bias, bribe, corrupt, lead astray, prejudice, suborn, tempt.

influential adjective
1 *an influential person.* authoritative, dominant, important, leading, powerful.
2 *an influential idea.* compelling, convincing, effective, far-reaching, moving, persuasive, significant, telling.
OPPOSITES: SEE **unimportant**.

influx noun
an influx of imports. flood, flow, inflow, inundation, invasion, rush, stream.

inform verb
to inform someone of the facts. advise, apprise, enlighten, [*informal*] fill in, give information to, instruct, leak, notify, [*informal*] put in the picture, teach, tell, tip off.
to inform against *to inform against a wanted man.* accuse, betray, complain about, denounce, give information about, [*informal*] grass on, incriminate, inculpate, report, [*informal*] sneak on, [*informal*] split on, [*informal*] tell of, [*informal*] tell tales about.

informal adjective
1 *an informal greeting. informal clothes. an informal party.* approachable, casual, comfortable, cosy, easy, easygoing, everyday, familiar, free and easy, friendly, homely, natural, ordinary, relaxed, simple, unceremonious, unofficial, unpretentious, unsophisticated.
2 *informal language.* chatty, colloquial, personal, slangy.
3 *an informal design.* asymmetrical, flexible, fluid, intuitive, irregular, spontaneous.
OPPOSITES: SEE **formal**.

information noun
1 *information about what is happening.* announcement, briefing, bulletin, communication, enlightenment, facts, instruction, message, news, report, statement, [*old-fashioned*] tidings, [*informal*] tip-off.
2 *information gathered for a purpose.* data, database, dossier, evidence, intelligence, knowledge, statistics.

informative adjective
an informative booklet. communicative, enlightening, factual, giving information, helpful, illuminating, instructive, revealing, useful.
OPPOSITES: SEE **evasive**.

infrequent adjective
an infrequent guest. infrequent buses. exceptional, intermittent, irregular, occasional, [*informal*] once in a blue moon, rare, spasmodic, uncommon, unusual.
OPPOSITES: SEE **frequent** adjective.

infuriate verb SEE **anger** verb.

ingenious adjective
[Don't confuse with *ingenuous*.] *an ingenious plan.* artful, astute, brilliant, clever, complex, crafty, creative, cunning, imaginative, inspired, intricate, inventive, original, resourceful, shrewd, skilful, subtle.
OPPOSITES: SEE **unimaginative**.

ingenuous adjective
[Don't confuse with *ingenious*.] *an ingenuous beginner.* artless, childlike, frank, guileless, honest, innocent, naïve, open, plain, simple, trusting, uncomplicated, unsophisticated.
OPPOSITES: SEE **sophisticated**.

ingratitude noun
ungratefulness.
OPPOSITES: SEE **thanks**.

ingredient noun
component, constituent, element, part.

inhabit verb
to inhabit a place. [*old-fashioned*] abide in, dwell in, live in, make your home in, occupy, people, populate, possess, reside in, settle in, set up home in.

inhabitant noun
citizen, [*old-fashioned*] denizen, dweller, inmate, native, occupant, occupier, [*plural*] population, resident, settler, tenant, [*plural*] townsfolk, [*plural*] townspeople.

inhabited adjective
an inhabited island. colonized, lived-in, occupied, peopled, populated, settled.
OPPOSITES: SEE **uninhabited**.

inherit verb
to inherit property. be the inheritor of [SEE **inheritor**], be left, [*informal*] come into, receive as an inheritance [SEE **inheritance**], succeed to.

inheritance noun
a small inheritance from uncle's will. bequest, estate, fortune, heritage, legacy.

inheritor noun
the inheritor of an estate. beneficiary, heir, heiress, [*formal*] legatee, recipient, successor.

inhibited adjective
too inhibited to join the fun. bashful, diffident, formal, frustrated, full of inhibitions [SEE **inhibition**], guarded, [*informal*] prim and proper, repressed, reserved, self-conscious, shy, tense, undemonstrative, unemotional, [*informal*] uptight.
OPPOSITES: SEE **uninhibited**.

inhibition noun
1 [*usually plural*] *Try to overcome your inhibitions.* diffidence, [*informal*] hang-ups, repression, reserve, self-consciousness, shyness.
2 *There's no inhibition on your freedom here.* bar, barrier, check, impediment, interference, restraint.

inhospitable adjective
1 *an inhospitable person.* SEE **unfriendly**.
2 *an inhospitable place.* SEE **desolate**.

inhuman adjective
inhuman feelings. barbaric, barbarous, bestial, blood-thirsty, brutish, cruel, diabolical, fiendish, heartless, SEE **inhumane**, merciless, pitiless, ruthless, savage, unkind, unnatural.
OPPOSITES: SEE **human**.

inhumane adjective
inhumane treatment of animals. cold-hearted, cruel, hard, heartless, inconsiderate, SEE **inhuman**, insensitive, uncaring, uncharitable, uncivilized, unfeeling, unkind, unsympathetic.
OPPOSITES: SEE **humane**.

iniquitous adjective
SEE **wicked**.

initial adjective
an initial payment. an initial reaction. beginning, commencing, earliest, first, inaugural, introductory, opening, original, preliminary, starting.
OPPOSITES: SEE **final**.

initiate verb
to initiate negotiations. SEE **begin**.

initiative verb
Show some initiative. ambition, drive, dynamism, enterprise, [*informal*] get-up-and-go, inventiveness, lead, leadership, originality, resourcefulness.

inject verb
to inject into a vein. insert, introduce, make an injection.

injection noun
The nurse gave me an injection. [*informal*]
fix, inoculation, [*informal*] jab,
vaccination.

injure verb
break, crush, cut, damage, deface, disfigure,
harm, hurt, ill-treat, mar, ruin, spoil,
vandalize, SEE **wound** verb.

injury noun
damage, harm, hurt, mischief (*did him a
mischief*), SEE **wound** noun.

injustice noun
The injustice of the decision angered me. bias,
discrimination, dishonesty, favouritism,
illegality, inequality, inequity, oppression,
partiality, prejudice, unfairness,
unlawfulness, wrongness.
OPPOSITES: SEE **justice**.

inner adjective
inner walls. inner feelings. central,
concealed, hidden, innermost, inside,
interior, internal, intimate, inward, mental,
middle, private, secret.
OPPOSITES: SEE **outer**.

innocent adjective
1 *The trial proved he was innocent.* blameless,
free from blame, guiltless.
OPPOSITES: SEE **guilty**.
2 *innocent babes.* angelic, chaste, faultless,
[*informal*] green, harmless, honest,
incorrupt, inexperienced, ingenuous,
inoffensive, naïve, pure, righteous, simple-
minded, sinless, spotless, untainted,
virtuous.

innovation noun
*We propose to introduce some innovations
next year.* change, departure, new feature,
novelty, reform, revolution.

innumerable adjective
innumerable stars. countless, SEE
infinite, many, numberless, uncountable,
untold.

inoffensive adjective
SEE **harmless**.

inorganic adjective
inorganic fertilizers. artificial, chemical,
dead, inanimate, unnatural.
OPPOSITES: SEE **organic**.

inquest noun
1 *an inquest to determine how someone died.*
hearing, inquiry.
2 [*informal*] *an inquest into why we lost the
game.* discussion, exploration,
investigation, [*informal*] post-mortem,
probe, review.

inquire verb
SEE **ask**.

inquiry, **inquisition** nouns
SEE **investigation**.

inquisitive adjective
*I want to know simply because I'm
inquisitive!* curious, inquiring, interested,
interfering, meddling, nosy, probing, prying,
questioning, sceptical, snooping.
to be inquisitive SEE **pry**.
an inquisitive person SEE **busybody**.

insane adjective
SEE **mad**.

insanitary adjective
SEE **unhealthy**.

insanity noun
SEE **madness**.

inscription noun
the inscription on a memorial. engraving,
epigraph, superscription, wording, writing.

insect noun
[*informal*] creepy-crawly.

VARIOUS INSECTS: ant, aphid, bee, beetle,
black-beetle, blackfly, bluebottle,
bumble-bee, butterfly, cicada,
cockchafer, cockroach, Colorado beetle,
crane-fly, cricket, daddy-long-legs,
damsel-fly, dragonfly, earwig, firefly, fly,
glow-worm, gnat, grasshopper, hornet,
ladybird, locust, mantis, mayfly, midge,
mosquito, moth, sawfly, termite, tsetse fly,
wasp, weevil.

OTHER FORMS OF AN INSECT: caterpillar,
chrysalis, grub, larva, maggot.
There are many crawling creatures
commonly called *insects* which, strictly
speaking, are not insects: e.g. arachnid,
centipede, earthworm, mite, slug, spider,
woodlouse, worm.

---

insecure adjective
1 *an insecure foothold.* loose, precarious,
rocky, shaky, uncertain, unsafe, unstable,
unsteady, unsupported, weak, wobbly.
2 *an insecure feeling.* SEE **anxious**, exposed,
underconfident, vulnerable.
OPPOSITES: SEE **secure** adjective.

insensitive adjective
1 *It's insensitive to joke about people's
misfortunes.* callous, SEE **cruel**, imperceptive,
obtuse, tactless, [*informal*] thick-skinned,
thoughtless, uncaring, unfeeling,
unsympathetic.
OPPOSITES: SEE **tactful**.
2 *an insensitive spot on your skin.*
anaesthetized, dead, numb,

unresponsive, without feeling.
OPPOSITES: SEE **sensitive**.

inseparable adjective
always together, attached, indissoluble,
indivisible, integral.

insert verb
to insert a wedge. to insert papers in a file.
drive in, embed, implant, interleave (*pages
in a book*), introduce, [*informal*] pop in, push
in, put in, tuck in.

inside noun
bowels (*the bowels of the earth*), centre,
contents, core, heart, indoors, interior,
middle.
OPPOSITES: SEE **outside** noun.

insignificant adjective
inconsiderable, irrelevant, lightweight,
meaningless, negligible, small, trivial, SEE
unimportant, unimpressive, valueless,
worthless..

insincere adjective
insincere compliments. deceitful, deceptive,
devious, dishonest, disingenuous, false,
feigned, flattering, hollow, hypocritical,
lying, [*informal*] mealy-mouthed,
mendacious, [*informal*] phoney, pretended,
[*informal*] put on, sycophantic, [*informal*]
two-faced, untrue.
OPPOSITES: SEE **sincere**.

insist verb
He insisted he was innocent. assert, aver,
declare, emphasize, maintain, state, stress,
swear, take an oath, vow.
to insist on *She insists on obedience.*
command, demand, enforce, [*informal*] put
your foot down, require, stipulate.

insistent adjective
an insistent rhythm. insistent requests.
assertive, demanding, emphatic, forceful,
importunate, peremptory, persistent,
relentless, repeated, unrelenting,
unremitting, urgent.

insolence noun
Teachers don't like insolence from pupils.
arrogance, boldness, [*informal*] cheek,
defiance, disrespect, effrontery,
forwardness, impertinence, impudence,
incivility, insubordination, [*informal*] lip,
presumptuousness, rudeness.
OPPOSITES: SEE **politeness**.

insolent adjective
an insolent stare. arrogant, bold, brazen,
[*informal*] cheeky, contemptuous,
disdainful, disrespectful, forward,
impertinent, impolite, impudent, insulting,
presumptuous, rude, saucy, shameless,
sneering, uncivil.
OPPOSITES: SEE **polite**.

insoluble adjective
an insoluble problem. baffling, enigmatic,
incomprehensible, inexplicable,
mysterious, mystifying, puzzling, strange,
unaccountable, unanswerable,
unfathomable, unsolvable.
OPPOSITES: SEE **soluble**.

inspect verb
to inspect damage. to inspect someone's work.
check, examine, [*informal*] give it the once
over, investigate, make an inspection of,
scrutinize, study, survey, vet.

inspection noun
check, check-up, examination, [*informal*]
going-over, investigation, review, scrutiny,
survey.

inspector noun
1 *An inspector checked the standard of work.*
controller, examiner, investigator, official,
scrutineer, superintendent, supervisor,
tester.
2 *a police inspector.* SEE **policeman**.

inspiration noun
1 *the inspiration behind a poem.* creativity,
enthusiasm, genius, imagination, influence,
motivation, muse, spur, stimulus.
2 *I had a sudden inspiration.* brainwave,
idea, thought.

inspire verb
The crowd inspired us to play well. animate,
arouse, [*informal*] egg on, encourage,
enthuse, galvanize, influence, motivate,
prompt, reassure, spur, stimulate, stir,
support.

instability noun
emotional instability. instability in prices.
capriciousness, change, changeableness,
fickleness, fluctuation, flux, impermanence,
inconstancy, insecurity, mutability,
precariousness, shakiness, transience,
uncertainty, unpredictability, unreliability,
unsteadiness, [*informal*] ups-and-downs,
vacillation, variability, variations,
weakness.
OPPOSITES: SEE **stability**.

install verb
1 *to install central heating.* establish, fix,
introduce, put in, set up.
2 *He installed himself in the best chair.*
ensconce, place, plant, position, situate,
station.
OPPOSITES: SEE **remove**.

instalment noun
1 *We pay for the TV in instalments.* payment,
rent, rental.
2 *an instalment of a serial.* chapter, episode,
part.

instance noun
Give me an instance of what you mean. case,
example, illustration, occurrence, sample.

instant adjective
an instant reply. direct, fast, immediate,
instantaneous, prompt, quick, rapid,
speedy, swift, unhesitating, urgent.

instant noun
The shooting star was gone in an instant.
flash, moment, point of time, second, split
second, [*informal*] tick, [*informal*]
twinkling.

instigate verb
to instigate a riot. activate, begin, bring
about, cause, encourage, foment, generate,
incite, initiate, inspire, kindle, prompt,
provoke, set up, start, stimulate, stir up,
urge, [*informal*] whip up.

instigator noun
the instigator of a riot. agitator, fomenter,
inciter, initiator, inspirer, leader, mischief-
maker, provoker, ringleader, trouble-maker.

instinct noun
People do some things by instinct. feel,
feeling, guesswork, hunch, impulse,
inclination, instinctive urge [SEE **instinctive**],
intuition, presentiment, sixth-sense,
tendency, urge.

instinctive adjective
an instinctive reaction. automatic,
[*informal*] gut (*gut feeling*), impulsive,
inborn, inherent, innate, intuitive,
involuntary, natural, reflex, spontaneous,
unconscious, unreasoning, unthinking.
OPPOSITES: SEE **deliberate** adjective.

institution noun
1 *the institution of a new set of rules.* creation,
establishing, formation, founding,
inauguration, inception, initiation,
introduction, launching, opening, setting
up.
2 *an institution for blind people.* academy,
college, establishment, foundation, home,
hospital, institute, SEE **organization**, school,
[*informal*] set-up.
3 *Sunday dinner is a regular institution in
our house.* convention, custom, habit,
practice, ritual, routine, tradition.

instruct verb
1 *The teacher instructed us in a new
technique.* SEE **teach**.
2 *He instructed us to wait.* SEE **command** verb.

instruction noun
1 *He gave us instruction in the use of the
equipment.* SEE **teaching**.
2 *Obey instructions!* SEE **command** noun.

instructive adjective
an instructive book. didactic, edifying,
educational, enlightening, helpful,
illuminating, improving, informative,
revealing.

instructor noun
SEE **teacher**.

instrument noun
*surgical instruments. mathematical
instruments.* apparatus, appliance,
contraption, device, equipment, gadget,
implement, machine, mechanism, tool,
utensil.
MUSICAL INSTRUMENTS: SEE **music**.

insubordinate adjective
*Many teachers dislike insubordinate
children.* defiant, disobedient, SEE
impertinent, insurgent, mutinous,
rebellious, riotous, seditious, undisciplined,
unruly.
OPPOSITES: SEE **obedient**.

insufficient adjective
insufficient supplies. deficient, inadequate,
meagre, poor, scanty, scarce, short, sparse,
unsatisfactory.
OPPOSITES: SEE **excessive**, **sufficient**.

insulate verb
to insulate water-pipes. cocoon, cover,
enclose, isolate, lag, protect, surround, wrap
up.

insult noun
I was offended by his insults. abuse, cheek,
contumely, impudence, insulting behaviour
[SEE **insulting**], rudeness, slander, slight, snub.
OPPOSITES: SEE **compliment** noun.

insult verb
abuse, affront, be insulting to [SEE **insulting**],
[*informal*] call someone names, [*informal*]
cock a snook at, mock, offend, outrage,
patronize, revile, slander, slight, sneer at,
snub, [*informal*] thumb your nose at, vilify.
OPPOSITES: SEE **compliment** verb.

insulting adjective
insulting remarks. abusive, condescending,
contemptuous, disparaging, insolent,
mocking, offensive, patronizing, SEE **rude**,
scornful, scurrilous, slanderous, [*informal*]
snide.
OPPOSITES: SEE **complimentary**.

insure verb
to insure yourself against loss or accident.
cover, indemnify, protect, take out
insurance.

intact adjective
SEE **undamaged**.

intangible adjective
The scent of flowers is an intangible quality.
abstract, airy, disembodied, elusive,

ethereal, impalpable, incorporeal,
indefinite, insubstantial, invisible, unreal,
vague.
OPPOSITES: SEE **tangible**.

integral adjective
1 *The boiler is an integral part of the heating
system.* constituent, essential,
indispensable, intrinsic, irreplaceable,
necessary, requisite.
2 *The equipment is supplied as an integral
unit.* complete, full, indivisible, whole.

integrate verb
We tried to integrate the two groups.
amalgamate, blend, bring together, combine,
consolidate, desegregate, fuse, harmonize,
join, merge, mix, put together, unify, unite,
weld.
OPPOSITES: SEE **separate** verb.

integrity noun
You can trust his integrity. fidelity, goodness,
SEE **honesty**, honour, incorruptibility,
loyalty, morality, principle, reliability,
righteousness, sincerity, uprightness,
virtue.
OPPOSITES: SEE **dishonesty**.

intellectual adjective
1 *an intellectual student.* academic,
[*informal*] bookish, cerebral, cultured,
highbrow, SEE **intelligent**, scholarly,
studious, thoughtful.
2 *an intellectual book.* cultural, deep,
difficult, educational, highbrow, improving,
thought-provoking.

intelligence noun
1 *Use your intelligence!* ability, acumen,
[*informal*] brains, brightness, brilliance,
capacity, cleverness, discernment, genius,
insight, intellect, judgement, mind,
[*informal*] nous, perceptiveness, quickness,
reason, sense, understanding, wisdom, wit
(*He didn't have the wit to ask*), wits.
2 *They received intelligence of an impending
invasion.* data, facts, information,
knowledge, news, notification, report,
[*informal*] tip-off, warning.
3 *Our intelligence discovered the enemy's
position.* espionage, secret service, spies.

intelligent adjective
an intelligent student. intelligent work. able,
acute, alert, astute, brainy, bright, brilliant,
clever, discerning, intellectual, knowing,
penetrating, perceptive, perspicacious,
profound, quick, rational, sagacious, sharp,
shrewd, [*informal*] smart, trenchant, wise,
[*informal*] with it.
OPPOSITES: SEE **stupid**.

intelligible adjective
an intelligible message. clear,
comprehensible, decipherable, legible,
logical, lucid, meaningful, plain,

straightforward, unambiguous,
understandable.
OPPOSITES: SEE **incomprehensible**.

intend verb
1 *What do you intend to do?* aim, aspire,
contemplate, design, have in mind, mean,
plan, plot, propose, purpose, scheme.
2 *The gift was intended to please you.* design,
destine, put forward, set up.

intense adjective
1 *intense pain.* acute, agonizing, extreme,
fierce, great, keen, severe, sharp, strong,
violent.
OPPOSITES: SEE **slight** adjective.
2 *intense emotions.* ardent, burning, deep,
eager, earnest, fanatical, impassioned,
passionate, powerful, profound, serious,
towering, vehement.
OPPOSITES: SEE **cool** adjective.

intensify verb
*The heat intensified. They intensified the
pressure.* add to, aggravate, become greater,
boost, build up, deepen, emphasize, escalate,
fire, fuel, heighten, increase, magnify, make
greater, quicken, raise, redouble, reinforce,
sharpen, [*informal*] step up, strengthen.
OPPOSITES: SEE **reduce**.

intensive adjective
intensive effort. intensive enquiries.
[*informal*] all-out, concentrated, detailed,
exhaustive, high-powered, thorough,
unremitting.

intent adjective
intent on what you're doing. absorbed,
attentive (to), committed (to),
concentrating, determined, eager,
engrossed, keen, occupied, preoccupied, set,
steadfast, watchful.

intention noun
What is your intention? aim, ambition,
design, end, goal, intent, object, objective,
plan, point, purpose, target.

intentional adjective
an intentional foul. calculated, conscious,
deliberate, designed, intended, planned,
prearranged, premeditated, wilful.
OPPOSITES: SEE **unintentional**.

intercept verb
*I intercepted the messenger before he delivered
the message.* ambush, block, catch, check,
cut off, deflect, head off, interrupt, obstruct,
stop, thwart, trap.

interest noun
1 *Did he show any interest?* attention,
attentiveness, care, commitment, concern,
curiosity, involvement, notice, regard.
2 *The information was of no interest.*

consequence, importance, moment, note, significance, value.
3 *What are your main interests?* activity, diversion, hobby, pastime, preoccupation, pursuit, relaxation.

interest verb
Astronomy interests me. appeal to, arouse the curiosity of, attract, capture the imagination of, concern, divert, engage, engross, entertain, SEE **excite**, fascinate, intrigue, involve, stimulate, [*informal*] turn on.
OPPOSITES: SEE **bore**.

interested adjective
1 *an interested listener. interested in your work.* absorbed, attentive, curious, engrossed, enthusiastic, excited, fascinated, intent, keen, preoccupied, responsive.
OPPOSITES: SEE **uninterested**.
2 *Don't consult the owner of the damaged car: she's an interested party.* SEE **biased**, concerned, involved, partial.
OPPOSITES: SEE **unbiased**.

interesting adjective
[Things and experiences can be *interesting* in many ways. Only some of the possible synonyms are given here.] *an interesting problem. interesting conversation.* absorbing, challenging, curious, engaging, engrossing, entertaining, exciting, fascinating, important, intriguing, piquant, [*often ironic*] riveting, stimulating, unpredictable, unusual, varied.
OPPOSITES: SEE **boring**.

interfere verb
to interfere in someone's affairs. be a busybody, butt in, interrupt, intervene, intrude, meddle, molest, obtrude, [*informal*] poke your nose in, pry, snoop, tamper.
to interfere with *to interfere with the smooth running of something.* block, get in the way of, hamper, hinder, impede, obstruct.

interfering adjective
an interfering busybody. curious, meddlesome, nosy, prying, snooping.

interlude noun
SEE **interval**.

intermediate adjective
an intermediate position. average, [*informal*] betwixt and between, half-way, mean, medial, median, middle, midway, [*informal*] neither one thing nor the other, neutral, [*informal*] sitting on the fence, transitional.

intermittent adjective
an intermittent fault in a machine. fitful, irregular, occasional, [*informal*] on and off, periodic, recurrent, spasmodic, sporadic.
OPPOSITES: SEE **continual**.

intern verb SEE **imprison**.

internal adjective
the internal parts of something. inner, inside, interior, intimate, private.
OPPOSITES: SEE **outside** adjective.

international adjective
international travel. global, inter-continental, worldwide.

interpret verb
Can you interpret this old writing? clarify, construe, decipher, decode, elucidate, explain, expound, gloss, make clear, paraphrase, render (*into another language*), rephrase, reword, translate, understand.

interpretation noun
What's your interpretation of her behaviour? definition, explanation, gloss, reading, understanding, version.

interpreter noun
linguist, translator.

interrogate verb SEE **question** verb.

interrupt verb
1 *Interrupt if you have any questions.* [*informal*] barge in, break in, butt in, cut in, heckle, intervene, punctuate (*He punctuated the lecture with questions*).
2 *A fire alarm interrupted work.* break in on, break off, call a halt to, cause an interruption in [SEE **interruption**], cut (someone) off, cut short, disrupt, disturb, hold up, stop, suspend.
3 *The new houses interrupt our view.* get in the way of, interfere with, intrude upon, obstruct, spoil.

interruption noun
an interruption in service. break, check, disruption, division, gap, halt, hiatus, pause, stop, suspension.

intersect verb
motorways intersect. bisect each other, converge, criss-cross, cross, divide, meet, pass across each other.

interval noun
1 *an interval between events, places, etc.* break, [*informal*] breather, breathing-space, delay, distance, gap, hiatus, lapse, lull, opening, pause, respite, rest, space, wait.
2 *an interval in a play or concert.* adjournment, interlude, intermission, recess.

intervene verb
1 *A week intervened before I saw her again.* come between, happen, intrude, occur.
2 *to intervene in a quarrel.* arbitrate, butt in, intercede, interfere, interrupt, mediate, [*informal*] step in.

interview verb
A reporter interviewed eyewitnesses. ask questions, examine, interrogate, question.

intimate adjective
1 *an intimate relationship.* affectionate, close, familiar, SEE **friendly**, informal, loving, sexual.
2 *intimate details.* confidential, detailed, exhaustive, personal, private, secret.

intimidate verb
The strong often intimidate the weak. browbeat, bully, coerce, cow, daunt, frighten, hector, make afraid, menace, persecute, scare, terrify, terrorize, threaten.

intolerable adjective
intolerable pain. excruciating, impossible, insufferable, insupportable, unbearable, unendurable.
OPPOSITES: SEE **tolerable**.

intolerant adjective
intolerant of other people's views. bigoted, chauvinistic, dogmatic, illiberal, narrow-minded, opinionated, prejudiced, racialist, racist, sexist.
OPPOSITES: SEE **tolerant**.

intoxicated adjective
SEE **drunk**.

intricate adjective
intricate machinery. intricate negotiations. complex, complicated, convoluted, delicate, detailed, elaborate, [*informal*] fiddly, involved, sophisticated, tangled, tortuous.
OPPOSITES: SEE **simple**.

intrigue noun
a political intrigue. SEE **plot** noun.

intrigue verb
Science intrigues me. SEE **interest** verb.

intrinsic adjective
The brooch has little intrinsic value. basic, essential, fundamental, inborn, in-built, inherent, native, natural, proper, real.

introduce verb
1 *to introduce someone to a friend.* acquaint, make known, present.
2 *to introduce a radio programme.* announce, give an introduction to, lead into, preface.
3 *to introduce something new.* add, SEE **begin**, bring in, bring out, broach, create, establish, initiate, offer, pioneer, set up, start.

introduction noun
1 *an introduction to a book or song.* foreword, [*informal*] intro, introductory part [SEE **introductory**], [*informal*] lead-in, opening, overture, preamble, preface, prelude, prologue.
2 *the introduction of a new bus service.* SEE **beginning**.

introductory adjective
an introductory offer. introductory chapters of a book. early, first, inaugural, initial, opening, prefatory, preliminary, preparatory, starting.
OPPOSITES: SEE **final**.

introverted adjective
an introverted character. contemplative, introspective, inward-looking, meditative, pensive, quiet, reserved, retiring, self-contained, shy, thoughtful, unsociable, withdrawn.
OPPOSITES: SEE **extroverted**.

intrude verb
to intrude on a private conversation. break in, butt in, eavesdrop, encroach, gatecrash, interfere, interrupt, intervene, join uninvited.

intruder noun
1 *intruders at a party.* eavesdropper, gatecrasher, infiltrator, interloper, snooper, [*informal*] uninvited guest.
2 *an intruder on your property.* burglar, housebreaker, invader, prowler, raider, robber, thief, trespasser.

intuitive adjective
SEE **instinctive**.

invade verb
to invade enemy territory. SEE **attack** verb, descend on, encroach on, enter, impinge on, infest, infringe, march into, occupy, overrun, penetrate, raid, subdue, violate.

invalid adjective
1 *an invalid passport.* false, null and void, out-of-date, unacceptable, unusable, void, worthless.
2 *an invalid argument.* fallacious, illogical, incorrect, irrational, unconvincing, unfounded, unreasonable, unscientific, unsound, untrue.
OPPOSITES: SEE **valid**.

invaluable adjective
[Note: *invaluable* is NOT the opposite of *valuable*.] *Your help was invaluable.* incalculable, inestimable, precious, priceless, useful, SEE **valuable**.
OPPOSITES: SEE **worthless**.

invariable adjective
an invariable rule. certain, constant, eternal, even, immutable, inflexible, permanent, predictable, reliable, rigid, solid, stable, steady, unalterable, unchangeable, unchanging, unvarying.
OPPOSITES: SEE **variable**.

invasion noun
1 *an invasion by an enemy.* SEE **attack** noun, encroachment, incursion, inroad, onslaught, raid, violation.

2 *an invasion of ants.* colony, flood, horde, infestation, spate, stream, swarm, throng.

invent verb
to invent something new. be the inventor of [SEE **inventor**], coin [= *to invent a new word*], conceive, concoct, construct, contrive, [*informal*] cook up, create, design, devise, discover, [*informal*] dream up, fabricate, imagine, improvise, make up, originate, plan, put together, think up, trump up (*to trump up charges against someone*).

invention noun
1 *The system is my own invention.* brainchild, coinage, contrivance, creation, design, discovery, figment (*of the imagination*).
2 *She let us see her new invention.* contraption, device, gadget.
3 *His work is full of lively invention.* creativity, genius, imagination, ingenuity, inspiration, inventiveness, originality.
4 *Her story was pure invention.* deceit, fabrication, fantasy, fiction, lies.

inventive adjective
an inventive mind. inventive work. creative, enterprising, fertile, imaginative, ingenious, innovative, inspired, original, resourceful.
OPPOSITES: SEE **imitative**.

inventor noun
the inventor of something new. architect, author, [*informal*] boffin, creator, designer, discoverer, maker, originator.

invert verb
capsize, overturn, reverse, turn upside down, upset.

invest verb
to invest money. buy stocks and shares, put to work, save, use profitably.
to invest in SEE **buy**.

investigate verb
to investigate a crime or a problem. consider, examine, explore, follow up, gather evidence about, [*informal*] go into, inquire into, look into, probe, research, scrutinize, study, [*informal*] suss out.

investigation noun
an investigation into a crime or problem. enquiry, examination, inquiry, inquisition, inspection, [*informal*] post-mortem, [*informal*] probe, research, scrutiny, study, survey.

invigorating adjective
an invigorating cold shower. bracing, enlivening, exhilarating, fresh, health-giving, healthy, refreshing, rejuvenating, revitalizing, stimulating.
OPPOSITES: SEE **boring, tiring**.

invincible adjective
an invincible army. indestructible, indomitable, invulnerable, strong, unbeatable, unconquerable.
OPPOSITES: SEE **vulnerable, weak**.

invisible adjective
an invisible repair. concealed, covered, disguised, hidden, imperceptible, inconspicuous, obscured, out of sight, secret, undetectable, unnoticeable, unnoticed, unseen.
OPPOSITES: SEE **visible**.

invite verb
1 *We invite you to join in.* ask, encourage, request, summon, urge.
2 *Shops want to invite our custom.* attract, entice, solicit, tempt.

invoke verb
to invoke someone's help. appeal to, call for, cry out for, entreat, implore, pray for, solicit, supplicate.

involuntary adjective
Blinking is an involuntary movement. automatic, conditioned, impulsive, instinctive, reflex, spontaneous, unconscious, unintentional, unthinking.
OPPOSITES: SEE **deliberate** adjective.

involve verb
1 *What does your job involve?* comprise, contain, embrace, entail, hold, include, incorporate, take in.
2 *Conserving resources involves us all.* affect, concern, interest, touch.
3 *Don't involve me in your dubious activities!* embroil, implicate, include, incriminate, inculpate, mix up.

involved adjective
1 *an involved problem.* complex, complicated, confusing, convoluted, difficult, elaborate, intricate, [*informal*] knotty, tangled.
OPPOSITES: SEE **simple**.
2 *involved in your work.* active, busy, caught up, committed, concerned, dedicated, employed, keen, occupied.
OPPOSITES: SEE **apathetic**.

invulnerable adjective
The dangerous drivers are those who think they're invulnerable. indestructible, SEE **invincible**, protected, safe, secure, unwoundable.
OPPOSITES: SEE **vulnerable**.

ironic adjective
I was being ironic when I said their dreadful play was brilliant. derisive, double-edged, ironical, mocking, sarcastic, satirical, wry.

irony noun
I don't think they saw the irony in my comments. double meaning, hidden meaning, sarcasm, satire.

irrational adjective
irrational behaviour. irrational argument.
absurd, arbitrary, biased, crazy, emotional,
emotive, illogical, insane, mad, nonsensical,
prejudiced, senseless, SEE **silly**, subjective,
unintelligent, unreasonable, unreasoning,
unsound, unthinking, wild.
OPPOSITES: SEE **rational**.

irregular adjective
1 *irregular intervals. an irregular rhythm.*
erratic, fitful, fluctuating, haphazard,
intermittent, occasional, random,
spasmodic, sporadic, unequal,
unpredictable, unpunctual, variable,
varying, wavering.
2 *irregular behaviour. an irregular
procedure.* abnormal, anomalous, eccentric,
exceptional, extraordinary, illegal,
improper, odd, peculiar, quirky,
unconventional, unofficial, unplanned,
unscheduled, unusual.
3 *an irregular surface.* broken, bumpy,
jagged, lumpy, patchy, pitted, ragged, rough,
uneven, up and down.
OPPOSITES: SEE **regular**.

irrelevant adjective
Omit irrelevant details. extraneous,
immaterial, inapplicable, inappropriate,
inessential, pointless, unconnected,
unnecessary, unrelated.
OPPOSITES: SEE **relevant**.

irreligious adjective
*If you don't go to church, you aren't
necessarily irreligious.* agnostic, atheistic,
godless, heathen, humanist, impious,
irreverent, pagan, ungodly, unrighteous,
wicked.
OPPOSITES: SEE **religious**.

irrepressible adjective
irrepressible high spirits. boisterous,
bouncy, ebullient, SEE **lively**, resilient,
uncontrollable, ungovernable, uninhibited,
unstoppable, vigorous.

irresistible adjective
an irresistible temptation. compelling,
inescapable, inexorable, not to be denied,
overpowering, overwhelming, persuasive,
SEE **powerful**, seductive, unavoidable.

irresolute adjective
irresolute about what to choose. doubtful,
fickle, flexible, [*informal*] hedging your
bets, SEE **hesitant**, indecisive, open to
compromise, tentative, undecided,
vacillating, wavering, weak, weak-willed.
OPPOSITES: SEE **resolute**.

irresponsible adjective
irresponsible driving. careless,
conscienceless, feckless, immature,
immoral, inconsiderate, negligent, rash,
reckless, selfish, shiftless, thoughtless,

unethical, unreliable, unthinking,
untrustworthy.
OPPOSITES: SEE **responsible**.

irreverent adjective
irreverent behaviour in church.
blasphemous, disrespectful, impious,
profane, SEE **rude**, sacrilegious.
OPPOSITES: SEE **reverent**.

irrevocable adjective
an irrevocable decision. binding, final, fixed,
hard and fast, immutable, irreversible,
settled, unalterable, unchangeable.

irritable adjective
an irritable mood. an irritable person. SEE
angry, bad-tempered, cantankerous,
choleric, cross, crotchety, dyspeptic, easily
annoyed, edgy, fractious, grumpy, ill-
tempered, impatient, irascible,
oversensitive, peevish, pettish, petulant,
[*informal*] prickly, querulous, [*informal*]
ratty, short-tempered, snappy, testy, tetchy,
touchy, waspish.
OPPOSITES: SEE **even-tempered**.

irritate verb
1 *Rudeness irritates me.* SEE **annoy**.
2 *These spots irritate.* cause irritation, itch,
tickle, tingle.

island noun
atoll, coral reef, isle, islet.
RELATED ADJECTIVE: insular.
group of islands archipelago.

isolate verb
1 *The police isolated the trouble-makers.*
cordon off, cut off, keep apart, segregate,
separate, single out.
2 *The hospital isolated the infectious patients.*
place apart, quarantine, set apart.

isolated adjective
1 *an isolated farmhouse.* deserted, desolate,
[*informal*] godforsaken, inaccessible,
lonely, [*informal*] off the beaten track,
outlying, out of the way, private, remote,
secluded, sequestered, solitary,
unfrequented.
OPPOSITES: SEE **accessible**.
2 *an isolated case of cheating.* abnormal,
exceptional, single, uncommon, unique,
untypical, unusual.
OPPOSITES: SEE **common** adjective.

issue noun
1 *political issues.* affair, argument,
controversy, dispute, matter, point,
problem, question, subject, topic.
2 *an issue of a magazine.* copy, edition,
instalment, number, printing, publication.
3 *We awaited the issue of the election.*
consequence, effect, end, impact, outcome,
repercussions, result, upshot.

issue verb
1 *Smoke issued from the chimney.* appear, come out, emerge, erupt, flow out, gush, leak, rise, spring.
2 *He issued a formal statement.* bring out, circulate, distribute, give out, print, produce, promulgate, publicize, publish, put out, release, send out, supply.

itch noun
1 *an itch in my foot.* irritation, need to scratch, tickle, tingling.
2 *an itch to do something.* ache, desire, hankering, impatience, impulse, longing, lust, need, restlessness, urge, wish, yearning, [*informal*] yen.

item noun
1 *items in a sale. an item on a list.* article, bit, component, contribution, entry, ingredient, lot (*in an auction*), object, single thing, thing.
2 *an item in a newspaper.* account, article, feature, piece, report.

Jj

jab verb
to jab someone in the ribs. elbow, SEE **hit** verb, nudge, poke, prod, stab, thrust.

jacket noun
1 OTHER COATS: SEE **coat** noun.
2 *a jacket for a book, an insulating jacket.* casing, coat, cover, covering, envelope, folder, sheath, skin, wrapper, wrapping.

jaded adjective
jaded by lack of success. bored, [*informal*] done in, exhausted, [*informal*] fagged, fatigued, [*informal*] fed up, listless, spent, tired out, weary.
OPPOSITES: SEE **lively**.

jagged adjective
a jagged edge. angular, barbed, broken, indented, irregular, ragged, rough, serrated, sharp, snagged, spiky, toothed, uneven, zigzag.
OPPOSITES: SEE **even** adjective.

jail SEE **gaol**.

jam noun
1 *a jam on the motorway.* blockage, bottleneck, crowd, crush, press, squeeze, throng, traffic jam.
2 *Help me out of a jam!* difficulty, dilemma, embarrassment, [*informal*] fix, [*informal*] hole, [*informal*] hot water, plight, predicament, quandary, tight corner, trouble.
3 *bread and jam.* conserve, jelly, marmalade, preserve.

jam verb
1 *They jammed us into a minibus.* cram, crowd, crush, pack, ram, squash, squeeze, stuff.
2 *Cars jammed the street.* block, [*informal*] bung up, congest, fill, obstruct, overcrowd, stop up.
3 *Jam the door open.* prop, stick, wedge.

jangle verb
VARIOUS SOUNDS: SEE **sound** noun.

jar noun
a glass jar. carafe, SEE **container**, crock, flagon, glass, jug, mug, pitcher, pot, urn, vessel.

jargon noun
I can't understand the technical jargon. cant, dialect, idiom, language, slang.

jarring adjective
a jarring noise. annoying, disagreeable, discordant, grating, grinding, harsh, [*informal*] jangling, raucous, unpleasant.

jaunt noun
to go on a pleasure jaunt. excursion, expedition, SEE **journey** noun, outing, tour, trip.

jaunty adjective
a jaunty tune, alert, breezy, bright, carefree, [*informal*] cheeky, debonair, frisky, lively, perky, sprightly.

jazzy adjective
1 *jazzy music.* animated, lively, rhythmic, spirited, swinging, syncopated, vivacious.
2 *jazzy colours.* bold, clashing, contrasting, flashy, gaudy, loud.

jealous adjective
1 *He's jealous because I won.* bitter, covetous, envious, [*informal*] green-eyed, grudging, jaundiced, resentful.
2 *He's jealous of his reputation.* careful, possessive, protective, vigilant, watchful.

jeer verb
to jeer at *It's unkind to jeer at the losers.* barrack, boo, disapprove of, hiss, gibe at, heckle, [*informal*] knock, laugh at, make fun of, mock, ridicule, scoff at, sneer at, taunt.
OPPOSITES: SEE **cheer** verb.

jeopardize verb SEE **endanger**.

jerk verb
Jerk the rope when you are ready. jog, jolt, move suddenly, pluck, pull, tug, tweak, twist, twitch, wrench, [*informal*] yank.

jerky adjective
jerky movements. bouncy, bumpy, convulsive, erratic, fitful, jolting, jumpy, rough, shaky, spasmodic, [*informal*] stopping and starting, twitchy, uncontrolled, uneven.
OPPOSITES: SEE **steady** adjective.

jest noun, verb SEE **joke** noun, verb.

jester noun
the king's jester. buffoon, clown, comedian, comic, SEE **entertainer**, fool, joker.

jet noun
a jet of water. flow, fountain, gush, rush, spout, spray, spurt, squirt, stream.

jetty noun
A boat tied up at the jetty. breakwater, groyne, landing-stage, mole, pier, quay, wharf.

jewel noun
gem, gemstone, precious stone.
VARIOUS JEWELS: SEE **jewellery**.

jewellery noun
gems, jewels, ornaments, [*informal*] sparklers, treasure.

ITEMS OF JEWELLERY: bangle, beads, bracelet, brooch, chain, charm, clasp, cufflinks, ear-ring, locket, necklace, pendant, pin, ring, signet-ring, tie-pin, watch-chain.

JEWELS AND JEWELLERY STONES: amber, cairngorm, carnelian or cornelian, coral, diamond, emerald, garnet, ivory, jade, jasper, jet, lapis lazuli, moonstone, onyx, opal, pearl, rhinestone, ruby, sapphire, topaz, turquoise.

METALS USED TO MAKE JEWELLERY: gold, platinum, silver.

---

jingle verb
coins jingling in his pocket. chink, clink, jangle, ring, tinkle.

job noun
1 *a well-paid job.* business, calling, career, employment, livelihood, occupation, position, post, profession, sinecure, trade, vocation, work.
2 *jobs in the house.* activity, assignment, chore, duty, errand, function, housework, pursuit, responsibility, role, stint, task, work.

SOME JOBS PEOPLE DO: accountant, actuary, air hostess, architect, SEE **artist**, astronaut, astronomer, banker, barber, barmaid or barman, barrister, beautician, blacksmith, bookmaker, bookseller, brewer, bricklayer, broadcaster, builder,

butler, cameraman, caretaker, carpenter, cashier, caterer, chauffeur, chef, chimney-sweep, cleaner, clergyman, clerk, coastguard, cobbler, commentator, composer, compositor, conductor, constable, cook, courier, croupier, curator.

decorator, dentist, designer, detective, dietician, diver, driver, docker, doctor, draughtsman, dressmaker, dustman, editor, electrician, engineer, SEE **entertainer**, estate agent, executive, farmer, farrier, fireman, fitter, forester, frogman, gamekeeper, gardener, glazier, groom, groundsman, gunsmith, hairdresser, handyman, hotelier, industrialist, interpreter, joiner, journalist.

labourer, lawyer, lecturer, lexicographer, librarian, lifeguard, lighterman, linguist, locksmith, longshoreman, lumberjack, machinist, manicurist, mannequin, manufacturer, mason, [*male*] masseur, [*female*] masseuse, mechanic, metallurgist, midwife, milkman, miller, milliner, miner, model, musician [SEE **music**], naturalist, night-watchman, nurse, nurseryman.

office worker, optician, parson, pathologist, pharmacist, photographer, platelayer, physiotherapist, pilot, plasterer, ploughman, plumber, policeman, politician, porter, postman, postmaster, postmistress, printer, probation officer, professor, programmer, projectionist, psychiatrist, psychologist, publisher, radiographer, radiologist, railwayman, receptionist, reporter.

saddler, sailor, salesperson, SEE **scientist**, secretary, shepherd, shoemaker, SEE **shopkeeper**, signalman, social worker, soldier, solicitor, stableman, steeplejack, stevedore, steward, stewardess, stockbroker, stoker, stonemason, stunt man, surgeon, surveyor, tailor, taxidermist, teacher, technician, telephonist, teller, test-pilot, traffic warden, translator, treasurer, typist, undertaker, [*male*] usher, [*female*] usherette, vet, [*male*] waiter, [*female*] waitress, warehouseman, woodman.

---

jog verb
1 *to jog someone's elbow.* SEE **hit** verb, jar, jerk, jolt, knock, nudge.
2 *to jog someone's memory.* prompt, refresh, remind, set off, stimulate, stir.
3 *to jog round the park.* exercise, run, trot.

join verb
1 *to join things together.* add, amalgamate, attach, combine, connect, couple, dock, dovetail, SEE **fasten**, fit, fix, knit, link, marry, merge, put together, splice, tack on, unite, yoke.
2 *Two rivers join here.* come together, converge, meet.

OPPOSITES: SEE **separate** verb.
3 *to join a crowd.* follow, go with, [*informal*]
latch on to, tag along with.
4 *to join a youth club.* affiliate with, become
a member of, enlist in, enrol in, participate
in, register for, sign up for, volunteer for.
OPPOSITES: SEE **leave** verb.

joint adjective
a joint effort. collective, combined, common,
communal, concerted, co-operative,
general, mutual, shared, united.
OPPOSITES: SEE **individual** adjective.

joint noun

JOINTS IN YOUR BODY: ankle, elbow, hip,
knee, knuckle, shoulder, vertebra, wrist.

joke noun
an amusing joke. [*informal*] crack, funny
story, [*informal*] gag, [*old-fashioned*] jape,
jest, pleasantry, pun, quip, wisecrack,
witticism.

joke verb
be facetious, clown, jest, have a laugh, make
jokes [SEE **joke** noun].

jolly adjective SEE **joyful, merry**.

jolt verb
1 *The car jolted over the rough track.* bounce,
bump, jar, jerk, jog, shake, twitch.
2 *The noise jolted us into action.* astonish,
disturb, nonplus, shock, startle, surprise.

jostle verb
The crowd jostled us. crowd in on, hustle,
press, push, shove.

journal noun
1 *a trade journal.* gazette, magazine,
monthly, newspaper, paper, periodical,
publication, weekly.
2 *the journal of a voyage.* account, chronicle,
diary, log, record.

journalist noun
a newspaper journalist. columnist,
contributor, correspondent, reporter,
writer.

journey noun
itinerary, peregrination, route, travels,
trip.

KINDS OF JOURNEY: crossing (*sea crossing*),
cruise, drive, excursion, expedition, flight,
hike, jaunt, joy-ride, mission, odyssey,
outing, passage (*a sea passage*), pilgrimage,
ramble, ride, run, safari, sail, tour, trek,
voyage, walk, wanderings.
SEE ALSO: **travel** noun.

jovial adjective SEE **joyful**.

joy noun
bliss, cheerfulness, delight, ecstasy, elation,
euphoria, exaltation, exultation, felicity,
gaiety, gladness, glee, happiness, hilarity,
joyfulness, jubilation, mirth, pleasure,
rapture, rejoicing, triumph.
OPPOSITES: SEE **sorrow** noun.

joyful adjective
a joyful occasion, a joyful welcome. cheerful,
delighted, ecstatic, elated, enraptured,
euphoric, exultant, gay, glad, gleeful, happy,
jocund, jolly, jovial, joyous, jubilant, merry,
overjoyed, pleased, rapturous, rejoicing,
triumphant.
OPPOSITES: SEE **sad**.

jubilee noun
anniversary, celebration, commemoration,
festival.

judge noun
1 *a judge at a sporting event.* adjudicator,
arbiter, arbitrator, referee, umpire.
2 *a judge in a lawcourt.* SEE **law**.
3 *a good judge of wines.* connoisseur, critic,
expert.

judge verb
1 *to judge someone in a lawcourt.* condemn,
convict, examine, pronounce judgement on
[SEE **judgement**], punish, sentence, try.
2 *The umpire judged that the ball was out.*
adjudicate, conclude, decide, decree, deem,
determine, pass judgement, rule.
3 *to judge others. to judge a work of art.*
appraise, assess, criticize, evaluate, give
your opinion of, rebuke, scold, sit in
judgement on.
4 *I judged that the eggs would be cooked.*
believe, consider, estimate, gauge, guess,
reckon, suppose.

judgement noun
1 *The court pronounced its judgement.*
arbitration, award, conclusion, conviction,
decision, decree, [*old-fashioned*] doom,
finding, outcome, penalty, punishment,
result, ruling, verdict.
2 *Use your judgement.* acumen, common
sense, discernment, discretion,
discrimination, expertise, good sense, SEE
intelligence, reason, wisdom.
3 *In my judgement, he was driving too fast.*
assessment, belief, estimation, evaluation,
idea, impression, mind, notion, opinion,
point of view, valuation.

judicial adjective
[Do not confuse with *judicious*.] *a judicial
decision.* legal, official.

judicious adjective
[Do not confuse with *judicial*.] *a judicious
change of policy.* appropriate, astute, SEE

clever, diplomatic, expedient, politic, prudent, sensible, shrewd, thoughtful, well judged, wise.

jug noun
carafe, SEE **container**, ewer, flagon, jar, pitcher, vessel.

juice noun
the juice of an orange. SEE **drink** noun, fluid, liquid, sap.

juicy adjective
juicy fruit. full of juice, lush, moist, soft, [*informal*] squelchy, succulent, wet.

jumble noun
a jumble of odds and ends. chaos, clutter, confusion, disorder, farrago, hotchpotch, mess, muddle.

jumble verb
Don't jumble the papers I've just sorted. confuse, disarrange, [*informal*] mess up, mix up, muddle, shuffle, tangle.
OPPOSITES: SEE **organize**.

jump noun
1 *a jump in the air.* bounce, bound, hop, leap, pounce, skip, spring, vault.
2 *The horse easily cleared the last jump.* ditch, fence, gap, gate, hurdle, obstacle.
3 *a jump in prices.* SEE **rise** noun.

jump verb
1 *to jump in the air.* bounce, bound, hop, leap, skip, spring.
2 *to jump a fence.* clear, hurdle, vault.
3 *to jump about.* caper, dance, frisk, frolic, gambol, prance.
4 *The cat jumped on the mouse.* SEE **attack** verb, pounce.
5 *I jumped the boring chapters.* SEE **omit**.
6 *The bang made me jump.* SEE **flinch**.

jumpy adjective
SEE **nervous**.

junction noun
a road junction. a junction between two routes. confluence (*of two rivers*), corner, crossroads, interchange, intersection, joining, meeting, T-junction.

junior adjective
junior rank. inferior, lesser, lower, minor, secondary, subordinate, subsidiary, younger.
OPPOSITES: SEE **senior**.

junk noun
a lot of old junk. clutter, debris, flotsam-and-jetsam, garbage, litter, lumber, oddments, odds and ends, refuse, rubbish, rummage, scrap, trash, waste.

just adjective
a just punishment. a just decision, apt, deserved, equitable, ethical, even-handed,

fair, fair-minded, honest, impartial, justified, lawful, legal, legitimate, merited, proper, reasonable, rightful, right-minded, unbiased, unprejudiced, upright.
OPPOSITES: SEE **unjust**.

justice noun
1 *Justice demands that women and men should be paid the same.* equity, fairness, honesty, impartiality, integrity, legality, right.
OPPOSITES: SEE **injustice**.
2 *Lawcourts exist to administer justice.* the law, legal proceedings, punishment, retribution, vengeance.

justifiable adjective
a justifiable course of action. acceptable, allowable, defensible, excusable, forgivable, justified, lawful, legitimate, pardonable, permissible, reasonable, understandable, warranted.
OPPOSITES: SEE **unjustifiable**.

justify verb
Don't try to justify his wickedness. condone, defend, [*informal*] exculpate, excuse, exonerate, explain, explain away, forgive, pardon, support, uphold, vindicate, warrant (*Nothing can warrant such cruelty*).

jut verb
The mantelpiece juts over the fireplace. extend, overhang, poke out, project, protrude, stick out.

juvenile adjective
1 [*uncomplimentary*] *juvenile behaviour.* babyish, childish, immature, infantile, puerile.
OPPOSITES: SEE **mature**.
2 *juvenile novels.* adolescent, young, youthful.

Kk

keen adjective
1 *a keen cutting-edge.* piercing, pointed, razor-sharp, sharp, sharpened.
OPPOSITES: SEE **blunt** adjective.
2 *a keen wit.* biting, cutting, incisive, lively, mordant, satirical, scathing, shrewd, sophisticated.
OPPOSITES: SEE **dull** adjective.
3 *keen eyesight.* acute, clear, perceptive, sensitive.
OPPOSITES: SEE **dim** adjective.
4 *a keen wind.* bitter, cold, extreme, icy, intense, penetrating, severe.

OPPOSITES: SEE **mild.**

5 *keen prices.* competitive, low, rockbottom.
OPPOSITES: SEE **exorbitant.**

6 *a keen pupil.* ambitious, anxious, assiduous, avid, bright, clever, committed, diligent, eager, enthusiastic, fervent, industrious, intelligent, intent, interested, motivated, quick, zealous.
OPPOSITES: SEE **apathetic.**

keep verb

1 *to keep something safe. to keep it for later.* conserve, guard, hang on to, hold, preserve, protect, put aside, put away, retain, safeguard, save, store, stow away, withhold.
OPPOSITES: SEE **lose, use** verb.

2 *to keep looking for something.* carry on, continue, do again and again, do for a long time, keep on, persevere in, persist in.
OPPOSITES: SEE **cease.**

3 *to keep a pet. to keep a shop.* be responsible for, care for, cherish, foster, guard, have, have charge of, look after, manage, mind, own, tend, watch over.

4 *to keep a family.* feed, maintain, pay for, provide for, support.

5 *to keep your birthday.* celebrate, commemorate, mark, observe, [*formal*] solemnize.

6 *How long does milk keep?* be preserved, be usable, last, stay good.

7 *I won't keep you.* block, check, curb, delay, detain, deter, get in the way of, hamper, hinder, hold up, impede, obstruct, prevent, restrain, retard.

to keep to *Keep to the rules!* abide by, adhere to, be ruled by, conform to, honour, obey, recognize, submit to.

keeper noun

the keeper of a museum. curator, custodian, gaoler, guard, guardian, warden, warder.

key noun

1 *the key to a problem.* answer, clue, indicator, pointer, secret, solution.

2 *a key to a map.* explanation, glossary, guide, index.

keyboard noun

KEYBOARD INSTRUMENTS: accordion, celesta, clavichord, clavier, harmonium, harpsichord, organ, piano, spinet, virginals.

kick verb

1 *to kick a ball.* boot, heel, SEE **hit** verb, punt.

2 [*informal*] *to kick a habit.* SEE **cease.**

kidnap verb

abduct, carry off, run away with, seize, snatch.

kill verb

annihilate, assassinate, be guilty of the killing of [SEE **killing** noun], be the killer of [SEE **killer**], [*informal*] bump off, butcher, cull [= *kill animals selectively*], decimate [see note under *decimate*], destroy, [*informal*] dispatch, [*informal*] do away with, execute, exterminate, [*informal*] finish off, [*informal*] knock off, liquidate, martyr, massacre, murder, put down, put to death, slaughter, slay, take life.

WAYS TO KILL: behead, brain, choke, crucify, decapitate, disembowel, drown, electrocute, eviscerate, garrotte, gas, guillotine, hang, knife, lynch, poison, pole-axe, shoot, smother, stab, starve, stifle, stone, strangle, suffocate, throttle.

killer noun

assassin, butcher, cut-throat, destroyer, executioner, exterminator, gunman, murderer, slayer.

killing noun

annihilation, assassination, bloodshed, butchery, carnage, decimation [see note under *decimate*], destruction, elimination, eradication, euthanasia, execution, extermination, extinction, fratricide, genocide, homicide, infanticide, liquidation, manslaughter, martyrdom, massacre, matricide, murder, parricide, patricide, pogrom, regicide, slaughter, suicide.

kind adjective

a kind action. a kind person. a kind remark. accommodating, affectionate, agreeable, altruistic, amenable, amiable, attentive, avuncular, beneficent, benevolent, benign, bountiful, brotherly, caring, charitable, comforting, compassionate, considerate, cordial, courteous, encouraging, fatherly, favourable, friendly, generous, genial, gentle, good-natured, good-tempered, gracious, helpful, hospitable, humane, indulgent, kind-hearted, kindly, lenient, loving, merciful, mild, motherly, neighbourly, nice, obliging, patient, philanthropic, pleasant, polite, public-spirited, sensitive, sisterly, soft-hearted, sweet, sympathetic, tactful, tender, thoughtful, understanding, unselfish, warm-hearted, well-intentioned, well-meaning, well-meant.
OPPOSITES: SEE **unkind.**

kind noun

a kind of dog. a kind of food. a kind of book. brand, breed, category, class, description, family, form, genre, genus, make, nature, race, set, sort, species, style, type, variety.

kindle verb
1 *to kindle a fire.* burn, fire, ignite, light, set fire to.
2 *to kindle strong emotions.* SEE **arouse**.

kink noun
a kink in a rope. bend, coil, knot, loop, tangle, twist.

kiosk noun
1 *a newspaper kiosk.* bookstall, booth, newsstand, stall.
2 *a telephone kiosk.* telephone box.

kit noun
games kit. a wine-making kit. a soldier's kit. apparatus, baggage, effects, equipment, gear, [*informal*] impedimenta, luggage, outfit, paraphernalia, rig, tackle, tools.

kitchen noun.

SOME KITCHEN EQUIPMENT: blender, cooker, SEE **crockery**, SEE **cutlery**, deep-freeze, dish rack, dishwasher, draining-board, extractor-fan, food-processor, freezer, fridge, grill, kettle, liquidizer, microwave-oven, mincer, mixer, oven, pantry, percolator, range, refrigerator, scales, sink, stove, thermos, toaster, tray, vacuum flask.

COOKING UTENSILS: SEE **cook**.

knack noun
a knack for making friends. a knack for mending machines. ability, adroitness, art, bent, dexterity, expertise, flair, genius, gift, skill, talent, trick.

knapsack noun
backpack, haversack, rucksack.

knead verb
to knead dough. manipulate, massage, pound, press, pummel, squeeze, work.

kneel verb
bend, bow, crouch, fall to your knees, genuflect, stoop.

knickers noun
[*old-fashioned*] bloomers, boxer-shorts, briefs, drawers, panties, pants, shorts, trunks, underpants.

knife noun

KINDS OF KNIFE: butter-knife, carving-knife, clasp-knife, cleaver, dagger, flick-knife, machete, penknife, pocket-knife, scalpel, sheathknife.

knife verb
to knife someone. SEE **kill**, slash, stab, wound.

knit verb
1 *to knit a pullover.* crochet, weave.
2 *to knit together.* bind, combine, connect, fasten, interweave, knot, mend, tie, unite.

knob noun
1 *a door knob.* handle.
2 boss, bulge, bump, lump, projection, protuberance, swelling.

knock verb
to knock against something. [*informal*] bash, buffet, bump, SEE **hit** verb, rap, smack, [*old-fashioned*] smite, strike, tap, thump.

knot noun
1 *a knot in a rope.*

VARIOUS KNOTS: bow, bowline, clovehitch, grannyknot, hitch, noose, reef-knot, sheephank, slipknot.

2 *a knot of people.* SEE **group** noun.

knot verb
to knot ropes together. bind, do up (*do up your shoelace*), entangle, entwine, SEE **fasten**, join, knit, lash, link, tie, untie.
OPPOSITES: SEE **untie**.

know verb
1 *to know facts. to know how to do something.* comprehend, have experience of, have in mind, remember, understand.
2 *to know that you are right.* be certain, have confidence.
3 *to know what something is. to know who someone is.* discern, distinguish, identify, make out, perceive, realize, recognize, see.
4 *to know a person.* be acquainted with, be familiar with, be a friend of.

knowing adjective
Her knowing smile showed that she understood. artful, astute, aware, clever, crafty, cunning, discerning, experienced, expressive, intelligent, meaningful, perceptive, shrewd, sly, well-informed, wily.
OPPOSITES: SEE **naïve**.

knowledge noun
1 *An encyclopaedia contains a lot of knowledge.* data, facts, information, learning, scholarship, science.
2 *She's got enough knowledge to do the job.* ability, awareness, background, competence, education, experience, familiarity, grasp, [*informal*] know-how, learning, lore, skill, talent, technique, training, understanding, wisdom.
OPPOSITES: SEE **ignorance**.

knowledgeable adjective
knowledgeable about antiques. aware,
conversant, educated, erudite, experienced,
familiar (with), informed, learned,
scholarly, versed (in), well-informed.
OPPOSITES: SEE **ignorant**.

Ll

label noun
a label on a parcel. docket, marker, sticker,
tag, ticket.

label verb
We labelled him as a troublemaker. brand,
call, categorize, class, classify, define,
describe, identify, mark, name, stamp.

laborious adjective
a laborious climb. laborious effort. arduous,
back-breaking, difficult, exhausting,
fatiguing, gruelling, hard, heavy, onerous,
stiff, strenuous, tiresome, tough, uphill,
wearisome.
OPPOSITES: SEE **easy**.

labour noun
1 *You deserve a reward for your labour.*
[*informal*] donkey-work, drudgery, effort,
exertion, industry, [*informal*] pains, toil,
SEE **work** noun.
2 *Because of increased orders, the firm took
on extra labour.* employees, [*old-fashioned*]
hands, workers, workforce.
3 [= *giving birth to a baby*] childbirth,
contractions, delivery, labour pains, [*old-
fashioned*] travail.

labour verb
drudge, exert yourself, [*informal*] slave
away, [*informal*] sweat, toil, SEE **work** verb,
work hard.

labyrinth noun
a labyrinth of corridors. complex, jungle,
maze, network, tangle.

lace noun
1 *lace curtains.* filigree, net, tatting.
2 *a lace for your shoe.* cord, string, thong.

lack noun
a lack of food. a lack of self-confidence.
absence, dearth, deprivation, famine, need,
paucity, privation, scarcity, shortage, want.
OPPOSITES: SEE **plenty**.

lack verb
The game lacked excitement. be deficient in,
be short of, be without, miss, need, require,
want.

lacking adjective
lacking in courage. defective, deficient,
inadequate, short, unsatisfactory, wanting,
weak.

ladder noun
fire-escape, step-ladder, steps.

laden adjective
laden with shopping. burdened, fraught, full,
hampered, loaded, oppressed, weighed
down.

lady noun
SEE **woman**.

ladylike adjective
ladylike behaviour. dainty, genteel, modest,
SEE **polite**, posh, prim and proper,
[*uncomplimentary*] prissy, refined,
respectable, well-bred.

lag verb
1 *to lag behind.* [*informal*] bring up the rear,
come last, dally, dawdle, drop behind, fall
behind, go too slow, hang about, idle, linger,
loiter, saunter, straggle, trail.
2 *to lag water-pipes.* insulate, wrap up.

laid-back adjective
SEE **easygoing**.

lair noun
an animal's lair. den, hide-out, hiding-place,
refuge, retreat, shelter.

lake noun
boating-lake, lagoon, lido, (*Scottish*) loch,
mere, pond, pool, reservoir, sea, tarn,
water.

lame adjective
1 *a lame person.* crippled, disabled, SEE
handicapped, incapacitated, maimed.
2 *a lame leg.* dragging, game (*a game leg*),
[*informal*] gammy, injured, limping, stiff.
3 *a lame excuse.* feeble, flimsy, inadequate,
poor, tame, thin, unconvincing, weak.

lame verb
The accident temporarily lamed him. cripple,
disable, incapacitate, make limp [SEE **limp**
verb], maim.

lament noun
a lament for the dead. dirge, elegy,
lamentation, monody, requiem,
threnody.

lament verb
*to lament the passing of someone or
something.* bemoan, bewail, complain about,
deplore, express your sorrow about, grieve
about, mourn, regret, shed tears for, wail,
weep.

lamentable adjective
SEE **regrettable**.

lamp noun
SEE **light** noun.

land noun
1 *Surveyors mapped out the lie of the land.*
geography, landscape, terrain, topography.
2 *your native land.* country, nation, region,
state, territory.
3 *land to grow things on.* farmland, earth,
ground, soil.
4 *land belonging to a person.* estate, grounds,
property.
5 *The sailors came to land.* coast, landfall,
shore, [*joking*] terra firma.

land verb
to land from an aircraft, ship, or vehicle.
alight, arrive, berth, come ashore,
disembark, dock, end a journey, get down,
reach landfall, touch down.

landing noun
1 *the landing of an aircraft or spacecraft.* re-
entry, return, touchdown.
2 *the landing of passengers.* SEE **arrival**,
disembarkation.

landlady, **landlord** nouns
1 *the landlady or landlord of a pub.* hotelier,
[*old-fashioned*] innkeeper, licensee,
publican.
2 *the landlady or landlord of rented property.*
landowner, letter, owner, proprietor.

landmark noun
1 *a landmark in the countryside.* feature,
high point, visible feature.
2 *a landmark in history.* milestone, new era,
turning point.

landscape noun
a painting of a landscape. countryside,
outlook, panorama, prospect, rural scene,
scene, scenery, view, vista.

language noun
1 *the language we speak. foreign languages.*
[*informal*] lingo, speech, tongue.
2 *language of particular people or of
particular situations.* argot, cant,
colloquialism, dialect, formal language,
idiolect, idiom, informal language, jargon,
journalese, lingua franca, patois, register,
slang, vernacular.

EVERYDAY LINGUISTIC TERMS: accent, active
verb or voice, adjective, adverb, clause,
conjunction, consonant, grammar,
indicative mood, noun, paragraph, passive
verb or voice, phrase, plural, predicate,
prefix, preposition, pronoun, SEE
punctuation, sentence, singular, subject,
subjunctive mood, suffix, syllable,
synonym, syntax, tense, verb, vocabulary,
vowel, word.

ASPECTS OF THE STUDY OF LANGUAGE:
etymology, lexicography, linguistics,
orthography, philology, phonetics,
psycholinguistics, semantics, semiotics,
sociolinguistics.

---

languid adjective
[*uncomplimentary*] *His languid manner
annoys me when there's work to be done.*
apathetic, [*informal*] droopy, feeble,
inactive, inert, lackadaisical, lazy,
lethargic, slow, sluggish, torpid,
unenthusiastic, weak.
OPPOSITES: SEE **energetic**.

languish verb
*He languished after his dog died. Our project
languished during the holidays.* become
languid [SEE **languid**], decline, flag, lose
momentum, mope, pine, slow down,
stagnate, suffer, sulk, waste away, weaken,
wither.
OPPOSITES: SEE **flourish** verb.

lank adjective
[*uncomplimentary*] *lank hair.* drooping,
lifeless, limp, long, straight, thin.

lanky adjective
[*uncomplimentary*] *a lanky figure.* angular,
awkward, bony, gangling, gaunt, lank, lean,
long, scraggy, scrawny, skinny, tall, thin,
ungraceful, weedy.
OPPOSITES: SEE **graceful**, **sturdy**.

lap noun
1 *Sit on my lap.* knees, thighs.
2 *a lap of a racetrack.* circle, circuit, course,
orbit.

lapse noun
1 *a lapse of memory. a lapse in behaviour.*
backsliding, error, fault, flaw, mistake,
relapse, shortcoming, slip, temporary
failure, weakness.
2 *a lapse in a training programme.* break,
gap, interruption, interval, lull, pause.

lapse verb
1 *to lapse from your normal standard of work.*
decline, deteriorate, drop, fall, slide, slip.
2 *My membership has lapsed.* become invalid
[SEE **invalid** adjective], expire, finish, run
out, stop.

large adjective
[The meaning of *large* is relative. You can
speak of *a large ant* and *a small elephant*,
but you are not really confused about which
is larger in size! The words listed here are
just some of the many words which can
mean *larger than average for its kind*.]
above average, abundant, ample, big, bold

(*bold handwriting*), broad, bulky, capacious, colossal, commodious, considerable, copious, elephantine, enormous, extensive, [*informal*] fat (*a fat increase*), formidable, gargantuan, generous, giant, gigantic, grand, great, heavy, hefty, high, huge, [*informal*] hulking, immeasurable, immense, impressive, incalculable, infinite, [*informal*] jumbo, [*informal*] kingsized, large, largish, lofty, long, mammoth, massive, mighty, [*informal*] monstrous, monumental, mountainous, outsize, overgrown, oversized, prodigious, [*informal*] roomy, sizeable, spacious, substantial, swingeing (*a swingeing increase*), tall, thick, [*informal*] thumping, [*informal*] tidy (*a tidy sum*), titanic, towering, tremendous, vast, voluminous, weighty, [*informal*] whacking, [*informal*] whopping, wide.
OPPOSITES: SEE **small**.

lash noun SEE **whip** noun.

last adjective
1 *last in the queue.* furthest, hindmost.
OPPOSITES: SEE **first**.
2 *Z is the last letter of the alphabet.* closing, concluding, final, terminal, terminating, ultimate.
OPPOSITES: SEE **initial**.
3 *What was his last record called?* latest, most recent, previous.
OPPOSITES: SEE **next**.

last verb
I hope the fine weather lasts. carry on, continue, endure, hold, hold out, keep on, linger, live, persist, remain, stay, survive, wear (*These jeans have worn well*).

lasting adjective
a lasting friendship. abiding, continuing, durable, enduring, indestructible, indissoluble, lifelong, long-lasting, long-lived, long-standing, permanent, stable, unchanging, undying, unending.
OPPOSITES: SEE **temporary**.

late adjective
1 *The bus is late.* behind-hand, belated, delayed, dilatory, overdue, slow, tardy, unpunctual.
OPPOSITES: SEE **early**.
2 *the late king.* dead, deceased, departed, former.

lately adverb
latterly, recently.

latent adjective
latent talent. dormant, hidden, invisible, potential, undeveloped, undiscovered.

lather noun
soapy lather. bubbles, foam, froth, suds.

latter adjective
The latter part of the speech became tedious. closing, concluding, last, later, recent, second.
OPPOSITES: SEE **former**.

laudable adjective
SEE **praiseworthy**.

laugh verb

WAYS TO EXPRESS AMUSEMENT: beam, burst into laughter [SEE **laughter**], chortle, chuckle, giggle, grin, guffaw, simper, smile, smirk, sneer, snigger, titter.

to laugh at SEE **ridicule** verb.

laughable adjective
The play was a tragedy, but the acting was laughable. absurd, derisory, SEE **funny**, ludicrous, preposterous, ridiculous.

laughing-stock noun
His eccentric ways made him a laughing-stock. butt, figure of fun, victim.

laughter noun
Their performance caused a lot of laughter. chuckling, giggling, guffaws, hilarity, [*informal*] hysterics, laughing, laughs, merriment, mirth, sniggering, tittering.

launch verb
1 *to launch a ship.* float.
2 *to launch a rocket.* blast-off, fire, propel, send off, set off.
3 *to launch a new business.* begin, embark on, establish, found, inaugurate, initiate, open, set up, start.

lavatory noun
cloakroom, convenience, latrine, [*informal*] loo, [*childish*] potty, [*old-fashioned*] privy, public convenience, toilet, urinal, water-closet, WC.

lavish adjective
a lavish supply of food. abundant, bountiful, copious, extravagant, exuberant, generous, liberal, luxuriant, luxurious, munificent, opulent, plentiful, prodigal, sumptuous, unstinting, wasteful.
OPPOSITES: SEE **economical**.

law noun
1 *the laws of the land.* act, bill [= *draft of a proposed law*], commandment, decree, edict, order, pronouncement, statute.
2 *the laws of a game.* code, principle, regulation, rule.
3 *a court of law.* justice, litigation.
RELATED ADJECTIVES: legal, litigious.

EVENTS IN A COURT OF LAW: action, case, court martial, hearing, inquest, lawsuit, litigation, proceedings, suit, trial.

PEOPLE INVOLVED IN LEGAL AFFAIRS: accused, advocate, attorney, bailiff, barrister, clerk, coroner, counsel for the defence, counsel for the prosecution, defendant, judge, juror, lawyer, magistrate, plaintiff, police, prosecutor, solicitor, usher, witness.

SOME EVERYDAY LEGAL TERMS: accusation, arrest, bail, the bar, the bench, charge, court, dock, evidence, judgement, jurisprudence, lawcourt, litigant, notary public, plea, probate, SEE **punishment**, remand, sentence, statute, sue, summons, testimony, tort, verdict.

law-abiding adjective
law-abiding citizens. compliant, decent, disciplined, good, honest, obedient, orderly, peaceable, peaceful, respectable, well-behaved.
OPPOSITES: SEE **lawless**.

lawful adjective
1 *It isn't lawful to steal.* allowable, allowed, authorized, just, permissible, permitted, right.
2 *Who's the lawful owner of this car?* documented, legal, legitimate, prescribed, proper, recognized, regular, rightful, valid.
OPPOSITES: SEE **illegal**.

lawless adjective
a lawless mob. anarchic, anarchical, badly behaved, chaotic, disobedient, disorderly, ill-disciplined, insubordinate, mutinous, rebellious, riotous, rowdy, seditious, turbulent, uncontrolled, undisciplined, ungoverned, unrestrained, unruly, wild.
OPPOSITES: SEE **law-abiding**.

lay verb
1 *Lay your work on the table. Lay the paint on thickly.* apply, arrange, deposit, leave, place, position, put down, rest, set down, set out, spread.
2 *Don't lay all the blame on her.* ascribe, assign, burden, impose, plant, [*informal*] saddle.
3 *We laid secret plans.* concoct, create, design, establish, organize, plan, set up.
[*Lay* is also past tense of the verb to *lie*: *I lay down yesterday evening for a rest.* It is often used wrongly as present tense. Do NOT say *Let's lay down and have a rest* but *Let's lie . . .*]

layer noun
1 *a layer of paint.* coat, coating, covering, film, sheet, skin, surface, thickness.

2 *a layer of rock.* seam, stratum, substratum.
in layers laminated, layered, sandwiched, stratified.

laze verb
to laze in the sun. be lazy [SEE **lazy**], do nothing, lie about, loaf, lounge, relax, sit about, unwind.

laziness noun
dilatoriness, idleness, inactivity, indolence, lethargy, loafing, lounging about, sloth, slowness, sluggishness.
OPPOSITES: SEE **industry**.

lazy adjective
1 *a lazy worker.* easily pleased, idle, inactive, indolent, languid, lethargic, listless, shiftless, [*informal*] skiving, slack, slothful, slow, sluggish, torpid, unenterprising, work-shy.
OPPOSITES: SEE **industrious**.
2 *a lazy holiday.* peaceful, quiet, relaxing.
OPPOSITES: SEE **energetic**.

lead noun
1 [pronounced *led*] *lead pipes.*
METALS: SEE **metal**.
2 [pronounced *leed*] *We looked to the captain for a lead.* direction, example, guidance, leadership.
3 [*informal*] *The police hoped for a lead on the crime.* clue, hint, line, tip, tip-off.
4 *She was in the lead from the start.* first place, front position, spearhead, vanguard.
5 *the lead in a play or film.* chief part, starring role, title role.
6 *an electrical lead.* cable, flex, wire.

lead verb
1 *to lead someone in a certain direction.* conduct, draw, escort, guide, influence, pilot, steer, usher.
OPPOSITES: SEE **follow**.
2 *to lead an expedition.* be in charge of, command, direct, govern, head, manage, preside over, rule, supervise.
3 *to lead in a race.* be in front, be in the lead, head the field.

leader noun

LEADERS IN VARIOUS SITUATIONS: ayatollah, boss, captain, chief, chieftain, commander, conductor, courier, demagogue, director, figure-head, godfather, guide, head, patriarch, premier, prime minister, principal, ring-leader, SEE **ruler**, superior, [*informal*] supremo.

leading adjective
a leading figure in politics. SEE **chief**
adjective, dominant, foremost, important,
inspiring, outstanding, prominent, well-
known.

leaf noun
1 *leaves of a plant.* blade (*of grass*), foliage,
frond, greenery.
2 *leaves in a book.* folio, page, sheet.

leaflet noun
an advertising leaflet. booklet, brochure,
circular, handout, pamphlet.

leak noun
a leak in a bucket. crack, drip, hole, opening,
perforation, puncture.

leak verb
1 *to leak water or oil.* drip, escape, exude,
ooze, percolate, seep, spill, trickle.
2 *to leak secrets.* disclose, divulge, give away,
let out, make known, pass on, reveal.

lean adjective
a lean figure. bony, emaciated, gaunt, lanky,
skinny, slender, slim, spare, thin, wiry.
OPPOSITES: SEE **fat** adjective.

lean verb
1 *to lean to one side.* bank, heel over, incline,
list, loll, slant, slope, tilt, tip.
2 *to lean against the fence.* prop yourself up,
recline, rest, support yourself.

leaning noun
*a leaning towards science. a leaning towards
vegetarianism.* bent, bias, inclination,
instinct, liking, partiality, penchant,
predilection, preference, propensity,
readiness, taste, tendency, trend.

leap verb
1 *to leap in the air.* bound, clear (*clear a
fence*), jump, leap-frog, spring, vault.
2 *to leap on someone.* ambush, attack,
pounce.

learn verb
At school, you learn facts and skills. acquire,
assimilate, become aware of, be taught [SEE
teach], discover, find out, gain, gain
understanding of, gather, grasp, master,
memorize, [*informal*] mug up, pick up,
remember, study, [*informal*] swot up.

learned adjective
a learned professor. academic, clever,
cultured, educated, erudite, highbrow,
intellectual, SEE **knowledgeable**, scholarly.

learner noun
apprentice, beginner, cadet, L-driver,
novice, pupil, scholar, starter, student,
trainee, tiro.

least adjective
*the least amount. least in importance. least
in number.* fewest, lowest, minimum,
negligible, poorest, slightest, smallest,
tiniest.

leather noun
chamois, hide, skin, suede.

leave noun
1 *Will you give me leave to speak?*
authorization, liberty, permission.
2 *leave from the army.* absence, free time,
holiday, sabbatical, time off, vacation.

leave verb
1 *I have to leave.* depart, go away, go out,
[*informal*] pull out, run away, say goodbye,
set off, take your leave, withdraw.
OPPOSITES: SEE **arrive, enter**.
2 *The rats left the sinking ship.* abandon,
desert, evacuate, forsake, vacate.
3 *I left my job.* [*informal*] chuck in, give up,
quit, relinquish, resign from, retire from,
[*informal*] walk out of.
4 *Leave it where it is.* allow (it) to stay, let
(it) alone, [*informal*] let (it) be.
5 *She left me some money in her will.*
bequeath, hand down, will.
6 *Leave the milk bottles by the front door.*
deposit, place, position, put down, set down.
to leave off SEE **stop** verb.
to leave out SEE **omit**.

lecture noun
1 *a lecture on science.* address, discourse,
lesson, speech, talk.
2 *a lecture on bad manners.* SEE **reprimand**
noun.

lecturer noun
a college lecturer. don, fellow, instructor,
professor, speaker, teacher, tutor.

ledge noun
projection, ridge, shelf, sill, step, window-
sill.

left adjective
1 *on the left side.* left-hand, port [= *left side
of a ship when you face the bow*].
2 *left in politics.* communist, Labour, leftist,
left-wing, liberal, Marxist, progressive,
radical, revolutionary, socialist.
OPPOSITES: SEE **right** adjective.

leg noun
1 lower limb, [*informal*] pin (*unsteady on
his pins*), shank.

PARTS OF YOUR LEG: ankle, calf, foot, hock,
knee, shin, thigh.

WORDS TO DESCRIBE PEOPLE'S LEGS: bandy,
bandy-legged, bow-legged, knock-kneed.

2 *a leg of a table.* prop, support, upright.
3 *a leg of a journey.* lap, part, section, stage.

legacy noun
a legacy bequeathed in a will. bequest, endowment, estate, inheritance.

legal adjective
1 *legal proceedings.* judicial.
2 *I'm the legal owner of my car.* aboveboard, allowable, allowed, authorized, constitutional, lawful, legalized, legitimate, licensed, permissible, permitted, regular, rightful, valid.
OPPOSITES: SEE **illegal**.

legalize verb
They won't ever legalize the drugs trade. allow, legitimize, license, make legal [SEE **legal**], normalize, permit, regularize.
OPPOSITES: SEE **ban** verb.

legendary adjective
1 *Unicorns are legendary beasts.* apocryphal, fabled, fabulous, fictional, fictitious, invented, made-up, mythical, non-existent, story-book.
OPPOSITES: SEE **real**.
2 *Presley is a legendary name in the pop world.* SEE **famous**.

legible adjective
legible handwriting. clear, decipherable, distinct, intelligible, neat, plain, readable.
OPPOSITES: SEE **illegible**.

legitimate adjective
1 *The solicitor said it was legitimate to sell the house.* SEE **legal**.
OPPOSITES: SEE **illegal**.
2 *Do you believe it's legitimate to copy his ideas?* ethical, just, justifiable, moral, proper, reasonable, right.
OPPOSITES: SEE **immoral**.
3 *a legitimate child = a child born within a legal marriage.*
OPPOSITES: SEE **illegitimate**.

leisure noun
Most people enjoy their leisure. ease, holiday time, liberty, recreation, relaxation, rest, spare time, time off.

leisurely adjective
a leisurely walk. easy, gentle, lingering, peaceful, relaxed, relaxing, restful, SEE **slow** adjective, unhurried.
OPPOSITES: SEE **brisk**.

lend verb
to lend money. advance, loan.
OPPOSITES: SEE **borrow**.

length noun
1 *the length of a piece of string.* distance, extent, measurement, stretch.

2 *the length of a piece of music.* duration, period, time.

lengthen verb
The days lengthen in spring. You can lengthen the ladder if you need to. draw out, enlarge, elongate, expand, extend, get longer, increase, make longer, prolong, pull out, stretch.
OPPOSITES: SEE **shorten**.

less adjective
fewer, smaller.
OPPOSITES: SEE **more**.

lessen verb
1 *The ointment will lessen the pain.* assuage, cut, deaden, decrease, lower, make less, minimize, mitigate, reduce, tone down.
2 *The pain lessened.* abate, become less, decline, decrease, die away, diminish, dwindle, ease off, moderate, slacken, subside, tail off, weaken.
OPPOSITES: SEE **increase** verb.

lesson noun
1 *Pupils are expected to attend lessons.* class, lecture, seminar, tutorial.
2 *Let that be a lesson to you!* example, moral, SEE **reprimand** noun, warning.

let verb
1 *You let it happen. Let him have it.* agree to, allow, consent to, give permission to, permit.
OPPOSITES: SEE **forbid**, **object** verb.
2 *a house to let.* hire, lease, rent.
to let go, **to let loose** *to let prisoners go. to let animals loose.* free, liberate, release.
to let off *to let off fireworks.* detonate, discharge, explode, fire, set off.
to let someone off *to let an accused person off.* acquit, excuse, exonerate.

lethal adjective
a lethal dose of a drug. deadly, fatal, mortal, poisonous.

lethargic adjective
The fumes made us feel lethargic. apathetic, inactive, languid, lazy, listless, SEE **sleepy**, slow, sluggish, torpid.
OPPOSITES: SEE **energetic**.

lethargy noun
apathy, laziness, listlessness, slowness, sluggishness, torpor.

letter noun
1 *the letters of the alphabet.* character, consonant, vowel.
2 *a letter to a friend.* [old-fashioned] billet-doux, card, SEE **communication**, [formal] dispatch, [formal or joking] epistle, message, [joking] missive, note, postcard.
letters correspondence, mail, post.

level adjective
1 *a level surface.* even, flat, flush, horizontal, plane, regular, smooth, uniform.
OPPOSITES: SEE **uneven.**
2 *level scores.* balanced, equal, even, matching, [*informal*] neck-and-neck, the same.

level noun
1 *floods at a dangerous level. prices at a high level.* altitude, depth, height, value.
2 *the first level of an exam.* grade, stage, standard.
3 *promotion to a higher level.* degree, echelon, plane, position, rank, [*informal*] rung on the ladder, standing, status.
4 *rooms on the ground level.* floor, storey.

level verb
1 *We levelled the ground to make a lawn.* bulldoze, even out, flatten, rake, smooth.
2 *An earthquake levelled the town.* demolish, destroy, devastate, knock down, lay low, raze.

lever verb
to lever open a box. force, prise, wrench.

liable adjective
1 *The drunken driver was held to be liable for the accident.* accountable, answerable, responsible.
2 *I'm liable to fall asleep in the evenings.* disposed, inclined, likely, predisposed, prone, ready, willing.
OPPOSITES: SEE **unlikely.**

liaison noun
1 *liaison between business interests.* communication, co-operation, liaising, links, mediation.
2 *a liaison between a man and a woman.* SEE **love** noun (**love affair**).

liar noun
deceiver, [*informal*] fibber, [*formal*] perjurer, [*informal*] story-teller.

liberal adjective
1 *a liberal supply of food.* abundant, ample, bounteous, bountiful, copious, generous, lavish, munificent, plentiful, unstinting.
OPPOSITES: SEE **mean** adjective.
2 *liberal attitudes.* broad-minded, charitable, easygoing, enlightened, fair-minded, humanitarian, indulgent, lenient, magnanimous, permissive, tolerant, unbiased, unprejudiced.
OPPOSITES: SEE **narrow-minded.**
3 *liberal political views.* progressive, radical.
OPPOSITES: SEE **conservative** adjective.

liberate verb
to liberate prisoners. discharge, emancipate, free, let out, loose, ransom, release, rescue, save, set free, untie.
OPPOSITES: SEE **enslave, imprison.**

liberty noun
liberty from slavery. liberty to do what you want. emancipation, freedom, independence, liberation, release.
at liberty SEE **free** adjective.

licence noun
1 *a TV licence.* certificate, document, permit, warrant.
2 *licence to do as you please.* SEE **permission.**

license verb
1 *The authorities license certain shops to sell tobacco.* allow, authorize, empower, entitle, give a licence to, permit.
2 *to license a car.* buy a licence for, make legal.

lid noun
the lid of a container. cap, cover, covering, top.

lie noun
His lies didn't fool us. deceit, dishonesty, disinformation, fabrication, falsehood, falsification, [*informal*] fib, fiction, invention, untruth.
OPPOSITES: SEE **truth.**

lie verb
1 *to lie in order to deceive.* be economical with the truth, bluff, SEE **deceive,** falsify the facts, [*informal*] fib, perjure yourself.
2 *to lie on a bed.* be horizontal, be prone [= *lie face downwards*], be supine [= *lie face upwards*], lean back, lounge, recline, repose, rest, sprawl, stretch out.
3 *The house lies in a valley.* be, be found, be located, be situated, exist.

life noun
1 *life on earth.* being, existence.
2 *full of life.* activity, animation, energy, [*informal*] go, liveliness, spirit, sprightliness, verve, vigour, vitality, vivacity, zest.
3 *a life of Elvis Presley.* autobiography, biography, story.

lifeless adjective
1 *a lifeless body.* comatose, dead, deceased, inanimate, inert, killed, motionless, unconscious.
OPPOSITES: SEE **living** adjective.
2 *lifeless desert.* arid, bare, barren, sterile.
OPPOSITES: SEE **fertile.**
3 *a lifeless performance.* apathetic, boring, flat, lack-lustre, lethargic, slow, unexciting.
OPPOSITES: SEE **animated.**

lifelike adjective
a lifelike image. authentic, convincing, natural, photographic, realistic, true-to-life.
OPPOSITES: SEE **unrealistic.**

lift verb
1 *to lift into the air.* buoy up, carry, elevate, hoist, jack up, pick up, pull up, raise, rear.
2 *The plane lifted off the ground.* ascend, rise, soar.

light adjective
1 *light to carry.* lightweight, SEE **portable**, underweight, weightless.
OPPOSITES: SEE **heavy**.
2 *a light and airy room.* SEE **bright**, illuminated, lit-up, well-lit.
OPPOSITES: SEE **dark**. [The adjective *light* has many other senses. We refer you to entries where you can find synonyms for some of the common ones.]
3 *light work.* SEE **easy**.
4 *light wind.* SEE **gentle**.
5 *a light touch.* SEE **delicate**.
6 *light colours.* SEE **pale** adjective.
7 *a light heart.* SEE **cheerful**.
8 *light traffic.* SEE **sparse**.

light noun
a shining light. beam, blaze, brightness, brilliance, effulgence, flare, flash, fluorescence, glare, gleam, glint, glitter, glow, halo, illumination, incandescence, luminosity, lustre, phosphorescence, radiance, ray, reflection, shine, sparkle, twinkle.
to give light, to reflect light be bright, be luminous, be phosphorescent, blaze, blink, burn, coruscate, dazzle, flash, flicker, glare, gleam, glimmer, glint, glisten, glitter, glow, radiate, reflect, scintillate, shimmer, shine, spark, sparkle, twinkle.

KINDS OF LIGHT: daylight, electric light, firelight, floodlight, half-light, moonlight, starlight, sunlight, torchlight, twilight.

THINGS WHICH GIVE LIGHT: arc light, beacon, bulb, candelabra, candle, chandelier, fire, fluorescent lamp, headlamp, headlight, illuminations, lamp, lantern, laser, lighter, lighthouse, lightship, match, moon, neon light, pilot light, searchlight, spotlight, standard lamp, star, street light, strobe or stroboscope, sun, torch, traffic lights.

---

light verb
1 *to light a fire.* begin to burn, fire, ignite, kindle, set alight, set fire to, put a match to, switch on.
OPPOSITES: SEE **quench**.
2 *The bonfire lit the sky.* brighten, cast light on, floodlight, illuminate, irradiate, lighten, light up, shed light on, shine on.
OPPOSITES: SEE **darken**, **obscure** verb.

light-hearted adjective
SEE **cheerful**.

like adjective SEE **similar**.

like verb
to like a person. to like food. admire, appreciate, approve of, be interested in, be fond of, be partial to, be pleased by, delight in, enjoy, find pleasant, [*informal*] go in for, have a high regard for, SEE **love** verb, prefer, relish, [*informal*] take to, welcome.
I (you, she, etc.) would like. SEE **want** verb.
OPPOSITES: SEE **dislike** verb.

likeable adjective
a likeable person. attractive, charming, congenial, endearing, SEE **friendly**, lovable, nice, personable, pleasant, pleasing.
OPPOSITES: SEE **hateful**.

likely adjective
1 *a likely result.* anticipated, expected, feasible, foreseeable, plausible, possible, predictable, probable, reasonable, unsurprising.
2 *a likely candidate for election.* appropriate, convincing, credible, favourite, fitting, hopeful, qualified, suitable, [*informal*] tipped to win.
3 *He's likely to be late.* apt, disposed, inclined, liable, prone, willing.
OPPOSITES: SEE **unlikely**.

likeness noun
1 *The photo is a good likeness of her.* copy, depiction, image, picture, portrait, replica, representation, reproduction, study.
2 *There's a strong likeness between the two sisters.* affinity, compatibility, congruity, correspondence, resemblance, similarity.
OPPOSITES: SEE **difference**.

liking noun
a liking for classical music. a liking for sweet things. affection, fondness, inclination, love, partiality, penchant, predilection, preference, propensity, [*informal*] soft spot, taste, weakness (*Chocolate is one of my weaknesses*).
OPPOSITES: SEE **dislike** noun.

limb noun
limbs of an animal. a limb of a tree. appendage, member, offshoot, projection.

VARIOUS LIMBS: arm, bough, branch, flipper, foreleg, forelimb, leg, wing.

---

limber verb
to limber up exercise, get ready, loosen up, prepare, warm up.

limit noun
1 *the limit of a territory.* border, boundary, bounds, brink, confines, edge, end, extent,

limit
extreme point, frontier, perimeter.
2 *a speed-limit. a limit on numbers.* ceiling,
curb, cut-off point, deadline [= *a time-limit*],
limitation, maximum, restraint, restriction,
threshold.

limit verb
to limit someone's freedom. to limit numbers.
check, circumscribe, confine, control, curb,
fix, put a limit on, ration, restrain, restrict.

limitation noun
1 *a limitation on numbers.* SEE **limit** noun.
2 *I know my limitations.* defect, deficiency,
inadequacy, weakness.

limited adjective
limited funds. limited space. circumscribed,
controlled, cramped, defined, determinate,
finite, fixed, inadequate, insufficient,
narrow, rationed, reduced, restricted, short,
small, unsatisfactory.
OPPOSITES: SEE **limitless**.

limitless adjective
limitless funds. limitless opportunities.
boundless, countless, endless, incalculable,
inexhaustible, infinite, never-ending,
renewable, unbounded, unending,
unimaginable, unlimited, vast.
OPPOSITES: SEE **limited**.

limp adjective
limp lettuce. [*informal*] bendy, drooping,
flabby, flexible, [*informal*] floppy, pliable,
sagging, slack, soft, weak, wilting, yielding.
OPPOSITES: SEE **rigid**.

limp verb
be lame, falter, hobble, hop, SEE **walk** verb.

line noun
1 *a dirty line round the bath. a line drawn on
paper.* band, borderline, boundary, contour,
contour line, dash, mark, streak, striation,
strip, stripe, stroke, trail.
2 *lines on a person's face.* crease, furrow,
groove, score, wrinkle.
3 *Hold the end of this line.* cable, cord, flex,
hawser, lead, rope, string, thread, wire.
4 *a line of cars. a line of police.* chain, column,
cordon, crocodile, file, procession, queue,
rank, row, series.
5 *a railway line.* branch, mainline, route,
service, track.

linger verb
1 *The smell of burning lingered.* continue,
endure, hang about, last, persist, remain,
stay, survive.
OPPOSITES: SEE **disappear**.
2 *Don't linger outside in this cold weather.*
dally, dawdle, delay, hang about, hover, idle,
lag, loiter, stay behind, wait about.
OPPOSITES: SEE **hurry** verb.

lining noun
*the lining of a garment. a lining of a
container.* inner coat, inner layer,
interfacing, liner, padding.

link noun
1 *a link between two things.* bond,
connection, connector, coupling, join, joint,
linkage, tie, yoke.
2 *links between nations. a link between two
groups.* alliance, association,
communication, liaison, partnership,
relationship, [*informal*] tie-up, twinning,
union.

link verb
1 *to link one object with another.* amalgamate,
attach, connect, couple, SEE **fasten**,
interlink, join, merge, network (*networked
microcomputers*), twin (*an English town
twinned with a French town*), unite, yoke.
OPPOSITES: SEE **isolate, separate** verb.
2 *to link one idea with another.* associate,
compare, make a link, relate, see a link.

lip noun
the lip of a cup. brim, brink, edge, rim.

liquid adjective
a liquid substance. aqueous, flowing, fluid,
molten, running, [*informal*] runny, sloppy,
[*informal*] sloshy, thin, watery, wet.
OPPOSITES: SEE **solid**.

liquid noun
He can only consume liquids. fluid, liquid
substance [SEE **liquid** adjective].

list noun
a list of names. catalogue, column, directory,
file, index, inventory, listing, register, roll,
shopping-list, table.

list verb
1 *to list your possessions.* catalogue, file,
index, itemize, make a list of [SEE **list** noun],
record, register, tabulate, write down.
2 *to list to one side.* heel, incline, lean, slope,
tilt, tip.

listen verb
Did you listen to what I said? attend to,
concentrate on, [*old-fashioned*] hark, hear,
heed, eavesdrop, lend an ear to, overhear,
pay attention to, take notice of.

listless adjective
listless in the heat. apathetic, enervated,
feeble, heavy, lackadaisical, languid, lazy,
lethargic, lifeless, sluggish, tired, torpid,
unenthusiastic, uninterested, weak, weary.
OPPOSITES: SEE **lively**.

literal adjective
[Do not confuse with *literary*.] *the literal
meaning of something.* close, plain, prosaic,
strict, unimaginative, word for word.

literary adjective
1 *literary writing.* highly regarded, imaginative, ornate, polished, recognized as literature, [*uncomplimentary*] self-conscious, sophisticated, stylish.
2 *literary tastes.* cultured, educated, erudite, literate, refined, well-read, widely read.

literate adjective
1 *a literate person.* able to read and write, SEE **educated**.
2 *literate writing.* accurate, correct, properly spelt, readable, well-written.

literature noun
1 *literature about local tourist attractions.* brochures, handouts, leaflets, pamphlets, papers.
2 *English literature.* books, writings.

KINDS OF LITERATURE: autobiography, biography, children's literature, comedy, crime fiction, criticism, drama, epic, essay, fantasy, fiction, folk-tale, journalism, myth and legend, novels, parody, poetry, prose, romance, satire, science fiction, tragedy, tragi-comedy.
OTHER KINDS OF WRITING: SEE **writing**.

---

lithe adjective
a lithe gymnast. agile, flexible, limber, lissom, loose-jointed, pliant, supple.

litter noun
Clear up the litter. bits and pieces, clutter, debris, garbage, jumble, junk, mess, odds and ends, refuse, rubbish, trash, waste.

litter verb
to litter a room with papers. clutter, fill with litter [SEE **litter** noun], make untidy, [*informal*] mess up, scatter, strew.

little adjective
SEE **small**.

live adjective
1 *live animals.* SEE **living** adjective.
2 *a live issue.* contemporary, current, important, pressing, relevant, topical, vital.

live verb
1 *Will these plants live through the winter?* continue, exist, flourish, last, remain, stay alive, survive.
OPPOSITES: SEE **die**.
2 *I can live on £20 a week.* [*informal*] get along, keep going, make a living, pay the bills, subsist.
to live in *I live in a flat.* dwell in, inhabit, occupy, reside in.

livelihood noun
SEE **job**.

lively adjective
lively kittens. a lively party. a lively expression. active, agile, alert, animated,

boisterous, bubbly, bustling, busy, cheerful, colourful, dashing, energetic, enthusiastic, exciting, expressive, exuberant, frisky, gay, SEE **happy**, high-spirited, irrepressible, jaunty, jolly, merry, nimble, [*informal*] perky, playful, quick, spirited, sprightly, stimulating, vigorous, vital, vivacious, [*informal*] zippy.
OPPOSITES: SEE **apathetic, tired**.

living adjective
living creatures. SEE **active**, alive, animate, breathing, existing, live, sentient, surviving, vigorous, vital.
OPPOSITES: SEE **dead, extinct**.

living noun
She makes a living from painting. income, livelihood, occupation, subsistence, way of life.

load noun
1 *a load of goods.* cargo, consignment, freight, [*formal*] lading, lorry-load, shipment, van-load.
2 *a heavy load of responsibility.* burden, millstone, onus, weight.

load verb
1 *We loaded the luggage into the car.* fill, heap, pack, pile, ply, stow.
2 *They loaded me with their shopping.* burden, encumber, weigh down.

loaded adjective
1 *loaded with gifts.* burdened, inundated, laden, piled high, weighed down.
2 *a loaded argument.* biased, distorted, emotive, one-sided, partial, prejudiced, unfair.

loafer noun
idler, [*informal*] good-for-nothing, layabout, [*informal*] lazybones, lounger, shirker, [*informal*] skiver, wastrel.

loan noun
I need a loan to buy a car. advance, credit, mortgage.

loathe verb
SEE **hate** verb.

loathsome adjective
SEE **hateful**.

lobby verb
to lobby your MP. persuade, petition, pressurize, try to influence, urge.

local adjective
1 *local amenities.* nearby, neighbourhood, neighbouring, serving the locality [SEE **locality**].
2 *a matter of local interest.* community, limited, narrow, parochial, particular, provincial, regional.
OPPOSITES: SEE **general, national**.

locality noun
There are good shops in our locality. area, catchment area, community, district, location, neighbourhood, parish, region, residential area, town, vicinity, zone.

localize verb
The authorities tried to localize the epidemic. concentrate, confine, contain, enclose, keep within bounds, limit, narrow down, pin down, restrict.
OPPOSITES: SEE **spread** verb.

locate verb
1 *I located the book I wanted in the library.* detect, discover, find, identify, [*informal*] run to earth, search out, track down, unearth.
OPPOSITES: SEE **lose**.
2 *They located the new offices in the middle of town.* build, establish, find a place for, found, place, position, put, set up, site, situate, station.

location noun
1 *Can you find the location on the map?* locale, SEE **locality**, place, point, position, site, situation, spot, venue, whereabouts.
2 *The film was shot in real locations.* background, scene, setting.

lock noun
1 *a lock on a door.* bolt, catch, clasp, latch, padlock.
2 *a lock of hair.* SEE **hair**.

lock verb
to lock a door. bolt, close, SEE **fasten**, seal, secure, shut.
to lock in, to lock up SEE **imprison**.

lodge verb
1 *to lodge homeless families in a hostel.* accommodate, billet, board, SEE **house** verb, put up.
2 *to lodge in a motel.* reside, stay.
3 *to lodge a complaint.* file, make formally, put on record, register, submit.

lodger noun
a lodger in a guest-house. boarder, guest, inmate, paying guest, resident, tenant.

lodgings noun
accommodation, apartments, billet, boarding-house, [*informal*] digs, lodging-house, [*informal*] pad, quarters, rooms, [*informal*] squat, temporary home.

lofty adjective
a lofty spire. SEE **high**.

log noun
1 *logs to burn.* timber, wood.
2 *the log of a voyage.* account, diary, journal, record.

logic noun
I admired the logic of his argument. clarity, logical thinking [SEE **logical**], rationality, reasoning, sense, validity.

logical adjective
a logical argument. clear, cogent, coherent, consistent, intelligent, methodical, rational, reasonable, sensible, sound, systematic, valid.
OPPOSITES: SEE **illogical**.

loiter verb
We'll be left behind if we loiter. be slow, dally, dawdle, hang back, linger, [*informal*] loaf about, [*informal*] mess about, skulk, [*informal*] stand about, straggle.

lone adjective
a lone walker on the hills. a lone voice. isolated, SEE **lonely**, separate, single, solitary, solo, unaccompanied.

lonely adjective
1 *I was lonely while my friends were away.* alone, forlorn, friendless, lonesome, neglected, SEE **sad**, solitary.
2 *a lonely farmhouse. a lonely road.* abandoned, desolate, distant, far-away, forsaken, isolated, [*informal*] off the beaten track, out of the way, remote, secluded, unfrequented, uninhabited.

long adjective
a long piece of rope. a long wait. drawn out, elongated, endless, extended, extensive, interminable, lasting, lengthy, longish, prolonged, protracted, slow, stretched, time-consuming, unending.

long verb
to long for [*informal*] be dying for (*I'm dying for a drink*), desire, fancy, hanker after, have a longing for [SEE **longing**], hunger after, [*informal*] itch for, lust after, pine for, thirst for, want, wish for, yearn for.

longing noun
appetite, craving, desire, hunger, [*informal*] itch, need, thirst, urge, wish, yearning, [*informal*] yen.

long-winded adjective
a long-winded speaker. boring, diffuse, dreary, dry, garrulous, lengthy, long, rambling, tedious, uninteresting, verbose, wordy.

look noun
1 *Give me a look. Take a look.* glance, glimpse, observation, peek, peep, sight, [*informal*] squint, view.
2 *She has a friendly look.* [*often plural*] *He's vain about his looks.* air, appearance, aspect, bearing, complexion, countenance, demeanour, expression, face, manner, mien.

look verb
1 **to look at** behold, [*informal*] cast your eye over, consider, contemplate, examine, eye, gape at, [*informal*] gawp at, gaze at, glance at, glimpse, goggle at, inspect, observe, ogle, peek at, peep at, peer at, read, regard, scan, scrutinize, see, skim through (*I'll just skim through the book*), squint at, stare at, study, survey, take a look at, take note of, view, watch.
2 *Our house looks south.* face, overlook.
3 *You look pleased.* appear, seem.
to look after SEE **care** verb (**to care for**).
to look for SEE **seek**.
to look into SEE **investigate**.
to look out *If you don't look out, you'll get wet.* be vigilant, beware, keep an eye open, keep an eye out, pay attention, watch out.

look-out noun
guard, sentinel, sentry, watchman.

loom verb
A castle loomed on the skyline. appear, arise, dominate, emerge, materialize, rise, stand out, stick up, threaten, tower.

loop noun
a loop in a rope. bend, circle, coil, curl, hoop, kink, noose, ring, turn, twist.

loop verb
Loop the rope round the post. bend, coil, curl, entwine, make a loop [SEE **loop** noun], turn, twist, wind.

loose adjective
1 *loose stones. loose wires.* detachable, detached, disconnected, insecure, loosened, movable, shaky, unattached, unfastened, unsteady, untied, wobbly.
2 *loose animals.* at large, free, roaming, uncaged, unconfined, unrestricted.
OPPOSITES: SEE **secure** adjective.
3 *loose clothing.* baggy, [*informal*] floppy, loose-fitting, slack, unbuttoned.
OPPOSITES: SEE **tight**.
4 *a loose agreement. a loose translation.* diffuse, general, ill-defined, imprecise, inexact, informal, vague.
OPPOSITES: SEE **precise**.

loosen verb
1 *Loosen the knots.* ease off, free, let go, loose, make loose, relax, release, slacken, undo, unfasten, unloose, untie.
2 *Check that the knots haven't loosened.* become loose, come adrift, open up.
OPPOSITES: SEE **tighten**.

loot noun
thieves' loot. booty, contraband, haul, [*informal*] ill-gotten gains, plunder, prize, spoils, [*informal*] swag, takings.

loot verb
Rioters looted the shops. pillage, plunder, raid, ransack, rifle, rob, steal from.

lop verb
SEE **cut** verb.

lopsided adjective
The lopsided load on the lorry looked dangerous. askew, asymmetrical, [*informal*] cock-eyed, crooked, tilting, unbalanced, uneven.

lose verb
1 *to lose something or someone.* be deprived of, be unable to find, cease to have, drop, find yourself without, forfeit, forget, leave behind, mislay, misplace, miss, stray from, suffer the loss of [SEE **loss**].
OPPOSITES: SEE **find**, **gain** verb.
2 *to lose in a game or race.* be defeated, capitulate, [*informal*] come to grief, fail, get beaten, [*informal*] get thrashed, suffer defeat.
OPPOSITES: SEE **win**.

losing adjective
SEE **defeated**.

loss noun
bereavement, damage, defeat, deficit, deprivation, destruction, disappearance, failure, forfeiture, impairment, privation.
OPPOSITES: SEE **gain** noun.
losses *losses in battle.* casualties, deaths, death toll, fatalities.

lost adjective
1 *lost property. lost animals.* abandoned, disappeared, gone, irrecoverable, left behind, mislaid, misplaced, strayed, untraceable, vanished.
2 *lost in thought.* absorbed, day-dreaming, dreamy, distracted, engrossed, preoccupied, rapt.

lot noun
1 **a lot of, lots of** *a lot of food. lots of money.* SEE **plenty**.
2 **the lot** *Give her the lot.* all, everything.
3 *a lot in an auction sale.* SEE **item**.
to draw lots SEE **choose**, **gamble** verb.

lotion noun
balm, cream, embrocation, liniment, ointment, salve.

loud adjective
loud noise. audible, blaring, booming, clamorous, clarion (*a clarion call*), deafening, ear-splitting, echoing, fortissimo, high, noisy, penetrating, piercing, raucous, resounding, reverberating, rowdy, shrieking, shrill, stentorian, strident, thundering, thunderous, uproarious, vociferous.
OPPOSITES: SEE **quiet**.

lounge verb
to lounge about. to lounge in a chair. be idle, be lazy, dawdle, hang about, idle, [*informal*] kill time, laze, loaf, lie around, loiter,

[*informal*] loll about, [*informal*] mess about, [*informal*] mooch about, relax, [*informal*] skive, slouch, slump, sprawl, stand about, take it easy, waste time.

lovable adjective
Teddy bears are lovable toys. adorable, appealing, attractive, charming, cuddly, enchanting, endearing, engaging, likeable, lovely, pleasing, taking, winning.
OPPOSITES: SEE **hateful**.

love noun
1 *Giving flowers is one way to show your love.* admiration, adoration, affection, ardour, desire, devotion, fondness, friendship, infatuation, liking, passion.
2 *My dearest love.* beloved, darling, dear, dearest, loved one, SEE **lover**.
in love with devoted to, enamoured with, fond of, infatuated with.
to make love court, flirt, have sexual intercourse [SEE **sex**], philander, woo.
love affair affair, courtship, intrigue, liaison, relationship, romance.
RELATED ADJECTIVES: amatory, erotic.

love verb
1 *to love someone.* admire, adore, be charmed by, be in love with [SEE **love** noun (**in love with**)], care for, cherish, desire, dote on, fancy, feel love for [SEE **love** noun], have a passion for, idolize, lust after, treasure, value, want, worship.
OPPOSITES: SEE **hate** verb.
2 *I love fish and chips.* SEE **like** verb.

loveless adjective
a loveless relationship. cold, frigid, heartless, passionless, undemonstrative, unfeeling, unloving, unresponsive.
OPPOSITES: SEE **loving**.

lovely adjective
a lovely day. lovely flowers. appealing, attractive, SEE **beautiful**, charming, delightful, enjoyable, fine, nice, pleasant, pretty, sweet.
OPPOSITES: SEE **nasty**.

lover noun
[*old-fashioned*] admirer, boyfriend, companion, concubine, [*male*] fiancé, [*female*] fiancée, [*old-fashioned*] follower, friend, gigolo, girlfriend, mistress, [*old-fashioned*] paramour, suitor, sweetheart, valentine, wooer.

lovesick adjective
frustrated, languishing, lovelorn, pining.

loving adjective
loving kisses. a loving nature. affectionate, amorous, ardent, demonstrative, devoted, doting, fatherly, fond, SEE **friendly**, kind,

maternal, motherly, passionate, paternal, tender, warm.
OPPOSITES: SEE **loveless**.

low adjective
1 *low land.* flat, low-lying, sunken.
OPPOSITES: SEE **high**.
2 *a low position.* abject, base, degraded, humble, inferior, junior, lower, lowly, menial, modest, servile.
OPPOSITES: SEE **superior**.
3 *low behaviour.* churlish, coarse, common, cowardly, crude, [*old-fashioned*] dastardly, disreputable, ignoble, SEE **immoral**, mean, nasty, vulgar, wicked.
OPPOSITES: SEE **noble**.
4 *low whispers.* muffled, muted, pianissimo, quiet, soft, subdued.
OPPOSITES: SEE **loud**.
5 *a low note.* bass, deep.
OPPOSITES: SEE **high**.

lower verb
1 *to lower a flag.* dip, drop, haul down, let down, take down.
2 *to lower prices.* bring down, cut, decrease, lessen, reduce, [*informal*] slash.
3 *to lower the volume.* abate, quieten, tone down, turn down.
OPPOSITES: SEE **raise**.
4 *He's too high-and-mighty to lower himself by coming out with us.* degrade, demean, discredit, disgrace, humiliate, stoop.

lowly adjective
a lowly position in life. base, humble, insignificant, low, lowborn, meek, modest.

loyal adjective
a loyal supporter. constant, dependable, devoted, dutiful, faithful, honest, patriotic, reliable, sincere, staunch, steadfast, true, trustworthy, trusty, unswerving.
OPPOSITES: SEE **disloyal**.

loyalty noun
allegiance, constancy, dependability, devotion, faithfulness, fealty, fidelity, honesty, patriotism, reliability, staunchness, steadfastness, trustworthiness.
OPPOSITES: SEE **disloyalty**.

lucid adjective
a lucid explanation. SEE **clear** adjective.

luck noun
1 *I found my watch by luck.* accident, [*informal*] break (*a lucky break*), chance, coincidence, destiny, fate, [*informal*] fluke, fortune.
2 *I had a bit of luck today.* good fortune, happiness, prosperity, success.

lucky adjective
1 *a lucky discovery.* accidental, chance, [*informal*] fluky, fortuitous, providential, timely, unintended, unintentional, unplanned, welcome.
2 *a lucky person.* favoured, fortunate, SEE **happy**, successful.
3 *3 is my lucky number.* auspicious.
OPPOSITES: SEE **unlucky**.

luggage noun
baggage, bags, belongings, boxes, cases, impedimenta, paraphernalia, things.

ITEMS OF LUGGAGE: bag, basket, box, briefcase, case, chest, hamper, handbag, hand luggage, haversack, holdall, knapsack, pannier, [*old-fashioned*] portmanteau, purse, rucksack, satchel, suitcase, trunk, wallet.

---

lukewarm adjective
1 *lukewarm water.* tepid, warm.
2 *a lukewarm response.* apathetic, cool, half-hearted, unenthusiastic.

lull noun
a lull in a storm. break, calm, gap, interval, [*informal*] let-up, pause, respite, rest, silence.

lull verb
to lull someone to sleep. calm, hush, pacify, quell, quieten, soothe, subdue, tranquillize.

lumber verb
1 [*informal*] *They lumbered me with the clearing up.* SEE **burden** verb.
2 *A rhinoceros lumbered towards them.* blunder, move clumsily, shamble, trudge.

luminous adjective
a luminous dial. glowing, luminescent, lustrous, phosphorescent, shining.

lump noun
1 *a lump of chocolate. a lump of soap.* ball, bar, bit, block, cake, chunk, clod, clot, [*informal*] dollop, gobbet, hunk, ingot, mass, nugget, piece, slab, [*informal*] wodge.
2 *a lump on the head.* bulge, bump, hump, knob, node, nodule, protrusion, protuberance, spot, swelling, tumour.

lunatic noun
SEE **madman**.

lunge verb
1 *to lunge with a sword.* jab, stab, strike, thrust.
2 *to lunge after someone.* charge, dash, dive, lurch, pounce, rush, throw yourself.

lurch verb
to lurch from side to side. heave, lean, list, lunge, pitch, plunge, reel, roll, stagger, stumble, sway, totter, wallow.

lure verb
to lure someone into a trap. allure, attract, bait, coax, decoy, draw, entice, inveigle, invite, lead on, persuade, seduce, tempt.

lurid adjective
1 *lurid colours.* SEE **gaudy**.
2 *lurid details.* SEE **sensational**.

lurk verb
to lurk in wait for prey. crouch, hide, lie in wait, lie low, skulk, wait.

luscious adjective
luscious peaches. appetizing, delicious, juicy, succulent, sweet, tasty.

lush adjective
1 *lush grass.* SEE **luxuriant**.
2 *lush surroundings.* SEE **luxurious**.

lust noun
1 *sexual lust.* carnality, lasciviousness, lechery, libido, licentiousness, passion, sensuality.
2 *a lust for power.* appetite, craving, desire, greed, itch, hunger, longing.

lustful adjective
carnal, lascivious, lecherous, libidinous, licentious, passionate, [*informal*] randy, sensual, SEE **sexy**.

luxuriant adjective
luxuriant growth. abundant, ample, copious, dense, exuberant, fertile, flourishing, green, lush, opulent, plenteous, plentiful, profuse, prolific, rich, teeming, thick, thriving, verdant.
OPPOSITES: SEE **barren**, **sparse**.

luxurious adjective
luxurious surroundings. comfortable, costly, expensive, grand, hedonistic, lavish, lush, magnificent, [*informal*] plush, rich, self-indulgent, splendid, sumptuous, voluptuous.
OPPOSITES: SEE **spartan**.

luxury noun
a life of luxury. affluence, comfort, ease, enjoyment, extravagance, hedonism, high living, indulgence, pleasure, relaxation, self-indulgence, splendour, sumptuousness, voluptuousness.

lying adjective
a lying witness. crooked, deceitful, dishonest, double-dealing, false, inaccurate, insincere, mendacious, perfidious, unreliable, untrustworthy, untruthful.
OPPOSITES: SEE **truthful**.

lying noun
deceit, dishonesty, falsehood, mendacity, [*formal*] perjury.

lyrical adjective
a lyrical tune. a lyrical description.
emotional, expressive, inspired, poetic,
song-like.

Mm

macabre adjective
He takes a macabre interest in graveyards.
eerie, ghoulish, SEE **gruesome**, morbid, sick,
unhealthy, weird.

machine noun
apparatus, appliance, contraption,
contrivance, device, engine, gadget,
instrument, SEE **machinery**, mechanism,
robot, tool.

machinery noun
1 *machinery in a factory.* equipment, gear,
machines [SEE **machine**], plant.
2 *machinery for electing a new leader.*
constitution, method, organization,
procedure, structure, system.

mackintosh noun
anorak, cape, mac, raincoat, sou'wester,
waterproof.
OTHER COATS: SEE **coat** noun.

mad adjective
[Many of these words are used informally.
Though they may be used jokingly, they are
often offensive.] *a mad person. mad
behaviour.* batty, berserk, bonkers,
certified, crackers, crazed, crazy, daft,
delirious, demented, deranged, disordered,
dotty, eccentric, fanatical, frantic, frenzied,
hysterical, insane, irrational, loony,
lunatic, maniacal, manic, mental, mentally
unstable, moonstruck, [*Latin*] non compos
mentis, nutty, off your head, off your rocker,
out of your mind, possessed, potty, [*formal*]
psychotic, queer in the head, round the
bend, round the twist, screwy, touched,
unbalanced, unhinged, unstable, up the pole,
wild.
OPPOSITES: SEE **sane**.

madden verb
The noise maddened me. anger, craze,
derange, enrage, exasperate, incense,
inflame, infuriate, irritate, make mad [SEE
mad], provoke, [*informal*] send round the
bend, unhinge, vex.

madman, **madwoman** nouns
[Though these words may be used jokingly,
they are often offensive.] [*informal*]
crackpot, [*informal*] crank, eccentric,

lunatic, mad person [SEE **mad**], maniac,
[*informal*] mental case, [*informal*] nutcase,
[*informal*] nutter, [*formal*] psychopath,
[*formal*] psychotic.

madness noun
delirium, derangement, eccentricity, frenzy,
hysteria, insanity, lunacy, mania, mental
illness, psychosis.

magazine noun
1 *a magazine to read.* comic, journal,
monthly, newspaper, pamphlet, paper,
periodical, publication, quarterly, weekly.
2 *a magazine of weapons.* ammunition dump,
arsenal, storehouse.

magic noun
1 *magic performed by witches.* black magic,
charms, enchantment, hocus-pocus,
incantation, [*informal*] mumbo-jumbo,
necromancy, occultism, sorcery, spell,
voodoo, witchcraft, witchery, wizardry.
2 *magic performed by a conjuror.* conjuring,
illusion, legerdemain, sleight of hand, trick,
trickery.
to do magic bewitch, cast spells, charm,
conjure, enchant, work miracles.

magician noun
conjuror, enchanter, enchantress, SEE
entertainer, illusionist, sorcerer, [*old-
fashioned*] warlock, witch, witch-doctor,
wizard.

magnetic adjective
a magnetic personality. alluring, SEE
attractive, captivating, charismatic,
charming, compelling, fascinating,
hypnotic, irresistible, seductive.
OPPOSITES: SEE **repulsive**.

magnetism noun
personal magnetism. allure, appeal,
attractiveness, charisma, charm,
fascination, lure, power, seductiveness.

magnificent adjective
*a magnificent palace. magnificent mountain
scenery.* SEE **beautiful**, excellent, glorious,
gorgeous, grand, grandiose, imposing,
impressive, majestic, marvellous, noble,
opulent, [*informal*] posh, regal, spectacular,
splendid, stately, sumptuous, superb,
wonderful.
OPPOSITES: SEE **ordinary**.

magnify verb
1 *to magnify an image.* amplify, augment,
[*informal*] blow up, enlarge, expand,
increase, intensify, make larger.
OPPOSITES: SEE **reduce**. 2 [*informal*] blow up
out of all proportion, dramatize, exaggerate,
inflate, make too much of, maximize, overdo,
overestimate, overstate.
OPPOSITES: SEE **minimize**.

mail noun
The postman brings the mail.
correspondence, letters, parcels, post.

mail verb
The shop mailed the book to me. dispatch,
forward, post, send.

maim verb
He was maimed in an accident. cripple,
disable, handicap, injure, mutilate, SEE
wound verb.

main adjective
*the main ingredients. the main point of a
story.* basic, biggest, cardinal, central, chief,
crucial, dominant, essential, foremost,
fundamental, greatest, important, largest,
leading, major, outstanding, predominant,
pre-eminent, prevailing, primary, prime,
principal, special, supreme, top (*the top
attraction*).
OPPOSITES: SEE **unimportant**.

mainly adverb
chiefly, especially, generally, in the main,
largely, mostly, normally, on the whole,
predominantly, primarily, principally,
usually.

maintain verb
1 *to maintain a constant speed.* carry on,
continue, hold to, keep up, retain,
stick to.
2 *to maintain a car in good order.* keep in
good condition, look after, preserve,
service, take care of.
3 *to maintain a family.* feed, keep, pay for,
provide for, support.
4 *to maintain that you are innocent.* affirm,
allege, argue, assert, aver, claim, contend,
declare, insist, proclaim, profess, state,
uphold.

maintenance noun
1 *the maintenance of a house or a car.* care,
conservation, looking after, preservation,
repairs, servicing, upkeep.
2 *He pays maintenance to his ex-wife.*
alimony, allowance, subsistence.

majestic adjective
a majestic palace. august, awe-inspiring,
awesome, dignified, distinguished, grand,
imperial, imposing, impressive, kingly,
lordly, magnificent, monumental, noble,
pompous, princely, regal, royal, SEE
splendid, stately.

major adjective
*major roadworks. a major city, a major
operation.* bigger, chief, considerable,
extensive, great, greater, important, key,
large, larger, leading, outstanding,
principal, serious, significant.
OPPOSITES: SEE **minor**.

majority noun
The majority voted to go back to work. bulk,
greater number, preponderance.
OPPOSITES: SEE **minority**.

make noun
What make is your car? brand, kind, model,
sort, type, variety.

make verb
1 *to make furniture. to make a success of
something.* assemble, beget, bring about,
build, compose, constitute, construct,
create, do, engender, erect, execute,
fabricate, fashion, forge, form, generate,
invent, make up, manufacture, mass-
produce, originate, produce, think up. [*Make*
is used in many other senses. We give only
a selection of them here.]
2 *to make a cake.* SEE **cook** verb.
3 *to make clothes.* knit, [*informal*] run up,
sew, weave.
4 *to make a sculpture.* carve, cast, model,
mould, shape.
5 *to make a speech.* deliver, pronounce,
speak, utter.
6 *to make someone captain.* appoint, elect,
nominate, ordain.
7 *to make a P into a B.* alter, change, convert,
modify, transform, turn.
8 *to make a fortune.* earn, gain, get, obtain,
receive.
9 *to make a good games player.* become,
change into, grow into, turn into.
10 *to make your objective.* accomplish,
achieve, arrive at, attain, catch, get to,
reach, win.
11 *2 and 2 make 4.* add up to, amount to,
come to, total.
12 *to make rules.* agree, arrange, codify,
establish, decide on, draw up, fix, write.
13 *to make someone happy.* cause to become,
render.
14 *to make trouble.* bring about, carry out,
cause, give rise to, provoke, result in.
15 *to make someone do something.* coerce,
compel, constrain, force, induce, oblige,
order, pressurize, prevail on, require.
to make fun of, SEE **ridicule**.
to make off SEE **depart**.
to make off with SEE **steal**.
to make sense of SEE **understand**.
to make up SEE **invent**.
to make up for SEE **compensate**.
to make up your mind SEE **decide**.

maker noun
architect, author, builder, creator,
manufacturer, originator, producer.

male adjective
male characteristics. SEE **manly**, **masculine**.
OPPOSITES: SEE **female**.
MALE HUMAN BEINGS: SEE **boy**, **man**.
MALE CREATURES: SEE **animal** noun.

malevolent adjective
SEE **malicious**.

malfunction noun SEE **fault** noun.

malice noun
animosity, [*informal*] bitchiness,
bitterness, [*informal*] cattiness, enmity,
hatred, hostility, ill-will, malevolence,
maliciousness, malignity, nastiness,
rancour, spite, spitefulness, vengefulness,
venom, viciousness, vindictiveness.

malicious adjective
malicious remarks. [*informal*] bitchy, bitter,
[*informal*] catty, evil, evil-minded, hateful,
ill-natured, malevolent, malignant,
mischievous, nasty, rancorous, revengeful,
sly, spiteful, vengeful, venomous, vicious,
villainous, vindictive, wicked.
OPPOSITES: SEE **benevolent, kind** adjective.

malignant adjective
1 *a malignant disease.* dangerous,
destructive, harmful, injurious, poisonous,
spreading, [*informal*] terminal,
uncontrollable, virulent.
OPPOSITE: benign.
2 *malignant intentions.* SEE **malicious**.

malnutrition noun
famine, hunger, starvation, undernourishment.

maltreat verb
SEE **harm** verb.

man noun
1 = *human beings of either sex.* SEE **mankind**.
2 = *male human being.* bachelor, boy,
[*informal*] bloke, boyfriend, [*informal*]
bridegroom, chap, [*informal*] codger, father,
fellow, gentleman, groom, [*informal*] guy,
husband, lad, lover, male, son, [*joking*]
squire, widower.

manage verb
1 *to manage a business. to manage a crowd.*
administer, be in charge of, be the manager
of [SEE **manager**], command, conduct,
control, cope with, deal with, direct,
dominate, govern, handle, lead, look after,
manipulate, mastermind, operate, oversee,
preside over, regulate, rule, run,
superintend, supervise, take control of, take
over.
2 *How much work can you manage before
dinner?* accomplish, achieve, bring about,
carry out, contrive, do, finish, perform,
succeed in, undertake.

manageable adjective
1 *a manageable size. a manageable quantity.*
acceptable, convenient, easy to manage [SEE
manage], governable, handy, neat,
reasonable.
OPPOSITES: SEE **awkward**.

2 *a manageable horse. a manageable crowd.*
amenable, disciplined, docile, SEE **obedient**,
tractable.
OPPOSITES: SEE **disobedient**.

manager noun
administrator, boss, SEE **chief**, controller,
director, executive, governor, head,
organizer, overseer, proprietor, ruler,
superintendent, supervisor.

mangle verb
*He was off work because he'd mangled his
hand in a machine.* crush, cut, damage,
disfigure, injure, lacerate, maim, maul,
mutilate, squash, tear, SEE **wound** verb.

manhandle verb
1 *We manhandled the piano up the stairs.*
carry, haul, heave, hump, lift, manœuvre,
move, pull, push.
2 *The muggers manhandled him.* [*informal*]
beat up, knock about, maltreat, mistreat,
misuse, [*informal*] rough up, treat roughly.

mania noun
a mania for collecting things. craze,
enthusiasm, fad, fetish, frenzy, hysteria,
infatuation, insanity, lunacy, madness,
obsession, passion, preoccupation.

maniac noun SEE **madman**.

manifesto noun
a party manifesto. declaration, policy,
statement.

manipulate verb
1 *to manipulate a crowd. to manipulate
election results.* control, engineer, guide,
handle, influence, manage, steer.
2 *to manipulate an injured person's leg.* feel,
massage, rub.

mankind noun
human beings, humanity, the human race,
man, men and women, people [SEE **person**].
RELATED ADJECTIVE: anthropological.

manly adjective
[*Manly* as a term of approval may have sexist
overtones.] SEE **brave**, heroic,
[*uncomplimentary*] macho, male, mannish,
masculine, strong, swashbuckling,
vigorous, virile.
OPPOSITES: SEE **effeminate**.

man-made adjective
man-made substances. artificial, imitation,
manufactured, simulated, synthetic,
unnatural.
OPPOSITES: SEE **natural**.

manner noun
1 *She does things in a professional manner.*
fashion, means, method, mode, procedure,
process, style, way.
2 *I don't like his cheeky manner.* air, attitude,
bearing, behaviour, character, conduct,
demeanour, disposition, look, mien.

good manners good behaviour, breeding, civility, conduct, courtesy, etiquette, gentility, politeness, refinement.

mannerism noun
an annoying mannerism. characteristic, habit, idiosyncrasy, peculiarity, quirk, trait.

manoeuvre noun
1 *Getting the car into the drive is a tricky manoeuvre.* move, operation.
2 *It was a clever manoeuvre to take his bishop.* dodge, gambit, move, plan, plot, ploy, ruse, scheme, stratagem, strategy, tactics, trick.
manoeuvres *army manoeuvres,* exercise, movement, operation, training.

manoeuvre verb
to manoeuvre something into position. engineer, guide, jockey, manipulate, move, navigate, negotiate, pilot, steer.

mansion noun
castle, château, manor, manor-house, palace, stately home, villa.

manual adjective
manual work. by hand, physical.

manufacture verb
to manufacture goods in a factory. assemble, build, fabricate, make, mass-produce, prefabricate, process, [*informal*] turn out.

manufactured adjective
1 *manufactured goods.* factory-made, mass-produced.
2 *manufactured substances.* artificial, man-made, synthetic.

manufacturer noun
factory-owner, industrialist, producer.

manure noun
compost, dung, fertilizer, [*informal*] muck.

manuscript noun
SEE **book** noun, document, papers, script.

many adjective
abundant, copious, countless, frequent, innumerable, multifarious, numberless, numerous, profuse, [*informal*] umpteen, untold, various.
OPPOSITES: SEE **few**.

map noun
chart, diagram, plan.
a book of maps atlas, roadbook.
the drawing of maps cartography.

mar verb SEE **spoil**.

marauder noun
bandit, buccaneer, invader, pirate, plunderer, raider.

march verb
Soldiers marched into town. file, parade, stride, troop, SEE **walk** verb.

margin noun
the margin of a piece of paper. the margin of a lake. border, boundary, SEE **edge** noun, frieze, perimeter, side, verge.

marginal adjective
of marginal importance. borderline, doubtful, minimal, negligible, peripheral, small, unimportant.

marine adjective
SEE **sea** adjective.

marine noun SEE **soldier**.

mariner noun
sailor, seafarer, seaman.

mark noun
1 *dirty marks. marks on your skin.* blemish, blot, blotch, dot, fingermark, [*plural*] graffiti, marking, print, scar, scratch, scribble, smear, smudge, smut, [*informal*] splotch, SEE **spot** noun, stain, [*formal*] stigma (*plural* stigmata), streak, trace, vestige.
2 *a mark of respect. a mark of good breeding.* characteristic, emblem, feature, hallmark, indication, sign, symbol, token.
3 *a manufacturer's mark.* badge, brand, device, label, seal, stamp, standard.

mark verb
1 *to mark a surface.* blemish, blot, brand, bruise, damage, deface, dirty, disfigure, draw on, make a mark on [SEE **mark** noun], mar, scar, scratch, scrawl over, scribble on, smudge, spot, stain, stamp, streak, tattoo, write on.
2 *to mark students' work.* appraise, assess, correct, evaluate, grade.
3 *Mark what I say.* attend to, heed, listen to, mind, note, notice, observe, take note of, [*informal*] take to heart, watch.

market verb
His firm markets furniture. SEE **advertise**, retail, sell, [*informal*] tout, trade, trade in.

marketable adjective
marketable goods. in demand, merchantable, saleable, sellable.

maroon verb
to maroon someone on an island. abandon, cast away, desert, forsake, isolate, leave, put ashore, strand.

marriage noun
1 *They celebrated 25 years of marriage.* matrimony, partnership, union, wedlock.
2 *Today is the anniversary of their marriage.* [*old-fashioned*] espousal, match, nuptials, wedding.

VARIOUS STATES OF MARRIAGE: bigamy, monogamy, polyandry, polygamy.

COMPARE: celibacy, divorce, separation.

RELATED ADJECTIVES: conjugal, marital, matrimonial, nuptial.

---

marry verb
1 *to marry a husband or wife.* espouse, [*informal*] get hitched, join in matrimony, [*informal*] tie the knot, wed.
2 *to marry two things together.* SEE **unite**.

marsh noun
bog, fen, marshland, mire, morass, mud, mudflats, quagmire, quicksands, saltings, saltmarsh, [*old-fashioned*] slough, swamp, wetland.

marshal verb
to marshal troops. to marshal your thoughts. arrange, assemble, collect, deploy, draw up, gather, group, line up, muster, organize, set out.

martial adjective
1 *a martial figure.* aggressive, bellicose, belligerent, militant, pugnacious, warlike.
OPPOSITES: SEE **peaceable**.
2 *martial law.* military.
OPPOSITES: SEE **civil**.
martial arts judo, karate, kung fu, taekwondo.

marvel noun
the marvel of space travel. miracle, wonder.

marvel verb
to marvel at *We marvelled at their skill.* admire, applaud, be amazed by, be astonished by, be surprised by, gape at, SEE **praise** verb, wonder at.

marvellous adjective
a marvellous scientific discovery. marvellous works of art. admirable, amazing, astonishing, excellent, extraordinary, [*informal*] fabulous, [*informal*] fantastic, glorious, incredible, magnificent, miraculous, phenomenal, praiseworthy, remarkable, sensational, spectacular, splendid, [*informal*] super, superb, surprising, unbelievable, wonderful, wondrous.
OPPOSITES: SEE **ordinary**.

masculine adjective
[*Masculine* and its synonyms may have sexist overtones, and therefore should be used with care.] *a masculine appearance. masculine behaviour.* boyish, [*informal*] butch, dynamic, gentlemanly, heroic, [*uncomplimentary*] macho, male, manly, mannish, muscular, powerful, strong, vigorous, virile.
OPPOSITES: SEE **feminine**.

mash verb
to mash something to a pulp. beat, crush, grind, mangle, pound, pulp, pulverize, smash, squash.

mask noun
a mask to cover your face. camouflage, cover, disguise, façade, front, screen, shield, veil, visor.

mask verb
We planted a tree to mask the ugly building. blot out, camouflage, cloak, conceal, cover, disguise, hide, obscure, screen, shield, shroud, veil.

mass adjective
a mass revolt. comprehensive, general, large-scale, popular, universal, wholesale, widespread.
the mass media SEE **communication**.

mass noun
1 *a mass of rubbish.* accumulation, body, bulk, [*informal*] chunk, concretion, conglomeration, [*informal*] dollop, heap, [*informal*] hunk, [*informal*] load, lot, lump, mound, pile, quantity, stack.
2 *a mass of people.* SEE **group** noun.

massacre verb SEE **kill**.

massage verb
The trainer massaged my injured leg. knead, manipulate, rub.

massive adjective SEE **huge**.

mast noun
aerial, flagpole, maypole, pylon, transmitter.

master noun
1 *the master of a dog.* keeper, owner, person in charge, proprietor.
2 *a schoolmaster.* SEE **teacher**.
3 *the master of a ship.* captain.
4 *a master at chess.* [*informal*] ace, expert, genius, mastermind, virtuoso.

master verb
[Some people regard the verb *master* as sexist.] 1 *to master the rules.* acquire, [*informal*] get off by heart, [*informal*] get the hang of, grasp, learn, understand.
2 *to master a wild horse.* break in, bridle, conquer, control, curb, defeat, dominate, [*informal*] get the better of, govern, manage, overcome, overpower, quell, regulate, rule, subdue, subjugate, suppress, tame, triumph over, vanquish.

mastermind noun
1 *the mastermind behind an undertaking.* architect, brains, creator, engineer, inventor, manager, originator, planner, prime mover.
2 [*informal*] *Ask the mastermind!* [*informal*] egghead, expert, genius, intellectual, master.

mastermind verb
She masterminded the whole operation. be
the mastermind behind [SEE **mastermind**
noun], carry through, direct, execute, SEE
manage, organize, plan.

masterpiece noun
*This piece of music is the composer's
masterpiece.* best work, chef-d'œuvre,
classic, [*informal*] hit, pièce de résistance.

mat noun
carpet, floor-covering, matting, rug.

match noun
1 *It was an exciting match on Saturday.*
competition, contest, game, test match, tie,
tournament.
2 *The jacket and tie are a good match.*
combination, complement, counterpart,
double, equivalent, fit, pair, similarity, tally,
twin.
3 *a love match.* friendship, marriage,
partnership, relationship, union.

match verb
1 *The tie matches my shirt.* agree with, be
compatible with, be the same colour (style,
etc.) as, be similar to, blend with, coincide
with, combine with, compare with,
correspond to, fit with, go with, harmonize
with, marry with, tally with, tone in with.
OPPOSITES: SEE **contrast** verb.
2 *We'll match you with a suitable partner.*
ally, combine, couple, fit, join, link up, mate,
put together, team.

matching adjective
a blue shirt with matching tie. alike,
appropriate, comparable, compatible, co-
ordinating, corresponding, equal,
equivalent, harmonizing, identical, similar,
toning, twin.
OPPOSITES: SEE **incongruous**.

mate noun
1 *a plumber's mate.* assistant, collaborator,
colleague, helper, partner.
2 *a mate for life.* husband, spouse, wife.
3 [*informal*] *He's a mate of mine.* SEE **friend**.

mate verb
Many birds mate in the springtime. become
partners, copulate, couple, have
intercourse, [*informal*] have sex [SEE **sex**],
marry, unite, wed.

material noun
1 *material to make a shirt.* SEE **cloth**, fabric,
textile.
2 *material for a story.* content, data, facts,
ideas, information, matter, notes, subject
matter.
3 *material to make a patio.* building
materials, stuff, substances, things.
VARIOUS BUILDING MATERIALS: SEE **building**.

mathematics noun
[*informal*] maths, number work.

BRANCHES OF MATHEMATICS: algebra,
arithmetic, calculus, geometry, statistics,
trigonometry.

EVERYDAY MATHEMATICAL TERMS: addition,
angle, area, binary system, concentric,
congruence, cosine, decimal, fraction,
decimal point, diagonal, diameter, division,
equation, equilateral, exponent, factor,
fraction, function, graph, index (*plural*
indices), locus, logarithm, matrix,
mensuration, minus, multiplication,
negative number, parallel, percentage,
perpendicular, plus, positive number,
radius, ratio, right angle, SEE **shape** noun,
sine, subtraction, sum, symmetry, tangent,
tessellation, theorem.

---

matted adjective
matted hair. knotted, tangled, uncombed,
unkempt.

matter noun
1 *mind over matter. colouring matter.* body,
material, stuff, substance.
2 *poisonous matter in a wound.* discharge,
pus, suppuration.
3 *The manager will deal with this matter.*
affair, business, concern, incident, issue,
situation, subject, thing, topic.
4 *What's the matter with the car?* difficulty,
problem, trouble, upset, worry, wrong
(*What's wrong?*).

matter verb
Will it matter if I'm late? be important, count,
make a difference, signify.

mature adjective
1 *mature for her age.* adult, advanced, full-
grown, grown-up, nubile, well-developed.
OPPOSITES: SEE **immature**.
2 *mature fruit.* mellow, ready, ripe.
OPPOSITES: SEE **unripe**.

maul verb
The lion mauled the keeper. claw, injure,
[*informal*] knock about, lacerate, mangle,
manhandle, mutilate, paw, treat roughly, SEE
wound verb.

maximize verb
1 *to maximize your profits.* SEE **increase** verb.
2 *to maximize your problems.* SEE **exaggerate**.
OPPOSITES: SEE **minimize**.

maximum adjective
maximum size. maximum speed. biggest, full,
fullest, greatest, highest, largest, most,
supreme, top.
OPPOSITES: SEE **minimum** adjective.

maximum noun
Temperatures usually reach their maximum after noon. ceiling, highest point, peak, top, upper limit, zenith.
OPPOSITES: SEE **minimum** noun.

maybe adverb
conceivably, perhaps, possibly.

maze noun
a maze of corridors. confusion, labyrinth, network, tangle, web.

meadow noun
field, [*poetic*] mead, paddock, pasture.

meagre adjective
SEE **scanty**.

meal noun
[*informal*] blow-out, repast, [*informal*] spread.

VARIOUS MEALS: banquet, barbecue, breakfast, buffet, dinner, [*informal*] elevenses, feast, high tea, lunch, luncheon, picnic, snack, supper, takeaway, tea, tea-break, [*old-fashioned*] tiffin.

COURSES OF A MEAL: [*informal*] afters, dessert, [*formal*] entrée, hors-d'œuvres, main course, pudding, starter, sweet.

---

mean adjective
1 *too mean to give a donation.* beggarly, [*informal*] cheese-paring, close, close-fisted, [*informal*] mingy, miserly, niggardly, parsimonious, [*informal*] penny-pinching, selfish, sparing, [*informal*] stingy, [*informal*] tight, tight-fisted.
OPPOSITES: SEE **generous**.
2 *a mean trick.* base, callous, churlish, contemptible, cruel, despicable, hard-hearted, malicious, nasty, shabby, shameful, [*informal*] sneaky, spiteful, unkind, vicious.
OPPOSITES: SEE **kind** adjective.
3 [*old-fashioned*] *a mean dwelling.* humble, inferior, insignificant, lowly, SEE **poor**, squalid, wretched.
OPPOSITES: SEE **superior**.

mean verb
1 *What does that sign mean?* betoken, communicate, connote, convey, denote, express, hint at, imply, indicate, portend, presage, say, signify, spell out, stand for, suggest, symbolize.
2 *I mean to work harder.* aim, desire, intend, plan, propose, purpose, want, wish.
3 *The job means working long hours.* entail, involve, necessitate.

meaning noun
1 *the meaning of a word.* connotation, definition, denotation, force, sense, signification.

2 *the meaning of a poem. the meaning of someone's behaviour.* explanation, gist, implication, interpretation, message, point, purport, purpose, significance, thrust.

meaningful adjective
a meaningful glance. meaningful discussions. eloquent, expressive, meaning, pointed, positive, pregnant, significant, suggestive, warning, worthwhile.
OPPOSITES: SEE **meaningless**.

meaningless adjective
1 *meaningless compliments.* empty, flattering, hollow, insincere, sycophantic, worthless.
2 *a meaningless message.* absurd, coded, incoherent, incomprehensible, inconsequential, nonsensical, pointless, senseless.
OPPOSITES: SEE **meaningful**.

means noun
1 *the means to do something. a means to an end.* ability, capacity, channel, course, fashion, machinery, manner, medium, method, mode, process, way.
2 *the means to pay for something. private means.* affluence, capital, finances, funds, income, money, resources, riches, wealth, [*informal*] wherewithal.

measurable adjective
a measurable amount. appreciable, considerable, perceptible, quantifiable, reasonable, significant.

measure noun
1 *full measure.* amount, capacity, distance, extent, length, magnitude, measurement, quantity, ration, size, unit, way.
2 *a measure of someone's ability.* criterion, standard, test, touchstone, yardstick.
3 *measures to curb crime.* act, action, bill, expedient, law, means, procedure, step.

UNITS USED IN MEASURING: BREADTH, DEPTH, DISTANCE, GAUGE, HEIGHT, LENGTH, WIDTH: centimetre, cubit, fathom, foot, furlong, inch, kilometre, light-year, metre, millimetre, parsec, yard.

AREA: acre, hectare, square centimetres (metres, etc.).

TIME: century, day, decade, hour, microsecond, millennium, minute, month, second, week, year.

CAPACITY, VOLUME: bushel, cubic centimetres (inches, etc.), gallon, hogshead, litre, millilitre, pint, quart.

WEIGHT: carat, drachm, gram, hundred-weight, kilo or kilogram, megaton, megatonne, milligram, ounce, pound, stone, ton, tonne.

SPEED, VELOCITY: kilometres per hour, knot, Mach number, miles per hour, [*informal*] ton.

QUANTITY: century [= *100*], dozen, gross, score.

TEMPERATURE: degree Celsius, degree centigrade, degree Fahrenheit.

INFORMAL MEASUREMENTS: armful, cupful, handful, mouthful, pinch, plateful, spoonful.

---

measure verb
He measured its size. assess, calculate, calibrate, compute, determine, gauge, judge, mark-out, plumb (*to plumb the depths of water*), quantify, survey, take measurements of, weigh.
to measure out *She measured out their daily ration.* allot, apportion, deal out, dispense, distribute, [*informal*] dole out, ration out, share out.

measurement noun
the measurements of a room. dimensions, extent, size.

meat noun
flesh.

KINDS OF MEAT: bacon, beef, chicken, game, gammon, ham, lamb, mutton, offal, oxtail, pork, poultry, tripe, turkey, veal, venison.

VARIOUS CUTS OR JOINTS OF MEAT: breast, brisket, chine, chops, chuck, cutlet, fillet, flank, leg, loin, oxtail, rib, rump, scrag, shoulder, silverside, sirloin, spare-rib, steak, topside, trotter.

KINDS OF PROCESSED MEAT: brawn, burger, corned beef, hamburger, mince, pasty, pâté, pie, potted meat, rissole, salted meat, sausage.

---

mechanical adjective
a mechanical process. automated, automatic, machine-driven, technological.
OPPOSITES: SEE **manual**.

medal noun
award, decoration, honour, medallion, prize, reward, trophy.

meddle verb
SEE **interfere**.

media noun
SEE **communication**.

mediate verb
to mediate in a dispute. act as mediator [SEE **mediator**], arbitrate, intercede, liaise, negotiate.

mediator noun
arbitrator, broker, go-between, intermediary, negotiator, peacemaker, referee, umpire.

medicinal adjective
a medicinal ointment. healing, medical, restorative, therapeutic.

medicine noun
1 *the study of medicine.* healing, surgery, therapeutics, treatment of diseases.
2 *medicine from the chemist's.* cure, dose, drug, medicament, medication, [*uncomplimentary*] nostrum, prescription, remedy, treatment.

SOME BRANCHES OF MEDICAL PRACTICE: anaesthesiology (*anaesthetics*), audiometrics (*hearing*), chiropody (*feet*), dentistry (*teeth*), dermatology (*skin*), dietetics (*diet*), family practice, general practice, geriatrics (*old age*), gynaecology (*women's illnesses*), homeopathy, immunology (*resistance to infection*), neurology (*nerves*), neurosurgery, obstetrics (*childbirth*), ophthalmology (*eyes*), orthopaedics (*bones & muscles*), osteopathy, paediatrics (*children*), pathology, plastic surgery, preventive or preventative medicine, psychiatry (*mind*), radiology (*X-rays*), surgery, SEE **therapy**.

PEOPLE WHO LOOK AFTER OUR HEALTH: acupuncturist, anaesthetist, audiometrician, chiropodist, chiropractor, dentist, dermatologist, dietician, doctor, general practitioner, gynaecologist, homeopath, hygienist, hypnotherapist, [*male*] masseur, [*female*] masseuse, medical practitioner, midwife, neurologist, nurse, obstetrician, oculist, optician, osteopath, paediatrician, physician, physiotherapist, plastic surgeon, psychiatrist, radiographer, sister, surgeon.

PLACES WHERE YOU GET MEDICAL TREATMENT: clinic, dispensary, health centre, health farm, hospital, infirmary, intensive-care unit, nursing home, operating theatre, outpatients' department, sickbay, surgery, ward.

VARIOUS MEDICINES, ETC.: anaesthetic, antibiotic, antidote, antiseptic, aspirin, capsule, embrocation, gargle, herbs, inhaler, iodine, linctus, lotion, lozenge, manipulation, massage, morphia, narcotic, ointment, pastille, penicillin, [*informal*] the pill, sedative, suppository, tablet, tonic, tranquilliser.

OTHER MEDICAL TERMS: bandage, biopsy, dressing, first aid, forceps, hypodermic syringe, immunization, injection, inoculation, lint, plaster, poultice, scalpel,

sling, splint, stethoscope, stretcher, syringe, thermometer, transfusion, transplant, tweezers, X-ray.
WORDS TO DO WITH ILLNESS: SEE **ill, illness**.

---

mediocre adjective
mediocre work. amateurish, average, commonplace, fair, indifferent, inferior, middling, moderate, [*informal*] neither one thing nor the other, [*informal*] nothing special, ordinary, passable, pedestrian, poorish, second-rate, [*informal*] so-so, undistinguished, unexciting, uninspired, unremarkable, weakish.

meditate verb
to meditate in silence. brood, cogitate, consider, contemplate, deliberate, mull things over, muse, ponder, pray, reflect, ruminate, think.

medium adjective
average, intermediate, mean, middle, middling, midway, moderate, normal, ordinary, usual.

medium noun
1 *a happy medium.* average, compromise, mean, middle, midpoint.
2 *This artist's favourite medium is water-colour.* form, means, method, vehicle, way.
3 *a medium who claims to communicate with the dead.* clairvoyant, seer, spiritualist.
the media [*Media* is plural, so we should speak not of *a media*, but of *the media*.] SEE **communication**.

meek adjective
meek acceptance of defeat. acquiescent, compliant, docile, forbearing, gentle, humble, long-suffering, lowly, mild, modest, obedient, patient, quiet, resigned, soft, spineless, tame, unassuming, unprotesting, weak.
OPPOSITES: SEE **aggressive**.

meet verb
1 *I met my friend in town.* [*informal*] bump into, chance upon, come across, confront, contact, encounter, face, happen on, have a meeting with [SEE **meeting**], [*informal*] run across, [*informal*] run into, see.
OPPOSITES: SEE **part** verb
2 *I'll meet you at the station.* come and fetch, greet, [*informal*] pick up, welcome.
3 *We all met in the hall.* assemble, collect, come together, congregate, convene, forgather, gather, have a meeting [SEE **meeting**], muster, rally.
4 *Two roads meet here.* come together, connect, converge, cross, intersect, join, link up, merge, unite.
5 *We met their demands.* acquiesce in, agree to, comply with, fulfil, [*informal*] measure up to, satisfy.

meeting noun
1 *a business meeting.* assembly, audience (*an audience with the king*), board meeting, briefing, cabinet meeting, committee, conclave, conference, congregation, congress, convention, council, discussion group, forum, gathering, [*informal*] powwow, prayer meeting, rally, seminar, service (*in church*), synod (*of the church*).
2 *a chance meeting.* confrontation, contact, encounter.
3 *an arranged meeting with someone.* appointment, assignation, date, engagement, [*informal*] get-together, rendezvous, [*old-fashioned*] tryst.
4 *the meeting of two routes.* confluence (*of rivers*), convergence, crossing, crossroads, intersection, junction.

melancholy adjective
a melancholy look on her face. a melancholy scene. cheerless, dejected, depressed, depressing, despondent, dispirited, dispiriting, [*informal*] down, down-hearted, gloomy, joyless, lifeless, low, lugubrious, melancholic, miserable, moody, mournful, sad, sombre, sorrowful, unhappy, woebegone, woeful.
OPPOSITES: SEE **cheerful**.

mellow adjective
1 *a mellow taste.* mature, mild, pleasant, rich, ripe, smooth, sweet.
2 *mellow light. mellow sounds. mellow surroundings.* agreeable, comforting, genial, gentle, happy, kindly, peaceful, reassuring, soft, subdued, warm.
OPPOSITES: SEE **harsh**.

melodious adjective
SEE **tuneful**.

melody noun
air, strain, theme, tune.

melt verb
The sun's warmth melts the snow. deliquesce, liquefy, soften, thaw, unfreeze.
to melt away *The crowds melted away.* dematerialize, disappear, disperse, dissolve, dwindle, evaporate, fade, pass away, vanish.

member noun
1 *a member of a club.* associate, fellow.
2 *the members of your body.* SEE **limb**.
to be a member SEE **belong**.

memorable adjective
1 *a memorable occasion.* distinguished, SEE **extraordinary**, impressive, indelible, ineradicable, outstanding, remarkable, striking, unforgettable.
2 *a memorable tune.* [*informal*] catchy, haunting.
OPPOSITES: SEE **commonplace**.

memorial noun
cairn, cenotaph, gravestone, headstone,
monument, plaque, tablet, SEE **tomb**.

memorize noun
to memorize facts. commit to memory,
[*informal*] get off by heart, SEE **learn**, learn
by rote, learn parrot-fashion, remember.

memory noun
1 *a bad memory.* ability to remember, recall,
retention.
2 *happy memories of our holiday.* impression,
recollection, remembrance, reminder,
reminiscence, souvenir.
3 *The memory of people we loved is always
with us.* fame, name, reputation.

menace verb
SEE **threaten**.

mend verb
1 *to mend the car. to mend clothes.* fix, put
right, rectify, renew, renovate, repair,
restore.

WAYS TO MEND THINGS: beat out (*to beat out
dents*), darn, glue, patch, replace parts, sew
up, solder, stick, stitch up, touch up, weld.

---

2 *to mend your ways.* amend, correct, cure,
improve, make better, reform, revise.

menial adjective
menial jobs. base, boring, degrading,
demeaning, humble, lowly, mean, servile,
slavish, subservient, unskilled, unworthy.

mental adjective
1 *mental arithmetic. mental effort.* abstract,
cerebral, intellectual, rational, theoretical.
2 *a mental condition.* emotional,
psychological, subjective, temperamental.

mentality noun
a criminal mentality. attitude, character,
disposition, frame of mind, [*informal*]
make-up, outlook, personality,
predisposition, propensity, psychology, way
of thinking.

mention verb
1 *to mention something casually.* allude to,
comment on, disclose, hint at, [*informal*] let
drop, let out, refer to, reveal, speak about,
touch on.
2 *The speaker mentioned all the prize-winners.*
acknowledge, cite, draw attention to,
enumerate, make known, name, point out.
3 *I mentioned that I might go out.* observe,
remark, say.

merchandise noun
commodities, goods, things for sale.

merchant noun
a timber merchant. dealer, retailer,
salesman, shopkeeper, stockist, supplier,
trader, tradesman, wholesaler.

merciful adjective
a merciful judge. merciful treatment.
benevolent, charitable, clement,
compassionate, forbearing, forgiving,
generous, gracious, humane, humanitarian,
kind, lenient, liberal, mild, pitying,
[*uncomplimentary*] soft, sympathetic,
tender-hearted, tolerant.
OPPOSITES: SEE **merciless**.

merciless adjective
a merciless judge. merciless punishment.
barbaric, callous, cruel, cut-throat, hard,
hard-hearted, harsh, heartless, inexorable,
inhuman, inhumane, intolerant, pitiless,
relentless, remorseless, ruthless, savage,
severe, stern, strict, unfeeling, unforgiving,
unkind, unrelenting, unremitting, vicious.
OPPOSITES: SEE **merciful**.

mercy noun
The attackers showed no mercy. charity,
clemency, compassion, feeling, forbearance,
forgiveness, grace, humanity, kindness,
leniency, love, pity, sympathy,
understanding.
OPPOSITES: SEE **cruelty**.

merge verb
1 *to merge two schools.* amalgamate, blend,
combine, come together, confederate, fuse,
integrate, join together, link up, mingle,
mix, put together, unite.
2 *motorways merge.* converge, join, meet.
OPPOSITES: SEE **separate** verb.

merit noun
1 *Your work has some merit.* asset,
excellence, goodness, importance, quality,
strength, talent, value, virtue, worth.
2 *a certificate of merit.* credit, distinction.

merit verb
Her performance merited first prize. be
entitled to, deserve, earn, incur, justify,
rate, warrant.

merriment noun
What's all the merriment about? amusement,
gaiety, hilarity, jocularity, joking, jollity,
joviality, laughter, levity, light-heartedness,
liveliness, mirth, vivacity.

merry adjective
a merry tune. bright, carefree, cheerful,
[*informal*] chirpy, festive, fun-loving, gay,
glad, SEE **happy**, hilarious, jocular, jolly,
jovial, joyful, joyous, light-hearted, lively,
rollicking, spirited, vivacious.
OPPOSITES: SEE **serious**.

mesh noun
a mesh of intersecting lines. lattice, net,
netting, network, tangle, tracery, web.

mess noun
1 *Clear up this mess.* chaos, clutter, SEE
confusion, SEE **dirt**, disorder, jumble, litter,

muddle, [*informal*] shambles, untidiness.
2 *I made a mess of it!* [*informal*] botch,
failure, [*informal*] hash, [*informal*] mix-up.
3 *I got into a mess.* difficulty, dilemma,
[*informal*] fix, [*informal*] jam, plight,
predicament, problem.

mess verb
to mess about [*informal*] *Stop messing
about and start work!* amuse yourself, loaf,
loiter, lounge about [SEE **lounge** verb],
[*informal*] monkey about, [*informal*] muck
about, play about.
to mess up SEE **muddle** verb.

message noun
announcement, bulletin, cable, SEE
communication, communiqué, dispatch,
letter, memo, memorandum, note, notice,
report, statement.

messenger noun
bearer, carrier, courier, dispatch-rider,
[*formal*] emissary, [*formal*] envoy, go-
between, [*poetic*] harbinger, herald,
postman, runner.

messy adjective
a messy appearance. blowzy, careless,
chaotic, cluttered, SEE **dirty**, dishevelled,
disorderly, filthy, grubby, mucky, muddled,
[*informal*] shambolic, slapdash, sloppy,
slovenly, unkempt, untidy.
OPPOSITES: SEE **neat**.

metal noun
a lump of metal ingot, nugget.

METALLIC ELEMENTS: aluminium, barium,
beryllium, bismuth, cadmium, calcium,
chromium, cobalt, copper, gold, iridium,
iron, lead, lithium, magnesium, manganese,
mercury, molybdenum, nickel, platinum,
potassium, silver, sodium, strontium, tin,
titanium, tungsten, uranium, zinc.

SOME METAL ALLOYS: brass, bronze,
gunmetal, pewter, solder, steel.

---

metallic adjective
1 *a metallic sheen.* gleaming, lustrous, shiny.
2 *a metallic sound.* clanking, clinking,
ringing.

method noun
1 *a method of doing something.* fashion,
[*informal*] knack, manner, means, mode,
plan, procedure, process, recipe, scheme,
style, technique, trick, way.
2 *method behind the chaos.* arrangement,
design, order, orderliness, organization,
pattern, routine, system.

methodical adjective
a methodical worker. businesslike, careful,
deliberate, disciplined, logical, meticulous,

neat, orderly, organized, painstaking,
precise, rational, regular, structured,
systematic, tidy.
OPPOSITES: SEE **arbitrary**, **careless**.

meticulous adjective
SEE **scrupulous**.

micro-organism noun
bacillus, [*plural*] bacteria, [*informal*] bug,
germ, microbe, virus.

microscopic adjective
SEE **tiny**.

middle adjective
the middle stump. central, half-way, inner,
inside, intermediate, intervening, mean,
medial, median, middle-of-the-road, midway,
neutral.

middle noun
the middle of the earth. the middle of the road.
centre, core, crown (*of the road*), focus,
heart, hub, inside, middle position [SEE
middle adjective], midpoint, midst (*in the
midst of the confusion*), nucleus.

middling adjective
a middling performance. average, fair,
[*informal*] fair to middling, indifferent,
mediocre, moderate, modest, [*informal*]
nothing to write home about, ordinary,
passable, run-of-the-mill, [*informal*] so-so,
unremarkable.
OPPOSITES: SEE **outstanding**.

midget adjective SEE **small**.

might noun
I banged at the door with all my might.
energy, force, power, strength, vigour.

mighty adjective
a mighty blow. a mighty figure. big,
enormous, forceful, great, hefty, SEE **huge**,
muscular, powerful, strong, vigorous.
OPPOSITES: SEE **weak**.

mild adjective
1 *a mild person.* amiable, docile, easygoing,
forbearing, gentle, good-tempered,
harmless, indulgent, kind, lenient, SEE
merciful, placid, [*uncomplimentary*] soft,
soft-hearted, understanding.
2 *mild weather.* balmy, calm, clement,
peaceful, pleasant, temperate, warm.
OPPOSITES: SEE **severe**.
3 *a mild flavour.* bland, delicate, faint,
mellow, subtle.
OPPOSITES: SEE **strong**.

militant adjective
[Do not confuse with *militaristic* or *military*.]
militant political views. active, aggressive,
assertive, attacking, positive.

militant noun
a political militant. activist, extremist,
[*informal*] hawk, partisan.

militaristic adjective
[Do not confuse with *militant.*] belligerent,
combative, fond of fighting, hostile,
pugnacious, warlike.
OPPOSITES: SEE **peaceable.**

military adjective
1 *military might. military personnel.* armed,
belligerent, enlisted, uniformed, warlike.
OPPOSITE: SEE **civilian.**
2 *military law.* martial.
OPPOSITES: SEE **civil.**

milk noun

KINDS OF MILK: condensed, dried, evaporated,
long-life, pasteurized, skimmed, UHT.

FOODS MADE FROM MILK: butter, cheese,
cream, curds, custard, dairy products,
junket, milk pudding, yoghurt.

milky adjective
a milky liquid. chalky, cloudy, misty,
opaque, whitish.
OPPOSITES: SEE **clear** adjective.

mill noun
a steel mill. factory, processing plant, works,
workshop.

mimic verb
Children often mimic their teachers. ape,
caricature, copy, do impressions of, echo,
imitate, impersonate, look like, parody,
parrot, pretend to be, simulate, sound like,
[*informal*] take off.

mincer noun
blender, food-processor, mincing machine.

mind noun
1 *Use your mind!* brain, cleverness,
[*informal*] grey matter, head, intellect,
intelligence, judgement, memory, mental
power, psyche, rationality, reasoning,
remembrance, sense, thinking,
understanding, wits.
RELATED ADJECTIVES: mental, psychological.
2 *He's changed his mind.* belief, intention,
opinion, outlook, point of view, view, way
of thinking, wishes.

mind verb
1 *Mind my things while I'm swimming.* attend
to, care for, guard, keep an eye on, look
after, watch.
2 *Mind the step.* be careful about, beware of,
heed, look out for, note, remember, take
notice of, watch out for.
3 *We won't mind if you're late.* be resentful,

bother, care, complain, disapprove,
grumble, object, take offence, worry.

mindless adjective
SEE **stupid.**

mine noun
a coal-mine. colliery, excavation, opencast
mine, pit, quarry, shaft, tunnel, working.

mine verb
to mine gold. dig for, excavate, extract,
quarry, remove.

mineral noun
minerals quarried out of the ground. metal,
ore, rock.

mingle verb
People mingled happily at the carnival.
associate, blend, circulate, combine, get
together, intermingle, merge, mix, move
about, [*informal*] rub shoulders, socialize.

miniature adjective SEE **tiny.**

minimal adjective
Modern cars require minimal servicing. SEE
minimum adjective, negligible, slightest.

minimize verb
1 *They banned smoking to minimize the
danger of fire.* SEE **reduce.**
2 *He always minimizes the difficulties.* gloss
over, make light of, play down, SEE
underestimate.
OPPOSITES: SEE **maximize.**

minimum adjective
minimum wages. minimum temperature.
bottom, least, littlest, lowest, minimal,
[*informal*] rock bottom, slightest, smallest.
OPPOSITES: SEE **maximum** adjective.

minimum noun
Keep expenses to the minimum. lowest level,
minimum amount (quantity, etc.) [SEE
minimum adjective], nadir.
OPPOSITES: SEE **maximum** noun.

minister noun
1 *a government minister.* SEE **government.**
2 *a minister of the church.* SEE **clergyman.**

minister verb
to minister to the sick. SEE **attend (attend to).**

minor adjective
a minor accident. a minor official.
inconsequential, inferior, insignificant,
lesser, little, petty, secondary, SEE **small,**
subordinate, trivial, unimportant.
OPPOSITES: SEE **major** adjective.

minority noun
Only a minority voted to strike. lesser
number, smaller number.
to be in a minority be outnumbered, lose.

mint adjective
in mint condition. brand-new, first-class,
fresh, immaculate, new, perfect,
unblemished, unmarked, unused.

mint verb
to mint coins. cast, coin, forge, make,
manufacture, stamp out, strike.

minuscule, minute adjectives
SEE **tiny.**

miracle noun
the miracle of birth. marvel, miraculous
event [SEE **miraculous**], mystery, wonder.

miraculous adjective
a miraculous cure. amazing, astonishing,
extraordinary, incredible, inexplicable,
magic, marvellous, mysterious,
preternatural, supernatural,
unaccountable, unbelievable, wonderful.

mirage noun
a mirage in the desert. delusion,
hallucination, illusion, vision.

mire noun
sinking in the mire. bog, SEE **dirt**, marsh,
morass, mud, ooze, quagmire, quicksand,
slime, swamp.

mirror noun
looking-glass, reflector.

misadventure noun
death by misadventure. accident, calamity,
catastrophe, disaster, ill fortune,
mischance, misfortune, mishap.

misanthropic adjective
*a misanthropic attitude towards your fellow
human beings.* cynical, mean, nasty, surly,
unfriendly, unpleasant, unsociable.
OPPOSITES: SEE **philanthropic.**

misbehave verb
behave badly, be mischievous [SEE
mischievous], be a nuisance, [*informal*] blot
your copybook, [*informal*] carry on, commit
an offence, default, disobey, do wrong, err,
fool about, make mischief, [*informal*] mess
about, [*informal*] muck about, offend,
[*informal*] play up, sin, transgress.

misbehaviour noun
delinquency, disobedience, horseplay,
indiscipline, insubordination, mischief,
mischief-making, misconduct, naughtiness,
rudeness, sin, vandalism, wrongdoing.

miscalculate verb
[*informal*] boob, err, [*informal*] get it
wrong, go wrong, make a mistake [SEE
mistake noun], misjudge, [*informal*] slip up.

miscarriage noun
1 *miscarriage of a baby.* abortion, premature
birth, termination of pregnancy.

2 *a miscarriage of justice.* breakdown, error,
failure, SEE **mistake** noun, perversion.

miscarry verb
1 *to miscarry in pregnancy.* [*informal*] lose
the baby, suffer a miscarriage [SEE
miscarriage].
2 *The project miscarried.* break down, come
to nothing, fail, fall through, go wrong,
misfire.
OPPOSITES: SEE **succeed.**

miscellaneous adjective
miscellaneous odds and ends. assorted,
different, diverse, heterogeneous, mixed,
motley (*a motley crowd*), multifarious,
sundry, varied, various.
OPPOSITES: SEE **homogeneous.**

mischief noun
1 *Don't get into mischief.* devilment, [*joking*]
devilry, escapade, misbehaviour,
misconduct, [*informal*] monkey business,
naughtiness, prank, scrape, trouble.
2 *Did you come to any mischief?* damage,
harm, hurt, injury, misfortune.

mischievous adjective
mischievous children. annoying, badly
behaved, boisterous, disobedient, fractious,
full of mischief [SEE **mischief**], impish, lively,
naughty, playful, [*informal*] puckish,
roguish, uncontrollable, [*informal*] up to no
good, wicked.

misconduct noun
SEE **misbehaviour.**

miserable adjective
1 *miserable after hearing bad news.* broken-
hearted, dejected, depressed, desolate,
despondent, disconsolate, distressed,
doleful, [*informal*] down, downcast, down-
hearted, forlorn, gloomy, glum, grief-
stricken, heartbroken, joyless, lonely,
melancholy, moping, mournful, SEE **sad**,
tearful, uneasy, unfortunate, unhappy,
unlucky, woebegone, wretched.
OPPOSITES: SEE **happy.**
2 *miserable living conditions.* abject,
destitute, disgraceful, distressing, heartbreaking, hopeless, impoverished, inhuman,
pathetic, pitiable, pitiful, SEE **poor**, sordid,
soul-destroying, squalid, uncivilized,
uncomfortable, vile, worthless, wretched.
OPPOSITES: SEE **affluent.**
3 *miserable weather.* SEE **bad**, cheerless,
depressing, dismal, dreary, grey.
OPPOSITES: SEE **bright.**
4 *He's a miserable old so-and-so!* churlish,
cross, disagreeable, discontented,
[*informal*] grumpy, ill-natured, mean,
miserly, morose, sulky, sullen, surly,
unfriendly, unhelpful.
OPPOSITES: SEE **cheerful.**

miserly adjective
avaricious, [*informal*] close, [*informal*]
close-fisted, covetous, economical, grasping,
mean, mercenary, mingy, niggardly,
parsimonious, penny-pinching, stingy,
[*informal*] tight, [*informal*] tight-fisted.
OPPOSITES: SEE **generous**.

misery noun
1 *You could see the misery on their faces.*
anguish, bitterness, depression, despair,
distress, gloom, grief, heartache,
heartbreak, melancholy, sadness, sorrow,
suffering, unhappiness, wretchedness.
2 *a life of misery.* adversity, affliction,
deprivation, destitution, hardship,
misfortune, need, oppression, penury,
poverty, privation, squalor, tribulation,
want.

misfire verb
The plan misfired. abort, fail, fall through,
[*informal*] flop, founder, go wrong,
miscarry.
OPPOSITES: SEE **succeed**.

misfortune noun
We had the misfortune of breaking down.
accident, adversity, affliction, bad luck, bane
(*the bane of my life*), calamity, catastrophe,
disappointment, disaster, hardship,
misadventure, mischance, mishap, reverse,
setback, tragedy, trouble, vicissitude.
OPPOSITES: SEE **luck**.

misguided adjective
SEE **mistaken**.

mishap noun
SEE **accident**.

misjudge verb
to misjudge a situation. get wrong, guess
wrongly, [*informal*] jump to the wrong
conclusion about, make a mistake about,
miscalculate, misinterpret, SEE
misunderstand, overestimate,
underestimate, undervalue.

mislay verb
I mislaid my purse. SEE **lose**.

mislead verb
Don't try to mislead us! bluff, confuse,
deceive, delude, fool, give misleading
information to [SEE **misleading**], give a wrong
impression to, hoax, hoodwink, [*informal*]
kid, [*informal*] lead up the garden path, lie
to, misinform, [*informal*] take for a ride,
take in, trick.

misleading adjective
misleading directions. ambiguous,
confusing, deceptive, dishonest, distorted,
equivocal, evasive, fallacious, false, SEE
lying, muddling, puzzling, specious,
spurious, unreliable, unsound, wrong.

miss verb
1 *to miss a bus.* be too late for, let go, lose.
2 *to miss a target.* be wide of, fail to hit, fall
short of.
3 *to miss an appointment.* avoid, be absent
from, forget, play truant from, [*informal*]
skip, [*informal*] skive off.
4 *to miss someone who is absent.* grieve for,
lament, long for, need, pine for, want, yearn
for.
to miss something out SEE **omit**.

misshapen adjective
a misshapen tree-trunk. crooked, deformed,
disfigured, distorted, grotesque, malformed,
monstrous, twisted, ugly, warped.
OPPOSITES: SEE **perfect** adjective.

missile noun

VARIOUS MISSILES: arrow, bomb, brickbat,
bullet, dart, grenade, projectile, rocket,
shell, shot, torpedo.

VARIOUS WEAPONS: SEE **weapons**.

missing adjective
missing children. absent, disappeared, lost,
mislaid, straying, unaccounted for.

mission noun
1 *a mission into the unknown.* expedition,
exploration, journey, sortie, voyage.
2 *a mission to help the starving.* SEE **campaign**.

mist noun
1 *mist in the air.* cloud, drizzle, fog, haze,
vapour.
2 *mist on the windows.* condensation, film,
steam.

mistake noun
[*informal*] bloomer, blunder, [*informal*]
boob, [*informal*] clanger, error, faux pas,
gaffe, [*informal*] howler, inaccuracy,
indiscretion, lapse, miscalculation,
miscarriage (*of justice*), misjudgement,
misprint, misspelling, misunderstanding,
omission, oversight, slip, slip-up, [*formal*]
solecism.

mistake verb
I mistook your message. confuse, get wrong,
[*informal*] get the wrong end of the stick,
misconstrue, misinterpret, misjudge,
misread, misunderstand, mix up.

mistaken adjective
a mistaken decision. erroneous, ill-judged,
inappropriate, incorrect, inexact,
misguided, misinformed, unfounded, unjust,
unsound, SEE **wrong** adjective.

mistreat verb
to mistreat animals. abuse, batter, harm,
hurt, ill-treat, ill-use, [*informal*] knock
about, misuse.

mistrust verb
I mistrust his judgement. be sceptical about, be wary of, disbelieve, distrust, doubt, fear, have misgivings about, question, suspect.
OPPOSITES: SEE **trust** verb.

misty adjective
misty windows. a misty view. bleary, blurred, blurry, clouded, cloudy, dim, faint, foggy, fuzzy, hazy, indistinct, opaque, shadowy, smoky, steamy, unclear, vague.
OPPOSITES: SEE **clear** adjective.

misunderstand verb
to misunderstand a message. get wrong, [*informal*] get the wrong end of the stick, have a misunderstanding about [SEE **misunderstanding**], misconstrue, mishear, misinterpret, SEE **misjudge**, misread, miss the point, mistake, mistranslate.
OPPOSITES: SEE **understand**.

misunderstanding noun
1 *a misunderstanding of the problem.* error, failure of understanding, misapprehension, misconception, misinterpretation, misjudgement, mistake, [*informal*] mix-up.
2 *a misunderstanding with someone.* argument, [*informal*] contretemps, difference of opinion, disagreement, dispute, SEE **quarrel** noun.

misuse verb
1 *Someone misused my tape-recorder.* damage, harm, mishandle, treat carelessly.
2 *He misused his dog shamefully.* abuse, batter, hurt, ill-treat, injure, [*informal*] knock about, mistreat, treat badly.
3 *She misused the club funds.* fritter away, misappropriate, squander, use wrongly, waste.

mix verb
1 *Mix the ingredients together. Oil and water won't mix.* amalgamate, blend, coalesce, combine, compound, confuse, diffuse, emulsify, fuse, homogenize, integrate, intermingle, join, jumble up, make a mixture [SEE **mixture**], meld, merge, mingle, mix up, muddle, put together, shuffle (*cards or papers*), unite.
OPPOSITES: SEE **separate** verb.
2 *He mixed with the wrong crowd.* SEE **socialize**.

mixed adjective
1 *mixed biscuits.* assorted, different, diverse, heterogeneous, miscellaneous, muddled, varied, various.
2 *a mixed team.* amalgamated, combined, composite, integrated, hybrid, joint, united.
3 *mixed feelings.* ambiguous, ambivalent, confused, equivocal, uncertain.

mixture noun
a mixture of ingredients. alloy (*of metals*), amalgam, association, assortment, blend, collection, combination, composite, compound, concoction, conglomeration, emulsion (*of a solid in a liquid*), fusion, [*informal*] hotchpotch, hybrid [= *a mixture of species or varieties*], jumble, medley, mélange, miscellany, mix, mongrel [= *a mixture of breeds*], pot-pourri, suspension (*of a solid in a liquid*), variety.

moan verb
1 VARIOUS SOUNDS: SEE **sound** noun.
2 *We moaned about the food.*
SEE **complain**.

mob noun
an angry mob. [*informal*] bunch, crowd, gang, SEE **group** noun, herd, horde, pack, rabble, riot, [*informal*] shower, swarm, throng.

mob verb
to mob a pop idol. besiege, crowd round, hem in, jostle, surround, swarm round, throng round.

mobile adjective
1 *a mobile caravan.* itinerant, movable, portable, travelling.
2 *It didn't take me long to get mobile after my accident.* able to move, active, agile, independent, moving about, [*informal*] on the go, [*informal*] up and about.
3 *mobile features.* changeable, changing, expressive, flexible, fluid, shifting.
OPPOSITES: SEE **immobile**.

mobilize verb
to mobilize support. activate, assemble, call up, enlist, gather, get together, levy, marshal, muster, organize, rally, stir up, summon.

mock verb
They mocked my pathetic attempts. deride, disparage, insult, jeer at, lampoon, laugh at, make fun of, parody, poke fun at, ridicule, satirize, scoff at, scorn, [*informal*] send up, sneer at, taunt, tease, travesty.

mockery noun
a mockery of the truth. lampoon, parody, satire, [*informal*] send-up, travesty.

mocking adjective
mocking insults. contemptuous, derisive, disparaging, disrespectful, insulting, irreverent, rude, sarcastic, satirical, scornful, taunting, teasing, uncomplimentary, unkind.
OPPOSITES: SEE **respectful**.

model noun
1 *scale models.* copy, dummy, effigy, image, imitation, miniature, replica, representation, toy.
2 *a model of a futuristic car.* archetype, [*informal*] mock-up, paradigm, pattern, prototype.

3 *a model of good behaviour.* byword,
example, ideal, paragon, yardstick.
4 *an out-of-date model.* design, mark, type,
version.

moderate adjective
1 *moderate prices. moderate opinions. a
moderate drinker.* average, cautious,
deliberate, fair, medium, middle, [*informal*]
middle-of-the-road, middling, modest,
normal, ordinary, rational, reasonable,
respectable, sensible, sober, steady,
temperate, usual.
2 *a moderate wind.* gentle, light, mild.
OPPOSITES: SEE **extreme** adjective.

moderate verb
1 *The storm moderated.* abate, become less
extreme, decline, decrease, die down, ease
off, subside.
2 *Please moderate the noise.* check, curb, keep
down, lessen, make less extreme, mitigate,
modify, modulate, regulate, restrain,
subdue, temper, tone down.

moderately adverb
moderately good. fairly, passably, [*informal*]
pretty, quite, rather, reasonably, somewhat,
to some extent.

moderation noun
*He always showed moderation in his
drinking.* caution, reasonableness, sobriety,
temperance.

modern adjective
modern music. modern architecture.
advanced, avant-garde, contemporary,
current, fashionable, forward-looking,
futuristic, the latest, new,
[*uncomplimentary*] newfangled, novel,
present, present-day, progressive, recent,
stylish, [*informal*] trendy, up-to-date, up-to-
the-minute, [*informal*] with it.
OPPOSITES: SEE **old**.

modernize verb
to modernize an old house. [*informal*] do up,
improve, make modern [SEE **modern**],
rebuild, refurbish, regenerate, renovate,
update.

modest adjective
1 *modest about your success.* humble, lowly,
meek, quiet, reserved, reticent,
unassuming, unpretentious.
OPPOSITES: SEE **conceited**.
2 *modest about getting undressed.* bashful,
coy, demure, shamefaced, shy.
3 *a modest dress.* chaste, decent, discreet,
plain, proper, seemly, simple.
OPPOSITES: SEE **indecent**.
4 *a modest sum of money.* SEE **moderate**
adjective.

modesty noun
1 *modesty about your success.* humbleness,
humility, reserve, reticence, self-
effacement.
2 *modesty about getting undressed.*
bashfulness, coyness, demureness, shyness.

modify verb
to modify the design of something. adapt,
adjust, alter, change, convert, improve, SEE
moderate verb, redesign, re-organize, revise,
transform, vary.

module noun
SEE **unit**.

moist adjective
affected by moisture [SEE **moisture**], clammy,
damp, dank, dewy, humid [*informal*]
muggy, rainy, [*informal*] runny, steamy,
watery, SEE **wet** adjective.
OPPOSITES: SEE **dry** adjective.

moisten verb
damp, dampen, humidify, make moist [SEE
moist], moisturize, soak, wet.
OPPOSITES: SEE **dry** verb.

moisture noun
condensation, damp, dampness, dankness,
dew, humidity, liquid, [*formal*]
precipitation, steam, vapour, water, wet,
wetness.

molest verb
Hooligans molested the bystanders. abuse,
annoy, assault, attack, badger, bother,
harass, harry, hassle, interfere with,
irritate, manhandle, mistreat, persecute,
pester, set on, tease, torment, vex, worry.

molten adjective
molten metal. liquefied, liquid, melted.

moment noun
1 *over in a moment.* flash, instant, [*informal*]
jiffy, minute, second, split second,
[*informal*] tick, [*informal*] trice, [*informal*]
twinkling of an eye.
2 *an important moment.* juncture, occasion,
opportunity, point in time, time.

momentary adjective
a momentary lapse of memory. brief,
ephemeral, fleeting, passing, quick, short,
temporary, transient, transitory.
OPPOSITES: SEE **permanent**.

momentous adjective
a momentous decision. critical, crucial,
decisive, epoch-making, fateful, historic, SEE
important, significant.
OPPOSITES: SEE **unimportant**.

monarchy noun
kingdom, realm.

money noun
[*informal*] bread, currency, [*informal*]
dough, finances, [*informal*] lolly, [*old-*

fashioned] lucre, riches, wealth, [*informal*] the wherewithal.
RELATED ADJECTIVES: financial, monetary, pecuniary.

FORMS IN WHICH YOU CAN SPEND MONEY:
bank-notes, cash, change, cheque, coins, coppers, credit card, credit transfer, notes, pennies, silver, sterling, traveller's cheque.

EVERYDAY TERMS FOR MONEY YOU OWE, OWN, PAY, OR RECEIVE: arrears, assets, capital, damages, debt, dividend, dowry, dues, duty, earnings, endowment, estate, expenditure, fortune, funds, grant, income, interest, investments, loan, mortgage, [*informal*] nest-egg, outgoings, patrimony, pay, pension, pocket-money, proceeds, profits, remittance, resources, revenue, salary, savings, takings, tax, wages, winnings.

---

money-box noun
cash-box, coffer, piggy-bank, safe, till.

mongrel noun
cross-breed, hybrid.

monk noun
brother, friar, hermit.

monkey noun

SOME KINDS OF MONKEY: ape, baboon, chimpanzee, gibbon, gorilla, marmoset, orang-utan.
RELATED ADJECTIVE: simian.

---

monopolize verb
to monopolize a conversation. control, [*informal*] corner, have a monopoly of, [*informal*] hog, keep for yourself, shut others out of, take over.
OPPOSITES: SEE **share** verb.

monotonous adjective
a monotonous voice. a monotonous landscape. boring, dreary, dull, featureless, flat, level, repetitive, tedious, toneless, unchanging, uneventful, unexciting, uniform, uninteresting, unvarying, wearisome.
OPPOSITES: SEE **interesting.**

monster noun
a frightening monster. abortion, beast, brute, freak, giant, monstrosity, monstrous creature or thing [SEE **monstrous**], mutant, ogre.

monstrous adjective
1 *a creature of monstrous size.* SEE **big,** colossal, elephantine, enormous, gargantuan, giant, gigantic, great, huge, hulking, immense, mammoth, mighty, titanic, towering, vast.

2 *a monstrous crime.* abhorrent, atrocious, cruel, dreadful, evil, gross, gruesome, heinous, hideous, [*informal*] horrendous, horrible, horrifying, inhuman, obscene, outrageous, repulsive, shocking, terrible, villainous, wicked.

monument noun
a monument to the dead. an ancient monument. cairn, cenotaph, cross, gravestone, headstone, mausoleum, memorial, obelisk, pillar, relic, reminder, shrine, tomb, tombstone.

mood noun
1 *in a good mood. in a bad mood.* disposition, humour, spirit, state of mind, temper, vein.
2 *the mood of a piece of music.* atmosphere, feeling, tone.

moody adjective
bad-tempered, capricious, changeable, cross, depressed, depressive, disgruntled, erratic, gloomy, grumpy, irritable, melancholy, miserable, morose, peevish, short-tempered, snappy, sulky, sullen, temperamental, [*informal*] touchy, unpredictable, unstable, volatile.

moor verb
to moor a boat. anchor, berth, SEE **fasten,** secure, tie up.

mope verb
He moped about because he wasn't invited to the party. be sad [SEE **sad**], brood, despair, grieve, languish, [*informal*] moon, pine, sulk.

moral adjective
1 *a moral person. moral principles.* blameless, chaste, decent, ethical, good, high-minded, honest, honourable, incorruptible, innocent, irreproachable, just, law-abiding, noble, principled, pure, responsible, right, righteous, sinless, trustworthy, truthful, upright, virtuous.
2 *a moral tale.* cautionary, didactic, moralistic, moralizing.
OPPOSITES: SEE **immoral.**

moral noun
What's the moral of the story? lesson, meaning, message, precept, principle.
morals SEE **morality.**

morale noun
The team's morale is high. cheerfulness, confidence, [*informal*] heart, mood, self-confidence, self-esteem, spirit, state of mind.

morality noun
I question the morality of some kinds of advertising. conduct, decency, ethics, ethos, goodness, honesty, ideals, integrity, morals, principles, scruples, standards, uprightness, virtue.
OPPOSITES: SEE **wickedness.**

moralize verb
lecture, philosophize, pontificate, preach,
sermonize.

morbid adjective
a morbid account of her death. brooding,
ghoulish, gloomy, grim, macabre,
melancholy, morose, pessimistic, [*informal*]
sick, unhappy, unhealthy, unpleasant,
unwholesome.
OPPOSITES: SEE **cheerful**.

more adjective
added, additional, extra, further, increased,
new, other, renewed, supplementary.
OPPOSITES: SEE **less**.

moreover adverb
also, besides, further, furthermore, too.

morose adjective
a morose expression. bad-tempered, churlish,
depressed, gloomy, glum, grim, humourless,
ill-natured, melancholy, moody, mournful,
pessimistic, SEE **sad**, saturnine, sour, sulky,
sullen, surly, taciturn, unhappy, unsociable.
OPPOSITES: SEE **cheerful**.

morsel noun
a morsel of food. bite, crumb, fragment,
mouthful, nibble, piece, scrap, small amount
[SEE **small**], taste, titbit.

mortal adjective
1 *mortal beings.* earthly, ephemeral, human,
passing, transient.
OPPOSITES: SEE **immortal**.
2 *a mortal sickness.* deadly, fatal, lethal,
terminal.
3 *mortal enemies.* deadly, implacable,
irreconcilable, remorseless, sworn (*sworn
enemy*), unrelenting.

mortal noun
We are mortals, not gods. human being,
mortal creature [SEE **mortal** adjective], SEE
person.

mortality noun
1 *We aren't gods: we must accept our
mortality.* corruptibility, humanity,
impermanence, transience.
OPPOSITES: SEE **immortality**.
2 *There is high mortality among young birds.*
death-rate, dying, fatalities, loss of life.
OPPOSITES: SEE **survival**.

mostly adverb
chiefly, commonly, generally, largely,
mainly, normally, predominantly,
primarily, principally, typically, usually.

moth-eaten adjective
a moth-eaten appearance. antiquated,
decrepit, mangy, SEE **old**, ragged, shabby,
[*informal*] tatty.

mother verb
He likes to mother the toddlers. care for,
cherish, comfort, cuddle, fuss over, love,
nurse, pamper, protect.

motherly adjective
a motherly person. caring, kind, SEE **loving**,
maternal, protective.

motif noun
a floral motif on the curtains. design, device,
ornament, pattern, SEE **symbol**, theme.

motion noun
SEE **movement**.

motionless adjective
motionless statues. motionless waters. at rest,
calm, frozen, immobile, inanimate, inert,
lifeless, paralysed, peaceful, resting,
stagnant, static, stationary, still, stock-still,
unmoving.
OPPOSITES: SEE **moving**.

motivate verb
What motivated her to do such a thing?
arouse, be the motivation of [SEE
motivation], encourage, incite, induce,
inspire, move, persuade, prompt, provoke,
push, spur, stimulate, stir, urge.

motivation noun
the motivation behind someone's achievement.
drive, encouragement, impulse, incentive,
inducement, inspiration, instigation, SEE
motive, provocation, push, spur, stimulus.

motive noun
the motive for a crime. aim, cause, grounds,
intention, SEE **motivation**, object, purpose,
rationale, reason, thinking.

motor verb
We motored into town. drive, go by car, SEE
travel verb.

mottled adjective
SEE **dappled**.

mould noun
mould on cheese. fungus, growth, mildew.

mould verb
to mould clay. cast, fashion, form, model,
[*informal*] sculpt, shape.

mouldy adjective
a mouldy smell. damp, decaying, fusty,
mildewed, musty, rotten, stale.

mound noun
SEE **pile** noun.

mount verb
1 *to mount the stairs. to mount into the air.*
ascend, climb, go up, rise, soar.
OPPOSITES: SEE **descend**.
2 *to mount a horse.* get astride, get on, jump
onto.
OPPOSITES: SEE **dismount**.
3 *My savings mounted. The excitement*

mounted. accumulate, get bigger, grow, increase, intensify, multiply, pile up, swell.
OPPOSITES: SEE **decrease** verb.

mountain noun
1 [*poetic*] alp, arête, [*Scottish*] ben, eminence, height, hill, mound, mount, peak, range, ridge, sierra, summit, volcano.
2 [*informal*] *a mountain of business to get through.* SEE **pile** noun.

mountainous adjective
1 *mountainous slopes.* alpine, daunting, high, hilly, precipitous, rocky, rugged, steep, towering.
2 *mountainous waves.* SEE **huge.**

mourn verb
He mourned for his dead dog. bewail, fret, go into mourning, grieve, lament, mope, pine, wail, weep.
OPPOSITES: SEE **rejoice.**

mournful adjective
a mournful cry. a mournful occasion. dismal, distressed, distressing, doleful, funereal, gloomy, grief-stricken, grieving, heartbreaking, heartbroken, lamenting, lugubrious, melancholy, plaintive, plangent, SEE **sad,** sorrowful, tearful, tragic, unhappy, woeful.
OPPOSITES: SEE **cheerful.**

mouth noun
1 [*slang*] gob, jaws, lips, palate.
RELATED ADJECTIVE: oral.
2 *the mouth of a cave. the mouth of a bottle.* aperture, doorway, entrance, exit, gateway, opening, orifice, outlet.
3 *the mouth of a river.* estuary, outlet.

mouthful noun
a mouthful of food. bite, gobbet, gulp, morsel, spoonful, swallow, taste.

movable adjective
movable furniture. adjustable, detachable, mobile, portable, transferable, transportable.
OPPOSITES: SEE **immobile.**

move noun
1 *What will the criminal's next move be?* act, action, deed, gambit, manœuvre, measure, movement, ploy, [*informal*] shift, step, stratagem, [*informal*] tack, tactic.
2 *It's your move next.* chance, go, opportunity, turn.

move verb
[Many words can be used as synonyms of *move.* We give some of the commoner ones.]
1 *to move about.* be agitated, be astir, budge, change places, change position, fidget, flap, roll, shake, shift, stir, swing, toss, tremble, turn, twist, twitch, wag, [*informal*] waggle, wave, [*informal*] wiggle.
2 *to move along.* cruise, fly, jog, journey, make headway, make progress, march, pass, proceed, SEE **travel** verb, **walk** verb.

3 *to move along quickly.* bolt, canter, career, dart, dash, flit, flounce, fly, gallop, hasten, hurry, hurtle, hustle, [*informal*] nip, race, run, rush, shoot, speed, stampede, streak, tear (*We tore home*), [*informal*] zip, [*informal*] zoom.
4 *to move along slowly.* amble, crawl, dawdle, drift, stroll.
5 *to move along gracefully.* dance, flow, glide, skate, skim, slide, slip, sweep.
6 *to move along awkwardly.* dodder, falter, flounder, lumber, lurch, pitch, shuffle, stagger, stumble, sway, totter, trip, trundle.
7 *to move along stealthily.* crawl, creep, edge, slink, slither.
8 *to move things from one place to another.* carry, export, import, shift, ship, relocate, transfer, transplant, transport, transpose.
9 *to move someone to do something.* encourage, impel, influence, inspire, persuade, prompt, stimulate, urge.
10 *to move someone's feelings.* affect, arouse, enrage, fire, impassion, rouse, stir, touch.
to move away budge, depart, go, leave, migrate, quit, start.
to move back back off, retreat, reverse, withdraw.
to move down descend, drop, fall, lower, sink, swoop.
to move in enter, penetrate.
to move round circulate, revolve, roll, rotate, spin, tour, turn, twirl, twist, wheel, whirl.
to move towards advance, approach, come, proceed, progress.
to move up arise, ascend, climb, mount, rise.

movement noun
1 *Animals are capable of movement.* action, activity, SEE **gesture** noun, motion.
2 *Has there been any movement in their attitude?* change, development, evolution, progress, shift, trend.
3 *a political movement.* campaign, crusade, group, organization, party.

movie noun
SEE **film.**

moving adjective
1 *a moving object.* active, alive, astir, dynamic, mobile, movable, on the move, travelling, under way.
OPPOSITES: SEE **motionless.**
2 *a moving story.* affecting, emotional, emotive, heart-warming, inspiring, pathetic, poignant, [*uncomplimentary*] sentimental, stirring, [*informal*] tear-jerking, touching.
OPPOSITES: SEE **unemotional.**

muck noun
dirt, dung, filth, grime, manure, mire, mud, ooze, rubbish, sewage, slime, sludge.

mucky adjective
dirty, filthy, foul, grimy, grubby, messy, muddy, soiled, sordid, squalid.
OPPOSITES: SEE **clean** adjective.

mud noun
clay, dirt, mire, muck, ooze, silt, slime, sludge, slurry, soil.

muddle noun
1 *There was a muddle over the arrangements.* bewilderment, confusion, misunderstanding, [*informal*] mix-up.
2 *My room is in a muddle.* clutter, disorder, jumble, mess, [*informal*] shambles, tangle, untidiness.

muddle verb
1 *You muddle me when you talk fast.* bewilder, confuse, disorientate, mislead, perplex, puzzle.
OPPOSITES: SEE **clarify**.
2 *Don't muddle the clothes in the drawer.* disarrange, disorder, disorganize, [*informal*] foul up, jumble, make a mess of, [*informal*] mess up, mix up, shuffle, tangle.
OPPOSITES: SEE **tidy** verb.

muddy adjective
1 *muddy shoes.* caked, dirty, filthy, messy, mucky, soiled.
OPPOSITES: SEE **clean** adjective.
2 *muddy ground.* boggy, marshy, sloppy, sodden, soft, spongy, waterlogged, SEE **wet** adjective.
OPPOSITES: SEE **firm** adjective, **dry** adjective
3 *muddy water.* cloudy, impure, misty, opaque.
OPPOSITES: SEE **clear** adjective.

muffle verb
1 *to muffle yourself up in cold weather.* cover, enclose, envelop, swathe, wrap up.
2 *to muffle a noise.* dampen, deaden, disguise, dull, make muffled [SEE **muffled**], mask, mute, quieten, silence, soften, stifle, suppress.

muffled adjective
a muffled sound. deadened, dull, fuzzy, indistinct, muted, unclear, woolly.
OPPOSITES: SEE **clear** adjective.

mug verb
assault, attack, beat up, jump on, molest, rob, set on, steal from.
to mug up SEE **learn**.

mugger noun
attacker, SEE **criminal** noun, hooligan, robber, ruffian, thief, thug.

muggy adjective
muggy weather. clammy, close, damp, humid, moist, oppressive, steamy, sticky, stuffy, sultry, warm.

multiple adjective
a multiple crash on the motorway. multiple injuries. complex, compound, double [= 2], involving many, numerous, plural, quadruple [= 4], quintuple [= 5], triple [= 3].

multiplicity noun
The accident was due to a multiplicity of causes. abundance, array, complex, diversity, number, plurality, profusion, variety.

multiply verb
1 double [= *multiply by 2*], quadruple [4], quintuple [5], triple [3], [*informal*] times.
2 *Mice multiply quickly.* become numerous, breed, increase, proliferate, propagate, reproduce, spread.

multitude noun
a multitude of people. a multitude of things to do. SEE **crowd** noun, host, large number, legion, lots, mass, myriad, swarm, throng.

mumble verb
SEE **talk** verb.

munch verb
bite, chew, chomp, crunch, SEE **eat**, gnaw.

mundane adjective
It was hard to return to mundane matters after such excitement. banal, common, commonplace, down-to-earth, dull, everyday, familiar, human, material, SEE **ordinary**, physical, practical, quotidian, routine, worldly.
OPPOSITES: SEE **extraordinary, spiritual**.

municipal adjective
municipal government. municipal affairs. borough, city, civic, community, district, local, public, urban.

mural noun
fresco, wall-painting.

murder noun
assassination, fratricide, homicide, infanticide, SEE **killing** noun, matricide, parricide, patricide, regicide.

murder verb
assassinate, SEE **kill**.

murderer noun
assassin, SEE **killer**.

murderous adjective
murderous bandits. barbarous, bloodthirsty, brutal, cruel, dangerous, deadly, ferocious, fierce, homicidal, pitiless, ruthless, savage, vicious, violent.

murky adjective
murky water. murky light. cloudy, dark, dim,
dull, foggy, gloomy, grey, misty, muddy,
obscure, sombre.
OPPOSITES: SEE **clear** adjective.

murmur noun, verb SEE **talk** verb.

muscular adjective
a muscular wrestler. athletic, [*informal*]
beefy, brawny, burly, hefty, [*informal*]
hulking, husky, powerful, robust, sinewy,
[*informal*] strapping, strong, sturdy, tough,
well-built, well-developed, wiry.
OPPOSITES: SEE **feeble**.

music noun
harmony, pleasant sound.

KINDS OF MUSIC: chamber music, choral
music, classical music, dance music, disco
music, folk-music, instrumental music, jazz,
orchestral music, plainsong, pop music,
ragtime, reggae, rock, soul, swing.

VARIOUS MUSICAL COMPOSITIONS: anthem,
ballad, blues, cadenza, calypso, canon,
cantata, canticle, carol, chant, concerto, SEE
dance noun, dirge, duet, étude, fanfare,
fugue, hymn, improvisation, intermezzo,
lullaby, march, musical, nocturne, nonet,
octet, opera, operetta, oratorio, overture,
prelude, quartet, quintet, rhapsody, rondo,
scherzo, sea shanty, septet, sextet, sonata,
SEE **song**, spiritual, symphony, toccata, trio.

FAMILIES OF MUSICAL INSTRUMENTS: brass,
keyboard, percussion, strings, woodwind.

MUSICAL INSTRUMENTS: accordion,
bagpipes, banjo, barrel organ, bassoon,
bugle, castanets, cello, clarinet, clavichord,
concertina, cor anglais, cornet, cymbals,
double-bass, drum, dulcimer, euphonium,
fiddle, fife, flute, French horn, glockenspiel,
gong, guitar.
harmonica, harmonium, harp, harpsichord,
horn, hurdy-gurdy, kettledrum, keyboard,
lute, lyre, mouth-organ, oboe, organ, piano,
piccolo, pipes, recorder, saxophone, sitar,
spinet, synthesizer, tambourine, timpani,
tom-tom, triangle, trombone, trumpet, tuba,
tubular bells, ukulele, viol, viola, violin,
virginals, xylophone, zither.

VARIOUS MUSICIANS: accompanist, bass,
bugler, cellist, clarinettist, composer,
conductor, contralto, drummer, fiddler,
flautist, guitarist, harpist, instrumentalist,
maestro, minstrel, oboist, organist,
percussionist, pianist, piper, singer, soloist,
soprano, tenor, timpanist, treble,
trombonist, trumpeter, violinist, virtuoso,
vocalist.

GROUPS OF MUSICIANS: band, choir, chorus,

consort, duet, duo, ensemble, group, nonet,
octet, orchestra, quartet, quintet, septet,
sextet, trio.

OTHER EVERYDAY MUSICAL TERMS: baton,
chord, chromatic scale, clef, counterpoint
(adjective contrapuntal), crotchet, diatonic
scale, discord, flat, harmony, key, melody,
metronome marking, minim, natural, note,
octave, pentatonic scale, pitch, polyphony,
quaver, rhythm, scale, semibreve,
semiquaver, semitone, sharp, stave, tempo,
theme, time signature, tone, tune, unison.

---

musical adjective
musical sounds. euphonious, harmonious,
lyrical, melodious, pleasant, sweet-
sounding, tuneful.

muster verb
Can we muster a team for Saturday?
assemble, call together, collect, convene,
gather, get together, group, marshal,
mobilize, rally, round up, summon.

musty adjective
a musty smell. airless, damp, dank, fusty,
mildewed, mouldy, smelly, stale, stuffy,
unventilated.

mutant noun
abortion, deviant, freak, monster,
monstrosity, sport.

mutation noun
a genetic mutation. alteration, change,
deviance, evolution, metamorphosis,
modification, transformation, variation.

mute adjective
dumb, silent, speechless, tongue-tied,
voiceless.

mutilate verb
*The soldier was horribly mutilated in the
explosion.* cripple, damage, disable,
disfigure, injure, lame, maim, mangle, SEE
wound verb.

mutinous adjective
a mutinous crew. SEE **rebellious**.

mutiny noun
a mutiny on board ship. SEE **rebellion**.

mutiny verb
SEE **rebel** verb.

mutter verb SEE **talk** verb.

mutual adjective
friends with mutual interests. common, joint,
reciprocal, reciprocated, shared.

muzzle verb
to muzzle someone. censor, gag, restrain,
silence, stifle, suppress.

mysterious adjective
a mysterious illness. mysterious powers.
arcane, baffling, curious, enigmatic,

incomprehensible, inexplicable, insoluble, magical, miraculous, SEE **mystical**, mystifying, obscure, perplexing, puzzling, secret, strange, uncanny, unexplained, unfathomable, unknown, weird.
OPPOSITES: SEE **straightforward**.

mystery noun
an insoluble mystery. enigma, miracle, mysterious happening [SEE **mysterious**], problem, puzzle, riddle, secret.

mystical adjective
a mystical experience. abnormal, metaphysical, SEE **mysterious**, occult, religious, spiritual, supernatural.
OPPOSITES: SEE **mundane**.

mystify verb
baffle, bamboozle, bewilder, perplex, SEE **puzzle** verb.

mythical adjective
mythical monsters. fabled, fabulous, fanciful, fictional, imaginary, invented, legendary, make-believe, mythological, non-existent, unreal.
OPPOSITES: SEE **real**.

N

nadir noun
bottom, lowest point.
OPPOSITES: SEE **zenith**.

nag verb
to nag about jobs to be done. badger, [*informal*] go on (*Stop going on about it!*), [*informal*] henpeck, keep complaining, pester, [*informal*] plague, scold.

nail noun
an iron nail. pin, stud, tack.

naïve adjective
too naïve to succeed in politics. artless, childlike, credulous, [*informal*] green, guileless, gullible, inexperienced, ingenuous, innocent, open, simple, simple-minded, [*uncomplimentary*] stupid, unsophisticated, unwary.
OPPOSITES: SEE **knowing**.

naked adjective
bare, denuded, disrobed, exposed, nude, stark naked, stripped, unclothed, uncovered, undressed.
OPPOSITES: SEE **clothed**.

name noun
1 *a person's name.* alias [= *assumed name*] [*formal*] appellation, Christian name, first

name, forename, given name, [*informal*] handle, identity, nickname, nom de plume, pen name, personal name, pseudonym, sobriquet, surname.
2 *the name of a book.* title.

name verb
1 *His parents named him Antony.* baptize, call, christen, dub, style.
2 *What did you name your story?* entitle, label.
3 *They named me as captain.* appoint, choose, designate, elect, nominate, select, single out, specify.

named adjective
named varieties of flowers. identified, known, specific, specified.

nameless adjective
1 *nameless heroes.* anonymous, unheard of, unidentified, unnamed.
2 *nameless horrors.* SEE **unspeakable**.

narrate verb
to narrate a story. chronicle, describe, recount, relate, report, tell.

narrative noun
a narrative of events. account, chronicle, history, story, tale, [*informal*] yarn.

narrow adjective
1 *a narrow line.* fine, slender, slim, thin.
2 *a narrow space.* close, confined, constricting, cramped, enclosed, limited, [*old-fashioned*] strait.
OPPOSITES: SEE **wide**.

narrow-minded adjective
a narrow-minded outlook. biased, bigoted, conservative, hidebound, illiberal, inflexible, insular, intolerant, narrow, old-fashioned, parochial, petty, prejudiced, prim, prudish, rigid, small-minded, straight, straight-laced.
OPPOSITES: SEE **broad-minded**.

nasty adjective
[The meaning of *nasty* is vague: it can refer to almost anything you don't like. The number of synonyms is virtually limitless, so we give just some of the commoner ones here, and refer you to some of the places where you may find more.] SEE **bad** (*a nasty person*), beastly, SEE **dangerous** (*a nasty weapon*), SEE **difficult** (*a nasty problem*), SEE **dirty** (*a nasty mess*), disagreeable, disgusting, distasteful, foul, hateful, horrible, loathsome, [*slang*] lousy, SEE **objectionable** (*a nasty smell*), obnoxious, SEE **obscene** (*a nasty film*), [*informal*] off-putting, repulsive, revolting, SEE **severe** (*a nasty illness*), sickening, SEE **unkind** (*nasty to animals*), SEE **unpleasant**.
OPPOSITES: SEE **nice**.

nation noun
1 *The nation mourned when the king died.* community, people, population, society.
2 *the nations of the world.* civilization, country, land, power, race, state, superpower.

national adjective
1 *national customs.* ethnic, popular, racial.
2 *a national emergency.* countrywide, general, nationwide, state, widespread.
OPPOSITES: SEE **local** adjective.

national noun
British nationals. citizen, native, resident, subject.

nationalistic adjective
nationalistic feelings. [*uncomplimentary*] chauvinist or chauvinistic, [*uncomplimentary*] jingoistic, loyal, patriotic, [*uncomplimentary*] xenophobic.

native adjective
1 *native inhabitants.* aboriginal, indigenous, local, original.
2 *native wit.* congenital, hereditary, inborn, inbred, inherent, inherited, innate, natural.

natural adjective
1 *the natural world.* normal, ordinary, predictable, regular, usual.
2 *natural feelings.* healthy, hereditary, human, inborn, inherited, innate, instinctive, intuitive, kind, maternal, native, paternal, proper, right.
3 *natural behaviour.* artless, authentic, genuine, sincere, spontaneous, unaffected, uncorrupted, unselfconscious, unsurprising.
4 *natural resources.* crude (*crude oil*), found in nature, raw, unadulterated, unprocessed, unrefined.
5 *a natural leader.* born, congenital, untaught.
OPPOSITES: SEE **unnatural**.

nature noun
1 *A naturalist loves nature.* countryside, natural environment, natural history, wildlife.
2 *He has a kind nature.* character, disposition, make-up, manner, personality, temperament.
3 *I collect coins, medals, and things of that nature.* description, kind, sort, species, type, variety.

naughty adjective
naughty children. SEE **bad**, badly-behaved, bad-mannered, boisterous, contrary, delinquent, disobedient, fractious, headstrong, impish, impolite, incorrigible, insubordinate, intractable, mischievous, obstinate, perverse, playful, rascally, rebellious, rude, self-willed, stubborn,

troublesome, uncontrollable, ungovernable, unmanageable, unruly, wayward, wicked, wilful.
OPPOSITES: SEE **well-behaved**.

nauseating, **nauseous** adjectives
SEE **sickening**.

nautical adjective
nautical dress. marine, maritime, naval, of sailors, seafaring, seagoing.

naval adjective
naval warfare. marine, maritime, nautical, of the navy.

navigate verb
1 *to navigate a ship.* captain, direct, drive, guide, handle, manœuvre, pilot, sail, steer.
2 [*informal*] *Who's going to navigate?* map-read.

navy noun
armada, convoy, fleet, flotilla.
RANKS IN THE NAVY: SEE **rank** noun.

near adjective
1 *near neighbours.* adjacent, adjoining, bordering, close, connected, nearby, neighbouring, next-door.
2 *My birthday is near.* approaching, coming, forthcoming, imminent, impending, [*informal*] round the corner.
3 *near friends.* close, dear, familiar, intimate, related.
OPPOSITES: SEE **distant**.

nearly adverb
It's nearly dinner time. about, almost, approaching, approximately, around, not quite, practically, roughly, virtually.

neat adjective
1 *a neat room.* clean, orderly, [*informal*] shipshape, [*informal*] spick and span, straight, tidy, uncluttered, well-kept.
2 *neat clothes.* dainty, elegant, pretty, smart, spruce, trim.
3 *a neat person. a neat job.* accurate, adroit, deft, expert, houseproud (*a houseproud person*), methodical, meticulous, precise, skilful.
OPPOSITES: SEE **untidy**.

neatness noun
SEE **tidiness**.

necessary adjective
necessary repairs. compulsory, essential, imperative, important, indispensable, inescapable, inevitable, mandatory, needed, needful, obligatory, required, requisite, unavoidable, vital.
OPPOSITES: SEE **unnecessary**.

necessity noun
1 *Is it a necessity, or can we do without it?* compulsion, essential, inevitability, [*informal*] must (*It's a must!*), need,

obligation, requirement, [*Latin*] sine qua non.
2 *Necessity compelled them to steal.* beggary, destitution, hardship, need, penury, poverty, privation, shortage, suffering, want.

need noun
1 SEE **necessity**.
2 *There's a great need for more shops in our area.* call, demand, requirement.

need verb
1 *We need £10.* be short of, lack, miss, require, want.
2 *We need your support.* crave, depend on, rely on.

needless adjective
SEE **unnecessary**.

needy adjective
SEE **poor**.

negative adjective
a negative attitude. antagonistic, contradictory, destructive, dissenting, grudging, nullifying, obstructive, opposing, pessimistic, rejecting, saying "no", uncooperative, unenthusiastic, unwilling.
OPPOSITES: SEE **positive**.

neglect noun
guilty of neglect. carelessness, dereliction of duty, inattention, indifference, negligence, slackness.

neglect verb
Don't neglect your work. disregard, forget, ignore, leave alone, let slide, miss, omit, overlook, pay no attention to, shirk, skip.

neglected adjective
1 *neglected by friends. feeling neglected.* abandoned, disregarded, forlorn, [*informal*] in limbo, overlooked, unappreciated, unloved.
2 *a neglected garden.* derelict, overgrown, uncared for, untended, unweeded.

negligent adjective
negligent work. a negligent attitude. careless, forgetful, inattentive, inconsiderate, indifferent, irresponsible, lax, offhand, reckless, remiss, slack, sloppy, slovenly, thoughtless, uncaring, unthinking.
OPPOSITES: SEE **careful**.

negligible adjective
a negligible amount. imperceptible, inconsiderable, insignificant, slight, small, SEE **tiny**, trifling, trivial, unimportant.
OPPOSITES: SEE **considerable**.

negotiate verb
to negotiate a price, to negotiate with an enemy. arbitrate, bargain, confer, discuss

terms, enter into negotiation [SEE **negotiation**], haggle, make arrangements, mediate, parley.

negotiation noun
arbitration, bargaining, conciliation, debate, diplomacy, discussion, mediation, transaction.

negotiator noun
ambassador, arbitrator, broker, conciliator, diplomat, go-between, intermediary, mediator.

neighbourhood noun
Are there many shops in your neighbourhood? area, community, district, environs, locality, place, region, surroundings, vicinity, zone.

neighbouring adjective
The cats from the neighbouring houses come to our garden. adjacent, adjoining, attached, bordering, close, closest, connecting, near, nearby, nearest, next-door.

neighbourly adjective
SEE **friendly**.

nervous adjective
I get nervous before an exam. afraid, agitated, anxious, apprehensive, edgy, excitable, fearful, fidgety, flustered, highly strung, insecure, [*informal*] jittery, jumpy, [*informal*] nervy, neurotic, on edge, restless, shaky, shy, strained, tense, timid, [*informal*] touchy, [*informal*] twitchy, uneasy, [*informal*] uptight, worried.
OPPOSITES: SEE **calm** adjective.

nestle verb
to nestle up against someone. cuddle, curl up, huddle, lie comfortably, nuzzle, snuggle.

net noun
a fish net. mesh, netting, SEE **network**.

net verb
1 *to net a fish.* SEE **catch** verb, enmesh, trammel.
2 *to net a big salary.* accumulate, bring in, clear, earn, get, make, receive.

network noun
1 *a network of lines.* crisscross pattern, grid, labyrinth, lattice, maze, mesh, net, netting, tracery, web.
2 *a railway network.* complex, organization, system.

neurosis noun
abnormality, anxiety, depression, mental condition, obsession, phobia.

neurotic adjective
Don't get neurotic about things that worry you. anxious, distraught, disturbed, maladjusted, mentally unbalanced, nervous, obsessive, overwrought, unstable.

neuter adjective
neuter gender. ambiguous, ambivalent, indeterminate, neither one thing nor the other, uncertain.
COMPARE: feminine, hermaphrodite, masculine.

neuter verb
to neuter an animal. castrate, [*informal*] doctor, geld, spay, sterilize.

neutral adjective
1 *a neutral referee.* detached, disinterested, dispassionate, fair, impartial, indifferent, non-aligned, non-partisan, objective, unbiased, uninvolved, unprejudiced.
OPPOSITES: SEE **prejudiced**.
2 *neutral colours.* characterless, colourless, dull, indefinite, indeterminate, intermediate, middle.
OPPOSITES: SEE **distinctive**.

neutralize verb
Alkalis neutralize acids. cancel out, counteract, counterbalance, invalidate, make ineffective, negate, nullify, offset.

new adjective
1 *a new banknote.* brand-new, clean, fresh, mint, unused.
2 *a new invention. new music.* advanced, contemporary, current, latest, modern, modernistic, [*uncomplimentary*] newfangled, novel, original, recent, revolutionary, [*informal*] trendy, up-to-date.
3 *new evidence. a new problem.* added, additional, changed, different, extra, just arrived, more, supplementary, unaccustomed, unexpected, unfamiliar, unknown.
OPPOSITES: SEE **old**.

news noun
news from abroad. news of a special event. advice, announcement, bulletin, communiqué, dispatch, headlines, information, intelligence, [*informal*] latest (*What's the latest?*), message, newscast, newsletter, notice, press-release, proclamation, report, rumour, statement, [*old-fashioned*] tidings, word.

newspaper noun
[*informal*] daily, gazette, journal, paper, periodical, [*uncomplimentary*] rag, tabloid.
OTHER MEDIA: SEE **communication**.

next adjective
1 *the next street.* adjacent, adjoining, closest, nearest, neighbouring.
OPPOSITES: SEE **distant**.
2 *the next bus.* following, soonest, subsequent, succeeding.
OPPOSITES: SEE **previous**.

nice adjective
1 *nice food. a nice view. a nice person.* [In this sense, the meaning of *nice* is vague: it can refer to almost anything you like. The number of synonyms is virtually limitless, so we give just some of the commoner ones here, and refer you to some of the places where you may find more.] acceptable, agreeable, amiable, attractive, SEE **beautiful**, SEE **delicious**, delightful, SEE **friendly**, SEE **good**, gratifying, SEE **kind** adjective, likeable, SEE **pleasant**, pleasing, satisfactory, welcome.
OPPOSITES: SEE **nasty**.
2 *a nice calculation. a nice distinction.* accurate, careful, delicate, discriminating, exact, fine, meticulous, precise, punctilious, scrupulous.
OPPOSITES: SEE **careless**.
3 *nice table-manners.* dainty, elegant, fastidious, [*uncomplimentary*] fussy, particular, [*informal*] pernickety, polished, refined, well-mannered.
OPPOSITES: SEE **inelegant**.

nickname noun
alias, SEE **name** noun, sobriquet.

night-clothes noun
night-dress, night-gown, [*informal*] nightie, [*old-fashioned*] night-shirt, pyjamas.

nimble adjective
nimble movements. acrobatic, active, agile, brisk, deft, dextrous, lively, [*informal*] nippy, quick, quick-moving, sprightly, spry, swift.

nip verb
1 *The teeth nipped my leg.* bite, clip, pinch, snag, snap at, squeeze.
2 [*informal*] *I nipped along to the shops.* SEE **go**.

nippy adjective
1 [*informal*] *a nippy car.* fast, SEE **nimble**, quick, rapid, speedy.
2 [*informal*] *nippy weather.* SEE **cold** adjective.

nobility noun
1 *nobility of character.* dignity, greatness, integrity, magnanimity, morality, nobleness, uprightness, virtue, worthiness.
2 *the nobility.* aristocracy, gentry, nobles [SEE **noble** noun], peerage.

noble adjective
1 *a noble family.* aristocratic, [*informal*] blue-blooded, courtly, élite, gentle, high-born, princely, royal, thoroughbred, titled, upper-class.
OPPOSITES: SEE **lowly**.
2 *a noble deed.* brave, chivalrous, courageous, gallant, glorious, heroic, honourable, magnanimous, upright, virtuous, worthy.

OPPOSITES: SEE **ignoble**.
3 *a noble edifice.* dignified, distinguished, elegant, grand, great, imposing, impressive, magnificent, majestic, SEE **splendid**, stately.
OPPOSITES: SEE **insignificant**.

noble noun
aristocrat, grandee, lady, lord, nobleman, noblewoman, peer, peeress.

nod verb
to nod your head. bend, bob, bow, SEE **gesture** verb.
to nod off SEE **sleep** verb.

noise noun
a dreadful noise. babble, [*informal*] ballyhoo, [*informal*] bedlam, blare, cacophony, clamour, clatter, commotion, din, discord, fracas, hubbub, hullabaloo, outcry, pandemonium, racket, row, rumpus, screaming, screeching, shrieking, shouting, tumult, uproar, yelling.
OPPOSITES: SEE **silence** noun.
VARIOUS WAYS TO MAKE NOISE: SEE **sound** noun.

noiseless adjective SEE **silent**.

noisy adjective
a noisy class of children. noisy traffic. blaring, boisterous, booming, cacophonous, chattering, clamorous, deafening, ear-splitting, fortissimo, loud, raucous, resounding, reverberating, rowdy, screaming, screeching, shrieking, shrill, strident, talkative, thunderous, tumultuous, uproarious, vociferous.
OPPOSITES: SEE **silent**.

nominal adjective
1 *He's the nominal head, but his deputy does the work.* formal, in name only, ostensible, supposed, theoretical.
2 *If we pay a nominal sum, the dog is ours.* minimal, small, token.

nominate verb
We nominated him as captain. appoint, choose, elect, name, select.

non-existent adjective
Unicorns are non-existent. fictitious, hypothetical, imaginary, imagined, legendary, made-up, mythical, unreal.
OPPOSITES: SEE **existing**.

nonsense noun
1 *She's talking nonsense.* [Most of these synonyms are used *informally*.] balderdash, bilge, boloney, bosh, bunk, bunkum, claptrap, codswallop, double Dutch, drivel, fiddlesticks, gibberish, gobbledegook, piffle, poppycock, rot, rubbish, stuff and nonsense, tommy-rot, tripe, twaddle.
2 *I thought from the start that her plan was a nonsense.* absurdity, inanity, mistake, nonsensical idea [SEE **nonsensical**].

nonsensical adjective
absurd, crazy, fatuous, foolish, inane, incomprehensible, illogical, impractical, irrational, laughable, ludicrous, meaningless, ridiculous, senseless, SEE **silly**, stupid, unreasonable.
OPPOSITES: SEE **sensible**.

non-stop adjective
1 *a non-stop train.* direct, express, fast.
OPPOSITE: stopping.
2 *non-stop chattering.* SEE **continual**.

noose noun
a noose in a rope. collar, halter, loop.

normal adjective
1 *normal temperature. a normal kind of day.* accepted, accustomed, average, common, commonplace, conventional, customary, established, everyday, familiar, habitual, natural, ordinary, predictable, prosaic, quotidian, regular, routine, [*informal*] run-of-the-mill, standard, typical, unsurprising, usual.
2 *a normal person.* balanced, healthy, rational, reasonable, sane, [*informal*] straight, well-adjusted.
OPPOSITES: SEE **abnormal**.

nose noun
1 nostrils, [*formal*] proboscis, snout.
RELATED ADJECTIVE: nasal.
ADJECTIVES DESCRIBING TYPES OF NOSE: aquiline, retroussé, Roman, snub.
2 *the nose of a boat.* bow, front, prow.

nose verb
to nose into a space. to nose into the traffic. enter cautiously, insinuate yourself, intrude, nudge your way in, penetrate, probe, push, shove.
to nose about *He was nosing about in my room!* interfere, look, meddle, pry, search, snoop.

nostalgia noun
nostalgia for the past. longing, memory, nostalgic feeling [SEE **nostalgic**], pining, regret, reminiscence, sentiment, sentimentality, yearning.

nostalgic adjective
nostalgic feelings about your childhood. emotional, maudlin, regretful, romantic, sentimental, wistful, yearning.

notable adjective
a notable example of something. a notable visitor. celebrated, conspicuous, distinguished, eminent, evident, extraordinary, famous, important, impressive, memorable, noted, noteworthy, noticeable, obvious, outstanding, pre-eminent, prominent, rare, remarkable, renowned, striking, uncommon, unusual, well-known.
OPPOSITES: SEE **ordinary**.

note noun
1 *I wrote her a note.* billet-doux, chit,
communication, [*joking*] epistle, jotting,
letter, [*informal*] memo, memorandum,
message.
2 *a note in a textbook.* annotation, cross-
reference, explanation, footnote, gloss.
3 *an angry note in her voice.* feeling, quality,
sound, tone.
4 *a £5 note.* bill, banknote.

note verb
1 *to note what is happening.* SEE **notice** verb.
2 *to note something on paper.* enter, jot down,
record, scribble, write down.

notebook noun
diary, exercise-book, jotter, writing-book.

noted adjective
SEE **famous**.

nothing noun
[*cricket*] duck, [*tennis*] love, [*football*] nil,
[*old-fashioned*] naught, nought, zero.

notice noun
1 *Didn't you see the notice?* advertisement,
announcement, handbill, handout,
intimation, leaflet, message, note, placard,
poster, sign, warning.
2 *She didn't take any notice of the signs.*
cognizance, heed, note, regard, warning.
to give someone notice SEE **dismiss**.

notice verb
to notice what is happening. detect, discern,
discover, feel, find, heed, mark, mind (*Mind
what I say*), note, observe, pay attention to,
register, remark, see, spy, take note of, take
notice of [SEE **notice** noun].

noticeable adjective
*a noticeable improvement in the weather. a
noticeable foreign accent.* appreciable,
audible, clear, conspicuous, detectable,
discernible, distinct, important, manifest,
marked, measurable, notable, obtrusive,
obvious, perceptible, plain, prominent,
pronounced, salient, significant, striking,
unmistakable, visible.
OPPOSITES: SEE **imperceptible**.

notify verb
*If you see anything suspicious, notify the
police.* acquaint, advise, alert, inform, make
known to, report to, tell, warn.

notion noun
*I had a notion that you were on holiday. He
has strange notions about religion.*
apprehension, belief, concept, fancy,
hypothesis, idea, impression, opinion,
sentiment, theory, thought, understanding,
view.

notorious adjective
a notorious criminal. disreputable, famous,
flagrant, known, infamous, obvious,
outrageous, overt, patent, scandalous,
shocking, talked about, undisguised,
undisputed, well-known, wicked.

nought noun
SEE **nothing**.

nourish verb
Food nourishes us. feed, maintain,
strengthen, support, sustain.

nourishing adjective
nourishing food. beneficial, good for you,
health-giving, nutritious, sustaining,
wholesome.

nourishment noun
diet, food, goodness, nutrient, nutriment,
nutrition, sustenance.

novel adjective
a novel way of doing something. different,
fresh, imaginative, innovative, new, odd,
original, rare, singular, startling, strange,
surprising, uncommon, unconventional,
unfamiliar, unusual.
OPPOSITES: SEE **familiar**.

novel noun
I like to read a novel. fiction, novelette,
romance, story.
OTHER KINDS OF WRITING: SEE **writing**.

novelty noun
1 *The novelty will soon wear off.* freshness,
newness, oddity, originality, strangeness,
surprise, unfamiliarity.
2 *novelties sold in holiday resorts.* curiosity,
gimmick, knick-knack, souvenir, trinket.

novice noun SEE **beginner**.

now adverb
at present, here and now, immediately,
nowadays, straight away.

nub noun
the nub of the problem. centre, core, crux,
essence, gist, heart, kernel, nucleus, point.

nucleus noun
centre, core, heart, middle.

nude adjective SEE **naked**.

nudge verb
to nudge someone with your elbow. bump, SEE
hit verb, jog, jolt, poke, prod, shove, touch.

nuisance noun
That dog's a nuisance. annoyance, bother,
inconvenience, irritation, [*informal*] pain,
pest, plague, trouble, vexation, worry.

nullify verb
to nullify an agreement. abolish, annul, SEE
cancel, do away with, invalidate, negate,
neutralize, repeal, rescind, revoke, stultify.

numb adjective
My leg's gone numb. anaesthetized,
[*informal*] asleep, cold, dead, deadened,
frozen, immobile, insensitive, paralysed,
suffering from pins and needles.
OPPOSITES: SEE **sensitive**.

numb verb
*The cold numbs my hands. The dentist's
injection numbed my mouth.* anaesthetize,
deaden, desensitize, freeze, immobilize,
make numb, paralyse.

number noun
1 *numbers written on paper.* digit, figure,
integer, numeral, unit.
RELATED ADJECTIVE: numerical.
2 *a large number.* aggregate, amount,
collection, crowd, multitude, quantity, sum,
total.
3 *a musical number.* item, piece, song.
4 *a special number of a magazine.* copy,
edition, impression, issue, printing,
publication.

numeral noun
digit, figure, integer, number.

numerous adjective
a numerous crowd. numerous people.
abundant, copious, countless, innumerable,
many, multitudinous, numberless, plentiful,
plenty of, several, uncountable, untold.
OPPOSITES: SEE **few, small**.

nun noun
abbess, mother-superior, prioress, sister.

nurse noun
1 *a medical nurse.* district-nurse, [*old-
fashioned*] matron, sister.
2 *a child's nurse.* nanny, nursemaid.

nurse verb
1 *to nurse a sick person.* care for, look after,
tend, treat.
2 *to nurse a baby.* breast-feed, feed, suckle.
3 *to nurse someone in your arms.* cherish,
cradle, cuddle, dandle, hold, hug, mother.

nursery noun
1 *a nursery for young children.* crèche,
kindergarten, nursery school.
2 *a nursery for growing plants.* garden
centre, market garden.

nurture verb
*to nurture the young. to nurture tender
plants.* bring up, cultivate, educate, feed,
look after, nourish, nurse, rear, tend, train.

nut noun
kernel.

KINDS OF NUT: almond, brazil, cashew,
chestnut, cob-nut, coconut, filbert, hazel,
peanut, pecan, pistachio, walnut.

---

nutrient noun
Provide plants with their proper nutrients.
fertilizer, SEE **nourishment**.

nutritious adjective SEE **nourishing**.

Oo

oath noun
1 *to swear an oath.* assurance, guarantee,
pledge, promise, undertaking, vow, word of
honour.
2 *a terrible oath.* blasphemy, curse,
exclamation, expletive, imprecation,
profanity, swear word.

obedient adjective
obedient servants. obedient animals.
acquiescent, amenable, biddable,
compliant, deferential, disciplined, docile,
dutiful, law-abiding, manageable,
submissive, subservient, tamed, tractable,
well-behaved, well-trained.
OPPOSITES: SEE **disobedient**.

obese adjective SEE **fat** adjective.

obey verb
1 *Obey the rules.* abide by, adhere to, be ruled
by, carry out, comply with, conform to,
execute, follow, heed, implement, keep to,
mind, observe, submit to.
2 *Soldiers are trained to obey.* acquiesce, be
obedient [SEE **obedient**], conform, do what
you are told, submit, take orders.
OPPOSITES: SEE **disobey**.

object noun
1 *What's that object you've found?* article,
body, item, thing.
2 *What is the object of this exercise?* aim, end,
goal, intent, intention, objective, point,
purpose, target.

object verb
*She objected to the smell. He objected against
the plan.* argue, be opposed, carp, complain,
demur, disapprove, dispute, dissent,
expostulate, [*slang*] grouse, grumble, make
an objection [SEE **objection**], mind, moan,
protest, quibble, raise questions,
remonstrate, take exception (to).
OPPOSITES: SEE **accept, agree**.

objection noun
The secretary noted our objection. challenge,
complaint, disapproval, opposition, outcry,
protest, query, question, quibble,
remonstration.

objectionable adjective
an objectionable smell. abhorrent,
detestable, disagreeable, disgusting,
dislikeable, displeasing, distasteful, foul,
hateful, insufferable, intolerable,
loathsome, nasty, nauseating, noisome,
obnoxious, odious, offensive, [*informal*]
offputting, repellent, repugnant, revolting,
sickening, unacceptable, undesirable, SEE
unpleasant, unwanted.
OPPOSITES: SEE **acceptable**.

objective adjective
objective evidence. an objective account.
detached, disinterested, dispassionate,
empirical, existing, factual, impartial,
impersonal, observable, outward-looking,
rational, real, scientific, unbiased,
unemotional, unprejudiced.
OPPOSITES: SEE **subjective**.

objective noun
*The objective is to get the ball into the net.
Our objective was the top of the hill.* aim,
ambition, aspiration, design, destination,
end, goal, intent, intention, object, point,
purpose, target.

obligation noun
an obligation to pay taxes. commitment,
compulsion, duty, liability, need,
requirement, responsibility.
OPPOSITES: SEE **option**.

oblige verb
to oblige someone to do something. coerce,
compel, constrain, force, make, require.

obliged adjective
1 *He's obliged to come.* bound, certain,
compelled, constrained, forced, required,
sure.
2 *I'm obliged to you for your kindness.*
appreciative, grateful, gratified, indebted,
thankful.

obliging adjective
Thank you for being so obliging.
accommodating, agreeable, civil,
considerate, co-operative, courteous,
friendly, helpful, kind, neighbourly, polite,
thoughtful, willing.
OPPOSITES: SEE **unhelpful**.

oblique adjective
1 *an oblique line.* angled, diagonal, inclined,
slanting, sloping, tilted.
2 *an oblique insult.* backhanded,
circumlocutory, SEE **evasive**, implicit,
indirect, roundabout.
OPPOSITES: SEE **direct** adjective.

obliterate verb
to obliterate your tracks. blot out, cancel,
cover over, delete, destroy, efface,
eradicate, erase, expunge, extirpate, leave
no trace of, rub out, wipe out.

oblivion noun
1 *Most of this composer's music has fallen
into oblivion.* disregard, extinction, neglect,
obscurity.
2 *After the accident I was in a state of
oblivion.* amnesia, coma, forgetfulness,
ignorance, insensibility, obliviousness,
unawareness, unconsciousness.

oblivious adjective
oblivious of what is going on. forgetful,
heedless, ignorant, insensible (to),
insensitive (to), unacquainted (with),
unaware, unconscious, uninformed (about),
unmindful, unresponsive (to).
OPPOSITES: SEE **aware**.

obnoxious adjective
SEE **objectionable**.

obscene adjective
obscene language. obscene books. bawdy,
[*informal*] blue, coarse, corrupting, crude,
depraved, dirty, disgusting, filthy, foul,
gross, immodest, immoral, improper,
impure, indecent, indecorous, indelicate,
[*informal*] kinky, lewd, nasty, SEE
objectionable, offensive, outrageous,
perverted, pornographic, prurient,
repulsive, rude, salacious, scurrilous,
shameless, shocking, [*informal*] sick,
smutty, suggestive, vile, vulgar.
OPPOSITES: SEE **decent**.

obscenity noun
*the obscenity of war. the obscenity of
pornography.* abomination, blasphemy,
coarseness, dirtiness, evil, filth, foulness,
immorality, impropriety, indecency,
lewdness, licentiousness, offensiveness,
outrage, pornography, profanity, vileness.

obscure adjective
1 *an obscure shape in the mist.* blurred,
clouded, concealed, covered, dark, dim,
hidden, inconspicuous, indefinable,
indistinct, masked, misty, murky, shadowy,
shady, shrouded, unclear, unlit,
unrecognizable, vague, veiled.
OPPOSITES: SEE **clear** adjective.
2 *an obscure poet.* forgotten, minor,
undistinguished, unheard of, unimportant,
unknown.
OPPOSITES: SEE **famous**.
3 *an obscure joke.* arcane, complex, cryptic,
enigmatic, esoteric, incomprehensible,
puzzling, recherché, recondite.
OPPOSITES: SEE **obvious**.

obscure verb
*Mist obscured the view. The complications
obscured the main point.* block out, blur,
cloud, conceal, cover, darken, disguise,
eclipse, envelop, hide, make obscure [SEE

obscure adjective], mask, screen, shade, shroud, veil.
OPPOSITES: SEE **clarify**.

obsequious adjective
obsequious flattery. abject, cringing, deferential, fawning, flattering, [*informal*] greasy, grovelling, ingratiating, menial, [*informal*] oily, servile, [*informal*] smarmy, subservient, sycophantic, unctuous.

observant adjective
an observant sentry. alert, astute, attentive, aware, careful, eagle-eyed, heedful, perceptive, percipient, quick, sharp-eyed, shrewd, vigilant, watchful.
OPPOSITES: SEE **inattentive**.

observation noun
1 *an astronomer's observation of the stars*. attention (to), examination, inspection, monitoring, scrutiny, study, surveillance, watching.
2 *Have you any observations?* comment, opinion, reaction, reflection, remark, response, statement, thought, utterance.

observe verb
1 *to observe an eclipse. to observe someone's behaviour*. contemplate, detect, discern, [*informal*] keep an eye on, look at, monitor, note, notice, perceive, regard, scrutinize, see, spot, spy, stare at, study, view, watch, witness.
2 *to observe the rules*. abide by, adhere to, comply with, conform to, follow, heed, honour, keep, obey, pay attention to, respect.
3 *to observe Christmas*. celebrate, commemorate, keep, remember, solemnize.
4 *I observed that it was a nice day*. comment, declare, explain, make an observation [SEE **observation**], mention, reflect, remark, say.

observer noun
bystander, commentator, eye-witness, onlooker, spectator, viewer, watcher, witness.

obsess verb
His hobby obsessed him. become an obsession with [SEE **obsession**], consume, dominate, grip, haunt, monopolize, plague, possess, rule, take hold of.

obsession noun
Don't let your hobby become an obsession. addiction, [*informal*] bee in your bonnet, fetish, fixation, [*informal*] hobby-horse, infatuation, mania, passion, preoccupation.

obsessive adjective
an obsessive interest in something. addictive, compulsive, consuming, dominating.

obsolescent adjective
an obsolescent design. dying out, going out of use, losing popularity, moribund, [*informal*] on the way out, waning.

obsolete adjective
an obsolete design. anachronistic, antiquated, antique, archaic, dated, dead, discarded, disused, extinct, old-fashioned, outdated, out-of-date, outmoded, primitive, superannuated, superseded, unfashionable.
OPPOSITES: SEE **current** adjective.

obstacle noun
an obstacle to be got over. bar, barricade, barrier, block, blockage, check, difficulty, hindrance, hurdle, impediment, obstruction, problem, snag, [*informal*] stumbling-block.

obstinate adjective
an obstinate refusal to co-operate. defiant, determined, dogged, firm, headstrong, inflexible, intractable, intransigent, [*informal*] mulish, obdurate, persistent, perverse, [*informal*] pig-headed, refractory, rigid, self-willed, [*informal*] stiff-necked, stubborn, tenacious, unreasonable, unyielding, wilful, wrong-headed.
OPPOSITES: SEE **amenable**.

obstruct verb
to obstruct progress. bar, block, check, curb, deter, frustrate, halt, hamper, hinder, hold up, impede, inhibit, interfere with, interrupt, [*formal*] occlude, prevent, restrict, retard, slow down, [*informal*] stonewall, stop, [*informal*] stymie, thwart.
OPPOSITES: SEE **help** verb.

obstruction noun SEE **obstacle**.

obtain verb
to obtain what you want. acquire, attain, be given, bring, buy, come by, come into possession of, earn, elicit, enlist (*She enlisted my help*), extort, extract, find, gain, get, get hold of, [*informal*] lay hands on, [*informal*] pick up, procure, purchase, receive, secure, win.

obtrusive adjective
The factory is an obtrusive eyesore. blatant, conspicuous, inescapable, interfering, intrusive, SEE **obvious**, out of place, prominent, ugly, unwanted, unwelcome.
OPPOSITES: SEE **inconspicuous**.

obvious adjective
an obvious accent. an obvious landmark. obvious favouritism. blatant, clear, conspicuous, distinct, evident, eyecatching, flagrant, glaring, gross (*gross negligence*), inescapable, intrusive, notable, noticeable, obtrusive, open, patent, perceptible, plain, prominent, pronounced, recognizable, self-

evident, unconcealed, undisguised, undisputed, unmistakable, visible.
OPPOSITES: SEE **hidden**.

occasion noun
1 *A party should be a happy occasion.* affair, celebration, ceremony, event, happening, incident, occurrence.
2 *If I can find the right occasion, I'll tell him.* chance, moment, opportunity, time.

occasional adjective
occasional showers. occasional moments of enthusiasm. casual, desultory, fitful, infrequent, intermittent, irregular, odd, [*informal*] once in a while, periodic, rare, scattered, spasmodic, sporadic, uncommon, unpredictable.
OPPOSITES: SEE **frequent** adjective, **regular**.

occult noun
the occult black magic, diabolism, sorcery, the supernatural, witchcraft.

occupation noun
1 *the occupation of a house.* lease, occupancy, possession, residency, tenancy, tenure, use.
2 *the occupation of a foreign country.* colonization, conquest, invasion, seizure, subjugation, [*informal*] take-over, usurpation.
3 *a full-time occupation.* business, calling, employment, job, [*informal*] line, post, profession, trade, vocation, work.
VARIOUS OCCUPATIONS: SEE **job**.
4 *a leisure occupation.* activity, hobby, pastime, pursuit.

occupied adjective
1 *occupied in your work.* absorbed, active, busy, engaged, engrossed, [*informal*] hard at it, involved.
2 *an occupied house.* inhabited, lived-in, tenanted.
3 *an occupied country.* conquered, defeated, overrun, subjugated.

occupy verb
1 *We occupy a council house.* dwell in, inhabit, live in, reside in.
2 *Troops occupied the town.* capture, conquer, garrison, invade, overrun, possess, take over, take possession of.
3 *The garden occupies her spare time.* absorb, engage, engross, fill, monopolize, preoccupy, take up, use, utilize.

occur verb
Earthquakes don't often occur in this part of the world. appear, arise, befall, be found, come about, come into being, crop up, develop, exist, happen, manifest itself, materialize, [*informal*] show up, take place, [*informal*] turn up.

occurrence noun
an unusual occurrence. affair, case, circumstance, development, event, happening, incident, manifestation, occasion, phenomenon, proceeding.

odd adjective
1 *odd numbers.* uneven.
OPPOSITES: SEE **even** adjective.
2 *an odd sock.* left over, remaining, single, spare, unmatched.
3 *odd jobs.* casual, irregular, miscellaneous, occasional, random, varied, various.
4 *odd behaviour.* abnormal, atypical, bizarre, [*informal*] cranky, curious, eccentric, freak, funny, incongruous, inexplicable, [*informal*] kinky, peculiar, puzzling, queer, singular, strange, uncharacteristic, uncommon, unconventional, unusual, weird.
OPPOSITES: SEE **normal**.

oddment noun
oddments left over from a jumble sale. bit, [*plural*] bits and pieces, fragment, leftover, [*plural*] odds and ends, offcut, remnant, scrap, unwanted piece.

odious adjective
SEE **hateful**.

odour noun
SEE **smell** noun.

offence noun
1 *a criminal offence.* crime, fault, infringement, misdeed, misdemeanour, outrage, peccadillo, sin, transgression, trespass, wrong, wrongdoing.
2 *The bad language caused offence to our neighbours.* anger, annoyance, disgust, displeasure, hard feelings, indignation, irritation, resentment, [*informal*] upset.

offend verb
1 *to offend someone.* affront, anger, annoy, cause offence [SEE **offence**], disgust, displease, give offence (to), insult, irritate, make angry, outrage, pain, provoke, rile, sicken, upset, vex.
to be offended be annoyed, [*informal*] take umbrage.
2 *to offend against the law.* do wrong, transgress, violate.

offender noun
criminal, culprit, delinquent, guilty party, malefactor, miscreant, sinner, transgressor, wrongdoer.

offensive adjective
offensive behaviour. offensive language. abusive, aggressive, annoying, antisocial, coarse, detestable, disagreeable, disgusting, displeasing, disrespectful, embarrassing, foul, impolite, improper, indecent, insulting, loathsome, nasty, nauseating,

objectionable, obnoxious, SEE **obscene**, [*informal*] offputting, revolting, rude, sickening, unpleasant, vile, vulgar.
OPPOSITES: SEE **pleasant**.

offer noun
He made me an offer. bid, proposal, proposition, suggestion, tender.

offer verb
1 *He offered me a cup of tea. The bank offered me a loan.* be willing to provide, extend, give the opportunity of, hold out, make available, make an offer of [SEE **offer** noun], proffer, put forward, suggest.
2 *She offered to come with me.* propose, [*informal*] show willing, volunteer.

offering noun
an offering in church. contribution, donation, gift, offertory, sacrifice.

offhand adjective
an offhand manner. aloof, SEE **casual**, curt, offhanded, perfunctory, unceremonious, uncooperative, uninterested.

office noun
1 *the manager's office.* bureau, room, workroom.
2 *The office of prime minister is a responsible one.* appointment, duty, function, occupation, place, position, post, responsibility, situation, work.

officer noun
1 *an officer in the armed services.* adjutant, aide-de-camp, CO, commandant, commanding officer.
VARIOUS RANKS: SEE **rank** noun.
2 *a police officer.* constable, policeman, policewoman.

official adjective
an official document. an official organization. accredited, approved, authentic, authoritative, authorized, bona fide, certified, formal, legitimate, licensed, proper, trustworthy.

official noun
We spoke to an official of the organization. agent, authorized person, [*uncomplimentary*] bureaucrat, SEE **chief** noun, executive, [*often uncomplimentary*] functionary, [*often uncomplimentary*] mandarin, officer, organizer, representative, responsible person.

TITLES OF VARIOUS OFFICIALS: bailiff, captain, clerk of the court, commander, commanding officer, commissioner, consul, customs officer, director, elder (*of the church*), equerry, governor, manager, managing director, marshal, mayor, mayoress, monitor, ombudsman, overseer, prefect, president, principal, proctor, proprietor, registrar, sheriff, steward, superintendent, supervisor, usher.

officiate verb
to officiate at a ceremony. be in charge, be responsible, have official authority, manage, preside.

officious adjective
an officious car-park attendant. SEE **bossy**, bumptious, [*informal*] cocky, impertinent, interfering, meddling, over-zealous, [*informal*] pushy, self-important.

offspring noun
Singular: baby, child, descendant, heir, successor. *Plural:* brood, family, fry, issue, litter, progeny, seed, spawn, young.

often adverb
again and again, constantly, frequently, generally, many times, regularly, repeatedly, time after time.
OPPOSITES: SEE **seldom**.

oil verb
to oil your bike. grease, lubricate.

oily adjective
oily food. fat, fatty, greasy.

ointment noun
an ointment for the skin. balm, cream, embrocation, emollient, liniment, lotion, paste, salve, unguent.

old adjective
1 *old buildings. an old car.* ancient, [*joking*] antediluvian, antiquated, antique, crumbling, decayed, decaying, decrepit, dilapidated, early, historic, medieval, obsolete, prehistoric, primitive, quaint, ruined, [*joking*] superannuated, venerable, veteran, vintage.
2 *old times.* bygone, forgotten, former, immemorial (*from time immemorial*), [*old-fashioned*] olden, past, prehistoric, previous, primeval, remote.
3 *old people.* aged, [*informal*] doddery, elderly, [*formal*] geriatric, grey-haired, hoary, [*informal*] in your dotage, oldish, [*informal*] past it, senile.
4 *old clothes.* moth-eaten, SEE **old-fashioned**, ragged, scruffy, shabby, worn, worn-out.
5 *old bread. old news.* dry, stale.
6 *old bus-tickets.* cancelled, expired, invalid, used.
7 *an old hand at the game.* experienced, expert, familiar, long-established, mature, practised, skilled, well-established.
OPPOSITES: SEE **new**, **recent**, **young**.

old-fashioned adjective
old-fashioned ways. anachronistic, antiquated, archaic, backward-looking, conventional, dated, fusty, hackneyed,

obsolete, old, outdated, out-of-date, out-of-touch, outmoded, passé, reactionary, time-honoured, traditional, unfashionable.
OPPOSITES: SEE **modern**.

omen noun
an omen of disaster. augury, auspice, foreboding, indication, portent, premonition, presage, prognostication, sign, warning.
to be an omen of SEE **foretell**.

ominous adjective
ominous signs of disaster. baleful, dire, fateful, forbidding, grim, inauspicious, menacing, portentous, sinister, threatening, unlucky, unpropitious.
OPPOSITES: SEE **auspicious**.

omission noun
an unfortunate omission. exclusion, gap, oversight.

omit verb
1 *to omit facts from a report.* cut, drop, edit out, eliminate, exclude, ignore, jump, leave out, miss out, overlook, pass over, reject, skip.
2 *to omit to do something.* fail, forget, neglect.

omnipotent adjective
all-powerful, almighty, supreme.

oncoming adjective
oncoming traffic. advancing, approaching, looming.

onlooker noun
SEE **observer**.

onslaught noun SEE **attack** noun.

opaque adjective
The diver couldn't see through the opaque water. cloudy, dark, dull, filmy, hazy, impenetrable, muddy, murky, obscure, turbid, unclear.
OPPOSITES: SEE **clear** adjective.

open adjective
1 *an open door. an open mouth.* ajar, gaping, unfastened, unlocked, wide, wide-open, yawning.
2 *open to the public.* accessible, available, exposed, public, revealed.
OPPOSITES: SEE **closed**.
3 *open space. the open road.* broad, clear, empty, extensive, uncrowded, unfenced, unobstructed, unrestricted.
OPPOSITES: SEE **enclosed**.
4 *an open nature. an open face.* artless, communicative, frank, honest, SEE **open-minded**, sincere, straightforward.
OPPOSITES: SEE **deceitful**.
5 *open defiance.* barefaced, blatant, candid, conspicuous, evident, flagrant, obvious, outspoken, overt, plain, unconcealed,

undisguised, visible.
OPPOSITES: SEE **concealed**.

open verb
1 *to open a door, bottle, letter, etc.* unblock, unbolt, unclose, uncork, undo, unfasten, unfold, unfurl, unlock, unroll, unseal, unwrap.
2 *The door opened. Her mouth opened.* become open [SEE **open** adjective], gape, yawn.
3 *to open a campaign. to open a new shop.* begin, commence, establish, [*informal*] get going, inaugurate, initiate, launch, set up, start.
OPPOSITES: SEE **close** verb.

opening adjective
the opening item in a concert. first, inaugural, initial, introductory.
OPPOSITES: SEE **final**.

opening noun
1 *an opening in a fence.* aperture, breach, break, chink, crack, cut, door, doorway, fissure, gap, gash, gate, gateway, hatch, hole, leak, mouth, orifice, outlet, rent, rift, slit, slot, space, split, tear, vent.
2 *the opening of a concert. the opening of a new era.* beginning, birth, commencement, dawn, inauguration, inception, initiation, launch, outset, start.
3 *The job provides a good opening for someone with initiative.* [*informal*] break, chance, opportunity.

open-minded adjective
SEE **unbiased**.

operate verb
1 *The device operates in all weathers.* act, function, go, perform, run, work.
2 *Can you operate this machine?* deal with, drive, handle, manage, use, work.
3 *The surgeon operated to remove her appendix.* do an operation, perform surgery.

operation noun
1 *a military operation. a business operation.* action, activity, campaign, effort, enterprise, exercise, manœuvre, movement, procedure, proceeding, process, transaction, undertaking.
2 *a surgical operation.* biopsy, surgery, transplant.

operational adjective
Is the new machinery operational yet? functioning, going, operating, usable, working.

operative adjective
[*informal*] *When I say "come quickly", the operative word is "quickly".* crucial, effective, important, key, principal, relevant, significant.

opinion

280

ordeal

opinion noun
I've got my own opinion. assessment,
attitude, belief, comment, conclusion,
conjecture, conviction, estimate, feeling,
guess, idea, impression, judgement, notion,
perception, point of view, theory, thought,
view.

opponent noun
an opponent in a debate. adversary,
antagonist, challenger, competitor,
contestant, enemy, foe, opposer, opposition,
rival.
OPPOSITES: SEE **ally** noun.

opportune adjective
an opportune moment. advantageous,
appropriate, auspicious, convenient,
favourable, lucky, propitious, right,
suitable, timely.
OPPOSITES: SEE **inconvenient**.

opportunity noun
*The weekend is a good opportunity for
shopping.* [*informal*] break, chance,
moment, occasion, opening, time.

oppose verb
to oppose someone's ideas. to oppose an enemy.
argue with, attack, be opposed to [SEE
opposed], challenge, combat, compete
against, confront, contest, contradict,
controvert, counter, counter-attack, defy,
disapprove of, face, fight, obstruct,
[*informal*] pit your wits against, quarrel
with, resist, rival, stand up to, [*informal*]
take a stand against, withstand.
OPPOSITES: SEE **support** verb.

opposed adjective
I'm opposed to the idea. against, antagonistic,
antipathetic, hostile, inimical, SEE **opposite**
adjective, unsympathetic.

opposite adjective
1 *the opposite view. the opposite theory.*
antithetical, conflicting, contradictory,
contrary, contrasting, converse, different,
incompatible, SEE **opposed**, opposing,
reverse.
2 *the opposite side of the road. your opposite
number.* corresponding, equivalent, facing,
matching, similar.

opposite noun
She says one thing and does the opposite.
antithesis, contrary, converse, reverse.

opposition noun
1 *We didn't expect so much opposition.*
antagonism, competition, disapproval,
resistance, scepticism, unfriendliness.
OPPOSITES: SEE **support** noun.
2 *We underestimated the strength of the
opposition.* SEE **opponent**.

oppress verb
The factory owners oppressed their workers.
abuse, afflict, crush, depress, enslave,
exploit, grind down, [*informal*] keep under,
persecute, subdue, subjugate, SEE **terrorize**,
[*informal*] trample on, tyrannize.

oppressed adjective
oppressed sections of the community. abused,
browbeaten, crushed, disadvantaged,
downtrodden, enslaved, exploited,
maltreated, misused, persecuted,
subjugated.
OPPOSITES: SEE **privileged**.

oppressive adjective
1 *an oppressive ruler.* brutal, cruel, despotic,
harsh, repressive, severe, tyrannical,
unjust.
2 *oppressive weather.* airless, close, heavy,
hot, humid, muggy, stifling, stuffy, sultry.

optical adjective

VARIOUS OPTICAL INSTRUMENTS: bifocals,
binoculars, field-glasses, glasses, lens,
magnifier, magnifying glass, microscope,
monocle, opera-glasses, periscope,
spectacles, sun-glasses, telescope.

---

optimistic adjective
optimistic about our chances. buoyant,
cheerful, confident, expectant, hopeful,
positive, sanguine.
OPPOSITES: SEE **pessimistic**.

optimum adjective
the optimum value of something. best,
highest, ideal, maximum, perfect, top.
OPPOSITE: worst.

option noun
You had the option of staying or leaving.
alternative, choice, possibility.
OPPOSITES: SEE **compulsion**.

optional adjective
optional extras. discretionary, dispensable,
elective, inessential, possible, unnecessary,
voluntary.
OPPOSITES: SEE **compulsory**.

oral adjective
an oral report. by mouth, said, spoken,
unwritten, verbal.
OPPOSITES: SEE **written**.

orbit noun
the orbit of a spacecraft. circuit, course, path,
revolution, trajectory.

ordain verb SEE **command** verb.

ordeal noun
a painful ordeal. difficulty, experience,
[*informal*] nightmare, suffering, test,
torture, trial, tribulation, trouble.

order noun

1 *alphabetical order. chronological order.* arrangement, array, classification, [*informal*] line-up, pattern, progression, sequence, series, succession.
2 *We restored order after the party.* neatness, system, tidiness.
3 *The army restored order after the riot.* calm, control, discipline, good behaviour, government, harmony, law and order, obedience, orderliness, organization, peace, quiet, rule.
OPPOSITES: SEE **disorder**.
4 *Keep your car in good order.* condition, state.
5 *The boss gives the orders.* command, decree, directive, edict, injunction, instruction.
6 *an order for a new carpet. an order for work to be done.* application, booking, commission, demand, mandate, request, requisition, reservation.

order verb

1 *to order things properly.* SEE **arrange**.
2 *She ordered us to be quiet.* [*old-fashioned*] bid, charge, command, compel, decree, direct, enjoin, instruct, ordain, require.
3 *He ordered a new magazine.* apply for, book, requisition, reserve.

orderly adjective

1 *orderly work.* careful, methodical, neat, organized, systematic, tidy, well-arranged, well-organized, well-prepared.
2 *orderly behaviour. an orderly crowd.* civilized, controlled, decorous, disciplined, law-abiding, peaceable, restrained, well-behaved.
OPPOSITES: SEE **disorderly**.

ordinary adjective

ordinary people. ordinary behaviour. accustomed, average, common, commonplace, conventional, customary, established, everyday, familiar, habitual, humble, [*informal*] humdrum, indifferent, mediocre, medium, middling, moderate, modest, mundane, nondescript, normal, orthodox, pedestrian, plain, prosaic, quotidian, reasonable, regular, routine, [*informal*] run-of-the-mill, satisfactory, simple, standard, stock (*a stock reply*), typical, undistinguished, unexceptional, unexciting, unimpressive, uninteresting, unsurprising, usual, well-known, workaday.
OPPOSITES: SEE **exceptional**.

organic adjective

1 *an organic substance.* animate, biological, growing, live, living, natural.
OPPOSITES: SEE **inorganic**.
2 *an organic whole.* evolving, integrated, organized, structured, systematic.

organism noun

a living organism. animal, cell, creature, living thing, plant.

organization noun

1 *Who was responsible for the organization of the outing?* arrangement, co-ordination, logistics, organizing, planning, regimentation, [*informal*] running.
2 *a business organization. a charitable organization.* alliance, association, body, business, club, company, concern, confederation, consortium, corporation, federation, firm, group, institute, institution, league, network, [*informal*] outfit, party, society, syndicate, union.

organize verb

1 *to organize into groups.* arrange, classify, group, put in order, rearrange, regiment, sort, sort out, structure, systematize, tidy up.
OPPOSITES: SEE **jumble** verb.
2 *to organize a party. to organize a demonstration.* co-ordinate, create, establish, make arrangements for, mobilize, orchestrate, plan, run, [*informal*] see to, set up.

organized adjective

an organized argument. organized effort. careful, clear, efficient, logical, methodical, neat, orderly, planned, regimented, scientific, structured, systematic, tidy, well-arranged, well-presented, well-run.
OPPOSITES: SEE **disorganized**.

orientate verb

to orientate yourself to a new situation. acclimatize, accustom, adapt, adjust, familiarize, orient, position.

origin noun

1 *the origin of life on earth. the origin of a rumour.* basis, beginning, birth, cause, commencement, creation, derivation, foundation, genesis, inauguration, inception, provenance, root, source, start.
OPPOSITES: SEE **end** noun.
2 *a millionaire of humble origin.* ancestry, background, descent, extraction, family, parentage, pedigree, start in life, stock.

original adjective

1 *the original inhabitants of a country.* aboriginal, archetypal, earliest, first, initial, native, primal, primitive, primordial.
OPPOSITES: SEE **recent**.
2 *an original idea. an original story.* creative, first-hand, fresh, imaginative, innovative, inspired, inventive, new, novel, resourceful, thoughtful, unconventional, unfamiliar, unique, unusual.
OPPOSITES: SEE **unoriginal**.

originate verb
1 *Where did the idea originate?* arise, be born, begin, commence, crop up, emanate, emerge, start.
2 *Who originated the idea?* be the inventor of, conceive, create, design, discover, give birth to, inaugurate, initiate, inspire, institute, introduce, invent, launch, pioneer.

ornament noun
accessory, adornment, bauble, decoration, embellishment, filigree, frill, frippery, garnish, gewgaw, SEE **jewel**, tracery, trimming, trinket.

ornament verb
adorn, beautify, deck, decorate, dress up, embellish, emblazon, emboss, embroider, festoon, garnish, [*uncomplimentary*] prettify, trim.

ornamental adjective
attractive, decorative, fancy, [*uncomplimentary*] flashy, pretty, showy.

ornate adjective
ornate decorations. [*formal*] baroque, decorated, elaborate, fancy, florid, flowery, fussy, ornamented, [*formal*] rococo.
OPPOSITES: SEE **plain** adjective.

orphan noun
foundling, stray, waif.

orthodox adjective
orthodox beliefs. the orthodox way to do something. accepted, approved, conformist, conventional, customary, established, mainstream, normal, official, ordinary, regular, standard, traditional, usual, well-established.
OPPOSITES: SEE **unconventional**.

oscillate verb
fluctuate, move to and fro, [*informal*] see-saw, swing, vacillate, vary, vibrate.

ostensible adjective
The ostensible reason wasn't the real reason. alleged, apparent, offered, outward, pretended, professed, [*informal*] put-on, reputed, specious, supposed, visible.
OPPOSITES: SEE **real**.

ostentation noun
I don't like the ostentation of their expensive life-style. affectation, display, exhibitionism, flamboyance, [*informal*] flashiness, pretentiousness, self-advertisement, show, showing off, [*informal*] swank.
OPPOSITES: SEE **modesty**.

ostracize verb
to ostracize someone you don't like. avoid, [*informal*] black, blackball, blacklist, boycott, cast out, cold-shoulder, [*informal*]

cut, [*informal*] cut dead, [*formal*] excommunicate, exile, expel, reject, [*informal*] send to Coventry, shut out.

oust verb
banish, eject, expel, [*informal*] kick out, remove, unseat.

outbreak noun
an outbreak of measles. an outbreak of vandalism. epidemic, [*informal*] flare-up, SEE **outburst**, plague, rash, upsurge.

outburst noun
an outburst of laughter. attack, eruption, explosion, fit, paroxysm, spasm, surge.

outcast noun
an outcast from society. castaway, exile, outlaw, outsider, pariah, refugee, untouchable.

outclass verb
SEE **surpass**.

outcome noun
SEE **result** noun.

outcry noun SEE **protest** noun.

outdated adjective
SEE **obsolete**.

outer adjective
1 *outer clothing.* exterior, external, outside, outward, superficial, surface.
2 *outer regions.* distant, further, outlying, peripheral, remote.
OPPOSITES: SEE **inner**.

outfit noun
1 *a complete water-skiing outfit.* SEE **equipment**.
2 *a new outfit of clothes.* costume, ensemble, [*informal*] get-up, suit, [*informal*] turn-out.

outgoing adjective
1 *an outgoing personality.* SEE **sociable**.
2 *the outgoing president.* ex-, former, last, past, retiring.
3 *the outgoing tide.* ebbing, falling, retreating.
OPPOSITES: SEE **incoming**.

outing noun
an outing to the seaside. excursion, expedition, jaunt, picnic, tour, trip.

outlaw noun
outlaws hiding in the mountains. bandit, brigand, criminal, deserter, desperado, fugitive, marauder, outcast, renegade, robber.

outlaw verb
SEE **prohibit**.

outlet noun
an outlet for waste water. channel, duct, exit, mouth, opening, orifice, vent, way out.

outline noun
1 *an outline of a scheme.* [*informal*] bare
bones, diagram, framework, plan, rough
idea, skeleton, sketch, summary.
2 *the outline of someone passing the window.*
figure, form, profile, shadow, shape,
silhouette.

outline verb
to outline your plans. delineate, draft, give
an outline of [SEE **outline** noun], rough out,
sketch, summarize.

outlook noun
1 *the outlook from my window.* aspect,
panorama, prospect, scene, sight, vantage-
point, view, vista.
2 *a person's mental outlook.* attitude, frame
of mind, point of view, standpoint,
viewpoint.
3 *the weather outlook.* expectations, forecast,
[*informal*] look-out, prediction, prognosis.

outlying adjective
outlying areas. distant, far-flung, far-off,
outer, remote.
OPPOSITES: SEE **central**.

out-of-date adjective SEE **old-fashioned**.

output noun
the output of a factory. production, yield.

outrage noun
1 *The way he treats his pets is an outrage.*
atrocity, crime, disgrace, outrageous act
[SEE **outrageous**], scandal, sensation.
2 *You can imagine our outrage when we heard
what he'd done.* anger, disgust, fury, horror,
indignation, resentment, revulsion, sense of
shock.

outrageous adjective
outrageous behaviour. outrageous prices.
abominable, atrocious, beastly, bestial,
criminal, disgraceful, disgusting, excessive,
execrable, extortionate, extravagant,
immoderate, infamous, iniquitous,
monstrous, nefarious, notorious, offensive,
preposterous, revolting, scandalous,
shocking, unreasonable, unspeakable,
unthinkable, vile, villainous, wicked.
OPPOSITES: SEE **reasonable**.

outside adjective
1 *outside walls.* exterior, external, outer,
outward, superficial, surface, visible.
2 *outside interference.* alien, extraneous,
foreign.

outside noun
the outside of a house. exterior, façade, shell,
skin, surface.
OPPOSITES: SEE **inside** noun.

outsider noun
Make outsiders feel welcome. alien, foreigner,
immigrant, interloper, intruder, newcomer,
non-resident, outcast, stranger, visitor.
OPPOSITES: SEE **member**, **resident** noun.

outskirts plural noun
the outskirts of the town. edge, fringe,
margin, outer areas, periphery, purlieus,
suburbs.
OPPOSITES: SEE **centre**.

outspoken adjective
SEE **frank**.

outstanding adjective
1 *an outstanding player. an outstanding
feature.* above the rest, celebrated,
conspicuous, distinguished, dominant,
eminent, excellent, exceptional,
extraordinary, great, important, impressive,
memorable, notable, noteworthy,
noticeable, predominant, pre-eminent,
prominent, remarkable, singular, special,
striking, unrivalled, well-known.
OPPOSITES: SEE **ordinary**.
2 *outstanding bills.* due, overdue, owing,
unpaid, unsettled.

outward adjective
outward appearances. apparent, evident,
exterior, external, noticeable, obvious,
ostensible, outer, outside, superficial,
surface, visible.

outwit verb
The fox outwitted the hounds. cheat, SEE
deceive, dupe, fool, hoax, hoodwink,
[*informal*] outsmart, [*informal*] take in,
trick.

oval adjective
egg-shaped, elliptical, ovoid.

overcast adjective
an overcast sky. black, cloudy, dark, dismal,
dull, gloomy, grey, leaden, lowering,
stormy, threatening.

overcome adjective
overcome by the heat. beaten, [*informal*] done
in, SEE **exhausted**, prostrate.

overcome verb
1 *to overcome an opponent.* SEE **defeat** verb.
2 *to overcome a problem.* SEE **deal** verb (**deal
with**).

overdue adjective
1 *The train is overdue.* belated, delayed, late,
slow, tardy, unpunctual.
OPPOSITES: SEE **early**.
2 *The gas bill is overdue.* outstanding, owing,
unpaid.

overeat verb
be greedy [SEE **greedy**], eat too much, gorge
yourself, gormandize, [*informal*] guzzle,
indulge yourself, [*informal*] make a pig of
yourself.

overeating noun
excess, gluttony, self-indulgence.
OPPOSITES: SEE **starvation**.

overflow verb
The lavatory cistern overflowed. brim over,
flood, pour over, run over, spill, well up.

overgrown adjective
1 *an overgrown schoolboy.* SEE **large**, outsize,
oversized.
2 *an overgrown garden.* rank, tangled, uncut,
unkempt, untidy, untrimmed, unweeded,
weedy, wild.

overhaul verb
1 *to overhaul an engine.* check over, examine,
inspect, renovate, repair, restore, service.
2 *The express overhauled a goods train.* SEE
overtake.

overhead adjective
an overhead walkway. aerial, elevated, high,
overhanging, raised.

overhear verb
to overhear a conversation. eavesdrop on,
listen in to.

overlook verb
1 *to overlook someone's wrongdoing.* condone,
disregard, excuse, forget, ignore, leave out,
let pass, miss, neglect, omit, pardon, pass
over, pay no attention to, [*informal*] turn a
blind eye to.
2 *My window overlooks the pie factory.* face,
front, have a view of, look at, look on to.

overpower verb
SEE **subdue**.

overpowering adjective
an overpowering urge. compelling,
irrepressible, irresistible, overwhelming,
powerful, uncontrollable.

overrun verb SEE **invade**.

oversee verb
SEE **supervise**.

oversight noun SEE **error**.

overt adjective
overt hostility. blatant, SEE **obvious**, open,
plain, unconcealed, undisguised.
OPPOSITES: SEE **secret** adjective.

overtake verb
Overtake the car in front. catch up with, leave
behind, outdistance, outpace, outstrip,
overhaul, pass.

overthrow verb
SEE **defeat** verb.

overtone noun
The word "witchcraft" has sinister overtones.
association, connotation, implication,
reverberation, suggestion.

overturn verb
1 *The boat overturned.* capsize, keel over, tip
over, turn over, turn turtle.
2 *The cat overturned the milk.* knock over,
spill, tip over, topple, upset.

overweight adjective
SEE **fat** adjective.

overwhelm verb
1 *to overwhelm the opposition.* SEE **defeat**
verb.
2 *A tidal-wave overwhelmed the town.* SEE
submerge.

overwhelming adjective
an overwhelming victory. crushing,
devastating, SEE **great**, landslide,
overpowering.

owe verb
to owe money be in debt, have debts.

owing adjective
I'll pay whatever is owing. due, outstanding,
overdue, owed, payable, unpaid, unsettled.
owing to because of, caused by, thanks to.

own verb
We own our house. be the owner of, have,
hold, possess.
to own up acknowledge your guilt, admit,
[*informal*] come clean, confess, [*informal*]
make a clean breast of it, [*informal*] tell all.

owner noun
the owner of property. free-holder, landlady,
landlord, possessor, proprietor.

Pp

pace noun
1 *Move forward two paces.* step, stride.
2 *The front runner set a quick pace.* gait,
[*informal*] lick, movement, quickness, rate,
speed, velocity.

pacify verb
*to pacify an angry person. to pacify someone's
anger.* appease, assuage, calm, conciliate,
humour, mollify, placate, propitiate, quell,
quieten, soothe, subdue, tame, tranquillize.
OPPOSITES: SEE **anger** verb.

pack noun
1 *a pack of goods.* bale, box, bundle, package,
packet, parcel.
2 *a pack to carry on your back.* back-pack,
haversack, kitbag, knapsack, rucksack.
3 *a pack of wolves.* SEE **group** noun.

pack verb
1 *to pack things in a box.* bundle, fill, load, package, put, put together, store, stow, wrap up.
2 *to pack things tightly. to pack people into a minibus.* compress, cram, crowd, huddle, jam, overcrowd, press, ram, squeeze, stuff, wedge.

pact noun
a pact with the enemy. agreement, alliance, armistice, arrangement, bargain, compact, contract, covenant, deal, entente, league, peace, settlement, treaty, truce, understanding.

pad verb
to pad something with soft material. cover, fill, line, pack, protect, stuff, upholster.

padding noun
1 *padding in an armchair.* filling, protection, upholstery, stuffing, wadding.
2 *padding in an essay.* prolixity, verbiage, verbosity, [*informal*] waffle, wordiness.

pagan adjective
pagan tribes. atheistic, godless, heathen, idolatrous, irreligious, unchristian.

page noun
a page of a book. folio, leaf, sheet, side.

pageantry noun
the pageantry of a royal wedding. ceremony, display, formality, grandeur, magnificence, pomp, ritual, show, spectacle, splendour.

pain noun
ache, affliction, agony, anguish, cramp, crick (*in the neck*), discomfort, distress, headache, hurt, irritation, ordeal, pang, smart, soreness, spasm, stab, sting, suffering, tenderness, throb, throes (*throes of childbirth*), toothache, torment, torture, twinge.
to suffer pain SEE **hurt** verb.

painful adjective
1 *painful torture.* agonizing, cruel, excruciating, severe.
2 *a painful wound.* aching, [*informal*] achy, hurting, inflamed, raw, smarting, sore, [*informal*] splitting (*a splitting headache*), tender.
3 *a painful experience.* distressing, hard to bear, harrowing, hurtful, nasty, [*informal*] traumatic, trying, unpleasant, upsetting.
4 *a painful decision.* difficult, hard, laborious, troublesome.
OPPOSITES: SEE **painless**.
to be painful SEE **hurt** verb.

pain-killer noun
anaesthetic, analgesic, anodyne, sedative.

painless adjective
a painless visit to the dentist. a painless decision. comfortable, easy, effortless, pain-free, simple, trouble-free, undemanding.
OPPOSITES: SEE **painful**.

painstaking adjective
SEE **careful**.

paint noun
colour, colouring, pigment, tint.

KINDS OF PAINT: acrylic, distemper, emulsion, enamel, gloss paint, lacquer, matt paint, oil-colour, oil-paint, pastel, primer, stain, tempera, undercoat, varnish, water-colour, whitewash.

---

paint verb
1 *to paint a wall. to paint a toy.* apply paint to, coat with paint, colour, cover with paint, decorate, enamel, gild, lacquer, redecorate, varnish, whitewash.
2 *to paint a picture.* delineate, depict, describe, portray, represent.

painting noun

KINDS OF PAINTED PICTURE: fresco, landscape, miniature, mural, oil-painting, portrait, still-life, water-colour.

OTHER KINDS OF PICTURE: SEE **picture** noun.

---

pair noun
a pair of friends. working as a pair. brace, couple, duet, duo, mates, partners, partnership, set of two, twins, twosome.

palace noun
castle, château, mansion, official residence, stately home.

palatable adjective
palatable food. acceptable, agreeable, appetizing, easy to take, eatable, edible, nice to eat, pleasant, tasty.
OPPOSITES: SEE **unpalatable**.

pale adjective
1 *a pale face.* anaemic, ashen, bloodless, colourless, drained, etiolated, ill-looking, pallid, pasty, [*informal*] peaky, sallow, sickly, unhealthy, wan, [*informal*] washed-out, [*informal*] whey-faced, white, whitish.
OPPOSITES: SEE **ruddy**.
2 *pale colours.* bleached, dim, faded, faint, light, pastel, subtle, weak.
OPPOSITES: SEE **bright**.

paling noun
fence, fencing, palisade, railing, stockade.

pall noun
1 *a pall on a coffin.* mantle, shroud, veil.
2 *a pall of smoke.* SEE **covering**.

pall verb
The novelty soon began to pall. become boring, become uninteresting, weary.

pallid adjective
SEE **pale** adjective.

paltry adjective
SEE **worthless**.

pamper verb
to pamper your pet. coddle, cosset, humour, indulge, mollycoddle, over-indulge, pet, spoil, spoon-feed.

pamphlet noun
a pamphlet about road safety. booklet, brochure, catalogue, folder, handout, leaflet, tract.

pandemonium noun
SEE **uproar**.

pander verb
to pander to *to pander to low tastes.* cater for, fulfil, gratify, indulge, please, provide, satisfy.

pane noun
glass, sheet of glass, window.

panel noun
1 *a wooden panel.* insert, rectangle, rectangular piece.
2 *a panel of experts.* committee, group, jury, team.
member of a panel expert, panellist, pundit.

pang noun
SEE **pain** noun.

panic noun
If a fire starts, we don't want any panic! alarm, consternation, SEE **fear** noun, [*informal*] flap, horror, hysteria, stampede, terror.

panic verb
Don't panic! become panic-stricken [SEE **panic-stricken**], [*informal*] flap, [*informal*] go to pieces, [*informal*] lose your head, over-react, stampede.

panic-stricken adjective
alarmed, disorientated, frantic, SEE **frightened**, horrified, hysterical, overexcited, panicky, terror-stricken, undisciplined, unnerved.
OPPOSITES: SEE **cool** adjective.

panorama noun
a beautiful panorama across the valley. landscape, perspective, prospect, scene, view, vista.

pant verb
to pant because you've been running. breathe quickly, gasp, puff, wheeze.

pantry noun
food cupboard, larder.

pants noun
1 briefs, knickers, panties, shorts, trunks, underpants.
2 SEE **trousers**.

paper noun
1 *a piece of paper.* folio, leaf, sheet.

KINDS OF PAPER: card, cardboard, cartridge paper, manila, notepaper, papyrus, parchment, postcard, stationery, tissue-paper, toilet-paper, tracing-paper, vellum, wallpaper, wrapping-paper, writing-paper.

---

2 *I keep important papers in a file.* certificates, deeds, documents, forms, records.
3 *a daily paper.* SEE **newspaper**.
4 *a scientific paper.* article, dissertation, essay, monograph, thesis, treatise.

parade noun
a military parade. a fancy dress parade. cavalcade, ceremony, column, display, march-past, motorcade, pageant, procession, review, show.

parade verb
to parade in front of the judges. assemble, file past, form up, line up, make a procession, march past, present yourself, process.

paradise noun
SEE **delight** noun, Eden, Elysium, heaven, nirvana, Utopia.

paradoxical adjective
It seems paradoxical to make weapons in order to maintain peace. absurd, anomalous, conflicting, contradictory, illogical, incongruous, self-contradictory.

parallel adjective
1 *parallel lines.* equidistant.
2 *a parallel example. parallel events.* analogous, corresponding, matching, SEE **similar**.

parallel noun
I saw a parallel between her situation and mine. analogy, comparison, correspondence, likeness, match, resemblance, similarity.

paralyse verb
The shock paralysed him. anaesthetize, cripple, deaden, desensitize, freeze, immobilize, incapacitate, lame, numb, petrify, stun.

paralysed adjective
a paralysed person. paralysed limbs. crippled, desensitized, disabled, SEE **handicapped**, immobile, immovable,

incapacitated, lame, numb, palsied,
paralytic, paraplegic, rigid, unusable,
useless.

paralysis noun
immobility, palsy, paraplegia.

parapet noun
battlement, fortification, rampart.

paraphernalia noun
*Can you move all your paraphernalia out of
the way?* baggage, belongings, effects,
equipment, gear, impedimenta, [*informal*]
odds and ends, stuff, tackle, things.

paraphrase verb
*to paraphrase something in simpler
language.* interpret, rephrase, reword,
rewrite, translate.

paraplegic adjective
SEE **paralysed**.

parcel noun
bale, bundle, carton, pack, package, packet.

parched adjective
1 *Plants won't grow in parched ground.* arid,
baked, barren, dehydrated, dry, lifeless,
scorched, sterile, waterless.
2 *I'm parched!* gasping, thirsty.

pardon noun
pardon for a condemned criminal.
absolution, amnesty, discharge,
forgiveness, mercy, reprieve.

pardon verb
to pardon a condemned person. absolve,
condone, [*formal*] exculpate, excuse,
exonerate, forgive, free, let off, overlook,
release, reprieve, set free, spare.

pardonable adjective
a pardonable mistake. allowable, excusable,
forgivable, justifiable, minor, negligible,
petty, understandable, venial (*a venial sin*).
OPPOSITES: SEE **unforgivable**.

pare verb
1 *to pare an apple.* peel, skin.
2 *to pare something down.* clip, SEE **cut** verb,
prune, reduce, trim.

parent noun
FAMILY RELATIONSHIPS: SEE **family**.

park noun

KINDS OF PARK: amusement park, arboretum,
botanical gardens, car-park, estate, nature
reserve, parkland, public gardens,
recreation ground, safari park, theme park.

park verb
to park a car. leave, place, position, station.

parliament noun
assembly, conclave, congress, convocation,
council, SEE **government**, the Houses of
Parliament, legislature, senate.

parody verb
ape, caricature, guy, SEE **imitate**, satirize,
[*informal*] send up, [*informal*] take off,
travesty.

parry verb
to parry a blow. avert, block, deflect, evade,
fend off, push away, repel, repulse, stave
off, ward off.

parsimonious adjective
SEE **stingy**.

part noun
1 *a part of a whole.* bit, branch, component,
constituent, department, division, element,
fraction, fragment, ingredient, particle,
piece, portion, ramification, scrap, section,
sector, segment, share, single item,
subdivision, unit.
2 *a part of a book or TV programme.* chapter,
episode.
3 *a part of a town or country.* area, district,
neighbourhood, quarter, region, sector.
4 *parts of your body.* limb, member, organ.
PARTS OF THE BODY: SEE **body**.
5 *a part in a play.* cameo, character, role.

part verb
1 *to part a child from its parents. to part a
branch from the trunk.* cut off, detach,
disconnect, divide, separate, sever, split,
sunder.
OPPOSITES: SEE **join** verb.
2 *to part from someone.* depart, go away,
leave, quit, say goodbye, split up, take your
leave, withdraw.

partial adjective
1 *Our play was only a partial success.*
imperfect, incomplete, limited, unfinished.
OPPOSITES: SEE **complete** adjective.
2 *a partial referee.* SEE **prejudiced**.
to be partial to *I'm partial to a drink at
bedtime.* appreciate, be fond of, be keen on,
enjoy, [*informal*] go for, like.

participate verb
to participate in a game. assist, be active, be
involved, co-operate, engage, help, join in,
partake, share, take part.

particle noun
1 *a particle of food.* bit, crumb, drop,
fragment, grain, iota, jot, morsel, piece,
scrap, shred, sliver, speck.
2 *a particle of matter.* atom, electron,
molecule, neutron.

particular adjective
1 *I recognized his particular way of talking.*
distinct, individual, peculiar, personal,
singular, specific, uncommon, unique,
unmistakable.
OPPOSITES: SEE **general**.
2 *I made a particular effort.* exceptional,
important, notable, outstanding, special,
unusual.
OPPOSITES: SEE **ordinary**.
3 *The cat's particular about food.* choosy,
discriminating, fastidious, finicky, fussy,
meticulous, nice, pernickety, selective.
OPPOSITES: SEE **undiscriminating**.

particulars plural noun
Give me the particulars. circumstances,
details, facts, information, [*slang*] low-
down.

parting noun
We were sad when it came to parting.
departure, going, leave-taking, leaving,
saying goodbye [SEE **goodbye**], separation,
splitting up.

partisan adjective
SEE **prejudiced**.

partition verb
to partition a country. divide, parcel out,
separate off, share out, split up, subdivide.

partner noun
1 *a business partner.* accomplice, ally,
assistant, [*joking*] bedfellow, collaborator,
colleague, companion, confederate, helper.
2 *a marriage partner.* consort, husband,
mate, spouse, wife.

partnership noun
1 *a business partnership.* affiliation, alliance,
combination, company, co-operative,
syndicate.
2 *partnership in crime.* association,
collaboration, complicity, co-operation.
3 *a marriage partnership.* marriage,
relationship, union.

party noun
1 *a Christmas party.* celebration, [*informal*]
do, festivity, function, gathering, [*informal*]
get-together, [*joking*] jollification,
merrymaking, [*informal*] rave-up.

VARIOUS KINDS OF PARTY: ball, banquet,
barbecue, birthday party, ceilidh,
Christmas party, dance, [*informal*] disco,
discothèque, feast, [*informal*] hen-party,
house-warming, orgy, picnic, reception,
reunion, social, [*informal*] stag-party, tea-
party, wedding.

---

2 *a political party.* alliance, association,
cabal, [*informal*] camp (*He went over to their*

camp), coalition, faction, SEE **group** noun,
league.

pass noun
1 *a mountain pass.* canyon, defile, gap, gorge,
ravine, valley, way through.
2 *a bus pass.* authority, authorization,
licence, permission, permit, ticket, warrant.

pass verb
1 *We watched the traffic pass.* go by, move on,
move past, proceed, progress, [*informal*]
thread your way.
2 *Try to pass the car in front.* go beyond,
outstrip, overhaul, overtake.
3 *The time passed slowly.* elapse, lapse,
[*informal*] tick by.
4 *The pain passed.* disappear, fade, go away,
vanish.
5 *Pass the books round.* circulate, deal out,
deliver, give, hand over, offer, present,
share, submit, supply, transfer.
6 *They passed a law. The judge passed
sentence.* agree, approve, authorize, confirm,
decree, enact, establish, ordain, pronounce,
ratify, validate.
7 *I pass!* [*informal*] give in, opt out, say
nothing, waive your rights.
to pass away SEE **die**.
to pass out SEE **faint** verb.

passable adjective
1 *a passable standard of work.* acceptable,
adequate, all right, fair, mediocre, middling,
moderate, ordinary, satisfactory, [*informal*]
so-so, tolerable.
OPPOSITES: SEE **unacceptable**.
2 *The road is passable again.* clear,
navigable, open, traversable, unblocked,
usable.
OPPOSITES: SEE **impassable**.

passage noun
1 *the passage of time.* advance, moving on,
passing, progress, progression.
2 *a sea passage.* crossing, SEE **journey** noun,
voyage.
3 *a secret passage.* corridor, passageway,
thoroughfare, tube, tunnel, way through.
4 *Wait in the passage!* entrance, hall,
hallway, lobby, vestibule.
5 *a passage of a book.* episode, excerpt,
extract, paragraph, piece, quotation, scene,
section.

passenger noun SEE **traveller**.

passing adjective
SEE **temporary**.

passion noun
a passion for adventure. appetite, ardour,
commitment, craving, desire, drive,
eagerness, emotion, enthusiasm, fervour,
frenzy, greed, [*informal*] heat (*in the heat of*

the moment), infatuation, love, lust, obsession, strong feeling, thirst, urge, zeal, zest.

passionate adjective
passionate feelings. ardent, avid, burning, committed, eager, emotional, enthusiastic, excited, fervent, fiery, frenzied, greedy, hot, impassioned, inflamed, intense, lustful, obsessive, sexy, strong, urgent, vehement, violent, zealous.
OPPOSITES: SEE **apathetic**.

passive adjective
a passive response. compliant, docile, impassive, inactive, long-suffering, non-violent, patient, resigned, submissive, unresisting.
OPPOSITES: SEE **active**.

past adjective
past events. bygone, earlier, ended, finished, former, gone, [*informal*] over and done with, previous.
OPPOSITES: SEE **future** adjective.

past noun
In the past, things were different. antiquity, days gone by, history, old days, olden days, past times [SEE **past** adjective]
OPPOSITES: SEE **future** noun.

pasta noun

KINDS OF PASTA: cannelloni, lasagne, macaroni, noodles, ravioli, spaghetti, tagliatelle, vermicelli.

paste noun
1 *adhesive paste.* adhesive, fixative, glue, gum.
2 *fish-paste.* pâté, spread.

pastiche noun
a pastiche of various styles. blend, composite, [*informal*] hodgepodge or hotchpotch, medley, mixture, motley collection, patchwork, selection.

pastime noun
What's your favourite pastime? activity, amusement, diversion, entertainment, game, hobby, occupation, recreation, relaxation, sport.
VARIOUS SPORTS AND GAMES: SEE **game** noun, **sport**.

pastoral adjective
1 *a pastoral scene.* agrarian, bucolic, country, farming, idyllic, outdoor, peaceful, rural, rustic.
OPPOSITES: SEE **urban**.
2 *a clergyman's pastoral duties.* caring, ecclesiastical, parochial, ministerial, priestly.

pasture noun
pasture for sheep or cattle. field, grassland, grazing, [*old-fashioned, poetic*] mead, meadow, paddock, pasturage.

pasty adjective SEE **pale** adjective.

pat verb
to pat with your hand. caress, dab, slap, tap, SEE **touch** verb.

patch verb
to patch a hole. cover, darn, fix, mend, reinforce, repair, sew up, stitch up.

patchy adjective
1 *patchy fog. patchy success.* [*informal*] bitty, changeable, changing, erratic, inconsistent, irregular, uneven, unpredictable, variable, varied, varying.
2 *patchy colours.* SEE **dappled**.
OPPOSITES: SEE **uniform** adjective.

path noun
alley, bridle-path, bridle-way, esplanade, footpath, footway, SEE **road**, route, pathway, pavement, [*American*] sidewalk, towpath, track, trail, walk, walkway, way.

pathetic adjective
a pathetic farewell. affecting, distressing, heartrending, lamentable, moving, piteous, pitiable, pitiful, poignant, SEE **sad**, touching, tragic.

pathos noun
The pathos of the situation brought tears to our eyes. emotion, feeling, pity, poignancy, sadness, tragedy.

patience noun
I waited with great patience. calmness, composure, endurance, equanimity, forbearance, fortitude, long-suffering, perseverance, persistence, resignation, restraint, self-control, stoicism, toleration.

patient adjective
1 *patient suffering. a patient animal.* accommodating, calm, composed, docile, easygoing, even-tempered, forbearing, long-suffering, mild, philosophical, quiet, resigned, self-possessed, serene, stoical, submissive, tolerant, uncomplaining.
2 *patient effort. a patient worker.* determined, diligent, persevering, persistent, steady, unhurried, untiring.
OPPOSITES: SEE **impatient**.

patriot noun
[*uncomplimentary*] chauvinist, loyalist, nationalist.

patriotic adjective
a patriotic person. [*uncomplimentary*] chauvinistic, [*uncomplimentary*] jingoistic, loyal, nationalistic, [*uncomplimentary*] xenophobic.

patriotism noun
[*uncomplimentary*] chauvinism,
[*uncomplimentary*] jingoism, loyalty,
nationalism, [*uncomplimentary*]
xenophobia.

patrol noun
1 *on patrol.* guard, policing, sentry-duty,
surveillance, watch.
2 *a night-patrol.* guard, look-out, sentinel,
sentry, watchman.

patrol verb
Police patrolled the area all night. be on
patrol [SEE **patrol** noun], guard, inspect,
keep a look-out, police, tour, walk the
beat.

patron noun
1 *a patron of the arts.* [*informal*] angel,
backer, benefactor, champion,
defender, helper, sponsor, subscriber,
supporter.
2 *a patron of a shop or restaurant.* client,
customer, frequenter, [*informal*] regular,
shopper.

patronize verb
1 *I patronize the local shops.* back, be a patron
of [SEE **patron**], encourage, frequent, shop at,
support.
2 *to patronize someone.* be patronizing
towards [SEE **patronizing**], talk down to.

patronizing adjective
a patronizing attitude. condescending,
disdainful, haughty, lofty, paternalistic,
snobbish, supercilious, superior.

pattern noun
1 *patterns on wallpaper.* arrangement,
decoration, design, device, figuration,
figure, motif, ornamentation, shape,
tessellation.
2 *a pattern to copy.* archetype, criterion,
example, guide, model, norm, original,
precedent, prototype, sample, specimen,
standard.

pause noun
a pause to get our breath back. break,
[*informal*] breather, check, delay, gap, halt,
interlude, intermission, interruption,
interval, lull, respite, rest, stand-still, stop,
stoppage, suspension, wait.

pause verb
*She paused uncertainly. We'll pause for a
rest.* break off, delay, halt, hang back, have
a pause [SEE **pause** noun], hesitate, rest, stop,
[*informal*] take a break, wait.

pave verb
to pave a path. asphalt, concrete, cover with
paving [SEE **paving**], flag, [*informal*] make
up, surface, tile.

paving noun

VARIOUS KINDS OF PAVING: cobbles,
concrete, crazy-paving, flagstones, paving-
stones, setts, tiles.

pay noun
How much pay do you get? earnings,
emoluments, fee, [*formal*] honorarium,
income, SEE **payment**, reimbursement,
salary, stipend, wages.

pay verb
1 *Did you pay a lot for your bike?* [*informal*]
cough up, [*informal*] fork out, give, hand
over, proffer, spend.
2 *They pay her a good wage.* grant,
remunerate.
3 *I'll pay my debts.* clear, [*informal*] foot,
meet, pay off, pay up, settle.
4 *He paid me for the glass he broke.* bear the
cost of, compensate, indemnify, pay back,
recompense, refund, reimburse, repay.
5 *Crime doesn't pay.* be profitable [SEE
profitable].
6 *She'll pay for her mistake!* SEE **suffer**.

payment noun
monthly payments. charge, cost,
expenditure, figure, outgoings, outlay, price,
rate, remittance.
OPPOSITES: SEE **income**.

KINDS OF PAYMENT: advance, alimony,
allowance, commission, compensation,
contribution, deposit, donation, fare, fee,
fine, instalment, loan, SEE **pay** noun, pocket-
money, premium, ransom, reward, royalty,
[*informal*] sub, subscription, subsistence,
supplement (*a supplement for first-class
travel*), surcharge, tip, toll, wage.

peace noun
1 *After the war, there was a period of peace.*
accord, agreement, amity, conciliation,
concord, friendliness, harmony, order.
OPPOSITES: SEE **war**.
2 *The two sides signed a peace.* alliance,
armistice, cease-fire, pact, treaty, truce.
OPPOSITES: declaration of war.
3 *the peace of the countryside. peace of mind.*
calmness, peace and quiet, peacefulness,
placidity, quiet, repose, serenity, silence,
stillness, tranquillity.
OPPOSITES: SEE **activity**, **noise**.

peaceable adjective
a peaceable community. amicable,
conciliatory, co-operative, friendly, gentle,
harmonious, mild, non-violent, pacific,
peace-loving, placid, understanding.
OPPOSITES: SEE **quarrelsome**.

peaceful adjective
a peaceful evening. peaceful music. balmy,
calm, easy, gentle, pacific, placid, pleasant,
quiet, relaxing, restful, serene, slow-moving,
soothing, still, tranquil, undisturbed,
unruffled, untroubled.
OPPOSITES: SEE **noisy, troubled**.

peak noun
1 *the peak of a mountain.* apex, brow, cap,
crest, crown, pinnacle, point, summit, tip,
top.
2 *snowy peaks.* SEE **mountain**.
3 *the peak of her career.* acme, climax, crisis,
culmination, height, highest point, zenith.

peal verb
The bells pealed. chime, ring, toll.

peculiar adjective
1 *There's a peculiar person snooping around.
That's a peculiar way to do it.* abnormal,
bizarre, curious, eccentric, funny, odd,
outlandish, out of the ordinary, quaint,
queer, quirky, surprising, strange,
uncommon, unconventional, unusual,
weird.
OPPOSITES: SEE **ordinary**.
2 *I recognized her peculiar way of writing.*
characteristic, different, distinctive,
identifiable, idiosyncratic, individual,
particular, personal, private, special,
singular, unique.
OPPOSITES: SEE **common** adjective.

peculiarity noun
We all have our peculiarities. abnormality,
characteristic, eccentricity, foible,
idiosyncrasy, mannerism, oddity, peculiar
feature [SEE **peculiar**], quirk, singularity,
speciality, trait, uniqueness.

pedantic adjective
1 *a pedantic use of long words.* academic,
bookish, formal, humourless, learned, old-
fashioned, pompous, scholarly,
schoolmasterly, stilted.
2 *pedantic observance of the rules.* inflexible,
[*informal*] nit-picking, precise, strict,
unimaginative.
OPPOSITES: SEE **informal**.

pedestal noun SEE **base** noun.

pedestrian adjective
1 *a pedestrian precinct.* pedestrianized,
traffic-free.
2 *a pedestrian performance.* SEE **ordinary**.

pedestrian noun
foot-traveller, walker.

pedigree adjective
a pedigree animal. pure-bred, thoroughbred.

pedigree noun
a dog's pedigree. ancestry, descent, SEE
family, family history, line.

peel noun
orange peel. rind, skin.

peel verb
to peel an orange. to peel off a covering.
denude, pare, skin, strip.

peep noun, verb
SEE **look** noun, verb.

peer verb
SEE **look** verb.

peer, peeress nouns
aristocrat, noble, nobleman, noblewoman,
titled person.
OPPOSITES: COMMONER.

TITLES OF BRITISH PEERS: baron, baroness,
duchess, duke, earl, lady, lord, marchioness,
marquis or marquess, viscount, viscountess.

peers 1 *the peers of the land.* the aristocracy,
the nobility, the peerage.
OPPOSITES: THE COMMONS.
2 *She's quite at ease with her peers.* equals,
fellows.

peevish adjective
SEE **irritable**.

peg verb
SEE **fasten**.

pellet noun
ball, pill.

pelt verb
to pelt someone with missiles. assail,
bombard, shower, SEE **throw**.

pen noun
1 *a pen for animals.* SEE **enclosure**.
2 *a pen to write with.* ball-point, biro, felt-
tipped pen, fountain pen.

penalize verb
SEE **punish**.

penalty noun
SEE **punishment**.

penance noun
to do penance for SEE **atone**.

pendent adjective
the pendent branches of a willow. dangling,
hanging, loose, pendulous, suspended,
swinging, trailing.

pending adjective
There's an inquiry pending. about to happen,
forthcoming, imminent, impending,
[*informal*] in the offing, undecided, waiting.

pendulous adjective
SEE **pendent**.

penetrate verb
1 *The drill can penetrate concrete.* bore
through, make a hole in, pierce, puncture.

2 *We penetrated their defences.* enter, get through, infiltrate, probe.
3 *Damp had penetrated the brick-work.* impregnate, permeate, pervade, seep into.

penitent adjective
penitent about his mistake. apologetic, conscience-stricken, contrite, regretful, remorseful, repentant, sorry.
OPPOSITES: SEE **unrepentant**.

penniless adjective SEE **poor**.

pensive adjective
SEE **thoughtful**.

penury noun
SEE **poverty**.

people noun
1 *Do you like being with other people?* folk, [*uncomplimentary*] hoi polloi, human beings, humanity, humans, individuals, mankind, mortals, persons.
2 *In an election, the people decide who will govern.* citizens, common people, community, electorate, nation, populace, population, the public, society.
3 *After living abroad for a time, he returned to his people.* clan, family, kith and kin, nation, race, relatives, tribe.

people verb
a strange world peopled by monsters. colonize, fill, inhabit, occupy, overrun, populate, settle.

perceive verb
1 *I perceived a shape on the horizon.* become aware of, catch sight of, detect, discern, distinguish, make out, notice, observe, recognize, see, spot.
2 *I began to perceive what she meant.* apprehend, comprehend, deduce, feel, gather, grasp, know, realize, sense, understand.

perceptible adjective
a perceptible drop in temperature. perceptible anger in his voice. appreciable, audible, detectable, distinct, evident, marked, noticeable, observable, obvious, palpable, perceivable, recognizable, visible.
OPPOSITES: SEE **imperceptible**.

perception noun
What is your perception of the problem? Ears and eyes are organs of perception. apprehension, awareness, cognition, comprehension, consciousness, discernment, insight, observation, recognition, sensation, sense, understanding, view.

perceptive adjective
[Do not confuse with *perceptible*.] *a perceptive judge of character.* acute, alert, astute, aware, clever, discriminating,

discerning, SEE **intelligent**, observant, penetrating, percipient, perspicacious, responsive, sensitive, sharp, sharp-eyed, shrewd, sympathetic, understanding.

perch verb
to perch on a fence. balance, rest, roost, settle, sit.

percussion noun
[*uncomplimentary*] kitchen department.

PERCUSSION INSTRUMENTS INCLUDE:
castanets, celesta or celeste, chime bars, cymbals, SEE **drum**, glockenspiel, gong, kettledrum, maracas, rattle, tambourine, [*plural*] timpani, triangle, tubular bells, vibraphone, wood block, xylophone.

OTHER MUSICAL INSTRUMENTS: SEE **music**.

perfect adjective
1 *a perfect example of something.* complete, excellent, faultless, finished, flawless, ideal, mint (*in mint condition*), unbeatable, undamaged, unexceptionable, whole.
2 *Nobody is perfect.* blameless, irreproachable, pure, spotless.
3 *a perfect fit. a perfect copy.* accurate, correct, exact, faithful, immaculate, impeccable, precise, tailor-made.
OPPOSITES: SEE **imperfect**.

perfect verb
to perfect your plans. bring to fruition, carry through, complete, consummate, finish, fulfil, make perfect [SEE **perfect** adjective], realize, [*informal*] see through (*When I've started a thing I like to see it through*).

perfection noun
1 *the perfection of a lovely jewel.* beauty, completeness, excellence, ideal, precision, wholeness.
2 *the perfection of our plans.* accomplishment, achievement, completion, consummation, end, fruition, fulfilment, realization.

perforate verb
to perforate something with a pin. bore through, drill, penetrate, pierce, prick, puncture.

perform verb
1 *to perform your duty.* accomplish, achieve, bring about, carry out, commit, complete, discharge, do, execute, finish, fulfil.
2 *to perform on the stage.* act, appear, dance, enact, play, present, produce, put on (*to put on a play*), render, represent, serenade, sing, take part.

performance noun
1 *a performance by actors or musicians.* acting, concert, début [= *a first performance*], impersonation,

interpretation, matinée, play, playing,
portrayal, première, presentation, preview,
production, rendition, representation,
show, sketch, turn.
MUSICAL TERMS: SEE **music**.
THEATRICAL TERMS: SEE **theatre**.
2 *a poor performance by our team.*
achievement, behaviour, conduct,
exhibition, exploit, feat.
3 *He put on a bit of a performance.* act,
deception, play-acting, pretence.

performer noun
actor, actress, artist, artiste, player, singer,
star, [*informal*] superstar, trouper.
VARIOUS ENTERTAINERS: SEE **entertainer**.

perfume noun
the perfume of roses. aroma, fragrance,
odour, scent, SEE **smell** noun, whiff.

perhaps adverb
conceivably, maybe, possibly.
OPPOSITES: SEE **definitely**.

peril noun SEE **danger**.

perilous adjective
SEE **dangerous**.

perimeter noun
the perimeter of a field. border, borderline,
boundary, bounds, circumference, confines,
edge, fringe, frontier, margin, periphery.

period noun
*a period of history. a period spent doing
something.* age, epoch, era, interval, phase,
season, session, spell, stage, stint, stretch,
term, SEE **time** noun, while.

periodical noun
SEE **magazine**.

peripheral adjective
1 *peripheral areas of town.* distant, on the
perimeter [SEE **perimeter**], outer, outermost,
outlying.
2 *Don't waste time on peripheral details.*
borderline, inessential, irrelevant,
marginal, minor, secondary, unimportant,
unnecessary.
OPPOSITES: SEE **central**.

perish verb
1 *Many birds perished in the cold weather.* be
destroyed, be killed, die, expire, fall, pass
away.
2 *There was a leak where the rubber hose had
perished.* crumble away, decay, decompose,
disintegrate, go bad, rot.

perishable adjective
perishable goods. biodegradable
(*biodegradable plastic*), destructible, liable to
perish [SEE **perish**], unstable.
OPPOSITES: SEE **lasting**.

perjury noun SEE **lying** noun.

perk noun
[*informal*] *She gets various perks in addition
to her wages.* benefit, bonus, extra, fringe
benefit, gratuity, [*informal*] perk, tip.

perky adjective
SEE **lively**.

permanent adjective
*a permanent job. a permanent relationship.
a permanent problem.* abiding, chronic,
constant, continual, continuous, durable,
enduring, everlasting, fixed, immutable,
incessant, incurable, indestructible,
ineradicable, irreparable (*irreparable
damage*), irreversible (*an irreversible
decision*), lasting, lifelong, long-lasting,
neverending, perennial, perpetual,
persistent, stable, steady, unalterable,
unchanging, unending.
OPPOSITES: SEE **temporary**.

permeate verb
The smell permeated the house. filter through,
flow through, impregnate, penetrate,
percolate, pervade, saturate, spread
through.

permissible adjective
Is it permissible to smoke? acceptable,
admissible, allowable, allowed, lawful,
legal, legitimate, permitted, proper, right,
sanctioned, valid.
OPPOSITES: SEE **forbidden**.

permission noun
We had her permission to leave. agreement,
approval, assent, authority, authorization,
consent, dispensation, [*informal*] go-ahead,
[*informal*] green light, leave, licence, SEE
permit noun, [*informal*] rubber stamp,
sanction.

permissive adjective
SEE **tolerant**.

permit noun
a permit to fish in the lake. authorization,
charter, licence, order, pass, passport,
ticket, visa, warrant.

permit verb
We don't permit smoking in the house. agree
to, allow, approve of, authorize, consent to,
endorse, give permission for [SEE
permission], license, [*old-fashioned*] suffer,
tolerate.

perpendicular adjective
at right angles, upright, vertical.

perpetrate verb
to perpetrate a crime. SEE **commit**.

perpetual adjective
*the perpetual cycle of life and death. a baby's
perpetual crying for attention.* abiding,

ceaseless, chronic, constant, continual, continuous, endless, eternal, everlasting, frequent, immortal, incessant, interminable, lasting, long-lasting, neverending, nonstop, ongoing, perennial, permanent, persistent, protracted, recurrent, recurring, repeated, unceasing, unchanging, unending, unfailing, unremitting.

perplex verb
The mystery perplexed us. baffle, bewilder, confound, confuse, disconcert, muddle, mystify, puzzle, [*informal*] stump, [*informal*] throw, worry.

persecute verb
to persecute people for their religious beliefs. badger, bother, bully, discriminate against, harass, hound, ill-treat, intimidate, maltreat, martyr, molest, oppress, pester, [*informal*] put the screws on, terrorize, torment, torture, tyrannize, victimize, worry.

persevere verb
If you persevere you'll succeed in the end. be diligent, be steadfast [SEE **steadfast**], carry on, continue, endure, [*informal*] hang on, [*informal*] keep at it, keep going, persist, [*informal*] plug away, [*informal*] soldier on, stand firm, [*informal*] stick at it.
OPPOSITES: SEE **cease, falter.**

persist verb
1 *If you persist, you'll succeed in the end.* SEE **persevere.**
2 *How long will this snow persist?* go on, keep on, last, linger, remain.
OPPOSITES: SEE **cease.**

persistent adjective
1 *a persistent cold. persistent rumours.* ceaseless, chronic, constant, continual, continuous, endless, eternal, everlasting, incessant, interminable, lasting, long-lasting, neverending, obstinate, permanent, perpetual, persisting, recurrent, recurring, repeated, unending, unrelenting, unrelieved, unremitting.
OPPOSITES: SEE **intermittent, temporary.**
2 *a persistent worker.* assiduous, determined, dogged, hard-working, indefatigable, patient, persevering, pertinacious, relentless, resolute, steadfast, steady, stubborn, tenacious, tireless, unflagging, untiring, unwavering, zealous.
OPPOSITES: SEE **lazy.**

person noun
adolescent, adult, baby, being, [*informal*] body, character, SEE **child,** [*joking*] customer (*a difficult customer*), figure, human, human being, individual, infant, SEE **man** noun, personage, soul, [*informal*] type, SEE **woman.**
SEE ALSO: **people.**

personable adjective SEE **good-looking.**

personal adjective
1 *personal characteristics.* distinct, distinctive, idiosyncratic, individual, inimitable, particular, peculiar, private, special, unique, your own.
OPPOSITES: SEE **general.**
2 *personal information.* confidential, intimate, private, secret.
OPPOSITES: SEE **public** adjective.
3 *personal remarks.* critical, derogatory, disparaging, insulting, offensive, pejorative, SEE **rude,** slighting.

personality noun
1 *She has an attractive personality.* character, disposition, identity, individuality, [*informal*] make-up, nature, [*formal*] psyche, temperament.
2 *She has great personality.* attractiveness, charisma, charm, magnetism.
3 *a show-business personality.* big name, celebrity, figure (*a well-known figure in show-business*), star, [*informal*] superstar.

personification noun
Santa Claus is the personification of Christmas. allegorical representation, embodiment, epitome, human likeness, incarnation, living image, manifestation.

personify verb
Santa Claus personifies the spirit of Christmas. allegorize, be the personification of [SEE **personification**], embody, epitomize, give a human shape to, incarnate, personalize, represent, symbolize.

personnel noun
the personnel who work in a factory. employees, manpower, people, staff, work-force, workers.

perspective noun
Birds see a garden from a different perspective. angle, outlook, point of view, slant, view, viewpoint.

perspire verb
sweat.

persuade verb
I persuaded him to accept my terms. bring round, cajole, coax, convert, convince, entice, induce, influence, inveigle, prevail upon, talk into, tempt, urge, use persuasion [SEE **persuasion**], wheedle (into), win over.
OPPOSITES: SEE **dissuade.**

persuasion noun
It took a lot of persuasion to convince him. argument, blandishment, cajolery, brainwashing, conditioning, enticement, exhortation, persuading [SEE **persuade**], propaganda, reasoning.

persuasive adjective
a persuasive argument. cogent, compelling, convincing, credible, effective, eloquent, forceful, influential, logical, plausible, reasonable, sound, strong, telling, valid, watertight.
OPPOSITES: SEE **incredible**.

pertinent adjective
SEE **relevant**.

perturb verb
The bad news perturbed us. agitate, alarm, bother, disconcert, distress, disturb, frighten, make anxious [SEE **anxious**], scare, shake, trouble, unsettle, upset, vex, worry.
OPPOSITES: SEE **reassure**.

pervade verb
The smell pervaded the whole building. affect, diffuse, fill, filter through, flow through, impregnate, penetrate, percolate, permeate, saturate, spread through, suffuse.

pervasive adjective
a pervasive smell. general, inescapable, insidious, permeating, pervading, prevalent, rife, ubiquitous, universal, widespread.

perverse adjective
It's perverse of him to buy hot dogs when we want ice-cream. contradictory, contrary, disobedient, fractious, headstrong, illogical, inappropriate, intractable, intransigent, obdurate, obstinate, [*informal*] pig-headed, rebellious, refractory, stubborn, tiresome, uncooperative, unhelpful, unreasonable, wayward, wilful, wrong-headed.
OPPOSITES: SEE **helpful, reasonable**.

perversion noun
1 *perversion of the truth.* corruption, distortion, falsification, misrepresentation, misuse, twisting.
2 *sexual perversion.* abnormality, depravity, deviance, deviation, immorality, impropriety, [*informal*] kinkiness, unnaturalness, vice, wickedness.

pervert verb
1 *to pervert the course of justice.* bend, distort, divert, perjure, subvert, twist, undermine.
2 *to pervert a witness.* bribe, corrupt, lead astray.

perverted adjective
perverted behaviour. perverted sexual practices. abnormal, corrupt, debauched, depraved, deviant, eccentric, immoral, improper, [*informal*] kinky, SEE **obscene**, sick, twisted, unnatural, warped, wicked, wrong.
OPPOSITES: SEE **natural**.

pessimistic adjective
pessimistic about our chances. cynical, defeatist, despairing, despondent, fatalistic, gloomy, hopeless, melancholy, morbid, negative, resigned, unhappy.
OPPOSITES: SEE **optimistic**.

pest noun
1 *Don't be a pest!* annoyance, bother, curse, irritation, nuisance, [*informal*] pain in the neck, trial, vexation.
2 *garden pests.* [*informal*] bug, [*informal*] creepy-crawly, insect, parasite, [*plural*] vermin.

pester verb
Don't pester me while I'm busy! annoy, badger, bait, besiege, bother, harass, harry, [*informal*] hassle, molest, nag, plague, torment, trouble, worry.

pet noun

CREATURES COMMONLY KEPT AS PETS: budgerigar, canary, cat, dog, ferret, fish, gerbil, goldfish, guinea-pig, hamster, mouse, parrot, pigeon, rabbit, rat, tortoise.
OTHER ANIMALS: SEE **animal** noun.

---

pet verb
Our dog loves you to pet him. caress, cuddle, fondle, kiss, pat, stroke, SEE **touch** verb.

petition noun
a petition to the government. appeal, entreaty, list of signatures, plea, request, suit, supplication.

petty adjective
1 *petty crime.* insignificant, minor, small, trifling, trivial, SEE **unimportant**.
OPPOSITES: SEE **important**.
2 *a petty attitude.* grudging, nit-picking, SEE **small-minded**, ungenerous.

pharmacy noun
Get your medicine from the pharmacy. chemists, dispensary, [*American*] drug-store.

phase noun
a phase of your life. a phase of an activity. development, period, season, spell, stage, step, SEE **time** noun.

phenomenal adjective
The winner of the qui had a phenomenal memory. amazing, exceptional, extraordinary, [*informal*] fantastic, incredible, notable, outstanding, remarkable, [*informal*] sensational, singular, unbelievable, unusual, [*informal*] wonderful.
OPPOSITES: SEE **ordinary**.

phenomenon noun
1 *Snow is a common phenomenon in winter.* circumstance, event, fact, happening, incident, occurrence, sight.

2 *They said the six-year old pianist was quite a phenomenon.* curiosity, marvel, phenomenal person or thing [SEE **phenomenal**], prodigy, wonder.

philanthropic adjective
She's known for her philanthropic work in the community. altruistic, beneficent, benevolent, bountiful, caring, charitable, generous, humane, humanitarian, SEE **kind** adjective, munificent.
OPPOSITES: SEE **misanthropic**.

philosophical adjective
1 *a philosophical debate.* abstract, academic, analytical, ideological, intellectual, learned, logical, metaphysical, rational, reasoned, theoretical, thoughtful, wise.
2 *philosophical in defeat.* calm, collected, composed, patient, reasonable, resigned, stoical, unemotional, unruffled.
OPPOSITES: SEE **emotional**.

philosophize verb
He philosophizes instead of actually doing something. analyse, be philosophical [SEE **philosophical**], moralize, pontificate, preach, rationalize, reason, sermonize, theorize, think things out.

philosophy noun
your philosophy of life. convictions, ideology, metaphysics, set of beliefs, values, wisdom.

phlegmatic adjective
a phlegmatic temperament. apathetic, cold, cool, frigid, impassive, imperturbable, lethargic, placid, slow, sluggish, stolid, undemonstrative, unemotional, unresponsive.
OPPOSITES: SEE **excitable**.

phobia noun
a phobia about spiders. anxiety, aversion, dislike, dread, SEE **fear** noun, [*informal*] hang-up, hatred, horror, neurosis, obsession, revulsion.

Phobia is related to Greek *phobos = fear*. There are a number of words for particular fears which end in *-phobia*, such as: acrophobia (*fear of heights*), agoraphobia (*open spaces*), anglophobia (*the English*), arachnophobia (*spiders*), claustrophobia (*enclosed spaces*), hydrophobia (*water*), nyctophobia (*the dark*), photophobia (*light*), xenophobia (*strangers*), zoophobia (*animals*).

---

phone verb
I phoned granny. call, dial, [*informal*] give a buzz, ring, telephone.

phoney adjective
[*slang*] *a phoney Welsh accent.* affected, artificial, assumed, bogus, cheating,

counterfeit, faked, false, fictitious, fraudulent, imitation, insincere, pretended, [*informal*] put-on, [*informal*] put-up (*a put-up job*), sham, synthetic, trick, unreal.
OPPOSITES: SEE **real**.

photocopy verb
copy, duplicate, photostat, print off, reproduce, [*informal*] run off.

photograph noun
enlargement, exposure, negative, photo, plate, positive, print, shot, slide, [*informal*] snap, snapshot, transparency.

photographic adjective
a photographic description. accurate, exact, faithful, graphic, lifelike, naturalistic, realistic, representational, true to life.

PHOTOGRAPHIC EQUIPMENT INCLUDES: box camera, ciné-camera, dark-room, developer, enlarger, exposure-meter, fixer, light-meter, Polaroid camera, reflex camera, SLR camera, telephoto lens, tripod, zoom lens.

---

phraseology noun
I liked her neat phraseology. diction, SEE **expression**, idiom, language, parlance, phrasing, style, turn of phrase, wording.

physical adjective
1 *physical contact.* bodily, carnal, corporal, corporeal.
2 *Ghosts have no physical existence.* earthly, fleshly, material, mortal, palpable, physiological, real, solid, substantial, tangible.
OPPOSITES: SEE **incorporeal, spiritual**.

physiological adjective
anatomical, bodily, physical.

physique noun
a person's physique. body, build, figure, form, frame, muscles, physical condition, shape.

pick noun
1 *Take your pick.* SEE **choice** noun, election, preference, selection.
2 *the pick of the bunch.* best, cream, élite, favourite, flower, pride.

pick verb
1 *Pick a partner. Pick your representative.* choose, decide on, elect, fix on, make a choice of, name, nominate, opt for, prefer, select, settle on, single out, vote for.
2 *to pick flowers.* collect, cull, cut, gather, harvest, pluck, pull off, take.

pictorial adjective
a pictorial representation of something. diagrammatic, graphic, illustrated, representational.

picture noun
a recognizable picture. delineation, depiction, image, likeness, outline, portrayal, profile, representation.

KINDS OF PICTURE: abstract, cameo, caricature, cartoon, collage, design, doodle, drawing, engraving, etching, film, fresco, [*plural*] graffiti, [*plural*] graphics, icon, identikit, illustration, landscape, montage, mosaic, mural, oil-painting, old master, painting, photofit, photograph, pin-up, plate (*photographic plate*), portrait, print, reproduction, self-portrait, sketch, slide, [*informal*] snap, snapshot, still life, transfer, transparency, triptych, trompe l'œil, video, vignette.

picture verb
1 *Historical scenes were pictured on the wall.* delineate, depict, evoke, illustrate, outline, portray, represent, show.

WAYS TO MAKE A PICTURE: caricature, doodle, draw, engrave, etch, film, paint, photograph, print, sketch, video.

2 *Can you picture what the world will be like in 100 years?* conceive, describe, dream up, envisage, imagine, think up, visualize.

picturesque adjective
1 *picturesque scenery.* attractive, SEE **beautiful**, charming, pleasant, pretty, quaint, scenic.
OPPOSITES: SEE **ugly**.
2 *picturesque language.* colourful, descriptive, expressive, graphic, imaginative, poetic, vivid.
OPPOSITES: SEE **prosaic**.

pie noun
flan, pasty, patty, quiche, tart, tartlet, turnover, vol-au-vent.

piece noun
1 *a piece of cake. a piece of wood.* bar, bit, bite, block, chip, chunk, crumb, division, [*informal*] dollop, fraction, fragment, grain, helping, hunk, length, lump, morsel, part, particle, portion, quantity, sample, scrap, section, segment, share, shred, slab, slice, snippet, speck, stick, tablet, [*informal*] titbit.
2 *a piece of a machine.* component, constituent, element, spare part, unit.
3 *a piece of music. a piece of writing. a piece of clothing.* article, composition, example, instance, item, number, passage, specimen, work.

pied adjective
dappled, flecked, mottled, particoloured, piebald, spotted, variegated.

pier noun
1 *Passengers disembark at the pier.* breakwater, SEE **dock** noun, jetty, landing-stage, quay, wharf.
2 *the piers of a bridge. a pier supporting a wall.* buttress, column, pile, pillar, support, upright.

pierce verb
bore through, drill through, enter, go through, impale, make a hole in, penetrate, perforate, prick, punch (*punch a hole in a ticket*), puncture, skewer, spike, spit, stab, stick into, transfix, wound.

piercing adjective
1 *a piercing scream.* deafening, high-pitched, SEE **loud**, penetrating, sharp, shrill.
2 *a piercing wind.* SEE **cold** adjective.

piety noun
the piety of the martyrs. devotion, devoutness, faith, godliness, holiness, piousness, religion, [*uncomplimentary*] religiosity, saintliness, sanctity.
OPPOSITES: SEE **impiety**.

pig noun
boar, hog, [*childish*] piggy, piglet, runt [= *smallest piglet in a litter*], sow, swine.

pigmy dwarf, midget.

pile noun
1 *a pile of rubbish.* accumulation, heap, hoard, mass, mound, [*informal*] mountain, quantity, stack.
2 *piles driven into the ground.* column, pier, post, support, upright.

pile verb
Pile everything in the corner. accumulate, amass, assemble, bring together, build up, collect, concentrate, gather, heap up, hoard, load, mass, stack up, store.

pilfer verb SEE **steal**.

pilgrimage noun SEE **journey** noun.

pill noun
Swallow the pills with a little water. capsule, pellet, tablet.

pillage verb
SEE **plunder** verb.

pillar noun
supporting pillars. baluster, column, pier, pilaster [= *ornamental pillar*], pile, post, prop, shaft, stanchion, support, upright.

pilot noun
1 *the pilot of an aircraft.* airman, [*old-fashioned*] aviator, flier.
2 *the pilot of a boat.* coxswain, helmsman, navigator, steersman.

pilot verb
He piloted us back to safety. conduct, convey, direct, drive, fly, guide, lead, navigate, steer.

pimple noun
boil, pustule, [*plural*] rash, spot, swelling, [*slang*] zit.

pin noun
[*old-fashioned*] bodkin, brooch, clip, drawing-pin, hat-pin, peg, safety-pin, tie-pin.

pin verb SEE **fasten**, pierce, transfix.

pinch verb
1 *to pinch something between your fingers.* crush, nip, squeeze, tweak.
2 [*informal*] *to pinch things from other people.* SEE **steal**.

pine verb
The dog pined when its master died. mope, mourn, sicken, waste away.
to pine for *In winter I pine for warm sunshine!* crave, hanker after, long for, miss, SEE **want** verb, yearn for.

pinnacle noun
1 *the pinnacle of your career.* acme, apex, climax, height, highest point, peak, summit, top, zenith.
2 *a tower topped with ornate pinnacles.* spire, steeple, turret.

pioneer noun
1 *pioneers who opened up new territories.* colonist, discoverer, explorer, settler.
2 *a pioneer of a new technique.* innovator, inventor, originator.

pioneer verb
to pioneer a new idea. [*informal*] bring out, develop, discover, experiment with, invent, launch, originate, set up, start.

pious adjective
1 [*complimentary*] *pious worshippers.* dedicated, devout, god-fearing, godly, holy, moral, religious, reverent, saintly, sincere, spiritual.
OPPOSITES: SEE **irreligious**.
2 [*uncomplimentary*] *I hate their pious moralizing.* [*informal*] holier-than-thou, hypocritical, insincere, sanctimonious, self-righteous, self-satisfied, unctuous.
OPPOSITES: SEE **sincere**.

pip noun
1 *an orange pip.* seed, stone.
2 *a pip on a dice, officer's uniform, etc.* mark, spot, star.
3 *At the last pip it will be exactly six o'clock.* bleep, blip, stroke.

pipe noun
a water pipe. conduit, duct, hose, hydrant, pipeline, piping, tube.

pirate noun
a pirate on the high seas. buccaneer, [*old-fashioned*] corsair, marauder, SEE **thief**.

pirate verb SEE **plagiarize**.

pistol noun SEE **gun**.

pit noun
1 *a deep pit.* abyss, chasm, crater, depression, excavation, hole, hollow, pothole.
2 *Miners work in a pit.* coal-mine, colliery, mine, quarry, shaft, working.

pitch noun
1 *black as pitch.* tar.
2 *the pitch of a roof.* angle, gradient, incline, slope, steepness, tilt.
3 *the pitch of a musical note.* height, tuning.
4 *a football pitch.* arena, ground, playing-field, stadium.

pitch verb
1 *to pitch a tent.* erect, put up, raise, set up.
2 *to pitch a stone into a pond.* bowl, [*informal*] bung, cast, [*informal*] chuck, fling, heave, hurl, lob, sling, throw, toss.
3 *to pitch into the water.* dive, drop, fall heavily, plunge, topple.
4 *to pitch about in a storm.* dip up and down, lurch, rock, roll, toss.

piteous adjective
piteous cries for help. affecting, distressing, heartbreaking, heartrending, miserable, moving, pathetic, pitiable, pitiful, SEE **sad**, touching, wretched.

pitfall noun
I tried to avoid the obvious pitfalls. catch, danger, difficulty, hazard, snag, trap.

pitiable adjective SEE **piteous**, **pitiful**.

pitiful adjective
1 *pitiful cries for help.* SEE **piteous**.
2 [*uncomplimentary*] *a pitiful attempt to stop the ball.* abject, contemptible, deplorable, hopeless, inadequate, incompetent, laughable, [*informal*] miserable, [*informal*] pathetic, pitiable, ridiculous, useless, worthless.
OPPOSITES: SEE **admirable**.

pitiless adjective
a pitiless attack. blood-thirsty, callous, cruel, hard, heartless, inexorable, SEE **merciless**, relentless, ruthless, unfeeling, unrelenting, unrelieved, unremitting.
OPPOSITES: SEE **merciful**.

pitted adjective
a pitted surface. dented, pock-marked, rough, scarred, uneven.
OPPOSITES: SEE **smooth** adjective.

pity noun
The thugs showed no pity. charity, clemency, compassion, feeling, forbearance,

forgiveness, grace, humanity, kindness, leniency, love, mercy, regret, softness, sympathy, tenderness, understanding, warmth.
OPPOSITES: SEE **cruelty**.

pity verb
I pitied anyone who was out in the storm. [*informal*] bleed for (*My heart bleeds for them*), commiserate with, [*informal*] feel for, feel or show pity for [SEE **pity** noun], sympathize with, weep for.

pivot noun
turning on a pivot. axis, axle, centre, fulcrum, hub, point of balance, swivel.

pivot verb
SEE **turn** verb.

placard noun
an advertising placard. advert, advertisement, bill, notice, poster, sign.

place noun
1 *a place on a map.* location, point, position, site, situation, [*informal*] spot, [*informal*] whereabouts.
2 *a nice place for a holiday.* area, country, district, locale, locality, neighbourhood, region, SEE **town**, venue, vicinity.
3 *your place in society.* degree, function, grade, SEE **job**, office, position, rank, station, status.

place verb
1 *Place your things on the table.* arrange, deposit, dispose, [*informal*] dump, lay, leave, locate, plant, position, put down, rest, set down, settle, situate, stand, station, [*informal*] stick.
2 *The judges placed me third.* grade, position, put in order, rank.
3 *I've heard the tune before, but I can't place it.* identify, locate, put a name to, put into context, recognize.

placid adjective
a placid temperament. collected, composed, cool, equable, even-tempered, imperturbable, level-headed, mild, phlegmatic, restful, sensible, stable, steady, unexcitable.

plagiarize verb
to plagiarize someone else's ideas. borrow, copy, [*informal*] crib, imitate, [*informal*] lift, pirate, reproduce, SEE **steal**.

plague noun
1 *bubonic plague.* blight, contagion, epidemic, SEE **illness**, infection, outbreak, pestilence.
2 *a plague of flies.* infestation, invasion, nuisance, scourge, swarm.

plague verb
The flies plagued us. Don't plague me with your questions. afflict, annoy, be a nuisance to, be a plague to, bother, disturb, irritate, molest, [*informal*] nag, persecute, pester, torment, trouble, vex, worry.

plain adjective
1 *a plain signal.* apparent, audible, certain, clear, comprehensible, definite, distinct, evident, legible, manifest, obvious, unambiguous, unmistakable, visible, well-defined.
OPPOSITES: SEE **unclear**.
2 *plain speech. the plain truth.* basic, blunt, candid, direct, downright, explicit, forthright, frank, honest, informative, outspoken, plain-spoken, prosaic, sincere, straightforward, unadorned, unequivocal, unvarnished.
OPPOSITES: SEE **evasive**.
3 *a plain appearance. plain cooking.* austere, everyday, frugal, homely, modest, ordinary, simple, unattractive, undecorated, unprepossessing, unpretentious, unremarkable, workaday.
OPPOSITES: SEE **attractive**, **elaborate** adjective.

plain noun
a wide plain. prairie, savannah, steppe.

plaintive adjective
a plaintive tune. doleful, melancholy, mournful, SEE **sad**, sorrowful, wistful.

plan noun
1 *a plan of the town.* [*informal*] bird's-eye view, chart, diagram, drawing, layout, map, representation, sketch-map.
2 *a carefully worked-out plan.* aim, blueprint, course of action, design, idea, intention, method, plot, policy, procedure, programme, project, proposal, proposition, scenario, scheme, strategy.

plan verb
1 *We planned our campaign.* arrange, concoct, contrive, design, devise, draw up a plan of [SEE **plan** noun], formulate, invent, map out, [*informal*] mastermind, organize, outline, plot, prepare, scheme, think out, work out.
2 *What do they plan to do next?* aim, conspire, contemplate, envisage, intend, mean, propose, think of.

plane noun
1 *raised to a higher plane.* SEE **level** noun.
2 [= *aircraft*] SEE **aircraft**.

planet noun
globe, orb, satellite, sphere, world.

PLANETS OF THE SOLAR SYSTEM: Earth,
Jupiter, Mars, Mercury, Neptune, Pluto,
Saturn, Uranus, Venus.

plank noun
beam, board, planking, timber.

planned adjective
*Was the meeting planned, or did it happen by
chance?* arranged, contrived, SEE **deliberate**
adjective, designed, masterminded,
organized, premeditated, [*informal*] set up,
thought out, worked out.
OPPOSITES: SEE **spontaneous**.

planning noun
You should do the planning in advance.
arrangement, design, drafting, forethought,
organization, preparation, setting up,
thinking out.

plant noun
plants greenery, growth, undergrowth,
vegetation.

KINDS OF PLANT: annual, SEE **bulb**, cactus, SEE
cereal, climber, fern, SEE **flower** noun, SEE
fungus, grass, SEE **herb**, lichen, moss,
perennial, seedling, shrub, SEE **tree**, SEE
vegetable, waterplant, weed.

PARTS OF A PLANT: bloom, blossom, branch,
bud, bulb, corm, SEE **flower** noun, frond,
fruit, [*formal*] inflorescence, leaf, [*formal*]
panicle, petal, pod, [*formal*] raceme, root,
seed, shoot, [*formal*] spadix, stalk, stem,
trunk, tuber, twig.

plant verb
to plant flowers. set out, sow, transplant.

plaster noun
1 *plaster on a wall.* mortar, stucco.
2 *a plaster to cover a wound.* dressing,
sticking-plaster.

plaster verb
to plaster a wall. coat, cover, daub.

plastic noun

KINDS OF PLASTIC: bakelite, celluloid,
polystyrene, polythene, polyurethane,
polyvinyl, PVC, vinyl.

plate noun
1 *plates piled with food.* dinner-plate, dish,
[*old-fashioned*] platter, side-plate, soup-
plate.
2 *a steel plate. plates of rock.* layer, panel,
sheet, slab, stratum.

plate verb
to plate one metal with a layer of another.
anodize, coat, cover, electroplate, galvanize
(*with zinc*), gild (*with gold*).

platform noun
The speakers sat on a platform. dais, podium,
rostrum, stage.

plausible adjective
a plausible excuse. acceptable, believable,
conceivable, credible, likely, persuasive,
possible, probable, reasonable, tenable.
OPPOSITES: SEE **implausible**.

play noun
1 *We all enjoy play.* amusement, diversion,
fun, [*informal*] fun and games, joking,
make-believe, playing, pretending,
recreation, sport.
VARIOUS GAMES AND SPORTS: SEE **game** noun,
sport.
2 *a play on TV.* drama, performance,
production.
THEATRICAL ENTERTAINMENTS: SEE **theatre**.
3 *play in the moving parts of a machine.*
freedom, freedom of movement, latitude,
leeway, looseness, tolerance.

play verb
1 *The children went to play.* amuse yourself,
caper, disport yourself, fool about, frisk,
frolic, gambol, have fun, [*informal*] mess
about, romp, sport.
2 *He won't play.* join in, participate, take part.
3 *I played him at snooker.* challenge, compete
against, oppose, vie with.
4 *Who played Mary in the nativity play?* act,
impersonate, perform, portray, pretend to
be, represent, take the part of.
5 *to play the piano.* make music on, perform
on, strum.
6 *to play records. to play a tape-recorder.* have
on, listen to, operate, put on, switch on.

player noun
1 *the players in a game.* competitor,
contestant, sportsman, sportswoman.
2 *players on stage.* actor, actress, entertainer,
instrumentalist, musician, performer,
soloist, [*joking*] Thespian.
VARIOUS PERFORMERS: SEE **music**, **theatre**.

playful adjective
a playful puppy. playful teasing. active,
cheerful, flirtatious, frisky, good-natured,
humorous, impish, [*informal*] jokey, joking,
lighthearted, lively, mischievous, puckish,
roguish, skittish, spirited, sportive,
sprightly, [*informal*] tongue-in-cheek,
vivacious, waggish.
OPPOSITES: SEE **serious**.

playground noun
play-area, recreation ground, school yard.

playing-field noun
arena, ground, pitch, recreation ground,
sports-ground.

playmate noun
SEE **friend**.

plea noun
a plea for mercy. appeal, entreaty, invocation, petition, prayer, request, supplication.
LEGAL TERMS: SEE **law**.

plead verb
He pleaded to be let off. appeal, ask, beg, entreat, implore, importune, petition, request, solicit.

pleasant adjective
[*Pleasant* can refer to anything which pleases you, and there are many possible synonyms. We give just some of the commoner ones here.] *pleasant food. pleasant weather. pleasant manners.* acceptable, affable, agreeable, amiable, attractive, balmy, beautiful, charming, cheerful, congenial, decent, delicious, delightful, enjoyable, entertaining, excellent, fine, friendly, genial, gentle, SEE **good**, gratifying, [*informal*] heavenly, hospitable, kind, likeable, lovely, mellow, mild, nice, palatable, peaceful, pleasing, pleasurable, pretty, relaxed, satisfying, soothing, sympathetic, warm, welcome, welcoming.
OPPOSITES: SEE **unpleasant**.

please verb
I did it to please you. amuse, content, delight, entertain, give pleasure to, gladden, gratify, make happy, satisfy.

pleased adjective
a pleased expression. [*informal*] chuffed, [*uncomplimentary*] complacent, contented, delighted, elated, euphoric, glad, grateful, gratified, SEE **happy**, satisfied, thankful, thrilled.
OPPOSITES: SEE **annoyed**.

pleasing, **pleasurable** adjectives
SEE **pleasant**.

pleasure noun
1 *I get pleasure from my garden.* bliss, comfort, contentment, delight, ecstasy, enjoyment, gladness, gratification, happiness, joy, rapture, satisfaction, solace.
2 *What are your favourite pleasures?* amusement, diversion, entertainment, fun, luxury, recreation, self-indulgence.

pleat noun
a pleat in a skirt. crease, flute, fold, gather, tuck.

pledge noun
1 *a pledge left at a pawn-broker's.* bail, bond, deposit, security, surety.
2 *a pledge of good faith.* assurance, guarantee, oath, pact, promise, undertaking, vow, word.

pledge verb
She pledged to give her support. agree, commit yourself, contract, give a pledge [SEE **pledge** noun], guarantee, promise, swear, undertake, vow.

plentiful adjective
a plentiful supply of food. abounding, abundant, ample, bounteous, bountiful, bristling, bumper (*a bumper crop*), copious, generous, inexhaustible, lavish, liberal, overflowing, plenteous, profuse, prolific.
OPPOSITES: SEE **scarce**.

plenty noun
plenty to do. plenty in the garden. abundance, affluence, cornucopia, excess, fertility, flood, fruitfulness, glut, more than enough, [*informal*] oodles, plentifulness, plethora, profusion, prosperity, sufficiency, superabundance, surfeit, surplus, wealth.
OPPOSITES: SEE **scarcity**.
plenty of *plenty of food.* abundant, ample, heaps of, [*informal*] lashings of, [*informal*] loads of, a lot of, lots of, [*informal*] masses of, much, [*informal*] oodles of, piles of, SEE **plentiful**.

pliable adjective
1 *pliable wire.* bendable, [*informal*] bendy, ductile, flexible, plastic, pliant, springy, supple.
2 *a pliable character.* compliant, easily influenced, easily led, easily persuaded, impressionable, responsive, suggestible, tractable.
OPPOSITES: SEE **rigid**

plod verb
1 *to plod through mud.* tramp, trudge, SEE **walk** verb.
2 *to plod through your work.* grind on, labour, persevere, SEE **work** verb.

plot noun
1 *a plot of ground.* allotment, area, estate, garden, lot, parcel, patch, smallholding, tract.
2 *the plot of a novel.* narrative, organization, outline, scenario, story, thread.
3 *a plot against the government.* cabal, conspiracy, intrigue, machination, plan, scheme.

plot verb
1 *to plot a route.* chart, draw, map out, plan, project.
2 *They plotted to rob a bank.* collude, conspire, have designs, intrigue, scheme.
3 *What are you two plotting?* [*informal*] brew, [*informal*] cook up, design, hatch.

plough verb
to plough a field. cultivate, till, turn over.

ploy noun SEE **trick** noun.

pluck verb
1 *to pluck fruit off a tree.* collect, gather, harvest, pick, pull off.
2 *to pluck a chicken.* denude, remove the feathers from, strip.
3 *to pluck something out of someone's hand.* grab, jerk, seize, snatch, tweak, yank.
4 *to pluck the strings of a violin.* play pizzicato, strum, twang.

plucky adjective
SEE **brave**.

plug verb
1 *to plug a leak.* block up, [*informal*] bung up, close, cork, fill, jam, seal, stop up, stuff up.
2 [*informal*] *to plug a record on radio.* advertise, mention frequently, promote.

plumage noun
feathers, plumes.

plummet verb SEE **plunge**.

plump adjective
a plump figure. buxom, chubby, dumpy, SEE **fat** adjective, overweight, podgy, portly, pudgy, rotund, round, squat, stout, tubby.
OPPOSITES: SEE **thin** adjective.

plunder noun
The robbers escaped with their plunder. booty, contraband, loot, pickings, prize, spoils, swag, takings.

plunder verb
Rioters plundered the shops. despoil, loot, pillage, raid, ransack, ravage, rifle, rob, sack, steal from.

plunge verb
1 *She plunged into the water.* dive, drop, fall, hurtle, jump, leap, nosedive, pitch, plummet, swoop, tumble.
2 *I plunged my hand in the water.* dip, immerse, lower, sink, submerge.
3 *He plunged his spear into the animal's side.* force, push, thrust.

poach verb
to poach game. hunt, steal.

pod noun
a pea-pod. case, hull, shell.

poem noun
poetry, rhyme, verse.

KINDS OF POEM: ballad, ballade, [*informal*] ditty, doggerel, eclogue, elegy, epic, epithalamium, free-verse, haiku, idyll, [*informal*] jingle, lay, limerick, lyric, nursery-rhyme, pastoral, ode, sonnet.
VERSE FORMS: SEE **verse**.

poet noun
bard, lyricist, minstrel, rhymer, sonneteer, versifier.
OTHER WRITERS: SEE **writer**.

poetic adjective
poetic language. emotive, [*uncomplimentary*] flowery, imaginative, lyrical, metrical, poetical.
OPPOSITES: SEE **prosaic**.

poignant adjective
a poignant moment of farewell. affecting, distressing, heart-breaking, moving, painful, pathetic, piquant, SEE **sad**, tender, touching.

point noun
1 *the point of a spear.* prong, sharp end, spike, tine, tip.
2 *a point on a map.* location, place, position, site, situation.
3 *a point of time.* instant, juncture, moment, second, stage, time.
4 *a decimal point.* dot, full stop, spot.
5 *the point of a story.* aim, crux, drift, end, essence, gist, goal, idea, intention, meaning, motive, nub, object, objective, purpose, subject, theme, use, usefulness.
6 *Honesty is one of his good points.* aspect, attribute, characteristic, facet, feature, peculiarity, quality, trait.

point verb
1 *She pointed the way.* draw attention to, indicate, point out, show, signal.
2 *She pointed us in the right direction.* aim, direct, guide, lead, steer.

pointed adjective
1 *a pointed stick.* SEE **sharp**.
2 *I didn't like her pointed remarks.* barbed, biting, edged, hinting, hurtful, insinuating, sarcastic, sharp, telling, trenchant.
OPPOSITES: SEE **bland**.

pointless adjective SEE **futile**.

poise noun
She showed considerable poise on her first public appearance. aplomb, assurance, balance, calmness, composure, coolness, dignity, equilibrium, presence, self-confidence, self-control, serenity, steadiness.

poise verb
He poised himself on a narrow ledge. balance, be poised [SEE **poised**], keep in balance, support, suspend.

poised adjective
1 *poised on the edge.* balanced, hovering, in equilibrium, steady.
2 *poised to begin.* keyed up, ready, set, waiting.
3 *a poised performer.* assured, calm, composed, cool, dignified, self-confident, suave, urbane.

poison noun
toxin, venom.

poison verb
1 *to poison someone.* SEE **kill.**
2 *Chemicals are poisoning the sea.*
contaminate, infect, pollute, taint.
3 *Propaganda can poison people's minds.*
corrupt, deprave, pervert, prejudice,
subvert, warp.

poisoned adjective
a poisoned wound. diseased, festering,
infected, septic.

poisonous adjective
a poisonous snake-bite. deadly, fatal, lethal,
mortal, noxious, toxic, venomous, virulent.

poke verb
to poke with a finger or a stick. dig, SEE **hit**
verb, jab, nudge, prod, stab, stick, thrust.

poky adjective
a poky little room. confined, cramped,
inconvenient, restrictive, SEE **small,**
uncomfortable.
OPPOSITES: SEE **spacious.**

polarize verb
*Opinions have polarized into two opposing
sides.* diverge, divide, move to opposite
positions, separate, split.

pole noun
1 [*plural*] *the poles of the earth.* extremes,
opposite ends.
2 *a long pole.* bar, column, flagpole, mast,
post, rod, shaft, spar, staff, stake, stick, stilt.

police noun
[*plural*] *Call the police.* constabulary,
[*informal*] the law, police force, policemen
[SEE **policeman**]

police verb
to police a football match. control, keep in
order, keep the peace at, monitor, patrol,
provide a police presence at, supervise,
watch over.

policeman, policewoman nouns
[*informal*] bobby, constable, [*informal*] cop,
[*informal*] copper, detective, inspector,
officer.

policy noun
1 *the library's policy on lost books.* approach,
code of conduct, guidelines, [*informal*] line,
practice, procedure, protocol, rules, stance,
strategy, tactics.
2 *the policy of a political party.* intentions,
manifesto, plan of action, platform,
programme, proposals.
3 *an insurance policy.* SEE **document.**

polish noun
1 *a lovely polish on the wood-work.*
brightness, brilliance, finish, glaze, gloss,

lustre, sheen, shine, smoothness, sparkle.
2 *I wish his manners had more polish.*
[*informal*] class, elegance, finesse, grace,
refinement, sophistication, style, suavity,
urbanity.

polish verb
to polish the furniture. to polish the cutlery.
brush up, buff up, burnish, French-polish,
rub down, rub up, shine, wax.

SUBSTANCES USED TO SMOOTH AND POLISH
THINGS: beeswax, Carborundum, emery,
emery-paper, furniture polish, glasspaper,
oil, sandpaper, shellac, varnish, wax.

---

polished adjective
1 *a polished surface.* bright, burnished,
glassy, gleaming, glossy, lustrous, shining,
shiny.
2 *polished manners.* cultured, elegant,
gracious, perfected, SEE **polite,** [*sometimes
uncomplimentary*] posh, refined,
sophisticated, suave, urbane.
OPPOSITES: SEE **rough.**

polite adjective
polite behaviour. polite language. acceptable,
attentive, chivalrous, civil, considerate,
correct, courteous, cultivated, deferential,
diplomatic, discreet, euphemistic, gallant,
genteel, gentlemanly, ladylike, obliging, SEE
polished, respectful, tactful, thoughtful,
well-bred, well-mannered, well-spoken.
OPPOSITES: SEE **rude.**

politics noun
*In a democracy, everyone should be involved
in politics.* diplomacy, government, political
affairs, political science, statesmanship.

VARIOUS POLITICAL POSITIONS: activist,
anarchist, capitalist, communist,
conservative, democrat, fascist, Labour,
leftist, left-wing, liberal, Marxist, moderate,
monarchist, nationalist, Nazi,
parliamentarian, radical, republican,
revolutionary, rightist, right-wing, socialist,
Tory, [*old-fashioned*] Whig.

VARIOUS POLITICAL SYSTEMS: anarchy,
capitalism, communism, democracy,
dictatorship, martial law, monarchy,
oligarchy, parliamentary democracy,
republic.

---

poll noun
1 *to go to the polls.* ballot, election, vote.
2 *an opinion poll.* census, plebiscite,
referendum, survey.

pollute verb
Chemicals pollute the rivers. contaminate,
defile, dirty, foul, infect, poison, soil, taint.

pomp noun
The coronation was conducted with great pomp. ceremonial, ceremony, display, formality, grandeur, magnificence, ostentation, pageantry, ritual, show, solemnity, spectacle, splendour.

pompous adjective
[*uncomplimentary*] *pompous language. a pompous manner.* affected, arrogant, bombastic, grandiose, haughty, [*informal*] high-faluting, long-winded, ostentatious, pontifical, posh, pretentious, self-important, sententious, showy, snobbish, [*informal*] stuck-up, supercilious.
OPPOSITES: SEE **modest**.

pond noun
a fish pond. lake, pool, puddle.

ponder verb
SEE **think**.

ponderous adjective
1 *a ponderous load.* bulky, burdensome, cumbersome, heavy, hefty, massive, unwieldy, weighty.
OPPOSITES: SEE **light** adjective.
2 *a ponderous style.* dull, heavy-handed, humourless, laboured, lifeless, long-winded, plodding, prolix, slow, stilted, stodgy, tedious, verbose.
OPPOSITES: SEE **lively**.

pony noun SEE **horse**.

pool noun
a pool of water. lake, mere, oasis, pond, puddle, swimming-pool, tarn.

poor adjective
1 *Poor people can't afford luxuries.* badly off, bankrupt, beggarly, [*informal*] broke, deprived, destitute, hard up, homeless, impecunious, impoverished, in debt, indigent, needy, penniless, penurious, poverty-stricken, [*informal*] skint, underpaid, underprivileged.
OPPOSITES: SEE **rich**.
2 *poor soil.* barren, exhausted, infertile, sterile, unproductive.
OPPOSITES: SEE **fertile**.
3 *a poor yield from the garden.* low, mean, SEE **scanty**, small, sparse, unprofitable, unrewarding.
OPPOSITES: SEE **plentiful**.
4 *goods of poor quality.* bad, cheap, deficient, faulty, imperfect, inadequate, inferior, low-grade, mediocre, paltry, second-rate, shoddy, substandard, unsatisfactory, useless, worthless.
OPPOSITES: SEE **superior**.
5 [*informal*] *The poor animals stood in the rain.* forlorn, hapless, luckless, miserable, pathetic, pitiable, sad, unfortunate, unhappy, unlucky, wretched.
OPPOSITES: SEE **happy**.

poorly adjective
I felt poorly. SEE **ill**.

popular adjective
a popular performer. popular styles. accepted, celebrated, famous, fashionable, favoured, favourite, [*informal*] in (*It's the in thing*), liked, lionized, loved, renowned, sought after, well-known, well-liked.
OPPOSITES: SEE **unpopular**.

popularize verb
1 *to popularize a new product.* make popular [SEE **popular**], promote, spread.
2 *to popularize Shakespeare's plays.* make easy, present in a popular way, simplify, [*informal*] tart up.

populate verb
In summer the town is populated mainly by holidaymakers. colonize, fill, inhabit, live in, occupy, overrun, settle.

population noun
the population of a country. citizens, community, inhabitants, natives, occupants, populace, residents.

populous adjective
a populous area. crowded, full, overpopulated, packed, swarming, teeming.

porous adjective
Porous substances will soak up liquid. absorbent, cellular, holey, permeable, pervious, spongy.

port adjective
the port side of a ship. lefthand (when facing forward).
OPPOSITES: SEE **starboard**.

port noun
The ship entered port. anchorage, SEE **dock**, dockyard, harbour, haven, marina, sea-port.

portable adjective
a portable tool-box. compact, convenient, easy to carry, handy, light, lightweight, manageable, mobile, movable, small, transportable.

porter noun
1 caretaker, door-keeper, doorman, gatekeeper, janitor, security guard.
2 baggage-handler, bearer, carrier.

portion noun
a small portion of pie. allocation, allowance, bit, fraction, fragment, helping, measure, part, piece, quantity, quota, ration, section, segment, serving, share, slice.

portrait noun
a portrait of a famous person. depiction, image, likeness, SEE **picture** noun, portrayal, profile, representation, self-portrait.

portray verb
The book portrays what life was like 1000 years ago. delineate, depict, describe, evoke, illustrate, SEE **picture** verb, represent, show.

pose noun
1 *The model adopted a suitable pose.* attitude, position.
2 *Don't take his behaviour seriously—it's only a pose.* act, affectation, façade, masquerade, posture, pretence.

pose verb
1 *to pose for a portrait.* model, sit.
2 *to pose in front of your friends.* adopt a pose [SEE **pose** noun], be a poser [SEE **poser**], posture, show off.
3 *to pose a question.* ask, posit, present, put forward, suggest.
to pose as *The burglar posed as the gas man.* impersonate, masquerade as, pass yourself off as, pretend to be.

poser noun
[*informal*] *I hate to see posers showing off.* exhibitionist, [*informal*] phoney, poseur, [*informal*] show-off.

posh adjective
[*informal*] *a posh party.* [*informal*] classy, elegant, fashionable, formal, lavish, ostentatious, showy, smart, snobbish, stylish, [*informal*] swanky, [*informal*] swish.

position noun
1 *Mark our position on the map.* locality, location, locus, place, point, reference, site, situation, spot, whereabouts.
2 *Having lost my money, I was in an embarrassing position.* circumstances, condition, predicament, state.
3 *I'll get cramp if I don't shift my position.* angle, posture.
4 *A referee adopts a neutral position.* attitude, opinion, outlook, perspective, standpoint, view, viewpoint.
5 *a responsible position in the firm.* appointment, degree, employment, function, grade, job, level, niche, occupation, rank, role, standing, station, status, title.

position verb
The captain positioned her players where she wanted them. arrange, deploy, dispose, locate, place, put, settle, situate, stand, station.

positive adjective
1 *He was positive that he was right.* affirmative, assured, certain, confident, convinced, decided, definite, emphatic, sure, unequivocal.
2 *I can show you positive evidence.* categorical, clear, conclusive, explicit, firm, incontestable, incontrovertible, irrefutable, real, undeniable.

3 *The counsellor gave me positive advice.* beneficial, constructive, helpful, optimistic, practical, useful, worthwhile.
OPPOSITES: SEE **negative**.

possess verb
1 *Do you possess a pen?* be in possession of, have, own.
2 *Foreign invaders possessed the country.* acquire, control, dominate, govern, occupy, rule, seize, take over.

possessions noun
assets, belongings, chattels, effects, estate, fortune, goods, property, riches, wealth.

possessive adjective
a possessive nature. clinging, domineering, jealous, proprietorial, protective, selfish.

possibility noun
a possibility of rain. the possibility of travelling to Mars. capability, chance, danger, feasibility, likelihood, opportunity, potential, potentiality, practicality, probability, risk.
OPPOSITES: SEE **impossibility**.

possible adjective
a possible outcome. a possible explanation. achievable, attainable, conceivable, credible, feasible, imaginable, likely, obtainable, plausible, potential, practicable, practical, probable, prospective, viable, workable.
OPPOSITES: SEE **impossible**.

post noun
1 *an upright post*

VARIOUS KINDS OF POST: baluster, bollard, capstan, column, gate-post, leg, newel, pier, pile, pillar, pole, prop, shaft, stake, stanchion, starting-post, strut, support, upright, winning-post.

---

2 *a sentry's post.* location, place, point, position.
3 *a post in a local business.* appointment, employment, SEE **job**, occupation, office, place, position, situation, work.
4 *Was there any post today?* airmail, cards, delivery, letters, mail, packets, parcels, postcards.

post verb
1 *to post information.* advertise, announce, display, pin up, put up, stick up.
2 *to post a letter.* dispatch, mail, send, transmit.

poster noun
We put up posters advertising sports day. advertisement, announcement, bill, display, notice, placard, sign.

posterity noun
What will posterity say about modern architecture? descendants, future generations, heirs, offspring, successors.

post-mortem noun
1 *a post-mortem on a dead body.* autopsy.
2 [*informal*] *a post-mortem on last week's disaster.* SEE **investigation**.

postpone verb
to postpone a meeting. to postpone a decision. adjourn, defer, delay, extend, hold over, put back, put off, [*informal*] put on ice, [*informal*] shelve, stay (*to stay judgement*), suspend.

postscript noun
a postscript to a letter. [*formal*] addendum, addition, afterthought, codicil (*to a will*), epilogue, [*informal*] PS.

posture noun
your physical posture. bearing, deportment, stance.

posy noun
a posy of flowers. bouquet, bunch, buttonhole, corsage, nosegay, spray.

pot noun
a cooking pot. pots and pans. basin, bowl, casserole, cauldron, container, crock, crucible, dish, jar, pan, saucepan, teapot, urn, vessel.

potent adjective
a potent drug. a potent smell. a potent influence. effective, forceful, formidable, influential, intoxicating (*potent drink*), overpowering, overwhelming, powerful, strong.
OPPOSITES: SEE **impotent, weak**.

potential adjective
1 *a potential champion.* budding, embryonic, future, likely, possible, probable, promising, prospective.
OPPOSITES: SEE **established**.
2 *a potential disaster.* imminent, impending, latent, looming, threatening.

potion noun
a health-giving potion. brew, concoction, dose, draught, drug, elixir, liquid, medicine, mixture, philtre, tonic.

pottery noun
ceramics, china, SEE **crockery**, crocks, earthenware, porcelain, stoneware.

pouch noun
a pouch to keep money in. bag, SEE **container**, purse, sack, wallet.

poultry noun

KINDS OF POULTRY: bantam, chicken, duck, fowl, goose, guinea-fowl, hen, pullet, turkey.

pounce verb
to pounce on *The cat pounced on the mouse.* ambush, attack, drop on, jump on, leap on, seize, snatch, spring at, swoop down on.

pound verb
I pounded the clay until it was soft. batter, beat, crush, grind, SEE **hit** verb, knead, mash, pulp, smash.

pour verb
1 *Water poured through the hole.* cascade, course, disgorge, flow, gush, run, spew, spill, spout, stream.
2 *I poured the milk out of the bottle.* decant, serve, tip.

poverty noun
He was rich, but is now reduced to poverty. bankruptcy, beggary, dearth, debt, destitution, hardship, indigence, lack, necessity, need, penury, privation, scarcity, shortage, want.
OPPOSITES: SEE **wealth**.

poverty-stricken adjective
SEE **poor**.

powder noun
dust, particles.

powder verb
1 *to powder a substance in a pestle and mortar.* atomize, crush, grind, pound, pulverize, reduce to powder.
2 *to powder a baby's bottom.* cover with powder, dust, sprinkle.

powdered adjective
1 *powdered stone.* crushed, granulated, ground, pulverized.
2 *powdered milk.* dehydrated, dried.

powdery adjective
a powdery substance. chalky, crumbly, disintegrating, dry, dusty, fine, friable, granular, loose, pulverized, sandy.
OPPOSITES: SEE **solid, wet** adjective.

power noun
1 *the power to do something.* ability, capability, competence, energy, faculty, force, might, muscle, skill, strength, talent, vigour.
2 *the power to arrest someone.* authority, privilege, right.
3 *the power of a tyrant.* [*informal*] clout, command, control, domination, influence, omnipotence, oppression, potency, rule, sovereignty, supremacy, sway.
OPPOSITES: SEE **impotence**.

powerful adjective
a powerful machine. a powerful ruler. a powerful argument. authoritative, cogent, commanding, compelling, consuming, convincing, dominant, dynamic, effective, effectual, energetic, forceful, influential, invincible, irresistible, high-powered, mighty, muscular, omnipotent, overpowering, overwhelming, persuasive, potent, sovereign, SEE **strong**, vigorous, weighty.
OPPOSITES: SEE **powerless, weak**.

powerless *powerless against the enemy's might.* defenceless, feeble, helpless, impotent, incapable, ineffective, ineffectual, unable, SEE **weak**.
OPPOSITES: SEE **powerful, strong**.

practicable adjective
a practicable plan. achievable, attainable, feasible, possible, practical, realistic, sensible, viable, workable.
OPPOSITES: SEE **impractical**.

practical adjective
1 *practical science.* applied, empirical, experimental.
2 *a practical approach.* businesslike, efficient, down-to-earth, hard-headed, matter-of-fact, [*informal*] no-nonsense, pragmatic, realistic, sensible, utilitarian.
OPPOSITES: SEE **theoretical**.
3 *a practical worker.* accomplished, capable, competent, expert, proficient, skilled.
4 *a practical tool.* convenient, functional, handy, usable, useful.
OPPOSITES: SEE **impractical**.
5 *a practical plan* SEE **practicable**.

practically adverb
We're practically there. almost, close to, just about, nearly, virtually.

practice noun
1 *What does the plan mean in practice?* action, actuality, application, effect, operation, reality, use.
2 *We need more practice.* [*informal*] dummy-run, exercise, preparation, rehearsal, [*informal*] run-through, training.
OPPOSITES: SEE **theory**.
3 *Smoking is still a common practice.* custom, habit, routine, tradition.

practise verb
1 *Keep practising.* do exercises, drill, exercise, prepare, rehearse, train, warm up.
2 *Practise what you preach.* apply, carry out, do, engage in, follow, perform, put into practice.

praise noun
Our praise embarrassed her. acclamation, accolade, admiration, adulation, applause, approval, commendation, compliment, congratulation, [*formal*] encomium, eulogy, homage, honour, ovation, panegyric, plaudits, testimonial, thanks, tribute.

praise verb
1 *to praise someone for an achievement. to praise a performance.* acclaim, admire, applaud, cheer, clap, commend, compliment, congratulate, [*informal*] crack up (*They cracked her up as one of our best actresses*), eulogize, exalt, extol, give a good review of, marvel at, offer praise to [SEE **praise** noun], pay tribute to, [*informal*] rave about, recommend, [*informal*] say nice things about, show approval of.
OPPOSITES: SEE **criticize**.
2 *to praise God.* adore, glorify, honour, [*formal*] laud, magnify, worship.
OPPOSITES: SEE **curse** verb.

praiseworthy adjective
a praiseworthy effort. admirable, commendable, creditable, deserving, SEE **good**, laudable, meritorious, worthy.
OPPOSITES: SEE **deplorable**.

prance verb
to prance about. caper, cavort, dance, frisk, frolic, gambol, jump, leap, play, romp, skip.

prayer noun
a prayer to God. collect, devotion, entreaty, invocation, litany, meditation, petition, supplication.

prayer-book noun
breviary, missal.

preach verb
1 *to preach in church.* deliver a sermon, evangelize, expound, proselytize, spread the Gospel.
2 *He's a fine one to preach about turning up on time!* expatiate, give moral advice, [*informal*] lay down the law, lecture, moralize, pontificate, sermonize, tell others what to do.

preacher noun
SEE **clergyman**, crusader, evangelist, minister, missionary, moralist, pastor, revivalist.

precarious adjective
dangerous, insecure, perilous, risky, rocky, shaky, uncertain, unsafe, unstable, unsteady, vulnerable, wobbly.
OPPOSITES: SEE **safe**.

precaution noun
What precautions can you take against flu? anticipation, defence, insurance, protection, provision, safeguard, safety measure.

precede verb
1 *A flag-bearer preceded the procession.* be in front of, come before, go before, lead.

2 *He preceded his speech with an announcement.* introduce, lead into, preface, prefix, start.
OPPOSITES: SEE **follow**.

precious adjective
SEE **valuable**.

precipice noun
The climber fell down a precipice. cliff, crag, drop, escarpment, precipitous face [SEE **precipitous**], rock.

precipitate verb
to precipitate a crisis. bring on, cause, encourage, expedite, further, hasten, induce, occasion, spark off, trigger off.

precipitous adjective
a precipitous hillside. abrupt, perpendicular, sharp, sheer, steep, vertical.

précis noun SEE **summary**.

precise adjective
1 *the precise time. precise instructions.* accurate, clear-cut, correct, defined, definite, distinct, exact, explicit, fixed, measured, right, specific, unambiguous, unequivocal.
OPPOSITES: SEE **imprecise**.
2 *precise workmanship.* careful, finicky, meticulous, punctilious, scrupulous.
OPPOSITES: SEE **careless**.

preclude verb
Does this agreement preclude changes later on? debar, exclude, make impossible, pre-empt, prevent, rule out.

precocious adjective
a precocious child. advanced, SEE **clever**, forward, mature, quick.
OPPOSITES: SEE **backward**.

preconception noun
I had no preconceptions about what to expect. assumption, expectation, prejudice, presupposition.

predator noun
hunter.

predatory adjective
predatory animals. predatory bands of robbers. acquisitive, covetous, greedy, hunting, marauding, pillaging, plundering, preying, rapacious, voracious.

predecessor noun
ancestor, antecedent, forebear, forefather, forerunner, precursor.

predestination noun
SEE **fate**.

predestined adjective
SEE **fated**.

predicament noun
How did you get out of that predicament? crisis, difficulty, dilemma, embarrassment, emergency, jam, [*informal*] mess, [*informal*] pickle, plight, problem, quandary.

predict verb
to predict the future. forebode, forecast, foresee, foretell, forewarn, prognosticate, prophesy, tell fortunes.

predictable adjective
a predictable disaster. certain, expected, foreseeable, likely, probable.
OPPOSITES: SEE **unpredictable**.

predisposition noun SEE **inclination**, **prejudice** noun.

predominant adjective SEE **chief** adjective.

predominate verb
Women still predominate in the nursing profession. be in the majority, dominate, hold sway, outnumber, outweigh, preponderate, prevail.

pre-empt verb
We pre-empted any criticism by admitting that we'd done a poor job. anticipate, forestall.

preface noun
the preface to a book. foreword, introduction, preamble, prelude, prologue.

preface verb
He prefaced his speech with an announcement. introduce, lead into, precede, prefix, start.

prefer verb
Which style do you prefer? advocate, [*informal*] back, choose, fancy, favour, [*informal*] go for, incline towards, like, like better, pick out, [*informal*] plump for, recommend, single out, think preferable [SEE **preferable**], vote for, SEE **want** verb.

preferable adjective
Vote for whoever you think is preferable. advantageous, better, better-liked, desirable, likely, nicer, preferred, recommended, wanted.
OPPOSITES: SEE **objectionable**.

preference noun
a preference for sweet things. What's your preference? choice, fancy, favouritism, inclination, liking, option, partiality, predilection, wish.

preferential adjective
preferential treatment. better, biased, favoured, privileged, showing favouritism, special.

prefix noun
OPPOSITE: suffix.

pregnancy noun
gestation.

pregnant adjective
1 *a pregnant woman.* carrying a child,
expectant, [*informal*] expecting, [*old-
fashioned*] with child.
2 *a pregnant remark.* SEE **meaningful**.

WORDS TO DO WITH PREGNANCY: abortion,
SEE **birth**, conception, gestation,
miscarriage, parturition, premature birth.

---

prejudice noun
racial prejudice. sexual prejudice. bias,
bigotry, chauvinism, discrimination,
dogmatism, fanaticism, favouritism,
intolerance, jingoism, narrow-mindedness,
partisanship, predisposition, racialism,
racism, sexism, unfairness, xenophobia.
OPPOSITES: SEE **impartiality**.

prejudice verb
1 *His dirty appearance prejudiced me against
him.* bias, incline, predispose, sway.
2 *Publicity might prejudice the result of the
trial.* influence, interfere with, prejudge,
sway.
3 *Will a criminal record prejudice your
chances of a job?* damage, harm, injure, ruin,
spoil, undermine.

prejudiced adjective
a prejudiced attitude. prejudiced remarks.
biased, bigoted, chauvinist, discriminatory,
illiberal, intolerant, jingoistic, leading (*a
leading question*), loaded, narrow-minded,
one-sided, partial, partisan, racist, sexist,
tendentious, unfair, xenophobic.
OPPOSITES: SEE **impartial**.

prejudicial adjective
*The news-report was prejudicial to the
defendant's case.* damaging, detrimental,
harmful, injurious, unfavourable.

preliminary adjective
*We'll go ahead if the preliminary survey is
encouraging.* earliest, early, experimental,
exploratory, first, inaugural, initial,
introductory, opening, prefatory,
preparatory, qualifying, (*qualifying rounds
of a competition*), tentative, trial.

prelude noun
*The first match was an exciting prelude to the
series.* beginning, [*informal*] curtain-raiser,
introduction, opener, opening, overture,
preamble, precursor, preface, preliminary,
preparation, prologue, start, starter,
[*informal*] warm-up.
OPPOSITES: SEE **epilogue**.

premature adverb
a premature birth. a premature decision.
abortive, before time, early, hasty,
precipitate, [*informal*] previous (*You were a
bit previous with your congratulations!*), too
early, too soon, untimely.
OPPOSITES: SEE **late**.

premeditated adjective
a premeditated crime. calculated, conscious,
considered, deliberate, intended,
intentional, planned, pre-arranged,
predetermined, pre-planned, wilful.
OPPOSITES: SEE **spontaneous**.

premonition noun
*I had a premonition that something nasty
would happen.* anxiety, fear, foreboding,
forewarning, indication, intuition,
misgiving, omen, portent, presentiment,
suspicion, warning, worry.

preoccupied adjective
1 *preoccupied in her work.* absorbed, engaged,
engrossed, immersed, interested, involved,
obsessed, sunk, taken up, wrapped up.
2 *You look preoccupied: what are you thinking
of?* absent-minded, day-dreaming, faraway,
inattentive, pensive, rapt, thoughtful.

preparation noun
[*often plural*] *preparations for Christmas.*
arrangement(s), getting ready, groundwork,
making provision, measure(s), organization.

prepare verb
1 *to prepare dinner. to prepare for visitors.*
arrange, SEE **cook** verb, devise, [*informal*]
do what's necessary, [*informal*] fix up, get
ready, make arrangements for, organize,
plan, process, set up.
2 *A teacher has to prepare pupils for exams.*
brief, coach, educate, equip, instruct,
rehearse, teach, train, tutor.

preposterous adjective
SEE **absurd**.

prerequisite noun
*It is a prerequisite of entry to the profession
that you pass the exams.* condition, essential,
necessity, precondition, qualification,
requirement, stipulation.

prescribe noun
1 *The doctor prescribed medicine.* advise,
recommend, suggest.
2 *The boss prescribed our duties.* assign,
dictate, fix, impose, lay down, ordain,
specify, stipulate.

prescription noun SEE **medicine**.

presence noun
1 *The boss requires your presence.*
attendance.
2 *I value the presence of friends when I'm sad.*
closeness, companionship, company,

nearness, propinquity, proximity.
3 *an actor with a commanding presence.* air,
appearance, bearing, demeanour,
impressiveness, personality.

present adjective
1 *Is everyone present?* at hand, here, in
attendance.
2 *Who's the present champion?* contemporary,
current, existing, extant.

present noun
1 *We live in the present, not in the past.*
[*informal*] here and now.
2 *She gave me a present.* contribution,
donation, gift, gratuity, offering, tip.

present verb
1 *to present prizes.* award, confer, donate,
give, hand over, offer.
2 *to present your work.* demonstrate, display,
exhibit, reveal, show.
3 *to present a guest.* introduce, make known.
4 *to present a play.* act, bring out, perform,
put on.

presentable adjective
a presentable appearance. acceptable, clean,
decent, neat, passable, proper, respectable,
satisfactory, tidy, tolerable, worthy.

presently adverb
shortly, soon.

preserve verb
1 *to preserve peace.* defend, guard, maintain,
perpetuate, protect, retain, safeguard,
secure, sustain, uphold.
OPPOSITES: SEE **destroy**.
2 *to preserve food. to preserve resources.*
conserve, keep, lay up, look after, save,
stockpile, store.

WAYS TO PRESERVE FOOD: bottle, can, chill,
cure, dehydrate, dry, freeze, freeze-dry,
irradiate, jam (*to jam fruit*), pickle,
refrigerate, salt, tin.

---

preside verb
to preside at a meeting. be in charge, officiate,
take charge.

press verb
1 *to press things together.* compress,
condense, cram, crowd, crush, force, gather,
[*informal*] jam, shove, squash, squeeze.
2 *to press a pair of trousers.* flatten, iron,
smooth.
3 *Press the bell.* depress, push.
4 *They pressed me to stay.* beg, bully, coerce,
constrain, dragoon, entreat, exhort,
implore, importune, [*informal*] lean on,
persuade, pressure, pressurize, put pressure
on, require, urge.

pressure noun
1 *the pressure of a load on your back.* burden,
force, heaviness, load, might, power, stress,
weight.
2 *air pressure in a tyre.* compression.
3 *the pressure of modern life.* adversity,
constraint, difficulty, [*informal*] hassle,
hurry, oppression, stress, urgency.

prestige noun
If we lose again, our prestige will suffer.
credit, esteem, fame, glory, good name,
honour, importance, [*informal*] kudos,
renown, reputation, standing.

prestigious adjective
SEE **reputable**.

presume verb
1 *I presume you want something to eat.*
assume, believe, conjecture, guess,
hypothesize, imagine, infer, postulate,
suppose, surmise, [*informal*] take it for
granted, think.
2 *She presumed to tell us what to do.* be
presumptuous enough [SEE **presumptuous**],
dare, make bold, [*informal*] take the liberty,
venture.

presumptuous adjective
It was presumptuous of him to take charge.
arrogant, bold, [*informal*] cheeky,
conceited, forward, impertinent, impudent,
insolent, over-confident, [*informal*] pushy,
shameless, unauthorized, unwarranted.

pretence noun
I saw through her pretence. act, acting,
affectation, charade, counterfeiting, deceit,
deception, disguise, dissembling,
dissimulation, façade, feigning, feint, guise,
hoax, insincerity, invention, lying, make-
believe, masquerade, pose, posing,
posturing, ruse, sham, show, simulation,
subterfuge, trickery, wile.

pretend verb
1 *Don't believe him—he was pretending. I
pretended to be someone else.* act, affect,
behave insincerely, bluff, counterfeit,
deceive, disguise, dissemble, dissimulate,
fake, feign, fool, hoax, hoodwink, imitate,
impersonate, [*informal*] kid, lie, mislead,
play a part, perform, pose, posture, profess,
purport, put on an act, sham, simulate, take
someone in, trick.
2 *Pretend you're on a desert island.* SEE
imagine.
3 *I don't pretend that I play well.* SEE **claim**
verb.

pretentious adjective
a pretentious show of knowledge. affected,
[*informal*] arty, conceited, grandiose,
inflated, ostentatious, [*informal*] over the
top, SEE **pompous**, showy.
OPPOSITES: SEE **modest**.

pretty adjective
pretty decorations. appealing, attractive, SEE
beautiful, charming, [*informal*] cute,
dainty, delicate, good-looking, lovely, nice,
pleasing, [*uncomplimentary*] pretty-pretty.
OPPOSITES: SEE **ugly**.

pretty adverb
[*informal*] *That's pretty good!* fairly,
moderately, quite, rather, somewhat,
tolerably.

prevail verb
1 *to prevail over an enemy.* SEE **win**.
2 *After a long argument, common sense
prevailed.* SEE **predominate**.

prevailing adjective
the prevailing fashion. accepted, chief,
common, current, dominant, familiar,
fashionable, general, influential, main,
mainstream, normal, ordinary, orthodox,
popular, predominant, prevalent, principal,
usual, widespread.
OPPOSITES: SEE **unusual**.

prevalent adjective
SEE **prevailing**.

prevaricate verb
Stop prevaricating and say what you think.
[*informal*] beat about the bush, be evasive
[SEE **evasive**], cavil, dither, equivocate,
hedge, [*informal*] hesitate, hum and haw,
quibble, [*informal*] shilly-shally, temporize,
vacillate, waver.

prevent verb
1 *to prevent a mishap.* anticipate, avert,
avoid, foil, forestall, frustrate, [*informal*]
head off, [*informal*] help (*I can't help
coughing*), inoculate against (*a disease*),
intercept, [*informal*] nip in the bud, pre-
empt, stave off, take precautions against,
thwart, ward off.
OPPOSITES: SEE **encourage**.
2 *to prevent someone from doing something.*
check, curb, deter, hamper, hinder, impede,
obstruct, save, stop.
OPPOSITES: SEE **help** verb.

preventative, **preventive** adjectives
preventive measures. deterrent, obstructive,
precautionary, pre-emptive.

previous adjective
looking back on previous events. antecedent,
earlier, foregoing, former, preceding, prior.
OPPOSITES: SEE **following**.

prey noun
The lion killed its prey. quarry, victim.

prey verb
to prey on *Owls prey on small animals.* eat,
feed on, hunt, kill.

price noun
1 *a reasonable price to pay.* amount, charge,
cost, [*informal*] damage (*What's the
damage?*), expenditure, expense, fare, fee,
figure, outlay, payment, rate, sum, terms,
toll, valuation, value, worth.

priceless adjective
1 *priceless jewels.* costly, dear, expensive,
inestimable, invaluable, irreplaceable,
precious, [*informal*] pricey, rare, valuable.
2 [*informal*] *a priceless joke.* SEE **funny**.

prick verb
1 *to prick with a pin.* bore into, jab, perforate,
pierce, punch, puncture, stab, sting.
2 *to prick someone into action.* SEE **goad**.

prickly adjective
1 *a prickly bush.* bristly, scratchy, sharp,
spiky, spiny, thorny.
2 [*informal*] *He's in a prickly mood.* SEE
irritable.

pride noun
1 *Display your work with pride.* delight,
dignity, gratification, happiness, honour,
pleasure, satisfaction, self-respect, self-
satisfaction.
2 *The new car is her pride and joy.* jewel,
treasured possession.
3 [*uncomplimentary*] *Pride goes before a fall.*
arrogance, being proud [SEE **proud**],
[*informal*] big-headedness, conceit, egotism,
haughtiness, megalomania, presumption,
self-esteem, self-importance, self-love,
smugness, snobbery, vainglory, vanity.
OPPOSITES: SEE **humility**.

priest noun SEE **clergyman**, Druid, lama.

priggish adjective
SEE **self-righteous**.

prim adjective
She's too prim to enjoy rude jokes! demure,
fastidious, SEE **narrow-minded**, [*informal*]
prissy, proper, prudish, starchy, strait-
laced.
OPPOSITES: SEE **broad-minded**.

primal adjective
primal forms of life. earliest, early, first,
original, primeval, primitive, primordial.

primarily adverb
basically, chiefly, especially, firstly,
fundamentally, generally, mainly, mostly,
predominantly, principally.

primary adjective
Our primary aim was to win. basic, chief,
dominant, first, foremost, fundamental,
greatest, important, initial, leading, main,
major, outstanding, paramount, prime,
principal, supreme, top.

prime adjective
1 *Our prime aim was to win.* SEE **primary.**
2 *prime beef. prime grade.* best, first-class,
select, top.

prime verb
to prime a pump. get ready, prepare.

primitive adjective
1 *primitive tribes.* ancient, barbarian, early,
prehistoric, primeval, savage, uncivilized,
uncultivated, unsophisticated.
OPPOSITES: SEE **civilized.**
2 *primitive technology.* backward, basic,
[*informal*] behind the times, crude,
elementary. SEE **obsolete,** rough,
rudimentary, simple, undeveloped.
OPPOSITES: SEE **advanced.**

principal adjective
What's your principal interest in life? basic,
chief, dominant, dominating, first, foremost,
fundamental, greatest, highest, important,
leading, main, major, outstanding,
paramount, pre-eminent, primary, prime,
supreme, top.

principle noun
1 *moral principles.* assumption, axiom,
belief, doctrine, dogma, ethic, ideal, maxim,
precept, proposition, rule, tenet, theory,
values.
2 [*plural*] *the basic principles of a subject.*
basics, elements, essentials, fundamentals,
laws.
3 *a person of principle.* high-mindedness,
honesty, honour, ideals, integrity, morality,
probity, scruples, standards, uprightness,
virtue.

print noun
1 *the print of feet in the sand.* impression,
imprint, indentation, mark, stamp.
2 *I like a book with clear print.* characters,
fount, lettering, letters, printing, type,
typeface.
3 *It's a print, not an original painting.* copy,
duplicate, engraving, lithograph,
photograph, reproduction.

prior adjective
SEE **previous.**

priority noun
Give priority to traffic on the main road.
greater importance, precedence, right-of-
way, seniority.

prise, prize verb
to prise off a lid. force, lever, wrench.

prison noun
sentenced to six months in prison. Borstal,
cell, confinement, custody, detention centre,
dungeon, gaol, house of correction,
imprisonment, jail, [*American*]
penitentiary, reformatory.

prisoner noun
captive, convict, detainee, hostage, inmate,
internee.

privacy noun
I enjoy the privacy of my own room.
concealment, isolation, quietness, seclusion,
secrecy, solitude.

private adjective
1 *private property.* individual, personal,
privately owned.
2 *private information.* classified,
confidential, intimate, secret.
3 *a private meeting.* clandestine, closed,
restricted.
4 *a private hideaway.* concealed, hidden, SEE
isolated, little-known, quiet, secluded,
sequestered, solitary, unknown.
OPPOSITES: SEE **public** adjective.

privilege noun
Club members enjoy special privileges.
advantage, benefit, concession, entitlement,
licence, right.

privileged adjective
The boss has a privileged position.
advantaged, élite, favoured, powerful,
special, superior.
OPPOSITES: SEE **oppressed.**

prize noun
a prize for coming first. award, jackpot,
reward, trophy, winnings.

prize verb
*Which of your possessions do you prize most
highly?* appreciate, approve of, cherish,
esteem, hold dear, like, rate, regard, revere,
treasure, value.

probable adjective
the probable result. believable, credible,
expected, feasible, likely, plausible,
possible, predictable, presumed.
OPPOSITES: SEE **improbable.**

probation noun
*New employees are on probation for three
months.* apprenticeship, test, trial period.

probe noun
a probe into a smuggling racket.
examination, inquiry, investigation,
research, scrutiny, study.

probe verb
1 *to probe a wound.* poke, prod.
2 *to probe the depths of the sea.* SEE **explore,**
penetrate, plumb (*the depths*).
3 *to probe a problem.* examine, go into,
inquire into, investigate, look into, research
into, scrutinize, study.

problem noun
1 *an intriguing problem to solve.* brainteaser,
conundrum, enigma, mystery, poser, puzzle,
question, riddle.

2 *a worrying problem to overcome.* burden, complication, difficulty, dilemma, dispute, [*informal*] headache, predicament, quandary, set-back, snag, trouble, worry.

problematic, **problematical** adjectives
There's no easy solution to such a problematical issue. complicated, controversial, debatable, difficult, enigmatic, hard to deal with, intractable, puzzling, taxing, worrying.
OPPOSITES: SEE **straightforward**.

procedure noun
What's the procedure for getting a licence? course of action, formula, method, [*Latin*] modus operandi, plan of action, practice, process, routine, scheme, strategy, system, technique, way.

proceed verb
After a rest, we proceeded. advance, carry on, continue, follow, go ahead, go on, make progress, move forward, [*informal*] press on, progress.

proceedings noun
1 *legal proceedings.* action, lawsuit.
2 *The secretary writes up the proceedings of the meeting.* [*informal*] doings, minutes, records, report, transactions.
3 [*informal*] *On sports day, a storm ended proceedings.* events, [*informal*] goings-on, happenings, matters, things.

proceeds plural noun
proceeds from an OXFAM collection. earnings, income, SEE **money**, profit, receipts, revenue, takings.

process noun
1 *a manufacturing process.* method, operation, SEE **procedure**, system, technique.
2 *the process of growing up.* course, development, evolution, experience, progression.

process verb
1 *to process crude oil.* alter, change, convert, deal with, make usable, prepare, refine, transform, treat.
2 [*informal*] *A cavalcade processed through town.* SEE **parade** verb.

procession noun
cavalcade, column, cortège, line, march, motorcade, pageant, parade.

proclaim verb
1 *to proclaim something publicly.* announce, assert, declare, give out, make known, profess, pronounce.
2 *to proclaim a public holiday.* SEE **decree** verb.

procrastinate verb
Stop procrastinating and do something. be indecisive, defer a decision, delay, [*informal*] dilly-dally, dither, [*informal*]

drag your feet, [*informal*] hum and haw, [*informal*] play for time, postpone, prevaricate, put things off, [*informal*] shilly-shally, stall, temporize.

procure verb SEE **obtain**.

prod verb
to prod with a stick. dig, goad, SEE **hit** verb, jab, nudge, poke, push, urge on.

prodigal adjective
SEE **wasteful**.

prodigy noun
a child prodigy. curiosity, freak, genius, marvel, phenomenon, rarity, sensation, talent, wonder.

produce noun
garden produce. crop, harvest, output, products, yield.

produce verb
1 *Can you produce evidence?* advance, bring out, disclose, display, exhibit, furnish, offer, present, put forward, reveal, show, supply, throw up.
2 *A factory produces goods. Farmers produce crops.* cause, compose, conjure up, construct, create, cultivate, develop, fabricate, form, generate, give rise to, grow, invent, make, manufacture, originate, provoke, result in, think up, turn out, yield.
3 *to produce children.* bear, beget, breed, give birth to, raise, rear.
4 *to produce a play.* direct.

product noun
1 *What kind of product does this factory make?* artefact, commodity, end-product, goods, merchandise, output, produce, production.
2 *Our plan was the product of much thought.* consequence, effect, fruit, outcome, result, upshot.

productive adjective
1 *productive work.* beneficial, busy, constructive, creative, effective, efficient, gainful (*gainful employment*), profitable, profitmaking, rewarding, useful, valuable, worthwhile.
2 *a productive garden.* fertile, fruitful, lush, prolific.
OPPOSITES: SEE **unproductive**.

profane adjective
SEE **blasphemous**.

profess verb
1 *He professed to be the gas man.* allege, claim, make out, pretend, purport.
2 *to profess your faith.* SEE **declare**.

profession noun
1 *Nursing is a worthwhile profession.* business, calling, career, employment, job,

line of work, occupation, trade, vocation, work.
2 *a profession of faith.* acknowledgement, confession, declaration, statement, testimony.

professional adjective
1 *professional advice.* competent, efficient, expert, paid, proficient, qualified, skilled, trained.
OPPOSITES: SEE **amateur**.
2 *a professional attitude.* conscientious, dutiful, responsible.
OPPOSITES: SEE **unprofessional**.

proficient adjective
SEE **competent**.

profile noun
1 *the profile of a person's face.* outline, SEE **picture** noun, shape, side view, silhouette.
2 *a profile of a famous personality.* account, biography, [*Latin*] curriculum vitae, sketch, study.

profit noun
a profit on your investment. advantage, benefit, excess, gain, interest, SEE **money**, return, surplus, yield.

profit verb
1 *It won't profit anyone to get angry.* benefit, further the interests of, SEE **help** verb, pay (*It doesn't pay to get angry*), serve.
2 *Did you profit from the sale?* earn money, gain, make money, receive a profit [SEE **profit** noun].
to profit by or **from** *You can sometimes profit from other people's mistakes.* capitalize on, [*informal*] cash in on, exploit, take advantage of, use.

profitable adjective
profitable employment. advantageous, beneficial, commercial, fruitful, gainful, lucrative, moneymaking, paying, productive, profitmaking, remunerative, rewarding, useful, valuable, worthwhile.
OPPOSITES: SEE **unprofitable**.

profiteering noun
Profiteering in a time of shortage is wrong. exploitation, extortion, overcharging.

profound adjective
1 *profound sympathy.* deep, heartfelt, intense, sincere.
OPPOSITES: SEE **insincere**.
2 *a profound discussion.* abstruse, erudite, imponderable, intellectual, knowledgeable, learned, philosophical, serious, thoughtful, wise.
OPPOSITES: SEE **facile**.

profuse adjective
SEE **plentiful**.

progeny noun
SEE **offspring**.

programme noun
1 *a published programme of events.* agenda, [*informal*] line-up, listing, plan, schedule, timetable.
2 *a television programme.* broadcast, performance, production, transmission.

progress noun
1 *scientific progress.* advance, breakthrough, development, gain, headway, improvement, march (*the march of time*), movement, progression, [*informal*] step forward.
2 *I traced their progress on a map.* journey, route, travels, way.

progress verb
Our plans are progressing. advance, [*informal*] come on, develop, [*informal*] forge ahead, improve, make progress [SEE **progress** noun], move forward, proceed, prosper.
OPPOSITES: SEE **regress, stagnate**.

progression noun
a progression of events. chain, row, sequence, series, string, succession.

progressive adjective
1 *a progressive increase in prices.* accelerating, continuing, continuous, escalating, growing, increasing, ongoing, steady.
OPPOSITES: SEE **erratic**.
2 *progressive ideas.* advanced, avant-garde, contemporary, enterprising, forward-looking, [*informal*] go-ahead, modernistic, radical, revolutionary, up-to-date.
OPPOSITES: SEE **conservative** adjective.

prohibit verb
to prohibit smoking. to prohibit non-members. ban, bar, censor, [*informal*] cut out, debar, disallow, exclude, forbid, hinder, [*formal*] interdict, make illegal, outlaw, place an embargo on, preclude, prevent, proscribe, restrict, rule out, shut out, stop, veto.
OPPOSITES: SEE **allow**.

prohibitive adjective
prohibitive prices. discouraging, excessive, SEE **exorbitant**, impossible, out of reach, unreasonable, unthinkable.

project noun
1 *a project to build a bypass.* design, enterprise, idea, plan, proposal, scheme, undertaking, venture.
2 *a history project.* activity, assignment, piece of research, piece of work, task.

project verb
1 *A narrow ledge projects from the cliff.* beetle, bulge, extend, jut out, overhang, protrude, stand out, stick out.
2 *The lighthouse projects a strong beam.* cast, flash, shine, throw out.

projectile noun
SEE **missile**.

proliferate verb SEE **multiply**.

prolific adjective
prolific crops. a prolific writer. abundant, copious, fertile, fruitful, productive, profuse, rich.
OPPOSITES: SEE **unproductive**.

prologue noun SEE **prelude**.

prolong verb
The game was prolonged by injuries. delay, draw out, extend, increase, lengthen, make longer, protract, [*informal*] spin out, stretch out.
OPPOSITES: SEE **shorten**.

prominent adjective
1 *prominent teeth.* bulging, jutting out, large, projecting, protruding, sticking out.
2 *a prominent landmark.* conspicuous, eye-catching, noticeable, obtrusive, obvious, pronounced, salient, significant.
OPPOSITES: SEE **inconspicuous**.
3 *a prominent politician.* celebrated, distinguished, eminent, familiar, famous, foremost, important, leading, major, much-publicized, noted, outstanding, recognizable, renowned, well-known.
OPPOSITES: SEE **unknown**.

promiscuous adjective
promiscuous sexual relationships. casual, haphazard, SEE **immoral**, indiscriminate, random, undiscriminating.
OPPOSITES: SEE **moral** adjective.

promise noun
1 *We had promises of help from many people.* assurance, commitment, [*formal*] covenant, guarantee, oath, pledge, undertaking, vow, word, word of honour.
2 *The young actor shows promise.* latent ability, potential, talent.

promise verb
1 *You promised me that you'd pay. She promised to come.* agree, assure, consent, contract, engage, give a promise [SEE **promise** noun], give your word, guarantee, pledge, swear, take an oath, undertake, vow.
2 *The clouds promise rain.* augur, forebode, indicate, presage, prophesy, suggest.

promising adjective
a promising debut. a promising newcomer. auspicious, budding, encouraging, hopeful, likely, propitious, talented, [*informal*] up-and-coming.

promontory noun
cape, foreland, headland, peninsula, point, projection, ridge, spit, spur.

promote verb
1 *to promote someone to a higher rank.* advance, elevate, exalt, give promotion [SEE **promotion**], move up, prefer, raise, upgrade.
OPPOSITES: SEE **demote**.
2 *A local firm promoted our festival.* back, boost, encourage, help, sponsor, support.
3 *to promote a new product.* advertise, make known, market, [*informal*] plug, popularize, publicize, [*informal*] push, sell.

promoter noun
backer, sponsor.

promotion noun
1 *promotion to a higher rank.* advancement, elevation, preferment, rise, upgrading.
2 *the promotion of a new product.* advertising, backing, encouragement, marketing, publicity, selling.

prompt adjective
a prompt reply. eager, efficient, immediate, instantaneous, on time, punctual, SEE **quick**, unhesitating, willing.
OPPOSITES: SEE **belated**.

prompt verb
If you forget what to say, I'll prompt you. advise, egg on, encourage, help, incite, inspire, jog the memory, motivate, nudge, persuade, prod, provoke, remind, spur, stimulate, urge.

prone adjective
1 *lying prone on the floor.* face down, on your front, prostrate.
OPPOSITES: SEE **supine**.
2 *She's prone to exaggerate. I'm prone to colds.* apt, disposed, given, inclined, liable, likely, predisposed, susceptible, vulnerable.
OPPOSITES: SEE **immune**.

prong noun
the prong of a fork. point, spike, spur, tine.

pronounce verb
1 *Try to pronounce the words clearly.* articulate, aspirate, enunciate, say, sound, speak, utter.
2 *The doctor pronounced me fit again.* announce, assert, declare, decree, judge, make known, proclaim.

pronounced adjective
a pronounced limp. clear, conspicuous, decided, definite, distinct, evident, marked, noticeable, obvious, prominent, striking, unmistakable.

pronunciation noun
The announcer's pronunciation is very clear. accent, articulation, diction, elocution, enunciation, inflection, intonation.

proof noun
proof of guilt. confirmation, corroboration, demonstration, evidence, facts, grounds, testimony, verification.

prop noun
a prop to lean on. buttress, crutch, post, strut, support.

prop verb
to prop a bike against a wall. lean, rest, stand.
to prop up *to prop up a wall.* buttress, hold up, reinforce, shore up, support.

propaganda noun
government propaganda. advertising, brainwashing, indoctrination, persuasion, publicity.

propagate verb
1 *to propagate lies.* disseminate, generate, multiply, pass on, produce, proliferate, spread, transmit.
2 *to propagate plants.* breed, grow from seed, increase, layer, reproduce, sow, take cuttings.

propel verb
The crowd propelled me forward. The spacecraft was propelled by a rocket. drive, force, impel, launch, move, pitchfork (*They pitchforked me into it*), push, send, shoot, spur, thrust, urge.

propeller noun
rotor, screw, vane.

proper adjective
1 *proper language. proper manners.* acceptable, becoming, decent, decorous, delicate, dignified, fitting, formal, genteel, gentlemanly, grave, in good taste, ladylike, modest, orthodox, polite, respectable, sedate, seemly, serious, solemn, suitable, tactful, tasteful.
2 *the proper thing to do. a proper price.* advisable, appropriate, conventional, correct, deserved, fair, fitting, just, lawful, legal, right, usual, valid.
OPPOSITES: SEE **improper**.

property noun
1 *I don't own much property.* assets, belongings, [*formal*] chattels, effects, fortune, goods, patrimony, possessions, riches, wealth.
2 *Keep off! Private property.* buildings, estate, land, premises.
3 *This chemical has unusual properties.* attribute, characteristic, feature, idiosyncrasy, peculiarity, quality, trait.

prophecy noun
a prophecy that came true. augury, forecast, prediction, prognosis, prognostication.

prophesy verb
She prophesied the tragic outcome. forecast, foresee, foretell, predict, prognosticate.

prophet noun
clairvoyant, forecaster, fortune-teller, oracle, seer, soothsayer.

proportion noun
1 *the proportion of girls to boys in a class.* balance, ratio.
2 *A large proportion of the audience cheered.* fraction, part, piece, quota, section, share.

proportionate adjective
The cost of the ticket is proportionate to the distance you travel. commensurate, comparable, corresponding, in proportion, proportional, relative.
OPPOSITES: SEE **disproportionate**.

proposal noun
a proposal to build a supermarket. bid, motion [= *a proposal made at a meeting*], offer, plan, project, proposition, recommendation, scheme, suggestion.

propose verb
1 *I proposed a change in the rules.* ask for, present, put forward, recommend, submit, suggest.
2 *Our friends propose to visit us.* aim, have in mind, intend, mean, offer, plan, purpose.
3 *They proposed me as a candidate in the election.* nominate, put up.

proposition noun
1 *I don't accept the proposition that the moon is made of cheese.* SEE **statement**.
2 *I made a proposition that we should adjourn the meeting.* SEE **proposal**.

proprietor noun
the proprietor of a shop. boss, manager, owner.

propriety noun
The sensitive matter was handled with great propriety. appropriateness, correctness, decency, decorum, delicacy, etiquette, good manners, politeness, seemliness, sensitivity, tact.
OPPOSITES: SEE **impropriety**.

prosaic adjective
a prosaic statement. clear, dry, dull, hackneyed, matter-of-fact, ordinary, pedestrian, plain, prosy, simple, straightforward, trite, unimaginative, uninspired, uninspiring, unvarnished.
OPPOSITES: SEE **poetic**.

prosecute verb
They prosecuted him for dangerous driving. accuse, bring to trial, charge, institute legal proceedings against, prefer charges against, sue, take legal proceedings against.

prosecution, prosecutor nouns
LEGAL TERMS: SEE **law**.

prospect noun
1 *a lovely prospect from the top of the hill.*
landscape, outlook, panorama, perspective,
scene, sight, spectacle, view, vista.
2 *the prospect of a change in the weather.*
chance, expectation, hope, likelihood,
possibility, probability, promise.

prospect verb
to prospect for gold. explore, quest, search,
survey.

prospective adjective
prospective changes. a prospective employee.
anticipated, coming, expected, forthcoming,
future, imminent, intended, likely,
negotiable, possible, potential, probable.

prospectus noun
a college prospectus. brochure, catalogue,
leaflet, manifesto, pamphlet, programme,
scheme, syllabus.

prosper verb
to prosper in business. become prosperous
[SEE **prosperous**], be successful, [*informal*]
boom, burgeon, do well, flourish, [*informal*]
get on, [*informal*] go from strength to
strength, grow, make good, progress,
strengthen, succeed, thrive.
OPPOSITES: SEE **fail**.

prosperity noun
Will this prosperity last? affluence,
[*informal*] bonanza, [*informal*] boom,
growth, plenty, profitability, success,
wealth.

prosperous adjective
a prosperous business. affluent, [*informal*]
booming, buoyant, flourishing,
moneymaking, profitable, prospering, rich,
successful, thriving, wealthy, well-off, well-
to-do.
OPPOSITES: SEE **unsuccessful**.

prostitute noun
[*old-fashioned*] bawd, call-girl, [*old-
fashioned*] courtesan, [*old-fashioned*]
harlot, [*old-fashioned*] strumpet, [*informal*]
tart, whore.

prostrate adjective
1 *lying prostrate.* SEE **prone**.
2 *prostrate with grief.* SEE **overcome** adjective.

protagonist noun
the protagonist of a play. chief actor,
contender, contestant, hero, heroine,
leading figure, principal.

protect verb
1 *to protect someone from danger.* defend,
escort, guard, harbour, insulate, keep safe,
preserve, provide cover (for), safeguard,
screen, secure, shield.
2 *Parents protect their young.* care for,
cherish, look after, mind, support, watch
over.
OPPOSITES: SEE **endanger**.

protection noun
*protection from the weather. protection
against enemies.* barrier, bulwark, cloak,
cover, defence, guard, guardianship,
insulation, preservation, safety, screen,
security, shelter, shield, tutelage.

protective adjective
1 *a protective cover.* defensive, insulating,
protecting, sheltering, shielding.
2 *protective parents.* careful, jealous,
paternalistic, possessive, solicitous,
watchful.

protector noun
benefactor, bodyguard, champion, defender,
guard, guardian, patron.

protest noun
1 *We made a protest against the referee's
decision.* complaint, cry of disapproval,
objection, outcry, protestation,
remonstrance.
2 *They held a big protest in the square.*
[*informal*] demo, demonstration, march,
rally.

protest verb
1 *We protested against his decision.* argue,
complain, cry out, expostulate, express
disapproval, fulminate, grouse, grumble,
make a protest [SEE **protest** noun], moan,
object, remonstrate.
2 *A big crowd protested in the square.*
demonstrate, [*informal*] hold a demo, march.
3 *He protested that he was innocent.* SEE
declare.

protracted adjective SEE **long** adjective.

protrude verb
His stomach protrudes above his waistband.
bulge, jut out, poke out, project, stand out,
stick out, swell.

proud adjective
1 *proud of his new car.* appreciative,
delighted (with), happy (with), pleased
(with), satisfied (with).
2 *a proud bearing.* dignified, honourable,
independent, self-respecting.
3 *He's too proud to mix with the likes of us!*
arrogant, boastful, bumptious, [*informal*]
cocky, conceited, disdainful, egotistical,
grand, haughty, [*informal*] high and
mighty, lordly, self-important, snobbish,
[*informal*] snooty, [*informal*] stuck-up,
[*informal*] toffee-nosed, vain.
OPPOSITES: SEE **humble** adjective.

provable adjective
demonstrable, verifiable.
OPPOSITES: SEE **unprovable**.

prove verb
to prove a theory. ascertain, attest,
authenticate, [*informal*] bear out, confirm,
corroborate, demonstrate, establish,
explain, justify, show to be true,
substantiate, test, verify.
OPPOSITES: SEE **disprove**.

proven adjective
a player of proven ability. accepted,
authenticated, certified, checked,
confirmed, corroborated, demonstrated,
established, proved, reliable, tested, tried,
trustworthy, undoubted, unquestionable,
valid, verified.

proverbial adjective
a proverbial remark. conventional, clichéd,
customary, famous, legendary, traditional,
well-known.

provide verb
We provide food and clothing for our families.
afford, allot, allow, arrange for, cater,
contribute, donate, endow, equip, [*informal*]
fork out, furnish, give, grant, lay on, lend,
make provision, produce, spare, supply.

providence noun
SEE **fate**.

providential adjective
SEE **lucky**.

provincial adjective
1 *a provincial area. provincial government.*
local, regional.
OPPOSITES: SEE **national** adjective.
2 [*uncomplimentary*] *City dwellers think
country folk have provincial attitudes.*
bucolic, insular, narrow-minded, parochial,
rural, rustic, small-minded,
unsophisticated.
OPPOSITES: SEE **cosmopolitan**.

provisional adjective
a provisional agreement. conditional,
interim, stop-gap, temporary, tentative.
OPPOSITES: SEE **permanent**.

provisions noun
food, foodstuff, groceries, rations,
requirements, stores, subsistence, supplies.

provocation noun
The dog won't attack without provocation.
[*informal*] aggravation, cause, challenge,
grievance, grounds, incitement,
inducement, justification, motivation,
reason, taunts, teasing.

provoke verb
1 *If you provoke the dog, it'll bite.* [*informal*]
aggravate, anger, annoy, arouse, encourage,
enrage, exasperate, goad, incense, incite,

inflame, infuriate, insult, irk, irritate,
offend, pique, rile, tease, torment, upset,
urge on, vex, worry.
OPPOSITES: SEE **pacify**.
2 *His jokes provoked a lot of laughter.* arouse,
bring about, cause, elicit, excite, generate,
give rise to, induce, inspire, kindle,
occasion, produce, promote, prompt, spark
off, stimulate, stir up.

prowess noun
1 *prowess in battle.* bravery, courage, daring,
heroism, spirit, valour.
2 *The dancers showed off their prowess.*
ability, accomplishment, adroitness,
aptitude, cleverness, competence,
excellence, expertise, genius, skill, talent.

prowl verb
to prowl about in the dark. creep, roam,
slink, sneak, steal, SEE **walk** verb.

proximity noun
We objected to the proximity of the pig-farm.
closeness, nearness, propinquity.

prudent adjective
It's prudent to keep money in a bank.
advisable, careful, cautious, discreet,
economical, far-sighted, politic, proper,
sensible, shrewd, thoughtful, thrifty, wise.
OPPOSITES: SEE **unwise**.

prudish adjective
a prudish attitude to sex. easily shocked,
illiberal, intolerant, narrow-minded, old-
fashioned, priggish, prim, [*informal*] prissy,
proper, puritanical, shockable, strait-laced,
strict.
OPPOSITES: SEE **broad-minded**.

pry verb
Don't pry into my affairs. be curious, be
inquisitive, delve, [*informal*] ferret,
interfere, meddle, [*informal*] nose about,
peer rudely, poke about, [*informal*] snoop,
[*informal*] stick your nose in.

prying adjective
*We pulled down the blind to keep out prying
eyes.* curious, impertinent, inquisitive,
interfering, meddlesome, [*informal*] nosy,
[*informal*] snooping, spying.
OPPOSITES: SEE **discreet**.

pseudonym noun
alias, assumed name, false name, [*French*]
nom de plume, pen-name, sobriquet.

psychic adjective
Some people are said to have psychic powers.
clairvoyant, extrasensory, mystic, occult,
psychical, supernatural, telepathic.

psychological adjective
a psychological condition. emotional, mental,
subconscious, subjective.
OPPOSITES: SEE **physiological**.

psychopath noun SEE **madman**.

pub noun
bar, [*old-fashioned*] hostelry, inn,
[*informal*] local, public house, saloon,
tavern.

public adjective
a public place. public knowledge. accessible,
common, communal, familiar, general,
known, national, open, popular, shared,
unconcealed, universal, unrestricted, well-
known.
OPPOSITES: SEE **private**.

public noun
the public. citizens, the community, the
country, the nation, people, the populace,
society, voters.

publication noun
1 *the publication of a book.* appearance,
issuing, printing, production.
2 *the publication of secret information.*
announcement, broadcasting, disclosure,
dissemination, promulgation, reporting.
3 *I bought his latest publication.*
KINDS OF PUBLICATION: SEE **book** noun,
magazine, **recording**.

publicity noun
1 *Did you see the publicity for our play?* SEE
advertisement.
2 *Famous people don't always enjoy publicity.*
attention, [*informal*] ballyhoo, fame,
limelight, notoriety.

publicize verb
SEE **advertise**.

publish verb
1 *to publish a book or magazine.* bring out,
circulate, issue, print, produce, release.
2 *to publish secrets.* announce, broadcast,
communicate, declare, disclose,
disseminate, divulge, [*informal*] leak, make
known, make public, proclaim, promulgate,
publicize, report, reveal, spread.

pudding noun
[*informal*] afters, dessert, sweet.

puff noun
1 *a puff of wind.* blast, breath, draught,
flurry, gust.
2 *a puff of smoke.* cloud, whiff.

puff verb
1 *By the end of the race I was puffing.* blow,
breathe heavily, gasp, pant, wheeze.
2 *The sails puffed out.* become inflated,
billow, distend, rise, swell.

pugnacious adjective
a pugnacious fighter. aggressive, bellicose,
belligerent, combative, excitable, hostile,
hot-tempered, militant, quarrelsome,
warlike.
OPPOSITES: SEE **placid**.

pull verb
1 *A locomotive pulls a train.* drag, draw, haul,
lug, tow, trail.
OPPOSITES: SEE **push**.
2 *You nearly pulled my arm off!* jerk, tug,
pluck, rip, wrench.
3 *The dentist pulled a tooth.* extract, pull out,
remove, take out.

pulp noun
fruit pulp. squashed to a pulp. mash, mush,
paste, purée.

pulp verb
to pulp food. crush, liquidize, mash, pound,
pulverize, purée, smash, squash.

pulsate verb
A regular rhythm pulsated in our ears. beat,
drum, oscillate, palpitate, quiver, throb,
tick, vibrate.

pulse noun
a regular pulse. beat, drumming, oscillation,
pulsation, rhythm, throb, ticking, vibration.

pummel verb
batter, beat, SEE **hit** verb, pound, thump.

pump verb
*The fire brigade pumped water out of the
cellar.* drain, draw off, empty, force, raise,
siphon.

punch verb
1 *to punch someone on the nose.* beat, clout,
cuff, SEE **hit** verb, jab, poke, prod, slog, strike,
thump.
2 *to punch a hole.* SEE **pierce**.

punctual adjective
The bus is punctual today. in good time,
[*informal*] on the dot, on time, prompt.
OPPOSITES: SEE **unpunctual**.

punctuation noun

PUNCTUATION MARKS: accent, apostrophe,
asterisk, bracket, caret, cedilla, colon,
comma, dash, exclamation mark, full stop,
hyphen, question mark, quotation marks,
semicolon, speech marks.

---

puncture noun
1 *a puncture in a tyre.* burst, hole, leak, pin-
prick, rupture.
2 *We had a puncture on the way home.* blow-
out, burst tyre, [*informal*] flat, flat tyre.

puncture verb
A nail punctured my tyre. deflate, let down,
SEE **pierce**, rupture.

punish verb
to punish someone for wrongdoing. chasten,
chastise, correct, discipline, exact
retribution (from), impose or inflict

punishment on [SEE **punishment**], [*informal*] make an example of, pay back, penalize, [*informal*] teach (someone) a lesson.

WAYS TO PUNISH PEOPLE: beat, cane, detain, SEE **execute**, exile, fine, flog, gaol or jail, give a hiding (to), imprison, [*old-fashioned*] keelhaul, pillory, put in the stocks, put on probation, scourge, send to prison, spank, torture, whip.

---

punishment noun
chastisement, correction, discipline, penalty, retribution, revenge.

VARIOUS PUNISHMENTS: beating, Borstal, the cane, capital punishment, confiscation, corporal punishment, detention, execution [SEE **execute**], fine, flogging, forfeit, gaol or jail, [*informal*] a hiding, imposition, pillory, prison, probation, spanking, the stocks, torture, whipping.

---

punitive adjective
They took punitive measures against the whole gang. penal, retaliatory, revengeful, vindictive.

puny adjective
SEE **feeble**.

pupil noun
a teacher's pupil. disciple, follower, learner, protégé, scholar, schoolboy, schoolchild, schoolgirl, student.

puppet noun
doll, dummy, glove-puppet, marionette.

purchase noun
1 *I put my purchases in a bag.* acquisition, [*informal*] buy (*That was a good buy*), investment.
2 *I can't get enough purchase to prise this lid off.* grasp, hold, leverage.

purchase verb
What can you purchase for £1? acquire, buy, get, invest in, obtain, pay for, procure, secure.

pure adjective
1 *pure alcohol. pure gold.* authentic, genuine, neat, real, straight, unadulterated, unalloyed, undiluted.
2 *pure food.* eatable, germ-free, hygienic, natural, pasteurized, uncontaminated, untainted, wholesome.
3 *pure water.* clean, clear, distilled, drinkable, fresh, potable, sterile, unpolluted.
OPPOSITES: SEE **impure**.
4 *a pure person.* chaste, good, innocent, irreproachable, modest, moral, sinless,

stainless, virginal, virtuous.
OPPOSITES: SEE **immoral**.
5 *pure nonsense. pure genius.* absolute, complete, perfect, sheer, total, true, unmitigated, utter.
6 *pure science.* abstract, theoretical.
OPPOSITES: SEE **applied**.

purgatory noun SEE **torment** noun.

purge verb
1 *to purge your bowels.* clean out, cleanse, empty, purify.
2 *to purge spies from the government.* eradicate, expel, get rid of, remove, root out.

purify verb
to purify water. clarify, clean, disinfect, distil, filter, make pure [SEE **pure**], refine, sterilize.

puritanical adjective
a puritanical dislike of self-indulgence. ascetic, austere, moralistic, narrow-minded, prim, prudish, self-denying, self-disciplined, severe, strait-laced, strict, temperate, unbending.
OPPOSITES: SEE **hedonistic**.

purpose noun
1 *a particular purpose in mind.* aim, ambition, aspiration, design, end, goal, hope, intention, motive, object, objective, outcome, plan, result, target, wish.
2 *a sense of purpose.* determination, devotion, firmness, persistence, resolution, resolve, steadfastness, zeal.
3 *What's the purpose of this gadget?* application, point, use, usefulness, value.

purposeful adjective
Her purposeful stare showed she meant business. calculated, decided, decisive, deliberate, determined, firm, positive, resolute, steadfast, unwavering.
OPPOSITES: SEE **hesitant**.

purposeless adjective
purposeless vandalism. aimless, gratuitous, pointless, senseless, unnecessary, useless, wanton.
OPPOSITES: SEE **useful**.

purposely adverb
consciously, deliberately, intentionally, knowingly, on purpose, wilfully.

purse noun
bag, handbag, pouch, wallet.

pursue verb
1 *Hounds pursue the fox.* chase, follow, go in pursuit of, harry, hound, hunt, run after, seek, shadow, tail, track down.
2 *She's pursuing a career in engineering.* aim for, aspire to, [*informal*] go for, strive for, try for.
3 *I pursue my hobbies at weekends.* carry on,

conduct, continue, engage in, follow up, inquire into, investigate, keep up with, persevere in, proceed with.

pursuit noun
1 *The hounds were in pursuit of the fox.* chase, [*informal*] hue and cry, hunt, tracking down, trail.
2 *What are your favourite pursuits?* activity, hobby, interest, occupation, pastime, pleasure.

push verb
1 *to push something away from you.* advance, drive, force, hustle, impel, jostle, poke, press, prod, propel, shove, thrust.
OPPOSITES: SEE **pull**.
2 *I pushed my things into a bag.* compress, cram, crowd, crush, insert, jam, pack, put, ram, squash, squeeze.
3 *They pushed him to work even harder.* browbeat, bully, coerce, compel, constrain, dragoon, hurry, importune, [*informal*] lean on, persuade, put pressure on, pressurize, urge.
4 *The firm is pushing its new product hard.* advertise, make known, market, [*informal*] plug, promote, publicize.

put verb
1 *Put the books on the shelf.* arrange, assign, consign, deploy, deposit, dispose, fix, hang, lay, leave, locate, park, place, [*informal*] plonk, position, rest, set down, situate, stand, station.
2 *to put a question.* express, formulate, frame, phrase, say, state, suggest, utter, voice, word, write.
3 *to put the blame on someone else.* cast, impose, inflict, lay.
to put down 1 *to put down a rebellion.* SEE **suppress**.
2 *to put down an animal.* SEE **kill**.
to put in *to put in new sparking-plugs.* SEE **insert** verb, **install**.
to put off *to put off a visit.* SEE **postpone**.
to put out *to put out a fire.* SEE **extinguish**.
to put right *to put damage right.* SEE **repair** verb.
to put up 1 *to put up a tent.* SEE **erect** verb.
2 *to put up prices.* SEE **raise**.
3 *to put up guests.* SEE **accommodate**.

putrid adjective
SEE **rotten**.

puzzle noun
Can you solve this puzzle? brainteaser, difficulty, dilemma, enigma, mystery, [*informal*] poser, problem, quandary, question.

KINDS OF PUZZLE: acrostic, anagram, conundrum, crossword, maze, riddle.

puzzle verb
1 *His coded message puzzled us.* baffle, bewilder, confuse, [*informal*] floor, [*informal*] flummox, mystify, nonplus, perplex, set thinking, stump, worry.
2 *We puzzled over the problem for hours.* SEE **think**.

puzzling adjective
a puzzling problem. baffling, bewildering, confusing, cryptic, enigmatic, impenetrable, inexplicable, insoluble, [*informal*] mind-boggling, mysterious, mystifying, perplexing, strange, unaccountable, unanswerable, unfathomable.
OPPOSITES: SEE **straightforward**.

pygmy adjective SEE **small**.

Qq

quadrangle noun
a quadrangle surrounded by buildings. cloisters, courtyard, enclosure, [*informal*] quad, yard.

quagmire noun
My wellingtons got stuck in a quagmire. bog, fen, marsh, mire, morass, mud, quicksand, [*old-fashioned*] slough, swamp.

quail verb
I quailed at the danger. back away, blench, cower, cringe, falter, flinch, quake, recoil, show fear, shrink, tremble, wince.

quaint adjective
a quaint thatched cottage. antiquated, antique, charming, curious, fanciful, fantastic, odd, old-fashioned, old-world, picturesque, [*informal*] twee, unusual, whimsical.

quake verb
The buildings quaked when the bomb went off. convulse, heave, move, quaver, quiver, rock, shake, shiver, shudder, sway, tremble, vibrate, wobble.

qualification noun
1 *the proper qualifications for a job.* ability, certification, competence, eligibility, experience, fitness, [*informal*] know-how, knowledge, quality, skill, suitability, training.
2 *I'd say without qualification that he's our best player.* condition, exception, limitation, proviso, reservation, restriction.

qualified adjective
1 *a qualified electrician.* certificated, chartered, competent, equipped, experienced, graduate, professional, skilled, trained.
OPPOSITES: SEE **amateur** adjective.
2 *qualified applicants for a job.* appropriate, eligible, suitable.
3 *qualified praise.* cautious, conditional, equivocal, guarded, half-hearted, limited, modified, reserved, restricted.
OPPOSITES: SEE **unconditional**.

qualify verb
1 *The driving test qualifies you to drive.* authorize, empower, entitle, equip, fit, permit, sanction.
2 *The first three runners qualify for the final.* become eligible, [*informal*] get through, pass.
3 *He qualified his praise with one criticism.* abate, lessen, limit, moderate, restrain, restrict, soften, temper, weaken.

quality noun
1 *top quality meat.* calibre, class, condition, excellence, grade, rank, sort, standard, value.
2 *She has many good qualities.* attribute, characteristic, feature, peculiarity, property, trait.

quandary noun
SEE **dilemma**.

quantity noun
a quantity of goods. a measurable quantity. aggregate, amount, bulk, consignment, dosage, dose, expanse, extent, length, load, lot, magnitude, mass, SEE **measure** noun, measurement, number, part (*1 part of sugar to 2 parts of flour*), pinch (*a pinch of salt*), portion, proportion, quantum, sum, total, volume, weight.

An almost infinite number of words indicating *quantity* can be formed using suffixes *-ful* and *-load*: e.g., armful, barrowload, bucketful, busload, cupful, handful, lorryload, mouthful, plateful, pocketful, spadeful, spoonful.

---

quarrel noun
a quarrel between rivals. altercation, argument, bickering, brawl, clash, conflict, confrontation, contention, controversy, difference, disagreement, discord, disharmony, dispute, dissension, division, feud, SEE **fight** noun, [*informal*] hassle, misunderstanding, row, [*informal*] ructions, rupture, [*informal*] scene, schism, [*informal*] slanging match, split, squabble, strife, [*informal*] tiff, vendetta, wrangle.

quarrel verb
Members of the rival teams often quarrel. argue [*informal*] be at loggerheads, be at odds, bicker, clash, conflict, contend, [*informal*] cross swords, differ, disagree, dissent, fall out, SEE **fight** verb, haggle, have a quarrel [SEE **quarrel** noun], [*informal*] row, squabble, wrangle.
to quarrel with *I can't quarrel with your decision.* complain about, disagree with, dispute, fault, object to, SEE **oppose**, [*informal*] pick holes in, query, question, take exception to.

quarrelsome adjective
a quarrelsome customer. aggressive, SEE **angry**, argumentative, bad-tempered, belligerent, cantankerous, contentious, cross, defiant, explosive, fractious, impatient, irascible, irritable, petulant, quick-tempered, [*informal*] stroppy, truculent.
OPPOSITES: SEE **peaceable**.

quarry verb
to quarry stone. dig out, excavate, extract, mine.

quarter noun
1 *the commercial quarter of a city.* area, district, division, locality, neighbourhood, part, sector, vicinity, zone.
2 [*plural*] *soldiers' quarters.* SEE **accommodation**, barracks, billet, housing, living quarters, lodgings.

quaver verb
1 *I quavered when I heard him shout.* falter, quake, quiver, shake, shudder, tremble, waver.
2 *His voice quavered.* pulsate, vibrate.

quay noun
a quay where ships tie up. berth, dock, harbour, jetty, landing-stage, pier, wharf.

queasy adjective
bilious, SEE **ill**, nauseous, [*informal*] poorly, [*informal*] queer, sick, unwell.

queer adjective
1 *A queer thing happened.* aberrant, abnormal, anomalous, atypical bizarre, curious, eerie, [*informal*] fishy, SEE **funny**, inexplicable, irrational, mysterious, odd, off-beat, outlandish, peculiar, puzzling, quaint, remarkable, [*informal*] rum, singular, strange, unaccountable, uncanny, uncommon, unconventional, unexpected, unnatural, unorthodox, unusual, weird.
2 [*informal*] *a queer person.* [*informal*] cranky, deviant, eccentric, SEE **mad**, questionable, [*informal*] shady (*a shady customer*), [*informal*] shifty, suspect, suspicious.
3 *I felt queer after eating too much.* SEE **ill**.
4 [= *homosexual*] SEE **homosexual**.

quell verb
to quell a riot. SEE **suppress**.

quench verb
1 *to quench a fire.* damp down, douse,
extinguish, put out, smother, snuff out.
OPPOSITES: SEE **light** verb.
2 *to quench your thirst.* allay, cool, satisfy,
slake.

query noun, verb SEE **question** noun, verb.

quest noun
a quest for treasure. crusade, expedition,
hunt, mission, search.

question noun
1 *Answer this question.* [*informal*]
brainteaser, conundrum, demand, enquiry,
inquiry, mystery, [*informal*] poser,
problem, puzzle, query, riddle.
2 *There's some question about whether he can
play.* argument, controversy, debate,
dispute, doubt, misgiving, SEE **objection**,
uncertainty.

question verb
1 *They questioned me about the accident.* ask,
[*formal*] catechize, cross-examine, cross-
question, debrief, examine, [*informal*] grill,
interrogate, interview, probe, [*informal*]
pump, quiz.
2 *He questioned the referee's decision.* argue
over, be sceptical about, challenge, dispute,
doubt, enquire about, impugn, inquire
about, object to [SEE **object** verb], oppose,
quarrel with, query.

questionable adjective
questionable evidence. arguable, borderline,
debatable, disputable, doubtful, dubious,
[*informal*] iffy, moot (*a moot point*), suspect,
uncertain, unclear, unprovable, unreliable.

questionnaire noun
[*formal*] catechism, opinion poll, question
sheet, quiz, survey, test.

queue noun
a queue of cars. column, file, line, line-up,
procession, row, string, tail-back.

queue verb
Please queue at the door. form a queue [SEE
queue noun], line up.

quibble verb
He quibbled about the price. carp, cavil,
equivocate, SEE **object** verb, [*informal*] split
hairs.

quick adjective
1 *a quick pace. a quick journey.* breakneck,
brisk, expeditious, express (*an express
train*), fast, [*old-fashioned*] fleet, hasty,
headlong, highspeed, hurried, [*informal*]
nippy, precipitate, rapid, [*informal*] smart
(*a smart pace*), [*informal*] spanking, speedy,
swift.

2 *quick movements.* adroit, agile, animated,
brisk, deft, dextrous, lively, nimble,
sudden.
OPPOSITES: SEE **slow** adjective.
3 *a quick rest.* brief, fleeting, momentary,
passing, perfunctory, short, shortlived,
temporary, transitory.
OPPOSITES: SEE **long** adjective.
4 *a quick reply.* abrupt, early, immediate,
instant, instantaneous, prompt, punctual,
ready, unhesitating.
OPPOSITES: SEE **belated**.
5 *a quick pupil.* acute, alert, apt, astute,
bright, clever, intelligent, perceptive,
quick-witted, sharp, shrewd, smart.
OPPOSITES: SEE **stupid**.

quicken verb
1 *Our speed quickened.* accelerate, hasten,
hurry, go faster, speed up.
2 *The appearance of a new character
quickened our interest.* SEE **arouse**.

quiet adjective
1 *a quiet engine.* inaudible, noiseless, silent,
soundless.
OPPOSITES: SEE **audible**.
2 *quiet music.* hushed, low, pianissimo, soft.
OPPOSITES: SEE **loud**.
3 *a quiet person. a quiet member of a group.*
reserved, retiring, taciturn,
uncommunicative, unforthcoming.
OPPOSITES: SEE **talkative**.
4 *a quiet personality. a quiet mood.* composed,
contemplative, contented, gentle,
introverted, meditative, meek, mild, modest,
peaceable, shy, thoughtful.
OPPOSITES: SEE **extroverted**.
5 *quiet weather.* calm, motionless, placid,
restful, serene, still, tranquil, untroubled.
OPPOSITES: SEE **turbulent**.
6 *a quiet road. a quiet place for a holiday.*
isolated, lonely, peaceful, private, secluded,
sequestered, undisturbed, unfrequented.
OPPOSITES: SEE **busy**.

quieten verb
1 *Please quieten the baby!* calm, compose,
hush, pacify, soothe, subdue, tranquillize.
2 *A silencer quietens the noise of the engine.*
deaden, dull, muffle, mute, reduce the
volume of, silence, soften, stifle, suppress,
tone down.

quip noun
SEE **joke** noun.

quirk noun SEE **peculiarity**.

quit verb
1 *to quit the house. It's time to quit.* abandon,
decamp, depart, desert, forsake, go away,
leave, walk out, withdraw.
2 *to quit your job.* abdicate, discontinue,
drop, give up, [*informal*] pack it in,

relinquish, renounce, repudiate, resign from.

quite adverb
[Take care how you use *quite*, as the two senses are almost opposite.] 1 *Yes, I have quite finished.* absolutely, altogether, completely, entirely, perfectly, totally, utterly, wholly.
2 *It was quite good, but far from perfect.* comparatively, fairly, moderately, [*informal*] pretty, rather, relatively, somewhat.

quits adjective
to be quits with someone. equal, even, level, repaid, revenged, square.

quiz verb
SEE **question** verb.

quota noun
a daily quota of food. allocation, allowance, assignment, portion, proportion, ration, share.

quotation noun
1 *a quotation from a book.* [*informal*] citation, [*informal*] clip (*a clip from a TV programme*), cutting (*a cutting from a newspaper*), excerpt, extract, passage, piece, reference.
2 *The garage gave us a quotation for repairing the car.* estimate, likely price, tender.
quotation marks inverted commas, speech marks.

quote verb
1 *to quote what someone has said or written.* cite, instance, mention, produce a quotation from [SEE **quotation**], refer to, repeat, reproduce.
2 *The builder quoted a figure of £10,000 for our extension.* estimate, tender.

Rr

rabble noun
a noisy rabble. crowd, gang, SEE **group** noun, herd, horde, mob, swarm, throng.

race noun
1 *a race of people.* clan, ethnic group, nation, people, tribe.
RELATED ADJECTIVES: ethnic, racial.
2 *the human race.* breed, genus, kind, species, variety.
3 *a running race.* chase, competition, contest, heat, rivalry.

COMPETITIVE RACES: cross-country, horse-race, hurdles, marathon, motor-race, regatta, relay race, road-race, rowing, scramble, speedway, sprint, steeple-chase, stock-car race, swimming, track race.

race verb
1 *I'll race you.* compete with, contest with, have a race with, try to beat.
2 *I raced home because I was late.* career, dash, fly, gallop, hasten, hurry, move fast, run, rush, sprint, tear, zoom.

racial adjective
racial characteristics. ethnic, national, tribal.

racialism, racism nouns
anti-Semitism, apartheid, bias, bigotry, chauvinism, discrimination, intolerance, prejudice, racial hatred, xenophobia.

rack noun
a plate rack. a luggage rack. frame, framework, shelf, stand, support.

racketeer noun
SEE **swindler**.

radiant adjective
1 *a radiant light.* SEE **bright**.
2 *a radiant smile.* SEE **beautiful, happy**.

radiate verb
The fire radiates heat. diffuse, emit, give off, glow, send out, shed, shine, spread, transmit.

radical adjective
1 *a radical inquiry.* basic, drastic, fundamental, thorough.
OPPOSITES: SEE **superficial**.
2 *radical political views.* extreme, extremist, far-reaching, revolutionary, [*uncomplimentary*] subversive.
OPPOSITES: SEE **moderate** adjective.

radio noun
receiver, set, [*informal*] transistor, transmitter, [*old-fashioned*] wireless.

rafter noun
rafters in the roof. beam, girder, joist.

rag noun
SEE **rags**.

rage noun
SEE **anger** noun.

ragged adjective
1 *ragged clothes.* frayed, in ribbons, old, patched, patchy, rent, ripped, shabby, shaggy, tattered, tatty, threadbare, torn, unkempt, worn out.
2 *a ragged line.* disorganized, erratic, irregular, uneven.

rags noun
[*plural*] bits and pieces, cloths, old clothes, remnants, scraps, shreds, tatters.

raid noun
a raid on an enemy. assault, attack, blitz, foray, incursion, inroad, invasion, onslaught, sortie, strike, swoop.

raid verb
1 *Police raided the gang's hideaway.* attack, descend on, invade, make a raid on [SEE **raid** noun], pounce on, rush, storm, swoop on.
2 *We raided the larder.* loot, pillage, plunder, ransack, rob, steal from.

raider noun
Raiders swooped down from the mountains. attacker, brigand, invader, looter, marauder, pillager, pirate, plunderer, ransacker, robber, rustler, thief.

rail noun
bar, rod.

railing noun
barrier, fence, paling.

railway noun
line, permanent way, [*American*] railroad, rails, track.

KINDS OF RAILWAY: branch line, cable railway, funicular, light railway, main line, metro, mineral line, monorail, mountain railway, narrow gauge, rack-and-pinion railway, rapid transit system, siding, standard gauge, tramway, tube, underground railway.

TRAINS AND ROLLING-STOCK: buffet-car, cable-car, carriage, coach, container wagon, diesel, dining-car, DMU, electric train, engine, express, freight train, goods train, goods van, goods wagon, guard's van, Inter-city, locomotive, shunter, sleeper, sleeping-car, steam-engine, steam-train, stopping train, tender, truck, tube-train, underground train, wagon.

PEOPLE WHO WORK ON THE RAILWAY: announcer, booking-clerk, crossing-keeper, driver, engineer, fireman, guard, plate-layer, porter, signalman, station manager, [*old-fashioned*] stationmaster, steward.

SOME OTHER RAILWAY TERMS: bogie, booking-office, buffer, compartment, corridor, coupling, cutting, footplate, gauge, halt, left-luggage office, level-crossing, luggage, trolley, marshalling yard, platform, points, sidings, signals, signal-box, sleepers, station, terminus, ticket-office, timetable, track, waiting-room.

---

rain noun
Take a mac to keep the rain off. cloudburst, deluge, downpour, drizzle, [*formal*] precipitation, raindrops, rainfall, rainstorm, shower, squall.

rain verb
It always seems to rain when we go on holiday. bucket, drizzle, pelt, pour, [*informal*] rain cats and dogs, spit, teem.

rainy adjective
a rainy day. damp, drizzly, pouring, showery, wet.

raise verb
1 *to raise your hand. to raise your head.* hold up, lift, put up, rear.
2 *to raise something to a higher position.* elevate, heave up, hoist, jack up, lift, pick up.
3 *to raise prices. to raise the volume on a radio.* augment, boost, increase, inflate, put up, [*informal*] up.
OPPOSITES: SEE **lower**.
4 *to raise someone to a higher rank.* exalt, prefer, promote, upgrade.
OPPOSITES: SEE **demote**.
5 *to raise a monument.* build, construct, create, erect, set up.
6 *to raise someone's hopes.* activate, arouse, awaken, build up, cause, encourage, engender, enlarge, excite, foment, foster, heighten, incite, kindle, motivate, provoke, rouse, stimulate, uplift.
OPPOSITES: SEE **destroy**.
7 *to raise animals and crops. to raise a family.* breed, bring up, care for, cultivate, educate, grow, look after, nurture, produce, propagate, rear.
8 *to raise money for charity.* collect, get, make, receive.
9 *to raise questions.* advance, broach, instigate, introduce, moot, originate, pose, present, put forward, suggest.

rake noun
1 *a garden rake.* SEE **tool**.
2 *the rake of a stage.* SEE **slope** noun.
3 [=*immoral person*] SEE **immoral (immoral person)**.

rally noun
1 *a political rally.* [*informal*] demo, demonstration, march, meeting, protest.
2 *a motor rally.* SEE **competition**.

rally verb
1 *to rally your supporters.* SEE **assemble**.
2 *to rally after an illness.* SEE **recover**.

ram verb
Our car rammed the one in front. bump, collide with, crash into, SEE **hit** verb, smash into, strike.

ramble verb
1 *to ramble in the hills.* hike, roam, rove, stroll, SEE **walk** verb.
2 *to ramble off the point.* digress, drift, maunder, wander.

rambling adjective
1 *a rambling route.* circuitous, indirect, labyrinthine, meandering, roundabout, tortuous, twisting, wandering, winding, zigzag.
OPPOSITES: SEE **direct** adjective.
2 *a rambling speech. a rambling speaker.* aimless, SEE **confused**, disconnected, discursive, disjointed, incoherent, unstructured, verbose, wordy.
OPPOSITES: SEE **coherent**.

ramp noun SEE **slope** noun.

rampage verb
Hooligans rampaged through the town. behave violently, go berserk, go wild, race about, run amok, run riot, rush about.

rampant adjective
unchecked, unrestrained, wild.

ramshackle adjective
a ramshackle old hut. broken down, decrepit, dilapidated, rickety, ruined, shaky, tumbledown, unsafe.
OPPOSITES: SEE **solid**.

random adjective
a random choice. accidental, aimless, arbitrary, casual, chance, fortuitous, haphazard, indiscriminate, irregular, unconsidered, unplanned, unpremeditated.
OPPOSITES: SEE **deliberate** adjective.

range noun
1 *a range of mountains.* chain, file, line, row, series, string.
2 *a wide range of goods. your range of knowledge.* area, compass, extent, field, gamut, limits, scope, selection, spectrum, variety.
3 *the range of a gun.* distance, limit, reach.

range verb
1 *His trophies were ranged on the shelf.* SEE **arrange**.
2 *Prices range from £10 to £15.* differ, extend, fluctuate, reach, vary.
3 *Sheep range over the hills.* roam, rove, stray, travel, wander.

rank noun
1 *Line up in single rank.* column, file, formation, line, order, row, series, tier.
2 *a high rank. a low rank.* caste, class, condition, degree, estate, grade, level, position, standing, station, status, title.

RANKS IN THE ARMED SERVICES: [within each group, these are listed in descending order of seniority]:

AIR FORCE: Marshal of the RAF, Air Chief Marshal, Air Marshal, Air Vice-Marshal, air commodore, group captain, wing-commander, squadron leader, flight-lieutenant, flying officer, pilot officer; warrant officer, flight sergeant, chief technician, sergeant, corporal, junior technician, senior aircraftman, leading aircraftman, aircraftman.

ARMY: Field Marshal, general, lieutenant general, major general, brigadier, colonel, lieutenant colonel, major, captain, lieutenant, second lieutenant or subaltern; warrant officer, staff sergeant, sergeant, corporal, lance-corporal, private.

NAVY: Admiral of the Fleet, admiral, vice-admiral, rear-admiral, commodore, captain, commander, lieutenant commander, lieutenant, sub-lieutenant; chief petty officer, petty officer, leading rating, able rating, ordinary rating.

ransack verb
1 *I ransacked the house looking for my purse.* comb, rummage through, scour, search, [*informal*] turn upside down.
2 *Rioters ransacked the shops.* loot, pillage, plunder, raid, ravage, rob, wreck.

rape verb
[*applied to the action of a man*] *to rape a woman.* assault, defile, force yourself on, [*old-fashioned*] ravish.

rapid adjective
rapid progress. breakneck, brisk, expeditious, express, fast, hasty, high-speed, headlong, hurried, [*informal*] nippy, precipitate, quick, smooth, speedy, swift, unchecked, uninterrupted.
OPPOSITES: SEE **slow** adjective.

rapids noun
swept along by the rapids. cataract, white water.

rapture noun
SEE **delight** noun.

rapturous SEE **happy**.

rare adjective
1 *a rare visitor. a rare example of something.* abnormal, curious, exceptional, infrequent, irreplaceable, occasional, odd, peculiar, scarce, singular, special, strange, surprising, uncommon, unusual.
OPPOSITES: SEE **common** adjective.
2 [*informal*] *We had a rare time.* SEE **good**.

rascal noun
[*Rascal* and its synonyms are often used informally or jokingly.] blackguard, SEE **criminal** noun, good-for-nothing, imp, knave, miscreant, ne'er-do-well, rapscallion, rogue, scallywag, scamp, scoundrel, trouble-maker, villain.

rash adjective
a rash decision. careless, foolhardy, hare-brained, hasty, headstrong, heedless, hot-headed, hurried, ill-advised, ill-considered, impetuous, imprudent, impulsive, incautious, injudicious, precipitate, reckless, risky, thoughtless, unthinking.
OPPOSITES: SEE **careful**.

rasping adjective
a rasping voice. croaking, croaky, grating, gravelly, gruff, harsh, hoarse, husky, raucous, rough.

rate noun
1 *We set out at a fast rate.* pace, speed, tempo, velocity.
2 *What's a reasonable rate for the job?* amount, charge, cost, fare, fee, figure, SEE **payment**, price, wage.

rate verb
How do you rate our chance of winning? appraise, assess, consider, estimate, evaluate, judge, measure, prize, put a price on, rank, regard, value, weigh.

rather adverb
1 *I was rather ill.* fairly, moderately, [*informal*] pretty, quite, relatively, slightly, somewhat.
2 *I'd rather have an apple than an orange.* preferably, sooner.

rating noun
Her performance would get a high rating from me. SEE **class** noun, evaluation, grade, grading, mark, placing, ranking.

ratio noun
The ratio of boys to girls is about 50:50. balance, correlation, fraction, percentage, proportion, relationship.

ration noun
You've had your ration of sweets! allocation, allowance, helping, measure, portion, quota, share.
rations *The expedition carried rations to last a month.* food, necessaries, necessities, provisions, stores, supplies.

ration verb
In time of war, the government may ration food supplies. allocate, allot, apportion, conserve, control, distribute fairly, dole out, give out a ration [SEE **ration** noun], limit, restrict, share equally.

rational adjective
a rational discussion. a rational decision. balanced, intelligent, judicious, logical, lucid, normal, reasonable, reasoned, sane, sensible, sound, thoughtful, wise.
OPPOSITES: SEE **irrational**.

rationalize verb
1 *I rationalized the silly arrangement of books in the library.* make rational [SEE **rational**], reorganize, [*informal*] sort out.
2 *I can't rationalize my absurd fear of insects.* be rational about [SEE **rational**], elucidate, explain, justify, think through.

raucous adjective
raucous laughter. harsh, grating, jarring, noisy, rough, shrill, strident.

ravage verb
The invaders ravaged the countryside. damage, despoil, destroy, devastate, lay waste, loot, pillage, plunder, raid, ransack, ruin, sack, wreck.

rave verb
1 *The head raved about our bad behaviour.* be angry [SEE **angry**], fulminate, fume, rage, rant, roar, storm.
2 *The papers raved about her success.* be enthusiastic [SEE **enthusiastic**].

ravenous adjective
The ravenous children ate everything on the table. famished, gluttonous, greedy, hungry, insatiable, ravening, starved, starving, voracious.

raw adjective
1 *raw food.* fresh, rare (*rare steak*), uncooked, underdone, wet (*wet fish*).
OPPOSITES: COOKED.
2 *raw materials.* crude, natural, unprocessed, unrefined, untreated.
OPPOSITES: SEE **processed**.
3 *a raw place on your skin.* bloody, chafed, grazed, inflamed, painful, red, rough, scraped, scratched, sore, tender, vulnerable.
4 *a raw recruit.* ignorant, SEE **inexperienced**, innocent, new, untrained.
OPPOSITES: SEE **experienced**.
5 *a raw wind.* SEE **cold** adjective.

ray noun
1 *a ray of light.* bar, beam, laser, shaft, stream.
2 *a ray of hope.* gleam, glimmer, hint, indication, sign.

razor noun
cut-throat razor, disposable razor, electric razor, safety razor.

reach noun
The shops are in easy reach. compass, distance, range, scope.

reach verb
1 *I reached the end. We reached our target.* achieve, arrive at, attain, get to, go as far as, [*informal*] make.
2 *I can't reach the handle.* grasp, get hold of, take, touch.
3 *You can reach me by phone.* communicate with, contact, get in touch with.
to reach out *Reach out your hand.* extend, hold out, put out, raise, stick out, stretch.

react verb
How did she react when you asked for money? act, answer, behave, reply, respond, retort.

reaction noun
a reaction to a question. a reaction to a stimulus. answer, backlash, [*informal*] come-back, feedback, reflex, rejoinder, reply, response, retort, [*joking*] riposte.

read verb
1 *to read a story.* [*informal*] dip into, glance at, interpret, peruse, pore over, scan, skim, study.
2 *I can't read your handwriting.* decipher, decode, make out, understand.

readable adjective
1 *a readable story.* compulsive, enjoyable, entertaining, gripping, interesting, well-written.
OPPOSITES: SEE **boring**.
2 *readable handwriting.* clear, decipherable, legible, neat, plain, understandable.
OPPOSITES: SEE **illegible**.

readily adverb
eagerly, easily, gladly, happily, voluntarily, willingly.

ready adjective
1 *Dinner is ready.* available, complete, convenient, done, finalized, finished, obtainable, prepared, set up, waiting.
OPPOSITES: unready.
2 *I'm ready to lend a hand.* disposed, eager, fit, [*informal*] game (*game for a laugh*), glad, inclined, keen, [*informal*] keyed up, liable, likely, minded, organized, pleased, poised, predisposed, primed, raring (*raring to go*), willing.
OPPOSITES: SEE **reluctant**.

real adjective
1 *real events. real people.* actual, certain, everyday, existing, factual, ordinary, palpable, SEE **realistic**, tangible, true, verifiable.
OPPOSITES: SEE **imaginary**.
2 *real wood. real gold.* authentic, genuine, natural, pure.
OPPOSITES: SEE **artificial**.
3 *a real work of art.* authenticated, bona fide, legitimate, unquestionable, valid.
OPPOSITES: SEE **imitation** adjective.
4 *a real friend.* dependable, positive,

reliable, sound, trustworthy, worthy.
OPPOSITES: SEE **unreliable**.

realism noun
1 *realism in a work of art.* authenticity, fidelity, truth to life, verisimilitude.
2 *realism in the way you deal with things.* clear-sightedness, common sense, objectivity, practicality, pragmatism.

realistic adjective
1 *a realistic portrait.* authentic, convincing, faithful, lifelike, natural, recognizable, representational, true to life, truthful.
2 *a realistic plan. a realistic assessment of the situation.* businesslike, clear-sighted, common-sense, down-to-earth, feasible, level-headed, logical, objective, possible, practicable, practical, pragmatic, rational, sensible, unemotional, viable, workable.
3 *realistic prices. realistic wages.* acceptable, adequate, fair, justifiable, moderate, reasonable.
OPPOSITES: SEE **unrealistic**.

reality noun
Stop day-dreaming and face reality. actuality, certainty, fact, [*informal*] nitty-gritty, the real world [SEE **real**], truth, verity.
OPPOSITES: SEE **fantasy**.

realize verb
1 *I suddenly realized what you meant.* accept, appreciate, apprehend, be aware of, [*informal*] catch on to, comprehend, grasp, know, recognize, see, sense, [*informal*] twig, understand, [*informal*] wake up to.
2 *It'll take years to realize my ambition.* accomplish, achieve, complete, fulfil, implement, obtain, perform.
3 *My old car realized a good price.* [*informal*] bring in, [*informal*] clear, earn, fetch, make, net, obtain, produce.

realm noun
SEE **country**, domain, empire, kingdom, monarchy.

reap verb
1 *to reap corn.* SEE **cut** verb, gather in, harvest, mow.
2 *to reap your reward.* collect, get, obtain, receive, win.

rear adjective
the rear legs of an animal. back, end, hind, hinder, hindmost, last, rearmost.
OPPOSITES: SEE **front** adjective.

rear verb
1 *Parents rear their families. Farmers rear cattle.* breed, bring up, care for, cultivate, feed, look after, nurture, produce, raise, train.
2 *The animal reared its head.* elevate, lift, raise.

rearrange verb SEE **change** verb, regroup, reorganize, switch round, swop round, transpose.

reason noun
1 *He had a good reason for his behaviour.* apology, argument, case, cause, excuse, explanation, grounds, incentive, justification, motive, occasion, pretext, rationale, vindication.
2 *Show some reason!* brains, common sense, [*informal*] gumption, intelligence, judgement, mind, [*informal*] nous, rationality, SEE **reasoning**, understanding, wisdom, wit.
3 *She tried to make him see reason.* logic, reasonableness, sanity, sense.

reason verb
1 *I reasoned that it was cheaper to go by bus.* calculate, conclude, consider, deduce, infer, judge, resolve, think, work out.
2 *I reasoned with him, but I couldn't persuade him.* argue, debate, discuss, expostulate, intellectualize, remonstrate, use reason.

reasonable adjective
1 *a reasonable person. reasonable behaviour.* calm, honest, intelligent, rational, realistic, sane, sensible, sincere, sober, thoughtful, unemotional, wise.
OPPOSITES: SEE **irrational**.
2 *a reasonable argument.* believable, credible, defensible, justifiable, logical, plausible, practical, reasoned, sound, tenable, viable.
OPPOSITES: SEE **absurd**.
3 *a reasonable price.* acceptable, average, cheap, fair, inexpensive, moderate, ordinary, proper.
OPPOSITES: SEE **excessive**.

reasoning noun
I don't follow your reasoning. analysis, argument, case, [*uncomplimentary*] casuistry, deduction, dialectic, hypothesis, line of thought, logic, proof, SEE **reason** noun, [*uncomplimentary*] sophistry, thinking.

reassure verb
to reassure someone who is worried. assure, bolster (up), calm, comfort, encourage, give confidence to, hearten, support.
OPPOSITES: SEE **threaten**.

reassuring adjective
a reassuring smile. reassuring signs of success. calming, caring, comforting, encouraging, favourable, hopeful, promising, supportive, sympathetic, understanding.
OPPOSITES: SEE **threatening**.

rebate noun SEE **refund** noun.

rebel adjective
rebel forces. breakaway, insubordinate, insurgent, malcontent, mutinous, SEE **rebellious**, revolutionary.

rebel noun
a rebel against authority. anarchist, apostate, dissenter, heretic, iconoclast, insurgent, malcontent, maverick, mutineer, nonconformist, revolutionary, schismatic.

rebel verb
to rebel against authority. be a rebel [SEE **rebel** noun], disobey, dissent, fight, [*informal*] kick (against), [*informal*] kick over the traces, mutiny, refuse to obey, revolt, rise up, [*informal*] run riot, [*informal*] take a stand.
OPPOSITES: SEE **obey**.

rebellion noun
rebellion in the ranks. disobedience, insubordination, insurgency, insurrection, mutiny, rebelliousness, resistance, revolt, revolution, rising, schism, sedition, uprising.

rebellious adjective
rebellious troops. a rebellious class of children. [*informal*] bolshie, breakaway, defiant, difficult, disaffected, disloyal, disobedient, insubordinate, insurgent, intractable, malcontent, mutinous, quarrelsome, rebel, refractory, resistant, revolting, revolutionary, seditious, uncontrollable, ungovernable, unmanageable, unruly, wild.
OPPOSITES: SEE **obedient**.

rebound verb
1 *The dart rebounded off the wall.* SEE **bounce**, ricochet, spring back.
2 *His wily plan rebounded on him.* [*informal*] backfire, [*informal*] boomerang, misfire, recoil.

rebuild noun
1 *to rebuild a town.* build again, reconstruct, redevelop, regenerate.
2 *to rebuild an old car.* make good, overhaul, reassemble, recondition, recreate, refashion, remake, renew, renovate, repair, restore.

rebuke noun, verb SEE **reprimand** noun, verb.

recall verb
1 *The garage recalled the faulty cars.* bring back, call in, withdraw.
2 *Try to recall what happened.* SEE **remember**.

recede verb
The flood gradually receded. decline, ebb, go back, regress, retire, retreat, return, shrink back, slacken, subside.

receipt noun
a receipt for goods bought. account,
acknowledgement, bill, proof of purchase,
ticket.
receipts gains, gate (*at a football match*),
income, proceeds, profits, takings.

receive verb
1 *to receive payment for something.* accept,
acquire, be given, be sent, collect, earn, get,
obtain, take.
OPPOSITES: SEE **give**.
2 *to receive an injury.* bear, experience,
suffer, sustain, undergo.
OPPOSITES: SEE **inflict**.
3 *to receive visitors.* accommodate, entertain,
greet, meet, welcome.

receiver noun
a radio receiver. apparatus, radio, set, tuner,
[*old-fashioned*] wireless.

recent adjective
recent events. recent innovations.
contemporary, current, fresh, modern, new,
novel, present-day, up-to-date.
OPPOSITES: SEE **old**.

receptacle noun
SEE **container**.

reception noun
1 *They gave us a friendly reception.* greeting,
welcome.
2 *a wedding reception.* SEE **party**.

receptive adjective
receptive to new ideas. amenable, favourable,
interested, kindly disposed, open, open-
minded, responsive, susceptible,
sympathetic, welcoming.

recess noun
1 *a recess in a wall.* alcove, apse, bay, cavity,
corner, hollow, indentation, niche, nook.
2 *a recess during a meeting.* adjournment,
break, breathing-space, interlude,
intermission, interval, respite, rest.

recession noun
an economic recession. decline, depression,
downturn, slump.

reciprocate verb
Did she reciprocate his love? exchange, give
the same in return, match, requite, return.

recital noun
1 *a piano recital.* concert, performance,
programme.
2 *a recital of events.* account, narration,
narrative, SEE **recitation**, repetition, story,
telling.

recitation noun
a recitation of a poem. declaiming, delivery,
narration, performance, [*old-fashioned*]
rendition, speaking, telling.

recite verb
to recite a poem. articulate, declaim, deliver,
narrate, perform, recount, rehearse, relate,
repeat, speak, tell.

reckless adjective
1 *reckless driving. reckless extravagance.*
brash, careless, [*informal*] crazy, daredevil,
foolhardy, [*informal*] harum-scarum, hasty,
heedless, imprudent, impulsive, inattentive,
incautious, irresponsible, [*informal*] mad,
madcap, negligent, rash, thoughtless,
unconsidered.
OPPOSITES: SEE **careful**.
2 *reckless criminals.* dangerous, desperate,
violent, wild.

reckon verb
1 *I reckoned up how much she owed me.* add
up, assess, calculate, compute, count,
estimate, evaluate, figure out, gauge,
number, total, work out.
2 [*informal*] *I reckon it's going to rain.* SEE
think.

reclaim verb
1 *to reclaim derelict land.* make usable,
regenerate, reinstate, restore, salvage, save.

recline verb
to recline on a sofa. lean back, lie, loll,
lounge, rest, sprawl, stretch out.

recluse noun
a recluse who never appears in public.
hermit, loner, solitary.

recognizable adjective
a recognizable figure. distinctive,
distinguishable, identifiable, known,
undisguised, unmistakable.

recognize verb
1 *to recognize a person. to recognize a
landmark.* discern, distinguish, identify,
know, name, perceive, pick out, [*informal*]
put a name to, recall, recollect, remember,
see, spot.
2 *The doctor recognized the symptoms.* detect,
diagnose, notice, perceive.
3 *I recognize my shortcomings.* accept,
acknowledge, admit to, be aware of, concede,
confess, grant, realize, understand.

recoil verb
1 *His wily plan recoiled on him.* SEE **rebound**.
2 *I recoiled when I saw blood.* blench, draw
back, falter, flinch, jerk back, quail, shrink,
wince.

recollect verb
SEE **remember**.

recollection noun
I have no recollection of what happened. SEE
memory.

recommend verb
1 *The doctor recommends a complete rest.*
advise, advocate, counsel, prescribe,
propose, suggest, urge.
2 *The critics recommend this film.* applaud,
approve of, commend, [*informal*] plug,
praise, speak well of, vouch for.

reconcile verb
*I managed to reconcile them after their
quarrel.* bring together, conciliate,
harmonize, placate, reunite.

reconnaissance noun
*The troops moved in after a reconnaissance
of the area.* examination, exploration,
inspection, investigation, observation,
reconnoitring, spying, survey.

record noun
1 *We kept a record of what we saw.* account,
chronicle, diary, dossier, file, journal, log,
minute (*minutes of a meeting*), narrative,
note, register, report.
2 [*plural*] *historical records.* annals,
archives, documents.
3 *a gramophone record.* album, disc, long-
playing record, LP, SEE **recording**, single.
4 *Her time in the last race was a school record.*
[*informal*] best, [*informal*] highest.

record verb
1 *I recorded what I saw in a notebook.* enter,
inscribe, log, minute, note, put down,
register, set down, write down.
2 *We recorded our performance on tape.* keep,
preserve, tape, tape-record, video.

recording noun
Have you heard their latest recording?
performance, release.

KINDS OF RECORDING: audio-tape, cassette,
compact disc, digital recording, mono
recording, quadraphonic recording, SEE
record noun, stereo recording, tape, tape-
recording, tele-recording, video, video-
cassette, video disc, video-tape.

---

recount verb
He recounted his adventures. describe, detail,
narrate, recite, relate, report, retail, tell.

recover verb
1 *to recover after an illness.* come round,
convalesce, get better, heal, improve, mend,
[*informal*] pull round, [*informal*] pull
through, rally, recuperate, revive.
2 *to recover something you have lost.* find, get
back, make good, recapture, reclaim,
recoup, regain, repossess, restore, retrieve,
salvage, trace, track down.

recovery noun
1 *recovery from an illness.* convalescence,
cure, healing, improvement, recuperation.

2 *the recovery of business after a recession.*
revival, upturn.
3 *recovery of something you had lost.*
recapture, reclamation, repossession,
restoration, retrieval, salvaging.

recreation noun
*We deserve some recreation after working
hard.* amusement, diversion, enjoyment,
entertainment, fun, games, hobby, leisure,
pastime, play, pleasure, relaxation.

recrimination noun
*I don't want any recriminations if this goes
wrong.* accusation, [*informal*] come-back,
retaliation, retort.

recruit noun
*a recruit in the services. a new recruit to the
firm.* apprentice, beginner, conscript,
learner, [*informal*] new boy, [*informal*] new
girl, new member, novice, tiro, trainee.
OPPOSITES: SEE **veteran** noun.

recruit verb
to recruit new staff. advertise for, engage,
enlist, enrol, mobilize, sign on, take on.

rectify verb
SEE **correct** verb.

recuperate verb
SEE **recover**.

recur verb
Go to the dentist if the pain recurs. come
again, persist, reappear, repeat, return.

recurrent adjective
a recurrent illness. recurrent problems.
chronic, SEE **continual**, cyclical, frequent,
intermittent, periodic, persistent, recurring,
regular, repeated.

recycle verb
to recycle waste. reclaim, recover, retrieve,
re-use, salvage, use again.

red adjective
red in the face. blushing, embarrassed,
flaming, florid, flushed, glowing, inflamed,
rosy, rubicund, ruddy.

VARIOUS SHADES OF RED: auburn, blood-red,
brick-red, cardinal red, carmine, carroty,
cerise, cherry, crimson, damask, flame-
coloured, magenta, maroon, pink, rose,
roseate, ruby, scarlet, vermilion, wine-
coloured.

---

redden verb
His face reddened with embarrassment.
blush, colour, flush, glow.

redeem verb
1 *He redeemed his watch from the
pawnbroker's.* buy back, reclaim, recover,
re-purchase.

2 *I redeemed some Premium Bonds.* cash in, exchange for cash, trade in.
to redeem yourself *After playing badly for weeks, he redeemed himself by scoring a goal.* SEE **atone**.

redo verb SEE **renew**, **repeat**.

reduce verb
1 *to reduce the amount or intensity or effect of something.* commute (*to commute a prison sentence*), curtail, cut, cut back, decimate [see note under *decimate*], decrease, detract from, devalue, dilute, diminish, [*informal*] dock (*to dock someone's wages*), halve, impair, lessen, lower, make less, minimize, moderate, narrow, shorten, shrink, [*informal*] slash, slim down, trim, truncate, weaken, whittle.
2 *Our supplies gradually reduced.* become less, contract, dwindle, shrink.
OPPOSITES: SEE **increase** verb.

reduction noun
1 *a reduction in amount or intensity or effect.* contraction, cutback, deceleration [= *reduction in speed*], decimation, decline, decrease, diminution, drop, impairment, lessening, limitation, loss, moderation, narrowing, remission, shortening, shrinkage, weakening.
2 *a reduction in price.* concession, cut, depreciation, devaluation, discount, rebate, refund.
OPPOSITES: SEE **increase** noun.

redundant adjective
redundant workers. Omit any redundant words in your essay. excessive, superfluous, surplus, too many, unnecessary, unwanted.
OPPOSITES: SEE **necessary**.

reel noun
a reel of cotton. bobbin, spool.

reel verb
I reeled after that knock on the head. lurch, rock, roll, spin, stagger, stumble, sway, totter, whirl, wobble.

refer verb
1 *I won't refer to your mistake.* allude to, cite, comment on, draw attention to, make reference to, mention, quote, speak of, touch on.
2 *They didn't have what I wanted, so they referred me to another shop.* direct, guide, recommend, send.
to refer to *If I can't spell a word, I refer to my dictionary.* consult, go to, look up, turn to.

referee noun
adjudicator, arbitrator, judge, umpire.

reference noun
1 *Which book does this reference come from?* allusion, citation, example, illustration,

instance, mention, quotation, remark.
2 *When you apply for jobs you need a reference.* recommendation, testimonial.

refine verb
1 *to refine raw materials.* clarify, distil, process, purify, treat.
2 *to refine your behaviour.* SEE **improve**.

refined adjective
1 *refined tastes.* civilized, courteous, cultivated, cultured, delicate, dignified, discerning, discriminating, elegant, fastidious, genteel, gentlemanly, ladylike, nice, polished, polite, [*informal*] posh, [*uncomplimentary*] pretentious, [*uncomplimentary*] prissy, sophisticated, subtle, tasteful, [*informal*] upper crust, urbane, well-bred, well brought-up.
OPPOSITES: SEE **vulgar**.
2 *refined oil.* distilled, processed, purified, treated.
OPPOSITES: SEE **crude**.

refinement noun
1 *refinement of manners.* breeding, [*informal*] class (*She's got real class*), courtesy, cultivation, delicacy, discrimination, elegance, finesse, gentility, polish, [*uncomplimentary*] pretentiousness, sophistication, style, subtlety, taste, urbanity.
2 *They've made some refinements in the design of the new model.* alteration, change, improvement, modification.

reflect verb
1 *A mirror reflects your image. Cat's-eyes reflect headlights.* mirror, return, send back, shine back, throw back.
2 *Their success reflects their hard work.* bear witness to, correspond to, demonstrate, echo, exhibit, indicate, match, reveal, show.
to reflect on *to reflect on past events.* brood on, [*informal*] chew over, consider, contemplate, meditate on, ponder, remind yourself of, reminisce about, ruminate, talk over, think about.

reflection noun
1 *a reflection in a mirror.* image, likeness.
2 *Their success is a reflection of their hard work.* demonstration, echo, indication, manifestation, result.
3 *Your exam failure is no reflection on your intelligence.* censure, criticism, discredit, reproach, shame, slur.
4 *a quiet time for reflection.* contemplation, deliberation, meditation, pondering, rumination, study, thinking, thought.

reflector noun
Cat's-eyes, looking-glass, mirror, reflective glass, reflective patch.

reflex adjective
a reflex action. SEE **involuntary**.

reform verb
1 *to reform your behaviour.* amend, become better, change, convert, correct, improve, make better, save.
2 *to reform a political system.* purge, reconstitute, regenerate, remodel, reorganize, revolutionize.

refrain verb
to refrain from *Please refrain from smoking.* abstain from, avoid, desist from, do without, eschew, forbear, [*informal*] quit, stop.

refresh verb
1 *The drink refreshed us.* cool, freshen, invigorate, quench the thirst of, rejuvenate, renew, restore, revitalize, revive.
2 *Let me refresh your memory.* jog, remind, prod, prompt, stimulate.

refreshing adjective
1 *a refreshing drink. a refreshing shower.* bracing, cool, enlivening, invigorating, restorative, reviving, stimulating, thirst-quenching, tingling.
OPPOSITES: SEE **cloying, exhausting**.
2 *a refreshing change.* different, fresh, interesting, new, novel, original, unexpected, unfamiliar, unforeseen, unpredictable, welcome.
OPPOSITES: SEE **boring**.

refrigerate verb
to refrigerate food. chill, cool, freeze, keep cold, SEE **preserve** verb.

refuge noun
The climbers found refuge from the blizzard. asylum, [*informal*] bolt-hole, cover, haven, hideout, hiding-place, protection, retreat, safety, sanctuary, security, shelter.

refugee noun
displaced person, exile, fugitive, outcast.

refund noun
If you are not satisfied, ask for a refund. rebate, repayment.

refund verb
to refund expenses. give back, pay back, recoup, reimburse, repay, return.

refusal noun
Our request was met with a refusal. [*informal*] brush-off, denial, negative reply, rebuff, rejection.
OPPOSITES: SEE **acceptance**.

refuse noun
Throw away the refuse. SEE **rubbish**.

refuse verb
1 *to refuse an invitation.* baulk at, decline, give a negative reply to, [*informal*] jib at, reject, say no to, spurn, turn down.

OPPOSITES: SEE **accept**.
2 *to refuse someone their rights.* deny, deprive of, withhold.
OPPOSITES: SEE **grant** verb.

refute verb
to refute an argument. counter, discredit, disprove, negate, prove wrong, rebut.

regain verb
to regain something you've lost. be reunited with, find, get back, recapture, reclaim, recoup, recover, repossess, retake, retrieve, return to, win back.

regal adjective
a regal figure. kingly, majestic, noble, princely, queenly, royal, SEE **splendid**, stately.

regard noun
1 *I quailed under his stern regard.* gaze, look, scrutiny, state.
2 *Give due regard to the warnings.* attention, care, concern, consideration, deference, heed, notice, respect, thought.
3 *I have a high regard for her ability.* admiration, affection, esteem, honour, love, respect.

regard verb
1 *to regard something closely.* contemplate, eye, gaze at, look at, observe, scrutinize, stare at, view, watch.
2 *We regard her as our best swimmer.* account, consider, deem, esteem, judge, reckon, respect, think, value.

regarding preposition
about, concerning, connected with, involving, on the subject of, with reference to, with regard to.

regardless adjective
regardless of danger. careless (about), heedless, indifferent (to), neglectful, uncaring (about), unconcerned (about), unmindful.

regenerate verb SEE **renew**.

region noun
The Arctic is a cold region. area, SEE **country**, district, expanse, land, locality, neighbourhood, place, province, quarter, territory, tract, vicinity, zone.

register noun
a register of names and addresses. catalogue, directory, file, index, ledger, list, record, roll.

register verb
1 *to register as a voter. to register as a member of a club.* enlist, enrol, enter your name, join, sign on.
2 *to register a complaint.* make official, present, record, set down, write down.
3 *Did you register what she was wearing?*

keep in mind, make a note of, mark, notice, take account of.
4 *His face registered pleasure.* express, indicate, reveal, show.

regress verb
Business tends to regress during a holiday. backslide, degenerate, deteriorate, fall back, go back, move backwards, retreat, retrogress, revert, slip back.
OPPOSITES: SEE **progress** verb.

regret noun
1 *regret for doing wrong.* compunction, contrition, guilt, penitence, pricking of conscience, remorse, repentance, self-accusation, shame.
2 *regret about someone's loss.* grief, sadness, sorrow, sympathy.

regret verb
1 *I regret that I lost my temper.* be regretful [SEE **regretful**], feel regret [SEE **regret** noun], repent, reproach yourself.
2 *I deeply regret the death of your friend.* be sad about, feel regret about [SEE **regret** noun], grieve over, lament, mourn.

regretful adjective
a regretful smile. apologetic, ashamed, conscience-stricken, contrite, disappointed, penitent, remorseful, repentant, SEE **sad**, sorry.
OPPOSITES: SEE **happy, unrepentant**.

regrettable adjective
a regrettable accident. deplorable, disappointing, distressing, lamentable, reprehensible, sad, shameful, undesirable, unfortunate, unhappy, unlucky, unwanted.

regular adjective
1 *regular intervals. a regular pattern.* consistent, constant, daily, equal, even, fixed, hourly, measured, monthly, ordered, predictable, recurring, repeated, rhythmic, steady, symmetrical, systematic, uniform, unvarying, weekly, yearly.
2 *the regular procedure. our regular postman.* accustomed, common, commonplace, conventional, customary, established, everyday, familiar, frequent, habitual, known, normal, official, ordinary, orthodox, prevailing, proper, routine, scheduled, standard, traditional, typical, usual.
3 *a regular supporter.* dependable, faithful, reliable.
OPPOSITES: SEE **irregular**.

regular noun
She's one of the regulars here. [*informal*] faithful, frequenter, habitué, regular customer [SEE **regular** adjective], patron.

regulate verb
1 *to regulate the traffic.* control, direct, govern, manage, order, organize, restrict, supervise.
2 *to regulate the temperature.* adjust, alter, change, get right, moderate, vary.

regulation noun
Obey the regulations. by-law, commandment, decree, directive, edict, law, order, requirement, restriction, rule, statute.

rehearsal noun
a rehearsal for a play. practice, preparation, [*informal*] run-through, [*informal*] try-out.

rehearse verb
to rehearse a play. go over, practise, prepare, [*informal*] run over (*Just run over the last scene*), try out.

rehearsed adjective
I'm sure his remarks were rehearsed, not impromptu. calculated, practised, pre-arranged, premeditated, prepared, thought out.
OPPOSITES: SEE **impromptu**.

reign verb
Which British monarch reigned the longest? be king, be queen, be on the throne, govern, have power, rule.

reinforce verb
1 *to reinforce a wall.* back up, bolster, buttress, fortify, give strength to, hold up, prop up, stiffen, strengthen, support, toughen.
2 *to reinforce an army.* add to, assist, help, increase the size of, provide reinforcements for, supplement.

reinforcements noun
additional troops, auxiliaries, back-up, help, reserves, support.

reinstate verb
The firm reinstated the man who was wrongly dismissed. recall, rehabilitate, restore, take back, welcome back.
OPPOSITES: SEE **dismiss**.

reject verb
1 *Good shops reject sub-standard goods.* discard, eliminate, exclude, jettison, scrap, send back, throw away, throw out.
2 *It's not nice to reject your friends.* dismiss, disown, [*informal*] drop, jilt, rebuff, renounce, repel, repudiate, repulse, spurn.
3 *to reject an invitation.* decline, refuse, say no to, turn down, veto.
OPPOSITES: SEE **accept**.

rejoice verb
Everyone rejoiced in their team's success. be happy [SEE **happy**], celebrate, delight, exult, glory, revel, triumph.
OPPOSITES: SEE **grieve**.

rejoinder noun SEE **answer** noun.

relapse noun
After making some progress, he suffered a relapse. deterioration, recurrence, set-back.

relapse verb
to relapse after making progress. degenerate, deteriorate, fall back, have a relapse, regress, revert, slip back, weaken.

relate verb
1 *to relate your adventures.* describe, detail, narrate, recite, recount, rehearse, report, tell.
2 *The police related the two crimes.* associate, compare, connect, consider together, join, link.
3 *I saw a TV programme which related to a book I'd just read.* be relevant [SEE **relevant**], concern, pertain, refer.
4 *The team members relate well to each other.* be friends, fraternize, have a relationship [SEE **relationship**], socialize.

related adjective
related crimes. related businesses. related facts. affiliated, akin, allied, associated, cognate, comparable, connected, interconnected, joined, linked, parallel, similar.
OPPOSITES: SEE **separate** adjective.

relation noun
1 *the relation between two people or things.* SEE **relationship**.
2 *All our relations came to the wedding.* SEE **relative** noun.

relationship noun
1 *the relationship between two people or things.* affinity, association, bond, connection, [*formal*] consanguinity, contrast, correlation, correspondence, kinship, link, parallel, ratio (= *relationship of one number to another*), similarity, tie.
2 *The twins have a close relationship.* attachment, closeness, SEE **friendship**, rapport, understanding.
3 [*informal*] *a sexual relationship.* affair, [*informal*] intrigue, [*informal*] liaison, love affair, romance, sexual relations.
FAMILY RELATIONSHIPS: SEE **family**.

relative noun
All our relatives came to the wedding. [*old-fashioned*] kinsman, [*old-fashioned*] kinswoman, [*plural*] kith and kin, member of the family, relation.
FAMILY RELATIONSHIPS: SEE **family**.

relax verb
1 *to relax your grip. to relax the pressure on something.* diminish, ease off, lessen, loosen, moderate, reduce, release, relieve, slacken, soften, unclench, unfasten, weaken.
OPPOSITES: SEE **increase, tighten**.
2 *to relax in front of the TV.* be easy, be

relaxed [SEE **relaxed**], feel at home, rest, unbend, unwind.

relaxed adjective
a relaxed atmosphere. a relaxed conversation. calm, carefree, casual, comfortable, contented, cosy, easygoing, friendly, good-humoured, happy, informal, [*informal*] laid-back, leisurely, light-hearted, nonchalant, reassuring, restful, serene, [*uncomplimentary*] SEE **slack** adjective, tranquil, unconcerned, unhurried, untroubled.
OPPOSITES: SEE **tense** adjective.

relay noun
1 *working in relays.* shift, turn.
2 *a live relay on TV.* broadcast, programme, transmission.

relay verb
to relay information. broadcast, communicate, pass on, send out, spread, transmit, televise.

release verb
1 *to release prisoners.* acquit, allow out, deliver, discharge, dismiss, emancipate, excuse, exonerate, free, let go, let loose, liberate, loose, pardon, rescue, save, set free, set loose, unleash, untie.
OPPOSITES: SEE **detain**.
2 *to release a missile.* fire off, launch, let fly, let off, send off.
3 *to release information.* circulate, disseminate, distribute, issue, make available, publish, send out.

relent verb
He was cross at first, but later he relented. become more lenient, give in, show pity, soften, weaken, yield.

relentless adjective
a relentless attack. relentless nagging. SEE **continual**, cruel, fierce, hard-hearted, implacable, incessant, inexorable, merciless, pitiless, remorseless, ruthless, unceasing, uncompromising, unfeeling, unforgiving, unmerciful, unrelieved, unremitting.
OPPOSITES: SEE **temporary**.

relevant adjective
Don't interrupt unless you have something relevant to say. appertaining, applicable, apposite, appropriate, apropos, apt, connected, essential, fitting, germane, linked, material, pertinent, related, relative, significant, suitable, to the point.
OPPOSITES: SEE **irrelevant**.

reliable adjective
reliable information. a reliable friend. a reliable car. certain, consistent, constant, dependable, devoted, efficient, faithful, loyal, predictable, proven, regular,

responsible, safe, solid, sound, stable, staunch, steady, sure, trustworthy, unchanging, unfailing.
OPPOSITES: SEE **unreliable**.

relic noun
a relic from the past. memento, reminder, remnant, souvenir, survival, token, vestige.

relief noun
The pills gave some relief from the pain. abatement, aid, alleviation, assistance, comfort, cure, diversion, ease, easement, help, [*informal*] let-up, mitigation, palliation, relaxation, release, remission, respite, rest.

relieve verb
to relieve pain. to relieve pressure on something. alleviate, anaesthetize, assuage, bring relief [SEE **relief**], calm, comfort, console, cure, diminish, dull, ease, SEE **help** verb, lessen, lighten, make less, mitigate, moderate, palliate, reduce, relax, soothe.
OPPOSITES: SEE **intensify**.

religion noun
1 *the religions of the world.* creed, cult, denomination, faith, sect.
2 *An evangelist preaches religion.* belief, doctrine, dogma, theology.
COMPARE: humanism.

SOME PRINCIPAL WORLD RELIGIONS: Buddhism, Christianity, Hinduism, Islam, Judaism, Sikhism, Taoism, Zen.

CHRISTIAN DENOMINATIONS: SEE **denomination**.

OTHER RELATED WORDS: SEE **church**, **clergyman**, **worship**.

---

religious adjective
1 *a religious service. religious writings.* devotional, divine, holy, sacramental, sacred, scriptural, theological.
OPPOSITES: SEE **secular**.
2 *a religious person.* committed, dedicated, devout, God-fearing, godly, pious, reverent, [*uncomplimentary*] religiose, righteous, [*uncomplimentary*] sanctimonious, spiritual.
OPPOSITES: SEE **irreligious**.
3 *a religious dispute. religious wars.* bigoted, doctrinal, fanatical, sectarian, schismatic.

relinquish verb
SEE **surrender**.

relish verb
She relishes a challenge. appreciate, delight in, enjoy, like, love, revel in.

reluctant adjective
I was reluctant to pay what they demanded. disinclined, grudging, hesitant, loath, unenthusiastic, SEE **unwilling**.
OPPOSITES: SEE **eager**.

rely verb
You can rely on me to do my best. [*informal*] bank on, count on, depend on, have confidence in, trust.

remain verb
Only half the audience remained at the end of the concert. be left, carry on, continue, endure, keep on, linger, live on, persist, stay, survive.

remainder noun
Use what you can now, and keep the remainder for later. balance, excess, extra, SEE **remains**, remnant, residue, rest, surplus.

remaining adjective
abiding, continuing, left over, persisting, residual, surviving, unused.

remains noun
1 *the remains of something that has been used, damaged, or destroyed.* crumbs, debris, dregs, fragments, [*informal*] left-overs, [*informal*] odds and ends, SEE **remainder**, remnants, residue, rubble, ruins, scraps, traces, vestiges, wreckage.
2 *historic remains.* heritage, relics.
3 *the remains of a dead animal.* ashes, body, carcass, corpse.

remark noun
The judge made a few remarks about our performance. comment, mention, observation, opinion, reflection, statement, thought, utterance, word.

remark verb
1 *He remarked that it was a nice day.* comment, declare, mention, note, observe, reflect, say, state.
2 *Did you remark anything unusual?* heed, mark, notice, observe, perceive, see.

remarkable adjective
a remarkable achievement. amazing, conspicuous, distinguished, exceptional, extraordinary, important, impressive, notable, noteworthy, out of the ordinary, outstanding, phenomenal, prominent, singular, special, strange, striking, surprising, [*informal*] terrific, [*informal*] tremendous, uncommon, unusual, wonderful.
OPPOSITES: SEE **ordinary**.

remedy noun
a remedy for a cold. a remedy for a problem. [*informal*] answer, antidote, corrective, cure, elixir, medicine, nostrum, palliative, panacea [= *a cure for everything*], prescription, relief, restorative, solution, therapy, treatment.

remedy verb
I remedied the fault in the car. alleviate, correct, counteract, cure, [*informal*] fix,

heal, help, mend, mitigate, palliate, put right, rectify, redress, relieve, repair, solve, treat.

remember verb
1 *Do you remember Uncle George?* have a memory of, have in mind, recall, recognize, recollect, summon up.
2 *Remember what I say!* keep in mind, learn, memorize, retain.
OPPOSITES: SEE **forget**.
3 *We sat for hours remembering old times.* be nostalgic about, hark back to, recall, reminisce about, review, tell stories about, think back to.

remind verb
Remind me to buy potatoes. give a reminder to [SEE **reminder**], jog the memory, prompt.

reminder noun
1 *a reminder of what you have to do or say.* aide-mémoire, cue, hint, [*informal*] memo, [*formal*] memorandum, mnemonic, nudge, prompt, [*informal*] shopping list.
2 *a reminder of the past.* memento, relic, souvenir.

reminiscence noun
reminiscences of childhood. account, anecdote, memoir, memory, recollection, remembrance.

reminiscent adjective
scenes reminiscent of the past. evocative, nostalgic, recalling, redolent, suggestive.

remiss adjective
SEE **negligent**.

remnants noun SEE **remains**.

remorse noun
remorse for wrongdoing. compunction, contrition, grief, guilt, penitence, pricking of conscience, regret, repentance, sadness, self-accusation, shame, sorrow.

remorseful adjective
SEE **repentant**.

remote adjective
1 *a remote corner of the world.* alien, cut off, desolate, distant, faraway, foreign, godforsaken, hard to find, inaccessible, isolated, lonely, out of reach, outlying, out of the way, secluded, solitary, unfamiliar, unfrequented, [*informal*] unget-at-able, unreachable.
OPPOSITES: SEE **accessible**.
2 *a remote chance of winning.* doubtful, implausible, improbable, negligible, outside, poor, slender, slight, small, unlikely.
OPPOSITES: SEE **likely**.
3 *a remote manner.* aloof, cold, cool, detached, haughty, preoccupied, reserved,

standoffish, uninvolved, withdrawn.
OPPOSITES: SEE **friendly**.

removal noun
1 *the removal of furniture from a house.* relocation, taking away, transfer, transportation.
2 *the removal of a tooth.* drawing, extraction, taking out, withdrawal.
3 *the removal of someone from a job or position.* dismissal, displacement, ejection, elimination, eradication, exile, expulsion, ousting, purge, purging.

remove verb
1 *to remove unwanted people or things.* abolish, abstract, amputate (*amputate a limb*), clear away, cut out, delete, depose (*depose a monarch*), detach, disconnect, dismiss, dispense with, displace, eject, eliminate, eradicate, erase, evict (*evict a tenant*), excise, exile, expel, expunge, [*informal*] get rid of, [*informal*] kick out, kill, oust, purge, root out, rub out, send away, separate, strike out (*strike out words in a document*), take out, throw out, turn out, uproot, wash off, wipe (*wipe a recording from a tape*), wipe out.
2 *to remove furniture.* carry away, convey, move, take away, transfer, transport.

rend verb SEE **tear** verb.

renegade noun
Faithful supporters were bitter about the renegades. apostate, backslider, defector, deserter, fugitive, mutineer, outlaw, rebel, runaway, traitor, turncoat.

renew verb
VARIOUS WAYS TO RENEW OLD THINGS: bring up to date, [*informal*] do up, [*informal*] give a face-lift to, improve, mend, modernize, overhaul, recondition, reconstitute, recreate, redecorate, redesign, redevelop, redo, refit, refresh (*refresh the paintwork*), refurbish, regenerate, reintroduce, rejuvenate, remake, remodel, renovate, repaint, repair, replace, replenish, restore, resume, revamp, revitalize, revive, touch up, transform, update.

renewal noun
1 *the renewal of life in the spring.* reawakening, rebirth, regeneration, renaissance, resumption, resurgence, resurrection, return, revival.
2 *renewal of the paintwork.* SEE **renovation**.
3 *renewal of your passport.* replacement, revalidation, updating.

renounce verb
1 *to renounce violence.* abandon, abjure, declare your opposition to, discard, disown, forsake, forswear, reject, repudiate, spurn.
2 *to renounce the throne.* abdicate, give up, quit, relinquish, resign.

renovation noun
the renovation of an old building.
improvement, modernization, overhaul,
reconditioning, redevelopment, refit,
refurbishment, renewal, repair, restoration,
transformation, updating.

renovate verb
SEE **renew**.

renowned adjective SEE **famous**.

rent noun
1 *I forgot to pay the rent for the TV.* fee, hire,
instalment, regular payment, rental.
2 *a rent in my jeans.* SEE **tear** noun.

rent verb
We rented a caravan for our holiday. charter,
hire, lease, let.

reorganize verb
*to reorganize a business. to reorganize your
time.* rearrange, redeploy, reshuffle,
restructure.

repair verb
to repair a damaged car. [*informal*] fix,
mend, overhaul, patch up, put right, rectify,
refit, SEE **renew**, service.

repay verb
1 *They repaid my expenses.* compensate, pay
back, recompense, refund, reimburse,
remunerate, settle.
2 [*uncomplimentary*] *She repaid his insult
with interest.* avenge, get even with,
[*informal*] get your own back for,
reciprocate, requite, retaliate, return,
revenge.

repeat verb
to repeat an action or an event or a saying.
do again, duplicate, echo, quote,
recapitulate, redo, re-echo, regurgitate,
rehearse, reiterate, replay, reproduce, re-
run, restate, retell, say again, show again.

repel verb
1 *to repel an attack.* check, drive away, fend
off, fight off, hold off, parry, push away,
rebuff, repulse, ward off.
2 *This oily material repels water.* be
impermeable to, exclude, keep out, reject,
resist.
OPPOSITES: SEE **attract**.
3 *Her callous attitude repels me.* disgust,
nauseate, offend, [*informal*] put off (*Her
attitude puts me off*), revolt, sicken,
[*informal*] turn off (*Her attitude turns me
off*).
OPPOSITES: SEE **delight** verb.

repellent adjective
SEE **repulsive**.

repent verb
to repent your sins. be repentant about [SEE
repentant], feel repentance for [SEE
repentance], regret, reproach yourself for.

repentance noun
contrition, guilt, penitence, regret, remorse,
self-accusation, self-reproach, sorrow.

repentant adjective
*He was repentant when he saw what he'd
done.* apologetic, ashamed, conscience-
stricken, contrite, grief-stricken, guilt-
ridden, guilty, penitent, regretful,
remorseful, sorry.
OPPOSITES: SEE **unrepentant**.

repetitive adjective
a repetitive job. a repetitive story. boring,
monotonous, recurrent, repeating,
repetitious, tautological, tedious,
unchanging, unvaried.

replace verb
1 *Replace the books on the shelf.* put back,
reinstate, restore, return.
2 *Who will replace the present prime minister?*
be a substitute for, come after, follow, oust,
succeed, supersede, supplant, take over
from, take the place of.
3 *It's time we replaced those tyres.* change,
provide a substitute for, renew.

replacement noun
a replacement for the regular teacher.
[*informal*] fill-in, proxy, stand-in,
substitute, successor, understudy
[= *replacement for an actor*].

replica noun
*a replica of a lunar-module. a replica of a
document.* clone, copy, duplicate, facsimile,
imitation, model, reconstruction,
reproduction.

reply noun
a reply to a letter or a question.
acknowledgement, answer, [*informal*]
come-back, reaction, rejoinder, response,
retort, [*joking*] riposte.

reply verb
to reply to *to reply to a letter or a question.*
acknowledge, answer, counter, react to,
respond to.

report noun
1 *a report in a newspaper. a report on an
investigation.* account, announcement,
article, communication, communiqué,
description, dispatch, narrative, news,
record, statement, story, [*informal*] write-
up.
2 *the report of a gun.* bang, blast, crack,
detonation, explosion, noise.

report verb
1 *I reported the results of my investigation.*
announce, circulate, communicate, declare,
describe, document, give an account of,
notify, present a report on [SEE **report** noun],
proclaim, publish, record, recount, reveal,
state, tell.

2 *Report to reception when you arrive.*
announce yourself, introduce yourself, make
yourself known, present yourself.
3 *I reported him to the police.* complain about,
SEE **denounce**, inform against, [*informal*]
tell of.

reporter noun
a newspaper reporter. correspondent,
journalist.

repose noun
a moment of repose in the midst of activity.
calm, comfort, ease, inactivity, peace,
peacefulness, poise, quiet, quietness,
relaxation, respite, rest, serenity, stillness,
tranquillity.

reprehensible adjective
reprehensible behaviour. SEE **bad**,
blameworthy, culpable, deplorable,
disgraceful, immoral, objectionable,
regrettable, remiss, shameful, unworthy,
wicked.
OPPOSITES: SEE **praiseworthy**.

represent verb
1 *Our pageant represented scenes from
history.* act out, delineate, depict, describe,
draw, enact, exhibit, illustrate, paint,
picture, portray, show.
2 *Santa Claus represents the spirit of
Christmas.* embody, epitomize, exemplify,
incarnate, personify, stand for, symbolize.
3 *Our spokesperson represents the views of us
all.* be an example of, express, present, speak
for.

representation noun
a representation of a goddess. depiction,
figure, icon, image, imitation, likeness,
model, picture, portrait, portrayal,
resemblance, statue.

representative noun
1 *a representative who speaks for someone
else.* delegate [= *a person representing a
group*], deputy, proxy, stand-in, substitute.
2 *a sales representative.* agent, [*informal*]
rep, salesman, salesperson, saleswoman,
[*informal*] traveller.
3 *a government representative.* ambassador,
consul, diplomat.

repress verb
to repress your feelings. [*informal*] bottle up,
control, crush, curb, inhibit, keep down,
quell, restrain, stifle, suppress.

repressed adjective
1 *a repressed person.* cold, frigid, inhibited,
neurotic, unbalanced.
2 *repressed emotions.* [*informal*] bottled up,
hidden, latent, subconscious, suppressed,
unconscious, unfulfilled.
OPPOSITES: SEE **uninhibited**.

repressive adjective
repressive laws. authoritarian, autocratic,
coercive, cruel, despotic, dictatorial, harsh,
illiberal, oppressive, restricting, severe,
totalitarian, tyrannical, undemocratic,
unenlightened.
OPPOSITES: SEE **liberal**.

reprieve verb
to reprieve a condemned prisoner. forgive, let
off, pardon, set free, spare.

reprimand noun
*The teacher gave the class a severe
reprimand.* admonition, censure, [*informal*]
dressing-down, [*informal*] going-over,
lecture, lesson, rebuke, reproach, reproof,
scolding, [*informal*] talking-to, [*informal*]
telling-off, [*informal*] ticking-off, [*informal*]
wigging.

reprimand verb
to reprimand a wrongdoer. admonish,
censure, chide, condemn, criticize,
lecture, [*informal*] rap, rate,
rebuke, reprehend, reproach,
reprove, scold, [*informal*] slate,
[*informal*]take to task, [*informal*] teach
(someone) a lesson, [*informal*] tell off,
[*informal*] tick off, upbraid.
OPPOSITES: SEE **congratulate**.

reprisal noun
a reprisal against the attackers. counter-
attack, retaliation, retribution, revenge,
vengeance.

reproach verb
to reproach someone you disapprove of.
censure, criticize, SEE **reprimand** verb, show
disapproval of, upbraid.
OPPOSITES: SEE **praise** verb.

reproachful adjective
a reproachful frown. censorious, critical,
disapproving, reproving, scornful,
withering.

reproduce verb
1 *to reproduce a document.* copy, counterfeit,
duplicate, forge, imitate, mimic, photocopy,
print, redo, reissue, SEE **repeat**, reprint,
simulate.
2 *to reproduce your own kind.* breed,
increase, multiply, procreate, produce
offspring, propagate, spawn.

reproduction noun
1 *the reproduction of animals or plants.*
breeding, increase, multiplying, procreation,
propagation.
2 *a reproduction of an original picture.* copy,
duplicate, facsimile, fake, forgery,
imitation, likeness, print, replica.

reptile noun

SOME REPTILES: alligator, basilisk,
chameleon, crocodile, lizard, salamander,
snake, tortoise, turtle.

repugnant adjective
SEE **repulsive**.

repulse verb
SEE **repel**.

repulsive adjective
repulsive behaviour. a repulsive appearance.
abhorrent, disagreeable, disgusting,
distasteful, foul, hateful, hideous,
loathsome, nauseating, objectionable,
obnoxious, odious, offensive, [*informal*] offputting, repellent, repugnant, revolting,
sickening, SEE **ugly**, unattractive,
unpleasant, unsightly, vile.
OPPOSITES: SEE **attractive**.

reputable adjective
a reputable business. dependable, esteemed,
famous, highly regarded, honoured,
prestigious, reliable, respectable, respected,
trustworthy, unimpeachable, [*informal*]
upmarket, well thought of.
OPPOSITES: SEE **disreputable**.

reputation noun
a good reputation for reliability. character,
fame, name, prestige, recognition, renown,
repute, standing.

reputed adjective
reputed to be of good quality. alleged,
believed, considered, famed, reckoned,
regarded, rumoured, said, supposed,
thought.

request noun
He didn't listen to our request. appeal,
application, call, demand, entreaty,
petition, plea, prayer, question, requisition,
[*formal*] suit, supplication.

request verb
*We requested help. He requested to see my
licence.* adjure, appeal (for), apply (for), ask,
beg, call (for), claim, demand, desire,
entreat, implore, importune, invite,
[*formal*] petition, pray for, require,
requisition, seek, solicit, [*formal*]
supplicate.

require verb
1 *We required 3 runs to win.* be short of,
depend on, lack, need, want.
2 *The officer required me to show my licence.*
command, compel, direct, force, instruct,
make, oblige, order, SEE **request** verb.

requisition verb
*to requisition vehicles to deal with an
emergency.* appropriate, commandeer,
occupy, seize, take over.

rescue noun
*the rescue of a prisoner. a heroic rescue at
sea.* deliverance, liberation, recovery,
release, relief, salvage.

rescue verb
1 *to rescue someone from captivity.* deliver,
extricate, free, liberate, ransom, release,
save, set free.
2 *I rescued my belongings from the flood.*
bring away, recover, retrieve, salvage.

research noun
research into the causes of disease.
experimentation, exploration, inquiry,
investigation, [*informal*] probe, searching,
study.

resemblance noun
the resemblance of twins. affinity, closeness,
correspondence, likeness, similarity,
similitude.

resemble verb
Twins usually resemble each other. be similar
to, look like, mirror, [*informal*] take after.

resent verb
to resent someone else's success. begrudge, be
resentful about [SEE **resentful**], dislike, envy,
grudge, grumble at, object to, [*informal*]
take exception to, [*informal*] take umbrage
at.

resentful adjective
*resentful feelings about someone else's
success.* aggrieved, SEE **angry**, annoyed,
bitter, displeased, embittered, envious,
grudging, hurt, indignant, jaundiced,
jealous, malicious, offended, [*informal*]
peeved, [*informal*] put out, spiteful,
unfriendly, ungenerous, upset, vexed,
vindictive.

resentment noun
feelings of resentment. SEE **anger** noun,
animosity, bitterness, discontent, grudge,
hatred, hurt, ill-will, indignation,
malevolence, malice, pique, rancour, spite,
unfriendliness, vexation, vindictiveness.

reserve noun
1 *a reserve of food.* fund, hoard, reservoir,
savings, stock, stockpile, store, supply.
2 *reserves for a game of football.* deputy,
[*plural*] reinforcements, replacement,
stand-by, [*informal*] stand-in, substitute,
understudy.
3 *a wildlife reserve.* enclave, game park,
preserve, protected area, reservation,
safari-park, sanctuary.
4 *Overcome your reserve and join in.*
aloofness, caution, modesty, reluctance,

reticence, self-consciousness, self-effacement, shyness, timidity.

reserve verb
1 *Reserve some food to eat later.* earmark, hoard, hold back, keep, keep back, preserve, put aside, retain, save, set aside, stockpile, store up.
2 *We reserved seats on the train.* [*informal*] bag, book, order, pay for.

reserved adjective
too reserved to speak up for herself. aloof, bashful, cautious, cool, demure, diffident, discreet, distant, modest, quiet, restrained, reticent, retiring, secretive, self-conscious, self-effacing, shy, silent, [*uncomplimentary*] standoffish, taciturn, timid, uncommunicative, undemonstrative, unforthcoming, withdrawn.
OPPOSITES: SEE **demonstrative**.

reside verb
to reside in dwell in, have as a home, inhabit, live in, lodge in, occupy, settle in.

residence noun
your permanent residence. [*old-fashioned*] abode, address, [*formal*] domicile, dwelling, habitation, home, SEE **house** noun.

resident noun
the residents of an area. citizen, denizen, inhabitant, [*informal*] local, native.

residue noun
SEE **remainder**.

resign verb
to resign your job. abdicate, forsake, give up, leave, quit, relinquish, renounce, stand down from, surrender, vacate.

resigned adjective
resigned about your problems. calm, [*uncomplimentary*] defeatist, long-suffering, patient, philosophical, reasonable, stoical, submissive.

resilient adjective
1 *Rubber is a resilient material.* bouncy, elastic, firm, plastic, pliable, rubbery, springy, supple.
OPPOSITES: SEE **brittle**.
2 *a resilient person.* adaptable, buoyant, irrepressible, strong, tough, unstoppable.
OPPOSITES: SEE **vulnerable**.

resist verb
to resist arrest. to resist temptation. avoid, be resistant to [SEE **resistant**], counteract, defy, SEE **fight** verb, oppose, prevent, refuse, stand up to, withstand.

resistant adjective
resistant to heat. resistant to temptation. hostile, impervious, invulnerable, opposed,

repellent, unaffected (by), unresponsive, unsusceptible, unyielding.
OPPOSITES: SEE **susceptible**.

resolute adjective
resolute opposition. resolute courage. adamant, bold, committed, constant, courageous, decided, decisive, determined, dogged, firm, immovable, [*uncomplimentary*] inflexible, [*uncomplimentary*] obstinate, relentless, resolved, staunch, steadfast, strong-minded, strong-willed, [*uncomplimentary*] stubborn, unbending, undaunted, unflinching, unswerving, unwavering.
OPPOSITES: SEE **irresolute**.

resolve verb
We resolved to start our own business. agree, conclude, decide formally, determine, elect, make a firm decision, opt, pass a resolution, settle, undertake, vote.

resonant adjective
a resonant voice. the resonant sound of a gong. booming, echoing, full, resounding, reverberant, reverberating, rich, ringing, sonorous, vibrant.

resort noun
Use violence only as a last resort. alternative, course of action, expedient, option, recourse, refuge.

resort verb
I don't want to resort to violence. adopt, [*informal*] fall back on, make use of, turn to, use.

resound verb
Our voices resounded in the cave. boom, echo, resonate, reverberate, ring, vibrate.

resourceful adjective
a resourceful inventor. clever, creative, enterprising, imaginative, ingenious, innovative, inspired, inventive, original, talented.
OPPOSITES: SEE **unimaginative**.

resources noun
1 *financial resources.* assets, capital, funds, SEE **money**, reserves, riches, wealth.
2 *natural resources.* materials, raw materials.

respect noun
1 *We remained silent as a sign of respect.* admiration, awe, consideration, deference, esteem, homage, honour, liking, love, regard, reverence, tribute, veneration.
2 *My work isn't perfect in every respect.* aspect, characteristic, detail, facet, feature, particular, point, way.

respect verb
Everyone respects her for her courage. admire, esteem, honour, pay homage to,

revere, reverence, show respect to [SEE
respect noun], think well of, value,
venerate.
OPPOSITES: SEE **scorn** verb.

respectable adjective
1 *respectable people*. decent, honest,
honourable, law-abiding, respected,
upright, worthy.
2 *respectable clothes*. clean, modest,
presentable, proper.
OPPOSITES: SEE **disreputable**.

respectful adjective
a respectful greeting. civil, courteous,
deferential, dutiful, gracious, humble,
polite, proper, reverent, reverential,
[*uncomplimentary*] servile, subservient.
OPPOSITES: SEE **rude**.

respective adjective
We all returned to our respective homes.
individual, own, particular, personal,
several, specific.

respond verb
to respond to *to respond to a question*.
acknowledge, answer, counter, give a
response to [SEE **response**], react to, reply to.

response noun
a response to a question. acknowledgement,
answer, [*informal*] come-back,
counterblast, feedback, reaction, rejoinder,
reply, retort, [*joking*] riposte.

responsible adjective
1 *A teacher is responsible for her class*.
accountable, answerable, in charge of.
2 *I was responsible for the damage*. culpable,
guilty, liable.
3 *We need a responsible person as treasurer*.
concerned, conscientious, dependable,
diligent, dutiful, ethical, honest, law-
abiding, loyal, mature, moral, reliable,
sensible, sober, steady, thinking, thoughtful,
trustworthy, unselfish.
OPPOSITES: SEE **irresponsible**.

responsive adjective
a responsive audience. responsive pupils.
alert, alive, aware, impressionable,
interested, open, perceptive, receptive,
sympathetic, warm-hearted, willing.
OPPOSITES: SEE **uninterested**.

rest noun
1 *a rest from work. a rest on the sofa*. break,
[*informal*] breather, breathing-space,
comfort, ease, holiday, idleness, inactivity,
interlude, intermission, interval, leisure,
[*informal*] lie-down, lull, nap, pause, quiet,
relaxation, relief, repose, siesta, time off,
vacation.
2 *a rest for a telescope*. base, holder, prop,
stand, support.

rest verb
1 *to rest on the sofa. to rest from your labours*.
be still, doze, have a rest [SEE **rest** noun],
idle, laze, lie back, lie down, lounge, nod off,
recline, relax, sleep, slumber, snooze,
[*informal*] take a nap.
2 *Rest the ladder against the wall*. lean, place,
prop, stand, support.
3 *Everything rests on the committee's decision*.
depend, hang, hinge, rely, turn.

restaurant noun
bistro, brasserie, buffet, café, cafeteria,
canteen, carvery, diner, dining-room,
eating-place, grill, snack-bar, steak-house.

restful adjective
a restful holiday. calm, comfortable,
leisurely, peaceful, quiet, relaxing,
soothing, tranquil, undisturbed, unhurried,
untroubled.
OPPOSITES: SEE **exhausting**.

restless adjective
1 *restless animals*. agitated, anxious, edgy,
excitable, fidgety, impatient, jittery, jumpy,
nervous, restive, worried.
OPPOSITES: SEE **relaxed**.
2 *a restless night*. disturbed, interrupted,
sleepless, troubled, uncomfortable,
unsettled.
OPPOSITES: SEE **restful**.

restore verb
1 *to restore something you have borrowed*.
give back, put back, replace, return.
2 *to restore an old building*. clean, [*informal*]
do up, fix, [*informal*] make good, mend,
rebuild, recondition, reconstruct, refurbish,
renew, renovate, repair, touch up.
3 *to restore good relations with the
neighbours*. bring back, re-establish,
rehabilitate, reinstate, reintroduce, revive.

restrain verb
*Please restrain your dog. Restrain your
laughter*. bridle, check, confine, control,
curb, fetter, govern, handcuff, harness, hold
back, inhibit, keep back, keep under control,
muzzle, pinion, rein in, repress, restrict,
stop, straitjacket, subdue, suppress, tie up.

restrained adjective
*In spite of his anger, his remarks were
restrained*. calm, controlled, discreet, low-
key, mild, moderate, muted, quiet,
repressed, reserved, reticent, soft, subdued,
temperate, undemonstrative, understated,
unemotional.
OPPOSITES: SEE **uninhibited**.

restrict verb
1 *to restrict someone's freedom*. circumscribe,
control, cramp, inhibit, limit, regulate.
2 *The prisoners were restricted in their cells*.
confine, enclose, imprison, keep, SEE

restrain, shut.
OPPOSITES: SEE **free** verb.

restriction noun
1 *restrictions on your freedom.* check, constraint, control, curb, curfew, inhibition, limitation, restraint.
2 *a speed restriction.* ban, limit, regulation, rule, stipulation.

result noun
1 *The water shortage is a result of the hot weather.* consequence, effect, end-product, issue, outcome, product, repercussion, sequel, upshot.
2 *the result of a trial.* decision, judgement, verdict.
3 *the result of a game.* score.

result verb
What resulted from your interview? arise, come about, culminate, develop, emanate, emerge, ensue, eventuate, follow, happen, issue, occur, proceed, spring, stem, take place, turn out.
to result in *I hope it doesn't result in tears!* achieve, bring about, cause, give rise to, lead to, provoke.

resume verb
to resume after a break. begin again, carry on, continue, [*informal*] pick up the threads, proceed, recommence, reconvene, re-open, restart.

resurrect verb
to resurrect an old railway line. bring back, SEE **renew**, restore, resuscitate, revitalize, revive.

retain verb
1 *Please retain your ticket.* [*informal*] hang on to, hold, hold back, keep, reserve, save.
OPPOSITES: SEE **surrender**.
2 *Throughout the crisis he retained his composure.* keep control of, maintain, preserve.
OPPOSITES: SEE **lose**.
3 *He retains everything he reads.* keep in mind, learn, memorize, remember.
OPPOSITES: SEE **forget**.

retaliate verb
to retaliate against someone who hurt you. [*informal*] get even (with), [*informal*] get your own back, hit back, make a counter-attack, pay back, repay, revenge yourself, seek retribution, strike back, take revenge.

reticent adjective
SEE **reserved**.

retire verb
to retire from work. to retire from a fight. give up, leave, quit, resign, SEE **withdraw**.

retiring adjective
SEE **reserved**.

retort noun
a sharp retort. answer, comeback, quip, recrimination, rejoinder, reply, response, retaliation, [*joking*] riposte.

retort verb
He retorted rudely. answer, counter, react, reply, respond, retaliate, return.

retract verb
1 *A snail can retract its horns.* draw in, pull back, pull in.
2 *to retract an accusation.* abandon, cancel, disclaim, disown, [*informal*] have second thoughts about, recant, renounce, repeal, repudiate, rescind, reverse, revoke, withdraw.

retreat noun
1 *We made a quick retreat.* departure, escape, evacuation, exit, flight, withdrawal.
2 *a secluded retreat in the hills.* asylum, den, haven, [*informal*] hide-away, hideout, hiding-place, refuge, resort, sanctuary, shelter.

retreat verb
The army retreated. back away, back down, climb down, depart, fall back, go away, leave, move back, retire, [*informal*] run away, [*informal*] turn tail, withdraw.

retribution noun
The victim's family sought retribution. compensation, recompense, redress, reprisal, retaliation, revenge, vengeance.
OPPOSITES: SEE **forgiveness**.

retrieve verb
to retrieve something you lost. fetch back, find, get back, recapture, recoup, recover, regain, repossess, rescue, restore, return, salvage, save, trace, track down.

retrospective adjective
a retrospective glance. backward-looking, looking behind.

return noun
1 *We look forward to your return.* arrival, re-entry, homecoming, reappearance.
2 *After the flood there was a slow return to normality.* re-establishment (of), regression, restoration (of), reversion.
3 *We must avoid a return of the problem.* recrudescence, recurrence.
4 *I want a good return on my investment.* gain, income, interest, profit.

return verb
1 *I'll see you when you return.* come back, reappear, reassemble, reconvene, re-enter, retrace your steps.
2 *to return someone or something to their place of origin.* convey, deliver, repatriate,

replace, restore, send back.
3 *Things soon returned to their original state.*
go back, regress, revert.
4 *The problem may return.* happen again,
recur.
5 *Please return the money I lent you.* give
back, refund, reimburse, repay.

reveal verb
to reveal the truth. announce, bare, betray,
communicate, confess, declare, disclose,
display, divulge, exhibit, expose, [*informal*]
give the game away, lay bare, leak, make
known, proclaim, produce, publish, show,
show up, [*informal*] spill the beans, tell,
uncover, unfold, unmask, unveil.
OPPOSITES: SEE **hide** verb.

revel verb
We were revelling all night. carouse,
celebrate, [*informal*] have a spree, have fun,
make merry.

revelation noun
The revelation of what he'd done amazed me.
announcement, confession, disclosure,
discovery, exposé, exposure, news,
publication, revealing, unmasking.

revelry noun
The revelry continued all night. carousing,
celebration, conviviality, debauchery,
festivity, fun, [*joking*] jollification,
[*informal*] junketing, merrymaking, orgy,
party, revelling, revels, roistering,
[*informal*] spree.

revenge noun
His cruel heart was set on revenge. reprisal,
retaliation, retribution, vengeance,
vindictiveness.

revenge verb
to revenge a wrong. avenge, [*informal*] get
your own back for, repay, retaliate, take
revenge for.

revenue noun
the revenue from a business. income, SEE
money, proceeds, profits, receipts.

reverberation noun
the reverberation of a gong. echo, resonance,
ringing, rumble, vibration.

revere verb
We revere our heroes. admire, adore, feel
reverence for [SEE **reverence**], honour,
idolize, pay homage to, praise, respect,
reverence, value, venerate, worship.
OPPOSITES: SEE **despise**.

reverence noun
reverence for our heroes. admiration,
adoration, awe, deference, devotion, esteem,
homage, praise, respect, veneration,
worship.

reverent adjective
reverent worshippers. a reverent silence.
adoring, awed, awe-struck, deferential,
devout, pious, respectful, reverential,
solemn.
OPPOSITES: SEE **irreverent**.

reverie noun SEE **dream** noun.

reverse adjective
the reverse side. back, contrary, opposite,
rear.

reverse noun
1 *He says one thing and does the reverse.*
antithesis, contrary, converse, opposite.
2 *We suffered a number of reverses last year.*
defeat, failure, SEE **misfortune**, reversal, set-
back, [*informal*] upset.

reverse verb
1 *to reverse a sequence.* change, invert,
transpose, turn round.
2 *to reverse a car.* back, drive backwards, go
backwards, go into reverse.
3 *to reverse a decision.* countermand, negate,
overturn, repeal, rescind, retract, revoke,
undo.

review noun
1 *a review of the year.* look back, reappraisal,
recapitulation, reconsideration, re-
examination, report, study, survey.
2 *a book or record review.* appreciation,
criticism, critique, notice, [*informal*] write-
up.

review verb
to review the evidence. appraise, assess,
consider, evaluate, [*informal*] go over,
inspect, recapitulate, reconsider, re-
examine, scrutinize, study, survey,
[*informal*] weigh up.

revise verb
1 *to revise your opinions. to revise a draft.*
adapt, alter, change, correct, edit, emend,
improve, modify, [*informal*] polish up,
reconsider, [*informal*] redo, [*informal*]
rehash, rephrase, revamp, reword, rewrite,
update.
2 *to revise for an exam.* [*informal*] cram,
learn, study, [*informal*] swot.

revival noun
a revival of interest in old crafts.
reawakening, rebirth, recovery,
renaissance, renewal, restoration,
resurgence, resurrection, return,
revitalization, upsurge.

revive verb
1 *He soon revived after his black-out.*
awaken, come back to life, [*informal*] come
round, [*informal*] come to, rally, recover,
rouse.
2 *A cold drink revived us.* bring back to life,
[*informal*] cheer up, freshen up, invigorate,

refresh, renew, restore, resuscitate,
revitalize.
OPPOSITES: SEE **weaken, weary** verb.

revolt verb
to revolt against authority. disobey, mutiny,
rebel, riot, rise up.

revolting adjective
SEE **disgusting.**

revolution noun
1 *a political revolution.* civil war, coup, coup
d'état, mutiny, SEE **rebellion**, reformation,
revolt, rising, uprising.
2 *a revolution of the earth.* circuit, orbit,
rotation, turn.
3 *Computers have created an economic
revolution.* change, reorganization,
reorientation, shift, transformation,
[*informal*] turn-about, upheaval, [*informal*]
upset, [*informal*] U-turn.

revolutionary adjective
revolutionary ideas. avant-garde,
challenging, experimental, extremist,
innovative, new, novel, progressive, radical,
seditious, subversive, [*informal*] unheard
of, upsetting.
OPPOSITES: SEE **conservative** adjective.

revolve verb
Wheels revolve. Planets revolve round the sun.
circle, gyrate, orbit, pirouette (*Dancers
pirouette*), rotate, spin, swivel, turn, twirl,
wheel, whirl.

reward noun
a reward for bravery. a reward for hard work.
award, bonus, bounty, compensation,
decoration, honour, medal, payment, prize,
recompense, remuneration, return.
OPPOSITES: SEE **punishment.**

reward verb
1 *to reward someone for bravery.* decorate,
honour.
2 *to reward someone for hard work.*
compensate, give a reward to [SEE **reward**
noun], recompense, remunerate, repay.
OPPOSITES: SEE **punish.**

rewarding adjective
Nursing is said to be a rewarding job.
fulfilling, gratifying, satisfying,
worthwhile.
OPPOSITES: SEE **thankless.**

rhetorical adjective
[*nowadays usually uncomplimentary*] *a
rhetorical style.* artificial, bombastic,
[*informal*] flowery, high-flown, insincere,
oratorical, ornate, pretentious, verbose,
wordy.
OPPOSITES: SEE **simple.**

rhythm noun
a steady rhythm. accent, beat, metre,
movement, pattern, pulse, tempo, throb.

rhythmic adjective
a rhythmic beat. metrical, predictable,
regular, repeated, steady, throbbing.
OPPOSITES: SEE **irregular.**

ribbon noun
1 *a ribbon for her hair.* braid, head-band,
tape.
2 *a ribbon of colour.* band, strip, stripe.

rich adjective
1 *a rich industrialist.* affluent, [*informal*]
flush, [*informal*] loaded, moneyed, opulent,
[*joking*] plutocratic, prosperous, wealthy,
[*informal*] well-heeled, well-off, well-to-do.
2 *rich furnishings.* costly, elaborate,
expensive, lavish, luxurious, splendid,
sumptuous, valuable.
3 *rich agricultural land.* fertile, fruitful,
lush, productive.
4 *a rich harvest.* abundant, copious,
plenteous, plentiful, prolific, teeming.
5 *rich colours.* deep, full, strong, vivid,
warm.
OPPOSITES: SEE **poor.**
a rich person billionaire, capitalist,
millionaire, plutocrat, tycoon.

riches noun
SEE **wealth.**

rid verb
to rid the town of rats. clear, free, purge.
to get rid of dispense with, eject, evict,
expel, remove, throw out.

riddle noun
1 *Can you solve this riddle?* conundrum,
mystery, [*informal*] poser, problem, puzzle,
question.
2 *She sifted the soil in a riddle.* sieve.

riddle verb
1 *to riddle out large bits with a sieve.* filter,
screen, sieve, sift, strain.
2 *to riddle something with holes.* [*informal*]
pepper, perforate, pierce, puncture.

ride verb
1 *to ride a horse.* control, handle, manage, sit
on.
2 *to ride on a bike.* be carried, free-wheel,
pedal, SEE **travel** verb.

ridge noun
There's a good view from the ridge. bank,
edge, embankment, escarpment, SEE **hill.**

ridicule noun
*We had to put up with the ridicule of local
youths.* badinage, banter, derision, jeering,
laughter, mockery, raillery, [*informal*]
ribbing, sarcasm, satire, scorn, sneers,
taunts, teasing.

ridicule verb
Don't ridicule them because of their appearance. be sarcastic about, be satirical about, caricature, chaff, deride, guy, jeer at, joke about, lampoon, laugh at, make fun of, make jokes about, mock, parody, pillory, [*informal*] poke fun at, [*informal*] rib, scoff at, [*informal*] send up, sneer at, subject (someone) to ridicule [SEE **ridicule** noun], taunt, tease.

ridiculous adjective
a ridiculous comedy. ridiculous behaviour. absurd, amusing, comic, [*informal*] crazy, [*informal*] daft, eccentric, farcical, foolish, funny, grotesque, hilarious, illogical, irrational, laughable, ludicrous, mad, nonsensical, preposterous, senseless, silly, stupid, unbelievable, unreasonable, weird, [*informal*] zany.
OPPOSITES: SEE **sensible, serious**.

rift noun
a rift in a rock. a rift in a friendship. breach, break, chink, cleft, crack, division, fracture, gap, opening, separation, split.

right adjective
1 *the right thing to do.* decent, ethical, fair, honest, honourable, just, law-abiding, lawful, moral, principled, responsible, righteous, upright, virtuous.
2 *the right answer. the right word.* accurate, apposite, appropriate, apt, correct, exact, factual, faultless, fitting, genuine, precise, proper, suitable, true.
3 *Have we come the right way?* best, convenient, good, normal, recommended, sensible, usual.
OPPOSITES: SEE **wrong** adjective.
4 *your right side.* right-hand, starboard [= *right side of a ship when you face the bow*].
5 *right in politics.* conservative, fascist, reactionary, right-wing, Tory.

right noun
1 *the right to free speech.* entitlement, facility, freedom, liberty, prerogative, privilege.
2 *a teacher's right to give orders. a chemist's right to sell medicines.* authority, commission, franchise, influence, licence, position, power.

right verb
1 *to right something which was overturned.* make perpendicular, pick up, set upright, stand upright, straighten.
OPPOSITES: SEE **overturn**.
2 *to right a wrong.* correct, make amends for, put right, rectify, redress, remedy, repair, set right.

righteous adjective
It is not only the righteous who go to church. blameless, God-fearing, good, guiltless, just, law-abiding, moral, pure,

[*uncomplimentary*] SEE **sanctimonious**, upright, virtuous.
OPPOSITES: SEE **sinful**.

rightful adjective
the rightful owner of a car. authorized, just, lawful, legal, legitimate, licensed, proper, real, true, valid.
OPPOSITES: SEE **illegal**.

rigid adjective
1 *a rigid board. a rigid framework. a rigid expression.* adamant, firm, hard, inflexible, solid, stiff, unbending, wooden.
2 *a rigid disciplinarian.* harsh, intransigent, stern, strict, stubborn, uncompromising, unkind, unyielding.
OPPOSITES: SEE **flexible**.

rigorous adjective
1 *rigorous training.* conscientious, demanding, exacting, hard, painstaking, rigid, stringent, structured, thorough, tough, unsparing.
OPPOSITES: SEE **easygoing**.
2 *a rigorous climate.* extreme, harsh, inclement, inhospitable, severe, unfriendly, unpleasant.
OPPOSITES: SEE **mild**.

rim noun
the rim of a cup. brim, brink, circumference, edge, lip.

ring noun
1 *in the shape of a ring.* band, circle, hoop, loop.
2 *a boxing-ring.* arena.
3 *a smuggling ring.* association, band, gang, SEE **group** noun, mob, organization, syndicate.

ring verb
1 *The police ringed the area.* circle, encircle, enclose, encompass, surround.
2 *The bell rang.* chime, clang, clink, jangle, peal, ping, resonate, resound, reverberate, sound the knell, tinkle, toll.
3 *Ring me tomorrow evening.* call, [*informal*] give a buzz, phone, ring up, telephone.

rinse verb
to rinse in clean water. bathe, clean, sluice, swill, wash.

riot noun
a riot in the streets. anarchy, brawl, chaos, commotion, demonstration, disorder, disturbance, hubbub, insurrection, lawlessness, mass protest, mutiny, pandemonium, revolt, rioting, rising, [*informal*] rumpus, [*informal*] shindy, turmoil, unrest, uproar, violence.

riot verb
The discontented crowd rioted. [*informal*] go wild, mutiny, rampage, rebel, revolt, rise up, run riot.

riotous adjective
a riotous party. anarchic, boisterous,
disorderly, lawless, mutinous, noisy,
rampageous, rebellious, rowdy, uncivilized,
uncontrollable, undisciplined,
ungovernable, unrestrained, unruly,
violent, wild.
OPPOSITES: SEE **orderly.**

rip verb SEE **tear** verb.

ripe adjective
ripe fruit. mature, mellow, ready to use.

ripen verb
These pears need to ripen. age, become riper,
develop, mature, mellow.

ripple verb
Wind rippled the surface of the water. agitate,
disturb, make waves on, ruffle, stir.

rise noun
1 *a rise in the ground.* ascent, bank, climb,
elevation, SEE **hill**, incline, ramp, slope.
2 *a rise in wages, temperature, etc.* escalation,
increase, increment, jump, leap, upsurge,
upswing, upturn, upward movement.

rise verb
1 *to rise into the air.* arise, ascend, climb, fly
up, go up, jump, leap, levitate, lift, lift off,
mount, soar, spring, take off.
2 *to rise from bed.* get up, stand up.
3 *Prices have risen.* escalate, grow, increase.

risk noun
1 *a risk of frost.* chance, likelihood,
possibility.
2 *Starting a business involves financial risk.*
danger, gamble, hazard, peril, speculation,
uncertainty, venture.

risk verb
He risked his capital starting the business.
chance, dare, gamble, hazard, jeopardize,
speculate, venture.

risky adjective
SEE **dangerous.**

ritual noun
a religious ritual. ceremonial, ceremony,
formality, liturgy, practice, rite, sacrament,
service, solemnity, tradition.

rival noun
sporting rivals. adversary, challenger,
competitor, contender, contestant, enemy,
opponent, opposition.

rival verb
The new shop rivals the shop down the road.
be as good as, compare with, compete with,
contend with, contest, emulate, equal,
match, oppose, struggle with, vie with.
OPPOSITES: SEE **co-operate.**

rivalry noun
rivalry between two teams. antagonism,
competition, competitiveness, opposition.
OPPOSITES: SEE **co-operation.**

river noun SEE **stream** noun.

PARTS OF A RIVER: channel, confluence, delta,
estuary, lower reaches, mouth, source,
tributary, upper reaches.

---

road noun
roadway, route, way.

ROADS AND PATHWAYS: alley, arterial road,
avenue, boulevard, bridle-path, bridle-way,
bypass, by-road, byway, cart-track,
causeway, clearway, crescent, cul-de-sac,
drive, driveway, dual carriageway,
esplanade, footpath, [*American*] freeway,
highway, lane, motorway, one-way street,
path, pathway, pavement, ring road, service
road, side-road, side-street, slip-road, street,
thoroughfare, tow-path, track, trail, trunk-
road, [*old-fashioned*] turnpike, walk,
walkway.

SURFACES FOR ROADS AND PATHS: asphalt,
cobbles, concrete, crazy paving,
flagstones, gravel, paving stones, Tarmac,
tiles.

---

roam verb
Sheep roam over the hills. meander, prowl,
ramble, range, rove, stray, travel, SEE **walk**
verb, wander.

rob verb
to rob a shop. to rob someone in the street.
[*informal*] con, defraud, loot, [*informal*]
mug, [*informal*] mulct, pick (someone's)
pocket, pilfer from, pillage, plunder,
ransack, steal from [SEE **steal**].

robber noun
bandit, brigand, burglar, [*informal*] con-
man, embezzler, fraud, highwayman, looter,
mugger, pickpocket, pirate, shop-lifter,
swindler, thief.
OTHER CRIMINALS: SEE **criminal** noun.

robbery noun
burglary, confidence trick, embezzlement,
fraud, [*informal*] hold-up, larceny,
mugging, pillage, plunder, shop-lifting,
stealing, [*informal*] stick-up, theft.
OTHER CRIMES: SEE **crime.**

robe noun
bath-robe, dress, dressing-gown, frock,
gown, habit (*a monk's habit*), house-coat.

robust adjective
1 *a robust physique.* athletic, brawny, hardy, healthy, muscular, powerful, rugged, sound, strong, vigorous.
2 *a robust machine.* durable, serviceable, sturdy, tough.
OPPOSITES: SEE **weak**.

rock noun
1 *a lorry-load of rock.* ore, stone.
2 *We clambered over the rocks.* boulder, crag, outcrop, scree.

PRINCIPAL TYPES OF ROCK: igneous, metamorphic, sedimentary.

SOME KINDS OF ROCK: basalt, chalk, clay, flint, gneiss, granite, gravel, lava, limestone, marble, obsidian, pumice, quartz, sandstone, schist, shale, slate, tufa, tuff.

rock verb
1 *to rock to and fro.* move gently, sway, swing.
2 *The ship rocked in the storm.* lurch, pitch, reel, roll, shake, toss, totter.

rocky adjective
1 *rocky terrain.* barren, inhospitable, pebbly, rough, rugged, stony.
2 *a rocky chair.* SEE **unsteady**.

rod noun
bar, baton, cane, dowel, pole, rail, shaft, spoke, staff, stick, strut, wand.

rogue noun
rogues and criminals. [*old-fashioned*] blackguard, charlatan, cheat, [*informal*] con-man, SEE **criminal** noun, fraud, [*old-fashioned*] knave, mischievous person [SEE **mischievous**], [*informal*] quack, rascal, ruffian, scoundrel, swindler, villain.

role noun
1 *an actor's role.* character, part, portrayal.
2 *What's her role in this business?* contribution, duty, function, job, position, post, task.

roll noun
1 *a roll of paper.* cylinder, drum, scroll.
2 *a roll of honour.* catalogue, index, inventory, list, record, register.

roll verb
1 *The wheels began to roll.* gyrate, move round, revolve, rotate, run, spin, turn, twirl, whirl.
2 *to roll up a carpet, a sail, etc.* coil, curl, furl, make into a roll, twist, wind, wrap.
3 *to roll a cricket pitch.* flatten, level out, smooth, use a roller on.
4 *The ship rolled in the storm. A drunk rolled along the street.* lumber, lurch, pitch, reel, rock, stagger, sway, toss, totter, wallow, welter.
to roll in, to roll up SEE **arrive**.

romance noun
1 *a historical romance.*
KINDS OF WRITING: SEE **writing**.
2 *the romance of travel.* adventure, excitement, fascination, glamour.
3 *Are those two having a romance?* affair, attachment, intrigue, liaison, love affair, relationship.

romantic adjective
1 *a romantic setting for a love affair.* colourful, dream-like, exotic, glamorous, idyllic, picturesque.
2 *a romantic novel.* emotional, escapist, heart warming, nostalgic, reassuring, sentimental, [*uncomplimentary*] sloppy, tender, unrealistic.
3 *romantic notions of changing the world.* [*informal*] head in the clouds, idealistic, impractical, improbable, quixotic, starry-eyed, unworkable, Utopian, visionary.
OPPOSITES: SEE **realistic**.

romp verb
The children romped in the playground. caper, cavort, dance, frisk, frolic, leap about, play, prance, run about.

roof noun

MATERIALS USED FOR ROOFS: asbestos, corrugated iron, felt, pantiles, shingles, slates, thatch, tiles.

room noun
1 *Give me more room.* [*informal*] elbow-room, freedom, latitude, leeway, scope, space, territory.
2 *a room in a house.* [*old-fashioned*] chamber.

VARIOUS ROOMS: ante-room, attic, audience chamber, bathroom, bedroom, boudoir, cell, cellar, chapel, classroom, cloakroom, conservatory, corridor, dining-room, dormitory, drawing-room, dressing-room, gallery, guest-room, hall, kitchen, kitchenette, laboratory, landing, larder, laundry, lavatory, library, living-room, loft, lounge, music-room, nursery, office, outhouse, pantry, parlour, passage, play-room, porch, salon, saloon, scullery, sick-room, sitting-room, spare-room, state-room, store-room, studio, study, toilet, utility room, waiting-room, ward, washroom, WC, workroom, workshop.

roomy adjective
a roomy car. SEE **big**, capacious, commodious, large, sizeable, spacious, voluminous.
OPPOSITES: SEE **cramped**.

root noun
1 *the root of a plant.* radicle, rhizome, rootlet, tuber.
2 *the root of a problem.* basis, bottom (*I want to get to the bottom of this*), origin, seat, source, starting-point.

rope noun
cable, cord, halyard, hawser, lanyard, lariat, lasso, line, string.

rot noun
The damp has caused some rot. corrosion, decay, decomposition, deterioration, disintegration, dry rot, mouldiness, wet rot.

rot verb
Most substances eventually rot. become rotten [SEE **rotten**], corrode, crumble, decay, decompose, degenerate, deteriorate, disintegrate, go bad, perish, putrefy, spoil.

rotary adjective
rotary movement. gyrating, revolving, rotating, rotatory, spinning, turning, twirling, twisting, whirling.

rotate verb
to rotate on an axis. gyrate, have a rotary movement, pirouette, pivot, reel, revolve, spin, swivel, turn, turn anticlockwise, turn clockwise, twiddle, twirl, twist, wheel, whirl.

rotten adjective
1 *rotten wood. rotten ironwork.* corroded, crumbling, decayed, decaying, decomposed, disintegrating, [*of iron, etc.*] rusty, unsound.
2 *rotten food.* foul, mouldering, mouldy, [*informal*] off (*The fish is off*), perished, putrid, smelly, tainted, unfit for consumption.
OPPOSITES: SEE **sound** adjective.

rough adjective
1 *a rough surface.* broken, bumpy, coarse, craggy, irregular, jagged, pitted, rocky, rugged, stony, uneven.
OPPOSITES: SEE **even** adjective.
2 *rough skin.* bristly, callused, chapped, coarse, hairy, harsh, leathery, scratchy, shaggy, unshaven, wrinkled.
OPPOSITES: SEE **smooth** adjective.
3 *a rough sea.* choppy, stormy, tempestuous, turbulent, violent, wild.
OPPOSITES: SEE **calm** adjective.
4 *a rough voice.* grating, gruff, harsh, hoarse, husky, rasping, raucous, unpleasant.
OPPOSITES: SEE **soft**.
5 *a rough crowd. rough manners.* badly behaved, bluff, blunt, brusque, churlish, ill-bred, impolite, loutish, SEE **rowdy**, rude,

surly, [*informal*] ugly, uncivil, uncivilized, undisciplined, unfriendly.
OPPOSITES: SEE **polite**.
6 *rough work.* amateurish, careless, clumsy, crude, hasty, imperfect, inept, [*informal*] rough and ready, unfinished, unpolished, unskilful.
OPPOSITES: SEE **skilful**.
7 *a rough estimate.* approximate, imprecise, inexact, vague.
OPPOSITES: SEE **exact** adjective.

roughly adverb
about, approximately, around, close to, nearly.

round adjective
1 *a round shape.* bulbous, circular, curved, cylindrical, globular, spherical.
2 *a round figure.* ample, SEE **fat** adjective, full, plump, rotund, rounded, well-padded.

round noun
a round in a competition. bout, contest, game, heat, stage.

roundabout adjective
a roundabout route. circuitous, devious, indirect, long, meandering, rambling, tortuous, twisting, winding.
OPPOSITES: SEE **direct** adjective.

round-shouldered adjective
humpbacked, hunchbacked, stooping.

rouse verb
1 *to rouse someone from sleep.* arouse, awaken, call, get up, wake up.
2 *to rouse someone to a frenzy.* agitate, animate, excite, incite, inflame, provoke, stimulate, stir up.

rousing adjective
SEE **exciting**.

rout verb
We routed the opposition. conquer, crush, SEE **defeat** verb, overwhelm.

route noun
Which route shall we take? course, direction, itinerary, journey, path, road, way.

routine noun
1 *a normal routine.* course of action, custom, [*informal*] drill (*Follow the usual drill*), habit, method, pattern, practice, procedure, system, way.
2 *The skaters performed their new routine.* act, performance, programme.

row noun
1 [Rhymes with *crow*.] *Arrange them in a row.* chain, column, cordon, file, line, queue, rank, sequence, series, string.
2 [Rhymes with *cow*.] *I heard his row all down the street.* SEE **noise**, [*informal*] racket,

rumpus, tumult, uproar.
3 [Rhymes with *cow*.] *They don't speak to each other since their row.* altercation, argument, controversy, disagreement, dispute, fight, SEE **quarrel** noun, [*informal*] ructions, [*informal*] slanging match, squabble.

rowdy adjective
a rowdy crowd. badly behaved, boisterous, disorderly, ill-disciplined, irrepressible, lawless, SEE **noisy**, obstreperous, riotous, rough, turbulent, undisciplined, unruly, violent, wild.
OPPOSITES: SEE **quiet**.

royal adjective
a royal palace. by royal command. imperial, kingly, majestic, princely, queenly, regal, stately.

royalty noun

MEMBERS OF ROYALTY: consort, Her or His Majesty, Her or His Royal Highness, king, monarch, prince, princess, queen, queen mother, regent, sovereign.
OTHER RULERS: SEE **ruler**.

---

rub verb
1 *to rub a sore place and make it better.* caress, knead, massage, smooth, stroke.
2 *to rub a place and damage it.* abrade, chafe, graze, scrape, wear away.
3 *to rub something clean.* polish, scour, scrub, wipe.
to rub out blot out, cancel, delete, erase, expunge, obliterate, remove, wipe out.

rubbish noun
1 *Throw away that rubbish.* debris, dross, flotsam and jetsam, garbage, junk, leavings, [*informal*] leftovers, litter, lumber, muck, [*informal*] odds and ends, offcuts, refuse, rubble, scrap, trash, waste.
2 *Don't talk rubbish!* SEE **nonsense**.

rubble noun
The building collapsed into a pile of rubble. broken bricks, debris, fragments, remains, ruins, wreckage.

ruddy adjective
a ruddy complexion. fresh, flushed, glowing, healthy, SEE **red**, sunburnt.

rude noun
rude language. rude behaviour. a rude person. abrupt, abusive, bad-mannered, bad-tempered, blasphemous, blunt, boorish, brusque, cheeky, churlish, coarse, common, condescending, contemptuous, crude, discourteous, disparaging, disrespectful, foul, graceless, gross, ignorant, ill-bred, ill-mannered, impertinent, impolite, improper, impudent, in bad taste, inconsiderate,

indecent, insolent, insulting, loutish, mocking, naughty, oafish, SEE **obscene**, offensive, offhand, patronizing, peremptory, personal (*Don't make personal remarks*), saucy, scurrilous, shameless, tactless, unchivalrous, uncivil, uncomplimentary, uncouth, ungracious, [*old-fashioned*] unmannerly, unprintable, vulgar.
OPPOSITES: SEE **polite**.
to be rude to abuse, SEE **insult** verb, offend, sneer at, snub.

rudeness noun
I'm sick of her rudeness. abuse, [*informal*] backchat, bad manners, boorishness, [*informal*] cheek, churlishness, condescension, contempt, discourtesy, disrespect, ill-breeding, impertinence, impudence, incivility, insolence, insults, oafishness, tactlessness, uncouthness, vulgarity.

rudimentary adjective
He has only a rudimentary knowledge of the subject. basic, crude, elementary, embryonic, immature, introductory, preliminary, primitive, provisional, undeveloped.
OPPOSITES: SEE **advanced**.

rudiments noun
the rudiments of a subject. basic principles, basics, elements, essentials, foundations, fundamentals, principles.

ruffian noun
[*informal*] brute, bully, desperado, gangster, hoodlum, hooligan, lout, mugger, SEE **rogue**, scoundrel, thug, [*informal*] tough, villain, [*informal*] yob.

ruffle verb
1 *A breeze ruffled the water.* agitate, disturb, ripple, stir.
2 *She ruffled his hair.* derange, dishevel, [*informal*] mess up, rumple, tousle.
OPPOSITES: SEE **smooth** verb.

rugged adjective
1 *rugged mountains.* bumpy, craggy, irregular, jagged, rocky, rough, uneven.
2 *rugged good looks.* burly, husky, muscular, robust, rough, strong, sturdy, tough, unpolished, weather-beaten.

ruin noun
1 *the ruin of a business.* bankruptcy, breakdown, collapse, [*informal*] crash, destruction, downfall, end, failure, fall, ruination, undoing, wreck.
2 [*often plural*] *the ruins of a building.* debris, havoc, remains, rubble, ruined buildings [SEE **ruined**], wreckage.

ruin verb
The storm ruined the flowers. damage,
demolish, destroy, devastate, flatten,
overthrow, shatter, spoil, wreck.
ruined adjective
a ruined castle. crumbling, derelict,
dilapidated, fallen down, in ruins,
ramshackle, ruinous, tumble-down,
uninhabitable, unsafe, wrecked.
rule noun
1 *rules of conduct. the rules of a game.* code,
convention, custom, law, practice, precept,
principle, regulation, routine.
2 *under foreign rule.* administration,
authority, command, control, domination,
dominion, empire, government, influence,
jurisdiction, management, mastery, power,
regime, reign, sovereignty, supremacy,
sway.
rule verb
1 *to rule a country.* administer, command,
control, direct, dominate, govern, lead,
manage, reign over, run.
2 *Elizabeth I ruled for many years.* be ruler
[SEE **ruler**], reign.
3 *The umpire ruled that the batsman was out.*
adjudicate, decide, decree, determine, find,
judge, pronounce, resolve.
to rule out SEE **exclude**.
ruler noun

VARIOUS RULERS: autocrat, caesar, SEE **chief**
noun, demagogue, dictator, doge, emir,
emperor, empress, governor, kaiser, king,
lord, monarch, potentate, president, prince,
princess, queen, rajah, regent, satrap,
sovereign, sultan, suzerain, triumvirate [=
three people ruling jointly], tyrant, tsar,
viceroy.

---

rumour noun
The scandalous story was only a rumour.
gossip, hearsay, prattle, scandal, whisper.
run noun
1 *a run across the park.* canter, dash, gallop,
jog, marathon, race, sprint, trot.
2 *a run in the car.* drive, SEE **journey** noun,
joyride, ride, [*informal*] spin.
3 *a run of bad luck.* chain, sequence, series,
stretch.
run verb
1 *We ran as fast as our legs could carry us.*
bolt, canter, career, dash, gallop, hare, hurry,
jog, race, rush, scamper, scoot, scurry,
scuttle, speed, sprint, tear, trot.
2 *The buses don't run on Sundays.* go,
operate, ply, provide a service, travel.
3 *The car runs well.* behave, function,
perform, work.

4 *Water ran down the wall.* cascade, dribble,
flow, gush, leak, pour, spill, stream,
trickle.
5 *The government is supposed to run the
country's affairs.* administer, conduct,
control, direct, govern, look after, maintain,
manage, rule, supervise.
to run away abscond, [*informal*] beat it,
bolt, depart, elope, SEE **escape** verb,
[*informal*] take to your heels, [*informal*]
turn tail.
runner noun
1 *a runner in a race.* athlete,
competitor, entrant, jogger, participant,
sprinter.
2 *The commanding officer sent a
runner to headquarters.* courier, messenger.
3 *a runner of a plant.* offshoot, shoot,
sprout.
runny adjective
fluid, free-flowing, liquid, thin, watery.
OPPOSITES: SEE **viscous**.
rupture verb SEE **burst**.
rural adjective
*I like to get away from the town into rural
surroundings.* agricultural, bucolic,
countrified, pastoral, rustic, sylvan.
rush noun
1 *a rush to get things finished.* haste, hurry,
pressure, race, scramble, urgency.
2 *a rush of water.* cataract, flood, gush,
spate.
3 *a rush of people or animals.* charge,
onslaught, panic, stampede.
rush verb
to rush home. to rush in with good news.
bolt, burst, canter, career, charge, dash,
fly, gallop, hare, hasten, hurry, jog,
move fast, race, run, scamper, scramble,
scurry, scuttle, shoot, speed, sprint,
stampede, [*informal*] tear, trot, [*informal*]
zoom.
rustic adjective
SEE **rural**.
rusty adjective
1 *rusty iron.* corroded, oxidized, rotten,
tarnished.
2 [*informal*] *My French is a bit rusty.* dated,
forgotten, unused.
rut noun
a rut in a path. channel, furrow, groove,
indentation, pothole, track, trough.
ruthless *a ruthless attack. ruthless
criminals.* brutal, cruel, dangerous,
ferocious, fierce, SEE **pitiless**, vicious,
violent.

Ss

sabotage noun
Terrorists were responsible for the sabotage.
deliberate destruction, disruption,
treachery, vandalism, wilful damage,
wrecking.

sabotage verb
to sabotage a machine. cripple, damage,
destroy, disable, put out of action,
vandalize, wreck.

sack verb
1 *to sack someone from a job.* [*informal*] axe,
discharge, dismiss, [*informal*] fire, give
(someone) notice, [*informal*] give (someone)
the sack, lay off [= *to discharge temporarily*],
make redundant.
2 *to sack a town.* SEE **plunder** verb.

sacred adjective
The Koran is a sacred book. blessed,
consecrated, dedicated, divine, godly,
hallowed, holy, religious, revered,
sacrosanct, venerated.
OPPOSITES: SEE **secular**.

sacrifice verb
1 *I sacrificed my weekend to finish the job.*
abandon, forgo, give up, let go, lose,
relinquish, surrender.
2 *to sacrifice an animal to the gods.* kill, offer
up, slaughter.

sacrilege noun
blasphemy, desecration, godlessness,
impiety, irreverence, profanity,
ungodliness.
OPPOSITES: SEE **piety**.

sad adjective
1 *sad faces. sad emotions.* [*informal*] blue,
broken-hearted, careworn, cheerless,
crestfallen, dejected, depressed, desolate,
despairing, desperate, despondent,
disappointed, disconsolate, discontented,
discouraged, disgruntled, dismal,
dispirited, dissatisfied, distracted,
distraught, distressed, doleful, dolorous,
[*informal*] down, downcast, down-hearted,
dreary, forlorn, gloomy, glum, grave, grief-
stricken, grieving, grim, guilty,
heartbroken, [*informal*] heavy, heavy-
hearted, homesick, hopeless, in low spirits,
[*informal*] in the doldrums, joyless,
lachrymose, lonely, [*informal*] long-faced,
[*informal*] low, lugubrious, melancholy,
miserable, moody, moping, morose,
mournful, pathetic, penitent, pessimistic,
piteous, pitiable, pitiful, plaintive, poignant,
regretful, rueful, serious, sober, sombre,

sorrowful, sorry, tearful, troubled, unhappy,
upset, wistful, woebegone, woeful,
wretched.
2 *sad news. a sad event.* calamitous,
deplorable, depressing, disastrous,
discouraging, distressing, grievous, heartbreaking, heart-rending, lamentable,
morbid, moving, painful, regrettable,
[*informal*] tear-jerking, touching, tragic,
unfortunate, unsatisfactory, unwelcome,
upsetting.
OPPOSITES: SEE **happy**.

sadden verb
Our friend's illness saddened us. [*informal*]
break (someone's) heart, depress,
disappoint, discourage, dishearten, dismay,
dispirit, distress, grieve, make sad [SEE **sad**],
upset.
OPPOSITES: SEE **cheer** verb.

sadistic adjective SEE **cruel**.

safe adjective
1 *Is your house safe against burglars?*
defended, foolproof, guarded, immune,
impregnable, invulnerable, protected,
secure.
OPPOSITES: SEE **vulnerable**.
2 *We got home safe in spite of the storm.*
[*informal*] alive and well, [*informal*] all
right, [*informal*] in one piece, intact, sound,
undamaged, unharmed, unhurt, uninjured,
unscathed.
OPPOSITES: SEE **damaged**.
3 *She's a safe driver.* cautious,
circumspect, dependable, reliable,
trustworthy.
4 *The dog's quite safe.* docile, friendly,
harmless, innocuous, tame.
5 *The water's safe to drink. The food's safe to
eat.* drinkable, eatable, good, non-
poisonous, non-toxic, potable, pure,
uncontaminated, wholesome.
OPPOSITES: SEE **dangerous**.

safeguard verb SEE **protect**.

safety noun
1 *The airline does all it can to ensure
passengers' safety.* immunity,
invulnerability, protection, security.
2 *The nurse assured me of the safety of the
drug.* harmlessness, reliability.

sag verb
The rope sags in the middle. be limp, dip,
droop, fall, flop, hang down, sink, slump.

sail verb
1 *to sail a boat.* captain, navigate, pilot,
skipper, steer.
2 *to sail in a boat.* cruise, paddle, punt, row,
steam, SEE **travel** verb.

sailor noun
mariner, seaman.

VARIOUS SAILORS: able seaman, bargee,
boatman, boatswain or bosun, captain, cox
or coxswain, [*plural*] crew, helmsman, mate,
midshipman, navigator, pilot, rating,
rower, yachtsman.
RANKS IN THE NAVY: SEE **rank** noun.

---

saintly adjective
angelic, blessed, SEE **good**, holy, innocent,
pure, religious, sinless, virtuous.
OPPOSITES: SEE **devilish**.

sake noun
Do it for my sake. advantage, behalf, benefit,
gain, good, interest, welfare.

salad noun

VEGETABLES OFTEN EATEN IN SALADS:
beetroot, celery, chicory, cress, cucumber,
lettuce, mustard and cress, onion, potato,
radish, tomato, watercress.
OTHER VEGETABLES: SEE **vegetable**.

---

salary noun
a salary of £15,000 a year. earnings,
emolument, income, pay, payment,
remuneration, stipend, wages.

sale noun
KINDS OF SALE: auction, bazaar, closing-down
sale, fair, jumble sale, market, winter sales.

salt adjective
salt water. brackish, briny, saline, salted,
salty, savoury.
OPPOSITES: **fresh**.

salute verb SEE **greet**.
WAYS TO GESTURE: SEE **gesture** verb.

salvage verb
to salvage waste materials. conserve,
preserve, reclaim, recover, recycle, rescue,
retrieve, re-use, save, use again.

salvation noun
1 [*theological*] *the salvation of souls.*
redemption, saving.
OPPOSITES: DAMNATION.
2 *When I lost my cash, my credit card was my
salvation.* deliverance, escape, help,
preservation, rescue, way out.

same adjective
1 *That's the same person who came yesterday.*
actual, identical, selfsame.
2 *Make it the same shape. Come on the same
date next year.* analogous, comparable,
consistent, corresponding, duplicate, equal,

equivalent, indistinguishable,
interchangeable, matching, parallel,
similar, synonymous [= *having the same
meaning*], twin, unaltered, unchanged,
uniform, unvaried.
OPPOSITES: SEE **different**.

sample noun
a sample of your work. demonstration,
example, foretaste, free sample,
illustration, indication, instance, model,
pattern, representative piece, selection,
specimen.

sample verb
We sampled the food. inspect, take a sample
of [SEE **sample** noun], taste, test, try.

sanctimonious adjective
[*uncomplimentary*] *sanctimonious
preaching.* holier-than-thou, hypocritical,
insincere, moralizing, pious, SEE **righteous**,
self-righteous, sententious, [*informal*]
smarmy, smug, superior, unctuous.
OPPOSITES: SEE **modest**.

sanction verb
SEE **authorize**.

sanctuary noun
The hunted fox found sanctuary in a wood.
asylum, haven, protection, refuge, retreat,
safety, shelter.

sane adjective
a sane person. a sane decision. balanced,
[*informal*] compos mentis, level-headed,
lucid, normal, rational, reasonable,
sensible, sound, stable.
OPPOSITES: SEE **mad**.

sanguine adjective
SEE **optimistic**.

sanitary adjective
sanitary conditions in a hospital. aseptic,
clean, disinfected, germ-free, healthy,
hygienic, pure, salubrious, sterilized,
uncontaminated, unpolluted.
OPPOSITES: INSANITARY, SEE **unhealthy**.

sanitation noun
You need proper sanitation on a camp-site.
drainage, drains, lavatories, sanitary
arrangements, sewage disposal, sewers.

sarcastic adjective
sarcastic jokes. a sarcastic manner. SEE **comic**
adjective, contemptuous, cutting,
demeaning, derisive, disparaging, hurtful,
ironical, mocking, SEE **sardonic**, satirical,
scathing, sharp, sneering, taunting,
vitriolic, withering.

sardonic adjective
sardonic humour. acid, biting, black (*black
comedy*), SEE **comic** adjective, cynical,
heartless, malicious, mordant, SEE **sarcastic**,
wry.

sash noun
a sash round the waist. band, belt, cummerbund, girdle, waistband.

satire noun
a satire on human folly. burlesque, caricature, invective, irony, lampoon, mockery, parody, SEE **ridicule** noun, satirical comedy [SEE **satirical**], [*informal*] send-up, [*informal*] spoof, [*informal*] take-off, travesty.

satirical adjective
a satirical comedy. SEE **comic** adjective, critical, disparaging, disrespectful, ironic, irreverent, mocking, SEE **sarcastic**.

satirize verb
to satirize someone's faults. be satirical about [SEE **satirical**], burlesque, caricature, SEE **criticize**, deride, lampoon, laugh at, make fun of, mock, parody, ridicule, [*informal*] send up, [*informal*] take off, travesty.

satisfaction noun
I get satisfaction from my hobby. comfort, contentment, enjoyment, fulfilment, gratification, happiness, pleasure, pride, self-satisfaction, sense of achievement.
OPPOSITES: SEE **dissatisfaction**.

satisfactory adjective
satisfactory work. acceptable, adequate, [*informal*] all right, competent, fair, [*informal*] good enough, passable, pleasing, satisfying, sufficient, suitable, tolerable, [*informal*] up to scratch.
OPPOSITES: SEE **unsatisfactory**.

satisfy verb
to satisfy a need. to satisfy someone's curiosity. appease, assuage, content, fulfil, gratify, make happy, meet, pacify, please, put an end to, quench (*your thirst*), sate, satiate, settle, slake (*your thirst*), supply.
OPPOSITES: SEE **frustrate**.

saturate verb
to saturate a sponge with water. drench, impregnate, permeate, soak, steep, suffuse, wet.

sauce noun

KINDS OF SAUCE: bread sauce, cranberry sauce, custard, curry, gravy, horse-radish sauce, ketchup, mayonnaise, mint sauce, salad cream, sweet and sour.

---

saucepan noun
cauldron, pan, pot, skillet, stockpot.

savage adjective
1 *savage tribes.* barbarian, barbaric, cannibal, heathen, pagan, primitive, uncivilized, uncultivated, uneducated.
OPPOSITES: SEE **civilized**.

2 *savage beasts.* fierce, undomesticated, untamed, wild.
OPPOSITES: SEE **domesticated**.
3 *a savage attack.* angry, atrocious, barbarous, beastly, bestial, blistering, blood-thirsty, bloody, brutal, callous, cold-blooded, cruel, diabolical, ferocious, heartless, inhuman, merciless, murderous, pitiless, ruthless, sadistic, unfeeling, vicious, violent.
OPPOSITES: SEE **humane**.

save verb
1 *to save money.* collect, conserve, hold back, hold on to, hoard, invest, keep [*informal*] put by, put in a safe place, reserve, retain, scrape together, set aside, [*informal*] stash away, store up, take care of.
OPPOSITES: SEE **squander**.
2 *to save fuel.* be sparing with, economize on, use wisely.
OPPOSITES: SEE **waste** verb.
3 *to save people or property from a wreck.* free, liberate, recover, release, rescue, retrieve, salvage, set free.
4 *to save someone from danger.* defend, guard, keep safe, preserve, protect, safeguard, screen, shield.
5 *I saved him from making a fool of himself.* check, deter, prevent, stop.

saving noun
You can make a saving if you buy in a sale. cut, discount, economy, reduction.
savings *I put my savings in the bank.* nest-egg, reserves, resources, riches, wealth.

savoury adjective
We often follow the savoury course with a sweet course. appetizing, piquant, salty, SEE **tasty**.
OPPOSITES: SEE **sweet** adjective.

say verb
Did you hear what I said? affirm, allege, announce, answer, articulate, assert, [*informal*] come out with, comment, communicate, convey, declare, disclose, divulge, ejaculate, enunciate, exclaim, express, intimate, maintain, mention, mouth, pronounce, read aloud, recite, rejoin, remark, repeat, reply, report, respond, retort, reveal, speak, state, suggest, SEE **talk** verb, utter.

saying noun
an old Chinese saying. adage, aphorism, apophthegm, axiom, [*informal*] catch-phrase, catchword, cliché, dictum, epigram, expression, formula, maxim, motto, phrase, precept, proverb, quotation, remark, [*old-fashioned*] saw, slogan, statement, tag, truism, watchword.

scab noun
a scab on a wound. clot of blood, crust, sore.

scale noun
1 *scales on a fish.* flake, plate.
2 *scale in a kettle.* crust, deposit, encrustation, [*informal*] fur.
3 *a scale on a measuring instrument.* [*formal*] calibration, gradation.
4 *the social scale.* hierarchy, ladder, order, ranking, spectrum.
5 *a musical scale.* chromatic scale, diatonic scale, major scale, minor scale, sequence, series.
6 *the scale of a map.* proportion, ratio.
7 *We were amazed by the huge scale of the building.* SEE **size**.
scales *bathroom scales.* balance, weighing-machine.

scale verb
to scale a ladder. ascend, climb, mount.

scamper verb
to scamper home. dash, hasten, hurry, run, rush, scuttle.

scan verb
1 *to scan the horizon.* examine, eye, gaze at, look at, scrutinize, search, stare at, study, survey, view, watch.
2 *to scan a newspaper.* glance at, read quickly, skim.

scandal noun
1 *It's a scandal when food is wasted.* disgrace, embarrassment, notoriety, outrage, reproach, sensation, shame.
2 *The newspapers shouldn't print such scandal.* calumny, gossip, libel, rumour, slander, [*informal*] tittle-tattle.

scandalous adjective
1 *a scandalous waste of money.* disgraceful, improper, infamous, notorious, outrageous, shameful, shocking, wicked.
2 *a scandalous lie.* defamatory, libellous, scurrilous, slanderous, untrue.

scanty adjective
1 *a scanty supply of food.* inadequate, insufficient, meagre, mean, [*slang*] measly, [*informal*] mingy, scant, scarce, [*informal*] skimpy, small, sparing, sparse, stingy.
OPPOSITES: SEE **plentiful**.
2 *scanty clothes.* barely adequate, indecent, revealing, [*informal*] see-through, thin.

scar noun
The cut left a scar. blemish, mark, scab, SEE **wound** noun.

scar verb
The wound scarred his face. brand, damage, deface, disfigure, leave a scar on, mark, spoil.

scarce adjective
Water was scarce during the drought. [*informal*] few and far between, [*informal*] hard to find, inadequate, infrequent, in short supply, insufficient, lacking, meagre, rare, scant, scanty, sparse, [*informal*] thin on the ground, uncommon, unusual.
OPPOSITES: SEE **plentiful**.

scarcely adverb
barely, hardly, only just.

scarcity noun
a scarcity of water. dearth, famine, inadequacy, insufficiency, lack, paucity, poverty, rarity, shortage, want.
OPPOSITES: SEE **plenty**.

scare noun
The bang gave us a nasty scare. alarm, SEE **fright**, jolt, shock.

scare verb
1 *The bang scared us.* alarm, dismay, shake, shock, startle, unnerve.
2 *The ruffians tried to scare us.* bully, cow, daunt, dismay, SEE **frighten**, intimidate, make afraid, menace, panic, terrorize, threaten.
OPPOSITES: SEE **reassure**.

scary adjective
SEE **frightening**.

scathing adjective
SEE **critical**.

scatter verb
1 *to scatter a crowd.* break up, disband, disintegrate, dispel, disperse, divide, send in all directions.
2 *to scatter seeds.* broadcast, disseminate, intersperse [= *scatter between other things*], shed, shower, sow, spread, sprinkle, strew, throw about.
OPPOSITES: SEE **gather**.

scatter-brained adjective
absent-minded, careless, crazy, disorganized, forgetful, frivolous, inattentive, muddled, [*informal*] not with it, [*informal*] scatty, SEE **silly**, thoughtless, unreliable, unsystematic, vague.

scavenge verb
to scavenge in a rubbish heap. forage, rummage, scrounge, search.

scene noun
1 *the scene of a crime.* locale, locality, location, place, position, setting, site, situation, spot.
2 *a beautiful scene.* landscape, outlook, panorama, picture, prospect, scenery, sight, spectacle, view, vista.
3 *the scene for a play.* backdrop, scenery, set, stage.
4 *a scene from a play.* act, [*informal*] clip, episode, part, section, sequence.

5 *He made a scene because he didn't win.*
argument, [*informal*] carry-on, commotion,
disturbance, fuss, quarrel, row, [*informal*]
to-do.

scenic adjective
a scenic journey. attractive, beautiful, lovely,
panoramic, picturesque, pretty,
spectacular.

scent noun
1 *the scent of flowers.* fragrance, odour,
perfume, redolence, SEE **smell** noun.
2 *a bottle of scent.* after-shave, eau de
Cologne, lavender water, perfume.
3 *The dog followed the scent.* trail.

sceptical adjective
I was sceptical about the truth of his story.
cynical, disbelieving, distrustful, doubting,
dubious, incredulous, mistrustful,
questioning, suspicious, uncertain,
unconvinced, unsure.
OPPOSITES: SEE **confident**.

scepticism noun
agnosticism, cynicism, disbelief, distrust,
doubt, incredulity, lack of confidence,
suspicion.
OPPOSITES: SEE **faith**.

schedule noun
a schedule of events. agenda, calendar, diary,
itinerary, list, plan, programme, scheme,
timetable.

schedule verb
When are we scheduled to arrive? appoint,
arrange, book, fix a time, organize, plan,
programme, timetable.

scheme noun
1 *a proper scheme for running the business.*
idea, method, plan, procedure, project,
proposal, system.
2 *a dishonest scheme to make money.*
conspiracy, [*informal*] dodge, intrigue,
machinations, manœuvre, plot, [*informal*]
ploy, [*informal*] racket, ruse, scheming,
stratagem.
3 *a colour scheme.* arrangement, design.

scheme verb
Two boys schemed together. collude,
conspire, intrigue, plan, plot.

scholarly adjective
SEE **academic**.

scholarship noun
1 *a scholarship to study at college.* award,
bursary, exhibition, grant.
2 *a woman of great scholarship.* academic
achievement, education, erudition,
intellectual attainment, knowledge,
learning, wisdom.

school noun

KINDS OF SCHOOL: academy, boarding-
school, coeducational school, college,
comprehensive school, grammar school,
high school, infant school, junior school,
kindergarten, nursery school, play group,
preparatory school, primary school, public
school, secondary school.

PARTS OF A SCHOOL: assembly hall, cafeteria,
common room, dormitory, classroom,
cloakroom, foyer, gymnasium, hall,
laboratory, library, office, playground,
playing-field, reception, refectory, staff
room, stock room.

PEOPLE WHO HELP RUN A SCHOOL: assistant,
caretaker, groundsman, headmaster,
headmistress, head teacher, librarian,
monitor, peripatetic teacher, prefect,
principal, secretary, [*plural*] staff, SEE
teacher, technician, tutor.

science noun

SOME BRANCHES OF SCIENCE AND
TECHNOLOGY: acoustics, aeronautics,
agricultural science, anatomy,
anthropology, artificial intelligence,
astronomy, astrophysics, behavioural
science, biochemistry, biology, biophysics,
botany, chemistry, climatology, computer
science, cybernetics, dietetics, domestic
science, dynamics, earth science, ecology,
economics, electronics, engineering,
entomology, environmental science, food
science, genetics, geographical science,
geology, geophysics, hydraulics.
information technology, life science,
linguistics, materials science, mathematics,
mechanics, medical science [SEE **medicine**],
metallurgy, meteorology, microbiology,
mineralogy, ornithology, pathology,
pharmacology, physics, physiology,
political science, psychology, robotics,
sociology, space technology, sports science,
telecommunications, thermodynamics,
toxicology, veterinary science, zoology.

scientific adjective
a scientific investigation. analytical,
methodical, organized, precise, systematic.

scientist noun
[*informal*] boffin, researcher, scientific
expert, technologist.

scold verb
to scold someone for wrongdoing. admonish,
berate, blame, castigate, censure, chide,

criticize, find fault with, [*informal*] lecture, [*informal*] nag, rebuke, reprimand, reproach, reprove, [*informal*] tell off, [*informal*] tick off, upbraid.

scoop verb
to scoop out a hole. dig, excavate, gouge, hollow, scrape, shovel.

scope noun
1 *That kind of work is beyond my scope.* ambit, capacity, compass, competence, extent, limit, range, reach, sphere, terms of reference.
2 *scope for expansion.* chance, [*informal*] elbow-room, freedom, latitude, leeway, liberty, opportunity, outlet, room, space.

score verb
1 *to score points in a game.* SEE **achieve,** add up, [*informal*] chalk up, earn, gain, [*informal*] knock up, make, win.
2 *to score a line on a surface.* cut, engrave, gouge, incise, mark, scrape, scratch, slash.

scorn noun
They viewed my cooking with scorn. contempt, derision, detestation, disdain, disgust, dislike, disparagement, disrespect, mockery, ridicule.
OPPOSITES: SEE **admiration.**

scorn verb
They scorned my efforts. be scornful about [SEE **scornful**], deride, despise, disapprove of, disdain, dislike, dismiss, hate, insult, jeer at, laugh at, look down on, make fun of, mock, reject, ridicule, [*informal*] scoff at, sneer at, spurn, taunt.
OPPOSITES: SEE **admire.**

scornful adjective
scornful laughter. condescending, contemptuous, derisive, disdainful, dismissive, disrespectful, insulting, jeering, mocking, patronizing, sarcastic, satirical, scathing, sneering, [*informal*] snide, [*informal*] snooty, supercilious, taunting, withering (*a withering look*).
OPPOSITES: SEE **admiring, flattering.**

scoundrel noun
[*Scoundrel* and synonyms are mostly used *informally.*] blackguard, blighter, good-for-nothing, heel, knave, miscreant, ne'er-do-well, rascal, rogue, ruffian, scallywag, scamp, villain.

scour verb
1 *to scour a saucepan.* buff up, burnish, clean, polish, rub, scrape, scrub, wash.
2 *I scoured the house looking for my purse.* comb, forage (through), hunt through, ransack, rummage through, search, [*informal*] turn upside down.

scout verb
Wait here while I scout round. explore, get information, investigate, look about, reconnoitre, search, [*informal*] snoop, spy.

scramble verb
1 *to scramble over rocks.* clamber, climb, crawl, move awkwardly.
2 *to scramble for food.* compete, contend, fight, jostle, push, scuffle, strive, struggle, tussle, vie.

scrap noun
1 *a scrap of food. a scrap of cloth.* bit, crumb, fraction, fragment, iota, mite, morsel, particle, piece, rag, shred, snippet, speck.
2 *a pile of scrap.* junk, litter, odds and ends, refuse, rubbish, salvage, waste.
3 *Two dogs had a scrap.* SEE **fight** noun.

scrap verb
1 *We scrapped our plan when we worked out the cost.* abandon, cancel, discard, [*informal*] ditch, drop, give up, jettison, throw away, write off.
2 *Those two are always scrapping.* SEE **fight** verb.

scrape verb
1 *to scrape your skin.* abrade, bark, graze, lacerate, scratch, scuff.
2 *to scrape something clean.* clean, file, rasp, rub, scour, scrub.

scrappy adjective
scrappy work. bitty, disjointed, fragmentary, hurriedly put together, imperfect, incomplete, inconclusive, sketchy, slipshod, unfinished, unpolished, unsatisfactory.
OPPOSITES: SEE **perfect** adjective.

scratch noun
1 *scratches on the furniture.* gash, groove, line, mark, scoring, scrape.
2 *a scratch on your skin.* graze, laceration, SEE **wound** noun.

scratch verb
to scratch a car. to scratch your skin. claw at, cut, damage the surface of, gouge, graze, incise, lacerate, mark, rub, scarify, score, scrape.

scream noun, verb
bawl, cry, howl, roar, screech, shout, shriek, squeal, wail, yell.

screen noun
a dividing screen. blind, curtain, partition.

screen verb
1 *We planted a hedge to screen the manure heap.* camouflage, cloak, conceal, cover, disguise, guard, hide, mask, protect, safeguard, shade, shelter, shield, shroud, veil.
2 *All employees were screened before being appointed.* examine, investigate, vet.

screw verb
1 *to screw something down.* SEE **fasten**.
2 *to screw something into a spiral shape or with a spiral movement.* SEE **twist** verb.

scribble verb SEE **write**.

scribe noun
amanuensis, secretary, writer.

script noun
1 *cursive script.* handwriting.
2 *the script of a play.* screenplay, text, words.

scripture noun
Bible, Koran, sacred writings, Word of God.

scrounge verb
The stray cat scrounged scraps. beg, cadge.

scruffy adjective
a scruffy appearance. scruffy clothes.
bedraggled, dirty, dishevelled, disordered,
dowdy, messy, ragged, scrappy, shabby,
slatternly, slovenly, tatty, ungroomed,
unkempt, untidy, worn out.
OPPOSITES: SEE **smart** adjective.

scruples noun
Don't trust him—he has no scruples about cheating. compunction, conscience, doubts,
hesitation, misgivings, qualms.

scrupulous adjective
1 *a scrupulous worker. scrupulous attention to detail.* SEE **careful**, conscientious, diligent,
fastidious, meticulous, minute, painstaking,
precise, punctilious, rigorous, strict,
systematic, thorough.
2 *a scrupulous businessman. scrupulous honesty.* ethical, fair-minded, honest,
honourable, just, moral, proper, upright.
OPPOSITES: SEE **unscrupulous**.

scrutinize verb SEE **examine**.

scrutiny noun
She subjected my work to close scrutiny.
examination, inspection, investigation,
search, study.

sculpture noun
three-dimensional art.

KINDS OF SCULPTURE: bas-relief, bronze,
bust, carving, caryatid, cast, effigy, figure,
figurine, maquette, moulding, plaster cast,
statue.

---

sculpture verb
to sculpture a statue. carve, cast, chisel, form,
hew, model, mould, [*informal*] sculpt,
shape.

scum noun
scum on dirty water. film, foam, froth,
impurities.

sea adjective
sea creatures. a sea voyage. a sea port.
aquatic, marine, maritime, nautical, naval,
oceangoing, oceanic, saltwater, seafaring,
seagoing.

sea noun
[*joking*] the briny, [*poetic*] the deep, lake,
ocean.

seal noun
1 sea-lion, walrus.
2 *the royal seal.* crest, emblem, impression,
sign, stamp, symbol.

seal verb
1 *to seal a lid. to seal an envelope.* close,
fasten, lock, secure, shut, stick down.
2 *to seal a leak.* make airtight, make
waterproof, plug, stop up.
3 *to seal an agreement.* authenticate,
[*informal*] clinch, conclude, confirm,
decide, finalize, ratify, settle, sign, validate.

seam noun
1 *the seam of a garment.* join, stitching.
2 *a seam of coal.* layer, stratum, thickness,
vein.

seaman noun SEE **sailor**.

seamy adjective
SEE **sordid**.

search noun
a search for the things we'd lost. a search for intruders. check, examination, hunt,
inspection, investigation, look, quest,
scrutiny.

search verb
1 *I searched for the things we'd lost.* explore,
ferret about, hunt, look, nose about, poke
about, prospect, pry, seek.
2 *Security staff search all passengers.* check,
examine, [*informal*] frisk, inspect,
investigate, scrutinize.
3 *I searched the house for my purse.* comb,
ransack, rifle, rummage through, scour.

searching adjective
searching questions. deep, intimate, minute,
penetrating, probing, sharp, thorough.
OPPOSITES: SEE **superficial**.

seaside noun
a day at the seaside. beach, coast, coastal
resort, sands, sea-coast, sea-shore, shore.

season noun
the festive season. the holiday season. period,
phase, time.

season verb
1 *to season food.* add seasoning to, flavour, salt, spice.
2 *to season wood.* harden, mature.

seasoning noun
I don't add much seasoning to my food. additives, condiments, flavouring.

KINDS OF SEASONING: dressing, herbs, mustard, pepper, relish, salt, SEE **sauce**, spice, vinegar.

---

seat noun

KINDS OF SEAT: armchair, bench, chair, chaise longue, couch, deck-chair, pew, pillion, place, pouffe, reclining chair, rocking-chair, saddle, settee, settle, sofa, squab, stall, stool, throne, window seat.

ITEMS OF FURNITURE: SEE **furniture**.

---

seat verb
to seat yourself SEE **sit**.

secluded adjective
a secluded existence. a secluded beach. cloistered, concealed, cut off, inaccessible, isolated, lonely, private, remote, screened, sequestered, sheltered, shut away, solitary, unfrequented, unvisited.

seclusion noun
the seclusion of your own home. the seclusion of a hermit. concealment, isolation, loneliness, privacy, retirement, shelter, solitariness.

second adjective
You won't get a second chance. additional, alternative, another, duplicate, extra, further, repeated, SEE **secondary**, subsequent.

second noun
1 *The pain only lasted a second.* flash, instant, [*informal*] jiffy, moment, [*informal*] tick, [*informal*] twinkling.
2 *a second to a boxer in a fight.* assistant, helper, supporter.

second verb
1 *to second a proposal. to second someone in a fight.* assist, back, encourage, give approval to, help, promote, side with, support.
2 [pronounced se-*cond*] *to second someone to another job.* move, relocate, transfer.

secondary adjective
1 *of secondary importance.* inferior, lesser, lower, minor, second-rate, subordinate, subsidiary.
2 *a secondary line of attack.* auxiliary, extra,

reinforcing, reserve, second, supplementary, supportive.

second-rate adjective
a second-rate performance. commonplace, indifferent, inferior, low-grade, mediocre, middling, ordinary, poor, second-best, second-class, undistinguished, unexciting, uninspiring.

secret adjective
secret messages. secret meetings. arcane, clandestine, classified, concealed, confidential, covert, cryptic, disguised, hidden, [*informal*] hushed up, [*informal*] hush-hush, inaccessible, intimate, invisible, occult, personal, private, secluded, SEE **secretive**, stealthy, undercover, underground, undisclosed, unknown, unpublished.
OPPOSITES: SEE **open** adjective.

secretary noun
amanuensis, clerk, filing-clerk, personal assistant, scribe, shorthand-typist, stenographer, typist, word-processor operator.

secretive adjective
secretive about his private life. close-lipped, enigmatic, furtive, mysterious, quiet, reserved, reticent, shifty, tight-lipped, uncommunicative, unforthcoming, withdrawn.
OPPOSITES: SEE **communicative**.

sect noun
a religious sect. cult, denomination, faction, SEE **group** noun, party.

section noun
a section of a more complex whole. bit, branch, chapter (*of a book*), compartment, component, department, division, fraction, fragment, instalment, part, passage (*from a book or piece of music*), portion, SEE **sector**, segment, slice, stage (*of a journey*), subdivision, subsection.

sector noun
a sector of a town. area, district, division, part, quarter, region, SEE **section**, zone.

secular adjective
the secular authorities. secular music. civil, earthly, lay, mundane, non-religious, [*formal*] temporal, worldly.
OPPOSITES: SEE **religious**.

secure adjective
1 *Is the house secure against burglars?* defended, foolproof, guarded, impregnable, invulnerable, protected, safe.
2 *During the storm we remained secure indoors.* snug, unharmed, unhurt, unscathed.
3 *Is that hook secure?* fast, firm, fixed, immovable, solid, steady, tight, unyielding.

secure verb
SEE **fasten**.

security noun
SEE **safety**.

sedate adjective
The procession moved at a sedate pace. calm, collected, composed, cool, decorous, deliberate, dignified, grave, level-headed, quiet, sensible, serene, serious, slow, sober, solemn, staid, tranquil.
OPPOSITES: SEE **lively**.

sedate verb
The nurse sedated the patient. calm, put to sleep, tranquillize, treat with sedatives.

sedative noun
anodyne, barbiturate, narcotic, opiate, sleeping-pill, tranquillizer.

sedentary adjective
People in sedentary jobs need to take exercise. immobile, inactive, seated, sitting down.
OPPOSITES: SEE **active**.

sediment noun
sediment at the bottom of a bottle. deposit, dregs, lees, [*formal*] precipitate, remains, [*informal*] sludge.

seduce verb
to seduce someone into wicked ways. allure, beguile, corrupt, debauch, decoy, deprave, entice, inveigle, lead astray, lure, mislead, tempt.

seductive adjective
a seductive dress. seductive music. alluring, appealing, SEE **attractive**, bewitching, captivating, enticing, irresistible, provocative, [*informal*] sexy, tempting.
OPPOSITES: SEE **repulsive**.

see verb
1 *What did you see?* [*old-fashioned*] behold, discern, discover, distinguish, [*old-fashioned*] espy, glimpse, identify, look at, make out, mark, note, notice, observe, perceive, recognize, sight, spot, spy, view, witness.
2 *I can see what you mean.* appreciate, comprehend, fathom, follow, grasp, know, realize, take in, understand.
3 *I see problems ahead.* anticipate, conceive, envisage, foresee, foretell, imagine, picture, visualize.
4 *I'll have to see what I can do.* consider, decide, investigate, reflect on, think about, weigh up.
5 *Did you see the game on Saturday?* attend, be a spectator at, watch.
6 *She's going to see him again tonight.* go out with, have a date with, meet, visit.
7 *Shall I see you home?* accompany, conduct, escort.
8 *The homeless see much misery.* endure, experience, go through, suffer, undergo.
9 *Guess who I saw in town!* encounter, face, meet, run into, visit.

seed noun
1 *a seed from which something will grow.* egg, germ, ovule, ovum, semen, [*plural*] spawn, sperm, spore.
2 *a seed in a fruit.* pip, stone.

seek verb
to seek something you've lost. to seek revenge. ask for, aspire to, beg for, desire, hunt for, inquire after, look for, pursue, search for, solicit, strive after, want, wish for.

seem verb
She isn't as well as she seems. appear, feel, give an impression of being, look, pretend, sound.

seep verb
Oil seeped through the crack. dribble, drip, exude, flow, leak, ooze, percolate, run, soak, trickle.

segregate verb
They segregated visitors from the home supporters. cut off, isolate, keep apart, put apart, separate, set apart.
OPPOSITES: SEE **integrate**.

segregation noun
1 *racial segregation.* apartheid, discrimination, separation.
2 *the segregation of sick animals.* isolation, quarantine.

seize verb
1 *to seize something in your hands.* catch, clutch, grab, grasp, grip, hold, pluck, snatch, take.
2 *to seize a person by force.* abduct, apprehend, arrest, capture, [*informal*] collar, detain, [*informal*] nab, take prisoner.
3 *to seize a country.* annex, invade.
4 *to seize property.* appropriate, commandeer, confiscate, hijack, impound, steal, take away.
OPPOSITES: SEE **release** verb.

seizure noun
to suffer a seizure. apoplexy, attack, convulsion, epileptic fit, fit, paroxysm, spasm, stroke.

seldom adverb
infrequently, rarely.
OPPOSITES: SEE **often**.

select adjective
Only a select few were invited. choice, chosen, élite, exclusive, first-class, [*informal*] hand-picked, preferred, privileged, rare, selected, special, top-quality.
OPPOSITES: SEE **ordinary**.

select verb
to select a representative. to select your purchases. appoint, choose, decide on, elect, nominate, opt for, pick, prefer, settle on, single out, vote for.

selection noun
1 *There's a wide selection to choose from.* assortment, SEE **range** noun, variety.
2 *Make your selection.* choice, option, pick.

selective adjective
She's very selective in what she watches on TV. careful, [*informal*] choosy, discerning, discriminating, particular, specialized.
OPPOSITES: SEE **undiscriminating**.

self-confident adjective
Try to look self-confident at the interview. assertive, assured, bold, collected, cool, fearless, poised, positive, self-assured, self-possessed, sure of yourself.
OPPOSITES: SEE **self-conscious**.

self-conscious adjective
self-conscious in front of an audience. awkward, bashful, blushing, coy, diffident, embarrassed, ill at ease, insecure, nervous, reserved, self-effacing, sheepish, shy, uncomfortable, unnatural.
OPPOSITES: SEE **self-confident**.

self-control noun
He showed great self-control when they were teasing him. calmness, composure, coolness, patience, restraint, self-command, self-discipline, will-power.

self-employed adjective
a self-employed journalist. free-lance, independent.

self-esteem noun
SEE **pride**.

self-indulgent adjective
a self-indulgent pursuit of pleasure. dissipated, epicurean, extravagant, greedy, hedonistic, intemperate, pleasure-loving, profligate, SEE **selfish**, sybaritic.
OPPOSITES: SEE **abstemious**.

self-interest noun
SEE **selfishness**.

selfish adjective
It's selfish to keep it all to yourself. demanding, egocentric, egotistic, grasping, greedy, mean, mercenary, miserly, self-centred, self-indulgent, self-seeking, [*informal*] stingy, thoughtless, worldly.
OPPOSITES: SEE **unselfish**.

selfishness noun
egotism, greed, meanness, miserliness, self-indulgence, self-interest, self-love, self-regard, [*informal*] stinginess, thoughtlessness.
OPPOSITES: SEE **unselfishness**.

selfless adjective SEE **unselfish**.

self-respect noun
SEE **pride**.

self-righteous adjective
Don't feel self-righteous just because you gave an odd coin to charity. complacent, [*informal*] holier-than-thou, pious, pompous, priggish, proud, sanctimonious, self-important, self-satisfied, sleek, smug, vain.

self-supporting adjective
a self-supporting community. independent, self-contained, self-reliant, self-sufficient.

sell verb
1 *What does this shop sell?* deal in, [*informal*] keep, offer for sale, retail, stock, trade in (*He trades in electrical goods*), traffic in, vend.

VARIOUS WAYS TO SELL THINGS: auction, barter, give in part-exchange, hawk, [*informal*] knock down, peddle, [*informal*] put under the hammer, sell off, tout, trade-in (*He traded-in his old car*).

2 *If business is slack, we must sell our product more attractively.* advertise, market, merchandise, package, promote, [*informal*] push.

seller noun
vendor.

PEOPLE WHO SELL THINGS: agent, barrowboy, costermonger, dealer, [*old-fashioned*] hawker, market-trader, merchant, pedlar, [*informal*] rep, representative, retailer, salesman, saleswoman, shopkeeper, stockist, storekeeper, street-trader, supplier, trader, tradesman, traveller, wholesaler.
PARTICULAR SHOPS: SEE **shop**.

send verb
1 *to send a parcel. to send a cheque.* convey, dispatch, post, remit, transmit.
2 *to send a rocket to the moon.* direct, fire, launch, propel, shoot.
to send away banish, dismiss, exile, expel.
to send out belch, broadcast, discharge, emit, give off.

senile adjective
SEE **old**.

senior adjective
a senior position. a senior member of the team. chief, higher, major, older, principal, revered, superior, well-established.
OPPOSITES: SEE **junior**.

sensation noun
1 *a tingling sensation in my fingers.*
awareness, feeling, sense.
2 *The robbery caused a sensation.* SEE
commotion, excitement, furore, outrage,
scandal, surprise, thrill.

sensational adjective
1 *a sensational account of a murder. the
sensational experience of hang-gliding.*
blood-curdling, breathtaking, exciting, hair-
raising, lurid, shocking, startling,
stimulating, thrilling, violent.
2 [*informal*] *a sensational football result.*
amazing, SEE **extraordinary**, fabulous,
fantastic, great, marvellous, remarkable,
spectacular, superb, surprising,
unexpected, wonderful.

sense noun
1 *She has no sense of shame.* awareness,
consciousness, faculty, feeling, intuition,
perception, sensation.
YOUR FIVE SENSES ARE: hearing, sight, smell,
taste, touch.
2 *If you had any sense you'd stay at home.*
brains, cleverness, gumption, intellect,
intelligence, judgement, logic, [*informal*]
nous, reason, reasoning, understanding,
wisdom, wit.
3 *Did you grasp the sense of her message?*
denotation, [*informal*] drift, gist, import,
interpretation, meaning, point, significance.
to make sense of SEE **understand**.

sense verb
*I sensed that he was bored. The machine
senses any change of temperature.* be aware
(of), detect, discern, feel, guess, notice,
perceive, realize, respond to, suspect,
understand.
WAYS IN WHICH WE SENSE THINGS: SEE **feel**,
hear, **see**, **smell**, **taste** verbs.

senseless adjective
1 *a senseless thing to do.* SEE **stupid**.
2 *knocked senseless.* SEE **unconscious**.

sensible adjective
1 *a sensible person. a sensible decision.* calm,
common-sense, cool, discriminating,
intelligent, judicious, level-headed, logical,
prudent, rational, realistic, reasonable,
sane, serious-minded, sound,
straightforward, thoughtful, wise.
OPPOSITES: SEE **stupid**.
2 *sensible clothes.* comfortable, functional,
[*informal*] no-nonsense, practical, useful.

sensitive adjective
1 *sensitive to light.* affected (by), responsive,
susceptible.
2 *sensitive to someone's problems.*
considerate, perceptive, sympathetic, tactful,
thoughtful, understanding.
3 *Take care what you say—he's very sensitive.*

emotional, hypersensitive, thin-skinned,
touchy.
4 *a sensitive skin.* delicate, fine, fragile,
painful, soft, tender.
5 *a sensitive subject.* confidential,
controversial, secret.
OPPOSITES: SEE **insensitive**.

sensual adjective
sensual pleasures. animal, bodily, carnal,
fleshly, physical, self-indulgent, SEE **sexual**,
voluptuous, worldly.

sensuous adjective
a sensuous description. sensuous music.
affecting, appealing, beautiful, emotional,
lush, rich, richly embellished.

sentence verb
The judge sentenced the convicted man.
condemn, pass judgement on, pronounce
sentence on.

sentiment noun
1 *What are your sentiments about experiments
on animals?* attitude, belief, idea,
judgement, opinion, thought, view.
2 *The reader communicated the sentiment of
the poem most powerfully.* emotion, feeling.

sentimental adjective
1 *Old family photographs make me
sentimental.* emotional, nostalgic, romantic,
soft-hearted, tearful, tender, [*informal*]
weepy.
2 [*uncomplimentary*] *I hate sentimental
words on birthday cards.* gushing, indulgent,
insincere, maudlin, mawkish, [*informal*]
mushy, overdone, over-emotional,
[*informal*] sloppy, [*informal*] soppy,
[*informal*] sugary, tear-jerking, [*informal*]
treacly, unrealistic.
OPPOSITES: SEE **cynical, unemotional**.

sentinel, sentry nouns
guard, look-out, picket, watchman.

separate adjective
1 *They kept visiting supporters separate from
ours.* apart, cut off, divided, divorced, fenced
off, isolated, segregated.
2 *We all have separate jobs to do. We work in
separate buildings.* detached, different,
discrete, distinct, free-standing, unattached,
unconnected, unrelated.
3 *The islanders have their own separate
government.* autonomous, free, independent,
particular.

separate verb
1 *to separate people or things or places from
each other.* break up, cut off, detach,
disconnect, disentangle, disjoin, dissociate,
divide, fence off, hive off, isolate, keep apart,
part, segregate, set apart, sever, split,
sunder, take apart.
OPPOSITES: SEE **unite**.

2 *Our paths separated.* diverge, fork.
OPPOSITES: SEE **merge**.
3 *to separate grain from chaff.* abstract, filter out, remove, sift out, winnow.
OPPOSITES: SEE **mix**.
4 *to separate from your spouse.* become estranged, divorce, part company, [*informal*] split up.

separation noun
1 *the separation of one thing from another.* amputation, cutting off, detachment, disconnection, dissociation, division, parting, removal, segregation, severance, splitting.
OPPOSITES: SEE **connection**.
2 *the separation of a married couple.* [*informal*] break-up, divorce, estrangement, rift, split.

septic adjective
a septic wound. festering, infected, inflamed, poisoned, purulent, putrefying, suppurating.

sequel noun
the sequel of an event or story. consequence, continuation, [*informal*] follow-up, outcome, result, upshot.

sequence noun
1 *an unbroken sequence of events.* chain, concatenation, cycle, procession, progression, SEE **series**, succession, train.
2 *a sequence from a film.* episode, scene, section.

serene adjective
a serene mood. serene music. calm, contented, imperturbable, peaceful, placid, pleasing, quiet, tranquil, unclouded, unruffled, untroubled.
OPPOSITES: SEE **agitated**.

series noun
1 *a series of events.* arrangement, chain, concatenation, course, cycle, line, order, procession, programme, progression, range, row, run, sequence, set, string, succession, train.
2 *a television series.* mini-series, serial, [*informal*] soap, soap-opera.

serious adjective
1 *a serious expression.* dignified, grave, grim, humourless, long-faced, pensive, sedate, sober, solemn, staid, stern, thoughtful, unsmiling.
OPPOSITES: SEE **cheerful**.
2 *a serious discussion. serious literature.* deep, earnest, heavy, important, intellectual, profound, sincere, weighty.
OPPOSITES: SEE **frivolous**.
3 *a serious accident. a serious illness.* acute, appalling, awful, calamitous, critical, dangerous, dreadful, frightful, ghastly, grievous, hideous, horrible, nasty, severe,

shocking, terrible, unfortunate, unpleasant, violent.
OPPOSITES: SEE **trivial**.
4 *a serious worker.* careful, committed, conscientious, diligent, hard-working.
OPPOSITES: SEE **lax**.

servant noun
assistant, attendant, [*informal*] dogsbody, drudge, [*joking*] factotum, [*joking*] flunkey, helper, hireling, menial, [*informal*] skivvy, slave, vassal.

VARIOUS SERVANTS: au pair, barmaid, barman, batman, butler, chamber-maid, [*informal*] char, charwoman, chauffeur, commissionaire, cook, [*informal*] daily, errand boy, footman, home help, housekeeper, housemaid, kitchenmaid, lackey, lady-in-waiting, maid, manservant, page, parlourmaid, retainer, [*plural*] retinue, scout, slave, steward, stewardess, valet, waiter, waitress.

serve verb
1 *to serve the community.* aid, assist, attend, further, help, look after, minister to, work for.
2 *to serve in the armed forces.* be employed, do your duty.
3 *to serve food. to serve at table.* [*informal*] dish up, distribute, give out, officiate, wait.
4 *to serve in a shop.* assist, be an assistant, sell goods.

service noun
1 *Would you do me a small service?* assistance, benefit, favour, help, kindness, office.
2 *He spent his life in the service of the same firm.* attendance (on), employment, ministering (to), work (for).
3 *a bus service.* business, organization, provision, system, timetable.
4 *a service for a car.* check-over, maintenance, overhaul, repair, servicing.
5 *a religious service.* ceremony, liturgy, meeting, rite, worship.

VARIOUS CHURCH SERVICES: baptism, christening, communion, compline, Eucharist, evensong, funeral, Lord's Supper, marriage, Mass, matins, Requiem Mass, vespers.

service verb
to service a car. check, maintain, mend, overhaul, repair, tune.

servile adjective
servile self-abasement. abject, [*informal*] boot-licking, craven, cringing, fawning, flattering, grovelling, humble, ingratiating,

menial, obsequious, slavish, submissive, subservient, sycophantic, unctuous.
OPPOSITES: SEE **bossy**.

serving noun
a serving of food. helping, plateful, portion, ration.

servitude noun
SEE **slavery**.

session noun
1 *The court is in session.* assembly, conference, discussion, hearing, meeting, sitting.
2 *a session at the swimming-baths.* period, time.

set noun
1 *a set of people. a set of tools.* batch, bunch, category, class, clique, collection, SEE **group** noun, kind, series, sort.
2 *a TV set.* apparatus, receiver.
3 *a set for a play.* scene, scenery, setting, stage.

set verb
1 *to set something in place.* arrange, assign, deploy, deposit, dispose, lay, leave, locate, lodge, park, place, plant, [*informal*] plonk, position, put, rest, set down, set out, settle, situate, stand, station.
2 *to set a gate-post in concrete.* embed, fasten, fix.
3 *to set a watch.* adjust, correct, put right, rectify, regulate.
4 *to set a question in an exam.* ask, express, formulate, frame, phrase, put forward, suggest, write.
5 *Has the jelly set?* become firm, congeal, [*informal*] gel, harden, [*informal*] jell, stiffen, take shape.
6 *to set a target. to set a date.* allocate, allot, appoint, decide, designate, determine, establish, identify, name, ordain, prescribe, settle.
to set free SEE **liberate**.
to set off 1 *We set off on a journey.* SEE **depart**.
2 *They set off a bomb.* SEE **explode**.
to set up SEE **establish**.

set-back noun
We were delayed by a set-back. [*informal*]
blow, complication, difficulty, disappointment, [*informal*] hitch, misfortune, obstacle, problem, reverse, snag, upset.

setting noun
1 *a beautiful setting for a picnic.* background, context, environment, location, place, position, site, surroundings.
2 *a setting for a drama.* backcloth, backdrop, scene, scenery, set.

settle verb
1 *to settle something in place.* SEE **set** verb.
2 *They plan to settle here.* become established, colonize, immigrate, make your home, move to, occupy, people, set up home, stay.
3 *We settled on the sofa. A bird settled on the fence.* alight, come to rest, land, light, [*informal*] make yourself comfortable, [*informal*] park yourself, pause, rest, sit down.
4 *Wait until the dust settles.* calm down, clear, compact, go down, sink, subside.
5 *We settled what to do.* agree, choose, decide, establish, fix.
6 *They settled their differences.* conclude, deal with, end, reconcile, resolve, square.
7 *I settled the bill.* pay.

settlement noun
1 *a business settlement.* SEE **arrangement**.
2 *a human settlement.* colony, community, encampment, kibbutz, SEE **town**, village.

settler noun
colonist, immigrant, newcomer, pioneer, squatter.

sever verb
to sever a limb. to sever a relationship. amputate, break, break off, SEE **cut** verb, cut off, disconnect, end, part, remove, separate, split, terminate.

several adjective
assorted, different, a few, many, miscellaneous, a number of, sundry, various.

severe adjective
1 *a severe ruler. a severe look.* cold-hearted, cruel, disapproving, forbidding, grim, hard, harsh, oppressive, pitiless, relentless, stern, strict, unkind, unsmiling, unsympathetic.
OPPOSITES: SEE **kind** adjective.
2 *a severe frost. severe flu.* acute, bad, drastic, extreme, great, intense, keen, serious, sharp, troublesome, violent.
OPPOSITES: SEE **mild**.
3 *severe conditions. a severe test of stamina.* arduous, dangerous, demanding, difficult, nasty, spartan, stringent, taxing, tough.
OPPOSITES: SEE **easy**.
4 *a severe style of dress.* austere, chaste, plain, simple, unadorned.
OPPOSITES: SEE **ornate**.

sew verb
to sew up a hole in your jeans. darn, mend, repair, stitch, tack.

sewage noun
effluent, waste.

sewing noun
dressmaking, embroidery, mending, needlepoint, needlework, tapestry.

sex noun
a person's sex. gender, sexuality.
to have sexual intercourse be intimate,
consummate marriage, copulate, couple,
fornicate, [*informal*] have sex, make love,
mate, rape, unite.

KINDS OF SEXUALITY: bisexual,
hermaphrodite, heterosexual,
homosexual.

WORDS TO DESCRIBE SEXUAL ACTIVITY: [*old-
fashioned*] carnal knowledge,
coitus, consummation of marriage,
copulation, coupling, fornication, incest,
intercourse, intimacy, love-making,
masturbation, mating, orgasm,
perversion, rape, seduction, sexual
intercourse, union.

---

sexist adjective
[*informal*] chauvinist, SEE **prejudiced**.

sexual adjective
sexual feelings. carnal, erotic, physical,
sensual, SEE **sexy**, venereal (*venereal
diseases*).

sexy adjective
1 *a sexy person.* attractive, desirable,
[*informal*] dishy, flirtatious, seductive,
sensual, [*informal*] sultry, voluptuous.
2 *sexy feelings.* amorous, erotic, lascivious,
lecherous, libidinous, lustful, passionate,
[*informal*] randy.
3 *sexy talk. sexy books.* aphrodisiac, erotic,
SEE **obscene**, pornographic, provocative,
[*informal*] raunchy, suggestive, titillating,
[*informal*] torrid.

shabby adjective
shabby clothes. dingy, dirty, dowdy, drab,
faded, frayed, grubby, [*informal*] moth-
eaten, ragged, [*informal*] scruffy, seedy,
tattered, [*informal*] tatty, threadbare,
unattractive, worn, worn-out.
OPPOSITES: SEE **smart** adjective.

shade noun
1 *the shade of a tree.* SEE **shadow** noun.
2 *a shade to keep the sun off.* blind, canopy,
covering, parasol, screen, shelter, shield,
umbrella.
3 *a pale shade of blue.* colour, hue, tinge, tint,
tone.

shade verb
1 *I shaded my eyes from the sun.* conceal,
hide, mask, protect, screen, shield, shroud,
veil.
2 *I shaded the background with a pencil.*
block in, cross-hatch, darken, fill in, make
dark.

shadow noun
1 *I sat in the shadow of a tree.* darkness,
dimness, gloom, [*formal*] penumbra, semi-
darkness, shade, [*formal*] umbra.
2 *The sun casts shadows.* outline, shape.

shadow verb
The detective shadowed the suspect. follow,
hunt, [*informal*] keep tabs on, keep watch
on, pursue, stalk, [*informal*] tag onto, tail,
track, trail, watch.

shadowy adjective
a shadowy figure. dim, faint, ghostly, hazy,
indistinct, nebulous, obscure,
unrecognizable, vague.

shady adjective
1 *a shady spot under a tree.* cool, dark, dim,
gloomy, shaded, shadowy, sheltered,
sunless.
OPPOSITES: SEE **sunny**.
2 *a shady character.* dishonest, disreputable,
dubious, [*informal*] fishy, shifty,
suspicious, untrustworthy.
OPPOSITES: SEE **honest**.

shaft noun
1 *a wooden shaft.* arrow, column, handle,
pillar, pole, post, rod, stem, stick.
2 *a shaft of light.* beam, ray.
3 *a mine-shaft.* mine, pit, working.

shake verb
1 *An explosion made the house shake.*
convulse, heave, jump, quake, quiver, rattle,
rock, shiver, shudder, sway, throb, totter,
tremble, vibrate, waver, wobble.
2 *I shook my watch to get it going again.*
agitate, brandish, flourish, jar, jerk,
[*informal*] jiggle, [*informal*] joggle, jolt,
twirl, twitch, wag, [*informal*] waggle, wave,
[*informal*] wiggle.

shaky adjective
1 *shaky hands.* quivering, shaking,
trembling.
2 *a shaky table.* flimsy, frail, ramshackle,
rickety, rocky, unsteady, weak, wobbly.
3 *a shaky voice.* faltering, nervous,
quavering, tremulous.
OPPOSITES: SEE **steady** adjective.
4 *a shaky start.* insecure, precarious,
uncertain, under-confident, unimpressive,
unpromising, unreliable, unsound.

shallow adjective
1 *shallow water.* [Surprisingly, there are no
convenient synonyms for this common
sense of *shallow*.]
2 *a shallow person, shallow arguments.*
facile, foolish, frivolous, glib, insincere,
puerile, silly, simple, slight, superficial,
trivial, unconvincing, unscholarly,
unthinkable.
OPPOSITES: SEE **deep**.

sham verb SEE **pretend**.

shambles noun
1 slaughter-house.
2 [*informal*] *My room is a shambles.* chaos, confusion, disorder, mess, muddle.

shame noun
1 *the shame of being found out.* degradation, discredit, disgrace, dishonour, embarrassment, guilt, humiliation, ignominy, mortification, opprobrium, remorse, stain, stigma.
2 [*informal*] *It's a shame to treat a dog so badly!* outrage, pity, scandal.

shame verb
They shamed him into admitting everything. discomfit, disconcert, disgrace, embarrass, humble, humiliate, make ashamed [SEE **ashamed**], [*informal*] show up.

shameful adjective
a shameful defeat. a shameful crime. base, contemptible, degrading, discreditable, disgraceful, dishonourable, humiliating, ignominious, inglorious, outrageous, reprehensible, scandalous, unworthy, SEE **wicked**.
OPPOSITES: SEE **honourable**.

shameless adjective
He's shameless about his cheating and lying. barefaced, bold, brazen, cheeky, cool, defiant, flagrant, hardened, impenitent, impudent, incorrigible, insolent, rude, unabashed, unashamed, unrepentant.
OPPOSITES: SEE **ashamed**.

shape noun
configuration, figure, form, format, model, mould, outline, pattern, silhouette.

FLAT SHAPES: circle, diamond, ellipse, heptagon, hexagon, lozenge, oblong, octagon, oval, parallelogram, pentagon, polygon, quadrant, quadrilateral, rectangle, rhomboid, rhombus, ring, semicircle, square, trapezium, trapezoid, triangle.

THREE-DIMENSIONAL SHAPES: cone, cube, cylinder, decahedron, hemisphere, hexahedron, octahedron, polyhedron, prism, pyramid, sphere.

---

shape verb
The sculptor shaped the stone. carve, cast, cut, fashion, form, frame, give shape to, model, mould, [*informal*] sculpt, sculpture, whittle.

shapeless adjective
1 *a shapeless mass.* amorphous, formless, indeterminate, irregular, nebulous, undefined, unformed, vague.
OPPOSITE: defined.
2 *a shapeless figure.* [*informal*] dumpy, unattractive, unshapely.
OPPOSITES: SEE **shapely**.

shapely adjective
a shapely figure. attractive, [*informal*], [*sexist*] curvaceous, elegant, graceful, trim, [*informal*], [*sexist*] voluptuous, well-proportioned.
OPPOSITES: SEE **shapeless**.

share noun
Everyone got a share of the cake. allocation, allowance, bit, cut, division, fraction, helping, part, piece, portion, proportion, quota, ration, [*informal*] whack.

share verb
1 *We shared the food equally.* allocate, allot, apportion, deal out, distribute, divide, [*informal*] go halves or shares (with), halve, partake of, portion out, ration out, share out, split.
2 *If we share the work we'll finish quickly.* be involved, co-operate, join, participate, take part.

sharp adjective
1 *a sharp knife. a sharp point.* cutting, fine, jagged, keen, pointed, razor-sharp, sharpened, spiky.
OPPOSITES: SEE **blunt** adjective.
2 *a sharp corner. a sharp drop.* abrupt, acute, angular, hairpin (*a hairpin bend*), precipitous (*a precipitous drop*), steep, sudden, surprising, unexpected.
OPPOSITES: SEE **gradual**.
3 *a sharp picture.* clear, defined, distinct, focused, well-defined.
OPPOSITES: SEE **blurred**.
4 *a sharp frost.* extreme, heavy, intense, serious, severe, violent.
OPPOSITES: SEE **slight** adjective.
5 *a sharp pain.* acute, excruciating, painful, stabbing, stinging.
6 *a sharp tongue.* acerbic, acid, acidulous, barbed, biting, caustic, critical, hurtful, incisive, mocking, mordant, sarcastic, sardonic, scathing, trenchant, unkind, vitriolic.
OPPOSITES: SEE **kind** adjective.
7 *a sharp taste or smell.* acid, acrid, bitter, caustic, pungent, sour, tangy, tart.
OPPOSITES: SEE **bland**.
8 *a sharp mind.* acute, alert, astute, bright, clever, cute, discerning, incisive, intelligent, observant, perceptive, quick, quick-witted, shrewd, [*informal*] smart.
OPPOSITES: SEE **stupid**.
9 *a sharp sound.* clear, high, penetrating,

piercing, shrill.
OPPOSITES: SEE **muffled**.

sharpen verb
to sharpen a knife. file, grind, hone, make
sharp, strop, whet.
OPPOSITES: SEE **blunt** adjective.

shatter verb
to shatter a window. blast, break, break up,
burst, crack, destroy, disintegrate, explode,
pulverize, shiver, smash, splinter, split,
wreck.

shear verb
to shear sheep. clip, SEE **cut** verb, strip, trim.

sheath noun
a sheath for a sword. casing, covering,
scabbard, sleeve.

shed noun
a garden shed. hut, lean-to, outhouse,
potting-shed, shack, shelter, storehouse.

shed verb
A lorry shed its load. I shed a few tears. cast
off, discard, drop, let fall, scatter, shower,
spill, throw off.

sheen noun
a nice sheen on the furniture. brightness,
burnish, gleam, gloss, lustre, patina, polish,
shine.

sheep noun
ewe, lamb, mutton [= *meat from sheep*], ram,
wether.

sheepish adjective
a sheepish look. abashed, ashamed, bashful,
coy, embarrassed, guilty, mortified, self-
conscious, shamefaced, shy, timid.
OPPOSITES: SEE **shameless**.

sheer adjective
1 *sheer nonsense.* absolute, complete, out-
and-out, pure, total, unmitigated,
unqualified, utter.
2 *a sheer cliff.* abrupt, perpendicular,
precipitous, vertical.
3 *sheer silk.* diaphanous, fine, flimsy,
[*informal*] see-through, thin, transparent.

sheet noun
1 *sheets for a bed.*
OTHER BEDCLOTHES: SEE **bedclothes**.
2 *a sheet of paper.* folio, leaf, page.
3 *a sheet of glass.* pane, panel, plate.
4 *a sheet of ice on a pond.* coating, covering,
film, layer, skin.
5 *a sheet of water.* area, expanse, surface.

shelf noun
ledge, shelving.

shell noun
1 *a hard outer shell.* carapace [= *shell of a
tortoise*], case, casing, covering, crust,
exterior, husk, outside, pod.
2 *a shell from a gun.* SEE **ammunition**.

shell verb
to shell the enemy. attack, barrage, bomb,
bombard, fire at, shoot at, strafe.

shellfish noun
bivalve, crustacean, mollusc.

VARIOUS SHELLFISH: barnacle, clam, cockle,
conch, crab, crayfish, cuttlefish, limpet,
lobster, mussel, oyster, prawn, scallop,
shrimp, whelk, winkle.

shelter noun
1 *Where can we find shelter from the wind?*
asylum, cover, haven, lee, protection, refuge,
safety, sanctuary.
2 *a shelter against the wind.* barrier, cover,
fence, hut, roof, screen, shield.
3 *an air-raid shelter.* bunker.

shelter verb
1 *The fence sheltered us from the wind.* defend,
guard, protect, safeguard, screen, shade,
shield.
2 *Is it wrong to shelter a criminal?*
accommodate, give shelter to [SEE **shelter**
noun], harbour, hide.

sheltered adjective
1 *a sheltered spot.* enclosed, on the leeward
side, protected, quiet, screened, shielded,
snug, windless.
OPPOSITES: SEE **windswept**.
2 *a sheltered life.* cloistered, isolated, limited,
lonely, unadventurous, unexciting,
withdrawn.
OPPOSITES: SEE **adventurous**.

shield noun
1 *a shield against the wind.* barrier, defence,
guard, protection, safeguard, screen,
shelter.
2 *a warrior's shield.* buckler, [*in heraldry*]
escutcheon.

shield verb
to shield someone from danger. cover, defend,
guard, keep safe, protect, safeguard, screen,
shade, shelter.

shift verb
to shift your position. SEE **change** verb, **move**
verb.

shifty adjective
I didn't trust his shifty expression. crafty,
deceitful, devious, dishonest, evasive,
furtive, scheming, secretive, [*informal*]
shady, [*informal*] slippery, sly, tricky,
untrustworthy, wily.
OPPOSITES: SEE **straightforward**.

shine verb
1 SEE **light** noun **(give light)**.
2 *What do you shine at?* be clever, do well, excel.
3 [*informal*] *to shine your shoes.* SEE **polish** verb.

shingle noun
1 *shingle on the beach.* gravel, pebbles, stones.
2 *shingles on the roof.* tile.

shining adjective
1 *a shining light.* brilliant, glittering, glowing, luminous, radiant, SEE **shiny**, sparkling.
2 *a shining example.* conspicuous, eminent, glorious, outstanding, praiseworthy, resplendent, splendid.

shiny adjective
a shiny surface. bright, burnished, dazzling, gleaming, glistening, glossy, lustrous, polished, reflective, rubbed, shining, sleek.
OPPOSITES: SEE **dull** adjective.

ship noun
VARIOUS SHIPS: SEE **vessel**.

shirk verb
to shirk your duty. avoid, dodge, duck, evade, get out of, neglect.
to shirk work be lazy, malinger, [*informal*] skive, slack.

shiver verb
to shiver with cold. quake, quaver, quiver, shake, shudder, tremble, twitch, vibrate.

shock noun
1 *the shock of an explosion.* blow, collision, concussion, impact, jolt.
2 *His sudden death was a great shock.* blow, bombshell, SEE **surprise** noun.
3 *in a state of shock.* dismay, distress, fright, [*formal*] trauma, upset.

shock verb
1 *The unexpected news shocked us.* alarm, amaze, astonish, astound, confound, daze, dismay, distress, frighten, [*informal*] give someone a turn, jolt, numb, paralyse, scare, shake, stagger, startle, stun, stupefy, surprise, [*formal*] traumatize, unnerve.
2 *The bad language shocked us.* appal, disgust, horrify, offend, outrage, repel, revolt, scandalize.

shocking adjective
1 *a shocking experience.* alarming, distressing, frightening, SEE **painful**, staggering, traumatic, unnerving, upsetting.
2 *shocking bad language.* SEE **outrageous**.

shoddy adjective
1 *shoddy goods.* cheap, flimsy, gimcrack, inferior, jerry-built, nasty, poor quality, rubbishy, tawdry, trashy.

OPPOSITES: SEE **superior**.
2 *shoddy work.* careless, messy, negligent, slipshod, sloppy, slovenly, untidy.
OPPOSITES: SEE **careful**.

shoe noun
[*plural*] footwear.

KINDS OF SHOE: boot, bootee, brogue, clog, espadrille, [*plural*] galoshes, gumboot, [*informal*] lace-up, moccasin, plimsoll, pump, sabot, sandal, [*informal*] slip-on, slipper, trainer, wader, wellington.

shoot noun
shoots of a plant. branch, bud, new growth, offshoot, sprout, twig.

shoot verb
1 *to shoot a gun.* aim, discharge, fire.
2 *to shoot animals. to shoot someone in the street.* aim at, bombard, fire at, gun down, hit, SEE **hunt** verb, SEE **kill** verb, open fire on, [*informal*] pick off, shell, snipe at, strafe, [*informal*] take pot-shots at.
3 *He shot out of his chair.* dart, dash, hurtle, leap, move quickly, rush, streak.
4 *Plants shoot in the spring.* bud, grow, put out shoots, spring up, sprout.

shop noun
boutique, cash-and-carry, department store, [*old-fashioned*] emporium, establishment, market, retailer, seller, store, wholesaler.

VARIOUS SHOPS AND BUSINESSES: antique shop, baker, bank, barber, betting shop, bookmaker, bookshop, building society, butcher, café, chandler, chemist, clothes shop, confectioner, creamery, dairy, delicatessen, DIY, draper.

electrician, estate agent, fish and chip shop, fishmonger, florist, furniture store, garden-centre, greengrocer, grocer, haberdasher, hairdresser, hardware store, health-food shop, herbalist, hypermarket, insurance brokers, ironmonger, jeweller.

launderette, market, newsagent, off-licence, outfitters, pawnbroker, pharmacy, post office, poulterer, radio and TV shop, shoemaker, stationer, supermarket, tailor, take-away, tobacconist, toyshop, video-shop, vintner, watchmaker.

shopkeeper noun
dealer, merchant, retailer, salesgirl, salesman, saleswoman, stockist, storekeeper, supplier, trader, tradesman.

shore noun
the shore of a lake or the sea. bank, beach, coast, edge, foreshore, sands, seashore, seaside, shingle, [*old-fashioned*] strand.

short adjective
1 *a short piece of string.* [There is no obvious synonym for *short* in this sense.]
OPPOSITES: SEE **long** adjective.
2 *a short person.* diminutive, dumpy, dwarfish, little, [*of a woman*] petite, small, squat, stubby, stumpy, tiny, [*informal*] wee, undergrown.
OPPOSITES: SEE **tall**.
3 *a short visit.* brief, cursory, curtailed, ephemeral, fleeting, momentary, passing, quick, temporary, transient, transitory.
OPPOSITES: SEE **long** adjective.
4 *a short book.* abbreviated, abridged, compact, concise, shortened, succinct, terse.
OPPOSITES: SEE **long** adjective.
5 *During the drought water was in short supply.* deficient, inadequate, insufficient, lacking, limited, meagre, scanty, scarce, sparse, wanting.
OPPOSITES: SEE **plentiful**.
6 *He was short with me when I asked for a loan.* abrupt, bad-tempered, blunt, brusque, cross, curt, gruff, grumpy, impolite, irritable, laconic, sharp, snappy, testy, unfriendly, unkind, unsympathetic.
OPPOSITES: SEE **friendly**.

shortage noun
a shortage of water during drought. absence, dearth, deficiency, insufficiency, lack, paucity, poverty, scarcity, shortfall, want.
OPPOSITES: SEE **plenty**.

shortcoming noun
Bad language is one of his shortcomings. defect, failing, fault, foible, imperfection, vice, weakness.

shorten verb
I shortened my story because it was too long. abbreviate, abridge, compress, condense, curtail, cut down, cut short, précis, prune, reduce, summarize, telescope, trim, truncate.
OPPOSITES: SEE **lengthen**.

shot noun
1 *a shot from a gun.* ball, bang, blast, bullet, crack, discharge, pellet, round, [*informal*] slug.
2 *He's a good shot.* marksman.
3 *a shot at goal.* attempt, effort, endeavour, [*informal*] go (*Have a go!*), hit, kick, stroke, try.
4 *The photographer took some unusual shots.* angle, photograph, picture, scene, sequence, snap.

shout verb
bawl, bellow, [*informal*] belt (*Belt it out!*), call, cheer, clamour, cry out, exclaim, rant, roar, scream, screech, shriek, talk loudly, vociferate, yell, yelp.
OPPOSITES: SEE **whisper** verb.

shouting noun SEE **clamour** noun.

shove verb
They shoved me out of the way. barge, crowd, drive, elbow, hustle, jostle, SEE **push**, shoulder.

shovel verb
I shovelled the snow off the path. clear, dig, scoop, shift.

show noun
1 *a show at the theatre.* SEE **entertainment**, performance, production.
2 *an art show. a dog show.* competition, display, exhibition, presentation.
3 *a show of strength.* appearance, demonstration, façade, illusion, impression, pose, pretence, threat.

show verb
1 *We showed our work in public.* display, exhibit, open up, present, produce, reveal.
2 *My knee showed through a hole in my jeans.* appear, be seen, be visible, emerge, materialize, stand out.
3 *She showed me the way.* conduct, direct, guide, indicate, point out.
4 *He showed me great kindness.* bestow (upon), confer (upon), treat with.
5 *The photo shows us at work.* depict, give a picture of, illustrate, picture, portray, represent.
6 *She showed me how to do it.* describe, explain, instruct, make clear, teach, tell.
7 *The tests showed that I was right.* attest, demonstrate, evince, exemplify, manifest, prove, witness (to).
to show off SEE **boast**.

shower verb
A passing bus showered mud over us. deluge, rain, spatter, splash, spray, sprinkle.

show-off noun
[*informal*] big-head, boaster, braggart, conceited person [SEE **conceited**], egotist, exhibitionist, [*informal*] poser, poseur, [*informal*] showman.

showy adjective
showy clothes. bright, conspicuous, flamboyant, flashy, garish, gaudy, [*informal*] loud, lurid, ostentatious, pretentious, striking, trumpery.
OPPOSITES: SEE **restrained**.

shred noun
not a shred of evidence. bit, iota, jot, piece, scrap, snippet, trace.
shreds *torn to shreds.* rags, ribbons, strips, tatters.

shred verb
cut to shreds, grate, tear.

shrewd adjective
a shrewd politician. artful, astute, [*informal*] canny, clever, crafty, cunning, discerning, discriminating, ingenious, intelligent, knowing, observant, perceptive, quick-witted, sharp, sly, smart, wily, wise.
OPPOSITES: SEE **stupid**.

shriek noun, verb
SEE **scream**.

shrill adjective
a shrill voice. ear-splitting, high, high-pitched, penetrating, piercing, piping, screaming, sharp, strident, treble.
OPPOSITES: SEE **gentle**, **sonorous**.

shrink verb
1 *The pond shrank during the drought. The laundry has shrunk my jumper.* become smaller, contract, decrease, diminish, dwindle, lessen, make smaller, narrow, reduce, shorten, SEE **shrivel**.
OPPOSITES: SEE **expand**.
2 *The dog shrank when the cat spat at him.* back off, cower, cringe, flinch, hang back, quail, recoil, retire, wince, withdraw.

shrivel verb
The plants shrivelled in the heat. become parched, dehydrate, droop, dry out, dry up, SEE **shrink**, wilt, wither, wrinkle.

shroud verb
Mist shrouded the top of the mountain. cloak, conceal, cover, enshroud, envelop, hide, mask, screen, swathe, veil, wrap up.

shrub noun
bush, tree.

COMMON SHRUBS: azalea, berberis, blackthorn, broom, bryony, buddleia, camellia, daphne, forsythia, gorse, heather, hydrangea, japonica, jasmine, lavender, lilac, myrtle, privet, rhododendron, rosemary, rue, viburnum.

---

shudder verb
I shuddered when I heard the gory details. be horrified, convulse, quake, quiver, shake, shiver, squirm, tremble.

shuffle verb
1 *I shuffled upstairs in my slippers.* SEE **walk** verb.
2 *to shuffle cards.* jumble, mix, mix up, rearrange, reorganize.

shun verb
SEE **avoid**.

shut verb
Shut the door. bolt, close, fasten, latch, lock, push to, replace, seal, secure, slam.
to shut in, to shut up confine, detain, enclose, imprison, incarcerate, keep in.
to shut out ban, bar, exclude, keep out, prohibit.

shutter noun
Close the shutter. blind, louvre, screen.

shy adjective
I was too shy to call out. backward, bashful, cautious, chary, coy, diffident, hesitant, inhibited, modest, [*informal*] mousy, nervous, reserved, reticent, retiring, self-conscious, self-effacing, timid, timorous, wary.
OPPOSITES: SEE **assertive**.

sick adjective
1 *unable to work because she was sick.* ailing, bedridden, diseased, SEE **ill**, indisposed, infirm, [*informal*] laid up, [*informal*] poorly, [*informal*] queer, sickly, unwell.
2 *He feels sick.* bilious, likely to vomit, nauseous, queasy.
3 *We're sick of their rude behaviour.* annoyed (by), disgusted (by), distressed (by), nauseated (by), sickened (by), upset (by).
4 *I'm sick of that tune.* bored (with), [*informal*] fed up (with), glutted (with), sated (with), tired, weary.
to be sick SEE **vomit**.

sicken verb
The sight of people fighting sickens me. disgust, nauseate, repel, revolt, [*informal*] turn off.

sickening adjective
sickening cruelty. bestial, disgusting, distressing, foul, hateful, inhuman, loathsome, nasty, nauseating, nauseous, offensive, repulsive, revolting, SEE **unpleasant**, vile.

sickly adjective
1 *a sickly child.* ailing, delicate, feeble, frail, SEE **ill**, pallid, [*informal*] peaky, unhealthy, weak.
OPPOSITES: SEE **healthy**.
2 *sickly sweetness. sickly sentiment.* cloying, nasty, nauseating, obnoxious, syrupy, treacly, unpleasant.
OPPOSITES: SEE **refreshing**.

sickness noun
1 *a bout of sickness.* biliousness, nausea, queasiness, vomiting.
2 VARIOUS ILLNESSES: SEE **illness**.

side noun
1 *the sides of a cube.* face, facet, elevation, flank, surface.
2 *the side of a road, pool, etc.* border, boundary, brim, brink, edge, fringe, limit, margin, perimeter, rim, verge.
3 *I saw both sides of the problem.* angle, aspect, perspective, slant, standpoint, view, viewpoint.
4 *The two sides attacked each other.* army, camp, faction, team.

sideways adjective
1 *sideways movement.* indirect, lateral, oblique.
2 *a sideways glance.* covert, sidelong, sly, [*informal*] sneaky, unobtrusive.

siege noun
blockade.

sieve noun
colander, riddle, screen, strainer.

sieve verb
Sieve out the lumps. filter, riddle, separate, sift, strain.

sift verb
1 *to sift flour.* SEE **sieve** verb.
2 *to sift the evidence.* analyse, examine, investigate, review, scrutinize, sort out, winnow.

sight noun
1 *the power of sight.* eyesight, seeing, vision, visual perception.
2 *We live within sight of the power-station.* field of vision, range, view, visibility.
3 *The sight of home brought tears to his eyes.* appearance, glimpse, look.
4 *The procession was an impressive sight.* display, exhibition, scene, show, showpiece, spectacle.

sight verb
The look-out sighted a ship. behold, discern, distinguish, glimpse, make out, notice, observe, perceive, recognize, see, spot.

sign noun
1 *signs of a change in the weather.* augury, forewarning, hint, indication, intimation, omen, pointer, portent, presage, warning.
2 *a sign to begin.* cue, SEE **gesture** noun, signal, [*informal*] tip-off.
3 *a sign that someone was here.* clue, [*informal*] giveaway, proof, reminder, spoor (*of an animal*), trace, vestige.
4 *The flowers are a sign of our love.* manifestation, marker, symptom, token.
5 *We painted a sign for our sweet-stall.* advertisement, notice, placard, poster, publicity, signboard.
6 *Do you recognize the British Rail sign?* badge, cipher, device, emblem, insignia, logo, mark, symbol, trademark.

sign verb
Sign your name. autograph, endorse, inscribe, write.

signal noun
1 *I gave a clear signal.* communication, cue, SEE **gesture** noun, [*informal*] go-ahead, indication, sign, [*informal*] tip-off, token, warning.

VARIOUS SIGNALS: alarm-bell, beacon, bell, burglar-alarm, buzzer, flag, flare, gong, green light, indicator, light, lights, password, red light, reveille, rocket, semaphore signal, siren, smokesignal, [*old-fashioned*] tocsin, trafficator, traffic-lights, warning-light, whistle, winker.

2 *They sent a signal to say all was well.* cable, telegram, transmission.

signal verb
I signalled that I was ready. beckon, communicate, flag, gesticulate, SEE **gesture** verb, give or send a signal [SEE **signal** noun], indicate, motion, sign, wave.

signature noun
a signature on a cheque. autograph, endorsement, mark, name.

significance noun
the significance of wearing a red poppy. force, implication, importance, meaning, message, point, purport, relevance, sense, signification, usefulness.

significant adjective
1 *a significant remark.* eloquent, expressive, indicative, knowing, meaningful, pregnant, revealing, symbolic, [*informal*] tell-tale.
2 *a significant moment in history.* big, considerable, SEE **important**, influential, newsworthy, noteworthy, salient, serious, sizeable, valuable, vital, worthwhile.
OPPOSITES: SEE **insignificant**.

signify verb
1 *A green light signifies "all clear".* be a sign of [SEE **sign** noun], betoken, bode, connote, denote, imply, mean, portend, presage, represent, say, spell, stand for, symbolize.
2 *Signify your agreement by raising your hand.* announce, communicate, convey, express, indicate, intimate, make known, signal, tell, transmit.

silence noun
1 *the silence of the night.* calm, hush, peace, quiet, quietness, stillness.
OPPOSITES: SEE **noise**.
2 *We couldn't understand her silence.* dumbness, muteness, reticence, taciturnity, uncommunicativeness.
OPPOSITES: SEE **verbosity**.

silence verb
1 *The gang silenced witnesses by intimidation.* gag, keep quiet, make silent, muzzle, shut up, suppress.
2 *The silencer is supposed to silence the engine noise.* deaden, muffle, mute, quieten.

silent adjective
1 *a silent engine.* inaudible, muffled, muted, noiseless, soundless.
2 *a silent audience.* attentive, hushed, quiet, rapt, restrained, still.
OPPOSITES: SEE **noisy**.
3 *a silent person.* dumb, laconic, [*informal*] mum (*Keep mum!*), mute, reserved, reticent, speechless, taciturn, tongue-tied, uncommunicative, unforthcoming, voiceless.
OPPOSITES: SEE **talkative**.

silhouette noun SEE outline noun.

silky adjective
A cat has silky fur. fine, satiny, sleek, smooth, soft, velvety.

silly adjective
silly behaviour. a silly plan. absurd, asinine, brainless, childish, crazy, daft, [*informal*] dopey, [*informal*] dotty, fatuous, feather-brained, feeble-minded, flighty, foolish, [*old-fashioned*] fond (*fond hopes*), frivolous, grotesque, [*informal*] half-baked, hare-brained, idiotic, illogical, immature, inane, infantile, irrational, [*informal*] jokey, laughable, ludicrous, mad, meaningless, mindless, misguided, naïve, nonsensical, playful, pointless, preposterous, ridiculous, scatter-brained, [*informal*] scatty, senseless, shallow, simple (*He's a bit simple*), simpleminded, simplistic, [*informal*] soppy, stupid, thoughtless, unintelligent, unreasonable, unsound, unwise, wild, witless.
OPPOSITES: SEE **serious, wise**.

silt noun
silt at the bottom of an estuary. [*formal*] alluvium, deposit, mud, sediment, slime, sludge.

similar adjective
similar in appearance. akin, alike, analogous, comparable, compatible, congruous, corresponding, equal, equivalent, homogeneous, identical, indistinguishable, like, matching, parallel, related, resembling, the same, uniform, well-matched.
OPPOSITES: SEE **dissimilar**.

similarity noun
the similarity of twins. affinity, closeness, congruity, correspondence, likeness, resemblance, sameness, similitude, uniformity.
OPPOSITES: SEE **difference**.

simple adjective
1 *a simple person. a simple life-style.* artless, guileless, homely, honest, humble, innocent, lowly, modest, [*uncomplimentary*] naïve, natural, sincere, straightforward, unaffected, uncomplicated, unpretentious, unsophisticated.
OPPOSITES: SEE **sophisticated**.
2 *a simple explanation.* basic, clear, direct, easy, elementary, foolproof, intelligible, lucid, understandable.
OPPOSITES: SEE **complicated**.
3 *a simple dress.* austere, classical, plain, stark, unadorned.
OPPOSITES: SEE **ornate**.

simplify verb
They simplified the way we pay taxes. clarify, make simple, prune, streamline.
OPPOSITES: SEE **complicate**.

simplistic adjective
a simplistic view of things. facile, inadequate, naïve, oversimple, shallow, silly, superficial.
OPPOSITES: SEE **sophisticated**.

simulate verb
1 *to simulate a crashlanding.* SEE **reproduce**.
2 *to simulate drunkenness.* SEE **pretend**.

simultaneous adjective
I can't attend two simultaneous events. coinciding, concurrent, contemporaneous, parallel, synchronized, synchronous.

sin noun
sin against God. blasphemy, depravity, error, evil, guilt, immorality, impiety, iniquity, offence, sacrilege, sinfulness, transgression, [*formal*] trespass, ungodliness, unrighteousness, vice, wickedness, wrong, wrongdoing.

sin verb
blaspheme, do wrong, err, go astray, misbehave, offend, transgress.

sincere adjective
sincere beliefs. candid, earnest, frank, genuine, guileless, heartfelt, honest, open, real, serious, simple, straightforward, true, truthful, unaffected, wholehearted.
OPPOSITES: SEE **insincere**.

sincerity noun
I trust her sincerity. candour, directness, frankness, genuineness, honesty, honour, integrity, openness, straightforwardness, trustworthiness, truthfulness.

sinful adjective
sinful behaviour. bad, blasphemous, corrupt, damnable, depraved, erring, evil, fallen, guilty, immoral, impious, iniquitous, irreligious, sacrilegious, ungodly, unholy, unrighteous, wicked, wrong.
OPPOSITES: SEE **righteous**.

sing verb
chant, croon, descant, hum, intone,
serenade, trill, warble, yodel.
MUSIC FOR SINGING: SEE **song**.

singe verb
blacken, SEE **burn** verb, char, scorch.

singer noun
songster, vocalist.

VARIOUS SINGERS: alto, baritone, bass,
[*plural*] choir, choirboy, choirgirl,
chorister, [*plural*] chorus, coloratura,
contralto, crooner, folk singer, minstrel,
precentor, opera singer, pop star, prima
donna, soloist, soprano, tenor, treble,
troubadour.

---

single adjective
1 *I got all my things into a single suitcase.*
exclusive, individual, isolated, one, only,
personal, separate, sole, solitary, unique.
OPPOSITE: plural.
2 *a single person.* celibate, [*informal*] free,
unattached, unmarried.
OPPOSITES: SEE **married**.

single-handed adjective
I can't shift the piano single-handed. alone,
independently, unaided, without help.

singular adjective
1 [*as grammatical term*]
OPPOSITE: plural.
2 *a singular happening.* abnormal, curious,
extraordinary, odd, peculiar, remarkable,
uncommon, unusual.

sinister adjective
1 *a sinister leer. a sinister groan.* disquieting,
disturbing, evil, forbidding, frightening,
menacing, ominous, threatening, villainous,
upsetting.
2 *sinister motives.* bad, corrupt, criminal,
dishonest, illegal, questionable, [*informal*]
shady, suspect.

sink verb
1 *The sun sinks in the west.* decline, descend,
disappear, drop, fall, go down, go lower, set,
slip down, subside.
2 *Our spirits sank.* diminish, droop, dwindle,
ebb, fail, fall, weaken.
3 *The ship sank.* become submerged, founder,
go down.
4 *The attackers sank the ship.* scupper,
scuttle.

sinner noun
offender, reprobate, transgressor,
wrongdoer.

sip noun, verb SEE **drink** noun, verb.

sit verb
1 *to sit on a chair.* be seated, perch, rest, seat
yourself, settle, squat.

2 *to sit for your portrait.* pose.
3 *to sit an exam.* be a candidate in, [*informal*]
go in for, take, write.
4 *Parliament does not sit over Christmas.*
assemble, be in session [SEE **session**],
convene, meet.

site noun
a site for a new building. campus, ground,
location, place, plot, position, setting,
situation, spot.

sitting-room noun
drawing-room, living-room, lounge.

situate verb
The house is situated in the park. build,
establish, found, locate, place, position, put,
set up, site, station.

situation noun
1 *The house is in a pleasant situation.*
locality, location, place, position, setting,
site, spot.
2 *I was in an awkward situation when I lost
my money.* circumstances, condition, plight,
position, predicament.
3 *She applied for a situation in the new firm.*
employment, job, position, post.

size noun
amount, area, breadth, bulk, capacity, depth,
dimensions, extent, gauge, height,
immensity, largeness, length, magnitude,
measurement, proportions, scale, volume,
width.
UNITS OF SIZE: SEE **measure** noun.

sizeable adjective
sizeable helpings. SEE **big**, considerable,
decent, generous, largish, significant,
worthwhile.

skeleton noun
bones, frame, framework, structure.

PRINCIPAL BONES IN YOUR BODY: backbone,
carpus, coccyx, cranium, digit, femur,
fibula, humerus, jaw, metacarpus, patella,
pelvis, radius, rib, sacrum, scapula, skull,
tarsal, tibia, ulna, vertebra.
SEE ALSO: **joint** noun.

---

sketch noun
1 *a quick sketch of someone.* description,
design, diagram, draft, drawing, outline, SEE
picture noun, plan, skeleton, vignette.
2 *a comic sketch on TV.* SEE **performance**,
playlet, scene, skit, turn.

sketch verb
to sketch with crayons. depict, draw, portray,
represent.
to sketch out *I sketched out my plan.* draft,
give the gist of, outline, rough out.

sketchy adjective
a sketchy essay. bitty, imperfect, incomplete, perfunctory, rough, scrappy, undeveloped, unfinished.
OPPOSITES: SEE **perfect** adjective.

skid verb
to skid on a slippery road. aquaplane, glide, go out of control, slide, slip.

skilful adjective
a skilful carpenter. skilful work. able, accomplished, adept, adroit, apt, artful, brilliant, [*informal*] canny, capable, clever, competent, consummate, crafty, cunning, deft, dextrous, experienced, expert, gifted, handy, ingenious, masterly, practised, professional, proficient, shrewd, smart, talented, versatile.
OPPOSITES: SEE **unskilful**.

skill noun
the skill of a carpenter. ability, accomplishment, adroitness, aptitude, art, capability, cleverness, competence, craft, cunning, deftness, dexterity, experience, expertise, gift, handicraft, ingenuity, knack, mastery, professionalism, proficiency, prowess, shrewdness, talent, technique, training, versatility, workmanship.

skilled adjective
experienced, qualified, SEE **skilful**, trained, versed.

skim verb
1 *to skim across ice or water.* aquaplane, coast, glide, move lightly, plane, skate, ski, skid, slide, slip.
2 *to skim through a book.* look through, read quickly, scan, skip.

skimpy adjective
SEE **scanty**.

skin noun
1 *the skin of an animal, fruit, etc.* casing, coat, coating, covering, [*formal*] epidermis, exterior, film, fur, hide, husk, membrane, outside, peel, pelt, rind, shell, surface.
2 *a person's skin.* SEE **complexion**.

skin verb
to skin an orange. to skin an animal. flay, pare, peel, strip.

skinny adjective
a skinny figure. emaciated, lanky, scraggy, SEE **thin** adjective.

skip noun SEE **container**.

skip verb
1 *to skip and play.* bound, caper, cavort, dance, frisk, gambol, hop, jump, leap, prance, spring.
2 *to skip the boring bits.* forget, ignore, leave out, miss out, neglect, overlook, pass over, skim through.

3 *to skip lessons.* be absent from, cut, miss, play truant from.

skirmish noun, verb SEE **fight** noun, verb.

skirt verb
The path skirts the playing-field. avoid, border, bypass, circle, encircle, go round, pass round, [*informal*] steer clear of, surround.

skit noun
burlesque, parody, satire, sketch, spoof, [*informal*] take-off.

sky noun
The rocket rose into the sky. air, atmosphere, [*poetic*] blue, [*poetic*] firmament, [*poetic*] heavens, space, stratosphere, [*poetic*] welkin.

slab noun
a slab of rock, cake, etc. block, chunk, hunk, lump, piece, slice, wedge.

slack adjective
1 *slack ropes.* limp, loose.
OPPOSITES: SEE **tight**.
2 *a slack attitude.* disorganized, easygoing, flaccid, idle, lax, lazy, listless, negligent, permissive, relaxed, unbusinesslike, uncaring, undisciplined.
OPPOSITES: SEE **businesslike**.
3 *slack trade.* inactive, quiet, slow, slowmoving, sluggish.
OPPOSITES: SEE **busy**.

slacken verb
1 *to slacken the tension in ropes.* ease off, loosen, relax, release.
2 *The pace slackened in the second half.* abate, decrease, ease, lessen, lower, moderate, reduce, slow down.

slake verb
to slake your thirst. allay, cool, quench, satisfy.

slam verb
to slam a door. bang, shut.

slander noun
The slander in the papers ruined his reputation. backbiting, calumny, defamation, denigration, insult, libel, lie, misrepresentation, obloquy, scandal, slur, smear.

slander verb
to slander someone. blacken the name of, defame, denigrate, disparage, libel, malign, misrepresent, smear, spread tales about, tell lies about, traduce, vilify.

slanderous adjective
slanderous rumours. abusive, cruel, damaging, defamatory, disparaging, false, hurtful, insulting, libellous, malicious, scurrilous, untrue, vicious.

slang noun
argot, cant, jargon.

slant noun
1 *Rest the ladder at a slant.* angle, diagonal, gradient, incline, list, rake, ramp, slope, tilt.
2 *I didn't like the slant they gave to the news.* bias, distortion, emphasis, imbalance, perspective, prejudice, viewpoint.

slant verb
Her handwriting slants backwards. be at an angle, be skewed, incline, lean, shelve, slope, tilt.

slanting adjective
a slanting line. angled, askew, diagonal, inclined, listing, oblique, raked, skewed, slantwise, sloping, tilted.

slap verb SEE **hit** verb.

slash verb
SEE **cut** verb.

slaughter noun
bloodshed, butchery, carnage, SEE **killing**, massacre, murder.

slaughter verb
to slaughter men on a battlefield. annihilate, butcher, SEE **kill**, massacre, murder, slay.

slaughter-house noun
abattoir, [*old-fashioned*] shambles.

slave noun
drudge, serf, SEE **servant**, thrall, vassal.

slave verb
We slaved away all day. drudge, exert yourself, labour, [*informal*] sweat, toil, SEE **work** verb.

slavery noun
bondage, captivity, enslavement, serfdom, servitude.
OPPOSITES: SEE **freedom**.

slavish adjective
1 *slavish submission.* abject, cringing, fawning, grovelling, humiliating, menial, obsequious, servile, submissive.
OPPOSITES: SEE **proud**.
2 *a slavish imitation.* close, flattering, strict, sycophantic, unimaginative, unoriginal.
OPPOSITES: SEE **independent**.

slay verb
assassinate, bump off, butcher, destroy, dispatch, execute, exterminate, [*informal*] finish off, SEE **kill**, martyr, massacre, murder, put down, put to death, slaughter.

sleazy adjective
a sleazy night-club. dirty, disreputable, mucky, seedy, slovenly, sordid, squalid, unprepossessing.

sledge noun
bob-sleigh, sled, sleigh, toboggan.

sleek adjective
1 *The cat had a sleek coat.* brushed, glossy, shiny, silky, smooth, soft, velvety, well-groomed.
OPPOSITES: SEE **unkempt**.
2 *The cat had a sleek look.* complacent, contented, self-satisfied, smug, thriving, well-fed.

sleep noun
cat-nap, coma, dormancy, doze, [*informal*] forty winks, hibernation, [*informal*] kip, [*informal*] nap, rest, [*informal*] shut-eye, siesta, slumber, snooze.

sleep verb
cat-nap, [*informal*] doss down, doze, [*informal*] drop off, drowse, hibernate, [*informal*] nod off, rest, slumber, snooze, [*informal*] take a nap.

sleepiness noun
drowsiness, lethargy, somnolence, torpor.

sleeping adjective
asleep, comatose, dormant, hibernating, [*informal*] in the land of Nod, [*informal*] off, [*informal*] out like a light, resting, slumbering, unconscious.

sleepless adjective
sleepless through the night. awake, disturbed, insomniac, restless, wakeful, watchful, wide awake.

sleepy adjective
sleepy after a big meal. comatose, [*informal*] dopey, drowsy, heavy, lethargic, ready to sleep, sluggish, somnolent, soporific, tired, torpid, weary.

slender adjective
a slender figure. graceful, slight, SEE **slim** adjective, svelte, thin.
OPPOSITES: SEE **fat** adjective.

slice verb
carve, SEE **cut** verb.

slick adjective
a slick bit of deception. adroit, artful, clever, cunning, deft, dextrous, glib, plausible, quick, smart, smooth, [*informal*] tricky, wily.
OPPOSITES: SEE **clumsy**.

slide verb
to slide over a slippery surface. aquaplane, coast, glide, glissade, skate, ski, skid, skim, slip, slither, toboggan.

slight adjective
1 *a slight improvement.* imperceptible, insignificant, minor, negligible, slim (*a slim chance*), superficial, tiny, trifling, trivial, unimportant.

2 *a slight figure*. delicate, feeble, flimsy, fragile, frail, sickly, slender, SEE **slim** adjective, thin, weak.
OPPOSITES: SEE **big**.

slightly adverb
slightly warm. hardly, moderately, only just, scarcely.
OPPOSITES: SEE **very**.

slim adjective
1 *a slim figure*. fine, graceful, lean, narrow, slender, slight, svelte, sylphlike, SEE **thin** adjective, trim.
2 *a slim chance of winning*. SEE **slight** adjective.

slim verb
become slimmer, diet, lose weight, reduce.

slime noun
muck, mucus, mud, ooze, sludge.

sling verb
I slung the rubbish on the tip. cast, chuck, fling, heave, hurl, lob, pelt, pitch, shy, throw, toss.

slink verb
He slunk away in disgrace. creep, edge, move guiltily, slither, sneak, steal.

slip noun
I made a silly slip. accident, [*informal*] bloomer, blunder, error, fault, inaccuracy, indiscretion, lapse, miscalculation, mistake, oversight, [*informal*] slip of the pen/tongue, [*informal*] slip-up.

slip verb
1 *I slipped on the wet floor*. aquaplane, coast, glide, glissade, move out of control, skate, skid, ski, skim, slide, slip, slither.
2 *She slipped into the room without being noticed*. creep, edge, move quietly, slink, sneak, steal.

slippery adjective
Take care: the floor is slippery. glassy, greasy, icy, lubricated, oily, [*informal*] slippy, slithery, smooth.

slit noun
a slit in a fence. *a slit made with a knife*. breach, break, chink, crack, cut, fissure, gap, gash, hole, incision, opening, rift, slot, split, tear, vent.

slit verb SEE **cut** verb.

slither verb
The snake slithered away. creep, glide, slide, slink, SEE **slip** verb, snake, worm.

slogan noun
an advertising slogan. catchphrase, catchword, jingle, motto, SEE **saying**.

slope noun
an upwards slope. *a downwards slope*. ascent, bank, camber, cant, declivity, descent, dip, fall, gradient, hill, incline, rake, ramp, rise, scarp, slant, tilt.

slope verb
The beach slopes gently. bank, fall, rise, shelve.

sloppy adjective
1 *a sloppy mixture*. liquid, messy, runny, slushy, splashing about, watery, wet.
2 *sloppy work*. SEE **slovenly**.
3 *a sloppy love-story*. SEE **sentimental**.

slot noun
Put a coin in the slot. break, chink, crack, cut, fissure, gap, gash, groove, hole, incision, opening, rift, slit, split.

slothful adjective SEE **lazy**.

slouch verb
Don't slouch in that slovenly way! droop, loaf, lounge, shamble, slump, stoop.

slovenly adjective
slovenly work. *a slovenly appearance*. careless, disorganized, hasty, messy, shoddy, slapdash, slatternly, sloppy, thoughtless, untidy.
OPPOSITES: SEE **careful**.

slow adjective
1 *slow progress*. careful, cautious, dawdling, delayed, deliberate, dilatory, gradual, leisurely, lingering, loitering, measured, moderate, painstaking, plodding, protracted, sluggish, steady, tardy, unhurried.
OPPOSITES: SEE **fast** adjective.
2 *a slow learner*. backward, dense, dim, dull, obtuse, stupid, [*informal*] thick.
3 *a slow worker*. idle, lazy, sluggish.
to be slow dally, dawdle, delay, [*informal*] hang about, idle, lag behind, linger, loiter, move slowly, straggle, [*informal*] take your time, trail behind.

slow verb
to slow down brake, decelerate, go slower, reduce speed.

sludge noun
mud, ooze, silt, slime, slurry, slush.

sluggish adjective
a sluggish response. dull, idle, lazy, lethargic, lifeless, listless, phlegmatic, slothful, SEE **slow** adjective, torpid, unresponsive.
OPPOSITES: SEE **lively**.

slump noun
a slump in trade. collapse, crash, decline, depression, downturn, drop, fall, recession, trough.
OPPOSITES: SEE **boom** noun.

slump verb
1 *Trade slumped after Christmas.* collapse, decline, drop, fall off, plummet, plunge, sink, worsen.
OPPOSITES: SEE **prosper**.
2 *He slumped across his desk.* be limp, collapse, droop, flop, loll, sag, slouch.

sly adjective
a sly trick. artful, [*informal*] catty, conniving, crafty, cunning, deceitful, devious, [*informal*] foxy, furtive, guileful, knowing, scheming, secretive, [*informal*] shifty, [*informal*] sneaky, [*informal*] snide, stealthy, surreptitious, tricky, underhand, wily.
OPPOSITES: SEE **straightforward**.

smack verb
to smack someone on the wrist. SEE **hit** verb, pat, slap, spank.

small adjective
1 *a small person. small things.* [*informal*] baby, compact, concise, diminutive, [*informal*] dinky, dwarf, exiguous, fractional, infinitesimal, lilliputian, little, microscopic, midget, [*informal*] mini, miniature, minuscule, minute, petite (*a petite woman*), [*informal*] pint-sized, [*informal*] poky (*a poky room*), portable, pygmy, short, [*informal*] teeny, tiny, toy, undersized, [*informal*] wee, [*informal*] weeny.
2 *small helpings.* inadequate, insufficient, meagre, mean, measly, scanty, stingy.
3 *a small problem.* SEE **trivial**.
OPPOSITES: SEE **big**.

small-minded adjective
small-minded objections. bigoted, grudging, hidebound, illiberal, intolerant, mean, narrow-minded, old-fashioned, parochial, petty, prejudiced, selfish, trivial.
OPPOSITES: SEE **broad-minded**.

smart adjective
1 *a smart pace.* brisk, [*informal*] cracking, fast, forceful, quick, rapid, [*informal*] rattling, speedy, swift.
OPPOSITES: SEE **slow** adjective.
2 *a smart idea.* acute, artful, astute, bright, clever, crafty, [*informal*] cute, ingenious, intelligent, shrewd.
OPPOSITES: SEE **stupid**.
3 *a smart appearance.* chic, clean, dapper, [*informal*] dashing, elegant, fashionable, modish, [*informal*] natty, neat, [*informal*] posh, [*informal*] snazzy, spruce, stylish, tidy, trim, well-dressed.
OPPOSITES: SEE **dowdy**.

smash verb
1 *to smash an egg.* SEE **break** verb, crumple, crush, demolish, destroy, shatter, squash, wreck.

2 *to smash into a wall.* bang, bash, batter, bump, collide, crash, hammer, SEE **hit** verb, knock, pound, ram, slam, strike, thump, wallop.

smear noun
1 *a smear of grease.* mark, smudge, streak.
2 *a smear on his good name.* SEE **slander** noun.

smear verb
1 *He smeared paint over the canvas.* dab, daub, plaster, rub, smudge, spread, wipe.
2 *The papers smeared his reputation.* attack, malign, SEE **slander** verb, vilify.

smell noun
aroma, bouquet, fragrance, incense, nose, odour, perfume, [*informal*] pong, redolence, reek, scent, stench, stink, whiff.

smell verb
1 *Smell these roses.* scent, sniff.
2 *Those onions smell.* [*informal*] pong, reek, stink, whiff.

smelling adjective
[*Smelling* is usually used not on its own but in combination with other words: *strong-smelling*, *sweet-smelling*, etc.] 1 *pleasant-smelling.* aromatic, fragrant, musky, odorous, perfumed, redolent, scented.
2 *strong˄ or unpleasant-smelling.* fetid, foul, [*informal*] high, malodorous, musty, noisome, [*informal*] off, pongy, pungent, putrid, rank, reeking, rotten, smelly, stinking, [*informal*] whiffy.
OPPOSITES: SEE **odourless**.

smelly adjective
SEE **smelling**.

smile noun, verb
beam, grin, SEE **laugh**, leer, simper, smirk, sneer.

smoke noun
1 *clouds of smoke.* air pollution, exhaust, fog, fumes, gas, smog, steam, vapour.
2 *She offered me a smoke.* cheroot, cigar, cigarette, [*informal*] fag, pipe, tobacco.

smoke verb
1 *The fire was smoking.* emit smoke, fume, reek, smoulder.
2 *He smokes cigars.* inhale, puff at.

smooth adjective
1 *a smooth lawn.* even, flat, horizontal, level.
2 *a smooth sea.* calm, glassy, peaceful, placid, quiet, restful, unruffled.
3 *a cat's smooth coat. a smooth finish on the car.* glossy, polished, shiny, silken, silky, sleek, soft, velvety.
4 *a smooth ride. smooth progress.* comfortable, easy, steady, uneventful, uninterrupted.
5 *a smooth taste.* agreeable, bland, mellow, mild, pleasant.

6 *a smooth mixture.* creamy, flowing, runny.
OPPOSITES: lumpy.
7 *a smooth manner. a smooth talker.*
convincing, facile, glib, insincere, plausible,
polite, self-assured, self-satisfied, smug,
sophisticated, suave, untrustworthy,
urbane.
OPPOSITES: SEE **rough**.

smooth verb
to smooth a rough surface. even out, file,
flatten, iron, level, level off, plane, polish,
press, roll out, sand down, sandpaper.

smother verb
*to smother a fire. to smother someone with a
pillow.* choke, cover, SEE **kill**, snuff out, stifle,
strangle, suffocate, throttle.

smoulder verb
SEE **burn** verb, smoke.

smudge verb
1 *I smudged the ink.* blur, smear, streak.
2 *I smudged the paper.* blot, dirty, mark,
stain.

smug adjective
a smug expression. complacent, conceited,
pleased, priggish, self-righteous, self-
satisfied, sleek, superior.
OPPOSITES: SEE **humble** adjective.

snack noun
bite, [*informal*] elevenses, [*informal*]
nibble, refreshments.

snack-bar noun
buffet, café, cafeteria, fast-food restaurant.

snag noun
An unexpected snag delayed our plan.
complication, difficulty, hindrance, hitch,
obstacle, problem, setback, [*informal*]
stumbling-block.

snake noun
serpent.

VARIOUS SNAKES: adder, anaconda, boa
constrictor, cobra, copperhead, flyingsnake,
grass snake, mamba, python, rattlesnake,
sand snake, sea snake, sidewinder, tree
snake, viper.

---

snap verb
1 *A twig snapped.* SEE **break** verb, crack.
2 *The dog snapped at me.* bite, nip, snatch.
3 *She snapped at us.* SEE **angry** **(be angry)**.

snare noun
ambush, booby-trap, [*old-fashioned*] gin,
noose, trap.

snare verb
to snare animals. catch, decoy, ensnare, net,
trap.

snatch verb
The muggers snatched her handbag. catch,
clutch, grab, grasp, pluck, seize, take,
wrench away, wrest away.

sneak verb
1 *I sneaked in without anyone seeing.* creep,
move stealthily, prowl, slink, stalk, steal.
2 [*informal*] *She sneaked on me.* [*informal*]
grass, inform (against), report, [*informal*]
tell tales (about).

sneaky adjective
[*informal*] *a sneaky way of getting an
advantage.* cheating, contemptible, crafty,
deceitful, despicable, devious, dishonest,
furtive, [*informal*] low-down, mean, nasty,
shady, [*informal*] shifty, sly, sneaking,
treacherous, underhand, unorthodox,
untrustworthy.
OPPOSITES: SEE **straightforward**.

sneer adjective
boo, hiss, hoot, jeer, SEE **laugh**, scoff.
to sneer at be contemptuous of, be scornful
of [SEE **scornful**], denigrate, mock, ridicule,
[*informal*] sniff at, taunt.

sneering adjective
SEE **scornful**.

sniff verb
1 *to sniff the roses.* SEE **smell** verb.
2 *to sniff because you have a cold.* [*informal*]
sniffle, snivel, snuffle.

snigger verb
to snigger at a rude joke. chuckle, giggle, SEE
laugh, snicker, titter.

snip noun, verb
SEE **cut** noun, verb.

snipe verb
A gunman sniped at them from the roof. fire,
SEE **shoot** verb, [*informal*] take pot-shots.

snippet noun
snippets of information. fragment, morsel,
particle, piece, scrap, shred, snatch (*a
snatch of a song*).

snivel verb
*He began to snivel when he heard his
punishment.* blubber, cry, grizzle, grovel,
sniff, sob, weep, whimper, whine, [*informal*]
whinge.

snobbish adjective
*too snobbish to eat convenience foods. a
snobbish attitude to art.* condescending,
disdainful, élitist, haughty, patronizing,
pompous, [*informal*] posh, presumptuous,
pretentious, [*informal*] snooty, [*informal*]
stuck-up, superior, [*informal*] toffee-nosed.
OPPOSITES: SEE **unpretentious**.

snoop verb
Don't snoop into my affairs! be inquisitive
[SEE **inquisitive**], interfere, intrude, meddle,
[*informal*] nose about, pry, sneak, spy,
[*informal*] stick your nose (into).

snout noun
an animal's snout. face, muzzle, nose,
proboscis, trunk.

snub verb
She snubbed him by ignoring his question. be
rude to, brush off, cold-shoulder, disdain,
humiliate, insult, offend, [*informal*] put
(someone) down, rebuff, reject, scorn,
[*informal*] squash.

snug adjective
1 *snug in bed.* comfortable, [*informal*] comfy,
cosy, relaxed, safe, secure, soft, warm.
2 *The jacket was a snug fit.* close-fitting,
exact, well-tailored.

soak verb
1 *to soak something in liquid.* bathe, drench,
[*informal*] dunk, immerse, [*in cooking*]
marinate, pickle, souse, steep, submerge,
wet thoroughly.
2 *Rain soaked the pitch.* make soaked [SEE
soaked], penetrate, permeate, saturate.
3 *A sponge soaks up water.* absorb, take up.

soaked, soaking adjectives
drenched, dripping, sodden, soggy, sopping,
waterlogged, SEE **wet** adjective, wet through.
OPPOSITES: SEE **dry** adjective.

soar verb
An eagle soared overhead. ascend, climb,
float, fly, glide, hover, rise, tower.

sob verb
SEE **weep**.

sober adjective
1 *He got drunk, but you stayed sober. I spent
time in sober reflection.* calm, clear-headed,
composed, in control, lucid, rational,
sensible, steady.
OPPOSITES: SEE **drunk, irrational**.
2 *a sober life-style.* abstemious, moderate,
plain, restrained, self-controlled, staid,
temperate, unexciting.
OPPOSITES: SEE **self-indulgent**.
3 *a sober occasion. sober colours.* dignified,
dull, grave, peaceful, quiet, sedate, serene,
serious, solemn, sombre, subdued.
OPPOSITES: SEE **frivolous**.

sociable adjective
a sociable crowd of people. affable,
approachable, [*old-fashioned*] clubbable,
companionable, convivial, extroverted,
friendly, gregarious, hospitable,
neighbourly, outgoing, SEE **social** adjective,
warm, welcoming.
OPPOSITES: SEE **unfriendly**.

social adjective
1 *Humans are supposed to be social creatures.*
civilized, collaborative, friendly,
gregarious, organized, SEE **sociable**.
OPPOSITES: SEE **solitary**.
2 *We organized some social events.*
communal, community, group, public.
OPPOSITES: SEE **individual** adjective.

social noun
a Christmas social. dance, disco, [*informal*]
do, gathering, [*informal*] get-together, SEE
party, reception, reunion, soirée.

socialize verb
She's got lots of friends: she likes to socialize.
associate, be sociable [SEE **sociable**],
entertain, fraternize, get together, join in,
mix, relate.

society noun
1 *We are part of human society.* civilization,
community, nation, the public.
2 *We enjoy the society of our friends.*
camaraderie, companionship, company,
fellowship, friendship.
3 *a secret society.* association, brotherhood,
club, fraternity, group, league,
organization, sisterhood, union.

sodden adjective
SEE **soaked**.

sofa noun
chaise longue, couch, SEE **seat** noun, settee.

soft adjective
1 *soft rubber. soft spongecake. soft clay.*
crumbly, cushiony, elastic, flabby, flexible,
floppy, limp, malleable, mushy, plastic,
pliable, pulpy, spongy, springy, squashy,
supple, tender, yielding.
2 *a soft bed.* comfortable, cosy.
OPPOSITES: SEE **hard**.
3 *a soft texture.* downy, feathery, fleecy,
furry, silky, sleek, smooth, velvety.
OPPOSITES: SEE **rough**.
4 *a soft voice. soft music. soft lighting.* faint,
dim, low, mellifluous, muted, peaceful,
soothing, subdued.
OPPOSITES: SEE **bright, loud**.
5 [*informal*] *a soft teacher.* compassionate,
easygoing, indulgent, kind, lenient,
permissive, sympathetic, tenderhearted,
understanding.
OPPOSITES: SEE **severe**.
6 *a soft breeze. a soft touch.* delicate, gentle,
light, mild.
OPPOSITES: SEE **violent**.
7 [*informal*] *a soft job. a soft option.* easy,
undemanding.
OPPOSITES: SEE **difficult**.

soften verb
1 *to soften your tone.* deaden, decrease, lower,
make quieter, moderate, muffle, quieten,
subdue, tone down.

2 *to soften a blow.* alleviate, buffer, cushion, deflect, reduce the impact of, temper.
OPPOSITES: SEE **intensify**.
3 *to soften ingredients before mixing a cake.* dissolve, fluff up, lighten, liquefy, make softer, melt.
OPPOSITES: SEE **harden**.

soil noun
the soil in the garden. earth, ground, humus, land, loam, marl, topsoil.

soil verb
Don't soil your hands with that filthy stuff. contaminate, defile, dirty, make dirty, pollute, stain, tarnish.

soiled adjective
SEE **dirty** adjective.

soldier noun
cavalryman, centurion, commando, conscript, [SEE **fighter**], guardsman, gunner, infantryman, lancer, marine, mercenary, NCO, officer, paratrooper, private, regular, rifleman, sapper, sentry, serviceman, trooper, [*plural*] troops, warrior.
RANKS IN THE ARMY: SEE **rank** noun.

sole adjective
the sole survivor. exclusive, individual, lone, one, only, single, solitary, unique.

solemn adjective
1 *a solemn expression.* earnest, glum, grave, grim, sedate, serious, sober, sombre, staid, thoughtful, unsmiling.
OPPOSITES: SEE **cheerful**.
2 *a solemn occasion.* awe-inspiring, ceremonious, dignified, formal, grand, holy, important, imposing, impressive, pompous, religious, stately.
OPPOSITES: SEE **frivolous**.

solicitor noun
lawyer.

solid adjective
1 *solid rock. frozen solid.* compact, dense, firm, fixed, hard, rigid, stable, unbending, unyielding.
OPPOSITES: SEE **fluid, powdery, soft**.
2 *solid gold.* pure, unalloyed, unmixed.
OPPOSITE: alloyed.
3 *a solid piece of furniture.* robust, sound, steady, SEE **strong**, sturdy, well-made.
OPPOSITES: SEE **flimsy**.
4 *solid evidence.* concrete, genuine, physical, proven, real, tangible, weighty.
OPPOSITES: SEE **hypothetical**.
5 *solid support from friends.* complete, dependable, like-minded, reliable, trustworthy, unanimous, undivided, united.
OPPOSITES: SEE **unreliable**.

solidarity noun
cohesion, harmony, like-mindedness, unanimity, unity.
OPPOSITES: SEE **disunity**.

solidify verb
The liquid solidifies as it cools down. cake, clot, coagulate, congeal, SEE **harden**, set.

solitary adjective
1 *a solitary existence.* alone, anti-social, cloistered, companionless, friendless, isolated, lonely, unsociable.
OPPOSITES: SEE **social** adjective.
2 *a solitary survivor.* one, only, single, sole.
3 *a solitary place.* desolate, hidden, isolated, out-of-the-way, remote, secluded, sequestered, unfrequented.

solitude noun
the solitude of the wilderness. isolation, loneliness, privacy, remoteness, retirement, seclusion.

soluble adjective
1 *soluble in water.* dispersing, dissolving.
2 *a soluble problem.* explicable, manageable, solvable, tractable, understandable.
OPPOSITES: SEE **insoluble**.

solution noun
1 *a solution of salt in water.* blend, compound, mixture.
2 *the solution to a problem.* answer, elucidation, explanation, key, resolution, solving.

solve verb
to solve a riddle. answer, [*informal*] crack, decipher, elucidate, explain, find the solution to, interpret, work out.

sombre adjective
sombre colours. a sombre expression. cheerless, dark, dim, dismal, doleful, drab, dull, gloomy, grave, lugubrious, melancholy, mournful, SEE **sad**, serious, sober.
OPPOSITES: SEE **cheerful**.

somewhat adverb
somewhat annoyed. fairly, moderately, [*informal*] pretty, quite, rather, [*informal*] sort of.

song noun
lyric.

MUSIC FOR SINGING: air, anthem, aria, ballad, blues, calypso, cantata, canticle, carol, chant, chorus, descant, ditty, folk-song, hymn, jingle, lied, lullaby, madrigal, musical, number, nursery rhyme, opera, oratorio, pop song, psalm, reggae, rock, serenade, shanty, soul, spiritual, wassail.
OTHER MUSICAL TERMS: SEE **music**.

sonorous adjective
a sonorous voice. deep, full, loud, powerful, resonant, resounding, rich, ringing.
OPPOSITES: SEE **quiet, shrill**.

soon adverb
[*old-fashioned*] anon, presently, quickly, shortly.

sooner adverb
1 *I wish you'd come sooner.* before, earlier.
2 *I'd sooner have an apple than sweets.* preferably, rather.

soothe verb
Quiet music soothes my nerves. allay, appease, assuage, calm, comfort, compose, ease, mollify, pacify, quiet, relieve, salve, settle, still, tranquillize.

soothing adjective
1 *soothing ointment.* balmy, comforting, emollient, healing, mild, palliative.
2 *soothing music.* calming, gentle, peaceful, pleasant, relaxing, restful.

sooty adjective
SEE **dirty** adjective.

sophisticated adjective
1 *sophisticated behaviour. sophisticated clothes.* adult, cosmopolitan, cultivated, cultured, fashionable, [*informal*] grown-up, mature, [*informal*] posh, [*uncomplimentary*] pretentious, refined, stylish, urbane, worldly.
OPPOSITES: SEE **naïve, simple**.
2 *sophisticated ideas, sophisticated machinery.* advanced, clever, complex, complicated, elaborate, hard to understand, ingenious, intricate, involved, subtle.
OPPOSITES: SEE **primitive, simple**.

sorcerer noun
conjuror, enchanter, magician, necromancer, sorceress, [*old-fashioned*] warlock, witch, witchdoctor, wizard.

sorcery noun
black magic, charms, conjuring, incantations, magic, necromancy, the occult, spells, voodoo, witchcraft, wizardry.

sordid adjective
1 *sordid surroundings. sordid details.* dirty, disreputable, filthy, foul, mucky, nasty, seamy, [*informal*] sleazy, [*informal*] slummy, squalid, ugly, undignified, SEE **unpleasant**, wretched.
OPPOSITES: SEE **pleasant**.
2 *sordid dealings on the stock-exchange.* avaricious, corrupt, covetous, degenerate, dishonourable, immoral, mercenary, rapacious, selfish, [*informal*] shabby, shameful, unethical.
OPPOSITES: SEE **honourable**.

sore adjective
a sore wound. a sore place on your skin. aching, chafing, hurting, inflamed, painful, raw, red, sensitive, smarting, tender.

sore noun
I put ointment on the sores. abscess, boil, carbuncle, gall, gathering, graze, inflammation, laceration, pimple, rawness, spot, ulcer, SEE **wound** noun.

sorrow noun
1 *the sorrow of parting.* affliction, anguish, dejection, depression, desolation, despair, desperation, despondency, disappointment, discontent, disgruntlement, dissatisfaction, distress, [*poetic*] dolour, gloom, glumness, grief, heartache, heartbreak, heaviness, homesickness, hopelessness, loneliness, melancholy, misery, misfortune, mourning, sad feelings [SEE **sad**], sadness, suffering, tearfulness, tribulation, trouble, unhappiness, wistfulness, woe, wretchedness.
OPPOSITES: SEE **happiness**.
2 *She expressed her sorrow for what she had done.* apologies, feeling of guilt, penitence, regret, remorse, repentance.
OPPOSITES: impenitence.

sorrowful adjective
sorrowful feelings. a sorrowful expression. broken-hearted, concerned, dejected, disconsolate, distressed, doleful, grief-stricken, heartbroken, long-faced, lugubrious, melancholy, miserable, mournful, regretful, rueful, SEE **sad**, saddened, sombre, SEE **sorry**, sympathetic, tearful, unhappy, upset, woebegone, woeful, wretched.
OPPOSITES: SEE **happy**.

sorry adjective
1 *I'm sorry for what I did.* apologetic, ashamed, conscience-stricken, contrite, guilt-ridden, penitent, regretful, remorseful, repentant, shamefaced.
OPPOSITES: SEE **unrepentant**.
2 *We were sorry for the girl who came last.* compassionate, merciful, pitying, sympathetic, understanding.

sort noun
1 *Pop is my sort of music. The club welcomes all sorts of people.* brand, category, class, description, form, genre, group, kind, make, set, quality, type, variety.
2 *a sort of dog. a sort of wild flower.* breed, class, family, genus, race, species.

sort verb
to sort things into sets. arrange, assort, catalogue, categorize, classify, divide, file, grade, group, organize, put in order, tidy.
OPPOSITES: SEE **mix**.
to sort out 1 *Sort out the things you need.*

choose, [*informal*] put on one side, segregate, select, separate, set aside.
2 *I sorted out their problem.* attend to, clear up, cope with, deal with, find an answer to, grapple with, handle, manage, resolve, solve, tackle.

soulful adjective
a soulful expression. a soulful performance. deeply felt, eloquent, emotional, expressive, heartfelt, inspiring, moving, passionate, profound, sincere, spiritual, stirring, uplifting.
OPPOSITES: SEE **soulless.**

soulless adjective
a soulless performance. cold, insincere, mechanical, perfunctory, routine, spiritless, superficial, trite, unemotional, unfeeling, uninspiring, unsympathetic.
OPPOSITES: SEE **soulful.**

sound adjective
1 *in a sound condition.* fit, healthy, hearty, robust, secure, solid, strong, sturdy, undamaged, well, whole.
OPPOSITES: SEE **damaged, ill.**
2 *sound advice.* coherent, convincing, correct, logical, prudent, rational, reasonable, reasoned, sensible, wise.
OPPOSITES: SEE **silly.**
3 *a sound business.* dependable, established, recognized, reliable, reputable, safe, trustworthy, viable.
OPPOSITES: SEE **disreputable.**

sound noun
noise, timbre.
RELATED ADJECTIVES: [= *to do with sound*]: acoustic, sonic.

VARIOUS SOUNDS: [Most of these words can be used either as nouns or as verbs] bang, bark, bawl, bay, bellow, blare, bleat, bleep, boo, boom, bray, buzz, cackle, caw, chime, chink, chirp, chirrup, chug, clack, clamour, clang, clank, clap, clash, clatter, click, clink, cluck, coo, crack, crackle, crash, creak, croak, croon, crow, crunch, cry.
drone, echo, fizz, grate, grizzle, groan, growl, grunt, gurgle, hiccup, hiss, honk, hoot, howl, hum, jabber, jangle, jeer, jingle, lisp, low, miaow, moan, moo, murmur, neigh, patter, peal, ping, pip, plop, pop, purr, quack, rattle, reverberation, ring, roar, rumble, rustle.
scream, screech, shout, shriek, sigh, sizzle, skirl, slam, slurp, snap, snarl, sniff, snore, snort, sob, splutter, squawk, squeak, squeal, squelch, swish, throb, thud, thunder, tick, ting, tinkle, toot, trumpet, twang, tweet, twitter, wail, warble, whimper, whine, whinny, whir, whistle, whiz, whoop, woof, yap, yell, yelp, yodel, yowl.
SEE ALSO: **music, noise, talk** verb.

sound verb
1 *The signal sounded.* become audible, be heard, make a noise, resound, reverberate.
2 *They sounded the signal.* cause, create, make, make audible, produce, pronounce, utter.
3 *to sound the depth of a river. to sound out public opinion.* examine, investigate, measure, plumb, probe, test, try.

soundless adjective
SEE **silent.**

sour adjective
1 *sour fruit.* acid, bitter, pungent, sharp, tangy, tart, unripe, vinegary.
OPPOSITES: SEE **sweet** adjective.
2 *a sour temper. sour comments.* acerbic, bad-tempered, bitter, cynical, disagreeable, grudging, grumpy, ill-natured, irritable, jaundiced, peevish, snappy, testy, unpleasant.
OPPOSITES: SEE **kind** adjective.

source noun
1 *the source of a rumour.* author, cause, derivation, initiator, originator, starting-point.
2 *the source of a river.* beginning, head, origin, spring, start.

souvenir noun
a souvenir of a holiday. keepsake, memento, reminder.

sovereign adjective
1 *sovereign power.* absolute, dominant, supreme.
2 *a sovereign state.* autonomous, independent, self-governing.

sovereign noun
emperor, empress, king, monarch, queen, SEE **ruler.**

sow verb
to sow seeds. broadcast, plant, scatter, seed, spread.

space adjective
space exploration. extraterrestrial, interplanetary, interstellar, orbiting.

WORDS TO DO WITH TRAVEL IN SPACE: astronaut, blast-off, booster rocket, capsule, cosmonaut, count-down, heatshield, module, orbit, probe, re-entry, retro-rocket, rocket, satellite, spacecraft, spaceship, space-shuttle, spacestation, spacesuit, splash-down, sputnik.

space noun
1 *interstellar space*. emptiness, endlessness, ionosphere, infinity, stratosphere, the universe.
ASTRONOMICAL TERMS: SEE **astronomy**.
2 *space to move about*. [*informal*] elbowroom, freedom, leeway, room, scope.
3 *an empty space*. area, blank, break, chasm, concourse, distance, gap, hiatus, hole, interval, lacuna, opening, place, vacuum.

spacious adjective
a spacious house. ample, SEE **big**, capacious, commodious, extensive, large, open, roomy, sizeable.
OPPOSITES: SEE **poky, small**.

span noun
a span of time. We could look along the whole span of the lake. breadth, compass, distance, duration, extent, length, reach, scope, stretch, width.

span verb
to span a river. arch over, bridge, cross, extend across, pass over, reach over, straddle, stretch over, traverse.

spank verb
SEE **hit** verb, slap, smack.

spare adjective
spare players. spare food. additional, extra, inessential, leftover, odd, remaining, superfluous, surplus, unnecessary, unneeded, unused, unwanted.
OPPOSITES: SEE **necessary**.

spare verb
1 *The judge did not spare the guilty man*. be merciful to, forgive, free, [*informal*] let off, pardon, release, reprieve, save.
2 *Can you spare something for charity?* afford, allow, give, give up, manage (*£10 is all I can manage*), part with, provide, sacrifice.

sparing adjective
sparing with his money. careful, [*informal*] close, economical, frugal, mean, miserly, prudent, stingy, thrifty.
OPPOSITES: SEE **generous, wasteful**.

spark noun
a spark of light. flash, flicker, gleam, glint, sparkle.

sparkle verb
SEE **light** noun (**give light**).

sparkling adjective
1 *sparkling jewels*. brilliant, flashing, glinting, glittering, scintillating, shining, shiny, twinkling.
OPPOSITES: SEE **dull** adjective.
2 *sparkling drinks*. aerated, bubbling, bubbly, carbonated, effervescent, fizzy, foaming.
OPPOSITES: SEE **flat, still** adjectives.

sparse adjective
sparse vegetation. inadequate, light (*light traffic*), meagre, scanty, scarce, scattered, thin, [*informal*] thin on the ground.
OPPOSITES: SEE **dense**.

spartan adjective
spartan conditions. abstemious, ascetic, austere, bare, bleak, frugal, hard, harsh, plain, rigorous, severe, simple, stern, strict.
OPPOSITES: SEE **luxurious**, PAMPERED.

spasm noun
a spasm of coughing. a muscular spasm. attack, contraction, convulsion, fit, jerk, paroxysm, seizure, [*plural*] throes, twitch.

spasmodic adjective
a spasmodic fault on our TV. erratic, fitful, intermittent, irregular, occasional, [*informal*] on and off, sporadic.
OPPOSITES: SEE **continual, regular**.

spate noun
a spate of water. cataract, flood, gush, rush, torrent.

spatter verb
The bus spattered water over us. pepper, scatter, shower, slop, splash, spray, sprinkle.

speak verb
articulate, communicate, converse, deliver a speech, discourse, enunciate, express yourself, hold a conversation, [*informal*] pipe up, pronounce words, say something, soliloquize, talk, tell, use your voice, utter, verbalize, vocalize.
FOR A LONGER LIST OF SYNONYMS: SEE **talk** verb.
to speak about allude to, comment on, discuss, mention, refer to, relate.
to speak to address, harangue, lecture.

speaker noun
a speaker at a meeting. lecturer, orator, spokesperson.

spear noun
assegai, harpoon, javelin, lance, pike.

special adjective
1 *a special occasion. a special visitor*. distinguished, exceptional, extraordinary, important, infrequent, momentous, notable, [*informal*] out-of-the-ordinary, rare, red-letter (*a red-letter day*), significant, uncommon, unusual.
OPPOSITES: SEE **ordinary**.
2 *Petrol has a special smell*. characteristic, distinctive, memorable, unique, unmistakable.
OPPOSITES: SEE **common** adjective.
3 *my special chair*. especial, individual, particular, personal.
4 *a special tool for cutting glass*. proper, specific, specialized, tailor-made.

specialist noun
1 *a science specialist. a specialist in antiques.*
authority, connoisseur, expert, fancier (*a
pigeon fancier*), professional, researcher.
2 *a medical specialist.* consultant.

speciality noun
What's your speciality? expertise, forte,
[*informal*] line (*What's your line?*), special
knowledge or skill, strength, strong point.

specialized adjective
specialized knowledge. esoteric, expert,
specialist, unfamiliar.
OPPOSITES: SEE **general**.

species noun
a species of animal. breed, class, genus, kind,
race, sort, type, variety.

specific adjective
I need specific information, not rumours.
clear-cut, definite, detailed, exact, explicit,
particular, precise, special.
OPPOSITES: SEE **general**.

specify verb
Specify your requirements. be specific about
[SEE **specific**], define, detail, enumerate,
identify, itemize, list, name, particularize,
[*informal*] spell out, stipulate.

specimen noun
a specimen of your handwriting. example,
illustration, instance, model, pattern,
representative, sample.

speck noun
a speck of dirt. bit, dot, fleck, grain, mark,
mite, particle, speckle, spot, trace.

speckled adjective
speckled with patches of colour. blotchy,
brindled, dappled, dotted, flecked, freckled,
mottled, patchy, spotted, spotty, stippled.

spectacle noun
*a colourful spectacle. the spectacle of a
coronation.* ceremonial, ceremony,
colourfulness, display, exhibition,
extravaganza, grandeur, magnificence,
ostentation, pageantry, parade, pomp, show,
spectacular effects [SEE **spectacular**],
splendour.

spectacular adjective
a spectacular display. SEE **beautiful**,
breathtaking, colourful, dramatic,
elaborate, eye-catching, impressive,
magnificent, [*uncomplimentary*]
ostentatious, sensational, showy, splendid,
stunning.

spectator noun
[*plural*] audience, bystander, [*plural*] crowd,
eye-witness, looker-on, observer, onlooker,
passer-by, viewer, watcher, witness.

speculate verb
1 *We speculated as to whether they would
marry.* conjecture, hypothesize, make
guesses, reflect, surmise, theorize, wonder.
2 *He speculates on the stock exchange.* gamble,
hope to make profit, invest speculatively.

speculative adjective
1 *speculative rumours.* based on guesswork,
conjectural, [*informal*] gossipy,
hypothetical, suppositional, theoretical,
unfounded, uninformed.
OPPOSITES: SEE **knowledgeable**.
2 *speculative investments.* chancy, [*informal*]
dicey, [*informal*] dodgy, hazardous,
[*informal*] iffy, risky, uncertain,
unpredictable, unsafe.
OPPOSITES: SEE **safe**.

speech noun
1 *clear speech.* articulation, communication,
declamation, delivery, elocution,
enunciation, pronunciation, speaking,
talking, using words, utterance.
2 *a speech to an audience.* address, discourse,
disquisition, harangue, homily, lecture,
oration, paper (*to give a paper*), presentation,
sermon, [*informal*] spiel, talk.
3 *a speech in a play.* dialogue, lines,
monologue, soliloquy.

speechless adjective
speechless with rage. dumb, dumbfounded,
dumbstruck, inarticulate, [*informal*] mum,
mute, nonplussed, silent, thunderstruck,
tongue-tied.
OPPOSITES: SEE **talkative**.

speed noun
1 *What speed were you going?* pace, rate,
tempo (*the tempo of a piece of music*),
velocity.
2 *I was amazed by her speed.* alacrity,
celerity, fleetness, haste, hurry, quickness,
rapidity, swiftness.

speed verb
1 *We sped along.* [*informal*] belt, [*informal*]
bolt, canter, career, dart, dash, flash, flit,
fly, gallop, hasten, hurry, hurtle, move
quickly, [*informal*] nip, [*informal*] put your
foot down, race, run, rush, shoot, sprint,
stampede, streak, tear, [*informal*] zoom.
2 *She was speeding when the police stopped
her.* break the speed limit, go too fast.
to speed up accelerate, go faster, increase
speed, quicken, spurt.

spell noun
1 *a magic spell.* bewitchment, charm,
conjuration, conjuring, enchantment,
incantation, magic formula, sorcery,
witchcraft.
2 *the spell of the theatre.* allure, charm,
fascination, glamour, magic.

3 *a spell of fine weather.* interval, period, phase, season, session, stint, stretch, term, time, turn.

spellbound adjective
spellbound by the music. bewitched, captivated, charmed, enchanted, enthralled, entranced, fascinated, hypnotized, mesmerized, transported.

spend verb
1 *I spent all my money.* [*informal*] blue, consume, [*informal*] cough up, exhaust, [*informal*] fork out, fritter, [*informal*] get through, invest, [*informal*] lash out, pay out, [*informal*] shell out, [*informal*] splurge, squander.
2 *We spent all our time talking.* fill, occupy, pass, use up, waste.

sphere noun
1 ball, globe, orb, spheroid.
2 *He's an expert in his own limited sphere.* area, department, domain, field, milieu, province, range, scope, subject, territory.

spherical adjective
a spherical object. ball-shaped, globular, rotund, round, spheroidal.

spice noun
spices used in cooking. flavouring, piquancy, seasoning.

SOME COMMON SPICES: allspice, bayleaf, capsicum, cardamom, cassia, cayenne, chilli, cinnamon, cloves, coriander, curry powder, ginger, grains of paradise, juniper, mace, nutmeg, paprika, pepper, pimento, poppy seed, saffron, sesame, turmeric.

spicy adjective
a spicy smell. spicy food. highly flavoured, hot, piquant, pungent, seasoned.
OPPOSITES: SEE **bland**.

spike noun
He tore his jeans on a spike. barb, nail, point, projection, prong, tine (*the tines of a fork*).

spill verb
1 *to spill milk.* overturn, slop, splash about, tip over, upset.
2 *Milk spilled out of the bottle.* brim, flow, overflow, run, pour.

spin verb
1 *A wheel spins on an axle.* gyrate, pirouette, revolve, rotate, swirl, turn, twirl, twist, wheel, whirl.
2 *Alcohol makes my head spin.* reel, swim.

spine noun
1 backbone, spinal column, vertebrae.
2 *A hedgehog has sharp spines.* bristle, needle, point, quill, spike.

spine-chilling adjective
SEE **frightening**.

spineless adjective
a spineless coward. cowardly, faint-hearted, feeble, helpless, irresolute, [*informal*] soft, timid, unheroic, weak, weedy.
OPPOSITES: SEE **brave**.

spinney noun SEE **wood**.

spin-off noun SEE **by-product**.

spinster noun
SEE **unmarried**.

spiny adjective
SEE **prickly**.

spiral adjective
coiled, turning.
OTHER CURVING SHAPES: SEE **curved**.

spiral noun
coil, screw, whorl.

spiral verb
SEE **twist** verb.

spirit noun
1 *a person's spirit.* mind, psyche, soul.
OPPOSITES: SEE **body**.
2 *supernatural spirits.* apparition, [*informal*] bogy, demon, devil, genie, ghost, ghoul, gremlin, hobgoblin, imp, incubus, nymph, phantasm, phantom, poltergeist, [*poetic*] shade, shadow, spectre, [*informal*] spook, sprite, sylph, vision, visitant, wraith, zombie.
3 *It took some time to get into the spirit of the party.* atmosphere, essence, feeling, mood.
4 *The athletes had great spirit.* animation, bravery, cheerfulness, confidence, courage, daring, determination, energy, enthusiasm, fortitude, [*informal*] go, [*informal*] guts, heroism, morale, motivation, optimism, pluck, valour, verve, will-power.

spirited adjective
a spirited performance. spirited opposition. active, animated, assertive, brave, courageous, daring, energetic, frisky, gallant, intrepid, lively, plucky, positive, sparkling, sprightly, vigorous.
OPPOSITES: SEE **spiritless**.

spiritless adjective
a spiritless performance. apathetic, cowardly, defeatist, despondent, dispirited, dull, lacklustre, languid, lifeless, listless, melancholy, negative, unenthusiastic.
OPPOSITES: SEE **spirited**.

spiritual adjective
Are spiritual or worldly values more important? devotional, eternal, heavenly, holy, incorporeal, other-worldly, religious, sacred, unworldly.
OPPOSITES: SEE **physical**.

spit noun
1 *spit dribbling down his face.* dribble, saliva, spittle, [*formal*] sputum.
2 *a spit of land.* SEE **promontory**.

spit verb
to spit something out. eject, spew.

spite noun
They showed their spite by not co-operating. animosity, animus, [*informal*] bitchiness, bitterness, [*informal*] cattiness, grudge, hate, hostility, ill-feeling, malevolence, malice, malignity, rancour, resentment, spleen, vindictiveness.

spiteful adjective
spiteful remarks. acid, [*informal*] bitchy, bitter, [*informal*] catty, cruel, cutting, hateful, hostile, hurtful, ill-natured, malevolent, malicious, nasty, poisonous, rancorous, resentful, revengeful, sharp, [*informal*] snide, sour, venomous, vicious, vindictive.

splash verb
1 *The bus splashed water over us.* shower, slop, [*informal*] slosh, spatter, spill, splatter, spray, sprinkle, squirt, wash.
2 *We splashed about in the water.* bathe, dabble, paddle, wade.

splendid adjective
1 *a splendid banquet. splendid clothes. splendid surroundings.* beautiful, brilliant, costly, dazzling, elegant, glittering, glorious, gorgeous, grand, great, handsome, imposing, impressive, lavish, luxurious, magnificent, majestic, marvellous, noble, ornate, palatial, [*informal*] posh, regal, resplendent, rich, royal, stately, sublime, sumptuous, [*informal*] super, superb, supreme, wonderful.
2 *splendid work.* admirable, excellent, first-class, SEE **good**.

splendour noun
Tourists love the splendour of a royal occasion. brilliance, ceremony, display, glory, grandeur, magnificence, majesty, ostentation, pomp, richness, show, spectacle, stateliness, sumptuousness.

splinter noun
a splinter of wood. chip, flake, fragment, shaving, [*plural*] shivers, sliver.

splinter verb
He splintered the door when he kicked it. SEE **break** verb, chip, crack, fracture, shatter, shiver, smash, split.

split noun
1 *a split in a tree. a split in my jeans.* break, cleavage, cleft, crack, fissure, SEE **opening** noun, rent, rift, rupture, slash, slit, tear.
2 *a split in a political party. a split in a marriage.* breach, difference, dissension,

divergence of opinion, division, divorce, estrangement, SEE **quarrel** noun, schism, separation.

split verb
1 *We split into two teams.* break up, divide, separate.
2 *The axe split the log. I split my jeans.* burst, chop, cleave, crack, SEE **cut** verb, rend, rip open, slice, splinter, tear.
3 *We split the profits.* allocate, allot, apportion, distribute, divide, halve, share.
4 *The roads split here.* branch, diverge, fork.

spoil verb
1 *Don't spoil that neat work. She spoilt her reputation.* blight, blot, blotch, bungle, damage, deface, destroy, disfigure, [*informal*] dish, harm, injure, [*informal*] make a mess of, mar, [*informal*] mess up, ruin, stain, undermine, undo, upset, vitiate, worsen, wreck.
OPPOSITES: SEE **improve**.
2 *Soft fruit spoils quickly.* become useless, decompose, go bad, go off, perish, putrefy, rot.
3 *Grandad spoils the little ones.* coddle, cosset, indulge, make a fuss of, mollycoddle, over-indulge, pamper.

spoken adjective
Her spoken French is excellent. oral, unwritten, verbal.
OPPOSITES: SEE **written**.

sponge verb
1 *to sponge down the car.* clean, mop, rinse, swill, wash, wipe.
2 [*informal*] *to sponge on your friends.* cadge (from), scrounge (from).

spongy adjective
spongy rubber. absorbent, porous, soft, springy.
OPPOSITES: SEE **solid**.

sponsor noun
Our team's sponsor donated the new equipment. backer, benefactor, donor, patron, promoter.

sponsor verb
to sponsor someone in a race. to sponsor an arts festival. back, be a sponsor of, finance, fund, help, promote, subsidize, support.

sponsorship noun
We were able to go ahead under the sponsorship of a local firm. aegis, [*plural*] auspices, backing, benefaction, guarantee, patronage, promotion, support.

spontaneous adjective
1 *a spontaneous display of affection.* extempore, impromptu, impulsive, unconstrained, unforced, unplanned, unpremeditated, unprepared, unrehearsed, voluntary.

2 *a spontaneous reaction.* automatic,
instinctive, involuntary, natural, reflex.
OPPOSITES: SEE **premeditated**.

spoon noun
dessert-spoon, ladle, tablespoon, teaspoon.

sport noun
1 *Sport can help you keep healthy.* exercise,
games, pastime, play, recreation.
2 *They were having a bit of sport at my
expense.* amusement, diversion,
entertainment, fun, joking, merriment,
raillery, teasing.

VARIOUS SPORTS: aerobics, American
football, angling, archery, Association
football, SEE **athletics**, badminton, baseball,
basketball, billiards, bobsleigh, bowls,
boxing, bullfighting, canoeing, climbing,
cricket, croquet, cross-country, curling.
darts, decathlon, discus, fishing, football,
gliding, golf, gymnastics, hockey, hurdling,
ice-hockey, javelin, jogging, keep-fit,
lacrosse, marathon, SEE **martial (martial
arts)**, mountaineering, netball, orienteering,
pentathlon, [*informal*] ping-pong, polo,
pool, pot-holing, quoits.
racing [SEE **race** noun], rock-climbing, roller-
skating, rounders, rowing, Rugby, running,
sailing, shot, show-jumping, skating, skiing,
skin-diving, sky-diving, snooker, soccer,
sprinting, squash, street-hockey, surfing or
surfriding, SEE **swimming**, table-tennis,
tennis, tobogganing, trampolining, volley-
ball, water-polo, water-skiing, windsurfing,
SEE **winter sports**, wrestling, yachting.

PLACES WHERE SPORTS TAKE PLACE: arena,
boxing-ring, circuit, course, court, field,
golf-course, ground, gymnasium, ice-rink,
links, pitch, playingfield, race-course, race-
track, stadium.

---

sporting adjective
a sporting gesture. considerate, fair,
generous, honourable, sportsmanlike.

sportsperson noun
contestant, participant, player, sportsman,
sportswoman.

spot noun
1 *a dirty spot on your clothing.* blemish, blot,
blotch, discoloration, dot, fleck, mark,
smudge, speck, speckle, stain.
2 *a spot on the skin.* birthmark, boil, freckle,
impetigo [= *skin disease causing spots*],
mole, naevus, pimple, rash [= *spots*], sty,
whitlow.
3 *a spot of rain.* bead, blob, drop.
4 *a nice spot for a picnic.* locality, location,
place, point, position, site, situation.

spot verb
1 *My overalls were spotted with paint.* blot,
discolour, fleck, mark, mottle, smudge,
spatter, speckle, stain.
2 *I spotted a rare bird.* SEE **see**.

spotless adjective
1 *spotless laundry.* SEE **clean** adjective,
unmarked.
2 *a spotless reputation.* blameless,
immaculate, innocent, irreproachable,
pure, unblemished, unsullied, untarnished,
[*informal*] whiter than white.

spotty adjective
a spotty face. blotchy, freckled, mottled,
pimply, speckled, spotted.

spouse noun
[*joking*] better half, [*old-fashioned*]
helpmate, husband, partner, wife.

spout noun
Water poured from the spout. fountain,
gargoyle, geyser, jet, lip (*of a jug*), nozzle,
outlet, rose (*of a watering-can*), spray.

spout verb
Water spouted through the hole. discharge,
erupt, flow, gush, jet, pour, shoot, spurt,
squirt, stream.

sprawl verb
1 *We sprawled on the lawn.* flop, lean back,
lie, loll, lounge, recline, relax, slouch,
slump, spread out, stretch out.
2 *The village sprawled across the valley.* be
scattered, spread, straggle.

spray noun
1 *a spray of water.* droplets, fountain, mist,
shower, splash, sprinkling.
2 *a spray of flowers.* arrangement, bouquet,
branch, bunch, corsage, posy, sprig.
3 *a paint spray.* aerosol, atomizer, spray-gun,
sprinkler.

spray verb
The bus sprayed mud over us. scatter,
shower, spatter, splash, spread in droplets,
sprinkle.

spread verb
1 *to spread things on a table. to spread out a
map.* arrange, display, lay out, open out,
unfold, unroll.
2 *The epidemic spread. The stain spread.*
broaden, enlarge, expand, extend, get bigger
or longer or wider, lengthen, [*informal*]
mushroom, proliferate, widen.
3 *to spread butter.* apply, cover a surface
with.
4 *to spread news.* advertise, broadcast,
circulate, diffuse, disperse, disseminate,
distribute, divulge, give out, make known,
pass on, pass round, proclaim, promulgate,
publicize, publish, scatter, transmit.

sprightly adjective
a sprightly 90-year-old. active, agile,
animated, brisk, energetic, lively, nimble,
[*informal*] perky, playful, quickmoving,
spirited, spry, vivacious.
OPPOSITES: SEE **lethargic.**

spring noun
1 *a clock's spring.* coil, mainspring.
2 *a spring in your step.* bounce, buoyancy,
elasticity, give, liveliness.
3 *a spring of water.* fount, fountain, geyser,
source (*of a river*), spa, well.

spring verb
1 *He sprang over the gate.* bounce, bound,
hop, jump, leap, pounce, vault.
2 *Weeds sprang up.* appear, develop, emerge,
germinate, grow, shoot up, sprout.

springy adjective
bendy, elastic, flexible, pliable, resilient,
spongy, stretchy, supple.
OPPOSITES: SEE **rigid.**

sprinkle verb
*to sprinkle salt on food. to sprinkle water
about.* drip, dust, pepper, scatter, shower,
spatter, splash, spray, strew.

sprout verb
The seeds began to sprout. bud, develop,
emerge, germinate, grow, shoot up, spring
up.

spruce verb
to spruce yourself up. SEE **tidy** verb.

spur noun
Applause is a spur to greater effort.
encouragement, impetus, incentive,
inducement, motive, prompting, stimulus.

spur verb
The applause spurred us to greater efforts.
egg on, encourage, incite, prick, prod,
prompt, provide a spur [SEE **spur** noun],
stimulate, urge.

spurn verb
SEE **reject.**

spurt verb
1 *Water spurted from the hole.* SEE **squirt.**
2 *She spurted ahead.* SEE **speed** verb (**speed
up**).

spy noun
a spy working for the enemy. contact, double
agent, infiltrator, informer, mole, private
detective, secret agent, snooper, undercover
agent.

spy verb
1 *to spy for the enemy.* be a spy [SEE **spy** noun],
be engaged in spying [SEE **spying**],
eavesdrop, gather intelligence, inform,
snoop.
2 *I spy with my little eye.* SEE **see.**

spying noun
counter-espionage, detective work,
eavesdropping, espionage, intelligence,
snooping.

squabble verb SEE **quarrel** verb.

squalid adjective
squalid surroundings. dingy, dirty,
disgusting, filthy, foul, mucky, nasty,
poverty-stricken, repulsive, run-down,
[*informal*] sleazy, slummy, sordid, ugly,
uncared for, unpleasant, unsalubrious.
OPPOSITES: SEE **clean** adjective.

squander verb
to squander your money. [*informal*] blow,
[*informal*] blue, dissipate, [*informal*]
fritter, misuse, spend unwisely, [*informal*]
splurge, use up, waste.
OPPOSITES: SEE **save.**

square noun
1 SEE **shape** noun.
2 *a market square.* piazza, plaza.
3 [*informal*] *Don't be a square!* conformist,
conservative, conventional person, die-
hard, [*informal*] old fogy, [*informal*] stick-
in-the-mud, traditionalist.
marked in squares chequered, criss-
crossed.

squash verb
1 *Don't squash the strawberries.* compress,
crumple, crush, flatten, mangle, mash,
pound, press, pulp, smash, stamp on, tread
on.
2 *We all squashed into the room.* crowd, pack,
squeeze.
3 *They squashed the uprising.* control, put
down, quell, repress, suppress.
4 *She squashed him with a withering look.*
humiliate, [*informal*] put down, silence,
snub.

squashy adjective
squashy fruit. mashed up, mushy, pulpy,
shapeless, soft, spongy, squelchy, yielding.
OPPOSITES: SEE **firm** adjective.

squat adjective
a squat figure. burly, dumpy, plump, podgy,
short, stocky, thick, thickset.
OPPOSITES: SEE **slender.**

squat verb
to squat on the ground. crouch, sit.

squeamish adjective
squeamish about dirty things. [*informal*]
choosy, fastidious, finicky, particular, prim,
[*informal*] prissy, scrupulous.

squeeze verb
1 *He squeezed my hand.* clasp, compress,
crush, embrace, enfold, exert pressure on,
grip, hug, pinch, press, squash, wring.
2 *They squeezed us into a little room.* cram,

crowd, push, ram, shove, stuff, thrust, wedge.

squint verb
1 be cross-eyed, have a squint.
2 *I squinted through the keyhole.* SEE **look** verb.

squirm verb
The worm squirmed. twist, wriggle, writhe.

squirt verb
Water squirted out. They squirted water at us. ejaculate, gush, jet, send out, shoot, spit, spout, spray, spurt.

stab verb
to stab with a dagger. bayonet, cut, injure, jab, SEE **pierce**, stick, thrust, wound.

stability noun
balance, equilibrium, firmness, permanence, solidity, soundness, steadiness, strength.
OPPOSITES: SEE **instability**.

stabilize verb
to stabilize a ship. to stabilize a political regime. balance, give stability to [SEE **stability**], keep upright, make stable [SEE **stable**], settle.
OPPOSITES: SEE **undermine**, **upset**.

stable adjective
1 *Make sure the tripod is stable.* balanced, firm, fixed, solid, sound, steady, strong.
2 *a stable relationship.* constant, continuing, durable, established, lasting, permanent, predictable, steadfast, unchanging, unwavering.
OPPOSITES: SEE **changeable, unsteady**.

stack noun
1 *a stack of books.* heap, mound, mountain, pile, quantity.
2 *a stack of hay.* [*old-fashioned*] cock, haycock, rick, stook.
3 *a tall stack.* chimney, pillar.

stack verb
Stack the books on the table. accumulate, assemble, build up, collect, gather, heap, load, mass, pile.

staff noun
1 *She carried a staff as a sign of her authority.* cane, crosier, pole, rod, sceptre, stave, stick.
2 *the staff of a business.* assistants, crew, employees, personnel, officers, team, workers, workforce.

stage noun
1 *the stage in a theatre.* apron, dais, performing area, platform, proscenium.
2 *a stage of a journey. a stage in your life.* juncture, leg, period, phase, point, time.

stage verb
to stage a play. to stage a demonstration. arrange, [*informal*] get up, mount, organize, perform, present, produce, put on, set up, stage-manage.

stagger verb
1 *He staggered under the heavy load.* falter, lurch, reel, stumble, sway, totter, walk unsteadily, waver, wobble.
2 *The price staggered us.* alarm, amaze, astonish, astound, confuse, dismay, dumbfound, flabbergast, shake, shock, startle, stun, stupefy, surprise, worry.

stagnant adjective
stagnant water. motionless, stale, standing, static, still.
OPPOSITES: flowing.

stagnate verb
to stagnate in the same job for years. achieve nothing, become stale, deteriorate, idle, languish, stand still, stay still, vegetate.
OPPOSITES: SEE **progress** verb.

stain noun
1 *What's that stain on your shirt?* blemish, blot, blotch, discoloration, mark, smear, spot.
2 *a wood stain.* colouring, paint, pigment, tint, varnish.

stain verb
1 *to stain something with dirty marks.* blacken, blemish, blot, contaminate, defile, dirty, discolour, make dirty, mark, smudge, soil, sully, taint, tarnish.
2 *to stain wood.* colour, dye, paint, tinge, tint, varnish.

stair noun
one stair at a time. riser, step, tread.
stairs escalator, flight of stairs, staircase, stairway, steps.

stake noun
1 *a wooden stake.* paling, pile, pole, post, spike, stave, stick.
2 *the stake you risk when you gamble.* bet, pledge, wager.

stale adjective
1 *stale bread.* dry, hard, mouldy, old, tasteless.
2 *stale ideas.* hackneyed, out-of-date, overused, uninteresting, unoriginal, worn out.
OPPOSITES: SEE **fresh**.

stalk noun
the stalk of a plant. branch, shoot, stem, trunk, twig.

stalk verb
1 *The lion stalked its prey.* follow, hound, hunt, pursue, shadow, tail, track, trail.

2 *I stalked up and down.* prowl, rove, stride, strut, SEE **walk** verb.

stall verb
Stop stalling! delay, hang back, hesitate, pause, [*informal*] play for time, postpone, prevaricate, put off, stop, temporize.

stalwart adjective
stalwart supporters. dependable, faithful, reliable, robust, staunch, strong, sturdy, tough, trustworthy, valiant.
OPPOSITES: SEE **feeble**.

stamina noun
I don't have the stamina to run long distances. energy, resilience, staying-power.

stammer verb
falter, splutter, stumble, stutter, SEE **talk** verb.

stamp verb
1 *to stamp your foot.* bring down, strike, thump.
2 *to stamp a mark on something.* brand, engrave, impress, imprint, mark, print.
to stamp on *to stamp on a cigarette stub.* crush, trample, tread on.
to stamp out *to stamp out crime.* eliminate, end, eradicate, extinguish, put an end to, [*informal*] scotch, suppress.

stampede noun
a stampede towards the exit. charge, dash, rout, rush, sprint.

stampede verb
The cattle stampeded. bolt, career, charge, dash, gallop, panic, run, rush, sprint, tear.

stand noun
1 *a stand to put something on.* base, pedestal, rack, support, tripod, trivet.
2 *a newspaper stand.* booth, kiosk, stall.

stand verb
1 *Stand when the visitor comes.* get to your feet, get up, rise.
2 *A tree stands by our gate.* be, be situated, exist.
3 *They stood the monument on a hill.* erect, locate, position, put up, set up, situate, station.
4 *I stood my books on a shelf.* arrange, deposit, place, set upright.
5 *My offer still stands.* be unchanged, continue, remain valid, stay.
6 *I can't stand smoking in the house.* abide, bear, endure, put up with, suffer, tolerate, [*informal*] wear.
to stand by *She stood by her friends.* adhere to, be faithful to, stay with, stick to, support.
to stand for *What do your initials stand for?* be a sign for, denote, indicate, mean, represent, signify, symbolize.
to stand out *He stands out in a crowd.* be obvious, be prominent, catch the eye, show, stick out.

to stand up for *Stand up for yourself.* champion, defend, fight for, help, look after, protect, shield, side with, speak up for, support.
to stand up to *They bravely stood up to the attack.* clash with, confront, defy, face up to, oppose, resist, withstand.

standard adjective
a standard procedure. a standard size. accepted, accustomed, approved, average, basic, common, conventional, customary, established, everyday, familiar, habitual, normal, official, ordinary, orthodox, popular, recognized, regular, routine, set, staple (*a staple diet*), typical, usual.
OPPOSITES: SEE **abnormal**.

standard noun
1 *a high standard.* achievement, benchmark, criterion, example, gauge, grade, guideline, ideal, level, measure, measurement, model, norm, pattern, rule, sample, specification, touchstone, yardstick.
2 *the standard of a regiment.* banner, colours, ensign, flag, pennant.

standardize verb
Standardize your results. Standardize the presentation of your work. average out, conform to a standard, equalize, normalize, regiment, stereotype.

stand-in noun
SEE **substitute** noun.

standpoint noun
Can you understand my standpoint? angle, attitude, belief, opinion, perspective, point of view, position, stance, vantage-point, view, viewpoint.

standstill noun
We came to a standstill. [*informal*] dead end, deadlock, halt, [*informal*] hold-up, impasse, stalemate, stop, stoppage.

star noun
1 asteroid, lodestar, nova, shooting star, sun, supernova.
RELATED ADJECTIVES: astral, stellar.
2 *the shape of a star.* asterisk, pentagram.
3 *a TV star.* attraction, big name, celebrity, [*informal*] draw, idol, SEE **performer**, starlet, superstar.

starboard adjective
starboard side of a ship. right-hand (when facing forward).
OPPOSITES: port.

stare verb
Why are you staring? gape, gaze, glare, goggle, look fixedly, peer.
to stare at contemplate, examine, eye, scrutinize, study, watch.

starry adjective
a starry sky. clear, glittering, star-filled, twinkling.
OPPOSITE: starless.

start noun
1 *the start of something new.* beginning, birth, commencement, creation, dawn, establishment, inauguration, inception, initiation, institution, introduction, launch, onset, opening.
OPPOSITES: SEE **finish** noun.
2 *the start of a journey.* point of departure, setting out.
3 *Having a rich mother gave her a start in life.* advantage, opportunity.
4 *The explosion gave me a nasty start.* jump, shock, surprise.
to give someone a start SEE **startle**.

start verb
1 *to start something new.* activate, begin, commence, create, embark on, engender, establish, found, [*informal*] get cracking on, give birth to, inaugurate, initiate, instigate, institute, introduce, launch, open, originate, pioneer, set up.
OPPOSITES: SEE **finish** verb.
2 *The train is ready to start.* depart, [*informal*] get going, leave, move off, set off, set out.
OPPOSITES: SEE **stop** verb.
to make someone start SEE **startle**.

startle verb
The explosion startled us. agitate, alarm, catch unawares, frighten, give you a start, jolt, make you start, scare, shake, shock, surprise, take by surprise, upset.
OPPOSITES: SEE **calm** verb.

startling adjective
SEE **surprising**.

starvation noun
dying of starvation. deprivation, famine, hunger, malnutrition, undernourishment, want.
OPPOSITES: SEE **overeating**, **plenty**.

starving adjective
starving refugees. emaciated, famished, hungry, ravenous, starved, underfed, undernourished.

state noun
1 *in an excellent state.* [*plural*] circumstances, condition, fitness, health, mood, situation.
2 [*informal*] *He was in such a state!* agitation, excitement, [*informal*] flap, panic, plight, predicament, [*informal*] tizzy.
3 *a sovereign state.* SEE **country**, nation.

state verb
to state the obvious. affirm, announce, assert, communicate, declare, express, formulate, proclaim, put into words, report, say, SEE **speak**, submit, voice.

stately adjective
a stately ceremony. dignified, elegant, formal, grand, imposing, impressive, majestic, noble, pompous, regal, royal, solemn, splendid.
OPPOSITES: SEE **informal**.

statement noun
an official statement. account, announcement, assertion, bulletin, comment, communication, communiqué, declaration, explanation, message, notice, proclamation, proposition, report, testament, testimony, utterance.

static adjective
1 *a static caravan.* fixed, immobile, motionless, SEE **stationary**, still, unmoving.
OPPOSITES: SEE **mobile**.
2 *static sales figures.* constant, invariable, stable, stagnant, steady, unchanging.
OPPOSITES: SEE **variable**.

station noun
1 *your station in life.* calling, class, employment, occupation, place, position, post, rank, situation, standing, status.
2 *a fire station. a police station.* base, depot, headquarters, office.
3 *a radio station.* channel, company, transmitter, wavelength.
4 *a railway station.* halt, platform, stopping-place, terminus.

station verb
We stationed a look-out on the roof. assign, garrison, locate, place, position, put, situate, stand.

stationary adjective
stationary cars. at a standstill, at rest, halted, immobile, immovable, motionless, parked, standing, static, still, stock-still, unmoving.
OPPOSITES: SEE **moving**.

statistics noun
data, figures, information, numbers.

statue noun
SEE **sculpture** noun.

stature noun
1 *a woman of average stature.* build, height, size, tallness.
2 *a politician of international stature.* esteem, greatness, importance, prominence, recognition, significance, SEE **status**.

status noun
your status in society or in your job. class, degree, eminence, grade, importance, level, position, prestige, rank, standing, title.

staunch adjective
a staunch supporter. constant, dependable, faithful, firm, loyal, reliable, sound,

stalwart, steadfast, strong, true,
trustworthy, unswerving.
OPPOSITES: SEE **unreliable**.

stave verb
to stave off SEE **avert**.

stay verb
1 *to stay in one place.* [*old-fashioned*] abide,
carry on, continue, endure, [*informal*] hang
about, hold out, keep on, last, linger, live on,
loiter, persist, remain, survive, [*old-fashioned*] tarry, wait.
OPPOSITES: SEE **depart**.
2 *to stay in a hotel.* be accommodated, be a
guest, be housed, board, dwell, live, lodge,
reside, settle, [*old-fashioned*] sojourn, stop,
visit.
3 *to stay judgement.* SEE **postpone**.

steadfast adjective
steadfast support. committed, constant,
dedicated, dependable, faithful, firm, loyal,
patient, persevering, reliable, resolute,
staunch, steady, unchanging, unfaltering,
unflinching, unswerving, unwavering.
OPPOSITES: SEE **unreliable**.

steady adjective
1 *Is the ladder steady? Baby isn't steady on
her feet yet.* balanced, confident, fast, firm,
immovable, poised, safe, secure, settled,
solid, stable.
2 *a steady supply of water.* ceaseless,
consistent, constant, continuous,
dependable, incessant, non-stop, regular,
reliable, uninterrupted.
3 *a steady rhythm.* even, invariable, regular,
repeated, rhythmic, smooth, unbroken,
unchanging, uniform, unhurried,
unremitting, unvarying.
4 *a steady friend.* devoted, faithful, loyal,
serious, SEE **steadfast**.
OPPOSITES: SEE **unsteady**.

steady verb
to steady a rocking boat. balance, hold,
secure, stabilize.

steal verb
1 *to steal someone's property.* appropriate,
burgle, embezzle, [*informal*] filch, hijack,
[*informal*] knock off, [*informal*] lift, loot,
[*informal*] make off with, misappropriate,
[*informal*] nick, pick someone's pocket,
pilfer, pillage, [*informal*] pinch, pirate,
plagiarize [= *to steal someone else's ideas*],
plunder, poach, purloin, [*informal*] rip
someone off, rob, shop-lift, [*informal*]
sneak, [*informal*] snitch, [*informal*] swipe,
take, thieve, walk off with.
SEE ALSO: **stealing**.
2 *I stole quietly upstairs.* creep, move
stealthily, slink, sneak, tiptoe, SEE **walk**
verb.

stealing noun

VARIOUS KINDS OF STEALING: burglary,
embezzlement, fraud, hijacking,
housebreaking, larceny, looting,
misappropriation, mugging, [*formal*]
peculation, pilfering, pillage, piracy,
plagiarism [= *stealing someone else's ideas*],
plundering, purloining, robbery, scrumping,
shop-lifting, theft, thieving.
OTHER CRIMES: SEE **crime**.

stealthy adjective
stealthy movements. concealed, covert,
disguised, furtive, inconspicuous, quiet,
secret, secretive, [*informal*] shifty, sly,
sneaky, surreptitious, underhand,
unobtrusive.
OPPOSITES: SEE **blatant**.

steamy adjective
1 *steamy windows.* cloudy, hazy, misty.
2 *a steamy atmosphere.* close, damp, humid,
moist, muggy, sultry, sweaty.

steep adjective
a steep cliff. a steep rise. abrupt, headlong,
precipitous, sharp, sheer, sudden, vertical.
OPPOSITES: SEE **gradual**.

steer verb
to steer a vehicle. be at the wheel of, control,
direct, drive, guide, navigate, pilot.

stem noun
the stem of a plant. shoot, stalk, trunk, twig.

stench noun
SEE **smell** noun.

step noun
1 *I took a step forward.* footstep, pace, stride.
2 *a step into the unknown.* advance,
movement, progress, progression.
3 *She explained the next step in the process.*
action, manœuvre, measure, phase, stage.
4 *I stood on the step.* doorstep, rung, stair,
tread (*the treads of a staircase*).

step verb
Don't step in the mud! put your foot, stamp,
trample, tread, SEE **walk** verb.
to step in *The boss stepped in to sort things
out.* SEE **intervene**.
to step up *They stepped up the pressure.* SEE
increase verb.

stereotyped adjective
a stereotyped character in a play. clichéd,
conventional, hackneyed, predictable,
standard, standardized, stock, typecast,
unoriginal.
OPPOSITES: SEE **individual** adjective.

sterile adjective
1 *sterile soil.* arid, barren, dry, infertile,
lifeless, unproductive.
OPPOSITES: SEE **fertile**.

2 *sterile bandages.* antiseptic, aseptic, clean, disinfected, germ-free, hygienic, sterilized, uninfected.
OPPOSITES: SEE **infected**, unsterilized.
3 *a sterile attempt to reach agreement.* abortive, fruitless, hopeless, pointless, unfruitful, unprofitable, useless.
OPPOSITES: SEE **fruitful**.

sterilize verb
1 *to sterilize medical equipment. to sterilize food.* clean, decontaminate, disinfect, fumigate, make sterile [SEE **sterile**], pasteurize, purify.
OPPOSITES: SEE **infect**.
2 *to sterilize animals so that they cannot reproduce.* castrate, geld, neuter, perform a vasectomy, spay.

stern adjective
a stern rebuke. a stern disciplinarian. austere, authoritarian, dour, forbidding, grim, hard, harsh, inflexible, rigid, rigorous, severe, strict, unbending, unrelenting.
OPPOSITES: SEE **lenient**.

stew noun
stew for dinner. casserole, goulash, hash, hot-pot, ragout.

stew verb
to stew meat. boil, braise, casserole, simmer.

steward, stewardess nouns
1 *a steward on a ship.* attendant, SEE **servant**, waiter.
2 *a steward at a racecourse.* marshal, officer, official.

stick noun
dry sticks used for firewood. branch, stalk, twig.

VARIOUS KINDS OF STICK: bar, baton, cane, club, cudgel, hockey-stick, pole, rod, staff, truncheon, walking-stick, wand.

---

stick verb
1 *to stick a pin in. to stick someone in the ribs.* dig, jab, poke, prod, punch, puncture, stab, thrust.
2 *to stick something with glue. to stick together.* adhere, affix, agglutinate, bind, bond, cement, cling, coagulate, SEE **fasten**, fuse together, glue, weld.
3 *His head stuck between the railings.* become trapped, jam, wedge.
to stick at [*informal*] *Stick at it!* SEE **persevere**.
to stick in *The pin won't stick in.* go in, pass through, penetrate, pierce.
to stick out *A shelf stuck out above my head.* jut, overhang, project, protrude.
to stick up *The spire sticks up above the trees.* loom, rise, stand out, tower.
to stick up for SEE **defend**.

sticky adjective
1 *sticky tape.* adhesive, glued, gummed, self-adhesive.
OPPOSITES: NON-ADHESIVE.
2 *sticky fingers.* gluey, [*informal*] gooey, gummy, tacky.
OPPOSITES: SEE **clean** adjective.

stiff adjective
1 *stiff cardboard. stiff clay.* firm, hard, heavy, inflexible, rigid, solid, solidified, thick, unbending, unyielding, viscous.
OPPOSITES: SEE **soft**.
2 *stiff joints.* arthritic, immovable, painful, paralysed, rheumatic, taut, tight.
OPPOSITES: SEE **supple**.
3 *a stiff task. stiff opposition.* arduous, difficult, exacting, hard, laborious, powerful, severe, strong, stubborn, tiring, touch, uphill.
OPPOSITES: SEE **easy**.
4 *a stiff manner.* awkward, clumsy, cold, formal, graceless, inelegant, starchy, stilted, tense, ungainly, unnatural, wooden.
OPPOSITES: SEE **relaxed**.
5 *a stiff penalty.* excessive, harsh, merciless, pitiless, relentless, rigorous, strict.
OPPOSITES: SEE **lenient**.

stiffen verb
become stiff [SEE **stiff**], congeal, harden, set, solidify, thicken, tighten.

stifle verb
1 *The heat stifled us.* asphyxiate, choke, smother, strangle, suffocate, throttle.
2 *We stifled our laughter.* check, curb, dampen, deaden, muffle, repress, restrain, silence, stop, suppress.

stigma noun
the stigma of prison. blot, disgrace, dishonour, reproach, shame, slur, stain.

still adjective
1 *a still evening.* calm, hushed, noiseless, peaceful, placid, quiet, restful, serene, silent, tranquil, untroubled, windless.
OPPOSITES: SEE **stormy, turbulent**.
2 *Keep still!* immobile, inert, lifeless, motionless, stagnant (*stagnant water*), static, stationary, unmoving.
OPPOSITES: SEE **moving**.

still verb
She stilled my fears. He stilled the audience by raising his hand. allay, appease, calm, lull, make still [SEE **still** adjective], pacify, quieten, settle, silence, soothe, subdue, tranquillize.
OPPOSITES: SEE **agitate**.

stimulate verb
to stimulate interest. to stimulate people to greater effort. activate, arouse, encourage, excite, fan, fire, foment, galvanize, goad, incite, inflame, inspire, invigorate, prompt,

provoke, quicken, rouse, spur, stir up, titillate, urge, whet.
OPPOSITES: SEE **discourage**.

stimulating adjective
a stimulating discussion. stimulating company. challenging, exciting, exhilarating, inspiring, interesting, intoxicating, invigorating, provoking, rousing, stirring, thought-provoking.
OPPOSITES: SEE **boring**.

stimulus noun
a stimulus to greater effort. encouragement, fillip, goad, incentive, inducement, inspiration, prompting, provocation, spur.
OPPOSITES: SEE **discouragement**.

sting verb
1 *Some insects can sting you.* bite, nip, SEE **wound** verb.
2 *The salt water stings.* SEE **hurt** verb, smart, tingle.

stingy adjective
1 *a stingy miser.* avaricious, cheese-paring, close, close-fisted, covetous, mean, mingy, miserly, niggardly, parsimonious, penny-pinching, tight-fisted, ungenerous.
OPPOSITES: SEE **generous**.
2 *stingy helpings.* inadequate, insufficient, meagre, [*informal*] measly, scanty, SEE **small**.
OPPOSITES: SEE **big**.

stink noun, verb SEE **smell** noun, verb.

stir verb
1 *Stir yourself!* SEE **move** verb.
2 *Stir the ingredients thoroughly.* agitate, beat, blend, mix, whisk.
3 *The music stirred us.* affect, arouse, challenge, electrify, excite, exhilarate, fire, impress, inspire, move, rouse, stimulate, touch.
to stir up *Don't stir up any trouble!* awaken, cause, incite, instigate, kindle, provoke, set off.

stirring adjective
stirring music. a stirring speech. affecting, dramatic, emotional, exciting, heady, impassioned, moving, rousing, spirited, stimulating, thrilling.
OPPOSITES: SEE **boring**.

stitch verb
to stitch a hole in your jeans. darn, mend, repair, sew, tack.

stock adjective
a stock response. accustomed, common, conventional, customary, expected, ordinary, predictable, regular, set, standard, staple, stereotyped, traditional, unoriginal, usual.
OPPOSITES: SEE **unexpected**.

stock noun
1 *a stock of provisions.* hoard, reserve, reservoir, stockpile, store, supply.
2 *the stock in a shop.* commodities, goods, merchandise, wares.
3 *the stock on a cattle farm.* animals, beasts, cattle, flocks, herds, livestock.
4 *descended from ancient stock.* ancestry, blood, breed, descent, extraction, family, forebears, line, lineage, parentage.

stock verb
The local shop stocks most things. deal in, handle, [*informal*] keep, keep in stock, provide, sell, supply, trade in.

stocky adjective
a stocky figure. compact, dumpy, short, solid, squat, stubby, sturdy, thickset.
OPPOSITES: SEE **thin** adjective.

stodgy adjective
1 *stodgy food.* filling, heavy, indigestible, lumpy, soggy, solid, starchy.
OPPOSITES: SEE **appetizing**.
2 *a stodgy lecture.* boring, dull, [*informal*] stuffy, tedious, turgid, unexciting, unimaginative, uninteresting.
OPPOSITES: SEE **lively**.

stoical adjective
a stoical response to pain. calm, impassive, imperturbable, long-suffering, patient, philosophical, phlegmatic, resigned, stolid, uncomplaining.
OPPOSITES: SEE **excitable**.

stoke verb
to stoke a fire. fuel, keep burning, mend, put fuel on, tend.

stolid adjective
a dependable, stolid member of the team. heavy, impassive, SEE **stoical**, unemotional, unexciting, unimaginative, wooden.
OPPOSITES: SEE **lively**.

stomach noun
abdomen, belly, [*informal*] guts, [*informal*] insides, [*uncomplimentary*] paunch, [*informal*] tummy.
OTHER PARTS OF YOUR BODY: SEE **body**.

stomach-ache noun
colic, [*informal*] colly-wobbles, [*childish*] tummy-ache.

stone noun
1 *stones on the beach.* boulder, cobble, [*plural*] gravel, pebble, rock, [*plural*] scree.
KINDS OF STONE: SEE **rock** noun.
2 *stones used by builders.* block, flagstone, sett, slab.
3 *a stone to commemorate the fallen.* memorial, monolith, obelisk.
4 *a precious stone.* gem, SEE **jewel**.

stony adjective
1 *a stony beach.* pebbly, rocky, rough, shingly.
2 *a stony silence. a stony response.* cold, expressionless, frigid, hard, heartless, hostile, icy, indifferent, pitiless, steely, stony-hearted, uncaring, unemotional, unfeeling, unforgiving, unfriendly, unresponsive.
OPPOSITES: SEE **emotional**.

stooge noun
butt, dupe, [*informal*] fallguy, lackey, puppet.

stool noun
SEE **seat** noun.

stoop verb
1 *I stooped to go under the barrier.* bend, bow, crouch, duck, hunch your shoulders, kneel, lean, squat.
2 *She wouldn't stoop to be seen with the likes of us.* condescend, deign, lower yourself, sink.

stop noun
1 *Everything came to a stop.* cessation, conclusion, end, finish, halt, shut-down, standstill, stoppage, termination.
2 *a stop on a journey.* break, destination, pause, resting-place, station, stopover, terminus.
3 *a stop at a hotel.* [*old-fashioned*] sojourn, stay, visit.

stop verb
1 *to stop what you are doing.* break off, call a halt to, cease, conclude, cut off, desist from, discontinue, end, finish, [*informal*] knock off, leave off, [*informal*] pack in, pause, quit, refrain from, rest from, suspend, terminate.
OPPOSITES: SEE **start** verb.
2 *to stop traffic. to stop something happening.* bar, block, check, curb, delay, frustrate, halt, hamper, hinder, immobilize, impede, intercept, interrupt, [*informal*] nip in the bud, obstruct, put a stop to, stanch or staunch, stem.
3 *to stop in a hotel.* be a guest, have a holiday, [*old-fashioned*] sojourn, spend time, stay, visit.
4 *to stop a gap.* [*informal*] bung up, close, fill in, plug, seal.
5 *Wait for the bus to stop.* come to rest, draw up, halt, pull up.
6 *Stop the thief!* arrest, capture, catch, detain, hold, seize.

stopper noun
a stopper in a bottle. bung, cork, plug.

storage noun
SEE **storehouse**.

store noun
1 *a store of supplies.* accumulation, cache,

fund, hoard, quantity, reserve, reservoir, stock, stockpile, SEE **storehouse**, supply.
2 *a grocery store.* outlet, retail business, retailers, SEE **shop**, supermarket.

store verb
to store food for future use. accumulate, deposit, hoard, keep, lay by, lay up, preserve, put away, reserve, save, set aside, [*informal*] stash away, stockpile, stock up, stow away.

storehouse noun

PLACES TO STORE THINGS: armoury, arsenal, barn, cellar, cold-storage, depot, granary, larder, pantry, repository, safe, silo, stockroom, storage, store-room, strong-room, treasury, vault, warehouse.

storey noun
[Don't confuse with *story*.] *a building with six storeys.* deck, floor, level, stage, tier.

storm noun
The forecast predicts a storm. disturbance, onslaught, outbreak, stormy weather [SEE **stormy**], tempest, tumult, turbulence.
OPPOSITES: SEE **calm** noun.

KINDS OF STORM: blizzard, cyclone, deluge, dust-storm, gale, hurricane, rainstorm, sandstorm, squall, thunderstorm, tornado, typhoon, whirlwind.

stormy adjective
stormy seas. stormy weather. angry, blustery, choppy, gusty, raging, rough, squally, tempestuous, thundery, tumultuous, turbulent, violent, wild, windy.
OPPOSITES: SEE **calm** adjective.

story noun
1 *the story of my life. Tell me a story.* account, chronicle, fiction, history, narration, narrative, plot, scenario, tale, yarn.
2 *a story in a newspaper.* article, [*informal*] exclusive, feature, news item, report.

VARIOUS KINDS OF STORY: anecdote, children's story, crime story, detective story, fable, fairy-tale, fantasy, folk-tale, legend, mystery, myth, novel, parable, romance, saga, science fiction or SF, thriller, [*informal*] whodunit.

storyteller noun
author, narrator, raconteur, teller.

stout adjective
1 *stout rope.* reliable, robust, sound, strong, sturdy, substantial, thick, tough.
OPPOSITES: SEE **weak**.

2 *a stout person.* [*informal*] beefy, [*informal*]
chubby, SEE **fat** adjective, heavy, overweight,
plump, portly, solid, stocky, tubby, well-
built.
OPPOSITES: SEE **thin** adjective.

stove noun
boiler, cooker, fire, furnace, heater, oven,
range.

stow verb
1 *I stow unwanted things in the attic.* SEE
store verb.
2 *Stow the luggage in the car.* SEE **load** verb.

straggle verb
Some of the runners straggled behind.
dawdle, fall behind, lag, loiter, ramble,
scatter, spread out, stray, string out, trail,
wander.

straight adjective
[Do not confuse with *strait.*] 1 *a straight line.*
a straight road. aligned, direct, smooth,
undeviating, unswerving.
OPPOSITES: SEE **crooked**.
2 *Put the room straight.* neat, orderly,
organized, right, [*informal*] shipshape,
tidy.
OPPOSITES: SEE **untidy**.
3 *a straight sequence.* consecutive,
continuous, non-stop, perfect, sustained,
unbroken, uninterrupted, unrelieved.
4 *straight talking.* SEE **straightforward**.
straight away at once, directly,
immediately, instantly, now, without delay.

straighten verb
to straighten out disentangle, make
straight, sort out, SEE **tidy** verb, unbend,
untwist.

straightforward adjective
straightforward talk. a straightforward
person. blunt, candid, direct, easy,
forthright, frank, genuine, honest,
intelligible, lucid, open, plain, simple,
sincere, straight, truthful, uncomplicated.
OPPOSITES: SEE **devious**.

strain noun
He's been under great strain. anxiety,
difficulty, hardship, pressure, stress,
tension, worry.

strain verb
1 *We strained at the ropes.* haul, pull, stretch,
tighten, tug.
2 *I strained to hear what he said.* attempt,
endeavour, exert yourself, make an effort,
strive, struggle, try.
3 *Don't strain yourself.* exhaust, tire out,
weaken, wear out, weary.
4 *I strained my neck.* damage, hurt, injure,
rick, sprain, twist, wrench.
5 *to strain solids out of a liquid.* filter,
percolate, riddle, separate, sieve, sift.

strained adjective
a strained expression. strained good humour.
artificial, drawn, embarrassed, false, forced,
self-conscious, stiff, tense, tired,
uncomfortable, uneasy, unnatural.
OPPOSITES: SEE **relaxed**.

strainer noun
colander, filter, riddle, sieve.

strand noun
one strand of a rope. fibre, filament, string,
thread, wire.

strand verb
to strand someone on an island. abandon,
desert, forsake, leave stranded [SEE
stranded], maroon.

stranded adjective
1 *a stranded ship.* aground, beached,
grounded, [*informal*] high and dry,
shipwrecked, stuck.
2 *stranded in London without any money.*
abandoned, alone, deserted, forsaken,
helpless, in difficulties, left, lost, marooned,
without help.

strange adjective
1 *a strange event. strange goings-on.*
abnormal, astonishing, atypical, bizarre,
curious, eerie, exceptional, extraordinary,
[*informal*] funny, irregular, odd, out of the
ordinary, peculiar, queer, rare, remarkable,
singular, surprising, uncommon,
unexpected, unheard of, unique, unnatural,
untypical, unusual.
2 *We have strange neighbours.* [*informal*]
cranky, eccentric, sinister, unconventional,
weird, [*informal*] zany.
3 *The experts agreed it was a strange problem.*
baffling, bewildering, inexplicable,
insoluble, mysterious, mystifying,
perplexing, puzzling, unaccountable.
4 *We travelled to some strange places.* alien,
exotic, foreign, little-known, off the beaten
track, outlandish, remote, unexplored,
unmapped.
5 *Eating the local food was a strange*
experience. different, fresh, new, novel,
unaccustomed, unfamiliar.
OPPOSITES: SEE **familiar**, **ordinary**.

stranger noun
I'm a stranger here. alien, foreigner, guest,
newcomer, outsider, visitor.

strangle verb
asphyxiate, choke, garotte, smother, stifle,
SEE **strangulate**, suffocate, throttle.

strangulate verb
compress, constrict, squeeze, SEE **strangle**.

strangulation noun
asphyxiation, garotting, suffocation.

strap noun
band, belt, strop, tawse, thong, webbing.

strategy noun
a strategy to beat the opposition. approach, manœuvre, method, plan, plot, policy, procedure, programme, scheme, tactics.

stray verb
1 *Don't stray in the hills.* get lost, go astray, meander, move about aimlessly, ramble, range, roam, rove, straggle, wander.
2 *Don't stray from the point.* deviate, digress, diverge, drift.

streak noun
1 *a streak of dirt on the window.* band, line, smear, stain, strip, stripe, vein.
2 *a streak of selfishness in her character.* component, element, trace.

streak verb
1 *Rain streaked the new paint.* mark with streaks, smear, smudge, stain.
2 [*informal*] *Cars streaked past.* dash, flash, fly, gallop, hurtle, move at speed, rush, speed, sprint, tear, zoom.

streaky adjective
lined, smeary, smudged, streaked, striated, stripy, veined.

stream noun
1 *a rippling stream.* beck, brook, burn, SEE **channel** noun, [*poetic*] rill, river, rivulet, streamlet, watercourse.
2 *A stream of water poured through the hole.* cataract, current, flood, flow, gush, jet, outpouring, rush, spate, surge, tide, torrent.

stream verb
Water streamed through the hole. cascade, course, flood, flow, gush, issue, pour, run, spill, spout, spurt, squirt, surge, well.

streamer noun
banner, flag, pennant, pennon, ribbon.

streamlined adjective
a car with a streamlined body. aerodynamic, efficient, graceful, sleek, smooth.
OPPOSITE: air-resistant.

strength noun
physical strength. brawn, capacity, condition, energy, fitness, force, health, might, muscle, power, robustness, stamina, sturdiness, toughness, vigour.
OPPOSITES: SEE **weakness**.

strengthen verb
1 *to strengthen your muscles.* build up, fortify, harden, increase, make stronger, tone up, toughen.
2 *to strengthen a fence.* bolster, brace, buttress, prop up, reinforce, support.
3 *We need more evidence to strengthen our case.* back up, consolidate, corroborate, enhance, justify, substantiate.
OPPOSITES: SEE **weaken**.

strenuous adjective
1 *strenuous efforts.* active, committed, determined, dynamic, energetic, herculean, laborious, resolute, spirited, strong, tireless, unremitting, vigorous.
OPPOSITES: SEE **apathetic, casual**.
2 *strenuous work.* arduous, demanding, difficult, exhausting, gruelling, hard, punishing, stiff, taxing, tough, uphill.
OPPOSITES: SEE **easy**.

stress noun
1 *a time of stress.* anxiety, difficulty, hardship, pressure, strain, tension, trauma, worry.
2 *Put a stress on the important words.* accent, beat, emphasis, importance, weight.

stress verb
He stressed the importance of keeping fit. accentuate, assert, emphasize, insist on, lay stress on, put the stress on, repeat, underline.

stressful adjective
a stressful period in my life. anxious, difficult, tense, traumatic, worrying.
OPPOSITES: SEE **easy**.

stretch noun
1 *a stretch in prison.* period, spell, stint, term, time.
2 *a stretch of road.* distance, length.
3 *a stretch of countryside.* area, expanse, sweep, tract.

stretch verb
1 *to stretch something to make it longer or bigger or wider.* crane (*to crane your neck*), distend, draw out, elongate, expand, extend, flatten out, inflate, lengthen, open out, pull out, spread out, swell, tauten, tighten.
2 *The lake stretches into the distance.* be unbroken, continue, disappear, extend, go, spread.

stricken adjective
SEE **troubled**.

strict adjective
1 *strict rules.* absolute, binding, [*informal*] hard and fast, inflexible, invariable, rigid, stringent, tight, unchangeable.
OPPOSITES: SEE **flexible**.
2 *strict discipline. a strict teacher.* austere, authoritarian, autocratic, firm, harsh, merciless, [*informal*] no-nonsense, rigorous, severe, stern, stringent, tyrannical, uncompromising.
OPPOSITES: SEE **lax, lenient**.
3 *the strict truth.* accurate, complete, correct, exact, perfect, precise, right, scrupulous, true.
OPPOSITES: SEE **approximate** adjective.

stride verb SEE **walk** verb.

strident adjective
a strident cry. strident voices. clamorous,
grating, harsh, jarring, loud, noisy,
raucous, screeching, shrill.
OPPOSITES: SEE **soft**.

strife noun SEE **conflict** noun.

strike noun
an industrial strike. industrial action,
stoppage, withdrawal of labour.

strike verb
1 *I struck my head.* SEE **hit** verb.
2 *The invaders struck without warning.* SEE
attack verb.
3 *The clock struck one.* chime, ring.
4 *The workforce threatened to strike.*
[*informal*] come out, [*informal*] down tools,
stop work, take industrial action, withdraw
your labour.

striking adjective
a striking contrast. a striking hair-do.
arresting, conspicuous, distinctive,
impressive, memorable, noticeable, obvious,
outstanding, prominent, showy, stunning,
telling, unmistakable, unusual.
OPPOSITES: SEE **inconspicuous**.

string noun
1 *a length of string.* cord, line, rope, twine.
2 *a string of cars waiting at the lights.* file,
line, procession, queue, row, succession.
3 *a string of coincidences.* chain, progression,
sequence, series.

MUSICAL INSTRUMENTS WITH STRINGS:
banjo, cello, clavichord, double-bass,
[*informal*] fiddle, guitar, harp, harpsichord,
lute, lyre, piano, sitar, spinet, ukulele, viola,
violin, zither.
OTHER INSTRUMENTS: SEE **music**.

---

stringent adjective SEE **strict**.

strip noun
*a strip of carpet. a strip of wood. a strip of
land.* band, belt, lath, line, narrow piece,
ribbon, shred, slat, sliver, stripe, swathe.

strip verb
1 *to strip clothes, vegetation, paint, etc., off
something.* clear, defoliate, denude, divest,
[*old-fashioned*] doff, flay [= *strip skin off*],
peel, remove, skin, take.
OPPOSITES: SEE **cover** verb.
2 *to strip to the waist.* bare yourself, expose
yourself, lay yourself bare, uncover
yourself.
OPPOSITES: SEE **dress** verb.

stripe noun
football shirts with red and white stripes.
band, bar, line, [*formal*] striation, strip.

striped adjective
banded, barred, lined, streaky, striated,
stripy.

strive verb
SEE **try** verb.

stroke noun
1 *a stroke with a cricket bat.* SEE **hit** noun.
2 *You can't change the world at a single
stroke.* action, blow, effort, move.
3 *a stroke of the pen.* flourish, line, mark,
movement, sweep.
4 [= *medical condition*] apoplexy, seizure.

stroke verb
to stroke the cat. caress, fondle, pass your
hand over, pat, pet, rub, touch.

stroll noun, verb SEE **walk** noun, verb.

strong adjective
1 *a strong person.* athletic, [*informal*] beefy,
[*informal*] brawny, burly, fit, [*informal*]
hale and hearty, hardy, hefty, mighty,
muscular, powerful, [*informal*] strapping,
sturdy, tough, well-built, wiry.
2 *a strong structure. strong materials.*
durable, hard, hardwearing, heavy-duty,
impregnable (*an impregnable fortress*),
indestructible, permanent, reinforced,
resilient, robust, sound, stout, substantial,
thick, unbreakable, well-made.
3 *strong government. strong efforts.*
aggressive, assertive, decisive, dependable,
determined, [*uncomplimentary*] SEE
dictatorial, domineering, fearless, firm,
forceful, herculean, loyal, reliable, resolute,
stalwart, staunch, steadfast, [*informal*]
stout, strong-minded, strong-willed, true,
unflinching, unswerving, vehement,
vigorous, violent.
4 *a strong army.* formidable, invincible,
large, numerous, unconquerable, well-
armed, well-equipped, well-trained.
5 *a strong light.* bright, brilliant, clear,
dazzling, glaring.
6 *a strong taste or smell.* highly-flavoured,
hot, noticeable, obvious, overpowering,
prominent, pronounced, pungent, spicy,
unmistakable.
7 *strong drink.* alcoholic, concentrated,
intoxicating, potent, undiluted.
8 *strong evidence.* clear-cut, cogent,
compelling, convincing, evident,
persuasive, plain, solid, undisputed.
9 *strong convictions.* committed, deep-rooted,
deep-seated, eager, earnest, enthusiastic,
fervent, fierce, genuine, intense, keen,
zealous.
OPPOSITES: SEE **weak**.

stronghold noun
bastion, bulwark, castle, citadel, fort,
fortress, garrison.

structure noun
1 *the structure of a poem. the structure of a living cell.* arrangement, composition, constitution, design, [*informal*] make-up, organization, plan, shape.
2 *a structure of steel and stone.* SEE **building**, construction, edifice, erection, fabric, framework, pile, superstructure.

struggle noun
1 *a struggle to get things finished.* challenge, difficulty, effort, endeavour, exertion, labour, problem.
2 *a struggle against an enemy or opponent.* SEE **fight** noun.

struggle verb
1 *to struggle to get free.* endeavour, exert yourself, labour, make an effort, move violently, strain, strive, toil, try, work hard, wrestle, wriggle about, writhe about.
2 *to struggle with an enemy.* SEE **fight** verb.

stub noun
a cigarette stub. the stub of a tree. butt, end, remains, remnant, stump.

stubbly adjective
a man with a stubbly chin. bristly, prickly, rough, unshaven.

stubborn adjective
a stubborn donkey. stubborn opposition. defiant, difficult, disobedient, dogged, headstrong, inflexible, intractable, intransigent, mulish, obdurate, obstinate, opinionated, persistent, [*informal*] pig-headed, recalcitrant, refractory, rigid, self-willed, uncontrollable, uncooperative, unmanageable, unreasonable, unyielding, wilful.
OPPOSITES: SEE **obedient**.

stuck adjective
1 *stuck in the mud.* bogged down, fast, fastened, fixed, immovable.
2 *stuck on a problem.* baffled, beaten, held up, [*informal*] stumped.

stuck-up adjective
[*informal*] *a stuck-up snob.* arrogant, [*informal*] big-headed, bumptious, [*informal*] cocky, conceited, condescending, [*informal*] high-and-mighty, patronizing, proud, self-important, snobbish, [*informal*] snooty, supercilious, [*informal*] toffee-nosed.
OPPOSITES: SEE **modest**.

student noun
learner, pupil, postgraduate, scholar, undergraduate.

studious adjective
a studious pupil. academic, bookish, brainy, earnest, hard-working, intellectual, scholarly, serious-minded, thoughtful.

study verb
1 *We studied the evidence.* analyse, consider, contemplate, enquire into, examine, give attention to, investigate, learn about, look closely at, peruse, pore over, read carefully, research, scrutinize, survey, think about.
2 *to study for an examination.* [*informal*] cram, learn, [*informal*] mug up, read, [*informal*] swot, work.

stuff noun
1 *What's this stuff in the jar?* matter, substance.
2 *stuff to make a skirt.* cloth, fabric, material, textile.
3 [*informal*] *That's my stuff in the drawer.* articles, belongings, [*informal*] clobber, [*formal*] effects, [*informal*] gear, junk, objects, [*informal*] paraphernalia, possessions, [*informal*] tackle, things.

stuff verb
1 *I stuffed everything into a suitcase.* compress, cram, crowd, force, jam, pack, push, ram, shove, squeeze, stow, tuck.
2 *to stuff a cushion.* fill, pad.

stuffing noun
1 *stuffing in a cushion.* filling, padding, quilting, wadding.
2 *stuffing in a roast chicken.* forcemeat, seasoning.

stuffy adjective
a stuffy room. airless, close, fetid, fuggy, fusty, heavy, humid, muggy, musty, oppressive, stale, steamy, stifling, suffocating, sultry, unventilated, warm.
OPPOSITES: SEE **airy**.

stumble verb
1 *to stumble as you walk.* blunder, flounder, lurch, reel, stagger, totter, trip, tumble, SEE **walk** verb.
2 *to stumble in your speech.* falter, hesitate, stammer, stutter, SEE **talk** verb.

stun verb
1 *The blow stunned him.* daze, knock out, knock senseless, make unconscious.
2 *The terrible news stunned us.* amaze, astonish, astound, bewilder, confound, confuse, dumbfound, flabbergast, numb, shock, stagger, stupefy.

stunt noun
exploit, feat, trick.

stupendous adjective
stupendous strength. a stupendous achievement. amazing, colossal, enormous, exceptional, extraordinary, huge, incredible, marvellous, miraculous, notable, phenomenal, prodigious, remarkable, [*informal*] sensational,

singular, special, staggering, stunning, tremendous, unbelievable, wonderful.
OPPOSITES: SEE **ordinary**.

stupid adjective
1 [Note that all these words can be insulting, and some will be more insulting than others. Many are used only *informally*.] *a stupid person*. brainless, clueless, cretinous, dense, dim, dopey, drippy, dull, dumb, feeble-minded, foolish, gormless, half-witted, idiotic, ignorant, imbecilic, ineducable, irrational, irresponsible, lacking, mindless, moronic, naïve, obtuse, puerile, senseless, silly, simple, slow, slow in the uptake, slow-witted, subnormal, thick, thick-headed, thick-skulled, thick-witted, unintelligent, unthinking, unwise, vacuous, witless.
2 *a stupid thing to do*. absurd, asinine, crack-brained, crass, crazy, fatuous, [*informal*] feeble, futile, [*informal*] half-baked, ill-advised, inane, irrelevant, laughable, ludicrous, [*informal*] lunatic, [*informal*] mad, nonsensical, pointless, rash, reckless, ridiculous, thoughtless, unjustifiable.
OPPOSITES: SEE **intelligent**.
a stupid person SEE **fool** noun.

stupidity noun
I could hardly believe her stupidity. absurdity, crassness, denseness, dullness, [*informal*] dumbness, fatuousness, folly, foolishness, idiocy, imbecility, inanity, lack of intelligence, lunacy, madness, naïvety, silliness, slowness.
OPPOSITES: SEE **intelligence**.

sturdy adjective
1 *a sturdy person*. athletic, brawny, burly, hardy, healthy, hefty, husky, muscular, powerful, robust, stalwart, stocky, [*informal*] strapping, strong, vigorous, well-built.
OPPOSITES: SEE **weak**.
2 *a sturdy pair of shoes*. durable, solid, sound, substantial, tough, well-made.
OPPOSITES: SEE **flimsy**.

style noun
1 *a style of writing*. custom, habit, idiosyncrasy, manner, method, phraseology, register, tone, way, wording.
2 *the latest style in clothes*. cut, design, fashion, mode, pattern, taste, type, vogue.
3 *She dresses with great style*. chic, dress sense, elegance, flair, flamboyance, panache, refinement, smartness, sophistication, stylishness, taste.

stylish adjective
stylish clothes. chic, [*informal*] classy, contemporary, [*informal*] dapper, elegant, fashionable, modern, modish, [*informal*] natty, [*informal*] posh, smart, [*informal*]

snazzy, sophisticated, [*informal*] trendy, up-to-date.
OPPOSITES: SEE **dowdy**.

subconscious adjective
subconscious awareness. intuitive, repressed, subliminal, unacknowledged, unconscious.
OPPOSITES: SEE **conscious**.

subdue verb
1 *to subdue the opposition*. beat, conquer, control, crush, defeat, master, overcome, overpower, overrun, quell, subject (*to subject a country*), subjugate, vanquish.
2 *to subdue your excitement*. check, curb, hold back, keep under, quieten, repress, restrain, suppress.

subdued adjective
1 *a subdued mood*. depressed, downcast, grave, reflective, repressed, restrained, serious, silent, sober, solemn, thoughtful.
OPPOSITES: SEE **excitable**.
2 *subdued music*. hushed, muted, peaceful, placid, quiet, soft, soothing, toned down, unobtrusive.
OPPOSITES: SEE **loud**.

subject noun
1 *a British subject*. citizen, dependant, national, passport-holder.
2 *a subject for discussion*. affair, business, issue, matter, point, question, theme, topic.

SUBJECTS WHICH STUDENTS STUDY:
anatomy, archaeology, architecture, art, astronomy, biology, business, chemistry, classics, computing, craft, design, divinity, domestic science, drama, economics, education, electronics, engineering, English, environmental science, ethnology, etymology.
geography, geology, heraldry, history, languages, Latin, law, linguistics, literature, mathematics, mechanics, SEE **medicine**, metallurgy, metaphysics, meteorology, music, natural history, oceanography, ornithology.
penology, pharmacology, pharmacy, philology, philosophy, photography, physics, physiology, politics, psychology, religious studies, SEE **science**, scripture, social work, sociology, sport, surveying, technology, theology, topology, zoology.

subjective adjective
a subjective reaction to something. biased, emotional, [*informal*] gut (*a gut reaction*), idiosyncratic, instinctive, intuitive, personal, prejudiced.
OPPOSITES: SEE **objective** adjective.

sublimate verb
to sublimate your emotions. divert, purify, redirect, refine.

sublime adjective
a sublime religious experience. ecstatic, elated, elevated, exalted, lofty, noble, spiritual, transcendent.
OPPOSITES: SEE **base** adjective.

submerge verb
1 *The flood submerged the village.* cover, drown, engulf, flood, immerse, inundate, overwhelm, swamp.
2 *The submarine submerged.* dive, go under, subside.

submission noun
1 *the submission of a wrestler.* capitulation, giving in, surrender.
2 *The judge accepted counsel's submission.* argument, claim, contention, idea, presentation, proposal, suggestion, theory.

submissive adjective
submissive acceptance of someone else's authority. acquiescent, compliant, deferential, docile, humble, meek, obedient, passive, resigned, [*uncomplimentary*] SEE **servile**, supine, tame, tractable, unassertive, uncomplaining, [*uncomplimentary*] weak.
OPPOSITES: SEE **assertive**.

submit verb
1 *to submit to an opponent.* accede, capitulate, give in, [*informal*] knuckle under, surrender, yield.
2 *to submit work to a teacher.* give in, hand in, present.
3 *to submit your views.* advance, offer, put forward, propound, SEE **state** verb, suggest.

subordinate adjective
subordinate rank. inferior, junior, lesser, lower, menial, minor, secondary, subservient, subsidiary.
OPPOSITES: SEE **superior**.

subordinate noun
He likes ordering subordinates about. assistant, dependant, employee, inferior, junior, menial, servant, [*informal*] underling.

subscribe verb
to subscribe to 1 *to subscribe to a good cause.* contribute to, donate to, give to, support.
2 *to subscribe to a magazine.* be a subscriber to, buy regularly, pay a subscription to.
3 *to subscribe to a theory or a course of action.* advocate, agree with, approve of, believe in, condone, endorse, [*informal*] give your blessing to.

subscriber noun
patron, regular customer, sponsor, supporter.

subscription noun
a club subscription. fee, SEE **payment**, regular contribution.

subsequent adjective
I made a guess, but subsequent events proved me wrong. consequent, ensuing, following, later, next, resulting, succeeding.
OPPOSITES: SEE **previous**.

subside verb
1 *The flood subsided. The pain subsided.* abate, decline, decrease, diminish, dwindle, ebb, fall, go down, lessen, melt away, moderate, recede, shrink, slacken, wear off.
2 *I subsided into a comfortable chair.* collapse, settle, sink.
OPPOSITES: SEE **rise** verb.

subsidiary adjective
of subsidiary importance. ancillary, auxiliary, contributory, lesser, minor, secondary, SEE **subordinate** adjective.

subsidize verb
Their parents subsidized their trip abroad. aid, back, finance, fund, promote, sponsor, support, underwrite.

subsidy noun
Public transport needs a subsidy from taxes. backing, financial help, grant, sponsorship, support.

substance noun
1 *What is this substance?* chemical, material, matter, stuff.
2 *the substance of an argument.* essence, gist, meaning, subject-matter, theme.

substandard adjective
substandard workmanship. [*informal*] below par, disappointing, inadequate, inferior, poor, shoddy, unworthy.

substantial adjective
1 *a substantial door.* durable, hefty, solid, sound, strong, sturdy, well-made.
OPPOSITES: SEE **flimsy**.
2 *a substantial amount of money.* big, considerable, generous, large, significant, sizeable, worthwhile.
OPPOSITES: SEE **small**.

substitute adjective
1 *a substitute player.* acting, deputy, relief, reserve, standby, surrogate, temporary.
2 *a substitute ingredient.* alternative, ersatz, imitation.

substitute noun
deputy, locum [= *substitute doctor*], proxy [= *substitute voter*], relief, replacement, reserve, stand-in, stopgap, supply [= *substitute teacher*], surrogate, understudy.

substitute verb
1 *to substitute one thing for another.* change, exchange, interchange, replace, [*informal*]

swop, [*informal*] switch.
2 [*informal*] *to substitute for an absent colleague.* act as a substitute [SEE **substitute** noun], deputize, stand in, understudy.

subtle adjective
1 *subtle flavours.* delicate, elusive, faint, mild, slight, unobtrusive.
2 *a subtle hint.* gentle, indirect, tactful, understated.
3 *a subtle argument.* clever, SEE **cunning**, ingenious, refined, shrewd, sophisticated.
OPPOSITES: SEE **obvious**.

subtract verb
to subtract one number from another. debit, deduct, remove, take away.
OPPOSITES: SEE **add**.

suburban adjective
the suburban areas of a town. residential, outer, outlying.

suburbs noun
the suburbs of a city. fringes, outer areas, outskirts, residential areas, suburbia.

subversive adjective
subversive ideas. subversive propaganda. challenging, disruptive, questioning, revolutionary, seditious, undermining, unsettling.
OPPOSITES: SEE **orthodox**.

subway noun
tunnel, underpass.

succeed verb
1 *If you work hard you will succeed.* accomplish your objective, be successful, do well, flourish, [*informal*] make it, prosper, thrive.
2 *The plan succeeded.* be effective, [*informal*] catch on, produce results, work.
OPPOSITES: SEE **fail**.
3 *Elizabeth II succeeded George VI.* come after, follow, replace, take over from.

success noun
1 *How do you measure success?* accomplishment, achievement, attainment, fame, prosperity.
2 *The success of the plan depends on your co-operation.* completion, effectiveness, successful outcome.
3 *The plan was a success.* [*informal*] hit, [*informal*] sensation, triumph, victory, [*informal*] winner.
OPPOSITES: SEE **failure**.

successful adjective
1 *a successful business.* effective, flourishing, fruitful, lucrative, productive, profitable, profit-making, prosperous, rewarding, thriving, well-off.
2 *a successful team.* unbeaten, victorious, winning.
OPPOSITES: SEE **unsuccessful**.

succession noun
a succession of disasters. chain, line, procession, progression, run, sequence, series, string.

successive adjective
We had rain on seven successive days. consecutive, in succession, uninterrupted.

successor noun
the successor to the throne. heir, inheritor, replacement.

succinct adjective
SEE **concise**.

succulent adjective
succulent fruit. fleshy, juicy, luscious, moist, rich.

succumb verb SEE **surrender**.

suck verb
to suck up *to suck up liquid.* absorb, draw up, pull up, soak up.

sudden adjective
1 *a sudden decision.* abrupt, hasty, hurried, impetuous, impulsive, quick, rash, [*informal*] snap, swift, unconsidered.
OPPOSITES: SEE **slow** adjective.
2 *a sudden happening.* acute (*an acute illness*), sharp, startling, surprising, unexpected, unforeseen, unlooked for.
OPPOSITES: SEE **expected**.

suds noun
bubbles, foam, froth, lather, soapsuds.

suffer verb
1 *to suffer pain.* bear, cope with, endure, experience, feel, go through, put up with, stand, tolerate, undergo.
2 *Did you suffer when you were ill?* experience pain [SEE **pain** noun], hurt.
3 *He suffered for his crime.* be punished, make amends, pay.

suffering noun
SEE **pain**.

sufficient adjective
sufficient money to live on. adequate, enough, satisfactory.
OPPOSITES: SEE **insufficient**.

suffix noun
OPPOSITE: prefix.

suffocate verb
asphyxiate, choke, SEE **kill**, smother, stifle, strangle, throttle.

sugar noun

FORMS OF SUGAR: brown sugar, cane sugar, caster sugar, demerara, glucose, granulated sugar, icing sugar, lump sugar, molasses, sucrose, SEE **sweets**, syrup, treacle.

sugar verb
SEE **sweeten**.

sugary adjective
1 *a sugary taste.* SEE **sweet** adjective.
2 *sugary sentiments.* cloying, SEE **sentimental**, sickly.

suggest verb
1 *I suggest we go home.* advise, advocate, moot, move, propose, propound, put forward, raise, recommend.
2 *Her face suggests that she's bored.* communicate, hint, imply, indicate, insinuate, intimate, mean, signal.

suggestion noun
1 *I made a suggestion.* offer, plan, proposal, recommendation.
2 *a suggestion of cheating.* hint, suspicion, trace.

suggestive adjective
1 *suggestive images in a poem.* evocative, expressive, thought-provoking.
2 *suggestive jokes.* SEE **indecent**.

suicidal adjective
1 *a suicidal mood.* SEE **depressed**.
2 *a suicidal mission.* hopeless, [*informal*] kamikaze, self-destructive.

suit noun
1 *a suit to wear.*
VARIOUS ITEMS OF CLOTHING: SEE **clothes**.
2 *a suit of cards.* set.
SUITS IN A PACK OF CARDS: clubs, diamonds, hearts, spades.

suit verb
1 *What you suggest suits me.* be suitable for [SEE **suitable**], gratify, please, satisfy.
2 *Their offer suits our requirements.* accommodate, conform to, fit in with, harmonize with, match, tally with.
3 *That colour suits you.* become, fit, look good on.

suitable adjective
a suitable present for granny. acceptable, applicable, apposite, appropriate, apt, becoming, congenial, convenient, fit, fitting, handy, pertinent, proper, relevant, satisfactory, seemly, timely, well-chosen, well-judged, well-timed.
OPPOSITES: SEE **unsuitable**.

sulk verb
to sulk after a defeat. be sullen [SEE **sullen**], brood, mope.

sulky adjective
a sulky look. SEE **sullen**.

sullen adjective
1 *a sullen expression.* bad-tempered, churlish, cross, disgruntled, grudging, moody, morose, petulant, resentful, sad, silent, sour, stubborn, sulky, surly, uncommunicative, unfriendly, unhappy, unsociable.
OPPOSITES: SEE **cheerful**.
2 *a sullen sky.* brooding, cheerless, dark, dismal, dull, gloomy, grey, sombre.
OPPOSITES: SEE **bright**.

sultry adjective
sultry weather. close, hot, humid, [*informal*] muggy, oppressive, steamy, stifling, stuffy, warm.
OPPOSITES: SEE **cool** adjective.

sum noun
Add up the sum. aggregate, amount, number, quantity, reckoning, result, score, tally, total, whole.

summarize verb
1 *to summarize evidence.* make a summary of [SEE **summary** noun], outline, [*informal*] recap, recapitulate, review, sum up.
2 *to summarize a story.* abridge, condense, précis, reduce, shorten.
OPPOSITES: SEE **elaborate** verb.

summary noun
1 *a summary of the main points.* abstract, digest, outline, recapitulation, resumé, review, summation, summing-up.
2 *a summary of a story.* abridgement, condensation, précis, reduction, synopsis.

summery adjective
summery weather. bright, SEE **hot**, sunny, tropical, warm.
OPPOSITES: SEE **wintry**.

summit noun
1 *the summit of a mountain.* apex, crown, head, height, peak, pinnacle, point, top.
OPPOSITES: SEE **base** noun.
2 *the summit of your success.* acme, apogee, high point, zenith.
OPPOSITES: SEE **nadir**.

summon verb
1 *to summon someone to attend.* command, demand, invite, order, send for, [*formal*] subpoena.
2 *to summon a meeting.* assemble, call, convene, convoke, gather together, muster, rally.

sumptuous *a sumptuous banquet.* costly, dear, expensive, extravagant, grand, lavish, luxurious, magnificent, opulent, [*informal*] posh, rich, splendid, superb.
OPPOSITES: SEE **mean** adjective.

sun noun
sunlight, sunshine.
RELATED ADJECTIVE: solar.

sunburnt adjective
blistered, bronzed, brown, peeling, tanned, weatherbeaten.

sundry adjective
SEE **various**.

sunken adjective
a sunken area. concave, depressed, hollow, hollowed, low.

sunless adjective
a sunless day. cheerless, cloudy, dark, dismal, dreary, dull, gloomy, grey, overcast.
OPPOSITES: SEE **sunny**.

sunny adjective
a sunny day. bright, clear, cloudless, fine, summery, sunlit.
OPPOSITES: SEE **sunless**.

sunrise noun
dawn, daybreak.

sunset noun
dusk, evening, [*poetic*] gloaming, nightfall, sundown, twilight.

sunshade noun
awning, canopy, parasol.

suntan noun
sunburn, tan.

super adjective
SEE **good**.

superannuation noun
annuity, pension.

superb adjective
SEE **splendid**.

superficial adjective
1 *a superficial wound*. exterior, on the surface, shallow, skin-deep, slight, surface, unimportant.
OPPOSITES: SEE **deep**.
2 *a superficial examination*. careless, casual, cursory, desultory, hasty, hurried, inattentive, [*informal*] nodding (*a nodding acquaintance*), passing, perfunctory.
OPPOSITES: SEE **thorough**.
3 *superficial arguments*. facile, frivolous, lightweight, simple-minded, simplistic, sweeping (*sweeping generalizations*), trivial, unconvincing, uncritical, unscholarly, unsophisticated.
OPPOSITES: SEE **analytical**.

superfluous adjective
superfluous possessions. excess, excessive, needless, redundant, spare, surplus, unnecessary, unwanted.
OPPOSITES: SEE **necessary**.

superhuman adjective
superhuman efforts. herculean, heroic, phenomenal, prodigious.

superior adjective
1 *superior in rank*. greater, higher, more important, senior.
2 *superior quality*. better, choice, exclusive, fine, first-class, first-rate, select, top, unrivalled.
3 *a superior attitude*. arrogant, condescending, disdainful, haughty, [*informal*] high-and-mighty, lofty, patronizing, self-important, smug, snobbish, [*informal*] snooty, stuck-up, supercilious.
OPPOSITES: SEE **inferior**.

supernatural adjective
supernatural powers, supernatural manifestations. abnormal, ghostly, inexplicable, magical, metaphysical, miraculous, mysterious, mystic, occult, paranormal, preternatural, psychic, spiritual, uncanny, unearthly, unnatural, weird.
SUPERNATURAL BEINGS: SEE **spirit**.

superstar noun
big name, celebrity, idol, SEE **performer**, star.

superstition noun
My fear of Friday 13th is just superstition. delusion, illusion, myth, [*informal*] old wives' tale, superstitious belief [SEE **superstitious**].

superstitious adjective
superstitious beliefs. groundless, illusory, irrational, mythical, traditional, unfounded, unprovable.
OPPOSITES: SEE **scientific**.

supervise verb
to supervise a task. administer, be in charge (of), be the supervisor (of) [SEE **supervisor**], conduct, control, direct, invigilate [= *supervise an exam*]. lead, look after, manage, organize, oversee, preside over, run, superintend, watch over.

supervision noun
the supervision of a production line. the supervision of an exam. administration, conduct, control, invigilation, management, organization, oversight, surveillance.

supervisor noun
administrator, SEE **chief** noun, controller, director, foreman, [*informal*] gaffer, head, inspector, invigilator, leader, manager, organizer, overseer, superintendent, timekeeper.

supine adjective
lying supine on the floor. face upwards, on your back.
OPPOSITES: SEE **prone**.

supplant verb
to supplant a leader. displace, oust, replace, [*informal*] step into the shoes of, [*informal*] topple, unseat.

supple adjective
supple leather. supple limbs. bending,
[*informal*] bendy, elastic, flexible, graceful,
limber, lithe, plastic, pliable, pliant, soft.
OPPOSITES: SEE **brittle, rigid**.

supplement noun
1 *a supplement to travel first class.* additional
payment, excess, surcharge.
2 *a newspaper supplement.* addendum,
addition, SEE **appendix, extra, insert**.

supplement verb
I do odd jobs to supplement my income. add
to, augment, boost, complement, reinforce,
[*informal*] top up.

supplementary adjective
*a supplementary fare. supplementary
information.* accompanying, additional,
auxiliary, complementary, extra.

supplier noun
dealer, provider, purveyor, retailer, seller,
shopkeeper, vendor, wholesaler.

supply noun
a supply of sweets. quantity, reserve,
reservoir, stock, stockpile, store.
supplies *supplies for the weekend.*
equipment, food, necessities, provisions,
rations, shopping.

supply verb
to supply goods. contribute, donate, equip,
feed, furnish, give, handover, pass on,
produce, provide, purvey, sell, stock.

support noun
1 *Thank you for your support.* aid, approval,
assistance, backing, contribution, co-
operation, donation, encouragement,
friendship, help, interest, loyalty,
patronage, protection, reassurance,
reinforcement, sponsorship, succour.
2 *a support to lean or rest on.* bracket,
buttress, crutch, foundation, pillar, post,
prop, sling, stanchion, stay, strut, trestle,
truss.

support verb
1 *to support a weight.* bear, bolster, buttress,
carry, give strength to, hold up, prop up,
provide a support for, reinforce, shore up,
strengthen, underlie, underpin.
2 *to support someone in trouble.* aid, assist,
back, champion, comfort, defend,
encourage, give support to [SEE **support**
noun], rally round, reassure, speak up for,
stand by, stand up for, take (someone's)
part.
3 *to support a family.* bring up, feed, finance,
fund, keep, maintain, nourish, provide for,
sustain.
4 *to support a charity.* be a supporter of [SEE
supporter], be interested in, contribute to,
espouse (*to espouse a cause*), follow, give to,

patronize, pay money to, sponsor, subsidize,
work for.
5 *to support a point of view.* advocate, agree
with, argue for, confirm, corroborate,
defend, endorse, explain, justify, promote,
substantiate, uphold, verify.
OPPOSITES: SEE **undermine**.

supporter noun
1 *a football supporter.* enthusiast, [*informal*]
fan, fanatic, follower.
2 *a supporter of an idea. a supporter of a
political party.* adherent, advocate, apologist
(for), champion, defender, seconder,
upholder, voter.
3 *a supporter of someone in a job or in a
contest.* ally, collaborate, helper, [*old-
fashioned*] henchman, second.

supportive adjective
a supportive group of friends. caring,
concerned, encouraging, helpful, interested,
kind, loyal, positive, reassuring,
sympathetic, understanding.
OPPOSITES: SEE **subversive**.

suppose verb
1 *I suppose you want some food.* accept,
assume, believe, conclude, conjecture,
expect, guess, infer, judge, postulate,
presume, speculate, surmise, think.
2 *Just suppose you had lots of money.* fancy,
fantasize, imagine, hypothesize, maintain,
pretend.

supposed adjective
No one has ever seen the supposed monster.
alleged, assumed, conjectural, hypothetical,
imagined, presumed, putative, reported,
reputed, rumoured.
to be supposed to *I'm supposed to start
work at 8.30.* be due to, be expected to, be
meant to, be required to, have a duty to,
need to, ought to.

suppress verb
1 *to suppress a rebellion.* conquer, crush,
overcome, overthrow, put an end to, put
down, quash, quell, stamp out, stop, subdue.
2 *to suppress the truth. to suppress your
feelings.* bottle up, censor, conceal, cover up,
SEE **hide** verb, [*informal*] keep quiet about,
repress, restrain, silence, smother.

supremacy noun
*No one could challenge her supremacy in
gymnastics.* dominance, domination, lead,
predominance, pre-eminence, sovereignty.

supreme adjective
*Her supreme moment was winning a gold
medal.* best, consummate, crowning,
culminating, greatest, highest,
incomparable, matchless, outstanding,
paramount, predominant, pre-eminent,
prime, principal, superlative, surpassing,

top, ultimate, unbeatable, unbeaten, unparalleled, unrivalled, unsurpassable, unsurpassed.

surcharge noun SEE **supplement** noun.

sure adjective
1 *I'm sure that I'm right.* assured, confident, convinced, decided, definite, persuaded, positive, resolute.
2 *He's sure to come.* bound, certain, compelled, obliged, required.
3 *a sure fact.* accurate, clear, convincing, guaranteed, indisputable, inescapable, inevitable, precise, proven, true, unchallenged, undeniable, undisputed, undoubted, verifiable.
4 *a sure ally.* dependable, effective, faithful, firm, infallible, loyal, reliable, safe, secure, solid, steadfast, steady, trustworthy, trusty, unerring, unfailing, unswerving.
OPPOSITES: SEE **uncertain**.

surface noun
1 *the outer surface.* coat, covering, crust, exterior, façade, outside, shell, skin, veneer.
OPPOSITES: SEE **centre**.
2 *A cube has six surfaces.* face, facet, plane, side.
3 *a working surface.* top, worktop.

surface verb
1 *I surfaced the wood with plastic.* coat, cover, veneer.
2 *The submarine surfaced. A problem surfaced.* appear, [*informal*] come to light, come up, emerge, materialize, rise, [*informal*] pop up.

surfeit noun
a surfeit of rich food. excess, glut, over-indulgence, superfluity.

surge verb
1 *Water surged around them.* billow, eddy, gush, heave, make waves, roll, swirl.
2 *The crowd surged forward.* move irresistibly, push, rush, stampede, sweep.

surgery noun
1 *She underwent surgery.* biopsy, operation.
2 *I visited the doctor's surgery.* clinic, consulting room, health centre, infirmary, medical centre, sick-bay.

surly adjective
a surly mood. a surly answer. bad-tempered, churlish, cross, [*informal*] crusty, gruff, [*informal*] grumpy, ill-natured, irascible, miserable, morose, peevish, rude, sulky, sullen, testy, uncivil, unfriendly, ungracious.
OPPOSITES: SEE **friendly**.

surmount verb SEE **deal** verb (**deal with**).

surpass verb
The success of the sale surpassed our expectations. beat, better, do better than, eclipse, exceed, excel, outclass, outdo, outshine, outstrip, overshadow, top, transcend.

surplus noun
If you've had all you want, give the surplus to others. balance, excess, extra, remainder, residue, superfluity, surfeit.

surprise noun
1 *Imagine our surprise when she walked in.* alarm, amazement, astonishment, consternation, dismay, incredulity, wonder.
2 *Her arrival was a complete surprise.* [*informal*] bolt from the blue, [*informal*] bombshell, [*informal*] eye-opener, shock.

surprise verb
1 *The news surprised us.* alarm, amaze, astonish, astound, disconcert, dismay, shock, stagger, startle, stun, [*informal*] take aback, take by surprise, [*informal*] throw (*The unexpected news threw me*).
2 *The security officer surprised him opening the safe.* capture, catch out, [*informal*] catch red-handed, come upon, detect, discover, take unawares.

surprised adjective
I admit that I was surprised. alarmed, amazed, astonished, astounded, disconcerted, dumbfounded, flabbergasted, incredulous, nonplussed, shocked, speechless, staggered, startled, stunned, taken aback, taken by surprise, thunderstruck.

surprising adjective
a surprising turn of events. alarming, amazing, astonishing, astounding, disconcerting, extraordinary, incredible, [*informal*] offputting, shocking, staggering, startling, stunning, sudden, unexpected, unforeseen, unlooked for, unplanned.
OPPOSITES: SEE **predictable**.

surrender verb
1 *to surrender to an enemy.* capitulate, [*informal*] cave in, collapse, concede, fall, [*informal*] give in, resign, submit, succumb, [*informal*] throw in the towel, [*informal*] throw up the sponge, yield.
2 *to surrender your ticket.* give, hand over, relinquish.
3 *to surrender your rights.* abandon, cede, give up, renounce, waive.

surreptitious adjective
a surreptitious look at the answers. concealed, covert, crafty, disguised, furtive, hidden, secretive, shifty, sly, [*informal*] sneaky, stealthy, underhand.
OPPOSITES: SEE **blatant**.

surround verb
The park is surrounded by houses. besiege, beset, encircle, encompass, engulf, girdle, hedge in, hem in, ring, skirt.

surroundings noun
You work more happily in pleasant surroundings. ambience, area, background, context, environment, location, milieu, neighbourhood, setting, vicinity.

surveillance noun
Police maintained a 24-hour surveillance on the building. check, observation, scrutiny, supervision, vigilance, watch.

survey noun
a traffic survey, a land survey. appraisal, assessment, census, count, evaluation, examination, inspection, investigation, scrutiny, study, [*formal*] triangulation.

survey verb
to survey the damage after an accident. appraise, assess, estimate, evaluate, examine, inspect, investigate, look over, scrutinize, study, view, weigh up.

survival noun
Commercial exploitation of resources threatens our survival. continuance, continued existence.

survive verb
1 *You can't survive without water.* carry on, continue, endure, keep going, last, live, persist, remain.
OPPOSITES: SEE **die**.
2 *He survived the disasters which plagued him.* come through, live through, outlast, outlive, weather, withstand.
OPPOSITE: succumb to.

susceptible adjective
susceptible to colds. disposed, given, inclined, liable, predisposed, prone, sensitive, vulnerable.
OPPOSITES: SEE **resistant**.

suspect adjective
1 *His evidence was suspect.* doubtful, inadequate, questionable, unconvincing, unreliable, unsatisfactory.
OPPOSITES: SEE **satisfactory**.
2 *a suspect character.* dubious, suspected, SEE **suspicious**.

suspect verb
1 *I suspect his motives.* call into question, distrust, doubt, mistrust.
2 *I suspect that he's lying.* believe, conjecture, consider, guess, imagine, infer, presume, speculate, suppose, surmise, think.

suspend verb
1 *to suspend something from a hook, etc.* dangle, hang, swing.
2 *to suspend a meeting.* adjourn, break off, defer, delay, discontinue, interrupt, postpone, put off.
3 *to suspend someone from school or from a job.* debar, dismiss, expel, send down.

suspense noun
The suspense was unbearable. anticipation, anxiety, drama, excitement, expectancy, expectation, tension, uncertainty, waiting.

suspicion noun
1 *a suspicion that she was lying.* apprehension, distrust, doubt, feeling, guess, [*informal*] hunch, impression, misgiving, presentiment, qualm, uncertainty, wariness.
2 *a suspicion of a smile on his face.* hint, shadow, suggestion, tinge, touch, trace.

suspicious adjective
1 *suspicious of the evidence.* [*informal*] chary, disbelieving, distrustful, doubtful, incredulous, mistrustful, sceptical, unconvinced, uneasy, wary.
OPPOSITES: SEE **credulous**.
2 *a suspicious character.* disreputable, dubious, [*informal*] fishy, peculiar, questionable, shady, suspect, suspected, unreliable, untrustworthy.
OPPOSITES: SEE **straightforward**.

sustain verb SEE **support** verb.

sustenance noun
SEE **food**.

swallow verb
consume, SEE **drink** verb, **eat**.
to swallow up *Fog swallowed them up.* absorb, enclose, enfold, envelop, SEE **swamp** verb.

swamp noun
bog, fen, marsh, marshland, mire, morass, mud, mudflats, quagmire, quicksand, saltmarsh, [*old-fashioned*] slough, wetlands.

swamp verb
A huge wave swamped the ship. deluge, drench, engulf, flood, inundate, overwhelm, sink, submerge, swallow up.

swampy adjective
swampy ground. boggy, marshy, miry, muddy, soft, soggy, unstable, waterlogged, wet.
OPPOSITES: SEE **dry** adjective.

swank verb SEE **boast**.

swap verb SEE **exchange** verb.

swarm noun
a swarm of bees. SEE **group** noun.

swarm verb
People swarm to watch an accident. cluster, congregate, crowd, flock, mass, move in a swarm, throng.
to swarm with *The kitchen swarmed with ants.* abound, be alive with, be infested with, be invaded by, be overrun with, crawl, teem.

swarthy adjective
a swarthy complexion. brown, dark, dusky, tanned.

sway verb
1 *to sway in the breeze.* bend, lean from side to side, rock, roll, swing, wave.
2 *Nothing I can say will sway them.* affect, change the mind of, govern, influence, persuade.

swear verb
1 *He swore that he would tell the truth.* affirm, attest, declare, give your word, pledge, promise, state on oath, take an oath, testify, vow.
2 *She swore when she hit her finger.* blaspheme, curse, use swearwords [SEE **swearword**].

swearword noun
blasphemy, curse, expletive, [*informal*] four-letter word, oath, obscenity, profanity.
swearwords bad language, foul language, swearing.

sweat verb
perspire, swelter.

sweaty adjective
sweaty hands. clammy, damp, moist, perspiring, sticky, sweating.

sweep verb
1 *Sweep the floor.* brush, clean, clear, dust.
2 *The bus swept past.* SEE **move** verb.

sweeping adjective
1 *sweeping changes.* comprehensive, extensive, far-reaching, indiscriminate, radical, wholesale.
OPPOSITES: SEE **limited**.
2 *a sweeping statement.* broad, general, oversimplified, simplistic, superficial, uncritical, undiscriminating, unqualified, unscholarly.
OPPOSITES: SEE **analytical**.

sweet adjective
1 *a sweet taste. a sweet smell.* cloying, fragrant, luscious, mellow, perfumed, sickly, sugary, sweetened, syrupy.
OPPOSITES: SEE **acid**, **acrid**, **bitter**, **savoury**.
2 *sweet sounds.* [*often joking*] dulcet (*dulcet tones*), euphonious, harmonious, heavenly, melodious, musical, pleasant, silvery, soothing, tuneful.
OPPOSITES: SEE **discordant**.
3 *a sweet nature.* affectionate, attractive, charming, dear, endearing, engaging, gentle, gracious, lovable, lovely, nice, pretty, unselfish, winning.
OPPOSITES: SEE **selfish**, **ugly**.

sweet noun
[= *the sweet course of a meal*] [*informal*] afters, dessert, pudding.

sweets [*old-fashioned*] bon-bons, [*American*] candy, confectionery, [*childish*] sweeties, [*old-fashioned*] sweetmeats.

VARIOUS SWEETS: acid drop, barley sugar, boiled sweet, bull's-eye, butterscotch, candy, candyfloss, caramel, chewing-gum, chocolate, fondant, fruit pastille, fudge, humbug, liquorice, lollipop, marshmallow, marzipan, mint, nougat, peppermint, rock, toffee, Turkish delight.

---

sweeten verb
1 *to sweeten your coffee.* make sweeter, sugar.
2 *to sweeten someone's temper.* appease, calm, mellow, mollify, pacify, soothe.

sweetheart noun
SEE **lover**.

swell verb
1 *The balloon swelled as it filled with air.* balloon, become bigger, billow, blow up, bulge, dilate, distend, enlarge, expand, fatten, grow, inflate, puff up, rise.
2 *We invited friends to swell the numbers in the audience.* augment, boost, build up, extend, increase, make bigger.
OPPOSITES: SEE **shrink**.

swelling noun
a painful swelling. blister, bulge, bump, hump, inflammation, knob, lump, protuberance, tumescence, tumour.

sweltering adjective
SEE **hot**.

swerve verb
The car swerved to avoid a hedgehog. change direction, deviate, dodge about, swing, take avoiding action, turn aside, veer, wheel.

swift adjective
a swift journey. a swift reaction. agile, brisk, fast, [*old-fashioned*] fleet, fleet-footed, hasty, hurried, nimble, [*informal*] nippy, prompt, SEE **quick**, rapid, speedy, sudden.
OPPOSITES: SEE **slow** adjective.

swill verb
1 *Swill the car with clear water.* bathe, clean, rinse, sponge down, wash.
2 [*informal*] *They sat there swilling champagne.* SEE **drink** verb.

swim verb
to swim in the sea. bathe, dive in, float, go swimming, [*informal*] take a dip.

swimming-bath noun
baths, leisurepool, lido, swimming-pool.

swim-suit noun
bathing-costume, bathing-dress, bathing-suit, bikini, swim-wear, trunks.

swindle noun
I don't want to get involved in a swindle.
cheat, chicanery, [*informal*] con, deception,
double-dealing, fraud, [*informal*] racket,
[*informal*] rip-off, [*informal*] sharp
practice, [*informal*] swizz, trickery.

swindle verb
He swindled us out of a lot of money.
[*informal*] bamboozle, cheat, [*informal*] con,
deceive, defraud, [*informal*] do, double-
cross, dupe, [*informal*] fiddle, [*informal*]
fleece, fool, hoax, hoodwink, [*informal*]
rook, trick, [*informal*] welsh (*to welsh on a
bet*).

swindler noun
charlatan, cheat, cheater, [*informal*] con-
man, counterfeiter, double-cross,
extortioner, forger, fraud, hoaxer, impostor,
mountebank, quack, racketeer, [*informal*]
shark, trickster, [*informal*] twister.

swing noun
a swing in public opinion. change,
fluctuation, movement, oscillation, shift,
variation.

swing verb
1 *He swung from the end of a rope.* be
suspended, dangle, flap, hang loose, rock,
sway, swivel, turn, twirl, wave about.
2 *The car swung from one side of the road to
the other.* SEE **swerve.**
3 *During the election, support swung to the
opposition.* change, fluctuate, move across,
oscillate, shift, transfer, vary.

swipe verb
1 *to swipe with a bat.* SEE **hit** verb.
2 [*informal*] *She swiped my pen.* SEE **steal.**

swirl verb
The water swirled round. boil, churn, eddy,
move in circles, spin, surge, twirl, twist,
whirl.

switch verb
to switch places. change, exchange, replace,
shift, substitute, [*informal*] swap.

swivel verb
to swivel round. gyrate, pirouette, pivot,
revolve, rotate, spin, swing, turn, twirl,
wheel.

swollen adjective
big, bulging, distended, enlarged, fat, full,
inflated, puffy, tumescent.

swoop verb
The owl swooped down. descend, dive, drop,
fall, fly down, lunge, plunge, pounce.

sword noun
blade, broadsword, cutlass, foil, rapier,
sabre, scimitar.

sycophantic adjective
SEE **flattering.**

syllabus noun
course, curriculum, outline, programme of
study.

symbol noun
1 *A crown is a symbol of royal power.* badge,
emblem, figure, ideogram, ideograph,
image, insignia, logo, monogram, motif,
pictogram, pictograph, sign.
2 *symbols used in writing.* character, letter.

symbolic adjective
a symbolic image. a symbolic gesture.
allegorical, emblematic, figurative,
meaningful, metaphorical, representative,
significant, suggestive, token (*a token
gesture*).

symbolize verb
Easter eggs symbolize the renewal of life. be
a sign of, betoken, communicate, connote,
denote, indicate, mean, represent, signify,
stand for, suggest.

symmetrical adjective
a symmetrical design. balanced, even,
regular.
OPPOSITES: SEE **asymmetrical.**

sympathetic adjective
sympathetic about someone's problems.
benevolent, caring, charitable, comforting,
compassionate, concerned, consoling,
friendly, humane, interested, kind,
merciful, pitying, soft-hearted, sorry,
supportive, tender, tolerant, understanding,
warm.
OPPOSITES: SEE **unsympathetic.**

sympathize verb
to sympathize with *to sympathize with
someone in trouble.* be sorry for, be
sympathetic towards [SEE **sympathetic**],
comfort, commiserate with, console,
empathize with, feel for, identify with, pity,
show sympathy for [SEE **sympathy**],
understand.

sympathy noun
*She showed no sympathy when I described my
problem.* affinity, commiseration,
compassion, condolences, consideration,
empathy, feeling, fellow-feeling, kindness,
mercy, pity, tenderness, understanding.

symptom noun
A rash is one of the symptoms of measles.
feature, indication, manifestation, mark,
sign, warning.

symptomatic adjective
*Do you think violence is symptomatic of our
times?* characteristic, indicative,
suggestive, typical.

synonym noun
OPPOSITES: antonym.

synthesize verb
SEE **combine**.

synthetic adjective
Nylon is a synthetic material. artificial, concocted, ersatz, fabricated, fake [*informal*] made-up, man-made, manufactured, mock, simulated, unnatural.
OPPOSITES: SEE **authentic, natural**.

system noun
1 *a railway system.* network, organization, [*informal*] setup.
2 *a system for getting your work done.* arrangement, logic, method, methodology, order, plan, practice, procedure, process, routine, rules, scheme, structure, technique, theory.
3 *a system of government.* constitution, philosophy, principles, regime, science.

systematic adjective
a systematic worker. systematic organization. businesslike, logical, methodical, ordered, orderly, organized, planned, scientific, structured.
OPPOSITES: SEE **unsystematic**.

Tt

table noun
1 coffee-table, dining-table, gate-leg table, kitchen table.
OTHER FURNITURE: SEE **furniture**.
2 *a table of information.* catalogue, chart, diagram, graph, index, list, register, schedule, tabulation, timetable.

tablet noun
1 *a tablet of soap.* bar, block, chunk, piece, slab.
2 *The doctor prescribed some tablets.* capsule, medicine, pellet, pill.

taboo adjective
a taboo subject. banned, disapproved of, forbidden, prohibited, proscribed, unacceptable, unmentionable, unnameable.

tabulate verb
to tabulate information. arrange as a table, catalogue, list, set out in columns.

tacit adjective
tacit agreement. implicit, implied, silent, understood, unspoken, unvoiced.

taciturn adjective
SEE **silent**.

tack noun
1 drawing-pin, nail, pin, tin-tack.
2 *a tack in a garment.* stitch.
3 *You're on the wrong tack.* approach, SEE **direction**, policy, procedure.

tack verb
1 *to tack down a carpet.* nail, pin.
WAYS TO FASTEN THINGS: SEE **fasten**.
2 *to tack up a hem.* sew, stitch.
to tack on SEE **add**.

tackle noun
1 *fishing tackle.* apparatus, equipment, gear, implements, kit, outfit, [*joking*] paraphernalia, rig, tools.
2 *a football tackle.* attack, block, challenge, interception, intervention.

tackle verb
1 *to tackle a problem.* address yourself to, attempt, attend to, combat, confront, cope with, deal with, face up to, grapple with, handle, manage, set about, sort out, undertake.
2 *to tackle an opposing player.* attack, challenge, intercept, stop, take on.

tact noun
He showed tact in dealing with their embarrassment. consideration, delicacy, diplomacy, discretion, sensitivity, tactfulness, thoughtfulness, understanding.

tactful adjective
a tactful reminder. appropriate, considerate, delicate, diplomatic, discreet, judicious, polite, sensitive, thoughtful.
OPPOSITES: SEE **tactless**.

tactical adjective
a tactical manœuvre. calculated, deliberate, planned, politic, prudent, shrewd, skilful, strategic.

tactics noun
The manager explained the tactics for the next game. approach, campaign, course of action, manœuvring, plan, ploy, policy, procedure, scheme, strategy.

tactless adjective
a tactless reference to her illness. blundering, boorish, clumsy, gauche, heavy-handed, hurtful, impolite, inappropriate, inconsiderate, indelicate, indiscreet, inept, insensitive, misjudged, SEE **rude**, thoughtless, uncouth, undiplomatic, unkind.
OPPOSITES: SEE **tactful**.

tag noun
a price tag. docket, label, marker, slip, sticker, tab, ticket.

tag verb
to tag items in a database. to tag goods with price-labels. identify, label, mark, ticket.
to tag along *We tagged along at the end of the queue.* SEE **follow**, join, [*informal*] latch on, trail, unite.

tail noun
an animal's tail. the tail of a queue. back, end, extremity, rear, tailend.

tail verb
to tail a car. follow, pursue, shadow, stalk, track, trail.
to tail off *Our enthusiasm tailed off when we got tired.* decline, decrease, dwindle, lessen, peter out, reduce, slacken, subside, wane.

taint verb
1 *to taint food or water.* adulterate, contaminate, dirty, infect, poison, pollute, soil.
2 *to taint someone's reputation.* blacken, dishonour, ruin, slander, smear, stain.

take verb
[*Take* has many meanings and uses. We give just the commoner ones here.] 1 *Take my hand.* clutch, grab, grasp, hold, pluck, seize, snatch.
2 *They took prisoners.* abduct, arrest, capture, catch, corner, detain, ensnare, entrap, secure.
3 *Someone took my pen.* appropriate, move, pick up, pocket, remove, SEE **steal**.
4 *Take 2 from 4.* deduct, eliminate, subtract, take away.
5 *My car takes four people.* accommodate, carry, contain, have room for, hold.
6 *We took him home.* accompany, bring, [*informal*] cart, conduct, convey, escort, ferry, fetch, guide, lead, transport.
7 *We took a taxi.* catch, engage, hire, make use of, travel by, use.
8 *She took science at college.* have lessons in, learn about, read, study.
9 *I can't take rich food. I won't take any more insults.* abide, accept, bear, brook, consume, drink, eat, endure, have, receive, [*informal*] stand, [*informal*] stomach, suffer, swallow, tolerate, undergo, withstand.
10 *It took a lot of courage to own up.* necessitate, need, require, use up.
11 *She took a new name.* adopt, assume, choose, select.
to take aback SEE **surprise** verb.
to take after SEE **resemble**.
to take against SEE **dislike** verb.
to take back SEE **withdraw**.
to take in 1 *The trick took me in.* SEE **deceive**.
2 *I hope you took in all I said.* SEE **understand**.
to take life SEE **kill**.
to take off 1 *Take off your clothes.* SEE **remove**.
2 *The mimic took off the prime minister.* SEE **imitate**.

to take on SEE **undertake**.
to take part *We took part in the organization.* SEE **participate**.
to take place SEE **happen**.

take-over noun
a business take-over. amalgamation, combination, incorporation, merger.

takings noun
the takings of a shop. earnings, gains, gate [= *takings at a football match*], income, proceeds, profits, receipts, revenue.

tale noun
She told us her tale. account, anecdote, narration, narrative, relation, report, [*slang*] spiel, story, yarn.

talent noun
musical talent. sporting talent. ability, accomplishment, aptitude, brilliance, capacity, expertise, flair, genius, gift, knack, [*informal*] know-how, prowess, skill.

talented adjective
a talented player. able, accomplished, artistic, brilliant, SEE **clever**, distinguished, expert, gifted, inspired, skilful, skilled, versatile.
OPPOSITES: SEE **unskilful**.

talk noun
1 *talk between two or more people.* chat, confabulation, conference, conversation, dialogue, discussion, gossip, intercourse, palaver, words.
2 *a talk to an audience.* address, discourse, harangue, lecture, oration, presentation, sermon, speech.

talk verb
1 *As far as we know, animals can't talk.* address each other, articulate ideas, commune, communicate, confer, converse, deliver a speech, discourse, enunciate, exchange views, have a conversation, negotiate, [*informal*] pipe up, pronounce words, say something [SEE **say**], speak, tell, use language, use your voice, utter, verbalize, vocalize.
2 *Can you talk French?* communicate in, express yourself in, pronounce, speak.
3 *The police tried to get him to talk.* confess, give information, [*informal*] grass, inform, [*informal*] let on, [*informal*] spill the beans, [*informal*] squeal, [*informal*] tell tales.
to talk about allude to, comment on, discuss, mention, refer to, relate.

VERBS EXPRESSING DIFFERENT MODES OF TALKING: SEE **answer**, argue, SEE **ask**, assert, complain, declaim, declare, ejaculate, exclaim, fulminate, harangue, object, plead, read aloud, recite, soliloquize, [*informal*] speechify.

WORDS EXPRESSING DIFFERENT WAYS OF
TALKING: [many of these words are used
both as nouns and as verbs; many are used
informally]babble, baby-talk, bawl, bellow,
blab, blarney, blether, blurt out, breathe
(*Don't breathe a word!*), burble, call out,
chat, chatter, chin-wag, chit-chat, clamour,
croak, cry, drawl, drone, gabble, gas, gibber,
gossip, grunt, harp, howl, intone, jabber,
jaw, jeer, lisp, maunder, moan, mumble,
murmur, mutter, natter, patter, prattle,
pray, preach, rabbit, rant, rasp, rave, roar,
scream, screech, shout, shriek, slur, snap,
snarl, speak in an undertone, splutter,
spout, squeal, stammer, stutter, tattle, tittle-
tattle, utter, vociferate, wail, whimper,
whine, whinge, whisper, witter, yell.

talkative adjective
a talkative person. articulate, [*informal*]
chatty, communicative, effusive, eloquent,
expansive, garrulous, glib, gossipy, long-
winded, loquacious, prolix, unstoppable,
verbose, vocal, voluble, wordy.
a talkative person chatter-box, [*informal*]
gas-bag, gossip, [*informal*] wind-bag.

tall adjective
a tall skyscraper. SEE **big**, giant, high, lofty,
towering.
OPPOSITES: SEE **short**.

tame adjective
1 *tame animals.* amenable, biddable,
compliant, disciplined, docile,
domesticated, gentle, manageable, meek,
obedient, safe, subdued, submissive,
tractable.
OPPOSITES: SEE **wild**.
2 *a tame story.* bland, boring, dull, feeble,
flat, lifeless, tedious, unadventurous,
unexciting, uninspiring, uninteresting.
OPPOSITES: SEE **exciting**.

tame verb
1 *to tame a wild animal.* break in, discipline,
domesticate, house-train, make tame [SEE
tame adjective], master, train.
2 *to tame your passions.* conquer, curb,
humble, keep under, quell, repress, subdue,
subjugate, suppress, temper.

tamper verb
to tamper with alter, [*informal*] fiddle
about with, interfere with, make
adjustments to, meddle with, tinker with.

tan noun
I got a tan on holiday. sunburn, suntan.

tan verb
to tan in the sun. burn, bronze, brown,
colour, darken, get tanned [SEE **tanned**].

tang noun
The flavour has quite a tang to it. acidity,
[*informal*] bite, piquancy, pungency,
savour, sharpness.

tangible adjective
tangible evidence. actual, concrete, definite,
material, palpable, physical, positive,
provable, real, solid, substantial, touchable.
OPPOSITES: SEE **intangible**.

tangle noun
a tangle of string. coil, confusion, jumble,
jungle, knot, mass, muddle, twist, web.

tangle verb
1 *to tangle string or ropes.* confuse, entangle,
entwine, [*informal*] foul up, interweave,
muddle, ravel, [*informal*] snarl up, twist.
OPPOSITES: SEE **disentangle**.
2 *A fish was tangled in the net.* catch, enmesh,
ensnare, entrap, trap.
3 *Don't tangle with those criminals.* become
involved with, confront, cross.

tangy adjective
a tangy taste. acid, appetizing, bitter, fresh,
piquant, pungent, refreshing, sharp, spicy,
strong, tart.
OPPOSITES: SEE **bland**.

tank noun
1 *a water tank.* basin, cistern, reservoir.
OTHER CONTAINERS: SEE **container**.
2 *a fish tank.* aquarium.

tanned adjective
brown, sunburnt, suntanned, weather-
beaten.

tantalize verb
The delicious smell tantalized us. entice,
frustrate, [*informal*] keep on tenterhooks,
lead on, provoke, taunt, tease, tempt,
titillate, torment.

tap noun
a water tap. [*American*] faucet, stop-cock,
valve.

tap verb
I tapped on the door. SEE **hit** verb, knock, rap,
strike.

tape noun
I tied the parcel with tape. band, binding,
braid, ribbon, strip.

taper verb
to taper to a point. attenuate, become
narrower, narrow, thin.
to taper off *The conversation tapered off.* SEE
decrease verb.

target noun
1 *Our target was to raise £100.* aim, ambition,
end, goal, hope, intention, objective,
purpose.
2 *Who was the target of their criticism?* butt,
object, quarry, victim.

tariff noun
1 *a hotel's tariff.* charges, menu, price-list,
schedule.

2 *a tariff on imports.* customs, duty, excise, levy, tax, toll.

tarnish verb
1 *Acid rain tarnished the metal.* blacken, corrode, discolour.
2 *The slander tarnished his reputation.* blemish, blot, dishonour, mar, spoil, stain, sully.

tart adjective
the tart taste of lemons. acid, biting, piquant, pungent, sharp, sour, tangy.
OPPOSITES: SEE **bland, sweet** adjective.

tart noun
flan, pastry, pie, quiche, tartlet.

task noun
We were given several tasks to do. activity, assignment, burden, business, chore, duty, employment, enterprise, errand, imposition, job, mission, requirement, undertaking, work.

taste noun
1 *the taste of strawberries.* character, flavour, savour.
2 *I gave her a taste of my apple.* bit, bite, morsel, mouthful, nibble, piece, sample, titbit.
3 *We share the same tastes in music.* appreciation, choice, inclination, judgement, liking, preference.
4 *She is a person of taste.* breeding, culture, discernment, discretion, discrimination, education, elegance, fashion sense, finesse, good judgement, perception, polish, refinement, sensitivity, style.
in bad taste SEE **tasteless.**
in good taste SEE **tasteful.**

taste verb
Taste a bit of this! nibble, relish, sample, savour, sip, test, try.

WORDS TO DESCRIBE HOW THINGS TASTE:
acid, bitter, creamy, fresh, fruity, hot, luscious, meaty, mellow, peppery, piquant, pungent, rancid, refreshing, salty, savoury, sharp, sour, spicy, stale, strong, sugary, sweet, tangy, tart, SEE **tasteless**, SEE **tasty,** unpalatable.

---

tasteful adjective
tasteful clothes. a tasteful choice of colours. artistic, attractive, cultivated, dignified, discerning, discreet, discriminating, elegant, fashionable, in good taste, judicious, proper, refined, restrained, sensitive, smart, stylish, well-judged.
OPPOSITES: SEE **tasteless.**

tasteless adjective
1 *tasteless food.* bland, characterless, flavourless, insipid, mild, uninteresting,

watered down, watery, weak.
OPPOSITES: SEE **tasty.**
2 *a tasteless choice of colours. a tasteless joke.* crude, garish, gaudy, graceless, improper, inartistic, in bad taste, indelicate, inelegant, injudicious, [*informal*] kitsch, ugly, unattractive, undiscriminating, unfashionable, unimaginative, unpleasant, unseemly, unstylish, SEE **vulgar.**
OPPOSITES: SEE **tasteful.**

tasty adjective
tasty food. appetizing, delicious, flavoursome, [*informal*] mouthwatering, [*informal*] nice, piquant, savoury, [*informal*] scrumptious.
OTHER WORDS TO DESCRIBE HOW THINGS TASTE:
SEE **taste** verb.
OPPOSITES: SEE **tasteless.**

tattered adjective
tattered clothes. frayed, ragged, ripped, tatty, threadbare, torn, worn out.
OPPOSITES: SEE **smart** adjective.

tatters noun
Her clothes were in tatters. rags, ribbons, shreds, torn pieces.

tatty adjective
tatty clothes. frayed, old, patched, ragged, ripped, scruffy, shabby, tattered, torn, threadbare, untidy, worn out.
OPPOSITES: SEE **new.**

taunt verb SEE **ridicule** verb.

taut adjective
Make sure the rope is taut. firm, stretched, tense, tight.
OPPOSITES: SEE **slack** adjective.

tautology noun
duplication, pleonasm, repetition.

tavern noun
[*old-fashioned*] *They had a drink at the tavern.* [*old-fashioned*] alehouse, bar, [*joking*] hostelry, inn, [*informal*] local, pub, public house.

tawdry adjective
tawdry ornaments. a tawdry imitation. cheap, common, eye-catching, fancy, [*informal*] flashy, garish, gaudy, inferior, meretricious, poor quality, raffish, showy, tasteless, tatty, vulgar, worthless.
OPPOSITES: SEE **superior.**

tax noun
charge, imposition, levy, tariff.

tax verb
1 *to tax income, goods, etc.* impose a tax on, levy a tax on.
2 *The problem taxed me severely.* burden, exhaust, make heavy demands on, overwork, SEE **tire.**

taxi noun
cab, [*old-fashioned*] hackney carriage, minicab.

teach verb

VARIOUS WAYS TO TEACH THINGS TO OTHERS: advise, brainwash, coach, counsel, demonstrate to, discipline, drill, educate, enlighten, familiarize with, ground (someone) in, impart knowledge to, implant knowledge in, inculcate habits in, indoctrinate, inform, instruct, lecture, school, train, tutor.

---

teacher noun

VARIOUS TEACHERS: adviser, coach, counsellor, demonstrator, don, educator, governess, guide, guru, headteacher, housemaster, housemistress, instructor, lecturer, maharishi, master, mentor, mistress, pedagogue, preacher, preceptor, professor, pundit, schoolmaster, schoolmistress, school-teacher, trainer, tutor.

---

teaching noun
1 VARIOUS KINDS OF TEACHING: advice, brainwashing, briefing, coaching, computer-aided learning, counselling, demonstration, distance learning, grounding, guidance, indoctrination, instruction, lecture, lesson, practical (*a science practical*), preaching, rote learning, schooling, seminar, training, tuition, tutorial, work experience, workshop (*a writing workshop*).
2 *the teachings of holy scripture.* doctrine, dogma, gospel, precept, principle, tenet.

team noun
1 *a football team.* club, [*informal*] line-up, side.
2 *working as a team.* SEE **group** noun.

tear noun
1 [rhymes with *fear*] *tears in his eyes.* droplet, tear-drop.
tears [*informal*] blubbering, crying, sobs, weeping.
to shed tears SEE **weep**.
2 [rhymes with *bear*] *a tear in my jeans.* cut, gap, gash, hole, opening, rent, rip, slit, split.

tear verb
The barbed wire tore my jeans. claw, gash, lacerate, mangle, pierce, rend, rip, rupture, scratch, shred, slit, snag, split.

tearful adjective
tearful children. a tearful farewell.
[*informal*] blubbering, crying, emotional, lachrymose, SEE **sad**, sobbing, weeping, [*informal*] weepy.

tease verb
The cat scratches if you tease her. [*informal*] aggravate, annoy, bait, chaff, goad, irritate, laugh at, make fun of, mock, [*informal*] needle, pester, plague, provoke, [*informal*] pull someone's leg, [*informal*] rib, SEE **ridicule** verb, tantalize, taunt, torment, vex, worry.

teasing noun
I was annoyed by their teasing. badinage, banter, joking, mockery, provocation, raillery, [*informal*] ribbing, ridicule, taunts.

technical adjective
1 *technical data. technical details.* esoteric, expert, professional, specialized.
2 *technical skill.* engineering, mechanical, scientific.

technician noun
engineer, mechanic, skilled worker, [*plural*] technical staff.

technique noun
the technique you need to do a task. art, craft, craftsmanship, dodge, expertise, facility, knack, [*informal*] know-how, manner, means, method, mode, procedure, proficiency, routine, skill, system, trick, way, workmanship.

technological adjective
technological equipment. advanced, automated, computerized, electronic, scientific.

tedious adjective
a tedious journey. a tedious lecture. boring, dreary, dull, [*informal*] humdrum, irksome, laborious, long-winded, monotonous, slow, tiresome, tiring, unexciting, uninteresting, wearisome.
OPPOSITES: SEE **interesting**.

tedium noun
We played games to relieve the tedium of the journey. boredom, dreariness, dullness, long-windedness, monotony, slowness, tediousness.

teem verb
The pond teemed with tadpoles. abound (in), be full (of), be infested, be overrun (by), [*informal*] crawl, seethe, swarm.

teenager noun
adolescent, boy, girl, juvenile, minor, youngster, youth.

teetotaller noun
abstainer, non-drinker.
OPPOSITES: SEE **drunkard**.

telepathic adjective
If you know what I'm thinking, you must be telepathic. clairvoyant, psychic.

telephone verb
Telephone us if you can't come. [*informal*]
buzz, call, dial, [*informal*] give (someone) a
call, phone, ring.
OTHER WAYS OF COMMUNICATING: SEE
communication.

telescopic adjective
a tripod with telescopic legs. adjustable,
collapsible, expanding, extending,
retractable.

televise verb
They televise a lot of snooker these days.
broadcast, relay, send out, transmit.

television noun
monitor, receiver, [*informal*] telly,
[*informal*] the box, [*informal*] the small
screen, video.
OTHER WAYS OF COMMUNICATING: SEE
communication.

___

TELEVISION PROGRAMMES: cartoon, chat
show, comedy, commercial, documentary,
drama, SEE **entertainment**, film, interview,
mini series, movie, news, panel game, play,
quiz, serial, series, [*informal*] sitcom,
situation comedy, [*informal*] soap, soap
opera, sport.

___

tell verb
1 *Tell the whole story.* announce,
communicate, describe, disclose, divulge,
explain, impart, make known, narrate,
portray, recite, recount, rehearse, relate,
reveal, speak, utter.
2 *Tell me the time.* acquaint (someone) with,
advise, inform, notify.
3 *Can you tell the difference?* calculate,
comprehend, decide, discover, discriminate,
distinguish, identify, notice, recognize, see.
4 *He told me I could trust him.* assure, promise.
5 *Tell them to stop.* command, direct,
instruct, order.
to tell someone off SEE **reprimand** verb.

temper noun
1 *in a good temper. in a bad temper.* attitude,
disposition, humour, mood, state of mind,
temperament.
2 *He sometimes flies into a temper.* fit (of
anger), fury, [*informal*] paddy, passion,
rage, tantrum.
3 *Try to keep your temper.* calmness,
composure, coolness, sang-froid, self-
control.
4 *Beware of his temper.* anger, irascibility,
irritability, peevishness, petulance,
surliness, unpredictability, volatility,
wrath.

temper verb
to temper your opposition to something. SEE
moderate verb.

temperament noun
a melancholy temperament. character, [*old-
fashioned*] complexion, disposition, [*old-
fashioned*] humour, nature, personality,
spirit, temper.

temperamental adjective
1 *a temperamental aversion to work.*
characteristic, congenital, constitutional,
inherent, innate, natural.
2 *temperamental moods.* capricious,
changeable, emotional, erratic, excitable,
fickle, highly strung, impatient,
inconsistent, inconstant, irritable,
mercurial, moody, neurotic, passionate,
touchy, unpredictable, unreliable,
[*informal*] up and down, variable, volatile.

temperate adjective SEE **moderate**
adjective.

tempest noun
SEE **storm** noun.

tempestuous adjective
SEE **stormy**.

temple noun
a temple of the gods. SEE **worship** noun (**place
of worship**).

tempo noun
the tempo of a piece of music. pace, rhythm,
speed.

temporal adjective
temporal affairs. earthly, impermanent,
materialistic, mortal, mundane, passing,
secular, sublunary, terrestrial, transient,
transitory, worldly.
OPPOSITES: SEE **spiritual**.

temporary adjective
1 *a temporary building. a temporary
arrangement.* brief, ephemeral, evanescent,
fleeting, impermanent, interim, makeshift,
momentary, passing, provisional, short,
short-lived, short-term, stop-gap, transient,
transitory.
OPPOSITES: SEE **permanent**.
2 *temporary captain.* acting.

tempt verb
I tempted the mouse with a bit of cheese.
allure, attract, bait, bribe, coax, decoy,
entice, fascinate, inveigle, lure, persuade,
seduce, tantalize, woo.

temptation noun
*He succumbed to the temptations of the big
city.* allurement, appeal, attraction, draw,
enticement, fascination, lure, pull,
seduction.

tempting adjective
SEE **attractive**.

tenacious adjective
a tenacious hold on something. determined,
dogged, firm, intransigent, obdurate,

obstinate, pertinacious, resolute, single-minded, strong, stubborn, tight, unshakeable, unswerving, unwavering, unyielding.
OPPOSITES: SEE **weak**.

tenant noun
the tenant of a rented flat. inhabitant, leaseholder, lessee, lodger, occupant, resident.

tend verb
1 *A shepherd tends sheep.* attend to, care for, cherish, cultivate, guard, keep, look after, manage, mind, protect, watch.
2 *Doctors tend the sick.* nurse, treat.
3 *I tend to fall asleep in the evening.* be disposed to, be inclined to, be liable to, have a tendency to [SEE **tendency**], incline.

tendency noun
a tendency to be lazy. bias, disposition, inclination, instinct, leaning, liability, partiality, penchant, predilection, predisposition, proclivity, propensity, readiness, susceptibility, trend.

tender adjective
1 *tender meat.* eatable, edible.
OPPOSITES: SEE **tough**.
2 *tender plants.* dainty, delicate, fleshy, fragile, frail, soft, succulent, vulnerable, weak.
OPPOSITES: SEE **hardy**.
3 *a tender wound.* aching, painful, sensitive, smarting, sore.
4 *a tender love-song.* emotional, moving, poignant, romantic, sentimental, touching.
OPPOSITES: SEE **cynical**.
5 *tender care.* affectionate, caring, compassionate, concerned, considerate, fond, gentle, humane, kind, loving, merciful, pitying, soft-hearted, sympathetic, tender-hearted, warm-hearted.
OPPOSITES: SEE **callous**.

tense adjective
1 *tense muscles.* strained, stretched, taut, tight.
2 *a tense atmosphere.* anxious, apprehensive, edgy, excited, exciting, fidgety, highly strung, jittery, jumpy, [*informal*] nail-biting, nerve-racking, nervous, restless, stressed, [*informal*] strung up, touchy, uneasy, [*informal*] uptight, worried, worrying.
OPPOSITES: SEE **relaxed**.

tension noun
1 *the tension of guy ropes.* strain, stretching, tautness, tightness.
OPPOSITE: slackness.
2 *the tension of waiting for an answer.* anxiety, apprehension, excitement, nervousness, stress, suspense, unease, worry.

tent noun
KINDS OF TENT: bell tent, bigtop, frame tent, marquee, ridge tent, tepee, trailer tent, wigwam.

tentative adjective
1 *a tentative attempt.* cautious, diffident, doubtful, halfhearted, hesitant, indecisive, indefinite, nervous, timid, uncertain, [*informal*] wishy-washy.
2 *a tentative enquiry.* experimental, preliminary, provisional, speculative, uncommitted.
OPPOSITES: SEE **decisive**.

tenuous adjective
a tenuous connection. a tenuous line of argument. fine, flimsy, insubstantial, slight, SEE **thin** adjective, weak.
OPPOSITES: SEE **strong**.

tepid adjective
tepid bath-water. lukewarm, warm.

term noun
1 *a term in prison.* duration, period, season, span, spell, stretch, time.
2 *a school term.* [*American*] semester, session.
3 *a technical term. a foreign term.* epithet, expression, phrase, saying, title, word.
terms 1 *the terms of an agreement.* conditions, particulars, provisions, specifications, stipulations.
2 *a hotel's terms.* charges, fees, prices, rates, tariff.

terminal adjective
a terminal illness. deadly, fatal, final, incurable, killing, lethal, mortal.

terminal noun
1 *a computer terminal.* VDU, work-station.
2 *a passenger terminal.* SEE **airport**, destination, terminus.
3 *an electrical terminal.* connection, connector.

terminate verb
SEE **end** verb.

termination noun SEE **end** noun.

terminus noun
destination, terminal, termination.

terrace noun
a terrace in the garden. patio, paved area.

terrain noun
They made slow progress across difficult terrain. country, ground, land, landscape, SEE **territory**, topography.

terrestrial adjective
terrestrial beings. earthly, mundane, ordinary.

terrible adjective
a terrible accident. terrible living-conditions.
appalling, distressing, dreadful, fearful,
frightful, ghastly, hideous, horrible,
horrific, horrifying, insupportable,
intolerable, loathsome, nasty, outrageous,
revolting, shocking, unbearable,
unpleasant, vile.

terrific adjective
[Like *terrible*, *terrific* is related to Latin
terrere meaning *to frighten* and to our
English word *terror*. However, the meaning
of *terrific* is now vague. It is used informally
to describe anything which is extreme in its
own way, e.g. *We faced a terrific problem.*
SEE **extreme**; *My fish was a terrific size.* SEE
big; *We had a terrific time.* SEE **excellent**; *There
was a terrific storm.* SEE **violent**.]

terrified adjective
afraid, appalled, dismayed, SEE **frightened**,
horrified, horror-struck, panicky, petrified,
terror-stricken, unnerved.
OPPOSITES: SEE **calm** adjective.

terrify verb
appal, dismay, SEE **frighten**, horrify, petrify,
scare, shock, terrorize, unnerve.

terrifying adjective
blood-curdling, dreadful, SEE **frightening**,
hair-raising, horrifying, petrifying,
[*informal*] scary, spine-chilling, traumatic,
unnerving.

territory noun
enemy territory. area, colony, SEE **country**,
[*old-fashioned*] demesne, district, dominion,
enclave, jurisdiction, land, preserve,
province, region, sector, sphere [sphere of
influence], state, terrain, tract, zone.

terror noun
alarm, consternation, dread, SEE **fear** noun,
[*informal*] funk, fright, horror, panic,
shock, trepidation.

terrorist noun
assassin, SEE **criminal** noun, gunman,
hijacker.

terrorize verb
*A criminal gang terrorized the
neighbourhood.* browbeat, bully, coerce,
cow, SEE **frighten**, intimidate, menace,
persecute, terrify, threaten, torment,
tyrannize.

terse adjective
a terse comment. SEE **brief** adjective, brusque,
concise, crisp, curt, epigrammatic, incisive,
laconic, pithy, short, [*informal*] snappy,
succinct, to the point.
OPPOSITES: SEE **verbose**.

test noun
You have to pass a test before you get the job.
appraisal, assessment, audition, [*informal*]
check-over, evaluation, examination,
interrogation, investigation, probation,
quiz, trial.

test verb
*to test a theory. to test the quality of a product
or a substance. to test a candidate.* analyse,
appraise, assay, assess, audition, check,
evaluate, examine, experiment with,
inspect, interrogate, investigate, [*informal*]
put someone through their paces, put to the
test, screen, question, try out.

testify verb
to testify in a court of law. affirm, attest, bear
witness, declare, give evidence, state on
oath, swear, vouch, witness.

testimonial noun
a testimonial for an applicant for a job.
character reference, commendation,
recommendation, reference.

testimony noun
testimony given in court. affidavit,
declaration, deposition, evidence,
statement, submission, witness.
LEGAL TERMS: SEE **law**.

tether noun
an animal's tether. chain, cord, halter, lead,
leash, rope.

tether verb
to tether an animal. chain up, SEE **fasten**,
keep on a tether, restrain, rope, secure, tie
up.

text noun
1 *the text of a document.* argument, contents,
matter, wording.
2 *a literary text.* book, textbook, work, SEE
writing.
3 *the text of a sermon. a text from the Bible.*
motif, passage of scripture, sentence, theme,
topic, verse.

textiles noun
SEE **cloth**, fabric, material, stuff.

texture noun
the soft texture of velvet. composition,
consistency, feel, quality, touch.

thankful adjective
thankful to be home. appreciative, contented,
grateful, happy, pleased, relieved.
OPPOSITES: SEE **ungrateful**.

thankless adjective
a thankless task. unappreciated,
unrecognized, unrewarded, unrewarding.
OPPOSITES: SEE **rewarding**.

thanks noun
acknowledgement, appreciation,
gratefulness, gratitude, recognition,
thanksgiving.

thaw verb
The snow thawed. become liquid, defrost,
melt, soften, uncongeal, unfreeze, unthaw,
warm up.
OPPOSITES: SEE **freeze**.

theatre noun
auditorium, drama studio, hall, opera-house,
playhouse.

THEATRICAL ENTERTAINMENTS: ballet,
comedy, drama, farce, masque, melodrama,
mime, music hall, nativity play, opera,
operetta, pantomime, play, tragedy.

KINDS OF PERFORMANCE: command
performance, dress rehearsal, first night,
last night, matinée, première, preview,
production, rehearsal, show.

THEATRE PEOPLE: actor, actress, backstage
staff, ballerina, dancer, director, dresser,
make-up artist, performer, player, producer,
prompter, stage-manager, understudy,
usher or usherette.

PARTS OF A THEATRE: back-stage, balcony,
box-office, circle, dressing-room, foyer,
front of house, gallery, [*informal*] the gods,
[*old-fashioned*] pit, stage, stalls.

---

theatrical adjective
1 *I made my first theatrical appearance in a
Shakespeare play.* dramatic, histrionic.
2 *He made the announcement in a theatrical
manner.* demonstrative, exaggerated,
melodramatic, ostentatious, pompous, self-
important, showy, stagy, stilted, unnatural.

theft noun SEE **stealing**.

theme noun
1 *the theme of a talk.* argument, idea, issue,
keynote, matter, subject, text, thesis, topic.
2 *a musical theme.* air, melody, motif,
[*formal*] subject, tune.

theoretical adjective
theoretical knowledge. abstract, academic,
conjectural, doctrinaire, hypothetical,
ideal, notional, pure (*pure science*),
speculative, unproven, untested.
OPPOSITES: SEE **applied, empirical**.

theorize verb
to theorize about a problem. conjecture, form
a theory, hypothesize, speculate.

theory noun
1 *My theory would explain what happened.*
argument, assumption, belief, conjecture,
explanation, guess, hypothesis, idea, notion,

speculation, supposition, surmise, thesis,
view.
2 *the theory of musical composition.* laws,
principles, rules, science.
OPPOSITES: SEE **practice**.

therapeutic adjective
*When I was sad, music had a therapeutic
effect.* beneficial, corrective, curative,
healing, helpful, restorative.
OPPOSITES: SEE **harmful**.

therapist noun
healer, physiotherapist, psychotherapist.

therapy noun
cure, healing, remedy, tonic, treatment.

SOME KINDS OF THERAPY: chemotherapy,
group therapy, hydrotherapy,
hypnotherapy, occupational therapy,
physiotherapy, psychotherapy,
radiotherapy.
OTHER MEDICAL TREATMENT: SEE **medicine**.

---

therefore adverb
accordingly, consequently, hence, so, thus.

thesis noun
1 *She argued a convincing thesis.* argument,
hypothesis, idea, premise or premiss,
proposition, theory, view.
2 *He wrote a thesis about his research.*
disquisition, dissertation, essay,
monograph, paper, tract, treatise.

thick adjective
1 *a thick book. thick rope. a thick line.* broad,
[*informal*] bulky, chunky, fat, stout, sturdy,
substantial, wide.
2 *thick snow. thick cloth.* deep, heavy.
3 *a thick crowd.* dense, impenetrable,
numerous, packed, solid.
4 *The place was thick with photographers.*
covered, filled, swarming, teeming.
5 *thick mud. thick cream.* clotted, coagulated,
concentrated, condensed, heavy, stiff,
viscous.
OPPOSITES: SEE **thin** adjective.

thickness noun
1 *a thickness of paint.* coating, layer.
2 *a thickness of rock.* seam, stratum.

thief noun
bandit, burglar, SEE **criminal** noun,
embezzler, highwayman, housebreaker,
looter, mugger, pickpocket, pirate, plagiarist
[= *person who steals other people's ideas*],
poacher, robber, shop-lifter, stealer, swindler.

thieve verb
SEE **steal**.

thin adjective
1 *a thin figure.* anorexic, attenuated, bony,
emaciated, flat-chested, gaunt, lanky, lean,

narrow, rangy, scraggy, scrawny, skeletal, skinny, slender, slight, slim, small, spare, spindly, underweight, wiry.
OPPOSITES: SEE **fat** adjective.
2 *thin cloth.* delicate, diaphanous, filmy, fine, flimsy, insubstantial, light, sheer (*sheer silk*), wispy.
3 *thin gravy.* dilute, flowing, fluid, runny, watery.
4 *a thin crowd.* meagre, scanty, scarce, scattered, sparse.
OPPOSITES: SEE **thick**.
5 *a thin atmosphere.* rarefied.
OPPOSITES: SEE **dense**.
6 *a thin excuse.* feeble, implausible, tenuous, unconvincing.
OPPOSITES: SEE **convincing**.

thin verb
to thin paint. dilute, water down, weaken.
to thin out 1 *The crowd thinned out.* become less dense, diminish, disperse. 2 *to thin out seedlings. to thin out a hedge.* make less dense, prune, trim, weed out.

thing noun
1 *a thing you can touch or hold.* artefact, article, body, device, entity, implement, item, object.
2 *a thing that happens.* affair, circumstance, deed, event, eventuality, happening, incident, occurrence, phenomenon.
3 *a thing on your mind. things you want to say.* concept, detail, fact, factor, idea, point, statement, thought.
4 *a thing you have to do.* act, action, job, task.
5 [*informal*] *He's got a thing about snakes.* [*informal*] hang-up, obsession, phobia, preoccupation.
things 1 *Put your things in the back of the car.* baggage, belongings, clothing, equipment, [*informal*] gear, luggage, possessions, [*informal*] stuff. 2 *Things improved when I found a place to live.* circumstances, conditions, life.

think verb
1 *I thought about my mistakes.* attend, brood, cogitate, concentrate, consider, contemplate, deliberate, give thought (to), meditate, [*informal*] mull over, muse, ponder, [*informal*] rack your brains, reason, reflect, ruminate, use your intelligence, work things out, worry.
2 *He thinks that science can explain everything.* accept, admit, be convinced, believe, conclude, deem, have faith, judge.
3 *I think she's angry.* assume, believe, be under the impression, estimate, feel, guess, imagine, presume, reckon, suppose, surmise.
to think out *She thought out how to do it.* analyse, answer, calculate, puzzle out, work out.
to think up *We thought up a plan.* conceive,

concoct, create, design, devise, [*informal*] dream up, imagine, improvise, invent, make up.

thinker noun
Plato was one of the world's great thinkers. [*informal*] brain, innovator, intellect, philosopher.

thinking adjective
She said that all thinking people would agree with her. educated, intelligent, rational, reasonable, sensible, thoughtful.
OPPOSITES: SEE **stupid**.

thirst noun
1 *a thirst for water.* drought, dryness, thirstiness.
2 *a thirst for knowledge.* appetite, craving, desire, eagerness, hunger, itch, longing, love (of), lust, passion, urge, wish, yearning.

thirst verb
to thirst after. be thirsty for [SEE **thirsty**], crave, have a thirst for, hunger after, long for, need, strive after, want, wish for, yearn for.

thirsty adjective
1 *thirsty after a long walk.* dehydrated, dry, [*informal*] gasping (for a drink), panting, parched.
2 *thirsty for adventure.* avid, eager, greedy, itching, longing, yearning.

thorn noun
thorns on a rose-bush. barb, needle, prickle, spike, spine.

thorny adjective
a thorny bush. barbed, bristly, prickly, scratchy, sharp, spiky, spiny.
OPPOSITE: thornless.

thorough adjective
1 *a thorough piece of work.* assiduous, attentive, careful, comprehensive, conscientious, diligent, efficient, exhaustive, full, [*informal*] indepth, methodical, meticulous, observant, orderly, organized, painstaking, scrupulous, systematic, thoughtful, watchful.
OPPOSITES: SEE **superficial**.
2 [*informal*] *He's a thorough rascal!* absolute, arrant, complete, downright, out-and-out, perfect, thoroughgoing, total, unmitigated, unqualified, utter.

thought noun
1 *deep in thought.* [*informal*] brainwork, brooding, [*informal*] brown study (*in a brown study*), cogitation, concentration, consideration, contemplation, day-dreaming, deliberation, introspection, meditation, musing, pensiveness, reasoning, reflection, reverie, rumination, study, thinking, worrying.
2 *a clever thought.* belief, concept,

conception, conclusion, conjecture, conviction, idea, notion, opinion.
3 *We had no thought of staying so long.* aim, design, expectation, intention, objective, plan, purpose.
4 *It was a nice thought to give them flowers.* attention, concern, kindness, solicitude, thoughtfulness.

thoughtful adjective
1 *a thoughtful expression.* absorbed, abstracted, anxious, attentive, brooding, contemplative, dreamy, grave, introspective, meditative, pensive, philosophical, rapt, reflective, serious, solemn, studious, wary, watchful, worried.
2 *a thoughtful piece of work.* careful, conscientious, diligent, exhaustive, methodical, meticulous, observant, orderly, organized, painstaking, scrupulous, systematic, thorough.
3 *a thoughtful kindness.* attentive, caring, concerned, considerate, friendly, good-natured, helpful, SEE **kind** adjective, obliging, public-spirited, solicitous, unselfish.
OPPOSITES: SEE **thoughtless**.

thoughtless adjective
1 *thoughtless stupidity.* absent-minded, careless, forgetful, hasty, heedless, ill-considered, impetuous, inadvertent, inattentive, injudicious, irresponsible, mindless, negligent, rash, reckless, [*informal*] scatter-brained, SEE **stupid**, unobservant, unthinking.
2 *a thoughtless insult.* cruel, heartless, impolite, inconsiderate, insensitive, rude, selfish, tactless, uncaring, undiplomatic, unfeeling, SEE **unkind**.
OPPOSITES: SEE **thoughtful**.

thrash verb
1 *to thrash with a stick.* SEE **whip** verb.
2 [*informal*] *to thrash your opponents.* SEE **defeat** verb.

thread noun
threads in a piece of cloth. fibre, filament, hair, strand.
KINDS OF THREAD: cotton, silk, thong, twine, wool, yarn.

thread verb
to thread beads. put on a thread, string together.

threadbare adjective
threadbare clothes. frayed, old, ragged, shabby, tattered, tatty, worn, worn-out.

threat noun
1 *threats against his life.* menace, warning.
2 *a threat of snow.* danger, forewarning, omen, portent, presage, risk, warning.

threaten verb
1 *A gang of hooligans threatened us.* browbeat, bully, SEE **frighten**, intimidate,

make threats against, menace, pressurize, terrorize.
2 *The forecast threatened rain.* forebode, foreshadow, forewarn of, give warning of, portend, presage, warn of.
3 *An avalanche threatened the town.* endanger, imperil, jeopardize.
OPPOSITES: SEE **reassure**.

threatening adjective
threatening stormclouds. forbidding, grim, menacing, minatory, ominous, sinister, stern, unfriendly, worrying.
OPPOSITES: SEE **reassuring**.

three noun
[= *a group of three.*] triad, trio, triplet, triumvirate.
RELATED ADJECTIVES: SEE **triple**.

thrifty adjective
thrifty with your money. careful, economical, frugal, parsimonious, provident, prudent, sparing.
OPPOSITES: SEE **extravagant**.

thrill noun
the thrill of a fun-fair. adventure, [*informal*] buzz, excitement, [*informal*] kick, pleasure, sensation, suspense, tingle, tremor.

thrill verb
The music thrilled us. delight, electrify, excite, rouse, stimulate, stir, titillate.
OPPOSITES: SEE **bore** verb.

thriller noun
crime story, detective story, mystery, [*informal*] whodunit.

thrilling adjective
thrilling feats. electrifying, exciting, extraordinary, gripping, [*informal*] hair-raising, rousing, sensational, spectacular, stimulating, stirring.
OPPOSITES: SEE **boring**.

thrive verb
Tomato plants thrive in my greenhouse. be vigorous, burgeon, develop strongly, do well, flourish, grow, prosper, succeed.
OPPOSITES: SEE **die**.

throat noun
gullet, neck, oesophagus, uvula, wind pipe.
RELATED ADJECTIVE: guttural.

throb verb
Blood throbs through our veins. beat, palpitate, pound, pulsate, pulse.

throng noun, verb SEE **crowd** noun, verb.

throttle verb
asphyxiate, choke, SEE **kill**, smother, stifle, strangle, suffocate.

throw verb
1 *to throw a ball. to throw stones at something.* bowl, [*informal*] bung, cast,

[*informal*] chuck, fling, heave, hurl, launch, lob, pelt, pitch, project, propel, put (*to put the shot*), [*informal*] shy, [*informal*] sling, toss.
2 *The horse threw the rider.* dislodge, shake off, throw off, unseat.
3 [*informal*] *The unexpected question threw me.* SEE **disconcert**.
to throw away SEE **discard**.
to throw out SEE **expel**.

throwaway adjective
1 *throwaway plastic cups.* cheap, disposable.
2 *a throwaway remark.* casual, offhand, passing, unimportant.

thrust verb
1 *to thrust someone or something forward.* drive, force, press, propel, push, send, shove, urge.
2 *to thrust with a dagger.* jab, lunge, plunge, poke, prod, stab, stick.

thug noun
[*informal*] bully-boy, SEE **criminal** noun, delinquent, gangster, hooligan, killer, mugger, ruffian, [*informal*] tough, trouble-maker, vandal, [*informal*] yob.

thump noun, verb
SEE **hit**

thunder noun, verb
WORDS FOR THE SOUND OF THUNDER: clap, crack, peal, roll, rumble.

thunderous adjective
SEE **loud**.

thus adverb
accordingly, consequently, hence, so, therefore.

thwart verb
to thwart someone's wishes. foil, frustrate, hinder, impede, obstruct, prevent, stand in the way of, stop.

ticket noun
1 *an entry ticket.* coupon, pass, permit, token, voucher.
2 *a price ticket.* docket, label, marker, tab, tag.

tickle verb
1 *to tickle someone with your fingertips.* SEE **touch** verb.
2 *My foot tickles.* SEE **itch** verb.

ticklish adjective
1 *Are you ticklish?* [*informal*] giggly, responsive to tickling, sensitive.
2 *a ticklish problem.* awkward, delicate, difficult, risky, [*informal*] thorny, touchy, tricky.

tide noun
the tides of the sea. current, drift, ebb and flow, movement, rise and fall.

tidiness noun
I admire her tidiness. meticulousness, neatness, order, orderliness, organization, system.
OPPOSITES: SEE **disorder**.

tidings noun
[*old-fashioned*] *good tidings.* SEE **news**.

tidy adjective
1 *tidy in appearance.* neat, orderly, presentable, shipshape, smart, spick and span, spruce, straight, trim, uncluttered, well-groomed.
2 *tidy in your habits.* businesslike, careful, house-proud, methodical, meticulous, organized, systematic.
OPPOSITES: SEE **untidy**.

tidy verb
Please tidy your room. arrange, clean up, groom (*your hair*), make tidy [SEE **tidy** adjective], neaten, put in order, set straight, smarten, spruce up, straighten, titivate.
OPPOSITES: SEE **muddle** verb.

tie verb
1 *to tie something with string.* bind, SEE **fasten**, hitch, interlace, join, knot, lash, truss up.
OPPOSITES: SEE **untie**.
2 *to tie with an opponent in a game.* be equal, be level, draw.
to tie up *to tie up a boat or an animal.* anchor, moor, secure, tether.

tier noun
seats arranged in tiers. level, line, rank, row, stage, storey, terrace.

tight adjective
1 *a tight fit.* close, close-fitting, fast, firm, fixed, immovable, secure, snug.
2 *a jar with a tight lid.* airtight, hermetic, impervious, sealed, watertight.
3 *tight controls.* inflexible, precise, rigorous, severe, strict, stringent.
4 *tight ropes.* rigid, stiff, stretched, taut, tense.
5 *a tight space.* compact, constricted, crammed, cramped, crowded, dense, packed.
OPPOSITES: SEE **loose**.
6 [*informal*] *tight with her money.* SEE **miserly**.

tighten verb
1 *to tighten your grip.* clamp down, constrict, hold tighter, squeeze, tense.
2 *to tighten a rope.* pull tighter, stretch, tauten.
3 *to tighten a screw.* give another turn to, make tighter, screw up.
OPPOSITES: SEE **loosen**.

tight-fisted adjective
SEE **miserly**.

tilt verb
1 *to tilt to one side*. careen, incline, keel over, lean, list, slant, slope, tip.
2 *to tilt with lances*. SEE **fight** verb, joust, thrust.

timber noun
a house built of timber. beams, boarding, boards, deal, lath, logs, lumber, planking, planks, posts, softwood, trees, tree trunks, SEE **wood**.

time noun
1 [= *a moment in time*] date, hour, instant, juncture, moment, occasion, opportunity.
2 [= *a length of time*] duration, period, phase, season, semester, session, spell, stretch, term, while.
3 *the time of Elizabeth I*. age, days, epoch, era, period.
4 *Keep time with the music*. beat, rhythm, tempo.
RELATED ADJECTIVE: chronological.

UNITS OF TIME: aeon, century, day, decade, eternity, fortnight, hour, instant, leap year, lifetime, minute, month, second, week, weekend, year.

DEVICES FOR MEASURING TIME: calendar, chronometer, clock, digital clock, digital watch, hour-glass, stop-watch, sundial, timepiece, timer, watch, wrist-watch.

SPECIAL TIMES OF THE YEAR: Advent, autumn, Christmas, Easter, equinox, Hallowe'en, hogmanay, Lent, midsummer, midwinter, New Year, Passover, Ramadan, solstice, spring, summer, Whitsun, winter, Yom Kippur, yuletide.

TIMES OF THE DAY: SEE **day**.

---

time verb
I timed my arrival to coincide with hers. choose a time for, estimate, fix a time for, judge, schedule, timetable.

timely adjective
appropriate, apt, fitting, suitable.

timetable noun
a timetable of events. agenda, calendar, diary, list, programme, roster, rota, schedule.

timid adjective
Don't be timid—dive in at the deep end! afraid, apprehensive, bashful, cowardly, coy, diffident, faint-hearted, fearful, [*informal*] mousy, nervous, pusillanimous, reserved, retiring, sheepish, shrinking, shy, spineless, tentative, timorous, unadventurous, unheroic.
OPPOSITES: SEE **bold**.

timorous adjective SEE **timid**.

tinge noun, verb SEE **colour** noun, verb.

tingle noun
1 *a tingle under the skin*. itch, itching, pins and needles, prickling, stinging, tickle, tickling.
2 *a tingle of excitement*. quiver, sensation, shiver, thrill.

tinker verb
Don't tinker with the TV. fiddle, interfere, meddle, [*informal*] mess about, [*informal*] play about, tamper, try to mend, work amateurishly.

tinny adjective
[*informal*] *a tinny old car*. cheap, inferior, poor-quality.

tinsel noun
decorated with tinsel. glitter, sparkle, tin foil.

tint noun, verb SEE **colour** noun, verb.

tiny adjective
a tiny insect, a tiny amount. diminutive, imperceptible, infinitesimal, insignificant, microscopic, midget, [*informal*] mini, miniature, minuscule, minute, negligible, pygmy, SEE **small**, [*informal*] teeny, unimportant, [*informal*] wee, [*informal*] weeny.
OPPOSITES: SEE **big**.

tip noun
1 *the tip of a pen or pencil*. end, extremity, nib, point, sharp end.
2 *the tip of a mountain or iceberg*. apex, cap, crown, head, peak, pinnacle, summit, top.
3 *a tip for the waiter*. gift, gratuity, money, [*informal*] perk, present, reward, service-charge.
4 *useful tips on how to do it*. advice, clue, hint, information, suggestion, warning.
5 *a rubbish tip*. dump, rubbish-heap.

tip verb
1 *to tip to one side*. careen, incline, keel over, lean, list, slant, slope, tilt.
2 *to tip something from a container*. dump, empty, pour out, spill, unload.
3 *to tip a waiter*. give a tip to, remunerate, reward.
to tip over *A wave tipped the boat over*. capsize, knock over, overturn, topple, turn over, upset.

tire verb
The long game tired us. drain, enervate, exhaust, fatigue, [*informal*] finish, make tired [SEE **tired**], overtire, tax, wear out, weary.
OPPOSITES: SEE **refresh**.

tired adjective
[*informal*] dead beat, [*informal*] dog-tired, [*informal*] done in, drawn [= *looking tired*],

drained, drowsy, exhausted, [*informal*]
fagged, fatigued, flagging, footsore, jaded,
[*informal*] jet-lagged, [*slang*] knackered,
listless, [*informal*] shattered, sleepy, spent,
travel-weary, wearied, weary, [*informal*]
whacked, worn out.
tired of *I'm tired of all this noise.* bored with,
[*informal*] fed up with, impatient with, sick
of, [*informal*] sick and tired.

tiredness noun
drowsiness, exhaustion, fatigue, inertia, jet-
lag, lassitude, lethargy, listlessness,
sleepiness, weariness.

tireless adjective
a tireless worker. determined, diligent,
energetic, indefatigable, persistent,
sedulous, unceasing, unflagging, untiring.
OPPOSITES: SEE **lazy**.

tiresome adjective
tiresome interruptions. annoying,
bothersome, distracting, exasperating,
irksome, irritating, petty, troublesome,
unwelcome, vexing, wearisome.
OPPOSITES: SEE **welcome** adjective.

tiring adjective
tiring work. demanding, difficult,
exhausting, fatiguing, hard, laborious,
taxing, wearying.
OPPOSITES: SEE **refreshing**.

tissue noun
1 *bodily tissue.* material, structure, stuff,
substance.
2 *paper tissue.* tissue paper, tracing paper.

title noun
1 *the title of a picture or story.* caption,
heading, name.
2 *a person's title.* appellation, designation,
form of address, office, position, rank, status.
3 *the title to an inheritance.* claim,
entitlement, ownership, prerogative, right.

TITLES YOU USE BEFORE SOMEONE'S NAME:
Baron, Baroness, Count, Countess, Dame, Dr
or Doctor, Duchess, Duke, Earl, Lady, Lord,
Marchioness, Marquis, Master, Miss, Mr,
Mrs, Ms, Professor, Rev or Reverend, Sir,
Viscount, Viscountess.

OTHER TITLES: SEE **rank** noun, **royalty**.TITLES
YOU USE WHEN ADDRESSING PEOPLE:
madam or madame, my lady, my lord, sir,
sire, your grace, your honour, your majesty.

---

title verb
to title a story. entitle, give a title to, name.

titled adjective
a titled family. aristocratic, noble.

titter verb
chuckle, giggle, SEE **laugh**, snigger.

toast verb
1 *to toast bread.* brown, grill.
2 *to toast a guest at a banquet.* drink a toast
to, drink the health of, raise your glass to.

tobacco noun

FORMS IN WHICH PEOPLE USE TOBACCO:
cigar, cigarette, pipe-tobacco, plug, snuff.

---

together adverb
all at once, at the same time, collectively,
concurrently, consecutively, continuously,
co-operatively, hand in hand, in chorus, in
unison, jointly, shoulder to shoulder, side
by side, simultaneously.
OPPOSITES: independently, separately.

toil noun
[*informal*] donkey work, drudgery, effort,
exertion, industry, labour, SEE **work** noun.

toil verb
drudge, exert yourself, [*informal*] keep at it,
labour, [*informal*] plug away, [*informal*]
slave away, struggle, [*informal*] sweat, SEE
work verb.

toiletries plural noun

THINGS USED IN PERFORMING YOUR TOILET:
SEE **cosmetics**, hair conditioner, lotion,
moisturizer, rinse, shampoo, soap, talcum
powder.

---

token noun
1 *a token of our affection.* evidence,
expression, indication, mark, proof,
reminder, sign, symbol, testimony.
2 *a bus-token.* counter, coupon, voucher.

tolerable adjective
1 *tolerable noise. tolerable pain.* acceptable,
bearable, endurable, sufferable,
supportable.
OPPOSITES: SEE **intolerable**.
2 *tolerable food. a tolerable performance.*
adequate, all right, fair, mediocre, middling,
[*informal*] OK, ordinary, passable,
satisfactory.

tolerance noun
1 *tolerance towards those who do wrong.*
broad-mindedness, charity, forbearance,
lenience, openness, permissiveness.
2 *tolerance of others' opinions.* acceptance,
sufferance, sympathy (towards), toleration,
understanding.

tolerant adjective
tolerant of people's mistakes. charitable,
easygoing, fair, forbearing, forgiving,
generous, indulgent, [*uncomplimentary*] lax,
lenient, liberal, magnanimous, open-
minded, patient, permissive,

[*uncomplimentary*] soft, sympathetic, understanding, unprejudiced, willing to forgive.
OPPOSITES: SEE **intolerant**.

tolerate verb
1 *I can't tolerate this toothache!* abide, bear, endure, [*informal*] lump (*You'll have to lump it!*), [*informal*] put up with, [*informal*] stand, [*informal*] stick, [*informal*] stomach, suffer, [*informal*] take (*I can't take any more*), undergo.
2 *They don't tolerate smoking in the house.* accept, admit, brook, condone, countenance, make allowances for, permit, sanction, [*informal*] wear (*You can ask, but I'm sure they won't wear it*).

toll noun
a toll to cross the bridge. charge, duty, fee, levy, payment, tax.

tomb noun
burial-place, catacomb, crypt, grave, gravestone, mausoleum, SEE **memorial**, sepulchre, tombstone, vault.

tone noun
1 *an angry tone in her voice.* accent, expression, feel, inflection, intonation, manner, modulation, note, quality, sound, timbre.
2 *eerie music to create the right tone for a mystery.* atmosphere, character, effect, feeling, mood, spirit, style, vein.

tone verb
to tone down SEE **soften**.
to tone in SEE **harmonize**.

toneless adjective
a toneless voice. SEE **monotonous**.

tongue-tied adjective
He can't explain because he gets tongue-tied. dumb, inarticulate, mute, silent, speechless.

tonic noun
You need a tonic after being ill. boost, cordial, [*formal*] dietary supplement, fillip, [*informal*] pick-me-up, restorative.

tool noun
a tool for every job. apparatus, appliance, contraption, contrivance, device, gadget, hardware, implement, instrument, invention, machine, utensil, weapon.

CARPENTER'S TOOLS: auger, awl, brace and bit, bradawl, chisel, clamp, cramp, drill, file, fretsaw, gimlet, glass-paper, hack-saw, hammer, jigsaw, mallet, pincers, plane, pliers, power-drill, rasp, sander, sandpaper, saw, spokeshave, T-square, vice, wrench.

GARDENING TOOLS: billhook, dibber, fork, grass-rake, hoe, lawn mower, mattock, rake, roller, scythe, secateurs, shears, sickle, spade, strimmer, trowel.

COOKING UTENSILS: SEE **cook** verb.

VARIOUS OTHER TOOLS: axe, bellows, chain-saw, chopper, clippers, crowbar, cutter, hatchet, jack, ladder, lever, penknife, pick, pickaxe, pitchfork, pocket-knife, scissors, screw-driver, shovel, sledge-hammer, spanner, tape-measure, tongs, tweezers.

---

tooth noun

VARIOUS TEETH: canine, eyetooth, fang, incisor, molar, tusk, wisdom tooth.
false teeth bridge, denture, dentures, plate.

RELATED ADJECTIVE: dental.

DENTAL PROBLEMS: caries, cavity, decay, plaque, toothache.

---

toothed adjective
a toothed edge. cogged, indented, jagged.

top adjective
top marks. top speed. the top performance. best, first, foremost, greatest, highest, leading, maximum, most, topmost, winning.
OPPOSITES: SEE **bottom** adjective.

top noun
1 *the top of a mountain.* apex, crest, crown, head, peak, pinnacle, summit, tip, vertex.
2 *the top of the table.* surface.
3 *the top of her fame.* acme, apogee, culmination, height, zenith.
4 *the top of a jar.* cap, cover, covering, lid.
OPPOSITES: SEE **bottom** noun.

top verb
1 *I topped the cake with chopped nuts.* cover, decorate, finish off, garnish.
2 *Our charity collection topped last year's record.* beat, be higher than, better, cap, exceed, excel, outdo, surpass.

topic noun
a topic for discussion. issue, matter, question, subject, talking-point, theme, [*formal*] thesis.

topical adjective
topical news. contemporary, current, recent, up-to-date.

topple verb
1 *The gale toppled our TV aerial.* knock down, overturn, throw down, tip over, upset.
2 *He toppled off the wall.* fall, overbalance, tumble.
3 *The opposition eventually toppled the prime minister.* oust, overthrow, unseat.

torch noun
bicycle lamp, [*old-fashioned*] brand, electric lamp, flashlight, [*old-fashioned*] link.

torment noun
the torment of toothache. affliction, agony, anguish, distress, misery, SEE **pain** noun, persecution, plague, purgatory, scourge, suffering, torture.

torment verb
My bad tooth was tormenting me. We were tormented by flies. afflict, annoy, bait, be a torment to, bedevil, bother, bully, distress, harass, hurt, inflict pain on, intimidate, [*informal*] nag, pain, persecute, pester, plague, tease, torture, vex, victimize, worry.

torrent noun
a torrent of water. cascade, cataract, deluge, downpour, flood, flow, gush, rush, spate, stream, tide.

torrential adjective
a torrential downpour. heavy, soaking, violent.
torrential rain cloudburst, deluge, rainstorm.

tortuous adjective
a tortuous route. a tortuous explanation. circuitous, complicated, convoluted, crooked, devious, indirect, involved, meandering, roundabout, twisted, twisting, winding, zigzag.
OPPOSITES: SEE **straightforward**.

torture noun
1 *Many political prisoners experience torture in prison.* cruelty, degradation, humiliation, inquisition, persecution, torment.
2 *the torture of toothache.* affliction, agony, anguish, distress, misery, plague, scourge, suffering.

torture verb
1 *to torture a prisoner.* be cruel to, brainwash, bully, cause pain to, degrade, dehumanize, humiliate, hurt, inflict pain on, intimidate, persecute, rack, torment, victimize.
2 *I was tortured by doubts.* afflict, agonize, annoy, bedevil, bother, distress, harass, [*informal*] nag, pester, plague, tease, vex, worry.

toss verb
1 *to toss something into the air.* bowl, cast, [*informal*] chuck, fling, flip (*to flip a coin*), heave, hurl, lob, pitch, shy, sling, throw.
2 *to toss about in a storm. to toss about in bed.* bob, lurch, move restlessly, pitch, reel, rock, roll, shake, twist and turn, wallow, welter, writhe.

total adjective
1 *The bill shows the total amount.* complete, comprehensive, entire, full, gross (*gross*

income), overall, whole.
2 *Our play was a total disaster.* absolute, downright, perfect, sheer, thorough, unmitigated, unqualified, utter.

total noun
Add up the figures and tell me the total. aggregate, amount, answer, lot, sum, totality, whole.

total verb
1 *Our shopping totalled £37.* add up to, amount to, come to, make.
2 *to total a list of figures.* add up, calculate, count, find the total of, reckon up, totalize, [*informal*] tot up, work out.

totalitarian adjective
a totalitarian regime. authoritarian, dictatorial, oneparty, oppressive, tyrannous, undemocratic, unrepresentative.
OPPOSITES: SEE **democratic**.

totter verb
We tottered unsteadily off the ship. dodder, falter, reel, stagger, SEE **walk** verb.

touch noun
1 *the sense of touch.* feeling, touching.
2 *I felt a touch on the arm.* caress, contact, dab, pat, stroke, tap.
3 *Working with animals requires a special touch.* ability, feel, flair, knack, manner, sensitivity, skill, style, technique, understanding, way.
4 *There's a touch of frost in the air.* hint, suggestion, suspicion, tinge, trace.
RELATED ADJECTIVE: tactile.

touch verb
1 *to touch physically.* brush, caress, contact, cuddle, dab, embrace, feel, finger, fondle, graze, handle, SEE **hit** verb, kiss, manipulate, massage, nuzzle, pat, paw, pet, push, rub, stroke, tap, tickle.
2 *to touch someone emotionally.* affect, concern, disturb, influence, inspire, move, stir, upset.
3 *Our speed touched 100 m.p.h.* attain, reach, rise to.

touched adjective
1 *I was touched by her kindness.* affected, moved, responsive (to), stirred, sympathetic (towards).
2 [*informal*] *He's a bit touched.* SEE **mad**.

touching adjective
a touching scene. affecting, SEE **emotional**, moving, tender.

touchy adjective
Be careful what you say because he's touchy. edgy, irascible, irritable, jittery, jumpy, nervous, quick-tempered, sensitive, snappy, temperamental, thin-skinned.

tough adjective
1 *tough shoes.* durable, hard-wearing, indestructible, lasting, stout, unbreakable, well-made.
OPPOSITES: SEE **delicate**.
2 *a tough physique.* [*informal*] beefy, brawny, burly, hardy, muscular, robust, stalwart, strong, sturdy.
3 *tough opposition.* invulnerable, merciless, obstinate, resilient, resistant, resolute, ruthless, stiff, stubborn, tenacious, unyielding.
OPPOSITES: SEE **weak**.
4 *tough meat.* chewy, hard, gristly, leathery, rubbery, uneatable.
OPPOSITES: SEE **tender**.
5 *a tough climb.* arduous, difficult, exacting, exhausting, gruelling, hard, laborious, stiff, strenuous.
6 *a tough problem.* baffling, intractable, [*informal*] knotty, puzzling, [*informal*] thorny.
OPPOSITES: SEE **easy**.

toughen verb
harden, make tougher, reinforce, strengthen.

tour noun
a sight-seeing tour. circular tour, drive, excursion, expedition, jaunt, journey, outing, ride, trip.

tour verb
to tour the beauty spots. do the rounds of, explore, go round, make a tour of, SEE **travel** verb, visit.

tourist noun
The cathedral was full of tourists. holiday-maker, sightseer, traveller, tripper, visitor.

tournament noun
a tennis tournament. championship, competition, contest, match, meeting, series.

tow verb
to tow a trailer. drag, draw, haul, pull, trail, tug.

tower noun

KINDS OF TOWER: belfry, castle, fort, fortress, keep, minaret, skyscraper, steeple, turret.

tower verb
The castle towers above the village. dominate, loom, rear, rise, stand out, stick up.

towering adjective
1 *a towering figure.* colossal, gigantic, high, imposing, lofty, mighty, soaring, SEE **tall**.
2 *a towering rage.* extreme, fiery, SEE **intense**, overpowering, passionate, violent.

town noun
borough, city, conurbation, municipality, SEE **settlement**.

PLACES IN A TOWN: bank, SEE **building**, café, car-park, cinema, college, concerthall, council-house, factory, filling station, flats, garage, ghetto, hotel, SEE **house** noun, housing estate, industrial estate, leisure-centre, library, museum, office block, park, police station, post office, [*informal*] pub, recreation ground, residential area, restaurant, SEE **road**, school, SEE **shop**, shopping centre, snack-bar, sports-centre, square, station, suburb, supermarket, theatre, warehouse.

toxic adjective
toxic fumes. dangerous, deadly, harmful, lethal, noxious, poisonous.
OPPOSITES: SEE **harmless**.

toy adjective
a toy car. imitation, model, [*informal*] pretend, scaled down, SEE **small**, small-scale.

trace noun
traces left by an animal. evidence, footprint, [*informal*] giveaway, hint, indication, mark, remains, sign, spoor, track, trail, vestige.

trace verb
1 *I traced my lost relatives.* detect, discover, find, get back, recover, retrieve, seek out.
2 *The hounds traced the fox across the field.* SEE **track** verb.
3 *to trace a picture.* copy, draw, go over, make a copy of, mark out, sketch.

track noun
1 *an animal's tracks.* footmark, footprint, mark, scent, spoor, trace, trail.
2 *a cross-country track.* bridle-path, bridle-way, cart-track, footpath, path, SEE **road**, way.
3 *a racing track.* circuit, course, dirt-track, race-track.
4 *a railway track.* SEE **railway**.

track verb
The hunters tracked the deer. chase, dog, follow, hound, hunt, pursue, shadow, stalk, tail, trace, trail.
to track down discover, find, get back, recover, retrieve, trace.

trade noun
1 *international trade.* barter, business, buying and selling, commerce, dealing, exchange, industry, market, trading, traffic, transactions.
2 *trained in a trade.* calling, craft, employment, SEE **job**, [*informal*] line

(*What's your line?*), occupation, profession, pursuit, work.

trade verb
be involved in trade [SEE **trade** noun], do business, market goods, retail, sell, traffic (in).
to trade in *to trade in your old car.* exchange, offer in part exchange, swop.

trader, **tradesman** nouns
market traders. local tradesmen. dealer, merchant, retailer, roundsman, salesman, seller, shopkeeper, stockist, supplier, trafficker [= *trader in something illegal or suspect*], vendor.
SHOPS AND BUSINESSES: SEE **shop**.

tradition noun
1 *It's a tradition to give gifts at Christmas.* convention, custom, habit, institution, practice, routine.
2 *Popular tradition portrays Richard III as a hunchback.* belief, folklore.

traditional adjective
1 *a traditional Christmas dinner.* accustomed, conventional, customary, established, familiar, habitual, historic, normal, orthodox, regular, time-honoured, typical, usual.
OPPOSITES: SEE **unconventional**.
2 *traditional stories.* folk, handed down, oral, popular, unwritten.
OPPOSITES: SEE **literary**.

traffic noun
1 *road traffic.* movement, transport, transportation.
VARIOUS VEHICLES: SEE **vehicle**.
2 *traffic in drugs.* SEE **trade** noun.

traffic verb SEE **trade** verb.

tragedy noun
1 *"Romeo and Juliet" is a tragedy by Shakespeare.*
KINDS OF WRITING: SEE **writing**.
2 *It was a tragedy when their dog was killed.* affliction, blow, calamity, catastrophe, disaster, misfortune.
OPPOSITES: SEE **comedy**.

tragic adjective
1 *a tragic accident.* appalling, awful, calamitous, catastrophic, depressing, dire, disastrous, dreadful, fatal, fearful, ill-fated, lamentable, terrible, unfortunate, unlucky.
2 *a tragic expression on her face.* bereft, distressed, grief-stricken, hurt, pathetic, piteous, pitiful, SEE **sad**, sorrowful, woeful, wretched.
OPPOSITES: SEE **comic** adjective.

trail noun
1 *The hounds followed the fox's trail.* evidence, footprints, mark, scent, signs, spoor, traces.
2 *a nature trail.* path, pathway, SEE **road**, route, track.

trail verb
1 *to trail something behind you.* dangle, drag, draw, haul, pull, tow.
2 *to trail someone.* chase, follow, hunt, pursue, shadow, stalk, tail, trace, track down.
3 *to trail behind.* SEE **dawdle**.

train noun SEE **railway**.

train verb
1 *to train a football team.* coach, educate, instruct, prepare, teach, tutor.
2 *to train hard.* do exercises, exercise, [*informal*] get fit, practise, prepare yourself, rehearse, [*informal*] work out.

trainee noun
apprentice, beginner, cadet, learner, [*informal*] L-driver, novice, pupil, starter, student, tiro, unqualified person.

trainer noun
coach, instructor, teacher, tutor.

traitor noun
a traitor to a cause. apostate, betrayer, blackleg, collaborator, defector, deserter, double-crosser, informer, [*informal*] Judas, quisling, renegade, treacherous person [SEE **treacherous**], turncoat.

tramp noun
1 *a long tramp across country.* SEE **walk** noun.
2 *a homeless tramp.* beggar, [*informal*] destitute person, [*informal*] dosser, [*informal*] down and out, homeless person, traveller, vagabond, vagrant, wanderer.

tramp verb
We tramped across the hills. [*informal*] footslog, hike, march, plod, stride, toil, traipse, trek, trudge, SEE **walk** verb, [*slang*] yomp.

trample verb
Don't trample on the flowers. crush, flatten, squash, stamp on, tread on, walk over.

trance noun
lost in a trance. day-dream, daze, dream, ecstasy, hypnotic state, reverie, spell, stupor, unconsciousness.

tranquil adjective
1 *a tranquil lake.* calm, peaceful, placid, quiet, restful, serene, still, undisturbed, unruffled.
OPPOSITES: SEE **stormy**.
2 *a tranquil mood.* collected, composed, dispassionate, [*informal*] laid-back, sedate, sober, unemotional, unexcited, untroubled.
OPPOSITES: SEE **excited**.

transaction noun
a business transaction. SEE **deal** noun.

transfer verb
to transfer from one place to another. carry, change, convey, displace, ferry, hand over,

move, relocate, remove, second (*seconded to another job*), take, transplant, transport, transpose.

transform verb
We transformed the attic into a games room. adapt, alter, SEE **change** verb, convert, metamorphose, modify, rebuild, reconstruct, remodel, revolutionize, transfigure, translate, [*joking*] transmogrify, transmute, turn.

transformation noun
a transformation in her appearance. alteration, SEE **change** noun, conversion, improvement, metamorphosis, revolution, transfiguration, transition, [*informal*] turn-about.

transgression noun
SEE **sin** noun.

transient adjective
transient visitors. a transient glimpse. brief, evanescent, fleeting, impermanent, momentary, passing, [*informal*] quick, short, temporary, transitory.
OPPOSITES: SEE **permanent**.

transit noun
goods damaged in transit. journey, movement, passage, shipment, transportation, travel.

transition noun
the transition from childhood to adulthood. alteration, SEE **change** noun, change-over, evolution, movement, progress, progression, shift, transformation, transit.

translate verb
to translate words into English. SEE **change** verb, convert, decode, express, interpret, make a translation, paraphrase, render, transcribe.

translation noun
gloss, interpretation, paraphrase, rendering, transcription, version.

translator noun
interpreter, linguist.

transmission noun
1 *the transmission of a TV programme.* broadcast, diffusion, dissemination, relaying, sending out.
2 *the transmission of goods.* carriage, conveyance, dispatch, shipment, transportation.

transmit verb
to transmit a message. to transmit radio signals. broadcast, communicate, convey, dispatch, disseminate, emit, pass on, relay, send.
OPPOSITES: SEE **receive**.

transparent adjective
transparent material. clear, crystalline, diaphanous, filmy, gauzy, limpid, pellucid, [*informal*] see-through, sheer, translucent.

transplant verb
to transplant seedlings. move, relocate, reposition, shift, transfer, uproot.

transport noun
public transport. conveyance, haulage, shipping, transportation.

KINDS OF TRANSPORT: SEE **aircraft**, barge, boat [SEE **vessel**], bus, cable-car, cable railway, canal, car, chair-lift, coach, cycle, ferry, horse, lorry, Metro, minibus, [*old-fashioned*] omnibus, SEE **railway**, road transport [SEE **vehicle**], sea, ship [SEE **vessel**], space-shuttle, taxi, train, tram, van, waterways.

WAYS TO TRAVEL: SEE **travel** noun.

---

transport verb
to transport goods. bring, carry, convey, fetch, haul, move, shift, ship, take, transfer.

transpose verb
to transpose letters in a word. change, exchange, move round, rearrange, reverse, substitute, swap, switch, transfer.

trap noun
a trap to catch someone or something. ambush, booby-trap, gin, mantrap, net, noose, snare.

trap verb
to trap an animal. to trap a criminal. ambush, arrest, capture, catch, corner, ensnare, entrap, snare.

trappings noun
The judge wore a wig and all the trappings of his position. accessories, accompaniments, accoutrements, adornments, decorations, equipment, finery, fittings, [*informal*] gear, ornaments, [*joking*] paraphernalia, [*informal*] things, trimmings.

trash noun
garbage, junk, litter, refuse, rubbish, waste.

travel noun
They say that travel broadens the mind. globe-trotting, moving around, [*joking*] peregrination, travelling.

KINDS OF TRAVEL: cruise, drive, excursion, expedition, exploration, flight, hike, holiday, journey, march, migration, mission, outing, pilgrimage, ramble, ride, safari, sail, sea-passage, tour, trek, trip, visit, voyage, walk.

WAYS TO TRAVEL: aviate, circumnavigate the world, commute, cruise, cycle, drive, emigrate, fly, free-wheel, [*informal*] gad about, [*informal*] gallivant, hike, hitch-hike, march, migrate, motor, navigate, paddle (*paddle a canoe*), pedal, pilot, punt, ramble, ride, roam, [*poetic*] rove, row, sail, shuttle, steam, tour, trek, voyage, walk, wander.

---

travel verb
to travel to work. to travel to foreign lands. go, journey, move, proceed, progress, [*old-fashioned*] wend.

traveller noun
1 astronaut, aviator, cosmonaut, cyclist, driver, flyer, migrant, motor-cyclist, motorist, passenger, pedestrian, sailor, voyager, walker.
2 [= *person travelling on business or to work*] commuter, [*informal*] rep, representative, salesman, saleswoman.
3 [= *person travelling for adventure or pleasure*] explorer, globe-trotter, hiker, hitch-hiker, holiday-maker, pilgrim, rambler, stowaway, tourist, tripper, wanderer, wayfarer.
4 [= *person for whom travelling is a way of life*] gypsy, itinerant, nomad, tinker, tramp, vagabond.

travelling adjective
travelling tribes. itinerant, migrant, migratory, mobile, nomadic, peripatetic, roaming, roving, touring, vagrant, wandering.

treacherous adjective
1 *a treacherous ally.* deceitful, disloyal, double-crossing, double-dealing, duplicitous, faithless, false, perfidious, sneaky, unfaithful, untrustworthy.
OPPOSITES: SEE **loyal**.
2 *treacherous weather conditions.* dangerous, deceptive, hazardous, misleading, perilous, risky, shifting, unpredictable, unreliable, unsafe, unstable.
OPPOSITES: SEE **reliable**.

treachery noun
treachery against an ally. betrayal, dishonesty, disloyalty, double-dealing, duplicity, faithlessness, infidelity, perfidy, SEE **treason**, untrustworthiness.
OPPOSITES: SEE **loyalty**.

tread verb
to tread carefully.
OTHER WAYS TO WALK: SEE **walk** verb.
to tread on *She trod on my foot.* crush, squash underfoot, stamp on, step on, trample, walk on.

treason noun
treason against your country. betrayal, mutiny, rebellion, sedition, SEE **treachery**.
OPPOSITES: SEE **loyalty**.

treasure noun
hidden treasure. fortune, gold, hoard, jewels, riches, treasure trove, valuables, wealth.

treasure verb
She treasures the brooch granny gave her. adore, appreciate, cherish, esteem, guard, keep safe, love, prize, value, venerate, worship.

treat noun
a birthday treat. entertainment, gift, outing, pleasure, surprise.

treat verb
1 *to treat someone kindly.* attend to, behave towards, care for, look after, use.
2 *to treat a subject thoroughly.* consider, deal with, discuss, tackle.
3 *to treat a patient. to treat a wound.* cure, dress, give treatment to [SEE **treatment**], heal, medicate, nurse, prescribe medicine for, tend.
4 *to treat food to kill germs.* process.
5 *I didn't have any money, but they were kind enough to treat me.* entertain, give (someone) a treat, pay for, provide for.

treatment noun
1 *the treatment of prisoners. the treatment of a problem.* care, conduct, dealing (with), handling, management, organization, use.
2 *the treatment of illness.* cure, first aid, healing, nursing, remedy, therapy.

treaty noun
a peace treaty. agreement, alliance, armistice, compact, concordat, contract, convention, covenant, [*informal*] deal, entente, pact, peace, [*formal*] protocol, settlement, truce, understanding.

tree noun
SOME TYPES OF TREE: bonsai, conifer, cordon, deciduous, espalier, evergreen, pollard, standard.
small tree bush, half-standard, shrub.
young tree sapling.
RELATED ADJECTIVE: arboreal.

VARIOUS TREES: ash, banian, bay, baobab, beech, birch, cacao, cedar, chestnut, cypress, elder, elm, eucalyptus, fir, fruit-tree [SEE **fruit**], gum-tree, hawthorn, hazel, holly, horse-chestnut, larch, lime, maple, oak, olive, palm, pine, plane, poplar, redwood, rowan, sequoia, spruce, sycamore, tamarisk, tulip tree, willow, yew.

---

trek noun, verb
SEE **travel** noun, verb.

tremble verb
to tremble with cold. quake, quaver, quiver, shake, shiver, shudder, vibrate, waver.

tremendous adjective
1 *a tremendous explosion.* alarming, appalling, awful, fearful, fearsome, frightening, frightful, horrifying, shocking, terrible, terrific.
2 [*informal*] *a tremendous helping of potatoes.* SEE **big**.
3 [*informal*] *a tremendous piece of music.* SEE **excellent**.
4 [*informal*] *a tremendous achievement.* SEE **remarkable**.

tremor noun
a tremor in someone's voice. agitation, hesitation, quavering, quiver, shaking, trembling, vibration.
an earth tremor SEE **earthquake**.

tremulous adjective
1 *We waited in tremulous anticipation.* agitated, anxious, excited, frightened, jittery, jumpy, nervous, timid, uncertain.
OPPOSITES: SEE **calm** adjective.
2 *I opened the important letter with tremulous fingers.* quivering, shaking, shivering, trembling, [*informal*] trembly, vibrating.
OPPOSITES: SEE **steady** adjective.

trench noun SEE **ditch** noun.

trend noun
1 *an upward trend in prices.* bias, direction, inclination, leaning, movement, shift, tendency.
2 *the latest trend in clothes.* [*informal*] fad, fashion, mode, style, [*informal*] thing (*It's the latest thing*), way.

trendy adjective
[*informal*] *trendy clothes.* contemporary, fashionable, [*informal*] in (*the in fashion*), latest, modern, stylish, up-to-date.
OPPOSITES: SEE **old-fashioned**.

trepidation noun SEE **fear** noun.

trespass verb
to trespass on someone's property. encroach, enter illegally, intrude, invade.

trial noun
1 *a legal trial.* case, court martial, examination, hearing, tribunal.
2 *a trial of a new product.* attempt, experiment, test, testing, [*informal*] try-out.
3 *Appearing in public can be a trial for shy people.* affliction, burden, difficulty, hardship, ordeal, problem, tribulation, trouble, worry.

triangular adjective
three-cornered, three-sided.

tribe noun
a close-knit tribe. clan, dynasty, family, group, horde, nation, people, race, stock.

tribute noun
Her friends read moving tributes to her courage. accolade, appreciation, commendation, compliment, eulogy, panegyric, testimony.
to pay tribute to *They paid tribute to her courage.* applaud, celebrate, commend, SEE **honour** verb, pay homage to, praise, respect.

trick noun
1 *a conjuring trick.* illusion, legerdemain, magic, sleight of hand.
2 *a deceitful trick.* cheat, [*informal*] con, deceit, deception, fraud, hoax, imposture, manœuvre, ploy, pretence, ruse, scheme, stratagem, stunt, subterfuge, swindle, trap, SEE **trickery**, wile.
3 *I never learned the trick of standing on my head.* art, craft, device, dodge, expertise, gimmick, knack, [*informal*] know-how, secret, skill, technique.
4 *He has a trick of repeating himself.* characteristic, habit, idiosyncrasy, mannerism, peculiarity, way.
5 *She played a trick on me.* joke, [*informal*] leg-pull, practical joke, prank.

trick verb
He tricked me into buying rubbish. [*informal*] bamboozle, bluff, catch out, cheat, [*informal*] con, deceive, defraud, [*informal*] diddle, dupe, fool, hoax, hoodwink, [*informal*] kid, mislead, outwit, [*informal*] pull (someone's) leg, swindle.

trickery noun
bluffing, cheating, chicanery, deceit, deception, dishonesty, fraud, [*informal*] hocus-pocus, [*informal*] jiggery-pokery, [*informal*] skulduggery, swindling, SEE **trick** noun.

trickle verb
Water trickled from a crack. dribble, drip, flow slowly, leak, ooze, percolate, run, seep.
OPPOSITES: SEE **gush** verb.

tricky adjective
1 *a tricky customer.* SEE **deceitful**.
2 *a tricky manœuvre.* SEE **complicated**.

trifling adjective
a trifling amount. SEE **trivial**.

trigger verb
to trigger off SEE **activate**.

trill verb
birds trilling in the garden. SEE **sing**, twitter, warble, whistle.

trim adjective
a trim garden. a trim figure. compact, neat,
orderly, [*informal*] shipshape, smart,
spruce, tidy, well-groomed, well-kept.
OPPOSITES: SEE **untidy**.

trim verb
to trim a hedge. clip, crop, SEE **cut** verb, shape,
shear, tidy.

trip noun
a trip to the seaside. excursion, expedition,
jaunt, journey, outing, tour, visit, voyage.
to make a trip SEE **travel** verb.

trip verb
1 *to trip along lightly.* run, skip, SEE **walk**
verb.
2 *to trip over something.* catch your foot, fall,
stagger, stumble, totter, tumble.

trite adjective
a trite remark. SEE **commonplace**.

triumph noun
1 *a triumph over our opponents.* conquest,
knock-out, victory, [*informal*] walk-over,
win.
2 *The pudding I made was a triumph.*
accomplishment, achievement, [*informal*]
hit, master-stroke, [*informal*] smash hit,
success.

triumph verb
We triumphed in the end. be victorious,
prevail, succeed, win.
to triumph over SEE **defeat** verb.

triumphant adjective
1 *We cheered the triumphant team.*
conquering, dominant, successful,
victorious, winning.
OPPOSITES: SEE **unsuccessful.**.
2 *The losers didn't like our triumphant
laughter.* boastful, [*informal*] cocky, elated,
exultant, gleeful, gloating, immodest, joyful,
jubilant, proud.
OPPOSITES: SEE **modest**.

trivial adjective
trivial details. [*informal*] fiddling,
[*informal*] footling, frivolous,
inconsequential, inconsiderable,
insignificant, little, minor, negligible,
paltry, pettifogging, petty, [*informal*]
piffling, silly, slight, small, superficial,
trifling, trite, unimportant, worthless.
OPPOSITES: SEE **important**.

troop noun SEE **group** noun.
troops *armed troops.* SEE **armed services**.

troop verb
We trooped along the road. march, parade,
SEE **walk** verb.

trophy noun
1 [*plural*] *trophies of war.* booty, loot,
mementoes, rewards, souvenirs, spoils.
2 *a sporting trophy.* award, cup, medal, prize.

tropical adjective
a tropical climate. equatorial, SEE **hot**.
OPPOSITES: arctic, SEE **cold** adjective.

trot noun, verb SEE **run** noun, verb.

trotter noun SEE **foot**.

trouble noun
1 *personal troubles.* adversity, affliction,
anxiety, burden, difficulty, distress, grief,
hardship, SEE **illness**, inconvenience, misery,
misfortune, pain, problem, sadness, sorrow,
suffering, trial, tribulation, unhappiness,
vexation, worry.
2 *trouble in the crowd.* bother, commotion,
conflict, discontent, discord, disorder,
dissatisfaction, disturbance, fighting, fuss,
misbehaviour, misconduct, naughtiness,
row, strife, turmoil, unpleasantness, unrest,
violence.
3 *engine trouble.* break-down, defect, failure,
fault, malfunction.
4 *I took a lot of trouble to get it right.* care,
concern, effort, exertion, labour, pains,
struggle, thought.

trouble verb
You look sad—is something troubling you?
afflict, annoy, bother, cause trouble to,
concern, distress, disturb, grieve, hurt,
inconvenience, interfere with, molest, pain,
perturb, pester, plague, threaten, torment,
upset, vex, worry.
OPPOSITES: SEE **reassure**.

troubled adjective
a troubled conscience. troubled times.
anxious, disturbed, fearful, [*informal*]
fraught, guilt-ridden, insecure, perturbed,
restless, stricken, uncertain, uneasy,
unhappy, vexed, worried.
OPPOSITES: SEE **peaceful**.

trouble-maker noun
agitator, SEE **criminal** noun, culprit,
delinquent, hooligan, mischief-maker,
offender, rabble-rouser, rascal, ring-leader,
ruffian, vandal, wrongdoer.

troublesome adjective
troublesome insects. troublesome neighbours.
annoying, badly behaved, bothersome,
disobedient, disorderly, distressing,
inconvenient, irksome, irritating, naughty,
[*informal*] pestiferous, pestilential, rowdy,
tiresome, trying, uncooperative, unruly,
upsetting, vexing, wearisome, worrisome,
worrying.
OPPOSITES: SEE **helpful**.

trousers noun

KINDS OF TROUSERS: [*informal*] bags,
breeches, corduroys, culottes, denims,
dungarees, jeans, jodhpurs, [*old-fashioned*]
knickerbockers, [*informal*] Levis, overalls,
[*American*] pants, plus fours, shorts, ski-
pants, slacks, [*Scottish*] trews, trunks.
OTHER GARMENTS: SEE **clothes**.

truant noun
a truant from school or work. absentee,
deserter (*from the army*), dodger,
malingerer, runaway, shirker, [*informal*]
skiver.
to play truant be absent, desert, malinger,
[*informal*] skive, stay away.

truce noun
a truce between two warring sides. armistice,
cease-fire, moratorium, pact, peace,
suspension of hostilities, treaty.

true adjective
1 *a true happening. true facts. a true copy.*
accurate, actual, authentic, confirmed,
correct, exact, factual, faithful, genuine,
proper, real, right, veracious, veritable.
2 *a true friend. true love.* constant,
dependable, devoted, faithful, firm, honest,
honourable, loyal, reliable, responsible,
sincere, steady, trustworthy, trusty.
OPPOSITES: SEE **false**.
3 *Are you the true owner of this car?*
authorized, legal, legitimate, rightful, valid.
4 *the true aim of a marksman. a true
alignment.* accurate, exact, perfect, precise,
[*informal*] spot-on, unerring, unswerving.
OPPOSITES: SEE **inaccurate**.

truncheon noun
a policeman's truncheon. baton, club, cudgel,
staff, stick.

trunk noun
1 *a tree trunk.* bole, shaft, stalk, stem.
2 *a person's trunk.* body, frame, torso.
3 *an elephant's trunk.* nose, proboscis.
4 *a clothes' trunk.* box, case, chest, coffer,
crate, suitcase.
trunks *swimming trunks.* briefs, shorts, SEE
trousers.

trust noun
1 *The dog has trust in his owner.* belief,
certainty, confidence, credence, faith,
reliance.
2 *a position of trust.* responsibility,
trusteeship.

trust verb
1 *We trust you to do your duty.* bank on,
believe in, be sure of, count on, depend on,
have confidence in, have faith in, rely on.
OPPOSITES: SEE **distrust**.

2 *I trust you are well.* assume, expect, hope,
imagine, presume, suppose, surmise.
OPPOSITES: SEE **doubt** verb.

trustful adjective
Small children are often very trustful.
credulous, gullible, innocent, trusting,
unquestioning, unsuspecting, unwary.
OPPOSITES: SEE **suspicious**.

trustworthy adjective
a trustworthy friend. constant, dependable,
faithful, honest, honourable, [*informal*] on
the level, loyal, reliable, responsible,
[*informal*] safe, sensible, steadfast, steady,
straightforward, true, [*old-fashioned*]
trusty, truthful, upright.
OPPOSITES: SEE **deceitful**.

truth noun
1 *Tell the truth.* facts, reality.
2 *I doubt the truth of her story.* accuracy,
authenticity, correctness, exactness,
factuality, integrity, reliability,
truthfulness, validity, veracity, verity.
3 *an accepted truth.* axiom, fact, maxim,
truism.
OPPOSITES: SEE **lie** noun.

truthful adjective
1 *a truthful person.* candid, credible,
forthright, frank, honest, reliable, sincere,
[*informal*] straight, straightforward,
trustworthy, veracious.
2 *a truthful answer.* accurate, correct,
proper, right, true, valid.
OPPOSITES: SEE **dishonest**.

try noun
Have a try! attempt, [*informal*] bash,
[*informal*] crack, effort, endeavour,
experiment, [*informal*] go, [*informal*] shot,
[*informal*] stab, test, trial.

try verb
1 *Try to do your best.* aim, attempt,
endeavour, essay, exert yourself, make an
effort, strain, strive, struggle, venture.
2 *We tried a new method.* [*informal*] check
out, evaluate, examine, experiment with,
investigate, test, try out, undertake.

tub noun
barrel, bath, butt, cask, drum, keg, pot, vat.

tube noun
tubes to carry liquids. capillary, conduit,
cylinder, duct, hose, main, pipe, spout,
tubing.

tuck verb
Tuck your shirt into your jeans. cram, gather,
insert, push, put away, shove, stuff.

tuft noun
a tuft of grass. bunch, clump, cluster, tuffet,
tussock.

tug verb
1 *We tugged the cart behind us.* drag, draw, haul, heave, lug, pull, tow.
2 *I tugged at the rope.* jerk, pluck, twitch, wrench, yank.

tumble verb
1 *I tumbled into the water.* collapse, drop, fall, flop, pitch, stumble, topple, trip up.
2 *I tumbled everything into a heap.* disarrange, jumble, mix up, roll, rumple, shove, spill, throw carelessly, toss.

tumbledown adjective
a tumbledown cottage. badly maintained, broken down, crumbling, decrepit, derelict, dilapidated, ramshackle, rickety, ruined, shaky.

tumult noun
SEE **uproar**.

tumultuous adjective
tumultuous applause. agitated, boisterous, confused, excited, hectic, passionate, tempestuous, turbulent, unrestrained, unruly, uproarious, violent, wild.
OPPOSITES: SEE **calm** adjective.

tune noun
air, melody, song, strain, theme.

tune verb
to tune a violin. to tune an engine. adjust, regulate, set, temper.

tuneful adjective
tuneful music. [*informal*] catchy, mellifluous, melodious, musical, pleasant, singable.
OPPOSITES: SEE **tuneless**.

tuneless adjective
tuneless music. atonal, boring, cacophonous, discordant, dissonant, harsh, monotonous, unmusical.
OPPOSITES: SEE **tuneful**.

tunnel noun
burrow, gallery, hole, mine, passage, passageway, shaft, subway, underpass.

tunnel verb
A rabbit tunnelled under the fence. burrow, dig, excavate, mine.

turbulent adjective
1 *turbulent emotions.* agitated, boisterous, confused, disordered, excited, hectic, passionate, restless, seething, turbid, unrestrained, violent, volatile, wild.
2 *a turbulent crowd.* badly behaved, disorderly, lawless, obstreperous, riotous, rowdy, undisciplined, unruly.
3 *turbulent weather.* blustery, bumpy (*a bumpy flight*), choppy (*choppy seas*), rough, stormy, tempestuous, violent, wild, windy.
OPPOSITES: SEE **calm** adjective.

turgid adjective
a turgid style of writing. affected, bombastic, flowery, fulsome, grandiose, high-flown, over-blown, pompous, pretentious, stilted, wordy.
OPPOSITES: SEE **lucid**.

turmoil noun
The place was in turmoil until we organized ourselves. [*informal*] bedlam, chaos, commotion, confusion, disorder, disturbance, ferment, [*informal*] hubbub, [*informal*] hullabaloo, pandemonium, riot, row, rumpus, tumult, turbulence, unrest, upheaval, uproar, welter.
OPPOSITES: SEE **calm** noun.

turn noun
1 *a turn of a wheel.* circle, cycle, revolution, rotation, spin, twirl, whirl.
2 *a turn in the road.* angle, bend, corner, curve, deviation, hairpin bend, junction, loop, twist.
3 *a turn in someone's fortunes.* change of direction, reversal, shift, turning-point, [*informal*] U-turn.
4 *a player's turn in a game.* chance, [*informal*] go, innings, opportunity, shot.
5 *a comic turn in a concert.* SEE **performance**.
6 [*informal*] *He had a bad turn and had to go to hospital.* SEE **illness**.

turn verb
1 *to turn round a central point as a wheel does.* circle, gyrate, hinge, move in a circle, orbit, pivot, revolve, roll, rotate, spin, spiral, swivel, twirl, twist, whirl, yaw.
2 *to turn left or right.* change direction, corner, deviate, divert, go round a corner, negotiate a corner, steer, swerve, veer, wheel.
3 *to turn a wire round a stick.* bend, coil, curl, loop, twist, wind.
4 *We turned the attic into a games room.* adapt, alter, change, convert, make, modify, remake, remodel, transfigure, transform.
5 *The snake turned this way and that.* squirm, twist, wriggle, writhe.
to turn away *They turned uninvited guests away.* decline, dismiss, exclude, send away, [*informal*] send packing.
to turn down 1 *I turned the invitation down.* decline, refuse, reject, spurn. 2 *Turn down the heat.* decrease, lessen, reduce.
to turn into *Tadpoles turn into frogs.* become, be transformed into, change into, metamorphose into.
to turn off 1 *We turned off the main road.* branch off, deviate from, leave. 2 *Turn off the water. Turn off the light.* cut off, disconnect, put off, shut off, stop, switch off, turn out. 3 [*informal*] *She turned me off with her bossy*

manner. alienate, irritate, put off, repel.
4 [*informal*] *He was so boring that I turned
off.* lose interest, stop listening.
to turn on 1 *Turn on the water. Turn on the
light.* connect, start, put on, switch on. 2
[*informal*] *He quite turned her on with his
flattering grin.* attract, excite, [*informal*] get
going, stimulate.
to turn out 1 *How did your party turn out?*
befall, emerge, happen, result. 2 *We had to
turn out an intruder.* eject, evict, expel,
[*informal*] kick out, remove, throw out. 3 *The
factory turns out hundreds of items each day.*
make, manufacture, produce. 4 *Turn out the
light.* SEE **turn off**.
to turn over 1 *The boat turned over.* capsize,
flip, invert, keel over, overturn, turn turtle,
turn upside down. 2 *I turned the problem
over.* consider, contemplate, deliberate, mull
over, ponder, reflect on, think about, weigh
up.
to turn up 1 *I turned up some interesting facts.*
[*informal*] dig up, disclose, discover,
expose, find, reveal, show up, unearth.
2 *Some friends turned up unexpectedly.*
appear, arrive, come, [*informal*] drop in,
materialize, [*informal*] pop up, visit. 3 *Turn
up the volume.* amplify, increase, raise.

turning noun
a turning in the road. SEE **corner** noun.

turning-point noun
a turning-point in your life. crisis,
crossroads, new direction, revolution,
watershed.

tussle noun, verb SEE **fight** noun, verb.

twig noun
branch, offshoot, shoot, spray, stalk, stem,
stick.

twilight noun
dusk, evening, [*poetic*] eventide, [*poetic*]
gloaming, gloom, halflight, nightfall,
sundown, sunset.

twin adjective
twin statuettes on the mantelpiece. balancing,
corresponding, duplicate, identical,
indistinguishable, matching, paired,
similar, symmetrical.
OPPOSITES: SEE **contrasting**.

twin noun
*This statue is a twin of the one in the antique
shop.* clone, double, duplicate, [*informal*]
lookalike, match, pair.

twinge noun
a twinge in your tooth. SEE **pain** noun.

twinkle verb
SEE **light** noun (**give light**).

twirl verb
1 *The dancers twirled faster and faster.*
gyrate, pirouette, revolve, rotate, spin, turn,
twist, wheel, whirl.
2 *I twirled my umbrella.* brandish, twiddle,
wave.

twist noun
1 *a twist in a rope. a twist in the road.* bend,
coil, curl, kink, knot, loop, tangle, turn,
zigzag.
2 *an unexpected twist to a story.* revelation,
surprise ending.

twist verb
1 *to twist and turn.* bend, coil, corkscrew,
curl, curve, loop, revolve, rotate, screw,
spin, spiral, turn, weave, wind, wreathe,
wriggle, writhe, zigzag.
2 *The ropes became twisted.* entangle,
entwine, intertwine, interweave, tangle.
3 *to twist the lid off a jar.* jerk, wrench, wrest.
4 *to twist something out of shape.* buckle,
contort, crinkle, crumple, distort, warp,
wrinkle.
5 *to twist the meaning of something.* alter,
change, falsify, misquote, misrepresent.

twisted adjective
1 *a twisted rope. a twisted shape.* bent, coiled,
contorted, corkscrew, crumpled, deformed,
distorted, knotted, looped, misshapen,
screwed up, tangled, warped.
2 *a twisted message.* garbled, misreported,
misrepresented, misunderstood.
3 *a twisted mind.* SEE **perverted**.

twisty adjective
[*informal*] *a twisty road.* bendy, crooked,
curving, indirect, serpentine, tortuous,
twisting, winding, zigzag.
OPPOSITES: SEE **straight**.

twitch noun
a nervous twitch. blink, convulsion, flutter,
jerk, jump, spasm, tic, tremor.

twitch verb
1 *Our dog's legs twitch while he's asleep.*
fidget, flutter, jerk, jump, start, tremble.
2 *to twitch at a rope.* SEE **tug** verb.

two noun
couple, duet, duo, pair, twosome.
RELATED ADJECTIVES: binary, bipartite,
double, dual, duple, paired, SEE **twin**
adjective, twofold.

type noun
1 *Things of the same type are classed together.*
category, class, classification, description,
designation, form, genre, group, kind, mark,
set, sort, species, variety.
2 *Job is often quoted as a type of patient
suffering.* embodiment, epitome, example,
model, pattern, personification, standard.
3 *a book printed in large type.* characters,

[*formal*] font or fount, letters, lettering, print, printing, type-face.

typical adjective
1 *a typical Chinese dinner.* characteristic, distinctive, particular, representative, special.
OPPOSITES: SEE **atypical.**
2 *a typical day.* average, conventional, normal, ordinary, orthodox, predictable, standard, stock, unsurprising, usual.
OPPOSITES: SEE **unusual.**

tyrannical adjective
a tyrannical ruler. absolute, authoritarian, autocratic, [*informal*] bossy, cruel, despotic, dictatorial, domineering, harsh, high-handed, imperious, oppressive, overbearing, ruthless, severe, tyrannous, unjust.
OPPOSITES: SEE **liberal.**

tyrant noun
autocrat, despot, dictator, [*informal*] hard taskmaster, oppressor, SEE **ruler,** slave-driver.

Uu

ubiquitous adjective
[*Ubiquitous* is related to Latin *ubique* = *everywhere.*] common, commonplace, pervasive, SEE **universal.**

ugliness noun
deformity, hideousness, repulsiveness, unsightliness.
OPPOSITES: SEE **beauty.**

ugly adjective
1 *ugly monsters.* deformed, disfigured, disgusting, frightful, ghastly, grisly, grotesque, gruesome, hideous, [*informal*] horrid, ill-favoured, misshapen, monstrous, nasty, objectionable, SEE **repulsive,** revolting.
2 *an ugly room. an ugly piece of furniture.* displeasing, inartistic, inelegant, plain, tasteless, unattractive, unpleasant, unsightly.
OPPOSITES: SEE **beautiful.**
3 *ugly storm clouds. in an ugly mood.* SEE **angry,** dangerous, forbidding, hostile, menacing, ominous, sinister, threatening, unfriendly.

ultimate adjective
1 *We scored in the ultimate minutes of the game.* closing, concluding, eventual, extreme, final, last, terminal.

2 *The ultimate cause of the fire was an electrical fault.* basic, fundamental, primary, root.

umpire noun
adjudicator, arbiter, arbitrator, judge, linesman, moderator, [*informal*] ref, referee.

---

un- The prefix *un-* can be attached to a vast number of words. Sometimes it simply signifies *not* (*happy/unhappy*; *safe/unsafe*); sometimes it has the effect of reversing the action indicated by a verb (*do/undo*; *lock/unlock*). The number of words beginning with *un-* is almost unlimited: we don't have space to include all of them.

---

unacceptable adjective
unacceptable work. an unacceptable level of pollution. inadequate, inadmissible, inappropriate, insupportable, intolerable, unsatisfactory, unsuitable.
OPPOSITES: SEE **acceptable.**

unaccompanied adjective
an unaccompanied traveller. alone, lone, sole, solo (*a solo performer*), unescorted.

unaccustomed adjective
SEE **strange.**

unadventurous adjective
1 *an unadventurous spirit.* cautious, cowardly, spiritless, SEE **timid,** unimaginative.
2 *an unadventurous life.* cloistered, limited, protected, sheltered, unexciting.
OPPOSITES: SEE **adventurous, enterprising.**

unalterable adjective
SEE **immutable.**

unasked adjective, adverb
It's not often someone does you a favour unasked. spontaneous(ly), unbidden, uninvited, unprompted, unsolicited, voluntary (voluntarily).

unattached adjective
[*informal*] available, free, independent, single, uncommitted, unmarried, [*informal*] unspoken for.
OPPOSITES: SEE **engaged, married.**

unattractive adjective
repulsive, SEE **ugly,** uninviting, unprepossessing.
OPPOSITES: SEE **attractive.**

unauthorized adjective
The train made an unauthorized stop. abnormal, illegal, irregular, unlawful, unusual.

unavoidable adjective
1 *an unavoidable accident.* certain, destined, fated, inescapable, inevitable, sure.

2 *an unavoidable payment.* compulsory,
mandatory, necessary, obligatory,
required.
OPPOSITES: SEE **unnecessary**.

unaware adjective
SEE **ignorant**.

unbalanced adjective
1 *an unbalanced shape.* asymmetrical,
irregular, lopsided, off-centre, uneven.
2 *an unbalanced argument.* biased, bigoted,
one-sided, partial, partisan, prejudiced,
unfair, unjust.
3 *an unbalanced mind.* SEE **mad**.
OPPOSITES: SEE **balanced**.

unbearable adjective
unbearable pain. an unbearable snob.
insufferable, insupportable, intolerable,
unacceptable, unendurable.
OPPOSITES: SEE **tolerable**.

unbeatable adjective
SEE **invincible**.

unbelievable adjective
SEE **incredible**.

unbend verb
1 *to unbend something that has been bent.*
straighten, uncurl, untwist.
OPPOSITES: SEE **bend** verb.
2 [*informal*] *to unbend in front of the TV in
the evening.* loosen up, relax, rest, unwind.

unbiased adjective
an unbiased opinion. disinterested,
enlightened, even-handed, fair, impartial,
independent, just, neutral, non-partisan,
objective, open-minded, reasonable,
[*informal*] straight, unbigoted, undogmatic,
unprejudiced.
OPPOSITES: SEE **biased**.

unbreakable adjective
SEE **indestructible**.

uncaring adjective
SEE **callous**.

unceasing adjective
SEE **continual**.

uncertain adjective
1 *The outcome of the trial is uncertain.*
ambiguous, arguable, conjectural,
imprecise, incalculable, inconclusive,
indefinite, indeterminate, speculative,
unclear, unconvincing, undecided,
undetermined, unforeseeable, unknown,
unresolved.
2 *I'm uncertain what to believe.* agnostic,
ambivalent, doubtful, dubious, [*informal*]
hazy, insecure, [*informal*] in two minds,
self-questioning, unconvinced, undecided,
unsure, vague, wavering.
3 *My chance of success is uncertain.*
[*informal*] chancy, hazardous, [*informal*]

iffy, problematical, questionable, risky,
[*informal*] touch and go.
4 *Our climate is uncertain.* changeable,
erratic, fitful, inconstant, irregular,
precarious, unpredictable, unreliable,
variable.
OPPOSITES: SEE **certain**.

unchanging adjective
SEE **constant**.

uncharitable, unchristian adjectives
SEE **unkind**.

uncivilized adjective
uncivilized behaviour. anarchic, antisocial,
badly behaved, barbarian, barbaric,
barbarous, disorganized, illiterate,
Philistine, primitive, savage, uncultured,
uneducated, unenlightened,
unsophisticated, wild.
OPPOSITES: SEE **civilized**.

unclear adjective
unclear evidence. unclear meaning.
ambiguous, cryptic, doubtful, dubious,
hazy, imprecise, obscure, puzzling, SEE
uncertain, vague.
OPPOSITES: SEE **clear** adjective.

unclothed adjective
SEE **naked**.

uncomfortable adjective
1 *uncomfortable surroundings. an
uncomfortable bed.* SEE **bleak**, comfortless,
cramped, hard, inconvenient, lumpy,
painful.
OPPOSITES: SEE **comfortable**.
2 *uncomfortable clothes.* formal, restrictive,
stiff, tight, tight-fitting.
3 *an uncomfortable silence.* awkward,
distressing, SEE **embarrassing**, nervous,
restless, troubled, uneasy, worried.

uncommon adjective
SEE **unusual**.

uncomplimentary adjective
uncomplimentary remarks. censorious,
critical, deprecatory, depreciatory,
derogatory, disapproving, disparaging,
pejorative, SEE **rude**, scathing, slighting,
unfavourable, unflattering.
OPPOSITES: SEE **complimentary**.

unconcealed adjective
SEE **obvious**.

unconcerned adjective
SEE **callous**.

unconditional adjective
unconditional surrender. absolute,
categorical, complete, full, outright, total,
unequivocal, unlimited, unqualified,
unreserved, unrestricted, whole-hearted,
[*informal*] with no strings attached.
OPPOSITES: SEE **conditional**.

uncongenial adjective
I can't work in uncongenial surroundings.
alien, antipathetic, disagreeable,
incompatible, unattractive, unfriendly,
unpleasant, unsympathetic.
OPPOSITES: SEE **congenial**.

unconscionable adjective
1 *an unconscionable rogue.* SEE **unscrupulous**.
2 *He kept me waiting an unconscionable time.*
SEE **unjustifiable**.

unconscious adjective
1 *unconscious after a knock on the head.*
anaesthetized, comatose, concussed,
[*informal*] dead to the world, insensible,
[*informal*] knocked out, oblivious,
[*informal*] out for the count, senseless,
sleeping.
2 *unconscious of her effect on others.* blind
(to), oblivious, unaware, unwitting.
3 *unconscious humour.* accidental,
inadvertent, unintended, unintentional.
4 *an unconscious reaction.* automatic,
impulsive, instinctive, involuntary, reflex,
spontaneous, unthinking.
5 *your unconscious desires.* repressed,
subconscious, subliminal, suppressed.
OPPOSITES: SEE **conscious**.

uncontrollable adjective
SEE **rebellious**.

unconventional adjective
*unconventional ideas. an unconventional
appearance.* abnormal, atypical, [*informal*]
cranky, eccentric, exotic, futuristic,
idiosyncratic, inventive, non-conforming,
non-standard, odd, off-beat, original,
peculiar, progressive, revolutionary,
strange, surprising, unaccustomed,
unorthodox, [*informal*] way-out, wayward,
weird, zany.
OPPOSITES: SEE **conventional**.

unconvincing adjective
SEE **incredible**.

uncooperative adjective
an uncooperative partner. lazy, obstructive,
recalcitrant, selfish, unhelpful, unwilling.
OPPOSITES: SEE **co-operative**.

uncover verb
1 *to uncover something which has been
concealed.* bare, disclose, disrobe, expose,
reveal, show, strip, take the wraps off,
undress, unmask, unveil, unwrap.
2 *to uncover something which was lost.* come
across, detect, dig up, discover, exhume,
locate, unearth.
OPPOSITES: SEE **cover** verb.

undamaged adjective
The goods survived the journey undamaged.
faultless, [*informal*] in one piece, intact,
mint (*in mint condition*), perfect, safe, sound,

unharmed, unhurt, unimpaired, uninjured,
unscathed, whole, [*informal*] without a
scratch.
OPPOSITES: SEE **damaged**.

undecided adjective
1 *The outcome is still undecided.* SEE
uncertain.
2 *an undecided manner.* SEE **hesitant**.

undefended adjective
*The army withdrew and left the post
undefended.* defenceless, exposed, helpless,
insecure, unarmed, unfortified, unguarded,
unprotected, vulnerable, weaponless.
OPPOSITES: SEE **secure** adjective.

undemanding adjective
undemanding work. SEE **easy**.

undemonstrative adjective
SEE **aloof**.

undeniable adjective
SEE **indisputable**.

underclothes noun
lingerie, underclothing, undergarments,
underwear, [*informal*] undies.

VARIOUS UNDERGARMENTS: bra, braces,
brassière, briefs, camiknickers, corset,
drawers, garter, girdle, knickers, panties,
panti-hose, pants, petticoat, slip,
suspenders, tights, trunks, underpants,
underskirt, vest.

OTHER GARMENTS: SEE **clothes**.

---

undercurrent noun
an undercurrent of hostility. atmosphere,
feeling, hint, sense, suggestion, trace,
undertone.

underestimate verb
to underestimate difficulties. belittle,
dismiss, disparage, minimize, misjudge,
underrate, undervalue.
OPPOSITES: SEE **exaggerate**.

undergarment noun
SEE **underclothes**.

undergo verb
to undergo an operation. bear, be subjected
to, endure, experience, go through, put up
with, submit yourself to, suffer, withstand.

underground adjective
1 *an underground store.* subterranean.
2 *an underground society.* SEE **secret**
adjective.
underground railway metro, tube.

undergrowth noun
undergrowth in the woods. brush, bushes,
ground cover, plants, vegetation.

underhand adjective
SEE **sly**.

underline verb
SEE **emphasize**.

undermine verb
1 *to undermine a wall.* burrow under, dig
under, erode, excavate, mine under,
sabotage, tunnel under, undercut.
OPPOSITES: underpin, SEE **support** verb.
2 *to undermine someone's confidence.* destroy,
ruin, sap, weaken, wear away.
OPPOSITES: SEE **boost** verb.

underprivileged adjective
deprived, destitute, disadvantaged,
impoverished, needy, SEE **poor**.

undersized adjective
SEE **small**.

understand verb
1 *to understand what something means.*
appreciate, apprehend, comprehend,
[*informal*] cotton on to, decipher, decode,
fathom, follow, gather, [*informal*] get,
[*informal*] get to the bottom of, grasp,
interpret, know, learn, make out, make
sense of, master, perceive, realize,
recognize, see, take in, [*informal*] twig.
2 *She understands animals.* empathize with,
sympathize with.

understanding noun
1 *a person of quick understanding.* ability,
acumen, brains, cleverness, discernment,
insight, intellect, intelligence, judgement,
penetration, perceptiveness, sense, wisdom.
2 *an understanding of a problem.*
appreciation, apprehension, awareness,
cognition, comprehension, grasp,
knowledge.
3 *friendly understanding between two people.*
accord, agreement, compassion, consensus,
consent, consideration, empathy, fellow
feeling, harmony, kindness, mutuality,
sympathy, tolerance.
4 *a formal understanding between two
parties.* arrangement, bargain, compact,
contract, deal, entente, pact, settlement,
treaty.

understate verb
to understate a problem. belittle, [*informal*]
make light of, minimize, [*informal*] play
down, [*informal*] soft-pedal.
OPPOSITES: SEE **exaggerate**.

undertake verb
1 *to undertake to do something.* agree,
consent, guarantee, pledge, promise.
2 *to undertake a task.* accept responsibility
for, address, approach, attempt, attend to,
begin, commence, commit yourself to, cope

with, deal with, embark on, grapple with,
handle, manage, tackle, take on, take up, try.

undertaking noun
SEE **enterprise**.

underwater adjective
underwater exploration. subaquatic,
submarine, undersea.

underwear noun
SEE **underclothes**.

undeserved adjective
undeserved punishment. unearned, unfair,
unjustified, unmerited, unwarranted.

undesirable adjective
SEE **objectionable**.

undignified adjective
an undignified rush to be first. indecorous,
inelegant, ridiculous, unbecoming,
unseemly.
OPPOSITES: SEE **dignified**.

undisciplined adjective
an undisciplined rabble. anarchic, chaotic,
disobedient, disorderly, disorganized,
intractable, rebellious, uncontrolled,
unruly, unsystematic, untrained, wild,
wilful.
OPPOSITES: SEE **disciplined**.

undiscriminating adjective
an undiscriminating audience. easily
pleased, imperceptive, superficial,
thoughtless, uncritical, undiscerning,
unselective.
OPPOSITES: SEE **discriminating**.

undisguised adjective
SEE **blatant**.

undisputed adjective
SEE **indisputable**.

undistinguished adjective
SEE **ordinary**.

undo verb
1 *to undo a fastening. to undo a parcel.* detach,
disconnect, disengage, loose, loosen, open,
part, separate, unbind, unbuckle, unbutton,
unchain, unclasp, unclip, uncouple,
unfasten, unfetter, unhook, unleash, unlock,
unpick, unpin, unscrew, unseal, unshackle,
unstick, untether, untie, unwrap, unzip.
OPPOSITES: SEE **fasten**.
2 *to undo someone's good work.* annul, cancel
out, destroy, mar, nullify, quash (*to quash a
decision*), reverse, ruin, spoil, undermine,
vitiate, wipe out, wreck.

undoubted adjective
SEE **indisputable**.

undoubtedly adverb
certainly, definitely, doubtless, indubitably,
of course, surely, undeniably,
unquestionably.

undress verb
disrobe, divest yourself, [*informal*] peel off,
shed your clothes, strip, take off your clothes,
uncover yourself.
OPPOSITES: SEE **dress** verb.

undressed adjective
SEE **naked**.

unearth verb
SEE **uncover**.

uneasy adjective
1 *an uneasy night.* disturbed, restive,
restless, uncomfortable, unsettled.
OPPOSITES: SEE **comfortable**.
2 *an uneasy feeling.* anxious, apprehensive,
awkward, concerned, distressing, edgy,
fearful, insecure, jittery, nervous, tense,
troubled, upsetting, worried.
OPPOSITES: SEE **secure** adjective.

uneconomic adjective
SEE **unprofitable**.

uneducated adjective
SEE **ignorant**.

unemotional adjective
1 *a doctor's unemotional approach to illness.*
clinical, cool, dispassionate, impassive,
objective.
2 *an unemotional reaction to a tragedy.*
apathetic, cold, frigid, hard-hearted,
heartless, indifferent, unfeeling, unmoved,
unresponsive.
OPPOSITES: SEE **emotional**.

unemployed adjective
jobless, on the dole, out of work, redundant.
OPPOSITES: SEE **working**.

unending adjective
SEE **endless**.

unenthusiastic adjective
SEE **apathetic**.

unequal adjective
1 *unequal contributions from two
participants.* different, differing, disparate,
dissimilar, uneven, varying.
OPPOSITES: SEE **equal**.
2 *unequal treatment of contestants by the
referee.* biased, prejudiced, unjust.
3 *an unequal contest.* ill-matched, one-sided,
unbalanced, uneven, unfair.

unequalled adjective
an unequalled reputation. incomparable,
inimitable, matchless, peerless, supreme,
surpassing, unmatched, unparalleled,
unrivalled, unsurpassed.

uneven adjective
1 *an uneven surface.* bent, broken, bumpy,
crooked, irregular, jagged, jerky, pitted,
rough, rutted, undulating, wavy.
OPPOSITES: SEE **smooth** adjective.

2 *an uneven rhythm.* erratic, fitful,
fluctuating, inconsistent, spasmodic,
unpredictable, variable, varying.
OPPOSITES: SEE **consistent**.
3 *an uneven load.* asymmetrical, lopsided,
unsteady.
4 *an uneven contest.* ill-matched, one-sided,
unbalanced, unequal, unfair.
OPPOSITES: SEE **balanced**.

unexpected adjective
an unexpected meeting. accidental, chance,
fortuitous, sudden, surprising, unforeseen,
unhoped for, unlooked for, unplanned,
unpredictable, unusual.
OPPOSITES: SEE **expected**.

unfair adjective
SEE **unjust**.

unfaithful adjective
deceitful, disloyal, double-dealing,
duplicitous, faithless, false, fickle,
inconstant, perfidious, traitorous,
treacherous, treasonable, unreliable,
untrue, untrustworthy.
OPPOSITES: SEE **faithful**.

unfaithfulness noun
1 *unfaithfulness to your country or your
party.* duplicity, perfidy, treachery, treason.
2 *unfaithfulness to a husband or wife.*
adultery, infidelity.

unfamiliar adjective
SEE **strange**.

unfashionable adjective
dated, obsolete, old-fashioned, [*informal*]
out (*Bright colours are out this year*),
outmoded, passé, superseded, unstylish.
OPPOSITES: SEE **fashionable**.

unfasten verb SEE **undo**.

unfavourable adjective
1 *unfavourable criticism. unfavourable
winds.* adverse, attacking, contrary, critical,
disapproving, discouraging, hostile, ill-
disposed, inauspicious, negative, opposing,
uncomplimentary, unfriendly, unhelpful,
unkind, unpromising, unpropitious,
unsympathetic.
2 *an unfavourable reputation.* bad,
undesirable, unenviable, unsatisfactory.
OPPOSITES: SEE **favourable**.

unfinished adjective
imperfect, incomplete, rough, sketchy,
uncompleted, unpolished.
OPPOSITES: SEE **perfect** adjective.

unfit adjective
1 *A drunkard is unfit to drive. A slum is unfit
to live in.* ill-equipped, inadequate,
incapable, incompetent, unsatisfactory,
useless.
2 *The film was unfit for children's viewing.*

improper, inappropriate, unbecoming, unsuitable, unsuited.
3 *You won't play well if you're unfit.* feeble, flabby, SEE **ill**, out of condition, unhealthy.
OPPOSITES: SEE **fit** adjective.

unforeseen adjective
SEE **unexpected**.

unforgettable adjective
SEE **memorable**.

unforgivable adjective
an unforgivable mistake. inexcusable, mortal (*a mortal sin*), reprehensible, shameful, unjustifiable, unpardonable, unwarrantable.
OPPOSITES: SEE **forgivable**.

unfortunate adjective
SEE **unlucky**.

unfounded adjective
SEE **groundless**.

unfrequented adjective
SEE **inaccessible**.

unfriendly adjective
an unfriendly welcome. unfriendly people. aggressive, aloof, antagonistic, antisocial, cold, cool, detached, disagreeable, distant, forbidding, hostile, ill-disposed, impersonal, indifferent, inhospitable, menacing, nasty, obnoxious, offensive, reserved, rude, sour, stand-offish, [*informal*] starchy, stern, threatening, uncivil, uncongenial, unenthusiastic, unkind, unneighbourly, unsociable, unsympathetic, unwelcoming.
OPPOSITES: SEE **friendly**.

ungainly adjective
SEE **awkward**.

ungovernable adjective
SEE **rebellious**.

ungrateful adjective
I won't give her any more if she's ungrateful. displeased, ill-mannered, selfish, unappreciative, unthankful.
OPPOSITES: SEE **grateful**.

unhappy adjective
1 *unhappy because things are not going well.* SEE **sad**.
2 *an unhappy accident.* SEE **unlucky**.

unhealthy adjective
1 *unhealthy animals.* ailing, delicate, diseased, SEE **ill**, infected, [*informal*] poorly, sick, sickly, suffering, unwell, weak.
2 *unhealthy conditions.* deleterious, dirty, harmful, insalubrious, insanitary, polluted, unhygienic, unwholesome.
OPPOSITES: SEE **healthy**.

unhelpful adjective
an unhelpful shop-assistant. disobliging, inconsiderate, negative, slow, uncivil, uncooperative, unwilling.
OPPOSITES: SEE **obliging**.

unhurried adjective
SEE **leisurely**.

unhygienic adjective
SEE **unhealthy**.

unidentifiable adjective
camouflaged, disguised, hidden, SEE **unidentified**, unrecognizable.
OPPOSITES: SEE **identifiable**.

unidentified adjective
an unidentified benefactor. anonymous, incognito, nameless, unfamiliar, unknown, unnamed, unrecognized, unspecified.
OPPOSITES: SEE **named**.

uniform adjective
a uniform appearance. consistent, homogeneous, identical, indistinguishable, regular, the same, similar, single, unvarying.
OPPOSITES: SEE **different**.

unify verb
unified by a common purpose. amalgamate, bring together, combine, consolidate, fuse, harmonize, integrate, join, merge, unite, weld together.
OPPOSITES: SEE **separate** verb.

unimaginable adjective
SEE **inconceivable**.

unimaginative adjective
an unimaginative story. banal, boring, derivative, dull, hackneyed, inartistic, obvious, ordinary, pedestrian, prosaic, stale, trite, uninspired, uninteresting, unoriginal.
OPPOSITES: SEE **imaginative**.

unimportant adjective
unimportant news. an unimportant mistake. ephemeral, immaterial, inconsequential, inessential, insignificant, irrelevant, lightweight, minor, negligible, peripheral, petty, secondary, slight, SEE **small**, trifling, trivial, uninteresting, unremarkable, worthless.
OPPOSITES: SEE **important**.

uninhabited adjective
an uninhabited island. abandoned, deserted, empty, uncolonized, unoccupied, unpeopled, vacant.
OPPOSITES: SEE **inhabited**.

uninhibited adjective
uninhibited language. abandoned, casual, frank, informal, natural, open, relaxed, spontaneous, unrepressed, unreserved, unrestrained, unselfconscious.
OPPOSITES: SEE **inhibited**.

uninspired adjective
SEE **unimaginative**.

unintelligent adjective
SEE **stupid**.

unintelligible adjective
SEE **incomprehensible**.

unintentional adjective
an unintentional insult. accidental,
fortuitous, inadvertent, involuntary,
unconscious, unintended, unplanned,
unwitting.
OPPOSITES: SEE **intentional**.

uninterested adjective
uninterested pupils. apathetic, bored,
incurious, indifferent, lethargic, passive,
phlegmatic, unconcerned, unenthusiastic,
uninvolved, unresponsive.
OPPOSITES: SEE **interested**.

uninteresting adjective
an uninteresting book. an uninteresting voice.
boring, dreary, dry, dull, flat, monotonous,
obvious, SEE **ordinary**, predictable, tedious,
unexciting, uninspiring, vapid, wearisome.
OPPOSITES: SEE **interesting**.

uninterrupted adjective
SEE **continuous**.

uninvited adjective
uninvited guests. unasked, unbidden,
unwelcome.

union noun
1 *a union of two organizations or parties.* SEE
alliance, amalgamation, association,
coalition, conjunction, integration, joining
together, merger, unification, unity.
2 *a union of two substances.* amalgam, blend,
combination, compound, fusion, mixture,
synthesis.
3 *a union of two people.* marriage,
matrimony, partnership, wedlock.

unique adjective
[Many people consider that *unique* correctly
means *being the only one of its kind*, and
that sense 2 is incorrect.] 1 [= *being the only
one of its kind*] *She's proud of her ring because
of its unique design.* distinctive, lone,
[*informal*] one-off, peculiar, single, singular,
unparalleled.
2 [*informal = rare, unusual*] SEE **unusual**.

unit noun
1 UNITS OF MEASUREMENT: SEE **measure** noun.
2 *a complete unit.* entity, item, whole.
3 *You can buy extra units to add on when you
can afford them.* component, constituent,
element, module, part, piece, portion,
section, segment.

unite verb
1 *The manager decided to unite two
departments.* amalgamate, blend, bring

together, coalesce, combine, confederate,
consolidate, couple, federate, fuse,
harmonize, incorporate, integrate, join, link,
marry, merge, unify, weld together.
OPPOSITES: SEE **separate** verb.
2 *Everyone united to support the appeal for
charity.* ally, associate, collaborate,
conspire, co-operate, go into partnership,
join forces.
3 *to unite in marriage* SEE **marry**.

united adjective
a united decision. a united effort. agreed,
common, collective, concerted, corporate,
harmonious, joint, unanimous, undivided.
OPPOSITES: SEE **disunited**.

universal adjective
universal peace. all-round, common, general,
global, international, total, ubiquitous,
widespread, worldwide.

universe noun
cosmos, the heavens.
ASTRONOMICAL TERMS: SEE **astronomy**.

unjust adjective
an unjust decision. biased, bigoted,
indefensible, inequitable, one-sided, partial,
partisan, prejudiced, undeserved, unfair,
unjustified, unlawful, unmerited,
unreasonable, unwarranted, wrong,
wrongful.
OPPOSITES: SEE **just**.

unjustifiable adjective
unjustifiable severity. excessive,
immoderate, indefensible, inexcusable,
unacceptable, unconscionable,
unforgivable, SEE **unjust**, unreasonable,
unwarrantable.
OPPOSITES: SEE **justifiable**.

unkind adjective
[There are many other words you can use in
addition to those listed here: SEE **angry**,
critical, **cruel**, etc.] *unkind criticism. unkind
treatment of animals.* [*informal*] beastly,
callous, cold-blooded, cruel, discourteous,
disobliging, hard, hard-hearted, harsh,
heartless, hurtful, ill-natured, impolite,
inconsiderate, inhumane, insensitive,
malevolent, malicious, mean, merciless,
nasty, pitiless, relentless, ruthless, sadistic,
savage, selfish, severe, spiteful, stern,
tactless, thoughtless, uncaring,
uncharitable, unchristian, unfeeling,
unfriendly, unpleasant, unsympathetic,
vicious.
OPPOSITES: SEE **kind** adjective.

unknown adjective
1 *unknown intruders.* anonymous, disguised,
incognito, mysterious, nameless, strange,
unidentified, unnamed, unrecognized,
unspecified.
OPPOSITES: SEE **named**.

2 *unknown territory.* alien, foreign, uncharted, undiscovered, unexplored, unfamiliar, unmapped.
OPPOSITES: SEE **familiar**.
3 *an unknown actor.* humble, insignificant, little-known, lowly, obscure, undistinguished, unheard of, unimportant.
OPPOSITES: SEE **famous**.

unlawful adjective
SEE **illegal**.

unlike adjective
SEE **dissimilar**.

unlikely adjective
1 *an unlikely story.* dubious, far-fetched, implausible, improbable, incredible, suspect, suspicious, [*informal*] tall (*a tall story*), unbelievable, unconvincing.
2 *an unlikely possibility.* distant, doubtful, faint, [*informal*] outside, remote, slight.
OPPOSITES: SEE **likely**.

unlimited adjective
SEE **boundless**.

unload verb
We unloaded the cases at the station. discharge, drop off, [*informal*] dump, empty, offload, take off, unpack.
OPPOSITES: SEE **load** verb.

unlock verb
SEE **open** verb.

unlucky adjective
1 *an unlucky mistake.* accidental, calamitous, chance, disastrous, dreadful, tragic, unfortunate, untimely, unwelcome.
2 *an unlucky person.* [*informal*] accident-prone, hapless, luckless, unhappy, unsuccessful, wretched.
3 *13 is supposed to be an unlucky number.* cursed, ill-fated, ill-omened, ill-starred, inauspicious, jinxed, ominous, unfavourable.
OPPOSITES: SEE **lucky**.

unmanageable adjective
SEE **rebellious**.

unmarried adjective
[*informal*] available, celibate, single, unwed.
an unmarried person [*male*] bachelor, [*female*] spinster.

unmistakable adjective
SEE **obvious**.

unnatural adjective
1 *unnatural happenings.* abnormal, bizarre, eerie, extraordinary, fantastic, freak, inexplicable, magic, magical, odd, queer, strange, supernatural, unaccountable, uncanny, unusual, weird.
2 *unnatural feelings.* callous, cold-blooded, cruel, hard-hearted, heartless, inhuman,

inhumane, monstrous, perverse, perverted, sadistic, savage, stony-hearted, unfeeling, unkind.
3 *unnatural behaviour. an unnatural accent.* actorish, affected, bogus, fake, feigned, insincere, mannered, [*informal*] phoney, pretended, [*informal*] pseudo, [*informal*] put on, self-conscious, stagey, stiff, stilted, theatrical, unspontaneous.
4 *unnatural materials.* artificial, fabricated, imitation, man-made, manufactured, simulated, synthetic.
OPPOSITES: SEE **natural**.

unnecessary adjective
Let's get rid of all the unnecessary things lying around. dispensable, excessive, expendable, extra, inessential, needless, non-essential, redundant, superfluous, surplus, uncalled for, unjustified, unneeded, unwanted, useless.
OPPOSITES: SEE **necessary**.

unobtrusive adjective
SEE **inconspicuous**.

unofficial adjective
an unofficial warning. friendly, informal, [*informal*] off the record, private, unauthorized, unconfirmed, unlicensed.
OPPOSITES: SEE **official** adjective.

unoriginal adjective
an unoriginal joke. banal, borrowed, conventional, copied, [*informal*] corny, derivative, hackneyed, old, orthodox, second-hand, stale, traditional, unimaginative, uninspired, uninventive.
OPPOSITES: SEE **original**.

unorthodox adjective
SEE **unconventional**.

unpaid adjective
1 *unpaid bills.* due, outstanding, owing.
2 *unpaid work.* unremunerative, voluntary.

unpalatable adjective
unpalatable food. disgusting, inedible, nauseating, sickening, tasteless, unappetizing, SEE **unpleasant**.
OPPOSITES: SEE **palatable**.

unparalleled adjective
SEE **unequalled**.

unpardonable adjective
SEE **unforgivable**.

unperturbed adjective
SEE **untroubled**.

unplanned adjective
SEE **spontaneous**.

unpleasant adjective
[*Unpleasant* can refer to anything which displeases you: there are far more synonyms than we can give here.] abhorrent,

abominable, antisocial, appalling, awful, SEE
bad, bad-tempered, bitter, coarse, crude,
detestable, diabolical, dirty, disagreeable,
disgusting, displeasing, distasteful,
dreadful, evil, fearful, fearsome, filthy, foul,
frightful, ghastly, grim, grisly, gruesome,
harsh, hateful, [*informal*] hellish, hideous,
horrible, horrid, horrifying, improper,
indecent, irksome, loathsome, [*informal*]
lousy, malevolent, malicious, mucky, nasty,
nauseating, objectionable, obnoxious,
odious, offensive, repellent, repugnant,
repulsive, revolting, rude, shocking,
sickening, sickly, sordid, sour, spiteful,
squalid, terrible, ugly, unattractive,
uncouth, undesirable, unfriendly, unkind,
unpalatable, unsavoury, unwelcome,
upsetting, vexing, vicious, vile, vulgar.
OPPOSITES: SEE **pleasant**.

unpopular adjective
*an unpopular choice. an unpopular
government.* despised, disliked, hated,
minority (*minority interests*), rejected,
shunned, unfashionable, unloved,
unwanted.
OPPOSITES: SEE **popular**.

unprecedented adjective
SEE **exceptional**.

unpredictable adjective
unpredictable weather. changeable,
uncertain, unexpected, unforeseeable, SEE
variable.
OPPOSITES: SEE **predictable**.

unprejudiced adjective
SEE **unbiased**.

unpretentious adjective
*Although she was wealthy, she lived in an
unpretentious house.* humble, modest, plain,
simple, straightforward, unaffected,
unassuming, unostentatious,
unsophisticated.
OPPOSITES: SEE **pretentious**.

unproductive adjective
1 *unproductive work.* ineffective, fruitless,
futile, pointless, unprofitable, unrewarding,
useless, valueless, worthless.
2 *an unproductive garden.* arid, barren,
infertile, sterile, unfruitful.
OPPOSITES: SEE **productive**.

unprofessional adjective
*an unprofessional attitude towards your
work.* amateurish, SEE **casual**, incompetent,
inefficient, irresponsible, lax, negligent,
unethical, unseemly, unskilled, unworthy.
OPPOSITES: SEE **professional**.

unprofitable adjective
an unprofitable business. loss-making,
uncommercial, uneconomic, unproductive,
unremunerative, unrewarding.
OPPOSITES: SEE **profitable**.

unprotected adjective
SEE **helpless**.

unprovable adjective SEE **questionable**,
undemonstrable, unsubstantiated,
unverifiable.
OPPOSITES: SEE **provable**.

unpunctual adjective
behind-hand, delayed, late, overdue, tardy,
unreliable.
OPPOSITES: SEE **punctual**.

unqualified adjective
1 *an unqualified worker.* SEE **amateur**
adjective.
2 *an unqualified refusal.* SEE **absolute**.

unquestionable adjective
SEE **indisputable**.

unreal adjective
SEE **imaginary**.

unrealistic adjective
1 *an unrealistic portrait.* non-
representational, unconvincing, unlifelike,
unnatural, unrecognizable.
2 *an unrealistic suggestion.* fanciful,
idealistic, impossible, impracticable,
impractical, over-ambitious, quixotic,
romantic, silly, unworkable.
3 *unrealistic prices.* SEE **exorbitant**.
OPPOSITES: SEE **realistic**.

unreasonable adjective
1 *an unreasonable person.* SEE **irrational**.
2 *an unreasonable argument.* SEE **absurd**.
3 *unreasonable prices.* SEE **excessive**.

unrecognizable adjective
SEE **unidentifiable**.

unreliable adjective
1 *unreliable evidence.* deceptive, false,
implausible, inaccurate, misleading,
suspect, unconvincing.
2 *an unreliable friend.* changeable, fallible,
fickle, inconsistent, irresponsible,
undependable, unpredictable, unsound,
unstable, untrustworthy.
OPPOSITES: SEE **reliable**.

unrepentant adjective
an unrepentant criminal. brazen, confirmed,
hardened, impenitent, incorrigible,
incurable, inveterate, irredeemable,
shameless, unashamed, unblushing,
unreformable, unregenerate.
OPPOSITES: SEE **repentant**.

unripe adjective
unripe fruit. immature, sour, unready.
OPPOSITES: SEE **ripe**.

unrivalled adjective
SEE **unequalled**.

unruly adjective
SEE **disobedient**.

unsafe adjective
SEE **dangerous**.

unsatisfactory adjective
an unsatisfactory result. disappointing,
displeasing, dissatisfying, frustrating,
inadequate, incompetent, inefficient,
insufficient, [*informal*] not good enough,
poor, unacceptable, unhappy, unsatisfying,
[*informal*] wretched.
OPPOSITES: SEE **satisfactory**.

unscathed adjective
SEE **safe**.

unscrupulous adjective
unscrupulous cheating. dishonest,
dishonourable, SEE **immoral**, improper, self-
interested, shameless, unconscionable.
OPPOSITES: SEE **scrupulous**.

unseen adjective
SEE **invisible**.

unselfish adjective
altruistic, caring, charitable, considerate,
disinterested, generous, humanitarian,
kind, magnanimous, philanthropic, public-
spirited, self-effacing, selfless, self-
sacrificing, thoughtful, ungrudging,
unstinting.
OPPOSITES: SEE **selfish**.

unselfishness noun
altruism, consideration, generosity,
kindness, magnanimity, philanthropy, self-
denial, selflessness, thoughtfulness.
OPPOSITES: SEE **selfishness**.

unsettle verb SEE **disturb**.

unsightly adjective
SEE **ugly**.

unskilful adjective
unskilful work. amateurish, bungled,
clumsy, crude, incompetent, inept, inexpert,
maladroit, [*informal*] rough and ready,
shoddy, unprofessional.
OPPOSITES: SEE **skilful**.

unskilled adjective
an unskilled worker. inexperienced, SEE
unskilful, unqualified, untrained.
OPPOSITES: SEE **skilled**.

unsociable adjective
SEE **unfriendly**.

unsolicited adjective
SEE **unasked**.

unsophisticated adjective
unsophisticated tastes. [*uncomplimentary*]
childish, childlike, ingenuous, innocent,
lowbrow, naïve, plain, provincial, simple,
simple-minded, straightforward,
unaffected, uncomplicated, unostentatious,
unpretentious, unrefined, unworldly.
OPPOSITES: SEE **sophisticated**.

unsound adjective
SEE **weak**.

unspeakable adjective
unspeakable horrors. SEE **dreadful**,
indescribable, inexpressible, nameless,
unutterable.

unstable adjective SEE **changeable**,
unsteady.

unsteady adjective
1 *unsteady on your legs. an unsteady
structure.* flimsy, frail, insecure, precarious,
rickety, [*informal*] rocky, shaky, tottering,
unbalanced, unsafe, unstable, wobbly.
2 *an unsteady trickle of water.* changeable,
erratic, inconstant, intermittent, irregular,
variable.
3 *the unsteady light of a candle.* flickering,
fluctuating, quavering, quivering,
trembling, tremulous, wavering.
OPPOSITES: SEE **steady** adjective.

unstinting adjective
SEE **generous**.

unsuccessful adjective
1 *an unsuccessful attempt.* abortive, failed,
fruitless, futile, ill-fated, ineffective,
ineffectual, loss-making, sterile, unavailing,
unlucky, unproductive, unprofitable,
unsatisfactory, useless, vain.
2 *unsuccessful contestants in a race.* beaten,
defeated, losing.
OPPOSITES: SEE **successful**.

unsuitable adjective
an unsuitable choice. ill-chosen, ill-judged,
ill-timed, inapposite, inappropriate,
incongruous, inept, irrelevant, mistaken,
unbefitting, unfitting, unhappy,
unsatisfactory, unseasonable, unseemly,
untimely.
OPPOSITES: SEE **suitable**.

unsure adjective
SEE **uncertain**.

unsurpassed adjective
SEE **unequalled**.

unsuspecting adjective
SEE **credulous**.

unsympathetic adjective
an unsympathetic response. apathetic, cold,
cool, dispassionate, hard-hearted, heartless,
impassive, indifferent, insensitive, neutral,
reserved, uncaring, uncharitable,
unconcerned, unfeeling, uninterested,
unkind, unmoved, unpitying,
unresponsive.
OPPOSITES: SEE **sympathetic**.

unsystematic adjective
an unsystematic worker. unsystematic work.
anarchic, chaotic, confused, disorderly,
disorganized, haphazard, illogical, jumbled,

muddled, [*informal*] shambolic, [*informal*]
sloppy, unmethodical, unplanned,
unstructured, untidy.
OPPOSITES: SEE **systematic**.

unthinkable adjective
SEE **incredible**.

unthinking adjective
SEE **thoughtless**.

untidy adjective
1 *untidy work. an untidy room.* careless,
chaotic, cluttered, confused, disorderly,
disorganized, haphazard, [*informal*]
higgledy-piggledy, in disarray, jumbled,
littered, [*informal*] messy, muddled,
[*informal*] shambolic, slapdash, [*informal*]
sloppy, slovenly, [*informal*] topsy-turvy,
unsystematic, upside-down.
2 *untidy hair. an untidy appearance.*
bedraggled, blowzy, dishevelled, disordered,
rumpled, scruffy, shabby, tangled, tousled,
uncared for, uncombed, ungroomed,
unkempt.
OPPOSITES: SEE **tidy** adjective.

untie verb
to untie a rope. cast off [= *to untie a boat*],
disentangle, free, loosen, release, unbind,
undo, unfasten, unknot, untether.

untrained adjective
SEE **unskilled**.

untried adjective
an untried formula. experimental,
innovatory, new, novel, unproved,
untested.
OPPOSITES: SEE **established**.

untroubled adjective
untroubled progress. carefree, SEE **peaceful**,
straightforward, undisturbed,
uninterrupted, unruffled.

untrue adjective
SEE **false**.

untrustworthy adjective
SEE **dishonest**.

untruthful adjective SEE **lying**.

unused adjective
The shop may take back any unused items.
blank, clean, fresh, intact, mint (*in mint
condition*), new, pristine, unopened,
untouched, unworn.

unusual adjective
unusual events. unusual things. abnormal,
atypical, curious, [*informal*] different,
exceptional, extraordinary, [*informal*]
funny, irregular, odd, out of the ordinary,
peculiar, queer, rare, remarkable, singular,
SEE **strange**, surprising, uncommon,
unconventional, unexpected, unfamiliar,

[*informal*] unheard of, [*informal*] unique,
unnatural, untypical, unwonted.
OPPOSITES: SEE **usual**.

unwanted adjective
SEE **unnecessary**.

unwary adjective
SEE **careless**.

unwelcome adjective
unwelcome guests. disagreeable,
unacceptable, undesirable, unwanted.
OPPOSITES: SEE **welcome** adjective.

unwell adjective SEE **ill**.

unwieldy adjective
SEE **awkward**.

unwilling adjective
unwilling helpers. averse, backward,
disinclined, grudging, half-hearted,
hesitant, ill-disposed, indisposed, lazy,
loath, opposed, reluctant, resistant, slow,
uncooperative, unenthusiastic, unhelpful.
OPPOSITES: SEE **willing**.

unwise adjective
unwise advice. an unwise thing to do.
[*informal*] daft, foolhardy, foolish, ill-
advised, ill-judged, illogical, imperceptive,
impolitic, imprudent, inadvisable,
indiscreet, inexperienced, injudicious,
irrational, irresponsible, mistaken, obtuse,
perverse, rash, reckless, senseless, short-
sighted, silly, SEE **stupid**, thoughtless,
unintelligent, unreasonable.
OPPOSITES: SEE **wise**.

unworthy adjective
A person who cheats is an unworthy winner.
despicable, discreditable, dishonourable,
disreputable, ignoble, inappropriate,
shameful, undeserving, unsuitable.
OPPOSITES: SEE **worthy**.

unwritten adjective
an unwritten message. oral, spoken, verbal,
[*informal*] word-of-mouth.
OPPOSITES: SEE **written**.

upbringing noun
the upbringing of children. breeding,
bringing up, care, education, instruction,
nurture, raising, rearing, teaching, training.

update verb
to update information. to update a design.
amend, bring up to date, correct, modernize,
review, revise.

upgrade verb
to upgrade a computer system. enhance,
expand, improve, make better.

upheaval noun SEE **commotion**.

uphill adjective
an uphill struggle. arduous, difficult,
exhausting, gruelling, hard, laborious, stiff,
strenuous, taxing, tough.

uphold verb SEE **support** verb.

upkeep noun
The upkeep of a car is expensive. care, keep,
maintenance, running, preservation.

uplifting adjective
an uplifting experience. civilizing, edifying,
educational, enlightening, ennobling,
enriching, good, humanizing, improving,
spiritual.
OPPOSITES: SEE **degrading**.

upper adjective
an upper floor. elevated, higher, raised,
superior, upstairs.

uppermost adjective
the uppermost level. SEE **dominant**, highest,
supreme, top, topmost.

upright adjective
1 *an upright position.* erect, perpendicular,
vertical.
OPPOSITES: SEE **horizontal**.
2 *an upright judge.* conscientious, fair, good,
high-minded, honest, honourable,
incorruptible, just, moral, principled,
righteous, [*informal*] straight, true,
trustworthy, upstanding, virtuous.
OPPOSITES: SEE **corrupt** adjective.

uproar noun
*There was uproar when the referee gave his
controversial decision.* [*informal*] bedlam,
brawling, chaos, clamour, commotion,
confusion, din, disorder, disturbance,
furore, [*informal*] hubbub, [*informal*]
hullabaloo, [*informal*] a madhouse, noise,
outburst, outcry, pandemonium, [*informal*]
racket, riot, row, [*informal*] ructions,
[*informal*] rumpus, tumult, turbulence,
turmoil.

uproarious adjective
an uproarious comedy. SEE **funny**.

uproot verb
to uproot plants. destroy, eliminate,
eradicate, extirpate, get rid of, [*informal*]
grub up, pull up, remove, root out, weed out.

upset verb
1 *to upset a cup. to upset a boat.* capsize,
destabilize, overturn, spill, tip over, topple.
OPPOSITES: SEE **stabilize**.
2 *to upset someone's plans.* affect, alter,
change, confuse, defeat, disorganize,
disrupt, hinder, interfere with, interrupt,
jeopardize, overthrow, spoil.
OPPOSITES: SEE **assist**.
3 *to upset someone's feelings.* agitate, alarm,

SEE **annoy**, disconcert, dismay, distress,
disturb, excite, fluster, frighten, grieve,
irritate, offend, perturb, [*informal*] rub up
the wrong way, ruffle, scare, unnerve,
worry.
OPPOSITES: SEE **calm** verb.

upside-down adjective
1 *I can't read it if it's upside-down.* inverted,
[*informal*] topsy-turvy, upturned, wrong
way up.
2 *They left the room upside-down.* SEE **chaotic**.

up-to-date adjective
1 *up-to-date technology.* advanced, current,
latest, modern, new, present-day, recent.
2 *up-to-date clothes.* contemporary,
fashionable, [*informal*] in, modish, stylish,
[*informal*] trendy.
OPPOSITES: SEE **old-fashioned**.

upward adjective
an upward path. ascending, rising, SEE
uphill.

urban adjective
an urban area. built-up, densely populated,
metropolitan.

urbane adjective SEE **polite**, **sophisticated**.

urge noun
an urge to giggle. compulsion, desire,
eagerness, impulse, inclination, instinct,
[*informal*] itch, longing, wish, yearning,
[*informal*] yen.

urge verb
1 *to urge a horse over a fence.* compel, drive,
force, impel, press, propel, push, spur.
2 *I urge you to make a decision.* advise,
advocate, appeal to, beg, beseech, [*informal*]
chivvy, counsel, [*informal*] egg on,
encourage, entreat, exhort, implore, incite,
induce, invite, nag, persuade, plead with,
prompt, recommend, solicit, stimulate.
OPPOSITES: SEE **deter**.

urgent adjective
1 *business needing urgent attention. an
urgent problem.* acute, dire (*in dire need*),
essential, exigent, immediate, important,
inescapable, instant, necessary, pressing,
top-priority, unavoidable.
2 *urgent cries for help.* eager, earnest,
importunate, insistent, persistent,
persuasive.

usable adjective
1 *Is the lift usable today?* fit for use,
functional, functioning, operating,
operational, serviceable, working.
OPPOSITES: SEE **useless**.
2 *My ticket is usable only on certain trains.*
acceptable, current, valid.
OPPOSITES: SEE **invalid** adjective.

use noun
What's the use of this? advantage,
application, necessity, need, [*informal*]
point, profit, purpose, usefulness, utility,
value, worth.

use verb
1 *to use something for a particular purpose.*
administer, apply, employ, exercise, exploit,
make use of, utilize, wield.
2 *to use a tool or machine.* deal with, handle,
manage, operate, work.
3 *How much money did you use?* consume,
exhaust, expend, spend, use up, waste.
to use up SEE **consume**.

useful adjective
1 *useful advice.* advantageous, beneficial,
constructive, good, helpful, invaluable,
positive, profitable, salutary, valuable,
worthwhile.
2 *a useful tool.* convenient, effective,
efficient, handy, powerful, practical,
productive, utilitarian.
3 *a useful player.* capable, competent,
effectual, proficient, skilful, successful,
talented.
OPPOSITES: SEE **useless**.

useless adjective
1 *a useless search. useless advice.* fruitless,
futile, hopeless, pointless, unavailing,
unprofitable, unsuccessful, vain,
worthless.
2 *a useless machine.* [*informal*] broken down,
[*informal*] clapped out, dead, dud,
ineffective, inefficient, impractical,
unusable.
3 *a useless player.* incapable, incompetent,
ineffectual, lazy, unhelpful, unskilful,
unsuccessful, untalented.
OPPOSITES: SEE **useful**.

usual adjective
our usual route home. the usual price.
accepted, accustomed, average, common,
conventional, customary, everyday,
expected, familiar, general, habitual,
natural, normal, official, ordinary, orthodox,
predictable, prevalent, recognized, regular,
routine, standard, stock, traditional, typical,
unexceptional, unsurprising, well-known,
widespread, wonted.
OPPOSITES: SEE **unusual**.

usurp verb
to usurp someone's position or rights.
appropriate, assume, commandeer, seize,
steal, take, take over.

utensil noun
kitchen utensils. appliance, device, gadget,
implement, instrument, machine, tool.
VARIOUS TOOLS: SEE **tool**.

utilize verb
SEE **use** verb.

utmost adjective SEE **extreme** adjective.

utter adjective
utter exhaustion. SEE **absolute**.

utter verb
I didn't utter a word! SEE **speak**.

vacant adjective
1 *a vacant space.* available, bare, blank,
clear, empty, free, open, unfilled, unused,
usable, void.
2 *a vacant house.* deserted, uninhabited,
unoccupied, untenanted.
OPPOSITES: SEE **occupied**.
3 *a vacant look.* absent-minded, abstracted,
blank, dreamy, expressionless, far away,
inattentive, SEE **vacuous**.
OPPOSITES: SEE **alert** adjective.

vacate verb
to vacate a room. abandon, depart from,
evacuate, give up, leave, quit, withdraw
from.

vacation noun
holiday, leave, time off.

vacuous adjective
a vacuous expression on his face. apathetic,
blank, empty-headed, expressionless, inane,
mindless, SEE **stupid**, uncomprehending,
unintelligent, vacant.
OPPOSITES: SEE **alert** adjective.

vacuum noun
emptiness, space, void.

vagrant noun
beggar, destitute person, [*informal*] down-
and-out, homeless person, itinerant, tramp,
traveller, vagabond, wanderer, wayfarer.

vague adjective
1 *vague remarks. a vague plan.* ambiguous,
ambivalent, broad (*broad generalizations*),
confused, equivocal, evasive, general,
generalized, imprecise, indefinite, inexact,
loose, nebulous, uncertain, unclear,
undefined, unspecific, unsure, [*informal*]
woolly.
2 *a vague shape in the mist.* amorphous,
blurred, dim, hazy, ill-defined, indistinct,
misty, shadowy, unrecognizable.
3 *a vague person.* absent-minded, careless,
disorganized, forgetful, inattentive, scatter-
brained, thoughtless.
OPPOSITES: SEE **definite**.

vain adjective
1 *vain about your appearance*. arrogant, boastful, [*informal*] cocky, conceited, egotistical, haughty, narcissistic, proud, self-important, self-satisfied, [*informal*] stuck-up, vainglorious.
OPPOSITES: SEE **modest**.
2 *a vain attempt*. abortive, fruitless, futile, ineffective, pointless, senseless, unavailing, unproductive, unrewarding, unsuccessful, useless, worthless.
OPPOSITES: SEE **successful**.

valiant adjective SEE **brave**.

valid adjective
a valid excuse. a valid ticket. acceptable, allowed, approved, authentic, authorized, bona fide, convincing, current, genuine, lawful, legal, legitimate, official, permissible, permitted, proper, ratified, reasonable, rightful, sound, suitable, usable.
OPPOSITES: SEE **invalid** adjective.

validate verb
You need an official signature to validate the order. authenticate, authorize, certify, endorse, legalize, legitimize, make valid, ratify.

valley noun
canyon, chasm, coomb, dale, defile, dell, dingle, glen, gorge, gulch, gully, hollow, pass, ravine, vale.

valour noun SEE **bravery**.

valuable adjective
1 *valuable jewellery*. costly, dear, expensive, generous (*a generous gift*), precious, priceless.
2 *valuable advice*. advantageous, beneficial, constructive, esteemed, good, helpful, invaluable [NB *invaluable* is not used as an opposite of *valuable*], positive, prized, profitable, treasured, useful, valued, worthwhile.
OPPOSITES: SEE **worthless**.

value noun
1 *the value of an antique*. cost, price, worth.
2 *the value of keeping fit*. advantage, benefit, importance, merit, significance, use, usefulness.

value verb
1 *The jeweller valued my watch*. assess, estimate the value of, evaluate, price, [*informal*] put a figure on.
2 *I value your advice*. appreciate, care for, cherish, esteem, [*informal*] have a high regard for, [*informal*] hold dear, love, prize, respect, treasure.

valueless adjective
SEE **worthless**.

vandal noun
barbarian, delinquent, hooligan, looter, marauder, Philistine, raider, ruffian, savage, thug, troublemaker.

vanish verb
The crowd vanished. clear, clear off, disappear, disperse, dissolve, dwindle, evaporate, fade, go away, melt away, pass.
OPPOSITES: SEE **appear**.

vanity noun SEE **pride**.

vanquish verb SEE **conquer**.

vapour noun
fog, fumes, gas, haze, miasma, mist, smoke, steam.

variable adjective
variable moods. capricious, changeable, erratic, fickle, fitful, fluctuating, fluid, inconsistent, inconstant, mercurial, mutable, shifting, temperamental, uncertain, unpredictable, unreliable, unstable, unsteady, [*informal*] up-and-down, vacillating, varying, volatile, wavering.
OPPOSITES: SEE **invariable**.

variation noun
a variation from the usual. alteration, change, deviation, difference, discrepancy, diversification, elaboration, modification, permutation, variant.

varied adjective
SEE **various**.

variety noun
1 *Variety is the spice of life*. alteration, change, difference, diversity, unpredictability, variation.
2 *a variety of things*. array, assortment, blend, collection, combination, jumble, medley, miscellany, mixture, multiplicity.
3 *a variety of baked beans. a variety of dog*. brand, breed, category, class, form, kind, make, sort, species, strain, type.

various adjective
balloons of various colours. assorted, contrasting, different, differing, dissimilar, diverse, heterogeneous, miscellaneous, mixed, [*informal*] motley (*a motley crowd*), multifarious, several, sundry, varied, varying.
OPPOSITES: SEE **similar**, **unchanging**.

vary verb
1 *The temperature varies during the day*. change, differ, fluctuate, go up and down.
2 *You can vary the temperature by turning the knob*. adapt, adjust, alter, convert, modify, reset, transform, upset.

vast adjective
a vast desert. vast amounts of money. SEE **big**,
boundless, broad, enormous, extensive,
great, huge, immeasurable, immense, large,
limitless, massive, measureless, never-
ending, unbounded, unlimited, wide.
OPPOSITES: SEE **small**.

vault noun
a wine vault. the vaults of a bank. basement,
cavern, cellar, crypt, repository,
strongroom, undercroft.

vault verb
to vault a fence. bound over, clear, hurdle,
jump, leap, leap-frog, spring over.

veer verb
The car veered across the road. change
direction, dodge, swerve, tack, turn, wheel.

vegetable noun

VARIOUS VEGETABLES: asparagus, bean,
beet, beetroot, broad bean, broccoli,
Brussels sprout, butter bean, cabbage,
carrot, cauliflower, celeriac, celery,
courgette, kale, kohlrabi, leek, marrow,
onion, parsnip, pea, potato, pumpkin,
runner bean, shallot, spinach, sugar beet,
swede, tomato, turnip, zucchini.

SALAD VEGETABLES: SEE **salad**.

---

vegetate verb
be inactive, do nothing, [*informal*] go to
seed, idle, lose interest, stagnate.

vegetation noun
foliage, greenery, growing things, growth,
plants, undergrowth, weeds.

vehement adjective
a vehement denial. animated, ardent, eager,
enthusiastic, excited, fervent, fierce,
forceful, heated, impassioned, intense,
passionate, powerful, strong, urgent,
vigorous, violent.
OPPOSITES: SEE **apathetic**.

vehicle noun
conveyance.

VARIOUS VEHICLES: ambulance, armoured
car, articulated lorry, breakdown vehicle,
[*informal*] buggy, bulldozer, bus, cab,
camper, SEE **car**, caravan, carriage, cart,
[*old-fashioned*] charabanc, chariot, coach,
container lorry, SEE **cycle**, double-decker
bus, dump truck, dustcart, estate car, fire-
engine, float, gig, go-kart, [*old-fashioned*]
hackney carriage, hearse, horse-box, jeep,
juggernaut, lorry, milk float, minibus,
minicab, moped, motor car, [*old-fashioned*]
omnibus, panda car, pantechnicon, patrol-
car, [*old-fashioned*] phaeton, pick-up,

removal van, rickshaw, scooter, sedan-
chair, side-car, single-decker bus, sledge,
snowplough, stagecoach, steam-roller, tank,
tanker (*oil tanker*), taxi, traction-engine,
tractor, trailer, tram, transporter, trap,
trolley-bus, truck, [*old-fashioned*] tumbrel,
van, wagon.

PARTS OF A MOTOR VEHICLE: accelerator,
accumulator, air-filter, axle, battery, big-
end, bodywork, bonnet, boot, brake, bumper,
carburettor, chassis, choke, clutch, cockpit,
cylinder, dashboard, diesel engine, dipstick,
distributor, engine, exhaust, fascia, fog-
light, fuel tank, gear, gearbox, headlight,
ignition, indicator, milometer, mudguard,
oil filter, piston, plug, radiator, rev counter,
safety belt or seat-belt, shock-absorber,
sidelight, silencer, spare wheel, sparking-
plug or spark plug, speedometer, starter,
steering-wheel, stop-light, tachograph,
tachometer, tail-light, throttle,
transmission, tyre, wheel, windscreen,
windscreen-wiper, wing.

---

veil verb
SEE **cover** verb.

vein noun
1 artery, blood vessel, capillary.
2 *in a sentimental vein.* SEE **mood**.

veneer noun
coating, covering, layer, surface.

vengeance noun
vengeance for an injury or insult. reprisal,
retaliation, retribution, revenge,
[*informal*] tit for tat.

vengeful adjective
avenging, bitter, rancorous, revengeful,
spiteful, unforgiving, vindictive.
OPPOSITES: SEE **forgiving**.

venomous adjective
SEE **poisonous**.

vent noun
a vent in a garment. a fresh-air vent.
aperture, cut, duct, gap, hole, opening,
outlet, passage, slit, split.

ventilate verb
to ventilate a room. aerate, air, freshen.

venture verb
1 *to venture a small wager. to venture an
opinion.* chance, dare, gamble, put forward,
risk, speculate, stake, wager.
2 *to venture out.* dare to go, risk going.

venue noun
a venue for a sporting event. meeting-place,
location, rendezvous.

verbal adjective
1 *verbal communication.* lexical, linguistic.
OPPOSITE: non-verbal.

2 *a verbal message.* oral, spoken, unwritten, word-of-mouth.
OPPOSITES: SEE **written**.

verbatim adjective
a verbatim account of what was said. exact, literal, precise, word for word.

verbose adjective
a verbose speaker. diffuse, garrulous, long-winded, loquacious, pleonastic, prolix, rambling, repetitious, talkative, tautological, unstoppable, wordy.
OPPOSITES: SEE **concise**.

verbosity noun
We became bored with his verbosity.
[*informal*] beating about the bush, circumlocution, diffuseness, garrulity, long-windedness, loquacity, periphrasis, pleonasm, prolixity, repetition, tautology, verbiage, wordiness.

verdict noun
the verdict of the jury. adjudication, assessment, conclusion, decision, finding, judgement, opinion, sentence.
LEGAL TERMS: SEE **law**.

verge noun
1 *the verge of the road.* bank, edge, hard shoulder, kerb, margin, roadside, shoulder, side, wayside.
2 *on the verge of a discovery.* brink.

verify verb
to verify someone's story. ascertain, authenticate, check out, confirm, corroborate, demonstrate the truth of, establish, prove, show the truth of, substantiate, support, uphold, validate.
OPPOSITES: SEE **discredit**, **disprove**.

versatile adjective
a versatile player. adaptable, all-round, gifted, resourceful, skilful, talented.

verse noun
a story in verse. lines, metre, rhyme, stanza.

VARIOUS VERSE FORMS: blank verse, Chaucerian stanza, clerihew, couplet, free verse, haiku, hexameter, limerick, ottava rima, pentameter, quatrain, rhyme royal, sestina, sonnet, Spenserian stanza, terza rima, triolet, triplet, vers libre, villanelle.

VARIOUS METRICAL FEET: anapaest, dactyl, iamb, spondee, trochee.

VARIOUS KINDS OF POEM: SEE **poem**.

version noun
1 *an unbiased version of what happened.* account, description, portrayal, report, story.
2 *a modern version of the Bible.* adaptation, interpretation, paraphrase, rendering, translation.
3 *The car is an up-dated version of our old one.* design, form, kind, [*formal*] mark, model, type, variant.

vertical adjective
1 *a vertical position.* erect, perpendicular, upright.
2 *a vertical drop.* precipitous, sheer.
OPPOSITES: SEE **horizontal**.

vertigo noun
dizziness, giddiness.

very adverb
acutely, enormously, especially, exceedingly, extremely, greatly, highly, [*informal*] jolly, most, noticeably, outstandingly, particularly, really, remarkably, [*informal*] terribly, truly, uncommonly, unusually.
OPPOSITES: SEE **slightly**.

vessel noun
1 [= *container*] SEE **container**.
2 *vessels in the harbour.* boat, craft, ship.

VARIOUS VESSELS: aircraft-carrier, barge, bathysphere, battleship, brigantine, cabin cruiser, canoe, catamaran, clipper, coaster, collier, coracle, corvette, cruise-liner, cruiser, cutter, destroyer, dhow, dinghy, dredger, dugout, ferry, freighter, frigate, galleon, galley, gondola, gunboat.
houseboat, hovercraft, hydrofoil, hydroplane, ice-breaker, junk, kayak, ketch, landing-craft, launch, lifeboat, lighter, light-ship, liner, longboat, lugger, man-of-war, merchant ship, minesweeper, motor boat, narrow-boat, oil-tanker, [*old-fashioned*] packet-ship, paddle-steamer, pedalo, pontoon, powerboat, pram, privateer, punt.
quinquereme, raft, rowing-boat, sailing-boat, sampan, schooner, skiff, sloop, smack, speed-boat, steamer, steamship, sub or submarine, super-tanker, tanker, tender, torpedo boat, tramp steamer, trawler, trireme, troop ship, tug, warship, whaler, wind-jammer, yacht, yawl.

PARTS OF A VESSEL: aft, amidships, anchor, binnacle, boom, bow, bridge, bulwark, conning-tower, crow's nest, deck, fo'c'sle or forecastle, funnel, galley, gunwale, helm, hull, keel, mast, oar, paddle, poop, port, porthole, propeller, prow, quarterdeck, rigging, rudder, sail, scull, starboard, stern, tiller.

veteran noun
a veteran of a war. experienced soldier, old soldier, survivor.
OPPOSITES: SEE **recruit** noun.

veto noun
We couldn't act because of the boss's veto on new schemes. ban, embargo, prohibition, refusal, rejection, [*informal*] thumbs down.
OPPOSITES: SEE **approval**.

veto verb
The boss vetoed our proposal. ban, bar, blackball, disallow, dismiss, forbid, prohibit, refuse, reject, rule out, say no to, turn down, vote against.
OPPOSITES: SEE **approve**.

vex verb SEE **annoy**.

viable adjective
a viable plan. achievable, feasible, operable, possible, practicable, practical, realistic, usable, workable.
OPPOSITES: SEE **impractical**.

vibrant adjective
vibrant with energy. alert, alive, dynamic, electric, energetic, living, pulsating, quivering, resonant, thrilling, throbbing, trembling, vibrating, vivacious.
OPPOSITES: SEE **lifeless**.

vibrate verb
The machine vibrated as the engine turned faster. judder, oscillate, pulsate, quake, quiver, rattle, reverberate, shake, shiver, shudder, throb, tremble, wobble.

vibration noun
juddering, oscillation, pulsation, quivering, rattling, reverberation, shaking, shivering, shuddering, throbbing, trembling, tremor, wobbling.

vice noun
1 *The police wage war on crime and vice.* corruption, depravity, evil, evil-doing, immorality, iniquity, sin, venality, wickedness, wrongdoing.
2 *His worst vice is his continual chattering.* bad habit, blemish, defect, failing, fault, imperfection, shortcoming, weakness.

vicinity noun
A taxi-driver ought to know the vicinity. area, district, environs, locality, neighbourhood, outskirts, precincts, proximity, purlieus, region, sector, territory, zone.

vicious adjective
1 *a vicious attack.* atrocious, barbaric, barbarous, beastly, blood-thirsty, brutal, callous, cruel, diabolical, fiendish, heinous, hurtful, inhuman, merciless, monstrous, murderous, pitiless, ruthless, sadistic, savage, unfeeling, vile, violent.

2 *a vicious character.* SEE **bad**, [*informal*] bitchy, [*informal*] catty, depraved, evil, heartless, immoral, malicious, mean, perverted, rancorous, sinful, spiteful, venomous, villainous, vindictive, vitriolic, wicked.
3 *a vicious animal.* aggressive, bad-tempered, dangerous, ferocious, fierce, snappy, untamed, wild.

victim noun
1 *a victim of an accident.* casualty, fatality, injured person, patient, sufferer, wounded person.
2 *a sacrificial victim.* martyr, offering, prey, sacrifice.

victimize verb
Don't victimize the weak. bully, cheat, discriminate against, exploit, intimidate, oppress, persecute, [*informal*] pick on, terrorize, torment, treat unfairly, [*informal*] use (*She was just using him*).

victor noun
SEE **winner**.

victorious adjective
the victorious team. champion, conquering, first, leading, prevailing, successful, top, top-scoring, triumphant, unbeaten, undefeated, winning.
OPPOSITES: SEE **defeated**.

victory noun
We celebrated our team's victory. achievement, conquest, knockout, mastery, success, superiority, triumph, [*informal*] walk-over, win.
OPPOSITES: SEE **defeat** noun.

vie verb
SEE **compete**.

view noun
1 *the view from the top of the hill.* aspect, landscape, outlook, panorama, perspective, picture, prospect, scene, scenery, spectacle, vista.
2 *I had a good view of what happened.* look, sight, vision.
3 *My view is that we should ban smoking.* attitude, belief, conviction, idea, notion, opinion, perception, thought.

view verb
1 *to view a scene.* behold, consider, contemplate, examine, eye, gaze at, inspect, observe, perceive, regard, scan, stare at, survey, witness.
2 *to view TV.* look at, see, watch.

viewer noun
[*plural*] audience, observer, onlooker, spectator, watcher, witness.

viewpoint noun
Our visitor saw the problem from a foreign viewpoint. angle, perspective, point of view, position, slant, standpoint.

vigilant adjective
Be vigilant! alert, attentive, awake, careful, observant, on the watch, on your guard, [*informal*] on your toes, wakeful, watchful, wide-awake.
OPPOSITES: SEE **negligent**.

vigorous adjective
a vigorous game. a vigorous player. active, animated, brisk, dynamic, energetic, flourishing, forceful, full-blooded, healthy, lively, lusty, potent, red-blooded, robust, spirited, strenuous, strong, virile, vital, zestful.
OPPOSITES: SEE **feeble**.

vigour noun
animation, dynamism, energy, force, forcefulness, gusto, health, life, liveliness, might, potency, power, robustness, spirit, stamina, strength, verve, [*informal*] vim, virility, vitality, zeal, zest.

vile adjective
a vile crime. contemptible, degenerate, depraved, despicable, disgusting, evil, filthy, foul, horrible, loathsome, low, nasty, nauseating, obnoxious, offensive, odious, perverted, repellent, repugnant, repulsive, revolting, sickening, ugly, vicious, wicked.

villainous adjective
SEE **wicked**.

vindictive adjective
vindictive retaliation. malicious, nasty, punitive, rancorous, revengeful, spiteful, unforgiving, vengeful, vicious.
OPPOSITES: SEE **forgiving**.

vintage adjective
a vintage wine. a vintage Presley record. choice, classic, fine, good, high-quality, mature, old, venerable.

violate verb
1 *to violate a rule.* break, contravene, defy, disobey, disregard, flout, ignore, infringe, transgress.
2 *to violate someone's privacy.* abuse, disturb, invade.
3 [*of a man*] *to violate a woman.* assault, dishonour, force yourself on, rape, ravish.

violation noun
the violation of a rule. breach, contravention, defiance, flouting, infringement, offence (against), transgression.

violent adjective
1 *a violent explosion. a violent reaction.* acute, damaging, dangerous, destructive, devastating, explosive, ferocious, fierce, forceful, furious, hard, harmful, intense, powerful, rough, savage, severe, strong, swingeing, tempestuous, turbulent, uncontrollable, vehement, wild.
2 *violent criminals. violent behaviour.* barbaric, berserk, blood-thirsty, brutal, cruel, desperate, headstrong, homicidal, murderous, riotous, rowdy, ruthless, unruly, vehement, vicious, wild.
OPPOSITES: SEE **gentle**.

virile adjective
a virile man [*uncomplimentary*] macho, manly, masculine, potent, vigorous.

virtue noun
1 *We respect virtue and hate vice.* decency, goodness, high-mindedness, honesty, honour, integrity, morality, nobility, principle, rectitude, righteousness, sincerity, uprightness, worthiness.
2 *sexual virtue.* abstinence, chastity, innocence, purity, virginity.
3 *This car's main virtue is that it's cheap to run.* advantage, asset, good point, merit, [*informal*] redeeming feature, strength.
OPPOSITES: SEE **vice**.

virtuous adjective
virtuous behaviour. blameless, chaste, ethical, exemplary, God-fearing, good, [*uncomplimentary*] goody-goody, high-principled, honest, honourable, innocent, irreproachable, just, law-abiding, moral, praiseworthy, pure, right, righteous, [*uncomplimentary*] smug, spotless, trustworthy, unimpeachable, upright, worthy.
OPPOSITES: SEE **wicked**.

viscous adjective
a viscous liquid. gluey, sticky, syrupy, thick, viscid.
OPPOSITES: SEE **runny**.

visible adjective
visible signs of weakness. apparent, clear, conspicuous, detectable, discernible, distinct, evident, manifest, noticeable, obvious, perceptible, plain, recognizable, unconcealed, undisguised, unmistakable.
OPPOSITES: SEE **invisible**.

vision noun
1 *The optician said I had good vision.* eyesight, sight.
2 *He claims to have seen a vision.* apparition, day-dream, delusion, fantasy, ghost, hallucination, illusion, mirage, phantasm, phantom, spectre, spirit.
3 *Statesmen need to be people of vision.* farsightedness, foresight, imagination, insight, spirituality, understanding.

visionary adjective
a visionary scheme for the future. fanciful, farsighted, futuristic, idealistic,

imaginative, impractical, prophetic, quixotic, romantic, speculative, transcendental, unrealistic, Utopian.

visionary noun
The ideas of a visionary may seem impractical to us. dreamer, idealist, mystic, poet, prophet, romantic, seer.

visit noun
1 *a visit to friends.* call, stay.
2 *an official visit.* visitation.
3 *a visit to London.* day out (in), excursion, outing, trip.

visit verb
to visit friends. call on, come to see, [*informal*] descend on, [*informal*] drop in on, go to see, [*informal*] look up, make a visit to, pay a call on, stay with.
to visit repeatedly frequent, haunt.

visitor noun
1 *We had visitors to dinner.* caller, [*plural*] company, guest.
2 *The town is full of visitors.* holiday-maker, sightseer, tourist, tripper.
3 *a visitor from another land.* alien, foreigner, migrant, traveller, visitant.

vista noun
landscape, outlook, panorama, prospect, scene, scenery, view.

visual adjective
visual effects. eye-catching, optical.

visualize verb
I can't visualize what heaven is like. conceive, dream up, envisage, imagine, picture.

vital adjective
1 *the vital spark of life.* alive, animate, dynamic, life-giving, live, living.
OPPOSITES: SEE **dead**.
2 *vital information.* current, crucial, essential, fundamental, imperative, important, indispensable, necessary, relevant.
OPPOSITES: SEE **inessential**.

vitality noun
full of vitality. animation, dynamism, energy, exuberance, [*informal*] go, life, liveliness, [*informal*] sparkle, spirit, sprightliness, vigour, [*informal*] vim, vivacity, zest.

vitriolic adjective
vitriolic criticism. abusive, acid, biting, bitter, caustic, cruel, destructive, hostile, hurtful, malicious, savage, scathing, vicious, vindictive, virulent.

vivacious adjective
SEE **lively**.

vivid adjective
1 *vivid colours.* bright, brilliant, colourful,

[*uncomplimentary*] gaudy, gay, gleaming, glowing, intense, shiny, showy, striking, strong, vibrant.
2 *a vivid description.* clear, graphic, imaginative, lifelike, lively, memorable, powerful, realistic.
OPPOSITES: SEE **dull**.

vocabulary noun
1 *I speak French, but my vocabulary is limited.* diction, lexis, words.
2 *The vocabulary in your French book gives the meanings of words.* dictionary, glossary, lexicon, word-list.

vocal adjective
1 *vocal sounds.* oral, said, spoken, sung, voiced.
2 *Usually she's quiet, but today she was quite vocal.* outspoken, SEE **talkative**, vociferous.

vocalist noun
SEE **singer**.

vogue noun
the latest vogue in clothes. craze, fashion, rage, style, taste, trend.

voice noun
I recognized her voice. accent, inflection, singing, sound, speaking, speech, tone.

void adjective
SEE **empty** adjective.

volatile adjective
1 *Petrol is a volatile liquid.* explosive, unstable.
2 *Beware of his volatile moods!* changeable, fickle, inconstant, lively, SEE **temperamental**, unpredictable, [*informal*] up and down, variable.
OPPOSITES: SEE **stable**.

voluble adjective
SEE **talkative**.

volume noun
1 *an encyclopaedia in ten volumes.* book, [*old-fashioned*] tome.
KINDS OF BOOK: SEE **book** noun.
2 *the volume of a container.* amount, bulk, capacity, dimensions, mass, quantity, size.

voluminous adjective
SEE **large**.

voluntary adjective
1 *voluntary work.* optional, unpaid, willing.
OPPOSITES: SEE **compulsory**.
2 *a voluntary act.* conscious, deliberate, intended, intentional.
OPPOSITES: SEE **involuntary**.

volunteer verb
to volunteer to clear up. be willing, offer, propose, put yourself forward.

vomit verb
be sick, [*informal*] bring up, disgorge,
[*informal*] heave up, [*informal*] puke,
regurgitate, retch, [*informal*] sick up,
[*informal*] spew up, [*informal*] throw up.

voracious adjective
1 *a voracious appetite.* SEE **greedy.**
2 *a voracious reader.* SEE **eager.**

vote noun
a democratic vote. ballot, election, plebiscite,
poll, referendum, show of hands.

vote verb
to vote in an election. ballot, cast your vote.
to vote for choose, elect, nominate, opt for,
pick, return, select, settle on.

voucher noun
a voucher to be exchanged for goods. coupon,
ticket, token.

vow noun
a solemn vow. assurance, guarantee, oath,
pledge, promise, undertaking, word of
honour.

vow verb
She vowed to be good. give an assurance, give
your word, guarantee, pledge, promise,
swear, take an oath.

voyage noun, verb SEE **travel** noun, verb.

vulgar adjective
1 *vulgar language.* churlish, coarse, foul,
gross, ill-bred, impolite, improper, indecent,
indecorous, low, SEE **obscene**, offensive,
rude, uncouth, ungentlemanly, unladylike.
OPPOSITES: SEE **polite.**
2 *a vulgar colour scheme.* common, crude,
gaudy, inartistic, in bad taste, inelegant,
insensitive, lowbrow, plebeian, tasteless,
tawdry, unrefined, unsophisticated.
OPPOSITES: SEE **tasteful.**

vulnerable adjective
1 *The defenders were in a vulnerable position.*
at risk, defenceless, exposed, unguarded,
unprotected, weak, wide open.
OPPOSITES: SEE **invulnerable.**
2 *He has a vulnerable nature.* easily hurt,
sensitive, thin-skinned.
OPPOSITES: SEE **resilient.**

Ww

wad noun
a wad of bank-notes. bundle, lump, mass,
pad, roll.

waffle noun
[*informal*] *Cut the waffle and get to the point.*
evasiveness, padding, prevarication, SEE
verbosity, wordiness.

waft verb
The scent wafted on the breeze. drift, float,
travel.

wag verb
A dog wags its tail. move to and fro, shake,
[*informal*] waggle, wave, [*informal*] wiggle.

wage noun
weekly wages. earnings, income, SEE **pay**
noun, pay packet.

wage verb
to wage war. carry on, conduct, engage in,
fight, undertake.

wager noun, verb SEE **bet** noun, verb.

wail verb
caterwaul, complain, cry, howl, lament,
moan, shriek, waul, weep, [*informal*] yowl.

waist noun
a belt round the waist. middle, waistline.

wait noun
*a long wait for the bus. a wait before taking
action.* SEE **delay** noun, halt, hesitation,
hiatus, [*informal*] hold-up, interval, pause,
postponement, rest, stay.

wait verb
1 *We waited for a signal.* [*old-fashioned*]
bide, SEE **delay** verb, halt, [*informal*] hang
about, hesitate, hold back, keep still, linger,
mark time, pause, remain, rest, stay, stop,
[*old-fashioned*] tarry.
2 *to wait at table.* serve.

waive verb
to waive your right to something. abandon,
disclaim, dispense with, forgo, give up,
relinquish, renounce, surrender.
OPPOSITES: SEE **enforce.**

wake noun
1 [= *funeral*] SEE **funeral.**
2 *the wake of a ship.* path, track, trail,
turbulence, wash.

wake verb
1 *A loud noise woke me.* arouse, awaken, call,
disturb, rouse, waken.
2 *I usually wake at about 7.* become
conscious, [*informal*] come to life, get up,
rise, [*informal*] stir, wake up.

walk noun
1 *He had a characteristic walk.* gait.
2 *a walk in the country.* [*joking*]
constitutional, hike, [*old-fashioned*]
promenade, ramble, saunter, stroll, traipse,
tramp, trek, trudge, [*informal*] turn (*I'll
take a turn in the garden*).

3 *I made a paved walk in the garden.* aisle, alley, path, pathway, pavement.

walk verb
1 *I walk to work.* be a pedestrian, travel on foot.
2 *Don't walk on the flowers.* stamp, step, trample, tread.

VARIOUS WAYS TO WALK: amble, crawl, creep, dodder, [*informal*] foot-slog, hike, hobble, limp, lope, lurch, march, mince, [*slang*] mooch, pace, pad, paddle, parade, [*old-fashioned*] perambulate, plod, promenade, prowl, ramble, saunter, scuttle, shamble, shuffle, slink, stagger, stalk, steal, step, [*informal*] stomp, stride, stroll, strut, stumble, swagger, tiptoe, [*informal*] toddle, totter, traipse, tramp, trample, trek, troop, trot, trudge, waddle, wade.

walker noun
hiker, pedestrian, rambler.

wall noun

KINDS OF WALL: barricade, barrier, bulkhead, bulwark, dam, dike, divider, embankment, fence, fortification, hedge, obstacle, paling, palisade, parapet, partition, rampart, screen, seawall, stockade.

wallet noun
notecase, pocket-book, pouch, purse.

wallow verb
1 *to wallow in mud.* flounder, lie, roll about, stagger about, wade, welter.
2 *to wallow in luxury.* glory, indulge yourself, luxuriate, revel, take delight.

wan adjective
SEE **pale** adjective.

wander verb
1 *to wander about the hills.* go aimlessly, meander, ramble, range, roam, rove, stray, travel about, walk, wind.
2 *to wander off course.* curve, deviate, digress, drift, err, stray, swerve, turn, twist, veer, zigzag.

wandering adjective
1 *wandering tribes.* homeless, itinerant, nomadic, peripatetic, rootless, roving, strolling, travelling, vagrant, wayfaring.
2 *wandering thoughts.* drifting, inattentive, rambling, straying.

wane verb
The evening light waned. My enthusiasm waned after a while. decline, decrease, dim,

diminish, dwindle, ebb, fade, fail, [*informal*] fall off, lessen, shrink, subside, taper off, weaken.

want noun
1 *The hotel staff try to satisfy all your wants.* demand, desire, need, requirement, wish.
2 *We had to abandon our project for want of a few pounds.* absence, lack, need.
3 *Why do we tolerate want when so many are rich?* dearth, famine, hunger, insufficiency, penury, poverty, privation, scarcity, shortage.

want verb
We can't always have what we want. covet, crave, demand, desire, fancy, hanker (after), [*informal*] have a yen (for), hunger (for), [*informal*] itch (for), like [often *would like (I would like a drink)*], long (for), pine (for), please (*You can take what you please*), prefer, [*informal*] set your heart on, wish (for), yearn (for).

war noun
1 *wars between nations.* conflict, fighting, hostilities, military action, strife, warfare.
2 *a war against crime.* campaign, crusade.
to wage war SEE **fight** verb.

VARIOUS KINDS OF ACTION IN WAR: ambush, assault, attack, battle, blitz, blockade, bombardment, campaign, counter-attack, espionage, guerrilla warfare, hostilities, invasion, manœuvre, negotiation, operation, resistance, retreat, siege, skirmish, surrender, withdrawal.

ward verb
to ward off *to ward off an attack.* avert, beat off, block, check, deflect, fend off, forestall, parry, push away, repel, repulse, stave off, thwart, turn aside.

warder noun
a prison warder. gaoler, guard, jailer, keeper, prison officer.

warehouse noun
depository, depot, store, storehouse.

wares plural noun
wares for sale. commodities, goods, merchandise, produce, stock.

warlike adjective
SEE **belligerent.**

warm adjective
1 *warm weather.* close, SEE **hot**, subtropical, sultry, summery, temperate, warmish.
OPPOSITES: SEE **cold** adjective.
2 *warm water.* lukewarm, tepid.
3 *warm clothes.* cosy, thermal, thick, winter, woolly.
4 *a warm welcome.* affable, affectionate,

cordial, enthusiastic, fervent, friendly, genial, kind, loving, sympathetic, warm-hearted.
OPPOSITES: SEE **unfriendly**.

warm verb SEE **heat** verb, make warmer, melt, raise the temperature (of), thaw, thaw out.
OPPOSITES: SEE **chill** verb.

warn verb
to warn someone of danger. advise, alert, caution, forewarn, give a warning [SEE **warning**], inform, notify, raise the alarm, remind, [informal] tip off.

warning noun
1 warning of impending trouble. She just turned up without warning. advance notice, augury, forewarning, hint, indication, notice, omen, premonition, presage, sign, signal, threat, [informal] tip-off.
2 They let him off with a warning. admonition, advice, caveat, caution, reprimand.

VARIOUS WARNING SIGNALS: alarm, alarm-bell, beacon, bell, fire-alarm, flashing lights, fog-horn, gong, hooter, red light, siren, traffic-lights, whistle.

---

warp verb
warped floor-boards. become deformed, bend, buckle, contort, curl, curve, distort, kink, twist.

warrant noun
a search-warrant. authority, authorization, SEE **document**, licence, permit, voucher.

warrior noun
SEE **fighter**.

wary adjective
wary of possible dangers. a wary approach. alert, apprehensive, attentive, careful, cautious, chary, circumspect, distrustful, heedful, observant, on the look-out (for), suspicious, vigilant, watchful.
OPPOSITES: SEE **reckless**.

wash noun
I have a wash as soon as I get up. [joking] ablutions, bath, rinse, shampoo, shower.

wash verb
1 to wash the car. to wash clothes. SEE **clean** verb, cleanse, launder, mop, rinse, scrub, shampoo, sluice, soap down, sponge down, swab down, swill, wipe.
2 to wash yourself. bath, bathe, [old-fashioned] make your toilet, [joking] perform your ablutions, shower.
3 The sea washes against the cliff. flow, splash.

waste adjective
1 waste materials. discarded, extra, superfluous, unused, unwanted.
2 waste land. bare, barren, derelict, empty, overgrown, run-down, uncared for, uncultivated, undeveloped, wild.

waste noun
1 The disposal of waste is a problem in big cities. debris, effluent, garbage, junk, litter, refuse, rubbish, scraps, trash.
2 waste left after you've finished something. dregs, excess, leavings, [informal] left-overs, offcuts, remnants, scrap, unusable material, unwanted material, wastage.

waste verb
to waste resources. be prodigal with, dissipate, fritter, misspend, misuse, squander, use wastefully [SEE **wasteful**], use up.
OPPOSITES: SEE **conserve** verb.
to waste away He wasted away when he was ill. become emaciated, become thin, become weaker, mope, pine, weaken.

wasteful adjective
a wasteful use of resources. excessive, expensive, extravagant, improvident, imprudent, lavish, needless, prodigal, profligate, reckless, thriftless, uneconomical.
OPPOSITES: SEE **economical**.

wasteland noun=waste land [SEE **waste** adjective].

watch noun
chronometer, clock, digital watch, stop-watch, timepiece, timer, wrist-watch.

watch verb
1 to watch what someone does. to watch TV. attend to, concentrate on, contemplate, eye, gaze at, heed, keep your eyes on, look at, mark, note, observe, pay attention to, regard, see, stare at, take notice of, view.
2 Watch the baby while I pop out for a minute. care for, defend, guard, keep an eye on, keep watch on, look after, mind, protect, safeguard, shield, supervise, tend.

watcher noun
[plural] audience, [informal] looker-on, observer, onlooker, spectator, viewer, witness.

watchful adjective
SEE **observant**.

watchman noun
caretaker, custodian, guard, look-out, night-watchman, security guard, sentinel, sentry.

watchword noun
SEE **saying**.

water noun

VARIOUS KINDS OF WATER: bath-water, brine, distilled water, drinking water, rainwater, sea-water, spa water, spring water, tap water.

VARIOUS STRETCHES OF WATER: brook, lake, lido, ocean, pond, pool, river, sea, SEE **stream** noun.

RELATED ADJECTIVES: aquatic, hydraulic.

water verb
to water the garden. dampen, douse, drench, flood, hose, irrigate, moisten, soak, souse, sprinkle, wet.
to water something down dilute, thin, weaken.

waterfall noun
cascade, cataract, chute, rapids, torrent, white water.

waterproof adjective
waterproof material. damp-proof, impermeable, impervious, water-repellent, water-resistant, watertight, weatherproof.

waterproof noun
Take a waterproof—it's going to be wet. cape, groundsheet, mackintosh, [*informal*] mac, raincoat, sou'wester.

watertight adjective
a watertight container. hermetic, sealed, sound, SEE **waterproof** adjective.
OPPOSITES: SEE **leaky**.

waterway noun SEE **channel** noun.

watery adjective
1 *a watery liquid. watery gravy.* aqueous, characterless, dilute, fluid, liquid, [*informal*] runny, [*informal*] sloppy, tasteless, thin, watered down, weak.
2 *watery eyes.* damp, moist, tear-filled, tearful, [*informal*] weepy, wet.

wave noun
1 *waves on the sea.* billow, breaker, crest, ridge, ripple, roller, surf, swell, tidal wave, undulation, wavelet, [*informal*] white horse.
2 *a wave of enthusiasm.* flood, outbreak, surge, upsurge.
3 *a new wave in the world of fashion.* advance, tendency, trend.
4 *a wave of the hand.* flourish, gesticulation, gesture, shake, signal.

wave verb
to wave your arms about. brandish, flail about, flap, flourish, flutter, move to and fro, shake, sway, swing, twirl, undulate, waft, wag, waggle, wiggle.
VARIOUS WAYS TO GESTURE: SEE **gesture** verb.

waver verb
to waver when confronted by danger. to waver on the brink. become unsteady, change, falter, SEE **hesitate**, quake, quaver, quiver, shake, shiver, shudder, sway, teeter, totter, tremble, vacillate, wobble.

wavy adjective
a wavy line. curling, curly, curving, rippling, sinuous, undulating, winding, zigzag.
OPPOSITES: SEE **straight**.

way noun
1 *the way home.* direction, journey, SEE **road**, route.
2 *a long way.* distance, length, measurement.
3 *the way to do something.* approach, avenue, course, knack, manner, means, method, mode, path, procedure, process, system, technique.
4 *I was not used to American ways.* custom, fashion, habit, practice, routine, style, tradition.
5 *Her funny ways take some getting used to.* characteristic, eccentricity, idiosyncrasy, oddity, peculiarity.
6 *It's all right in some ways.* aspect, circumstances, detail, feature, particular, respect.

waylay verb
He waylaid me on my way to the meeting. accost, ambush, attack, buttonhole, detain, intercept, lie in wait for, surprise.

wayward adjective
a wayward child. disobedient, headstrong, SEE **naughty**, obstinate, self-willed, stubborn, uncontrollable, uncooperative, wilful.
OPPOSITES: SEE **co-operative**.

weak adjective
1 *weak materials. a weak structure.* brittle, decrepit, delicate, feeble, flawed, flimsy, fragile, frail, inadequate, insubstantial, rickety, shaky, slight, substandard, tender, thin, unsafe, unsound, unsteady.
2 *a weak constitution.* anaemic, debilitated, delicate, enervated, exhausted, feeble, flabby, frail, helpless, ill, infirm, listless, low (*feeling low today*), [*informal*] poorly, puny, sickly, slight, thin, wasted, weakly, [*uncomplimentary*] weedy.
3 *a weak leader.* cowardly, fearful, impotent, indecisive, ineffective, ineffectual, irresolute, poor, powerless, pusillanimous, spineless, timid, timorous, weak-minded.
4 *a weak position.* defenceless, exposed, unguarded, unprotected, vulnerable.
5 *a weak excuse.* feeble, lame, unconvincing, unsatisfactory.

6 *weak tea.* dilute, diluted, tasteless, thin, watery.
OPPOSITES: SEE **strong**.

weaken verb
1 *to weaken the strength of someone or something.* debilitate, destroy, diminish, emasculate, enervate, enfeeble, erode, impair, lessen, lower, make weaker, reduce, ruin, sap, soften, undermine, [*informal*] water down.
2 *Our resolve weakened.* abate, become weaker, decline, decrease, dwindle, ebb, fade, flag, give way, wane.
OPPOSITES: SEE **strengthen**.

weakness noun
1 *a weakness in the design of something.* blemish, defect, error, failing, fault, flaw, imperfection, mistake, shortcoming.
2 *a weakness in the foundations.* flimsiness, fragility, frailty, inadequacy, softness.
3 *a feeling of weakness.* debility, feebleness, SEE **illness**, impotence, infirmity, lassitude, vulnerability.
OPPOSITES: SEE **strength**.
4 *a weakness for chocolates.* fondness, inclination, liking, penchant, predilection, [*informal*] soft spot.

wealth noun
1 *Most of his wealth is in stocks and shares.* affluence, assets, capital, fortune, [*old-fashioned*] lucre, SEE **money**, opulence, possessions, property, prosperity, riches, [*old-fashioned*] substance (*a man of substance*).
OPPOSITES: SEE **poverty**.
2 *a wealth of information.* abundance, SEE **plenty**, profusion, store.

wealthy adjective
affluent, [*informal*] flush, [*informal*] loaded, moneyed, opulent, [*joking*] plutocratic, prosperous, rich, [*informal*] well-heeled, well-off, well-to-do.
OPPOSITES: SEE **poor**.

weapons plural noun
armaments, munitions, ordnance, weaponry.

TYPES OF WEAPON: artillery, automatic weapons, biological weapons, chemical weapons, firearms, missiles, nuclear weapons, small arms, strategic weapons, tactical weapons.

VARIOUS WEAPONS: airgun, arrow, atom bomb, ballistic missile, battering-ram, battleaxe, bayonet, bazooka, blowpipe, blunderbuss, bomb, boomerang, bow and arrow, bren-gun, cannon, carbine, catapult, claymore, cosh, crossbow, CS gas, cudgel, cutlass.
dagger, depth-charge, dirk, flame-thrower,

foils, grenade, [*old-fashioned*] halberd, harpoon, H-bomb, howitzer, incendiary bomb, javelin, knuckleduster, lance, landmine, laser beam, longbow, machete, machine-gun, mine, missile, mortar, musket, mustard gas, napalm bomb, pike, pistol, pole-axe.
rapier, revolver, rifle, rocket, sabre, scimitar, shotgun, [*informal*] sixshooter, sling, spear, sten-gun, stiletto, sub-machinegun, sword, tank, teargas, time-bomb, tomahawk, tommygun, torpedo, truncheon, warhead, water-cannon.

PLACES WHERE WEAPONS ARE STORED: armoury, arsenal, depot, magazine.

---

wear verb
1 *to wear clothes.* be dressed in, clothe yourself in, dress in, have on, present yourself in, put on, wrap up in.
2 *Constant tramping in and out wears the carpet.* damage, fray, injure, mark, scuff, wear away, weaken.
3 *This carpet has worn well.* endure, last, [*informal*] stand the test of time, survive.
to wear away abrade, corrode, eat away, erode, grind down, rub away.

weariness noun
SEE **tiredness**.

wearisome adjective
wearisome business. boring, dreary, exhausting, monotonous, repetitive, tedious, tiring, SEE **troublesome**.
OPPOSITES: SEE **stimulating**.

weary adjective SEE **tired**.

weary verb SEE **tire**.

weather noun
climate, the elements, meteorological conditions.
RELATED ADJECTIVE: meteorological.

FEATURES OF WEATHER: blizzard, breeze, cloud, cyclone, deluge, dew, downpour, drizzle, drought, fog, frost, gale, hail, haze, heatwave, hoar-frost, hurricane, ice, lightning, mist, rain, rainbow, shower, sleet, slush, snow, snowstorm, squall, storm, sunshine, tempest, thaw, thunder, tornado, typhoon, whirlwind, wind.

WORDS USED TO DESCRIBE WEATHER: autumnal, blustery, breezy, bright, brilliant, chilly, clear, close, cloudless, cloudy, SEE **cold**, drizzly, dry, dull, fair, fine, foggy, foul, freezing, frosty, grey, hazy, SEE **hot**, humid, icy, inclement, misty, overcast, pouring, rainy, rough, showery, slushy, snowy, spring-like, squally, stormy, sultry,

summery, sunless, sunny, sweltering, teeming, thundery, torrential, turbulent, wet, wild, windy, wintry.
SOME METEOROLOGICAL TERMS: anticyclone, depression, front, isobar, isotherm, temperature.

weatherman noun
forecaster, meteorologist.

weave verb
1 *to weave threads.* braid, criss-cross, entwine, interlace, intertwine, interweave, knit, plait, sew.
2 *to weave a story.* compose, create, make, plot, put together.
3 *to weave your way through a crowd.* tack, [*informal*] twist and turn, wind, zigzag.

web noun
a web of intersecting lines. crisscross, lattice, mesh, net, network.

wedding noun
marriage, matrimony, [*joking*] nuptials.

PEOPLE AT A WEDDING: best man, bride, bridegroom, bridesmaid, groom, page, registrar, usher, wedding guests.
OTHER WORDS TO DO WITH WEDDINGS: confetti, honeymoon, reception, registry office, service, trousseau, wedding-ring.

wedge verb
Wedge the door open. SEE **fasten**, jam, stick.

weed noun
wild flower, wild plant, unwanted plant.

weedy adjective
1 *a weedy garden.* overgrown, rank, unkempt, untidy, unweeded, wild.
2 [*uncomplimentary*] *a weedy child.* SEE **weak**.

weep verb
blubber, cry, [*informal*] grizzle, moan, shed tears, snivel, sob, wail, whimper.

weigh verb
1 *to weigh something on scales.* measure the weight of.
2 *We weighed the evidence.* consider, evaluate, SEE **weigh up**.
3 *His evidence weighed with the jury.* be important, count, have weight.
to weigh down *weighed down with troubles. weighed down with shopping.* afflict, burden, depress, load, make heavy, overload, weight.
to weigh up *We weighed up the pros and cons.* assess, consider, evaluate, examine, give thought to, meditate on, mull over, ponder, study, think about.

weighing-machine noun
balance, scales, spring-balance, weighbridge.

weight noun
1 *a great weight to bear.* burden, heaviness, load, mass, pressure, strain.
UNITS OF WEIGHT: SEE **measure** noun.
2 *The boss's support lent weight to our campaign.* authority, emphasis, gravity, importance, seriousness, significance, substance.

weighty adjective
1 *a weighty load.* SEE **heavy**.
2 *a weighty problem.* SEE **serious**.

weird adjective
1 *a weird atmosphere in the dungeon.* creepy, eerie, ghostly, mysterious, scary, [*informal*] spooky, supernatural, unaccountable, uncanny, unearthly, unnatural.
OPPOSITES: SEE **natural**.
2 *a weird style of dress.* abnormal, bizarre, [*informal*] cranky, curious, eccentric, [*informal*] funny, grotesque, odd, outlandish, peculiar, queer, quirky, strange, unconventional, unusual, [*informal*] way-out, [*informal*] zany.
OPPOSITES: SEE **conventional**.

welcome adjective
a welcome rest. acceptable, agreeable, gratifying, much-needed, [*informal*] nice, pleasant, pleasing, pleasurable.
OPPOSITES: SEE **unwelcome**.

welcome noun
a friendly welcome. greeting, hospitality, reception.

welcome verb
1 *She welcomed us at the door.* greet, receive.
WORDS USED TO WELCOME PEOPLE: SEE **greeting**.
2 *We welcome constructive criticism.* accept, appreciate, approve of, delight in, like, want.

welcoming adjective
SEE **friendly**.

welfare noun
Nurses look after the welfare of patients. good, happiness, health, interests, prosperity, well-being.

well adjective
You look well. fit, healthy, hearty, lively, robust, sound, strong, thriving, vigorous.

well noun
1 *water from a well.* artesian well, borehole, oasis, shaft, spring, waterhole, wishing-well.
2 *oil from a well.* gusher, oil well.

well-behaved adjective
a well-behaved class. co-operative, disciplined, docile, dutiful, good, hard-working, law-abiding, manageable,

[*informal*] nice, SEE **obedient**, polite, quiet, well-trained.
OPPOSITES: SEE **naughty**.

well-built adjective
a well-built young person. athletic, big, brawny, burly, hefty, muscular, powerful, stocky, [*informal*] strapping, strong, sturdy, upstanding.
OPPOSITES: SEE **small**.

well-known adjective
a well-known person. SEE **famous**.

well-meaning adjective
[usually implies *kind but misguided*] *His well-meaning remarks misfired.* good-natured, SEE **kind** adjective, obliging, sincere, well-intentioned, well-meant.
OPPOSITES: SEE **malicious**.

well-off adjective SEE **wealthy**.

wet adjective
1 *wet clothes. wet grass.* awash, bedraggled, clammy, damp, dank, dewy, drenched, dripping, moist, muddy, saturated, sloppy, soaked, soaking, sodden, soggy, sopping, soused, spongy, submerged, waterlogged, watery, wringing.
2 *wet weather.* drizzly, humid, misty, pouring, rainy, showery.
WORDS TO DESCRIBE WEATHER: SEE **weather** noun.
3 *wet paint.* runny, sticky, tacky.
OPPOSITES: SEE **dry** adjective.

wet noun
Come in out of the wet. dampness, drizzle, rain.

wet verb
Wet the soil before you plant the seeds. dampen, douse, drench, irrigate, moisten, saturate, soak, spray, sprinkle, steep, water.
OPPOSITES: SEE **dry** verb.

wheel noun

KINDS OF WHEEL: bogie, castor, cog-wheel, spinning-wheel, steering-wheel.

PARTS OF A WHEEL: axle, hub, rim, spoke, tyre.

wheel verb
Gulls wheeled overhead. SEE **circle** verb, gyrate, move in circles.
to wheel round *He wheeled round when he heard her voice.* change direction, swerve, swing round, turn, veer.

wheeze verb
breathe noisily, cough, gasp, pant, puff.

whet verb
1 *to whet a knife.* SEE **sharpen**.
2 *to whet someone's appetite.* SEE **stimulate**.

whiff noun
a whiff of cigar smoke. breath, hint, puff, SEE **smell** noun.

whim noun
an unaccountable whim. caprice, desire, fancy, impulse, quirk, urge.

whimper, whine verbs
complain, cry, [*informal*] grizzle, groan, moan, snivel, wail, weep, whimper, [*informal*] whinge.

whip noun

VARIOUS INSTRUMENTS USED FOR WHIPPING: birch, cane, cat, cat-o'-nine-tails, crop, horsewhip, lash, riding-crop, scourge, switch.

whip verb
1 *to whip someone as a punishment.* beat, birch, cane, flagellate, flog, SEE **hit** verb, lash, scourge, [*informal*] tan, thrash.
2 *to whip cream.* beat, stir vigorously, whisk.

whirl verb
The dancers whirled round. SEE **circle** verb, gyrate, pirouette, reel, revolve, rotate, spin, swivel, turn, twirl, twist, wheel.

whirlpool noun
eddy, vortex.

whirlwind noun
cyclone, tornado, vortex.

whisk verb
to whisk eggs for an omelette. beat, mix, stir, whip.

whiskers noun
whiskers on a man's face. bristles, hairs, moustache.

whisper noun
1 *She spoke in a whisper.* murmur, undertone.
2 *I heard a whisper that they were engaged.* gossip, hearsay, rumour.

whisper verb
Keep quiet—don't even whisper. breathe, murmur, SEE **talk** verb.

whistle noun
the sound of a whistle. hooter, pipe, pipes, siren.

white adjective
white sheets. clean, spotless.

SHADES OF WHITE: cream, ivory, off-white, SEE **pale** adjective, snow-white, snowy, whitish.

whiten verb
blanch, bleach, etiolate, fade, lighten, pale.

whole adjective
1 *She told us the whole story.* complete, entire, full, total, unabbreviated, unabridged, uncut, unedited, unexpurgated.
OPPOSITES: SEE **incomplete**.
2 *When we unpacked it, the clock was still whole.* in one piece, intact, integral, perfect, sound, unbroken, undamaged, undivided, unharmed, unhurt.
OPPOSITES: SEE **fragmentary**.

wholesale adjective
1 *wholesale trade.*
OPPOSITES: retail.
2 *wholesale destruction.* comprehensive, extensive, general, global, indiscriminate, mass, total, universal, widespread.

wholesome adjective
wholesome food. a wholesome atmosphere. good, healthgiving, healthy, hygienic, nourishing, nutritious, salubrious, sanitary.
OPPOSITES: SEE **unhealthy**.

whorl noun
coil, spiral, turn, twist.

wicked adjective
a wicked deed. a wicked person. [*informal*] awful, bad, base, dissolute, SEE **evil** adjective, guilty, incorrigible, indefensible, insupportable, intolerable, irresponsible, lost (*a lost soul*), machiavelian, mischievous, naughty, nefarious, offensive, rascally, scandalous, shameful, sinful, sinister, spiteful, [*informal*] terrible, ungodly, unprincipled, unrighteous, vicious, vile, villainous, wrong.
OPPOSITES: SEE **moral** adjective.
a wicked person criminal, mischief-maker, sinner, villain, wretch.

wickedness noun
enormity, SEE **evil** noun, guilt, heinousness, immorality, infamy, irresponsibility, [*old-fashioned*] knavery, misconduct, naughtiness, sinfulness, spite, turpitude, unrighteousness, vileness, villainy, wrong, wrongdoing.

wide adjective
1 *a wide river. a wide area.* broad, expansive, extensive, large, panoramic (*a panoramic view*), spacious, vast, yawning.
2 *wide sympathies.* all-embracing, broadminded, catholic, comprehensive, eclectic, encyclopaedic, inclusive, wide-ranging.
3 *wide trousers.* baggy, flared.
OPPOSITES: SEE **narrow**.
4 *I welcomed her with arms open wide.* extended, open, outspread, outstretched.
5 *The shot was wide.* off-course, off-target.

widen verb
1 *to widen an opening.* broaden, dilate, distend, make wider, open out, spread, stretch.
2 *to widen the scope of a business.* enlarge, expand, extend, increase.

widespread adjective
Disease was widespread. common, endemic, extensive, far-reaching, general, global, pervasive, prevalent, rife, universal, wholesale.
OPPOSITES: SEE **unusual**.

width noun
beam (*of a ship*), breadth, diameter (*of a circle*), distance across, girth (*of a horse*), span (*of a bridge*), thickness.

wield verb
1 *to wield a tool or weapon.* brandish, flourish, handle, hold, manage, ply, use.
2 *to wield influence.* employ, exercise, have, possess.

wild adjective
1 *wild animals. wild flowers.* free, natural, uncultivated, undomesticated, untamed.
OPPOSITES: cultivated, SEE **domesticated**.
2 *wild tribes.* barbaric, barbarous, savage, uncivilized.
OPPOSITES: SEE **civilized**.
3 *wild country.* deserted, desolate, [*informal*] godforsaken, overgrown, remote, rough, rugged, uncultivated, unenclosed, unfarmed, uninhabited, waste.
OPPOSITES: SEE **cultivated**.
4 *wild behaviour.* aggressive, berserk, boisterous, disorderly, ferocious, fierce, frantic, hysterical, lawless, mad, noisy, obstreperous, out of control, rabid, rampant, rash, reckless, riotous, rowdy, savage, uncontrollable, uncontrolled, undisciplined, ungovernable, unmanageable, unrestrained, unruly, uproarious, violent.
OPPOSITES: SEE **restrained**.
5 *wild weather.* blustery, stormy, tempestuous, turbulent, violent, windy.
OPPOSITES: SEE **calm** adjective.
6 *wild enthusiasm.* eager, excited, extravagant, uninhibited, unrestrained.
7 *wild notions.* crazy, fantastic, impetuous, irrational, SEE **silly**, unreasonable.
8 *a wild guess.* inaccurate, random, unthinking.

wilderness noun
an uncultivated wilderness. desert, jungle, waste, wasteland, wilds (*out in the wilds*).

wile noun
SEE **trick** noun.

wilful adjective
1 *wilful disobedience.* [*informal*] bloody-minded, calculated, conscious, deliberate,

intended, intentional, premeditated, voluntary.
OPPOSITES: SEE **accidental**.
2 *a wilful character*. determined, dogged, headstrong, intransigent, obdurate, obstinate, perverse, self-willed, stubborn, uncompromising.
OPPOSITES: SEE **amenable**.

will noun
1 *the will to succeed*. aim, desire, determination, inclination, intention, purpose, resolution, resolve, volition, will-power, wish.
2 *a last will and testament*. SEE **document**.

will verb
1 *We willed her to keep going*. encourage, influence, inspire, wish.
2 *He willed his fortune to his housekeeper*. bequeath, leave, pass on.

willing adjective
1 *willing to help*. content, disposed, eager, [*informal*] game (*I'm game for anything*), inclined, pleased, prepared, ready.
2 *willing workers*. amenable, compliant, consenting, co-operative, enthusiastic, helpful, obliging.
OPPOSITES: SEE **unwilling**.

wilt verb
The plants wilted in the heat. become limp, droop, fade, fail, flag, flop, languish, sag, shrivel, weaken, wither.
OPPOSITES: SEE **flourish** verb.

wily adjective
Foxes are supposed to be wily creatures. artful, astute, clever, crafty, cunning, deceptive, designing, devious, furtive, guileful, ingenious, knowing, scheming, shifty, shrewd, skilful, sly, tricky, underhand.
OPPOSITES: SEE **straightforward**.

win verb
1 *to win in a game or battle*. be victorious, be the winner [SEE **winner**], come first, SEE **conquer**, overcome, prevail, succeed, triumph.
OPPOSITES: SEE **lose**.
2 *to win a prize. to win someone's admiration*. achieve, acquire, [*informal*] carry off, [*informal*] come away with, deserve, earn, gain, get, obtain, [*informal*] pick up, receive, secure, [*informal*] walk away with.

wind noun
1 *a blustery wind. a gentle wind*. air-current, blast, breath, breeze, cyclone, draught, gale, gust, hurricane, monsoon, puff, squall, tornado, whirlwind, [*poetic*] zephyr.
2 *wind in the stomach*. flatulence, gas.
wind instruments SEE **brass**, **woodwind**.

wind verb
1 *to wind thread on to a reel*. coil, curl, curve, furl, loop, roll, turn, twine.
2 *The road winds up the hill*. bend, curve, meander, ramble, snake, twist, [*informal*] twist and turn, zigzag.

winding adjective
a winding road. bending, [*informal*] bendy, circuitous, curving, [*informal*] in and out, indirect, meandering, rambling, roundabout, serpentine, sinuous, snaking, tortuous, [*informal*] twisting and turning, zigzag.
OPPOSITES: SEE **straight**.

window noun

KINDS OF WINDOW: casement, dormer, double-glazed window, embrasure, fanlight, French window, light, oriel, pane, sash window, skylight, shop window, stained-glass window, windscreen.

windswept adjective
a windswept moor. bare, bleak, desolate, exposed, unprotected, windy.
OPPOSITES: SEE **sheltered**.

windy adjective
1 *windy weather*. blowy, blustery, boisterous, breezy, draughty, gusty, squally, stormy.
OPPOSITES: SEE **calm** adjective.
2 *a windy corner*. SEE **windswept**.

wine noun

SOME KINDS OF WINE: beaujolais, Burgundy, champagne, chianti, claret, dry wine, hock, Madeira, malmsey, [*informal*] plonk, port, red wine, rosé, sherry, sweet wine, vintage, white wine.

OTHER DRINKS: SEE **drink** noun.

wink verb
1 *to wink an eye*. bat (*didn't bat an eyelid*), blink, flutter.
OTHER GESTURES: SEE **gesture** verb.
2 *The lights winked on and off*. flash, flicker, sparkle, twinkle.

winner noun
[*informal*] champ, champion, conqueror, first, medallist, victor.

winning adjective
1 *the winning team*. champion, conquering, first, leading, prevailing, successful, top, top-scoring, triumphant, unbeaten, undefeated, victorious.
OPPOSITES: SEE **defeated**.
2 *a winning smile*. SEE **charming**.

winter noun

WINTER SPORTS: bob-sleigh, ice-hockey, skating, skiing, sledging, tobogganing.

wintry adjective
wintry weather. SEE **cold** adjective.
OPPOSITES: SEE **summery**.

wipe verb
to wipe things clean. brush, clean, dry, dust, mop, polish, rub, scour, sponge, swab, wash.
to wipe out SEE **destroy**.

wire noun
a length of wire. cable, coaxial cable, flex, lead, [*plural*] wiring.

wiry adjective
a wiry figure. lean, sinewy, strong, thin, tough.

wisdom noun
astuteness, common sense, discernment, discrimination, good sense, insight, SEE **intelligence**, judgement, penetration, prudence, reason, sagacity, sense, understanding.

wise adjective
1 *a wise judge.* astute, discerning, enlightened, erudite, informed, SEE **intelligent**, judicious, knowledgeable, penetrating, perceptive, perspicacious, philosophical, prudent, rational, reasonable, sagacious, sage, sensible, shrewd, thoughtful, understanding, well-informed.
2 *a wise decision.* advisable, appropriate, fair, just, proper, right, sound.
OPPOSITES: SEE **unwise**.
a wise person philosopher, pundit, sage.

wish noun
What's your dearest wish? aim, ambition, aspiration, craving, desire, fancy, hankering, hope, longing, objective, request, want, yearning, [*informal*] yen.

wish verb
I wish that they'd be quiet. ask, hope.
to wish for *What do you most wish for?* aspire to, covet, crave, desire, fancy, hanker after, long for, want, yearn for.

wisp noun
a wisp of hair. a wisp of cloud. shred, strand, streak.

wispy adjective
wispy material. wispy clouds. flimsy, fragile, gossamer, insubstantial, light, streaky, thin.

wistful adjective
SEE **sad**.

wit noun
1 *a comedian's wit.* banter, cleverness, comedy, facetiousness, humour, ingenuity, jokes, puns, quickness, quips, repartee, witticisms, wordplay.
2 *She is quite a wit.* comedian, comic, humorist, jester, joker, [*informal*] wag.
3 *I didn't have the wit to understand.* SEE **intelligence**.

withdraw verb
1 *to withdraw an objection. to withdraw your troops.* call back, cancel, recall, remove, rescind, take away, take back.
2 *The attackers withdrew.* back away, draw back, fall back, leave, move back, retire, retreat, run away.
OPPOSITES: SEE **advance** verb.
3 *Some competitors withdrew at the last minute.* back out, [*informal*] chicken out, [*informal*] cry off, drop out, pull out.
OPPOSITES: SEE **enter**.

withdrawn adjective
SEE **reserved**.

wither verb
Plants withered in the drought. become dry, become limp, dehydrate, desiccate, droop, dry out, dry up, fail, flag, flop, sag, shrink, shrivel, waste away, wilt.
OPPOSITES: SEE **thrive**.

withhold verb
to withhold information. conceal, hide, hold back, keep back, keep secret, repress, retain, suppress.

withstand verb
to withstand an attack. bear, brave, cope with, defy, endure, hold out against, last out against, oppose, [*informal*] put up with, resist, stand up to, survive, tolerate, weather (*to weather a storm*).
OPPOSITES: SEE **surrender**.

witness noun
a witness of an accident. bystander, eye-witness, looker-on, observer, onlooker, spectator, watcher.
to bear witness SEE **testify**.

witness verb
1 *to witness an accident.* attend, behold, be present at, look on, observe, see, view, watch.
2 *to witness in a lawcourt.* SEE **testify**.

witty adjective
a witty storyteller. amusing, clever, comic, facetious, funny, humorous, ingenious, intelligent, quick-witted, sharp-witted, waggish.
OPPOSITES: SEE **stupid**.

wizard noun SEE **magician**, sorcerer, [*old-fashioned*] warlock.

wizardry noun SEE **magic** noun.

wobble verb
be unsteady, heave, move unsteadily, oscillate, quake, quiver, rock, shake, sway, teeter, totter, tremble, vacillate, vibrate, waver.

wobbly adjective
a wobbly stone. insecure, loose, rickety, rocky, shaky, teetering, tottering, unbalanced, unsafe, unstable, unsteady.
OPPOSITES: SEE **steady** adjective.

woe noun SEE **sorrow** noun.

woebegone, woeful SEE **sad**.

woman noun
bride, [*old-fashioned*] dame, [*old-fashioned*] damsel, daughter, dowager, female, girl, girlfriend, [*uncomplimentary*] hag, [*uncomplimentary*] harridan, housewife, hoyden, [*uncomplimentary, old-fashioned*] hussy, lady, lass, [*formal*] madam or Madame, maid, [*old-fashioned*] maiden, matriarch, matron, mistress, mother, [*uncomplimentary*] termagant, [*uncomplimentary*] virago, virgin, widow, wife.

wonder noun
1 *We gasped with wonder.* admiration, amazement, astonishment, awe, bewilderment, curiosity, fascination, respect, reverence, surprise, wonderment.
2 *It was a wonder that she recovered.* marvel, miracle.

wonder verb
I wonder if dinner is ready? ask yourself, be curious about, conjecture, ponder, question yourself, speculate, think.
to wonder at *We wondered at their skill.* admire, be amazed by, feel wonder at [SEE **wonder** noun], gape at, marvel at.

wonderful adjective
1 *She made a wonderful recovery.* amazing, astonishing, astounding, extraordinary, incredible, marvellous, miraculous, phenomenal, remarkable, surprising, unexpected, [*old-fashioned*] wondrous.
OPPOSITES: SEE **normal**.
2 [*informal*] *The food was wonderful.* SEE **excellent**.

woo verb
1 [*old-fashioned*] *to woo a girlfriend or boyfriend.* court, make love to.
2 *The shop is wooing new customers.* attract, bring in, coax, cultivate, persuade, pursue, seek, try to get.

wood noun
1 *We went for a walk in the wood.* afforestation, coppice, copse, forest, grove, jungle, orchard, plantation, spinney, thicket, trees, woodland, woods.
2 *A carpenter works with wood.* blockboard, chipboard, deal, planks, plywood, timber.

KINDS OF WOOD OFTEN USED TO MAKE THINGS: balsa, beech, cedar, chestnut, ebony, elm, mahogany, oak, pine, rosewood, sandalwood, sapele, teak, walnut.

wooded adjective
a wooded hillside. afforested, silvan, timbered, tree-covered, woody.

wooden adjective
1 *wooden furniture.* timber, wood.
2 *a wooden performance.* emotionless, expressionless, hard, inflexible, lifeless, rigid, stiff, unbending, unemotional, unnatural.
OPPOSITES: SEE **lively**.

woodwind noun

WOODWIND INSTRUMENTS: bassoon, clarinet, cor anglais, flute, oboe, piccolo, recorder.

OTHER INSTRUMENTS: SEE **music**.

woodwork noun
carpentry, joinery.

woody adjective
1 *a woody substance. a woody plant.* fibrous, hard, ligneous, tough, wooden.
2 *a woody hillside.* afforested, silvan, timbered, tree-covered, wooded.

woolly adjective
1 *a woolly jumper.* wool, woollen.
2 *a woolly teddybear.* cuddly, downy, fleecy, furry, fuzzy, hairy, shaggy, soft.
3 *woolly ideas.* ambiguous, blurry, confused, hazy, ill-defined, indefinite, indistinct, uncertain, unclear, unfocused, vague.

word noun
1 *A thesaurus is a book of words.* expression, term.
LINGUISTIC TERMS: SEE **language**.
2 *Have you had any word from granny?* SEE **news**.
3 *You gave me your word.* SEE **promise** noun.

wording noun
the wording of a letter. choice of words, diction, expression, language, phraseology, phrasing, style, terminology.

wordy adjective
a wordy lecture. a wordy speaker. diffuse, garrulous, longwinded, loquacious,

pleonastic, prolix, rambling, repetitious, talkative, tautological, unstoppable, verbose.
OPPOSITES: SEE **brief** adjective.

work noun
1 *He hates hard work.* [*informal*] donkey-work, drudgery, effort, exertion, [*informal*] fag, [*informal*] graft, [*informal*] grind, industry, labour, [*informal*] plod (*It was sheer plod*), slavery, [*informal*] slog, [*informal*] spadework, [*informal*] sweat, toil.
2 *He set me work to do.* assignment, chore, commission, homework, housework, job, project, task, undertaking.
3 *What work do you do?* business, employment, job, livelihood, living, occupation, profession, trade.
VARIOUS KINDS OF WORK: SEE **job**.

work verb
1 [*informal*] beaver away, be busy, drudge, exert yourself, [*informal*] fag, [*informal*] grind away, [*informal*] to keep your nose to the grindstone, labour, make efforts, [*informal*] peg away, [*informal*] plug away, [*informal*] potter about, slave, sweat, toil.
2 *She works her staff hard.* drive, exploit.
3 *Does your watch work? I hope my plan works.* act, be effective, function, go, operate, perform, run, succeed, thrive.
to work out *to work out answers.* SEE **calculate**.

worker noun
[In British society, *worker* is usually seen as being opposite to *manager* or *owner*.] artisan, coolie, craftsman, employee, [*old-fashioned*] hand, labourer, member of staff, member of the working class, navvy, operative, operator, peasant, practitioner, servant, slave, tradesman, working man, working woman, workman.
WORKERS IN SPECIFIC JOBS: SEE **job**.

working adjective
1 *a working woman.* employed, in work, practising.
OPPOSITES: SEE **unemployed**.
2 *Is the machine working?* functioning, going, in use, in working order, operational, running, usable.
OPPOSITES: SEE **faulty**.

workmanship noun
We admired the blacksmith's workmanship. art, artistry, competence, craft, craftsmanship, expertise, handicraft, handiwork, skill, technique.

workshop noun
factory, mill, smithy, studio, workroom.

world noun
earth, globe, planet.

worldly adjective
worldly things. a worldly outlook. avaricious, earthly, greedy, material, materialistic, mundane, physical, selfish, temporal.
OPPOSITES: SEE **spiritual**.

worn adjective
worn at the elbows. frayed, moth-eaten, SEE **old**, ragged, [*informal*] scruffy, shabby, tattered, [*informal*] tatty, thin, threadbare, worn-out.

worried adjective
worried about your work. worried about a sick relative. afraid, agitated, anxious, apprehensive, bothered, concerned, distressed, disturbed, edgy, fearful, nervous, nervy, neurotic, obsessed (by), overwrought, perplexed, perturbed, solicitous, tense, troubled, uneasy, unhappy, upset, vexed.

worry noun
1 *She's in a constant state of worry.* agitation, anxiety, apprehension, distress, fear, neurosis, tension, uneasiness, vexation.
2 *She has a lot of worries.* burden, care, concern, misgiving, problem, [*informal*], [*plural*] trials and tribulations, trouble.

worry verb
1 *Don't worry me while I'm busy.* agitate, annoy, [*informal*] badger, bother, distress, disturb, [*informal*] hassle, irritate, molest, nag, perplex, perturb, pester, plague, tease, torment, trouble, upset, vex.
2 *He worries about money.* agonize, be worried [SEE **worried**], brood, exercise yourself, feel uneasy, fret.

worrying adjective
worrying symptoms. disquieting, distressing, disturbing, perturbing, SEE **troublesome**.
OPPOSITES: SEE **reassuring**.

worsen verb
1 *to worsen a situation.* aggravate, exacerbate, make worse.
2 *My temper worsened as the day went on.* become worse, decline, degenerate, deteriorate, get worse.
OPPOSITES: SEE **improve**.

worship noun
the worship of an idol. adoration, adulation, deification, devotion, glorification, idolatry, love, praise, reverence (for), veneration.

PLACES OF WORSHIP: abbey, basilica, cathedral, chapel, church, meeting house, minster, mosque, oratory, pagoda, sanctuary, synagogue, tabernacle, temple.

---

worship verb

1 *She worships her grandad.* adore, be devoted to, deify, dote on, hero-worship, idolize, lionize, look up to, love, revere, reverence, venerate.
2 *to worship God.* glorify, laud, [*old-fashioned*] magnify, praise, pray to.

worth noun

What's the worth of this? cost, importance, merit, price, quality, significance, use, usefulness, utility, value.
to be worth be priced at, cost, have a value of.

worthless adjective

worthless junk. worthless advice. frivolous, futile, [*informal*] good-for-nothing, hollow, insignificant, meaningless, meretricious, paltry, pointless, poor, [*informal*] rubbishy, [*informal*] trashy, trifling, trivial, trumpery, unimportant, unusable, useless, valueless.
OPPOSITES: SEE **valuable, worthwhile**.

worthwhile adjective

a worthwhile sum of money. a worthwhile effort. advantageous, beneficial, biggish, considerable, good, helpful, important, invaluable, meaningful, noticeable, productive, profitable, rewarding, significant, sizeable, substantial, useful, valuable, SEE **worthy**.
OPPOSITES: SEE **worthless**.

worthy adjective

a worthy cause. a worthy winner. admirable, commendable, creditable, decent, deserving, good, honest, honourable, laudable, meritorious, praiseworthy, reputable, respectable, worthwhile.
OPPOSITES: SEE **unworthy**.

wound noun

disfigurement, hurt, injury, scar.

wound verb

Several were wounded in the accident. cause pain to, damage, disfigure, harm, hurt, injure.

KINDS OF WOUND: amputation, bite, bruise, burn, cut, fracture, gash, graze, laceration, lesion, mutilation, scab, scald, scar, scratch, sore, sprain, stab, sting, strain, weal, welt.

WAYS TO WOUND: bite, blow up, bruise, burn, claw, cut, fracture, gash, gore, graze, SEE **hit** verb, impale, knife, lacerate, maim, make sore, mangle, maul, mutilate, scald, scratch, shoot, sprain, stab, sting, strain, torture.

---

wrangle noun, verb SEE quarrel noun, verb.

wrap verb

We wrapped it in brown paper. bind, bundle up, cloak, cocoon, conceal, cover, encase, enclose, enfold, envelop, hide, insulate, lag, muffle, pack, package, shroud, surround, swaddle, swathe, wind.
OPPOSITES: SEE **uncover**.

wrath noun

SEE **anger** noun.

wreathe verb

wreathed in flowers. adorn, decorate, encircle, festoon, intertwine, interweave, twist, weave.

wreck noun

1 *a broken wreck.* shipwreck, SEE **wreckage**.
2 *the wreck of all our hopes.* demolition, destruction, devastation, overthrow, ruin, termination, undoing.

wreck verb

1 *The ship was wrecked on the rocks. He wrecked his car.* break up, crumple, crush, demolish, destroy, shatter, shipwreck, smash, [*informal*] write off.
2 *The storm wrecked our picnic.* ruin, spoil.

wreckage noun

bits, debris, [*informal*] flotsam and jetsam, fragments, pieces, remains, rubble, ruins.

wrench verb

to wrench a lid off. to wrench something out of shape. force, jerk, lever, prize, pull, strain, tug, twist, wrest, wring, [*informal*] yank.

wrestle verb SEE fight verb, grapple, struggle, tussle.

wretched adjective

1 *a wretched look on his face.* SEE **miserable**.
2 [*informal*] *The wretched car won't start!* SEE **unsatisfactory**.

wriggle verb

The snake wriggled away. snake, squirm, twist, waggle, wiggle, worm, writhe, zigzag.

wring verb

1 *to wring someone's hand.* clasp, grip, shake.
2 *to wring water out of wet clothes.* compress, crush, press, squeeze, twist.
3 *to wring a promise out of someone.* coerce, exact, extort, extract, force, wrench, wrest.

wrinkle noun

wrinkles in cloth. wrinkles in your face. corrugation, crease, crinkle, [*informal*] crow's feet [= *wrinkles at the side of your eyes*], dimple, fold, furrow, gather, line, pleat, pucker, ridge.

wrinkle verb
Don't wrinkle the carpet. crease, crinkle, crumple, fold, furrow, make wrinkles (in), pucker up, ridge, ruck up, rumple.
OPPOSITES: SEE **smooth** verb.

wrinkled adjective
a wrinkled face. a wrinkled surface. corrugated, creased, crinkly, crumpled, furrowed, lined, pleated, ridged, rumpled, shrivelled, wavy, wizened, wrinkly.

write verb
to write a shopping list. to write your thoughts. to write a book. compile, compose, copy, correspond [= *to write letters*], doodle, draft, draw up, engrave, inscribe, jot down, note, pen, print, record, scrawl, scribble, set down, take down, transcribe, type.

TOOLS YOU WRITE WITH: ballpoint, Biro, chalk, crayon, felt-tip, fountain-pen, ink, pen, pencil, typewriter, word-processor.

THINGS YOU WRITE ON: blackboard, card, exercise book, form, jotter, notepaper, pad, paper, papyrus, parchment, postcard, stationery, writing-paper.

writer noun
1 [= *person who writes things down*]
amanuensis, clerk, copyist,
[*uncomplimentary*] pen-pusher, scribe, secretary, typist.
2 [= *person who creates literature or music*]
author, [*joking*] bard, composer,
[*uncomplimentary*] hack, poet.

VARIOUS WRITERS: biographer, columnist, copy-writer, correspondent, diarist, dramatist, essayist, ghost-writer, journalist, leader-writer, librettist, novelist, playwright, poet, reporter, scriptwriter.

writhe verb
to writhe in agony. coil, contort, jerk, squirm, struggle, thrash about, thresh about, twist, wriggle.

writing noun
1 *Can you read this writing?* calligraphy, characters, copperplate, cuneiform, handwriting, hieroglyphics, inscription, italics, letters, longhand, notation, penmanship, printing, runes, scrawl, screed, scribble, script, shorthand.
2 *The children were busy at their writing.* authorship, composition.
writings *the writings of Shakespeare.* literary texts, literature, texts, works.

KINDS OF WRITING: article, autobiography, biography, children's literature, comedy, copy-writing, correspondence, crime story, criticism, detective story, diary, documentary, drama, editorial, epic, epistle, essay, fable, fairy story or fairy-tale, fantasy, fiction, folk-tale.

history, journalism, legal document, legend, letter, libretto, lyric, monograph, mystery, myth, newspaper column, non-fiction, novel, parable, parody, philosophy, play, SEE **poem**, propaganda, prose, reportage, romance.

saga, satire, science fiction, scientific writing, scriptwriting, SF, sketch, story, tale, thriller, tragi-comedy, tragedy, travel writing, treatise, trilogy, TV script, verse, [*informal*] whodunit, yarn.

written adjective
written evidence. documentary, [*informal*] in black and white, inscribed, in writing, set down, transcribed, typewritten.
OPPOSITES: SEE **unwritten**.

wrong adjective
1 *He was wrong to steal. Cruelty to animals is wrong.* SEE **bad**, base, blameworthy, corrupt, criminal, crooked, deceitful, dishonest, dishonourable, evil, felonious, illegal, illicit, immoral, iniquitous, irresponsible, naughty, reprehensible, sinful, unethical, unlawful, unprincipled, unscrupulous, vicious, villainous, wicked.
2 *a wrong answer. a wrong decision.* erroneous, fallacious, false, imprecise, improper, inaccurate, incorrect, inexact, misinformed, mistaken, unacceptable, unfair, unjust, untrue, wrongful.
3 *I put on the wrong coat. He came the wrong way.* abnormal, inappropriate, incongruous, inconvenient, unconventional, unsuitable, worst.
4 *What's wrong with the car? There's something wrong here.* amiss, broken down, defective, faulty, out of order, unusable.
OPPOSITES: SEE **right** adjective.

wrong verb
I wronged him when I accused him without evidence. abuse, be unfair to, cheat, do an injustice to, harm, hurt, maltreat, misrepresent, mistreat, traduce, treat unfairly.

wrongdoer noun
convict, criminal, crook, culprit, delinquent, evildoer, law-breaker, malefactor, mischief-maker, miscreant, offender, sinner, transgressor.

wrongdoing noun
crime, delinquency, disobedience, evil, immorality, indiscipline, iniquity, malpractice, misbehaviour, mischief, naughtiness, offence, sin, sinfulness, wickedness.

wry adjective
1 *a wry smile.* askew, awry, bent, crooked, distorted, twisted.
2 *a wry sense of humour.* droll, dry, ironic, mocking, sardonic.

Yy

yard noun
a back yard. court, courtyard, enclosure, garden, [*informal*] quad, quadrangle.

yarn noun
1 *yarn woven into cloth.* SEE **thread** noun.
2 [*informal*] *a sailor's yarn.* anecdote, narrative, story, tale.

yawning adjective
a yawning hole. gaping, open, wide.

yearly adjective
a yearly payment. annual.

yearn verb SEE **long** verb.

yellow adjective

SHADES OF YELLOW: amber, chrome yellow, cream, gold, golden, orange, tawny.

OTHER COLOURS: SEE **colour** noun.

---

yield noun
1 *a good yield from our fruit-trees.* crop, harvest, produce, product.
2 *a good yield from my investment.* earnings, income, interest, profit, return.

yield verb
1 *to yield to your opponent.* acquiesce, bow, capitulate, [*informal*] cave in, cede, concede, defer, give in, give way, submit, succumb, surrender, [*informal*] throw in the towel, [*informal*] throw up the sponge.
2 *Our fruit-trees yield a big crop.* bear, grow, produce, supply.
3 *This investment yields a high interest.* earn, generate, pay out, provide, return.

yoke verb
to yoke things together. SEE **link** verb.

young adjective
1 *young plants. young animals, young birds.* baby, early, growing, immature, newborn, undeveloped, unfledged, youngish, youthful.
2 *They're young for their age.* babyish, boyish, childish, girlish, immature, infantile, juvenile, puerile.

YOUNG PEOPLE: adolescent, baby, boy, [*uncomplimentary*] brat, child, girl, infant, juvenile, [*informal*] kid, lad, lass, [*informal*] nipper, teenager, toddler, [*uncomplimentary*] urchin, youngster, youth.

YOUNG ANIMALS: bullock, calf, colt, cub, fawn, foal, heifer, kid, kitten, lamb, leveret, piglet, puppy, whelp, yearling.

YOUNG BIRDS: chick, cygnet, duckling, fledgling, gosling, nestling, pullet.

YOUNG FISH: elver [= *young eel*], [*plural*] fry, grilse [= *young salmon*].

YOUNG PLANTS: cutting, sapling, seedling.

---

young noun
Parents have an instinct to protect their young. brood, family, issue, litter, offspring, progeny.

youth noun
1 *Grown-ups look back on their youth.* adolescence, babyhood, boyhood, childhood, girlhood, growing up, immaturity, infancy, [*informal*] teens.
2 [*often uncomplimentary*] *a noisy crowd of youths.* adolescent, boy, juvenile, [*informal*] kid, [*informal*] lad, stripling, teenager, youngster.

youthful adjective
1 *a youthful audience* SEE **young** adjective.
2 [*complimentary*] *youthful in appearance,* fresh, lively, sprightly, vigorous, well-preserved, young-looking.
3 [*uncomplimentary*] *youthful behaviour.* babyish, boyish, childish, girlish, immature, inexperienced, infantile, juvenile, puerile.

Zz

zeal noun
SEE **enthusiasm**.

zealous adjective
a zealous official. conscientious, diligent, eager, earnest, enthusiastic, fanatical, fervent, keen, passionate.
OPPOSITES: SEE **apathetic**.

zenith noun
1 *The sun was at its zenith.* highest point,
meridian.
2 *He's at the zenith of his career.* acme, apex,
climax, height, peak, pinnacle, top.
OPPOSITES: SEE **nadir**.

zero noun SEE **nothing**.

zest noun
We tucked into the food with zest. eagerness,
energy, enjoyment, enthusiasm, liveliness,
pleasure, zeal.

zigzag adjective
a zigzag route. bendy, crooked, [*informal*]
in and out, indirect, meandering,
serpentine, twisting, winding.

zigzag verb
The road zigzags up the hill. bend, curve,
meander, snake, tack (*to tack against the
wind*), twist, wind.

zodiac noun
astrological signs.

SIGNS OF THE ZODIAC: Aquarius [*Water-
Carrier*], Aries [*Ram*], Cancer [*Crab*],
Capricorn [*Goat*], Gemini [*Twins*], Leo
[*Lion*], Libra [*Scales*], Pisces [*Fish*],
Sagittarius [*Archer*], Scorpio [*Scorpion*],
Taurus [*Bull*], Virgo [*Virgin*].

---

zone noun
No one may enter the forbidden zone. area,
district, locality, neighbourhood, region,
sector, sphere, territory, tract, vicinity.

zoo noun
menagerie, safari-park, zoological gardens.
VARIOUS ANIMALS: SEE **animal** noun.

zoom verb
[*informal*] *She zoomed home with her good
news.* dash, hurry, hurtle, SEE **move** verb,
race, rush, speed, [*informal*] whiz,
[*informal*] zip.